"Wayne Grudem and I have always been on the same page, both in theology and in theological method. *Christian Ethics: An Introduction to Biblical Moral Reasoning* has all the excellent features of his *Systematic Theology*: biblical fidelity, comprehensiveness, clarity, practical application, and interaction with other writers. His exhortations drive the reader to worship the triune God. I hope the book gets the wide distribution and enthusiastic response that it deserves."

John Frame, Professor of Systematic Theology and Philosophy Emeritus,
Reformed Theological Seminary, Orlando, Florida

"This work by Wayne Grudem is the best text yet composed in biblical Christian ethics, and I mean that several ways. It is more comprehensive, more insightful, and more applicable than any comparable work and is sure to be a classroom classic. But what I like most is how Grudem unites a scholar's mind with a disciple's heart more committed to pleasing Christ than contemporaries, and more zealous for strengthening the church than impressing the world."

Daniel R. Heimbach, Fellow, L. Russ Bush Center for Faith and Culture;
Senior Professor of Christian Ethics, Southeastern Baptist Theological Seminary

"Wayne Grudem has a rare gift in making complex theological and ethical concepts accessible. He also has encyclopedic knowledge and an organized, analytical mind. All this is fully evident in this important book, which provides an invaluable resource to both scholars and practitioners."

Peter S. Heslam, Senior Fellow, University of Cambridge; Director, Transforming Business

"Wayne Grudem is a master at cutting into meaty intellectual topics, seasoning them, and serving them up in flavorful, bite-sized morsels for the ordinary person to savor and digest. Don't let the size of this book deter you! This rich feast will help you figure out what the Bible says about how to live today. Dig in. Taste the wisdom that is sweeter than honey. Eat from the bread that will bring health to your spirit and life to your bones."

Mary Kassian, author, *Girls Gone Wise*

"So much in the field of ethics today merely describes the issues and the alternatives. The very idea that there is a 'right' answer to anything is anathema. In such a stagnant climate, Wayne Grudem's *Christian Ethics* is a breath of fresh air. It demonstrates how the Bible provides specific answers to particular questions. However, this is not merely a compendium of his personal views on issues. Where his views are at odds with other views, even within evangelical Christianity, he explains those alternatives to his readers and invites comparison. Readers are challenged to think and are given the material they need to do so in a God-honoring way. We are in Grudem's debt for this massive labor of love."

John Kilner, Professor of Bioethics and Contemporary Culture, Forman Endowed
Chair of Ethics and Theology, Trinity Evangelical Divinity School; Director of Bioethics
Programs, Trinity International University

"Wayne Grudem has done it again. His *Systematic Theology* has equipped countless Christians, churches, and pastors in the truth of God's Word in a clear, accessible, and faithful manner. Now his *Christian Ethics* promises to do the same in helping us apply God's Word to our lives. In a time when obedience is often minimized in the name of grace, this book equips us to delight in God's will for our lives in response to grace."

C.J. Mahaney, Senior Pastor, Sovereign Grace Church of Louisville

"Through this encyclopedic treatment of applied ethics, Wayne Grudem shows how his method of whole-Bible hermeneutics can help Christians sort through the thorny ethical issues of the day. From the beginning of life to the end of life, and everywhere in between, Grudem demonstrates what faithfulness looks like in a God-centered, Scripture-centered life. Read with an open Bible and an open heart."

C. Ben Mitchell, Graves Professor of Moral Philosophy, Union University, Jackson, Tennessee

"Insightful, encyclopedic, biblical, and distinctively evangelical, this new book from Wayne Grudem is a massive contribution to Christian ethics. It will stand as one of the most important and definitive works of this generation. Readers should engage it chapter by chapter, and then keep it close at hand for continuing consultation."

R. Albert Mohler, Jr., President, The Southern Baptist Theological Seminary

"This is the best all-around book on Christian ethics I'm aware of, and I plan to require it as the primary textbook for my course on biblical ethics. Grudem writes in his characteristic style: clear, logical, accessible, and (usually!) persuasive."

Andy Naselli, Assistant Professor of New Testament and Theology, Bethlehem College & Seminary; Elder, Bethlehem Baptist Church

"This nearly exhaustive treatment of Christian ethics is destined to become the standard evangelical text for many years to come. It is wide-ranging, thoughtful, and unafraid to engage with controversial issues and with those who take a different approach. Regardless of whether one can side with Grudem on each topic, all of us can benefit immensely from his lucid presentation. There is hardly an ethical issue he doesn't address, and I will be consulting his work regularly for wisdom and guidance on a variety of matters that the church faces in a morally decadent and confused world. Highly recommended!"

Sam Storms, Senior Pastor, Bridgeway Church, Oklahoma City, Oklahoma

CHRISTIAN ETHICS

CHRISTIAN ETHICS

AN INTRODUCTION TO BIBLICAL MORAL REASONING

WAYNE GRUDEM

CROSSWAY®

WHEATON, ILLINOIS

Christian Ethics: An Introduction to Biblical Moral Reasoning

Copyright © 2018 by Wayne Grudem

Published by Crossway
        1300 Crescent Street
        Wheaton, Illinois 60187

Cover design: Derek Thornton, Faceout Studios

Cover image: Stocksy

First printing 2018

Printed in the United States of America

Unless otherwise indicated, all Scripture quotations are from the ESV® Bible (The Holy Bible, English Standard Version®), copyright © 2001 by Crossway, a publishing ministry of Good News Publishers. Used by permission. All rights reserved.

For other Scripture versions cited, please see Appendix B.

All emphases in Scripture quotations have been added by the author.

Hardcover ISBN: 978-1-4335-4965-6
ePub ISBN: 978-1-4335-4968-7
PDF ISBN: 978-1-4335-4966-3
Mobipocket ISBN: 978-1-4335-4967-0

Library of Congress Cataloging-in-Publication Data
Names: Grudem, Wayne A., author.
Title: Christian ethics: an introduction to biblical moral reasoning / Wayne Grudem.
Description: Wheaton: Crossway, 2018. | Includes bibliographical references and index.
Identifiers: LCCN 2017024129 (print) | LCCN 2018014341 (ebook) | ISBN 9781433549663 (pdf) | ISBN 9781433549670 (mobi) | ISBN 9781433549687 (epub) | ISBN 9781433549656 (hc)
Subjects: LCSH: Christian ethics.
Classification: LCC BJ1251 (ebook) | LCC BJ1251 .G78 2018 (print) | DDC 241—dc23
LC record available at https://lccn.loc.gov/2017024129

Crossway is a publishing ministry of Good News Publishers.

LSC   26   25   24   23   22   21   20   19   18
14   13   12   11   10   9   8   7   6   5   4   3   2   1

For Hannah, Ava, and Will,
in the hope that when you grow up the world will be a better place—
a world in which the will of God
is more fully understood and obeyed "on earth as it is in heaven" (Matthew 6:10)

CONTENTS

PART 1:
INTRODUCTION

PART 2:
PROTECTING GOD'S HONOR

"You shall have no other gods before me."
"You shall not make for yourself a carved image."
"You shall not take the name of the Lord your God in vain."
"Remember the Sabbath day."
"You shall not bear false witness."

PART 3:
PROTECTING HUMAN AUTHORITY

"Honor your father and your mother."

PART 4:
PROTECTING HUMAN LIFE

"You shall not murder."

PART 5:
PROTECTING MARRIAGE

"You shall not commit adultery."

PART 6:
PROTECTING PROPERTY

"You shall not steal."

PART 7:
PROTECTING PURITY OF HEART

"You shall not covet."

ABBREVIATIONS

ANF *The Ante-Nicene Fathers*. Edited by Alexander Roberts and James Donaldson. 1885–1887. 10 vols. Repr., Peabody, MA: Hendrickson, 1994

BDAG Bauer, Walter, Frederick William Danker, William F. Arndt, and F. Wilbur Gingrich. *A Greek-English Lexicon of the New Testament and Other Early Christian Literature*. 3rd ed. Chicago: University of Chicago Press, 2000

BDB Brown, Francis, S. R. Driver, and Charles Briggs. *A Hebrew and English Lexicon of the Old Testament*. Oxford: Clarendon, 1968

BECNT Baker Exegetical Commentary on the New Testament

CEV Contemporary English Version

cf. compare

chap. chapter

CSB Christian Standard Bible

DCH *Dictionary of Classical Hebrew*. Edited by David J. A. Clines. 9 vols. Sheffield, UK: Sheffield Phoenix Press, 1993–2014

EBC Expositor's Bible Commentary

ESV English Standard Version

et al. and others

HALOT Koehler, Ludwig, and Walter Baumgartner. *The Hebrew and Aramaic Lexicon of the Old Testament*. Study Edition. 2 vols. Leiden: Brill, 2001

HCSB Holman Christian Standard Bible

ICC International Critical Commentary

JETS *Journal of the Evangelical Theological Society*

KJV King James Version

LSJ	Liddell, Henry George, Robert Scott, Henry Stuart Jones. *A Greek-English Lexicon*. 9th ed. Oxford, UK: Clarendon, 1996
LXX	Septuagint
mg.	margin or marginal notes
n.	note
n.s.	new series
NAC	New American Commentaries
NASB	New American Standard Bible
NCV	New Century Version
NET	The NET Bible
NICNT	New International Commentary on the New Testament
NICOT	New International Commentary on the Old Testament
NIDOTTE	*New International Dictionary of Old Testament Theology and Exegesis*. Edited by Willem A. VanGemeren. 5 vols. Grand Rapids, MI: Zondervan, 1997
NIGTC	New International Greek Testament Commentaries
NIV	New International Version
NKJV	New King James Version
NLT	New Living Translation
NPNF[1]	*Nicene and Post-Nicene Fathers*, Series 1. Edited by Philip Schaff. 14 vols. 1886–1889. Repr., Peabody, MA: Hendrickson, 1994
NRSV	New Revised Standard Version
para.	paragraph
PNTC	Pillar New Testament Commentary
RSV	Revised Standard Version
sect.	section
TNIV	Today's New International Version
TNTC	Tyndale New Testament Commentaries
TOTC	Tyndale Old Testament Commentaries
trans.	translated by
TrinJ	*Trinity Journal*
vol.	volume

WBC	Word Biblical Commentary
WCF	Westminster Confession of Faith
WLC	Westminster Larger Catechism
WTJ	*Westminster Theological Journal*

ILLUSTRATIONS

Tables

Figures

PREFACE

I have written this book for Christians who want to understand what the Bible teaches about how to obey God faithfully in their daily lives. I hope the book will be useful not only for college and seminary students who take classes in Christian ethics, but also for all other Christians who seek, before God, to be "filled with the knowledge of his will in all spiritual wisdom and understanding," with the result that they will live "in a manner worthy of the Lord, fully pleasing to him: bearing fruit in every good work and increasing in the knowledge of God" (Col. 1:9–10).

This book as a whole is an invitation to experience the great blessing of God that comes from walking daily in paths of obedience, knowing more of the joy of God's presence, and experiencing his favor on our lives (see chap. 4). It is an invitation to delight in the goodness and beauty of God's moral standards because we understand that delight in those standards is really delight in the infinitely good moral character of God himself (see chap. 2). To delight in God's moral standards should lead us to exclaim with the psalmist, "Oh how I love your law! It is my meditation all the day" (Ps. 119:97).

But this book also contains a challenge. I am concerned that teaching about ethics has been neglected in many evangelical churches today—partly because the issues seem complex, partly because pastors do not want to be accused of sounding "legalistic," and partly because the surrounding non-Christian culture is hostile to Christian moral values, so anyone who teaches biblical ethics is likely to be criticized by unbelievers. Therefore, I hope this book will help to meet a need among Christians today for more biblical ethical understanding. The challenge in the book is for Christians today to live lives of personal holiness, lives that will often be distinctly different from those of others in the secular culture that surrounds us, not being "conformed to this world" but rather being "transformed by the renewal of your mind, that by testing you may discern what is the will of God, what is good and acceptable and perfect" (Rom. 12:2).

I cannot claim to live up to all of the ethical standards described in this book, nor can anyone else who reads it or teaches from it. Jesus said, "You therefore must be perfect, as your heavenly Father is perfect" (Matt. 5:48), and that includes not only moral perfection in our *actions*, but also unfailing perfection in our *motives* and *heart attitudes*—something that no one is capable of in this life. Who could ever claim to have perfectly obeyed even the two commandments that Jesus called the greatest: to love God and to love our neighbor?

> You shall love the Lord your God with all your heart and with all your soul and with all your mind. This is the great and first commandment. And a second is like it: You shall love your neighbor as yourself. On these two commandments depend all the Law and the Prophets. (Matt. 22:37–40)

But we press on. Knowing our weaknesses and failures, we can still say with the apostle Paul, "Forgetting what lies behind and straining forward to what lies ahead, *I press on toward the goal* for the prize of the upward call of God in Christ Jesus" (Phil. 3:13–14).

If we do this, we can hope that our lives will increasingly give glory to God as we seek to honor him and reflect his character in all that we do. "But the path of the righteous is like the light of dawn, which shines brighter and brighter until full day" (Prov. 4:18).

This book is similar in its method to my earlier book *Systematic Theology*,[1] because both books seek to explain "what the whole Bible teaches" about various specific topics. However, *Systematic Theology* dealt with theological topics such as the Trinity, the person of Christ, the atonement, and salvation, while this book deals with ethical topics such as lying and telling the truth, war, abortion, euthanasia, racial discrimination, divorce and remarriage, homosexuality, stewardship of money, wise use of the environment, and many other topics.[2]

In the subtitle, I have called this book "An Introduction to Biblical Moral Reasoning" because I have tried to make it understandable even for Christians who have never studied Christian ethics before. I have avoided using technical terms without first explaining them. And most of the chapters can be read on their own, so that someone can begin at any chapter and grasp its content without having read the earlier material.

Yet this book, despite its size, is still an *introduction* to Christian ethics. Entire books have been written about the topics covered in most of the chapters in this book, and expansive academic articles have been written about many of the passages that I quote in this book. Therefore, each chapter is capable of opening out into additional study in more breadth or more depth for those who are interested. The bibliographies at the end of each chapter give some help in that direction.

The following six distinctive features of this book grow out of my convictions about what Christian ethics is and how it should be taught:

1. A Clear Biblical Basis for Ethics. Because I believe that ethics should be explicitly based on the teachings of Scripture, in each chapter I have attempted to show where the Bible gives support for the ethical principles under consideration. In fact, because I believe that the words of Scripture themselves have power and authority greater than

---

[1] Wayne Grudem, *Systematic Theology: An Introduction to Biblical Doctrine* (Leicester, UK: Inter-Varsity, and Grand Rapids, MI: Zondervan, 1994).

[2] The next several paragraphs are adapted from ibid., 15–20, with permission of the publishers.

any human words, I have not just given Bible references; I have frequently *quoted* Bible passages at length so that readers can easily examine for themselves the scriptural evidence and in that way be like the noble Bereans, who were "examining the Scriptures daily to see if these things were so" (Acts 17:11). This conviction about the unique nature of the Bible as God's words has also led me to include a Scripture memory passage at the end of each chapter.

2. Clarity in the Explanation of Ethical Teachings. I do not believe that God intended the study of biblical ethics to result in confusion and frustration. A student who comes out of a course in ethics filled only with moral uncertainty and a thousand unanswered questions is hardly "able to give instruction in sound doctrine and also to rebuke those who contradict it" (Titus 1:9). Therefore, I have tried to state the ethical conclusions of this book clearly and to show where in Scripture I find convincing evidence for those positions. I do not expect that everyone reading this book will agree with me at every point of ethics; I do think that every reader will understand the positions for which I am arguing and where Scripture supports those positions.

I think it is only fair to readers of this book to say at the beginning what my convictions are regarding several ethical issues that are disputed within evangelical Christianity. I hold to a conservative view of biblical inerrancy, very much in agreement with the "Chicago Statement" of the International Council on Biblical Inerrancy[3] (chap. 3). While I agree that Christians are justified by faith alone and not by works, I also believe that our obedience is still important to God, that it brings us much joy and blessing, and that sin is still harmful in various ways (chap. 5). I think that the Bible is the only absolute source of moral standards for us, but I also believe that, subject to Scripture, it is right to give consideration to subjective perceptions of the guidance of the Holy Spirit in our daily lives (chap. 6). Because of God's promises to us, I argue that we will never be put in a situation where we are forced to choose the "lesser sin" (chap. 7). Regarding the use of the Old Testament for ethics, I argue that the entire Mosaic covenant has been abrogated and is no longer binding on us, but we can still gain wisdom from it if we bear in mind that it was God's plan for the people of Israel for a previous era in history (chap. 8).

I conclude from many passages of Scripture that it is never right to lie, in the sense of affirming in speech or writing something we believe to be false (chap. 12). I hold that men and women are equal in value before God, but that God has entrusted the husband with a unique leadership role in marriage (chap. 15). I argue that capital punishment is morally right in some cases (chap. 18), that some wars are morally acceptable as "just wars" (chap. 19), that it is morally right to use physical force to defend ourselves or others from harm in many situations (chap. 20), that abortion is always morally wrong except to save the life of the mother (chap. 21), and that euthanasia is always wrong if it involves murdering a terminally ill patient, but that "letting die" is sometimes morally

---

[3] The "Chicago Statement on Biblical Inerrancy" can be found in my *Systematic Theology*, 1203–7.

right (chap. 22). I conclude that drunkenness is always wrong, but that Scripture does not prohibit moderate use of alcohol, though I recognize good reasons why some Christians may choose total abstinence; in addition, I am opposed to laws that would legalize recreational marijuana (chap. 27).

I argue that some forms of birth control are morally acceptable (chap. 29) and that there are only two legitimate grounds for divorce, adultery and desertion, in which cases remarriage is morally acceptable (chap. 32). I argue that Scripture always views homosexual conduct as morally wrong, and that recent attempts to say that Scripture does not condemn contemporary, faithful homosexual relationships are unpersuasive (chap. 33).

I believe that God approves private ownership of property (chap. 34) and that he also intends that in the process of subduing the earth human beings will enjoy increased prosperity, but I disagree with the distinctive teachings of the "prosperity gospel" movement (chap. 36). Regarding solutions to poverty, I believe that charitable donations and government welfare programs are important to meet urgent needs, but the only long-term solution to poverty will come not through increased generosity but only by the poor being enabled to have productive jobs by which they can support themselves for life (chap. 37). I advocate wise use of the environment, not destructive misuse, and I also give reasons to think that all of the earth's natural resources will continue to be abundant for the foreseeable future. I argue that we should continue to use fossil fuels (coal, oil, natural gas) as good gifts from God, and that the use of them will not cause dangerous man-made global warming (chap. 41).

This does not mean that I ignore other viewpoints. Where there are differences on these issues within evangelical Christianity, I have tried to represent the other positions fairly, to explain why I disagree with them, and to give references to the best available defenses of the opposing positions. In several cases I have included an extended analysis of a highly influential book from an alternative position. I have also made it easy for students to find treatments of each topic in other evangelical texts by including, at the end of each chapter, the page numbers where that topic is treated in 13 other ethics textbooks.

3. Application to Life. Much of ethics is about application to life, explaining how God wants us to live in ways that honor him. Therefore, I have included much material on application within many of the chapters. In addition, I have added "Questions for Personal Application" at the end of each chapter, as well as a hymn related to the topic of the chapter, so that the study of ethics can be accompanied by worship in God's presence.

4. Focus on the Evangelical World. I do not think that a true system of ethics can be constructed from within what we may call the "liberal" theological tradition—that is, by people who deny the absolute truthfulness and internal consistency of the Bible or who do not think that the words of the Bible are God's very words (see the discussion of the authority of the Bible in chap. 3). For this reason, the other writers with whom I interact in this book are mostly within what is called the larger "conservative evangelical" tradition. I write as an evangelical and for evangelicals. This does not mean that those in the liberal tradition have nothing valuable to say about ethics; it simply means that disagreements with them almost always boil down to differences over the nature of the Bible and its authority. The degree of ethical agreement that can be reached by people with widely divergent bases of authority is quite limited. In addition, the world of conservative evangelical scholarship today is so rich and diverse that it affords ample opportunity for exploration of different viewpoints and insights into Scripture. (At several points I have also added interaction with Roman Catholic teaching, particularly the teaching of the *Catechism of the Catholic Church*,[4] because Roman Catholicism continues to exercise a significant influence worldwide.)

5. Hope for Progress in the Unity of the Church on Ethical Issues. Although I listed above several issues on which various viewpoints exist among evangelicals, I believe that there is still much hope for the evangelical church to attain deeper and more unified ethical understanding on many of these issues. Jesus is still at work perfecting his church "so that he might present the church to himself in splendor, without spot or wrinkle or any such thing, that she might be holy and without blemish" (Eph. 5:27), and he has given gifts to equip the church "until we all attain to the unity of the faith and of the knowledge of the son of God" (Eph. 4:13). Though present ethical disagreements may discourage us, these Scriptures remain true, and we should not abandon hope of greater agreement.

6. A Sense of the Urgent Need for Greater Ethical Understanding in the Whole Church. I am convinced that there is an urgent need in the church today for much greater understanding of Christian ethics. My perception is that there is much confusion and uncertainty about ethics among evangelicals today. Not only pastors and teachers need to understand ethics in greater depth—the whole church does as well. It is not that Christians today lack the ability to understand ethics; it is just that they must have access to teaching on it in an understandable form. Once that happens, I think many Christians will find that understanding (and living) the ethical teachings of Scripture is one of their greatest joys.

Many people have helped me in the writing of this book, beginning with the students who took ethics classes from me, a new professor, at Bethel College in St. Paul, Minnesota (1977–1981); the many students in my ethics classes at Trinity Evangelical Divinity School, Deerfield, Illinois (1981–2001); and finally the students who took the ethics classes that I taught at Phoenix Seminary in Arizona (2001–2017, and I hope continuing for many years to come). In many cases, the positions that I finally adopted in this book have come as a result of correction, modification, or supplementation from thoughtful interaction with these wonderful students over the last 40 years.

In addition, I wish to thank the members of the Christian Essentials class, the adult

---

[4] *Catechism of the Catholic Church*, 2nd ed. (New York: Doubleday, 1997).

Bible class that I taught at Scottsdale Bible Church for 12 years (2002–2014). During that time, I taught through the entire sequence of topics in this book and profited immensely from thoughtful interaction with the members of that class. Those class members and many other friends (including some special "prayer partners") have been praying for me as I worked on this project for several years. I am grateful to God for answering those prayers and giving me strength and diligence to complete this project.

I wish to thank Professor John Frame, whose class in Christian ethics significantly influenced my thinking when I was a student at Westminster Seminary in 1971–1973. Although it is impossible to acknowledge my indebtedness to him at every point in this book, it is appropriate to express gratitude to him here and to say that he has probably influenced my thinking on ethical topics more than anyone else. Many of his former students, as well as readers of his excellent book *The Doctrine of the Christian Life*, will recognize echoes of his teaching in the following pages. In fact, his outstanding work *The Doctrine of the Christian Life*[5] has been the primary textbook that I have used in my ethics classes for the past several years. (Prior to its publication, I used another truly excellent book, *Ethics for a Brave New World*,[6] by my former colleagues John Feinberg and Paul Feinberg at Trinity Evangelical Divinity School.)

Many people helped me with specialized knowledge in certain chapters, especially David Horner regarding the importance of character and the goal of ethics in chapter 4; Tim Kimmel regarding blessings for obedience in chapter 5; Garry Friesen regarding his view of guidance in chapter 6; John DelHousaye and Peter Gurry regarding recent studies in Greek grammar in chapter 6; John Stemberger regarding theonomy in chapter 8; Al Fadi regarding Islamic art in chapter 10; Jacque Chadwick with medical issues in chapters 22, 29, and 30; Michael Herrod and Steve Oman regarding various legal issues in chapter 24 and elsewhere; Jason DeRouchie regarding sexual ethics in chapter 28; Steve Eriksson, Joe Gordon, and Janice Noland regarding singleness in chapter 28; Wayne Lehsten regarding statistics on divorce in chapter 32; Denny Burk regarding homosexuality and transgenderism in chapter 33; Lars Kierspel regarding rabbinic backgrounds in chapter 33; and Vijay Raj and Cal Beisner regarding environmental statistics in chapter 41. In addition, the wisdom and economic knowledge of my previous coauthor Barry Asmus continued to influence my thinking in the material on economics in chapters 34–41.[7] Andy Naselli read the entire manuscript and made numerous suggestions that significantly strengthened the book. And I am deeply grateful to Greg Bailey of Crossway, who edited the entire manuscript with meticulous care, improving many sentences, strengthening many arguments, correcting many footnotes and Scripture refer-

[5] John M. Frame, *The Doctrine of the Christian Life: A Theology of Lordship* (Phillipsburg, NJ: P&R, 2008).

[6] John S. Feinberg and Paul D. Feinberg, *Ethics for a Brave New World*, 2nd ed. (Wheaton, IL: Crossway, 2010).

[7] See Wayne Grudem and Barry Asmus, *The Poverty of Nations: A Sustainable Solution* (Wheaton, IL: Crossway, 2013).

ences, and improving the organization of the material in many chapters. The book is much better because of his skillful work.

Jenny Miller typed several of the chapters with her usual care and precision, and Dan McCurley and Jeff Phillips also did excellent work in typing many of the remaining chapters. For the past several months, Phil Hoshiwara and Michael Alling, my student assistants at Phoenix Seminary, have worked many long hours in carefully proofreading the various chapters, typing the bibliographies, and helping in several other ways. Previous student assistants Josh McCoy, Jason Miller, and Danny Malakowsky also helped with research tasks and computer maintenance. Scott Bauer compiled the cross-references to 13 other ethics texts and helped with other research in various chapters. Brenda Dinell typed those same cross-references and the hymns, and added the Scripture memory passages, at the end of each chapter. Mitch Miller helped me with additional bibliographical research. Mary Lisa Urban helped me improve my skills in using Naturally Speaking software. During the final months of preparing the manuscript, Eric Wildgen and Ryan Carpenter provided additional valuable help in research and proofreading. I am also grateful to Holly DelHousaye, who helped me to see the wisdom of making this book a higher priority than other planned writing projects; to Darryl Gregg, for setting up the lighting in my study; and to Trent Poling, for once again providing me with timely help for a baffling software problem.

I also wish to thank Stan Gundry, senior vice president and editor-in-chief at Zondervan, for graciously granting me permission to adapt several sections from my Zondervan books *Systematic Theology: An Introduction to Biblical Doctrine* and *Politics—According to the Bible: A Comprehensive Resource for Understanding Modern Political Issues in Light of Scripture* for use in this book. It is inevitable that some topics traditionally treated in ethics courses (such as capital punishment, war, abortion, and euthanasia) will overlap with a book on a Christian view of politics, but I have tried to keep the focus in this book on biblical and ethical considerations, and I frequently refer readers to the longer treatments of the actual political questions that are found in *Politics—According to the Bible*. There is less overlap between this book and my *Systematic Theology*, but I have adapted some sections from that book in my treatment of topics such as aging and death, and in the introductory material in the preface and chapters 1 and 3. I am also grateful to Inter-Varsity Press of the United Kingdom for similarly granting me permission to use this material from *Systematic Theology*.

In the summer of 2014, I spent several weeks at the Tyndale House library in Cambridge, England, working on this book. Conversations about my work with Peter Williams, David Instone-Brewer, Dirk Jongkind, Peter Heslam, and Jonathan Chaplin were helpful to me during that time. Librarian Simon Sykes cheerfully helped me with various arrangements in the library, and Brad Green graciously made it possible for me to have a quiet desk in the crowded library.

Once again, as with my book *Politics—According to the Bible*, I owe a great debt of gratitude to Craig Osten, who accurately and quickly provided me with excellent assistance in researching a large number of specific factual details that I needed for many of the chapters. And Phil Hoshiwara accurately compiled the glossary for the entire book.

In 2006, my friend C. J. Mahaney approached me about a plan that would enable me to teach half-time at Phoenix Seminary (spring terms only), giving me eight months a year to write. The leadership at Phoenix Seminary agreed, and C. J. then raised the funding to make this possible for the first three years (2007–2010). Since then, I have been able to continue on a half-time schedule, and this is now the seventh book that I have written or coedited as a result of that plan. I am deeply grateful to C. J. for his 2006 idea, for it changed the entire course of my life for the last 10 years.

I am also deeply grateful to my friends Bret Edson, Brad Edson, Brad Routh, and their colleagues at Marketplace One, who have believed in this book from the beginning and who provided financial support that enabled me to continue to be free from teaching during the fall semesters and that also covered some research-related expenses. And I am grateful to President Darryl DelHousaye and Academic Dean Bing Hunter at Phoenix Seminary, who continue to encourage me in my writing.

After I was diagnosed with Parkinson's disease in December 2015, my son Alexander Grudem moved back home to help me complete this book. He had earned an MA in Christian studies at Regent College, Vancouver, and that academic background enabled him to provide me with substantial assistance. He read through every chapter, made helpful suggestions again and again, and also provided me with a digest of alternative viewpoints from other ethics books in many chapters. The book is much better as a result of his work. (And as I write this in May 2017, I am thankful to God that my Parkinson's symptoms remain remarkably mild and have shown only slow progression.)

Finally, I am thankful to God for the remarkable help of my amazing and wonderful wife, Margaret, who prays for me many times a day and who will always pray for me specifically when I tell her that I am "stuck" in attempting to write a certain section. She protects me from disruptions, brings meals into my study when I am working, encourages me to persevere when I am discouraged or frustrated, and simply contributes joy to our life together in so many ways. She has seen the importance of this book from the beginning, and has continued to support and encourage me as I worked on it.

> An excellent wife who can find?
>> She is far more precious than jewels.
> The heart of her husband trusts in her,
>> and he will have no lack of gain.
> She does him good, and not harm,
>> all the days of her life. (Prov. 31:10–12)

I am sure that this book, like all merely human books, has mistakes and oversights, and probably some faulty arguments as well. If I knew where they were, I would try to correct them! Therefore, I would be grateful if any interested readers would send me suggestions for changes and corrections. I do not guarantee that I can acknowledge each letter, but I will give consideration to the material in every one, so far as I am able, and will make corrections where I can.

> Oh give thanks to the LORD, for he is good;
>> for his steadfast love endures forever! (Ps. 118:29)

Not to us, O LORD, not to us, but to your name give glory. (Ps. 115:1)

WAYNE GRUDEM

PHOENIX SEMINARY

7901 EAST SHEA BLVD.

SCOTTSDALE, AZ 85260

USA

Great peace have those who love your law;
nothing can make them stumble.

Psalm 119:165

Part **1**

INTRODUCTION

Chapter 1

INTRODUCTION TO CHRISTIAN ETHICS

What is Christian ethics?

Why should Christians study ethics?

How should we study it?

Why should we base our study of ethics on everything the Bible says rather than on a few major ethical principles from Scripture?

A. DEFINITION OF CHRISTIAN ETHICS

1. Definition for This Book. For purposes of this book the following definition of Christian ethics will be used:

> **Christian ethics** is any study that answers the question, "What does the whole Bible teach us about which acts, attitudes, and personal character traits receive God's approval, and which do not?"[1]

This definition indicates that our study of Christian ethics will be God-centered and Bible-centered. This book will attempt, for each ethical topic, to collect and synthesize the teaching of all the relevant Bible passages about that topic and then to apply that teaching wisely to various life situations.

My approach here is similar to the approach I took in my book *Systematic Theology*, in which I defined systematic theology as "Any study that answers the question,

---

[1] This definition of Christian ethics is adapted from John M. Frame, *The Doctrine of the Christian Life: A Theology of Lordship* (Phillipsburg, NJ: P&R, 2008), 10.

'What does the whole Bible teach us today?' about any given topic."[2] But, as I explained there:

> The emphasis of systematic theology is on what God wants us to *believe* and to *know*, while the emphasis in Christian ethics is on what God wants us to *do* and what *attitudes* he wants us to have. . . . Thus theology focuses on ideas while ethics focuses on situations in life. Theology tells us how we should think while ethics tells us how we should live.[3]

This book, then, is about how to live one's life as a Christian today.

This first chapter has several parallels to chapter 1 in my book *Systematic Theology*. This is because my approach is similar: I am asking what the whole Bible says about various topics in both books.

2. Relationship to Other Disciplines. The emphasis of this book will not be on *historical ethics* (a study of how Christians in different periods of history have understood various ethical topics) or *philosophical ethics* (studying ethical topics largely without appeal to the Bible, using the tools and methods of philosophical reasoning and analyzing what can be known about moral right and wrong from observing the world).

These two subjects, which are worthwhile for Christians to pursue, are sometimes also included in a broader definition of the term *Christian ethics*. In fact, some consideration of historical and philosophical matters will be found at points throughout this book. This is because the study of history informs us of the insights gained and the mistakes made previously by others in understanding ethics, especially in the light of Scripture. And the study of philosophy helps us understand theories of moral right and wrong that are common in our culture and have been common in other cultures throughout history, and often helps us reason carefully about difficult ethical situations. But these two areas of study are not the focus of this volume, which emphasizes interacting directly with the biblical text in order to understand what the Bible itself teaches us about various ethical topics. Even though historical and philosophical studies do contribute to our understanding of ethical questions, my conviction (which I will explain in chap. 3) is that only Scripture has the final authority to define which actions, attitudes, and personal character traits receive God's approval and which

---

[2] Wayne Grudem, *Systematic Theology: An Introduction to Biblical Doctrine* (Leicester, UK: Inter-Varsity, and Grand Rapids, MI: Zondervan, 1994), 21.

[3] Ibid., 26. In that same book, I defined Christian ethics with different wording: "Christian ethics is any study that answers the question, 'What does God require us to do and what attitudes does he require us to have today?' with regard to any given situation." Ibid. My new definition in this book shifts the emphasis from what God *requires* to what he *approves*, because there are countless specific actions in life (such as enjoying a beautiful sunset or spontaneously singing a hymn of praise) that God does not actually require of us at that moment, but which he certainly approves. I also added personal character traits (sometimes called virtues) to the definition after some conversations with David Horner of Talbot School of Theology, in which he called my attention to the frequent New Testament emphasis on the importance of Christian virtues (see chap. 4).

ones do not, and therefore it is appropriate to spend significant time analyzing the teaching of Scripture itself.

My emphasis in this book is also different from a third approach that I will call *theological ethics*. Rather than seeking to understand and apply what the *whole Bible* teaches us about how to live (which is my approach), theological ethics begins with *a few major Christian doctrines* and then reasons from those doctrines to ethical conclusions. For example, Oliver O'Donovan starts with the doctrine of the resurrection of Christ and reasons from it to several significant ethical conclusions.[4] Another example is Richard B. Hays, who starts with the New Testament doctrines of community, cross, and new creation, and then reasons to ethical conclusions.[5] I agree that the doctrines they use as starting points are clearly emphasized in the New Testament, but rather than limiting our study to what can be deduced from those doctrines, in this book I will attempt to take into account the teachings of the whole Bible on each ethical topic—and that will include taking into account biblical passages that contain ethical teachings that could not be directly derived from those important doctrines.

While I agree that a study of the ethical implications of various Christian doctrines can and does bring beneficial insights into our ethical responsibilities, my concern is that the results of such studies are necessarily more limited in scope, more tentative, and more subject to bias in favor of the personal ethical conclusions of the practitioner, because they do not work on the basis of the richness of all the biblical data or face the constraints of having to be subject to every relevant passage rather than just those passages clearly related to the chosen themes.

Christian ethics, as I have defined my task here, also differs from *Old Testament ethics*[6] and *New Testament ethics*.[7] These two disciplines emphasize careful study of various ethical themes in the Old Testament or in the New Testament, but place less emphasis on attempting to draw together the teachings of the *whole Bible* on various topics as they apply to Christians today. At various points, I will make use of the careful work that has been done by specialists in Old Testament ethics or New Testament ethics, and I will then attempt to use that material to draw conclusions about what the whole Bible says to us today about various topics.

---

[4] See Oliver O'Donovan's widely acclaimed book *Resurrection and Moral Order: An Outline for Evangelical Ethics*, 2nd ed. (Leicester, UK: Apollos, and Grand Rapids, MI: Eerdmans, 1994), for this approach.

[5] See the widely influential book by Richard B. Hays, *The Moral Vision of the New Testament: Community, Cross, New Creation: A Contemporary Introduction to New Testament Ethics* (New York: HarperSanFrancisco, 1996). Hays's book appeals to far more biblical texts, especially New Testament texts, than O'Donovan's, while O'Donovan's method of argument is more distinctly philosophical. But for both authors the starting point is not the entire Bible viewed as a noncontradictory unity, but certain major theological themes drawn from the Bible.

[6] See, for example, Walter C. Kaiser Jr., *Toward Old Testament Ethics* (Grand Rapids, MI: Zondervan, 1983); Christopher J. H. Wright, *Old Testament Ethics for the People of God* (Downers Grove, IL: InterVarsity Press, 2004); Gordon J. Wenham, *Story as Torah: Reading Old Testament Narrative Ethically* (Grand Rapids, MI: Baker, 2000); Gordon J. Wenham, *Psalms as Torah: Reading Biblical Song Ethically* (Grand Rapids, MI: Baker, 2012).

[7] See, for example, Thomas R. Schreiner, *40 Questions about Christians and Biblical Law* (Grand Rapids, MI: Kregel, 2010); Frank Thielman, *The Law and the New Testament: The Question of Continuity*, Companions to the New Testament (New York: Herder & Herder, 1999); Frank Thielman, *Paul and the Law: A Contextual Approach* (Downers Grove, IL: InterVarsity Press, 1994).

3. Major Categories for Ethical Study. This book is organized into seven broad areas that cover seven areas of ethical decisions. Although I do not think that the old covenant is morally binding on us today (because we are now under the new covenant; see chap. 8), we still need to use some kind of system to organize the study of ethical topics, and I find that the Ten Commandments provide a helpful structure for such a study. In using this structure, I am following in a long line of Christian writers on ethics who have done so.[8] The broad categories that I employ follow the structure of the Ten Commandments (Ex. 20:1–17) in the following way:[9]

Part 1: Introduction
Part 2: Protecting God's Honor
    Commandment 1: "You shall have no other gods before me."
    Commandment 2: "You shall not make for yourself a carved image."
    Commandment 3: "You shall not take the name of the LORD your God
        in vain."
    Commandment 9: "You shall not bear false witness."
    Commandment 4: "Remember the Sabbath day."
Part 3: Protecting Human Authority
    Commandment 5: "Honor your father and your mother."
Part 4: Protecting Human Life
    Commandment 6: "You shall not murder."
Part 5: Protecting Marriage
    Commandment 7: "You shall not commit adultery."
Part 6: Protecting Property
    Commandment 8: "You shall not steal."
Part 7: Protecting Purity of Heart
    Commandment 10: "You shall not covet."

B. ETHICAL SYSTEMS: SECULAR AND CHRISTIAN

Because my goal in this book is *to show what the whole Bible teaches Christians* about how to live a life that is pleasing to God, I will not focus much attention on secular theories of ethics, for secular ethical systems do not claim to be subject to the moral

---

[8] Others who structure their treatment of Christian ethics after the pattern of the Ten Commandments include John Calvin, *Institutes of the Christian Religion*, ed. John T. McNeill, trans. Ford Lewis Battles, Library of Christian Classics, vols. 20–21 (Philadelphia: Westminster, 1960; based on 1559 edition), 2.8 (367–423); WLC (1647), Questions 98–148; Charles Hodge, *Systematic Theology*, 3 vols. (1871–1873; repr., Grand Rapids, MI: Eerdmans, 1970), 3:259–465; Frame, *The Doctrine of the Christian Life*; David W. Jones, *An Introduction to Biblical Ethics*, B&H Studies in Christian Ethics (Nashville: B&H, 2013); and Robertson McQuilkin and Paul Copan, *An Introduction to Biblical Ethics: Walking in the Way of Wisdom*, 3rd ed. (Downers Grove, IL: InterVarsity Press, 2014).

[9] See chap. 8, p. 255, for a discussion of the structure and numbering of the Ten Commandments.

authority of the Bible. However, it is useful here to give a brief overview of secular ethical systems. I have adapted and condensed the following overview from the clear discussion by Scott B. Rae in his book *Moral Choices: An Introduction to Ethics*.[10]

1. Deontological Systems. The word *deontological* is based on the Greek verb *dei*, used in the sense "it is necessary, it should be done."[11] Deontological systems are ethical systems based on *rules* for right and wrong, what ought to be done and ought not to be done.

Deontological systems can be secular (if the rules are based only on human reason and intuition) or Christian (if the rules come from God's Word, the Bible). All Christian ethical systems take God's commands in the Bible as rules that define right and wrong human conduct, and therefore all Christian ethical systems are deontological.

2. Teleological Systems. The word *teleological* is based on the Greek noun *telos*, meaning "end, goal, outcome."[12] Teleological systems are ethical systems based on seeking the best *results* for an action.

The most common secular teleological theory is *utilitarianism*, which involves seeking the greatest good for the greatest number of people. Most modern arguments about various political issues are based on utilitarian considerations.

Another secular teleological theory is *ethical egoism*, which involves seeking whatever is best for yourself personally, a position that is clearly contrary to Jesus's teaching, "You shall love your neighbor as yourself" (Matt. 22:39). The twentieth-century writer Ayn Rand promoted ethical egoism.

In contrast to secular teleological systems, a Christian ethical system should have a God-centered teleological aspect to it, because the Bible tells us that the result we should seek is the glory of God: "So, whether you eat or drink, or whatever you do, do all to the glory of God (1 Cor. 10:31).

3. Relativism. Ethical relativism is the belief that there is no absolute right and wrong, and so ethical decisions should be based on what is commonly accepted in each person's culture (*cultural relativism*) or on each individual's personal preferences (*individual relativism*). In the area of sexual ethics, the dominant view in today's popular culture (television, movies, music, literature, higher education) is individual relativism ("What's right for you is right for you, and what's right for me is right for me.")

A particular kind of ethical relativism is called *ethical emotivism*. This is the view that there is no such thing as right and wrong, but when people claim that something

---

[10] Scott B. Rae, *Moral Choices: An Introduction to Ethics*, 3rd ed. (Grand Rapids, MI: Zondervan, 2009), 15–18; 63–103. Rae includes a substantial critique of the secular versions of each of these ethical systems. See also John S. Feinberg and Paul D. Feinberg, *Ethics for a Brave New World*, 2nd ed. (Wheaton, IL: Crossway, 2010), 28–40; Frame, *The Doctrine of the Christian Life*, 41–125; and Arthur F. Holmes, *Ethics: Approaching Moral Decisions*, Contours of Christian Philosophy, 2nd ed. (Downers Grove, IL: InterVarsity Press, 2007).

[11] BDAG, 213–214.

[12] BDAG, 998, meaning 3.

is morally right or morally wrong, they are merely saying that they like one thing and do not like the other thing. They're just expressing their emotions with ethical language.

Another view that is similar to ethical relativism is called *antinomianism*. The word *antinomian* is based on the Greek prefix *anti-* (meaning "against") and the noun *nomos* (meaning "law").[13] An antinomian would say that we are not subject to any moral laws. Some of Paul's opponents were apparently antinomian and were teaching, "Why not do evil that good may come?" (Rom. 3:8).

One particular type of relativism that has gained much influence is called *situation ethics*. This is the view that there are no absolutely right or wrong actions, but a person should always do the most loving thing based on the facts in each new situation. This view was made popular by the 1966 book *Situation Ethics*[14] by Joseph Fletcher, an Episcopal priest (later an atheist) and ethics professor at Harvard Divinity School and the University of Virginia.[15]

Because the Bible does teach that there is absolute right and wrong, Christian ethics cannot accept ethical relativism. However, as we will see later, careful Christian decision-making will always take into account the factual details about the specific situation under consideration (see chap. 6).

4. Virtue Ethics. Theories of virtue ethics emphasize not whether specific actions are right or wrong, but the moral character of the individual. In virtue ethics, the primary concern is whether you are a virtuous person. In political elections, questions of a candidate's character are often important, and in those cases some emphasis on virtue ethics plays an important role.

A Christian ethical system should emphasize virtue ethics because the Bible teaches that we should seek to develop a Christlike character: Paul says that God predestined us "to be conformed to the image of his Son" (Rom. 8:29), and he also says, "Be imitators of me, as I am of Christ" (1 Cor. 11:1). Peter, in fact, uses the common Greek word for "virtue" (*aretē*, meaning "virtue, moral excellence") when he tells Christians to "make every effort to supplement your faith with *virtue*" (2 Pet. 1:5). For this reason, I include a long list of Christlike character traits in the discussion of the goal of Christian ethics in chapter 4.

5. Conclusion. A system of Christian ethics based on the Bible does not fit neatly into any one of these categories alone. Rather, if our ethical system is derived from the Bible,

---

[13] BDAG, 677, meaning 2.

[14] Joseph Fletcher, *Situation Ethics: The New Morality* (Philadelphia: Westminster Press, 1966).

[15] I have categorized Fletcher's view as an example of *ethical relativism* because he denies that there are any absolutely right or wrong actions, and even murder, adultery, stealing, or lying might be the most loving thing to do in certain situations. On the other hand, Fletcher's position could also be viewed as an example of *teleological* ethics, because his view holds that the most loving thing to do in each situation is what brings the greatest good for the greatest number of people—and therefore he favors seeking the best results from our actions.

it will be *deontological* (it will define right and wrong based on the rules God gives in Scripture) and also *teleological* (it will seek a good result, namely, doing all for the glory of God), and it will also include a component of *virtue ethics* (it will seek to develop Christlike character in each person).

A Christian approach to ethics will also exercise caution about adopting conclusions from the secular versions of these ethical systems, because all secular systems assume that ethical principles must be developed by human beings using only human observation, reasoning, and intuition, whereas a Christian approach believes that the Bible's ethical teachings are not merely the result of human thinking but have been revealed by God himself.

However, a Christian ethical system will not adopt *moral relativism*, for the Bible does teach that there is absolute right and wrong as defined by God himself.

C. WHY SHOULD CHRISTIANS STUDY ETHICS?

Why should Christians study Christian ethics? That is, why should we engage in the process of collecting and summarizing the teachings of many individual Bible passages on particular ethical questions? Why is it not sufficient simply to continue reading the Bible regularly every day of our lives?

1. The Basic Reason. In answering these questions, we must be careful not to propose a reason to study Christian ethics that implies that we can somehow "improve" on the Bible by doing a better job of organizing its ethical teachings or explaining them in a better way than the Bible itself has done. If we do this, we may be implicitly denying the clarity or sufficiency of Scripture (see chap. 2).

The basic reason that we should study ethics is to better know God's will for us. The New Testament tells us in several places that we should live in obedience to God's will. For example, Jesus taught that his followers should keep his commandments:

> Go therefore and make disciples of all nations, baptizing them in the name of the Father and of the Son and of the Holy Spirit, *teaching them to observe all that I have commanded you.* (Matt. 28:19–20)

> If you love me, you will *keep my commandments.* (John 14:15)

> If you *keep my commandments,* you will abide in my love, just as I have kept my Father's commandments and abide in his love. (John 15:10; see also Rom. 13:9; 1 Cor. 7:19; 1 John 2:3–4; 3:22, 24; 5:2–3; Rev. 12:17; 14:12)

But in order to keep Jesus's commandments, we have to know what they are and understand how they apply to us today, including their Old Testament background and their further explanation in the New Testament Epistles.[16] That is the study of Christian ethics.

The New Testament Epistles also give instructions to readers that sound very much like calls to study ethics:

> Do not be conformed to this world, but be transformed by the renewal of your mind, that by testing *you may discern what is the will of God*, what is good and acceptable and perfect. (Rom. 12:2)

> *Try to discern what is pleasing to the Lord.* (Eph. 5:10)

> And it is my prayer that your love may abound more and more, *with knowledge and all discernment*, so that you may *approve what is excellent*, and so be pure and blameless for the day of Christ, filled with the fruit of righteousness that comes through Jesus Christ, to the glory and praise of God. (Phil. 1:9–11)

> We have not ceased to pray for you, asking that you may be *filled with the knowledge of his will in all spiritual wisdom and understanding*, so as to walk in a manner worthy of the Lord, fully pleasing to him, bearing fruit in every good work and increasing in the knowledge of God. (Col. 1:9–10)

> For this very reason, make every effort to supplement your faith with *virtue, and virtue with knowledge.* (2 Pet. 1:5)

> For this is the love of God, that we *keep his commandments.* And his commandments are not burdensome. (1 John 5:3)

2. The Benefits That Come from Studying Christian Ethics. Someone might object at this point that, yes, Jesus and the New Testament writers tell us to learn and keep God's commandments, but why does that have to be done in this way, by collecting and study-

---

[16] What is included in teaching "all" that Jesus commanded? In a narrow sense, to teach all that Jesus commanded is simply to teach the content of the oral teaching of Jesus that is recorded in the four Gospels.

However, in a broader sense, "all that Jesus commanded" includes the interpretation and application of his life and teachings, because the first verse of the book of Acts implies that it contains a narrative of what Jesus *continued* to do and teach through the apostles after his resurrection. "All that Jesus commanded" can also include the Epistles, since they were written under the supervision of the Holy Spirit and were also considered to be a "command of the Lord" (1 Cor. 14:37; see also John 14:26; 16:13; 1 Thess. 4:15; 2 Pet. 3:2; Rev. 1:1–3). Thus, in a larger sense, "all that Jesus commanded" includes all of the New Testament.

Furthermore, when we consider that the New Testament writings endorse Jesus's absolute confidence in the authority and reliability of the Old Testament Scriptures as God's words (see chap. 3), and when we realize that the New Testament Epistles also endorse this view of the Old Testament as the absolutely authoritative words of God, then it becomes evident that we cannot teach "all that Jesus commanded" without including all of the Old Testament (rightly understood in the various ways in which it applies to the new covenant age in the history of redemption) as well. In this broad sense, "all that Jesus commanded" includes the whole Bible when it is rightly understood and applied to the lives of believers living in the New Testament age (also called the new covenant age; see chaps. 3 and 8 below).

ing groups of Bible texts that bear on particular topics? Why (someone might object) can I not learn what God's will is, and learn about obeying Jesus's commandments, simply by reading through the Bible over and over? Why read a book on ethics or take a specific class in Christian ethics?

In reply, I agree that there is great benefit in regular Bible reading, especially in reading completely through the entire Bible again and again. By doing this, many Christians throughout history have led wonderful lives that truly brought glory to God, showed love to other people, demonstrated high standards of personal integrity, and resulted in a spiritual harvest of much fruit for the kingdom of God.

However, there are significant benefits that come from studying ethical topics in a focused way *in addition to* reading the Bible straight through or just studying individual passages or books.

a. Gaining a More Accurate Understanding of Ethics: Every Christian reading this book already has a set of ethical convictions, opinions, and ideas about what is morally right and wrong. These ethical beliefs have come from various sources—from an internal moral instinct (which God gives to every human being: Rom. 1:32; 2:14–16), family training, schools, traditions, and cultural beliefs. Christians also have formed ethical beliefs from their own Bible reading, from listening to sermons, and from conversations with friends.

But my hope is that this book will help Christians gain more accuracy in their ethical views, in three ways:

(1) Changing from Instinctive to Informed Ethical Convictions: I hope that Christians who already have ethical views that are consistent with Scripture will move from having *instinctive convictions* to having *well-informed convictions*. For example, a person reading chapter 21 might move from an instinctive conviction that abortion is morally wrong to a well-informed conviction, including knowledge of how various Bible passages and medical facts support that conviction. Such a reader would also gain a better understanding of some broader matters, such as how to apply different Scripture passages to various medical situations, and whether there are any situations to which the passages might not apply.

(2) Changing from Imprecise to Accurate Ethical Convictions: I hope that Christians who have a somewhat vague and *imprecise understanding* of an issue (for example, divorce and remarriage, covered in chap. 32) will come to a more *accurate* and well-defined understanding of how the teachings of the Bible apply to that issue (for example, to various specific marriage, divorce, and remarriage situations).

(3) Changing from Unbiblical to Biblical Ethical Convictions: I hope that Christians who have an *incorrect understanding* of the Bible's moral standards (as I will argue many Christians do with respect to lying and telling the truth, discussed in chap. 12) will be persuaded to change their views and come to a moral conviction that is more faithful to Scripture.

Because of the large number of topics covered in a study of ethics and because of the great detail with which these topics are analyzed, it is inevitable that someone studying an ethics text or taking a course in ethics for the first time will have many personal beliefs challenged or modified, refined or enriched. It is of utmost importance, therefore, that each person beginning such a course firmly resolve in his or her mind to abandon as false any idea that is found to be clearly contradicted by the teaching of Scripture. But it is also important for each person to resolve not to believe any ethical position simply because this book or some other book or teacher says that it is true, unless the book or the instructor can convince the student from the text of Scripture itself. It is Scripture alone, not "conservative evangelical tradition" or the views of respected theologians or any other human authorities, that must function as the normative authority for our understanding of what God approves.

b. Using Our Time Wisely: Because we have limited lifetimes here on earth, we simply do not have enough time to carry out a detailed study of an important ethical topic every time a question arises. For example, if someone wonders what the whole Bible teaches about marriage and divorce, I could tell him, "Just keep reading your Bible and you'll find out." But if this questioner begins reading at Genesis 1:1, it will be a long time before he finds the passages that address divorce in Matthew 19 and 1 Corinthians 7, and by that time he will have many questions about other topics: animal sacrifices, capital punishment, wealth and poverty, and so forth.

Because of these time limitations, if we are to learn what the whole Bible teaches about ethical topics, we need to make use of the work of others who have searched through Scripture and proposed summaries on these various topics. Armed with such a study, I could send the person who asked me about divorce and remarriage to a list of about five key passages and one or two chapters in books that discuss that topic, and I could briefly summarize the common arguments for the two or three major positions. A basic overview and summary of that question can be read in an evening.[17]

c. Preparing to Face Real-Life Temptations: Training in sound principles of biblical ethics is best done before we are suddenly faced with a temptation and have to make a decision quickly (for example, a temptation to accept a bribe or tell a lie). In the Bible, Joseph had received some prior training in God's moral standards that gave him the resolve to flee immediately out of the house when Potiphar's wife grabbed his garment and said, "Lie with me" (Gen. 39:12). Jesus himself had "increased in wisdom" (Luke

---

[17] For example, see "Divorce and Remarriage" in the *ESV Study Bible* (Wheaton, IL: Crossway, 2008), 2545–47. (I was the primary author of this article.) Similar brief overviews of 12 additional ethical topics are found on pp. 2535–60.

2:52) throughout his childhood and had "learned obedience" (Heb. 5:8) during his first 30 years before he faced the temptations of Satan in the wilderness (Luke 4:1–13). Studying ethics in advance equips us to make wise ethical decisions when new situations suddenly confront us.

d. Gaining a Better Ability to Make Wise Ethical Decisions about New Matters Later: Studying Christian ethics helps us to *make better decisions later* on new questions of ethics that arise. We cannot know what new ethical controversies will develop in the churches in which we will live and minister 10, 20, or 30 years from now, if the Lord does not return before then. These new ethical controversies will sometimes include questions that no one has examined very extensively before. Christians will be asking, "What does the whole Bible say about this subject?"

Such new ethical questions seem to occur in every generation. For example, previous generations did not have to face questions about human cloning, embryonic stem cell research, surrogate motherhood, in vitro fertilization, methods of birth control, Internet privacy rights, and global warming. And questions about the roles of husbands and wives in marriage, and the roles of men and women in the church, have been far more controversial since the 1960s than at any previous time in history.

Whatever new ethical controversies arise in future years, those who have learned Christian ethics well (and also have learned systematic theology) will be much better able to address them. The reason for this is that everything that the Bible says is somehow related to everything else the Bible says (for it all fits together in a consistent way, at least within God's own understanding of reality, and in the nature of God and creation as they really are). Thus, the new questions will be related to much that has already been learned from Scripture. The more thoroughly we have learned that earlier material, the better able we will be to deal with new questions.

A helpful analogy at this point is that of a jigsaw puzzle.[18] If the puzzle represents what the whole Bible teaches us about every ethical question, then a course in Christian ethics represents filling in the border and several large sections of the puzzle. But we will never know everything that the Bible teaches about everything, so our jigsaw puzzle will have many gaps, many pieces that remain to be put in. Solving a new real-life problem is analogous to filling in another section of the jigsaw puzzle: the more pieces one has in place correctly to begin with, the easier it is to fit new pieces in, and the less apt one is to make mistakes.

In this book the goal is to enable Christians to put into their "ethical jigsaw puzzle" as many pieces with as much accuracy as possible, and then to encourage them to go on putting in more and more correct pieces for the rest of their lives. The teachings found in this book will act as guidelines to help in the future as Christians continue to fill in other areas that pertain to all aspects of obedience to God in all aspects of life.

---

[18] I also used the analogy of a jigsaw puzzle for studying systematic theology; see Grudem, *Systematic Theology*, 29.

e. Growing toward Christian Maturity and Personal Holiness: There is no doubt in the minds of the New Testament authors that growing in our knowledge of biblical ethics, coupled with heartfelt obedience to what we are learning, is a major part of growing to maturity in our Christian faith.

The author of Hebrews explains that mature Christians are those who have many years of practice in learning and obeying sound ethical teachings: "But solid food is for *the mature,* for those who have their powers of discernment *trained by constant practice to distinguish good from evil*" (Heb. 5:14).

Paul tells believers that he wants them to grow in their ethical discernment and in their obedience:

> As you received from us *how you ought to walk and to please God,* just as you are doing, that you *do so more and more.* . . . For this is the will of God, your sanctification. (1 Thess. 4:1–3)

A major part of growing in Christian maturity is growing in personal holiness of life, a New Testament emphasis that is too seldom heard in many churches today. The author of Hebrews tells Christians to "*strive for* peace with everyone, and for the *holiness* without which no one will see the Lord" (Heb. 12:14).

Other passages also emphasize the need for Christians to grow in holiness of life:

> Let us cleanse ourselves from every defilement of body and spirit, *bringing holiness to completion* in the fear of God. (2 Cor. 7:1)

> Put on the new self, created after the likeness of God in true righteousness and *holiness*. (Eph. 4:24)

> He disciplines us for our good, *that we may share his holiness.* (Heb. 12:10)

> Since all these things are thus to be dissolved, what sort of people ought you to be *in lives of holiness* and godliness. (2 Pet. 3:11)

The more we know about God and what he asks of his children, the better we will pray for his help and wisdom, and the more readily we will obey him. Studying Christian ethics rightly will make us more mature Christians and will result in greater personal holiness in our lives. If it does not do this, we are not studying it in the way God intends.

f. Evangelism: When Christians live in the midst of secular cultures that excuse and even glorify all kinds of sin, it is easy for them to feel embarrassed about mentioning Christian ethical standards to unbelievers and to feel reluctant to preach about biblical moral standards in church, lest non-Christians who are visiting become offended.

But that is not the perspective of the Bible. God's moral standards are regularly viewed as a wonderful means of evangelism. Even in the time of the old covenant, Moses told the people of Israel that the nations around them would hear of God's wise laws and would be amazed:

> See, I have taught you statutes and rules, as the LORD my God commanded me, that you should do them in the land that you are entering to take possession of it. Keep them and do them, for *that will be your wisdom and your understanding in the sight of the peoples, who, when they hear all these statutes, will say, "Surely this great nation is a wise and understanding people."* For what great nation is there that has a god so near to it as the LORD our God is to us, whenever we call upon him? And *what great nation is there, that has statutes and rules so righteous as all this law* that I set before you today? (Deut. 4:5–8)

In the New Testament, the apostles often included a call to repent of sins in their evangelistic messages, as Paul did in his presentation to Greek philosophers in Athens:

> The times of ignorance God overlooked, but now *he commands all people everywhere to repent*, because he has fixed a day on which he will judge the world in righteousness by a man whom he has appointed; and of this he has given assurance to all by raising him from the dead. (Acts 17:30–31)[19]

Peter knew that his hearers were often surrounded by hostile unbelievers who mocked and persecuted them, but he reminded them that their good conduct was a testimony that God would use to bring some of them to salvation (that is the most likely sense of "glorify God on the day of visitation"):[20]

> Beloved, I urge you as sojourners and exiles to abstain from the passions of the flesh, which wage war against your soul. *Keep your conduct among the Gentiles honorable*, so that when they speak against you as evildoers, they may see your good deeds and *glorify God on the day of visitation.* (1 Pet. 2:11–12)

Proclamation of God's moral standards to unbelievers is an essential component of evangelism for two reasons: (1) Unless they know God's moral standards, unbelievers will not be convicted that they have sinned against those standards, and therefore they will not repent of their sins and will not be saved. Preaching about God's moral standards leads unbelievers to be convicted of their sins, repent of their sins, and call out to Christ for forgiveness (see John 16:8 on the Holy Spirit's role in this). (2) Unbelievers still have a conscience that, by God's common grace, often bears witness that the moral

---

[19] See also Paul's conversation with Felix in Acts 24:24–25 and Paul's long list of specific sins in his summary of the gospel message in Rom. 1:18–3:20. I discuss the New Testament emphasis on a call for repentance from sin in evangelistic preaching in *"Free Grace" Theology: 5 Ways It Diminishes the Gospel* (Wheaton, IL: Crossway, 2016), 41–48.

[20] See Wayne Grudem, *The First Epistle of Peter: An Introduction and Commentary*, TNTC (Leicester, UK: Inter-Varsity, and Grand Rapids, MI: Eerdmans, 1988), 116–17.

standards that they are mocking and violating are, in fact, *good and true moral standards* to which they will be held accountable (see Rom. 1:32; 2:14–15).

Therefore, Christians should not be embarrassed about the Bible but should joyfully teach and graciously advocate its moral teachings as good—in fact, *wonderful*—standards that come from God himself.

D. MAJOR AND MINOR ETHICAL ISSUES

It is appropriate to ask what the difference is between a "major ethical issue" and a "minor ethical issue." I have found the following guideline useful:

> A major ethical issue is one that has a wide and long-lasting effect on our lives and the lives of others, and a minor ethical issue is one that has little effect on our lives and the lives of others.

According to this guideline, major ethical issues include such matters as marriage and divorce, homosexuality, abortion, and stewardship of money. By contrast, one's views on cremation, vegetarianism, and how parents speak to their children about Santa Claus seem to me to be minor issues.

Of course, individual issues will fall along a spectrum from major to minor, and Christian churches and other organizations often have to make wise judgment calls about which issues they will count significant enough to be used as a basis for membership or leadership roles. The importance of an issue might even vary according to the historical circumstances and needs of the church at any given time. Christians will need to ask God to give them mature wisdom and sound judgment as they try to determine to what extent an ethical issue should be considered "major" in their particular circumstances.

E. SOME OBJECTIONS TO THIS KIND OF STUDY OF CHRISTIAN ETHICS

1. Objection: "The Moral Teachings of the Bible are Inconsistent and Contradictory." Some scholars dismiss as simplistic or even naive any approach that claims that the teachings of the Bible can be understood in such a way that they do not contradict one another. For example, in a widely used textbook for Christian ethics, Robin Gill says:

> Once the literal infallibility of every verse in the Bible is rejected, and contradictions and factual and moral errors, anachronisms and inconsistencies are claimed, the exponent of Christian ethics can no longer adequately base moral claims on particular proof-texts in the manner of Augustine, Luther, and, even at times, Aquinas.[21]

---

[21] Robin Gill, *A Textbook of Christian Ethics*, 4th ed. (London: Bloomsbury T&T Clark, 2014), 10–11.

Four points can be made in response to this argument:

1. The objection is usually based on a different view of the nature of the Bible, namely, a nonevangelical or theologically "liberal" view that the writings of the Bible are *merely human words* that bear witness to an experience of God, and they are not also the very words of God. If they are merely human writings, then inconsistencies and contradictions are to be expected, as is the case among all other human writings from various authors and cultures.

But the claims of the Bible itself oppose this view. It insists that "*all Scripture* is breathed out by God and profitable for teaching, for reproof, for correction, and for training in righteousness" (2 Tim. 3:16), and it claims that the words of the Lord are internally consistent, for "the *sum* of your word is truth, and every one of your righteous rules endures forever" (Ps. 119:160).[22] From that perspective, we are right to begin with the expectation that God would not speak to us in inconsistent or contradictory ways. When the Bible's statements are combined, the result, the "sum," is "truth."

In personal conversation, it is important to ask the person making this objection to give specific examples to show exactly what "contradictions" and "moral and factual errors" he is referring to, or if he even has any specific ones in mind. This objection is sometimes made by those who—perhaps unconsciously—have adopted from modern Western culture a skeptical view of the possibility of finding universally true conclusions about *anything*, even about God and his moral standards in the Bible.

This type of skepticism regarding theological truth is especially common in the modern university world, where "ethics"—if it is studied at all—is not considered from the perspective of seeking to understand and submit to Scripture, but only from the perspectives of different theories of *philosophical ethics* and *historical ethics* (including perhaps a historical study of the various ideas that were believed by Christians such as Augustine and Martin Luther in previous generations). These fields of study (which have their own validity) can be comfortably carried out by taking into account only *human* writings and *human* reason, operating without a belief in a divinely authoritative Bible as our source for ethical standards.

But in this kind of intellectual climate in a secular university the study of "Christian ethics" as defined in this chapter would be considered impossible, because the Bible would be assumed to be merely the work of many *human authors* who wrote out of diverse cultures over the course of more than a thousand years. Therefore, trying to find "what the whole Bible teaches" about any ethical topic would be thought nearly as hopeless as trying to find "what all philosophers teach" or "what all politicians think" about some question. The answer in all cases would be assumed to be not one view but many diverse and often conflicting views.

Such a skeptical viewpoint from a secular worldview must be rejected by evangelicals

---

[22] The Hebrew word translated "sum" in Ps. 119:160 is *ro'sh*, which here takes the meaning "sum" (BDB, 911, meaning 7), indicating the result when things are added together or combined, as in the expression, "Take a *census* of [KJV, "take the *sum* of"] all the congregation of the people of Israel" (Num. 1:2).

who see Scripture as the product of human *and* divine authorship, and therefore as a collection of writings that teach noncontradictory truths about God and the kind of conduct that he approves for the human beings he created.

2. A belief in the internal consistency of Scripture can hardly be thought to be simplistic or naive, for that was exactly the belief of the greatest thinkers in the history of the Christian church for the first 18 centuries (as Gill's reference to Augustine, Luther, and Aquinas indicates). Even following the advent of modern biblical criticism in the early 1800s, thousands of competent evangelical scholars up to the present day have held this view.

3. The claim that Scripture is internally inconsistent is too often only briefly asserted or simply assumed in discussions, with little detailed analysis. Yes, there are varying emphases that at first seem to create tensions between different parts of Scripture, such as between James and Paul on faith and works, or between Jesus's command to turn the other cheek (Matt. 5:39) and Paul's teaching that the government official is to "bear the sword" (Rom. 13:4), but a simple rehearsal of those tensions does not constitute a persuasive argument showing that they cannot be resolved. In fact, much of the remainder of this book is concerned with seeking honest and reasonable resolutions to such tensions between passages that inform specific ethical issues.

4. In God's mind, his moral standards are all consistent with one another. Therefore, if we have accurately understood the teachings of God in Scripture, we should expect our conclusions to "fit together" and be mutually consistent. Internal consistency, then, is an argument for, not against, any individual results of Christian ethics.

2. Objection: "We Should Base the Study of Ethics on the Broad Principles of Scripture, Not on All the Specific Rules." A second objection to the kind of approach I take in this book comes from authors such as David P. Gushee and Glen H. Stassen, who use a scheme of four levels of biblical teachings:

1. Particular judgments
2. Rules
3. Principles
4. Basic convictions[23]

According to Gushee and Stassen, (1) the *particular judgments* tell what a specific person should do in a specific situation, such as, "Andrew should carry this Roman soldier's pack two miles." (2) The *rules* tell what to do in all such situations, such as, "And if anyone forces you to go one mile, go with him two miles" (Matt. 5:41, assuming a legal background in which Roman soldiers could compel citizens to carry burdens in this way). Rules give the reasons that support the particular judgments. (3) The

---

[23] David P. Gushee and Glen H. Stassen, *Kingdom Ethics: Following Jesus in Contemporary Context*, 2nd ed. (Grand Rapids, MI: Eerdmans, 2016), 65–85; see summary graph on 70.

principles are more general and do not tell us what to do in specific situations, but give the reasons that support the rules. The principle that supports "go with him two miles" is "Love your enemies" (v. 44) or perhaps "You shall love your neighbor as yourself" (22:39). (4) The *basic convictions* are beliefs about "God's character, activity, and will, and about our nature as participants in that will."[24] No reasons are needed to support basic convictions, for they are found in God. The basic conviction that supports loving one's enemy is that God "makes his sun rise on the evil and on the good, and sends rain on the just and on the unjust" (Matt. 5:45).

On first impression, those levels seem useful. It is hard to deny that the Bible contains various kinds of more specific directions and more general ethical statements, and these four categories seem to be one helpful way of classifying them.[25] In addition, I think that Gushee and Stassen are right to insist that the *principles* of biblical ethics do not hang on thin air or mere human invention but are grounded in *basic convictions* about the character of God himself.[26]

My objection to Gushee and Stassen, however, is that they claim that sometimes the *rules* of Scripture should be broken, and this can be justified by the broader *principles*. They write:

> Exceptions are considered as a last, not first, resort. An exception is legitimate only if it is grounded in a principle or another rule that Jesus taught or that is found in Scripture.[27]

Gushee and Stassen say that an ethical system that claims that we should always obey all the rules of Scripture is "legalism." They say such an approach "reads the Bible looking for rules" and "sees God primarily as the rule-giver." They also say the reason some people advocate such "legalism" is fear: "Legalists fear that exceptions to rules open the door to disastrous moral relativism and moral subjectivism."[28]

In spite of their objections, I maintain throughout this book that Christians today should obey *all* the rules *and all* the principles of Scripture that rightly apply to us in our specific situations. My belief is not based on a fear of moral relativism (as they say it must be). My conviction comes rather from the belief that the Bible itself claims that

---

[24] Ibid., 69.

[25] Where did Gushee and Stassen get these four levels of moral norms? They tell us, "Our approach to this issue is influenced heavily by philosophical efforts to clarify what people mean when they talk about morality," and they point especially to philosophical ethicists Henry David Aiken and James Gustafson as the source for their understanding of the four levels in Christian ethics. Ibid., 65. My objection is not that these categories derive from philosophical ethics but that the way Gushee and Stassen use this classification to give permission to disobey some of the Bible's "rules" seems foreign to the entire emphasis of Scripture on being completely obedient to all that God commands us.

[26] See their perceptive critique of modern secular ethical theories: "Contemporary philosophical ethics . . . rejects rooting principles in any theological basic conviction. Thus the principles exist, but, in our view, without a satisfactory support system to nourish them." Ibid., 73–74.

[27] Ibid., 72.

[28] Ibid.

all the ethical teachings of Scripture are God's authoritative words to human beings, and our task is to understand them rightly and to learn which ones of them apply to us in our specific situations today.[29] That is what I will attempt to do in this book, because it is not just *some* of Scripture (such as the broad principles and some rules), but "*all* Scripture" that Paul says is profitable for our moral instruction (2 Tim. 3:16).

I do not think that our task as Christian ethics teachers is to say that *sometimes* people are free to disobey *some* of God's specific rules that are addressed to people in *the same or substantially the same situation* that they are in. Saying that we may sometimes disobey makes it far too easy for Christians to stop struggling with difficult questions of how to apply certain scriptural "rules" that are unpopular today and just abandon those rules altogether in favor of some scriptural "principle" that can be found to nullify it.

For example, what about the rule "Whoever spares the rod hates his son, but he who loves him is diligent to discipline him" (Prov. 13:24)? For people who are uncomfortable with spanking disobedient children today, the approach of "obey the principles but not all the rules" would allow them to abandon it by appealing to the broader principle "Fathers, do not provoke your children to anger" (Eph. 6:4).

What about the rule "Wives, submit to your own husbands, as to the Lord" (Eph. 5:22)? If this seems uncomfortable today, then people can abandon it by an appeal to the scriptural principles of equality in the image of God (Gen. 1:27) and the principle that "there is no male and female, for you are all one in Christ Jesus" (Gal. 3:28).

What about the rule that the governmental authority is to use force ("the sword") to punish evil, according to Romans 13:4: "He does not bear the sword in vain. For he is the servant of God, an avenger who carries out God's wrath on the wrongdoer"? Someone who is uncomfortable with such a use of force can abandon the rule by appeal to the principle "You shall love your neighbor as yourself" (Matt. 22:39), or even to another rule, such as "Do not resist the one who is evil. But if anyone slaps you on the right cheek, turn to him the other also" (5:39).

In this way, *any rule in Scripture* could be overcome by a creative interpreter, once the guideline of "obey the principles but not all the rules" is accepted. Scripture is so rich, so full of ethical teaching, that some "principle" could always be claimed to nullify a particular "rule."

But there is no guideline in the New Testament that says we are to follow just the principles, not all the rules. The authors of the New Testament Epistles assume that their readers are under obligation to obey *everything they write*, whether it is a general principle or a specific command. This is the case for a broad principle such as "You shall love your neighbor as yourself" (Rom. 13:9) and it is also the case for specific commands ("rules") such as "Pay . . . taxes to whom taxes are owed" (v. 7) or "Do not get drunk with wine, for that is debauchery" (Eph. 5:18).

At this point, the "broad principle" advocate might respond that there are so many

---

[29] I give a more extensive discussion of the problem of legalism in chap. 4, p. 117.

rules in Scripture that is it impossible to be consistent and obey all of them. I will reply more fully below, in a discussion of whether at times we are forced to choose the "lesser sin,"[30] but at this point two things may be said briefly:

1. Jesus obeyed all the rules and principles that applied to him fully and without exception. This was what frustrated his opponents so greatly: though the Pharisees were highly rule oriented and highly trained in Old Testament law, they could find no occasion when Jesus broke even the slightest of Old Testament rules. They could not answer his challenge, "Which one of you convicts me of sin?" (John 8:46).[31] Therefore, the rules of Scripture do not necessarily conflict.

2. In the rest of this book, I will attempt to explain in detail how all the rules and principles of Scripture can be understood to apply in a consistent way to numerous real-life ethical situations. The objection "This cannot be done," if it is to be persuasive, would have to demonstrate that this book argues incorrectly about the meaning of some passages and some of the rules, and that other books like this through the history of the church have done the same.

3. Objection: "People Who Claim to Base Ethics on the Whole Bible as the Words of God in Reality Use Only a 'Canon within the Canon' to Develop Their Positions." The "canon" of Scripture is an accepted list of all the books that belong in the Bible. The idea of a "canon within the canon" is the claim that some people use a "personal canon"—one's favorite sections of Scripture, such as the teachings of Jesus or the writings of Paul—as the basis for ethical conclusions, rather than using all the books of the Bible (the whole canon).

Robin Gill gives voice to this objection:

> It is difficult for even the most literalistic biblicist not to be operating in practice a "canon within the Canon". That is, it is difficult to treat all parts of the Bible with equal seriousness and attention and not to be biblically selective.[32]

In response, I would say:

1. In this book, I have not (at least not consciously) favored certain passages or parts of the Bible and ignored or minimized others. When treating specific topics, I have made an effort to interact with all the passages that might seem to be in tension with the viewpoint I have advocated. For example, when arguing for the moral goodness of private ownership of property, I have also attempted to treat fairly the "all things in common" passages in Acts (Acts 2:44–45; 4:32–37; see p. 898). When arguing for the moral legitimacy of the police and military power of civil government from Romans

---

[30] See chap. 7.

[31] On several occasions, Jesus broke later rabbinic additions to the Sabbath commandment, and this caused conflict with his Jewish opponents, but he did not break the actual Old Testament Sabbath commandment as understood according to its true meaning and God's original intent (see Mark 2:23–28).

[32] Gill, *A Textbook of Christian Ethics*, 11.

13, I have also treated the "turn the other cheek" passage in the Sermon on the Mount (Matt. 5:39; see p. 431). That does not mean that I have concluded that these passages must remain in irreconcilable tension, for with each issue I propose a solution that views these passages as consistent and complementary. But it does mean that I am not ignoring those other passages by a process of selecting some kind of favorite "canon within the canon." And many other evangelical ethicists have taken an approach similar to mine in their writings.[33]

2. Most of my ethical conclusions in this book are not obscure, marginal viewpoints but are consistent with the positions advocated by the vast majority of recognized evangelical Protestant ethics writers since the Protestant Reformation in the 16th century. All of these authors have implicitly or explicitly expressed an intention to reflect faithfully the testimony of *all* of Scripture, not just certain favorite portions. To object that all of these writers have somehow deceived themselves and unknowingly operated with a "canon within the canon" comes close to saying that it is impossible for any mature Christian teacher ever to interpret the Bible rightly on ethical issues. But that argument suggests that God has not given us a Bible that *any* of his people are able to understand rightly. In other words, such an argument is in the end a denial of the important doctrine of the clarity of Scripture.[34]

3. Some passages of Scripture are more directly and evidently relevant for ethical study than others, and they will of course receive greater emphasis in this book. Just as a book about the Bible's teaching on creation will give much attention to Genesis 1–3, a book about worship will give much attention to the Psalms, and a book about spiritual gifts will give much attention to 1 Corinthians 12–14, so a book about ethics will need to give more attention to passages of Scripture where ethical themes are emphasized, such as the Ten Commandments, Proverbs, the Sermon on the Mount, and several of the Epistles, such as Romans, 1 Corinthians, Ephesians, James, 1 Peter, and 1 John. However, such an emphasis does not show that I am operating with a canon within the canon. It is simply a necessary procedure because of the nature of the subject matter.

F. HOW SHOULD CHRISTIANS STUDY CHRISTIAN ETHICS?

How then should we study Christian ethics? The answers are similar to what I wrote in *Systematic Theology* about how we should study theology, because in both kinds of study we are seeking to learn what the whole Bible says about a particular topic (whether a

---

[33] See, for example, the ethics textbooks in the bibliography to this chapter by authors John Jefferson Davis, John S. Feinberg and Paul D. Feinberg, John M. Frame, Norman L. Geisler, Carl F. H. Henry, David Clyde Jones, Walter C. Kaiser Jr., Robertson McQuilkin and Paul Copan, John Murray, Scott B. Rae, and Cornelius Van Til. Such an approach was also taken by theologians who wrote about ethics in previous generations, such as Richard Baxter, John Calvin, and Charles Hodge.

[34] See chap. 3, p. 90, for a discussion of the clarity of Scripture.

theological or an ethical topic). The Bible itself provides some guidelines as to how we should study its teachings.

1. We Should Study Christian Ethics with Prayer. If studying Christian ethics is simply a certain way of studying the Bible, then the passages in Scripture that talk about the way in which we should study God's Word give us guidance in this task. Just as the psalmist prays in Psalm 119:18, "Open my eyes, that I may behold wondrous things out of your law," so we should pray and seek God's help in understanding his Word. Paul tells us in 1 Corinthians 2:14, "The natural person does not accept the things of the Spirit of God, for they are folly to him, and he is not able to understand them because they are spiritually discerned." Studying ethics is a spiritual activity in which we need the help of the Holy Spirit.

No matter how intelligent a student is, if that student does not continue to pray for God to give him or her an understanding mind and a believing and humble heart, and if the student does not maintain a personal walk with the Lord, then he or she will misunderstand and disbelieve the teachings of Scripture, ethical error will result, and the mind and heart of the student will be changed not for the better but for the worse. Students of Christian ethics should resolve at the beginning to keep their lives free from any conscious disobedience to God or any known sin that would disrupt their relationship with him. They should resolve to maintain their own personal devotional lives with great regularity. They should continually pray for wisdom and understanding of Scripture.

Since it is the Holy Spirit who gives us the ability to understand Scripture rightly, we need to realize that the proper thing to do, particularly when we are unable to understand some passage or some doctrine of Scripture, is to pray for God's help. Often what we need is not more data but more insight into the data we already have available. This insight is given only by the Holy Spirit (cf. 1 Cor. 2:14; Eph. 1:17–19).

2. We Should Study Christian Ethics with Humility. Peter tells us, "Clothe yourselves, all of you, with humility toward one another, for 'God opposes the proud, but gives grace to the humble'" (1 Pet. 5:5). Those who study Christian ethics will learn many things about the teachings of Scripture that are perhaps not known or not known well by other Christians in their churches or by relatives who are older in the Lord than they are. They may also find that they understand things about Scripture that some of their church officers do not understand, and that even their pastor has perhaps forgotten or never learned well.

In all of these situations, it would be easy to adopt an attitude of pride or superiority toward others who have not made such a study. But how ugly it would be if anyone were to use this knowledge of God's Word simply to win arguments, to put down a fellow Christian in conversation, or to make another believer feel insignificant in the Lord's work. James's counsel is good for us at this point: "Let every person be quick to hear, slow to speak, slow to anger, for the anger of man does not produce the righteousness of God" (James 1:19–20). He tells us that one's understanding of Scripture is to be imparted in humility and love:

> Who is wise and understanding among you? By his good conduct let him show his works in the *meekness of wisdom.* . . . But the wisdom from above is first pure, then peaceable, gentle, open to reason, full of mercy and good fruits, impartial and sincere. And a harvest of righteousness is sown in peace by those who make peace. (James 3:13, 17–18)

The need for humility in studying ethics is also emphasized in Psalm 25:

> Good and upright is the Lord;
>> therefore he instructs sinners in the way.
> He leads *the humble* in what is right,
>> and teaches *the humble* his way. (vv. 8–9)

Christian ethics rightly studied will not lead to the knowledge that "puffs up" (1 Cor. 8:1) but to humility and love for others.

3. We Should Study Christian Ethics with Reason. Jesus and the New Testament authors will often quote a passage of Scripture and then draw logical conclusions from it (see, for example, Matt. 22:43–45; John 10:34–36; Rom. 10:10–11; 1 Tim. 5:17–18; and many other passages). They *reason* from Scripture. Their pattern of reasoning tells us that it is not wrong to use human understanding, human logic, and human reason to draw conclusions from the statements of Scripture. Nevertheless, when we reason and draw what we think to be correct logical deductions from Scripture, we sometimes make mistakes. The *deductions* we draw from the statements of Scripture are not equal to the *statements of Scripture* themselves in certainty or authority, for our ability to reason and draw conclusions is not the ultimate standard of truth—only Scripture is.

What then are the limits on our use of our reasoning abilities to draw deductions from the statements of Scripture? The fact that reasoning to conclusions that go beyond the mere statements of Scripture is appropriate and even necessary for studying Scripture, and the fact that Scripture itself is the ultimate standard of truth, combine to indicate to us that *we are free to use our reasoning abilities to draw deductions from any passage of Scripture so long as these deductions do not contradict the clear teaching of some other passage of Scripture.*[35]

For example, we might read Paul's instruction "Let every person be subject to the governing authorities" (Rom. 13:1) and conclude that we have an obligation to obey everything that the government tells us to do. But then we discover several narrative passages in which government authorities commanded God's people to sin against him;

---

[35] This guideline is also adopted from Professor John M. Frame, from whom I learned it when I took classes from him at Westminster Seminary (see preface, p. 28).

however, God's people disobeyed the authorities, and the scriptural narratives view that disobedience with approval: see Exodus 1:15–22 (the Hebrew midwives); Esther 4:16 (Esther going into the king's presence uninvited); Daniel 3 (Shadrach, Meshach, and Abednego refusing to bow to the golden image); Daniel 6 (Daniel praying to God in disobedience to the king's command); Matthew 2:8, 12 (the wise men disobeying King Herod); and Acts 4:18–20; 5:29 (the apostles preaching the gospel). Therefore, we conclude that our first inference was incorrect, and to "be subject" to the government does not mean we must obey a governmental command to sin against God.

This principle (that we should not allow deductions from one passage of Scripture to contradict some other passage of Scripture) puts a safeguard on our use of what we think to be valid logical deductions from Scripture. Our supposedly logical deductions may be erroneous, but Scripture itself cannot be erroneous. When the psalmist says, "The *sum* of your word is truth; and every one of your righteous ordinances endures forever" (Ps. 119:160), he implies that God's words are true not only individually but also when viewed together as a whole. Viewed collectively, their "sum" is also "truth." Ultimately, there is no internal contradiction either in Scripture or in God's own thoughts.

4. We Should Study Christian Ethics with Help from Others. We need to be thankful that God has put teachers in the church ("And God has appointed in the church first apostles, second prophets, third *teachers* ... ," 1 Cor. 12:28). We should allow those with gifts of teaching to help us understand Scripture. This means that we should make use of books on Christian ethics that have been written by some of the teachers whom God has given to the church over the course of its history. It also means that our study of ethics should include talking with other Christians about the things we study. Among those with whom we talk will often be some with gifts of teaching, who can explain biblical truth clearly and help us understand it more easily. In fact, some of the most effective learning in Christian ethics courses in colleges and seminaries occurs outside the classroom in informal conversations among students who are attempting to understand the Bible's ethical teachings for themselves.

5. We Should Study Christian Ethics by Collecting and Understanding All the Relevant Passages of Scripture on Any Topic. This point was mentioned in our definition of Christian ethics at the beginning of the chapter, but the actual process needs to be described here. How does one go about making an ethical summary of what all the passages of Scripture on a certain topic teach?

For topics covered in this book, many people will think that studying this book and reading the Bible passages noted in the chapters is enough. But some people will want to do further study of Scripture on a particular topic or study some topic not covered here. How could a student go about using the Bible to research its teachings on some other subject, perhaps one not discussed explicitly in any Christian ethics textbook?

The process would look like this:

1. Find all the relevant passages. The best tool for this step is a good Bible-search program (or a printed concordance) that will enable a person to look up key words and find the passages in which the subject is treated.

For example, in studying a biblical approach to wealth and poverty, one will need to find all the passages containing words such as *wealth, wealthy, rich, riches, poverty,* and *poor.* Already this would be a long list, and if the list is too long to be manageable, the student will have to skim the word-search results without looking up the passages, or will have to divide the search into smaller sections or limit it in some other way. Then the student can find other passages by casting the net even wider, skimming over word-search results on other terms, such as *gold, silver, money, treasure, hunger, hungry, destitute, afflicted,* and so forth.

Passages can also be found by thinking through the overall history of the Bible and then turning to sections where there would be information on the topic at hand. For example, on the issue of wealth and poverty, a student would want to read passages about Solomon's wealth, Abraham's wealth, and Job's times of both wealth and poverty, as well as New Testament passages about Jesus's poverty (Matt. 8:20) and Paul's apparent indifference to his own wealth or poverty (Phil. 4:11–13).

Then, in addition to doing word searches and reading other passages that one can find on the subject, checking any related sections in some Christian ethics books will often bring to light other passages that have been missed.

2. The second step is to read, make notes on, and try to summarize the points made in the relevant passages. Sometimes a theme will be repeated often and the summary of the various passages will be relatively easy. At other times, some passages will be difficult to understand, and the student will need to take some time to study each one in depth (just by reading the passage in context over and over, or by using specialized tools such as commentaries and dictionaries) until a satisfactory understanding is reached.

3. Finally, the teachings of the various passages should be summarized into one or more points that the Bible affirms about that subject. The summary does not have to take the exact form of anyone else's conclusions on the subject, because we each may organize the subject differently or emphasize different things, or even see things in Scripture that others have missed.

At this point it is also helpful to read related sections, if any can be found, in several Christian ethics books. This provides a useful check against error and oversight, and often makes us aware of alternative perspectives and arguments that may cause us to modify or strengthen our position. If a student finds that others have argued for strongly differing conclusions, then these other views need to be stated fairly and then answered. Sometimes other ethics books will alert us to historical or philosophical considerations that have been raised in the history of the church, and these will provide additional insights or warnings against error. (At the end of each chapter in this book I have added a listing of the page numbers where the same topic is treated in up to 13 other evangelical textbooks on Christian ethics, which should make it much easier for a student to consult a number of other books on the same topic.)

The process outlined above is possible for any Christian who can read his or her Bible and can use a search program or simply look up words in a concordance. Of course, people will become faster and more accurate in this process with time and Christian maturity, but it would be a tremendous help to the church if Christians generally would give much more time to searching out topics in Scripture for themselves and drawing conclusions in the manner outlined above. The joy of discovery of biblical themes would be richly rewarding. Especially pastors and those who lead Bible studies would find added freshness in their understanding of Scripture and in their teaching.

6. We Should Study Christian Ethics with Rejoicing and Praise. The study of ethics is not merely a theoretical exercise of the intellect. It is a study of the amazingly good moral standards given by the living God and of the remarkable blessings of living in obedience to his commands. We cannot study this subject dispassionately! We must love all that God is, all that he says, and all that he does. "You shall love the LORD your God with all your heart" (Deut. 6:5).

God is not only seeking that we do the right actions in following his commandments. He also wants us to enjoy him, to enjoy living in fellowship with him, and to enjoy pleasing him in all that we do. He wants us to find deep and lasting joy and fulfillment in living ethical lives. This is, in fact, the only path to deep and lasting happiness in life—to live lives that are pleasing to God, walking every day in close fellowship with him:

> Enoch *walked* with God, and he was not, for God took him. (Gen. 5:24)[36]

> By faith Enoch was taken up so that he should not see death, and he was not found, because God had taken him. Now before he was taken he was commended as *having pleased God*. (Heb. 11:5)

The Bible contains many words of praise to God for the excellence and wisdom of his moral standards and the blessings that come from walking in his ways. Therefore, in the study of the ethical teachings of God's Word, it should not surprise us if we often find our hearts spontaneously breaking forth in expressions of praise and delight like those of the psalmists:

> *Blessed* is the man
>   who walks not in the counsel of the wicked,
> nor stands in the way of sinners,
>   nor sits in the seat of scoffers;
> but his *delight* is in the law of the LORD,
>   and on his law he meditates day and night. (Ps. 1:1–2)

---

[36] The LXX at Gen. 5:24 says Enoch was "pleasing" to God, using *euaresteō*, "to be pleasing," as its translation of the Hebrew verb *hālak*, "to walk," which occurs here in the hithpael stem with an iterative meaning, "to go to and fro, to walk about" (HALOT, 248), suggesting a pattern of walking with God over time. Heb. 11:5 echoes the LXX since it also uses *euaresteō* to say that Enoch "pleased God."

The law of the LORD is perfect,
  reviving the soul;
the testimony of the LORD is sure,
  making wise the simple;
the precepts of the LORD are right,
  rejoicing the heart;
the commandment of the LORD is pure,
  enlightening the eyes;
the fear of the LORD is clean,
  enduring forever;
the rules of the LORD are true,
  and righteous altogether.
More to be desired are they than gold,
  even much fine gold;
sweeter also than honey
  and drippings of the honeycomb.
Moreover, by them is your servant warned;
  in keeping them there is *great reward.* (Ps. 19:7–11)

Blessed are those whose way is blameless,
  who walk in the law of the LORD!
Blessed are those who keep his testimonies,
  who seek him with their whole heart,
who also do no wrong,
  but walk in his ways! (Ps 119:1–3)

In the way of your testimonies I *delight*
  as much as in *all riches.* (Ps. 119:14)

How *sweet* are your words to my taste,
  sweeter than honey to my mouth! (Ps. 119:103)

Your testimonies are my heritage forever,
  for they are *the joy of my heart.* (Ps. 119:111)

QUESTIONS FOR PERSONAL APPLICATION

The questions at the end of each chapter focus on application to life. Because I think ethical study is to be felt at the emotional level as well as understood at the intellectual level, in many chapters I have included some questions about how a reader *feels* regarding a point of ethics. I think these questions will prove valuable for those who take the time to reflect on them.

1. In what ways (if any) has this chapter changed your understanding of what Christian ethics is? What was your attitude toward the study of Christian ethics before reading this chapter? What is your attitude now?

2. What is likely to happen to a church or denomination that gives up learning Christian ethics for a generation or longer? Has that been true of your church?

3. Are there any topics listed in the table of contents for which a fuller understanding would help to solve a personal difficulty in your life at the present time? What are the spiritual and emotional dangers that you personally need to be aware of in studying Christian ethics?

4. Pray for God to make this study of Christian ethics a time of spiritual growth and deeper fellowship with God, and a time in which you personally grow to please him in your conduct of life more than ever before.

SPECIAL TERMS

canon within the canon
Christian ethics
deontological systems
historical ethics
major ethical issue
minor ethical issue
philosophical ethics
relativism
situation ethics
teleological systems
theological ethics
virtue ethics

BIBLIOGRAPHY

In the bibliographies following each chapter, I have emphasized works written from a conservative evangelical position (broadly defined). This is because the purpose of this section is to give the student ready access to other treatments of each topic by ethics writers who share my general convictions about the nature of Scripture—that all of it is totally truthful and that it is God's unique and absolutely authoritative Word to us. Once we step outside of that conviction, the basis for making ethical decisions is far different.

I have also included some Roman Catholic resources (especially the *Catechism of the Catholic Church*) because of the great influence of the Roman Catholic Church in almost every society in the world.

In addition, in some chapters that deal extensively with the evaluation of facts from the world around us (such as racial discrimination, self-defense, wealth and poverty, and stewardship of the environment), I have also included some books by secular writers that are relevant to those topics.

Sections in Other Ethics Texts

At the end of each chapter, I have listed page numbers in 13 other commonly used ethics texts where the same topic is covered. (Full bibliographical information for these 13 books is provided in this chapter only.)

Clark, David K., and Robert V. Rakestraw, eds. *Readings in Christian Ethics*. 2 vols. Grand Rapids, MI: Baker, 1994, 1:17–66.

Davis, John Jefferson. *Evangelical Ethics: Issues Facing the Church Today*. 4th ed. Phillipsburg, NJ: P&R, 2015, 1–16.

Feinberg, John S., and Paul D. Feinberg. *Ethics for a Brave New World*. 2nd ed. Wheaton, IL: Crossway, 2010, 21–62.

Frame, John M. *The Doctrine of the Christian Life: A Theology of Lordship*. Phillipsburg, NJ: P&R, 2008, 3–384.

Geisler, Norman L. *Christian Ethics: Contemporary Issues and Options*. 2nd ed. Grand Rapids, MI: Baker, 2010, 15–130.

Gushee, David P., and Glen H. Stassen. *Kingdom Ethics: Following Jesus in Contemporary Context*. 2nd ed. Grand Rapids, MI: Eerdmans, 2016, 3–94.

Hays, Richard B. *The Moral Vision of the New Testament: Community, Cross, New Creation: A Contemporary Introduction to New Testament Ethics*. San Francisco: HarperSanFrancisco, 1996, 1–312.

Holmes, Arthur F. *Ethics: Approaching Moral Decisions*. Contours of Christian Philosophy. 2nd ed. Downers Grove, IL: InterVarsity Press, 2007, 11–58.

Jones, David Clyde. *Biblical Christian Ethics*. Grand Rapids, MI: Baker, 1994, 11–16.

Kaiser, Walter C., Jr. *What Does the Lord Require? A Guide for Preaching and Teaching Biblical Ethics*. Grand Rapids, MI: Baker, 2009, 9–18.

McQuilkin, Robertson, and Paul Copan. *An Introduction to Biblical Ethics: Walking in the Way of Wisdom*. 3rd ed. Downers Grove, IL: InterVarsity Press, 2014, 13–23.

Murray, John. *Principles of Conduct: Aspects of Biblical Ethics*. Grand Rapids, MI: Eerdmans, 1957, 11–26.

Rae, Scott B. *Moral Choices: An Introduction to Ethics*. 3rd ed. Grand Rapids, MI: Zondervan, 2009, 11–23.

Other Works

Anderson, Kerby. *Christian Ethics in Plain Language*. Nelson's Plain Language Series. Nashville: Nelson Reference & Electronic, 2005.

Atkinson, David J., and David H. Field, eds. *New Dictionary of Christian Ethics and Pastoral Theology*. Leicester, UK: Inter-Varsity, and Downers Grove, IL: InterVarsity Press, 1995.

Baxter, Richard. *A Christian Directory*. Morgan, PA: Soli Deo Gloria, 1673; repr., 1996.

Calvin, John. *Institutes of the Christian Religion*. John T. McNeill, ed. Ford Lewis Battles, trans. Library of Christian Classics, vols. 20–21. Philadelphia: Westminster, 1960.

Catechism of the Catholic Church. 2nd ed. New York: Doubleday, 1997.

Douma, Jochem. *The Ten Commandments: Manual for the Christian Life*. Phillipsburg, NJ: P&R, 1996.

Eckman, James P. *Biblical Ethics: Choosing Right in a World Gone Wrong*. Biblical Essentials Series. Wheaton, IL: Crossway, 2004.

Fairbairn, Patrick. *The Revelation of Law in Scripture*. Phillipsburg, NJ: P&R, 1996.

Fletcher, Joseph. *Situation Ethics: The New Morality*. Louisville, KY: Westminster John Knox, 1966.

Gill, Robin. *A Textbook of Christian Ethics*. 4th ed. London: Bloomsbury T&T Clark, 2014.

Gosnell, Peter W. *The Ethical Vision of the Bible: Learning Good from Knowing God*. Downers Grove, IL: InterVarsity Press, 2014.

Grenz, Stanley J., and Jay T. Smith. *Pocket Dictionary of Ethics*. Downers Grove, IL: InterVarsity Press, 2003.

Grenz, Stanley J. *The Moral Quest: Foundations of Christian Ethics*. Downers Grove, IL: InterVarsity Press, 1997.

Henry, Carl F. H., ed. *Baker's Dictionary of Christian Ethics*. Grand Rapids, MI: Baker, 1973.

———. *Christian Personal Ethics*. Grand Rapids, MI: Eerdmans, 1957.

Hodge, Charles. *Systematic Theology*. Vol. 3, *Soteriology*. Peabody, MA: Hendrickson, 1999.

Hughes, Philip Edgcumbe. *Christian Ethics in Secular Society*. Grand Rapids, MI: Baker, 1983.

Jones, David W. *An Introduction to Biblical Ethics*. B&H Studies in Christian Ethics. Nashville: B&H, 2013.

Jones, Mark. *Antinomianism: Reformed Theology's Unwelcome Guest?* Phillipsburg, NJ: P&R, 2013.

Kaiser, Walter C., Jr. *Toward Old Testament Ethics*. Grand Rapids, MI: Zondervan, 1983.

Lutzer, Erwin W., and Mark M. Hanna. *The Necessity of Ethical Absolutes*. Christian Free University Curriculum. Grand Rapids, MI: Zondervan, 1981.

MacArthur, John. *Right Thinking in a World Gone Wrong*. Eugene, OR: Harvest House, 2009.

Mitchell, C. Ben. *Ethics and Moral Reasoning: A Student's Guide*. Reclaiming the Christian Intellectual Tradition. Wheaton, IL: Crossway, 2013.

Mitchell, Craig Vincent. *Charts of Christian Ethics*. ZondervanCharts. Grand Rapids, MI: Zondervan, 2006.

Myers, Jeff, and David A. Noebel. *Understanding the Times: A Survey of Competing Worldviews*. Understanding the Times Series. Manitou Springs, CO: Summit Ministries, 2015.

Myers, Jeff. *Understanding the Culture: A Survey of Social Challenges*. Colorado Springs: David C. Cook, 2015.

Noebel, David A. *Understanding the Times: The Religious Worldviews of Our Day and the Search for Truth*. Eugene, OR: Harvest House, 1994.

O'Donovan, Oliver. *Ethics as Theology*. Vol. 1, *Self, World, and Time*. Grand Rapids, MI: Eerdmans, 2013.

———. *Resurrection and Moral Order: An Outline for Evangelical Ethics*. 2nd ed. Leicester, UK: Apollos, and Grand Rapids, MI: Eerdmans, 1994.

Piper, John. *Desiring God: Meditations of a Christian Hedonist*. Portland, OR: Multnomah, 1986.

Poythress, Vern S. *The Lordship of Christ: Serving Our Savior All of the Time, in All of Life, with All of Our Heart*. Wheaton, IL: Crossway, 2016.

Rae, Scott B. *Doing the Right Thing: Making Moral Choices in a World Full of Options*. Grand Rapids, MI: Zondervan, 2013.

Rushdoony, Rousas John. *The Institutes of Biblical Law*. Phillipsburg, NJ: Presbyterian and Reformed, 1973.

Ryken, Philip Graham. *Written in Stone: The Ten Commandments and Today's Moral Crisis*. Wheaton, IL: Crossway, 2003.

Van Til, Cornelius. *In Defense of the Faith*. Vol. 3, *Christian Theistic Ethics*. Philadelphia: Westminster Theological Seminary, 1971.

Wilkens, Steve. *Christian Ethics: Four Views*. Downers Grove, IL: InterVarsity Press, 2017.

SCRIPTURE MEMORY PASSAGE

Students have repeatedly mentioned that one of the most valuable parts of any of their courses in college or seminary has been the Scripture passages they were required to memorize. "I have stored up your word in my heart, that I might not sin against you" (Ps. 119:11). In each chapter, therefore, I have included an appropriate memory passage so that instructors may incorporate Scripture memory into the course requirements wherever possible. (Scripture memory passages at the end of each chapter are taken from the ESV.)

Colossians 1:9–10: And so, from the day we heard, we have not ceased to pray for you, asking that you may be filled with the knowledge of his will in all spiritual wisdom and understanding, so as to walk in a manner worthy of the Lord, fully pleasing to him: bearing fruit in every good work and increasing in the knowledge of God.

HYMN

Christian ethics at its best will result in praise, because God's moral commands flow from his character, and his character is holy, righteous, infinitely good, and most beautiful. The author of Psalm 119 realized this, for he exclaimed, "Oh how I love your law! It is my meditation all the day" and "My lips will pour forth praise, for you teach me your statutes" (Ps. 119:97, 171).

I will argue in chapter 4 that the kind of life that glorifies God is "a life of obedience to God, lived in personal relationship with God." But regular times of worship are an important help in refreshing and deepening our day-by-day relationship with God, and hymns of praise are also a wonderful means of expressing the joy we feel when we are aware of God's presence.

It is appropriate, therefore, at the end of each chapter to include a hymn, often one that is related to the subject of that chapter. In a classroom setting, the hymn can be sung together at the beginning or end of class. Alternatively, an individual reader can sing it privately or simply meditate quietly on the words.

For almost every chapter the words of the hymns were found in *Great Hymns of the Faith*,[37] but most of them are found in many other common hymnals. Unless otherwise noted, the words of these hymns are now in the public domain and no longer subject to copyright restrictions: therefore, they may be freely copied for public use.

Why have I used so many old hymns? Although I personally like many of the more recent worship songs that have come into wide use, when I began to select hymns that would correspond to the great ethical teachings of Scripture, I realized that the great hymns of the church throughout history have a richness and breadth that is still unequaled. Perhaps this can be a challenge to modern songwriters to study these chapters and then write songs reflecting the teaching of Scripture on the respective subjects.

"Holy, Holy, Holy"

Holy, holy, holy, Lord God Almighty!
Early in the morning our song shall rise to thee;
Holy, holy, holy! Merciful and mighty!
God in three persons, blessed Trinity!

Holy, holy, holy! All the saints adore thee,
Casting down their golden crowns around the glassy sea;
Cherubim and seraphim falling down before thee,
Who wert, and art, and evermore shalt be.

Holy, holy, holy! Though the darkness hide thee,
Though the eye of sinful man thy glory may not see,

[37] John W. Peterson, ed., *Great Hymns of the Faith* (Grand Rapids, MI: Zondervan, 1969).

Only thou art holy; there is none beside thee
Perfect in pow'r, in love, and purity.

Holy, holy, holy! Lord God Almighty!
All thy works shall praise thy name, in earth and sky and sea;
Holy, holy, holy! Merciful and mighty!
God in three persons, blessed Trinity!

AUTHOR: REGINALD HEBER, 1826

Chapter 2

THE ULTIMATE BASIS FOR ETHICS: THE MORAL CHARACTER OF GOD

Where did the Bible's ethical standards come from?

Why should we think they are valid?

Do these ethical standards apply to all

people in all societies at all times?

I wrote in chapter 1 that in this book we would study ethics by asking, "What does the whole Bible teach?" about various ethical topics. But that leaves another question unanswered: Where did the Bible's ethical standards come from?

A. THE BASIS OF THE BIBLE'S ETHICAL STANDARDS IS THE MORAL CHARACTER OF GOD

1. God's Character Is Good. When the Bible talks about God's moral character, it talks about God as being "good." For example:

> *You are good* and do good;
> teach me your statutes. (Ps. 119:68)

> The Rock, his work is perfect,
> for *all his ways are justice.*
> A God of faithfulness, and without iniquity,
> just and upright is he. (Deut. 32:4)

> *Just and true are your ways,*
>> O King of the nations!
> Who will not fear, O Lord,
>> and glorify your name?
> For you alone are holy.
>> All nations will come and worship you. (Rev. 15:3–4)

In these and many other passages, the Bible emphasizes that God's moral character is good. He is a God who is good, and also loving, just, merciful, faithful, truthful, and holy.

In addition, God approves of and actually delights in his own moral character. He is the One who is the "blessed" God, that is, the One who is supremely happy in himself (1 Tim. 1:11; 6:15).[1] In fact, when his Word declares that he is "good," it implies that he considers his own character to be worthy of approval.

2. God Approves of Creatures Who Conform to His Moral Character. Many other passages in Scripture show that God desires and approves of moral creatures who conform to his moral character. Just as God is loving, just, merciful, faithful, truthful, holy, and so forth, so he also desires that we act in ways that are loving, just, merciful, faithful, truthful, holy, and so forth. These are the qualities that God approves of in himself, and therefore these are the moral qualities that he approves of in his creatures as well. Just as he delights to contemplate his own moral excellence, he delights to see his moral excellence reflected in the creatures he has made.[2]

Here are some biblical passages showing that God delights to see his character reflected in our lives:

But as he who called you is holy, you also *be holy* in all your conduct. (1 Pet. 1:15)

Be merciful, even as your Father is merciful. (Luke 6:36)

We love because he first loved us. (1 John 4:19)

Therefore *be imitators of God*, as beloved children. (Eph. 5:1)

---

[1] The word *blessed* in these verses translates the Greek adjective *makarios*, which means "blessed, happy" (BDAG, 610–611).

[2] Once we accept the idea that God's own moral character is good, it is easier to answer the following question: "(1) Are God's moral standards right because he commands them or (2) does he command them because they are right?"

Both statements are true, if they are properly understood. (1) We must be careful not to imagine that God could command anything that is contrary to his moral character, and so we must not imagine that God could arbitrarily command anything we might imagine. If God's moral character is infinitely good, then he cannot command anything except what is right and good, and that means that anything he commands is right because he commands it. (2) We must be careful not to imagine that there is some higher standard of "good" or "right" outside of God to which he decides to conform. If we understand that the only absolute standard of good and right is God's own character, then we can also say that he commands things because they are right (they conform to his moral character).

You therefore must *be perfect*, as your heavenly Father is perfect. (Matt. 5:48)

Do not lie to one another, seeing that you have put off the old self with its practices and have put on the new self, which is being renewed in knowledge *after the image of its creator.* (Col. 3:9–10)

Paul's idea is that our "new self" is becoming more like God, and therefore we should imitate God's truthfulness.

Beloved, we are God's children now, and what we will be has not yet appeared; but we know that when he appears *we shall be like him*, because we shall see him as he is. And everyone who thus hopes in him *purifies himself as he is pure.* (1 John 3:2–3)

Putting this another way, we are to live in the same way that Jesus lived, to walk as he walked:

Be imitators of me, as I am of Christ. (1 Cor. 11:1)

And *walk in love, as Christ loved us* and gave himself up for us. (Eph. 5:2)

Whoever says he abides in him ought to walk in the same way in which he walked. (1 John 2:6)

For to this you have been called, because Christ also suffered for you, *leaving you an example*, so that you might follow in his steps. (1 Pet. 2:21)

John Murray, professor of systematic theology at Westminster Seminary in Philadelphia from 1930 to 1966, rightly observes:

In the last analysis, why must we behave in one way and not in another? . . . The ultimate standard of right is the character or nature of God. The basis of ethics is that God is what he is, and we must be conformed to what he is in holiness, righteousness, truth, goodness, and love. . . . God made man in his own image and after his likeness. Man must, therefore, be like God.[3]

B. GOD COULD NOT HAVE MADE OTHER MORAL STANDARDS

Because the moral standards that God gives us are grounded in his moral character, he could not have made other moral standards for us than the ones that he made. He could not have commanded us that it was right to hate people rather than to love them,

---

[3] John Murray, *Principles of Conduct: Aspects of Biblical Ethics* (Grand Rapids, MI: Eerdmans, 1957), 177.

to lie rather than to tell the truth, to murder rather than to protect life, to be unjust rather than just, and so forth.

However, one word of clarification is important here. When I speak of God's moral standards, *I do not mean to include the temporary regulations* that God gave the people of Israel in the time of Moses, such as the regulations about clean and unclean foods or the requirements for various kinds of animal sacrifices. Rather, I am referring to the abiding moral standards that have been applicable to all people for all periods of history (for further discussion of the laws in the Mosaic covenant, see chap. 8).

C. GOD'S ABIDING MORAL STANDARDS AS FOUND IN THE BIBLE APPLY TO ALL PEOPLE IN ALL CULTURES IN ALL PERIODS OF HISTORY

If God's moral standards flow from his unchanging moral character, then it follows that these are the moral standards by which God will hold all people everywhere accountable. Several passages indicate that God will one day be the Judge of the entire earth:

Shall not the *Judge of all the earth* do what is just? (Gen. 18:25)

He comes to judge the earth.
He will judge the world in righteousness,
and the peoples in his faithfulness. (Ps. 96:13)

When Paul spoke to the pagan Greek philosophers on the Areopagus in Athens, he was speaking to an audience that had no knowledge of the moral standards of the God of Israel (even if some had a passing acquaintance with Jewish religion, Paul could not have assumed such knowledge on the part of any of his hearers). Even to this audience Paul proclaimed that the one true God, "the God who made the world and everything in it," is the God who "has fixed a day on which he will *judge the world* in righteousness by a man whom he has appointed; and of this he has given assurance to all by raising him from the dead" (Acts 17:24, 31). These pagan Greek philosophers, Paul said, would be judged by God according to his eternal, universal moral standards.

Similarly, in Romans 1, Paul teaches that Gentiles (most of whom have no knowledge of God's written moral standards in the Jewish Bible) will be held accountable to God because they are "without excuse" when they do not honor God as God or give thanks to him (vv. 20–21). Paul says that such Gentile sinners "know God's righteous decree that those who practice such things deserve to die," but they "not only do them but give approval to those who practice them" (v. 32). Moreover, they "know" these standards because "the work of the law is written on their hearts" (2:15).

Of course, these statements do not mean that any unbeliever can live up to God's moral standards and merit God's approval for his or her life, for "all have sinned and fall short of the glory of God" (Rom. 3:23). These proclamations of accountability to God's moral laws are given for the purpose of persuading people to repent of their sins and trust in Christ for forgiveness: "For the wages of sin is death, but the free gift of God is eternal life in Christ Jesus our Lord" (6:23).

Peter says something similar in speaking about hostile unbelievers who are mocking and slandering faithful Christians:

> They are surprised when you do not join them in the same flood of debauchery, and they malign you; *but they will give account* to him who is ready to judge the living and the dead. (1 Pet. 4:4–5)

The conclusion from these passages is that even people who do not believe in the God of the Bible or agree that his moral standards have divine authority on their lives will be judged by the God of all the earth. And the moral standards for which they will be held accountable are those that are found in God's "law," which is perfectly revealed in Scripture and also written on people's hearts and consciences (though imperfectly perceived).

D. GOD'S MORAL CHARACTER AND THE PROBLEM OF HOW WE CAN MOVE FROM "IS" TO "OUGHT"

In a famous 1958 essay, British philosopher Elizabeth Anscombe argued that without a concept of a divine lawgiver, it is difficult (or perhaps impossible) to give any explanation of why something is *morally* right or wrong.[4] She wrote:

> To have a *law* conception of ethics is to hold that what is needed for conformity with the virtues . . . is required by divine law. Naturally it is not possible to have such a conception unless you believe in God as a law-giver. . . . It remains impossible to infer *"morally ought"* from "is" sentences. . . . And where one does not think there is a judge or a law, the notion of a verdict may retain its psychological effect, but not its meaning.[5]

Anscombe did not think that English moral philosophers in the previous hundred years had made any progress in moving from statements of fact about the world ("is" sentences) to statements of moral right and wrong ("ought" sentences), for they had simply concentrated on discussions of the results of actions (the consequences) without adequately demonstrating why any consequences should be considered morally right or wrong.

I think Anscombe was correct to argue that once the idea of a divine lawgiver is removed and we are left with just human observation, reason, and intuition, there is no

---

[4] G. E. M. Anscombe, "Modern Moral Philosophy," *Philosophy* 33, no. 124 (January 1958): 1–16.
[5] Ibid., 5–7. Emphasis in original.

satisfactory way to prove that something is, in fact, morally right or wrong. (Human beings can *think* or *feel instinctively* that an action is right or wrong, but why should that be enough reason to say that it is actually morally right or wrong? By what standard can moral right and wrong be established?)

Someone might argue that it is right to do an action that brings about *good results*. But how can we define what a good result is? Someone might suggest that a good result is one that increases happiness for us or other people, or that brings about the greatest amount of happiness for people. But that does not really solve the problem. What gives us the basis for saying that it is good to bring about happiness? Just because people *like* to be happy does not provide a convincing answer for why happiness "ought" to be or why it is a morally good thing. Many people say they "like" things that other people would say are morally evil. How can we find something *outside of ourselves* that will provide a final answer to the question of why something "ought to be"?[6]

The Bible has a clear answer. It teaches us that when people assume that nothing exists in the world except human beings and the material creation that we perceive with our senses, they have an incorrect assumption about what "is" in the universe. That is because they have excluded from consideration the most important thing that exists in the universe, the most important being that "is," namely, God himself. He is "the God who made the world and everything in it," and he is the "Lord of heaven and earth," and he "does not live in temples made by man" (Acts 17:24).

Furthermore, this God of the Bible is not just a vague, abstract idea, an impersonal supreme being, but he is an eternal person who has a moral character. His moral character is part of what "is" in the universe, and always has been and always will be. His approval of and delight in the excellence of his own moral character is also part of what "is" in the universe. There can be no higher standard of moral right and wrong than God's moral character.

John Frame, I think rightly, presents the following argument:

> Argument 2:
> Premise: X is morally right.
> Conclusion: We ought to do X.

Frame then says,

> Argument 2 is not a fallacy because there are oughts in both the premise and the conclusion. That which is "morally right" is equivalent to "what we ought to do." Argument 2 . . . can be described as "deducing a value

---

[6] Anscombe was not the first to say that it is impossible for human beings, apart from any idea of God, to reason from "is" to "ought" statements; that point had been made forcefully in 1740 by British philosopher David Hume. See the perceptive analysis of David Hume's argument in John M. Frame, *The Doctrine of the Christian Life: A Theology of Lordship* (Phillipsburg, NJ: P&R, 2008), 60–63.

from a fact," but . . . the fact in the premise is, we might say, a moral fact. So we should formulate the naturalistic fallacy more precisely as follows: One may deduce moral conclusions from moral facts, but not from non-moral facts.[7]

Then Frame asks us to consider the following argument, in which God's speaking is considered part of what "is" in the universe:

> Argument 3:
> Premise: God says stealing is wrong.
> Conclusion: Stealing is wrong.

Frame says of this argument:

> The Christian claims that this argument does not commit the naturalistic fallacy, because the premise is a moral fact, not a non-moral fact. There is an ought implicit in the premise. If God says something, it is never a mere fact; it is also a norm. God's word bears his Lordship attributes of control, authority, and presence, and his authority makes whatever he says normative for us. So whatever he says, we are obligated to believe, and whatever he commands, we are obligated to do. Whatever God says, then, is normative. If he says something, there is an *ought* attached to it. Argument 3 does not commit the naturalistic fallacy, then, because it is an argument from moral facts to moral conclusion.[8]

Therefore, in studying Christian ethics, we are not limited to our own observations of human conduct, instinct, and reasoning, for *God also is part of what exists*, and so are his words. In those words he has given us moral laws that define what "ought" and "ought not" to be, what is morally right and wrong. *What ought to be* is God's moral character and also whatever he approves of in his creatures as consistent with his moral character.

We should also understand, however, the viewpoint of non-Christians. If there is no God (as many people believe today), then it follows that all claims about "moral values" are *merely human inventions*. And if all our claims about moral right and wrong are just human inventions, then how can any one person have the right to say that his moral values are better than anyone else's?

Following that line of reasoning today, many people in modern societies assume that no one can know any such thing as absolute right and wrong. This conviction leads them to be frustrated and even angry at people (such as Christians who believe the Bible) who claim that they *do* know what is right and wrong for all people.

---

[7] Ibid., 60–61.
[8] Ibid., 61.

Non-Christians see this as an arrogant attempt on the part of Christians to say that everyone else should obey our personal moral standards (which they do not think came from God, for they think we made them up and then claimed that God gave them to us).

Christians, however, see this situation from a different perspective. We do not believe that the biblical authors or modern-day Christians *invented* the moral standards of the Bible for themselves, like the moral standards that other people claim for themselves. We believe, rather, that the Bible is correct when it claims that these words have been *revealed to us by the one true God* who created the entire universe and who rules over it as its sovereign Lord. But it is still helpful for us to understand how these different perspectives today lead to very different ways of evaluating claims to know absolute moral right and wrong.

E. GOD'S MORAL STANDARDS WILL NEVER CEASE TO BE VALID FOR US

Since God's moral standards flow from his character, which is unchanging, we can conclude that these standards will also apply to us in the age to come. God will never, throughout all eternity, tell us that it is right to serve other gods, to dishonor our fathers and mothers, to murder, to commit adultery, to steal, or to bear false witness. The abiding moral standards that God has given in his Word will be valid for all eternity, and obeying them will give joy to our hearts and glory to God forever.

QUESTIONS FOR PERSONAL APPLICATION

1. Before reading this chapter, had you ever thought about God delighting in his own moral character? Does it make you feel happy to think of God giving eternal, unlimited approval to his own moral character?
2. When you think of God's moral standards being grounded in his moral character, does that make you feel secure? Are you glad that God's unchanging, eternal moral character is the source of the moral standards in Scripture?
3. Does it make you uncomfortable to say that God's moral standards in the Bible apply to all people in all cultures in all periods of history? If so, why do you think you feel that way?
4. One day in the future, when your life in this age has ended and you find yourself with Christ in heaven, how do you think your heart will feel about the moral commands of Scripture? Do you feel that way about those commands today?
5. Do you think that this chapter will deepen your day-by-day relationship with God? Why or why not?

SPECIAL TERMS

"is" statements
"ought" statements

BIBLIOGRAPHY

Sections in Other Ethics Texts

(see complete bibliographical data, p. 64)

Clark and Rakestraw, 1:67–112
Davis, 1–6
Feinberg, John and Paul, 30–35
Frame, 131–384
Geisler, 15–21, 123–27
Gushee and Stassen, 3–20
Holmes, 71–82
McQuilkin and Copan, 180–83
Murray, 27–44, 229–42
Rae, 24–58

Other Works

Webster, J. B. "God." In *New Dictionary of Christian Ethics and Pastoral Theology*, edited by David J. Atkinson and David H. Field, 3–9. Leicester, UK: Inter-Varsity, and Downers Grove, IL: InterVarsity Press, 1995.

SCRIPTURE MEMORY PASSAGE

Ephesians 5:1–2: Therefore be imitators of God, as beloved children. And walk in love, as Christ loved us and gave himself up for us, a fragrant offering and sacrifice to God.

HYMN

"Immortal, Invisible, God Only Wise"

Immortal, invisible, God only wise,
In light inaccessible hid from our eyes,
Most blessed, most glorious, the Ancient of Days,
Almighty, victorious, thy great name we praise.

Unresting, unhasting, and silent as light,
Nor wanting, nor wasting, thou rulest in might;
Thy justice like mountains high soaring above
Thy clouds which are fountains of goodness and love.

Great Father of glory, pure Father of light,
Thine angels adore thee, all veiling their sight;
All praise we would render; O help us to see
'Tis only the splendor of light hideth thee!

AUTHOR: WALTER CHALMERS SMITH, 1867

Chapter 3

OUR SOURCE OF ETHICAL STANDARDS: THE BIBLE

Is the Bible supposed to teach us how to live?

How do we know it is true and trustworthy?

Can everybody understand it?

In chapter 2, I argued that the only satisfactory ultimate basis for ethical standards is the eternal, unchanging moral character of God. Before anything else existed, God existed. He *is*. And one aspect of his eternal existence is his eternal moral character. Because of that moral character, certain kinds of actions, attitudes, and personal character traits are pleasing to God, and other kinds of actions, attitudes, and character traits are not. Those actions, attitudes, and personal characteristics that receive God's approval are ones that are morally *right*, and they *ought* to be approved by us. Those actions, attitudes, and personal characteristics that receive God's disapproval are ones that are morally *wrong*, and they *ought not* to be approved.

But how can we find out what God considers to be right and wrong? We can learn that from the Bible. One of the purposes of the Bible is to enable us to know which actions, attitudes, and personal character traits receive God's approval, and which ones do not. In other words, one of the reasons God gave us the Bible was to teach us about his views of moral right and wrong—to teach us ethics![1]

---

[1] I say this is one of the purposes of the Bible because there are also other purposes, such as teaching us the way of salvation, teaching us about God's great acts of redemptive history, teaching us about his magnificent character, and enabling us to enjoy the great blessing of personal communication from him as he speaks to us in his Word.

A. THE BIBLE WAS GIVEN TO TEACH US HOW TO LIVE

Several passages in both the Old Testament and the New Testament affirm that one of the purposes of the Bible is to teach us how to live.

In the Old Testament, this is seen in passages that speak of walking in the law of the Lord (where "walking" is a metaphor for living one's life):

> Blessed is the man
>> who *walks not* in the counsel of the wicked,
> nor stands in the way of sinners,
>> nor sits in the seat of scoffers;
> but *his delight is in the law of the Lord*,
>> and on his law he meditates day and night. (Ps. 1:1–2)

Much of Psalm 119 is devoted to this theme of living in accordance with the words of God or with the law of the Lord:

> Blessed are those whose way is blameless,
>> who *walk in the law of the Lord*!
> Blessed are those who *keep his testimonies*,
>> who seek him with their whole heart,
> who also do no wrong,
>> but *walk in his ways*!
> You have commanded *your precepts*
>> to be kept diligently.
> Oh that my ways may be steadfast
>> in *keeping your statutes*!
> Then I shall not be put to shame,
>> having my eyes fixed on *all your commandments*. (Ps. 119:1–6)

> How can a young man keep his way pure?
>> By guarding it *according to your word*. (Ps. 119:9)

> *Your word* is a lamp to my feet
>> and *a light to my path*. (Ps. 119:105)

In the New Testament we have a similar affirmation, that the words of Scripture are useful for teaching us how to live or, as Paul says, for "training in righteousness":

> All Scripture is breathed out by God and profitable for teaching, for reproof, for correction, and for *training in righteousness*, that the man of God may be complete, equipped for every good work. (2 Tim. 3:16–17)

But this is not the only passage that affirms this truth. When the apostles taught from church to church, much of their teaching had to do with ethical matters, how to live as Christians in this world. For example:

> Finally, then, brothers, we ask and urge you in the Lord Jesus, that as *you re-ceived from us how you ought to walk and to please God*, just as you are doing, that you do so more and more. (1 Thess. 4:1)

The entire book of James treats many practical ethical issues, and so does 1 Peter. There are many other such passages that give instruction on right and wrong conduct of life (see Rom. 12–15; 1 Cor. 1:10; 3:3–4, 5–14; 16:1–2; 2 Cor. 7:1; 8:1–9:15; Gal. 5:13–6:10; Eph. 4:1–6:9; Phil. 2:12–13; Col. 1:9–10; 3:1–4:6; 2 Thess. 3:6–12; much of 1 Timothy, 2 Timothy, Titus, and Philemon; Heb. 12:1–13:19).

Therefore, in studying the Bible for ethical purposes, it will be necessary to collect, understand, and synthesize all the relevant Bible passages on a topic. At first this might sound difficult, but we should have hope that it can be done, for many millions of believers throughout history have already done this, seeking to follow Scripture every day of their lives. And God himself wants us to understand his commandments so that we can obey him rightly. "For this is the love of God, that we keep his commandments. And his commandments are not burdensome" (1 John 5:3).[2]

B. THREE OBJECTIONS TO USING THE BIBLE TO LEARN HOW TO LIVE

Here are three objections to the idea that we should use the Bible to learn how to live in a way that is pleasing to God:

1. Objection: "Don't Offend Visitors." Some Christians might object to pastors who emphasize teaching people to obey the commands of Scripture. They would claim that pastors should not preach much about sin and obedience because it will drive away visitors who are seeking to come to know Christ. Preaching about God's commandments, they would argue, is failing to be "seeker-sensitive" in our churches.[3]

---

[2] See also my discussion later in this chapter on the clarity of Scripture (p. 90).

[3] One of the most prominent examples of a seeker-sensitive church is Willow Creek Community Church in Illinois. G. A. Pritchard, a scholar with expertise in the sociology of religion, devoted an entire year to an extensive sociological analysis of Willow Creek and expressed the following concern: "Hybels's relevant teaching that God wants to meet individuals' needs and make them fulfilled unduly shapes his gospel message. The holiness of God and the convicting nature of God's moral law are obscured.... It is not that Hybels does not speak of God's holiness and the need to repent, it is merely that the message of God's transcendent holiness is flooded by the broader emphasis on God's immanent compassionate love." *Willow Creek Seeker Services: Evaluating a New Way of Doing Church* (Grand Rapids, MI: Baker, 1996), 263. Pritchard notes that the Willow Creek leadership has made some attempts to correct this imbalance in emphasis (41–42), but he does not see a lasting correction. (Pritchard's book was published several years ago, and I do not know if his analysis reflects current practice at Willow Creek.) Significantly, Pritchard then adds, "Willow Creek is

My response is that we have in the New Testament many detailed examples of how Jesus wants pastors to teach their churches. Those examples are found particularly in the Epistles, which are the very words of the apostles *giving instruction to the New Testament churches*. These Epistles were supposed to be read aloud in the churches! (See 2 Cor. 1:13; Eph. 3:4; Col. 4:16; 1 Thess. 5:27; also note how the opening verses of the Epistles often show that they are addressed to an entire church, as in Rom. 1:7; 1 Cor. 1:2; Gal. 1:2; Eph. 1:1, etc.)

It is impossible to ignore the fact that *the Epistles are full of moral instruction*, teaching people how they should live as Christians in the light of God's moral teachings, and the Epistles show us a pattern for how pastors and teachers should instruct their churches. This is true not only in Paul's epistles, but also strikingly true in epistles such as James, 1 Peter, and 1 John. In addition, Jesus commanded his apostles that in their ministries they should teach people "to observe all that I have commanded you" (Matt. 28:20). I conclude that pastors who avoid teaching people to obey the moral commandments of Scripture are failing to follow this command of Jesus and the clear pattern laid down in the New Testament as a whole.

Therefore, I disagree with the idea that pastors should avoid teaching their people to obey the moral commands of Scripture. I agree that churches should be sensitive to the needs and concerns of visitors (see 1 Cor. 14:16, 23–25; James 2:2–4), but such sensitivity must never lead to a watering down of the moral standards of God as found in Scripture.

The claim that we should not preach about repentance from sin to non-Christian "seekers" is certainly inconsistent with the pattern of the New Testament. In speaking to complete unbelievers from an entirely pagan background in Athens, Paul proclaimed:

> The times of ignorance God overlooked, but now *he commands all people everywhere to repent*, because he has fixed a day on which he will judge the world in righteousness by a man whom he has appointed; and of this he has given assurance to all by raising him from the dead. (Acts 17:30–31)

In fact, a failure to proclaim God's holiness and his moral standards will ultimately become a hindrance to evangelism. How will non-Christians ever genuinely repent of their sins if they don't know God's moral standards as revealed in Scripture?

How tragic it would be for a pastor to come to the end of his life and discover that, because of an excessive desire to avoid offending visitors, he had not been wholly faithful to his calling as a pastor-teacher because he had too often failed to proclaim to his

---

not alone in the problem I have depicted. The American evangelical church generally has lost a vision of the Lord's holiness" (271). Pritchard spends several pages detailing the harmful results of teaching that obscures God's holiness and our need for repentance and obedience (263–71).

In previous decades, Pastor Robert Schuller (1926–2015) of the Crystal Cathedral in Garden Grove, California, was criticized because he avoided preaching about sin.

people "the whole counsel of God" (Acts 20:27); had failed to boldly proclaim God's Word as profitable for "training in righteousness" (2 Tim. 3:16); and had left a lifetime legacy of shallow, immature Christians who had not been regularly challenged "to walk in a manner worthy of the Lord, fully pleasing to him: bearing fruit in every good work and increasing in the knowledge of God" (Col. 1:10).[4]

2. Objection: "There Is No 'Third Use' of the Law." Another objection arises in connection with a dispute over the so-called "third use" of the moral law of God. The three uses of God's law have traditionally been understood as follows:

1. To restrain sin in civil society
2. To convict unbelievers of sin and drive them to Christ for salvation
3. To instruct believers in obedience

This idea of three uses of God's moral law was expressed by John Calvin in his *Institutes of the Christian Religion* in 1559:[5]

> Let us survey briefly the function and use of what is called the "moral law."...
> It consists of three parts: [One] function of the law is this: at least by fear of punishment to restrain certain men who are untouched by any care for what is just and right unless compelled by hearing the dire threats in the law.... This constrained and forced righteousness is necessary for the public community of men.[6]

> [Another] part is this:... it warns, informs, convicts, and lastly condemns, every man of his own unrighteousness.... This means that, dismissing the stupid opinion of their own strength... they flee to his mercy.... For God's mercy is revealed in Christ to all who seek and wait upon it with true faith.[7]

---

[4] Someone might answer that, by largely avoiding messages about God's holiness, our sin, and our need to live in obedience to Christ each day, seeker-sensitive churches have brought many hundreds more people to trust in Christ. But that objection fails to take into account the consequences in the second, third, and fourth generation of believers who should follow from the life of a mature Christian. Shallow Christians do not bear fruit "thirtyfold and sixtyfold and a hundredfold" (Mark 4:20) in subsequent generations. God's purpose in the world is not merely to bring the largest number of people to trust in Christ for salvation and remain shallow, immature Christians, but rather that the earth would be filled with God-glorifying people who "walk in a manner worthy of the Lord, fully pleasing to him: bearing fruit in every good work and increasing in the knowledge of God" (Col. 1:10).

[5] John Calvin, *Institutes of the Christian Religion*, ed. John T. McNeill, trans. Ford Lewis Battles, Library of Christian Classics, vols. 20–21 (Philadelphia: Westminster, 1960), 2.7.6–12 (354–61). In Calvin's discussion, what he calls the "first" use is convicting people of sin and driving them to Christ for salvation, and what he calls the "second" use is restraining sin in civil society, but I have switched the order of his paragraphs in order to follow what are more commonly called the "first" and "second" uses in more recent ethical discussions.

[6] Ibid., 2.7.6–10 (354–59).

[7] Ibid., 2.7.6–8 (354–57).

> *The third and principal use* . . . finds its place among believers in whose hearts the Spirit of God already lives and reigns. . . . Here is the best instrument for them to learn more thoroughly each day the nature of the Lord's will to which they aspire, and confirm them in the understanding of it. . . . Again, because we need not only teaching but also exhortation, the servant of God will also avail himself of this benefit of the law: by frequent meditation upon it to be aroused to obedience, be strengthened in it, and be drawn back from the slippery path of transgression.[8]

Sometimes it is claimed that support for the "third use of the law" (to instruct believers) is missing or underemphasized in Lutheran writings.[9] However, David W. Jones thinks this emphasis is clearly present there. He says, "Some have claimed Luther denied the third use of the law; however, a review of his writings, as well as Lutheran confessions, does not support this claim."[10] My own conclusion is that few if any recognized Christian leaders today oppose this "third use" of the law.

3. Objection: "The Bible Is about the Gospel, Not about How to Live." Yet another objection comes from those who insist that the Bible is about "the gospel" and not about teaching us how to live as Christians.

But this objection is not consistent with what the apostle Paul says about the purpose of Scripture. Immediately after affirming that the Scriptures "are able to make you wise for salvation through faith in Christ Jesus" (2 Tim. 3:15), Paul adds a more comprehensive statement of the purpose of Scripture:

> All Scripture is breathed out by God and profitable for teaching, for reproof, for correction, and for *training in righteousness,* that the man of God may be complete, *equipped for every good work.* (2 Tim. 3:16–17)

Paul does not say that the Bible was given *only* to teach us the good news that Jesus died for our sins. He says that the purpose of Scripture also includes "training in righteousness" so that every Christian, in following the teachings of Scripture, might be "equipped for every good work."

In addition, Jesus himself taught, "If you love me, *you will keep my commandments*" (John 14:15), and his Great Commission, which he gave to his disciples at the very end of Matthew's Gospel, told them not only to make new disciples and baptize, but also that they should be "teaching" those new disciples "to observe all that I have commanded you" (Matt. 28:20). But where are we to find Jesus's commandments if

---

[8] Ibid., 2.7.12 (360–61).

[9] See a thoughtful discussion, with reference to the Lutheran Formula of Concord, in John M. Frame, *The Doctrine of the Christian Life: A Theology of Lordship* (Phillipsburg, NJ: P&R, 2008), 183–92.

[10] David W. Jones, *An Introduction to Biblical Ethics*, B&H Studies in Christian Ethics (Nashville: B&H, 2013), 61n21.

not in the Bible? To teach people to obey Jesus's commandments is to teach them to obey the Bible.

In answering the question of whether the Bible is mainly about "the gospel," we must specify what is meant by *gospel*, a term that can be used in a narrow or broad sense. In a narrow sense, *gospel* can be defined as referring to the simple message "Believe in the Lord Jesus, and you will be saved" (Acts 16:31). If we define *gospel* in that narrow sense, then that is the central message of the Bible, but not the only message. The Bible also teaches us much about living the Christian life.

In a broader sense, *gospel* is an English translation of the Greek word *euangelion*, which means "good news." This good news includes all that God did in past history (since Genesis 1) in preparation for the Messiah; all that he has done in Christ, who is our Messiah; and all that he is doing now and will do in the future in our lives and in the whole world as a result of the redemptive work of Christ. For someone who trusts in Christ, *everything* that the entire Bible says to us is part of the good news of the gospel, understood in a broader sense. And that good news includes much material about obedience to God in our daily lives.

Our task as pastors and Christian teachers is not simply to teach *one aspect* of the Bible, even as important an aspect as the command to believe in Christ for salvation, but rather to teach *everything* that the Bible teaches, just as Paul said that his responsibility was to declare "the whole counsel of God" (Acts 20:27).

In conclusion, should Christians today teach and preach about the moral standards of God as revealed in Scripture? Absolutely yes! John Frame rightly says:

> The notion that we should conduct our lives completely apart from the admonitions of God's Word is a terrible notion. To ignore God's revelation of his righteousness is sinful. To read Scripture, but to refuse to allow its commands to influence one's conduct, is the essence of sin.[11]

When Christians live in the midst of secular or even hostile religious cultures today, it is important that Christian leaders continue to teach Christian ethics as found in Scripture. This may be a challenging task in hostile cultures, but pastors who fail to regularly teach their congregations to live in obedience to the moral commands of Scripture are not obeying Jesus's command to be "teaching them to observe all that I have commanded you" (Matt. 28:20), and they will one day stand before God as those who failed to faithfully teach "the whole counsel of God" (Acts 20:27). The members of their congregations will not grow up "to mature manhood, to the measure of the stature of the fullness of Christ" (Eph. 4:13), but will remain "children" in the faith, "tossed to and fro by the waves and carried about by every wind of doctrine, by human cunning, by craftiness in deceitful schemes" (v. 14).

---

[11] Frame, *The Doctrine of the Christian Life*, 190.

C. FOUR CHARACTERISTICS OF THE BIBLE

Before we begin to discuss the teachings of the Bible on specific ethical topics, it will be helpful to understand four primary characteristics of the Bible and how each of them relates to Christian ethics:

1. Authority of Scripture
2. Clarity of Scripture
3. Necessity of Scripture
4. Sufficiency of Scripture[12]

1. Authority: The Bible Alone, and the Entire Bible, Is the Word of God Written. With respect to ethics, the authority of Scripture is important because it tells us that the Bible is our only absolute authority for defining moral right and wrong.

a. How Can We Know That the Bible Is the Word of God? In another book, I devoted 50 pages to a discussion of why the writings that we have in the Bible are the correct ones and why it is appropriate to believe that the words of the Bible (in the original manuscripts) are the written words of God.[13] What follows is a brief summary of that argument.

(1) The Bible Itself Claims to Be God's Words: Before a person decides whether or not to trust the Bible as the very words of God, an important first step is to investigate *what the Bible claims about itself* (whether or not someone accepts those claims as true is a second question). An important step in understanding *any* piece of literature is to ask what kind of literature it claims to be, whether or not one accepts those claims in the end.

In the case of the Bible, there are frequent claims that it is to be taken as the written words of God. The most frequently cited verse in that regard is in 2 Timothy: "All Scripture is *breathed out by God* and profitable for teaching, for reproof, for correction, and for training in righteousness" (3:16).

Here the word *Scripture* (Greek, *graphē*) must refer to the Old Testament, for that is what the word *graphē* refers to in every one of its 51 occurrences in the New Testament.[14] Therefore, Paul affirms that all of the Old Testament writings are "breathed out by God" (Greek, *theopneustos*, "God-breathed"). Since it is *writings* that are said to be "breathed out," this breathing must be understood as a metaphor for speaking the words of Scripture. Thus, in this verse, Paul states in brief form what was evident from the

---

[12] The material in the rest of this chapter is a summary of chaps. 4–8 in Wayne Grudem, *Systematic Theology: An Introduction to Biblical Doctrine* (Leicester, UK: Inter-Varsity, and Grand Rapids, MI: Zondervan, 1994), 73–138. Used with permission of the publishers.

[13] See Grudem, *Systematic Theology*, 54–104, with reference to other literature on this topic.

[14] In two cases, 1 Tim. 5:18 and 2 Pet. 3:16, *graphē* also includes some of the New Testament writings along with the Old Testament writings. See the discussion of these verses at the end of this section.

claims of many passages in the Old Testament: that the Old Testament writings should be regarded as God's own words in written form. This verse claims that God is the One who spoke (and still speaks) every word of the Old Testament, even though he used human agents to write these words down.

Similarly, in speaking of "Scripture," Peter says, "No prophecy was ever produced by the will of man, but men spoke from God as they were *carried along by the Holy Spirit*" (2 Pet. 1:21). Peter is saying that the Old Testament writers were speaking from God, for they were guided and directed by the Holy Spirit in what they wrote.

When Jesus was tempted by Satan in the wilderness, he referred to the Old Testament Scriptures and said, "Man shall not live by bread alone, but by *every word that comes from the mouth of God*" (Matt. 4:4). Jesus was saying that the Old Testament Scriptures are words that come from the mouth of God. Many other passages like this could be cited (see Matt. 1:22; 19:5; Luke 1:70; 24:25; John 5:45–47; Acts 3:18, 21).

But what about the New Testament? At two places in the New Testament we see other New Testament writings being called "Scripture" along with the Old Testament writings. In writing to Timothy, Paul quotes Jesus's words "The laborer deserves his wages" (taken from Luke 10:7) and refers to them as "Scripture" (1 Tim. 5:18). Paul, who traveled extensively with Luke as his companion, is quoting Luke's Gospel as "Scripture," as God's Word. Peter also speaks of all of Paul's writings as "Scripture," because he refers to "all his letters" as part of "the . . . Scriptures" (2 Pet. 3:16).

Therefore, the New Testament authors were consciously treating some of the writings of the New Testament as equal to the Old Testament Scriptures in authority. It is not surprising, therefore, that Paul says of his letter to the church at Corinth, "The things I am writing to you are *a command of the Lord*" (1 Cor. 14:37).[15]

(2) We Become Convinced of the Bible's Claims to Be God's Words as We Read the Bible: It is one thing to affirm that the Bible *claims* to be the words of God; it is another thing to be convinced that those claims are true. People ultimately come to the conviction that the words of the Bible are God's words only when the Holy Spirit speaks *in* and *through* the words of the Bible to their hearts and gives them an inner assurance that these are the words of our Creator speaking to us. All of the most logical arguments or most persuasive evidence in the world will not convince an unwilling person that the Bible is the Word of God.

Paul says:

> The natural person does not accept the things of God, for they are folly to him, and he is not able to understand them because they are spiritually discerned. (1 Cor. 2:14)

---

[15] For the objection that Paul distinguishes his own words from the words of the Lord in 1 Corinthians 7:12, see Grudem, *Systematic Theology*, 76–77. Briefly, Paul is distinguishing Jesus's earthly teaching about a subject from the authoritative teaching that Paul, under the Lord's authority, also has the right to give.

Apart from the work of the Spirit of God in his or her heart, a person will not receive or accept spiritual truths, particularly the truth that the words of Scripture are in fact the words of God. This is analogous to what happened when people on earth listened to Jesus and knew that his words were true. He said, "*My sheep hear my voice*, and I know them, and they follow me" (John 10:27).

This means that if anyone is going to come to believe that the Bible is the Word of God, that person must spend at least some time reading the Bible for himself or herself, preferably after saying a short prayer to God asking that, if the words are God's words, God will make that known to him or her. The Holy Spirit does not speak to our hearts about the truthfulness of Scripture apart from the words of Scripture themselves, but in and through those words.

(3) Other Evidence Is Useful but Not Finally Convincing: Does this mean that it is unimportant to consider evidence from historical sources, from archaeology, from internal consistency, and from the personal testimony of others in history who have challenged the Bible and then come to believe in it? It does not mean that at all. Such arguments and evidence can be useful in overcoming people's objections to the Bible and in showing that the Bible is historically accurate and internally consistent.[16] But all of that evidence, though significant in a preliminary way, will not match the power of hearing and recognizing the voice of our Creator himself speaking to our hearts in the very words of the Bible.

(4) If the Words of the Bible Are God's Own Words, to Disbelieve or Disobey Any Part of Scripture Is to Disbelieve or Disobey God: If all the words of Scripture are the very words of God for us, then we have an obligation to understand them, believe them, and obey them. They are more important than any other written words in the history of the world.

What God said about his words through Isaiah is still applicable to us today: "But this is the one to whom I will look: he who is humble and contrite in spirit and trembles at my word" (Isa. 66:2).

This is why Peter encourages his readers to remember "the commandment of the Lord and Savior through your apostles" (2 Pet. 3:2), probably referring to the writings of the apostles that were already circulating in the churches at that time.

(5) Written Scripture Is Our Authority, Not Something in the Background to Scripture: Sometimes Bible teachers can become fascinated by something they learned about various beliefs in the background in the New Testament writings. They might begin to talk about the teachings of the rabbis around the time of Jesus on some particular

---

[16] For an extensive collection of arguments showing the accuracy and reliability of the Bible, see Josh McDowell and Sean McDowell, *Evidence That Demands a Verdict: Life-Changing Truth for a Skeptical World* (Nashville: Thomas Nelson, 2017); see also the detailed annotations in the *ESV Study Bible* (Wheaton, IL: Crossway, 2008).

topic, the beliefs that Jewish people held about the universe at the time of Moses, the (supposed) "church situation" to which Matthew was writing his Gospel, or "what Jesus really said in the Aramaic language" (which, they claim, is different from what the Gospels tell us).

In all of those cases people are trying to substitute other ideas for the authority of the words of Scripture themselves. But our authority is not what various Jewish people thought or practiced at a certain point in history, or something that a scholar's speculations claim that Jesus must have said, or some imagined church situation to which a Gospel author was writing. Our authority is *the text of Scripture itself*, not any ideas that supposedly lie "behind" the text of Scripture.

I am not saying that discussions of those other issues are useless, because they can sometimes clarify details about the historical background in which the biblical events occurred. But our reconstructions of those beliefs and situations are tentative and always somewhat uncertain. In addition, we have no guarantee that the biblical authors agreed with those ideas, for the books of the Bible often were written to differ with and correct ideas current at that time. Our authority is the written words of Scripture themselves, not anything other than those words.

b. The Bible's Authority Is Higher Than All Other Authorities for Ethics: If the Bible alone is the Word of God written for our benefit and given to us, then we must count it a higher authority than all other sources of authority in ethical discussions. This is the position commonly affirmed by evangelical Christian ethicists.[17] Specifically, the Bible is a higher authority than these other five sources of authority that are sometimes claimed:

(1) Tradition: The Bible is a higher authority than human tradition, or any ideas that have been held by the majority of teachers throughout the history of the church. The study of church history can help us understand how Christians in other centuries thought about ethical topics, but the views of those earlier Christians are not a higher authority than the Bible itself.

(2) Reason: The Bible is also a higher authority than human reason. Though our reason is a useful tool for understanding and applying the teachings of the Bible, our reasoning abilities are limited and imperfect, and cannot match the authority of the Word of God.

(3) Experience: The authority of the Bible is also higher than the authority of our experiences in life. Reflection on our experiences can help us understand situations better,

---

[17] For example, John Jefferson Davis says, "The teachings of Scripture are the final court of appeal for ethics. Human reason, church tradition, and the natural and social sciences may aid moral reflection, but divine revelation, found in the canonical Scriptures of the Old and New Testaments, constitutes the 'bottom line' of the decision-making process." *Evangelical Ethics: Issues Facing the Church Today*, 4th ed. (Phillipsburg, NJ: P&R, 2015), 3. Similar statements are found in John S. Feinberg and Paul D. Feinberg, *Ethics for a Brave New World*, 2nd ed. (Wheaton, IL: Crossway, 2010), 37; and Frame, *The Doctrine of the Christian Life*, 146–47.

but our conclusions from those experiences are simply human conclusions, and cannot match the authority of God's own words.

(4) Expected Results: The Bible is also a higher authority than any results that we expect from events in life. The supposedly "good" results that come from lying at an interview in order to get a job, or from cheating on a test in order to pass a course, do not mean that those actions are right.

(5) Subjective Impressions: God's Word is also a higher authority than any subjective impressions we might have of God's will for us. A young Christian man should not put a subjective impression that it is God's will for him to marry his non-Christian girlfriend above the biblical moral standards that Christians are to marry "only in the Lord" (1 Cor. 7:39) and that we are not to be "unequally yoked with unbelievers" (2 Cor. 6:14).

However, the opposite mistake would be to ignore these sources of information. Human tradition, especially the tradition of the Christian church, human reason, our experience of life and the wisdom that comes from it, our reasonable expectations of the results of our actions, and our subjective impressions of God's will can all be valuable in making ethical decisions so long as we do not treat them as a higher authority than the Word of God or as an equal authority to it (see further discussion in chap. 6, beginning at p. 156).

2. Clarity: God Gave Us a Bible That Is Able to Be Understood.[18] The doctrine of the clarity of Scripture, briefly stated, means that God gave us a Bible that is able to be understood. (However, that statement needs careful explanation and clarification.) With regard to ethics, this is important because it means that the Bible is able to be understood *in what it teaches about moral right and wrong.* This should give us hope in studying ethics.

a. Scriptural Support for the Clarity of Scripture: Many passages point to a quality of Scripture by which it is able to be understood. Moses told the people of Israel, regarding the words that were in the book of Deuteronomy:

> And these words that I command you today shall be on your heart. *You shall teach them diligently to your children,* and shall talk of them when you sit in your house, and when you walk by the way, and when you lie down, and when you rise. (Deut. 6:6–7)

If all of the parents in Israel were expected to teach the words of Scripture to their children, this implies that ordinary people were able to understand the words rightly, at

---

[18] The material in this section is adapted from Wayne Grudem, "The Perspicuity of Scripture" (the John Wenham Lecture for the Tyndale Fellowship, Cambridge, UK, July 2009), *Themelios* 34, no. 3 (2009): 288–308, and also from Grudem, *Systematic Theology,* 105–15, with permission of the publishers.

least for the most part. And it even implies that children were able to understand them and learn from them, at least to some extent.

It was not only the wise and highly educated people in Israel who could understand God's words, for the "law of the LORD is perfect, reviving the soul; the testimony of the LORD is sure, *making wise the simple*" (Ps. 19:7; see also 119:130).

The New Testament has a similar emphasis. Jesus never responds to any questions with a hint of blaming the Old Testament Scriptures for being unclear. Instead, Jesus's responses always assume that the blame for any misunderstanding of the teachings of Scripture is not to be placed on the Scriptures themselves, but on those who fail to grasp or accept what is written:

Have you not read what David did . . . ? (Matt. 12:3)

Have you not read in the Law . . . ? (Matt. 12:5)

Have you never read in the Scriptures . . . ? (Matt. 21:42; see also 19:4; 22:29; 22:31; John 3:10)

In addition, most of the New Testament Epistles are written not to church leaders but to the ordinary people in all the churches:

To the church of God that is in Corinth. (1 Cor. 1:2)

To the churches of Galatia. (Gal. 1:2; see also Phil. 1:1; Col. 4:16; 1 Tim. 4:13)

Some sections of the Epistles even assume that *children* are in the audience, listening to Paul's letters as they are read aloud, and understanding at least part of what is written:

Children obey your parents in the Lord, for this is right. (Eph. 6:1; cf. Col. 3:20)

The appropriate conclusion from these passages is that Scripture repeatedly affirms that it is able to be understood: not only certain passages or statements, and not only the teaching on certain topics—such as the basic way of salvation—but the meaning of the whole of Scripture on many topics.[19] These are affirmations about the nature of Scripture in general. And these affirmations are apparently grounded in the deep

[19] The Westminster Confession of Faith (1646) affirms the clarity of Scripture with respect to those things "which are necessary to be known, believed, and observed for salvation" (1.7). The inclusion of "observed" makes me think that "salvation" might be intended in a broader sense ("the entire experience of the blessings of salvation throughout our lives") rather than a narrow sense ("initial saving faith"), but I am not sure about this. In any case, I do not see in the Scripture passages just mentioned any warrant for restricting the clarity of Scripture to certain topics or certain types of passages. And the Westminster Confession of Faith does not deny that Scripture is clear with respect to other matters. Interestingly, Frame says, "Scripture, then, is clear enough to make us responsible for carrying out our present duties to God." *The Doctrine of the Christian Life*, 150.

assumption that the Scriptures are communications from a God who desires and is able to communicate clearly to his people.

b. Important Qualifications to Clarity. The Bible is a large and complex set of writings that are the product of the infinite wisdom and knowledge of God. Because this is the kind of communication found in the Bible, some necessary qualifications must apply to the affirmations of Scripture's clarity.

(1) Scripture Is Able to Be Understood, but Not All at Once. Understanding Scripture is a process. Those who are blessed by God follow the righteous man in Psalm 1, who "meditates day and night" on God's law (Ps. 1:2; see also Josh. 1:8; Ps. 119:15, 23, 48, 78; cf. 1 Cor. 2:6–7; 2 Cor. 1:13; Heb. 5:14).

(2) Scripture Is Able to Be Understood, but Not without Effort. This follows from the previous statement. If we are expected to meditate on Scripture, this implies that we will be continually learning about it throughout our lives, and that will take some effort. For example, "Ezra had set his heart to *study* the Law of the LORD" (Ezra 7:10). And Peter says there are "some things" in Paul's writings "that are hard to understand" (2 Pet. 3:15–16)—not that they are impossible to grasp, but that understanding takes some effort.

(3) Scripture Is Able to Be Understood, but Not without Ordinary Means. The Westminster Confession of Faith (1646) says that even "the unlearned, in a due use of the ordinary means, may attain unto a sufficient understanding" of many things in Scripture.[20] The "ordinary means" include reading and studying a translation of the Bible in one's own language, and reading and listening to teachers and commentaries on the Bible. They may also include the use of tools such as concordances, Hebrew and Greek dictionaries, and books with background information on the various biblical writings.

(4) Scripture Is Able to Be Understood, but Not without a Willingness to Obey It. James tells his readers, "Be doers of the Word and not hearers only, deceiving yourselves" (James 1:22). Presumably James means that if one hears the Word without doing what it says, that hearer will be deceived; he or she will misunderstand. Other passages express a similar idea (see Ps. 119:34; John 8:43; 1 Cor. 3:1–3).

(5) Scripture Is Able to Be Understood, but Not without the Help of the Holy Spirit. Paul says "the natural person does not accept the things of the Spirit of God, for they are folly to him, and he is not able to understand them because they are spiritually discerned" (1 Cor. 2:14; see also 2 Cor. 3:14–16; Col. 4:3–4). But in contrast to such a "natural person" Paul tells the Corinthians that Christians have received "the Spirit who is from God, *that we might understand* the things freely given us by God" (1 Cor. 2:12).

---

[20] WCF, 1.7.

This implies that we need to pray for the Holy Spirit's help to enable us to understand Scripture rightly. (See also Ps. 119:18, 27, 34, 73; Luke 24:44–45; John 14:26.)

(6) Scripture Is Able to Be Understood, but Not without Some Misunderstanding. The clarity of Scripture is a property of Scripture, not a property of its readers.[21] The doctrine of the clarity of Scripture affirms that Scripture *can* be understood rightly by various readers, not that it *will* always be understood rightly by them. The disciples failed to understand some of Jesus's teachings, for Luke tells us that "they did not understand this saying" (Luke 9:45), and John says that "as yet they did not understand the Scripture, that he must rise from the dead" (John 20:9). In fact, there will be some who willfully misunderstand and distort what Scripture says, for Peter says, regarding some of Paul's writings, that "the ignorant and unstable" twist them "to their own destruction, as they do the other Scriptures" (2 Pet. 3:16; see also 2 Pet. 3:3–6).

Therefore, the clarity of Scripture guarantees that the Bible can be understood rightly, not that all believers will understand it rightly.

(7) Scripture Is Able to Be Understood, but Never Completely. Although we do understand Scripture at some level, even from childhood, we grow in our understanding as we progress through the Christian life. The writer of Hebrews mentions that some teaching is "solid food" for the "mature" (Heb. 5:14; see also 1 Cor. 3:1–4). We will never exhaust the wisdom of God contained in Scripture, for God's thoughts are higher than our thoughts "as the heavens are higher than the earth" (Isa. 55:9).

These seven qualifications, however, do not at all nullify the doctrine of the clarity of Scripture. The Bible is still understandable. Some parts can be understood more easily and quickly than others, but these qualifications are appropriate for a large and complex document coming from a person who has infinite wisdom and who wants us to spend a lifetime learning from him in personal relationship with him.

c. Objections to the Clarity of Scripture. We can briefly mention that biblical scholars coming from a nonevangelical perspective will often be reluctant to affirm a doctrine of the clarity of Scripture. First, scholars speaking from the perspective of *theological liberalism* will not think of the Bible as God's Word and internally consistent, but will think of it as "a fallible human record of religious thought and experience rather than a divine revelation of truth and reality."[22] According to this view, Scripture contains numerous conflicting meanings because it was written by numerous human authors who lived in widely differing Hebrew, Greek, and Roman cultures, and who had different

---

[21] I am grateful to Gregg Allison for first emphasizing to me how the focus of this doctrine must be on the nature of Scripture, not the misunderstandings of its various readers. See Gregg Allison, "The Protestant Doctrine of the Perspicuity of Scripture: A Reformulation on the Basis of Biblical Teaching" (PhD thesis, Trinity Evangelical Divinity School, Deerfield, Illinois, 1995).

[22] J. I. Packer, "Liberalism and Conservatism in Theology," *New Dictionary of Theology*, ed. Sinclair B. Ferguson and David F. Wright (Leicester, UK: Inter-Varsity, and Downers Grove, IL: InterVarsity, 1988), 385.

ideas of God and different experiences of him. From this perspective, any claim that the overall message of the Bible as a whole on certain ethical topics is understandable and clear would seem to lack any basis in fact. That is because, without a conviction as to the divine authorship of Scripture, there is no reason to assume that the conclusions of the authors would be internally consistent instead of conflicting and contradictory.

But this objection is based on a denial of the frequent claims of Scripture itself to be not merely human words but the very words of God, as we noted above.

Another objection comes from *postmodern hermeneutics*, a viewpoint that claims there is no absolute truth and no single meaning in a text. Rather, meaning depends on the assumptions and purposes that a reader brings to a text.[23] Therefore, *claims* to know what Scripture means on any topic are just disguised attempts to exert power over others. Mark Thompson notes that this postmodern understanding of truth has developed the suspicion, stated earlier by Friedrich Nietzsche (1844–1900), "that all claims to know what is true are in reality covert attempts to manipulate people."[24]

But such a denial that the meaning of Scripture can be known is ultimately an attack on the character of God—his goodness, his power, and his ability to communicate clearly to his people. And it is surely inconsistent with the many passages we examined above on the understandability of Scripture to ordinary people.

In addition, scriptural authors frequently base an argument on the idea that a text in Scripture means one thing but not another. "It was *not* after, *but* before he was circumcised" (Rom. 4:10, referring to the scriptural story about Abraham). The words of Genesis "were *not* written for his sake alone, *but* for ours also" (Rom. 4:23–24; see also Heb. 2:5–6; 4:8; 11:3).

The doctrine of the clarity of Scripture also differs from *Roman Catholic teaching*, which says that, with regard to properly interpreting Scripture, "The task of interpretation has been entrusted to the bishops in communion with the successor of Peter, the Bishop of Rome."[25] However, neither the teachings of Jesus nor the New Testament Epistles give any hint that believing readers need an authoritative interpreter of Scripture such as the bishop of Rome (that is, the pope). As noted above, Moses expected ordinary people to teach the Scriptures to their children; Jesus held everyone responsible for having a right understanding of Scripture; and Paul wrote many of his epistles to entire churches, even addressing some sections to children, and thus assuming that they would be listening and understanding.

d. Positive Implications of the Clarity of Scripture. The clarity of Scripture encourages us that we can teach biblical ethics to Christians today. Scholars in col-

---

[23] See the extensive discussions of postmodern hermeneutics in Grant R. Osborne, *The Hermeneutical Spiral: A Comprehensive Introduction to Biblical Interpretation* (Downers Grove, IL: InterVarsity Press, 1991), and Kevin J. Vanhoozer, *Is There a Meaning in This Text?* (Grand Rapids, MI: Zondervan, 1998).

[24] Mark D. Thompson, *A Clear and Present Word: The Clarity of Scripture*, New Studies in Biblical Theology (Nottingham, UK: Apollos, and Downers Grove, IL: InterVarsity Press, 2006), 33.

[25] *Catechism of the Catholic Church*, 2nd ed. (New York: Doubleday, 1997), 32 (sec. 85).

leges and seminaries, as well as pastors in churches, are not limited to studying only "Mosaic ethics," "Old Testament ethics," or "Pauline ethics" (all of which are valuable in their own right), but we should also be preaching and writing about "what the whole Bible teaches about ethical questions" with clear application to ordinary people's lives today.

In fact, the doctrine of the clarity of Scripture is absolutely essential if the Bible is to have any effective authority in people's lives. Without the clarity of Scripture someone could say, "I believe fully in the absolute divine authority of Scripture—but I have no idea what it requires me to believe or how it requires me to live." In this way, if Scripture has no clarity, its authority is effectively nullified in real life.

3. Necessity: The Bible Is Necessary for Knowing God's Declarations of Right and Wrong. With regard to Christian ethics, the necessity of Scripture is important because it tells us that we need the Bible in order to have any certain knowledge of God's will with respect to moral right and wrong.

Elsewhere I define the necessity of Scripture in a broader sense as follows:

> **The necessity of Scripture** means that the Bible is necessary for knowing the gospel, for maintaining spiritual life, and for knowing God's will, but is not necessary for knowing that God exists or for knowing something about God's character and moral laws.[26]

In that longer discussion in my book *Systematic Theology*, I examine passages that talk about the necessity of reading the Bible (or somehow learning the Bible's message) for knowing the gospel (this includes passages such as Rom. 10:13–17; John 3:18; 14:6; Acts 4:12; 1 Tim. 2:5–6). I also argue there that the Bible is necessary for maintaining spiritual life (see Matt. 4:4, quoting Deut. 8:3; see also Deut. 32:47; 1 Pet. 2:2).

However, in this book, and for purposes of studying ethics, our primary concern has to do with the necessity of the Bible for "knowing God's will." In terms of that focus, we can say that *the Bible is necessary for knowing God's declarations of right and wrong.*

a. The Study of Natural Law Has Some Value. Before I focus on the necessity of the Bible, however, I must affirm that people can indeed know *something* of God's moral laws apart from the Bible. Even without the specific moral teachings of the Bible, human beings have consciences that give them an *inward sense of right and wrong.* In addition, people are able to observe the way many other people act and the way everything functions in the world, and then they can *reason* about those observations and draw *conclusions about human nature* and about the right and wrong actions that are appropriate to human nature. The set of moral conclusions resulting from this type of study is known as "natural law."

---

[26] Grudem, *Systematic Theology*, 116.

Here is the definition of natural law as given by Gregg Allison:

> The rule, in accordance with God's moral law for human conduct, that is found in human nature. It is known by human beings through reason and enables them to discern right from wrong.[27]

Allison then goes on to explain, "Particularly important in Catholic theology, natural law is embraced cautiously by some Protestants."[28]

My own position is that the study of natural law has some value and carries some persuasive force with most people. Therefore, in several of the following chapters I will use arguments not only from the Bible but also from human reason and observations, apart from the Bible, about the consequences of various actions. I do not consider such arguments to be equal to the Bible in authority, but they can provide some supplemental confirmation of the rightness of our conclusions about biblical moral teachings.

The value of the study of natural law is evident when we realize that every person ever born has been given a conscience by God and therefore has some knowledge of right and wrong. This knowledge is not perfect, but it gives an approximation of God's moral will with more or less accuracy. Paul says that Gentiles who do not have the written law of God "show that the *work of the law is written on their hearts*, while their *conscience* also bears witness, and their conflicting thoughts accuse or even excuse them" (Rom. 2:15). In fact, Paul develops a long argument to show the moral guilt of all human beings before God, even those who do not "honor him as God or give thanks to him" (1:21), because they willfully do what they know is wrong:

> Though *they know God's righteous decree* that those who practice such things deserve to die, they not only do them but give approval to those who practice them. (Rom. 1:32; cf. all of Rom. 1:18–32; see also Ps. 19:1; Acts 14:16–17)

Therefore, we can conclude that all people ever born have *some* knowledge of God's will in their consciences. But this knowledge is often indistinct and cannot give certainty. In fact, if there were *no* written Word of God in the world, we *could not* gain certainty about God's will through other means, such as conscience, advice from others who are wise, and the use of human reasoning and common sense. These all might give an *approximation* of God's will in more or less reliable ways, but from these means alone no certainty about God's will could ever be attained, at least in a fallen world where sin distorts our perception of right and wrong, brings faulty reasoning into our thinking

---

[27] Gregg Allison, *The Baker Compact Dictionary of Theological Terms* (Grand Rapids, MI: Baker, 2016), 144. See also Arthur F. Holmes, "Natural Law," in *New Dictionary of Christian Ethics and Pastoral Theology*, ed. David J. Atkinson and David H. Field (Leicester, UK: Inter-Varsity, and Downers Grove, IL: InterVarsity, 1995), 619–21; J. Budziszewski, *Written on the Heart: The Case for Natural Law* (Downers Grove, IL: IVP Academic, 1997).

[28] Ibid.

processes, and causes us from time to time to suppress the testimony of our consciences (see Jer. 17:9; Rom. 2:14–15; 1 Cor. 8:10; Heb. 5:14; 10:22; also 1 Tim. 4:2; Titus 1:15). Therefore, natural law also has significant limitations when compared to the clear and explicit moral teachings of God's very words in the Bible.

b. The Bible Alone Contains God's Explicit Teachings about Moral Right and Wrong. In the Bible alone, by contrast, we have something more than the general impressions of our consciences and the conclusions we can develop by observing and reasoning about human nature. In the Bible, we have clear and definite verbal statements about God's will:

> The secret things belong to the LORD our God, but the *things that are revealed* belong to us and to our children forever, *that we may do all the words of this law.* (Deut. 29:29)

God has revealed his *words* to us in the Bible so that we might obey his laws and thereby do his will. To be "blameless" in God's sight is to "walk in the law of the LORD" (Ps. 119:1). To love God is to "keep his commandments" (1 John 5:3). If we are going to have a certain knowledge of God's will concerning right and wrong, then we must attain it through study of his commandments, which are found in the Bible.

If God's moral standards are defined explicitly only in the words of the Bible, then we would expect that secular studies of philosophical ethics, studies that do not explicitly subject themselves to the words of Scripture, would produce only tentative and conflicting results. And that is exactly what we find. The field of philosophical ethics throughout history has produced no consensus about how to know what kinds of actions and attitudes should be considered morally right and morally wrong.

The implication of the doctrine of the necessity of Scripture for our study of ethics is that we need to pay very careful attention to the teachings of Scripture and to take great care that we are interpreting it rightly. In addition, we should not be too surprised that ethicists who do not affirm the absolute divine authority of Scripture fail to reach agreement with Christians who do affirm it, or with each other, about a large number of ethical topics.

4. Sufficiency: God's Word Gives Us Substantial Freedom Regarding Numerous Ethical Decisions.

a. Scriptural Evidence for the Sufficiency of Scripture. The sufficiency of Scripture is important for ethics because it tells us that God has given us a limited number of ethical requirements in Scripture and has left us with substantial freedom in areas to which the Bible does not speak.

In an earlier publication, I define the sufficiency of Scripture in a broader way:

> **The sufficiency of Scripture** means that Scripture . . . contains all the words of God we need for salvation, for trusting him perfectly, and for obeying him perfectly.[29]

In that discussion, I examine texts that affirm that the Bible instructs people for salvation (2 Tim. 3:15; James 1:18; 1 Pet. 1:23). But for purposes of this book, we will focus on the sufficiency of Scripture for studying ethics. Once again, Paul's well-known statement about the nature of Scripture is most appropriate:

> All Scripture is breathed out by God and profitable for teaching, for reproof, for correction, and for training in righteousness, that the man of God[30] may be *complete, equipped for very good work.* (2 Tim. 3:16–17)

One purpose for which God caused Scripture to be written is to train us that we might be "equipped for every good work." This applies to all of life. If there is any "good work" that God wants a Christian to do, this passage indicates that God has made provision in his Word for training the Christian in it. Thus, there is no "good work" that God wants us to do other than those that are taught (at least in a broad sense) somewhere in Scripture: it is written to equip us for *every* good work.

A similar teaching is found in Psalm 119:

> Blessed are those whose way is *blameless,*
> who walk in the law of the LORD! (v. 1)

To simply "walk in the law of the LORD" is to be "blameless" before God. This again is an indication that all that God requires of us is recorded in his written Word: to do all that the Bible commands us is to be blameless in God's sight.

b. Implication: We Can Find All That God Has Said on Particular Topics and Answers to Our Ethical Questions in the Bible. The sufficiency of Scripture enables us to focus our search for God's words to us on the Bible alone, which saves us from searching through all the writings of Christians throughout history, all the teachings of the church, or all of our subjective feelings and impressions[31] in order to discover what God requires

---

[29] Grudem, *Systematic Theology*, 127. I have omitted a section of the definition that dealt with various periods in redemptive history, but that was not essential to the heart of the definition.

[30] The phrase "man of God" repeats a common Old Testament expression that refers to God's messengers, but the intention of the passage is to speak about the sufficiency of Scripture for training all of God's people, and certainly both men and women.

[31] This is not meant to imply that subjective impressions of God's will are useless or that they should be ignored. That would suggest almost a deistic view of God's (non)involvement in the lives of his children and a rather mechanical, impersonal view of guidance. God can and indeed does use subjective impressions of his will to remind and encourage us, and often to prompt our thoughts in the right direction in the many rapid decisions that we make throughout the day—and it is Scripture itself that tells us about these subjective factors in guidance (see Acts 16:6–7; Rom. 8:9, 14, 16; Gal. 5:16–18, 25). See further discussion in chap. 6, p. 161.

of us. This means that we can reach clear conclusions on many teachings of Scripture. For example, though it requires some work, it is possible to find all the biblical passages that are directly relevant to the matters of marriage and divorce, the responsibilities of parents to children, or the relationship between a Christian and civil government. Moreover, the sufficiency of Scripture gives us confidence that we *will be able to find* what God requires us to do in various areas. In many areas of ethics, we can attain confidence that we, together with the vast majority of Christians throughout history, have found and correctly formulated what actions, attitudes, and personal characteristics God approves. Simply stated, this doctrine tells us that it is possible to study ethics and find answers to many of our questions.

On this point we differ from Roman Catholic ethicists, who argue that we have not found all that God says to us about any particular subject until we have also consulted the official teaching of the church throughout its history. We would respond that although the history of the church may help us to *understand* what God says to us in the Bible, never in church history has God *added* to the teachings or commands of Scripture. Nowhere in church life, outside of Scripture, has God *added* anything that he requires us to believe or do. Scripture is sufficient to equip us for "every good work," and to walk in its ways is to be "blameless" in God's sight.

We also differ from nonevangelical theologians, who are not convinced that the Bible is God's Word in any unique or absolutely authoritative sense, and who therefore would also search many other early Christian writings in an attempt to learn not so much *what God said* to mankind but rather *what many early Christians experienced* in their relationship with God. They would not expect to arrive at a unified conclusion about what God wants us to think or do on any specific question, but to discover a variety of opinions and viewpoints on major unifying ideas.[32] So all of the viewpoints held by Christians in any of the early churches would be potentially valid for Christians today. To this we would reply that our search for answers to ethical questions is not an attempt to find what various believers have thought in the history of the church, but a quest to find and understand what God himself says to us in his own words, which are found only in Scripture.

c. Practical Applications of the Sufficiency of Scripture. This doctrine has several practical applications to our Christian lives. These include the following:

1. *The sufficiency of Scripture should encourage us as we try to discover what God would have us to do in particular situations.* Everything God wants to tell us about a question is to be found in Scripture. This does not mean that the Bible answers all the questions that we might think to ask, for "The secret things belong to the Lord our God" (Deut. 29:29). But it does mean that when we are facing a problem of genuine importance to

---

[32] The widely used ethics textbook by Robin Gill follows this pattern. It is a compilation of numerous extracts from the writings of Christian authors throughout history on various ethical topics. See Robin Gill, *A Textbook of Christian Ethics*, 4th ed. (London: Bloomsbury T&T Clark, 2014).

our Christian lives, we can approach the Bible with the confidence that God will use it to guide us.

Of course, Scripture does not speak directly to every question. (For example, we would be disappointed if we tried to find from Scripture what "order of worship" to follow on Sunday mornings or when we should eat our meals during the day.) In those cases, we may conclude that God has not required us to think or to act in any certain way (except, perhaps, in terms of more general principles regarding our attitudes and goals).

2. The sufficiency of Scripture reminds us that *we are to add nothing to Scripture*, and that *we are to consider no other writings of equal value to Scripture*. Almost all cults and sects violate this principle. Mormons, for example, profess to believe the Bible, but they also claim divine authority for *The Book of Mormon*. Since such claims violate God's commands not to add to his words, we should not think that any additional words from God will be found in these writings.

3. The sufficiency of Scripture shows us that *no modern revelations from God are to be placed on a level equal to Scripture in authority*. Throughout the history of the church, and especially in the modern charismatic movement, people have claimed that God has given revelations through them for the church. However we may evaluate such claims,[33] we must never regard such revelations as equal to Scripture.[34] Rather, we must insist that God does not require us to obey any moral directives that come to us through such means but are not confirmed by Scripture.[35] Whenever other documents have been placed alongside Scripture (whether extrabiblical Christian literature of the first century, the accumulated teachings of the Roman Catholic Church, or various cult publications), the result has always been a de-emphasis on the teachings of the Bible itself and the teaching of some things contrary to Scripture. The church must constantly remain aware of this danger.

4. The sufficiency of Scripture reminds us that *nothing is sin that is not forbidden by Scripture either explicitly or by implication*. To walk in the law of the Lord is to be "blameless" (Ps. 119:1). Therefore, we are not to add prohibitions to those already stated in Scripture. There may be unusual situations when it would be wrong, for example, for a Christian to drink coffee or Coca-Cola or to go to movie theaters (see 1 Corinthians 8–10), but these activities should not be seen as sinful in themselves unless a

---

[33] See Grudem, *Systematic Theology*, 1039–42, on the possibility of some kinds of revelation from God continuing today when the canon is closed, and especially 1049–61 on the gift of prophecy.

[34] In fact, the more responsible spokesmen for the modern charismatic movement seem generally to agree with this caution: see Wayne Grudem, *The Gift of Prophecy in the New Testament and Today* (Wheaton, IL: Crossway, 2000), 90–92, 209–14.

[35] I do not wish to imply at this point that I am adopting a "cessationist" view of spiritual gifts (that is, a view that certain gifts, such as prophecy and speaking in tongues, ceased when the apostles died). I only wish at this point to state that there is a danger in explicitly or even implicitly giving these gifts a status that effectively challenges the authority or the sufficiency of Scripture in Christians' lives. More detailed discussions of these gifts are given in Grudem, *Systematic Theology*, 1049–88, and in Grudem, *The Gift of Prophecy in the New Testament and Today*.

specific teaching or general principle of Scripture can be shown to prohibit them for all believers for all time.[36]

There is always a tendency among believers to begin to neglect the regular daily searching of Scripture for guidance and to begin to live by written (or unwritten) rules or traditions concerning what to do or not do in the Christian life. But whenever we add to the list of sins that are prohibited by Scripture itself, there will be harm to the church and to the lives of individual believers. The Holy Spirit will not empower obedience to rules that do not have God's approval from Scripture, nor will believers generally find delight in obeying commands that do not accord with the laws of God written on their hearts.

In some cases, Christians may repeatedly and earnestly plead with God for "victory" over supposed sins that are in fact not sins at all, yet no "victory" will be given, for the attitude or action is not displeasing to God. Great discouragement in prayer and general frustration in the Christian life may be the result. In other cases, continued disobedience to these new "sins" will result, along with a false sense of guilt and a resulting alienation from God. And there may arise an increasingly uncompromising and legalistic insistence on these new rules on the part of those who *do* follow them, disrupting genuine fellowship among believers. Finally, evangelism will often be stifled, for the silent proclamation of the gospel that comes from the lives of believers will at least *seem* to outsiders to include the additional requirement that one must fit this uniform pattern of life in order to become a member of the body of Christ.

One example of such an addition to the commands of Scripture is found in the Roman Catholic Church's opposition to "artificial" methods of birth control, a policy that finds no valid support in Scripture. Widespread disobedience, alienation, and false guilt have been the result.

5. The sufficiency of Scripture also tells us that *God requires nothing of us that is not commanded in Scripture either explicitly or by implication.* So we should focus our search for God's will on Scripture instead of seeking guidance through prayer for changed circumstances or altered feelings, or looking for direct guidance from

---

[36] Of course, human societies such as nations, churches, families, and so on can make rules for the conduct of their own affairs (such as "Children in this family may not watch television on weeknights"). No such rule can be found in Scripture, nor is it likely that such a rule could be demonstrated by implication from the principles of Scripture. Yet obedience to these rules is required by God because Scripture tells us to be subject to governing authorities (Rom. 13:1–7; 1 Pet. 2:13–3:6). A denial of the sufficiency of Scripture would occur only if someone attempted to give the rule a generalized application outside of the situation in which it should appropriately function ("No member of our church should watch TV on weeknights" or "No Christian should watch TV on weeknights"). In such a case, it becomes not a rule for conduct in one specific situation but a moral command apparently intended to apply to all Christians no matter what their situation. We are not free to add such rules to Scripture and to attempt to impose them on all the believers over whom we have influence, nor can the church as a whole attempt to do this. (Here again, Roman Catholics would differ and would say that God gives to the church the authority to impose moral rules in addition to Scripture on all the members of the church.)

the Holy Spirit apart from Scripture. If someone *claims* to have a message from God telling us what we ought to do, we need never assume that it is sin to disobey such a message—unless it can be confirmed by the application of Scripture itself to our situation.

The discovery of this great truth could bring tremendous joy and peace to thousands of Christians who have spent hours seeking God's will outside of Scripture, only to be left uncertain about whether they have found it. In fact, many Christians today have very little confidence in their ability to discover God's will with any degree of certainty. Thus, there is little striving to do God's will (for who can know it?) and little growth in holiness before God in their lives.

The opposite ought to be true. Christians who are convinced of the sufficiency of Scripture should begin eagerly to seek and find God's will in the Bible. They should be growing in obedience to him and knowing great freedom and peace in their Christian lives. Then they would be able to say with the psalmist:

> I will keep your law continually,
>> forever and ever,
> *and I shall walk in a wide place,*
>> *for I have sought your precepts.* . . .
> *Great peace have those who love your law;*
>> nothing can make them stumble. (Ps. 119:44–45, 165)

QUESTIONS FOR PERSONAL APPLICATION

1. Do you feel offended when your pastor preaches about the importance of seeking to avoid sin in your life or the importance of living in obedience to God's moral commands? Would you prefer that he avoid those topics or at least minimize them in his Bible teaching?

2. If you are a pastor or a Bible study leader, are there certain sins mentioned in the Bible that you mostly avoid talking about? If so, do you think that contributes to the spiritual health of your congregation?

3. If children do not learn in church about God's moral standards, what influences will play the strongest role in forming their personal moral convictions?

4. When you read the Bible, does it seem to you (honestly!) to have more authority than any other book?

5. What convinced you to believe that the words of the Bible are the very words of God?

6. After reading about the authority, clarity, necessity, and sufficiency of Scripture, which of these qualities were you most encouraged and even excited to learn about? Why?

SPECIAL TERMS

authority of Scripture
clarity of Scripture
the gospel
natural law
necessity of Scripture
postmodern hermeneutics
seeker-sensitive services
sufficiency of Scripture
theological liberalism
third use of the law

BIBLIOGRAPHY

Sections in Other Ethics Texts

(see complete bibliographical data, p. 64)

Clark and Rakestraw, 1:179–248, 67–112
Feinberg, John and Paul, 40–49
Frame, 131–236
Geisler, 125–27
Gushee and Stassen, 43–63
Holmes, 59–70
Jones, 59–76
McQuilkin and Copan, 29–93
Rae, 28–51

Other Works

Budziszewski, J. *Written on the Heart: The Case for Natural Law.* Downers Grove, IL: InterVarsity Press, 1997.

Gooding, David W., and John Lennox. *The Bible and Ethics.* Coleraine, Northern Ireland: The Myrtlefield Trust, 2015.

MacArthur, John, ed. *Think Biblically! Recovering a Christian Worldview.* Wheaton, IL: Crossway, 2003.

Mangalwadi, Vishal. *The Book That Made Your World: How the Bible Created the Soul of Western Civilization.* Nashville: Thomas Nelson, 2011.

Naselli, Andrew David, and J. D. Crowley. *Conscience: What It Is, How to Train It, and Loving Those Who Differ.* Wheaton, IL: Crossway, 2016.

Pritchard, G. A. *Willow Creek Seeker Services: Evaluating a New Way of Doing Church.* Grand Rapids, MI: Baker, 1996.

Scott, Stuart, and Heath Lambert, eds. *Counseling the Hard Cases: True Stories Illustrating the Sufficiency of God's Resources in Scripture.* Nashville: B&H Academic, 2012.

Sinton, V. M. "Gospel and Ethics." In *New Dictionary of Christian Ethics and Pastoral Theology,* edited by David J. Atkinson and David H. Field, 414–15. Leicester, UK: Inter-Varsity, and Downers Grove, IL: InterVarsity Press, 1995.

SCRIPTURE MEMORY PASSAGE

2 Timothy 3:16–17: All Scripture is breathed out by God and profitable for teaching, for reproof, for correction, and for training in righteousness, that the man of God may be complete, equipped for every good work.

HYMN

"Teach Me Thy Way, O Lord"

Teach me Thy Way, O Lord, Teach me Thy Way!
Thy guiding grace afford—Teach me Thy Way!
Help me to walk aright, more by faith, less by sight;
Lead me with heav'nly light—Teach me Thy Way!

When I am sad at heart, Teach me Thy Way!
When earthly joys depart, Teach me Thy Way!
In hours of loneliness, in times of dire distress,
In failure or success, Teach me Thy Way!

When doubts and fears arise, Teach me Thy Way!
When storms o'er spread the skies, Teach me Thy Way!
Shine thru the cloud and rain, thru sorrow, toil and pain;
Make Thou my pathway plain—Teach me Thy Way!

Long as my life shall last, Teach me Thy Way!
Where'er my lot be cast, Teach me Thy Way!
Until the race is run, until the journey's done,
Until the crown is won, Teach me Thy Way!

AUTHOR: B. MANSELL RAMSEY, 1849–1923

ALTERNATIVE HYMN

"The Law of the Lord Is Perfect"

The law of the Lord is perfect,
converting the soul.

The testimony of the Lord is sure,
making wise the simple.

Refrain:
More to be desired are they than gold,
yea than much fine gold.
Sweeter also than honey
and the honeycomb.

The statutes of the Lord are right,
rejoicing the heart.
The commandments of the Lord are pure,
enlight'ning the eyes.

The fear of the Lord is clean,
enduring forever.
The judgments of the Lord are true,
and righteous altogether.

AUTHOR: ANONYMOUS (FROM PS. 19:7–11)

Chapter 4

THE GOAL OF ETHICS: LIVING FOR THE GLORY OF GOD

Why should Christian ethics include more than learning about right actions?

Why is it important to develop Christlike character?

Why should we consider the results of our actions?

How is the study of ethics related to our personal relationship with God?

A. A LIFE LIVED FOR THE GLORY OF GOD

What is the overall goal of studying ethics? It should be to fulfill our ultimate purpose, which is to glorify God.

In the Old Testament, God speaks in this way about his sons and daughters:

> whom I created *for my glory*,
> whom I formed and made. (Isa. 43:7; see also v. 21)

The New Testament similarly affirms that before the foundation of the world God predestined people to be saved "so that we who were the first to hope in Christ might be *to the praise of his glory*" (Eph. 1:12). Because God created us to glorify him, it makes perfect sense that the New Testament should tell us, "Whether you eat or drink, or whatever you do, *do all to the glory of God*" (1 Cor. 10:31).

In summary of this perspective, the Westminster Larger Catechism says:

Question 1: What is the chief and highest end of man?

Answer: Man's chief and highest end is to glorify God, and fully to enjoy him forever.

B. THREE PERSPECTIVES ON A LIFE LIVED FOR THE GLORY OF GOD

It might at first seem quite abstract to say to people, "You should live for the glory of God." Exactly what does that mean? What does a life lived for God's glory look like?

The Bible is a rich treasure house of material that helps us answer these questions in specific ways. For purposes of this book, we will focus on what the Bible says with regard to three perspectives on a life lived for the glory of God: (1) our *personal character*, (2) the *results* that come from our lives, and (3) our actual *behavior*, our conduct of life.

It should not surprise us that God is concerned with more than just our behavior. He is interested in us as whole persons, not just in the individual actions that we do. He wants us not merely to *do* morally good *actions*, but he also wants us to *be* morally good *people*. Also, he wants our lives to have morally good results, results that please him and honor him. The following three sections of this chapter discuss those perspectives in more detail.[1]

In summary, a life lived for the glory of God will be one that has:

1. a character that glorifies God: a Christlike character.
2. results that glorify God: a life that bears abundant fruit for God's kingdom.
3. behavior that glorifies God: a life of obedience to God, lived in personal relationship with God.

C. THE CHARACTER GOAL: A LIFE CONFORMED TO THE IMAGE OF CHRIST

One division of ethical study is called "virtue ethics" (see chap. 1, p. 42). This is a study of what character qualities people should strive for. "Virtues" in ethics are habitual

---

[1] Readers of John M. Frame's book *The Doctrine of the Christian Life: A Theology of Lordship* (Phillipsburg, NJ: P&R, 2008) will recognize some similarity to his use of three perspectives on ethical life: What I call character is similar to his "existential" category; what I call results is similar to his "situational" category; and what I call behavior is similar to his "normative" category. My goal is to use terms that are readily understandable by ordinary readers and that capture the broad sweep of biblical testimony regarding the kind of life God wants us to live. These three perspectives are one helpful way of summarizing the biblical teaching. (Frame's three perspectives do that as well.) And both Frame and I would acknowledge that the categories are not absolutely distinct from one another, for many parts of the biblical testimony could fit rather well into either one category or another of these three. They are three "perspectives" (a favorite Frame word) on the whole of a life lived for the glory of God.

inward dispositions to act, feel, respond, and think in morally good ways.[2] I will sometimes refer to such virtues as "character traits."

The Bible is certainly concerned with developing moral virtue in Christian believers, for dozens of passages talk about desirable personal character traits that Christians should try to show in their lives. Peter says that Christians should make every effort to add to their Christian faith "virtue" (2 Pet. 1:5), and here he uses the Greek word (*aretē*), which was commonly used among Greek philosophers to talk about desirable traits that people should strive to incorporate into their own lives.

This does not mean that the ethical values of the Bible are the same as the ethical values of pagan Greek philosophy, however. R. C. Roberts explains:

> Some things that are true of Christian hope may not be true of Marxist hope; what is true of Christian peace may not be true of Stoic equanimity; what is true of Christian courage may not be true of Aristotelian courage. The way a mature Christian handles his fear (namely, his courage) will essentially involve his belief that God is present and trustworthy; thus it will depend on the practice of prayer and the experience of the Holy Spirit. Since the Aristotelian neither practices prayer, nor believes that God is present, nor has any experience of the Holy Spirit, his courage is not the same trait as the Christian's.[3]

1. Our Character Goal Is to Be Conformed to the Image of Christ. Paul says this about Christians: "Those whom he foreknew he also predestined to be *conformed to the image of his Son*" (Rom. 8:29). The purpose for which God chose us is that we would be conformed to the image of Christ, that is, that we would be like Christ in our character and our actions. Paul similarly says, "Just as we have borne the image of the man of dust, we shall also *bear the image of the man of heaven*" (1 Cor. 15:49), and the "man of heaven" in this passage is Christ. We will bear his image, which means we will be like him.

2. Becoming Like Christ Is a Lifelong Process.[4] Many passages in the New Testament talk about a lifelong process of becoming like Christ. "Be imitators of me,

---

[2] I am grateful to David Horner for helping me think about a clear definition of virtues (though I am responsible for this form of the definition). M. A. Reid explains that virtues and vices are "habitual inner tendencies, or dispositions, to perform morally good or bad acts." "Vice," in *New Dictionary of Christian Ethics and Pastoral Theology*, ed. David J. Atkinson and David H. Field (Leicester, UK: Inter-Varsity, and Downers Grove, IL: InterVarsity, 1995), 874. But virtues also include tendencies or dispositions to think and feel in morally good ways: see R. C. Roberts, "Virtue, Virtues," in Atkinson and Field, *New Dictionary of Christian Ethics and Pastoral Theology*, who says that a person's virtues "determine his or her concerns, desires, emotions and perceptions of virtually everything, as well as his or her actions" (p. 881).

[3] R. C. Roberts, "Character," in Atkinson and Field, *New Dictionary of Christian Ethics and Pastoral Theology*, 66.

[4] This section is adapted from Wayne Grudem, *Systematic Theology: An Introduction to Biblical Doctrine* (Leicester, UK: Inter-Varsity, and Grand Rapids, MI: Zondervan, 1994), 845–46, with permission of the publishers.

as I am of Christ," writes Paul (1 Cor. 11:1), implying that even mature believers among Paul's readers still needed to be encouraged to seek to imitate him, just as he continued to seek to imitate Christ. John reminds us, "Whoever says he abides in him ought to walk in the same way in which he walked" (1 John 2:6). Our lives ought to so reflect what his life was like that we bring honor to him in everything we do (Phil. 1:20).

For this reason, the New Testament pictures the Christian as one who strives to imitate Christ in all of his or her actions: "Welcome one another *as Christ has welcomed you*" (Rom. 15:7); "Husbands, love your wives, *as Christ loved the church*" (Eph. 5:25); "*As the Lord has forgiven you*, so you also must forgive" (Col. 3:13); "He laid down his life for us, and we ought to lay down our lives for the brothers" (1 John 3:16). Throughout our lives, we are to "run . . . the race that is set before us, looking to Jesus, the founder and perfecter of our faith" (Heb. 12:1–2; see also Eph. 5:2; Phil. 2:5–11; 1 Thess. 1:6; 1 John 3:7; 4:17). By contrast, disobedience holds Christ up to contempt (Heb. 6:6).

Our imitation of Christ is especially evident in suffering. Christians are called to endure suffering patiently "because Christ also suffered for you, leaving you an example, so that you might *follow in his steps*" (1 Pet. 2:21). Paul wanted to "share his [Christ's] sufferings, becoming *like him in his death*" (Phil. 3:10; see also 2 Cor. 1:5; 4:8–11; Heb. 12:3; 1 Peter 4:13).

Furthermore, our suffering is connected with sharing in Christ's glory when he returns: "We suffer with him in order that we may also be glorified with him" (Rom. 8:17). This is probably so because it is through suffering and difficulty that God makes us more Christlike, growing us to maturity in him (Eph. 4:13, 15; James 1:2–4; Heb. 5:8–9).

Also, since Christ perfectly obeyed his Father even in the face of great suffering, so our obedience, trust, and patience in suffering more fully portray what Christ was like, and so bring more honor to him. It gives us great comfort to know that we are experiencing only what he has already experienced, and that he therefore understands what we are going through and listens sympathetically to our prayers (Heb. 2:18; 4:15–16; 12:11). As the outcome of a life of obedience, we are able to share in Christ's glory: "The one who conquers, I will grant him to sit with me on my throne, as I also conquered and sat down with my Father on his throne" (Rev. 3:21).

Our imitation of Christ is no mere mimicking of his actions, however. The far deeper purpose is that in imitating him we are becoming more and more like him: *when we act like Christ we become like Christ*. We grow up to maturity in Christ (Eph. 4:13, 15; Heb. 5:8–9; James 1:2–4) as we are "being transformed into the same image from one degree of glory to another" (2 Cor. 3:18). The final result is that we shall become perfectly like Christ, just as God has predestined us (Rom. 8:29; 1 Cor. 15:49), and "when he appears *we shall be like him*" (1 John 3:2). When this happens, Christ will be fully glorified in us (2 Thess. 1:10–12; John 17:10).

Yet in all of this we never lose our individual personhood. We become perfectly *like* Christ, but *we do not become Christ*, and we are not absorbed into Christ or lost forever as individuals. Rather, it is we as real individuals who shall still know as we are known (1 Cor. 13:12); it is we who shall see him as he is (1 John 3:2); it is we who shall worship him, see his face, have his name on our foreheads, and reign with him for ever and ever (Rev. 22:3–5). Just as the Father, Son, and Holy Spirit are exactly like one another in character (John 14:7, 9), yet remain distinct persons, so we can become more and more like Christ and still be distinct individuals with different gifts and different functions (Eph. 4:15–16; 1 Cor. 12:4–27).

In fact, the more like Christ we become, the more truly ourselves we become (Matt. 10:39; John 10:3; Rev. 2:17; Ps. 37:4). If we forget this, we will tend to neglect the diversity of gifts in the church and will want to make everyone like ourselves. We will also tend to deny any ultimate importance for ourselves as individuals. A proper biblical perspective will allow each believer to say not only, "We Christians are important to Christ," but also, "*I* am important to Christ: he knows my name, he calls me by name, and he gives me a new name which is mine alone" (see John 10:3; Rev. 2:17).

3. A Partial List of Christlike Character Traits or "Virtues." This section contains a fairly extensive (but not exhaustive) list of the character traits that the New Testament Epistles encourage people to imitate in the process of becoming like Christ.[5] For the sake of brevity, I have confined this list to the character traits named in the New Testament Epistles, but more could be added from the Gospels, especially the Sermon on the Mount, such as "poor in spirit" (Matt. 5:3) or "those who hunger and thirst for righteousness" (v. 6). In fact, the entire life of Christ in the Gospels could be a source for even more character traits than those found in this list. (The longer I worked on this list, the more I realized that even this list of 27 items is incomplete, and more character traits could still be added.)[6]

We can grow in these character traits through a combination of our own effort and the power of the Holy Spirit.[7] The first verse in the list below reminds us that these character traits are "the fruit of the Spirit" (Gal. 5:22), so they are produced by the power of the Holy Spirit working in us. But we cannot be passive in this process, but should seek these qualities with habitual effort: "strive for . . . holiness" (Heb. 12:14; see also Rom. 8:13; Phil. 2:12–13; 1 John 3:3). Peter tells Christians to "make every effort" to grow in character traits that accord with virtue and godliness (2 Pet. 1:5).

---

[5] In compiling the following list, I began with the fruit of the Spirit in Gal. 5:22–23, then added "hope" from the love chapter in 1 Cor. 13:13. After that, the list follows the order of the New Testament canon, except where I inserted verses that used the same English word but a different Greek word.

[6] An entire Bible study series could be constructed from this list, using a word study for each character trait and examining several or all of the verses in which each Greek term is used.

[7] See the section, "God and Man Cooperate in Sanctification," in Grudem, *Systematic Theology*, 753–56.

English Word	Greek Word or Words	New Testament Passage
Love	*agapē*	"But the fruit of the Spirit is *love*, joy, peace, patience, kindness, goodness, faithfulness, gentleness, self-control; against such things there is no law" (Gal. 5:22–23).
Joy	*chara*	Gal. 5:22
Peace	*eirēnē*	Gal. 5:22
Patience	*makrothymia*	Gal. 5:22
Kindness	*chrēstotēs*	Gal. 5:22
Goodness	*agathōsynē*	Gal. 5:22
Faithfulness	*pistis*	Gal. 5:22
Gentleness (or meekness) Greek word with similar meaning: gentle	*praütēs* *epieikēs**	Gal. 5:23 "not a drunkard, not violent but *gentle*, not quarrelsome, not a lover of money" (1 Tim. 3:3).
Self-control Greek word with similar meaning: self-controlled (prudent, thoughtful)	*egkrateia* *sōphrōn*	Gal. 5:23 "Therefore an overseer must be above reproach, the husband of one wife, sober-minded, *self-controlled*, respectable, hospitable, able to teach" (1 Tim. 3:2).
Hope	*elpis*	"So now faith, *hope*, and love abide, these three; but the greatest of these is love" (1 Cor. 13:13).
Endurance	*hypomonē*	"Not only that, but we rejoice in our sufferings, knowing that suffering produces *endurance*" (Rom. 5:3).
Hospitality	*philoxenia*	"Contribute to the needs of the saints and seek to show *hospitality*" (Rom. 12:13).
Courage (confidence) Greek word with similar meaning: courage (boldness)	*tharreō/tharseō* *parrēsia*	"So we are always of *good courage*. We know that while we are at home in the body we are away from the Lord. . . . Yes, we are of *good courage*, and we would rather be away from the body and at home with the Lord" (2 Cor. 5:6, 8). "It is my eager expectation and hope that I will not be at all ashamed, but that with full *courage* now as always Christ will be honored in my body, whether by life or by death" (Phil. 1:20).

English Word	Greek Word or Words	New Testament Passage
Purity	*hagnotēs*	"[We commend ourselves] by *purity*, knowledge, patience, kindness, the Holy Spirit, genuine love . . ." (2 Cor. 6:6).
Generosity Greek word with similar meaning: Generosity	*haplotēs* *eumetadotos*	"You will be enriched in every way to be *generous* in every way, which through us will produce thanksgiving to God" (2 Cor. 9:11). "They are to do good, to be rich in good works, to be *generous* and ready to share" (1 Tim. 6:18).
Humility	*tapeinophrosynē*	"With all *humility* and gentleness, with patience, [bear] with one another in love" (Eph. 4:2).
Truthfulness	*alētheia*	"Therefore, having put away falsehood, let each one of you speak the *truth* with his neighbor, for we are members one of another" (Eph. 4:25).
Tenderheartedness (compassion)	*eusplagxnos*	"Be kind to one another, *tenderhearted*, forgiving one another, as God in Christ forgave you" (Eph. 4:32).
Reasonableness (forbearance, graciousness, courtesy; see also "gentleness" above.)	*epieikēs*†	"Let your *reasonableness* be known to everyone. The Lord is at hand" (Phil. 4:5).
Contentment	*autarkēs*	"I have learned in whatever situation I am to be *content*" (Phil. 4:11).
Compassion	*oiktirmos*	"Put on then, as God's chosen ones, holy and beloved, *compassionate* hearts, kindness, humility, meekness, and patience" (Col. 3:12).
Gratitude	*eucharisteō*	"*Give thanks* in all circumstances; for this is the will of God in Christ Jesus for you" (1 Thess. 5:18).
Sober-mindedness	*nēphalios*	"Therefore an overseer must be above reproach, the husband of one wife, *sober-minded*, self-controlled, respectable, hospitable, able to teach" (1 Tim. 3:2).
Godliness	*eusebeia*	"But as for you, O man of God, flee these things. Pursue righteousness, *godliness*, faith, love, steadfastness, gentleness" (1 Tim. 6:11).

English Word	Greek Word or Words	New Testament Passage
Mercy	*eleos*	"But the wisdom from above is first pure, then peaceable, gentle, open to reason, full of *mercy* and good fruits, impartial and sincere" (James 3:17).
Holiness	*hagios*	"As he who called you is holy, you also be *holy* in all your conduct, since it is written, 'You shall be holy, for I am holy'" (1 Pet. 1:15–16).
Sympathy	*sympathēs*	"Finally, all of you, have unity of mind, *sympathy*, brotherly love, a tender heart, and a humble mind" (1 Pet. 3:8).

* This term takes different senses in different contexts; see item "Reasonableness."
† This word takes different meanings in different contexts; see item "Gentleness."

Table 4.1 Christian Character Traits

4. "Vices" Are the Opposite of Christlike Virtues. I will not provide here a long list of vices that are named by the New Testament, but they occur in several places. Here is one example:

> Now the works of the flesh are evident: sexual immorality, impurity, sensuality, idolatry, sorcery, enmity, strife, jealousy, fits of anger, rivalries, dissensions, divisions, envy, drunkenness, orgies, and things like these. I warn you, as I warned you before, that those who do such things will not inherit the kingdom of God. (Gal. 5:19–21)

And here is another list:

> They were filled with all manner of unrighteousness, evil, covetousness, malice. They are full of envy, murder, strife, deceit, maliciousness. They are gossips, slanderers, haters of God, insolent, haughty, boastful, inventors of evil, disobedient to parents, foolish, faithless, heartless, ruthless. Though they know God's righteous decree that those who practice such things deserve to die, they not only do them but give approval to those who practice them. (Rom. 1:29–32)

In previous generations, and particularly in the Middle Ages, Christians developed a list of the "Seven Deadly Sins," which was a summary of vices that oppose God and Christlike character in our lives. Here is one form of the list: (1) pride, (2) envy, (3) wrath, (4) sloth, (5) avarice, (6) lust, and (7) gluttony.[8]

---

[8] Reid, "Vice," 874.

5. Implications for Studying Ethics, for Pastoral Ministry, and for Parenting. The realization that God's purpose is to develop a Christlike character in us has significant implications not only for studying ethics, but also for practical concerns such as pastoral ministry and the task of parenting children. If God's purpose is the development of character, then, for our personal study of ethics, *our goal must never be right actions alone.* Our goal must be also to develop a Christlike character that is pleasing to God. This is consistent with the Bible's teaching, for we read that "the LORD sees not as man sees: man looks on the outward appearance, but the LORD looks on the heart" (1 Sam. 16:7).

Pastors also must realize that in their preaching and personal counseling, it is not enough to persuade people to take the right actions when facing particularly difficult situations. God's purpose in such situations is also to develop a Christlike character in the person's heart.

This also is significant for parents who are raising children. It is perhaps too easy to focus on encouraging children to be obedient, emphasizing merely outward behavior. But "the LORD looks on the heart" (1 Sam. 16:7). Therefore, the goal of parents, in addition to raising their children be obedient, must be to pray, counsel, encourage, and admonish—and live—in such a way that their children's character will grow to maturity and Christlikeness as well.

This does not mean that behavior is unimportant. In fact, there is a mutually reinforcing interaction between character and actions. If people repeatedly tell the truth, they develop a habit of truthfulness and they develop a more truthful character. Then, if their hearts are more committed to truthfulness, they will more often tell the truth, and they will enjoy truthfulness, even delight in it. Similar results would follow from performing acts of kindness, developing habits of self-discipline, and so forth. Good behavior builds character, and character leads to good behavior. Paul tells Timothy, "*Train* yourself for godliness" (1 Tim. 4:7), and the author of Hebrews says that "mature" Christians are "those who have their powers of discernment *trained* by constant practice to distinguish good from evil" (Heb. 5:14).[9]

Therefore, any course on Christian ethics should aim not only at imparting greater *understanding* of right and wrong conduct but also at *personal transformation* so that each student (or each reader of a book on ethics) will develop a more Christlike character through the course and will *become* more like Christ. This is ultimately a work of the Holy Spirit, but the Holy Spirit most often works through old-fashioned spiritual disciplines such as regular Bible reading, private and corporate prayer, worship, sound Bible teaching, and fellowship with God's people.

As I indicated above, such growth in one's Christlike character of life is a gradual process. It is a kind of "walk" that continues throughout life (see Ps. 1:1–2). The path of

---

[9] In both verses, the Greek verb translated as "train" is *gymnazō*, "train, undergo discipline," a word that was commonly used of athletic exercises (BDAG, 208).

that "walk" should be one of continual growth, as in the image of a sunrise that grows brighter and brighter:

> But the path of the righteous is like the light of dawn,
>   which shines brighter and brighter until full day. (Prov. 4:18)

D. THE RESULTS GOAL: A LIFE THAT BEARS ABUNDANT FRUIT FOR GOD'S KINGDOM

God is not only concerned about our character. He is also concerned that our lives have productive results, or (to use an agricultural metaphor) that our lives would be like plants that bear much "fruit" for the purposes of God's kingdom.

Jesus tells us that we are to pray daily for God's kingdom to "come" or to advance on the earth: "*Your kingdom come,*[10] your will be done, on earth as it is in heaven" (Matt. 6:10). He also tells us that we are to seek the good of the kingdom of God: "But *seek first the kingdom of God* and his righteousness, and all these things will be added to you" (v. 33).

Jesus talks much about bearing fruit[11] in our lives:

> I am the vine; you are the branches. Whoever abides in me and I in him, he
>   it is that *bears much fruit,* for apart from me you can do nothing. (John 15:5)

By contrast, someone who falls away from Christ is like a branch that "does not bear fruit" (John 15:2). Such a person "is thrown away like a branch and withers; and the branches are gathered, thrown into the fire, and burned" (v. 6).

Paul uses the metaphor of constructing a building to talk about the same idea. He says that he had "laid a foundation" in his missionary work, and now other people are building on that foundation. The work that each person builds could be like "gold, silver, precious stones" or like "wood, hay, straw," and it will all be tested by fire on the judgment day: "The fire will test what sort of work each one has done. If the work that anyone has built on the foundation survives, he will receive a reward" (1 Cor. 3:10–14).

---

[10] The force of the third-person singular imperative *elthetō* ("may it come") is made more explicit by the NET: "*May* your kingdom come." However, most translations are reluctant to tamper with the traditional wording of the Lord's Prayer in this verse. The force of the request is the same in either case: it is a prayer that God's kingdom (his rule and reign in people's hearts and lives) would be continually advancing in the earth day after day.

[11] In Gal. 5:22–23, the "fruit of the Spirit" refers to character traits or virtues that the Holy Spirit produces within each individual Christian. But in John 15:5, Jesus is using "fruit" in a different sense, to refer to the advancement of the work of God's kingdom on earth through *results* such as more people coming to trust in Christ, churches being planted and growing, people living lives of obedience to God and lives that honor him, and ultimately entire societies and nations being transformed by the power of the Word of God and the work of the Holy Spirit. Other passages use the image of "fruit" to refer to results that advance the work of the kingdom of God; see, for example, Matt. 7:17–20; 13:23; John 15:1–8, 16; Phil. 1:22; 4:17; Col 1:10; James 3:17.

These and many other passages show that God wants our work to be productive, to bring about good results for advancing his kingdom here on earth during this lifetime.

Therefore, a life lived according to God's ethical teachings in Scripture is not only one that has a Christlike character, but also one that has positive *results*, results that advance the purposes of God and the work of his kingdom here on earth, and in that way bring glory to God.

E. THE BEHAVIORAL GOAL: A LIFE OF OBEDIENCE, LIVED IN PERSONAL FELLOWSHIP WITH GOD

1. The Importance of Obedience to God's Commands. In addition to caring about our *character* and about the *results* of our actions, God is concerned with our actions themselves, our behavior. Many passages in the New Testament talk about the importance of obedience to God's commands. "If you love me, you will *keep my commandments*" (John 14:15). And again, "For this is the love of God, that we *keep his commandments*. And his commandments are not burdensome" (1 John 5:3).

Therefore, in addition to seeking to live lives that conform to the image of Christ (the character goal) and that bear abundant fruit for God's kingdom (the results goal), it is also of the utmost importance that we seek to live lives of *obedience to God's commands*, doing so *in daily personal fellowship with God* (the behavioral goal).[12]

The commandments of God that we are to obey are found in the Bible:

> All Scripture is breathed out by God and profitable for teaching, for *reproof*, for *correction*, and for *training in righteousness*. (2 Tim. 3:16)

Obedience to Scripture is a complex task because the Bible is a large and complex book, and life itself is complex. Therefore, much of the rest of this book will be devoted to seeking out what kinds of behavior God commands of us in different situations (such as marriage and divorce, telling the truth, stewardship of possessions, work and leisure, and so forth). In this chapter, however, we will consider the question of obedience to God in more general terms.

2. Authentic Obedience Requires Ongoing Personal Fellowship with God. We must not think that obedience to God's commands is something we can do "on our own," apart from God, with God watching from a distance. Rather, all of our obedience must be done in continual fellowship with God. If we do not obey in this way, God will not be pleased, our lives will lack joy, and we will eventually tire of keeping rules and will go astray.

David understood this kind of life lived in continual fellowship with God day and night:

---

[12] These three goals all influence one another in positive ways, for a Christlike *character* produces *obedience* to God and *fellowship* with God, and obedience and fellowship lead to positive *results* for God's kingdom. But obedience also develops character, and results reinforce obedience, and so forth.

> I bless the LORD *who gives me counsel*;
>> in the night also my heart instructs me.
> I have set the LORD always before me;
>> because *he is at my right hand*, I shall not be shaken.
> Therefore my heart is glad, and my whole being rejoices;
>> my flesh also dwells secure. (Ps. 16:7–9)

Jesus spoke of this kind of life in terms of "abiding" in him:

> I am the vine; you are the branches. *Whoever abides in me and I in him*, he it
> is that bears much fruit, for apart from me you can do nothing. (John 15:5)

The apostle Paul also spoke of this kind of life, lived in personal fellowship with Christ:

> I have been crucified with Christ. It is no longer I who live, but *Christ who
> lives in me*. And the life I now live in the flesh I live by faith in the Son of God,
> who loved me and gave himself for me. (Gal. 2:20)

One aspect of that personal relationship is having God's power working in us, for apart from his power within, we will be unable to live in obedience to him:

> Therefore, my beloved, *as you have always obeyed*, so now, not only as in my
> presence but much more in my absence, work out your own salvation with
> fear and trembling, for *it is God who works in you*, both to will and to work
> for his good pleasure. (Phil. 2:12–13)

If we neglect this crucial component of regular fellowship with God, our Christian lives can easily degenerate into bleak days of dour obedience as we grit our teeth and seek to "follow all the rules" as best we can, hoping that some good will eventually come from it. But this is not the joyful kind of Christian life that the New Testament portrays.

3. The Joys and Blessings of Obedience. The New Testament contains many promises of joys and blessings that result from our obedience to God. In fact, these promises are so numerous that I have taken an entire chapter to discuss them (see chap. 5). At this point, I can mention one clear example from Jesus's teachings, showing a direct correlation between obeying his commandments and enjoying an ongoing, daily experience of his love:

> If you keep my commandments, *you will abide in my love*, just as I have kept
> my Father's commandments and abide in his love. (John 15:10)

4. The Dangers of Legalism. While obedience to God is very important in a Christian's life, there are two major errors to avoid in discussing obedience. As I mentioned in chapter 1, there is a viewpoint that denies the importance of obedience, and it is called *antinomianism*. (The term comes from Greek, *anti-*, "against," and *nomos*, "law.") An antinomian is one who thinks that obedience to God is not important or who places very little emphasis on obedience to God in the Christian life.

But there is also an opposite error to antinomianism. People who place much emphasis on obedience to God can fall into some wrongful attitudes or practices, all of which fall under the general category of *legalism*.

a. Legalism Regarding Justification: The fact that we are justified[13] by faith alone is at the heart of the gospel: "We know that a person is not justified by works of the law but through faith in Jesus Christ, so we also have believed in Christ Jesus, in order to be *justified by faith in Christ and not by works of the law*, because by works of the law no one will be justified" (Gal. 2:16). One form of legalism is the teaching that we are justified by works instead of by faith alone. (The word *legalism* itself does not occur in Scripture, but this is, I think, its most common meaning in theological discussions.)

b. Legalism in Adding to the Commands of Scripture: Another form of legalism is adding to the moral requirements of Scripture. For example, if someone were to say that Christians still have to follow the Mosaic laws about holiday observances and unclean foods, this would be adding to the moral requirements of Scripture for Christians in the New Testament age. Paul rebuked the Christians in the churches of Galatia: "You observe days and months and seasons and years! I am afraid I may have labored over you in vain" (Gal. 4:10–11; see also Col. 2:16–17).

The Pharisees at the time of Jesus added many rules to the moral requirements found in the Old Testament laws, but Jesus rebuked them: "And he said to them, 'You have a fine way of rejecting the commandment of God in order to establish your tradition'" (Mark 7:9; see also vv. 10–13).

Some Christian groups in previous generations made rules (or conveyed strong expectations) that their members should avoid movies, social dancing, and playing cards, for example, even though it is unlikely that these prohibitions can be supported from Scripture.

But we should not smugly think that the tendency to add to the rules of Scripture disappeared with earlier generations. Even today, in various churches or Christian groups, the preferences or personal life decisions of influential leaders can turn into a kind of legalism. The expectations of behavior tend to become legalistic regarding such things as: haircut styles; shaving styles; music preferences (regarding either worship music or secular music); food preferences (organic or nonorganic); babies (when to have them, how many to have, and how many to adopt); how much money a person

---

[13] Justification is "An instantaneous legal act of God in which he (1) thinks of our sins as forgiven and Christ's righteousness as belonging to us, and (2) declares us to be righteous in his sight." Grudem, *Systematic Theology*, 1246.

should earn and give away; how expensive a car or house a person should own; schooling choices (home school vs. Christian school vs. public school); how much a person should exercise or weigh; how much time a person should spend with his or her family; which sports teams a person should cheer for; which church activities a person should participate in; and whether a person should allow his or her children to engage in trick-or-treating at Halloween and to believe in Santa Claus at Christmas.[14]

There are certainly wise and unwise choices to be made in many of these areas. But wisdom from God might lead Christians to different conclusions in these areas according to their different circumstances, preferences, stages in life, and sense of calling from God.

c. Legalism in Attitudes: People can become legalistic in their attitudes toward one another. This would include having a critical, judgmental attitude toward others rather than a gracious and forgiving attitude. Paul says, *"Be kind to one another, tenderhearted, forgiving one another, as God in Christ forgave you"* (Eph. 4:32). But some people habitually seem to have a critical spirit, and by their words, body language, and facial expressions they project negative judgments, accusations, and condemnation toward others. (Many times others can sense this even if the critical person does not say a word.[15]) Such a critical spirit is inconsistent with a Christlike character, for it fails to imitate his love, mercy, and compassion for others.

Such critical people will rarely give affirmations, genuine words of encouragement, or compliments to others (because so few people meet their high standards!). When we spend time with such legalistic people, they tend to make us feel guilty, inferior, or just not good enough. People with such a critical spirit will often move from church to church, never being able to find a congregation that quite meets their high standards. Such people need to consider that they are probably the ones who do not "walk in the light," and as a result they cannot say to any church, "we have fellowship with one another" (1 John 1:7).

Another kind of legalistic attitude is pride. Although James says, "God opposes the proud, but gives grace to the humble" (James 4:6), there is a kind of prideful legalism that tends to make its proponents self-righteous. They aren't aware of their own faults because they are good at justifying to themselves everything they do. They don't recognize their own spiritual neediness, nor do they ever admit that they are wrong, in a genuine, heartfelt way. Such pride is the opposite of Christlike humility (one of the character traits mentioned earlier in this chapter).

In interpersonal situations, such prideful people will often inwardly be hoping that they will be shown to be more righteous, more holy, more intelligent, or more

---

[14] A helpful discussion of how to approach a variety of such matters where Christians have different convictions of "conscience" about them is found in Andrew David Naselli and J. D. Crowley, *Conscience: What It Is, How to Train It, and Loving Those Who Differ* (Wheaton, IL: Crossway, 2016). They provide a long list of such issues on 80–81.

[15] Some legalistic people seem to spend much of their time online, always eager to criticize others while hiding behind Internet anonymity.

doctrinally sound than everyone else (and they will also be hoping that others will slip up in some way). But Paul says, "Do nothing from selfish ambition or conceit, but in humility count others more significant than yourselves" (Phil. 2:3). They will seldom or never experience a truly repentant, deeply contrite heart (as in Ps. 51:17).

Their sense of their own superior judgment is so strong that they will never really submit to legitimate authority or recognize that the decision of the larger group might be wiser than their own viewpoint. They have not trusted in what James calls "the wisdom from above":

> But the wisdom from above is first pure, then peaceable, gentle, open to reason, full of mercy and good fruits, impartial and sincere. And a harvest of righteousness is sown in peace by those who make peace. (James 3:17–18)

Yet another kind of legalistic attitude is seen in people who withhold forgiveness and hold grudges. They think that they need to personally guarantee that others "suffer" for the wrongs that they have done to them, rather than being willing to leave it all to God, as Paul says: "Beloved, *never avenge yourselves,* but leave it to the wrath of God, for it is written, 'Vengeance is mine, I will repay,' says the Lord" (Rom. 12:19; see also Matt. 6:12; 18:23–35). They can also manifest such a legalistic attitude in thinking that they have to be personally responsible for convicting others of sin rather than praying and trusting the Holy Spirit to do what only he can do (see John 16:8).

Sometimes a legalistic attitude can show itself as the opposite of pride. Some legalistic people can turn their legalism upon themselves and become excessively self-condemning, always feeling like spiritual failures, always suspecting that they are never doing enough for God rather than thinking of themselves "with sober judgment, each according to the measure of faith that God has assigned" (Rom. 12:3).[16]

d. Legalism in Emphasis: In addition to legalism in doctrinal matters and legalism in attitudes, there can also be a legalism in people's emphases. Some people can major on minor things, always being picky and judgmental about minor details that might even be wrong but that should be overlooked because they are none of any other person's business. Jesus warns against this:

> Why do you see the speck that is in your brother's eye, but do not notice the log that is in your own eye? Or how can you say to your brother, "Let me take the speck out of your eye," when there is the log in your own eye? You hypocrite, first take the log out of your own eye, and then you will see clearly to take the speck out of your brother's eye. (Matt. 7:3–5; see also 23:23–24)

Another kind of mistake in emphasis can occur in focusing on outward conduct and

---

[16] I realize that earlier in this verse Paul is encouraging *proud* people to think with "sober judgment" about themselves, but I think that his counsel would also apply to those who have too negative a view of themselves.

appearance (such as clothing, physical beauty, or attractiveness) but neglecting inward heart attitudes and moral character. Parents can easily make this mistake in training their children to be obedient without giving adequate attention to the development of the children's hearts and their personal walks with God. Another warning from Jesus is appropriate:

> Woe to you, scribes and Pharisees, hypocrites! For you clean the outside of the cup and the plate, but inside they are full of greed and self-indulgence. (Matt. 23:25; see also 1 Pet. 3:3–4 and 1 Sam. 16:7)

F. SUMMARY: THE GOAL OF CHRISTIAN ETHICS SHOULD BE TO LIVE FOR THE GLORY OF GOD

To summarize this chapter, the appropriate goal of Christian ethics is a life that is lived for the glory of God. This can be divided into three aspects:

1. The *Character Goal* That Glorifies God Is to Live a Life Conformed to the Image of Christ. This is what it means to acquire and practice genuine "virtue" in our lives. Because of this goal, when considering specific ethical topics later in this book, particularly in the "questions for personal application," I will often consider what character traits are especially related to the topic under discussion. In addition, I will sometimes ask how to enjoy obeying God in this area of life, because part of a virtuous Christian character is to keep God's commandments with our hearts: "Let your heart keep my commandments" (Prov. 3:1).

2. The *Results Goal* That Glorifies God Is to Live a Life That Bears Abundant Fruit for God's Kingdom. Because of this goal, in discussing specific ethical topics I will often consider what results we should seek in order to advance the kingdom of God in this area of life.

3. The *Behavioral Goal* That Glorifies God Is to Live a Life of Obedience to God in Personal Relationship with God. Because of this goal, in the chapters that follow I will discuss morally good and bad actions related to particular topics, and how these actions must be done "before God" and in fellowship "with God."

QUESTIONS FOR PERSONAL APPLICATION

1. If the goal of ethics is to have (1) a character that glorifies God, (2) results in one's life that glorify God, and (3) behavior that glorifies God, which of these three do you think you most need to focus on while reading this book?
2. As you look over the list of Christlike character traits in this chapter, can you name some in which you are aware that the Holy Spirit has brought about growth over the last several years? Where would you like to see more growth?

3. When you were growing up, what did your parents do (if anything) to encourage you to grow not only in obedient behavior but also in Christlike character? If you yourself have children, what kinds of things do you do to encourage such character development?

4. In accordance with the prayer, "Your kingdom come" (Matt. 6:10), what are some of the changes that would happen in your life and in the lives of people around you if the presence of God's kingdom (his rule and reign in people's lives) came to be more fully experienced?

5. Do you notice a connection in your own life between personal obedience to God and daily fellowship with him?

6. Are you aware of any areas in your life where you have been acting in a legalistic way toward yourself or others? Do you think the culture of your church, even unintentionally, may project a legalism that goes beyond the moral requirements of Scripture in some areas?

SPECIAL TERMS

legalism
Seven Deadly Sins
vices
virtue ethics
virtues

BIBLIOGRAPHY

Sections in Other Ethics Texts

(see complete bibliographical data, p. 64)

Clark and Rakestraw, 1:247–310
Frame, 911–29
Gushee and Stassen, 21–42
Holmes, 122–30, 131–41
Jones, 17–58, 77–102
McQuilkin and Copan, 123–32
Rae, 31–34

Other Works

Ferguson, Sinclair B. *The Whole Christ: Legalism, Antinomianism, and Gospel Assurance.* Wheaton, IL: Crossway, 2016.

Horton, Michael. *Calvin on the Christian Life: Glorifying and Enjoying God Forever.* Wheaton, IL: Crossway, 2014.

Jones, Mark. *Antinomianism: Reformed Theology's Unwelcome Guest?* Phillipsburg, NJ: P&R, 2013.

Mathis, David. *Habits of Grace: Enjoying Jesus through the Spiritual Disciplines.* Wheaton, IL: Crossway, 2016.

Miller, Paul E. *A Loving Life: In a World of Broken Relationships.* Wheaton, IL: Crossway, 2014.

Naselli, Andrew David, and J. D. Crowley. *Conscience: What It Is, How to Train It, and Loving Those Who Differ.* Wheaton, IL: Crossway, 2016.

Poythress, Vern S. *The Lordship of Christ: Serving Our Savior All of the Time, in All of Life, with All of Our Heart.* Wheaton, IL: Crossway, 2016.

Roberts, R. C. "Character." In *New Dictionary of Christian Ethics and Pastoral Theology,* edited by David J. Atkinson and David H. Field, 65–71. Leicester, UK: Inter-Varsity, and Downers Grove, IL: InterVarsity Press, 1995.

SCRIPTURE MEMORY PASSAGE

1 Corinthians 10:31: So, whether you eat or drink, or whatever you do, do all to the glory of God.

HYMN

"O to Be Like Thee"

O to be like Thee! blessed Redeemer,
This is my constant longing and prayer;
Gladly I'll forfeit all of earth's treasures,
Jesus, Thy perfect likeness to wear.

Refrain:
O to be like Thee! O to be like Thee,
Blessed Redeemer, pure as Thou art!
Come in Thy sweetness, come in Thy fullness;
Stamp Thine own image deep on my heart.

O to be like Thee! full of compassion,
Loving, forgiving, tender and kind;
Helping the helpless, cheering the fainting,
Seeking the wand'ring sinner to find.

O to be like Thee! lowly in spirit,
Holy and harmless, patient and brave;

Meekly enduring cruel reproaches,
Willing to suffer others to save.

O to be like Thee! Lord, I am coming
Now to receive th' anointing divine;
All that I am and have I am bringing
Lord, from this moment all shall be Thine.

O to be like Thee! while I am pleading,
Pour out Thy Spirit, fill with Thy love;
Make me a temple meet for Thy dwelling,
Fit me for life and heaven above.

AUTHOR: THOMAS O. CHISHOLM, 1866–1960

Chapter 5

THE JOYS AND BLESSINGS OF OBEDIENCE TO GOD AND THE HARMFUL CONSEQUENCES OF SIN

(A DISCUSSION OF MOTIVES FOR OBEDIENCE)

Even though our sins are forgiven, what additional blessings come to our lives when we obey God and avoid sin?
Will there be negative consequences if we continue in willful sin?

Imagine for a moment that you are facing some kind of specific temptation:

> You are tempted to deal dishonestly with some money at work, or in a situation with a relative, or on your tax return.
> You are walking in late for a meeting and you are tempted to tell a small lie ("The traffic was unexpectedly heavy") to make an excuse for yourself.
> You are away on a business trip and other people have left the room, and you are tempted to linger too long in a conversation with a person of the opposite sex who is not your spouse.
> You are tempted to visit an Internet site that has pornography.
> Your boss wants you to sign a form that you know is untruthful.

You hear some interesting gossip and you don't know if it is true but you are tempted to pass it on to someone else.

Someone at work has been promoted over you, and you are tempted to lie about that person just to get even.

You are tempted to have another drink (if you drink at all) even though you know you've had enough.

You know that God has been prompting you to phone or visit another person, or perhaps has been calling you into some ministry, but you are tempted not to obey.

You are tempted to be dishonest about some details regarding an item you are returning to a store.

Innumerable situations like these come up in ordinary life. The question is, *does it really make any difference* what we do? You might even be tempted to rationalize by saying, "Hasn't God already forgiven me? This probably won't make any difference to anything at all."

The answer is yes, it does make a difference, and that difference is what we will discuss in this chapter. First, we will talk about the joys and blessings that come with obedience to God in daily life. Later in the chapter (p. 138), we will discuss sin and the harmful consequences that come from it, even sin in the life of a Christian.

A. THE JOYS AND BLESSINGS OF OBEDIENCE TO GOD

1. The Joy and Blessing of Deeper Fellowship with God. Jesus speaks about a direct correlation between obeying his commandments and an ongoing, daily experience of his love:

> If you keep my commandments, *you will abide in my love,* just as I have kept my Father's commandments and abide in his love. (John 15:10)

He also speaks about a connection between keeping his word (that is, obeying his commandments) and enjoying personal fellowship with the Father and the Son:

> Jesus answered him, "If anyone loves me, he will *keep my word,* and my Father will love him, and we will come to him and *make our home with him.*" (John 14:23)[1]

---

[1] Leon Morris says of John 14:23: "John is not thinking of the second coming, nor of the postresurrection appearances, but of that state of believers in which they experience the immediate presence of the Deity." *The Gospel according to John,* NICNT (Grand Rapids, MI: Eerdmans, 1995), 581.

But personal fellowship with God and with Christ (and the Holy Spirit) also means that we will experience the deepest joy possible in this life, the joy of God's very presence:[2]

> In your presence there is *fullness of joy*;
> at your right hand are pleasures forevermore. (Ps. 16:11)

> Oh, taste and see that the LORD is good!
> Blessed is the man who takes refuge in him! (Ps. 34:8)

> How precious is your steadfast love, O God!
> The children of mankind take refuge in the shadow of your wings.
> They feast on the abundance of your house,
> and *you give them drink from the river of your delights*. (Ps. 36:7–8)

Such joy in God's presence is also experienced in another way when we delight in the excellent character of God's nature as revealed in his moral laws:

> The precepts of the LORD are right,
> *rejoicing* the heart;
> the commandment of the LORD is pure,
> enlightening the eyes;
> the fear of the LORD is clean,
> enduring forever;
> the rules of the LORD are true,
> and righteous altogether.
> *More to be desired are they than gold*,
> even much fine gold;
> *sweeter also than honey*
> and drippings of the honeycomb. (Ps. 19:8–10)

2. The Joy and Blessing of Bringing Glory to God by Imitating His Character on Earth. Paul told us, "Be imitators of God, as beloved children" (Eph. 5:1), indicating that God wants to see his character reflected in our daily lives. Jesus said that our good actions will result in glory to God: "Let your light shine before others, so that they may see your good works and *give glory to your Father who is in heaven*" (Matt. 5:16).[3]

3. The Joy and Blessing of Expressing Our Love to God by Our Actions. All Christians have in their hearts a love for God and a sense of gratitude for all that he has done for them. It is natural that this love and gratitude will find expression in actions that are

---

[2] John Piper discusses extensively the idea of glorifying God *by enjoying* him (!) in his widely influential book *Desiring God: Meditations of a Christian Hedonist* (Portland, OR: Multnomah, 1986).

[3] See chap. 4, p. 108, for more on the idea of imitating God's character in our conduct.

pleasing to God. This is why Jesus says, "*If you love me*, you will keep my commandments" (John 14:15; see also 14:21; 1 John 5:3).

4. The Joy and Blessing of Pleasing God.[4] Sometimes Christians can become so fearful of teaching justification by works that they make an opposite mistake and fail to teach that, once we are justified by faith alone in Christ alone, we should seek to do *good works* (see Eph. 2:10; Titus 2:14; Heb. 10:24) that are pleasing to God. This emphasis is much more frequent in the New Testament than we might realize, because the New Testament authors often encourage Christian believers (not non-Christians) to *try to please God* by what they do:

> So whether we are at home or away, we make it our aim *to please him*. (2 Cor. 5:9; cf. Gal. 1:10)

> Try to discern *what is pleasing to the Lord*. (Eph. 5:10)

> It is God who works in you, both to will and to work for *his good pleasure*. (Phil. 2:13)

> I am well supplied, having received from Epaphroditus the gifts you sent, a fragrant offering, a sacrifice acceptable and *pleasing to God*. (Phil. 4:18)

> Walk in a manner worthy of the Lord, *fully pleasing to him*: bearing fruit in every good work and increasing in the knowledge of God. (Col. 1:10)

> Children, obey your parents in everything, *for this pleases the Lord*. (Col. 3:20)

> We speak, not to please man, but *to please God* who tests our hearts. (1 Thess. 2:4)

> We ask and urge you in the Lord Jesus, that as you received from us how you ought to walk and *to please God*, just as you are doing, that you do so more and more. (1 Thess. 4:1)

> If a widow has children or grandchildren, let them first learn to show godliness to their own household and to make some return to their parents, for *this is pleasing in the sight of God*. (1 Tim. 5:4)

> Now before he [Enoch] was taken he was commended as having *pleased God*. (Heb. 11:5)

---

[4] This section is adapted from Wayne Grudem, "Pleasing God by Our Obedience: A Neglected New Testament Teaching," in *For the Fame of God's Name: Essays in Honor of John Piper*, ed. Sam Storms and Justin Taylor (Wheaton, IL: Crossway, 2010), 272–92, with permission of the publisher.

Do not neglect to do good and to share what you have, for such sacrifices are *pleasing to God*. (Heb. 13:16)

[May God] equip you with everything good that you may do his will, working in us *that which is pleasing in his sight*, through Jesus Christ, to whom be glory forever and ever. Amen. (Heb. 13:21)

And whatever we ask we receive from him, because we keep his commandments and do *what pleases him*. (1 John 3:22)

The supreme pattern of a life pleasing to God is found in Jesus Christ himself. He alone could say, "He [God the Father] has not left me alone, for *I always do the things that are pleasing to him*" (John 8:29). And at Jesus's baptism the voice of the Father came from heaven saying, "This is my beloved Son, with whom I am *well pleased*" (Matt. 3:17; cf. Matt. 12:18; 17:5; Mark 1:11; Luke 3:22; 2 Pet. 1:17).

Sometimes Christians wrongly assume that they can do *absolutely nothing* in this life that will please God. They think that God counts even their faithful obedience as *totally* worthless, totally unworthy of his approval, and this can lead to feelings of complete insignificance. But that assumption is surely wrong, both because the New Testament so frequently speaks about "pleasing" God and because such an assumption tends to deny the genuine goodness of the work that Christ has done in redeeming us and making us acceptable before him. Such a view would maximize our sinfulness to the extent that it is even greater than Christ's redemptive work, "who gave himself for us to redeem us from all lawlessness and to *purify* for himself a people for his own possession who are zealous for *good works*" (Titus 2:14).

I suspect that just as Satan accuses Christians and wants them to feel false guilt and false accusation, so he also seeks to keep them from the great joy of knowing the favor of God in their daily activities, of knowing that God is pleased with their obedience. In this way, he seeks to hinder our personal relationship with God, for the ability to take pleasure in another person is an essential component of any genuine personal relationship.

Is Christ not capable of producing in us works that are genuinely *good works*? Is Paul wrong when he says that we have been created for good works?

For we are his workmanship, created in Christ Jesus *for good works*, which God prepared beforehand, that we should walk in them. (Eph. 2:10; see also Matt. 5:16; 1 Tim. 6:18; Titus 2:14)

When the New Testament Epistles talk about the obedience of believers after they have been justified, such works are called not "bad works" but "good works"! Though these works are imperfect, they are certainly not one hundred percent evil and sinful, especially when they proceed from faith and are motivated by a love for God and for other people.

The Westminster Confession of Faith speaks of God's acceptance of our good works, imperfect though they are:

> Notwithstanding, the persons of believers being accepted through Christ, *their good works also are accepted in Him*; not as though they were in this life wholly unblameable and unreproveable in God's sight; but that He, looking upon them in His Son, is pleased to accept and reward that which is sincere, although accompanied with many weaknesses and imperfections.[5]

Paul can even use the language of "worthiness" in speaking of the conduct of obedient believers before God, implying that our conduct can actually be "worthy" of God's approval:

> I therefore, a prisoner for the Lord, urge you to walk in a manner *worthy* [Greek, *axiōs*, "worthily, in a manner worthy of"] of the calling to which you have been called. (Eph. 4:1)

> Walk in a manner *worthy* of the Lord, fully pleasing to him, bearing fruit in every good work and increasing in the knowledge of God. (Col. 1:10; cf. Phil. 1:27; 1 Thess. 2:12; 2 Thess. 1:11)

We may conclude that God delights in our good works, that he is pleased with them, and that he accepts them in Christ. Thus, another benefit of obedience in the Christian life is that we are doing things that are pleasing to God himself.

5. The Joy and Blessing of Making Angels Happy. Scripture indicates that the angels of God rejoice when they see God's good purposes being worked out in our lives. This is the probable meaning of Jesus's words, "There will be more *joy in heaven* over one sinner who repents than over ninety-nine righteous persons who need no repentance" (Luke 15:7).[6]

Paul reminded Timothy that angels were watching his conduct, because he commanded Timothy "in the presence of God and of Christ Jesus and of *the elect angels*" that he should "keep these rules without prejudging, doing nothing from partiality" (1 Tim. 5:21).

Peter said that "angels long to look" into the "things that have now been announced to you" (1 Pet. 1:12), which probably included the specific ways in which the preaching of the gospel and its subsequent teaching applied to the situations of Christians to whom Peter was writing.[7]

Therefore, Christians should obey God with a consciousness that angels are watching and will rejoice in their obedience (see also Eph. 3:10; Heb. 12:22).

---

[5] WCF, 16.6, emphasis added.

[6] This joy probably also includes the joy of believers who have died and are already in heaven.

[7] See discussion in Wayne Grudem, *The First Epistle of Peter: An Introduction and Commentary* (Leicester, UK: Inter-Varsity, and Grand Rapids, MI: Eerdmans, 1988), 72–73.

6. The Joy and Blessing of Becoming a Vessel for "Honorable Use" by God. Paul explains that Christians who are working to advance God's kingdom on earth are like different kinds of vessels in a large house:

> Now in a great house there are not only vessels of gold and silver but also of wood and clay, some for honorable use, some for dishonorable. Therefore, *if anyone cleanses himself from what is dishonorable, he will be a vessel for honorable use,* set apart as holy, *useful* to the master of the house, ready for every good work. (2 Tim. 2:20–21)

The application to ethics is that if we occupy ourselves with things that are dishonoring to God, we will still remain in his house (we will still be Christians), but like the bucket used to scrub the floor or the bowl used to feed the dog, we will be like vessels of "wood and clay" for "dishonorable" use. But if we live in a purer way, cleansing our lives from things that are dishonoring to God, then we can become vessels "for honorable use," like the "vessels of gold and silver" that are used for important occasions. Then we will be "ready for every good work."

7. The Joy and Blessing of Being an Effective Witness to Unbelievers. Peter reminded his readers, many of whom were facing intense opposition from non-Christians, "keep your conduct among the Gentiles honorable" (1 Pet. 2:12). He said this because the good deeds of Christians will have a positive result in the lives of their non-Christian critics—it is possible that those critics will become Christians and eventually "glorify God" at the final judgment:

> Keep your conduct among the Gentiles honorable, so that when they speak against you as evildoers, *they may see your good deeds* and *glorify God* on the day of visitation. (1 Pet. 2:12; see also 1 Pet. 3:1)

8. The Joy and Blessing of Having God's Eyes and Ears More Attentive to Us. Peter writes about the additional blessings that come from habits of speech and obedience in the lives of Christians:

> Whoever desires to love life
>   and see good days,
> let him keep his tongue from evil
>   and his lips from speaking deceit;
> let him turn away from evil and do good;
>   let him seek peace and pursue it.
> *For the eyes of the Lord are on the righteous,*
>   *and his ears are open to their prayer.*
> But the face of the Lord is against those who do evil. (1 Pet. 3:10–12)

Peter is not speaking here about blessings that come to all Christians by virtue of the forgiveness and righteousness that we have in Christ, but about special blessings that result from our obedience, because he says that if we desire these blessings we have to keep our "tongue from evil" and our "lips from speaking deceit," and we have to "turn away from evil and do good."[8]

However, Peter does not imply that Christians who are obedient to God will have a trouble-free life, for he frequently mentions the persecution and hostile opposition that many of his readers are facing (see 1 Pet. 1:7; 2:12, 15, 19–21; 3:9, 13–17; 4:1, 4, 12–19; 5:8–10; see also Paul's frequent hardships in 2 Cor. 11:23–29).

James also indicates that a life of obedience to God results in a more powerful, more effective prayer life, for "the prayer of a *righteous person* has great power as it is working" (James 5:16). James does not simply say that "your prayers" (that is, the prayers of all of you Christians) or the prayers of a "believer" have this power, but the prayer of a *"righteous* person," most likely indicating a characteristic of a person's conduct of life.[9]

John also speaks about confidence before God in prayer based on a clear conscience and actual obedience in life:

> Beloved, *if our heart does not condemn us*, we have confidence before God; and whatever we ask we receive from him, *because we keep his commandments* and do what pleases him. (1 John 3:21–22)

Numerous passages in the Old Testament speak in a similar way, such as this one:

> The steps of a man are established by the LORD,
>   *when he delights in his way.* (Ps. 37:23)

9. The Joy and Blessing of Closer Fellowship with Other Christians. John explains that "walking in the light" (John's expression for living a life of moral purity) results in increased fellowship with other Christians:

> But *if we walk in the light*, as he is in the light, *we have fellowship with one another*, and the blood of Jesus his Son cleanses us from all sin. (1 John 1:7)

---

[8] Another reason that shows he is speaking about blessings that God gives to those who act in obedience to him is that he is quoting from Ps. 34:12–16, and that psalm clearly advocates righteous conduct as a means for God's people to obtain special blessings from him (see Ps. 34:2, 5, 7–10, 13–15, 18, 22). For further argument showing that Peter is primarily speaking about blessings in this lifetime, not heavenly blessings in the age to come, see ibid., 147–50.

[9] In this context, it does not seem that he is referring to all those who are "righteous" through the imputation of Christ's righteousness at the point of justification (as in 2 Cor. 5:21; Phil. 3:19). Both senses of "righteous" are found in the New Testament: several passages speak of Christians as "righteous" because Christ's righteousness has been imputed to them by faith, while other passages speak of people as "righteous" because their behavior, in general, has been characterized by obedience to God's moral laws. Passages that speak of people as "righteous" (*dikaios*) in this second sense include Matt. 9:13; 27:19; Mark 2:17; 6:20; Luke 1:6; 2:25; 5:32; 15:7; 18:9; Rom. 5:7; James 5:6; 1 Pet. 3:12, 18; 4:18; 2 Pet. 2:7, 8; 1 John 3:7; Rev. 22:11.

10. The Joy and Blessing of a Clear Conscience. Paul tells Timothy to train people to keep a good conscience before God, for he says, "The aim of our charge is love that issues from a pure heart *and a good conscience* and a sincere faith" (1 Tim. 1:5). He likewise tells Timothy that he should be carrying on his ministry by "holding faith and a *good conscience*," and he warns that by rejecting their consciences, "some have made shipwreck of their faith" (v. 19). But a good conscience depends on walking in obedience to God and resisting temptations to sin.[10]

11. The Joy and Blessing of God's Peace. Paul connects the idea of others imitating his conduct with having God's peace in their lives, for he says, "What you have learned and received and heard and seen in me—*practice these things, and the God of peace will be with you*" (Phil. 4:9). This echoes the words of Isaiah:

> Oh that you had paid attention to my commandments!
>> Then your peace would have been like a river,
>> and your righteousness like the waves of the sea. (Isa. 48:18; cf. v. 22)

12. The Joy and Blessing of Discovering by Experience That God's Commands Really Are Beneficial for Our Lives. Sometimes the New Testament authors use the Greek verb *dokimazō* in the sense of "testing something by trying it out, putting it to use, and thereby proving it."[11] This is the sense in Romans 12:2:

> Do not be conformed to this world, but be transformed by the renewal of your mind, that *by testing you may discern* [Greek, *dokimazō*] what is the will of God, *what is good and acceptable and perfect.*

This means that as Christians live in obedience to God's will in their lives, they will discover more and more that this way of life is "good and acceptable and perfect" for them. Obedience to God is the pathway to a "good" life for a Christian.[12]

13. The Joy and Blessing of Experiencing Freedom from Slavery to Sin. Paul writes:

> So you also must consider yourselves dead to sin and alive to God in Christ Jesus. Let not sin therefore reign in your mortal body, to make you obey its passions.... For sin will have no dominion over you, since you are not under law but under grace. (Rom. 6:11–14)

---

[10] An extensive study of conscience is Andrew David Naselli and J. D. Crowley, *Conscience: What It Is, How to Train It, and Loving Those Who Differ* (Wheaton, IL: Crossway, 2016).

[11] The actual definition from the BDAG *Lexicon* is "to make a critical examination of something to determine genuineness, put to the test, examine; to draw a conclusion about worth on the basis of testing, prove, approve" (BDAG, 255).

[12] This idea of proving in practice that obedience to God is beneficial for our lives is also seen in Eph. 5:10 and Phil. 1:9–10.

One of the joys of obedience to God is recognizing a victory over sin or temptation that has come as a result of our new life in Christ.

14. The Joy and Blessing of Avoiding God's Painful Discipline. The New Testament Epistles speak of God's fatherly "discipline" that comes to those who begin to live in disobedience to him. Jesus says to the church in Laodicea, "Those whom I love, *I reprove and discipline*, so be zealous and repent" (Rev. 3:19). And the author of Hebrews warns his readers about God's fatherly discipline, writing, "For the moment, all discipline seems painful rather than pleasant, but later it yields the peaceful fruit of righteousness to those who have been trained by it" (Heb. 12:11; see also 1 Cor. 11:29–30; Eph. 4:30).[13]

15. The Joy and Blessing of Greater Assurance of Salvation. John explains that obedience to God's commandments is one of the means of gaining additional assurance that we have come to "know" Christ in a personal, saving relationship, for he says, "And by this we know that we have come to know him, *if we keep his commandments*" (1 John 2:3).

Similarly, Peter says that one means that believers can use to "confirm [their] calling and election" (2 Pet. 1:10) is to add to their initial saving faith several qualities of moral goodness in their conduct of life:

> For this very reason, make every effort to supplement your faith with virtue, and virtue with knowledge, and knowledge with self-control, and self-control with steadfastness, and steadfastness with godliness, and godliness with brotherly affection, and brotherly affection with love. (2 Pet. 1:5–7)

Then Peter adds:

> Therefore, brothers, be all the more diligent *to confirm your calling and election, for if you practice these qualities you will never fall.* (2 Pet. 1:10)

16. The Joy and Blessing of Experiencing More of a Foretaste of Life in Heaven. Peter writes that "we are waiting for new heavens and a new earth *in which righteousness dwells*" (2 Pet. 3:13), indicating that our life in heaven will be one of perfect obedience to God's commandments. Therefore, a life of obedience to God's commandments in this present age allows us to experience more of a foretaste of what heaven will be like. There will be no sin or disobedience to God in the heavenly city to come, because "*nothing unclean will ever enter it*, nor anyone who does what is detestable or false" (Rev. 21:27).

17. The Joy and Blessing of Increased Heavenly Reward. Paul says that one of his motivations for seeking to live in obedience to God is the hope of receiving greater heavenly reward:

---

[13] See further discussion of God's discipline in our lives in chap. 5, p. 135.

So whether we are at home or away, we make it our aim to please him. For we must all appear before the judgment seat of Christ, *so that each one may receive what is due for what he has done in the body*, whether good or evil. (2 Cor. 5:9–10)

Other passages that talk about degrees of reward for believers in the life to come include Luke 19:17, 19; Romans 14:10–12; 1 Corinthians 3:12–15; 4–5; Colossians 3:25; Revelation 11:18.[14]

B. PRACTICAL QUESTIONS ABOUT THESE BLESSINGS

The preceding list indicates that God promises to give us much more joy and blessing in connection with obedience to him than Christians usually realize.[15] However, two questions naturally arise in terms of practical application:

1. How Long until Lost Blessings Will Be Restored? Someone might ask, "What if I give in to a temptation and choose to sin willfully, and then as a result I begin to miss out on some of these blessings from God? If I repent of my sin, how long will it be until I can experience those blessings again?" Several points must be made in response to this question:

1. We should not think that all of God's blessings will be lost all at once, for God is a wise father who seeks our good, so he will discipline us in ways that seem good to him. In addition, his discipline will always be filled with a measure of mercy and grace.

2. God's corrective discipline will stop when we turn away from the temptation and begin to walk once again in obedience. This is evident from the way Paul wrote to the Christians at Corinth, who had been abusing the Lord's Supper in the disgraceful, unthinking and irreverent way they were celebrating it. He told them that God was disciplining them as a result: "That is why many of you are weak and ill, and some have died" (1 Cor. 11:30).

However, in the very next sentence Paul told them that God's discipline would stop (and presumably the illnesses and deaths would end) if they understood and began to

---

[14] See also Dan. 12:2; Matt. 6:20–22; 19:21; Luke 6:22–23; 12:18–21, 32, 42–48; 14:13–14; 1 Cor. 3:8; 9:18; 13:3; 15:19, 29–32, 58; Gal. 6:9–10; Eph. 6:7–8; Col. 3:23–24; 1 Tim. 6:18; Heb. 10:34, 35; 11:10, 14–16, 26, 35; 1 Pet. 1:4; 2 John 8; Rev. 11:18; 22:12; see also Matt. 5:46; 6:2–6, 16–18, 24; Luke 6:35. Taken from Wayne Grudem, *Systematic Theology: An Introduction to Biblical Doctrine* (Leicester, UK: Inter-Varsity, and Grand Rapids, MI: Zondervan, 1994), 1144n4.

[15] I have not made much use of Old Testament passages about the blessings that God promises for obedience. The emphasis of the new covenant is more spiritual and less physical and material in nature than the blessings for obedience promised in Deuteronomy 28:1–14 or the curses for disobedience promised in Deuteronomy 28:15–68. Those blessings and curses belonged to the old covenant established through Moses for the people of Israel at that time, but the pattern of God giving additional blessing for obedience and giving discipline for disobedience is similar.

act in an appropriate way with the Lord's Supper, for he says, "But if we judged ourselves truly, we would not be judged" (1 Cor. 11:31). He was telling them that if they stopped the sin, God would stop the disciplinary judgment.

Still, the consequences from some sinful act might continue for a longer period of time. An alcoholic who has been abusing alcohol for a long time might continue to have harmful physical consequences in his own body for example.

3. Remember that "the LORD is merciful and gracious, slow to anger and abounding in love" (Ps. 103:8). Moreover, "he does not deal with us according to our sins, nor repay us according to our iniquities" (v. 10). We commit many lesser sins for which God, in his patience, does not discipline us. (See the section below on greater and lesser sins.) James says, "We all stumble in many ways" (James 3:2).

4. God's purpose is not to harm us but to do us good in all circumstances (see Rom. 8:28) and to "restore" us to a place of effective ministry (Gal. 6:1) for the advancement of his kingdom. It is important always to remember that God's discipline is the discipline of a loving and wise father: "He disciplines us *for our good*, that we may share his holiness" (Heb. 12:10).

5. For those who have been entrusted with positions of Christian leadership, it is especially difficult to know when and *if* God will restore the same measure of stewardship or ministry responsibility in the work of his kingdom. When David repented regarding his sin with Bathsheba, God forgave him (2 Sam. 12:13; see also Psalm 51), but the child born to David and Bathsheba died (v. 19), and God never again restored the measure of blessing that David had known in his kingdom (see the multiple troubles David experienced in 2 Samuel 13–24; 1 Kings 1).

Similarly, because of the one sin of Moses in striking the rock rather than just speaking to it (Num. 20:8, 11), God did not allow him to enter the Promised Land (v. 12; see also Num. 27:12–14; Deut. 1:37; 32:48–52).[16] And when Saul wrongfully offered a sacrifice rather than waiting for Samuel to do it, God took away his kingdom (see 1 Sam. 13:13–14; see also 1 Sam. 15:22–23, 26, 28).

6. In human interpersonal relationships, it might take a long time for a person who has harmed others to regain their trust. Others might quickly *forgive* the person (Matt. 6:14–15), but forgiveness is something distinct from trust. Deep trust between human beings grows slowly over time and can be damaged in a moment.

For instance, Paul did not quickly want to welcome John Mark on his second missionary journey:

> But Paul thought best not to take with them one who had withdrawn from them in Pamphylia and not gone with them to the work. (Acts 15:38; cf. 13:13)

---

[16] From an earlier incident of getting water from the rock, it is likely that Moses was aware that God himself was standing before the people who were sitting before Moses as he stood on the rock (see Ex. 17:6), and therefore when Moses struck the rock, it was a shocking expression of anger and frustration with God himself. It was also a failure to obey exactly what God had told him to do.

However, John Mark apparently later regained Paul's trust, and they ministered together (see Col. 4:10; 2 Tim. 4:11).

7. God knows our hearts, and he will look with favor on a genuinely repentant, contrite heart:

> The sacrifices of God are a broken spirit;
> > a broken and contrite heart, O God, you will not despise. (Ps. 51:17; see
> > > also 1 Sam. 16:7; Pss. 7:9; 26:2; 51:10; Jer. 11:20)

In conclusion, we simply cannot know in advance when the blessings of obedience will be restored, and in what measure.

2. If I Am Obedient, Why Do I Still Suffer? Someone might ask, "What if I've been obedient to God but I am still suffering some kind of hardship?"

1. Difficulties and hardships are a normal part of the Christian life. We have only to think of the examples of Abraham, Joseph, Moses, David, and Job, or, in the New Testament, Paul and Jesus himself. We can often encounter difficulties and hardships at the same time blessings for obedience (listed above) are being poured out on us in great abundance. And many Christians have later discovered that their difficulties were blessings in disguise (see Rom. 8:28; also Gen. 50:20). God's purpose for us during our lifetimes on earth is not to bestow unlimited blessings on us, but to perfect our character so that we will be more like Christ and to draw us near to him in daily fellowship.

> Count it all joy, my brothers, when you meet trials of various kinds, for you know that the testing of your faith produces steadfastness. And let steadfastness have its full effect, that you may be perfect and complete, lacking in nothing. (James 1:2–4)

Peter encouraged first-century Christians that God's favor could be on them even in the midst of suffering:

> Beloved, do not be surprised at the fiery trial when it comes upon you to test you, as though something strange were happening to you. But rejoice insofar as you share Christ's sufferings, that you may also rejoice and be glad when his glory is revealed. If you are insulted for the name of Christ, you are blessed, because the Spirit of glory and of God rests upon you. (1 Pet. 4:12–14; see also 1 Pet. 1:6–7)

2. The suffering will certainly come to an end, sometimes sooner than we expect:

> And *after you have suffered a little while*, the God of all grace, who has called you to his eternal glory in Christ, will himself restore, confirm, strengthen, and establish you. (1 Pet. 5:10)

C. THE HARMFUL CONSEQUENCES OF SIN IN THE LIFE OF A CHRISTIAN

Some Christians object to talking very much about sin. Isn't the New Testament mainly about God's forgiveness and grace? Why should we focus on sin?

In fact, it is spiritually healthy for Christians to think about sin in their lives. A search on the English word *sin* (and other words with the same root, such as *sins* or *sinner*) shows that it occurs 440 times in the New Testament alone. And my copy of the Bible in the English Standard Version (ESV) has 235 pages in the New Testament. This means that the topic of sin is mentioned in one way or another about two times per page on average through the entire New Testament. We would neglect such a topic at our peril.

This means we need to talk about sin whether we are interacting with non-Christians, young Christians, or mature Christians. Non-Christians need to understand God's moral standards and come to a conviction of sin before they will reach genuine repentance for sin and come to saving faith in Christ for the forgiveness of those sins. But young Christians and mature Christians alike need to realize that God intends the entire Christian life to be one of growth and sanctification, which certainly involves progressively overcoming sin in our lives. This is how we grow to Christian maturity. Therefore, it is important to understand what sin is and how it affects us.

1. Definition of Sin.[17] Sin can be defined as follows:

> **Sin** is any failure to conform to the moral law of God in act, attitude, or nature.

This definition shows that sin consists not only of particular *actions*, such as stealing, lying, or committing murder, but also of *attitudes* that are contrary to what God requires of us.

This truth can be seen in the Ten Commandments, which prohibit not only sinful actions, but also wrong attitudes. For example, the seventh and eighth commandments ban adultery and stealing. Then the tenth commandment says, "You shall not covet your neighbor's house; you shall not covet your neighbor's wife, or his male servant, or his female servant, or his ox, or his donkey, or anything that is your neighbor's" (Ex. 20:17). With this commandment, God specifies that he also regards the *desire* to steal or to commit adultery as sin. Likewise, in the Sermon on the Mount, Jesus prohibits sinful attitudes such as anger (Matt. 5:22) and lust (v. 28). And when Paul talks about works of the flesh that are opposed to desires of the Spirit (Gal. 5:17), he lists attitudes such as "enmity, . . . jealousy, fits of anger" (v. 20). Even the commandment that Jesus identified as the greatest dictates not an action but an attitude—love for God: "You shall love the Lord your God with all your heart and with all your soul

---

[17] This section on the definition of sin is adapted from Grudem, *Systematic Theology*, 490–91, with permission of the publishers.

and with all your mind and with all your strength" (Mark 12:30). This means that a Christian who lives a life that is pleasing to God has moral purity not only in his actions, but also in his heart desires.

But sin is failure to conform to God's moral law not only in *action* and in *attitude*, but also in our *moral nature*, the internal character that is the essence of who we are as people. Before Christ redeemed us, we were sinners by nature. This is why Paul can say that "while *we were still sinners*, Christ died for us" (Rom. 5:8) and that we previously "were *by nature* children of wrath, like the rest of mankind" (Eph. 2:3). This means that an unbeliever, even if he or she is not committing sinful actions or actively nurturing sinful attitudes, is still a "sinner" in God's sight; his or her sinful nature does not conform to God's moral law.

2. Are There Greater and Lesser Sins? The question, "Are there greater and lesser sins?" must be answered carefully, because the answer depends on what a person means by "greater" and "lesser."

a. Understanding "Greater" and "Lesser" in Regard to Sin:

(1) In Terms of *Legal Standing before God*, There Are Not Greater and Lesser Sins: This is because *any one sin* makes a person to be a "sinner" and therefore guilty before God. Adam and Eve found this out when they violated only one commandment of God, "But of the tree of the knowledge of good and evil you shall not eat" (Gen. 2:17). Paul looks back on this sin and says that "the judgment following *one trespass* brought condemnation" (Rom. 5:16).

A similar teaching is found in Galatians: "Cursed be everyone who does not abide by *all things* written in the Book of the Law, and do them" (3:10, quoting Deut. 27:26). And another example is found in James: "For whoever keeps the whole law but fails *in one point* has become guilty of all of it" (2:10).

Therefore, in terms of legal standing before God, it is not helpful to speak of greater or lesser sins. Any one sin makes a person guilty before God.

(2) In Terms of *the Results That Come from the Sin*, There Are Greater and Lesser Sins: For example, it is sinful to covet my neighbor's laptop computer (see Ex. 20:17, "You shall not covet"). But it is more harmful to allow that sinful desire to lead to the actual act of stealing the computer from my neighbor. More harm comes to my neighbor (who has lost a computer), to our relationship, to me (for I have committed a crime), and to my relationship to God.

In a similar way, it is a sin to hate someone (Matt. 5:43–44; 22:39), but it is a much more harmful sin to actually murder the person. It is a sin to desire to commit adultery (5:27–28), but it is a much more harmful sin to actually commit adultery.[18]

---

[18] See Ezek. 8:6, 13, and 15 for other examples of "still greater abominations."

(3) In Terms of *the Kind of Command That Is Broken,* There Are Greater and Lesser Sins: Jesus implies that there are greater and lesser commandments in the Old Testament law when he says:

> Whoever relaxes one of the *least of these commandments* and teaches others to
> do the same will be called least in the kingdom of heaven. (Matt. 5:19)

Jesus also rebuked the scribes and Pharisees as "hypocrites" because they scrupulously paid attention to minor details about the tithing laws ("you tithe mint and dill and cumin") but neglected "*the weightier matters of the law*: justice and mercy and faithfulness" (Matt. 23:23).

(4) In Terms of *the Person Committing the Sin,* There Are Greater and Lesser Sins: A particular sin may grieve God more deeply and harm God's kingdom more if it is done by someone with greater responsibility, someone who has more extensive knowledge that it is wrong, or someone whom God has repeatedly warned in the past. James warns that teachers, who have been entrusted with more responsibility, will be judged more strictly:

> Not many of you should become teachers, my brothers, for you know that *we
> who teach will be judged with greater strictness*. (James 3:1)

Jesus indicates that those to whom much has been given will be held more accountable by God:

> And that servant who knew his master's will but did not get ready or act
> according to his will, will receive a severe beating. But the one who did not
> know, and did what deserved a beating, will receive a light beating. *Everyone
> to whom much was given, of him much will be required*, and from him to whom
> they entrusted much, they will demand the more. (Luke 12:47–48)

Jesus told Pilate, "He who delivered me over to you has the *greater sin*" (John 19:11), probably referring to the high priest Caiaphas, who had extensive knowledge of the Old Testament and who was entrusted with a high leadership position among the Jewish people.

The Old Testament contains several warnings to those who have been warned often by God and have not listened:

> He who is often reproved, *yet stiffens his neck*,
>   will suddenly be broken beyond healing. (Prov. 29:1)

> Yet they did not listen to me or incline their ear, *but stiffened their neck*. They
> did worse than their fathers. (Jer. 7:26; see also Num. 15:30).[19]

---

[19] Several Old Testament passages treat sins that are done "unintentionally" differently than sins that are done stubbornly or with a "stiff neck." See, for example, Lev. 4:2, 13, 22, 27; 5:15; cf. Heb. 9:7.

b. Practical Benefits of Understanding Greater and Lesser Sins: This distinction between greater and lesser sins should be helpful to us in terms of our relationships with other believers and family members. In the ordinary course of human relationships, there will inevitably be numerous minor offenses that a wise Christian will simply overlook. Peter probably had this in mind when he told Christians to "keep loving one another earnestly, since *love covers a multitude of sins*" (1 Pet. 4:8).

The knowledge that there can be greater and lesser sins will be especially beneficial in helping us to act wisely with respect to raising children, teaching in schools, relating to friends, managing departments or entire companies, counseling one another, and knowing when to initiate a process of church discipline. It should also be helpful to us personally in understanding things that are more and less important in our daily confession of sins to God (see 1 John 1:9).

However, even though there are lesser sins, we must still remember that sin of any kind is a serious thing in God's sight, and no sin will ever bring us his blessing.

3. What Are the Harmful Consequences of Willful Sin in a Christian's Life? Some things remain unchanged in the life of a born-again Christian even when he or she starts down a path of conscious, willful sin. As Christians, we know that our *justification* before God is unchanging: "There is therefore now *no condemnation* for those who are in Christ Jesus" (Rom. 8:1). In addition, our *adoption* is unchanging, for we remain God's children, members of his family: "Beloved, *we are God's children now* and what we will be has not yet appeared" (1 John 3:2). And Paul writes to the Christians in the churches of Galatia, "In Christ Jesus *you are all sons of God*, through faith" (Gal. 3:26; see also Gal. 4:4–7; 1 John 3:1; John 1:12). Just as an earthly father does not ordinarily kick a disobedient child out of the family, so God does not reject us from being his sons and daughters simply because we have sinned, even willfully.

However, in spite of these things that remain unchanged, several New Testament passages affirm that there are still some harmful consequences of willful, conscious sin in the life of a believer. I will discuss these passages in the following material. (The following New Testament passages that warn believers not to sin are concerned primarily with sins that the readers know about, for the New Testament authors could not have expected readers to take any action to avoid sins that they were not doing consciously or willfully, since they would not have even known about such sins.)[20]

---

[20] I admit that Christians also commit sins that they do not know to be sins, perhaps because their understanding of Scripture is inadequate or because the teaching they have received was misleading or insufficient. In addition, it is possible to sin through negligence, not willfully choosing to do something wrong but simply failing to notice or remember a need that we should have met. In the familiar words of confession in the Book of Common Prayer, "We have left undone those things which we ought to have done" (from the prayer of General Confession). The material in the following paragraphs also applies (to some extent) to unintentional sins, but our focus in this life should of course be on dealing with those sins of which we are aware.

a. As a Result of Willful Sin, *Our Fellowship with God Will Be Disrupted*: This is because we "grieve the Holy Spirit" (Eph. 4:30). Furthermore, we no longer have confidence before God when we pray or worship, for John writes, "*If our heart does not condemn us*, we have confidence before God" (1 John 3:21).

Such a disruption of fellowship with God was operative even for believers who were forgiven under the old covenant, for Isaiah writes as follows:

> Behold, the LORD's hand is not shortened, that it cannot save,
>   or his ear dull, that it cannot hear;
> but your iniquities have made a separation
>   between you and your God,
> *and your sins have hidden his face from you*
>   so that he does not hear. (Isa. 59:1–2).[21]

Similarly, Peter warns Christians to "turn away from evil and do good," because "the face of the Lord is against those who do evil" (1 Pet. 3:11–12). This is certainly a disruption of fellowship.

b. As a Result of Willful Sin, We Will Experience *God's Fatherly Displeasure*: I have taken the phrase "fatherly displeasure" from the Westminster Confession of Faith (1646), which includes this wise statement about the consequences of sin:

> God doth continue to forgive the sins of those that are justified; and, although they can never fall from the state of justification, yet they may, by their sins, fall under *God's fatherly displeasure*, and not have the light of his countenance restored unto them, until they humble themselves, confess their sins, beg pardon, and renew their faith and repentance. (11.5, emphasis added)

The phrase "God's fatherly displeasure" seems very appropriate. The word *fatherly* reminds us that we are still God's children and he still loves us as our heavenly Father. But the word *displeasure* reminds us that God is not pleased with the sins of his children. Any parent who has raised children will recognize at once how it is possible, at the very same moment, to love a child very deeply but simultaneously to be exceptionally displeased with what that child has done!

Paul talks about such divine displeasure when he warns Christians, "Do not *grieve the Holy Spirit of God*" (Eph. 4:30; see also Heb. 12:5–11).

c. As a Result of Willful Sin, We Might Experience *God's Fatherly Discipline*: The risen Lord Jesus speaks about his discipline that comes to disobedient Christians when he tells the straying church in Laodicea, "Those whom I love, I *reprove and discipline*, so be zealous and repent" (Rev. 3:19, see also Heb. 12:6, 10).

---

[21] See also Ps. 66:18, "If I had cherished iniquity in my heart, the LORD would not have listened."

d. As a Result of Willful Sin, We Will *Slide Backward in Our Sanctification*: Paul warns the Christians in Rome that if they willingly yield themselves to some kind of sin, they run the danger of becoming increasingly enslaved to that sin:

> Do you not know that if you present yourselves to anyone as obedient slaves, you are slaves of the one whom you obey, either of sin, which leads to death, or of obedience, which leads to righteousness? (Rom. 6:16)

Peter also warns his readers not to give into thoughts or activities that would nurture wrongful desires in their minds and hearts: "Beloved, I urge you as sojourners and exiles to abstain from the passions of the flesh, which *wage war against your soul*" (1 Pet. 2:11).

Here the Greek word for "wage war" is *strateuō*, a term that normally means "to serve as a soldier" (see 1 Cor. 9:7; 2 Tim. 2:4; James 4:1). Peter indicates that entertaining sinful desires is a dangerous activity because, in spiritual terms, these desires are "enemy soldiers" that will inflict harm on the Christian's "soul," making him or her spiritually weak and ineffective.

e. As a Result of Willful Sin, We Will Tend to *Become Less Fruitful* in Our Ministries and Our Christian Lives: Jesus tells his disciples that they are to "abide" in him—that is, to maintain the kind of close personal fellowship with him that is necessary for any fruitfulness in the Christian life:

> *Abide in me*, and I in you. As the branch cannot bear fruit by itself, unless it abides in the vine, neither can you, unless you *abide in me*. I am the vine; you are the branches. Whoever abides in me and I in him, he it is that bears much fruit, *for apart from me you can do nothing*. (John 15:4–5)

f. As a Result of Willful Sin, We Will *Lose Some Heavenly Reward*: Although our justification is by faith alone (Rom. 5:1; Gal. 2:16), our heavenly rewards are based on our conduct in this life. If we live lives of faith and obedience to God, we will receive abundant heavenly rewards in the life to come (see Matt. 6:19–21; Luke 19:17, 19; 1 Cor. 3:12–15). Paul explains this quite explicitly to the Christians at Corinth:

> For we must all appear before the judgment seat of Christ, so that each one may receive what is due for what he has done in the body, whether good or evil. (2 Cor. 5:10)[22]

4. Why Should Christians Pray for Forgiveness of Sins? It might at first seem puzzling that Jesus instructs his disciples (and, by implication, instructs us) to pray following the pattern of the Lord's Prayer, which includes the request "Forgive us our sins" (Luke 11:4) or "Forgive us our debts, as we also have forgiven our debtors" (Matt. 6:12). In this same

---

[22] For further discussion on degrees of reward in heaven, see Grudem, *Systematic Theology*, 1144–45.

prayer, we are directed to ask for "our daily bread" (v. 11; Luke 11:3), so it seems that this is a pattern for prayer that Jesus expects us to use every day of our lives.

John assumes this same pattern of regularly asking for forgiveness when he writes to Christian believers, "*If we confess our sins*, he is faithful and just to forgive us our sins and to cleanse us from all unrighteousness" (1 John 1:9).

But if God forgave all our sins at the moment we trusted in Christ for salvation, why do we need to continue to ask for forgiveness?

To answer this question correctly, we need to distinguish between two different senses of forgiveness, both of which are involved in our relationship to God. The first sense is forgiveness with respect to *legal guilt or innocence*, and therefore liability to eternal punishment for our sins. In that sense, we have been forgiven once for all from the moment we first trusted in Christ for salvation, the moment of our justification (see Rom. 5:1–2; 8:1). Therefore, when we pray daily for forgiveness we are *not* praying again for God to give us right legal standing before him (justification), because that has already been given to us once for all time and it never needs to be repeated.

However, there is a second sense of forgiveness having to do with a *restoration of personal fellowship* with God that has been disrupted by our sin. In that sense, we are right to ask for forgiveness each day. This is apparently the sense of David's request, "Restore to me the joy of your salvation" (Ps. 51:12). When we are aware that we have grieved the Holy Spirit of God by our sin (see Eph. 4:30) and that our hearts condemn us when we come into God's presence (see 1 John 3:21), then it is appropriate to ask that God would forgive us, that he would restore his close personal relationship with us, and that the Holy Spirit would once more manifest his presence and power with us (Rom. 8:4, 5, 14; Gal. 5:25; Eph. 5:18).

A human analogy might be helpful for understanding these two senses of forgiveness. Suppose that a teenage driver has to appear in court on a charge of speeding and reckless driving. When he arrives, he finds that the judge is his own father![23] And then suppose that, due to some legal technicality (perhaps the only witness does not show up in court, for example), the judge has to declare the teenage driver "not guilty." In that case, the teenage driver is "forgiven" in a *legal* sense. He is not guilty before the law and he has no penalty to pay. But when the judge returns home that evening, he will still be deeply displeased with his son. The son will need to ask the father to forgive him in a *personal relationship* sense even though he has already been forgiven in a legal sense.

Now God relates to us both as the Judge of the universe and as our loving Father. Though we were forgiven at justification by God acting as Judge, we still need daily to ask for forgiveness in a relational sense from God acting as our Father.

---

[23] I realize that this could not occur in a modern legal system, where the judge would have to send the case to another judge to avoid the appearance of bias.

D. THE POWER TO OBEY GOD

God doesn't merely give us motives to obey him and promise blessings for obedience. He also provides us with the spiritual and moral ability to obey him in increasing measure throughout our lives. He does this through the sanctifying work of the Holy Spirit within us. Several passages in the New Testament speak about this process.

Paul promises the Philippian Christians, "It is God who works in you, both *to will* and to work for his good pleasure" (Phil. 2:13). God works in us to enable us "to will" (that is, to desire, prefer, and decide to follow; Greek, *thelō*) the things that he would have us do.

Paul encourages the Christians in Rome to grow in their patterns of obedience by the power of the Holy Spirit, for he says, "If *by the Spirit* you put to death the deeds of the body, you will live" (Rom. 8:13). He also promises them, "Sin will have no dominion over you, since you are not under law but under grace" (6:14).

John promises his readers that if they confess their sins to God, he will not only forgive their sins, but also will work inwardly in them to "cleanse" them from sin. John says, "If we confess our sins, he is faithful and just to forgive us our sins and *to cleanse us from all unrighteousness*" (1 John 1:9).

Therefore, we should be encouraged in our attempts to live each day in obedience to God's moral teachings in his Word. He promises us not only moral guidance and direction, but also the spiritual and moral ability to increasingly follow those directions. We will never do so perfectly in this life, but it should encourage us greatly that he promises this inward moral strength and inward work in our hearts.[24]

QUESTIONS FOR PERSONAL APPLICATION

1. Does the idea of obeying God seem joyful and pleasant to you, or burdensome?
2. Have you ever felt an awareness that God is pleased with something that you have done? Does this happen often? If not, what do you think is hindering you from sensing God's pleasure?
3. Are there any areas of your life that you would like to "cleanse" in order to be "a vessel for honorable use"? (See 2 Tim. 2:21.)
4. Can you recall a specific period in your life when God's discipline was painful for a time but brought good results?
5. Do you agree that willful sin in our lives will hinder our daily fellowship with God?
6. Do you think it is possible to sense God's fatherly displeasure with you and his love for you at the same time?

---

[24] For further discussion of the process of sanctification in the Christian life, see Grudem, *Systematic Theology*, 746–62.

SPECIAL TERMS

fatherly displeasure
good works
greater sins
lesser sins

BIBLIOGRAPHY

Sections in Other Ethics Texts

(see complete bibliographical data, p. 64)

Frame, 403–4, 590–92
McQuilkin and Copan, 598–605
Murray, 181–242
Rae, 40–42

Other Works

Brown, C. A. "Obedience." In *New Dictionary of Christian Ethics and Pastoral Theology*, edited by David J. Atkinson and David H. Field, 636–37. Leicester, UK: Inter-Varsity, and Downers Grove, IL: InterVarsity Press, 1995.

Naselli, Andrew David and J. D. Crowley. *Conscience: What It Is, How to Train It, and Loving Those Who Differ.* Wheaton, IL: Crossway, 2016.

Parkyn, D. L. "Blessedness." In *New Dictionary of Christian Ethics and Pastoral Theology*, 196–97.

Piper, John. *Desiring God: Meditations of a Christian Hedonist.* Portland, OR: Multnomah, 1986.

Sproul, R. C. *Pleasing God.* Wheaton, IL: Tyndale, 1988.

SCRIPTURE MEMORY PASSAGE

2 Timothy 2:21: Therefore, if anyone cleanses himself from what is dishonorable, he will be a vessel for honorable use, set apart as holy, useful to the master of the house, ready for every good work.

HYMN

"Trust and Obey"

When we walk with the Lord in the light of his Word,
What a glory he sheds on our way!

While we do his good will, he abides with us still,
And with all who will trust and obey.

Refrain:
Trust and obey, for there's no other way
To be happy in Jesus, but to trust and obey.

Not a shadow can rise, not a cloud in the skies,
But his smile quickly drives it away;
Not a doubt or a fear, not a sigh nor a tear,
Can abide while we trust and obey.

Not a burden we bear, not a sorrow we share,
But our toil he doth richly repay;
Not a grief nor a loss, not a frown or a cross,
But is blest if we trust and obey.

But we never can prove the delights of his love
Until all on the altar we lay;
For the favor he shows, and the joy he bestows,
Are for them who will trust and obey.

Then in fellowship sweet we will sit at his feet,
Or we'll walk by his side in the way;
What he says we will do, where he sends we will go,
Never fear, only trust and obey.

AUTHOR: JAMES H. SAMMIS, D. 1919

Chapter 6

HOW TO KNOW GOD'S WILL: FACTORS TO CONSIDER IN MAKING ETHICAL DECISIONS

What factors should we consider in making ethical decisions?
What does it mean to be "led by the Holy Spirit"?

If we define Christian ethics as a study of the question "What does the whole Bible teach us about which acts, attitudes, and personal character traits receive God's approval, and which do not?" then it is possible to see every significant decision as a search to answer the question "How can I know God's will for me in this situation?" To know God's will is to know what actions, attitudes, and character traits he approves of in each situation.

A. DECISIONS CAN BE QUICK OR DRAWN-OUT, AND CAN INVOLVE MAJOR EVENTS OR SMALL DAILY ACTIVITIES

Some decisions must be made instantly. When Joseph was working in Potiphar's house in Egypt, one day Potiphar's wife "caught him by his garment, saying, 'Lie with me.' But he left his garment in her hand and fled and got out of the house" (Gen. 39:12; but notice also his earlier pattern of wise responses in vv. 7–10). Joseph had only an instant to respond, and he made a wise decision and fled.[1]

---

[1] In another case, Uzzah had an instant to decide and made the wrong decision. God had given a clear commandment that the people "must not touch the holy things, lest they die" (Num. 4:15, referring to the

149

Other decisions take more time. In this chapter I will explain multiple factors that can and should be considered when we have more time to make a decision and when the decision itself is important enough to consider in greater detail.

Sometimes knowing God's will involves major decisions, such as what career to aim for, what subject a student should choose as a college major, or whom to marry. Sometimes the question is whether to take a new job or stay in the present job, which church to join, or whether to volunteer for a charitable cause or church activity. Still other situations may involve difficult end-of-life decisions regarding a terminally ill family member. And yet other decisions relate to convictions about public-policy issues, such as abortion, capital punishment, euthanasia, war, marriage laws, or the legalization of marijuana.

At other times Christians desire to have God's wisdom regarding simpler, everyday decisions, such as which emails to respond to or delete, which phone calls to make or postpone, or how to schedule various tasks that have to be done on certain days.

For all such questions, whether large or small, the following process should be helpful (even if only parts of this process are used in some situations). But this process must be understood in connection with the previous chapters, particularly chapters 4 and 5.

Chapter 4 discussed the importance of developing a *Christlike character* and growing in the numerous Christian virtues named in the New Testament. As a Christian grows toward a Christlike character, he or she will be more inclined to make wise ethical decisions that accord with what is pleasing to God.

Chapter 5 discussed the joys and blessings of obedience to God, and the harmful consequences of sin, even in the lives of Christians. But if someone begins to acquire a Christlike character and godly wisdom, and truly longs to experience the joys and blessings of obedience, it is still necessary to know what factors need to be considered in making ethical decisions.

The next two sections will discuss *four dimensions of every action* and *nine sources of information* that should be considered in any moral decision.

B. FOUR DIMENSIONS OF EVERY ACTION

Human actions have at least four dimensions that need to be considered when decisions need to be made:

---

various furnishings for the tabernacle). But the magnitude of God's holiness behind that prohibition had not penetrated deeply enough into Uzzah's heart, because when King David and the people of Israel were bringing the ark of the covenant to Jerusalem, Uzzah actually touched the ark: "And when they came to the threshing floor of Nacon, *Uzzah put out his hand to the ark of God and took hold of it*, for the oxen stumbled. And the anger of the LORD was kindled against Uzzah, and God struck him down there because of his error, and he died there beside the ark of God" (2 Sam. 6:6–7). There was also a failure of leadership in this situation, because the ark was wrongly being carried on a cart rather than with poles placed through the rings on the corners of the ark (see Ex. 25.14–15; 2 Sam. 6:3–4).

1. The action itself
2. The person's attitudes about the action
3. The person's motives for doing the action (the reason why the person does something)
4. The results of the action

While the action itself, as soon as it is done, will be visible to others, a person's attitudes and motives will be mostly invisible, and the results of the action will also be mostly invisible because they have not happened yet.

We can consider these four dimensions to every action in more detail.

1. The Action Itself: The first question to ask is, Is this a morally good action? To decide that, we need to know the commands of Scripture regarding the action.

Some actions are clearly prohibited by Scripture. The Bible tells us not to murder (Ex. 20:13), not to commit adultery (v. 14), not to steal (v. 15), not to bear false witness (v. 16), and so on. Other actions are commanded. Scripture tells us to "honor your father and your mother" (v. 12). Elsewhere the Bible tells us that we are to "pay . . . taxes to whom taxes are owed" (Rom. 13:7).

But many actions that we have to consider are neither specifically commanded nor specifically prohibited by Scripture, such as whether to accept a particular job offer, which used car to purchase, which church to join, or whom to marry. For such decisions, we need to consider other dimensions of the action in question, and we need to consider all nine sources of information.

2. The Person's Attitudes about the Action. Because "the LORD looks on the heart" (1 Sam. 16:7), it is not enough for us simply to do morally right actions. God also wants the attitudes of our hearts to be right before him:

> Every way of a man is right in his own eyes,
>   but *the LORD weighs the heart.* (Prov. 21:2)

In some cases, an *action* can be right and the *results* can be morally good, but a person's *attitudes* might be wrong. For instance, if Julie's mother tells her that she has to clean her room before she can go out to play with friends, she might do the right action (clean the room in a hurry) and get the right results (a clean room) but with the wrong attitude (she slams the door and cleans the room in anger and with simmering resentment against her mother).

3. The Person's Motives for Doing the Action. Jesus taught us to beware of doing good actions with wrong motives, such as the desire to be praised by other people:

> Beware of practicing your righteousness before other people *in order to be seen by them,* for then you will have no reward from your Father who is in heaven.

Thus, when you give to the needy, sound no trumpet before you, as the hypocrites do in the synagogues and in the streets, that they may be praised by others.
Truly, I say to you, they have received their reward. (Matt. 6:1–2; cf. 23:5–7)

For example, consider a couple who are talking together about whether they should
agree to help with their church's youth ministry one night a week. If they honestly ask
themselves why they want to do this, they might find that their motives are very positive
ones, such as a desire to minister effectively to young people who come to their church,
to be involved in a church activity in which their children participate, to do some kind
of ministry together, to meet a need because of a shortage of volunteers at the time, or
because of other similar motives. They might just want to honor God in the way they
conduct their lives and to advance his kingdom, as Jesus taught: "Seek first the kingdom
of God and his righteousness, and all these things will be added to you" (Matt. 6:33).

On the other hand, they might find that their motives are not appropriate. They might
be thinking about helping in the youth ministry because a neighbor has been putting
pressure on them to do so and they are tired of telling him no, even though they do not
feel it is the right thing for them to do. Or they might want to become better known and
gain recognition from others in the church, which is a simple appeal to their pride. Or
they might be seeking an opportunity to observe the youth pastor so they can lodge more
criticisms against him with the church leaders! All of these would be wrong motives.

4. The Results of the Action. Other passages in Scripture encourage us to take thought
for the results of our actions. For example, Paul wanted the Christians at Corinth to
evaluate what was happening in their worship services to see if various activities actually
contributed to building up one another in the Lord:

What then, brothers? When you come together, each one has a hymn, a lesson,
a revelation, a tongue, or an interpretation. *Let all things be done for building up.* (1 Cor. 14:26)

To take another example, Paul was persuaded that the unclean foods in the Old Testament were no longer unclean for Christians to eat ("Nothing is unclean in itself," Rom.
14:14), and therefore the action of eating pork (for example) was not morally wrong
in itself. But it could bring a wrongful result, and in those cases it should not be done:

For *if your brother is grieved by what you eat,* you are no longer walking in
love. By what you eat, do not destroy the one for whom Christ died. So do
not let what you regard as good be spoken of as evil. (Rom. 14:15–16; see also
1 Cor. 8:13; 10:24)

In writing to the Corinthian church, Paul concluded a long section of advice with a
general requirement for them to consider the results of their actions: "Whether you eat
or drink, or whatever you do, do all to the glory of God" (1 Cor. 10:31).

We need to consider all four of these dimensions for any action: (1) the action itself, (2) attitudes, (3) motives, and (4) results. An action that is pleasing to God will follow the teachings of Scripture in all four of these areas.

5. Most Actions Contain a Mix of Different Attitudes, Motives, and Results. Even simple actions can involve a complex mixture of *attitudes*. Any parent who has been awakened in the middle of the night to care for a sick child will attest to feeling deep love for the child, but also perhaps mild irritation or even resentment at the interruption of a sound sleep, coupled with thankfulness to God for the privilege of being a parent, plus a slight tinge of anxiety about being able to do a good job at work the next day with less sleep or about whether the disturbance will wake the other children, plus a deep sense of peace at knowing God's presence, plus a renewed sense of gratitude for the sacrifices made by his or her own parents, plus perhaps a bit of weariness and discouragement because of having so many responsibilities, and so forth. Our hearts are complex, and we are capable of having multiple attitudes at once in any given situation.

Then our *motives* for an action might be mixed. While our primary motive for giving time or money to a church or charitable organization might be to further the work of the church and to earn heavenly rewards from God, there might also be a small bit of desire to gain recognition from others. It is often difficult to know our own hearts or to fully understand our motives for our actions.

As for *results*, while we can usually predict the most likely outcome of an action, it is seldom possible to predict the results with certainty or to know how extensive the results will be. Often people are surprised by the "unintended consequences" of their actions. For example, someone could make a business investment in a morally good project (a right action), with right attitudes and motives, but have bad results (the investment could fail and the principal be lost, perhaps because the investment was in a product for which there was no consumer demand).[2]

But these complexities do not mean that it is impossible to know or to evaluate the attitudes, motives, and results of an action. Usually we can know the dominant attitudes and dominant motives for an action (at least for ourselves). It is often possible to predict the most likely results that will come from an action. Therefore, we can analyze these four factors in considering any particular action or situation.

C. NINE SOURCES OF INFORMATION AND GUIDANCE

As I mentioned earlier in this chapter, sometimes there is no time to ponder a decision, and a person simply has to use his or her best judgment at the moment and make the decision quickly. But at other times there is more opportunity to ponder it, and in that

---

[2] A tragic biblical example of unforeseen results is Jephthah's foolish vow in Judg. 11:30–31.

case, several different sources of information should be considered, especially if the decision is quite significant.

Here are nine sources of information to consider:

1. Information from the Bible. Our first source of information about any ethical decision should be the teachings of the Bible. The Bible is our only source of inerrant and absolutely authoritative ethical guidance. The rest of this book is devoted to searching out the teachings of the Bible on numerous specific ethical topics.

2. Information from Studying the Situation. Jesus gives examples from ordinary life that illustrate how people typically learn more about a situation before they agree to a course of action:

> For which of you, desiring to build a tower, does not first sit down and count the cost, whether he has enough to complete it? Otherwise, when he has laid a foundation and is not able to finish, all who see it begin to mock him, saying, "This man began to build and was not able to finish." Or what king, going out to encounter another king in war, will not sit down first and deliberate whether he is able with ten thousand to meet him who comes against him with twenty thousand? And if not, while the other is yet a great way off, he sends a delegation and asks for terms of peace. (Luke 14:28–32)

Many decisions about medical care, colleges, job offers, marriage partners, ministry opportunities, political positions, and numerous other things require us to find more information about the actual facts of a situation before we are able to make a responsible choice.

Studying the situation should also include reflection on "what might be," which comes from our imagination. John Frame explains why imagination is a useful factor in ethical decisions. He defines imagination as "our ability to think of things that are not," then says that imagination is helpful in making ethical decisions because it "enables us to conceive of alternative courses of action as we ponder what to do in the future."[3]

3. Information about Oneself. It is important to understand oneself and one's specific role in the situation at hand. Paul encourages such sober self-reflection:

> For by the grace given to me I say to everyone among you not *to think of himself* more highly than he ought to think, but *to think with sober judgment,* each according to the measure of faith that God has assigned. (Rom. 12:3)

Therefore, a person should honestly ponder his or her own skills, interests, desires,

---

[3] John M. Frame, *The Doctrine of the Christian Life: A Theology of Lordship* (Phillipsburg, NJ: P&R, 2008), 369–70.

and sense of life calling from God in deciding whether to take a specific action or not. Advice from friends and spiritual leaders can be helpful in this regard (see next section).

4. Advice from Others. Christians can get helpful advice from other people regarding an ethical decision. Personal friends as well as spiritual leaders such as pastors can give useful advice. Paul encouraged the Christians in Rome (whom he had not yet met!) that they were able, in general, to give one another wise advice:

> I myself am satisfied about you, my brothers, that you yourselves are full of goodness, filled with all knowledge and *able to instruct one another*. (Rom. 15:14)

The Greek word translated as "able to instruct" is *noutheteō*, "to counsel about avoidance or cessation of an improper course of conduct, admonish, warn, instruct."[4] In a similar way, we read in the Old Testament, "In an abundance of counselors there is safety" (Prov. 11:14).

Reading books and articles about the subject of the decision is another important source of "advice from others," only in this case the others are not personally present but have written their advice and published it.

Finally, the historical teachings of the church can be another source of "advice from others" that is helpful in making ethical decisions. Many of the wisest Bible teachers in the history of the church have given extensive time and thought to the common ethical questions that confront people in each generation, and a tradition of accepted church teaching on some ethical questions has accumulated over time. Sometimes that tradition finds expression (for Protestants at least) in some of the longer statements of faith, such as the Westminster Confession of Faith and the Westminster Larger Catechism, the Heidelberg Catechism, or the Philadelphia Baptist Confession.

5. Changed Circumstances. When your circumstances change, might that be an indication of God's will for you? A correct evaluation will require wisdom to discern whether the circumstances indicate something of God's purposes for us, and this requires prayer for God to give us discernment to understand the circumstances correctly. But there are several examples of circumstantial guidance in Scripture.

A famous example of seeking guidance from changed circumstances is found in the story of Gideon putting out a fleece of wool overnight and asking God to cause the fleece to be wet with dew and the ground dry, and then the next night asking God to cause the fleece to be dry and the ground wet with dew (see Judg. 6:36–40). God granted Gideon's request on both nights.

However, it is not at all clear that the biblical narrative holds this up as an example to imitate. God had already told Gideon clearly what he should do and had already promised to give him victory (see Judg. 6:14–16), and Gideon was essentially saying to

---

[4] BDAG, 679.

God, "If you will do *what you have said you will do*, give me this sign." He was certainly not demonstrating faith in God's promise. Moreover, Gideon had understood God's promise clearly, for he said to God, "If you will save Israel by my hand, *as you have said*, behold I am laying a fleece of wool on the threshing floor" (vv. 36–37). Often in the book of Judges, the events are reported truthfully, but they are not always portrayed in the narrative as examples for us to imitate.

I am not aware of any New Testament example in which God's people similarly sought guidance through asking God to perform a specific miracle. However, there are some other examples in the New Testament of guidance by changed circumstances. When Jesus sent his 12 disciples out to preach, he instructed them that the response of the town would tell them whether to stay there or leave:

> And if anyone will not receive you or listen to your words, shake off the dust from your feet when you leave that house or town. (Matt. 10:14)

Circumstances also seem to have played a significant role in how Paul determined whether to stay in a city or depart during his missionary journeys. Whenever violent hostility arose against his preaching, he left that city and went on to the next one (see Acts 13:50–51; 14:5–6, 20; 16:40; 17:10, 14; 20:1, 3).

He did not face violent opposition in Athens, but when he received only a minimal response, he left there and went on to Corinth, where he stayed a year and six months (Acts 18:1, 11). But the positive circumstance of God's blessing on Paul's ministry did not always indicate that he should stay in a city. He found an "open door" for ministry in Ephesus and decided to stay there longer, but then he found an "open door" for ministry in Troas and decided not to stay. Here is the situation in Ephesus:

> But I will stay in Ephesus until Pentecost, *for a wide door for effective work has opened to me*, and there are many adversaries. (1 Cor. 16:8–9)

And here is the contrasting situation in Troas:

> When I came to Troas to preach the gospel of Christ, *even though a door was opened for me in the Lord*, my spirit was not at rest because I did not find my brother Titus there. *So I took leave of them and went on to Macedonia.* (2 Cor. 2:12–13)

In this second case, in spite of a door for ministry that was "opened for me in the Lord," Paul left Troas, because his spirit was deeply concerned to find Titus, whom he had sent on ahead of him. (A reading of the larger context of these events shows that it was not merely Paul's concern for Titus as an individual, but his deep concern for the well-being of the church at Corinth, and the expectation that Titus would bring him the news from Corinth that he was longing to hear.) Apparently Paul did take account of changed circumstances in seeking to know God's will for his ministry, but at Troas the circumstances included not only the open door for the gospel but also the absence of Titus. And Paul may have taken other factors into account as well.

I will not examine here in detail the numerous additional examples of decision making in the light of changed circumstances that are found in Scripture, but from these examples we can draw this conclusion: we should take changed circumstances into consideration, but changed circumstances are only one factor in a decision-making process, and we need to pray for wisdom from God in understanding how to evaluate these circumstances.

6. Conscience. Conscience is a person's instinctive inward sense of right and wrong. Peter encourages his readers that they should take care to have "a *good conscience*" (1 Pet. 3:16), and Paul said, "I always take pains to have a *clear conscience* toward both God and man" (Acts 24:16). He told the Christians in Rome that one reason they should be obedient to government was "for the sake of conscience" (Rom. 13:5).

This does not mean that conscience is always a reliable guide, because some people can have a "weak" conscience (1 Cor. 8:10), and when Paul says that he wants his hearers to develop a "good conscience" (1 Tim. 1:5),[5] he implies that others can have a bad conscience or one that is not as reliable. Nevertheless, conscience must be taken into account in making an ethical decision. Serious consequences come to those who reject the testimony of their consciences, for Paul said that Timothy should "wage the good warfare" while "holding faith and a good conscience." Then he added, "By rejecting this [that is, by rejecting their consciences],[6] some have made shipwreck of their faith" (vv. 18–19). Therefore, people reject the testimony of their consciences at great peril.

7. Heart. While conscience is an instinctive *inward sense* of right and wrong, the "heart" in Scripture is a broader concept, for the heart is seen as the inward center of a person's deepest moral and spiritual inclinations and convictions, especially in relationship to God.[7]

Believers in the new covenant age have God's laws written on their hearts in a fuller and deeper sense than in the old covenant. As part of the superiority of the new covenant over the old, God promises, "I will *put my laws on their hearts*, and write them on their minds" (Heb. 10:16; cf. 8:10). In addition, Paul assumes that Christians in general have become "obedient from the *heart*" to God's will (Rom. 6:17). But we should not think that our hearts are yet perfect, because Paul also says that his goal in ministry is that Christians would come to practice "love that issues from a *pure heart* and a good conscience and a sincere faith" (1 Tim. 1:5; see also 2 Thess. 3:5). Paul also says that

---

[5] Andrew David Naselli and J. D. Crowley discuss how a person can train his or her conscience in *Conscience: What It Is, How to Train It, and Loving Those Who Differ* (Wheaton, IL: Crossway, 2016), 55–83.

[6] The word *this* translates the Greek pronoun *hēn*, a feminine singular pronoun that refers back to "conscience" (*suneidēsis*), which is also feminine singular in Greek and the nearest antecedent.

[7] Non-Christians are said to have "an evil, unbelieving heart" (Heb. 3:12; see also Rom. 1:21, 24; 2 Pet. 2:14). However, by God's common grace, they still have some inward sense of right and wrong, because Paul says that every person still has, to some extent, an innate understanding of the moral standards of God's laws: "The work of the law is *written on their hearts*" (Rom. 2:15).

God "*tests our hearts*" (1 Thess. 2:4), assuming that Christians can have hearts that are more or less pure before God. (See also Prov. 4:23; 1 Cor. 4:5; Eph. 1:18; 6:6; 1 Thess. 3:13; James 3:14; 4:8).

As far as ethical guidance is concerned, sometimes Scripture speaks of people following their heart desires so as to do what is pleasing to God. Paul told the Christians in the church at Corinth that, regarding the giving of money to the Lord's work, "each one must give as he has decided *in his heart*" (2 Cor. 9:7). He also said that God "*put into the heart of Titus* the same earnest care I have for you" (8:16; see also Acts 7:23).

Even in the old covenant, David could write of a heart that had been to some measure transformed by God:

> Delight yourself in the Lord,
>   and he will give you the desires of your *heart*. (Ps. 37:4)

This indicates that the deep, heartfelt desires of a person who loves God and takes delight in him will often be the very desires that God wants that person to have, the desires that God will be pleased to grant. In this case, a person's desires indicate the will of God for that person.

A similar idea of deep inward desires that accord with God's will is found in other passages that do not specifically use the word *heart* (Hebrew, *lēb*; Greek, *kardia*) but carry a similar meaning:

> If anyone *aspires* [Greek, *oregō*, "to seek to accomplish, aspire, strive for"] to the office of overseer, he *desires* [Greek, *epithymeō*, "to have a strong desire, long for"] a noble task. (1 Tim. 3:1)

With respect to the remarriage of a woman whose first husband has died, Paul writes:

> A wife is bound to her husband as long as he lives. But if her husband dies, she is free to be married *to whom she wishes*, only in the Lord. (1 Cor. 7:39)

Here the Greek term for "wishes" is *thelō*, "to have a desire for something, wish to have, desire, want." Paul is saying that a widow has considerable freedom to marry anyone she wants to marry, as long as he is a Christian believer ("only in the Lord"). I do not think there is a convincing reason to refrain from applying this guideline to marriage decisions generally, even though here it is speaking specifically of widows who wish to remarry. The principle is that people should be married to someone they *want* to be married to.

In my 40 years of teaching theology to undergraduate and graduate students, I have found this principle to be important when students have come to me asking for counsel regarding decisions they have to make between job opportunities, career directions, or sometimes whether to make a commitment to marry a certain person or not. Again and again, after learning about the specific situation, I have found it helpful to ask, "What do you most deeply *want* to do? What is in your heart?"

I find this question helpful because in many situations the Lord has already put in the person's heart a deep desire to follow a particular course of action, and it would be foolish to ignore that desire. I am not saying that such a desire is always reliable, for James warns his readers (who are for the most part Christian believers) that they might have "bitter jealousy and selfish ambition" in their hearts (James 3:14), and some of them need to "purify [their] hearts" (4:8; see also 1:26; 5:5, 8). But in general, Christian believers have become "obedient from the heart" to God's teachings (Rom. 6:17), and I have found again and again that, for Christians who are walking in obedience to the Lord, staying in fellowship with him, and maintaining regular prayer and Bible reading, their heart desires should be a large factor in discerning God's will in particular situations. (But let me be clear that a person's heart desires are not the only factor to take into account, for the other sources of information discussed in this entire section must also be considered.)[8]

8. A Person's Human Spirit. A person's "spirit" (Greek, *pneuma*) is the nonmaterial part of a person, the part that survives when the person's physical body dies. A person's *human spirit* is not the same as the Holy Spirit, who lives within us and who is himself God, for Paul distinguishes between the Holy Spirit and our human spirits when he says, "*The Spirit* himself bears witness with *our spirit* that we are children of God" (Rom. 8:16).

Paul was guided by the uneasiness of his human spirit when he was in Troas looking for Titus to bring him news from the church at Corinth:

> When I came to Troas to preach the gospel of Christ, even though a door was opened for me in the Lord, *my spirit was not at rest* because I did not find my brother Titus there. So I took leave of them and went on to Macedonia. (2 Cor. 2:12–13)

In another situation, when Paul came to the city of Athens, we read that "*his spirit* was provoked within him as he saw that the city was full of idols" (Acts 17:16). This apparently indicates that Paul had a subjective sense that invisible, evil spiritual forces

---

[8] At this point someone might object that Jeremiah 17:9 says, "The heart is deceitful above all things, and desperately sick; who can understand it?" But I do not think that this description is intended to apply to Christian believers in the new covenant, where God has fulfilled his promise, "I will put my law within them, and I will write it on their hearts" (Jer. 31:33; see also 32:39). The author of Hebrews sees this passage as indicating one of the ways the new covenant is superior to the old, and the author sees it as fulfilled in the lives of believers under the new covenant, where God has written his laws on his people's hearts (see Heb. 8:10; 10:16). Therefore, the author of Hebrews says that Christians under the new covenant can "draw near" to God "with a *true heart* in full assurance of faith, with our *hearts* sprinkled clean from an evil conscience" (10:22). For this reason, I do not think that Jeremiah 17:9 should be used to describe the condition of the hearts of believers in general in the new covenant, who have become "obedient from the *heart*" (Rom. 16:7) to God's laws.

were active in Athens and were behind the outward physical evidences of idolatry that he saw as he walked through the city. The presence of evil in the invisible, spiritual realm registered in Paul not so much in his intellect and reason as in his subjective perception of what his spirit was sensing within him.

In a similar way, the Gospels sometimes say that Jesus perceived something "in his *spirit*" (Mark 2:8) or that he "was troubled in his *spirit*" (John 13:21).

Sometimes a person's human spirit can give indications of positive emotions, such as when Mary declared, "My soul magnifies the Lord, and *my spirit* rejoices in God my Savior" (Luke 1:46–47).

Therefore, in addition to a subjective perception about right and wrong from our own *consciences*, and in addition to the deep inward desires and convictions that we feel in our *hearts*, it is also appropriate to consider any sense of invisible spiritual dynamics in a situation that may register in our *human spirits*.

9. Guidance from the Holy Spirit. Yet another source of guidance is personal direction from the Holy Spirit. Such guidance was explicitly identified in Paul's second missionary journey:

> And they went through the region of Phrygia and Galatia, *having been forbidden by the Holy Spirit to speak the word in Asia*. And when they had come up to Mysia, they attempted to go into Bithynia, *but the Spirit of Jesus did not allow them*. (Acts 16:6–7; see also 8:29; 13:2; 15:28)

But is direct guidance from the Holy Spirit part of the life of all Christians, or was it unique to Paul and the other apostles in the book of Acts? I am convinced that the New Testament teaches that direct guidance from the Holy Spirit is a normal component of the life of Christians generally, and it is one of the factors we should take into account in seeking to know God's will.

Paul wrote to Christians in Rome, whom he had not yet met, about an experience of being led by the Holy Spirit that he seems to have thought of as characteristic of the lives of Christians in general:

> For *all who are led by the Spirit of God* are sons of God. (Rom. 8:14)

The Greek word here translated as "led" is *agontai*, the present passive indicative form of *agō*, which means "to direct the movement of an object from one position to another" or (in a spiritual sense) "to lead/guide morally or spiritually."[9] In this context, Paul is describing a quality that characterizes the lives of "sons of God" generally. His use of the present-tense verb conveys "imperfective aspect," inviting the reader to view the action without beginning or end, and this is consistent with the idea of an ongoing action that occurs regularly or repeatedly over time. This sense of the verse is made explicit

---

[9] BDAG, 16, meanings 1 and 3.

by the NASB translation, "For all *who are being led* by the Spirit of God, these are sons of God. (Rom. 8:14). Paul is not speaking of a person being guided merely by his or her own moral convictions or desires, but by the Holy Spirit himself, who is a person. Paul is speaking of personal guidance from the Holy Spirit to individuals, and he indicates that this experience is characteristic of the lives of all Christians.[10]

Elsewhere Paul writes to Christians in the churches of Galatia in a similar way:

> But I say, *walk by the Spirit*, and you will not gratify the desires of the flesh. (Gal. 5:16)

> But *if you are led by the Spirit*, you are not under the law. (Gal. 5:18)

> If we live by the Spirit, let us also *keep in step with the Spirit*. (Gal. 5:25)

All of these passages speak about an expectation that Christians in general will experience a measure of leading or guiding by the Holy Spirit, who will influence their evaluation of various choices and courses of action in a subjectively perceived way.[11]

10. We Can Perceive Subjective Factors in Guidance Separately or in Combination.
All of the last four factors listed above (the conscience, the heart, the human spirit, and guidance from the Holy Spirit) may be called "subjective factors" because we become aware of them instinctively, as something we feel or sense, rather than by logical analysis of ideas or by observation of facts in the natural world.

People who operate from a non-Christian, materialistic worldview would lump all four of these factors into the broad category of "feelings" or "emotions" because they do not have a category for the invisible guidance of the Holy Spirit or for thinking about our human spirits as real but invisible components of who we are as persons.[12]

I have listed these four factors separately because the Bible treats them as distinct factors, and we can often recognize them as distinct components of guidance (as the passages above indicate). However, there may be other times when we are simply aware of an overall instinctive sense of what to do in a situation (sometimes people informally

---

[10] See the appendix of this chapter, p. 177, for further discussion of Rom. 8:14 and Gal. 5:18.

[11] I have discussed elsewhere the question of guidance from the Holy Spirit that can come through other people when God brings to their minds something concerning you, and they then report that to you. This is something the New Testament would call the gift of "prophecy." See Wayne Grudem, *Systematic Theology: An Introduction to Biblical Doctrine* (Leicester, UK: Inter-Varsity, and Grand Rapids, MI: Zondervan, 1994), 1049–61, on the gift of prophecy; see also Wayne Grudem, *The Gift of Prophecy in the New Testament and Today*, rev. ed. (Wheaton, IL: Crossway, 2000). My understanding of Scripture is that such guidance through a gift of prophecy will continue to be valid for the entire church age until Christ returns, but caution is needed to guard against abuse of this gift. Paul says, "Do not quench the Spirit. *Do not despise prophecies, but test everything*; hold fast what is good" (1 Thess. 5:19–21).

[12] Jesus speaks of the Holy Spirit as "the Spirit of truth, whom the world cannot receive, because *it neither sees him nor knows him*" (John 14:17).

refer to this as a "gut feeling" about a decision) without being able to specifically evaluate each of these factors separately.

11. Objection: "Subjective Impressions Can Mislead People." It is certainly possible for people to make mistakes in the area of subjective guidance. A person's instinctive sense of what to do can at times be wrong, and I am not saying that Christians should always trust such subjective impressions. Other, more objective factors must also be taken into account, especially the first five factors I listed above: (1) information from the Bible, (2) information from studying the situation, (3) information about ourselves, (4) advice from others, and (5) observation of changed circumstances. And the teaching of the Bible must always have the highest priority. Christians can make the mistake of putting too much emphasis on guidance from subjective impressions.

But I am also concerned about another kind of mistake, the mistake of teaching people not to pay any attention to subjective impressions about what decision to make. This cannot be right, because God has made us as whole persons, including a conscience, a heart, and a human spirit, and has given us the ability to relate to him through the personal presence of the Holy Spirit.

Jesus says, "And I will ask the Father, and he will give you *another Helper*, to be with you forever" (John 14:16; see also 14:26; 15:26; 16:7; 1 John 2:1). The word translated as "Helper" is the Greek *paraklētos*, which is variously translated as "Helper" (ESV, NASB, NKJV), "Advocate" (NRSV, NET, NIV, NLT), "Comforter" (KJV), or "Counselor" (RSV, CSB). Jesus was saying he would give the Holy Spirit to be "another Helper" to be present with the disciples when he was no longer physically present to talk with them and teach them. All of these translations convey the idea of someone who engages in personal communication and personal interaction with the person being helped or counseled.

In response to the objection that subjective impressions can mislead people, we must recognize that we can also be misled regarding the more objective factors in guidance. We can be misled by misunderstanding the teaching of Scripture, by wrongly evaluating ourselves and our abilities, or by depending on wrong information about a situation. We can be misled by wrongfully interpreting past experience. And certainly we can be misled by sermons (which we can also apply wrongly) and by advice from others. Books and articles can mislead us as well, and sometimes the historical tradition of the church has made mistakes. Therefore, I don't find the objection that subjective impressions might mislead us to be a convincing reason not to consider subjective factors.

My conclusion is that we should pay attention to the four subjective factors as well as the first five objective factors in making decisions. God relates to us as *whole persons*, including our ability to perceive these subjective factors, not merely as people with intellectual abilities. And I must reemphasize that we should never follow any of these subjective impressions to disobey the clear teachings of Scripture.

D. THE DANGER OF MAKING THIS PROCESS TOO COMPLICATED

This chapter has discussed four dimensions to be considered regarding any action and nine factors to be considered in making ethical decisions. I have gone into such great detail because it is helpful for Christians to have a more extensive understanding of the individual factors that form our decision-making process as we seek to know God's will for our individual situations.

However, I do not think that God wants this decision-making process to seem impossible for Christians to follow regularly or so complicated that they are discouraged by it. God wants us to be able to have wisdom to make right decisions: "If any of you lacks wisdom, let him ask God, who gives generously to all without reproach, and it will be given him" (James 1:5).

In the actual course of a person's life, all of these factors can be taken into account quite quickly in most situations—sometimes even instantly and instinctively, without consciously considering each of these factors individually. Yet in other situations, thoughtfully and explicitly considering these different dimensions and factors will provide much greater insight and discernment. In this way, wise decision making can become a good habit for all Christians, a skill that that they exercise more and more naturally through the course of a day, as they increase in "knowledge and all discernment" so that they "approve what is excellent" (Phil. 1:9–10).

A helpful analogy is that of a golf professional teaching a beginner how to swing a golf club. The golf pro might first take a club in his hands, step up to the ball, and swing the club once, sending the ball straight and far, making it all look so easy. But when the golf lesson gets under way, the beginner realizes how complicated a proper golf swing really is. He must learn the proper position for his fingers and his hands in holding the club, the proper position for his feet, the direction his body needs to face, and the proper position of his knees, torso, arms, elbows, wrists, shoulders, and head. And he has to learn not just the starting position for all of these things, but the movements that they need to make in beginning the golf swing and then in hitting the ball and following through properly. It is a genuinely complex task!

What I have done in this chapter is something like breaking down the golf swing into great detail to talk about its individual parts. But these individual parts can be put together into a natural process that becomes part of the way a Christian habitually lives his or her life. I think this is what the author of Hebrews is intending when he speaks about mature Christians as "those who have their powers of discernment *trained by constant practice* to distinguish good from evil" (Heb. 5:14). The process no longer seems complicated. They just take the club in their hands, step up to the ball, and hit it well.

E. ACQUIRING WISDOM: THE PERSONAL SKILL NECESSARY FOR ETHICAL LIVING

Up to this point in this chapter, I have discussed the importance of considering whether an *action itself* is morally right or wrong, considering the person's *attitudes* toward that action, considering the person's *motives* for the action, and considering the *results* of the action. Then I listed nine possible sources of information to be considered when making a decision about any particular action. But how can we know that we will evaluate each of these factors correctly when we "consider" them? To "consider" these factors requires skill in making correct evaluations. How can we obtain that skill, and how can we improve it? This brings us to the topic of *wisdom*.

Presumably everyone reading this book wants to gain more insight into making right decisions about different ethical situations that arise in their lives. In biblical terms, the personal skill of making such right decisions falls under the category of wisdom.

For purposes of this book, I will use the following definition:

> **Wisdom** is the skill of understanding and applying the Bible rightly to each situation.

In fact, wisdom is necessary for rightly understanding everything I have discussed in the previous chapters and everything I will discuss in the remainder of the book. For example, in the earlier chapters, I argued that Christian ethics seeks to answer the question, "What does the whole Bible teach us about which acts, attitudes, and personal character traits receive God's approval, and which do not?" (chap. 1). But we need wisdom in order to answer that question correctly. I also argued that the ultimate source of ethical standards is the moral character of God (chap. 2) and that we learn about God's ethical standards from the Bible (chap. 3). But how can we understand the Bible correctly, and how can we know that we have applied it correctly to the specific situation at hand? I have defined wisdom as the skill of doing exactly that: *understanding* the Bible's teachings about ethics correctly and then rightly *applying* those teachings to various situations.[13]

This definition indicates that wisdom is not a mechanical process but *a skill*, one that is exercised by real human beings in real situations.[14] As with other skills, wisdom can

---

[13] Someone might object that, based on this definition, people without the Bible could not become wise. But even unbelievers have, by common grace, some understanding of God's moral standards, because Paul says that "the work of the law is written on their hearts" (Rom. 2:15). Therefore, unbelievers can have an approximation of God's wisdom in some areas of life even though they do not have the Bible or access to the teachings of the Bible (see the section on the necessity of Scripture in chap. 3, p. 95). Yet their understanding, not based on the Bible itself, will also include many errors, and will not equal the true biblical wisdom that is practiced in relationship to God himself.

[14] The idea of wisdom as a *skill* is also found in other evangelical ethics books. Scott B. Rae says, "This concept of a craft or skill is at the heart of the Hebrew concept of wisdom." *Moral Choices: An Introduction to Ethics*, 2nd ed. (Grand Rapids, MI: Zondervan, 2000), 74n6. (The chapter that contains this footnote was not included in the third edition of this book in 2009, however.) Robertson McQuilkin and Paul Copan say,

increase with time and with practice at making good decisions in different situations. Gaining mature wisdom is a process that increases over many years of godly living, and mature Christians are "those who have their powers of discernment *trained* by constant practice to distinguish good from evil" (Heb. 5:14). Children do not yet have much life experience, and as a result they are not as wise as we hope they will be later. Even Jesus grew in wisdom during his childhood:

> And Jesus *increased in wisdom* and in stature and in favor with God and man. (Luke 2:52)

John Frame speaks of the need for such a skill:

> To apply the Word of God to circumstances requires a kind of moral vision. Such applications require the ability to *see* the circumstances *in the light of* biblical principles. In moral quandaries, we often ask questions such as "Is this act murder?" Or "Is this act stealing?" For Christians, the challenge is to give biblical names to human actions. Sometimes it is obvious: taking money out of a friend's wallet without authorization is what the Bible calls stealing. Sometimes it is less obvious: is it murder to remove this terminal patient from life support?[15]

My definition of wisdom is very similar to what Frame calls "a kind of moral vision" and "the ability to see the circumstances in the light of biblical principles."

The Bible places an exceptionally high emphasis on the value of wisdom. The book of Proverbs in particular extols wisdom over and over again:

> Blessed is the one who finds *wisdom,*
> and the one who gets understanding,
> for the gain from her is better than gain from silver
> and her profit better than gold.
> She is more precious than jewels,
> and nothing you desire can compare with her. . . .
> Her ways are ways of pleasantness,
> and all her paths are peace. (Prov. 3:13–17)

"Wisdom is the skill for living rightly, which means that true wisdom is anchored in a correct view of reality. Skillful living begins with being properly aligned with the intrinsically relational, triune God." *An Introduction to Biblical Ethics: Walking in the Way of Wisdom,* 3rd ed. (Downers Grove, IL: InterVarsity Press, 2014), 17. See also the quotation from Frame in the following footnote.

[15] Frame, *The Doctrine of the Christian Life,* 356, emphasis in original. Frame says that Scripture often represents wisdom "as a skill, a knowing *how* rather than knowing *that.* . . . In James 3:13–17, wisdom is clearly ethical, the skill of godly living." Ibid., 351, emphasis in original. If my memory is correct, I also first learned to think of wisdom as the skill of applying Scripture rightly to specific situations from Frame's ethics class in 1973 at Westminster Seminary, but I could not find it defined in exactly that way in his book *The Doctrine of the Christian Life.*

But how can a person become wise? The Bible speaks frequently about that subject. It is not a simple matter of following certain steps, so that if you merely complete steps A, B, and C you will automatically get the right answer. Rather, Scripture speaks often about *the character of the person* who is making ethical decisions—what kind of person he or she must be in order to have wisdom.

For the rest of this section, we will look at the source of wisdom and the personal character traits that accompany wisdom.

1. Wisdom Comes from God. God is infinitely wise. His wisdom is so far superior to all human wisdom that Paul can call him "the only wise God" (Rom. 16:27; see also Rom. 11:33). While human beings may obtain some wisdom, the Bible says that in Christ "are hidden *all* the treasures of *wisdom* and knowledge" (Col. 2:3).

Therefore, if we are to obtain true wisdom, we must obtain it from God himself as we walk in a personal relationship with him. "The LORD gives wisdom" (Prov. 2:6; see also 1 Kings 3:12; 4:29; 10:24; Ps. 51:6; Eccles. 2:26; Dan. 2:21–23). James tells his readers that the way to get wisdom is to ask God for it:

> If any of you lacks wisdom, *let him ask God*, who gives generously to all without reproach, and it will be given him. (James 1:5)

Other passages in the New Testament speak of Christ as the source of wisdom for us (see Luke 21:15; 1 Cor. 1:24, 30; Col. 2:3), and still others speak of the role of the Holy Spirit in imparting wisdom to believers (see 1 Cor. 12:8; Eph. 1:17).

If wisdom is the skill of applying the Bible rightly to each situation, then wisdom requires *discernment into situations*, an ability not only to learn the facts of a situation but also to see into the heart of it, to understand what is really going on. In addition, wisdom requires *discernment into Scripture*, the ability to evaluate various passages and understand accurately how they apply. That is why Paul prays that the Philippian Christians might grow in their discernment:

> And it is my prayer that your love may abound more and more, with knowledge and all discernment [Greek, *aesthēsis*, "discernment, insight, capacity to understand"], so that you may approve what is excellent, and so be pure and blameless for the day of Christ. (Phil. 1:9–10)

Since Paul prays for God to give discernment to these Christians, it is right for us also to ask God for the same kind of discernment for ourselves and others.

In a similar way, Paul prays for the Christians in Colossae to be filled with the knowledge of God's will "in all *spiritual wisdom* and understanding" (Col. 1:9). And the author of Ecclesiastes tells us, "To the one who pleases him God has given wisdom and knowledge and joy" (Eccles. 2:26). These passages are a further indication that wisdom comes from God, that it is right to pray to God for wisdom, and that he is especially pleased to give it to those who walk in a personal relationship with him.

2. Wisdom Comes from Scripture. If God is the source of all true wisdom, then it is not surprising that God often uses the words of the Bible as the means by which he gives wisdom to us. When Moses was giving the people of Israel the written commands of God in Deuteronomy, he told them that they should "keep them and do them," for, he said, "*that will be your wisdom* and your understanding in the sight of the peoples" (Deut. 4:6).

It is not only a small group of highly trained scholars who can be made wise by Scripture, but all of God's people, even "the simple"—those who might not be highly trained or wise in the world's eyes—can be made wise by God's words:

> The law of the LORD is perfect,
>   reviving the soul;
> the testimony of the LORD is sure,
>   *making wise the simple.* (Ps. 19:7; see also Ps. 119:98–100, 130; Col. 3:16;
>   1 Tim. 3:15)

The wisdom that comes from God through Scripture is far different from the wisdom of the world. Paul makes this contrast between worldly wisdom and the wisdom of God very clear:

> Yet among the mature we do impart wisdom, although *it is not a wisdom of this age* or of the rulers of this age, who are doomed to pass away. But we impart a secret and hidden wisdom of God, which God decreed before the ages for our glory. (1 Cor. 2:6–7; see also Gen. 3:6; 1 Cor. 1:18–31; 2:1–16; 2 Cor. 1:12)

3. Wisdom Comes with a Fear of God. Scripture makes clear in several places that if we are to gain wisdom, we must begin with a fear of God:

> *The fear of the LORD is the beginning of wisdom*;
>   all those who practice it have a good understanding. (Ps. 111:10)

> *The fear of the LORD is the beginning of wisdom,*
>   and the knowledge of the Holy One is insight. (Prov. 9:10)

> *The fear of the LORD is instruction in wisdom,*
>   and humility comes before honor. (Prov. 15:33; see also Job 28:28)

The idea of the fear of the Lord is not an obscure topic in Scripture, for the expressions "fear of God," "fear God," "fear of the Lord," and "fear the Lord" occur 84 times in the Old and New Testaments (in the ESV).[16]

Sometimes Christians explain this "fear of the Lord" as "reverence for God," a some-

---

[16] In addition, there are other verses saying "fear him," referring to God.

what weaker concept than fear. But I am aware of no modern Bible version that translates Psalm 111:10 as "Reverence for the LORD is the beginning of wisdom," no doubt because the most common sense of the Hebrew word *yir'āh* in the Old Testament and the Greek word *phobos* in the New Testament (in verses such as Deut. 2:25; Jonah 1:10; Acts 9:31; 2 Cor. 5:11) is simply "fear."[17] While it is true that the sense "reverence" is appropriate in some contexts,[18] it does not seem to me to fit the passages about wisdom nearly as well.

It is important to affirm clearly that Christians should no longer fear eternal condemnation from God (see 1 John 4:18), for Christ has eternally saved us from final condemnation: "There is therefore now no condemnation for those who are in Christ Jesus" (Rom. 8:1). Still, there are other senses of "the fear of the Lord" that seem appropriate to the Christian life. For example, it is very appropriate for Christians to *fear displeasing God* or grieving the Holy Spirit (see Eph. 4:30, and chap. 5, p. 142). And it is very appropriate for Christians to *fear God's fatherly discipline* if they walk in willful disobedience to him (see Heb. 12:5–11 and chap. 5, p. 142). But fear of God's fatherly displeasure and fear of his fatherly discipline are far different from the terror of final judgment, from which we have been freed by Christ's sacrifice for our sin.

A healthy fear of God's displeasure and fear of his fatherly discipline are appropriate to acquiring wisdom. If we establish in our minds, at the beginning of a quest for wisdom, that we deeply want to avoid disobeying God or displeasing him, then we will be much more eager to learn his directions for our lives and to walk in obedience to those good commands.

By contrast, if we have *no fear* of displeasing God and *no fear* of his discipline, then we will not be as careful to seek to understand his ways, and we will likely not grow much in wisdom. This is because "the fear of the LORD is the beginning of wisdom" (Ps. 111:10).

Those who have *no* fear of God can engage in all sorts of horrible sin. At the culmination of nine verses in which Paul talks about the sins of Jews and Gentiles apart from God, he summarizes the problem in the last sentence by saying they have *no fear of God*:

> "None is righteous, no, not one;
>> no one understands;
>> no one seeks for God.
> All have turned aside; together they have become worthless;
>> no one does good,
>> not even one."
> "Their throat is an open grave;
>> they use their tongues to deceive."

---

[17] HALOT, 433–34; BDB, 432; BDAG, 1062.

[18] See BDB, 432, meaning 3, "fear of God, reverence, piety," and BDAG, 1062, meaning 2b, "reverence, respect." However, the meaning "reverence" does not occur in the more recent (2001) Hebrew lexicon HALOT, 433–34.

"The venom of asps is under their lips."
"Their mouth is full of curses and bitterness."
"Their feet are swift to shed blood;
in their paths are ruin and misery,
and the way of peace they have not known."
"*There is no fear of God before their eyes.*" (Rom. 3:10b–18, quoting
several passages from the Old Testament)

The Bible's emphasis on a spiritually beneficial fear of God suggests to us that it is important for churches to teach Christians about the value of fearing God. Such teaching would undoubtedly lead to more wisdom in our churches, and that would result in more holiness and purity, and more of God's blessing on our daily lives.

4. Wisdom Comes with Faith. Immediately after telling his readers that someone who lacks wisdom should "ask God" for it, James adds three verses (vv. 6–8) about the importance of asking in faith:

If any of you lacks wisdom, let him ask God, who gives generously to all without reproach, and it will be given him. *But let him ask in faith, with no doubting,* for the one who doubts is like a wave of the sea that is driven and tossed by the wind. For that person must not suppose that he will receive anything from the Lord; he is a double-minded man, unstable in all his ways. (James 1:5–8)

To "ask in faith" means to ask with a settled trust or confidence in one's mind that God will grant the wisdom that we have asked for. This is a specific example of the general principle about trusting in God that is found in Hebrews 11:

And without faith it is impossible to please him, for whoever would draw near to God *must believe* that he exists and *that he rewards those who seek him.* (Heb. 11:6)

Verses like this should be a great encouragement. When we ask for something that God has approved or promised in his Word (such as wisdom), we don't have to keep wondering whether it is pleasing to him to give us what we ask, for his Word tells us that it is.[19]

5. Wisdom Comes with Knowledge. If wisdom is understood as the skill of applying the Bible rightly to each situation, wisdom often comes after we have gained *more information* about the teaching of the Bible on a topic or more information about the actual situation.

The Bible speaks of *knowledge* as an important factor that must accompany wisdom.

---

[19] For more discussion of prayer, including how to think about unanswered prayers in the Christian life, see Grudem, *Systematic Theology,* 355–75.

"An intelligent heart acquires *knowledge*, and the ear of the wise seeks *knowledge*" (Prov. 18:15; see also Prov. 10:14). In Proverbs 8, when "Wisdom" calls and invites people to learn, she says, "Take my instruction instead of silver, and *knowledge* rather than choice gold, for wisdom is better than jewels" (Prov. 8:10–11). Several other passages in the Psalms and Proverbs connect wisdom and knowledge (see Ps. 119:66; Prov. 1:7; 2:6, 10; 15:2, 7; 18:15; 21:11; 22:17; 24:3–5). These passages indicate that a wise person will not only have the *skill* of applying the Bible rightly to each situation, but will also have *knowledge* about the Bible and about the situation (including himself or other people who are in the situation).

For example, a young couple seeking wisdom about how to raise their children might need to spend time searching out numerous Bible passages that teach us about parenting (there is a lot of material in Proverbs and elsewhere). That would give them more information (knowledge) about the Bible.

More information about a situation is often needed before we can make a wise decision. A person seeking wisdom about whether to take another job will need to find out a considerable amount of information about the potential job before he is able to make a wise decision. People who are buying a house will often hire a professional home inspector to give them more detailed information about the house before they buy it.

In addition, knowledge of the situation also must include knowledge about *ourselves*, for we are part of the situation. A woman who is thinking about starting a new business will need to honestly evaluate herself to determine whether she has skills and interests necessary to succeed in that particular kind of business (wise counsel from honest friends can be a great help here).

6. Wisdom Comes with Obedience to God. In the Bible, the "wicked" person is not wise, for "the words of his mouth are trouble and deceit; he has ceased to act wisely and do good" (Ps. 36:3). By contrast, people who are obedient to God are those who gain wisdom and exercise it in their actions:

> The mouth of *the righteous* utters *wisdom*,
>   and his tongue speaks justice. (Ps. 37:30)

In Proverbs 8, "Wisdom" calls out and says, "I walk in the way of *righteousness*, in the paths of justice" (Prov. 8:20). In the New Testament, James says that anyone who is a "hearer of the Word and not a doer" will quickly forget what he has heard, implying that he will not learn wisdom from reading the Bible unless he follows through and obeys it, for then he will not be a "hearer who forgets" but a "doer who acts" (James 1:23–25). James elsewhere connects wisdom with good conduct:

> *Who is wise* and understanding among you? *By his good conduct* let him show
>   his works in the meekness of wisdom. (James 3:13)[20]

---

[20] Other verses also connect wisdom with obedience to God or with personal integrity of character (see Prov. 11:3; 12:5; Eccles. 2:26).

One passage in Hebrews indicates that we can become better at making wise decisions by years of "practice" in distinguishing good from evil, with the implication that those who constantly make morally wise choices will gain skill in such discernment:

> But solid food is for the mature, for those who have their powers of discernment *trained by constant practice* to distinguish good from evil. (Heb. 5:14)

In this verse, "powers of discernment" translates the Greek term *aisthētērion* (plural), which means "capacity for discernment" with regard to "the ability to make moral decisions."[21]

7. Wisdom Comes with Accepting Counsel from Others. A common theme in Proverbs is that people who are wise listen to counsel from other people. This is probably because other people can help us understand Scripture or understand a situation more accurately:

> The way of a fool is right in his own eyes,
>   but *a wise man listens to advice.* (Prov. 12:15)

> With those who take advice is wisdom. (Prov. 13:10)

> Listen to advice and accept instruction,
>   that you may gain wisdom in the future. (Prov. 19:20; see also 15:31;
>   20:18; 24:6)

But it is important to choose carefully the people from whom we take advice. It is possible to choose wise or foolish companions for our source of wisdom, and the kind of companions we choose will affect whether we gain wisdom or not:

> Whoever walks with the wise becomes wise,
>   but the companion of fools will suffer harm. (Prov. 13:20)

There are repeated warnings in Proverbs to beware of counsel from people who do evil:

> My son, if sinners entice you,
>   do not consent. (Prov. 1:10; see also Prov. 16:29; 25:5)

8. Wisdom Comes with Humility. Another characteristic of people who gain wisdom is humility. "When pride comes, then comes disgrace, but *with the humble is wisdom*" (Prov. 11:2). Proud people have a wrong kind of "wisdom," a false wisdom whereby they consider themselves to be wise. Scripture warns against this repeatedly:

---

[21] See BDAG, 29.

> *Be not wise in your own eyes*;
>> fear the LORD, and turn away from evil. (Prov. 3:7; see also 26:12; Jer.
>> 9:23; Rom. 12:16)

In the New Testament, James says that a person who is "wise in understanding" should "show his works *in the meekness of wisdom*" (James 3:13). Then, after talking about the false kind of wisdom that comes from "selfish ambition," James goes on to describe the gentle persuasiveness of the humble wisdom that comes from God:

> But the wisdom from above is first pure, then peaceable, *gentle, open to reason*, full of mercy and good fruits, impartial and sincere. And a harvest of righteousness is sown in peace by those who make peace. (James 3:17–18)

9. Wisdom Brings Us Joy. For the person who finds wisdom from God, a valuable reward is the joy that comes with wisdom. "*Wisdom is pleasure* to a man of understanding" (Prov. 10:23; also note the joy that wisdom brings to God in Prov. 8:30).[22]

Elsewhere the author of Proverbs compares the joy of wisdom to the sweetness of honey:

> My son, *eat honey*, for it is good,
>> and the drippings of the honeycomb are sweet to your taste.
> Know that *wisdom is such to your soul*;
>> if you find it, there will be a future,
>> and your hope will not be cut off. (Prov. 24:13–14)

This means that when a person finds a wise solution to a puzzling situation, God will often give with that wisdom an inward sense of joy and delight, and even a sense of being "led by the Spirit of God" (Rom. 8:14).

F. APPENDIX: A RESPONSE TO GARRY FRIESEN'S BOOK *DECISION MAKING AND THE WILL OF GOD*

First published in 1980, with a revised edition in 2004, *Decision Making and the Will of God*[23] has had a significant influence on evangelical thinking about how to know God's will. Author Garry Friesen[24] denies that God directly guides individual Christians to an "individual will" for each person that is more specific than the "moral will of God"

---

[22] Other passages connecting wisdom with things that are joyful or pleasant include Prov. 2:10; 3:13; 8:11, 18–19; 16:16; Eccles. 8:1.

[23] Garry Friesen with J. Robin Maxson, *Decision Making and the Will of God*, rev. ed. (Colorado Springs: Multnomah, 2004). The cover of the 2004 edition says, "Over 250,000 copies sold."

[24] For simplicity I have decided to refer to the book as "Friesen's" even though it was written "with J. Robin Maxson," who evidently played a significant role in its composition and revision. But throughout most of the book Friesen speaks as the primary author.

revealed in the Bible.[25] Because Friesen denies that God ordinarily gives additional guidance to Christians through the subjective means that I discussed earlier in this chapter, it is appropriate to provide a more extensive interaction with his book at this point.

1. Friesen's "Bible and Wisdom Only" View of Guidance. Here is Friesen's summary of his argument:

1. Where God commands, we must obey.
2. Where there is no command, God gives us freedom (and responsibility) to choose.
3. Where there is no command, God gives us wisdom to choose.
4. When we have chosen what is moral and wise, we must trust the sovereign God to work all the details together for good.[26]

When Friesen speaks of God's commands, he means God's moral law as revealed to us in Scripture. Apart from the teaching of Scripture, he does not think that God ordinarily guides Christians in more specific ways that relate to individual decisions in their daily lives. In other words, God does not have a detailed "individual will" for each Christian to follow that is more specific than the moral commands of Scripture.[27]

Therefore, when Christians make individual decisions in daily life, if there is no command of Scripture that applies, then "God gives us freedom." However, within that freedom, we should use the *wisdom* that God gives us to evaluate different courses of action and make wise decisions.

Friesen does not deny subjective feelings or thoughts that point us in one direction or another. He acknowledges "the reality of inner impressions" and says that "everyone experiences internal hunches that point to some specific conclusion. . . . There are nu-

---

[25] However, Friesen does admit the possibility that "in rare cases God may supernaturally reveal (by voice, angel, or dream) a divine command to a specific person." Friesen, 221; see also 233, 235. But he insists that "bona fide instances of special guidance have been rare—even for the apostles." Ibid., 236. Such special guidance would be "self-evident" because it would be "supernaturally confirmed and in harmony with the Scriptures." Ibid., 237. In all of these cases, "the area of freedom was reduced for the recipient and the moral will of God was expanded: where God commands, we must obey." Ibid., 236. Therefore, he implies that such supernatural intervention is nothing that we should expect or seek, nor should we think that it is an ordinary part of the lives of Christian believers.

[26] These four points are a verbatim account of Friesen's summary. Ibid., 15.

[27] When Friesen speaks of the concept of an "individual will" in what he calls the "traditional view" of guidance, he is referring to the traditional idea that there is a unique, individual, *whole-life road map* or blueprint that God wants each Christian to discover. But in this discussion I am using the phrase "individual will" to refer not to a "whole-life road map" but to God's guidance for any specific individual decision in a believer's life.

However, it must be noted that Friesen includes a balanced and insightful discussion of God's secret "sovereign will" directing all the detailed events of our lives, but he says that this sovereign will of God can be known only after events have happened and should play no part in our decision-making process. Ibid., 201–19. I found this discussion quite helpful and have no objections to it. I agree that God's secret, sovereign will for the events of our lives cannot be known in advance, and therefore it cannot become part of our process in making decisions about courses of action that are still in the future.

merous occasions when an idea pops into a person's head apparently out of thin air."[28] He does not want Christians to ignore these subjective feelings, but to evaluate them by Scripture and wisdom.

However, he insists that God does not ordinarily use these subjective impressions to guide us any more specifically than the moral commands of Scripture would teach and wise reflection on the entire decision would indicate.[29] Therefore, we must evaluate subjective impressions that come to us, and "the basis for this evaluation is to be the moral will of God and wisdom."[30]

2. Friesen's Critique of the "Traditional View." Friesen critiques what he calls the "traditional view" of guidance, a view that claims that "for each of our decisions, God has an ideal plan that He will make known to the attentive believer."[31] Friesen says that, according to this view, "believers are expected to find it [God's detailed plan] as part of the Christian life." This "individual will" for each believer contains more specific guidance than God's "moral will" as revealed in the Bible, according to this view.[32] He says that those who follow this traditional view are always attempting to find "the dot,"[33] which is God's specific will for each decision, rather than operating within a larger circle of "freedom" in which God allows us to use wisdom and our own preferences to make decisions based on our understanding.

According to Friesen, this traditional view is not taught in Scripture. He analyzes the Scripture passages most frequently used to support the traditional view and concludes that they are not convincing.[34] He also points out that subjective impressions can never give certain knowledge of God's will.[35] In addition, he says that the traditional view must be abandoned in the many hundreds of small decisions we all make in the course of an ordinary day, for it is impossible to seek God's guidance for all of them.[36]

3. A Response to Friesen. There is much that I like about this book. Friesen's sections on the moral law of God, on God's sovereignty in our lives, and on the use of wisdom in decision making contain much valuable material on theology as it impacts practical Christian living. The entire book is a model of clarity in writing and in developing an extended argument. Throughout every section of the book, Friesen's desire to understand and submit to the authoritative teaching of Scripture is evident. In addition, some of his criticisms of what he calls the traditional view provide good warnings against excessive dependence on subjective factors in seeking to know God's will.

---

[28] Ibid., 264–65.

[29] Ibid.

[30] Ibid., 265.

[31] Ibid., 28.

[32] Friesen summarizes the "traditional view" on ibid., 27–35.

[33] See ibid., 29, 54–88, 110, 138.

[34] Ibid., 45–111.

[35] Ibid., 92–98.

[36] Ibid., 81–82, 110, 246–47.

However, I disagree with the "Bible and wisdom only" view of guidance that is at the heart of this book.

a. Friesen's Exclusion of Personal Guidance from God to Individual Believers Is Contrary to the Entire Pattern of Scripture from Genesis to Revelation: What seems to me most striking about Friesen's book is *the absence of any clear biblical evidence to prove the heart of his "Bible and wisdom only" position.* By that I mean that I do not think there is any passage of Scripture, or any combination of passages, that should lead us to think that God does not communicate directly with his people throughout all of history in individual, personal ways that occur *in addition to* his communication in and through the written words of Scripture.

If we look at the whole scope of biblical history, we see that from beginning to end God has a personal relationship with his people, a relationship in which he communicates directly and personally with them, and this communication is never limited to the words that he gave to all of his people in "the book of the covenant" or the writings of the canon of Scripture. God had a personal relationship and direct interpersonal communication with Adam and Eve, Cain and Abel, Enoch (who walked with God, Gen. 5:24), Noah, Abraham, Isaac, Jacob, Moses, David, Solomon, and many other Old Testament prophets and kings.[37]

In the person of Jesus, God the Son communicated individually and personally with many people while he was on earth. After the resurrection, the Lord Jesus or the Holy Spirit interacted personally with Paul not only on the Damascus road (Acts 9:4–6), but also in directing his second missionary journey (16:6–7), encouraging him in Corinth (18:9–10), confirming his decision to go to Jerusalem (19:21), showing him what would happen in Jerusalem (20:23), encouraging him in prison in Jerusalem (23:11), assuring him that he would arrive safely in Rome (this time by an angel, 27:23–24), telling him he would not heal his thorn in the flesh (2 Cor. 12:9), directing him to go to Jerusalem (Gal. 2:2), and standing by him at his trial in Rome (2 Tim. 4:17).

But this was true not only with Paul, for God gave direct guidance for Philip (Acts 8:26, 29), Ananias (9:10–16), Cornelius (10:3–6), Peter (10:13–20; 12:7–8), the church at Antioch (13:2), and the church in Jerusalem (15:28).

In addition, the New Testament promises that each individual believer will have a personal relationship with the Father, Son, and Holy Spirit:

> If anyone loves me, he will keep my word, and my Father will love him, and we will come to him and *make our home with him.* (John 14:23)

---

[37] Friesen writes, "In the Bible, no believer asks, 'What is God's individual will for me in this matter?'" Ibid., 48. But this is surely incorrect. For example, David often sought specific guidance from God: "Therefore David inquired of the LORD, 'Shall I go and attack these Philistines?' And the LORD said to David, 'Go and attack the Philistines and save Keilah'" (1 Sam. 23:2; see also 1 Sam. 23:4, 9–12; 30:8; 2 Sam. 2:1; 5:19, 23–24). There are many other examples, such as the people seeking guidance from God in Judg. 1:1; 20:18, 23, 27–28; 1 Sam. 10:22.

For all who are *led by the Spirit of God* are sons of God. (Rom. 8:14: the present indicative Greek verb *agontai* views this "leading" as an ongoing or regular process)[38]

But I say, *walk by the Spirit*, and you will not gratify the desires of the flesh. . . . But if you are *led by the Spirit* you are not under the law. (Gal. 5:16, 18; the present indicative Greek verb *agesthe* views this as an ongoing or regular process)

[I pray] that the God of our Lord Jesus Christ, the Father of glory, may give you the Spirit of wisdom and of revelation *in the knowledge of him.* (Eph. 1:17)

[I desire] that I may *know him* and the power of his resurrection, and may share his sufferings, becoming like him in his death. (Phil. 3:10)

Let those of us who are mature think this way, and if in anything you think otherwise, *God will reveal that also to you.* (Phil. 3:15)

Behold, I stand at the door and knock. If anyone hears my voice and opens the door, I will come into him *and eat with him*, and he with me. (Rev. 3:20)

Friesen attempts to explain many of these examples as special cases that do not establish a pattern for ordinary Christians today.[39] But my counterargument is this: look at the overall pattern of Scripture.

From beginning to end the Bible tells us of a God who relates *individually and personally* to his people. And now Friesen tells us, contrary to the experience of God's people throughout all of the Bible, that God no longer communicates personally and individually with any of his people except through the written words in the canon of Scripture.[40]

So Friesen's "Bible and wisdom only" view is asking us to believe (1) that throughout the Bible God communicated to his people both through written Scripture (as much as they had at any point) and through direct personal fellowship and interaction with people, and (2) that God now communicates *only* through the written words of the

---

[38] See below, p. 177, for my interaction with Friesen's explanation of leading by the Spirit in Rom. 8:14 and Gal. 5:18.

[39] See Friesen, 45–111: the prophets are different, Jesus is different, Paul is different, their experiences are different, and so forth. Friesen also says that instances of special guidance in the Bible are uncommon: "Even in the biblical record, special guidance is rare . . . bona fide instances of special guidance have been rare—even for the apostles." Ibid., 233–36. I disagree, because a phenomenon that occurs many dozens of times throughout all parts of the Bible can hardly be called "rare" in Scripture. The large number of examples of personal interactions with God that are recorded in Scripture should lead us to expect that this kind of interpersonal relationship between God and individual believers also occurred multiple other times that were not recorded.

[40] See the previous footnote for Friesen's qualification that there are rare exceptions.

canon, and no longer through direct personal fellowship and interaction with people. This is quite strange in light of the fact that the new covenant in which we now live is seen to be better in every way (see 2 Corinthians 3; Hebrews 8–9). But how can it be better if we have lost the elements of personal relationship with God and personal communication from him that characterized all periods of history that the Bible talks about. Where is *anything* in the Bible that would lead us to believe that?

I realize, of course, that the canon of Scripture is closed[41] and no more writings are to be added to the Bible. But that is not the question. The question is, what about communication from God to specific individuals that is not part of the canon? If the Bible is the "book of the covenant" that stipulates the terms of the relationship between God as King and us as his covenant people, then are we to say that *the King can never communicate with his people in any additional ways besides the covenant document*? Can a God who loves his people never communicate with them directly and personally?

Evangelical theologian Carl F. H. Henry rightly commented as follows:

> Any statement of evangelical experience that does not include the possibility both of communion with God and the communication of the particularized divine will to the surrendered life seems to me artificially restrictive.[42]

Surely the vast majority of Christians throughout all history have known and experienced the guidance of the Holy Spirit in making decisions, especially while they were praying and reading the words of Scripture, and they have known that this guidance included not only the directions, commands, and principles of Scripture, but also subjective impressions of God's will, as well as thoughts or specific memories that the Lord brings to mind. And this certainly implies the validity of thinking that there is a particularized or "individual will" of God for specific people in some specific situations.

Therefore, my first observation on Friesen's argument is to note how a position that *rules out all direct personal guidance from the Holy Spirit today* is so completely different from the whole course of biblical history and from the New Testament teaching on personal fellowship that we have with the Father, Son, and Holy Spirit.

In addition, there is no passage that teaches this position. Where is there a passage that says something like, "You should never think that God is leading you through a subjective sense of his guidance. Make your decisions based only on the Bible and your own wisdom"? No passage even comes close to that kind of teaching.

Perhaps I have missed something, but I do not think the passages that imply the expectation of a closed canon provide such support for Friesen's position, nor do the passages that speak of the sufficiency of Scripture for the purposes for which it was intended. In fact, I don't think there are any strong passages of Scripture at all that support the "Bible and wisdom only" view of guidance. The scriptural support for such a view is

---

[41] See Grudem, *Systematic Theology*, 54–72.
[42] Carl F. H. Henry, *Confessions of a Theologian* (Waco, TX: Word, 1986), 53.

very weak indeed, and this view is also contrary to the way God has related personally to his people throughout biblical history.

b. Friesen Wrongly Reduces the Leading of the Holy Spirit to the Moral Teaching of Scripture. In two separate verses Paul talks about the leading of the Holy Spirit as an experience common to all Christian believers:

> For all who are *led by the Spirit of God* are sons of God. (Rom. 8:14)

> But if you are *led by the Spirit*, you are not under the law. (Gal. 5:18)

Friesen says that in their context, these verses are "not dealing with daily decision making in non-commanded areas." Rather, in Romans 8:14, "the leading is guidance into the moral will of God to do what is pleasing to Him."[43] And in Galatians 5:18, "this leading is unquestionably related to the moral will of God as revealed in Scripture."[44]

However, this interpretation does not sufficiently account for the actual word that Paul uses for "led," which is the Greek verb *agō*, "to lead." This verb is common in the New Testament (it is used 69 times), and it gives a picture of someone specifically leading a person (or even an animal) from one location to another. Here are some examples of this same verb:

> Go into the village in front of you, and immediately you will find a donkey tied, and a colt with her. Untie them and *bring* [*agō*] them to me. (Matt. 21:2)

> And when they *bring* [*agō*] you to trial and deliver you over, do not be anxious beforehand what you are to say, but say whatever is given you in that hour, for it is not you who speak, but the Holy Spirit. (Mark 13:11)

> And Jesus, full of the Holy Spirit, returned from the Jordan and was *led* [*agō*] by the Spirit in the wilderness. (Luke 4:1; this is very close to the wording of Rom. 8:14 and Gal. 5:18, and it means guidance to specific locations in the wilderness. The parallel verse in Matt. 4:1 uses a cognate verb to say that Jesus "was *led up* [*apagō*] by the Spirit into the wilderness.")

> And he *took* [*agō*] him to Jerusalem and set him on the pinnacle of the temple and said to him, "If you are the Son of God, throw yourself down from here." (Luke 4:9)

> He went to him and bound up his wounds, pouring on oil and wine. Then he set him on his own animal and *brought* [*agō*] him to an inn and took care of him. (Luke 10:34)

---

[43] Friesen, 100.
[44] Ibid., 102.

He [Andrew] first found his own brother Simon and said to him, "We have found the Messiah" (which means Christ). He *brought* [*agō*] him to Jesus. Jesus looked at him and said, "You are Simon the son of John. You shall be called Cephas" (which means Peter). (John 1:41–42)

Then they *led* [*agō*] Jesus from the house of Caiaphas to the governor's head-quarters. (John 18:28)

Luke alone is with me. Get Mark and *bring* [*agō*] him with you, for he is very useful to me for ministry. (2 Tim. 4:11)

There are many similar examples, but the point should be clear. When first-century readers (who frequently used the verb *agō* to speak of one person leading or guiding another person from one place to another) saw that Paul used this verb to speak of being "led" by the Holy Spirit, they would have understood it to mean detailed, specific guidance in the various choices and decisions of everyday life.

In fact, in Galatians 5, Paul had just told his readers to "*walk* by the Spirit" (Gal. 5:16), and a few verses later he said, "If we live by the Spirit, let us also *keep in step* with the Spirit" (Gal. 5:25), two other verses that use the metaphor of walking through life to speak of guidance by the Holy Spirit. The entire passage sustains the image of one's daily conduct as a "walk" that is to be guided by the Holy Spirit.

I agree with Friesen that the context in both verses shows that those who are led by the Holy Spirit will not live in a pattern of sin against God's moral laws. However, that idea fits well in a context of specific guidance from the Holy Spirit, because Paul is saying that if you are led by the Holy Spirit, you will be following the desires of the Holy Spirit, and those desires will guide you to fulfill God's moral law: "Walk by the Spirit, *and you will not gratify the desires of the flesh*" (Gal. 5:16).

This does not mean that the leading of the Holy Spirit is *confined to* teaching us to follow God's moral law in Scripture, but it means that the leading of the Holy Spirit, in whatever detailed path of conduct he chooses, will always be *consistent* with the character of the Holy Spirit, and so will necessarily conform to God's moral law. But the leading of the Holy Spirit is a broader reality than just giving us a desire to follow those moral laws—it is an actual *leading* through the path of life.

c. Friesen Underestimates the Way the Life of Christ Is an Example for Us. Friesen concludes that "Christ was given specific guidance by the Father beyond the moral will of God . . . it did include whatever Christ said He was seeing and hearing the Father do (John 5:19, 30)."[45] But he says that we are not intended to imitate Christ in that aspect of his life:

---

[45] Ibid., 49–50.

Christ is declared to be our example, but the extent to which He is our model is not open-ended. He is our example in specific ways. . . . The areas in which believers are told to imitate Jesus Christ *concern the manner in which He fulfilled the moral will of God.* Just as Jesus obeyed His Father's moral will, so the sons and daughters of God should obey their Father's will. The difference is this: for the only begotten Son of God, His Father's will was revealed through a variety of means; for the born-anew sons of God, their Father's will is fully revealed in His Word, the Bible.[46]

However, it is doubtful that Friesen is correct in this limitation. Certainly we should imitate Jesus in the way he was obedient to God, but if that obedience included a pattern of regularly seeking the guidance of his heavenly Father, then should we not also imitate that pattern? John tells us, "Whoever says he abides in him ought to walk in the same way in which he walked" (1 John 2:6). We should live our lives in imitation of his entire pattern of life.

In addition, Jesus is our High Priest, and "we do not have a high priest who is unable to sympathize with our weaknesses, but one who in every respect has been tempted as we are, yet without sin" (Heb. 4:15). But if Jesus could call on God's specific guidance when facing difficult decisions, but we cannot do the same, then it does not seem he would be fully able "to sympathize with our weaknesses" as One who "in every respect has been tempted as we are."

d. Friesen's "Bible and Wisdom Only" Method of Guidance Tends to Hinder the Personal Relationship between Us and God. When believers regularly seek God's guidance for several daily decisions, and then wait expectantly for some indication of God's direction, this becomes a major component of their personal relationship with him. But in the "Bible and wisdom only" system, such personal interaction with God is excluded, and our sense of personal fellowship with him is diminished.

A pastor who is also a former seminary student of mine wrote to me that this had happened to him:

I personally went through a phase where I was persuaded of the [no subjective guidance today] position and it was harmful for my relationship with the Lord: it was as though I had shut off communication with him as a living being.[47]

Even if someone with Friesen's view prays, "Please, Lord, guide me in this decision," he can be asking only for further understanding of *Scripture* or more *wisdom* about the situation, all of which will still be processed entirely through his intelligence and logical

---

[46] Ibid., 50–51, emphasis in original.
[47] Personal letter from a former student.

analysis.[48] On this view, God does not give any *additional* guidance through subjective impressions that come through our thoughts, our consciences, our hearts, our spirits, or a perceived leading of the Holy Spirit.

But this would mean that God is not fully relating to us as whole persons. He is relating to us only through our intellects, and not through our consciences, our heart desires, or our spiritual perceptions. It is significant that, even in a section where Friesen talks about "practicing the presence" of God, none of the five ways he mentions includes any personal interaction between God and the believer.[49] He even seems to claim that less personal interaction with God is better in our daily lives ("less is better"[50]) because God does not see us as "immature children" who need to be guided in every decision, but as "adults" who are capable of making informed decisions on our own.[51]

e. Friesen Gives Several Helpful Warnings against Mistakes Made by Advocates of the "Traditional View." Friesen does not document any author who advocates what he calls the "traditional view" of guidance in the main argument of his book (though he does in Appendix 1 on pp. 426–40). However, he does include some useful warnings against popular abuses of dependence on subjective guidance.

For example, he notes that the traditional view must be abandoned in ordinary decision making through the day, because no one could possibly take the time to seek guidance about every tiny decision. He rightly notes that this means that God could not possibly expect us to seek his guidance on every routine decision.[52] This is a valid caution against a misunderstanding of guidance, and I would even agree that Friesen's analogy of God treating us as adults and not "immature children" is a valid argument in support of this caution. But I would also reply that it would still be possible to seek God's guidance on *some* decisions during an ordinary day and to be receptive to God's guidance even at times when we did not specifically seek it. (Here I would modify Friesen's analogy of not being "immature children" so that it contains the idea of a mature adult son relating conversationally through the day to his incredibly wise father who is walking with him.)

While I agree that Friesen is correct in saying that God does not have an "individual will" in addition to the moral commands of Scripture that we should seek out for every

---

[48] Friesen thinks it is an advantage to base guidance only on objective factors, because this enables us to have certainty regarding guidance, while depending on subjective factors will never give us certainty (see Friesen, 92, 249, 252). I do not find this criticism persuasive, however, because even on Friesen's view, how can we be certain that our "wisdom" has understood the situation rightly and has applied Scripture rightly to the situation? In addition, even if subjective impressions of God's will do not give objective certainty, they can give sufficient confidence for us to act on them. And if the subjective impression leads us to act in a way that is within what Friesen calls the area of "freedom," and if it is not unwise, then what objection could there be to following it? In response to this question, Friesen wrote in an email, "You will get no objection from me. The only exception is if you knew of something else that was wiser for the same decision." Email to me from Garry Friesen, Sept. 20, 2016, quoted by permission.

[49] Friesen, 270–71.

[50] Ibid., 275–77.

[51] Ibid., 275–76.

[52] Ibid., 46, 86, 110, 246–47.

minute detail of our lives, I also think that the pattern of Scripture from beginning to end shows that God *sometimes* has an "individual will" for a believer in a certain situation, and that he guides believers in specific directions that he wants them to go in those situations.[53] (And Friesen would agree that subjective impressions can help us think rightly about which decisions are wise and consistent with Scripture—he just does not think these impressions give *additional guidance* to what is in Scripture and what is wise.)

I also think Friesen is correct in arguing that Scripture does not show any expectation that we must seek additional guidance from God in most of the ordinary, routine decisions of life. It would be hopelessly paralyzing.[54] He rightly criticizes the view that if we miss God's special guidance at some particular point in life, we are consigned to living a life of God's "second-best."[55] And he rightly emphasizes that most of the choices we make throughout each day can and should be decided according to the teachings of Scripture and the use of our God-given wisdom (in fact, this entire ethics book is devoted to helping people make wise decisions in that way).

Therefore, while I disagree with Friesen's viewpoint when it excludes additional guidance from God through subjective means, his emphasis on the importance of making decisions based on the Bible and wisdom is a helpful emphasis. I just think it is only part of the picture.

Finally, I am happy to report that Friesen read an earlier draft of this chapter and wrote to me as follows:

> After reading your chapter several times, I am convinced that we are closer in viewpoint than you think and than I thought. You do not hold the traditional view. You hold something like the wisdom view with exceptions. Even those exceptions are very close to my own view. But, of course, there are differences.[56]

---

[53] In personal correspondence, Friesen agrees that God can sometimes give special individual guidance, but then he says, "This is miraculous direct revelation and must always be obeyed. In practice when one gets direct revelation, your 'freedom' is restricted and the commands grow by one. We only disagree on the commonness of the special individual guidance. The total list for me looks very small for 6000 years of history. But, God can give direct miraculous revelation for an individual decision anytime He wants." Email to me from Garry Friesen, September 20, 2016, quoted by permission.

My response is to say: (1) I am glad to hear that we agree that such subjective guidance is possible; (2) Friesen is correct to say that we differ on the frequency with which such guidance happens, because I would say that it happens millions of times a day in various places of the world in the lives of individual Christians, while Friesen would say it happens only rarely in history; and (3) Friesen would put such miraculous guidance in the same category of moral authority as Scripture, while I would not, because (a) there is always a measure of uncertainty today about whether a subjective sense is truly from God and whether we have understood it correctly, whereas there is no uncertainty about whether a passage of Scripture is from God, and for many moral commands of Scripture we can gain a high level of certainty that we have understood them correctly; and (b) such subjective guidance is given today for a specific individual at a specific place and time, but Scripture is given for all of God's people for all places and all times.

[54] See Friesen, 246–47.

[55] Ibid., 29, 200, 517.

[56] Email to me from Garry Friesen, Sept. 20, 2016, quoted by permission.

f. How Does Guidance Work in Practice? Some Examples from My Own Life. By way of summarizing my view, it might be helpful for me to describe how I understand God's guidance to work in my own life. Here is a typical day when I have classes to teach at Phoenix Seminary:

Activity	Do I Pray for God's Guidance about This Activity?
Get up, run, shower, eat breakfast	No
Read Bible and spend time in prayer	Yes, about the application of Scripture to my life, how to pray for specific people, how to think about the day's events and other upcoming decisions, and guidance about items on my "to do" list. (This is the most extended time of seeking guidance during my day.)
Drive to Phoenix Seminary	No (I take the same route every day). However, I may be praying about other matters as I drive.
Attend faculty meeting	Not regarding routine matters, but during some discussions I ask the Lord's guidance about the matter at hand, and whether I should speak or not.
Office hours	Yes, I often pray during conversations with students or outside visitors, asking the Lord for insight into matters discussed, and if and when I should stop and pray aloud for the person in my office.
Teach class	Not during prepared parts of my lecture, but sometimes I pray silently for guidance about how to answer a difficult student question or when to interrupt a student who is taking too much class time.
Drive home	No (I take the same route every day).
Eat supper	No (I like Margaret's cooking and I eat whatever she has prepared!).
Spend time with Margaret (go for a walk, watch something on TV, play cards, or run errands)	No
Go to bed	No

Table 6.1. God's Guidance in Everyday Decisions

This indicates a pattern in which I do not seek God's guidance for routine decisions through the day, but I do seek his guidance for nonroutine decisions.

On days when I have no classes to teach, I work at home. On those days, I pray in the morning about the ordering of tasks in my daily schedule, and often when I pray the Holy Spirit seems to give me more insight and understanding of the tasks on my list, or sometimes brings to mind passages of Scripture that apply exactly to my situation.

I also experience what I think is the Holy Spirit's guidance in other situations. For example, I recently spoke to a pastors' conference on the topic of one of my published books. I had spoken on that same topic several other times to groups of pastors with a sense of the Lord's blessing in the talks, and it was the same this time. But when I got home I realized that my heart was simply not eager to do any more conferences on this particular topic. I understood that perception in my heart to be an indication of the Holy Spirit's guidance, that he was leading me not to allocate time to speaking on this topic any more in the future.

During a recent meeting of the home fellowship group that Margaret and I participate in, I felt an unusually strong sense of the Lord's presence and blessing during our prayer time. I understood this to mean that my human spirit was perceiving an unusually strong manifestation of the Holy Spirit's presence as we prayed.[57]

On another occasion Margaret and I spent several months praying and seeking the Lord's guidance about which church we should join. Within 15 minutes' drive from our house we had visited several churches with biblically faithful preaching and kingdom-advancing ministries. Applying the moral teachings of the Bible and all the wisdom God had given us did not lead to a clear solution. In the end, we decided to affiliate with the church where we *spiritually* felt more "at home"—admittedly a subjective factor, but one that we understood to be guidance from the Holy Spirit. "For all who are led by the Spirit of God are sons of God" (Rom. 8:14).

g. A Comparison of Friesen's "Bible and Wisdom Only" View with My Understanding of the Holy Spirit's Guidance in Seeking to Know God's Will. At this point, we return to Friesen's summary of his view of guidance, with which we began. Next to each of Friesen's four points, I have put my own conclusions by way of comparison.

Friesen's View: God's Guidance Comes Only from the Bible and Wisdom	My View: God's Guidance Comes from the Bible, Wisdom, and Some Subjective Factors
1. Where God commands, we must obey.	1. Where God commands, we must obey.
2. Where there is no command, God gives us freedom (and responsibility) to choose.	2. Where there is no command, God gives us freedom (and responsibility) to choose, *and sometimes the Holy Spirit directly guides us by influencing our thoughts, bringing Scripture passages to mind, giving us insight and understanding, changing our desires, awakening our consciences, or imparting to our human spirits the presence and specific guidance of the Holy Spirit.*

---

[57] Sometimes our human spirits can perceive a hostile spiritual influence. I remember visiting an old European cathedral several years ago. As we walked into the darkened interior following a throng of other tourists, I suddenly felt a strong sense of spiritual evil, a sensation that was so powerful that I had to turn around and leave. I think the Lord was allowing me to sense in my spirit that the cathedral was no longer serving the purposes for which it was built.

Friesen's View: God's Guidance Comes Only from the Bible and Wisdom	My View: God's Guidance Comes from the Bible, Wisdom, and Some Subjective Factors
3. Where there is no command, God gives us wisdom to choose.	3. Where there is no command, God often gives us wisdom to choose, *and sometimes the Holy Spirit directly guides us in cases where the Bible and wisdom do not or cannot decide the issue.*
4. When we have chosen what is moral and wise, we must trust the sovereign God to work all the details together for good.*	4. When we have chosen what is moral and wise, we must trust the sovereign God to work all the details together for good.

* The four points in the left column are a verbatim account of Friesen's summary; Friesen, 15.

Table 6.2. Two Views on God's Guidance

QUESTIONS FOR PERSONAL APPLICATION

1. Have you ever had to make an instant decision, and you decided rightly? Wrongly? Can you tell what factors in your heart led to the instant decision that you made?
2. Can you think of a time when it seemed to you that a sudden change in circumstances indicated God's guidance about how you should make a decision? How did you know this?
3. Would you say today that you have "a clear conscience toward both God and man" (Acts 24:16)? Or is there something troubling your conscience? If so, what could you do to make it right?
4. Have the deep desires of your heart ever affected any decisions regarding your job or career direction, or a ministry commitment?
5. Are you ever aware of sensing something in your spirit? Can you give a specific example?
6. How do you know when the Holy Spirit is guiding you, if at all?
7. Who are some wise people you have known? How do you think they became wise?
8. Do you feel a fear of God right now? If so, can you explain how it affects your relationship with him? How does it give you wisdom?
9. Read James 1:5–6. How much faith would you say that you have right now that God will give you wisdom regarding a specific difficult decision?
10. Do you personally favor the "traditional view" of guidance, the "Bible and wisdom only" view, or the mixed view that was advocated in this chapter?

SPECIAL TERMS

"Bible and wisdom only" view of guidance
conscience

fear of God
heart
moral will of God
sovereign will of God
spirit
subjective impression

BIBLIOGRAPHY

Sections in Other Ethics Texts

(see complete bibliographical data, p. 64)

Clark and Rakestraw, 1:279–310
Feinberg, John and Paul, 52–61
Frame, 24–36
Geisler, 116–27
Gushee and Stassen, 442–48
Jones, 59–76
McQuilkin and Copan, 599–605
Rae, 104–20

Other Works

DeYoung, Kevin. *Just Do Something: A Liberating Approach to Finding God's Will.* Chicago: Moody, 2009.

Friesen, Garry, and J. Robin Maxson. *Decision Making and the Will of God.* Sisters, OR: Multnomah, 2004.

Howard, J. Grant, Jr. *Knowing God's Will and Doing It!* Grand Rapids, MI: Zondervan, 1976.

Huffman, Douglas S., ed. *How Then Should We Choose? Three Views on God's Will and Decision Making.* Grand Rapids, MI: Kregel, 2009.

Naselli, Andrew David, and J. D. Crowley. *Conscience: What It Is, How to Train It, and Loving Those Who Differ.* Wheaton, IL: Crossway, 2016.

O'Donovan, O. M. T. "Christian Moral Reasoning." In *New Dictionary of Christian Ethics and Pastoral Theology*, edited by David J. Atkinson and David H. Field, 122–27. Leicester, UK: Inter-Varsity, and Downers Grove, IL: InterVarsity Press, 1995.

Willard, Dallas. *In Search of Guidance: Developing a Conversational Relationship with God.* Ventura, CA: Regal, 1983.

SCRIPTURE MEMORY PASSAGE

James 1:5–6: If any of you lacks wisdom, let him ask God, who gives generously to all without reproach, and it will be given him. But let him ask in faith, with no doubting, for the one who doubts is like a wave of the sea that is driven and tossed by the wind.

HYMN

"Open My Eyes, That I May See"

Open my eyes, that I may see
Glimpses of truth Thou hast for me;
Place in my hands the wonderful key
That shall unclasp and set me free.

Refrain:
Silently now I wait for Thee,
Ready, my God, Thy will to see;
Open my eyes—illumine me,
Spirit divine!

Open my ears, that I may hear
Voices of truth Thou sendest clear;
And while the wave-notes fall on my ear,
Ev'rything false will disappear.

Open my mouth, and let me bear
Gladly the warm truth ev'rywhere;
Open my heart and let me prepare
Love with Thy children thus to share.

AUTHOR: CLARA H. SCOTT, 1841–1897

Chapter 7

CHRISTIANS WILL NEVER HAVE TO CHOOSE THE "LESSER SIN"

Is it right to tell a lie in order to protect a human life?

Does God really want us to obey every command of Scripture?

Will we ever face an impossible moral conflict?

Several Christian ethics books claim that people sometimes find themselves in situations that are so difficult that their only possible choices are sinful ones, and so they are forced to choose between disobeying one of God's moral commands or disobeying another. Therefore, the best they can do is choose the "lesser sin."[1]

The classic example is that of a Christian in Nazi Germany who is hiding Jews in the basement of his house. What should he do when Nazi soldiers come pounding on the door, demanding to know if he is concealing Jews? The householder knows that if the Jews are discovered, they will be dragged away to a concentration camp and likely put to death.

Is this an "impossible moral conflict," what is sometimes called a "tragic moral choice"? The dilemma is that if the householder tells the truth, he will be betraying innocent life, which surely is morally wrong. But if he lies and says he has no Jews hiding in the house, he will be committing the moral wrong of lying. In such a situation, isn't it better to *tell a lie* (the lesser sin) than to *betray innocent people* so that they die (a greater sin)?

---

[1] This chapter has been adapted from Wayne Grudem, "Christians Never Have to Choose the 'Lesser Sin,'" in *Redeeming the Life of the Mind: Essays in Honor of Vern Poythress*, ed. John M. Frame, Wayne Grudem, and John J. Hughes (Wheaton, IL: Crossway, 2017), 331–59, with permission of the publisher.

A. THE IMPOSSIBLE MORAL CONFLICT VIEW

Some Christian ethicists *do* support the impossible moral conflict view. In this first section of the chapter, I will examine the arguments of two influential ethics texts that support that view, written by (1) Norman Geisler and (2) John Feinberg and Paul Feinberg.

1. Norman Geisler. Geisler gives an extensive argument for what he calls "graded absolutism" in his 2010 book *Christian Ethics: Contemporary Issues and Options*. He writes, "Some personally unavoidable moral conflicts exist in which an individual cannot obey both commands."[2] In such situations, Geisler argues:

> God does not hold a person guilty for not keeping a lower moral law so long as one keeps the higher law. God exempts one from his duty to keep the lower law since he could not keep it without breaking a higher law.[3]

> For example, in falsifying to save a life, it is not the falsehood that is good (a lie as such is always wrong), but it is the act of mercy to save a life that is good. . . . In these cases God does not consider a person culpable for the concomitant regrettable act in view of the performance of the greater good. . . . Graded absolutism does not believe there are any exceptions to absolute laws, only exemptions.[4]

> When we follow the higher moral law, we are not held responsible for breaking the lower law.[5]

Geisler explains that in "graded absolutism,"[6] there are certain categories of moral laws that are higher than others. He gives three examples:

1. Love for God over love for humankind
2. Obey God over government
3. Mercy over veracity[7]

He makes clear that he does not believe that one should choose the lesser sin and *then ask forgiveness for sinning* (a position that he calls "conflicting absolutism"), because he argues that there is *no sin involved* in breaking a lesser moral law in order to obey a higher one. God does not hold the person guilty at all, so there is no need to pray for forgiveness in such cases.[8]

---

[2] Norman L. Geisler, *Christian Ethics: Contemporary Issues and Options*, 2nd ed. (Grand Rapids, MI: Baker, 2010), 102.

[3] Ibid., 104.

[4] Ibid., 109–10.

[5] Ibid., 111, 115.

[6] Sometimes Geisler's view is also called *hierarchicalism*, because it is based on a hierarchy of moral laws.

[7] Geisler, *Christian Ethics*, 104–5.

[8] See ibid., 83–96, for Geisler's explanation and rejection of conflicting absolutism. I do not deal with conflicting absolutism in this chapter. My objections to that position would be the same as my objections

Geisler gives several examples from Scripture and modern life to prove that sometimes we face moral conflicts in which we cannot possibly obey both commands.

a. Disobeying Civil Government: Geisler mentions some cases in which, he claims, people had to disobey the government in order to be faithful to God, and thus they had to violate one moral obligation in order to keep a higher one. He gives these examples:

1. The Hebrew midwives Shiphrah and Puah, who disobeyed when Pharaoh told them to kill the baby Hebrew boys (Ex. 1:15–22).
2. Shadrach, Meshach, and Abednego, who refused to bow down to the golden image that was made by King Nebuchadnezzar (Daniel 3).
3. Daniel, who disobeyed the king's command not to pray to anyone but the king (Daniel 6).[9]
4. The apostles, who disobeyed the Sanhedrin when they were commanded not to preach in the name of Jesus (Acts 4:18–20; see also 5:29).[10]

I agree with Geisler that the biblical narrative views with approval these actions of disobedience to the government in order to be faithful to God. But I disagree with Geisler's claim that these actions constituted disobedience to commands of God.

The Bible never tells people always to obey every command of a secular civil government. Instead, Paul wisely says, "Let every person *be subject to the governing authorities*" (Rom. 13:1). To "be subject" to a government in general does not mean that one always must obey every command of that government.

An important principle here is that individual passages of Scripture should be interpreted in the light of the whole teaching of Scripture. There are several passages in which God clearly gave approval to his people who disobeyed a government that was commanding them to carry out a sinful action.[11]

Therefore, the teaching of *all of Scripture*, when rightly understood, is that God tells his people to *be subject* to governing authorities, but that we have no obligation to obey when the government commands us to sin (that is, to disobey something that God commands us in Scripture).[12] No example in the Bible disproves this principle.

---

to Geisler's position: the Bible does not teach that we will ever be in a position where all our choices will be sinful ones.

[9] Geisler mentions these examples especially in ibid., 102–4; see also 77.

[10] Ibid., 105.

[11] See my longer discussion of this principle in chap. 16, p. 437. In addition to Geisler's examples, see also Est. 4:16 (Esther) and Matt. 2:8, 12 (the wise men from the East).

[12] Geisler attempts to prove that Scripture commands believers to obey every law of government by quoting the King James Version of 1 Pet. 2:13, which says we should submit to "*every ordinance* of man for the Lord's sake." Unfortunately, the Greek word that Peter uses is not one of the common words for "law" or "ordinance" (such as *nomos* or *dikaiōma*). Peter instead uses *ktisis*, which here has the meaning "system of established authority that is the result of some founding action, governance system, authority system" (BDAG, 573), resulting in the ESV translation, "Be subject for the Lord's sake to *every human institution*." In addition to the ESV, the NASB, NET, NRSV, and RSV also have "institution," while CSB, NIV, and NLT

Therefore, Geisler's list of cases in which people were approved for disobeying government fails to demonstrate that there are some moral conflicts in which individuals cannot obey both commands.

b. Disobeying Parents: Another example that Geisler returns to again and again is when Jesus, according to Geisler, either did not honor or did not obey his parents, in order to honor God (in Luke 2:41–49). Geisler says, "Jesus seemed to face real conflicts between obeying his heavenly Father and obeying his earthly parents (Luke 2)."[13] He says, "At age twelve, Jesus faced a conflict between his earthly parents and his heavenly Father."[14] And he later speaks of a time when Jesus did not keep a moral command "to obey parents."[15]

But once again it does not seem that Geisler has been precise enough in representing what Scripture actually teaches. Nowhere does the Bible say that Jesus was disobedient to his parents. If any moral wrongdoing is suggested in the passage at all, it is on the part of Jesus's parents, who left Jerusalem without being sure that Jesus was with them:

> And when the feast was ended, as they were returning, the boy Jesus stayed behind in Jerusalem. His parents did not know it, but supposing him to be in the group they went a day's journey, but then they began to search for him among their relatives and acquaintances, and when they did not find him, they returned to Jerusalem, searching for him. After three days they found him in the temple, sitting among the teachers, listening to them and asking them questions. (Luke 2:43–46)

To claim that Jesus was disobedient to his parents in this situation is to claim something that the text simply does not say.[16]

---

translate *ktisis* as "human authority." The NKJV alone among modern translations follows the KJV and retains "ordinance" here.

The correct meaning in 1 Pet. 2:13 is "be subject . . . to every *human institution*," because Peter goes on to give specific examples: "the emperor as supreme" and also "governors." Therefore, the verse does not command obedience to every "ordinance of man," but rather a general submission to legitimate government authority.

The other text that Geisler uses to argue that the Bible requires us to obey every law and command of government is Titus 3:1: "Remind them to be submissive to rulers and authorities, *to be obedient*, to be ready for every good work." But such a general command to be "obedient" must be understood in light of another verse that uses this same Greek word (*peitharcheō*): "But Peter and the apostles answered, 'We must *obey* [*peitharcheō*] God rather than men'" (Acts 5:29). The teaching of the New Testament as a whole shows that Christians are to be obedient to government except when government commands them to sin against God. God does not grant an "exemption" in such cases (as Geisler claims), because God never required obedience to *every* command of human government in the first place.

[13] Geisler, *Christian Ethics*, 76.

[14] Ibid., 94.

[15] Ibid., 104; see also 109.

[16] Geisler also says, "If parents teach a child to hate God, the child must disobey the parents in order to obey God." Ibid., 104. But this requires disobedience to Col. 3:20: "Children, obey your parents in everything, for this pleases the Lord." Here Geisler mistakenly isolates "obey your parents in everything" from the context, for Paul was writing to a church where the "children" listening would have had believing parents. Also, the

c. Working on the Sabbath: Geisler says that Jesus faced a "moral conflict" "between showing mercy and keeping the Sabbath (Mark 2:27)."[17]

But again Geisler's argument is based on a misunderstanding of the scriptural passage. The New Testament points out numerous cases where Jesus broke the restrictive interpretations and rules that had been added to the Sabbath command by Jewish tradition, but there is no instance in which he broke the Sabbath commandment itself when it is understood correctly, in the way that God intended it. Jesus makes this very point in this passage, for he corrects the Pharisees' wrongful understanding of the Sabbath law when he says, "The Sabbath was made for man, not man for the Sabbath" (Mark 2:27).[18]

Jesus never broke the Old Testament Sabbath commandment when it is rightly understood. Therefore, these examples from Jesus's ministry do not prove that Jesus ever faced an impossible moral conflict.

d. Lying:

(1) Rahab: Geisler claims there are some cases in which people in the Bible were obligated to tell lies in order to fulfill a higher moral law. He mentions the case of Rahab, the prostitute in Jericho who hid the Israelite spies and then lied about it to the king's representatives who came to her door (Josh. 2:4–6).[19]

I will discuss the case of Rahab further in the chapter on lying and telling the truth (see chap. 12, p. 321), but at this point it is sufficient to note that it is doubtful whether Scripture holds up Rahab's lie as an example for believers to imitate.[20] This is because the context shows clearly that she was hardly an example of moral excellence, for she was a Canaanite prostitute (Josh. 2:1), and she had no previous acquaintance with the

---

very next words are "for this pleases the Lord," so Paul's command must be understood in an overall context of seeking to please God, not hating God. The broader teaching of the whole Bible (including Matt. 19:29; Mark 10:29–30; Luke 14:26; Eph. 6:1) shows that Scripture does not teach children to always obey their parents, but to always obey their parents *except when parents tell them to disobey God.* Both Geisler and I would say the child should disobey a parental command to hate God, but Geisler would say this involves disobeying one scriptural command in order to obey another, while I would say that it is not disobeying any scriptural command, once the whole teaching of Scripture is understood. This is similar to the Bible's teaching on obedience to the authority of civil government.

[17] Ibid., 76; Geisler repeats this claim on 94 and 109.

[18] Jesus often corrected the overly strict interpretations of the Old Testament by the Jewish rabbis of his time: "Why do you break the commandment of God for the sake of your tradition?" (Matt. 15:3; see also v. 6). Regarding the specific passage to which Geisler refers, about plucking grain to eat on the Sabbath (Mark 2:23–27), D. A. Carson rightly observes (about the parallel passage in Matt. 12:1–8), "It is not even clear how they were breaking any OT law, where commandments about the Sabbath were aimed primarily at regular work. The disciples were not farmers trying to do some illicit work but were itinerant preachers casually picking some heads of grain. Indeed, apart from halakic interpretations, it is not at all obvious that any commandment of Scripture was being broken." D. A. Carson, "Matthew," in *Matthew & Mark (Revised Edition)*, vol. 9 in EBC, ed. Tremper Longman III and David E. Garland (Grand Rapids, MI: Zondervan, 2010), 325.

[19] Geisler, *Christian Ethics*, 105.

[20] See also an important supplement to my argument in Vern S. Poythress's insightful analysis of some significant differences between verbal lies and deceptive actions in "Why Lying Is Always Wrong: The Uniqueness of Verbal Deceit," *WTJ* 75 (2013): 83–95.

moral standards that God had given to Israel. While her faith and her courage were remarkable (and the New Testament affirms her for these things: see Heb. 11:31; James 2:25) later passages of Scripture conspicuously avoid mentioning her lie. In fact, John Calvin (1509–1564) wisely observed:

> As to the falsehood, we must admit that *though it was done for a good purpose, it was not free from fault.* For those who hold what is called a dutiful lie to be altogether excusable, do not sufficiently consider how precious truth is in the sight of God. Therefore, although our purpose be to assist our brethren . . . *it can never be lawful to lie*, because that cannot be right which is contrary to the nature of God. And God is truth.[21]

Similarly, the church father Augustine (354–430) said:

> But the fact that she lied is not wisely proposed for imitation, even if something prophetic is thus intelligently exposed for interpretation, and even though God was mindful to reward those good deeds of hers and clement in pardoning this bad one.[22]

(2) Hebrew Midwives in Egypt: Geisler also mentions the Hebrew midwives Shiphrah and Puah (Ex. 1:15–22) as examples of lying that God commends,[23] but the text does not establish that the midwives were actually lying. What is clear is that Pharaoh had commanded the midwives to kill all male Hebrew babies that were born, "but the midwives feared God and did not do as the king of Egypt commanded them, but let the male children live" (v. 17).

When challenged by Pharaoh, the midwives told him that the Hebrew women "give birth before the midwife comes to them" (Ex. 1:19), and there is no reason to doubt that this was true. In fact, it is entirely reasonable to think that when Pharaoh's plan became known to the Hebrew people, they delayed calling the midwives until after a child's birth, perhaps using other midwives or assisting one another in the birth process. God gave favor to the midwives for preserving the children's lives, but there is no proof that they lied in what they said to Pharaoh. Augustine said many centuries ago, "And so, it was not their deception that was rewarded, but their benevolence; the benignity of their intention, not the iniquity of their invention."[24]

---

[21] John Calvin, *Commentaries on the Book of Joshua*, trans. Henry Beveridge (repr., Grand Rapids, MI: Baker, 2005), 47, emphasis added.

[22] Augustine, *Treatises on Various Subjects,* vol. 16 of *The Fathers of the Church,* trans. Mary Sarah Muldowney (Washington: The Catholic University of America Press, 1952), 170, emphasis added. Also found in *To Consentius: Against Lying,* sec. 34 (NPNF[1], 3:497), emphasis added. John Murray comes to a similar conclusion: "Neither Scripture itself nor the theological inferences derived from Scripture provide us with any warrant for the vindication of Rahab's untruth." *Principles of Conduct: Aspects of Biblical Ethics* (Grand Rapids, MI: Eerdmans, 1957), 139.

[23] Geisler, *Christian Ethics*, 105.

[24] Augustine, *Treatises on Various Subjects*, 16:165; also found in *To Consentius: Against Lying,* sec. 32 (NPNF[1], 3:495).

e. Modern Example: Lying to Nazi Soldiers: As noted above, the classic hypothetical impossible moral conflict is that of Nazi soldiers at the door demanding to know whether you have hidden any Jews in your house. Geisler mentions lying to Nazi soldiers in order to save Jewish people as an example that proves mercy is a higher moral law than truthfulness.[25]

But when people find themselves in a situation like this there are always other options besides lying or divulging where the Jews are hidden. Silence is one option. Inviting the soldiers to come in and look around for themselves is another option. In a comparable situation, several other possible responses might present themselves, including offering hospitality and refreshments to the soldiers. In the story of Corrie ten Boom, whose family hid Jews in their home in the Netherlands during World War II, there is a remarkable account of God's providential protection of the people they had hidden (see my more extensive discussion of this situation in chap. 12, p. 326). Vern Poythress quotes Corrie ten Boom's story at some length in his article on why lying is always wrong.[26]

f. Modern Example: Leaving the Lights On: Geisler mentions another modern example, that of people who will leave some lights on in their homes when they go away to deter burglars from entering the house. Geisler says that people who do this "engage in intentional deception to save their property."[27]

But once again Geisler's argument is based on a misunderstanding of Scripture. Scripture does not prohibit *all* actions that are intended to mislead others (see Josh. 8:3–8; 1 Sam. 21:13; 2 Sam. 5:22–25), because in some cases such actions are different from a "lie," understood in the sense of affirming something that you believe to be false. Actions (such as leaving lights on at home) are neither true nor false; they are just things that happen, and they have ambiguous meanings.[28]

What Scripture forbids is bearing "false witness against your neighbor" (Ex. 20:16). In other cases, it commands us not to lie, when lying is understood as affirming in speech or writing something we believe to be false (see Eph. 4:25; Col. 3:9–10; 1 Tim. 1:10; Rev. 14:5; 21:8; 22:15).[29] Once again, taking into account the whole of Scripture, we see that this command is quite specific: it does not prohibit all deceptive actions, but it always prohibits us from telling lies in the sense of verbally affirming something that we know is not true.

Leaving lights on does not violate that command. Geisler's example is not sufficient to prove that we face impossible moral conflicts.

---

[25] Geisler, *Christian Ethics*, 106. Geisler mentions the specific case of Corrie ten Boom, but often in ethics discussions this hypothetical situation is presented without specific details.

[26] Poythress, "Why Lying Is Always Wrong," 90–92.

[27] Geisler, *Christian Ethics*, 80; see also 106.

[28] See Poythress, "Why Lying is Always Wrong," for several differences between speech and actions.

[29] See my extensive discussion of lying in chap. 12, p. 309.

g. Modern Example: Coming Late to Dinner: Similarly, a man who tells his wife that he will meet her for dinner at 6 p.m. and then stops to help a seriously injured person in a tragic auto accident while he is on the way[30] is not violating the command against lying. In the ordinary circumstances of life, people understand that a commitment to meet someone at a certain place and time contains an implicit qualification: ". . . unless unforeseen circumstances prevent me from doing so." In such a circumstance, no reasonable person would think that a husband who was late for dinner for such a reason had done something morally wrong or violated any ethical norm.[31]

h. Jesus Not Testifying on His Own Behalf: Geisler claims that Jesus faced a moral conflict at that time of his death. He says:

> Mercy and justice came into direct and unavoidable conflict. Should he speak in defense of the innocent (himself), as the law demands (Lev. 5:1), or should he show mercy to the many (humankind) by refusing to defend himself?[32]

> [Jesus] was squeezed between the demands of justice for the innocent (himself) and mercy for humankind (the guilty). He chose mercy for the many over justice for the one. This conflict . . . dramatizes the supremacy of mercy over justice in unavoidable moral conflicts.[33]

But Geisler is incorrect in his understanding of both aspects of this situation. Leviticus 5:1 says that if someone "hears a public adjuration to testify, and though he is a witness . . . yet does not speak, he shall bear his iniquity." But Jesus obeyed this, because Matthew's Gospel explicitly tells us that when the high priest commanded Jesus under oath to testify by saying, "I adjure you by the Living God, tell us if you are the Christ, the Son of God," Jesus did not remain silent but actually did answer in that case, saying, "You have said so" (Matt. 26:63–64, with evident allusion to the command in Lev. 5:1, which Jesus was keeping).

It is an entire misunderstanding of the nature of Jesus's trial to say that Jesus failed to fulfill the demands of justice for the innocent, for Jesus was not the judge or the Roman governor in this case. He was the innocent victim who was wrongly condemned by Pilate, a tremendous act of injustice. But Pilate committed the injustice. Jesus did not commit this injustice—he suffered the results of it!

This example surely is inadequate evidence for Geisler's claim that we sometimes face moral conflicts in which we cannot obey both commands. Jesus disobeyed no com-

---

[30] Geisler calls this "breaking a promise." *Christian Ethics*, 103.

[31] Geisler would say the husband broke the promise, but this was not sin because God gives an "exemption" when a lesser moral law is broken in order to obey a higher moral law. I would say that no moral law was broken.

[32] Geisler, *Christian Ethics*, 94.

[33] Ibid., 109.

mand of Scripture when he suffered and died for us, and it is demeaning to the great glory of Christ's sacrifice on the cross to think that he did so.

i. Murdering:

(1) Samson: Finally, Geisler mentions two other examples, both of which, he claims, demonstrate violations of the biblical prohibition against killing. First, there is the example of Samson,[34] who pushed with such force against the pillars of the Philistines' stadium that it collapsed on him and killed him, but also destroyed thousands of the Philistine enemies of Israel (Judg. 16:28–30). Geisler sees this as disobeying the command against murder, because Samson murdered himself (along with the wicked Philistines).

Geisler again misses the point of the passage. Nothing in God's moral law prohibited the Israelites from risking or even bravely sacrificing their own lives when going to battle against the nation's enemies (such as the oppressive Philistines). Samson's destruction of the Philistine stadium was a heroic act of self-sacrifice on Samson's part, and in some ways it even prefigured the death of Christ for us. But Samson's story is not an example of someone facing an impossible moral conflict in which he could not obey multiple commands.

(2) Abraham and Isaac: The other example that Geisler mentions is God's command that Abraham sacrifice his son Isaac (Genesis 22).[35] Geisler says, "The story of Abraham and Isaac (Gen. 22) contains a real moral conflict. 'Thou shall not kill' is a divine moral command (Ex. 20:13 KJV), and yet God commanded Abraham to kill his son Isaac."[36]

However, it is not necessary to believe that God commanded Abraham to kill Isaac and also commanded him not to kill Isaac at the same time. First, this would not fit Geisler's "graded absolutism" paradigm, because it would not be a case of disobeying a lesser moral law in order to obey a higher moral law. That is because the same moral law is involved on both sides: "Kill Isaac" versus "Don't kill Isaac." And this was not a case of obeying God over government, but, as Geisler presents it, a case of obeying God ("Kill Isaac") versus obeying God ("Don't kill Isaac"). Graded absolutism therefore gives us no help in such a situation.

Every interpreter agrees that this passage about Abraham and Isaac is remarkably difficult. The resolution that I find most helpful begins with the understanding that, while we cannot rightfully murder another human being, God himself has the right to take life, and he can rightfully take the life of any human being who has sinned ("The soul who sins shall die," Ezek. 18:4; "The wages of sin is death," Rom. 6:23). God also

---

[34] Ibid., 102.

[35] Ibid., 102, 104.

[36] Ibid., 102; see also 77, 104. Even though the Ten Commandments were not given until later (Exodus 20), people have had an instinctive knowledge that murder is wrong since the very beginning of creation, as we see in the story of Cain and Abel (Gen. 4:8–16).

has the right to authorize human beings to carry out this punishment for sin on other human beings, as he does with civil government (see Gen. 6:5–6; Rom. 13:4; see also chap. 18, p. 508).

Abraham's thoughts were probably in turmoil. On the one hand, he must have hoped that God would provide another solution, for he said to his servants, "Stay here with the donkey; I and the boy will go over there and worship *and come again to you*" (Gen. 22:5), and the Hebrew verb for "come" is plural (*wenāshûbāh*, literally, "we will return").

On the other hand, he also must have realized that God in his sovereignty has the right to command even the taking of a human life, and in such a case there would be no violation of the command "You shall not murder" (Ex. 20:13).[37] But somehow Abraham also realized that God would be able to restore Isaac to life, for we read, "He considered that God was able even to raise him from the dead, from which, figuratively speaking, he did receive him back" (Heb. 11:19).

In any case, this difficult passage does not support Geisler's claim that sometimes we must disobey a lesser moral law in order to obey a higher moral law.

Therefore, we can conclude that Geisler has not provided any convincing examples to prove his claim that "some personally unavoidable moral conflicts exist in which an individual cannot obey both commands."[38] There are simply no examples in Scripture where violating one of God's moral commands is viewed with approval.

After considering several arguments that we sometimes face impossible moral conflicts, David W. Jones rightly observes:

> One of the greatest arguments in favor of non-conflicting absolutism is a natural reading of the Bible. As was noted earlier, there are no univocal examples of moral conflict in Scripture. While proponents of both conflicting and graded absolutism cite alleged examples of moral conflict in the Bible, *none of these proof-texts are presented as moral conflicts in the narrative of Scripture itself*—either in their appearance or in their resolution. Indeed, it seems clear that the focus of the Bible is not on conflict between moral norms but on conflict between believers and moral norms, including the temptation to sin.[39]

2. John Feinberg and Paul Feinberg. The view that we will sometimes face situations of impossible moral conflict is also found in *Ethics for a Brave New World* by John Feinberg and Paul Feinberg,[40] a book that I find myself in agreement with in many sections. But on this issue I hold a different view. The Feinbergs say:

---

[37] Note that there was no violation of the command against murder when God later told the people of Israel to destroy the Canaanites in the conquest of Canaan (Deut. 20:16–18). In God's justice, he can require the taking of the life of sinful human beings.

[38] Geisler, *Christian Ethics*, 102.

[39] David W. Jones, *An Introduction to Biblical Ethics*, B&H Studies in Christian Ethics (Nashville: B&H, 2013), 100, emphasis added.

[40] John S. Feinberg and Paul D. Feinberg, *Ethics for a Brave New World*, 2nd ed. (Wheaton, IL: Crossway, 2010).

As to our own view, we agree that there are *prima facie* duties and that sometimes they conflict. We agree with both [W. D.] Ross and Geisler that obeying one and disobeying or neglecting the other is not sin. . . . If two duties mutually exclude one another, one cannot obey both. No one is free to do the impossible.[41]

What evidence do the Feinbergs give to prove that sometimes we have duties that conflict with each other so that we cannot obey both?

a. Coming Late to a Meeting: First, the Feinbergs give the following example:

> Suppose someone promises to meet someone else at 10 AM. However, while on his way he sees someone in danger whom he can help. If he stops to help, he cannot keep his promise to arrive at 10 AM. Ross suggests that in such a case the duty to render aid is paramount, and the duty not to break a promise appears trivial. The right course of action becomes obvious. In other cases, the actual duty will be harder to discern, but one must do so anyway.[42]

My response here is similar to the one I gave to Geisler's example of coming late to dinner (see above, p. 194). In ordinary societal interactions, people understand that a commitment to meet someone at a certain place and time contains an implicit qualification: ". . . unless unforeseen circumstances prevent me from doing so." The need to help someone in danger is just such an unforeseen circumstance, and no reasonable person would think that the person who helped someone in danger and missed a meeting had done any moral wrong.

Therefore, while I agree with Geisler and the Feinbergs that it is morally right to help the person in danger and arrive late for the 10 a.m. meeting, we would have different moral analyses of the reason it is right. They would argue that the *higher duty* to help the person in danger takes priority over the *lower duty* not to break a promise, and therefore the person who helps someone in danger does not sin when he fails to keep his promise. By contrast, I would say that the person is not sinning because his promise to meet someone at 10 a.m. contained an implied condition. Both the speaker and the hearer understood the promise to imply, "I will meet you at 10 a.m. unless unforeseen circumstances prevent me from doing so." Therefore, the one who stopped to help the person in danger did not break this conditional promise.

In fact, James tells Christians that they should make clear the conditional nature of promises to do something in the future:

> Come now, you who say, "Today or tomorrow we will go into such and such a town and spend a year there and trade and make a profit"—yet you do not

[41] Ibid., 39.
[42] Ibid.

know what tomorrow will bring. What is your life? For you are a mist that appears for a little time and then vanishes. *Instead you ought to say, "If the Lord wills, we will live and do this or that."* (James 4:13–15)

b. The Example of Christ: Another argument the Feinbergs give is that it is "unthinkable" that Jesus himself never faced situations in which two moral duties conflicted and it was impossible for him to obey both of them. Here is their key paragraph:

> Our belief that one is not guilty for failing to obey both conflicting duties also stems from an appeal to the example of Christ.[43] As Geisler argues, it is unthinkable that while on earth Christ never confronted a situation where two duties conflicted so as to make it impossible to do both. In fact, Scripture says he was tempted in all points, as we are (Heb. 4:15), and since we face such situations, he must have too. However, the same verse says that he was without sin; if that is so, it must be possible to confront such decisions, obey one duty, and not sin by neglecting or disobeying the other.[44]

The reasoning in this paragraph is as follows:

1. We face situations where two moral duties cannot both be obeyed.
2. Christ was tempted in every way as we are.
3. Therefore, Christ must have faced such situations also.

But where is the argument that proves step 1, that we face such situations of impossible moral conflict? There is none, other than the example of being late for a meeting, for which there is a good alternative explanation. The Feinbergs give no example from Scripture that shows that Christ disobeyed a moral law of God.

c. The Idea of Deciding among Some Broad General Duties That Sometimes Conflict Is Not Found in Scripture: The Feinbergs say that they agree with W. D. Ross that "there are certain *prima facie* duties that we all have."[45] (The expression *prima facie* here means "self-evident, obvious" and refers to duties that people instinctively realize to be valid.) Ross, in fact, lists seven such duties:

1. Fidelity
2. Reparation (repairing or making amends for harm done)
3. Gratitude
4. Beneficence (showing kindness to others)

---

[43] "Also" refers to their previous paragraph, which I quoted above, in which they say "if two duties mutually exclude one another, one cannot obey both. No one is free to do the impossible." But this paragraph does not give any further reasons for such situations; it simply asserts that such situations happen.

[44] Feinberg and Feinberg, *Ethics for a Brave New World*, 39.

[45] Ibid., 38.

5. Justice
6. Self-improvement
7. Nonmaleficence (not doing harm)[46]

For our purposes in studying Christian ethics, notice how far from the pattern of biblical teaching is the idea that Christians should ponder such a list of seven "self-evident duties" and then decide which one has priority in each situation. Philosophers who do not derive their standards of moral right and wrong from the Bible may speak of our moral obligations as deriving from such self-evident duties, but the Bible simply does not speak that way. Nowhere do the apostles teach people to "weigh carefully your self-evident duties and decide among them."

Rather, the biblical pattern is to teach people to study and meditate on *God's words* and to obey *all* of God's commandments to us:

> But his delight is in the law of the Lord,
>   and *on his law he meditates day and night.* (Ps. 1:2)

> Blessed are those whose way is blameless,
>   who walk in the law of the Lord!
> Blessed are those *who keep his testimonies,*
>   who seek him with their whole heart,
> who also do no wrong,
>   but walk in his ways! (Ps. 119:1–3)

> Then I shall not be put to shame,
>   having my eyes fixed on *all* your commandments. (Ps. 119:6)

> With my lips I declare
>   *all* the rules of your mouth. (Ps. 119:13)

> *All* your commandments are sure. (Ps. 119:86)

> Therefore I consider *all* your precepts to be right;
>   I hate every false way. (Ps. 119:128)

> My tongue will sing of your word,
>   for *all* your commandments are right. (Ps. 119:172)

In the New Testament, Jesus told the apostles that they should be teaching the people "to observe *all that I have commanded you*" (Matt. 28:20). And Paul writes that "*All Scripture* is breathed out by God and profitable . . . for training in righteousness" (2 Tim. 3:16).

---

[46] W. D. Ross, *The Right and the Good*, ed. Philip Stratton-Lake (Oxford: Clarendon, 2002), 21.

B. THE HARMFUL RESULTS OF THE IMPOSSIBLE MORAL CONFLICT VIEW

1. The "Impossible Moral Conflict" View Becomes a Slippery Slope That Encourages Christians to Sin More and More. Students who take ethics classes in colleges or seminaries are often persuaded to adopt an impossible moral conflict position that then leads downward on a slippery slope toward moral relativism.

It happens in this way: A college professor challenges students with some puzzling hypothetical situations that he has honed and refined over decades of teaching (such as lying to protect the Jews in your basement from the Nazis, stealing to feed a starving family, or fending off a drowning man in order to keep everyone else alive in an overcrowded lifeboat).[47] Many students leave the class persuaded that there really are no moral absolutes, because there are times when it is morally necessary to lie, to steal, or even to kill in order to save lives. (It does not much matter whether they adopt an explicit hierarchy of moral laws, as in Geisler's view, or a conviction that the greater obligation has to be worked out in each new situation, as in the Feinbergs' view.)

If they become convinced that love is a "basic conviction" that can at times override the rules and principles of the Bible, then loving conduct expressed in personal obligations to friends or in personal attachments to romantic relationships may easily seem more important to them than telling the truth, staying morally pure, or honoring their parents if they suddenly decide that they are in situations of impossible moral conflict where they cannot fulfill both obligations.

It can happen in a workplace situation, where a Christian may think that it is acceptable to tell a small lie to his or her employer to cover up for a friend who really needs to keep the job. This may seem acceptable because "mercy" is a higher moral law than "veracity."[48] Or a youth pastor may begin exaggerating and embellishing testimonies of answers to prayer because there is a higher moral obligation to advance the kingdom of God than to tell the truth, and these amazing stories, he thinks, will build up people's faith. Or a government official who is a Christian may be persuaded that it is acceptable to tell small lies and then bigger lies because the higher principle is seeking the good of the country (which, of course, is most advanced if he remains in office). In these and many other situations, such complicated rationalizations actually become a shortcut to immoral behavior.

In this way, the idea that we can face impossible moral conflicts becomes an intellectual wedge that persuades people to adopt a position that functions essentially like moral relativism—there are no absolute moral standards that always must be obeyed.

---

[47] Joseph Fletcher used several such examples with great impact in his influential book *Situation Ethics* (Philadelphia: Westminster, 1966), esp. 37, 75, 133, 136, 143, 163–66. His goal was to persuade readers that there are no absolute standards of right and wrong other than the standard of "love," which he understood to mean acting in a way that will bring the greatest good to the greatest number of people in each situation (see 59, 61, 64).

[48] Geisler, *Christian Ethics*, 104–5.

If it was important for God to teach us that we will sometimes face impossible moral conflicts in which he wants us to disobey one of his commands in order to obey another one, would he not have made that evident in several incontrovertible examples in the life of Jesus?

By contrast, there are many examples of Jesus saying he is without sin and of others not being able to find any sin in him:

> I always do the things that are pleasing to him [that is, his Father]. (John 8:29)

> Which one of you convicts me of sin? (John 8:46)

> If you keep my commandments, you will abide in my love, just as I have kept my Father's commandments and abide in his love. (John 15:10)

> He committed no sin, neither was deceit found in his mouth. (1 Pet. 2:22)[51]

Geisler has an alternative understanding of these verses. He claims that Jesus did violate lesser commands of God, but it was not actually sin because God always gave him an "exemption" from one command in order that he would be able to obey a greater command. Geisler says, "When we follow the higher moral law, we are not held responsible for breaking the lower law."[52] He also says, "God does not hold a person guilty for not keeping a lower moral law so long as one keeps the higher law,"[53] and that God's exemption eliminates the individual's culpability for not keeping the lower moral law.[54]

But Geisler's claim is supported by no explicit teaching anywhere in the New Testament. Nowhere do the apostles Paul, Peter, or John write to first-century Christians and say, "When you face a difficult situation with an impossible moral conflict, God will give you an exemption for violating one of his moral laws." This idea is entirely foreign to the thought of the New Testament.

In addition, Jesus was surrounded by first-century Jewish opponents who were watching his every action and listening to his every word, trying to trap him in disobedience to some command of God, and they could find none. If Jesus had broken a moral command of God in a difficult situation, they would have pounced on him immediately and accused him of wrongdoing. But they could find in his life nothing that violated any of God's commands. Jesus repeatedly affirmed the goodness and inviolability of all of God's words in Scripture: "Scripture cannot be broken" (John 10:35).

2. First Corinthians 10:13 Promises That We Will Never Face Impossible Moral Conflicts. In writing to Christians at Corinth who were facing pressure from their

---

[51] See also Luke 4:13; John 8:12; Acts 2:27; 3:14; 4:30; 7:52; 13:35; Rom. 8:3; 2 Cor. 5:21; Heb. 7:26; 1 Pet. 1:19; 3:18; 1 John 2:1; 3:5. The testimony of the New Testament to Jesus's sinlessness is overwhelming.

[52] Geisler, *Christian Ethics*, 115.

[53] Ibid., 104.

[54] Ibid., 104, 110–11.

non-Christian culture to participate in aspects of idol worship, Paul assured them that believers will never face a situation in which the circumstances will force them to do something contrary to one of God's moral standards:

> No temptation has overtaken you that is not common to man. God is faithful, and he will not let you be tempted beyond your ability, but *with the temptation he will also provide the way of escape*, that you may be able to endure it. (1 Cor. 10:13)

Geisler responds that this verse applies only to situations of "temptation," not to the entire life of Christians.[55] But that is hardly a convincing objection, because situations in which people claim an impossible moral conflict are by definition situations of temptation.[56] They are all situations in which Christians feel tremendous pressure from circumstances around them to disobey one of God's moral laws. But Paul says that in all of those situations God will provide "the way of escape," a way out of the temptation so that the Christian does not have to give in and break one of God's moral laws.

The proper approach in such difficult situations is not to give in to the temptation and break one of God's moral laws, but rather to pray for God's wisdom (see James 1:5) to understand how to escape from the situation without doing something that God counts as sin.

3. It Is Foreign to the Entire Fabric of Biblical Moral Teaching to Say That God Sometimes Wants Us to Disobey One of His Commandments. Where is there anything in Scripture that encourages us to find out which commands we might need to disobey in difficult times? There is nothing of that sort.[57] The repeated perspective of Scripture, rather, is to command us again and again to keep *all* the commands of God:

> The law of the LORD is perfect,
>   reviving the soul. . . .
> The precepts of the LORD are right,
>   rejoicing the heart;
> The commandment of the LORD is pure,
>   enlightening the eyes. . . .
> The rules of the LORD are true,
>   and righteous altogether. . . .

---

[55] Ibid., 76.

[56] The Greek word Paul uses for "temptation" in 1 Cor. 10:13 is *peirasmos*, "an attempt to make one do something wrong, temptation, enticement to sin" (BDAG, 793). It is used in Luke 4:13 to speak of "every *temptation*" that Satan brought against Jesus in the wilderness. But in several verses the word is also used to refer to "test, trial" (BDAG, 793). James 1:2 is an example: "Count it all joy, my brothers, when you meet *trials* of various kinds." All sorts of difficult situations are included in Paul's assurance about "no temptation" in 1 Cor. 10:13.

[57] Frame says, "In Scripture, we have a moral duty to do what is right, and never to do what is wrong." *The Doctrine of the Christian Life*, 231.

Moreover, by them is your servant warned;
> in keeping them there is great reward. (Ps. 19:7–11)

Blessed are those whose way is blameless,
> who walk in the law of the LORD!
Blessed are those who keep his testimonies,
> who seek him with their whole heart. (Ps. 119:1–2)

Then I shall not be put to shame,
> having my eyes fixed on *all your commandments*. (Ps. 119:6)

Lead me in the path of your commandments,
> for I delight in it. (Ps. 119:35)

And they were both righteous before God, walking blamelessly in *all the commandments and statutes of the Lord*. (Luke 1:6)

For whoever keeps the whole law but fails in one point has become accountable for all of it. (James 2:10)

The New Testament never encourages Christians to "choose the lesser sin" or to "realize they have an exemption from lesser moral laws of God in difficult situations," but rather tells them to flee from sin and temptation:

Flee from sexual immorality. (1 Cor. 6:18)

Therefore, my beloved, *flee* from idolatry. (1 Cor. 10:14)

But as for you, O man of God, *flee* these things. Pursue righteousness, godliness, faith, love, steadfastness, gentleness. (1 Tim. 6:11)

So *flee* youthful passions and pursue righteousness, faith, love, and peace, along with those who call on the Lord from a pure heart. (2 Tim. 2:22)

4. Passages on Greater and Lesser Commandments Never Encourage Us to Disobey the Lesser Ones. I agree that there are some Scripture passages that distinguish between greater and lesser commandments. But they never encourage any obedience to the greater commandments that would involve disobedience to the lesser commandments.

For example, Jesus rebuked the scribes and Pharisees for paying tithes on tiny bits of spices but neglecting "*the weightier matters of the law*: justice and mercy and faithfulness" (Matt. 23:23). But when we read the entire verse we find that, far from encouraging disobedience to the lesser matters of the law, Jesus was reminding them that they were responsible (under the old covenant) for obeying both the greater and lesser laws:

> Woe to you, scribes and Pharisees, hypocrites! For you tithe mint and dill and cumin, and have neglected the weightier matters of the law: justice and mercy and faithfulness. These you ought to have done, *without neglecting the others.* (Matt. 23:23)

In another place, Jesus talks about "the least of these commandments," implying that there are lesser and greater commandments. But again he warns against teaching people that it is acceptable to disobey even the least of the commandments:

> For truly, I say to you, until heaven and earth pass away, not an iota, not a dot, will pass from the Law until all is accomplished. Therefore *whoever relaxes one of the least of these commandments* and teaches others to do the same will be called least in the kingdom of heaven, but whoever does them and teaches them will be called great in the kingdom of heaven. (Matt. 5:18–19)

5. It Would Be Unjust of God to Give Us Contradictory Commands. If we actually will face situations of impossible moral conflict, and if our ultimate moral obligation is to God, then this means that God will put us in situations in which he will command us to do things that are contradictory, which would be inconsistent and unjust of him. John Frame explains, "On this view, the law of God itself is contradictory, for it requires contradictory behavior.... Surely the consistency of Scripture is an empty concept if Scripture can command us to do contradictory things."[58] This is not an acceptable position.

6. God's Wisdom and Providence. The "nonconflicting biblical commands" position is consistent with the infinite wisdom of God in the moral commands that he has given us, and it is consistent with his providential ordering of all the circumstances of our lives. Robert Rakestraw rightly observes:

> The character of God argues for [nonconflicting moral absolutism]. If God has given numerous moral absolutes, some of which genuinely conflict at times, it appears that there is conflict within the mind and moral will of God! . . . The character of God as perfect and consistent within his own moral nature appears to be jeopardized by any view which holds that God's absolutes genuinely conflict.[59]

7. Conclusion. My conclusion, based on these various considerations from Scripture, is that Christians will never face a situation of impossible moral conflict, a situation where all our choices are sinful ones. I agree with Frame when he writes, "So I must conclude that there are no tragic moral choices, no conflicts of duties."[60]

---

[58] Ibid., 232.

[59] Rakestraw, "Ethical Choices," 123. Jones also finds that "nonconflicting absolutism" is the "least problematic" of three options advocated by Christians (conflicting absolutism, graded absolutism, and nonconflicting absolutism). *An Introduction to Biblical Ethics*, 105.

[60] Frame, *The Doctrine of the Christian Life*, 233; see longer discussion on 230–34.

QUESTIONS FOR PERSONAL APPLICATION

1. Was this chapter an encouragement to you? Why or why not?
2. Have you ever faced a situation in which it seemed that all your choices were sinful in some way? What did you do? Looking back on the decision, do you think you made the right choice? If not, what do you now think would have been the right choice? What do you think Jesus would have done in such a situation?
3. Read 1 Corinthians 10:13. How does it make you feel about your future? About a decision that you are facing right now?

SPECIAL TERMS

graded absolutism
impossible moral conflict
nonconflicting biblical commands
nonconflicting moral absolutism
prima facie duty

BIBLIOGRAPHY

Sections in Other Ethics Texts

(see complete bibliographical data, p. 64)

Clark and Rakestraw, 1:113–78
Davis, 6–10
Feinberg, John and Paul, 36–40
Frame, 230–34
Geisler, 61–62, 83–95
Gushee and Stassen, 298–307
Jones, 125–52
Murray, 123–48, 202–28
Rae, 50–51

Other Works

Fletcher, Joseph. *Situation Ethics: The New Morality*. Louisville, KY: Westminster John Knox, 1997.
Fletcher, Joseph, and John Warwick Montgomery. *Situation Ethics: True or False? A Dialogue between Joseph Fletcher and John Warwick Montgomery*. Minneapolis: Bethany Fellowship, 1972.

Higginson, R. A. "Absolutes." In *New Dictionary of Christian Ethics and Pastoral Theology*, edited by David J. Atkinson and David H. Field, 134–35. Leicester, UK: Inter-Varsity, and Downers Grove, IL: InterVarsity Press, 1995.

Wilkens, Steve. *Beyond Bumper Sticker Ethics: An Introduction to Theories of Right and Wrong*. Downers Grove, IL: IVP Academic, 2011.

SCRIPTURE MEMORY PASSAGE

1 Corinthians 10:13: No temptation has overtaken you that is not common to man. God is faithful, and he will not let you be tempted beyond your ability, but with the temptation he will also provide the way of escape, that you may be able to endure it.

HYMN

"Yield Not to Temptation"

Yield not to temptation, for yielding is sin,
Each vict'ry will help you some other to win;
Fight manfully onward, dark passions subdue,
Look ever to Jesus—He'll carry you through.

Refrain:
Ask the Savior to help you,
Comfort, strengthen and keep you;
He is willing to aid you
He will carry you through.

Shun evil companions, bad language disdain,
God's name hold in rev'rence, nor take it in vain;
Be thoughtful and earnest, kind-hearted and true,
Look ever to Jesus—He'll carry you through.

To him that o'ercometh God giveth a crown,
Thru faith we will conquer tho often cast down;
He who is our Savior our strength will renew,
Look ever to Jesus—He'll carry you through.

AUTHOR: HORATIO R. PALMER, 1834–1907

Chapter 8

HOW SHOULD CHRISTIANS USE THE OLD TESTAMENT FOR ETHICAL GUIDANCE?

If the entire Mosaic covenant has been canceled, can we still gain wisdom from studying it?

How can we know which Old Testament laws contain wise guidance for us today, and which laws were only intended for Israel before the time of Christ?

The Old Testament is clearly part of our Bible. But sometimes it is not easy to know which of its laws Christians should try to follow today. The question is how Christians should use the Old Testament for ethical guidance. The answer is not a simple one, and therefore this chapter will be devoted to attempting to resolve the question.

The problem arises when we see that some Old Testament passages seem to fit so well into the teachings of Jesus and the New Testament authors while others do not. For example, Deuteronomy 6:5 says:

> You shall love the LORD your God with all your heart and with all your soul and with all your might.

Jesus quotes this verse in the New Testament (see Matt. 22:37; Mark 12:30; Luke 10:27). Likewise, Leviticus 19:18 says:

> You shall love your neighbor as yourself.

This verse is also quoted in the New Testament (see Matt. 19:19; 22:39; Mark 12:31; Rom. 13:9; Gal. 5:14; James 2:8). In addition, some of the Ten Commandments, such as the commands against murder, adultery, and stealing, are also found in the New Testament (see discussion below).

On the other hand, other Old Testament laws seem completely foreign to the teaching and practice of the New Testament, and some of them are explicitly nullified by New Testament teachings. The vast majority of Christians today would agree that the following laws are no longer obligatory for anyone today:

> And the pig, because it parts the hoof and is cloven-footed but does not chew the cud, is unclean to you. (Lev. 11:7)

> And on the day when you wave the sheaf, you shall offer a male lamb a year old without blemish as a burnt offering to the LORD. (Lev. 23:12)

> Whoever blasphemes the name of the LORD shall surely be put to death. All the congregation shall stone him. The sojourner as well as the native, when he blasphemes the Name, shall be put to death. (Lev. 24:16)

> Whoever strikes his father or his mother shall be put to death. (Ex. 21:15)

Because the Old Testament contains such a variety—some laws that seem perpetually valid and other laws that seem to be discontinued—Christians have come to several different solutions to the question of how to use the Old Testament for ethical guidance.[1] Finding a persuasive solution will require wisdom in understanding the role each section of the Old Testament plays in the ongoing history of God's work as revealed in the Bible (what is often called the "history of redemption").

My argument in the following pages will attempt to establish the following principle:

> The Mosaic covenant, which began when God gave the Ten Commandments at Mount Sinai (Exodus 20), was terminated when Christ died, and Christians now live instead under the provisions of the new covenant. However, the Old Testament is still a valuable source of ethical wisdom when it is understood in accordance with the ways in which the New Testament authors continue to use the Old Testament for ethical teaching and in light of the changes brought about by the new covenant.

A. THE MOSAIC COVENANT WAS TERMINATED AT THE DEATH OF CHRIST

One important way to gain an overview of the entire Bible is to view it in terms of the different *covenants* that God established with people, such as the covenant with Noah

---

[1] See David Dorsey, "The Law of Moses and the Christian: A Compromise," *JETS* 34, no. 3 (September 1991): 322–24. Dorsey mentions six categories of solutions to the question of how to apply the law of Moses today.

(Gen. 9:8–17), the covenant with Abraham (15:1–21; 17:1–27), or the covenant made at the time of Moses (see Ex. 19:5; 24:7–8). Each covenant was marked by a series of statements by God that defined the conditions under which he would relate to people during the time of that covenant. Therefore, I define a covenant in the following way:

> **A covenant** is an unchangeable, divinely imposed legal agreement between God and man that stipulates the conditions of their relationship.[2]

I discuss the various covenants in the Bible at some length in my book *Systematic Theology*.[3]

If we are going to understand how to interpret the Old Testament rightly for ethical guidance, it is crucial that we grasp the differences between the *old covenant* that God established with the people of Israel through Moses and the *new covenant* that was established by Christ.

1. Several Explicit Statements Teach That the Mosaic Covenant Has Come to an End.
The first mention of a "new covenant" in the Bible comes in the Old Testament itself, when God promises this through Jeremiah:

> Behold, the days are coming, declares the LORD, when I will make *a new covenant* with the house of Israel and the house of Judah. (Jer. 31:31)

Then, in the Gospels, we do not hear anything about the new covenant until the very end of Jesus's earthly ministry, at the Last Supper, when he says, "This cup that is poured out for you is the *new covenant* in my blood" (Luke 22:20; see also 1 Cor. 11:25). Jesus's words in Matthew's Gospel make the connection between the cup of wine and his death even more explicit: "For this is my blood of the covenant, which is poured out for many for the forgiveness of sins" (Matt. 26:28).

The precise time when the new covenant began was not at the Last Supper, however, but a few hours later when Jesus's blood was actually poured out and he died. The author of Hebrews says, "For a will [*diathēkē*] takes effect only at death, since it is not in force as long as the one who made it is alive" (Heb. 9:17). The Greek word used here (*diathēkē*) can mean either "will" or "covenant," and the author seems to be calling on his readers' knowledge that both senses are possible, because this statement supports his claim that Jesus "is the mediator of a new *covenant*" (v. 15). This, then, is clear testimony that the old covenant came to an end and the new covenant began at the time of the death of Christ.

Paul contrasts this new covenant with what he calls "the old covenant" (2 Cor. 3:14). It is important to recognize that he identifies that old covenant *not with the entire Old*

---

[2] Wayne Grudem, *Systematic Theology An Introduction to Biblical Doctrine* (Leicester, UK: Inter-Varsity, and Grand Rapids, MI: Zondervan, 1994), 515.

[3] See ibid., 515–25.

Testament period but with the covenant God made with the people of Israel under Moses, because he calls it "the ministry of death, carved in letters on stone" (a reference to the Ten Commandments in Exodus 20) and mentions the fading glory of Moses's face (2 Cor. 3:7). He also contrasts that old covenant with his present new covenant ministry, what he calls "the ministry of the Spirit" (v. 8). Paul says in this context that the old covenant "was being brought to an end" (vv. 11, 13).

A more detailed argument about the end of the Mosaic covenant comes in Hebrews 7–10. Hebrews 7 argues that Jesus has become "a priest forever, after the order of Melchizedek" (Heb. 7:17), not as part of the system of priests descended from Levi in the old covenant, what the author of Hebrews calls "the Levitical priesthood" (v. 11). But if Jesus has become a priest "after the order of Melchizedek, rather than one named after the order of Aaron" (v. 11), then a new system of laws has also been established, because the author claims it is quite evident that "when there is a change in the priesthood, there is necessarily *a change in the law* as well" (v. 12). In other words, we know that a new legal system (a new covenant) has taken effect because it is evident that a new priest has taken office, namely, Jesus, and he could not be a priest according to the laws of the old covenant, under which priests had to descend from Levi. Therefore, says the author, Jesus has become "the guarantor of *a better covenant*" (v. 22). The old legal system—the old covenant—has come to an end, and a new legal system—a better covenant—has taken effect.

Then the entire argument of Hebrews 8–10 establishes again and again that *the Mosaic covenant has been terminated* and that Christ has inaugurated the long-promised new covenant through his offering of himself and his ongoing high priestly ministry. The author explains that Christ's ministry inaugurating the new covenant is much better than the ministry of the old covenant:

> But as it is, Christ has obtained a ministry that is as much more excellent than the old as *the covenant he mediates is better*, since it is enacted on better promises. For if that *first covenant* had been faultless, there would have been no occasion to look for *a second*.
>
> For he finds fault with them when he says:
>
> "Behold, the days are coming," declares the Lord,
>> "when I will establish a *new covenant* with the house of Israel
>> and with the house of Judah,
> *not like the covenant* that I made with their fathers
>> on the day when I took them by the hand to bring them out of the
>> land of Egypt.
> For they did not continue in my covenant,
>> and so I showed no concern for them," declares the Lord.
> "For *this is the covenant that I will make* with the house of Israel
>> after those days," declares the Lord:

"I will put my laws into their minds,
 and write them on their hearts,
and I will be their God,
 and they shall be my people.
And they shall not teach, each one his neighbor
 and each one his brother, saying, 'Know the Lord,'
for they shall all know me,
 from the least of them to the greatest.
For I will be merciful toward their iniquities,
 and I will remember their sins no more."

In speaking of *a new covenant*, he makes *the first one obsolete*. And what is becoming obsolete and growing old is ready to vanish away. (Heb. 8:6–13)

Then the author says that "even the *first covenant* had regulations for worship and an earthly place of holiness" (Heb. 9:1), and he explains in detail something of the system of sacrifices offered by the old covenant priests. But then he also explains that Christ has entered the better heavenly temple as a priest: "Through the greater and more perfect tent (not made with hands, that is, not of this creation) he entered once for all into the holy places . . . by means of his own blood" (vv. 11–12). In other words, Jesus's sacrifice was made in the heavenly temple, not the earthly one of the old covenant, and this shows that the old covenant is obsolete.

What is the conclusion? A new covenant is in effect: "Therefore he is the mediator of a *new covenant*" (Heb. 9:15).

It is important to realize that the author of Hebrews is not saying that *some* old covenant laws are no longer binding on Christians (such as sacrificial laws or purity laws, for example), but that *the old covenant itself*, that *entire system of laws* that defined the relationship between God and his people, is no longer in effect. It is "obsolete" (Heb. 8:13).[4] Frank Thielman argues persuasively for this conclusion:

> The entire law is obsolete, moreover, and not simply the portion of the law that regulates the priesthood and the sacrifices. . . . In [Hebrews] 9:15–22 he makes the term "first covenant" synonymous with "every commandment spoken by Moses according to the law" (9:19). . . . The entire Mosaic covenant, therefore, and not merely a part of it, has been superseded by the new covenant: the change in priesthood has required not merely a change in some laws pertaining to the priesthood, but a different law entirely (7:12).[5]

---

[4] Dorsey says, "The NT . . . speaks of the law in quite monolithic terms. Legal obligation to only a portion of the corpus is nowhere suggested. If one is legally bound to the law, it is to the entire law, including every 'minor' stipulation, that he is bound." "The Law of Moses and the Christian," 330.

[5] Frank Thielman, *The Law and the New Testament: The Question of Continuity*, Companions to the New Testament (New York: Herder & Herder, 1999), 131. Thielman's entire argument on pp. 111–34 is a persuasive treatment of this question in Hebrews.

Other passages in the New Testament also teach or assume that the old covenant is no longer in effect. In Galatians 3, Paul argues that the system of laws established under the Mosaic covenant was temporary:

> Why then the law? It was added because of transgressions, *until the offspring should come* to whom the promise had been made. (Gal. 3:19)

In this context, Paul makes clear that the entire system of law[6] established under Moses no longer is applicable to us, because he says, "The law was our guardian until Christ came, in order that we might be justified by faith. *But now that faith has come, we are no longer under a guardian*, for in Christ Jesus you are all sons of God, through faith" (Gal. 3:24–26). In saying "we are no longer under a guardian" (v. 25), Paul makes clear that we are no longer under the detailed stipulations of the Mosaic Law.

In a similar way, Paul refers in Romans to the laws of the Mosaic covenant as "the law," and says:

> Likewise, my brothers, *you also have died to the law* through the body of Christ, so that you may belong to another, to him who has been raised from the dead, in order that we may bear fruit for God. (Rom. 7:4)

Then Paul says, "But now we are *released from the law* . . . so that we serve in the new way of the Spirit and not in the old way of the written code" (Rom. 7:6).

In 1 Corinthians, Paul says, "To those under the law I became as one under the law (*though not being myself under the law*) that I might win those under the law" (9:20).

In Ephesians, Paul says that the Mosaic covenant ("the law") has been terminated, and this is evident in the fact that God's people are no longer the Jewish people only, but are made up of both Jews and Gentiles who have trusted Christ. The division and the hostility that existed between Jews and Gentiles no longer exist in the church. Christ established this unity by abolishing all the laws that marked the Jews as a distinct people, laws that Paul calls "the law of commandments expressed in ordinances":

> For he himself is our peace, who has made us both one and has broken down in his flesh the dividing wall of hostility *by abolishing the law of commandments expressed in ordinances*, that he might create in himself one new man in place of the two, so making peace, and might reconcile us both to God in one body through the cross, thereby killing the hostility. (Eph. 2:14–16)

---

[6] I agree with Douglas Moo when he states that in Gal. 3:24 there is "no reason to think that 'law' . . . means anything different than what it plainly means throughout Galatians 2–4: the Mosaic law, the *tôrâ*, in its entirety. . . . 'Law' in the New Testament denotes the Mosaic law unless there are good reasons to the contrary." Response to Greg L. Bahnsen, "The Theonomic Reformed Approach to Law and Gospel," in *Five Views on Law and Gospel*, Counterpoints, series ed. Stanley N. Gundry (Grand Rapids, MI: Zondervan, 1996), 168–69. Moo is responding to Bahnsen's claim in the same volume (104) that "law" in this passage refers only to ceremonial laws in the Mosaic covenant.

The termination of the Mosaic Law was also clear in Paul's preaching in his very first missionary journey, when he declared to the Jews at Antioch in Pisidia that, by Jesus himself, "everyone who believes is freed from everything from which you could not be freed by the law of Moses" (Acts 13:39), thus implying that for those who believe in Jesus, the law of Moses is no longer in effect.

In fact, the end of the Mosaic covenant, with its system of sacrifices and priests who alone had access to God's presence, was shown dramatically at the moment Jesus died when "behold, the curtain of the temple was torn in two, from top to bottom" (Matt. 27:51; see also Mark 15:38; Luke 23:45). God was indicating that the old system of priests and sacrifices, by which no one but the high priest could enter into the Most Holy Place and come into God's presence, was at an end. Believers henceforth would come to God through Jesus Christ and his sacrifice, and would come into the presence of God himself in heaven rather than being limited to an earthly temple. The *system of laws under the Mosaic covenant*, perfectly suited for the period for which God intended it, was finished.

Thomas R. Schreiner affirms the same position:

> Paul argues that the entirety of the law has been set aside now that Christ has come. To say that the "moral" elements of the law continue to be authoritative blunts the truth that the entire Mosaic covenant is no longer in force for believers.[7]

Brian Rosner also argues extensively that Paul explicitly repudiates the Mosaic Law as law-covenant.[8]

2. Some Specific Legal Obligations under the Mosaic Covenant Are Explicitly Said to Be No Longer Required for Christians. In addition to several statements that the Mosaic covenant *in its entirety* has been terminated, the New Testament contains a number of passages showing that Christians are no longer bound by several specific provisions of the Mosaic Law. We will examine these passages in several categories and note how the New Testament often provides replacements for these laws that are appropriate to the new covenant.

a. Christians No Longer Must Offer Old Testament Sacrifices: As explained in the previous section, Hebrews 7–10 gives an extensive argument that now there is a new High Priest (Jesus), a new sacrifice (Jesus's sacrifice of himself), and a new temple (the temple in heaven). For Christians to offer sacrifices for their sins at the temple in Jerusalem would be to give a public signal that they think the sacrifice of Jesus was not sufficient.

---

[7] Thomas R. Schreiner, *40 Questions about Christians and Biblical Law* (Grand Rapids, MI: Kregel, 2010), 90. He also says, "Paul clearly teaches that Christians are no longer under the law covenant instituted under Moses." Ibid., 67.

[8] See Brian S. Rosner, *Paul and the Law: Keeping the Commandments of God*, New Studies in Biblical Theology, vol. 31 (Downers Grove, IL: InterVarsity Press, 2013). Rosner notes that it is striking that Paul "never once says that believers should walk according to the law." Ibid., 87.

But in the new covenant there are spiritual replacements for these physical sacrifices. Christians can "offer up a *sacrifice of praise* to God" (Heb. 13:15), and when they share with others in need and "do not neglect to do good and to *share what you have* . . . such *sacrifices* are pleasing to God" (v. 16). Paul uses similar sacrificial language when he writes that Christians should give their whole lives to God, saying, "Present your bodies as *a living sacrifice*, holy and acceptable to God, which is your spiritual worship" (Rom. 12:1). Paul also says that when the church at Philippi sent him a gift, this was "a fragrant offering, a *sacrifice* acceptable and pleasing to God" (Phil. 4:18). In addition, Christians themselves are a new temple, for Paul says, "*You are God's temple* and . . . God's Spirit dwells in you" (1 Cor. 3:16). And Peter also says that Christians are a new temple, "a spiritual house," and that they are "a holy priesthood, to offer *spiritual sacrifices* acceptable to God through Jesus Christ" (1 Pet. 2:5). There is no longer any need for priests descended from Levi because "you are a chosen race, a royal priesthood" (v. 9).

b. Christians No Longer Must Be Circumcised: Paul is adamant that if the Galatian Christians require circumcision as a sign of salvation, then they will have to be subject once again to the entire law of Moses, in which case the new covenant salvation earned by Christ will not be valid for them:

> Look: I, Paul, say to you that if you accept circumcision, Christ will be of no advantage to you. I testify again to every man who accepts circumcision that *he is obligated to keep the whole law.* You are severed from Christ, you who would be justified by the law; you have fallen away from grace. (Gal. 5:2–4)

When Paul began to preach from city to city that believers in Jesus Christ did not have to be circumcised, he was severely persecuted. But he refused to compromise the gospel in this way:

> But if I, brothers, still preach circumcision, why am I still being persecuted? In that case the offense of the cross has been removed. (Gal. 5:11)

In addition, the Jerusalem Council (Acts 15:1–29) came to a resolution that circumcision was not required for Christians, and thus clearly rebuked the claim of some Jewish Christians, who said, "Unless you are circumcised according to the custom of Moses, you cannot be saved" (v. 1).[9]

But just as with Old Testament sacrifices, so it is with circumcision: there is a spiritual counterpart in the new covenant. Paul can say to the Christians in Colossae, "*You were circumcised* with a circumcision made without hands, by putting off the body of

---

[9] Several other passages affirm that circumcision is not required for Christians (see 1 Cor. 7:18–19; Gal. 2:3; Phil. 3:2–3; Col. 2:11; Titus 1:10). We do read that Paul circumcised Timothy, but the verse goes on to explain that this was "because of the Jews that were in those places, for they all knew that his father was a Greek" (Acts 16:3). Paul had Timothy circumcised not to fulfill Old Testament law but so as to avoid giving unnecessary offense to Jewish people who knew that Timothy's mother was Jewish (v. 1).

flesh, by the circumcision of Christ" (Col. 2:11). He explains more fully in Romans that this circumcision is a change of heart, so that our hearts are no longer hardened toward God but responsive to the Holy Spirit, because "circumcision is a matter of the heart, by the Spirit, not by the letter" (Rom. 2:29; see also Jer. 4:4).

c. Christians No Longer Must Follow the Food Laws of the Old Testament: Mark says that Jesus "declared *all foods clean*" (Mark 7:19) when he taught that "whatever goes into a person from outside cannot defile him," but "what comes out of a person is what defiles him," such as "evil thoughts, sexual immorality, theft, murder, adultery, coveting," and so forth (vv. 18–21).

In a discussion about what foods Christians can eat, Paul says, "I know and am persuaded in the Lord Jesus that *nothing is unclean in itself*" (Rom. 14:14). He goes on to say:

> Do not, for the sake of food, destroy the work of God. *Everything is indeed clean*, but it is wrong for anyone to make another stumble by what he eats. (Rom. 14:20)

Paul tells the Corinthians that if they go to dinner at the home of an unbeliever, "eat whatever is set before you without raising any question on the ground of conscience" (1 Cor. 10:27). This would be unthinkable for a Jew under the Mosaic Law, who was bound by conscience to abide by Mosaic dietary rules.[10]

Paul's dramatic confrontation of Peter at Antioch came about over this very issue of Jewish dietary laws. Peter had been "eating with the Gentiles" (Gal. 2:12), no doubt eating some foods that were unclean by Mosaic dietary standards, but when "certain men came from James . . . [Peter] drew back and separated himself, fearing the circumcision party" (v. 12). So Paul spoke up:

> But when I saw that their conduct was not in step with the truth of the gospel, I said to Cephas before them all, "If you, though a Jew, live like a Gentile and not like a Jew, how can you force the Gentiles to live like Jews?" (Gal. 2:14)

Paul also writes to the Colossian Christians that they do not need to feel guilty about failing to observe Jewish dietary laws:

> Therefore let no one pass judgment on you in *questions of food and drink*, or with regard to a festival or a new moon or a Sabbath. These are a shadow of the things to come, but the substance belongs to Christ. (Col. 2:16–17)

Finally, Paul writes to Timothy that teaching people that they must abstain from certain foods is not part of the Christian faith but is the result of "deceitful spirits and teachings of demons" (1 Tim. 4:1), and it leads people to wrongly

---

[10] See also 1 Cor. 6:12; Titus 1:15.

> forbid marriage and require abstinence from foods that God created to be received with thanksgiving by those who believe and know the truth. For everything created by God is good, and nothing is to be rejected if it is received with thanksgiving, for it is made holy by the word of God and prayer. (1 Tim. 4:3–5)

It is clear, therefore, that Christians do not have to follow the food laws of the Mosaic covenant,[11] but should abstain from evil thoughts and deeds that come out of their hearts (Mark 7:18–21).

d. Christians No Longer Must Observe the Old Testament Sabbath and Other Old Testament Festivals: In several places, the New Testament is quite clear that observance of the Jewish Sabbath or other special days and festivals is no longer mandatory for Christians. Paul writes to the Romans:

> One person esteems *one day as better* than another, while another esteems *all days alike.* Each one should be fully convinced in his own mind. (Rom. 14:5)

Likewise, he writes to the Galatians:

> You observe *days* and months and seasons and years! I am afraid I may have labored over you in vain. (Gal. 4:10–11)

Paul explains quite explicitly in Colossians why Christians no longer have to observe special days and Jewish festivals. This is because these observances were looking forward to the full redemption that would come in the ministry of Jesus Christ. Once he arrived, those observances were no longer required:

> Therefore let no one pass judgment on you in questions of food and drink, or with regard to a *festival or a new moon or a Sabbath.* These are *a shadow of the things to come,* but the substance belongs to Christ. (Col. 2:16–17)

---

[11] Someone might object that the Jerusalem Council in Acts 15 decided to send a message to the church at Antioch that they should abstain from certain foods, for we read:

> For it has seemed good to the Holy Spirit and to us to lay on you no greater burden than these requirements: that you abstain from what has been sacrificed to idols, and from blood, and from what has been strangled, and from sexual immorality. If you keep yourselves from these, you will do well. Farewell. (Acts 15:28–29)

But this decision is best understood not as a partial imposition of the Mosaic laws on Christians, but as a wise and strategic concession so as not to give unnecessary offense to the Jewish people who would be listening to the gospel. This is clear when the list of things to abstain from is explained with this reason: "For from ancient generations Moses has had in every city those who proclaim him, for he is read every Sabbath in the synagogues" (Acts 15:21). In other words, there are many observant Jewish people in the synagogues, and eating certain foods will give needless offense. Thielman wisely says, "The Apostolic Decree more naturally plays the role of a pragmatic compromise.... The apostles and elders have made it easier for the most conservative Jewish Christians to associate with Gentile believers." *The Law and the New Testament,* 158; see also 174.

It is significant here that Paul includes "a Sabbath" in the same category as "food and drink" and "a festival or new moon,"[12] all of which were required in Jewish laws. But Paul explicitly says that no one should "pass judgment" on others for observing or not observing these things because they are just "a shadow."

Hebrews 4:1–11 develops a long argument that the Sabbath rest of the Old Testament was looking forward to the spiritual rest that would come with salvation in Christ in the New Testament, so that today "there remains a Sabbath rest for the people of God" (Heb. 4:9) and that Christians who trust in Christ actually enter into that spiritual Sabbath rest, "for whoever has entered God's rest has also rested from his works as God did from his" (v. 10). This is something that anyone can enter today, because he immediately adds, "Let us therefore strive to enter that rest" (v. 11). The Old Testament Sabbath day looked forward to the spiritual rest that Christ would earn for his people in his earthly ministry, death, and resurrection. (For further discussion of the way in which the Sabbath commandment applies to Christians today, see chap. 13, p. 342.)

e. Christians No Longer Must Follow Old Testament Laws Regulating the Civil Government of Israel: During the time of the Mosaic covenant established on Mount Sinai (Exodus 20), the people of Israel existed as a geographically and politically distinct nation among the nations of the world. For that reason, God gave rules for courts and judges, guidelines for the enforcement of laws by the police or army, lists of legal penalties, and other provisions that were necessary for the civil government of a nation to function.

But in the new covenant age, people become Christians from every nation. Christians are nowhere instructed to constitute or even attempt to constitute a geographically and politically distinct nation among the nations of the earth. Therefore, the New Testament instructs Christians to be subject to the civil governments under which they live:

> *Let every person be subject to the governing authorities.* For there is no authority except from God, and those that exist have been instituted by God. Therefore whoever resists the authorities resists what God has appointed, and those who resist will incur judgment. For rulers are not a terror to good conduct, but to bad. Would you have no fear of the one who is in authority? Then do what is good, and you will receive his approval, for he is God's servant for your good. But if you do wrong, be afraid, for he does not bear the sword in vain. For he is the servant of God, an avenger who carries out God's wrath on the wrongdoer. Therefore one must be in subjection, not only to avoid God's wrath but also for the sake of conscience. For because of this you also pay taxes, for the authorities are ministers of God, attending to this very thing. Pay to all what is owed to them: taxes to whom taxes are owed, revenue to whom

---

[12] Certain offerings were required in the old covenant at a new moon (Num. 29:6).

revenue is owed, respect to whom respect is owed, honor to whom honor is owed. (Rom. 13:1–7)

Be subject for the Lord's sake to every human institution, whether it be to *the emperor* as supreme, or to *governors* as sent by him to punish those who do evil and to praise those who do good. . . . Honor everyone. Love the brotherhood. Fear God. *Honor the emperor.*" (1 Pet. 2:13–14, 17)

Thielman rightly observes that Paul's "admonitions to submit to the Roman government (Rom. 13:1–7) implied the abrogation of the . . . civil parts of the law."[13]

Another indication that the civil government of the nation was to be distinct from the government over the church is that the early Christians chose their church leaders from among the people in the church, not from the Roman authorities ruling over the areas where they lived. Therefore, Paul sends instructions for choosing elders to Timothy (see 1 Tim. 3:1–7) and to Titus (see Titus 1:5–9), and does not suggest that the Roman government authorities should have any leadership roles in the church.

This arrangement seems so commonplace to us today, but it is in striking contrast to the system of government in the Mosaic covenant. There, Moses and later leaders such as Samuel, David, and Solomon were not only the leaders over the people of God (the old covenant "church"), but also the leaders of the government of the nation of Israel ("the state"). There was no separation of "church" and "state" in the Mosaic covenant. But the new covenant age is far different.

Schreiner agrees:

The notion that the civil laws for Israel should continue to function as the rules for nation-states today represents a fundamental misreading of the Scriptures. Believers are no longer under the law, for the law was given to Israel, which functioned as both a political and ecclesiastical community. No nation today occupies the place of Israel, for no nation can claim to be God's chosen nation.[14]

This distinction between the government of the church (the ecclesiastical government) and the government of the state (the civil government) was wonderfully established in principle by Jesus when his Jewish opponents (here, the Pharisees and Herodians) asked him, "Is it lawful to pay taxes to Caesar, or not?" (Matt. 22:17). Jesus's opponents were trying to trap him. If he said it was lawful to pay taxes to Caesar, they thought he would lose many followers among the Jews who hated their Roman oppressors. But if he said it was not lawful to pay taxes to Caesar, he could be accused of inciting rebellion against Rome and arrested. Then this incident followed:

---

[13] Thielman, *The Law and the New Testament*, 169. See also Schreiner, *40 Questions*, 92.

[14] Schreiner, *40 Questions*, 224.

> But Jesus, aware of their malice, said, "Why put me to the test, you hypocrites? Show me the coin for the tax." And they brought him a denarius. And Jesus said to them, "Whose likeness and inscription is this?" They said, "Caesar's." Then he said to them, "Therefore *render to Caesar the things that are Caesar's, and to God the things that are God's.*" When they heard it, they marveled. And they left him and went away. (Matt. 22:18–22)

By pointing out that Caesar's inscription was on the coin and then saying, "Render to Caesar the things that are Caesar's," Jesus clearly implied that paying taxes was right. It was an appropriate function of the Roman government to collect taxes, and Jesus's followers should comply with it.

But by mentioning two distinct categories, "the things that are Caesar's" and "the things that are God's," Jesus also implied that there is a realm of human activity that is outside of Caesar's control. The civil government does not rightfully rule over every aspect of life. There is another area of life, one in which the believer is responsible to God directly, not through the governing authority. Jesus did not specify which parts of life belong in each category, but by identifying the two categories he wisely established a foundation for distinguishing two different realms of human activity, each governed by different authorities.

Such a distinction between things that belong to Caesar and things that belong to God also provides an argument showing why no civil government today should attempt to enforce penalties for religious beliefs or activities (such as the Old Testament death penalty for blasphemy or for advocating the worship of other gods). It is not only that the entire Mosaic covenant has been terminated and no longer is enforceable today. It is also that, even if some parts of the Mosaic covenant can inform us about wise personal conduct today (see discussion below), these Mosaic laws do not show us what God intends for civil governments in the new covenant age, because no *civil* government simultaneously has authority over the spiritual life of the *church*.

3. Reasons Why the Mosaic Covenant Was Terminated. Some New Testament passages also explain why the Mosaic covenant was terminated when the new covenant began. Understanding these reasons is another factor that contributes to our ability to wisely apply old covenant teachings to our lives as Christians today.

a. The Mosaic Covenant Was Established by God Only for a Temporary Period: In his argument in Galatians 3, Paul uses the phrase "the law" to refer to the Mosaic covenant: "The law, which came 430 years afterward, does not annul a covenant previously ratified by God" (Gal. 3:17). According to Paul, the covenant under Moses came 430 years after the covenant with Abraham.

Then comes this key verse:

> Why then the law? It was added because of transgressions, *until the offspring should come* to whom the promise had been made. (Gal. 3:19)

Paul is saying here that the law was given by God for a certain time, that is, until Christ ("the offspring" that God promised to Abraham) would come.

In the next few verses, Paul makes clear that we are no longer under this Mosaic Law. He says, "The law was our guardian *until Christ came*, . . . but now that faith has come, we are no longer under a guardian" (Gal. 3:24–25). Therefore, we are no longer under the Mosaic Law. It was given to show us our sin and to restrain our sin (as a "guardian" and "because of transgressions") until Christ came.

b. The Mosaic Covenant Was Intended to Be Fulfilled by Christ: Paul says that "Christ is the end of the law for righteousness to everyone who believes" (Rom. 10:4). Here the word translated "end" is the Greek word *telos*, which can mean either "termination, conclusion" or "goal." Paul probably intends his readers to understand both senses. The law pointed to Christ as the One who would fulfill it, and Christ brought a termination to the law as a way of obtaining righteousness (see Rom. 10:3–6).

Jesus's teaching in the Sermon on the Mount contains a crucial passage on the relationship between him and the Old Testament law:

> Do not think that I have come to abolish the Law or the Prophets; I have not come to abolish them but to fulfill them. For truly, I say to you, until heaven and earth pass away, not an iota, not a dot, will pass from the Law until all is accomplished. (Matt. 5:17–18)

Jesus "fulfilled" the Old Testament law in several ways. He perfectly obeyed it, never once committing any violation of its laws (see Luke 4:13; John 8:46; Rom. 8:3; 2 Cor. 5:21; Heb. 4:15; 1 Pet. 2:22; 1 John 3:5).

In another sense, he "fulfilled" many of the Old Testament laws by actions that showed the true spiritual purpose for which they were intended. He fulfilled the sacrificial laws by becoming the perfect sacrifice. He fulfilled the laws and regulations about priests by becoming our Great High Priest. He fulfilled the law about circumcision by the "circumcision of Christ," which gives us new hearts that are responsive to God's will (see Col. 2:11). He fulfilled the Sabbath law by bringing us eternal spiritual rest (see Matt. 11:28; Heb. 4:9–10). And he fulfilled the Old Testament laws for civil government by establishing for himself a kingdom that is not of this world (John 18:36; see also Phil. 3:20).

c. The Mosaic Covenant Was Established to Govern God's People While They Constituted a Separate Jewish Nation before Christ Came, but It Was Not Intended for a Time When God's People Would Have No Nation of Their Own but Would Live as Citizens of All Nations: As mentioned above, the church does not constitute a separate nation or political entity, nor should it try to establish one for itself, but Christians are to "be subject to the governing authorities" (Rom. 13:1). There is now a difference between church and state, a difference between "the things that are Caesar's" and "the things that are God's." Therefore, the church does not exist as a nation set apart from all the other nations of the world. People from all nations now become part of the church worldwide.

d. The Mosaic Law Could Not Impart Spiritual Life or Empower People to Obey It: Paul explains a shortcoming of the Mosaic Law when he shows that it could not give true spiritual life:

> Is the law then contrary to the promises of God? Certainly not! For if a law had been given that could give life, then righteousness would indeed be by the law. (Gal. 3:21)

Paul implies the same thing when he contrasts the law with the new covenant work of the Spirit:

> For the law of the Spirit of life has set you free in Christ Jesus from the law of sin and death. For God has done *what the law, weakened by the flesh, could not do.* By sending his own Son in the likeness of sinful flesh and for sin, he condemned sin in the flesh, in order that the righteous requirement of the law might be fulfilled in us, who walk not according to the flesh but according to the Spirit. (Rom. 8:2–4)

For all of these reasons, then, God established the Mosaic covenant for a temporary purpose, and when that purpose was fulfilled in the life, death, and resurrection of Christ, the Mosaic covenant was no longer in effect. It was terminated.

B. THE MOSAIC COVENANT WAS STILL IN EFFECT DURING JESUS'S EARTHLY MINISTRY

1. A New Covenant Takes Effect Only at Death. As was explained in the earlier section (p. 211), the new covenant did not take effect until Christ died, "For a will [covenant] takes effect only at death" (Heb. 9:17).[15]

2. Jesus Never Violated Any Law of the Mosaic Covenant, though He Did Violate the Highly Detailed Additional Rules Made by the Rabbis, Especially Respecting the Sabbath. Jesus was "born under the law" (Gal. 4:4), and he was blameless for his entire life as far as the laws of God in the Old Testament were concerned. It is unthinkable that he could have directly violated any of the Mosaic laws and then been able to say to his hostile Jewish opponents, "Which of you convicts me of sin?" (John 8:46). He received no answer. (See also Luke 4:13; John 8:46; Rom. 8:3; 2 Cor. 5:21; Heb. 4:15; 1 Pet. 2:22; 1 John 3:5).

---

[15] Thielman also concludes that the new covenant was "instituted at Christ's death." *Theology of the New Testament: A Canonical and Synthetic Approach* (Grand Rapids, MI: Zondervan, 2005), 365.

For example, there is no record of Jesus eating pork, failing to offer the required sacrifices, or failing to observe the specified Jewish festivals.

Schreiner notes that Jesus "lived under the Old Testament law." He also says:

> Strictly speaking, Jesus does not clearly abolish the Sabbath, nor does he violate its stipulations. Yet the focus on regulations that is evident in Jubilees, Qumran, and the Mishnah is absent in Jesus's teaching.[16]

But Jesus was quick to criticize and contradict the overly harsh traditions that had been built up by the Jewish teachers but were not actually part of the Jewish Scriptures. He said, "*For the sake of your tradition* you have made void the Word of God" (Matt. 15:6). And when Jesus told his disciples to beware of the "leaven" of the Pharisees and Sadducees, "they understood that he did not tell them to beware of the leaven of bread, but of the *teaching* of the Pharisees and Sadducees" (16:12).

In fact, several passages in the Gospels show Jesus as completely obedient to Old Testament laws, when rightly understood.

For example, after he healed a victim of leprosy, he told the man, "Go, show yourself to the priest and offer the gift that Moses commanded, for a proof to them" (Matt. 8:4), thus telling him to fulfill the Old Testament law.

When some tax collectors challenged Peter that Jesus was not paying the two-drachma tax, Jesus told Peter how to pay it and thus comply with the law (Matt. 17:24–27). When he cleansed the temple, he was restoring the temple to its proper function, driving out those who had turned it into a hubbub of commercial activity and reminding them of its true purpose: "My house shall be called a house of prayer" (21:13).

He rebuked the scribes and Pharisees about scrupulous attention to detail, not saying that such attention was wrong when it concerned parts of the Old Testament law, but that they were putting too much focus on less important matters of the law:

> Woe to you, scribes and Pharisees, hypocrites! For you tithe mint and dill and cumin, and have neglected the weightier matters of the law: justice and mercy and faithfulness. These you ought to have done, *without neglecting the others*. (Matt. 23:23)

When Jesus said, "These you ought to have done, without neglecting the others," he implied that they should have pursued justice, mercy, and faithfulness, and *also* tithed their spices as they were doing. The law required both.

At the end of his ministry, Jesus ate a Passover meal with his disciples, as the Mosaic Law instructed (see Matt. 26:17–29).

---

[16] Schreiner, *40 Questions*, 211. Jubilees, the Qumran documents, and the Mishnah are Jewish writings that were produced later than the books of the Hebrew Old Testament.

3. But Much of Jesus's Teaching Was about the Kingdom of God, with Application Both to the Time of Jesus's Earthly Ministry and to the New Covenant Age. The expression "kingdom of God" occurs 53 times in the Gospels, and the equivalent expression "kingdom of heaven" occurs 32 times in the Gospel of Matthew, giving a total of 85 times this idea is mentioned in the Gospels. The kingdom of God is the reign of God in people's hearts and lives, and it was increasingly making its presence known throughout Jesus's earthly ministry. Although Jesus lived under the old covenant, the coming of the kingdom of God was like new wine that had to be put in fresh wineskins (Matt. 9:17). This helps us understand why so much of Jesus's teaching is directly applicable to our lives as Christians today, even though Jesus gave the teaching while he was still living under the period of the old covenant.

C. A CRITIQUE OF "THEONOMY"

An alternative view of the relevance of the Mosaic Law today is promoted by the followers of a position called "theonomy." (The word *theonomy* means "God's law" and is derived from two Greek words, *theos*, "God," and *nomos*, "law.") The most widely read advocate of theonomy is Greg Bahnsen, who articulated and defended his viewpoint in the book *Five Views on Law and Gospel*[17] and more extensively in his book *Theonomy in Christian Ethics*.[18] Bahnsen argues that the "moral" and "civil" laws of the Mosaic covenant remain in force today, and only the "ceremonial" portions of the law were abrogated by the coming of the new covenant (see my discussion of these three divisions of the law, p. 248). Here are some of his statements of this position:

> The *moral* instructions found in the law—God's commandments revealed in the Old Testament—have not been laid aside along with the redemptive instructions for circumcision, priesthood, sacrifice, and the temple.[19]

> God's holy and good law is never wrong in what it demands. It is "perfect" (Deut. 32:4; Ps. 19:7; James 1:25), just like the Lawgiver himself (Matt. 5:48). It is a transcript of his moral character.[20]

> If the moral stipulations of the Mosaic revelation are axiomatically good and universal in character and are upheld by Christ in their moral validity even in the least commandment, unless God reveals otherwise, then *all civil magistrates today must be guided and regulated by those laws*.[21]

---

[17] Bahnsen, "The Theonomic Reformed Approach to Law and Gospel," in *Five Views on Law and Gospel*, 93–143.
[18] Greg Bahnsen, *Theonomy in Christian Ethics* (Nutley, NJ: Craig, 1977).
[19] Bahnsen, "The Theonomic Reformed Approach to Law and Gospel," 99, emphasis in original.
[20] Ibid., 109.
[21] Ibid., 125, emphasis added.

> Civil magistrates . . . need God's law to inform them how and where God's wrath is to be worked out in the state. Magistrates who repudiate *the penal directives of that law* are therefore rebelling against being God's servants.[22]

> The civil precepts of the Old Testament (standing "judicial" laws) are a model of perfect social justice for all cultures, *even in the punishment of criminals.*[23]

Bahnsen's claim that the *moral laws* of the Mosaic covenant remain in force today is not unusual, for it is the position most commonly held by contemporary Reformed theologians, a position that is affirmed in the Westminster Confession of Faith (see 19.3, 4, 5, which I quote later, p. 249). But his claim that the *civil laws* of the Mosaic covenant should be enforced by civil governments today, *including the penalties* of those laws, has been extremely controversial and widely criticized, particularly with respect to his support for instituting the death penalty for a wide range of crimes as specified in the Mosaic covenant.

Bahnsen's position leads him to argue:

> Civil magistrates today are under *obligation to execute all those who commit capital crimes* as defined by God's authoritative law.[24]

He then goes on to specify the capital crimes that he thinks should be subject to the death penalty in modern societies, because they were capital crimes in the Mosaic covenant. He includes the following: murder, adultery, unchastity, sodomy, bestiality, homosexuality, rape, incest, incorrigibility in children (with reference to Ex. 21:15–17, striking or cursing one's father or mother, and Deut. 21:20–21, being a stubborn and rebellious son), Sabbath breaking, kidnapping, apostasy, witchcraft, sorcery, false pretension to prophecy, and blasphemy.[25] Bahnsen says, "The Lord looks with so much scorn upon these crimes that he commands the state to execute those who commit them."[26]

I disagree strongly with theonomy, for several reasons:

1. A Failure to Recognize the Termination of the Entire Mosaic Covenant. My argument in section A of this chapter (p. 210) constitutes a significant objection to theonomy. Bahnsen argues that the moral and civil laws of the Mosaic covenant are still obligatory today, but, as I argued above, the New Testament authors repeatedly affirm that *the entire Mosaic covenant has been terminated*, so we no longer live under that covenant. Bahnsen's claim that only certain parts of the Mosaic covenant have been terminated is not persuasive in light of the frequent New Testament claim that the entire Mosaic covenant itself has come to an end.

---

[22] Ibid., 132, emphasis added.
[23] Ibid., 142, emphasis added.
[24] Bahnsen, *Theonomy*, 442.
[25] Ibid., 445.
[26] Ibid.

Theonomists often claim Matthew 5:17–18 for support, arguing that Jesus did not "abolish" the Old Testament law, not even an iota or a dot of it:

> Do not think that I have come to abolish the Law or the Prophets; I have not come to abolish them but to fulfill them. For truly, I say to you, until heaven and earth pass away, not an iota, not a dot, will pass from the Law until all is accomplished. (Matt. 5:17–18)

But in this very passage Jesus explained what he was going to do instead of abolishing the Old Testament: He was going to "fulfill" it, and he did so in several ways (as I explained above, p. 222). It is clear that he did not *abolish* any part of the Old Testament, because it still remained the Bible that was used by the apostles in the early church (see 2 Tim. 3:16–17). But Jesus *fulfilled* the law by establishing a new covenant that superseded the old covenant, and that meant the old covenant was no longer in force, as the apostles clearly taught (see discussion above, p. 211).

I agree that "not an iota, not a dot" should be deleted from the Old Testament today, but we must interpret and apply it rightly by understanding that *the Mosaic covenant was given for the people of Israel for a particular time*, and its provisions are not directly binding on us or on civil governments today. We can still gain wisdom from every part of the Old Testament, but only when we read it with the knowledge that the Mosaic covenant is something in the past, something that has now been terminated.

2. A Failure to Recognize the Unique Historical and Governmental Context of the Mosaic Laws. Advocates of theonomy fail to recognize that God's wise laws for the civil government of Israel as a nation *then* are not necessarily God's wise laws for the civil governments of secular nations *now*. This is a fundamental error, a failure to recognize the uniqueness of the redemptive-historical context in which the Mosaic laws were given.

Bahnsen argues that "the Bible repeatedly illustrates that the pagan nations were judged by the same moral standard as the Mosaic law,"[27] but this does not establish Bahnsen's position. I agree that all people are accountable to God for the basic moral standards that he has written on every person's heart (see Rom. 2:14–15), but that fact, which all Christians everywhere acknowledge, does not demonstrate Bahnsen's claim, namely, that secular governments in the time of the Old Testament were responsible for enforcing *all the specific details of the civil laws and penalties given to Israel in the Mosaic covenant*. It is noteworthy that Bahnsen here gives no examples of God's prophets rebuking any Gentile nations for failure to carry out the specific civil penalties for crimes under the Mosaic Law (such as the death penalty for striking one's father or mother, for breaking the Sabbath, and so forth).

The entire historical context surrounding the establishment of the Mosaic covenant

---

[27] Bahnsen, "The Theonomic Reformed Approach to Law and Gospel," 112.

(Exodus 20–23) shows that these laws were given specifically to the nation of Israel for that period of time. Nothing in the rest of the Old Testament suggests that God expected Gentile rulers to enforce those laws in their nations as well, for they were not part of the Mosaic covenant. And nothing in the New Testament suggests that God expected the secular Roman Empire or any other government to enforce the detailed Mosaic laws that he had given specifically to the nation of Israel—in fact, as already noted, the New Testament repeatedly teaches that the Mosaic covenant has been terminated.

In addition, as I argued above (p. 219), enforcing penalties for religious crimes such as blasphemy and public apostasy is contrary to Jesus's teaching that in this present age "Caesar" (the civil government) does not have jurisdiction over "the things that are God's" (Matt. 22:21).

3. Harsh and Intemperate Attitudes. Vern Poythress, a remarkably gracious and generous critic of theonomy, nevertheless comments on an argumentative tendency among many supporters of theonomy:

> A considerable number of Christians have received the impression that in practice theonomists are contentious and quarrelsome, a continuous source of aggravation, fights, wounds, and church splits. . . . The repeated recurrence of the difficulties suggests . . . that something within the movement itself somehow unleashes or encourages sin of this particular kind.[28]

John Frame, another generous and sometimes appreciative critic, says something similar:

> I have come to the conclusion that theonomy is a good case study of how theological ideas should *not* be introduced. The sharp polemics of the theonomic movement (and, to be sure, of its critics in return) have been, in my view, quite unnecessary and indeed counterproductive to its own purposes.[29]

This has also been my personal experience with advocates of theonomy. I remember in particular observing from a distance a conversation between one of the world's leading representatives of the theonomy movement and another man who was disagreeing with him. Soon the conversation turned ugly, with the theonomist actually shouting angrily at the other man. As I turned away quietly, I thought, "This is not the wisdom that comes from above." The passage that came to mind was this:

> But *the wisdom from above* is first pure, then peaceable, gentle, open to reason, full of mercy and good fruits, impartial and sincere. And a harvest of righteousness is sown in peace by those who make peace. (James 3:17–18)

[28] Vern S. Poythress, *The Shadow of Christ in the Law of Moses* (Phillipsburg, NJ: P&R, 1991), 359.
[29] John M. Frame, *The Doctrine of the Christian Life: A Theology of Lordship* (Phillipsburg, NJ: P&R, 2008), 223.

If it is true that divisiveness, contentions, and church splits frequently follow in the wake of those who advocate theonomy, then it is appropriate also to evaluate this viewpoint from the standpoint of the fruit it bears: "You will recognize them by their fruits" (Matt. 7:16).[30]

4. Bringing Reproach on the Gospel. I doubt that supporters of theonomy realize the extent to which their writing and speaking, rather than advancing the gospel of Jesus Christ and Christian influence on government, actually have the effect of turning people away from the Christian gospel. To understand what I mean, consider the outrage and revulsion that nearly everyone in Western societies feels today toward radical Islam when its representatives actually execute people whom they find guilty of adultery or blasphemy against Mohammed. Many peaceful Muslims insist that "this is not what Islam really teaches," but they know that not everyone is fully convinced. Like it or not, the worldwide image of Islam as a whole is deeply tarnished by this behavior of radical Muslims.

We need to recognize that this reaction to the extremes of Islam is similar to the reaction of many non-Christians when they find that within the evangelical Christian movement there exists a contingent that actually advocates *the death penalty* for private consensual sexual acts such as adultery, fornication, and homosexual conduct,[31] and for religious crimes such as public blasphemy, apostasy (advocating false religions), and Sabbath breaking.[32] This extreme view receives a disproportionate amount of coverage in the secular media, distorting people's perception of Christians in general.

For this reason, it seems to me that the theonomy movement actually brings reproach on the gospel of Christ. Its emphasis on a divine requirement for civil governments to impose the death penalty on such a wide variety of sins is contrary to the nature of the church age, in which our task is to win people to Christ, not by the civil government penalizing public blasphemy and the promotion of other religions, but by persuasion and by the power of the gospel: "For God *did not send his Son into the world to condemn the world*, but in order that the world might be saved through him" (John 3:17).

Therefore, I wondered for a time whether I should even include a discussion of theonomy in this ethics book, because I did not want to give it any further visibility or

---

[30] I am not claiming that theonomists themselves are not Christians, but that their distinctive position is wrong, and one indication of that is the harmful fruit that it bears.

[31] I argue elsewhere that private sexual acts such as adultery, fornication, and homosexual conduct, while morally wrong according to biblical standards, should not be punished by civil laws. Earlier in the history of the United States, several states had laws against fornication (sex between unmarried opposite-sex partners), for example, but these laws were seldom or never enforced. See Wayne Grudem, *Politics—According to the Bible: A Comprehensive Resource for Understanding Modern Political Issues in Light of Scripture* (Grand Rapids, MI: Zondervan, 2010), 237–38.

[32] See, for example, how the theonomy movement is the target of non-Christian writers who quote its extreme positions in order to reject the idea of Christian influence on politics and government generally, as in Michelle Goldberg, *Kingdom Coming: The Rise of Christian Nationalism* (New York: W. W. Norton, 2007).

credibility. I finally decided I must do so because I consider it not just benignly mistaken but genuinely harmful to the cause of Christ in the work of proclaiming the gospel and bringing Christian influence to governments in this new covenant age.

At this point a theonomist might object, "But don't you believe that God's law is holy and wise, and that the Bible's teachings should influence civil governments today?" In response I would say that I do think that sins such as adultery, homosexuality, and blasphemy are violations of God's holy law (see chaps. 11, 28, and 33), and, like all other sins, they make people guilty before God and worthy of eternal punishment (Rom. 6:23). In addition, I have written an entire book advocating significant Christian influence on civil government today.[33] And elsewhere in this book I advocate the use of the death penalty for premeditated murder (see chap. 18). But I do that not on the basis of the Mosaic covenant (as theonomists do) but on the basis of the teachings of Genesis 9 and Romans 13 (which are not part of the Mosaic covenant). Therefore, my disagreement with theonomy is *not* a disagreement about the holiness or goodness of God's moral law, but about the direct applicability of the Mosaic covenant to civil governments today.[34]

D. THE NEW TESTAMENT AUTHORS TEACH US HOW TO USE THE OLD TESTAMENT FOR ETHICAL INSTRUCTION

How exactly did the New Testament authors come to understand how they should apply the Old Testament to questions of ethical conduct for Christians in the new covenant? The answer is that (1) the apostles were taught by Jesus during his earthly ministry and (2) they had additional guidance from the Holy Spirit after Jesus ascended to heaven.

1. Jesus Taught His Apostles How to Interpret the Old Testament Correctly for Ethics.

a. Some of Jesus's Teaching about the Old Testament Is Recorded in the Gospels: At several points in the Gospels we find Jesus teaching about how to interpret the Old Testament correctly, as when he said, "The Sabbath was made for man, not man for the Sabbath" (Mark 2:27). Another example is seen when he applied a statement from Isaiah 56:7, "My house shall be called a house of prayer," to his actions of cleansing the temple (Matt. 21:13).

The six sets of "antitheses" in Matthew 5:21–48 also show Jesus's teaching about the

---

[33] See Grudem, *Politics—According to the Bible*.

[34] For more extensive critiques of theonomy, see Poythress, *The Shadow of Christ in the Law of Moses*, 311–61; Frame, *The Doctrine of the Christian Life*, 217–24, 957–76; William S. Barker and W. Robert Godfrey, eds., *Theonomy: A Reformed Critique* (Grand Rapids, MI: Zondervan, 1991); H. Wayne House and Thomas Ice, eds., *Dominion Theology: Blessing or Curse? An Analysis of Christian Reconstructionism* (Sisters, OR: Multnomah, 1988); Norman L. Geisler, *Christian Ethics: Contemporary Issues and Options*, 2nd ed. (Grand Rapids, MI: Baker, 2010), 205–14; Christopher J. H. Wright, *Old Testament Ethics for the People of God* (Downers Grove, IL: InterVarsity Press, 2004), 403–8.

Old Testament. Jesus begins each topic with the statement "You have heard that it was said to those of old . . ." (Matt. 5:21) or a similar expression. These six units cover six topics: murder (vv. 21–26), adultery (vv. 27–30), divorce (vv. 31–32), oaths (vv. 33–37), retaliation (vv. 38–42), and loving one's enemies (vv. 43–48).

Some people think that Jesus is correcting Old Testament laws here, but it is significant that three of the six statements that "you have heard" contain alterations or additions to the Old Testament law. The most blatant of these is this:

> You have heard that it was said, "You shall love your neighbor and hate your enemy." (Matt. 5:43)

The Old Testament does say, "Love your neighbor," but it nowhere says, "Hate your enemy"![35] Jesus is quoting some Jewish tradition, some teaching of the rabbis, or perhaps even a popular saying that had arisen in the time after the completion of the Old Testament Scriptures.

Similarly, in the other five units, Jesus is *correcting popular misinterpretations and misunderstandings* of the teaching of the Old Testament. Even when he quotes the Old Testament exactly (as in "You have heard that it was said, 'You shall not commit adultery,'" Matt. 5:27), Jesus is correcting a superficial understanding of the commandment whereby people thought that it prohibited only the actual physical act of adultery, thus minimizing the force of the command. Jesus shows, however, that the command goes much deeper and requires purity of heart (see Matt. 5:28).[36]

Another reason we know that Jesus is not correcting the Old Testament itself in Matthew 5:21–48 is that the expression, "You have heard that it was said" (Matt. 5:21, 27, 33, 38, 43; cf. v. 31 with a similar expression), never occurs anywhere else in the teachings of Jesus or in the rest of the New Testament to introduce quotations from the Old Testament. And Jesus chooses his words very carefully. He does not even affirm that "it was said to those of old," but just *you have heard* that it was said to those of old" (vv. 21, 33). This expression is far different from the authoritative way in which Jesus and the New Testament authors normally quote Scripture, with such definitive statements as

---

[35] It is true that some passages in the Old Testament, particularly regarding the conquest of Canaan, include commands to put unbelieving enemies to death. But nowhere does God command the people of Israel to hate their enemies. This is simply not a statement of anything the Old Testament says.

[36] Douglas Moo objects: "It is unlikely that Jesus is asserting the 'true' meaning of the original prohibitions. Nothing in the Old Testament suggests that anger and lust were included in the prohibitions of, respectively, murder and adultery." "The Law of Christ as the Fulfillment of the Law of Moses: A Modified Lutheran View," in *Five Views on Law and Gospel*, series ed. Stanley N. Gundry (Grand Rapids, MI: Zondervan, 1996), 348. But coveting one's neighbor's wife was explicitly prohibited in the Ten Commandments (Ex. 20:17), and this surely implied a prohibition against lust, not merely against adultery. Similarly, the prohibition against coveting one's neighbor's ox or donkey "or anything that is your neighbor's" (v. 17) implied not only that stealing was wrong, but that it was wrong to *want* to steal. Therefore, it seems that the tenth commandment gave a clear signal that God was asking purity of heart as well as actions in all of the commandments, and Jesus was making that explicit.

"It is written" (4:4, and frequently in the New Testament), "Scripture says" (Rom. 9:17; 10:11), and so forth.[37]

Therefore, I agree with Schreiner's statement regarding Matthew 5:21–48: "In these particular verses Jesus corrected misinterpretations of the Mosaic law. . . . Jesus explicated the true meaning of the law and corrected erroneous interpretations."[38]

b. Some of Jesus's Teaching about the Old Testament Was Not Recorded in the Gospels but Is Reflected in the Teaching of the Apostles in Acts and the Epistles: After Jesus's resurrection, he continued to teach his disciples, as in the conversation on the road to Emmaus, in which, "beginning with Moses and all the Prophets, he interpreted to them in all the Scriptures the things concerning himself" (Luke 24:27). This is just one example of the way in which he appeared to his disciples and taught them during the 40 days after he rose from the grave:

> In the first book, O Theophilus, I have dealt with all that Jesus began to do and teach, until the day when he was taken up, *after he had given commands through the Holy Spirit to the apostles* whom he had chosen. He presented himself alive to them after his suffering by many proofs, appearing to them during forty days and *speaking about the kingdom of God.* (Acts 1:1–3)

In addition to this post-resurrection teaching, the disciples were able to draw on other teachings of Jesus that they had heard during his three years of earthly ministry. That no doubt included much more content than is recorded in the four Gospels alone.

---

[37] I do not find it to be a persuasive objection that Matthew elsewhere uses an aorist passive form of the same verb (*legō*) to note that Old Testament prophecies were fulfilled, as in Matt. 1:22: "All this took place to fulfill what the Lord had spoken [Greek, *to rhēthen*, aorist passive participle of *legō*] by the prophet." (I am differing at this point with my friend Frank Thielman in his otherwise excellent book *The Law and the New Testament*, 51–52, 73.)

I would say in response that such expressions are different in two important ways. First, Matthew specifies that something was actually said by a prophet or by the Lord through a prophet, not merely "you have heard" that it was said. Second, the form of expression is different, for all of Matthew's statements about prophecies use an aorist participle as a substantive with a definite article proceeding it (here, Greek *to rhēthen*). But in the statements in Matthew 5, the expression uses a finite verb: "you have heard that it was said [Greek, *hoti errethē*, aorist passive indicative third singular, different from a participle used as a substantive]." The expressions are different. Moreover, the word *legō* is extremely common (it appears 2,353 times in the New Testament), so its use to refer to Scripture in other kinds of expressions is not a weighty argument.

Therefore Jesus is not correcting the Old Testament in Matthew 5:21–48, for in three of the six units he gives statements that are found nowhere in the Old Testament, and he uses an introductory formula ("You have heard that it was said . . .") that does not specify anything written in Scripture and that nowhere else is used to introduce statements from Scripture.

[38] Schreiner, *40 Questions*, 165; see his fuller argument in 165–69, including discussion of the specific quotations. Other interpreters who agree that Jesus is not correcting the Old Testament itself but misinterpretations of the Old Testament include John Murray, *Principles of Conduct: Aspects of Biblical Ethics* (Grand Rapids, MI: Eerdmans, 1957), 157–80; also D. A. Carson, "Matthew," in *Matthew & Mark (Revised Edition)*, vol. 9 in EBC, ed. Tremper Longman III and David E. Garland (Grand Rapids, MI: Zondervan, 2010), 180–81.

In addition, Jesus had promised that the Holy Spirit would help them to remember accurately those things that he had taught them:

> But the Helper, the Holy Spirit, whom the Father will send in my name, he will teach you all things and *bring to your remembrance all that I have said to you*. (John 14:26)

2. The Apostles Had Further Teaching Directly from the Guidance of the Holy Spirit. Jesus not only promised that the Holy Spirit would enable the apostles to *remember* accurately what he had taught them; he also promised that the Holy Spirit would continue to teach them:

> When the Spirit of truth comes, *he will guide you into all the truth*, for he will not speak on his own authority, but *whatever he hears he will speak*, and he will declare to you the things that are to come. (John 16:13)

3. The Result Is That the Apostles Spoke with the Authority of the Lord. As a result of these influences, the apostles were abundantly equipped to understand the teaching of the Old Testament correctly and to apply it wisely to the question of living lives that are pleasing to God in the time of the new covenant. Sometimes they even claim explicitly that they are speaking with the Lord's authority, as when Paul writes to the church at Corinth:

> If anyone thinks that he is a prophet, or spiritual, he should acknowledge that *the things I am writing to you are a command of the Lord*. (1 Cor. 14:37)

Peter says something similar:

> You should remember the predictions of the holy prophets and *the commandment of the Lord and Savior through your apostles*. (2 Pet. 3:2)

4. "The Law of Christ" and Several Other Expressions in the New Testament Refer to the Entire Body of Christian Teaching about a Life Pleasing to God. Sometimes the New Testament writers refer to the collection of standards by which Christians should guide their daily lives as "the law of Christ." Paul says that he is not "under the law" (1 Cor. 9:20, referring to the law of Moses), but in the next verse he clarifies this by saying:

> To those outside the law I became as one outside the law (not being outside the law of God but under *the law of Christ*) that I might win those outside the law. (1 Cor. 9:21)

Elsewhere he says, "Bear one another's burdens, and so fulfill the *law of Christ*" (Gal. 6:2).

The content of this "law of Christ" is best understood to be all that Jesus had taught about ethical living, including both his teaching about the Old Testament and any additional teaching that gave more completeness to New Testament ethical instructions. It would also include Jesus's own life example, since the New Testament authors sometimes speak of imitating Christ in our conduct (see 1 Cor. 11:1; 1 Thess. 1:6; 1 John 2:6).[39] Therefore, "the law of Christ" under which New Testament Christians were to live forms a fitting new covenant counterpart to the "law of Moses" from which they were freed (see Acts 13:39).

Another expression representing this body of ethical teaching is "the law of God." Paul said he is not "outside the law of God" (1 Cor. 9:21; see also Rom. 7:22, 25, where Paul views the law of God positively).

Another expression is "the commandments of God." Paul says, "For neither circumcision counts for anything nor uncircumcision, but *keeping the commandments of God*" (1 Cor. 7:19). It is significant here that Paul dismisses circumcision as something not required, but views "keeping the commandments of God" as something different from the law about circumcision. This is another indication that "the commandments of God" for Paul did not mean the laws of the Mosaic covenant, but rather all the New Testament ethical teachings that are significant for the Christian life. (The idea of keeping God's "commandments" is also found in 1 John 3:22, 24; 5:2–3; 2 John 6; Rev. 12:17; 14:12).

Another way the New Testament speaks about its ethical teachings is to call them the "commandments" of Jesus. These expressions occur only in John's Gospel and John's Epistles, where they refer to Christian ethical standards:

> If you love me, *you will keep my commandments*. (John 14:15)

> *Whoever has my commandments and keeps them*, he it is who loves me. And he who loves me will be loved by my Father, and I will love him and manifest myself to him. (John 14:21)

> And by this we know that we have come to know him, if we keep *his commandments*. (1 John 2:3; see also v. 4)

James calls this set of standards for Christian conduct "the perfect law, the law of liberty" (James 1:25; see also 2:12). He also calls it "the royal law" (2:8).

5. Specific Ways in Which the New Testament Authors Understand the Entire Old Testament as a Valuable Source of Ethical Wisdom. Although the New Testament authors repeatedly affirm that Christians are no longer under the Mosaic covenant and the Mosaic Law, they also affirm a complementary truth, namely, that there is *much valuable wisdom* to be gained from the words of God in the Old Testament. And this is not merely man-centered "wisdom" of the type found in modern self-help books, but wisdom that understands the kinds of actions, attitudes, and personal character traits that are pleasing or displeasing to God for all time.[40]

---

[39] Thielman rightly says, "For Paul, therefore, the law of Christ was Jesus's own ethical teaching and example." *The Law and the New Testament*, 19.

[40] I find myself in substantial agreement with Dorsey, "The Law of Moses and the Christian," 321–34. Dorsey states his thesis boldly: "Legally, none of the 613 stipulations of the Sinaitic covenant are binding

In a famous passage, Paul explains that every part of Scripture, including the entire Old Testament, comes from God and is profitable for teaching us how to live:

> *All Scripture* is breathed out by God and *profitable* for teaching, for reproof, for correction, and *for training in righteousness*, that the man of God may be complete, equipped for every good work. (2 Tim. 3:16–17)

Elsewhere, after quoting Psalm 69:9 (part of the Wisdom Literature of the Old Testament), Paul broadens the scope of what he says is useful for us to include the entire Old Testament, saying it was all written "for our instruction":

> For *whatever was written in former days was written for our instruction*, that through endurance and through the encouragement of *the Scriptures* we might have hope. (Rom. 15:4)

Finally, in referring to a specific historical section of the Old Testament, Paul says:

> Now these things happened to them as an example, but *they were written down for our instruction*, on whom the end of the ages has come. (1 Cor. 10:11)

Paul apparently can take any section of the Old Testament Historical Books and Wisdom Literature (not just the legal codes) and say that it was written down in Scripture "for our instruction" in the New Testament age. And though Paul insists that the Mosaic covenant has been terminated, he also clearly affirms that "the law is holy, and the commandment is holy and righteous and good" (Rom. 7:12).

Therefore, all types of literature found in the Old Testament (Law, Historical Books, Wisdom Literature, Prophetic Books) can be useful for us in seeking to understand the kind of life that is pleasing to God. In the *laws* of the Mosaic covenant, God gave the people of Israel not only regulations about ritual sacrifices and practices that would mark them as distinct from the nations, but also instructions regarding the ordinary conduct of life. Inevitably, God's instructions included some commandments that applied *only to Israel* for that particular time and place, and other commandments (for example, commandments against murder, adultery, stealing, and lying) that defined God's boundaries of conduct for *human life generally*, for all people and all periods of human life on earth. The task of sorting out which commandments belonged to which categories was carried out by the apostles as they had been taught by Jesus and under the guidance of the Holy Spirit.[41]

---

upon NT Christians, including the so-called moral laws, while in a revelatory and pedagogical sense all 613 are binding upon us, including all the ceremonial and civic laws." Ibid., 325.

[41] Frame rightly says, "The student of the Mosaic law must think through each statute to determine what it means, asking why God gave that statute to Israel. Did God give it simply as justice? As a type of Christ? As a way to remind Israel of their special covenant? Or some combination of these? Students of the law must think through many possibilities." *The Doctrine of the Christian Life*, 217.

For three different evangelical approaches to an analysis of the abiding ethical teachings found in the detailed laws in Exodus, Leviticus, and Deuteronomy, see Walter C. Kaiser Jr., *Toward Old Testament Ethics*

The same is true in the Historical Books of the Old Testament. Although some of the material specifically concerns details of obedience to the laws about the temple, the sacrifices, and other things unique to the nation of Israel at that time, there is also much material that teaches about human life in general before God.[42]

In addition, the Wisdom Literature of the Old Testament (Job, Psalms, Proverbs, Ecclesiastes, Song of Solomon) contains much material that does not apply only to the people of Israel under the Mosaic covenant, but teaches about wise patterns of conduct for human life in general, lived in accountability to God. The same is true of the *Prophetic Books*.

Here are some guidelines developed from the various ways in which the New Testament authors derive ethical teachings from the Old Testament:

a. Genesis 1–Exodus 19: This Material Predates the Mosaic Covenant and Therefore Teaches Ethical Principles for All Time: The Mosaic covenant did not begin until God spoke the words of the Ten Commandments to the people of Israel (Ex. 20:1–17) and then gave additional laws through Moses (Exodus 20–23).[43] Then Moses sprinkled the blood of a sacrifice on the people and said, "Behold *the blood of the covenant* that the LORD has made with you in accordance with all these words" (24:8). At that point the Mosaic covenant was initiated.

The author of Hebrews agrees with this and makes it more explicit in this passage:

> Therefore *not even the first covenant was inaugurated without blood.* For when every commandment of the law had been declared by Moses to all the people, he took the blood of calves and goats, with water and scarlet wool and hyssop, and sprinkled both the book itself and all the people, saying, "*This is the blood of the covenant that God commanded for you.*" (Heb. 9:18–20)

It is important to remember that when the New Testament speaks about the "old covenant," it simply means the Mosaic covenant, and therefore it does not include the material from Genesis 1 to Exodus 19. When God promised through Jeremiah that he would establish "a new covenant," he contrasted this not with the covenant he made with Noah, for example, or with Abraham, but with "the covenant that I made with their fathers when I took them by the hand *to bring them out of the land of Egypt*" (Jer.

(Grand Rapids, MI: Zondervan, 1983), 96–137; Poythress, *The Shadow of Christ in the Law of Moses*, 75–221; Wright, *Old Testament Ethics for the People of God*.

[42] Gordon J. Wenham gives a detailed, thoughtful analysis of the ways in which Old Testament narratives function to give ethical instruction in his book *Story as Torah: Reading Old Testament Narrative Ethically* (Grand Rapids, MI: Baker, 2000). Wenham provides a similarly thoughtful analysis of the ethical teachings of the Psalms in his companion volume *Psalms as Torah: Reading Biblical Song Ethically* (Grand Rapids, MI: Baker, 2012).

[43] In some ways Exodus 19 could be counted as part of the Mosaic covenant, since the entire chapter is concerned with preparations for the people to meet with God at Mount Sinai, where the covenant was to be initiated. I have decided to classify Exodus 19 with the pre-Mosaic covenant material, but if someone wished to include it with the Mosaic covenant there would be no significant difference in the pattern of interpretation that I'm proposing here.

31:31–32)—that is, the Mosaic covenant. When Paul speaks of the "old covenant," he is referring specifically to the Mosaic covenant (2 Cor. 3:14; this is the covenant with Moses that was "carved in letters on stone," v. 7). And the author of Hebrews uses the expression "the first covenant" to refer specifically to the regulations contained in the Mosaic covenant (see Heb. 9:1, 18).

Therefore, even though the New Testament authors repeatedly affirm that the Mosaic covenant has been terminated, they never teach or imply that we are free from the moral principles taught in Genesis 1–Exodus 19. The story of God's purposes at creation (Genesis 1–2) and God's judgment at the fall (Genesis 3) are particularly important here, for they lay a foundation for understanding all subsequent human conduct.

At several points, the New Testament applies material from Genesis 1–Exodus 19 directly to people's lives, without any hint that the ethical standards found there are no longer applicable. For example, Jesus reaches all the way back to the creation narrative in Genesis 2 to teach about the nature of marriage:

> He answered, "Have you not read that he who created them from the beginning made them male and female, and said, 'Therefore a man shall leave his father and his mother and hold fast to his wife, and the two shall become one flesh'? So they are no longer two but one flesh. What therefore God has joined together, let not man separate." (Matt. 19:4–6, quoting Gen. 2:24)

Paul also quotes the creation narrative to explain to the Corinthian church why having sex with a prostitute is contrary to God's purposes in creation and morally wrong (1 Cor. 6:16, again quoting Gen. 2:24). In another place, Paul returns to Genesis 2 to explain that marriage between a man and a woman—as God intended it from the beginning—is a profound "mystery" and, when understood correctly, "refers to Christ and the church" (Eph. 5:31–32, again quoting Gen. 2:24).

Although Paul does not explicitly quote Genesis 9 when he discusses the authority of civil government, the thought in Genesis 9:5–6—that God himself will require human beings to act as his agents in carrying out punishment on murderers—is probably in the background of Paul's statement that the civil government in the days of the Roman Empire is "the servant of God, an avenger who carries out God's wrath on the wrongdoer" (Rom. 13:4; see also 1 Pet. 2:14).[44]

---

[44] See further discussion in chap. 16 regarding the authority of civil government and in chap. 18 regarding capital punishment.

Regarding Noah, John Jefferson Davis observes, "Legitimate distinctions can be made between the legislation given to Israel as a theocratic state under Moses and the more universal revelation given to the human race through Noah. The abrogation of the specifics of the Mosaic covenant (e.g., circumcision, dietary laws, animal sacrifice) for the New Testament church does not necessarily affect the moral and legal principles given through Noah. Noah stood at the head of a new human race after the flood, and stipulations of the Noahic covenant, such as the permission to eat meat and the promise of no further universal flood, applied not just to Noah and his family or to some limited ethnic group, but also, in principle, to all mankind." *Evangelical Ethics: Issues Facing the Church Today*, 4th ed. (Phillipsburg, NJ: P&R, 2015), 204.

Elsewhere the New Testament authors mention the sins of Cain in Genesis 4:8 as wrongful murder (1 John 3:12; Jude 11), refer to Sarah's obedience to Abraham in Genesis as an example for wives in the new covenant to follow (1 Pet. 3:6), and speak of the evil of the sexual immorality of Sodom and Gomorrah in Genesis 19 (Jude 7).

Therefore, the New Testament authors frequently refer to the pre-Mosaic material in Genesis and Exodus to teach ethical conduct for all people for all time.

b. Exodus 20:1–17: The New Testament Authors Reaffirm All of the Ten Commandments (except the Sabbath Commandment): The Ten Commandments are found in Exodus 20:1–17 (and restated in Deut. 5:6–21). Although Jesus talks about the Sabbath commandment in the Gospels, the New Testament authors never quote or affirm the Sabbath commandment as something applicable to new covenant Christians. But they quote or allude to the other commandments quite often.

(1) The First Commandment:

> You shall have no other gods before me. (Ex. 20:3)

The idea that God must have first allegiance in our lives is implied by the greatest commandment: "*You shall love the Lord your God* with all your heart and with all your soul and with all your mind" (Matt. 22:37; see also Jesus's reply to Satan in Matt. 4:10). This commandment is also affirmed when Paul points out how people sinned when they "worshiped and served the creature rather than the Creator" (Rom. 1:25) and when the New Testament writers frequently condemn idolatry (see 1 Cor. 5:10–11; 6:9; 10:7, 14; Gal. 5:20; Eph. 5:5; Col. 3:5; 1 Thess. 1:9; 1 John 5:21; Rev. 9:20; 16:2; 20:4; 21:8; 22:15; see also Acts 12:23).

(2) The Second Commandment:

> You shall not make for yourself a carved image, or any likeness of anything that is in heaven above, or that is in the earth beneath, or that is in the water under the earth. You shall not bow down to them or serve them, for I the LORD your God am a jealous God, visiting the iniquity of the fathers on the children to the third and the fourth generation of those who hate me, but showing steadfast love to thousands of those who love me and keep my commandments. (Ex. 20:4–6)

This command against carved images made as idols was affirmed when Paul was in Athens and "his spirit was provoked within him as he saw that *the city was full of idols*" (Acts 17:16)—here, not idols of the heart but physical carved images. This command is also affirmed when Paul says that Gentiles "exchanged the glory of the immortal God for *images* resembling mortal man and birds and animals and creeping things" (Rom. 1:23). In addition, many of the passages cited under point (1) above could fit in this category as well, since in most cases people were worshiping physical objects that represented deities.

(3) The Third Commandment:

> You shall not take the name of the LORD your God in vain, for the LORD will
> not hold him guiltless who takes his name in vain. (Ex. 20:7)

Paul affirms the evil of dishonoring God's name when he says of the Jews who do not
believe in Christ, "the name of God is *blasphemed* among the Gentiles because of you"
(Rom. 2:24). Such blasphemy that dishonors the name of God is also identified as a sin
in 1 Timothy 1:13, 20; James 2:7; 2 Peter 2:12; Jude 10; Revelation 13:1, 5, 6; 16:9, 11, 21;
17:3; compare the prohibition against "corrupting talk" in Ephesians 4:29.

(4) The Fourth Commandment:

> Remember the Sabbath day, to keep it holy. Six days you shall labor, and do all
> your work, but the seventh day is a Sabbath to the LORD your God. On it you
> shall not do any work, you, or your son, or your daughter, your male servant,
> or your female servant, or your livestock, or the sojourner who is within your
> gates. For in six days the LORD made heaven and earth, the sea, and all that is
> in them, and rested on the seventh day. Therefore the LORD blessed the Sab-
> bath day and made it holy. (Ex. 20:8–11)

The command to rest on the Sabbath day is never repeated as an obligation for
Christians after the beginning of the new covenant at the time of Christ's death.[45] How-
ever, there is another part to the commandment. This commandment also requires that
God's people work: "Six days shall you labor, *and do all your work*" (Ex. 20:9). There are
New Testament commands that reflect this requirement, such as Ephesians 4:28:

> Let the thief no longer steal, but *rather let him labor, doing honest work with
> his own hands*, so that he may have something to share with anyone in need.

Similar commands for Christians to engage in productive work are found in 1 Thessalonians 4:11–12 and 2 Thessalonians 3:6–12. (However, there is nothing particularly innovative about a command to work, since God commanded Adam and Eve to
"subdue" the earth [Gen. 1:28], and he put Adam in the garden "to work it and keep
it" [2:15]. See chap. 13 for a further discussion of the fourth commandment, p. 342.)

---

[45] In chap. 13 I discuss the question of whether people are still morally obligated to observe the Sabbath
commandment under the new covenant. My conclusion in that chapter is that the Sabbath commandment
is intended to be understood as a summary of all the later details about Mosaic holidays (including the
Sabbath year and jubilee year), ceremonies, and sacrifices that looked forward to the coming of Christ,
and therefore we are not morally obligated to obey it today, though it is wise to take regular periods of
worship and rest.

Some Reformed writers have argued that observance of the Sabbath is still required today because it was a
"creation ordinance" established by God at the time of the creation of Adam and Eve: see Murray, *Principles
of Conduct*, 30–35.

(5) The Fifth Commandment:

> Honor your father and your mother, that your days may be long in the land that the Lord your God is giving you. (Ex. 20:12)

Paul quotes this commandment explicitly in Ephesians:

> Children, obey your parents in the Lord, for this is right. "Honor your father and mother" (this is the first commandment with a promise), "that it may go well with you and that you may live long in the land." (Eph. 6:1–3)

Other passages in the New Testament also affirm the validity of a moral requirement to honor one's father and mother (see Rom. 1:30; 1 Tim. 1:9; 2 Tim. 3:2; see also Jesus's teaching in Matt. 15:4; 19:18).

(6) The Sixth Commandment:

> You shall not murder. (Ex. 20:13)

"Murder" is listed many times among catalogs of various sins in the New Testament (see Rom. 1:29; 13:9; 1 Tim. 1:9; James 2:11; 4:2; 1 John 3:12, 15; Rev. 9:21; 16:6; 18:24; 21:8; 22:15; see also Jesus's teaching in Matt. 5:21–26; 15:19; 19:18).

(7) The Seventh Commandment:

> You shall not commit adultery. (Ex. 20:14)

Paul quotes "You shall not commit adultery" among the commandments that are summed up in the love command in Romans 13:9. James also quotes this commandment directly (James 2:11).

But if we understand this commandment to forbid not only adultery in the narrow sense but sexual immorality in a broader sense, then many other passages in the New Testament reflect this moral standard and prohibit immoral sexual conduct (see Rom. 1:26–27; 2:22; 1 Cor. 5:1–5; 6:9, 13–20; 7:2; 10:8; Gal. 5:19; Col. 3:5; 1 Thess. 4:3; 1 Tim. 1:10; Heb. 12:16; 13:4; James 2:11; 2 Pet. 2:14; Jude 7; Rev. 2:20–22; 9:21; 14:8; 17:1–5; 18:3; 19:2; 21:8, 22:15; see also Jesus's teaching in Matt. 5:27–28; 15:19; 19:9, 18).

(8) The Eighth Commandment:

> You shall not steal. (Ex. 20:15)

Paul quotes this commandment directly in Romans 13:9, his summary of moral requirements that are fulfilled in the command to love one's neighbor. He also echoes this command when he says, "Let the thief no longer steal" (Eph. 4:28). But several other verses also prohibit theft of various kinds (see Rom. 2:22; 1 Cor. 5:11; 6:10; Heb. 10:34; Titus 2:10; James 5:4; Rev. 9:21; see also Jesus's teaching in Matt. 15:19; 19:18).

(9) The Ninth Commandment:

You shall not bear false witness against your neighbor. (Ex. 20:16)

Although this commandment is not quoted explicitly in the New Testament, if we understand it to be a general prohibition against speaking falsehood, then there are several passages that affirm this moral standard, beginning with the judgment on Ananias and Sapphira for lying to the Holy Spirit in Acts 5:1–11. And Paul says to the Ephesians, "Having *put away falsehood*, let each one of you speak the truth with his neighbor" (Eph. 4:25). Commands against speaking falsely, especially about other people, are found in Romans 1:30; Ephesians 5:3–4; Colossians 3:8–9; 1 Timothy 1:10; 5:13; James 4:11; 1 John 1:6; 2:4, 21, 27; 2 John 7; Revelation 21:8; 22:15; see also Jesus's teaching in Matthew 5:37; 15:19; 19:18.

(10) The Tenth Commandment:

You shall not covet your neighbor's house; you shall not covet your neighbor's wife, or his male servant, or his female servant, or his ox, or his donkey, or anything that is your neighbor's. (Ex. 20:17)

Paul quotes the command "You shall not covet" as something that is summed up in the commandment, "You shall love your neighbor as yourself" (Rom. 13:9). He also quotes this command in Romans 7:7 as teaching him what it was to covet, thereby awakening more sin and being used by sin to produce in him "all kinds of covetousness" (7:8). The sin of coveting is also mentioned elsewhere (see 1:29; Col. 3:5; 1 Tim. 6:5–10, 17–18; Heb. 13:5; James 4:2; 2 Pet. 2:14; see also Jesus's teaching in Luke 12:15). Not all of these passages use the word *covet*, but all contain the idea that it is sinful to have our hearts set on greater riches than God has entrusted to us.

What shall we conclude from these numerous New Testament affirmations of nine out of 10 of the moral standards found in the Ten Commandments (plus the work aspect of the Sabbath command)? It would not be correct to conclude that the New Testament authors thought these commandments were binding for Christians because they were part of the Mosaic covenant. That line of thinking would contradict the other passages that so clearly teach that the Mosaic covenant has been terminated and that the new covenant is now in effect (see discussion above).

It is better to conclude that the New Testament authors, guided by the teachings of Jesus and by the further leading of the Holy Spirit after Jesus's ascension into heaven, understood that God, in his wisdom, placed within the Ten Commandments some broad principles that would not only teach the people of Israel what kind of conduct is pleasing or displeasing to him, but *would also be useful for teaching others outside of*

Israel, and throughout all history, about such conduct. In short, the Ten Commandments radiate God's wisdom for all of human history.

Bruce Waltke points out that, even within the original context of Exodus, "The Ten Commandments are the most important teachings of the old covenant for several reasons," including the fact that they are given first at the establishment of the covenant; they alone are given directly by God rather than through Moses; they alone are deposited in the ark of the covenant; they are not restricted to geography or history; they are referred to as "the covenant" (Deut. 4:13; 9:9, 11); and they are addressed personally to each individual within the whole Jewish nation using second-person singular verbs.[46] Waltke says:

> The Ten Commandments are not bound by time and space. Thus, the Ten Commandments cannot be relativized to culture. They apply to all people of all nationalities and all time periods. They express God's fundamental moral stance.[47]

In one remarkable paragraph, Waltke explains how the Ten Commandments are grounded in the order that God established at creation:

> The creation narratives undergird the Ten Commandments, which epitomize the ethics of Israel's faith and mold the judicial system of Judeo-Christian nations. The narrative affirms the priority of the one true God, demanded by the first commandment. It also affirms that he exists apart from and is sovereign over all creation; thus, to reimage him in the form of an idol or as the goddess Sophia, as prohibited by the second commandment, is a detestable distortion of his glorious person. This sublime God will not tolerate the attaching of his glorious name to anything false; this truth supports the third commandment. The stipulation of the Sabbath in the fourth commandment is predicated on the day of rest in the climax of creation. Murder is prohibited because humans are made in the image of God, which gives them dignity. The ban on adultery is based on the moral order established by God, who gave Adam only one wife. The Creator gave the arable soil to all humanity to provide them with food and wealth (Gen. 1:29). To steal from the community what rightly belongs to all or to steal from an individual what that person has lawfully earned as his or her wage from working the creation must not be tolerated. One must also protect the reputation of every human being, for all are made in God's image.[48]

---

[46] Bruce K. Waltke, *An Old Testament Theology: An Exegetical, Canonical, and Thematic Approach* (Grand Rapids, MI: Zondervan, 2007), 412–14. Waltke points out, however, that in the new covenant age Christians are not required to observe a weekly Sabbath, though he still thinks it wise to do so (424–25).

[47] Ibid., 413–14. Waltke explains the moral teachings of each commandment in some detail on pp. 414–33.

[48] Ibid., 206. While Waltke connects the Sabbath commandment to God's day of rest in creation, it is interesting that, unlike the other commands, this one is not grounded in the need to protect the honor of God

We could add that, in addition to the creation narratives, the subsequent chapters in Genesis show the moral wrong involved in several of these sins, such as murder (Gen. 4:8–10; 9:5–6), adultery (12:17; 34:2; 39:9), and stealing (31:9). Therefore, *prior to the Mosaic covenant*, many of the moral standards found in the Ten Commandments found earlier expression in the historical narratives of Genesis.

It is also significant to notice what is *not* affirmed by the New Testament authors as a moral standard for Christian conduct in the new covenant. We find no affirmation of circumcision, the sacrifices of the Mosaic Law, the Sabbath commandment (interestingly), the Jewish holidays and festivals, the food laws, the laws related to purity of clothing, and the laws regulating farming practices. We find no hint of a desire for the civil government to establish laws regarding religious activities, and no encouragement for Christians to form a separate nation or any separate political entities.

It is best to conclude that the New Testament authors reaffirmed the moral standards found in nine of the Ten Commandments, not because they thought that some parts of the Mosaic covenant remained in force, but because they saw in these commandments clear statements of conduct that is pleasing to God for all people, for all of life.[49]

c. The Rest of the Old Testament: The New Testament Authors Apply Various Passages in Light of Five Significant Changes Brought about by the New Covenant: In order to understand what the New Testament authors are doing with other Old Testament passages, it is important to take into account five important changes that came with the new covenant:

(1) The Old Covenant Has Been Terminated: Therefore, Christians should first understand the laws of the Old Testament as regulations that were given *for the people of Israel then*, not as regulations that are legally binding on all people for all time. Once that principle is established, then individual Old Testament laws, as well as sections from the Historical Books, Prophetic Books, and Wisdom Literature, can be evaluated as sources of wisdom regarding the kind of life that is pleasing to God for all time.

(2) The Messiah Has Come and Offered a Final Sacrifice: Therefore, the laws that pertained to the temple system, the priesthood, and the sacrifices—all of which looked forward to Christ—have been fulfilled. This means that Christians obey these laws in

---

or the dignity of human beings created in the image of God. See also the thoughtful analysis of "creation ordinances" by Murray in *Principles of Conduct*, 27–148.

[49] Geisler gives an ordinary-life example to demonstrate that New Testament authors could reaffirm old covenant moral standards without implying that Christians are still under the legal authority of the old covenant laws: "Just because there are similar moral laws in the New Testament does not mean we are still under the Old Testament. There are also similar traffic laws in North Carolina and Texas. But when a citizen of North Carolina disobeys one of its traffic laws, he has not thereby broken the similar law in Texas. Since God's moral nature does not change from age to age, we should expect that many of the moral laws will be the same. But this does not mean that we are still bound by the Mosaic codification simply because Moses received them from the same God who inspired Paul and Peter." *Christian Ethics*, 209.

new ways. The people of God are now God's temple on earth ("You are God's temple and . . . God's Spirit dwells in you"; 1 Cor. 3:16; see also 2 Cor. 6:16), and Christians individually are temples of the Holy Spirit ("Your body is a temple of the Holy Spirit within you"; 1 Cor. 6:19). Because Jesus is our "great high priest" (Heb. 4:14), he has made us to be "a royal priesthood" (1 Pet. 2:9). Paul sees his evangelism among the Gentiles as "the priestly service of the gospel of God," and in this priestly work the Gentiles who come to Christ are themselves an "offering" that he presents to God (Rom. 15:16). Paul also sees the sacrifice of his own life in the service of the gospel as a "drink offering" that he is giving up to God (Phil. 2:17; 2 Tim. 4:6). And now Christians no longer offer animals in sacrifice on a physical altar in Jerusalem, but they offer up "a sacrifice of praise to God," and when they "do good" and "share what you have," these actions are also "sacrifices" that are "pleasing to God" (Heb. 13:15–16).

(3) God's Laws Are Now More Powerfully Written on the Hearts of His People: Therefore, the New Testament standards for ethical conduct place more emphasis on inward righteousness, without neglecting instructions regarding actual conduct.

I do not mean to imply that the Old Testament is unconcerned with matters of the heart. Many passages talk about the need for a pure heart before God (see Gen. 6:5; Ex. 20:17; Deut. 6:5; Pss. 24:4; 51:17; Prov. 4:23; etc.). But apparently under the old covenant the Holy Spirit did not commonly give people the same level of ability to obey God from the heart as he gives in the new covenant, for Jeremiah predicted that the "new covenant" would be different from the old covenant in this way:

> For this is the covenant that I will make with the house of Israel after those days, declares the LORD: *I will put my law within them, and I will write it on their hearts.* And I will be their God, and they shall be my people. And no longer shall each one teach his neighbor and each his brother, saying, "Know the LORD," for they shall all know me, from the least of them to the greatest, declares the LORD. For I will forgive their iniquity, and I will remember their sin no more. (Jer. 31:33–34)

Therefore, teachings about the details of a pure heart did not receive as much emphasis in the Mosaic laws as the lengthy directions about civil penalties for various crimes; the procedures for purity in farming; instructions about various diseases; and the extensive lists of clean and unclean foods, in addition to the many laws regarding the priesthood, sacrifices, and festivals.

Moreover, we simply do not find in the Old Testament any sections that are parallel to the emphasis of the New Testament on moral virtues such as love, humility, forgiveness, faith, joy, steadfastness, and so forth. To my knowledge the Old Testament has no compact set of instructions in virtue ethics[50] like these passages in the New Testament:

---

[50] See discussion of virtue ethics in chap. 1, p. 42.

But the fruit of the Spirit is love, joy, peace, patience, kindness, goodness, faithfulness, gentleness, self-control; against such things there is no law. (Gal. 5:22–23)

Let all bitterness and wrath and anger and clamor and slander be put away from you, along with all malice. Be kind to one another, tenderhearted, forgiving one another, as God in Christ forgave you. (Eph. 4:31–32)

Finally, brothers, whatever is true, whatever is honorable, whatever is just, whatever is pure, whatever is lovely, whatever is commendable, if there is any excellence, if there is anything worthy of praise, think about these things. What you have learned and received and heard and seen in me—practice these things, and the God of peace will be with you. (Phil. 4:8–9)

Put on then, as God's chosen ones, holy and beloved, compassionate hearts, kindness, humility, meekness, and patience, bearing with one another and, if one has a complaint against another, forgiving each other; as the Lord has forgiven you, so you also must forgive. And above all these put on love, which binds everything together in perfect harmony. And let the peace of Christ rule in your hearts, to which indeed you were called in one body. And be thankful. Let the word of Christ dwell in you richly, teaching and admonishing one another in all wisdom, singing psalms and hymns and spiritual songs, with thankfulness in your hearts to God. And whatever you do, in word or deed, do everything in the name of the Lord Jesus, giving thanks to God the Father through him. (Col. 3:12–17)

And we urge you, brothers, admonish the idle, encourage the fainthearted, help the weak, be patient with them all. See that no one repays anyone evil for evil, but always seek to do good to one another and to everyone. Rejoice always, pray without ceasing, give thanks in all circumstances; for this is the will of God in Christ Jesus for you. (1 Thess. 5:14–18)

There are many similar passages in the New Testament Epistles, and the frequency with which they appear brings to light a clear difference in emphasis from the lists of outward duties and requirements so prevalent in the Mosaic covenant (for other lists of virtues see: Rom. 12:1–2, 9–21; 13:1–7, 8–14; 1 Cor. 10:31; 13:4–7; 2 Cor. 6:3–9; Gal. 5:13–14; many parts of Ephesians 4–6; 1 Tim. 3:1–13; 6:6, 11; 2 Tim. 2:22–26; Titus 1:7–9; 2:1–14; James 3:13–18; 1 Pet. 3:8–17; 4:7–19; 2 Pet. 1:3–7; 3:11). Such a remarkable emphasis on attitudes of the heart and inward moral virtues is entirely fitting for the new covenant, for the message of this covenant is written "not on tablets of stone but on tablets of human hearts" (2 Cor. 3:3).

This change in emphasis from the outward, physical realm to the inward, spiritual realm is also seen with regard to marriage. In the Mosaic Law, God commanded, "You shall not intermarry with them [the Canaanites], giving your daughters to their sons or taking their daughters for your sons" (Deut. 7:3). Although Paul does not explicitly quote this passage, it likely provides the background to his directive that Christians should marry only other Christians, "But if her husband dies, she is free to be married to whom she wishes, only in the Lord" (1 Cor. 7:39), and his command "Do not be unequally yoked with unbelievers" (2 Cor. 6:14). The Old Testament command against marrying people from other nations (pertaining to the *physical* realm) becomes in the New Testament a command against marrying people from other religions (pertaining to the *spiritual* realm).

In the new ethics of the kingdom of God, people are made unclean not by unclean foods but by impure thoughts in the heart:

> It is not what goes into the mouth that defiles a person, but what comes out of the mouth; this defiles a person. . . . Do you not see that whatever goes into the mouth passes into the stomach and is expelled? But what comes out of the mouth proceeds from the heart, and this defiles a person. For out of the heart come evil thoughts, murder, adultery, sexual immorality, theft, false witness, slander. These are what defile a person. But to eat with unwashed hands does not defile anyone. (Matt. 15:11, 17–20)

The Old Testament requirement for abstaining from unclean foods has become in the new covenant a spiritual requirement for abstaining from unclean thoughts and an unclean heart. Such wise reapplication of Mosaic laws is apparently what Douglas Moo has in mind when he says, "The detailed stipulations of the Mosaic law often reveal principles that are part of God's word to his people in both covenants."[51]

(4) God's People No Longer Constitute a Separate Earthly Nation: Therefore, the laws governing the conduct of civil society are applied in new ways to the church.

The Old Testament contains several chapters with lists of specific crimes related to masters and slaves, parents and children, personal injury law, care for agricultural animals, protection of personal property and restitution in times of theft, and so forth (for example, see Exodus 21–23). These laws reflected God's wonderful wisdom for the conduct of the people of Israel at that time and place.

But the New Testament repeats no such definitions of crimes, the penalties to be imposed by judges, and so forth. Those provisions were appropriate to governing people's lives in the nation of Israel at that time. The New Testament seldom quotes any of this material, but when it does, *it applies this Old Testament "civil law" to life in the church.* For instance, the requirement that an accusation be brought by "two witnesses or . . . three witnesses" in a civil crime (Deut. 19:15) is applied by Jesus to issues of church

---

[51] Moo, "The Law of Christ as the Fulfillment of the Law of Moses," 376, with reference to "the fine, detailed application of such laws by Poythress, *The Shadow of Christ in the Law of Moses.*"

discipline (see Matt. 18:16) and is applied by Paul to accusations about wrongdoing by one person against another within the church (see 2 Cor. 13:1). God's wise principle for providing protection against false accusation is still important, but it is treated as a principle to be applied in church discipline cases.

The Old Testament civil law required the people of Israel to put to death by stoning someone who advocated a false religion, and then added, "So you shall purge the evil from your midst" (Deut. 17:7; similarly, for other crimes, see Deut. 19:19; 22:21, 24). But in the New Testament, Paul applies this requirement not so as to encourage capital punishment from a civil government, but to encourage church discipline and the exclusion from the church of someone guilty of incest ("Purge the evil person from among you," 1 Cor. 5:13).

When the Mosaic Law commanded, "You shall not muzzle an ox when it is treading out the grain" (Deut. 25:4), this directive was applied in an agricultural society to agricultural practices. But Paul sees in it a deeper concern that workers be rewarded for their work, including his own work as an apostle (1 Cor. 9:9), and to payment for ministers of the gospel generally (1 Tim. 5:18), for he quotes this passage from Deuteronomy 25 in discussions of both of those issues. The application of the civil law in the Old Testament thus takes on a new focus in the new covenant.

Another example of this transition is found in Isaiah:

> Depart, depart, go out from there;
>   touch no unclean thing;
> go out from the midst of her; purify yourselves,
>   you who bear the vessels of the LORD. (Isa. 52:11)

In this passage, God is calling his people through the words of Isaiah to leave the nation of Babylon, return to their own country, and live as a separate nation. But when Paul quotes this passage in 2 Corinthians 6:17, he applies it to the church, not telling it to become a separate political entity among the nations of the world, but telling Christians not to be "unequally yoked with unbelievers" and calling them to "cleanse [themselves] from every defilement of body and spirit, bringing holiness to completion in the fear of God" (2 Cor. 6:14, 7:1). A call for national separateness now becomes a call for separateness from sinful practices in individual lives.

On the other hand, consider the instruction about the Lord's discipline in Proverbs:

> My son, do not despise the LORD's discipline
>   or be weary of his reproof,
> for the LORD reproves him whom he loves,
>   as a father the son in whom he delights. (Prov. 3:11–12)

In this case, though Proverbs 3 was written during the time of the Mosaic covenant, there is nothing in these passages that ties them to the specific circumstances of the Mosaic covenant, so the author of Hebrews quotes them directly as "the exhortation that *addresses you* as sons" (Heb. 12:5–6). The New Testament authors can warn against the sins of Balaam (2 Pet. 2:15; Rev. 2:14), recall the courage and faith of Rahab (Heb. 11:31; James 2:25), encourage imitation of the steadfastness of Job (James 5:11), and teach about prayer from the prayer life of Elijah (v. 17) without any hesitation that they are quoting from the writings of the old covenant, because there is nothing in the examples they quote that would restrict their application to the specific circumstances of Israel during the old covenant age.

(5) Gentiles No Longer Have to Become Jews to Be Saved: God is now saving people from every nation and ethnic group on earth. Therefore, the laws marking the separateness of the Jews from other nations are now applied not in physical terms but in terms of inward spiritual realities.

This principle is seen, for example, in the New Testament emphasis on circumcision "of the heart, by the Spirit" (Rom. 2:29), which is "a circumcision made without hands . . . the circumcision of Christ" (Col. 2:11). And the Jewish dietary laws marking out clean and unclean foods previously distinguished the Jews from other nations of the earth, but in the new covenant, refusing to eat with Gentiles (and presumably partake of their food) meant that even Peter "stood condemned" and "was not in step with the truth of the gospel" (Gal. 2:11, 14). Paul challenged Peter: "How can you force the Gentiles to live like Jews?" (v. 14).

By the same reasoning, we would expect that the laws regarding specific clothing and agricultural practices, though cancelled with the termination of the Mosaic covenant, could still teach something of God's wisdom regarding purity of conduct in one's life. That would be a parallel kind of application for a Mosaic law such as this:

> You shall keep my statutes. You shall not let your cattle breed with a different kind. You shall not sow your field with two kinds of seed, nor shall you wear a garment of cloth made of two kinds of material. (Lev. 19:19)

Although such practices are neither explicitly abrogated in the New Testament nor explicitly applied to a Christian's conduct of life, they are similar to the food laws in that they gave visible evidence that Israel was a distinct people, set apart from other nations on the earth. In the new covenant, God's people show that they are a distinct people, not by obeying laws about food and clothing, but by moral purity in their lives. Paul says, "Do not be conformed to this world, but be transformed by the renewal of your mind, that by testing you may discern what is the will of God, what is good and acceptable and perfect" (Rom. 12:2; cf. 2 Cor. 6:14–18).

E. SHOULD WE CHARACTERIZE OLD TESTAMENT LAWS AS CIVIL, CEREMONIAL, AND MORAL?

In previous generations, biblical interpreters sometimes used a threefold categorization of Old Testament laws as civil, ceremonial, and moral to help distinguish which remained applicable in the new covenant (the moral laws) and which were discontinued (the civil laws and ceremonial laws). This approach is found, for example, in the Westminster Confession of Faith (1646) (the label "judicial" is used for what others call "civil" laws):

> Besides this law, commonly called *moral*, God was pleased to give to the people of Israel, as a church under age, *ceremonial* laws, containing several typical ordinances, partly of worship, prefiguring Christ, His graces, actions, sufferings, and benefits, and partly, holding forth diverse instructions of moral duties. All of which *ceremonial* laws are now abrogated under the New Testament.
>
> To them also, as a body politic, He gave sundry *judicial* laws, which expired together with the State of that people; not obliging any other now, further than the general equity thereof may require.
>
> The *moral* law doth forever bind all, as well justified persons as others, to the obedience thereof; and that, not only in regard of the matter contained in it, but also in respect of the authority of God the Creator, who gave it. Neither doth Christ, in the Gospel, any way dissolve, but much strengthens this obligation. (WCF, 19.3–5, emphasis added)[52]

The Thirty-Nine Articles of the Church of England (1571) also contain this distinction:

> The Old Testament is not contrary to the New: for both in the Old and New Testament everlasting life is offered to mankind by Christ, who is the only Mediator between God and Man, being both God and Man. Wherefore they are not to be heard, which feign that the old Fathers did look only for transitory promises. Although the Law given from God by Moses, as touching *Ceremonies and Rites*, do not bind Christian men, nor the *Civil* precepts thereof ought of necessity to be received in any commonwealth; yet notwithstanding, no Christian man whatsoever is free from the obedience of the Commandments which are called *Moral*. (The Thirty-Nine Articles, VII, emphasis added)

There is some benefit in this threefold distinction, because what are called "ceremonial laws" are generally taken to refer to the sacrificial system, the priesthood, and the temple, and the history of redemption shows that direct and literal obedience to these laws is no longer required because they have been fulfilled in Christ. In addition, the laws called "civil laws" (or "judicial laws") include those given for the governance of Israel as a nation, and a history-of-redemption perspective shows that those laws no longer

---

[52] See a similar distinction in these types of laws in Charles Hodge, *Systematic Theology*, 3 vols. (1871–1873; repr., Grand Rapids, MI: Eerdmans, 1970), 3:267–69.

should be used as a detailed guide for civil legislation today, when Christians no longer live in a separate national entity.

However, the categorization has some significant shortcomings:

1. These categories of laws are nowhere mentioned explicitly in the Old Testament or the New Testament, nor does the New Testament give any suggestion that we should analyze the Old Testament in terms of such categories when looking for ethical guidance.

2. It is incorrect to think that only some parts of the Mosaic Law have been terminated and other parts remain in force. This is contrary to the New Testament emphasis that the entire Mosaic covenant has come to an end and is no longer operative. Therefore, it seems misleading to teach that the "moral" laws of the Mosaic covenant remain in force.

3. It is not always clear which laws belong to which categories, and the assignment of laws to various categories can become a subjective and arbitrary process.[53] The categories overlap, since all laws are "moral" in some sense. So, for example, Paul understands that the Old Testament passages about the temple have a moral component that imparts wisdom to New Testament Christians, because our bodies are now "a temple of the Holy Spirit," and therefore we should refrain from sexual immorality (1 Cor. 6:18–20).

To take another example, here is a provision from the Mosaic Law:

> The wages of a hired worker shall not remain with you all night until the morning. (Lev. 19:13)

But when I teach a class at Phoenix Seminary, the seminary does not pay me on the spot before I go home that day. In fact, the seminary pays me only twice a month. Are my employers violating Leviticus 19:13? Does it not seem to be a *moral* law, concerned for the well-being of employees?

A better solution comes when we understand that the Mosaic Law is completely abrogated in its entirety, but that we can find wisdom in it as we seek to determine conduct that is pleasing to God. On that basis, we can see a wise principle of paying workers when you have agreed to pay them, so that they have their income when they rightfully expect to receive it.

Here is another law that appears to be a "moral" law because it is concerned for the physical safety of people:

---

[53] Frame says it bluntly: "So *moral* is just a label for those laws we believe to be currently normative, rather than a quality of the laws that leads to that conclusion. The same is true for the label *ceremonial*. . . . It seems as though theologians call certain laws 'ceremonial,' not because they share a certain subject matter, but rather because they are judged not appropriate to the new covenant." *The Doctrine of the Christian Life*, 214–15. In addition, Dorsey gives a long list of Mosaic laws pertaining to agricultural, economic, and marriage practices (and are these not *moral* questions?) that would be impossible to fulfill outside of geography and weather patterns similar to those of Palestine, and says that this suggests "that this corpus was never intended to be the normative body of laws governing the Christian Church, scattered as it is throughout every climate of the inhabited earth." "The Law of Moses and the Christian," 326.

When you build a new house, you shall make a parapet for your roof, that you may not bring the guilt of blood upon your house, if anyone should fall from it. (Deut. 22:8)

If we claim that the "moral" laws are still valid and binding on people today, then my home in Arizona (with a sloped roof, and no parapet or railing around the outside edges) is in violation of God's command!

Someone might object that this law in Deuteronomy 22 was written in a historical and cultural setting in which houses had flat roofs. People would entertain visitors on the roof at times, and at other times people would sleep on the roof. The parapet was necessary as a safeguard to keep people from accidentally falling off. But I actually have a flat roof over just one room of my house, and no one goes up on that flat roof for any reason (except to patch leaks). Now, the law does not say, "You shall make a parapet for your roof *if people go up on the roof.*" It just says, "You shall make a parapet for your roof." Am I breaking the law by not having a parapet around my flat roof? If we say that the "moral" laws of the Mosaic covenant are binding on us today, and this law commands a parapet for a flat roof, then it seems to me I should make a parapet for my flat roof.

Once again, a better approach is to recognize that the entire Mosaic covenant has come to an end and is no longer operative. We are no longer under any part of the Mosaic covenant as a binding law. But we can gain wisdom from it, and in this case, the wise conclusion would seem to be a recognition that God is pleased when we take reasonable precautions to protect the physical safety of others on our property. Examples would include removing the ice on a sidewalk in front of one's house or sprinkling sand on it during the winter (in cold climates) to prevent people from falling; installing a railing rather than leaving a completely open staircase going down into a basement; putting a fence around a swimming pool to prevent children from falling in; or actually adding a protective railing around a flat roof if people use it as an activity area (as does one of my neighbors).

My conclusion, therefore, is that, while the civil-ceremonial-moral distinction has some usefulness, it is not as helpful a tool for understanding how the Old Testament applies to New Testament ethical conduct as a process of (1) recognizing that the Mosaic covenant in its entirety has been terminated; (2) recognizing the specific differences between the old and new covenants; and then, in light of those differences, (3) seeking wisdom for life from the whole of the Old Testament, including all of its laws.

F. SUMMARY OF PRINCIPLES FOR USING THE OLD TESTAMENT FOR GUIDANCE TODAY

With this background, we are now able to draw some conclusions about the way the Old Testament should be used for understanding Christian ethics today. But first we need to examine three less satisfactory alternatives.

1. Three Inadequate Solutions.

a. Everything Not Cancelled by the New Testament Is Still Required: The first alternative is to say that everything in the Old Testament that is not specifically abrogated by New Testament teaching remains valid for us today. But that is an inappropriate approach, because it would require us to avoid wearing clothing made of two kinds of cloth and to avoid planting our fields with two kinds of seeds, both of which are prohibited in the Old Testament (Lev. 19:19) but not mentioned in the New Testament. This approach fails to recognize that the New Testament authors were not trying to give us an exhaustive list of laws that are no longer binding, but were teaching us by many examples the general principles by which we can understand the differences between the old and the new covenants.

b. Nothing Is Required Except What the New Testament Reaffirms: A second (and opposite) approach is to say that we are required to obey nothing in the Old Testament except what is affirmed in the New Testament. But this approach also fails to realize what the New Testament authors were doing. They give no indication that they were attempting to give us an exhaustive list of Old Testament rules that would teach us wise conduct. Instead, they teach about the major differences between the old and new covenants, and they give us a number of specific examples showing how those differences are to be applied in practical situations in everyday life. The approach of "nothing from the Old Testament is required except things that are reaffirmed in the New Testament" does not adequately appreciate the fact that the whole Old Testament is included in the statement "*All Scripture* is breathed out by God and profitable for teaching, for reproof, for correction, and *for training in righteousness*" (2 Tim. 3:16). If we understand clearly the differences between the covenants, then every verse in the Old Testament has the potential to teach us something about wise conduct for living the Christian life today.

c. Framing the Question in Terms of More Continuity or Discontinuity: A third approach is to ask whether the New Testament emphasizes more continuity or discontinuity with Old Testament ethics. But I do not think that asking this question is a helpful approach because there is both continuity and discontinuity, as we have seen above. Moreover, any decision about the overall emphasis cannot really decide for us the question of how to understand a specific law, because we still would not know if it falls in the more emphasized or less emphasized category.

2. A Better Solution: Understand Each Old Testament Ethical Teaching in Light of the Differences between the Old and New Covenants. A better approach is to learn from the New Testament authors how to apply Old Testament passages to ethical questions today by keeping in mind the differences between the old and new covenants and the place of each passage in the overall history of redemption in the Bible. Specifically, the pattern of New Testament teaching shows that we must keep in mind these principles:

a. Genesis 1–Exodus 19: This material predates the Mosaic covenant and teaches ethical principles for all time.

b. The Ten Commandments in Exodus 20:1–17: All of the commandments are reaffirmed by the New Testament (except the Sabbath commandment) and should be understood as teaching universal moral standards for all time.

c. The Rest of the Old Testament: This material contains God's wisdom for human conduct, but each passage must be understood in light of five changes that came with the new covenant:

(1) The Old Covenant Has Been Terminated: Therefore, old covenant laws should first be understood as regulations that were given for God's people then, not as regulations that are legally binding on all people for all time. Then each passage can be evaluated as a source of wisdom regarding the kind of life that is pleasing to God for all time.

(2) The Messiah Has Come and Offered a Final Sacrifice: Therefore, the Old Testament sacrificial system has been discontinued and we fulfill those laws in new ways, several of which are made explicit by the New Testament authors.

(3) God's Laws Are Now More Powerfully Written on the Hearts of His People: Therefore, God's standards for ethical conduct place more emphasis on the details of inward righteousness, without neglecting instructions regarding actual conduct.

(4) God's People No Longer Constitute a Separate Earthly Nation: Therefore, many Old Testament laws governing the conduct of civil society, including civil punishments, are applied in new ways to the church.

(5) Gentiles No Longer Have to Become Jews to Be Saved: Therefore, laws marking the separateness of the Jewish people from other ethnic groups (such as circumcision, food laws, and clothing laws) are now applied not to physical indications of separateness but to inward spiritual realities.

3. This Is the Task of a Lifetime. Finally, the New Testament authors frequently encourage Christians to *grow* in wisdom and discernment, which implies that skill in applying the Bible rightly to life is something that can increase throughout our lifetime. Paul tells Christians to "be transformed by the renewal of your mind, that by testing *you may discern what is the will of God*, what is good and acceptable and perfect" (Rom. 12:2). He prays for the Philippians, "that your love may *abound more and more, with knowledge and all discernment*, so that you may approve what is excellent, and so be pure and blameless for the day of Christ" (1:9–10). He prays for the Christians in Colossae, "that you may be filled with the knowledge of his will *in all spiritual wisdom and understanding*, so as to walk in a manner worthy of the

Lord, fully pleasing to him" (Col. 1:9–10). Other passages speak the same way (see Eph. 4:23; Col. 4:5; Heb. 5:14).

These passages, addressed to people who had been believers for several years, suggest that wisdom in how to live the Christian life—especially wisdom in the difficult task of applying the Old Testament rightly to ethical conduct today—is a trait that Christians can acquire and practice with increasing accuracy as they grow in Christian maturity. There is no simple formula that will enable us automatically to understand each passage correctly, but under the guidance of the Holy Spirit, and following the pattern of interpretation that we see in the New Testament authors, we are to seek wisdom from God to rightly understand the Old Testament, including those commands that are neither affirmed nor abrogated by specific teachings in the New Testament, and also including the Historical Books, the Wisdom Literature, and the Prophetic Books.

When we can do this wisely, we will be rightly understanding the entire Old Testament as "breathed out by God" and "profitable for teaching, for reproof, for correction, and for training in righteousness" (2 Tim. 3:16). In this way, the teacher of Christian ethics will be ready to use material from the Old Testament as well as the New, and thus will become a "scribe who has been trained for the kingdom of heaven" and who "is like a master of a house, who brings out of his treasure what is new and what is old" (Matt. 13:52).

It is my goal to keep these principles in mind and to seek to apply them rightly to many other specific parts of the Old Testament in the remaining chapters of this book.

G. ARE ANY NEW TESTAMENT COMMANDS CULTURALLY RELATIVE?

Up to this point, I have been considering how we can know when some commands in the Old Testament no longer need to be obeyed by people living in the new covenant age. A related question is whether there are any New Testament commands that are culturally relative, so that we need not obey them literally today, but only the deeper principles that they represent.

I discuss this question at some length in an appendix to this book (see p. 1227), but at this point I can summarize that discussion by saying that the only culturally relative New Testament commands addressed to Christians living under the new covenant are those that concern *physical actions that carry symbolic meanings*. There are at least three of these: (1) holy kiss (Rom. 16:16; 1 Cor. 16:20; 2 Cor. 13:12; 1 Thess. 5:26; 1 Pet. 5:14); (2) foot washing (John 13:14; cf. 1 Tim. 5:10); and (3) wives (or women) covering their heads in worship (1 Cor. 11:4–16). There may be two or three others (see p. 1186). The holy kiss was a physical expression that conveyed the idea of a welcoming greeting. Foot washing (in the way that Jesus modeled it in John 13) was a physical action that symbolized taking a servantlike attitude toward one another. Putting on a head covering was a physical action that symbolized something about a woman's status or role (most likely that she was a married woman, or possibly that she was a woman and not a man; others have proposed other interpretations, but all of them are attempts to explain what was symbolized by the head covering).

I do not think this needs to be seen as a difficult question. While there are some Christians who believe we should literally obey these commands, for most people in the evangelical world, deciding that a holy kiss is a greeting that can be manifested in another way is not a baffling problem in biblical interpretation. It is something that comes almost instinctively as people intuitively realize that there are differences in forms of greeting among different cultures. The same is true for foot washing and head covering.

H. APPENDIX: USING THE TEN COMMANDMENTS AS AN ORGANIZING PRINCIPLE FOR TREATING SPECIFIC ETHICAL TOPICS

There are several possible ways in which we could organize the topics to be treated in a course on Christian ethics. One system would be to organize topics *alphabetically*. This is the procedure used by dictionaries of Christian ethics.[54] In such a system, the topics treated under the letter A would include:

Abortion
Abuse
Adoption
Adultery
Affluence
Alcohol
and so forth

But is there a *logical* order in which to arrange topics?[55]

Another approach is to treat a *limited number* of controversial topics, arranging them in various orders according to the *preference of the individual author*. Most ethics textbooks will cover, for example, the following topics:

---

[54] See, for example, *New Dictionary of Christian Ethics and Pastoral Theology*, ed. David J. Atkinson and David H. Field (Leicester, UK: Inter-Varsity, and Downers Grove, IL: InterVarsity Press, 1995), and *Dictionary of Scripture and Ethics*, ed. Joel B. Green (Grand Rapids, MI: Baker, 2011).

[55] The question of arrangement of topics is somewhat easier in systematic theology, where a very common scheme is to organize the topics in the broad historical perspective of creation-fall-redemption, which is the historical organizing principle of the Bible. Therefore, in my own *Systematic Theology*, after beginning with the doctrine of the Word of God (which is our source of information about theology), I then treat the broad topics of God, his creation, the fall and sin, Christ's work of redemption, the application of redemption to our lives, the doctrine of the church, and the doctrine of the future. Others have organized theology according to the doctrine of the Trinity, following the major sections of the Nicene Creed as an organizing principle. But the topics covered in ethics do not easily fit into such schemes.

Issues of life and death (such as abortion, euthanasia, capital punishment)

Issues related to marriage and human sexuality (marriage, divorce, homosexuality, sexual immorality, human reproductive technology)

Issues related to war

Economic issues (wealth and poverty, economic justice, the environment)[56]

Yet another commonly used system throughout Christian history has been to organize the treatment of ethical topics *according to the Ten Commandments*. That is the
organizing principle used recently in textbooks by John Frame[57] and by Robertson
McQuilkin and Paul Copan,[58] and it was used historically by John Calvin[59] and Charles
Hodge[60] to organize their ethical teaching. This is also the organizing principle used to
teach ethical conduct in the Westminster Larger Catechism of 1648 (Questions 98–148)
and the Heidelberg Catechism of 1563 (Questions 92–115). I have chosen to use that
organizational system in this book as well.

**1. The Ten Commandments Provide a Useful Structure for Organizing Ethical
Topics:** Although the Mosaic covenant was terminated at the death of Christ, the
Ten Commandments (Ex. 20:1–17; Deut. 5:6–21) still provide a useful summary
of ethical topics. All of these commandments (except the Sabbath commandment)
are reaffirmed in the New Testament and should be thought of as part of the "law
of Christ," which should guide the lives of Christian believers in the new covenant.
Jesus refers to several of the commandments as a way of summarizing a person's
ethical obligations:

> You know the commandments: "Do not murder, Do not commit adultery, Do
> not steal, Do not bear false witness, Do not defraud, Honor your father and
> mother." (Mark 10:19)

Similarly, Paul quotes several of the commandments as moral obligations of Christians, but says they are also summarized in the love commandment:

---

[56] The following ethics texts treat most or all of these issues but arrange them in various orders: John S.
Feinberg and Paul D. Feinberg, *Ethics for a Brave New World*, 2nd ed. (Wheaton, IL: Crossway, 2010); Geisler,
Christian Ethics; Robin Gill, *A Textbook of Christian Ethics*, 4th ed. (London: Bloomsbury T&T Clark, 2014);
Richard B. Hays, *The Moral Vision of the New Testament: Community, Cross, New Creation: A Contemporary
Introduction to New Testament Ethics* (San Francisco: HarperSanFrancisco, 1996); Arthur F. Holmes, *Ethics:
Approaching Moral Decisions*, Contours of Christian Philosophy, 2nd ed. (Downers Grove, IL: InterVarsity
Press, 2007); Murray, *Principles of Conduct*; Scott B. Rae, *Moral Choices: An Introduction to Ethics*, 3rd ed.
(Grand Rapids, MI: Zondervan, 2009); David P. Gushee and Glen H. Stassen, *Kingdom Ethics: Following Jesus
in Contemporary Context*, 2nd ed. (Downers Grove, IL: InterVarsity Press, 2016).

[57] Frame, *The Doctrine of the Christian Life*.

[58] Robertson McQuilkin and Paul Copan, *An Introduction to Biblical Ethics: Walking in the Way of Wisdom*,
3rd ed. (Downers Grove, IL: InterVarsity Press, 2014).

[59] John Calvin, *Institutes of the Christian Religion*, ed. John T. McNeill, trans. Ford Lewis Battles, Library
of Christian Classics, vols. 20–21 (Philadelphia: Westminster, 1960), 2.8 (367–423).

[60] Hodge, *Systematic Theology*, 3:259–465.

The commandments, "You shall not commit adultery, You shall not murder, You shall not steal, You shall not covet," and any other commandment, are summed up in this word: "You shall love your neighbor as yourself." Love does no wrong to a neighbor; therefore love is the fulfilling of the law. (Rom. 13:9–10)

a. Scripture Contains Various Brief Summaries of Ethical Obligations: The Ten Commandments are not the only summary of ethical obligations in the Bible, for Jesus himself summarized our ethical obligations in only two commandments:

You shall love the Lord your God with all your heart and with all your soul and with all your mind. This is the great and first commandment. And a second is like it: You shall love your neighbor as yourself. On these two commandments depend all the Law and the Prophets. (Matt. 22:37–40)

Paul gave an even shorter summary of the Christian life, in only one commandment: "So, whether you eat or drink, or whatever you do, do all to the glory of God" (1 Cor. 10:31).

The Ten Commandments, like these other summaries, provide a useful overview of the moral obligations we have before God.

But we should never think that we can use the summaries to replace the teaching of all of Scripture regarding how to live a life that is pleasing to God. For example, if we had only the commands to love God and love other people, Christians would come up with hundreds of different ideas of what it means to love God and other people, and many of those ideas would be confusing or contradictory. For that reason God has given us much more information and guidance in "all Scripture," and it is all "profitable" for "training in righteousness" (2 Tim. 3:16).

b. Each Commandment Can Be Viewed with a Broad or Narrow Perspective: James provides interesting insight into the Ten Commandments when he says:

For whoever keeps the whole law but fails in one point has become guilty of all of it. For he who said, "Do not commit adultery," also said, "Do not murder." If you do not commit adultery but do murder, you have become a transgressor of the law. (James 2:10–11)

James's intention seems to be to understand the entire moral law of God as an organic whole. This means that if someone breaks one part of it, in some sense he has become "guilty" of breaking all of it (understood broadly).

For example, suppose someone were to steal a car. He has clearly broken the eighth commandment, "You shall not steal." But what about the other commandments? He has violated the first commandment (no other gods), because he has made possession of that car more important than submitting to God and trusting him. He has broken the second commandment (no worship of carved images) because he has made the car, which is part of the creation, more important to him than God, the Creator (see Col. 3:5). He has broken the third commandment (no taking God's name in vain) because he is a human being made in the image of God, and so he is to represent God on the earth, but in stealing he is representing God as doing something dishonorable and dishonest, and so he is harming God's reputation (see Prov. 30:9: "lest I be poor and steal and profane the name of my God").

Although the fourth commandment (the Sabbath commandment) is not retained under the new covenant, the Sabbath commandment also includes the statement "Six days shall you labor, and do all your work" (Ex. 20:9), but instead of working or worshiping God on the day of the theft, this man stole a car (see Eph. 4:28, where stealing is seen as the opposite of working to support oneself.)

He has certainly broken the fifth commandment (honoring one's father and mother) because when his crime becomes known, it will bring shame on his family, including his father and mother. He has broken the sixth commandment (no murder) because, while he did not kill another person, he did damage another person's life by taking away that person's car (cf. Matt. 5:21–22). He has broken the seventh commandment (no adultery) by committing spiritual adultery and being unfaithful to Christ, whom he should serve as Christ's bride (see John 3:29; Rev. 19:7; 22:17). He has broken the ninth commandment (no bearing false witness) because, in his actions and words, he is proclaiming that the car belongs to him, when in fact it does not. And he has certainly broken the tenth commandment (no coveting) because he coveted the car that did not belong to him, and that led him to steal it.

Therefore, "Whoever keeps the whole law but fails in one point has become guilty of all of it" (James 2:10).

The value of such a hypothetical exercise is that it helps us see the seriousness of sin, and how even one sin can be a complex action that affects many parts of our lives.

c. Using Each Commandment as an Organizing Principle: The table of contents of this book will show how I understand the Ten Commandments to be a useful framework for studying all ethical topics, because each commandment can serve as an organizing principle for several related topics. For example, the third commandment (no taking God's name in vain) can be used as a broad category to deal with all questions about purity of speech. We can discuss not only taking the Lord's name in vain in a specific sense, but also obscene or vulgar language, drama and movies (and what roles might not be appropriate for Christians to take), swearing oaths and making vows, and the values and dangers of humor in speech. (Related to this topic is the question of lying and telling the truth, which is more specifically addressed in the ninth commandment: no bearing false witness).

Under the seventh commandment (no committing adultery) I treat not only the question of adultery in the narrow sense, but also the definition of marriage, polygamy, sexual purity, birth control, reproductive technology, pornography, divorce and remarriage, and homosexuality.

In this way, the entire range of topics related to living the Christian life can be discussed in an organized and logical fashion. In addition, the need to discuss all 10 of the commandments encourages us to include some topics that are not traditionally treated in ethics textbooks (such as the question of pictures of God and Christ in relation to the second commandment or the question of obscene language in relation to the third commandment).

2. How Shall We Number the Ten Commandments? In this book I have used the most common traditional Protestant system for numbering the Ten Commandments:

1. You shall have no other gods before me.
2. You shall not make a carved image.
3. You shall not take God's name in vain.
4. Keep the Sabbath holy.
5. Honor your father and your mother.
6. You shall not murder.
7. You shall not commit adultery.
8. You shall not steal.
9. You shall not bear false witness.
10. You shall not covet.

But is this numbering system correct? Although the Bible refers to these commandments as the "Ten Words" or "Ten Commandments" (Ex. 34:28; Deut. 4:13; 10:4), no specific numbers are assigned to the distinct commandments themselves. Therefore, different numbering systems have been used.

Another common numbering system is the one used in the Roman Catholic Church (the one used by Lutherans is similar). This system combines the first two commandments of the common Protestant system into one commandment, and then separates the last commandment about coveting into two commandments, as follows:

1. You shall have no other gods and shall not make or worship carved images.
2. You shall not take God's name in vain.
3. Keep the Sabbath holy.
4. Honor your father and your mother.
5. You shall not murder.
6. You shall not commit adultery.
7. You shall not steal.
8. You shall not bear false witness.
9. You shall not covet your neighbor's wife.
10. You shall not covet your neighbor's goods.[61]

---

[61] This numbering is given in *Catechism of the Catholic Church*, 2nd ed. (New York: Doubleday, 1997), 551–52; see explanation of the history of this numbering system, which began with Augustine, on 557 (para. 2065).

The first system of numbering, the one followed in the Reformed Protestant tradition, seems to me to be preferable to the Roman Catholic and Lutheran systems. This is because it seems artificial to separate the command not to covet one's neighbor's house from the command not to covet one's neighbor's wife. The ideas are closely related and belong together under one commandment that prohibits coveting. This becomes even clearer when we see that the wording of the first part of the commandment differs between Exodus and Deuteronomy:

> You shall not covet your neighbor's *house*; you shall not covet your neighbor's *wife*. (Ex. 20:17)

> And you shall not covet your neighbor's *wife*. And you shall not desire your neighbor's *house*. (Deut. 5:21).[62]

As for the first two commandments (or the first one), it seems better to separate the commandment against having other gods from the command against making a carved image or worshiping it, and seeing these as two commands. Waltke rightly observes:

> Separating the first two commandments distinguishes between worshipping either Canaanite or foreign deities, who were thought of as powers that rule aspects of nature, and misrepresenting the character of true Deity. According to this second command, God cannot be compared to anything that exists. These are distinct notions.[63]

Therefore, I have decided to follow the traditional Protestant (non-Lutheran) order of numbering the commandments. But no major issue of doctrine or ethics is at stake in this question.

QUESTIONS FOR PERSONAL APPLICATION

1. Did this chapter change the way you view the Old Testament? If so, how?
2. Can you name some commands from the Old Testament that still seem to be "written on your heart" today? (See Jer. 31:33; Heb. 8:10.)
3. What are some commands of the Old Testament that are clearly not "written on your heart" today?

SPECIAL TERMS

ceremonial laws

---

[62] Because of this difference in order, the Roman Catholic tradition follows the order in Deuteronomy and makes the ninth commandment a prohibition against coveting your neighbor's wife, while the Lutheran tradition follows the order in Exodus and makes the ninth commandment a prohibition against coveting your neighbor's house.

[63] Waltke, *An Old Testament Theology*, 411.

civil laws
kingdom of God
law of Christ
moral laws
Mosaic covenant
new covenant
old covenant
theonomy

BIBLIOGRAPHY

Sections in Other Ethics Texts

(see complete bibliographical data, p. 64)

Clark and Rakestraw, 1:179–210
Feinberg, John and Paul, 42–49
Frame, 206–36
Hays, 291–312
Jones, 103–24
McQuilkin and Copan, 205–16
Murray, 149–201
Rae, 28–38

Other Works

Bahnsen, Greg L. *Theonomy in Christian Ethics*. Nutley, NJ: Craig Press, 1977.

Barker, William S., and W. Robert Godfrey, eds. *Theonomy: A Reformed Critique*. Grand Rapids, MI: Zondervan, 1991.

Carroll R. (Rodas), M. Daniel. "Old Testament Ethics." In *Dictionary of Scripture and Ethics*, edited by Joel B. Green, 561–65. Grand Rapids, MI: Baker, 2011.

Clowney, Edmund P. *How Jesus Transforms the Ten Commandments*, edited by Rebecca Clowney Jones. Phillipsburg, NJ: P&R, 2007.

Goldberg, Michelle. *Kingdom Coming: The Rise of Christian Nationalism*. New York: W. W. Norton, 2007.

Gundry, Stanley N., series ed. *Five Views on Law and Gospel*. Counterpoints. Grand Rapids, MI: Zondervan, 1996.

House, H. Wayne, and Thomas Ice. *Dominion Theology, Blessing or Curse?* Portland, OR: Multnomah, 1988.

Kaiser, Walter C., Jr. *Toward Old Testament Ethics*. Grand Rapids, MI: Zondervan, 1991.

Poythress, Vern S. *The Shadow of Christ in the Law of Moses*. Phillipsburg, NJ: P&R, 1991.

Rooker, Mark F. *The Ten Commandments: Ethics for the Twenty-First Century*. NAC Studies in Bible and Theology. Vol. 7. Nashville: B&H Academic, 2010.

Rosner, Brian S. *Paul and the Law: Keeping the Commandments of God*. New Studies in Biblical Theology. Vol. 31. Downers Grove, IL: InterVarsity Press, 2013.

Schreiner, Thomas R. *40 Questions about Christians and Biblical Law*. Grand Rapids, MI: Kregel, 2010.

Thielman, Frank. *Paul and the Law: A Contextual Approach*. Downers Grove, IL: Inter-Varsity Press, 1994.

———. *The Law and the New Testament: The Question of Continuity*. Companions to the New Testament. New York: Herder & Herder, 1999.

Waltke, Bruce K. *An Old Testament Theology: An Exegetical, Canonical, and Thematic Approach*. Grand Rapids, MI: Zondervan, 2007.

Wenham, Gordon J. *Psalms as Torah: Reading Biblical Song Ethically*. Grand Rapids, MI: Baker, 2012.

———. *Story as Torah: Reading Old Testament Narrative Ethically*. Grand Rapids, MI: Baker, 2004.

Wogaman, J. Philip. *Christian Ethics: A Historical Introduction*. Louisville: Westminster John Knox, 1993.

Wright, Christopher J. H. "Old Testament Ethics." In *New Dictionary of Christian Ethics and Pastoral Theology*, edited by David J. Atkinson and David H. Field, 48–56. Leicester, UK: Inter-Varsity, and Downers Grove, IL: InterVarsity Press, 1995.

———. *Old Testament Ethics for the People of God*. Downers Grove, IL: InterVarsity, 2004.

SCRIPTURE MEMORY PASSAGE

Hebrews 8:6: But as it is, Christ has obtained a ministry that is as much more excellent than the old as the covenant he mediates is better, since it is enacted on better promises.

HYMN

"How Firm a Foundation"

How firm a foundation, ye saints of the Lord,
Is laid for your faith in his excellent Word!
What more can he say than to you he hath said,
You who unto Jesus for refuge have fled?
You who unto Jesus for refuge have fled?

"Fear not, I am with thee, O be not dismayed;
I, I am thy God, and will still give thee aid;
I'll strengthen thee, help thee, and cause thee to stand,

Upheld by my righteous, omnipotent hand,
Upheld by my righteous, omnipotent hand.

"When through the deep waters I call thee to go,
The rivers of woe shall not thee overflow;
For I will be with thee thy troubles to bless,
And sanctify to thee thy deepest distress,
And sanctify to thee thy deepest distress.

"When through fiery trials thy pathway shall lie,
My grace, all sufficient, shall be thy supply;
The flame shall not hurt thee; I only design
Thy dross to consume, and thy gold to refine,
Thy dross to consume, and thy gold to refine.

"E'en down to old age all my people shall prove
My sovereign, eternal, unchangeable love;
And when hoary hairs shall their temples adorn,
Like lambs they shall still in my bosom be borne,
Like lambs they shall still in my bosom be borne.

"The soul that on Jesus hath leaned for repose,
I will not, I will not desert to his foes;
That soul, though all hell should endeavor to shake,
I'll never, no, never, no, never forsake,
I'll never, no, never, no, never forsake."

FROM: RIPPON'S *SELECTION OF HYMNS*, 1787

Part 2

PROTECTING GOD'S HONOR

"You shall have no other gods before me."
"You shall not make for yourself a carved image."
"You shall not take the name of the Lord your God in vain."
"Remember the Sabbath day."
"You shall not bear false witness."

Chapter 9

NO OTHER GODS

Why is a right relationship with God the first requirement for studying ethics?

What things are we tempted to value more than God today?

When God spoke the Ten Commandments from Mount Sinai, he began by identifying himself and what he had done:

> And God spoke all these words, saying, "I am the LORD your God, who brought you out of the land of Egypt, out of the house of slavery." (Ex. 20:1–2)

Then came the first commandment:

> You shall have no other gods before me. (Ex. 20:3)

A. THE MEANING OF THE COMMANDMENT

In the Hebrew text, the word *you* is a singular pronoun,[1] indicating that God is addressing the people of Israel as individuals who are accountable to him personally.

The phrase "before me" represents the Hebrew expression ʿal-pānāy (literally, "on/to/towards/against my face"[2]), and it is translated as either "before me" (ESV and most other English translations) or "besides me" (CSB; ESV mg., NIV, and NRSV mg.), but the sense is similar in both expressions. The intention of English translators in rendering it "before me" was to give the sense of "in my presence" (which captures the idea of the Hebrew "to my face"). In any case, "before me" does *not* mean "You shall have no other gods who rank higher than me," for then it would allow us to have some little

---

[1] Very literally, the Hebrew text reads, "There shall not be to you [lekā] other gods before me."

[2] The Septuagint in fact translates this phrase in Deuteronomy 5:7 as "before my face" (Greek, *pro prosōpou mou*).

"gods" that we could partially worship, obey, and trust, as in pagan polytheism. That is not the sense intended. We should understand the verse to mean "You shall have no other gods in my presence" or "before my face." This commandment is a reminder that we are always and everywhere in the presence of God, and that he will tolerate no other small gods at any place or any time in our lives.

The first commandment therefore reminds us that God deserves and requires our absolute reverence, trust, obedience, and love. This idea gains fuller expression in this very familiar passage:

> Hear, O Israel: The LORD our God, the LORD is one. You shall love the LORD your God with all your heart and with all your soul and with all your might. (Deut. 6:4–5)

God is the supreme, omnipotent, most holy Creator and Ruler of the universe, and he rightly demands that we honor him as such:

> I am the LORD; that is my name;
> *my glory I give to no other,*
> nor my praise to carved idols. (Isa. 42:8)

> For my name's sake I defer my anger,
> for the sake of my praise I restrain it for you,
> that I may not cut you off.
> Behold, I have refined you, but not as silver;
> I have tried you in the furnace of affliction.
> For my own sake, for my own sake, I do it,
> *for how should my name be profaned?*
> *My glory I will not give to another.* (Isa. 48:9–11)

B. WHY IS THIS THE FIRST COMMANDMENT?

1. A Right Relationship with God Is Necessary for a Right Understanding of Ethics and Right Ethical Living. This commandment searches our hearts. It is concerned with the kind of relationship with God that we have in our hearts, a relationship that only God can see. This commandment comes first because it reminds us that the rest of the commands to follow are not mere opinions invented by human imagination, but are commandments that issue from our Creator himself.

That is why God's Word says elsewhere:

> *The fear of the LORD is the beginning of wisdom;*
> all those who practice it have a good understanding.
> His praise endures forever! (Ps. 111:10)

Before we can rightly listen to, fully understand, or joyfully obey the other commandments, we must first come to the point where we know God and love him—and, indeed, fear him (in that we should fear displeasing him and fear incurring his fatherly discipline).[3] Then we will be ready to obey him rightly.

Because this command challenges our hearts at the deepest level, we should immediately realize that in this lifetime it is impossible to obey it perfectly, and so this command should also drive us to Christ for full forgiveness (see 1 John 1:9).

As noted above, the phrase "before me" reminds us that all of life is lived in the presence of God. I do not agree with the view that this commandment pictures a setting of temple worship, with the people of Israel gathered at the temple, where they would be "before God." If that were so, the commandment would say they should not have other competing gods *in the temple*. But the perspective of the Old Testament is that God's presence is not confined to the temple (or the "tabernacle," the tent that served as a sanctuary from the time of Moses):

> The eyes of the Lord are in every place,
>   keeping watch on the evil and the good. (Prov. 15:3; see also Psalm 139)

> For the eyes of the Lord run to and fro *throughout the whole earth*, to give strong support to those whose heart is blameless toward him. (2 Chron. 16:9).

The commandment calls us also to remember that our hearts are continually in God's presence, for he sees them always:

> For the Lord sees not as man sees: man looks on the outward appearance, but *the Lord looks on the heart*. (1 Sam. 16:7)

2. When Societies Ignore the First Commandment, Much Evil Follows. Whenever a society forsakes the idea that we live in the presence of God and that we are accountable to him for our actions, evil deeds multiply.

When Paul writes of the sinfulness of the entire world, he strings together several quotations from the Old Testament with the conclusion "there is *no fear of God* before their eyes." Here is the full passage:

> "None is righteous, no, not one;
>   no one understands;
>   no one seeks for God.
> All have turned aside; together they have become worthless;
>   no one does good,
>   not even one."
> "Their throat is an open grave;
>   they use their tongues to deceive."

---

[3] See discussion of fearing God in chap. 6, p. 166.

"The venom of asps is under their lips."
"Their mouth is full of curses and bitterness."
"Their feet are swift to shed blood;
    in their paths are ruin and misery,
and the way of peace they have not known."
    "*There is no fear of God before their eyes.*" (Rom. 3:10–18)

One of the passages that Paul quotes is from Psalm 36, which explains this process precisely. It connects reckless, wanton evil with a foolish assumption by a wicked person that God will not know his actions, so he will not be accountable to God:

Transgression speaks to the wicked
    deep in his heart;
there is no fear of God
    before his eyes.
For he flatters himself in his own eyes
    that his iniquity cannot be found out and hated.
The words of his mouth are trouble and deceit;
    he has ceased to act wisely and do good. (Ps. 36:1–3)

A similar theme is found in Psalm 94, where "the wicked" think they can get away with evil because they assume that God does not see what they are doing:

O LORD, how long shall the wicked,
    how long shall the wicked exult?
They pour out their arrogant words;
    all the evildoers boast.
They crush your people, O LORD,
    and afflict your heritage.
They kill the widow and the sojourner,
    and murder the fatherless;
and they say, "The LORD does not see;
    the God of Jacob does not perceive." (Ps. 94:3–7)

One historical example of this tendency for moral decline to follow when a society loses a common sense of accountability to God has been evident within my own lifetime. In 1971 (when I was 23 and a first-year seminary student), the United States Supreme Court gave a new interpretation to the concept of freedom of religion in the First Amendment to the Constitution. In the case Lemon v. Kurtzman, the court ruled that government actions "must not have the primary effect of advancing or inhibiting religion." It did not say "advancing or inhibiting the Christian religion" (or the "Catholic religion," the "Jewish religion," the "Presbyterian religion," and so forth), but "advancing or inhibiting *religion*" (generally), something the First Amendment never meant and was never intended to mean.[4]

There were many consequences, but one in particular was seen in public schools (which are an arm of government). Increasingly, schoolteachers and other officials were prohibited from making any positive affirmation of belief in God or accountability to God (even in a nonsectarian way). The result has been that, since 1971, American society has increasingly been populated by people who, throughout their formative years, have been educated *without any sense of a societal consensus that people are morally accountable to God for their actions*. Some people may think this a good thing, but I do not. I cannot prove that such a system of public education without any reference to God has *caused* the widespread moral decline that we see, but it is unquestionable that moral decline *has clearly followed* this court-imposed change in our educational system, and I believe it has been a significant causative factor. This same kind of absence of a sense of moral accountability to God is also propagated continually by most mass media and the entertainment industry. When societies ignore the first commandment, much evil follows.

3. The Concept of Doing Ethics "before God" Is Lacking in Secular Ethics Today. Although most secular universities and graduate schools now offer courses in topics such as business ethics, legal ethics, or medical ethics, these courses generally lack the idea of accountability to God or the idea that there are absolute ethical standards based on the moral character of our Creator (or the idea that we can know what these ethical standards are).

This is not to say that such courses are without value, but only that their conclusions are necessarily tentative (since there are no moral absolutes) and the motives they teach for behaving ethically are necessarily limited to seeking the best results (consequentialist ethics). There is some benefit, of course, in evaluating results, but secular approaches lack the much stronger motive of accountability to God for one's actions and the ethical clarity that comes from knowing what God himself has told us about right and wrong ethical choices.

4. Jesus Demands the Same Loyalty. The first commandment teaches us that only God himself has the right to demand our absolute love, trust, and obedience. But then we see in the New Testament that Jesus requires that we love him more than anyone or anything else, even our families or our lives:

> Whoever loves father or mother more than me is not worthy of me, and whoever loves son or daughter more than me is not worthy of me. And whoever

---

[4] This decision was partially supported by the 1947 decision Everson v. Board of Education, 330 U.S. 1 (1947), which I also think was mistaken and went far beyond what the Constitution required. See discussion in Wayne Grudem, *Politics—According to the Bible: A Comprehensive Resource for Understanding Modern Political Issues in Light of Scripture* (Grand Rapids, MI: Zondervan, 2010), 136–37.

does not take his cross and follow me is not worthy of me. Whoever finds his life will lose it, and whoever loses his life for my sake will find it. (Matt. 10:37–39)

This is evidence of Jesus's claim to be God, because he demands the same loyalty that only God himself is worthy to receive. This is why it is so significant that Christians worship Jesus. If Jesus is not God, then worshiping him would be idolatry. If Jesus is truly God, as he claimed, then worshiping him is an eternally appropriate way of obeying the first commandment.

C. APPLICATION TO LIFE: OTHER GODS TODAY

1. Polytheistic Religions. One evident violation of the first commandment would be any polytheistic religion, such as modern Hinduism, which is so prevalent in India. Hindu temples can have hundreds or even thousands of idols representing various Hindu deities.

Polytheism is not new, for Paul encountered it in Athens:

Now while Paul was waiting for them at Athens, his spirit was provoked within him as he saw that *the city was full of idols.* (Acts 17:16)

Paul's spirit was deeply troubled by the idols in Athens, because he saw that they were not just benign representations of alternative ideas about God, but they were profoundly sinful violations of the commandment "You shall have no other gods before me."

2. All False Religions. All religions that worship deities other than the one true God of the Bible are violating the first commandment. In ancient Babylon, three faithful young Jewish men refused to violate this commandment and worship a golden image of a Babylonian deity as the king commanded. The king was told:

There are certain Jews whom you have appointed over the affairs of the province of Babylon: Shadrach, Meshach, and Abednego. These men, O king, pay no attention to you; they do not serve your gods or worship the golden image that you have set up. (Dan. 3:12)

They were thrown into a burning fiery furnace for their disobedience, but God miraculously protected them (see Dan. 3:13–30).

In the New Testament age, there were many pagan temples devoted to various Greek and Roman deities in the Mediterranean world. Paul did not say that these other religions were harmless, but he said that the worshipers in these pagan religious temples were worshiping demons rather than the one true God:

No, I imply that *what pagans sacrifice they offer to demons and not to God*. I do not want you to be participants with demons. (1 Cor. 10:20; see also 2 Cor. 4:4, where Satan is called "the god of this world")

3. Atheism. Although atheism claims to believe in no deity at all, in actuality those who profess atheism are also violating the first commandment because they have put their own ideas about religion in a place of higher priority than worship and obedience to the one true God, who created both them and the entire universe. In this way, atheists have "other gods" (their own false ideas) in the presence of God, who sees all things.

4. Things That We Do Not Call "Gods" but That We Value, Love, Serve, and Trust More Than God Himself. If we begin to list all the things that we sometimes value, love, serve, and trust more than God, the list could cover all of life and could become very long indeed. Here are some examples:

a. Money: Jesus warns us against putting money before God:

> No one can serve two masters, for either he will hate the one and love the other, or he will be devoted to the one and despise the other. You cannot serve God and money. (Matt. 6:24)

b. Material Things That We Covet: Paul can say that covetousness is "idolatry" because it means that we seek joy, contentment, and security in things that we long to have rather than seeking these things in and from God, who has promised to care for our needs:

> Put to death therefore what is earthly in you: sexual immorality, impurity, passion, evil desire, and *covetousness, which is idolatry*. (Col. 3:5)

c. Food and Physical Pleasure: Paul speaks of people whose "god is their belly" (Phil. 3:19), by which he may be referring to people who put eating and satisfying their physical appetites above all other concerns. Another possibility is that he is using this concrete example to speak of people who put physical comfort and hedonistic pleasures above everything else in life. In either case, this is a false god that takes the place of the one true God.

d. Approval of Other People: It is a common temptation for Christians to seek the approval of other people, popularity, and even fame, and then to start treating those things as more important than serving God or Christ. Paul protests that if he did this he would not be truly serving Christ:

> For am I now seeking the approval of man, or of God? Or am I trying to please man? *If I were still trying to please man, I would not be a servant of Christ.* (Gal. 1:10)

Even the apostle Peter made this mistake at one point, for when "certain men came from James" he "drew back and separated himself, fearing the circumcision party" (Gal. 2:12). Avoiding the disapproval of overly strict Jewish believers became more important to Peter than being faithful to the gospel, and Paul rebuked him for it (see Gal. 2:14; see also 1 Sam. 15:24, where Saul says he sinned "because *I feared the people* and obeyed their voice").

e. Praise That Belongs Only to God: It is dangerous for a famous or popular person to accept too much praise from other human beings and to delight in it, as Herod Agrippa I found to his own destruction:

> On an appointed day Herod put on his royal robes, took his seat upon the throne, and delivered an oration to them. And the people were shouting, "The voice of a god, and not of a man!" Immediately *an angel of the Lord struck him down, because he did not give God the glory*, and he was eaten by worms and breathed his last. (Acts 12:21–23)

f. Semireligious or "Spiritual" Practices: When we realize that the first commandment requires us to trust in God above all else, this calls into question small superstitions that can easily become part of a person's life. This could involve trusting in "luck" or good fortune to grant us favor or success, or allowing ourselves to think that events "just happen" according to fate or destiny rather than by God's providential governance of the universe.

Similar semireligious substitutes for truly trusting in God include trusting in "karma" in the events of life or relying on horoscopes, fortune-tellers, or psychics. Related to this would be using Ouija boards to attempt to gain guidance, learn the future, or contact the unseen spiritual world. Then there are the common, seemingly "harmless" superstitions such as placing confidence in lucky numbers, lucky days, lucky codes, and so forth rather than trusting in God.

These things have been common in every age. John Calvin observed that "man's nature . . . is a perpetual factory of idols."[5]

g. Power: Sometimes in human experience, having power over other people becomes intoxicating, and the person who has gained that power longs for more and more. This desire for power then takes a more important place than God in that person's life.

h. Self: For many people, the greatest idol of all is self. They spend their days working above all for themselves rather than for God's glory and his kingdom, and the primary focus of their thought is always "What's best for me?"

---

[5] John Calvin, *Institutes of the Christian Religion*, ed. John T. McNeill, trans. Ford Lewis Battles, Library of Christian Classics, vols. 20–21 (Philadelphia: Westminster, 1960), 1.11.8 (108).

i. Other Things That We Trust More Than God: When we realize that in this commandment God demands our complete loyalty and trust, it makes us realize that too often in life we trust other things more than him. Such things can include our own talents and abilities, our friends, our retirement savings, a favorite political party (for the future of our country), exercising and eating a healthy diet (to protect our health), modern medicine and competent doctors (to cure our diseases), and plans for vacation, family events, or sporting events (for our happiness). I am not saying that these things are wrong in themselves, because many of them are actually good things. But our trust in them and our love of them can take the place of God. Therefore, they can become idols in our hearts.

Protestants disagree with their Roman Catholic friends regarding one further application of this commandment. Many Protestants understand the Roman Catholic practices of "veneration" of Mary and other saints, and prayers to Mary and to the saints, as offering worship to and placing trust in finite creatures rather than in God himself, and thus as violations of the first commandment. Roman Catholics, however, understand these practices differently.[6]

QUESTIONS FOR PERSONAL APPLICATION

1. Are you today truly loving God above all else—more than your family, your friends, and even your very life?

2. In an ordinary day, how often are you aware of living all of life "before God"?

3. Are you today seeking joy in God above all else, and finding joy in human friendships and other earthly joys only when you see them as gifts from him?

4. Are there "little gods" that you tend to worship more than God himself— things that you love to talk about more than God or things that you love to think about more during the day?

5. Do you sometimes think that things happen because of fate, luck, or some small superstitious practice?

6. Do you ever seek approval from other people more than from God?

7. Are you sometimes tempted to make up your own rules for ethics rather than following what you know to be the rules found in the Bible?

8. Have you studied ethics in a secular high school, university, or business setting? If so, how was it different from what you are learning in this book?

9. What personal virtues or character traits would be helpful in influencing you toward a fuller obedience to this commandment? (See list of character traits in chap. 4, p. 110.)

---

[6] See discussion in *Catechism of the Catholic Church*, 2nd ed. (New York: Doubleday, 1997), para. 969, 971, 975, 2673–79, 2682, 2683–84, 2692.

BIBLIOGRAPHY

Sections in Other Ethics Texts

(see complete bibliographical data, p. 64)

> Frame, 421–49
> McQuilkin and Copan, 189–94

Other Works

Beale, G. K. *We Become What We Worship: A Biblical Theology of Idolatry*. Downers Grove, IL: InterVarsity Press, 2008.

Bigney, Brad. *Gospel Treason: Betraying the Gospel with Hidden Idols*. Phillipsburg, NJ: P&R, 2012.

Fitzpatrick, Elyse M. *Idols of the Heart: Learning to Long for God Alone*. 2nd ed. Phillipsburg, NJ: P&R, 2016.

Goudzwaard, Bob. *Idols of Our Time*. Downers Grove, IL: InterVarsity Press, 1984.

Hardyman, Julian. *Idols: God's Battle for Our Hearts*. Leicester, UK: Inter-Varsity Press, 2010.

Idleman, Kyle. *Gods at War: Defeating the Idols That Battle for Your Heart*. Grand Rapids, MI: Zondervan, 2013.

Keller, Timothy. *Counterfeit Gods: The Empty Promises of Money, Sex, and Power, and the Only Hope That Matters*. New York: Dutton, 2009.

Powlison, David. "Revisiting Idols of the Heart and Vanity Fair." *Journal of Biblical Counseling* 27, no. 3 (2013): 37–68.

Rosner, Brian S. *Greed as Idolatry: The Origin and Meaning of a Pauline Metaphor*. Grand Rapids, MI: Eerdmans, 2007.

———. "Idolatry." In *Dictionary of Scripture and Ethics*, edited by Joel B. Green, 392–94. Grand Rapids, MI: Baker, 2011.

SCRIPTURE MEMORY PASSAGE

> **Exodus 20:1–3:** And God spoke all these words, saying, "I am the Lᴏʀᴅ your God, who brought you out of the land of Egypt, out of the house of slavery. You shall have no other gods before me."

HYMN

"All That Thrills My Soul"

> Who can cheer the heart like Jesus,
> By His presence all divine?

True and tender, pure and precious,
O how blest to call Him mine!

Refrain:
All that thrills my soul is Jesus,
He is more than life to me;
And the fairest of ten thousand
In my blessed Lord I see.

Love of Christ so freely given,
Grace of God beyond degree,
Mercy higher than the heaven,
Deeper than the deepest sea!

What a wonderful redemption!
Never can a mortal know
How my sin, tho red like crimson,
Can be whiter than the snow.

Ev'ry need His hand supplying,
Ev'ry good in Him I see;
On His strength divine relying,
He is all in all to me.

By the crystal flowing river
With the ransomed I will sing,
And forever and forever
Praise and glorify the King.[7]

AUTHOR: THORO HARRIS, 1874–1955

---

[7] Words and music by Thoro Harris. © 1931, renewed 1959 Nazarene Publishing House. All rights reserved. Used by permission.

10

NO CARVED IMAGES

Is all artwork prohibited, or only that which is used for worship?

Is it wrong to make images of God for artistic purposes?

What about pictures of Jesus Christ or the Holy Spirit?

The second commandment reads:

> You shall not make for yourself a carved image, or any likeness of anything that is in heaven above, or that is in the earth beneath, or that is in the water under the earth. You shall not bow down to them or serve them, for I the LORD your God am a jealous God, visiting the iniquity of the fathers on the children to the third and the fourth generation of those who hate me, but showing steadfast love to thousands of those who love me and keep my commandments. (Ex. 20:4–6)

A. THE MEANING OF THE COMMANDMENT

1. It Prohibits Making Carved Images of God the Father. The Hebrew word translated as "carved image" is *pesel*, a noun related to the verb *pāsal*, "to carve out, hew" something (often from wood or stone). It always refers to an object that is carved or chiseled out of wood, stone, or metal and then used as an object of worship—in other words, an idol.[1]

While the first commandment prohibits worshiping gods other than the one true God, this commandment prohibits worshiping the one true God in a way that makes us think of him as having a physical form like something in his creation. To think of God's

---

[1] Instead of rendering *pesel* as "carved image," some Bible translations simply render it as "idol" (NASB, NLT, NRSV). The KJV uses the expression "graven image," where "graven" is an older English word meaning "carved or sculpted." This Hebrew word is frequently used elsewhere in the Old Testament to refer not to just any carved artwork at all but to carved images used in worship.

very being as having a physical form is to diminish him, to dishonor him, to ignore the immense difference between the Creator and the creature.

Sometimes the people of Israel gave in to the temptation to invent physical images to represent the Lord God himself. This is not surprising. All of the ancient Near Eastern nations and cultures surrounding Israel had physical images of their gods. Perhaps the people of Israel felt their religion was inferior when they interacted with people from other nations. They could easily have faced questions like these: "Why is your religion so different? What kind of religion doesn't even know what its god looks like?"

For whatever reason, soon after the exodus from Egypt, the people of Israel provoked Aaron to make a physical object representing God himself:

> When the people saw that Moses delayed to come down from the mountain, the people gathered themselves together to Aaron and said to him, "Up, *make us gods* who shall go before us. As for this Moses, the man who brought us up out of the land of Egypt, we do not know what has become of him." (Ex. 32:1)

Aaron gave in to the pressure of the people and told them to bring him their gold jewelry, which they did:

> And he received the gold from their hand and fashioned it with a graving tool and made a golden calf. And they said, "These are your gods, O Israel, *who brought you up out of the land of Egypt!*" When Aaron saw this, he built an altar before it. And Aaron made a proclamation and said, "Tomorrow shall be *a feast to the Lord.*" (Ex. 32:4–5)

This was not an image of Baal or Dagon, pagan deities. It was intended as an image of the Lord God himself. And it brought the judgment of God on the people (see Ex. 32:7–35).

Similarly, at a later period, King Jeroboam made images of the Lord God:

> So the king took counsel and made two calves of gold. And he said to the people, "You have gone up to Jerusalem long enough. Behold *your gods*, O Israel, *who brought you up out of the land of Egypt.*" (1 Kings 12:28)

The more we think about the golden calf that Aaron and the people made (Exodus 32), the more hateful the action seems. They may have thought at first that the calf represented God's vitality, strength, and fertility, all valued qualities. But thinking of God like a calf horribly misrepresented the power of the God who created the whole universe (compared to the power of a single calf!), his omnipresence (compared to one calf in one place), and his infinite knowledge and wisdom (compared to the intelligence of a calf!), not to mention his moral holiness and purity, his love, his patience, his unchangeableness, his eternity, his justice, his wrath, his personhood, his interpersonal relationship skills, his ability to speak, and his Trinitarian existence. This golden calf was a horrible affront to God's honor. It was proclaiming that God is like something in the creation, but in fact he is the eternal, infinite Creator of all things; he is not a mere creature.

2. It Prohibits Making Carved Images of False Gods. But the command also prohibits making and worshiping images of other gods, such as the Baal image or the Asherah image (both mentioned in Judg. 6:25 and frequently in the Old Testament), or the image of Dagon, the Philistine deity (see 1 Sam. 5:2–7), for the commandment does not narrowly specify, "You shall not make for yourself a carved image *of me*." Instead, it prohibits making and worshiping all carved images that represent *any* deities whatsoever.

The wicked Jewish king Manasseh built such images of other gods:

> For he rebuilt the high places that his father Hezekiah had broken down, and he erected altars to the *Baals*, and made *Asheroth*, and worshiped all the host of heaven and served them. (2 Chron. 33:3)

When Solomon married many foreign wives, he also built temples and idols for the gods of these foreign women:

> Then Solomon built a high place for Chemosh the abomination of Moab, and for Molech the abomination of the Ammonites, on the mountain east of Jerusalem. And so he did for all his foreign wives, who made offerings and sacrificed to their gods. (1 Kings 11:7–8)

Worshiping such foreign deities violated the first commandment. But even if Solomon did not worship these idols, simply making them for his wives to worship was a violation of the second commandment, for he made these things as objects of worship.

The psalmist tells the truth about these images of false gods:

> The idols of the nations are silver and gold,
>   the work of human hands.
> *They have mouths, but do not speak;*
>   *they have eyes, but do not see;*
> they have ears, but do not hear,
>   nor is there any breath in their mouths.
> Those who make them become like them,
>   so do all who trust in them. (Ps. 135:15–18; see also the foolishness of
>   idolatry as described in Isa. 44:9–20)

B. THE REASON FOR THIS COMMANDMENT

1. The Reason for This Commandment Is God's Jealousy. The second commandment includes a reason: "You shall not make for yourself a carved image . . . you shall not bow down to them or serve them, *for I the LORD your God am a jealous God*" (Ex. 20:4–5).

God seeks to be known and honored for who he is, and he is displeased when anyone represents him falsely or dishonors him. But as we saw earlier with regard to the golden calf, *any* physical form dishonors God and misrepresents him, for he does not look like or act like any material thing in the creation. He is the infinite, all-powerful, omnipresent Creator, and there is nothing in creation that can adequately represent who he is. In New Testament terms, "God is spirit, and those who worship him must worship in spirit and truth" (John 4:24).

However, God did make one creature in the entire universe to represent himself, and that is man:

> So God created man *in his own image,*
>> in the image of God he created him;
>> male and female he created them. (Gen. 1:27)

Since man is created in God's image, we as human beings are to be the primary representatives of God on earth. We are more like God than anything else that he has made, and we are to rule over his creation (see Gen. 1:28) as his representatives in obedience to him. God did not make us to bow down to an image of a calf, a fish, a bird, or any other created animal.

In Deuteronomy 4, Moses gave the people more detailed discussion of this commandment, and said that the reason the Jewish people should not make carved images is that they "*saw no form*" when the Lord appeared to them at Mount Sinai (also called "Horeb"). God did not appear to them in a physical form:

> Therefore watch yourselves very carefully. *Since you saw no form* on the day that the Lord spoke to you at Horeb out of the midst of the fire, *beware lest you act corruptly by making a carved image for yourselves*, in the form of any figure, the likeness of male or female, the likeness of any animal that is on the earth, the likeness of any winged bird that flies in the air, the likeness of anything that creeps on the ground, the likeness of any fish that is in the water under the earth. And beware lest you raise your eyes to heaven, and when you see the sun and the moon and the stars, all the host of heaven, you be drawn away and bow down to them and serve them, things that the Lord your God has allotted to all the peoples under the whole heaven. (Deut. 4:15–19)

There are some common occurrences in human life that help us understand this attribute of God's jealousy. We find it troubling when someone lies about us, because we do not want others to think of us in a wrongful way. Or we find it quite troubling if someone takes a photo of us and then modifies it to make us look ugly, to show us committing some sinful act, or to misrepresent us in some other way.

How much greater sorrow—and anger—must the infinitely wise and pure Creator of all things experience when his creatures misrepresent him and dishonor him! This helps us understand that God's jealousy for his own honor is *a good thing*, and is one of his holy attributes. We should realize how important it is to God that we think of him rightly and how displeased he is when we think of him, speak of him, and portray him wrongly.

God did not want to be dishonored at the time of Moses (1440 BC) and he does not want to be dishonored today, or ever. Therefore, this commandment means that people of all cultures and all ages of history should not make sculptures or paintings attempting to represent the invisible God.

This assertion will likely cause many people to think of one of the most amazing artistic creations in the world, the magnificent series of paintings by Michelangelo on the ceiling of the Sistine Chapel in the Vatican. The ceiling radiates Michelangelo's artistic genius. Yet near the center is the famous portrait of God reaching out his finger to touch the outstretched finger of Adam at the moment God created him. This is a picture of the invisible God portrayed as a man. While I am amazed at Michelangelo's artistic skill, and while I believe his *motives* were good (to communicate the events of the Bible to people through his paintings),[2] I also think that this picture of God violates the second commandment. Especially in light of Deuteronomy 4:15–17, I do not think that God is pleased at being portrayed as an old man with white hair and a flowing beard.[3]

2. The Question of God's Fairness. This second commandment also contains a statement of consequences that come to the children and grandchildren of those who worship idols:

> You shall not make for yourself a carved image, or any likeness of anything that is in heaven above, or that is in the earth beneath, or that is in the water under the earth. You shall not bow down to them or serve them, for I the LORD your God am a jealous God, visiting the iniquity of the fathers on the children to the third and the fourth generation of those who hate me, but showing steadfast love to thousands of those who love me and keep my commandments. (Ex. 20:4–6)

People sometimes wonder how it can be fair for God to punish children and grandchildren for the sins of their fathers.

In response, it must be said that one of the most hateful aspects of sin is that it often brings lasting harm not only to the sinner but also to the people around him or her. We can observe this pattern in daily life: children of abusive parents are more likely to

---

[2] See chap. 6, p. 149, for the distinction between the motives for an action and the action itself.

[3] I have seen the Sistine Chapel ceiling on two occasions and was overwhelmed by its scale and beauty. I think it is possible to distinguish between (1) *creating* an image of God, (2) *worshiping* an image of God, and (3) *looking at* an image of God as an observer. I think (1) and (2) are wrong, but (3) is usually not wrong. I have also visited a large Hindu temple in India that had hundreds of idols, and in that case I thought that the artistic quality was poor. But I do not think it was wrong to observe this idol, so long as I did not begin to worship it or to think it was showing me what God is like (see Acts 17:16, 22–23).

become abusive themselves in adulthood, and children of alcoholic parents are more likely to become alcoholics. Even when such sinful behavior is not directly imitated by the next generation, often emotional scars remain, and the harm caused by sin carries on over more than one generation. It sometimes is seen even to "the fourth generation" (great-grandchildren).

But it also must be said that there is hope for people in every generation who will turn to God. We must not read verse 5 in isolation, but must take it in connection with verse 6. The passage shows two groups of people: "*those who hate me*" (v. 5) and "*those who love me* and keep my commandments" (v. 6). A person in the first, second, or third generation after a deeply sinful parent can turn to God in repentance, asking for forgiveness. In that case, the repentant person is transferred from the category of "those who hate me" to the category of "those who love me and keep my commandments," and the perpetuation of sin to the descendants of "those who hate" God (v. 5) no longer applies. Now this person is in the category of those to whom God shows "steadfast love to thousands,"[4] and he or she can begin to know increasing freedom from previous sinful patterns of behavior.

C. APPLICATION TO LIFE

1. This Commandment Also Prohibits Mental Images of God. When Jesus taught about some of the Ten Commandments, he explained that God is concerned not merely with obedience in our outward actions, but also with obedience in the depths of our hearts (see Matt. 5:21–30). This is because "man looks on the outward appearance, but the LORD looks on the heart" (1 Sam. 16:7; see also Ps. 51:10).

Therefore, we should not merely refrain from making actual wooden or metal statues to represent God. We also should refrain from *thinking of God* in such a way that we imagine him to have a physical body or to look like a man or some other part of creation. We should not think of God the Father as having any kind of physical form at all.[5]

How, then, should we think about God when we pray to him? Although it is not wrong to think about Jesus Christ as a man (see below), we should not think of God the Father in the form of "*any likeness* of anything that is in heaven above, or that is in the earth beneath, or that is in the water under the earth" (Ex. 20:4). We should simply think of him as a *spiritual presence*, a presence without a physical body. And we should think of the Holy Spirit in the same way, as a spiritual being who is *present* with us but who does not have a physical form.

---

[4] The phrase in v. 6 can also be translated, "to the thousandth generation" (ESV mg., NRSV); several other translations have "to a thousand generations" (HCSB, NET, NIV, NLT). The Hebrew text literally just says "to a thousand," but this follows immediately after the mention of "the third and the fourth generation," so these translations understand it to mean "to a thousand (generations)."

[5] Mormons contradict this teaching when they claim that even God the Father at one time had a physical body as a human being.

2. But This Commandment Does Not Prohibit Pictures of Christ. When we come to the question of Jesus Christ, we face a different situation. Surely it is not wrong to *think of Christ* as existing on earth in a human form, because *he did live on earth as a man* for about 33 years. Thinking of him in a human form *does not misrepresent him*, but rather represents him truthfully. Therefore, the biblical rationale for making no image of God—"Since you saw no form on the day that the LORD spoke to you at Horeb" (Deut. 4:15)—does not apply to Jesus. People did, in fact, see a human "form" when Jesus walked among them, for he existed in a true human body. It would be wrong to read the Gospel stories of Jesus and *not* to think of him as a real man with a human body.

But if it is not wrong to form *mental images* of Jesus in our minds, then it cannot be wrong to portray Christ as a man in things such as paintings and sculptures as well. I see nothing wrong with portraying Jesus as a man in children's Bible storybooks, in all kinds of artistic paintings, and so forth. I see nothing wrong with a baby portraying Jesus as a baby for a Christmas play in a church. And I see nothing wrong with an actor portraying Jesus in a film, so long as the actor does not portray him as sinning in any way and does not treat him in a disrespectful or untruthful manner. Jesus lived among us as a man, and it is right to think of him and portray him as a genuine man.

In our prayers, it is certainly acceptable to think of Jesus as a man still today, for he rose from the dead in his physical body (though it was a perfect resurrection body; see Luke 24:38–43, 50–51). Today he still exists in heaven as both God and man joined in one person, and Scripture encourages us to think of him as our "merciful and faithful high priest in the service of God" (Heb. 2:17). Moreover, we are to think of him as one who has been tempted as we are and therefore understands our situation:

> For we do not have a high priest who is unable to sympathize with our weaknesses, but one who *in every respect has been tempted as we are*, yet without sin. Let us then with confidence draw near to the throne of grace, that we may receive mercy and find grace to help in time of need. (Heb. 4:15–16)

3. This Commandment Does Not Prohibit All Visual Arts. Upon first reading this commandment, an interpreter might take verse 4—"You shall not make for yourself a carved image, or a likeness of anything that is heaven above, or that is in the earth beneath, or that is in the water under the earth"—to be a stand-alone command that prohibits all visual arts that depict living things in the natural world.[6]

But such a strict prohibition against all images of created things misunderstands the force of this commandment. Verse 4 should not be taken by itself apart from its connection to the first part of verse 5—"You shall not bow down to them or serve them." Taken together, the reason given for both (1) "You shall not make for yourself a carved

---

[6] One example of such a prohibition is found in Islam. Islamic expert Al Fadi informs me (in a personal email) that "Islam allows for geometrical or architectural style artwork" and calligraphy, but does not permit "any depiction of humans, animals, or any living things." For this reason, the only visual artwork seen in mosques is Arabic writing and geometrical designs.

image . . ." and (2) "You shall not bow down to them or serve them" is God's jealousy: "*for* I the LORD your God am a jealous God." God does not want people to make visual images in order to worship them or in order to convey the idea, "This is what God is like." Any physical form representing God will dishonor him. But that is as far as the commandment goes; it is not prohibiting *all* visual arts.

Another reason we know this command does not prohibit all artistic renderings of living things is that God himself commanded the people of Israel to make images of some parts of creation. For instance, he explicitly told them that parts of the lampstand in the tabernacle should be made to look like almond blossoms:

> You shall make a lampstand of pure gold . . . *three cups made like almond blossoms*, each with calyx and flower, on one branch, and three cups made like almond blossoms, each with calyx and flower, on the other branch—so for the six branches going out of the lampstand. (Ex. 25:31–33)

In addition, God commanded that the decorations on the priestly garments that Aaron would wear would include images of pomegranates:

> On its hem you shall make *pomegranates* of blue and purple and scarlet yarns, around its hem, with bells of gold between them, a golden bell and a pomegranate, a golden bell and a pomegranate, around the hem of the robe. (Ex. 28:33–34)

Even more surprising, perhaps, is a command to make images of invisible heavenly creatures, the cherubim. These images were to be covered with gold and were to overshadow the ark of the covenant in the Most Holy Place in the tabernacle:

> *And you shall make two cherubim of gold*; of hammered work shall you make them, on the two ends of the mercy seat. Make one cherub on the one end, and one cherub on the other end. Of one piece with the mercy seat shall you make the cherubim on its two ends. The cherubim shall spread out their wings above, overshadowing the mercy seat with their wings, their faces one to another; toward the mercy seat shall the faces of the cherubim be. (Ex. 25:18–20)

Therefore, if God *commanded* such artwork depicting representations of earthly and heavenly realities, he cannot be *prohibiting* such action in the second commandment. The second commandment means, "You shall not make a carved image or any likeness . . . in order to bow down to them or to portray me by means of them."

QUESTIONS FOR PERSONAL APPLICATION

1. Do you commonly have a mental image of God the Father when you pray to him? Of Jesus Christ? Of the Holy Spirit?

2. Are you glad that God is jealous for his own honor, or does this idea make you uncomfortable?
3. When you see Jesus Christ portrayed in paintings or movies, is this helpful or harmful to your spiritual life?

SPECIAL TERMS

> carved image
> mental image

BIBLIOGRAPHY

Sections in Other Ethics Texts

(see complete bibliographical data, p. 64)

> Frame, 450–63
> McQuilkin and Copan, 195–99

Other Works

Barrs, Jerram. *Echoes of Eden: Reflections on Christianity, Literature, and the Arts.* Wheaton, IL: Crossway, 2013.

Gaebelein, Frank Ely, and D. Bruce Lockerbie. *The Christian, the Arts, and Truth: Regaining the Vision of Greatness.* Portland, OR: Multnomah, 1985.

Rookmaaker, H. R. *Modern Art and the Death of a Culture.* Downers Grove, IL: InterVarsity, 1970.

Rosner, Brian S. "Idolatry." In *Dictionary of Scripture and Ethics*, edited by Joel B. Green, 392–94. Grand Rapids, MI: Baker, 2011.

Schaeffer, Francis A. *Art and the Bible: Two Essays.* L'abri Special. London: Hodder and Stoughton, 1973.

Thistlethwaite, David. *The Art of God and the Religions of Art.* Carlisle, England: Solway, 1998.

Wolterstorff, Nicholas. *Art in Action: Toward a Christian Aesthetic.* Grand Rapids, MI: Eerdmans, 1996, 2010.

SCRIPTURE MEMORY PASSAGE

Exodus 20:4–6: You shall not make for yourself a carved image, or any likeness of anything that is in heaven above, or that is in the earth beneath, or that is in the water under the earth. You shall not bow down to them or serve them, for I the Lord your God am a jealous God, visiting the iniquity of the fathers on the children to the third and the fourth generation of those who

hate me, but showing steadfast love to thousands of those who love me and
keep my commandments.

HYMN

"To God Be the Glory"

To God be the glory, great things He hath done!
So loved He the world that He gave us His son,
Who yielded His life an atonement for sin
And opened the Life-gate that all may go in.

Refrain:
Praise the Lord, Praise the Lord,
Let the earth hear His voice!
Praise the Lord, Praise the Lord,
Let the people rejoice!
O come to the Father thru Jesus the Son,
And give Him the glory—great things He hath done.

O perfect redemption, the purchase of blood!
To every believer the promise of God;
The vilest offender who truly believes,
That moment from Jesus a pardon receives.

Great things He hath taught us, great things He hath done,
And great our rejoicing thru Jesus the Son;
But purer and higher and greater will be
Our wonder, our transport, when Jesus we see.

AUTHOR: FANNY CROSBY, 1820–1915

Chapter 11

PURITY OF SPEECH

What does it mean to take God's name "in vain"?
What guidelines does Scripture give us regarding obscene
language, oaths, vows, and humorous speech?

The third commandment reads:

> You shall not take the name of the LORD your God in vain, for the LORD will not hold him guiltless who takes his name in vain. (Ex. 20:7)

A. THE MEANING OF THE COMMANDMENT

1. The Meaning of "Name." Today, a name is mostly a label to identify a person and to distinguish him or her from other people. We do not often think of it as describing the character of the person. But in the Bible, the "name" of a person often has to do with the person's character or reputation. Thus, Proverbs says:

> A *good name* is to be chosen rather than great riches,
>   and favor is better than silver or gold. (Prov. 22:1)

God, in fact, sometimes changed the names of people to designate new roles that they would have or to give more accurate descriptions of who they were:

> No longer shall your name be called Abram, but *your name shall be Abraham*, for I have made you the father of a multitude of nations. (Gen. 17:5; "Abraham" means "Father of a multitude")

> And God said to Abraham, "As for Sarai your wife, you shall not call her name Sarai, but *Sarah* shall be her name." (Gen. 17:15; "Sarah" means "Princess")

She will bear a son, and *you shall call his name Jesus*, for he will save his people from their sins. (Matt. 1:21; "Jesus" is the Greek form of the Hebrew name "Joshua," which means "The Lord saves")

Therefore, the "name" of God refers not only to his name (such as "God" or "the Lord") in a narrow sense, but also to *everything that is said about God* in terms of his character or reputation. This commandment tells us that it is very important to God how we speak about him.

2. The Meaning of "Take . . . in Vain." The phrase translated "take . . . in vain" represents a combination of two Hebrew words, the ordinary word *nāśā'*, meaning "to lift up, to carry," and the word *shāwe'*, meaning "emptiness, nothingness, vanity." In an extremely literal sense, the command could be translated, "You shall not lift up the name of the Lord your God to worthlessness (or emptiness, vanity)."

3. The Command Forbids Foolish or Worthless Uses of God's Name. Therefore, this command in its most basic meaning forbids using God's name (or any of God's names, such as "God," "the Lord," "Jesus," or "Christ") in a careless or irreverent way.

The way in which a society uses God's name is one reflection of the way the society thinks about God. The more a society strays from God, the more common it is to hear people using his name simply as a curse or as an expression of surprise, frustration, or disgust. Quite commonly the expression, "Oh, my God!" (or "OMG") is heard today even in children's conversation, and people will use "Jesus Christ!" as an all-purpose exclamation with no thought of Jesus himself anywhere in their minds.

But if in the Bible a name refers also to the *entire reputation of a person*, then this command also prohibits *any* false, unworthy, or irreverent speech about God. Therefore, this command challenges us to consider how we speak about God whenever we speak about him. Are we amazed enough that we can even *speak* the name of God at all?[1] Is there enough reverence in our hearts when we speak about him?

When we pray, do we have enough reverence for God, enough awe of his majesty? (I have tried for years to avoid "churchy" language and intonation in praying aloud with others, and as a result my prayers sound much like ordinary conversation, but I recognize the danger that my prayers can become too casual and can lack appropriate reverence).

There is also a danger in humor when it concerns God. Speaking personally, I am

---

[1] Some Jewish people will not even say the name of God today. They will refer to him vaguely as "The Almighty," "The One Above," or "Hashem," which is Hebrew for "the Name." See Rabbi Baruch S. Davidson, "Why Don't Jews Say G-d's Name," http://www.chabad.org/library/article_cdo/aid/1443443/jewish/Why-Do nt-Jews-Say-Gds-Name.htm. In addition, some observant Jews avoid casually writing any name of God because they fear that the written name might later be defaced, obliterated, or destroyed accidentally or by one who does not know better. See "Jewish Concepts: The Name of God," http://www.jewishvirtuallibrary.org /the-name-of-god. The Bible does not support this idea, because it uses the name of God many thousands of times, but one can appreciate the attempt to be reverent.

almost always uncomfortable when people tell jokes about God or Jesus, or say foolish or comical things that God is supposedly doing in the world.

Other violations of this commandment occur when people speak wrongfully about God and dishonor his reputation. Some say that God is evil, that he is unworthy of praise, or that he is unfair or unjust. Others promote false religions, teaching that God is distant or cruel, that he cannot be known, or that his Word (the Bible) is untrustworthy. Some actually mock God, and others deeply dishonor Jesus by portraying him in sinful ways in television programs, plays, movies, paintings, or sculptures.

Compare these violations of the commandment to the appropriate and proper reverence toward God that Moses showed:

> The LORD passed before him and proclaimed, "The LORD, the LORD, a God merciful and gracious, slow to anger, and abounding in steadfast love and faithfulness, keeping steadfast love for thousands, forgiving iniquity and transgression and sin, but who will by no means clear the guilty, visiting the iniquity of the fathers on the children and the children's children, to the third and the fourth generation." *And Moses quickly bowed his head toward the earth and worshiped.* (Ex. 34:6–8)

Or compare the response of Job after God revealed himself to him:

> I had heard of you by the hearing of the ear,
> but now my eye sees you;
> therefore I despise myself,
> and *repent in dust and ashes.* (Job 42:5–6)

Or compare the response of Isaiah when he saw the Lord in heaven:

> And I said: *"Woe is me! For I am lost; for I am a man of unclean lips, and I dwell in the midst of a people of unclean lips*; for my eyes have seen the King, the LORD of hosts!" (Isa. 6:5)

In the book of Revelation, the inhabitants of heaven are frequently seen falling before God and worshiping:

> And all the angels were standing around the throne and around the elders and the four living creatures, and *they fell on their faces before the throne and worshiped God.* (Rev. 7:11)

A more serious thing than careless use of God's name is intentional cursing of God or blasphemy against him. This was the temptation of Job when his wife said to him, "Curse God and die" (Job 2:9), but he resisted the temptation and "in all this Job did not sin with his lips" (v. 10). Yet when wicked evildoers in the book of Revelation experience

God's wrath being poured out on the earth, rather than repenting and giving God glory, they continue to curse him:

> They were scorched by the fierce heat, and *they cursed the name of God* who had power over these plagues. *They did not repent and give him glory.* . . . People gnawed their tongues in anguish and *cursed the God of heaven* for their pain and sores. They did not repent of their deeds. (Rev. 16:9–11)

4. In a Broader Sense, This Command Covers All of Life. When the Bible says that God created us "in his own image" (Gen. 1:27), it means that he made us to be like him and also to represent him on the earth.[2] This implies that our whole life "proclaims" something about our Creator, even when we don't say it in specific words. This is why God wants us to imitate his moral character in our lives (see discussion in chap. 10, p. 281).

The author of Proverbs 30 realized this and prayed that God would keep him from stealing because if he stole something it would dishonor God:

> [Feed me] lest I be poor and steal
>   and profane the name of my God. (Prov. 30:9)

Peter also encouraged his readers that the way that they responded to suffering would give them opportunity to glorify God:

> If you are insulted for the name of Christ, you are blessed, because the Spirit of glory and of God rests upon you. But let none of you suffer as a murderer or a thief or an evildoer or as a meddler. Yet *if anyone suffers as a Christian*, let him not be ashamed, but *let him glorify God in that name.* (1 Pet. 4:14–16)

The implication is that, in a broad sense, *every sin* committed by human beings violates the third commandment, because when a person sins, an image bearer of God is portraying him in an evil or sinful way. This is especially true for Christians, because we bear the name "Christian," and thus people more readily connect what we do with the reputation of our Lord, Jesus Christ.

In practical terms, this understanding of the commandment means that if I act in a fair and just way, I proclaim that God, my Creator and my Lord, is fair and just. If I act with kindness and mercy, I proclaim that God is kind and merciful. But if I tell lies, I proclaim that my God is a liar and cannot be trusted. If I am cruel and vindictive, I proclaim that my God is also cruel and vindictive. This perspective helps us understand why God takes sin so seriously and why it must be punished. All sin dishonors God.

---

[2] See Wayne Grudem, *Systematic Theology: An Introduction to Biblical Doctrine* (Leicester, UK: Inter-Varsity, and Grand Rapids, MI: Zondervan, 1994), 442–50.

B. CATEGORIES OF OFFENSIVE SPEECH

The commandment against taking God's name in vain naturally suggests that we consider the somewhat broader idea of the purity of our speech in general.[3] In this section, therefore, I will discuss three categories of speech that are thought to be offensive today, at least to some degree. (I will be discussing word usage in the English-speaking world, especially American English, so far as I understand it.) When I say these categories of speech are "thought to be offensive," I mean, for example, that these are expressions that usually would be avoided by newscasters and reporters on national television, and that would not (usually) be used by politicians in public speeches, by public school teachers in their lessons, or by pastors in their sermons. They are also words that most parents would teach their children not to say.

The three categories of such speech are:

1. Taking God's name in vain (that is, using God's name in a dishonorable way)
2. Cursing (expressing a wish that someone would be damned or condemned)
3. Using obscene or unclean language (using offensive words that have to do with bathroom activities or sexual activities)

1. Taking God's Name in Vain. In the category of "taking God's name in vain," I include any use of God's name in an irreverent or dishonorable way, as explained above. This kind of speech is directly prohibited by the third commandment. Such misuse of God's name should never be spoken by a Christian in any circumstances. To do so is a direct sin against God himself.

Because God's moral standards as revealed in the Bible are applicable to all the people God has created, not just to Christians, it is also wrong for non-Christians to engage in this kind of speech—God counts it as sin against himself. However, because I believe that "Caesar" should not have jurisdiction over "the things that are God's" (Matt. 22:21), I do not think that civil governments should enforce laws concerning religious beliefs and practices, but should protect freedom of religion. Therefore, I do not think that any civil government today should make laws against such public swearing or "blasphemy" against God.

As we saw earlier, the Mosaic covenant has been canceled and we now live under the new covenant. God's people today do not constitute a separate nation (as the people of Israel did in the Old Testament period), and therefore many of the laws that God gave for the civil government of the nation of Israel no longer should be enforced by civil governments today (see discussion in chap. 8, p. 219). The Mosaic Law against

---

[3] I do not intend to discuss all types of wrongful speech here, for that would require a much more extensive discussion. Other kinds of wrongful speech would include such things as gossip, slander, enticement to criminal activity, promotion of false religions, harsh or cruel speech, cursing other people, and insincere speech. James says, "If anyone does not stumble in what he says, he is a perfect man, able also to bridle his whole body" (James 3:2).

blasphemy is a good example of an old covenant law that God does not intend civil governments to enforce today:

> And speak to the people of Israel, saying, Whoever curses his God shall bear his sin. *Whoever blasphemes the name of the* Lord *shall surely be put to death.* All the congregation shall stone him. The sojourner as well as the native, when he blasphemes the Name, shall be put to death. (Lev. 24:15–16)

Returning to the question of personal speech by Christians, sometimes a highly scrupulous person will raise the question of whether it is also wrong to use common substitutes for God's name. For instance, someone might say, "Oh my gosh" instead of "Oh my God." Is this also a practice Christians should avoid?

There is room for differences of opinion here. When I hear someone say, "Oh my gosh," I generally understand it to mean that the person is trying to *avoid* using God's name in vain, and I appreciate that. I hear it as an attempt at reverence rather than an expression of irreverence. On the other hand, in my own speech, I find myself using other alternative expressions, such as "My goodness!" rather than "Oh my gosh," probably because of an instinct that "Oh my gosh" is still quite close to "Oh my God." Even so, it seems to me this is an area where there is a wide range of legitimate conclusions for Christians regarding their own personal speech.

The deciding factor here is understanding what words mean when they are spoken. The meaning of a word is what it *presently* means to the speaker and to the hearers, and this is sometimes different from its historical origin. To take an obvious example, for anyone speaking English today, the word *Tuesday* does not mean "Zeus's day," nor does the word *Thursday* mean "Thor's day," though those were the original meanings of the words. Therefore, the proper question is not whether "Oh my gosh" at one point was a substitute for "Oh my God." The proper question is whether it actually means "Oh my God" to people today when they hear it. I do not think that it does.

2. Cursing. Words in this category include wishes or expressions of condemnation or God's judgment on a person. In anger, someone might say, "D--- you!" or something even stronger, expressing a destination to which the speaker wishes the person would go.

The New Testament authors are quite clear that such curses on other people should have no place in a Christian's speech. Paul says:

> Bless those who persecute you; bless and *do not curse them.* (Rom. 12:14).[4]

James says something similar:

---

[4] James also indicates that it is wrong even for angels to pronounce curses on such evil beings as demons, for he says: "But when the archangel Michael, contending with the devil, was disputing about the body of Moses, he did not presume to pronounce a blasphemous judgment, but said, 'The Lord rebuke you'" (Jude 9).

> But no human being can tame the tongue. It is a restless evil, full of deadly poison. With it we bless our Lord and Father, and *with it we curse people who are made in the likeness of God*. From the same mouth come blessing and cursing. My brothers, *these things ought not to be so*. (James 3:8–10)

Finally, Peter holds up the example of Jesus, who refrained from cursing the people who were mistreating him and putting him to death:

> For to this you have been called, because Christ also suffered for you, leaving you an example, so that you might follow in his steps. He committed no sin, neither was deceit found in his mouth. *When he was reviled, he did not revile in return*; when he suffered, he did not threaten, but continued entrusting himself to him who judges justly. (1 Pet. 2:21–23)

But what if someone speaks a curse against us? Should we be afraid that a curse that someone shouts against us will actually bring us spiritual or physical harm? The writer of Proverbs assures us that it will have no effect on us:

> Like a sparrow in its flitting, like a swallow in its flying,
> *a curse that is causeless does not alight.* (Prov. 26:2)

When King David and his loyal supporters were fleeing Jerusalem before the military invasion by David's rebellious son Absalom, an obnoxious man named Shimei began cursing David and throwing stones at him from a distance (2 Sam. 16:5–8). Then David expressed hope that God would in fact bring him and his men blessing rather than the curses that Shimei was shouting against him:

> It may be that the LORD will look on the wrong done to me, and that *the LORD will repay me with good for his cursing today*. (2 Sam. 16:12)

Therefore, we should not fear that God or some demon will harm us just because some enemy has angrily spoken a curse against us.

However, people can still experience emotional wounding from being on the receiving end of angry words spoken by someone else, and in that case, healing from the emotional wounds will often require prayer, either prayer alone or prayer with someone else who can pray with and minister to the person who has been hurt: "There is one whose rash words are like sword thrusts, *but the tongue of the wise brings healing*" (Prov. 12:18).

If we are cursed, Peter is emphatic that we should not speak a curse in return, but should give blessing, and God will bless us in return:

> Do not repay evil for evil *or reviling for reviling, but on the contrary, bless*, for to this you were called, that you may obtain a blessing. (1 Pet. 3:9)

The key to being able to return blessing for cursing is to commit the entire situation into God's hands, including the question of just judgment for the wrongdoer. This is what Paul was doing when he said, "Alexander the coppersmith did me great harm; *the Lord will repay him* according to his deeds" (2 Tim. 4:14). I think this is also what Jesus was doing when he was wrongfully slandered and eventually crucified, for Peter tells us:

> When he was reviled, he did not revile in return; when he suffered, he did not threaten, but *continued entrusting himself to him who judges justly*. (1 Pet. 2:23).[5]

3. Using Obscene or Unclean Language. This third category is different from the first (taking God's name in vain, which is always wrong) and the second (cursing someone, which is always wrong). This category includes a set of words that a society generally finds to be offensive. These are words that many people avoid using because most hearers will think the words are obscene or "dirty."

In this case, the ethical questions include what kind of reputation we want to have, whether it is wise to seek a reputation for clean rather than unclean speech, and whether the use of obscene language will bring a measure of reproach on the gospel that we represent (it often will).

This kind of speech is probably what Paul had in mind when he said:

> Let there be no *filthiness* nor *foolish talk* nor *crude joking*, which are out of place, but instead let there be thanksgiving. (Eph. 5:4)

> Let no *corrupting talk* come out of your mouths, but only such as is good for building up, as fits the occasion, that it may give grace to those who hear. (Eph. 4:29)

Paul encourages "bondservants," who are working for others, that their conduct should be characterized by "showing all good faith, so that *in everything they may adorn the doctrine of God our Savior*" (Titus 2:10). Certainly this would include their speech.

He also encourages Christians to a high level of purity not just in their speech but even in their thought:

> Finally, brothers, whatever is true, whatever is honorable, whatever is just, whatever is pure, whatever is lovely, whatever is commendable, if there is any excellence, if there is anything worthy of praise, think about these things. (Phil. 4:8)

---

[5] This idea is similar to the sense of Paul's directions in Rom. 12:19 ("Never avenge yourself, but leave it to the *wrath of God*") when combined with Rom. 13:4, which says that the civil government authority "is the servant of God, an avenger who carries out *God's wrath* on the wrongdoer." When Christians have been seriously harmed by criminal activity, Paul encourages them not to seek personal vengeance but to seek just punishment for the wrongdoer through the agency of civil government.

What kinds of speech am I talking about when I say "obscene" or "unclean"? The answer depends not on the subject matter that is being discussed but on the actual words used to refer to the subject matter. Every language has a range of what are called "registers" in speech, from polite and formal speech, to more common speech, to vulgar or offensive speech. Table 11.1 contains some examples.

Subject Matter	Polite or Formal Speech	Common Speech	Vulgar or Obscene Speech (or Unclean or Offensive Speech)
Bathroom Functions	defecate urinate	poop pee	sh-- p---
Sexual Activity	engage in sexual intercourse	sleep with or have sex with	f---

Table 11.1. "Registers" in Speech

It seems to me that using the words in the right-hand column is in a different category from taking God's name in vain or cursing someone. The question is what type of reputation we are constructing for ourselves by our speech patterns if we use language that is thought to be vulgar or offensive.

Unlike taking God's name in vain or cursing someone, I am not willing to say that speaking the words in the right-hand column is always wrong for everybody in all circumstances. But using these words is somewhat analogous to other socially offensive things, such as walking around with grape jelly spilled on the middle of our shirt, or not using deodorant and emitting an offensive odor, or picking our noses in public. These words will give offense and make people think we have dirty mouths, and they will reflect on our reputations.[6] I suspect this is the kind of thing that Paul had in mind when he referred to "corrupting talk" and "crude joking" (Eph. 4:29; 5:4).

We also need to recognize that the appropriateness of words can vary from situation to situation. Different occupations and workplaces have different accepted standards of appropriate speech. Outside of actually being in each situation, it is hard to say in advance what exactly will be offensive and how offensive it will be.

Words are considered obscene or vulgar because the society generally *thinks of them* in that way. The words carry a connotation of a *desire to shock or give offense*. A person who uses these words is announcing something about the kind of person he or she wishes to be known to be.

Finally, when a subculture within a society deteriorates into more and more sinful activity, its language tends to be more and more unclean. A friend who was arrested for protesting at an abortion clinic spent four nights in the city jail. He later told me that as

---

[6] See my personal email to my friend John Piper on this topic at https://www.desiringgod.org/articles/wayne-grudem-on-offensive-language.

he listened to other prisoners' voices echoing through the cellblock during the night, he kept hearing speech that was filled with vulgar sexual references and bathroom talk. The prisoners' lives had degenerated into greater and greater sinfulness, and their language had similarly degenerated into greater and greater vulgarity.

C. DRAMA AND FILMS: THE QUESTION OF QUOTING OR PORTRAYING UNBELIEVERS

What if a Christian has a role portraying an unbeliever in a theater production or a movie? Would it be acceptable in that role to speak as an unbeliever would normally speak? Are there any limits on what is right for a Christian to say in such circumstances?

1. The Bible Quotes Unbelievers at Times. In various places, the Bible records accurately the false things that unbelievers say. Here are some examples:

> The fool says in his heart, "There is no God." (Ps. 14:1)

> For they were saying, "He has an unclean spirit." (Mark 3:30)

> Therefore I want you to understand that no one speaking in the Spirit of God ever says "Jesus is accursed!" and no one can say "Jesus is Lord" except in the Holy Spirit. (1 Cor. 12:3)

In each of these cases, there is no danger that the reader will think that the Bible is *approving* these statements. The untrue statements are quoted in contexts that show clear disapproval of the falsehoods that are being spoken. But the fact remains that these unbelievers are quoted explicitly in the Bible itself.

2. There Is a Difference between Pretending to Do an Action and Actually Doing the Action. An actor on stage or in a movie can *pretend* to kill someone with a sword or a gun, but the other actor doesn't die—it's just a *pretended murder*. Similarly, an actor can pretend to be a lying auto mechanic who cheats a customer, but in reality he is just "lying" to another actor. Both actors understand that it is a pretended action.

Some people would probably want to put the use of vulgar language by an actor in this category as well. Someone could argue that people will not think of the *actor* as someone who has unclean and corrupt speech, but will simply think of the *character* in the play or movie as using that kind of speech. On the other hand, it could be argued that people who know the actor as someone who customarily does not use crude words will think it a bit strange that such vulgar language is coming out of his mouth. There should be freedom for people to make individual decisions in this regard.

I think the same thing applies to an actor who says "D--- you" in a production. This probably falls into the category of pretending to curse another person, because the actor receiving the curse thinks of it only as a pretended action, not really directed at him or her in real life. But I can see room for people to come to different conclusions on this question.

But the question of an actor *taking God's name in vain* seems to me to fall into a different category. It is not like *pretending* to murder someone. Rather, it is *actually* taking God's name in vain. It is speaking of God or using his name in a deeply dishonoring and irreverent manner. This would be something like the difference between an actor in a play criticizing a *fictitious* president of the United States, using a name that no president has ever held, and an actor who criticizes the *current* president of the United States by name. In that case, it is no longer a pretend action within a play, but a real criticism of a living president. In the same way, taking God's name in vain is a real dishonor to the living God.

Therefore, I cannot see a justification for an actor taking God's name in vain, even while he or she is playing a role in a play or a movie.

3. There Is a Difference between Watching a Movie or Play and Acting in It. There is also a significant difference between *doing* something wrong and *watching* somebody else do something wrong. Many of Jesus's followers watched the most evil deed in history, the crucifixion of Christ, but they did not themselves do wrong by watching it (see Luke 23:49). Similarly, watching a movie portraying someone taking God's name in vain is not the same as actually speaking such words.

On the other hand, that does not mean it is always right to watch every movie or play that portrays evil. In this case, the primary ethical considerations can be identified by asking what *results* will come from watching, for example, a particular movie. Will it make you more callous and insensitive to misuse of God's name? Will it trouble your heart, as Paul found that "his spirit was provoked within him as he saw that the city [Athens] was full of idols" (Acts 17:16; cf. 2 Pet. 2:7–8, concerning Lot)? Will it have a positive or negative effect on your personal character?

Other results to consider are the effects on others. Will your presence or your financial support imply approval of something in a play or movie that you wouldn't ordinarily approve? Will it encourage others to think there is nothing wrong with the play or movie, since you were present to watch it? There is certainly room for people to reach different decisions on these matters, and to respect one another's decisions.

D. OATHS

1. Definition. An oath can be defined as follows:

An oath is an appeal for God's punishment if your statement is untruthful.

When a person swears an oath, it is as if he were saying, "If I am not telling the truth, I call on God himself to punish me for it."

2. Oaths in the Bible. The Bible contains many examples of oaths. For example, Paul says in his second letter to the Corinthians:

> But *I call God to witness against me*—it was to spare you that I refrained from coming again to Corinth. (2 Cor. 1:23)

There are other examples in Scripture of Paul taking oaths:

> For *God is my witness*, whom I serve with my spirit in the gospel of his Son, that without ceasing I mention you always in my prayers, asking that somehow by God's will I may now at last succeed in coming to you. (Rom. 1:9–10)

> For *God is my witness*, how I yearn for you all with the affection of Christ Jesus. (Phil. 1:8; see also Gal. 1:20; 1 Thess. 2:5, 10)

Jesus himself faced a situation in his trial when the high priest declared that he was putting Jesus under oath:

> But Jesus remained silent. And the high priest said to him, "*I adjure you by the living God*, tell us if you are the Christ, the Son of God." Jesus said to him, "You have said so. But I tell you, from now on you will see the Son of Man seated at the right hand of Power and coming on the clouds of heaven." (Matt. 26:63–64)

The word translated "adjure" is the Greek verb *exorkizō*, "to put someone under oath."[7] In this situation, Jesus answered truthfully and did not refuse to speak under oath.

In a remarkable passage, the author of Hebrews tells how *God himself* took an oath when he made a promise to Abraham:

> For when God made a promise to Abraham, since he had no one greater by whom to swear, *he swore by himself*, saying, "Surely I will bless you and multiply you." And thus Abraham, having patiently waited, obtained the promise. For people swear by something greater than themselves, and in all their disputes *an oath is final for confirmation*. So when God desired to show more convincingly to the heirs of the promise the unchangeable character of his purpose, *he guaranteed it with an oath*, so that by two unchangeable things, in which it is impossible for God to lie, we who have fled for refuge might have strong encouragement to hold fast to the hope set before us. (Heb. 6:13–18; cf. "The oath that he swore to our father Abraham," Luke 1:73)

3. It Is Morally Acceptable for Christians to Take Oaths. Although there are many such examples in the Bible of God's people taking oaths, and these occur in contexts

---

[7] In fact, several translations actually say "I put you under oath before the living God" (NKJV, NRSV; similar expressions are found in CSB, NET, NIV).

in which the oaths are viewed with approval, some people have still wondered if it is right for people to take oaths because of what Jesus said in the Sermon on the Mount[8] (some have gone so far as to claim that Jesus was *prohibiting* all oaths in this passage[9]):

> Again you have heard that it was said to those of old, "You shall not swear falsely, but shall perform to the Lord what you have sworn." But I say to you, *Do not take an oath at all*, either by heaven, for it is the throne of God, or by the earth, for it is his footstool, or by Jerusalem, for it is the city of the great King. And do not take an oath by your head, for you cannot make one hair white or black. Let what you say be simply "Yes" or "No"; anything more than this comes from evil. (Matt. 5:33–37)

I agree with the majority of commentators who believe that Jesus is not prohibiting all oaths (as we saw above, there are many oaths in Scripture itself). Rather, he is prohibiting oaths spoken in the context of people routinely telling lies to one another—and even saying that people can lie under certain oaths but not under other, differently worded oaths[10]—so that no one could be trusted. In other words, Jesus is rebuking a *misuse of oaths*, a situation in which people needed to swear oaths in order to be believed because nobody believed these people's ordinary words. They were practicing and excusing routine lying, and then saying that if someone said something under certain kinds of oaths, it had to be true.

An example of this practice can be seen in the harsh condemnation that Jesus gives to the scribes and Pharisees in Matthew 23:

> Woe to you, blind guides, who say, "If anyone swears by the temple, it is nothing, but if anyone swears by the gold of the temple, he is bound by his oath." You blind fools! For which is greater, the gold or the temple that has made the gold sacred? (vv. 16–17; cf. vv. 18–22)

---

[8] A Christian friend who was a police officer in England told me that among Christians on his police force, there was much discussion about whether swearing an oath in court was prohibited by Jesus's teaching. Police officers are often called upon to give testimony in court, and it is expected that they will do so under oath.

[9] For example, Jehovah's Witnesses refuse to salute the U.S. flag, a right that was upheld by the U.S. Supreme Court in West Virginia State Board of Education v. Barnette, 319 U.S. 624 (1942); see https://www.oyez.org /cases/1940–1955/319us624. Quakers will not swear to an oath in court, but only "affirm." See http://www.bbc .co.uk/religion/religions/christianity/subdivisions/quakers_1.shtml. However, when Presidents Herbert Hoover and Richard Nixon, both of whom came from Quaker backgrounds, took the presidential oath of office, they agreed to "solemnly swear" rather than "affirm." However, President Franklin Pierce, a Quaker, used the word "affirm." See Don Kennon, "The Sad Inaugural of Franklin Pierce," U.S. Capitol Historical Society, https://us chs.wordpress.com/2013/01/22/presidential-inaugural-quiz-follow-up-the-sad-inaugural-of-franklin-pierce/.

[10] Regarding Matt. 5:34, John Calvin says, "It was not his purpose either to slacken or tighten the law, but to bring back to a true and genuine understanding what had been quite corrupted by the false devisings of the Scribes and Pharisees. If we understand this, we will not think that Christ condemned oaths entirely." *Institutes of the Christian Religion*, ed. John T. McNeill, trans. Ford Lewis Battles, Library of Christian Classics, vols. 20–21 (Philadelphia: Westminster, 1960), 2.8.27 (392). See also D. A. Carson, "Matthew," in *Matthew & Mark (Revised Edition)*, vol. 9 in EBC, ed. Tremper Longman III and David E. Garland (Grand Rapids, MI: Zondervan, 2010), 187–88.

Therefore, in Matthew 5:33–37, Jesus is saying, "Do not take an oath at all" *if* you are such a habitual liar that you need to swear an oath in order for people to believe you. In such a situation, you should instead return to a practice of speaking truthfully at all times so that your word can always be trusted.

James probably has the same meaning in mind (and is probably echoing the teaching of Jesus) when he says:

> But above all, my brothers, do not swear, either by heaven or by earth or by any other oath, but let your "yes" be yes and your "no" be no, so that you may not fall under condemnation. (James 5:12)

These teachings of Jesus and James require us to be habitually faithful and truthful in all of our words, so that we will not have to swear oaths in order for people to believe anything we say.

In courtroom situations today, witnesses are regularly asked to solemnly swear that they are speaking the truth. In light of the frequent oaths found in Scripture, my conclusion is that it is morally right for Christians to swear oaths in such a courtroom situation, and even to do it in such a way that calls God to witness the truthfulness of what they say. For example, here is the form of the oath commonly used in Maricopa County, Arizona, where I live:

> You do solemnly swear the testimony you are about to give will be the truth, the whole truth, and nothing but the truth, so help you God?

Witnesses who answer yes to this question generally understand that they are subject to legal penalties for perjury if they violate this oath in their testimony. Beyond that, I don't know how many people are aware of the fact that the statement "So help you God" can be understood as a form of an oath by which they are calling on God to hold them to account if they do not tell the truth in their testimony.

Another form of oath that is common today is a promise, sworn by someone being installed as a public official, to be faithful in executing the duties of his or her office. Members of Congress, members of the Supreme Court, and even local city officials are often "sworn in" with some kind of oath, in which the person promises to faithfully discharge the duties of the office. Such oaths, at least traditionally, have been understood both as an appeal to God for help in fulfilling the office and as an appeal to God to hold the one taking the oath accountable if he or she is not faithful.

The oath of office taken by the president of the United States, as stated in the U.S. Constitution, is as follows:

> I do solemnly swear (or affirm) that I will faithfully execute the Office of President of the United States, and will to the best of my ability, preserve, protect and defend the Constitution of the United States.

At his first inauguration, George Washington voluntarily added, "So help me God," and other presidents have followed this tradition ever since.

People who are becoming naturalized citizens of the United States take an oath of loyalty to the country. The current form of the oath is fairly long and includes very serious promises:

> I hereby declare, on oath, that I absolutely and entirely renounce and abjure all allegiance and fidelity to any foreign prince, potentate, state, or sovereignty, of whom or which I have heretofore been a subject or citizen; that I will support and defend the Constitution and laws of the United States of America against all enemies, foreign and domestic; that I will bear true faith and allegiance to the same; that I will bear arms on behalf of the United States when required by the law; that I will perform noncombatant service in the Armed Forces of the United States when required by the law; that I will perform work of national importance under civilian direction when required by the law; and that I take this obligation freely without any mental reservation or purpose of evasion; so help me God.[11]

I do not know how many new citizens understand that they are calling on God to help them and to hold them accountable for fulfilling this oath. But I think that is what the words are intended to mean.

Foolish oaths that people make to do sinful things should not be carried out. For instance, more than 40 men in Jerusalem swore an oath to kill Paul:

> When it was day, the Jews made a plot and *bound themselves by an oath* neither to eat nor drink till they had killed Paul. There were more than forty who made this conspiracy. (Acts 23:12–13)

But their plot failed (Acts 23:16–24). Presumably they violated their oath and resumed eating again![12]

E. VOWS

1. Definition. For purposes of this book, I am using the following definition:

> **A vow** is a promise made to God to perform a certain action or behave in a certain way.

2. Vows in the Bible. As with oaths, vows are found frequently in Scripture. One

---

[11] See https://www.uscis.gov/us-citizenship/naturalization-test/naturalization-oath-allegiance-united -states-america.

[12] Similar to this is the oath (not a vow because it was not a promise to God) that Herod made to give the daughter of Herodias whatever she asked, and she asked for the head of John the Baptist (see Matt. 14:6–8).

familiar example is the vow made by childless Hannah, the mother of the prophet Samuel, before she was able to bear any children:

> And *she vowed a vow* and said, "O LORD of hosts, if you will indeed look on the affliction of your servant and remember me and not forget your servant, but will give to your servant a son, then I will give him to the LORD all the days of his life, and no razor shall touch his head." (1 Sam. 1:11)

Another example of a vow is the promise that Jacob made to God after God had appeared to him in a dream at Bethel:

> Then *Jacob made a vow*, saying, "If God will be with me and will keep me in this way that I go, and will give me bread to eat and clothing to wear, so that I come again to my father's house in peace, then the LORD shall be my God, and this stone, which I have set up for a pillar, shall be God's house. And of all that you give me I will give a full tenth to you." (Gen. 28:20–22)

Later in Jacob's life, God reminded him of this vow:

> I am the God of Bethel, where you anointed a pillar and *made a vow to me.* Now arise, go out from this land and return to the land of your kindred. (Gen. 31:13)

3. Vows Made to God Should Be Kept. The biblical law about vows is quite explicit in saying that people do not have to make vows to God, but if they do, they should fulfill them:

> *If you make a vow to the LORD your God, you shall not delay fulfilling it,* for the LORD your God will surely require it of you, and you will be guilty of sin. *But if you refrain from vowing, you will not be guilty of sin.* You shall be careful to do what has passed your lips, for you have voluntarily vowed to the LORD your God what you have promised with your mouth. (Deut. 23:21–23; cf. Num. 30:2; Eccles. 5:4–5)

4. Vows to Do Something Sinful Should Not Be Kept. However, we are not required to keep vows to God that we will do something sinful, because God would not want us to do something sinful in the first place. This principle shows the foolishness of the hardhearted Jewish people who rejected the warnings of the prophet Jeremiah and proclaimed that they were going to continue fulfilling their evil vows:

> As for the word that you have spoken to us in the name of the LORD, we will not listen to you. *But we will do everything that we have vowed,* make offerings to the queen of heaven and pour out drink offerings to her, as we did, both we and our fathers, our kings and our officials, in the cities of Judah and in

the streets of Jerusalem. For then we had plenty of food, and prospered, and saw no disaster. (Jer. 44:16–17)

When Jephthah was the leader of Israel, he made a foolish vow:

And Jephthah made a vow to the LORD and said, "If you will give the Ammonites into my hand, then whatever comes out from the doors of my house to meet me when I return in peace from the Ammonites shall be the LORD's, and I will offer it up for a burnt offering." (Judg. 11:30–31)

But when he returned home, his daughter came out of the door of his house (Judg. 11:34). The Bible says he fulfilled his vow with regard to his daughter (v. 39), but he should not have done so.[13] This vow is one of a series of misguided and wrongful actions taken by various leaders of Israel throughout the book of Judges.

5. Sometimes a Vow Can Be Nullified by a Human Authority. In the Mosaic Law, people sometimes needed the approval of the head of a household for a vow to be considered valid. For example:

If a woman vows a vow to the LORD and binds herself by a pledge, while within her father's house in her youth, and her father hears of her vow and of her pledge by which she has bound herself and says nothing to her, then all her vows shall stand, and every pledge by which she has bound herself shall stand. *But if her father opposes her* on the day that he hears of it, *no vow of hers, no pledge by which she has bound herself shall stand.* And the LORD will forgive her, because her father opposed her. (Num. 30:3–5; see also vv. 6–15)

One modern application of the wisdom of God revealed in this law would be the principle that parents have the right to free their children from foolish or impetuous vows or promises, if they do so within a reasonable time after they hear of the promise. (For example, "But I *promised* that I would go to that party tonight" or "But I *promised* that I would give Samantha a ride home.")

6. Wedding Vows. The most familiar form of a vow found in Western societies today is a wedding vow. In many wedding ceremonies, the vows are still understood not only as promises that the husband and wife make to one another, but also as promises made in the presence of God, and thus promises made to God as well as to one another.

Therefore, many wedding services open with a statement such as this:

We are gathered together here *in the sight of God*, and in the presence of this company, to join together this man and this woman in holy matrimony.

---

[13] Commentators differ over whether he actually offered her as a sacrifice on an altar or whether he restricted her from ever marrying, which is the more likely result.

Then, at some point, often when rings are exchanged, the bride and groom make a promise to each other "in the name of the Father, and of the Son, and of the Holy Spirit."

It would do much to strengthen the ties of marriage in Western societies if people who were getting married realized more clearly that they were asking God both to enable them to fulfill their promises and to hold them accountable for them. It is likely that he will do just that.

F. HUMOR

1. Laughter in Scripture. In several places, the Bible offers a positive view of laughter as an expression of joy and delight:

> And Sarah said, "*God has made laughter for me*; everyone who hears will laugh over me." (Gen. 21:6)

> Then our mouth was *filled with laughter*,
>   and our tongue with shouts of joy. (Ps. 126:2)

> [There is] a time to weep, and *a time to laugh*;
>   a time to mourn, and a time to dance. (Eccles. 3:4)

> Bread is made for *laughter*,
>   and wine gladdens life. (Eccles. 10:19)

> Blessed are you who weep now, for *you shall laugh*. (Luke 6:21)

In these verses and elsewhere, laughter is depicted as the spontaneous expression of joy and happiness in life. It is seen as a blessing from God.

2. Humor in Scripture. Several passages in Scripture seem to be intended in a humorous way (though because of long familiarity, the humor may not strike us as quite so funny as it did the original readers). For example:

> The sluggard buries his hand in the dish;
>   it wears him out to bring it back to his mouth. (Prov. 26:15)

> Why do you see the speck that is in your brother's eye, but do not notice the log that is in your own eye? (Matt. 7:3)

In one humorous incident, just after an angel had rescued Peter from prison, he went to the house of Mary, the mother of John Mark, where many people were praying for him:

> And when he knocked at the door of the gateway, a servant girl named Rhoda came to answer. Recognizing Peter's voice, in her joy she did not open the

gate but ran in and reported that Peter was standing at the gate. . . . But Peter continued knocking. (Acts 12:13–16)

3. Some Cautions about Humor. While Scripture generally views laughter and humor positively, there are also some warnings:

> Let there be no filthiness *nor foolish talk nor crude joking*, which are out of place, but instead let there be thanksgiving. (Eph. 5:4)

This verse does not forbid all humor, but it does forbid the kind that causes offense to other people or that encourages thoughts of immoral behavior (see Eph. 5:5).

Further caution regarding humor comes from considering the *results* of humor in our conversations. In some situations it is "a time to weep" and not "a time to laugh" (Eccles. 3:4). Sometimes humor can be used to excess and become just a waste of time. Sometimes humor is inappropriate because it will crowd out helpful conversations and thanksgiving to God. Sometimes humor can "quench the Spirit" (1 Thess. 5:19), for when the Holy Spirit is actively working in people's hearts (for example, during a sermon, during a counseling session, or during a small group prayer time), someone might be uncomfortable with the weighty, solemn, sober atmosphere of the conversation and suddenly crack a joke—thus changing the atmosphere instantly and thereby quenching the work of the Holy Spirit. Therefore, we need to recognize the danger of using too much humor in a worship service, while leading Bible studies, or during times set aside for prayer.

Sometimes Christians will face the difficult situation of finding themselves in the midst of a group where someone is telling an off-color joke or one that is irreverent. Does listening imply approval in that case?

Each situation like this is different, but often a Christian can show some slight indication of disapproval or reluctance to join fully in the laughter without acting overly judgmental or cutting off the relationship completely. Sometimes a mere shaking of the head or a perplexed or troubled facial expression will be enough, but if the humor continues, it may be necessary to leave the room. This is certainly a time to pray for the Holy Spirit's guidance about how to respond in each unique situation (but see also Eph. 5:11–14).

QUESTIONS FOR PERSONAL APPLICATION

1. How do you feel when people make fun of your name, call you by a disrespectful nickname, or even lie about you?
2. Do you think you feel enough instinctive reverence when you speak the name of God or of Jesus Christ?
3. If you were to begin to think that all of your actions "proclaim" something about your Creator, what specific changes might that prompt you to make in your life?

4. Have you ever sworn an oath or taken a vow? How did it seem different to you from ordinary speech?
5. What character traits (see p. 110) will be evident in the life of a person who takes the third commandment seriously?
6. How will this chapter change the way you speak, if at all?

SPECIAL TERMS

cursing
in vain
name
oath
obscene language
vow

BIBLIOGRAPHY

Sections in Other Ethics Texts

(see complete bibliographical data, p. 64)

Frame, 487–512
McQuilkin and Copan, 200–205

Other Works

Baker, William R. *Sticks & Stones: The Discipleship of Our Speech*. Downers Grove, IL: InterVarsity Press, 1996.

Field, D. H. "Speech and the Tongue." In *New Dictionary of Christian Ethics and Pastoral Theology*, edited by David J. Atkinson and David H. Field, 805–6. Leicester, UK: Inter-Varsity, and Downers Grove, IL: InterVarsity Press, 1995.

Hovey, Craig. "Speech Ethics." In *Dictionary of Scripture and Ethics*, edited by Joel B. Green, 744–46. Grand Rapids, MI: Baker, 2011.

Kassian, Mary A., and Betty Hassler. *Conversation Peace: Improve Your Relationships One Word at a Time*. Nashville: Broadman & Holman, 2004.

Mains, Karen Burton. *You Are What You Say: Cure for the Troublesome Tongue*. Grand Rapids, MI: Zondervan, 1988.

Mayhall, Carole. *Words That Hurt, Words That Heal*. Colorado Springs: NavPress, 1990.

Piper, John, and Justin Taylor, eds. *The Power of Words and the Wonder of God*. Wheaton, IL: Crossway, 2009.

Stowell, Joseph M. *The Weight of Your Words: Measuring the Impact of What You Say*. Chicago: Moody, 1998.

SCRIPTURE MEMORY PASSAGE

Exodus 20:7: You shall not take the name of the LORD your God in vain, for the LORD will not hold him guiltless who takes his name in vain.

HYMN

"May the Mind of Christ My Savior"

May the mind of Christ my Savior,
Live in me from day to day,
By His love and pow'r controlling
All I do and say.

May the Word of God dwell richly
In my heart from hour to hour,
So that all may see I triumph
Only thru His pow'r.

May the peace of God, my Father,
Rule my life in everything,
That I may be calm to comfort
Sick and sorrowing.

May the love of Jesus fill me,
As the waters fill the sea;
Him exalting, self abasing—
This is victory.

May I run the race before me,
Strong and brave to face the foe,
Looking only unto Jesus
As I onward go.

May His beauty rest upon me
As I seek the lost to win,
And may they forget the channel,
Seeing only Him.

AUTHOR: KATE B. WILKINSON, 1859–1928

LYING AND TELLING THE TRUTH

Is it ever right to lie?

Is there a difference between a spoken lie and actions that deceive people?

Does the Bible teach anything about plagiarism or punctuality?

The ninth commandment reads:

> You shall not bear false witness against your neighbor. (Ex. 20:16)

A. THE MEANING OF THE COMMANDMENT

The specific focus of this commandment is a "false witness" that someone would give in a courtroom situation (see similar wording, for example, in passages about "false witness" such as Deut. 19:18; Ps. 27:12; Prov. 14:5; 25:18). In addition, this false witness is borne not against a stranger but against "your neighbor," whom you should know especially well and whom you should love (Lev. 19:18).[1]

But this commandment is not intended to prohibit *only* this specific kind of false speech (false testimony against your neighbor in a courtroom). I think John Calvin was correct in his insight that the negative commandments in the Ten Commandments

---

[1] This chapter has been adapted from Wayne Grudem, "Why It Is Never Right to Lie: An Example of John Frame's Influence on My Approach to Ethics," in *Speaking the Truth in Love: The Theology of John Frame* (Festschrift for John Frame), ed. John J. Hughes (Phillipsburg, NJ: P&R, 2009; ISBN 978-1-59638-164-3), 778–801, with permission of P&R Publishing Co., P.O. Box 817, Phillipsburg, NJ 08865, www.prpbooks.com.

select particularly hateful and harmful examples of whole categories of wrongful actions, but God's intention in doing this is to shock us into realizing how evil *all of the actions in that general category* really are.[2] (See further discussion of Calvin's view on p. 318 on the meaning of "neighbor").

Therefore, it seems appropriate, under this commandment, to consider the question of lying and truthful speech in general.

I am discussing the ninth commandment here in the early part of this book (rather than treating it in sequential order, after the eighth commandment) for two reasons: (1) The topic of lying and telling the truth is closely connected to the topic of purity of speech, which was discussed in the previous chapter in our consideration of the third commandment, and so it seemed appropriate to group these two commands together. (2) In teaching ethics classes for the last 40 years, I have found that it works best to treat this topic early, because it raises issues that are relevant for many other topics that follow.

Sadly, lying has become a common part of ordinary life for many people today. A 2014 survey of more than 1,200 adults found that 76 percent said it is OK to lie sometimes. According to this survey, 21.7 percent of men admitted they had had lied on their résumés, compared with 16.3 percent of women. In addition, 37.4 percent of men and 43.6 percent of women had lied to their parents, and 21.5 percent of men and 21.6 percent of women had lied to their spouses or significant others.[3]

One 2014 British study found that people lie, on average, 10 times a week.[4] A 2002 study done at the University of Massachusetts-Amherst found that 60 percent of people cannot go longer than 10 minutes without telling a lie, and told an average of two to three lies during that time.[5] Another British survey, done in 2008, found that people lie four times a day, or 1,460 times a year, and by the age of 60 will have lied 88,000 times.[6] Such widespread dishonesty is a destructive cancer relentlessly eating away at the fabric of society.

B. A DEFINITION OF LYING

1. The Need for a Precise Definition. Discussions of lying often suffer from a lack of precision in defining at the outset exactly what is being discussed. In a narrow sense, lying includes only verbally affirming something you believe to be false. In a broad

---

[2] See John Calvin, *Institutes of the Christian Religion*, ed. John T. McNeill, trans. Ford Lewis Battles, Library of Christian Classics, vols. 20–21 (Philadelphia: Westminster, 1960), 2.8.20, 2.8.47 (1:376, 411–12).

[3] "Survey: Who's Telling the Truth," CreditDonkey, http://www.creditdonkey.com/lying.html. This study was conducted Aug. 8–12, 2014.

[4] "Lies have become an accepted part of British life, poll reveals," *The Telegraph*, Nov. 13, 2014, http://www.telegraph.co.uk/news/newstopics/howaboutthat/11230110/Lies-have-become-an-accepted-part-of-British-life-poll-reveals.html.

[5] "UMass researcher finds most people lie in everyday conversation," University of Massachusetts-Amherst, June 10, 2002, https://www.eurekalert.org/pub_releases/2002-06/uoma-urf061002.php.

[6] "No lie: People average 4 fibs a day," *WorldNetDaily*, Jan. 21, 2008, http://www.wnd.com/2008/01/45642/#t4C13ZksfVEjx8kc.99.

sense, some people think that "lying" refers to all kinds of deception, including not only *spoken and written statements*, but also *actions* intended to mislead or deceive others (such as leaving the lights on in a home in order to make burglars think someone is there), verbal statements that only *disclose a part* of what someone knows to be true, and *unintentional falsehoods*, statements that someone believes to be true, but which turn out to be false.

However, these broader definitions of lying include so many different categories that it makes discussion of this topic hopelessly complex and often leads to more confusion than clarity. In addition, I am not aware of any modern ethical thinker who argues that *all kinds of deception* are always wrong. Philosopher Christopher Tollefsen, who argues that lying is always wrong, says, "It seems extremely difficult to defend the view that deception as such is *always* wrong."[7] He quotes Augustine, who says, "Although everyone who lies wishes to hide what is true, yet not everyone who wishes to hide what is true, tells a lie."[8] In distinction from the broader category of "deception," Tollefsen defines lying as "an assertion contrary to the speaker's belief."[9] Such a narrow definition of lying seems to me to be a helpful focus, and it adds precision to the argument.

Another reason for focusing on verbal statements is that the Bible's own focus in this issue is on lying in this more narrow sense, the sense of *affirming in words* something you believe to be false (see the long list of passages in the following section).

Therefore, while a broader meaning of "lying" is used by some, it is not my meaning in this chapter. The main issue I will discuss in this chapter is the narrow question of *verbal affirmations* of something one believes to be false. Therefore, I will use this definition for lying:

Lying is affirming in speech or writing something you believe to be false.

2. Things Not Included in Lying. Several related acts are not included in this narrow definition:

1. *Silence.* This is saying nothing, so silence is not exactly an affirmation of anything; note Jesus's silence in Matt. 26:63.
2. *Nonverbal actions intended to mislead or deceive someone.* An action is something that happens; it is neither true nor false like a verbal affirmation. An example is leaving a light on in our house when we are away for a weekend. An observer might rightly conclude, "The Grudems left a light on," but that may or may not mean that we are at home.
3. *Ironic statements, especially in humor.* These are not truly affirmations when understood rightly.

[7] Christopher O. Tollefsen, *Lying and Christian Ethics*, New Studies in Christian Ethics, vol. 33 (New York: Cambridge University Press, 2014), 16.
[8] Ibid., 42, quoting Augustine, *To Consentius: Against Lying*, 23 (NPNF[1], 3:491).
[9] Tollefsen, *Lying and Christian Ethics*, 25.

4. *Hyperbole.* Hyperbolic statements are not intended to be taken as literally true; they use impossible exaggeration for rhetorical effect: I might say, "It took me *forever* to write this chapter." Similarly, Jesus said, "Take the *log* out of your own eye" (Matt. 7:5).

5. *Unintentional falsehoods.* For example, you may be misinformed and then affirm something that is actually false. But this is not something you believe to be false, so it does not fit the definition of lying given above.

I want to be clear that I am *not* making moral judgments about these other acts. People may argue about acts 1 to 5, saying that some of them are *seldom or never wrong*, while others are *often or perhaps always wrong* (depending on other factors). Those are interesting questions, but they are not my main purpose in this chapter. They are not the same as lying in the narrow sense of "affirming in speech or writing something you believe to be false," which is my concern here.

3. Deceptive Actions Are Not the Same as Verbal Lies. Some may argue against this narrow definition of lying, saying, for example, "Deceptive actions are the *same thing* as lying." But that is not a careful statement. Deceptive actions are in *some* ways similar to lying (their intent is to persuade someone to believe something untrue) and in *some* ways different from lying.

For example, actions are ambiguous and can have various meanings, while verbal affirmations ordinarily are not ambiguous. Also, the Bible treats deceptive actions and false affirmations differently, as I will indicate below. And lying involves a contradiction between what you think to be true and what you say, which does not occur in deceptive actions (a difference that was very significant to Augustine). The differences are important, and show at least that the two categories should be analyzed separately.

In a gracious and kind response to an earlier form of this chapter,[10] my friend and former professor John Frame wrote:

> I fail to see any morally relevant difference between intentionally misleading someone with the lips and misleading him with an action. . . . I agree that actions in themselves are neither true nor false. But they do sometimes mislead people, and often they are performed intentionally to deceive. If verbal misrepresentations are wrong, they are wrong because they deceive people we should not deceive. . . . So I fail to see how actions and words are different in this respect.[11]

Frame agrees that actions and words are different in some respects, but he argues that there is no "morally relevant difference" between deceiving with words and deceiving with actions, for both are wrong "because they deceive people."

---

[10] See my article, "Why It Is Never Right to Lie."
[11] John M. Frame, "Responses to Some Articles," in *Speaking the Truth in Love*, 973.

My reply is that there are two different and deeper reasons why lying is wrong. It is wrong (1) because God says over and over again that lying is wrong (see next section) and (2) because lying fails to imitate the character of God, who never lies because he cannot lie (Titus 1:2; Heb. 6:18). It cannot be the case that lying is wrong *simply because* lies deceive people, or we would have to argue that all kinds of deception are morally wrong—including deceptive maneuvers in warfare or in sports contests—a position that no modern Christian ethicist defends, and one that is not possible to defend persuasively from Scripture.

Vern Poythress gives an additional response to Frame when he argues for what he calls the "uniqueness of verbal action." Poythress says that "verbal communication is different from leaving a light on or setting an ambush or feigning a retreat" because:

> When no words are involved, physical actions have to be interpreted. . . . Words and utterances need interpretation too. But the interpretation is constrained by the regularities of language, the regularities in the meaning of words, and the regularities of personal communication. Statements can be true or false; by contrast, a football maneuver or a military maneuver is neither true nor false.[12]

In addition, there is the overwhelming testimony of Scripture on this topic. As numerous passages in the next section indicate, Scripture itself uses *lie* and *lying* quite often in the narrow sense of affirming in words something that one thinks to be false. This meaning is found in passages such as these:

> I am *speaking the truth* in Christ—I am *not lying*; my conscience bears me witness in the Holy Spirit. (Rom. 9:1)

> For this I was appointed a preacher and an apostle (*I am telling the truth, I am not lying*), a teacher of the Gentiles in faith and truth. (1 Tim. 2:7)

One further clarification is needed: I agree that there are a few actions that are understood to be exactly equivalent to affirming something in speech or writing. In modern American society, for example, nodding the head up and down is understood as equivalent to saying yes, and shaking the head back and forth is understood as equivalent to saying no. Another example would be an injured person who has lost his voice but who is able to point to the words *yes* and *no* on a board held in front of him. These might be called "verbal-equivalent actions." They are unambiguous ways to affirm or deny something, and they belong in the same category as "affirming something in speech or writing." They do not belong in my category 2 above: "Nonverbal actions intended to mislead or deceive someone."

---

[12] Vern S. Poythress, "Why Lying Is Always Wrong: The Uniqueness of Verbal Deceit," *WTJ* 75 (2013): 85–86.

4. Augustine, Calvin, and Others Define Lying in a Similar Way. The restriction of lying to a narrow sense is not new with me. The respected church father Augustine (AD 354–430), the most famous defender of the view that lying is always wrong, argued against lying only in the narrow sense that I have outlined above, that is, affirming in speech or writing something that one believes at the time to be untrue.[13] Thomas Aquinas (1225–1274) held a similar view,[14] as did Calvin (1509–1564).[15]

Westminster Seminary professor John Murray (1898–1975) took the same position in *Principles of Conduct*. After a discussion of several passages of Scripture (such as the stories of Rahab in Joshua 2 and the Egyptian midwives in Exodus 1), he concluded, "The upshot of our investigation has been that no instance demonstrates the propriety of untruthfulness under any exigency."[16] Murray defines a lie as follows:

> The person who is to be branded as a liar is the person who affirms to be true what he knows or believes to be false or affirms to be false what he knows or believes to be true.[17]

He later says, "The injunctions of Scripture which bear directly on the demand for truthfulness have reference to speech or utterance."[18]

C. NUMEROUS BIBLICAL STATEMENTS CONDEMN LYING

1. Extensive Biblical Testimony. The Bible has numerous passages that prohibit or condemn lying in the sense of verbally affirming something that you believe to be false. These passages condemn false speech (seeing it as characteristic of sinners who are far

---

[13] See the extensive discussion in Paul J. Griffiths, *Lying: An Augustinian Theology of Duplicity* (Grand Rapids, MI: Brazos, 2004). Griffiths represents Augustine's view as follows: "The lie is a verbal act, something we do with words" (25). And he says that for Augustine, "the lie is deliberately duplicitous speech, insincere speech that deliberately contradicts what its speaker takes to be true" (31). "Nonverbal actions cannot be lies" (33). "Silence—the refusal of speech—is also excluded" (33). "Error is excluded from the lie. . . . Jokes are not lies" (34). "Augustine's definition of the lie, then, excludes in principle nonverbal communication in general and silence in particular" (38). Augustine himself says, "That man lies, who has one thing in his mind and utters another in words, or by signs of whatever kind." *On Lying*, sec. 3 (NPNF¹, 3:458). He concludes *On Lying* by saying, "It clearly appears then . . . that those testimonies of Scripture have none other meaning than that we must never at all tell a lie; seeing that not any examples of lies, worthy of imitation, are found in the manners and actions of the Saints." *On Lying*, sec. 42 (NPNF¹, 3:476).

[14] See Tollefsen, *Lying and Christian Ethics*, 6–8, 44–56.

[15] John Calvin, *Institutes of the Christian Religion*, ed. John T. McNeill, trans. Ford Lewis Battles, Library of Christian Classics, vols. 20–21 (Philadelphia: Westminster, 1960), 2.8.47 (411–12); see also Calvin, *Commentaries on the Book of Joshua*, trans. Henry Beveridge (repr., Grand Rapids, MI: Baker, 2005), 47 (on Josh. 2:4).

[16] John Murray, *Principles of Conduct: Aspects of Biblical Ethics* (Grand Rapids, MI: Eerdmans, 1957), 146.

[17] Ibid., 133.

[18] Ibid., 135. As for actions intended to deceive, Murray later argues that there was no wrongdoing on the part of Joshua or the army of Israel when it retreated from the city of Ai, drawing its inhabitants into an ambush by actions intended to deceive. Ibid., 144; cf. Joshua 8.

from God) or approve of truthfulness in speech (seeing it as characteristic of righteous people). What follows is a sample of such passages, but many more could be added. The extent of this testimony of Scripture against lying constitutes a repeated warning from God that we should not take this matter lightly.

You shall not *bear false witness* against your neighbor. (Ex. 20:16)

My lips will not *speak falsehood*,
    and my tongue will not utter deceit. (Job 27:4; verbal speaking emphasized)

You destroy those who *speak lies*. (Ps. 5:6; verbal speaking emphasized)

Everyone *utters lies* to his neighbor;
    with flattering lips and a double heart they speak. (Ps. 12:2; verbal
        speaking emphasized)

The wicked are estranged from the womb;
    they go astray from birth, *speaking lies*. (Ps. 58:3; speaking emphasized)

But the king shall rejoice in God;
    all who swear by him shall exult,
    for the mouths of *liars* will be stopped. (Ps. 63:11; speaking emphasized)

No one who utters lies
    shall continue before my eyes. (Ps. 101:7; speaking emphasized)

I said in my alarm,
    "All mankind are *liars*." (Ps. 116:11)

I hate and abhor *falsehood*,
    but I love your law. (Ps. 119:163)

Deliver me, O LORD,
    from *lying lips*,
    from a deceitful tongue. (Ps. 120:2; speaking emphasized)

Rescue me and deliver me
    from the hand of foreigners,
whose *mouths speak lies*
    and whose right hand is a right hand of falsehood. (Ps. 144:11; speaking
        emphasized)

Truthful lips endure forever,
    but a *lying tongue* is but for a moment.
        (Prov. 12:19; speaking emphasized)

Lying lips are an abomination to the LORD,
>but those who act faithfully are his delight. (Prov. 12:22; speaking
>>emphasized)

The righteous hates *falsehood*,
>but the wicked brings shame and disgrace. (Prov. 13:5)

Remove far from me *falsehood and lying*;
>give me neither poverty nor riches;
>feed me with the food that is needful for me. (Prov. 30:8)

No one enters suit justly;
>no one goes to law honestly;
they rely on empty pleas, *they speak lies*,
>they conceive mischief and give birth to iniquity. (Isa. 59:4; speaking
>>emphasized)

They bend their tongue like a bow;
>*falsehood and not truth* has grown strong in the land;
for they proceed from evil to evil,
>and they do not know me, declares the LORD. (Jer. 9:3; speaking
>>emphasized)

Everyone deceives his neighbor,
>and *no one speaks the truth*;
they have taught their tongue to *speak lies*;
>they weary themselves committing iniquity. (Jer. 9:5; speaking emphasized)

Your rich men are full of violence;
>your inhabitants *speak lies*,
>and their tongue is deceitful in their mouth. (Mic. 6:12; speaking
>>emphasized)

But Peter said, "Ananias, why has Satan filled your heart to *lie* to the Holy Spirit and to keep back for yourself part of the proceeds of the land? . . . You have not *lied* to men but to God." (Acts 5:3–4; Ananias's sin was speaking something untrue)[19]

I am *speaking the truth* in Christ—I am *not lying*; my conscience bears me witness in the Holy Spirit. (Rom. 9:1; writing truthful words, not false ones, emphasized)

---

[19] The specific words of Ananias are not recorded in Acts 5, but Peter's statement shows that Ananias had said that he was donating the entire amount received for the land. However, this statement was false.

In what I am writing to you, before God, *I do not lie!* (Gal. 1:20; here is an example where lying would mean affirming in *writing* something that Paul believed to be false, but the focus would still be on a lie as a falsehood expressed in words)

Therefore, having *put away falsehood*, let each one of you *speak the truth* with his neighbor, for we are members one of another. (Eph. 4:25; falsehood is contrasted with speaking the truth)

Do not lie to one another, seeing that you have put off the old self with its practices and have put on the new self, which is being renewed in knowledge after the image of its creator. (Col. 3:9–10)

[The law is laid down for] the sexually immoral, men who practice homosexuality, enslavers, *liars*, perjurers, and whatever else is contrary to sound doctrine. (1 Tim. 1:10)

For this I was appointed a preacher and an apostle (*I am telling the truth, I am not lying*), a teacher of the Gentiles in faith and truth. (1 Tim. 2:7; writing truthful words, not false ones, emphasized)

In their mouth *no lie was found*, for they are blameless. (Rev. 14:5; speaking emphasized)

But as for the cowardly, the faithless, the detestable, as for murderers, the sexually immoral, sorcerers, idolaters, *and all liars*, their portion will be in the lake that burns with fire and sulfur, which is the second death. (Rev. 21:8)

Therefore, the Bible's moral standards regarding lying include not only the ninth commandment, but an entire collection of Old Testament and New Testament passages that prohibit speaking lies or falsehood. *And this is just a partial list!* Many similar passages condemn such things as lying, falsehood, liars, and those who "speak lies."

2. The Mention of "Neighbor" in Exodus 20:16 Does Not Narrow the Application of the Ninth Commandment or the Many Other Passages about Lying. John Frame suggests that the inclusion of the word *neighbor* in the ninth commandment—"You shall not bear false witness against your neighbor" (Ex. 20:16)—may mean that it does not prohibit all affirmations of falsehood. He writes, "What then is a lie? I would say that a lie is a word or act that intentionally deceives a neighbor in order to hurt him. It is false witness *against* a neighbor."[20] Later, addressing Bible passages that promote some deception, he writes:

---

[20] John M. Frame, *The Doctrine of the Christian Life: A Theology of Lordship* (Phillipsburg, NJ: P&R, 2008), 835, emphasis in original.

[These passages] all have to do with the promotion of justice against the wicked, especially when they seek innocent life. . . . The requirement to tell the truth is conditioned on a relationship, that of "neighbor." . . . I have questioned whether a neighborly relationship exists between a believer and someone who seeks to murder. . . . We have no obligation to tell the truth to people who, for example, seek innocent life.[21]

However, I am not persuaded that the wording of the ninth commandment, "You shall not bear false witness *against your neighbor*" (Ex. 20:16), is intended to show us that there are some people to whom we are allowed to lie. Another explanation of that wording is more likely.

Calvin explained the concrete references in the Ten Commandments by saying that God formulated the *positive* commands in a way that would be easier for us to accept. For example, "Honor your father and your mother" (Ex. 20:12) should lead us to conclude, more broadly, that we should be subject to all rightful authority (such as the civil government), but God phrased the requirement in terms of one's father and mother, and "By that subjection which is easiest to tolerate, the Lord therefore gradually accustoms us to all lawful subjection."[22]

By contrast, Calvin says that the things prohibited in the *negative* commands put forth the most hateful examples of that whole category of wrongdoing in order to shock us into appreciating how hateful they all are. Thus, concerning the seventh commandment, "You shall not commit adultery" (Ex. 20:14), Calvin says, "But he expressly forbids fornication, to which all lust tends, in order through the foulness of fornication . . . to lead us to abominate all lust."[23]

Therefore, Calvin realizes that "You shall not bear false witness against your neighbor" (Ex. 20:16) pictures a courtroom scene in which the "false witness" will likely harm the neighbor by causing loss of life or property, but the wording of the commandment in this way is *not meant to narrow the application to neighbors only*. Calvin says:

As he forbade cruelty, shamelessness, and avarice in the preceding commandments, *here he bars falsehood.* . . . For we must always come back to this: one particular vice is singled out from various kinds *as an example*, and the rest are brought under the same category, the one chosen being an especially foul vice.[24]

Therefore, there is an alternative to seeing "against your neighbor" as limiting the scope of the ninth commandment. A better understanding is that "You shall not bear false witness *against your neighbor*" is chosen as *a particularly hateful example* of lying,

---

[21] Ibid., 839.
[22] Calvin, *Institutes*, 2.8.35 (401).
[23] Ibid., 2.8.41 (405).
[24] Ibid., 2.8.47 (411–12).

because it concerns a courtroom setting in which someone intentionally speaks falsely against a neighbor (whom he or she should love!) in a way that will cost the neighbor his goods (perhaps to the witness's benefit) or even his life. By this God means to show us how hateful all lying is, not merely this kind of lying.

The other use of "neighbor" in the Ten Commandments confirms this understanding:

> You shall not covet *your neighbor's* house; you shall not covet *your neighbor's* wife, or his male servant, or his female servant, or his ox, or his donkey, or anything that is *your neighbor's*. (Ex. 20:17)

Surely we would not want to argue that the mention of "neighbor" narrows the application of this commandment, so that it is wrong to covet your *neighbor's* house or wife but acceptable to covet your *enemy's* house or wife!

Rightly understood, then, "You shall not covet your neighbor's house; you shall not covet your neighbor's wife" implies "You shall not covet *anybody else's* house; you shall not covet *anybody else's* wife." Similarly, "You shall not bear false witness against your neighbor" implies "You shall not bear false witness *at all*," or, to put it in terms of lying, "You shall not *speak lies* at all." And the numerous other passages of Scripture mentioned above also confirm this when they condemn lying in general but make no mention of a neighbor.

D. THE CHARACTER OF GOD AS THE BASIS FOR NOT LYING

1. God Cannot Lie. The biblical commands against lying are ultimately rooted in the character of God, who never lies:

> *God is not man, that he should lie,*
>   or a son of man, that he should change his mind.
> Has he said, and will he not do it?
>   Or has he spoken, and will he not fulfill it? (Num. 23:19)

> *Every word of God proves true*;
>   he is a shield to those who take refuge in him. (Prov. 30:5)

> In hope of eternal life, which *God, who never lies*, promised before the ages began. (Titus 1:2)

> [God guaranteed his promise with an oath] so that by two unchangeable things, in which *it is impossible for God to lie*, we who have fled for refuge might have strong encouragement to hold fast to the hope set before us. (Heb. 6:18)

This, then, is the ultimate reason why lying is wrong: it makes us unfaithful image bearers of God. The New Testament tells us, "Therefore *be imitators of God*, as beloved children" (Eph. 5:1), and when we speak truthfully we rightly portray God as One who speaks the truth. But if we lie, we are not rightly imitating God's own truthful speech. If we lie, we are falsely portraying God as One who lies as well, and that dishonors him.[25]

This connection between not lying and bearing God's image is seen in Paul's statement to the Colossians:

> *Do not lie to one another*, seeing that you have put off the old self with its practices and have put on the new self, which is being renewed in knowledge *after the image of its creator*. (Col. 3:9–10)

By contrast, the character of Satan is such that he lies according to his own nature:

> *You are of your father the devil*, and your will is to do your father's desires. He was a murderer from the beginning, and has nothing to do with the truth, because *there is no truth in him. When he lies, he speaks out of his own character, for he is a liar and the father of lies.* (John 8:44)

The ground for these ethical norms against lying, therefore, is found not in any human results (such as the benefit or harm that lying might do to someone else, or whether someone might be led to think something false), but in the fact that *our lying dishonors God.* God seeks creatures who rightly represent his image, whereas Satan consistently promotes all kinds of falsehood and lying speech.

2. Jesus Never Found It Necessary to Lie. A strong objection to the view that it is sometimes acceptable to lie comes from the life of Christ. The New Testament tells us that Christ "in every respect has been tempted as we are, yet without sin" (Heb. 4:15). He faced, at least in some form, every type of difficult ethical situations that we will ever find ourselves in. That means that if people today ever face a situation in which it seems that they have to lie, then Jesus also faced that same difficult situation. And if we are required to lie in such a situation, then Jesus was required to lie as well. This would mean that Jesus actually lied, actually affirmed something that he believed to be untrue. It seems necessary to conclude that, according to this position, Jesus actually affirmed a falsehood!

But this would be impossible for Jesus, for he was also God, and "it is impossible for God to lie" (Heb. 6:18). Therefore, Jesus never lied. And therefore we never have to lie

---

[25] Some passages in Scripture show that God sends a "lying spirit" (1 Kings 22:22; cf. Ezek. 14:19) to deceive people, or sends people a delusion "so that they may believe what is false" (2 Thess. 2:11). These are portrayed in Scripture as instances of divine judgment on sin. God sometimes sends evil agents to carry out judgments (as he sent the Babylonians to carry the Israelites into exile), but he never actually does evil himself. So apparently God can send a lying spirit or some kind of deception as a form of judgment on people, but he himself still never lies.

either. Jesus's own moral character and the truthfulness of all his words provide additional evidence that Scripture prohibits us from ever telling a lie. The character of God, who never lies, is manifested to us in the life of Jesus, who never told a lie.

In conclusion, based on the abundant testimony of Scripture about lying and the biblical testimony about the character of God, I believe it is never right to lie in the sense of affirming in speech or writing something that you believe to be false.

E. THE NARRATIVE EXAMPLES OF LYING IN SCRIPTURE DO NOT OVERTURN OUR CONCLUSION THAT LYING IS ALWAYS WRONG

In spite of the strong testimony of Scripture against lying, a number of ethical writers have argued that there are specific *narrative examples* in Scripture that show that God sometimes approved of human lies that were told for good purposes, particularly to save human life, therefore overturning our conclusion that lying is always wrong. It is necessary to examine some of these passages.

1. Rahab's Lie. It is admitted by all that Rahab lied to the men who were looking for the Hebrew spies:

> And Joshua the son of Nun sent two men secretly from Shittim as spies, saying, "Go, view the land, especially Jericho." And they went and came into the house of a prostitute whose name was Rahab and lodged there. And it was told to the king of Jericho, "Behold, men of Israel have come here tonight to search out the land." Then the king of Jericho sent to Rahab, saying, "Bring out the men who have come to you, who entered your house, for they have come to search out all the land." But the woman had taken the two men and hidden them. And she said, "True, the men came to me, but I did not know where they were from. And when the gate was about to be closed at dark, *the men went out. I do not know where the men went.* Pursue them quickly, for you will overtake them." But she had brought them up to the roof and hid them with the stalks of flax that she had laid in order on the roof. So the men pursued after them on the way to the Jordan as far as the fords. And the gate was shut as soon as the pursuers had gone out. (Josh. 2:1–7)

The question is whether this passage or later passages that mention Rahab (see below) show that God actually approved of Rahab's lie.

A careful examination of the context is important. It shows that Rahab was a "prostitute" (v. 2) who lived in the Canaanite city of Jericho. There is nothing in the historical context to indicate that she had any prior instruction in the moral standards required by the God of Israel (other than what she could know by common grace). We should not assume that Scripture intends to hold up an untrained, uninformed Canaanite prostitute as a model of ethical conduct. The text does not give us warrant to draw this conclusion.

Two New Testament passages commend her faith and her receiving the spies and sending them out safely, but they conspicuously avoid mentioning her lie:

> By faith Rahab the prostitute did not perish with those who were disobedient, *because she had given a friendly welcome to the spies*. (Heb. 11:31)

> And in the same way was not also Rahab the prostitute justified by works *when she received the messengers and sent them out by another way*? (James 2:25)

These verses certainly do praise Rahab. But they do not say anything like this:

> By faith Rahab the prostitute did not perish with those who were disobedient, *because she told a skillful lie* to save the spies.

> And in the same way was not also Rahab the prostitute justified by works when she received the messengers *and told a lie* to keep them safe.

Nowhere in Scripture is there any verse that speaks this way and contains an explicit approval of a lie, even one told to protect innocent life. There are dozens of statements in Scripture about lies, and they always condemn them.

Regarding Rahab's lie, Calvin rightly observes:

> As to the falsehood, we must admit that *though it was done for a good purpose, it was not free from fault*. For those who hold what is called a dutiful lie to be altogether excusable, do not sufficiently consider how precious truth is in the sight of God. Therefore, although our purpose be to assist our brethren . . . *it can never be lawful to lie*, because that cannot be right which is contrary to the nature of God. And God is truth.[26]

Augustine takes the same position:

> Therefore, touching Rahab in Jericho, because she entertained strangers, men of God, because in entertaining of them she put herself in peril, because she believed on their God, because she diligently hid them where she could, because she gave them most faithful counsel of returning by another way, let her be praised as meet to be imitated. . . . But *in that she lied . . . not as meet to be imitated*: . . . albeit that *God hath* those things memorably honored, *this evil thing mercifully overlooked*.[27]

Therefore, Scripture does not hold up Rahab's lie as an example for believers to imitate.

---

[26] Calvin, *Commentaries on the Book of Joshua*, 47, emphasis added.
[27] Augustine, *To Consentius: Against Lying*, sec. 34 (NPNF[1], 3:497), emphasis added.

2. The Hebrew Midwives in Egypt.

> Then the king of Egypt said to the Hebrew midwives, one of whom was named Shiphrah and the other Puah, "When you serve as midwife to the Hebrew women and see them on the birthstool, if it is a son, you shall kill him, but if it is a daughter, she shall live." But the midwives feared God and did not do as the king of Egypt commanded them, but let the male children live. So the king of Egypt called the midwives and said to them, "Why have you done this, and let the male children live?" The midwives said to Pharaoh, "Because the Hebrew women are not like the Egyptian women, for they are vigorous and give birth before the midwife comes to them." So God dealt well with the midwives. And the people multiplied and grew very strong. And because the midwives feared God, he gave them families. (Ex. 1:15–21)

Does this passage show that God approved of lying? At least two factors call this conclusion into question: (1) The statement of the midwives may in fact have been true, or true as a generalization. It is entirely reasonable that, when Pharaoh's plan became known to the Hebrew people, they often delayed calling the midwives until after they had given birth, perhaps using other midwives or perhaps assisting one another in the birth process. The midwives themselves may have been complicit in this plan, even teaching the Hebrew women how to help one another at the time of childbirth. (2) God's favor on the midwives is primarily or entirely because of what is said in verse 17 (they "let the male children live") and verse 21 (they "feared God"). If their statement to Pharaoh was a lie, they told it only to protect themselves from punishment, not to protect the Hebrew children, so it is hardly a good example of lying to protect another life.

Thus, this passage is not a clear commendation of lying. Augustine writes that God's favor on them "was not because they lied, but because they were merciful to God's people. That therefore which was rewarded in them was, not their deceit, but their benevolence."[28]

3. Elisha's Statement to the Syrian Soldiers. The king of Syria sent a band of soldiers to capture the prophet Elisha, but God miraculously protected him in the following way:

> And when the Syrians came down against him, Elisha prayed to the LORD and said, "Please strike this people with blindness." So he struck them with blindness in accordance with the prayer of Elisha. And Elisha said to them, *"This is not the way, and this is not the city. Follow me, and I will bring you to the man whom you seek." And he led them to Samaria.* As soon as they entered Samaria, Elisha said, "O LORD, open the eyes of these men, that they may see." So the

---

[28] Ibid., sec. 32 (NPNF¹, 3:495).

Lord opened their eyes and they saw, and behold, they were in the midst of Samaria. (2 Kings 6:18–20)

Then the king of Israel, who was in the city of Samaria, asked Elisha if he should kill the Syrian soldiers whom Elisha had captured (2 Kings 6:21), but Elisha told the king to feed them and send them on their way (v. 22).

Did Elisha lie to the Syrian army? He said, "This is not the way, and this is not the city" (2 Kings 6:19), but the words were actually ambiguous, somewhat enigmatic. What way? What city? (The one where God wanted them to go?) The Lord had "blinded" them (v. 18), so they decided to follow Elisha. The statement "I will bring you to the man whom you seek" (v. 19) was, again, somewhat enigmatic, but rather than leaving them, Elisha did in fact bring them to a place where they encountered him face to face. This is by no means a clear example of a falsehood approved by God. (And in any case, it was not told to save Elisha's life or anyone else's life, for the Syrian soldiers were already blinded and harmless.)

4. Other Passages Reporting Various Kinds of Deception. Frame mentions 16 other sets of passages "in which someone misleads an enemy, without incurring any condemnation, and sometimes even being commended."[29] He says:

> In these passages, there is deceit, and that deceit brings harm. But the harm comes to an enemy, not to a neighbor. . . . It does appear that the Bible passages listed above, which justify deception in certain cases, all have to do with the promotion of justice against the wicked, especially when they seek innocent life. . . . We should recall that in the ninth commandment the requirement to tell the truth is conditioned on a relationship, that of "neighbor."[30]

The passages fall into several categories, but none of them contains a clear lie (in the sense of a verbal affirmation of something the speaker believed to be false) that is approved by God. Some of the passages speak about *deceptive actions*, such as a military ambush at Ai (Josh. 8:3–8), a surprise attack (2 Sam. 5:22–25), or David pretending to be insane (1 Sam. 21:13). These deceptive actions do seem to be approved by God in these passages, but they do not fall into the category of a "lie" as I have defined it in this chapter.[31]

But are such deceptive actions sufficiently different from a "lie" (as defined in this

---

[29] Frame, *The Doctrine of the Christian Life*, 836. The 16 sets of passages are (1) Ex. 1:15–21; (2) Josh. 2:4–6; 6:17, 25; Heb. 11:31; James 2:25; (3) Josh. 8:3–8; (4) Judg. 4:18–21; 5:24–27; (5) 1 Sam. 16:1–5; (6) 1 Sam. 19:12–17; (7) 1 Sam. 20:6; (8) 1 Sam. 21:13; (9) 1 Sam. 27:10; (10) 2 Sam. 5:22–25; (11) 2 Sam. 15:34; (12) 2 Sam. 17:19–20; (13) 1 Kings 22:19–23; (14) 2 Kings 6:14–20; (15) Jer. 38:24–28; and (16) 2 Thess. 2:11.

[30] Ibid., 836, 839.

[31] Warfare often depends on actions intended to deceive the enemy. Another area of morally acceptable deceptive actions is athletic contests (such a football quarterback who fakes a pass and then runs with the ball), and another is games, such as chess.

chapter) that we are justified in putting them in a different category? I think they are, for several reasons: (1) Scripture treats them differently, always condemning lies but not always condemning such deceptive actions. (2) Actions are not true or false (as verbal affirmations are), but are just things that happen. (3) People instinctively treat them differently. If on a weekend I leave a light on in my house (to deter burglars by making them think I am home) and then my neighbor bumps into me while I am staying in a hotel in Tucson (two hours away), the neighbor will not think me to be a liar because he saw that my light was on before he came to Tucson. But if I tell my neighbor, "I'm going to stay home this weekend" and then the neighbor bumps into me in a hotel in Tucson, he will think that I lied to him. This is because (4) actions have ambiguous meanings, but propositions ordinarily do not.

I am not saying deceptive actions are never wrong (sometimes they surely are, especially in situations of trust, such as marriages or parent-child relationships), but that they belong in a distinct category, one that Scripture treats differently from verbal affirmations of things that one believes to be false.

Other passages that Frame mentions have to do with *God sending a deceptive spirit* or a lying spirit to wicked unbelievers (1 Kings 22:19–23; 2 Thess. 2:11). These passages raise difficult questions about God's providential use of evil agents to carry out judgment, but they do not necessarily show God's approval of the lies any more than God's ordaining that evil people would crucify Christ (Acts 2:23; 4:27–28) shows that God approved of their evil deeds: he did not (Acts 2:23).

Other passages simply *report that someone lied* (just as Scripture narratives *report* other sins, such as murder or adultery) without indicating God's approval of the lie (these passages include 1 Sam. 19:12–17, where Michal lies to protect David and herself; 1 Sam. 20:6, where David counsels Jonathan to lie; and 2 Sam. 17:19–20, where a woman lies to protect David's messengers).

In still other passages there are cases of what we might call *deceptive speech*, but it is not clear that anyone actually told a lie in the sense of affirming something he thought to be false. These passages include Judges 4:18–21, where Jael invites Sisera into her tent; 2 Samuel 15:34, where David tells Hushai to say he will be Absalom's servant (he was, but he was an unfaithful servant); and Jeremiah 38:24–28, where Jeremiah reports that he has made a request to the king (which he might actually have done).

One passage deals with *stating part of the truth.* In 1 Samuel 16:1–5, God told Samuel to mention part of the purpose of his journey, that is, to say he was going to Bethlehem to offer a sacrifice (which was true), but Samuel remained silent regarding the other thing he was going to do: anoint David as king. There was no affirmation of anything false, but since God commanded Samuel what to say, the passage seems to approve of some cases in which a person states part of the truth and remains silent on other matters.

But in none of these passages is it clear that someone told a lie and it was approved by God. Therefore, these narrative passages should not be used against the consistent testimony of many normative statements of Scripture that uniformly condemn lying as something that is always displeasing to God.

F. DO SOME CIRCUMSTANCES REQUIRE A PERSON TO LIE?

1. Is Lying in Order to Protect Life Acceptable? Are there some circumstances in which God requires us to tell a lie to bring about a good result, such as lying to save a person's life? Some authors argue that lying to protect innocent lives can be morally right. For example, Frame writes:

> So we have no obligation to tell the truth to people who, for example, seek innocent life. In many volumes and essays on ethics, authors refer to perhaps the most famous of all ethical dilemmas: During World War II, a Christian is sheltering Jews in his home, protecting them from the Nazis. SS officers come to the door and ask him directly whether he is hiding Jews. . . . In this case . . . I think the obligation is clearly to deceive the SS. . . . If there were any chance to mislead the SS officers, as Rahab misled the officers of her own people, I think the Christian should have availed himself of that strategy.[32]

What shall we say about such a difficult situation? Isn't it better to lie to protect these hidden Jews than tell the truth and bring about their deaths?[33]

Interestingly, in about AD 395, Augustine treated a similar situation of a bishop named Firmus who was hiding a righteous person who was fleeing from the corrupt emperor. When the emperor's messengers came to capture the person, the bishop refused to lie, but neither would he disclose the hiding place. The emperor's messengers apparently tried to force him to disclose the hiding place, and as a result, he "suffered many torments of body," but "he stood firm in his purpose," and eventually, by his courage, he obtained a pardon from the emperor for the man he was protecting. Augustine says, "What conduct could be more brave and constant?"[34] Augustine thought it would have been wrong to lie, even for the purpose of protecting a human life.

2. Real-Life Situations Offer Many More Options. It must be said that real-life situations are always more complex, and offer more options, than hypothetical situations

---

[32] Frame, *The Doctrine of the Christian Life*, 839–40.

[33] Others who argue for the moral validity of lying to protect life in such situations include Norman L. Geisler, *Christian Ethics: Contemporary Issues and Options*, 2nd ed. (Grand Rapids, MI: Baker, 2010), 112, and David P. Gushee and Glen H. Stassen, *Kingdom Ethics: Following Jesus in Contemporary Context*, 2nd ed. (Grand Rapids, MI: Eerdmans, 2016), 299–305.

[34] Augustine, *On Lying*, sec. 23 (NPNF[1], 3:468). Tollefsen notes that Augustine repeatedly brings up another argument: "If lying is permitted in order to achieve some great spiritual or temporal good, then why would adultery, or some other form of unchastity, not also be acceptable for the sake of the same good?" *Lying and Christian Ethics*, 39, with reference to Augustine, *On Lying*, sec. 23 (NPNF[1], 3:468).

sketched in a sentence or two in an ethics textbook. For example, telling the truth and lying are not the only options, since *silence* is always an option (though it may lead to suffering, as with the bishop whom Augustine used as an example).

A fourth option is saying any of a hundred different things that don't answer the question asked, such as, "I will not cooperate with any attempt to capture and kill Jewish people." Yes, that may mean the Nazi soldiers will force their way in and search around, but they probably would do that anyway. Who can say that they would even believe the Christian if he said no?

Vern Poythress recounts an actual historical example in which God honored the simple faith of a young Dutch woman who refused to tell a lie. During the German occupation of the Netherlands, Nazi soldiers were searching for physically able Dutch men whom they would capture and force to work in Nazi munitions factories. One day, two nephews of Corrie ten Boom came to her family's home, seeking to escape from Nazi soldiers. The family hid them in a small cellar that was under a trapdoor in the kitchen floor. The trapdoor was covered by a rug, and on top of the rug was a kitchen table. Then the following events took place:

> We dropped the door shut, yanked the rug over it, and pulled the table back in place. With trembling hands, Betsy, Cocky, and I threw a long tablecloth over it and started laying five places for tea.
>
> There was a crash in the hall as the front door burst open and a smaller crash close by as Cocky dropped a teacup. Two uniformed Germans ran into the kitchen, rifles leveled.
>
> "Stay where you are. Do not move."
>
> We heard boots storming up the stairs. The soldiers glanced around disgustedly at this room filled with women and one old man. . . .
>
> "Where are your men?" The shorter soldier asked Cocky in clumsy, thick-accented Dutch.
>
> "These are my aunts," she said, "and this is my grandfather. My father is at his school, and my mother is shopping, and—"
>
> "I didn't ask about the whole tribe!" the man exploded in German. Then in Dutch: "Where are your brothers?"
>
> Cocky stared at him a second, then dropped her eyes. My heart stood still. I knew how Nollie had trained her children—but surely, surely now of all times a lie was permissible!
>
> "Do you have brothers?" the officer asked again.
>
> "Yes," Cocky said softly. "We have three."
>
> "How old are they?"
>
> "Twenty-one, 19, and 18."
>
> Upstairs we heard the sounds of doors opening and shutting, the scrape of furniture dragged from walls.

"Where are they now?" the soldier persisted.

Cocky leaned down and began gathering up the broken bits of cup. The man jerked her upright. "Where are your brothers?"

"The oldest one is at the Theological College. He doesn't get home most nights because—"

"What about the other two?"

Cocky did not miss a breath.

"Why, they are under the table."

Motioning us all away from it with his gun, the soldier seized a corner of the cloth. At a nod from him the taller man crouched with his rifle cocked. Then he flung back the cloth.

At last the pent-up tension exploded: Cocky burst into spasms of high hysterical laughter. The soldiers whirled around. Was this girl laughing at them?

"Don't take us for fools!" the short one snarled. Furiously he strode from the room and minutes later the entire squad trooped out—not, unfortunately, before the silent soldier had spied and pocketed our precious packet of tea.[35]

This is a remarkable instance of God's providential protection. But blurting out the location of hidden people is certainly not the only thing that can be said. Poythress wisely suggests that such "Nazis at the door" situations can also become opportunities to share the gospel with the soldiers themselves, in words such as this:

> Can you understand that I accept the legitimate authority of human government, but I cannot cooperate in evil? If I were harboring Jews, would I tell you? You ought not to be asking about the Jews, but asking instead about how to be reconciled to the God who made you.[36]

Roman Catholic philosopher Christopher Tollefsen makes a similar suggestion:

> So one should refuse to answer, by keeping silent or by evading in some way the question. Still, the Nazi is a human being . . . and one cannot assume that his soul is beyond saving. . . . It would be responsive to the obligation to love, and the good of sociality, to tell him further that he is engaged in a wicked activity and to encourage his repentance.[37]

Some would argue that in this situation, evildoers such as murderers have "forfeited their right to the truth." I would probably agree with this (at least the truth regarding the hidden Jews), and so I would not tell the Nazis that truth (we have no general obligation to tell everything we know). But that does not mean that I would have to lie to them

---

[35] Corrie ten Boom with Elizabeth and John Sherrill, *The Hiding Place* (Grand Rapids, MI: Baker, 1984), 106–7. Poythress quotes this lengthy narrative (from a different edition) in "Why Lying Is Always Wrong," 90–91.

[36] Poythress, "Why Lying Is Always Wrong," 93.

[37] Tollefsen, *Lying and Christian Ethics*, 177.

either. A Christian in that situation should immediately pray for God's wisdom to know what to say without lying and without disclosing where the Jews are hidden.

Poythress points out that Jesus promises his disciples the Holy Spirit's help when they are tried before hostile government authorities, a somewhat analogous situation:

> You will be dragged before governors and kings for my sake, to bear witness before them and the Gentiles. When they deliver you over, do not be anxious how you are to speak or what you are to say, for *what you are to say will be given to you in that hour*. For it is not you who speak, but the Spirit of your Father speaking through you. (Matt. 10:18–20).[38]

3. Does the Hidden Jews Situation Present a "Tragic Moral Choice"? Some ethicists would use the example of Nazis searching for hidden Jews to argue for a "tragic moral choice," a case in which we have to commit a lesser sin (lying) to avoid a greater sin (murder, giving aid to a murderer, or at least not preventing a murder when we could do so). But I disagree with this viewpoint, because (as I argued in chap. 7, p. 201), according to the Bible's teachings, *there are no such tragic moral choices*, times when God wants us to disobey one of his commands in order to obey another.

This point is more significant than people first realize. I am concerned that in today's evangelical Christian world, carefully constructed "hard cases" too often are used as a wedge to open the door a crack, to induce people to admit that there are some situations in which it is morally right (and acceptable to God!) to disobey one of God's commands in Scripture. As I explained in chapter 7 (see p. 200), this was the position of Joseph Fletcher, whose 1966 book *Situation Ethics*[39] constructed all sorts of "hard cases" in which a person supposedly had to lie, murder, commit adultery, or steal in order to follow the greater principle of "love" for others (that is, doing good for others).

But such reasoning from "hard cases" quickly leads to easy rationalizations for many other sins. It is easy for people to progress from (1) it is *sometimes* right to lie to preserve a human life, to (2) it is right to lie when it does *more good than harm*, to (3) it is right to lie when you think it will bring a *good result*, to (4) it is sometimes right to break *other* commands of the Bible when it will do more good than harm.

The end result is a terribly weak personal ethical system that lacks any backbone, that ignores the commands of Scripture, and that simply seeks to bring about good results by whatever means (without getting caught). The whole system can slide quickly to moral relativism.

4. The Broader Results of Lying or Not Lying Are Also Important. As with all ethical questions, we need to ask what *results* will come from a given action. If a person lies (even to protect life), several results will follow:

---

[38] Cited in Poythress, "Why Lying Is Always Wrong," 92.

[39] Joseph Fletcher, *Situation Ethics: The New Morality* (Philadelphia: Westminster Press, 1966).

1. The other person's life might or might not be preserved. But the person who lied cannot be sure that different actions (remaining silent or giving other answers) would not have also preserved life (especially if he or she trusts in God's sovereign control over situations).
2. God will be dishonored, because a human being who bears God's image, and who represents God on the earth, told a lie and thus represented his Creator as a liar.
3. People will begin to think of the person who lied as (at least sometimes) a liar, someone whose words cannot always be trusted.
4. The moral character of the person who lied will be eroded, because in a difficult situation he or she failed to obey the biblical commands against lying.
5. It will become easier for the person who lied to lie in the future, because once a person thinks it is right to lie in some circumstances, lying will seem to be an easy solution in additional circumstances, and the person's lying will become more frequent.
6. Others may imitate the person's act of lying, multiplying these results in other situations.

But if a person remains silent or tells the truth (refusing to lie), then several good results will follow:

1. The person will have trusted God to bring about the right results, including protecting the other person's life.
2. God will be honored because the person's actions portrayed his or her Creator as One who tells only the truth.
3. People will begin to think of the person who told the truth as someone whose words can always be trusted.
4. The moral character of the person who did not lie will be strengthened, because in a difficult situation he or she faithfully obeyed the biblical commands against lying.
5. The person who refused to lie will be more likely to always tell the truth in the future, remembering that it was not necessary to lie in this difficult situation in the past.
6. The speaker's truthfulness may be imitated by others, multiplying these results in other situations. In this way the work of the kingdom of God will be advanced.

G. THE CONNECTION BETWEEN LYING AND A PERSON'S MORAL CHARACTER

1. Lying Accompanies Most Other Sins. It is significant that lying often accompanies other sins. The murderer, the adulterer, and the thief all lie to conceal their wrongdoing. And those who promote false religions often use falsehood to advance their views:

> Now the Spirit expressly says that in later times some will depart from the faith by devoting themselves to deceitful spirits and teachings of demons, through the insincerity of *liars* whose consciences are seared. (1 Tim. 4:1–2)

But if lying is often used to cover up other sins, then a society in which lying is unacceptable, and in which truthfulness is held in high regard, might expect to see a decrease in other wrongdoing as well. (Certainly parents who have raised children, or teachers who have taught elementary students, will testify that if lying can be eliminated, then much other bad conduct will be eliminated as well.)

2. Telling the Truth in Difficult Situations Requires Faith in God and Strong Moral Character. From early childhood, all human beings face circumstances in which they do something wrong and then are asked about it.

> "Victoria, did you eat the cookies that I told you not to eat?"

> "Billy, did you break Mommy's favorite coffee cup?"

And then later in an employment situation:

> "Ralph, Mr. Smith says he still has not received our payment. Did you put the check in the mail before it was picked up on Friday, as I asked you to do?"

Another example is when someone is involved in a traffic accident and is questioned by police:

> "Mr. Thompson, how fast were you going when you approached the intersection?"

The temptation in these situations is to lie, because we expect that telling the truth will bring us negative consequences. In order to resist that temptation, we need to trust God to care for us even if telling the truth brings us painful consequences for a time. We also need to recognize that obeying God when it is difficult builds moral character in us and strengthens our moral backbone. Even children can be taught these simple truths, so that they form a habit of telling the truth with courage and faith even when it is costly.

The following Scripture passages will be an encouragement in such situations:

> Those who honor me I will honor. (1 Sam. 2:30)

> And we know that for those who love God all things work together for good, for those who are called according to his purpose. (Rom. 8:28)

> And my God will supply every need of yours according to his riches in glory in Christ Jesus. (Phil. 4:19)

> Although he was a son, he learned obedience through what he suffered. (Heb. 5:8)

> But solid food is for the mature, for those who have their powers of discernment trained by constant practice to distinguish good from evil. (Heb. 5:14)

3. Lying or Truth Telling Are Indications of the Moral Character of the Speaker. Truthfulness and lying are often highly significant indicators of a person's inward moral character. In fact, truthfulness in speech may be the most frequent test of our integrity each day.

In ordinary life, people don't often encounter opportunities to murder, commit adultery, steal, or break other civil laws without a high probability of being found out and suffering serious consequences. But people do have opportunities many times every day to speak truthfully or to tell small lies (usually with little likelihood of being caught). For example, the expressions "I don't know," "I don't remember," "I thought you said XYZ," or "I forgot" can be outright lies, but who can ever prove it? Small exaggerations of events or distortions of details of fact can be spoken repeatedly in situations in which the hearers have no way of knowing that they are untrue. But in each case, God is dishonored and the liar's moral character is further eroded, his conscience is progressively hardened against God's law, and he becomes more open to committing other kinds of sin as well.

> O Lord, who shall sojourn in your tent?
>> Who shall dwell on your holy hill?
> He who walks blamelessly and does what is right
>> *and speaks truth in his heart.* (Ps. 15:1–2)

Each time a person speaks the truth or lies, he aligns himself either with God, "who never lies" (Titus 1:2), or with Satan, "a liar and the father of lies" (John 8:44).

A person who tells the truth (or remains silent), even in a difficult situation, faithfully represents his Creator as one who tells the truth and does not lie, and therefore becomes more closely conformed to the image of God. In addition, as noted above, telling the truth often requires inward trust in God to govern the circumstances and the outcome of the situation.

H. CONCLUSION ON LYING

If lying is understood to mean "affirming in speech or writing something you believe to be false," then the overall testimony of Scripture is that lying is always wrong in every situation and every circumstance of life, and this will be true for all eternity.

I. SEEKING AND LOVING THE TRUTH

1. The Positive Obligations Implied by the Ninth Commandment. When God gives us a command to not do something, it often implies that he wants us to do the opposite thing, and that is certainly the case with the ninth commandment. God wants us to speak the truth, believe the truth, and love the truth. Such love for the truth includes all the truth of the gospel and the entire Bible, and also truth about other people and about the world around us.

> O Lord, who shall sojourn in your tent?
>   Who shall dwell on your holy hill?
> He who walks blamelessly and does what is right
>   and *speaks truth in his heart*. (Ps. 15:1–2)

> Behold, you delight in *truth* in the inward being. (Ps. 51:6)

> *Buy truth*, and do not sell it;
>   buy wisdom, instruction, and understanding. (Prov. 23:23)

> These are the things that you shall do: *Speak the truth* to one another; render in your gates judgments that are true and make for peace. . . . Therefore *love truth* and peace. (Zech. 8:16, 19)

> Jesus said to him, "I am the way, *and the truth*, and the life. No one comes to the Father except through me." (John 14:6)

> Therefore, having put away falsehood, let each one of you *speak the truth* with his neighbor, for we are members one of another. (Eph. 4:25)

John Calvin understood this, for in connection with the ninth commandment, he wrote:

> We should faithfully help everyone as much as we can in affirming the truth, in order to protect the integrity of his [the other person's] name and possessions.[40]

The Westminster Larger Catechism likewise explains the positive duties implied by the ninth commandment as follows:

> The duties required in the ninth commandment are, the preserving and promoting of truth between man and man, and the good name of our neighbor, as well as our own; appearing and standing for the truth; and from the heart, sincerely, freely, clearly, and fully, speaking the truth, and only the truth, in

---

[40] Calvin, *Institutes*, 2.8.47 (411).

matters of judgment and justice, and in all other things whatsoever; a charitable esteem of our neighbors; loving, desiring, and rejoicing in their good name; . . . [several more illustrations follow]. (WLC, Question 144)

By way of practical application, we should love truth and seek to promote and defend truth in all areas of human knowledge. If called upon to give testimony in court, we should do so with a willing heart and complete honesty, so far as we are able, that the truth may be known. And in the area of academic studies, we should faithfully and accurately report the results of our research in every field of study, never giving in to any temptation to distort or skew the truth to support the results we prefer.

2. The Necessity of Responding to Slander. The Westminster Larger Catechism, in further explanation of the ninth commandment, says that it also requires "love and care of our own good name, and *defending it* when need requireth" (Question 144). It gives two Scripture references in support:

A good name is to be chosen rather than great riches,
    and favor is better than silver or gold. (Prov. 22:1)

Jesus answered, "I do not have a demon, but I honor my Father, and you dishonor me." (John 8:49)

The second passage illustrates a general pattern in Jesus's ministry: he always defended himself immediately and firmly against false accusations throughout his entire ministry (see, for example, his progressive silencing of the Pharisees and Sadducees in Matt. 22:22, 33, 46). The only exception was the unique situation when he was on trial leading up to his crucifixion at the end of his life (27:12, 14). In that situation, it was important that he submit to the Father's plan that he would die as a criminal, under false accusation, and that he fulfill the prophecy of Isaiah:

He was oppressed, and he was afflicted,
    yet *he opened not his mouth*;
like a lamb that is led to the slaughter,
    and like a sheep that before its shearers is *silent*,
    so he opened not his mouth. (Isa. 53:7; cf. Acts 8:32)

Too often today Christian leaders mistakenly allow their own names or the ministries they lead to be slandered relentlessly in the public eye while they give no response. This can be immensely damaging in an age when Internet accusations can multiply rapidly with no accountability for the authors. These silent Christian leaders perhaps think they are imitating the example of Jesus at his crucifixion, but they fail to appreciate the uniqueness of that situation, and so they fail to imitate the example of Jesus during his entire public ministry, when he immediately defended himself and answered false accusations. I do not mean that we must answer everything we hear or read, for sometimes a false accusation has little influence and is best ignored: "Do not take to heart all the things that people say, lest you hear your servant cursing you" (Eccles. 7:21). But when it seems that a false accusation will gain influence and do harm, it must be answered.

The apostle Paul showed a similar concern to protect the good name of his ministry, the good name of Christ, and the reputation of the gospel when he demanded that the city officials in Philippi come to the jail and publicly release him and Silas, thus showing public vindication of their innocence:

> But Paul said to them, "They have beaten us publicly, uncondemned, men who are Roman citizens, and have thrown us into prison; and do they now throw us out secretly? No! Let them come themselves and take us out." (Acts 16:37; cf. Mark 13:11)

J. OTHER SPECIFIC ISSUES RELATED TO TRUTH TELLING

1. Spying and Undercover Police Work. Based on the abundant testimony of Scripture, and on the arguments in the preceding discussion based on that testimony, I do not think it is ever right to lie in the sense of affirming in speech or writing something you believe to be false. But does that mean that a Christian could never work as a spy or as an undercover police officer?

My conclusion is that there are some actions that would be morally acceptable for a Christian working as a spy and other actions that would be morally wrong.

1. It cannot be wrong in general to work as a spy (to visit another country secretly for the purpose of gaining information about it), for God himself commanded Moses, "Send men to spy out the land of Canaan, which I am giving to the people of Israel" (Num. 13:2). Later, Joshua "sent two men secretly from Shittim as spies, saying, 'Go, view the land, especially Jericho'" (Josh. 2:1).

2. It cannot be wrong to conceal one's full identity, for Jesus himself lived as an ordinary human being for the first 30 years of his life, and the people in his village of Nazareth did not know that he was both God and man, but thought of him simply as "the carpenter" (Mark 6:3; see Matt. 13:53–58). Even his brothers (who had grown up with him in the same small first-century house) did not know that he was also fully God! "For not even his brothers believed in him" (John 7:5).

In another example, Joseph concealed his identity from his brothers when they first visited Egypt, and his actions are viewed with approval in the Genesis narrative:

> Now Joseph was governor over all the land. . . . Joseph saw his brothers and recognized them, but he treated them like strangers and spoke roughly to them. "Where do you come from?" he said. They said, "From the land of

Canaan, to buy food." And Joseph recognized his brothers, but they did not recognize him. (Gen. 42:6–8)

Similarly, David pretended to be insane after he fled to Achish the king of Gath:

So he changed his behavior before them and pretended to be insane in their hands and made marks on the doors of the gate and let his spittle run down his beard. Then Achish said to his servants, "Behold, you see the man is mad. Why then have you brought him to me?" (1 Sam. 21:13–14)

3. While I do not think it is morally right to lie about one's name, I also think there are some situations in which going by another name is morally acceptable. This commonly happens when people use nicknames, such as "Chip," "Rocky," "Slim" or (referring to the gigantic American football player William Perry) "The Refrigerator." Literary authors often use pseudonyms to conceal their identities, such as Mary Anne Evans writing under the name George Eliot. Well-known celebrities sometimes register under an assumed name at a hotel, to protect their privacy. And apparently Joseph was going by some other Egyptian name or title when his brothers appeared before him in Egypt (Gen. 42:6–11), for he did not reveal his true name to them until much later, when he declared to them, "*I am your brother, Joseph,* whom you sold into Egypt" (45:4).

In such a situation, if his brothers had asked him, "Are you [Egyptian name], governor of the land of Egypt?" it would have been truthful for him to answer yes, for that was the name he was using. But if they had asked him, "Are you Joseph our brother, the son of Jacob?" it would have been a lie for him to say no.

4. It is morally permissible at times to tell part of the reason you are doing something, without stating all of the reasons you are doing it. This is evident from the story in which the Lord told the prophet Samuel to go to Bethlehem and anoint David as king. But Saul was presently the king, and so Samuel answered the Lord, "How can I go? If Saul hears it, he will kill me." Then the Lord told Samuel, "Take a heifer with you and say, 'I have come to sacrifice to the LORD'" (1 Sam. 16:2).

It was true that Samuel was going to sacrifice to the Lord at Bethlehem, and he did that. Although that was not his primary purpose in going, it was still a truthful statement. From that we can conclude that there are times when stating part of the truth is morally acceptable, even when done to conceal a more important purpose for an action. In this case, the Lord himself commanded it, so we cannot say that it was morally wrong.

This example gives justification, for example, for Christians to say that their purpose in traveling to other countries is to teach English, even though a more important purpose may be to do evangelism among the people that they teach. And it gives justification for a spy to travel to another country as, for example, a computer consultant or a management consultant (if he or she actually does some of that work), even though going as a spy may be the primary motivation.

5. These considerations do not fully answer the question of whether a Christian can

work as a spy or as an undercover police officer, but they may be helpful in clarifying some of the issues involved.

2. Plagiarism. Plagiarism means publishing part of another author's work but claiming it as one's own. Plagiarism occurs in educational settings when a student turns in an essay or term paper containing a block of wording taken from someone else's writing without footnoting it or indicating that it is a quotation from someone else. Plagiarism occurs in journalism when a reporter or an opinion writer copies someone else's wordings or thoughts without attributing them to the other person. And plagiarism occurs in sermons when a pastor preaches blocks of material he has found in someone else's sermon as if they were his own original material.

All of these are examples of claiming (or intentionally giving the impression) that an author has himself or herself written the material, and that therefore the wording and ideas originated with him or her. But that is another form of lying because the author, by identifying himself or herself as the source of the work, is understood by readers and hearers as claiming, "These words and ideas originated with me." That is a false claim.

3. Punctuality. Some people are habitually late. Your friend says, "I'll meet you at Starbucks for coffee at 11 a.m. on Thursday." You arrive at 11 and wait, and then he walks in at 11:15 or 11:20 with a quick excuse about "heavy traffic" or something else. In fact, in one of my classes in a recent term, I had a student like that—he habitually came in five or 10 minutes after the class had started. I spoke privately to him about it, with little result. I expect that habit had been built up over decades.

I recognize that a habit of lateness does not fall into the category of a "major sin," such as murder, adultery, or perjury,[41] but it still has some significance. If your friend agreed to meet you at Starbucks at 11 a.m. and did not make a reasonable effort to keep his word, this is a failure in his obligation to be truthful in speech. After a while, people will begin to doubt whether this person is "trustworthy" (see Ex. 18:21; 1 Cor. 7:25) in other things that he says. Certainly God himself is trustworthy in all that he says (Ps. 93:5; 111:7; 1 Tim. 1:15; Rev. 22:6), and we should imitate his speech.

In addition, your friend has "stolen" some time from you, because if you knew he was going to arrive at 11:20, you would have chosen to do something other than sit at Starbucks and wait for those 20 minutes. In disrespecting your time, your friend did not seem to be following Jesus's teaching "You shall love your neighbor as yourself" (Matt. 22:39).

From 40 years of teaching experience, I know how disruptive it is when two or three students walk in late to my class, after I have already started my lecture. I generally try to ignore it and just go on with the class, but it disturbs other students and disrupts my train of thought, at least to some degree. I am sure that pastors and worship leaders feel the same about people who walk into a church service five, 10, or even 15 minutes late, and do so habitually. They probably think, "Nobody will care," but that is not exactly true.

---

[41] See the discussion of greater and lesser sins in chap. 5, p. 139.

Yes, I'm sure the pastor would rather have them come late than not come at all, but such tardiness is still disrespectful of the pastor and worship leader, and disruptive to those who are already there. A helpful question for a person who is habitually late to ask himself or herself is "What would happen to the church if everybody acted the same way I did?"[42]

I recognize that there are occasional circumstances that are entirely unpredictable and over which we have no control (such as a flat tire, a traffic accident, or a medical emergency), and I am not saying it is irresponsible to be late for an appointment in such circumstances. But such rare occasions are different from a habit of continual lateness. Reasonable punctuality may be a minor virtue, but I believe it is still a virtue.

4. Other Common Situations. My approach to other situations that occur in everyday life would be similar to the approach above, in every case maintaining the principle that it is never right to tell a lie. Therefore, for example, there is no such thing as a "little white lie," that is, a supposedly "harmless" lie told to persuade someone to go to a surprise birthday party, or told in order to conceal a Christmas present, and so forth. Other means of persuading the person to go to the surprise party should be used (many truthful things can be said that do not involve telling a lie).

What should a husband say when his wife asks if he likes a dress she has bought or her new haircut, but he does not think the dress or the haircut is attractive? Here I can give personal counsel (from 48 years of marriage): it is always better to tell the truth, and to do so following Ephesians 4:15, "speaking the truth *in love*." This will mean speaking with kindness, humility, and thoughtfulness, and also speaking truthfully. ("Well, it wouldn't be my favorite . . . but the color is nice," or something like that. Perhaps Matt. 10:19 could just barely apply here: "What you are to say will be given to you in that hour.") The result may be momentary disappointment, but in the long term a husband and wife will trust each other always to speak truthfully and with love and kindness, and the benefits to their marriage will be great.

What about responses to conventional idioms or habitual greetings, such as "How are you?" I think that "Fine" can cover many situations (both speaker and hearer understand it to apply rather broadly), and "I'm OK, thanks" can be a truthful answer in almost any situation. (Even in great distress, I can be "OK" because I am trusting the Lord.) At times, a more specific answer might be appropriate. These are not really difficult situations, and creative thought will no doubt lead to opportunities for even more beneficial answers.[43]

---

[42] Fair disclosure: I am writing this section as someone who struggled with punctuality for many years, and who still struggles somewhat. A major turning point came a few years ago with the simple decision to leave earlier for appointments. For example, our church was a 15-minute drive from our home. Therefore, for many years, we would leave home at 9:15 for a 9:30 service, and always walk in a few minutes late. Finally we decided to start leaving at 9 a.m. for the 9:30 service, and suddenly the drive became more relaxed, we felt free to greet people as we walked into the church, and we would be seated five to 10 minutes before the service started, allowing time to talk to others who were there. It was a simple solution, but it changed our Sunday mornings significantly.

[43] My friend C. J. Mahaney often answers, "I'm doing far better than I deserve," which leads to many interesting conversations!

QUESTIONS FOR PERSONAL APPLICATION

1. How has this chapter changed your view of lying?
2. How would a habit of truthfulness in speech enable you to more fully glorify God and advance the work of his kingdom here on earth?
3. Did this chapter make you realize that you have not been as careful about truthfulness in your speech as you should be? Do you think this will make any difference in your life going forward?
4. Do you think it is permissible to lie in order to save a life? Are there any other alternatives?
5. Do you know anyone whom you consider to be completely trustworthy in everything he or she says? What do you think of that person?
6. What character traits (see p. 110) are particularly appropriate to encourage truthfulness in speech?
7. Has there ever been a time when someone spoke falsely about you or spread false information about you, and you acted to correct the false information? Or when you remained silent about it? Looking back on that situation, is there anything you would do differently if you could?
8. Do you think there are any circumstances in which a "little white lie" is morally permissible?

SPECIAL TERMS

bearing false witness
hyperbole
lying
plagiarism
punctuality
tragic moral choice

BIBLIOGRAPHY

Sections in Other Ethics Texts

(see complete bibliographical data, p. 64)

Frame, 830–40
Geisler, 19–20
Gushee and Stassen, 288–307
Jones, 144–52
McQuilkin and Copan, 501–14
Murray, 123–48

Other Works

Griffiths, Paul J. *Lying: An Augustinian Theology of Duplicity*. Grand Rapids, MI: Brazos, 2004.

Hammond, Peter. *Character Assassins: Dealing with Ecclesiastical Tyrants and Terrorists*. Cape Town: Christian Liberty Books, 2004.

Hicks, P. A. "Truth." In *New Dictionary of Christian Ethics and Pastoral Theology*, edited by David J. Atkinson and David H. Field, 867–68. Leicester, UK: Inter-Varsity, and Downers Grove, IL: InterVarsity Press, 1995.

Komp, Diane M. *Anatomy of a Lie: The Truth about Lies and Why Good People Tell Them*. Grand Rapids, MI: Zondervan, 1998.

Lindskoog, Kathryn Ann. *Fakes, Frauds, & Other Malarkey: 301 Amazing Stories & How Not to Be Fooled*. Grand Rapids, MI: Zondervan, 1993.

Morey, Robert A. *A Bible Handbook on Slander and Gossip: How God Wants You to Deal with Slander and Gossip*. Maitland, FL: Xulon Press, 2009.

Stowell, Joseph M. *The Weight of Your Words: Measuring the Impact of What You Say*. Chicago: Moody Press, 1998.

Tollefsen, Christopher O. *Lying and Christian Ethics*. New Studies in Christian Ethics. Vol. 33. New York: Cambridge University Press, 2014.

SCRIPTURE MEMORY PASSAGE

Exodus 20:16: You shall not bear false witness against your neighbor.

HYMN

"I Need Thee Every Hour"

I need Thee ev'ry hour,
Most gracious Lord;
No tender voice like Thine
Can peace afford.

Refrain:
I need Thee, O I need Thee,
Every hour I need Thee!
O bless me now, my Savior—
I come to Thee!

I need Thee ev'ry hour,
Stay Thou near by;
Temptations lose their pow'r
When Thou art nigh.

I need Thee ev'ry hour,
In joy or pain;
Come quickly and abide,
Or life is vain.

I need Thee ev'ry hour,
Most Holy One;
O make me Thine indeed,
Thou blessed Son!

AUTHOR: ANNIE S. HAWKS, 1835–1918

Chapter 13

THE SABBATH COMMANDMENT

Why did the day of worship change from Saturday to Sunday?
Is it wrong to work on Sundays?

The fourth commandment reads:

> Remember the Sabbath day, to keep it holy. Six days you shall labor, and do all your work, but the seventh day is a Sabbath to the LORD your God. On it you shall not do any work, you, or your son, or your daughter, your male servant, or your female servant, or your livestock, or the sojourner who is within your gates. For in six days the LORD made heaven and earth, the sea, and all that is in them, and rested on the seventh day. Therefore the LORD blessed the Sabbath day and made it holy. (Ex. 20:8–11)

The wording of this commandment in Deuteronomy contains an additional reason to that given in Exodus:

> Observe the Sabbath day, to keep it holy, as the LORD your God commanded you. Six days you shall labor and do all your work, but the seventh day is a Sabbath to the LORD your God. On it you shall not do any work, you or your son or your daughter or your male servant or your female servant, or your ox or your donkey or any of your livestock, or the sojourner who is within your gates, that your male servant and your female servant may rest as well as you. *You shall remember that you were a slave in the land of Egypt, and the LORD your God brought you out from there with a mighty hand and an outstretched arm. Therefore the LORD your God commanded you to keep the Sabbath day.* (Deut. 5:12–15).[1]

---

[1] The added reason in Deuteronomy represents additional wording that God gave to Moses regarding this commandment, either at the time God first spoke the Ten Commandments from the mountain or in a subsequent revelation (the text does not tell us).

A. THE MEANING OF THE COMMANDMENT

1. A Day of Rest Was a Gift from God. For the Israelites, an agrarian people who had to work to get food "by the sweat of your face" (Gen. 3:19), this commandment announced a welcome gift from God: a day of rest from their labor at which they worked during the rest of the week. This day was also a time in which they could draw near to God in worship, a day that God "blessed" (Ex. 20:11). The commandment was not intended to impose onerous restrictions on human activity, such that obedience would come to be viewed as a dreadful burden, and even the ordinary conduct of life would result in harsh accusations and fearful guilt. Jesus understood this, for he said, "The Sabbath was made for man, not man for the Sabbath" (Mark 2:27).

The Lord spoke through Isaiah to explain how he intended the Sabbath to be a "delight":

> If you turn back your foot from the Sabbath,
>> from doing your pleasure on my holy day,
> *and call the Sabbath a delight*
>> and the holy day of the Lord honorable;
> if you honor it, not going your own ways,
>> or seeking your own pleasure, or talking idly;
> *then you shall take delight in the Lord,*
>> and I will make you ride on the heights of the earth;
> I will feed you with the heritage of Jacob your father,
>> for the mouth of the Lord has spoken. (Isa. 58:13–14)

2. Later Jewish Tradition Added Many Oppressive Rules. However, Jewish tradition that developed after the last Old Testament books were written added numerous detailed legalistic rules about what was considered forbidden "work" on the Sabbath day and what kinds of activities were permitted. Here are some examples of such detailed rules from the Mishnah:[2]

> If a kettle [holding hot water] was taken off [from a stove], cold water may not be put in it to be made hot; but enough may be put therein . . . to make [the hot water] lukewarm.[3]

---

[2] The Mishnah is a topically arranged collection of recognized rabbinic teachings about all the details of Jewish life. It was put in written form around AD 200, but much of the oral tradition that it represents dates from before the time of Christ. The Talmud, which came after the Mishnah, consists of each of the paragraphs from the Mishnah followed by extensive rabbinic discussions of their meanings. The Talmud is therefore much longer than the Mishnah. The section of the Mishnah that deals with Sabbath regulations (the tractate called Shabbath) is 21 pages long in Herbert Danby's English translation, while the corresponding section of the Babylonian Talmud (also called Shabbath) in an English translation covers 806 pages. See *The Babylonian Talmud: Seder Moed*, 4 vols., ed. I. Epstein (London: Soncino, 1938), 1.1–806.

[3] Herbert Danby, trans., *The Mishnah* (Oxford: Oxford University Press, 1933), 103 (Mishnah, Shabbath, 3.5).

He is culpable that writes two letters, whether with his right hand or with his left, whether the same or different letters, whether in different inks or in any language.[4]

If a gentile lighted a lamp an Israelite may make use of the light, but if he lighted it for the sake of the Israelite it is forbidden. If he filled [a trough] with water to give his cattle to drink, an Israelite may give his own cattle to drink after him, but if the gentile did it for the Israelite, it is forbidden.[5]

If a stone lay on the mouth of a jar, the jar may be turned on its side so that the stone falls off. If the jar was among other jars it may be lifted up and then turned on its side so that the stone falls off. . . . If a sponge has a leather hand-piece they may use it to wipe with [on the Sabbath], but if it has not they may not use it to wipe with.[6]

Therefore, while Jesus never actually violated the fourth commandment in its original intention, his Jewish adversaries were assuming the validity of many such additional rules when they accused him and his disciples of "doing what is not lawful to do on the Sabbath" (Matt. 12:2; see also Luke 14:3; John 5:10). When he healed on the Sabbath day (John 9:14) or when his disciples plucked heads of grain on the Sabbath and ate them (Mark 2:23), they were accused of violating the Sabbath, but Jesus and his disciples were in fact obeying the true sense of this commandment. In the post-Reformation period, those Reformed Protestants who thought the Sabbath commandment was still binding nevertheless taught that "works of necessity and mercy" were surely permitted by God on this day.[7]

B. THE SABBATARIAN POSITION: SUNDAY SHOULD BE TREATED LIKE THE SABBATH DAY IN THE OLD TESTAMENT

There is a long and highly respected tradition within the Christian church that sees Sunday as the New Testament counterpart to the Old Testament Sabbath day, and therefore subject to many of its requirements.

This was the position, for example, of the English Puritans, and it found expression in the Westminster Confession of Faith:

---

[4] Ibid., 111 (Mishnah, Shabbath, 12.3).

[5] Ibid., 115 (Mishnah, Shabbath, 16.8).

[6] Ibid., 118 (Mishnah, Shabbath, 21:2–3).

[7] I have taken the phrase "works of necessity and mercy" from the Westminster Larger Catechism, Question 117; the Westminster Confession of Faith uses the expression "duties of necessity and mercy" (21.8). John M. Frame, who argues for the abiding validity of the Sabbath commandment today, sensibly explains that, even on this view, "Works of necessity are not just works that are necessary to keep us alive. They are works that keep human life on an even keel." *The Doctrine of the Christian Life: A Theology of Lordship* (Phillipsburg, NJ: P&R, 2008), 548.

By a positive, moral, and perpetual commandment binding all men in all ages, He [God] hath particularly appointed one day in seven, for a Sabbath, to be kept holy unto Him; which, from the beginning of the world to the resurrection of Christ, was the last day of the week; and from the resurrection of Christ, was changed into the first day of the week, which, in Scripture, is called the Lord's Day, and is to be continued to the end of the world, as the Christian Sabbath. (WCF, 21.7)

How was this day to be observed? The confession said:

[People are to] observe an holy rest, all the day, from their own works, words, and thoughts about their worldly employment and recreations, . . . [and be] taken up, the whole time, in the public and private exercises of His worship, and in the duties of necessity and mercy. (WCF, 21.8)

Those who argue for this alternative position often call their position a "Sabbatarian" view, because it argues for keeping the Old Testament Sabbath, but doing it on Sunday instead of Saturday.

The arguments in favor of this position are:

1. God established a pattern of Sabbath keeping at creation:

And on the seventh day God finished his work that he had done, *and he rested on the seventh day* from all his work that he had done. *So God blessed the seventh day* and made it holy, because on it God rested from all his work that he had done in creation. (Gen. 2:2–3)

In addition, when God gave the Sabbath commandment in Exodus 20, he gave his pattern of activities in creation as the reason:

For in six days the LORD made heaven and earth, the sea, and all that is in them, and rested on the seventh day. Therefore the LORD blessed the Sabbath day and made it holy. (Ex. 20:11)

Therefore, it is argued, resting on the seventh day is a moral requirement established by God at creation (a "creation ordinance"), and that means that God requires all people in all ages to obey it, not just those living under the Mosaic covenant.

2. The fourth commandment is part of the Ten Commandments, and all of the Ten Commandments represent moral requirements from God that apply to all human life on earth for all periods of history. Therefore, we should not disregard the fourth commandment.

3. There is nothing in the New Testament that convincingly indicates the abrogation of the Old Testament Sabbath commandment. Therefore, it is still morally binding on people today.

This Sabbatarian position has been extensively defended by many writers in the Reformed tradition in particular, and the defenses by John Murray[8] and John Frame[9] are particularly forceful and well argued.[10] I also held this view for several years, and I deeply respect this view and several friends who sincerely hold to it.[11]

While my own position will be explained more fully in the following pages, at this point I can respond briefly to these arguments as follows: (1) there is no command in Genesis 1–2 to indicate that Adam and Eve were to observe the seventh day as a special day of rest and worship; (2) the Sabbath commandment seems to me to be different from the other commandments because it is the only one that encompasses Jewish holidays and the related system of sacrifices (therefore, it would be called a "ceremonial" law in the old moral-civil-ceremonial categorization of laws); and (3) since the fourth commandment is part of the Mosaic covenant, which has been terminated, I do not think there is a need to find a specific cancellation of this commandment in the New Testament. It is enough that there is no reaffirmation of it by New Testament authors. In addition, Hebrews 3–4 indicates that Christians in the new covenant now enter into and participate in that "rest" that God established at creation and that the people of Israel did not enter.

I will now turn to a fuller consideration of the reasons why I believe the Sabbath command is no longer in effect.

C. THE SABBATH COMMANDMENT IS NOT MORALLY BINDING ON PEOPLE TODAY

1. The Mosaic Covenant Has Been Terminated. As I argued extensively in chapter 8, New Testament writers affirm clearly that the Mosaic covenant has been terminated and is no longer binding on people today, since we live in the age of the new covenant (see Luke 22:20; Rom. 7:4, 6; 8:2; 10:4; 1 Cor. 9:20; 2 Cor. 3:6; Gal. 3:24–25; Eph. 2:15; Heb. 7:18–19; 8:6–13, and the section beginning at p. 210).

---

[8] John Murray, *Principles of Conduct: Aspects of Biblical Ethics* (Grand Rapids, MI: Eerdmans, 1957), 30–35.

[9] Frame, *The Doctrine of the Christian Life*, 513–74.

[10] See also the Sabbatarian arguments of Peter Masters at http://www.metropolitantabernacle.org/Christian-Article/Remember-the-Lords-Day-Is-there-Christian-Sabbath/Sword-and-Trowel-Magazine. In addition, there is a brief, clear presentation of alternative views published in the UK by the Fellowship of Independent Evangelical Churches: https://fiec.org.uk/docs/Sabbath_(All_in_the_Family).pdf.

[11] I personally held to and followed a Sabbatarian position during my four years of undergraduate study and three years of theological seminary. I remember many of those Sundays as wonderful days of worship and fellowship with God's people. I changed my viewpoint and adopted essentially the "wise but not required" position found in this chapter while preparing to teach an adult Bible class at my local Baptist church during my PhD studies.

My own personal practice now is not much different from what it was when I held a Sabbatarian view, because I generally do not do any academic work on Sundays, but spend time in church and with family members and friends. However, occasionally (perhaps once every eight to 10 weeks) I will do some academic work on Sunday evening, such as preparing for a Monday lecture or working to meet a writing deadline. When I held a Sabbatarian position, I would not have done this and would have thought it to be sinful. Now I do not think it is sinful, but I think I would be unwise to let it become a regular pattern.

Therefore, the fact that this commandment is part of the Ten Commandments does not by itself demonstrate that it continues to carry moral obligation for people today. The Ten Commandments belong to the old covenant, which is no longer in effect.

Why, then, have I followed the structure of the Ten Commandments in organizing this book on ethics? I have done so because nine of the Ten Commandments are reaffirmed or even quoted in the New Testament as having moral validity for Christians in the new covenant age as well. This indicates that these nine commandments (at least) were given by God to the Israelites not for the purpose of showing that Israel was visibly distinct from other nations, but because these nine commandments contained moral standards from God that were applicable to all of mankind for all of history. Their application was not limited just to Israel for a particular time.

2. Unlike the Other Nine Commandments, This One Is Never Reaffirmed for Christians in the New Covenant. The absence of any affirmation of the Sabbath commandment for new covenant Christians apparently indicates that the early apostles, guided by the teaching of Jesus while he was on earth and by the work of the Holy Spirit after that (John 14:26; 16:13), realized that the Sabbath commandment did not express God's moral standards for all humanity for all time, but established specific requirements for the people of Israel as a nation while they lived under the Mosaic covenant. While the rainbow was the sign of God's covenant with Noah (Gen. 9:12–15) and circumcision was the sign of God's covenant with Abraham (17:11), Bruce Waltke notes that "the Sabbath is the sign of the Mosaic covenant"[12] (see Ex. 31:13).

The Sabbath commandment looked forward to the coming of Christ and was fulfilled by his life and ministry. It promised physical rest to laborers, but Jesus offered a deeper, spiritual rest, a rest from our struggling to make ourselves right before God. Jesus said:

> Come to me, all who labor and are heavy laden, *and I will give you rest*. Take my yoke upon you, and learn from me, for I am gentle and lowly in heart, and *you will find rest for your souls*. For my yoke is easy, and my burden is light. (Matt. 11:28–30)

According to the author of Hebrews, to trust in Christ is to enter the true "Sabbath rest" (Heb. 4:9) that the Jewish people failed to attain:

> Therefore, while the promise of *entering his rest* still stands, let us fear lest any of you should seem to have failed to reach it. . . . *For we who have believed enter that rest*. . . . So then, there remains a Sabbath rest for the people of God. (Heb. 4:1, 3, 9)

---

[12] Bruce K. Waltke, *An Old Testament Theology: An Exegetical, Canonical, and Thematic Approach* (Grand Rapids, MI: Zondervan, 2007), 423.

Paul explicitly says that the Sabbath commandment was a "shadow," but that the shadow is fulfilled in Christ:

> Therefore let no one pass judgment on you in questions of food and drink, or with regard to a festival or a new moon or *a Sabbath*. These are *a shadow of the things to come, but the substance belongs to Christ.* (Col. 2:16–17)

3. The New Testament Explicitly Says That Christians No Longer Must Observe Sabbath Days. Paul realized that there was some controversy over the observance of special days such as the Sabbath (and perhaps other Jewish holidays) in the church at Rome, for he wrote to the Roman believers that they should respect one another's choices in this regard—in other words, the observance of such days was not something that God required, but something that people could do if they so wished:

> One person esteems *one day as better than another*, while another esteems *all days alike*. Each one should be fully convinced in his own mind. The one who observes the day, observes it in honor of the Lord. The one who eats, eats in honor of the Lord, since he gives thanks to God, while the one who abstains, abstains in honor of the Lord and gives thanks to God. (Rom. 14:5–6)

Even more explicit is his strong rebuke to the churches of Galatia; he tells them that he is shocked that they are still requiring people to observe special days:[13]

> *You observe days* and months and seasons and years! I am afraid I may have labored over you in vain. (Gal. 4:10–11)

This is why he could tell the Christians at Colossae,

> Let no one pass judgment on you in questions of food or drink, or with regard to a festival or a new moon *or a Sabbath*. (Col. 2:16)

Christians were free to make up their own minds as to how they wanted to act on the Sabbath day (or on Sunday) because there was no moral requirement from God or from Christ about it.

John Calvin understood this, for he wrote:

> But there is no doubt that by the Lord Christ's coming the ceremonial part of this commandment was abolished. . . . He is, I say, the true fulfillment of the Sabbath. . . . For this reason the apostle elsewhere writes that the Sabbath [Col. 2:16] was "a shadow of what is to come; but the body belongs to Christ" [Col. 2:17], that is, the very substance of truth. . . . This is not confined within

---

[13] Paul was not upset that Christians *voluntarily* observed special days (Rom. 14:5–6), but apparently some churches in Galatia were requiring such observance as part of attempting to be justified by "works of the law" (see Gal. 2:16; 3:10–11; 5:4).

a single day but extends throughout the whole course of our life, until, completely dead to ourselves, we are filled with the life of God. Christians ought therefore to shun completely the superstitious observance of days.[14]

Calvin then goes on to explain in what way we should still observe this Sabbath commandment:

> Although the Sabbath has been abrogated, there is still occasion for us: (1) to assemble on stated days for the hearing of the word, the breaking of the mystical bread, and for public prayers [cf. Acts 2:42]; (2) to give surcease from labor to servants and workmen.[15]

Several of Jesus's conflicts with his Jewish opponents over the Sabbath hinted that a change regarding this commandment was coming. We do not read of conflicts between Jesus and his opponents over the other nine commandments, but there were several conflicts about observing the Sabbath. We get the impression that he was deliberately provoking conflict over this law, as in this event recorded in Mark:

> Again he entered the synagogue, and a man was there with a withered hand. And they watched Jesus, to see *whether he would heal him on the Sabbath*, so that they might accuse him. And he said to the man with the withered hand, "Come here." *And he said to them, "Is it lawful on the Sabbath to do good or to do harm, to save life or to kill?"* But they were silent. And he looked around at them with anger, grieved at their hardness of heart, and said to the man, "Stretch out your hand." He stretched it out, and his hand was restored. The Pharisees went out and immediately held counsel with the Herodians against him, how to destroy him. (Mark 3:1–6).[16]

Other statements that treat the Sabbath command differently include "the Son of Man is lord of the Sabbath" (Matt. 12:8) and "my Father is working until now, and I am working" (John 5:17).

4. The Sabbath Commandment Summarized Many Other Commandments about Special Holidays and Other Ceremonies. Just as the law "You shall love your neighbor as yourself" (Lev. 19:18) was a summary of several commandments about human relationships (see Rom. 13:9; Gal. 5:14), so each of the Ten Commandments can be seen as a summary of other, more detailed laws regarding the broad topic areas that they specify.

---

[14] John Calvin, *Institutes of the Christian Religion*, ed. John T. McNeill, trans. Ford Lewis Battles, Library of Christian Classics, vols. 20–21 (Philadelphia: Westminster, 1960), 2.8.31 (397).

[15] Ibid., 2.8.32 (398).

[16] While I understand this event to hint at a change in the Sabbath law for new covenant believers, I recognize that those who think the Sabbath commandment is still valid for Christians today will see these conflicts as merely correcting overly strict Jewish traditions about the Sabbath, not as hinting at its forthcoming abolition.

Many of these more detailed laws are found in Exodus 21–23, chapters that immediately follow the Ten Commandments.

For example, the sixth commandment, "You shall not murder" (Ex. 20:13), can be seen as a summary of numerous other specific laws protecting human life (see 21:12–14, 20–25, 28–32). The seventh commandment, "You shall not commit adultery" (20:14), served as a summary of several detailed laws protecting sexual purity in marriage (see 22:16–17, 19; Lev. 18:1–30). The eighth commandment, "You shall not steal" (20:15), was a summary of several other specific laws regarding the protection of property (see 21:33–36; 22:1–15; 23:4–5).

In the same way, the Sabbath commandment can be seen as a summary of a number of other closely related commandments, both about the Sabbath day and about the Sabbath year, the Year of Jubilee, and other required holidays and sacrifices (Ex. 23:10–19; Lev. 25:1–22, 28, 40–41, 54). If the command about the Sabbath day requires the same observance by Christians today as it did by the Jewish people in the nation of Israel, then it is hard to see why the Sabbath year and the Year of Jubilee are not also morally binding on us today.

The Sabbath day also was closely connected to other Jewish feasts and special days in the Mosaic code. If we are required to observe the Sabbath day, then it is hard to understand why we should not also be obligated to observe these additional feasts and special days. These included the following:

- Feast of Unleavened Bread (or Passover, a seven-day holiday: Ex. 23:15; Lev. 23:5)
- Feast of Weeks (or Harvest, First Fruits, or Pentecost: Ex. 23:16; 34:22; Num. 28:26)
- Feast of Tabernacles (or Booths or Ingathering, an eight-day festival: Ex. 23:16; 34:22; Lev. 23:34; Deut. 16:13)
- Day of Blowing of Trumpets (Lev. 23:24; Num. 29:1)
- Day of Atonement (Lev. 23:26–31)

The New Testament authors understood this close connection between the Sabbath commandment and these other special days and festivals, for Paul groups the Sabbath law with laws about "a festival or a new moon" (Col. 2:16; the "new moon" was also a time for special offerings; Num. 29:6; Ezra 3:5; Ps. 81:3; Isa. 1:13). But Paul does not merely tell the Colossian Christians that they are free from moral obligation regarding these special Jewish days. He amalgamates them together with matters of "food and drink," and says that these are all regulations from the old covenant that have been fulfilled in Christ:

> Therefore let no one pass judgment on you in questions of *food and drink*, or with regard to a *festival* or a *new moon* or a *Sabbath*. These are a shadow of the things to come, but the substance belongs to Christ. (Col. 2:16–17)

It seems, then, that the Sabbath commandment, like the other Jewish holiday and food laws, was designed uniquely for the situation of Jewish people living in the nation of Israel during the time of the Mosaic covenant. (Sometimes this category of laws is called "ceremonial" laws, but see the earlier discussion at p. 248.) My conclusion is that, like the laws about clean and unclean foods and all the Jewish festivals, the Sabbath commandment was not intended by God as something to be followed by all people for all time.

D. WE SHOULD STILL GAIN WISDOM FROM THE FOURTH COMMANDMENT

Since "all Scripture" is "profitable . . . for training in righteousness" (2 Tim. 3:16; cf. Rom. 15:4), we should expect to be able to gain wisdom from even those parts of the Mosaic covenant that are not reaffirmed but explicitly abrogated for New Testament Christians. That is certainly true regarding the Sabbath commandment.

1. It Is Wise to Observe Regular Times of Prayer, Worship, Learning, and Fellowship with Other Believers. From the very first days after Jesus ascended into heaven, the early Christians "were continually in the temple blessing God" (Luke 24:53). Christians throughout the world and throughout history have naturally desired to gather together to pray, worship God, learn from his Word, and fellowship together. After Pentecost, "day by day" the early Christians were "attending the temple together and breaking bread in their homes . . . praising God and having favor with all the people" (Acts 2:46–47).

The New Testament Epistles contain dozens of "one another" verses indicating that Christians regularly and habitually met together for prayer, worship, instruction, and fellowship: "Welcome *one another*" (Rom. 15:7); "Greet *one another*" (16:16; also 1 Cor. 16:20; 2 Cor. 13:12; 1 Pet. 5:14); "When you come together to eat, wait for *one another*" (1 Cor. 11:33); "Comfort *one another*" (2 Cor. 13:11); "Addressing *one another* in psalms and hymns and spiritual songs" (Eph. 5:19); "Teaching and admonishing *one another*" (Col. 3:16); "Encourage *one another* and build *one another* up" (1 Thess. 5:11); "Confess your sins to *one another* and pray for *one another*" (James 5:16); "Show hospitality to *one another*" (1 Pet. 4:9); and "Love *one another*" (1 John 3:23).

Therefore, it is not surprising that the author of Hebrews reminds his readers not to neglect meeting together:

> And let us consider how to stir up one another to love and good works, *not neglecting to meet together*, as is the habit of some, *but encouraging one another*, and all the more as you see the Day drawing near. (Heb. 10:24–25)

The conclusion from these passages is that it is a normal part of the Christian life to meet together at regular times with other believers for prayer, worship, learning from the Scriptures, and encouragement. This is why Paul could write to entire churches and assume that the letter would be read aloud when Christians in those cities assembled together (see Col. 4:16; 1 Thess. 5:27). Because of these New Testament passages, it seems not only wise but also morally required for Christians to meet regularly with other believers.

If Christian ethics is the study of "which acts, attitudes, and personal character traits receive God's approval" (see chap. 1, p. 37), then we could state our conclusion in this way: God is pleased when Christians observe regular times of prayer, worship, learning, and fellowship with other believers.

2. On Which Day Should Christians Worship Together?

a. Any Day Is Acceptable because the Fourth Commandment Is No Longer Binding. For the people of Israel, the fourth commandment specified the seventh day (Saturday) as a day of rest, prayer, and worship: "Remember the Sabbath day, to keep it holy. . . . The seventh day is a Sabbath to the LORD your God" (Ex. 20:8, 10). But the Mosaic covenant has been terminated, and the fourth commandment is no longer binding on believers today.

On which day, then, should Christians worship? In one sense, any day would be acceptable. In fact, many early Christians apparently worshiped together *every* day (see Acts 2:4–6).

In contemporary Western societies, there is a common pattern in which Christians meet together in small groups in private homes on various days during the week. For example, the group of which my wife and I are a part has been meeting on Thursday evenings for several years. Then we also attend a large corporate worship service with the entire local church on Sunday mornings, but occasionally we attend a Saturday night service instead (which has the same format and content as the Sunday morning service).

b. The Most Frequent Pattern in the History of the Christian Church Has Been to Meet on Sunday. In the New Testament era, early Christians started a pattern of meeting on Sunday:

> *On the first day of the week*, when we were gathered together to break bread, Paul talked with them, intending to depart on the next day, and he prolonged his speech until midnight. (Acts 20:7)

> *On the first day of every week*, each of you is to put something aside and store it up, as he may prosper, so that there will be no collecting when I come. (1 Cor. 16:2)

This change to Sunday was most likely made to celebrate Christ's resurrection on the first day of the week, which was Sunday (Matt. 28:1; Luke 24:1; John 20:1), and this is also why the day called "the Lord's day" (Rev. 20:1) was most likely Sunday.

Shortly after the New Testament books were written, some early Christian writers also recorded a pattern of Sunday worship among Christians. For example:

> And *on the day called Sunday*, all who live in cities or in the country gather together to one place, and the memoirs of the apostles or the writings of the prophets are read ... then ... the president [the leader] verbally instructs, and exhorts to the imitation of these good things. Then we all rise together and pray ... bread and wine and water are brought. ... Sunday is the day on which we hold our common assembly, because it is the first day on which God ... made the world; and Jesus Christ our Savior on the same day rose from the dead.[17]

The early Christians seem to have called Sunday "the Lord's day." John said in Revelation, "I was in the Spirit *on the Lord's day*" (Rev. 1:10), and a very early Christian writing distinguishes this from the Sabbath day of the Jews, for Ignatius, bishop of Antioch, writes in about AD 110 that Christians were "no longer living for the Sabbath, but *for the Lord's day*."[18]

c. Regular Meeting and Rest Is Wise, but No Particular Day Is Required. At this point an important difference between the old covenant and the new covenant should be noted. In the Mosaic covenant, the Jewish people were *required* to rest and to worship every Saturday. Any violation of this commandment, even one time, resulted in severe punishment (see Ex. 31:15: "Whoever does any work on the Sabbath day shall be put to death"; see also Num. 15:32–36).

But the New Testament teaching on regular times of worship is very different. The primary statement about this tells us not to neglect meeting together:

> And let us consider how to stir up one another to love and good works, *not neglecting to meet together*, as is the habit of some, but encouraging one another, and all the more as you see the Day drawing near. (Heb. 10:24–25)

Therefore, it is wise, and even required of Christians, that we meet together with other believers regularly. But if for various reasons this is not possible or practicable

---

[17] Justin Martyr, *First Apology* (about AD 152), chap. 67 (ANF, 1:186).

[18] Ignatius, *Epistle to the Magnesians*, 9.1, in *The Apostolic Fathers*, trans. Kirsopp Lake, 2 vols. (Cambridge, MA: Harvard University Press, 1970), 1:205. See also *The Didache*, 14.1: "*On the Lord's Day* of the Lord come together, break bread and hold Eucharist, after confessing your transgressions that your offering may be pure." Ibid., 1:331. The dating of *The Didache* is uncertain; it may have been as early as AD 50–100.

However, we should note that this pattern of meeting *on Sunday* for worship is recorded in the New Testament and later as *something that Christians did* rather than *something that is commanded* for every Christian to do on exactly that day. Paul's direction that the Corinthians are to put something aside and store it up "on the first day of every week" (1 Cor. 16:2) is a command for regular weekly giving, and some may understand that as a requirement that Christians come together on the first day of the week (and give offerings), but it is also possible to understand the specification of the "first day of every week" as simply taking account of the fact that Paul knew that the church met on Sunday. It might not mean that he intended to command that they should meet only on Sundays, but to direct that when they *did* meet, they should take an offering regularly.

once in a while, there is no hint that we should be stoned to death or even face church discipline of some sort. Meeting together regularly is simply a wise pattern of life that the Lord tells us to observe.

The lack of a specification of any one particular day as the only one acceptable for rest and worship is also important for Christians today. For some Christians (such as pastors and other full-time staff members at churches), Sunday is their primary day of work during the week. Others have various secular jobs that require them periodically or regularly to work on Sundays. It seems appropriate for pastors to take another day than Sunday as a day of rest, and for those whose jobs require them to work on Sundays to take another day for both rest and worship with other believers. The new covenant gives believers this kind of freedom to seek various wise and appropriate ways to fulfill the expectation that they will meet for regular times of worship and take regular times of rest.

3. It Is Wise to Have Regular Days of Rest from Our Ordinary Work. In his wisdom, God required the Jewish people to rest from their ordinary work one day per week. This was a gift from God to his people. They were not to think of themselves as oppressed slaves, required to work until the point of exhaustion seven days a week. God gave them a day when they could be free from work, to rest, to worship, and to enjoy the presence of God and fellowship with each other.

Here again we notice the difference between the Mosaic covenant and the new covenant. Since the Mosaic covenant has been terminated, New Testament Christians do not *have to* rest on the seventh day (the Sabbath) or on any other specific day in seven.

Yet we still must recognize that we need periodic times of rest. We do not yet have perfect resurrection bodies that will not grow weak or old (see Rom. 8:23; 1 Cor. 15:23). Even Jesus became physically tired from time to time. When Jesus and his disciples came to Samaria, "Jesus, *wearied* as he was from his journey, was sitting beside the well" (John 4:6).

Therefore, it is *wise* (but not commanded) for Christians in the new covenant age also to take regular times of rest from their ordinary work. These times of rest are a gift from God that he allows us to enjoy freely without guilt, just as he gave the Old Testament Jewish people the Sabbath as a gift: "The Sabbath was made for man, not man for the Sabbath" (Mark 2:27).

The day of rest that people select may vary from person to person. There is no New Testament command that it must be Sunday (or Saturday). For many Christians, Sunday will be the best day, one that fits the schedules of their families and jobs. For other Christians, another day will be just as appropriate.

But taking a day of rest still remains a *wise* practice, not one that is commanded. There is no *command* directed to Christians in the new covenant that they must take periodic days of rest from work, so it is not a sin if we sometimes do not take such days. Rather, the practice of taking a day of rest is a deduction that seems wise from the pattern that God established for himself at creation and from the pattern of work and rest that he established for the Jewish people in the old covenant. Bruce Waltke observes:

> A person who feels inclined to work seven days a week should examine what god he or she worships. . . . But it is important to remind ourselves again that Sabbath is no longer a requirement.[19]

Therefore, my approach to this commandment is different from the other nine commandments. While it is *never* right to worship another God (the first commandment), to make a carved image of God (the second commandment), to take God's name in vain (the third commandment), or to dishonor parents, murder, commit adultery, steal, lie, or covet (the fifth through tenth commandments), there may be circumstances from time to time (such as the need to meet an impending deadline) when it would be wise to break the pattern and work all seven days, perhaps even for a week or two. "Let no one pass judgment on you . . . with regard to . . . a Sabbath" (Col. 2:16; see also Rom. 14:5–6). Yet this should not become a common or regular pattern of life.

For those who have authority over others in the workplace or in a family, it is wise to provide times of rest for them as well, and even for the animals who work in agricultural situations, as God commanded his people to do in the Mosaic covenant:

> Six days you shall do your work, but on the seventh day you shall rest; *that your ox and your donkey may have rest, and the son of your servant woman, and the alien*, may be refreshed. (Ex. 23:12)

One practical application of this verse is that employers should provide regular days off from work for their employees. It would even seem wise for parents to give children a day of rest from household responsibilities (where possible), and, in households where the mother is the one primarily responsible for preparing meals, that the family would seek creative ways to relieve her of that responsibility one day per week.

4. God Is Pleased with Both Our Work and Our Rest. God himself established a pattern of work plus rest when he worked for six days and then rested on the seventh day:

> For in six days the LORD made heaven and earth, the sea, and all that is in them, *and rested on the seventh day*. Therefore the LORD blessed the Sabbath day and made it holy. (Ex. 20:11)

Through this example, God was teaching his people that he was pleased *both when they worked* in a way that honored him *and when they rested* in a way that imitated and honored him as well.[20] Similarly today, God is pleased when we work at various jobs in obedience to him, and also when we rest from that work from time to time in order to worship him and enjoy the fruits of our labor.

---

[19] Waltke, *An Old Testament Theology*, 424–25.

[20] Waltke observes, "The Sabbath . . . is a reminder that God does not value humans by their ability to produce. We are not machines. We have worth apart from what we produce. It is a difficult lesson." *An Old Testament Theology*, 421.

5. It Is Wise to Take Longer Vacations from Time to Time. The Mosaic covenant also contained commandments for longer periods of rest from work. There was the Sabbath year (Lev. 25:1–7) and the Jubilee year (vv. 8–17), and also a series of feasts every year. For example, the Feast of Booths was a seven-day feast and a time of rejoicing:

> You shall keep the Feast of Booths *seven days*, when you have gathered in the produce from your threshing floor and your winepress. *You shall rejoice in your feast*, you and your son and your daughter, your male servant and your female servant, the Levite, the sojourner, the fatherless, and the widow who are within your towns. *For seven days you shall keep the feast to the* LORD *your God at the place that the* LORD *will choose*, because the LORD your God will bless you in all your produce and in all the work of your hands, *so that you will be altogether joyful*. (Deut. 16:13–15)

These feasts are not required for believers in the new covenant. They were part of the Mosaic covenant that has been terminated. But they do teach us that God, in his wisdom, gave his people some longer periods of rest from work.

A sound application would be that it is wise for us periodically to take longer periods of vacation time, such as a week or two, away from our normal work so that we can be refreshed. (In the Old Testament, the feasts were times not only of rest and refreshment, but also of enjoyment in the Lord's presence.)

Jesus also taught his disciples a pattern of periodic times of rest from their intensive ministry:

> The apostles returned to Jesus and told him all that they had done and taught. And he said to them, "Come away by yourselves to a desolate place *and rest a while*." For many were coming and going, and they had no leisure even to eat. And *they went away in the boat to a desolate place by themselves*. (Mark 6:30–32)

6. Regular Work Is Also a Blessing. The fourth commandment not only directed the Jewish people to remember the Sabbath day and refrain from work on that day each week, it also instructed them to work on the other six days: "*Six days you shall labor* and do all your work" (Ex. 20:9). This part of the fourth commandment reflects the purpose of God in the creation of man and woman in his image, for he commanded Adam and Eve to "fill the earth and subdue it, and have dominion" (Gen. 1:28), and he put the man "in the garden of Eden *to work it and keep it*" (2:15).

This requirement that we carry out productive work *is* reaffirmed for Christians in the new covenant, for Paul himself said, "If anyone is *not willing to work*, let him not eat" (2 Thess. 3:10), and he himself "*worked* night and day" in order to give Christians "an example to imitate" (vv. 8–9). In another place, Paul wrote:

Let the thief no longer steal, but rather *let him labor, doing honest work* with his own hands, so that he may have something to share with anyone in need. (Eph. 4:28; cf. 1 Thess. 4:11–12)

These passages teach us that productive work is a good thing, something that God gives us as a blessing and a privilege as well as a requirement.

Therefore, it is pleasing to God for Christians (indeed, for all people) to live lives of regular, productive, useful work (whether paid or unpaid) that brings benefits not only to the worker but also to other people and to the society as a whole.[21]

E. PRACTICAL QUESTIONS

1. Should Christians Support Sunday Closing Laws? In previous centuries, many countries and local jurisdictions had laws requiring stores and most businesses to remain closed on Sundays. These laws were largely a result of Christian influence on societies, reflecting the belief among many Christians that the fourth commandment is still binding on people today. But in the United States at least, and to some extent more recently in the UK, such laws have been either abolished or considerably relaxed.[22]

Because the Mosaic covenant has been terminated and is no longer binding on us today, and because there is no command in the New Testament for Christians (or people in general) to rest one day in seven, this seems to me to be a question of wisdom that especially focuses on the *results* of a law rather than a question of obedience or disobedience to any specific passage of Scripture. My own viewpoint is that the decision should be made by seeking a wise evaluation of what will bring about the best results for a society. There is certainly room for people, even Christians, to disagree about this question. "One person esteems one day as better than another, while another esteems all days alike" (Rom. 14:5).

My personal judgment is that governmental laws should allow considerable freedom in this area for individuals and businesses to decide as they think best, but also that it is

---

[21] Students in school are yet not working for monetary pay, but they are in a period of intensive training so that they may be able to work more productively when the schooling is completed, and in that sense they should see their studies as a kind of productive work in God's sight.

[22] In 1985, Christians in the UK mounted a large campaign to "Keep Sunday Special" in opposition to proposed government legislation that would have abolished many Sunday closing laws (see https://www.keepsundayspecial.org.uk/). The campaign gained widespread support, especially from churches, trade unions (labor unions), and small shop owners. The campaign supported the retention of Sunday closing laws, showing the benefits to families and to society as a whole of retaining a recognized day of rest for the entire nation. The campaign had a significant effect. Even in 1994, when the Sunday Trading Act liberalized the Sunday closing laws, large stores were still allowed to do business only for six hours on Sundays. See "Trading Hours for Retailers: The Law," https://www.gov.uk/trading-hours-for-retailers-the-law.

a wise pattern for many businesses to remain closed on Sunday (and for some, Saturday and Sunday).

For example, in the United States, where laws against retail stores opening on Sunday have almost universally disappeared, it is still true that many workplaces are completely closed. Schools, colleges, and universities do not offer classes on Sundays. All government offices are closed. Doctors', dentists', and lawyers' offices are closed. Nearly all corporate offices and business offices are closed.

On the other hand, nearly all retail shops (grocery stores, clothing stores, department stores) are open. Airplanes continue to fly on a regular schedule. Nearly all restaurants are open.[23] Somehow American society seems to have reached the conclusion that it is more convenient to run errands and eat in restaurants on weekends, when people's daily work responsibilities do not intrude as they do during the week.

There is wisdom in Jesus's statement regarding the Old Testament Sabbath that "the Sabbath was made for man, not man for the Sabbath." Although people *could* buy groceries and clothing on Saturday instead of Sunday, sometimes they find it more convenient to shop on Sundays for these things (as my wife and I do from time to time). And a frequent part of our enjoyment of a day of rest on Sunday is taking time to eat at a local restaurant with friends.

2. Should Christians Advocate a Six-Day Workweek? Because the fourth commandment says, "*Six days you shall labor*, and do all your work" (Ex. 20:9), some might wonder if there is something wrong with having a job that requires only five days of work in a week (usually Monday through Friday). Is this widespread pattern a concession to human laziness?

First, we must remember that this commandment belongs to the Mosaic covenant, which has been terminated. It does not belong to the new covenant and is not repeated in the new covenant age. Therefore, this is not a question of a scriptural command.

On the other hand, if we view the fourth commandment, in its historical context, as a source of wisdom that might find different applications in the new covenant age, it provides a useful warning against laziness when it says, "Six days shall you labor." God does expect us, as long as we are physically and mentally able, to *regularly engage in productive work* (see discussion above).

But that does not mean we have to do the same kind of work every day. People who have jobs that require them to work Monday through Friday often use Saturday for other kinds of useful work, such as house maintenance, grocery shopping, running other errands, engaging in activities related to raising children, and sometimes even

---

[23] One notable exception is the Chick-fil-A company, whose founder, S. Truett Cathy, made it a principle to close on Sundays based on his Christian convictions. This fast-food restaurant chain has more than 2,000 restaurants in 43 states (in 2016) and more than $6.8 billion in annual revenue: See Courtney O'Neil-Hill, "Top of the List: Atlanta's Top 50 Private Companies," *Atlanta Business Chronicle*, Oct. 14, 2016, https://www .bizjournals.com/atlanta/news/2016/10/14/top-of-the-list-atlantas-top-50-private-companies.html. Also see https://www.chick-fil-a.com/About/Who-We-Are.

working at a second job. The question is not whether people are working *at the same job* for six days a week, but whether they are regularly engaged in some kind of productive work (whether paid or unpaid) that brings benefit to others and to a society as a whole in some way.

In more primitive agricultural societies, the idea that someone could work only five days a week and complete all the tasks necessary for maintaining the farm animals and tending the crops would have been thought amazing. But in modern, developed economic systems, human productivity has multiplied many times over, in all spheres of work, including agricultural work, industrial production, information-based businesses, and the service economy. Hundreds of millions of people are now able to earn a decent living and support themselves by working only five days a week. This should not be thought of as a curse but rather as a blessing. This leaves freedom for people to carry out many other useful activities on the other two days of the week, including work with community, voluntary, and charitable associations, and time spent with families, hobbies, and other kinds of useful activity.

QUESTIONS FOR PERSONAL APPLICATION

1. Do you look forward to Sunday? Why or why not?
2. After reading this chapter, how do you think your pattern of activities on Sunday might change, if at all?
3. When you meet with other Christians on Sunday, do you sense God's approval? Do you notice any refreshing or strengthening of your spiritual life?
4. Do you think that you take enough time of regular rest from work? Too little? Too much?
5. If you are a parent, or if you have supervisory authority in your workplace, how do you know if you are giving those under your authority enough opportunity to rest from their work? How do you know if you are giving them too much opportunity to rest?
6. What character traits (see p. 110) would you expect to see nurtured by the way you observe Sunday?
7. What are some positive results in terms of glorifying God and advancing the work of his kingdom that you would hope to see as a result of the way you decide to spend your time on Sundays?

SPECIAL TERMS

Sabbatarian position
Sabbath
"wise but not required" position

BIBLIOGRAPHY

Sections in Other Ethics Texts

(see complete bibliographical data, p. 64)

> Frame, 513–74
> Jones, 144–52
> McQuilkin and Copan, 205–16
> Murray, 30–35

Other Works

Beckwith, Roger T., and Wilfrid Stott. *The Christian Sunday: A Biblical and Historical Study*. Grand Rapids, MI: Baker, 1980.

Carson, D. A., ed. *From Sabbath to Lord's Day: A Biblical, Historical and Theological Investigation*. Collegeville, MN: Wipf & Stock, 2000.

Dawn, Marva J. *Keeping the Sabbath Wholly: Ceasing, Resting, Embracing, Feasting*. Grand Rapids, MI: Eerdmans, 1999.

———. *The Sense of the Call: A Sabbath Way of Life for Those Who Serve God, the Church, and the World*. Grand Rapids, MI: Eerdmans, 2006.

Dennison, James T. *The Market Day of the Soul: The Puritan Doctrine of the Sabbath in England, 1532–1700*. Morgan, PA: Soli Deo Gloria, 2001.

Donato, Christopher John, ed. *Perspectives on the Sabbath: 4 Views*. Nashville: Broadman & Holman, 2011.

Edwards, Brian H. *The Ten Commandments for Today*. Revised ed. Leominster, UK: Day One, 2005.

Field, D. H. "Sabbath." In *New Dictionary of Christian Ethics and Pastoral Theology*, edited by David J. Atkinson and David H. Field, 754–55. Leicester, UK: Inter-Varsity, and Downers Grove, IL: InterVarsity Press, 1995.

Jewett, Paul King. *The Lord's Day: A Theological Guide to the Christian Day of Worship*. Grand Rapids, MI: Eerdmans, 1971.

Pipa, Joseph A, Jr. *The Lord's Day*. Fearn, Ross-shire, Scotland: Christian Focus, 1996.

Ratzlaff, Dale. *Sabbath in Christ*. Glendale, AZ: Life Assurance Ministries, 2010. A response to the Seventh-Day Adventist view.

Schreiner, Thomas R. "Good-Bye and Hello: The Sabbath Command for New Covenant Believers." In *Progressive Covenantalism: Charting a Course between Dispensational and Covenant Theologies*, edited by Stephen J. Wellum and Brent E. Parker, 159–88. Nashville: Broadman & Holman, 2016.

Sleeth, Matthew. *24/6: A Prescription for a Healthier, Happier Life*. Wheaton, IL: Tyndale, 2012.

Wells, Tom. *The Christian and the Sabbath*. West Chester, OH: Tom Wells, 2010.

Wells, Tom, and Fred G. Zaspel. *New Covenant Theology: Description, Definition, Defense.* Frederick, MD: New Covenant Media, 2002, chapters 13 and 14.

SCRIPTURE MEMORY PASSAGE

Exodus 20:8–11: Remember the Sabbath day, to keep it holy. Six days you shall labor, and do all your work, but the seventh day is a Sabbath to the LORD your God. On it you shall not do any work, you, or your son, or your daughter, your male servant, or your female servant, or your livestock, or the sojourner who is within your gates. For in six days the LORD made heaven and earth, the sea, and all that is in them, and rested on the seventh day. Therefore the LORD blessed the Sabbath day and made it holy.

HYMN

"Safely through Another Week"

Safely through another week God has brought us on our way;
Let us now a blessing seek, waiting in His courts today:
Day of all the week the best, emblem of eternal rest;
Day of all the week the best, emblem of eternal rest.

While we pray for pard'ning grace thru the dear Redeemer's name,
Show Thy reconciled face, take away our sin and shame;
From our worldly cares set free, may we rest this day in Thee;
From our worldly cares set free, may we rest this day in Thee.

Here we come Thy name to praise—let us feel Thy presence near;
May Thy glory meet our eyes while we in Thy house appear:
Here afford us, Lord, a taste of our everlasting feast;
Here afford us, Lord, a taste of our everlasting feast.

May Thy gospel's joyful sound conquer sinners, comfort saints;
May the fruits of grace abound, bring relief for all complaints:
Thus may all our Sabbaths prove, til we join the Church above;
Thus may all our Sabbaths prove, til we join the Church above.

AUTHOR: JOHN NEWTON, 1725–1807

Part 3

PROTECTING HUMAN AUTHORITY

"Honor your father and your mother."

Chapter 14

AUTHORITY OF PARENTS

Why does God want children to honor their parents?

Should adult children continue to be obedient to their parents?

Is spanking wrong?

What are the advantages of public schools,

Christian schools, and homeschooling?

The fifth commandment reads:

> Honor your father and your mother, that your days may be long in the land that the LORD your God is giving you. (Ex. 20:12)

This commandment is restated by Moses in Deuteronomy, where he gives an additional motivation for obedience:

> Honor your father and your mother, as the LORD your God commanded you, that your days may be long, *and that it may go well with you* in the land that the LORD your God is giving you. (Deut. 5:16)

A. THE MEANING OF THE COMMANDMENT

1. The Placement of This Commandment. The first four commandments deal primarily with our relationship to God. The last six deal primarily with human relationships, and they begin with instructions about the family. This is not accidental, because the family is the foundational building block for all of society. Parents have greater influence than anyone else on the next generation, and therefore on the future of societies and nations. If children truly honor their parents, they will learn from them how to live all of life in obedience to God[1] and will know his blessing on their lives, as a father explains to a son in Proverbs:

My son, do not forget my teaching,
    but let your heart keep my commandments,
for length of days and years of life
    and peace they will add to you. (Prov. 3:1–2)

2. The Meaning of "Honor." To "honor" one's father and mother means to treat them with respect, deference, and care; also, to treat them as worthy of honor, as important and significant. John Calvin observes that "there are three parts of the honor here spoken of: reverence, obedience, and gratefulness."[2] The people of Israel were commanded, "Every one of you shall *revere* his mother and father" (Lev. 19:3).

    Obedience to parents was surely included in the Old Testament understanding of this commandment, for elsewhere in the Mosaic covenant there were severe penalties for a "stubborn and rebellious son who will not obey the voice of his father or the voice of his mother" (Deut. 21:18; cf. Prov. 30:17) and for cursing one's father and mother (Ex. 21:15, 17; Lev. 20:9; Prov. 20:20). (As I explained in chap. 8, such penalties were commanded only for the people of Israel and only at that time, and are no longer applicable today.)

3. The Motivation: God's Reward of a Long Life. This commandment specifies a reward that comes with obedience:

Honor your father and your mother, *that your days may be long in the land* that the LORD your God is giving you. (Ex. 20:12)

    An additional reason, "and that it may go well with you," is added to the commandment in Deuteronomy 5:16, but John Frame rightly observes that this aspect of the blessing was already implied in Exodus 20:12: "Of course, long life is not a blessing without prosperity, so, as with the fourth commandment, Deuteronomy merely spells out what is already implicit in Exodus."[3] This, then, is a prominent example of what is taught in hundreds of passages in both the Old Testament and the New Testament: God gives blessing in this life in response to our obedience to him.[4]

4. New Testament Affirmation of This Commandment. The apostle Paul quite clearly affirms this commandment as applicable to all people for all time, not only for the na-

---

[1] That is, if the parents are Christian believers. But even if the parents are unbelievers, by God's common grace they will be better able to impart wisdom about life if their children honor them.

[2] John Calvin, *Institutes of the Christian Religion*, ed. John T. McNeill, trans. Ford Lewis Battles, Library of Christian Classics, vols. 20–21 (Philadelphia: Westminster, 1960), 2.8.36 (402).

[3] John M. Frame, *The Doctrine of the Christian Life: A Theology of Lordship* (Phillipsburg, NJ: P&R, 2008), 575.

[4] There are exceptions, when godly people who are living in holiness before God suddenly have their lives cut short. But in these cases, the promise finds far greater fulfillment in their new home in heaven (see Phil. 3:20; Heb. 11:15–16). See further discussion in chap. 5, beginning at p. 126.

tion of Israel under the Mosaic covenant. For example, he says that one of the sins of Gentiles who do not know God is that they are "disobedient to parents" (Rom. 1:30; cf. 2 Tim. 3:2). When speaking of people who are "lawless and disobedient," he includes "those who strike their fathers and mothers" (1 Tim. 1:9).

Furthermore, Paul explicitly quotes the fifth commandment in his instructions to the believers of Ephesus:

> Children, obey your parents in the Lord, for this is right. "*Honor your father and mother*" (this is the first commandment with a promise), "that it may go well with you and that you may live long in the land." (Eph. 6:1–3)

5. Broader Application of This Commandment. Calvin understood this commandment to represent, in a broader sense, God's requirement that we be subject to all legitimate human authority that is placed over us. He wrote:

> Now this precept of subjection strongly conflicts with the depravity of human nature which, swollen with the longing for lofty position, bears subjection grudgingly. Accordingly, he has put forward as an example that kind of superiority which is by nature most amiable and least invidious, because he could thus more easily soften and bend our minds to the habit of submission. By that submission which is easiest to tolerate, the Lord therefore gradually accustoms us to all lawful subjection.[5]

I agree with Calvin's insight regarding this commandment (and the validity of viewing each of the Ten Commandments as summaries of many other specific laws of God), but if someone chooses to disagree with this perspective, it will not really affect the following discussion of other specific human authorities, because those discussions are grounded in detailed teachings of Scripture on those individual topics. However, I have organized the topics that I treat in this book according to this general plan, so that all ethical questions related to submission to authority, and proper use of human authority, are treated in Part 3. Therefore, the immediately succeeding chapters will treat authority within marriage (chap. 15), the authority of civil government (chap. 16), and authority in the workplace, in schools, and in churches (chap. 17).

B. RESPONSIBILITIES OF CHILDREN

1. When Children Are Young, They Are Responsible to Obey Their Parents. Paul is very clear when he says, "Children, *obey your parents in the Lord*, for this is right" (Eph. 6:1), and then goes on to quote the fifth commandment:

---

[5] Calvin, *Institutes*, 2.8.35 (401). The Westminster Larger Catechism also understands this commandment to include obedience to all rightful human authority: see Questions 123–33.

"Honor your father and mother" (this is the first commandment with a promise), "that it may go well with you and that you may live long in the land." (Eph. 6:2–3)

He repeats this statement with only a slight modification in Colossians: "Children, obey your parents in everything, *for this pleases the Lord.*" (Col. 3:20).

Jesus exemplified such obedience when he was 12 years old: "And he went down with them and came to Nazareth and *was submissive to them*" (Luke 2:51).

However, this obedience to one's parents must never take precedence over obedience to God. Paul implies this when he says, "Obey your parents *in the Lord,*" indicating that loyalty to God takes priority even over obedience to one's parents.[6] Jesus also taught that one must not love a parent more than him: "Whoever loves father or mother more than me is not worthy of me" (Matt. 10:37). This is one example of a broader principle in Scripture that we are not to obey any human authority that commands us to sin against God (see the earlier discussion with respect to civil government, beginning at p. 189).

2. When Children Become Adults, They Must Still Honor Their Parents, but Are Not Required to Obey Them. Sometimes *adult* Christians read Ephesians 6:1 and think it tells them to obey their parents even when they are grown and have their own households. Doesn't it say, "Children, obey your parents in the Lord, for this is right"? But this interpretation is based on a misunderstanding of the context and of the Greek word translated as "children" in this verse.

The context shows that Paul is addressing different groups of people in the church of Ephesus. He addresses "wives" (Eph. 5:22–24) and "husbands" (vv. 25–33), then "children" (6:1–3) and "fathers" (v. 4), and then "bondservants" (vv. 5–8) and "masters" (v. 9). Not one of these sections addresses everybody in the church, for Paul's hearers would have recognized that if they belonged in one category (such as "wives"), then they did not belong in the other category ("husbands") within each pair of categories.

In addition, Paul does not say, "*All of you,* obey your parents," but rather, "*Children,* obey your parents." The category of "children" is different from the category of all people in the church. And Paul does not say, "All of you, obey your parents *for your entire lives,*" nor does he imply that.

The idea of an adult leaving his parents' household and forming a new household goes back as far as the creation narrative in Genesis, where we read:

Therefore a man shall *leave his father and his mother* and hold fast to his wife, and they shall become one flesh. (2:24)

The assumption here is that when a man and woman marry, they leave their parents'

---

[6] I knew a friend in college whose parents had prohibited him from reading the Bible when he was a high school student. He disobeyed them and read the Bible in his room secretly with a flashlight under the covers at night. Today he is the successful pastor of a large evangelical church.

households and establish a new household and a new family of their own. As children grow from childhood to adulthood, they should experience a gradual transition from a relationship of a small child to a parent, a relationship in which the parent continually gives directions that the child continually obeys, to an adult-adult relationship, in which the parent is more often giving counsel and advice (if asked) and less often giving demands, even though the child may still be living at home while approaching mature and independent adulthood.

The adult son or daughter should still submit to the authority of the parents *with respect to the conduct of the parents' household* while he or she is living in that household (or while visiting at any time in the future). In other words, an adult child should respect the authority of the husband and wife to whom the home belongs just as any adult visitor would. And this is only with respect to matters of conduct within that household, not with respect to all of life.

It is impossible to say exactly at what particular age a child becomes an adult and is no longer subject to the authority of his or her parents. Certainly by the time a person has grown up, married, and established his or her own household, he has reached full adulthood and is no longer subject to the authority of his parents. But wise parents will give a great amount of freedom to their adult children who are still living at home while working or attending school, allowing them to make decisions as seems best to them regarding the conduct of their entire lives outside of the home.

Adult children must remember that, while Paul's words about obedience in Ephesians 6:1 are addressed to children and not to adults in the congregation, the fifth commandment was not addressed to children only! "Honor your father and your mother" (Ex. 20:12) is something that God spoke to all the people of Israel, adults and children alike. Therefore, the fifth commandment should teach all people to show honor and respect to their parents in public and in private for their entire lives, even though at times this will be difficult.

3. When Parents Grow Older, Their Children Are Responsible to Care for Them as Necessary and as They Are Able. The early church faced a problem of how to care for widows whose husbands had died and who could no longer support themselves. Does the church have some responsibility to support them?

Paul's answer was yes, the church should care for such widows (see 1 Tim. 5:9–16), but before the church becomes involved, the children of the widows should first do their part:

> Honor widows who are truly widows. But *if a widow has children or grandchildren*, let them first learn to show godliness to their own household and to *make some return to their parents*, for this is pleasing in the sight of God. . . . But if anyone does not provide for his relatives, and especially for members of his household, he has denied the faith and is worse than an unbeliever. (1 Tim. 5:3–4, 8)

Sometimes such care will involve financial support. Sometimes it will also involve taking an aging parent or parents into one's home, helping to make wise provisions for part-time professional care, or helping them move to an assisted-living center. Different solutions will be appropriate for different families in different circumstances, but Paul's instructions make it clear that children have a significant amount of responsibility for somehow caring for their parents or seeing that they are well cared for, so far as the children are able to do this. Certainly regular visits, correspondence, and telephone conversations are an important part of responsibility toward older parents.

Jesus rebuked the Pharisees who were in the habit of telling people that they could avoid the obligation to care for their parents by giving money to the temple instead:

> And he said to them, "You have a fine way of *rejecting the commandment of God* in order to establish your tradition! For Moses said, 'Honor your father and your mother'; and, 'Whoever reviles father or mother must surely die.' But you say, 'If a man tells his father or his mother, "Whatever you would have gained from me is Corban"' (that is, given to God)—*then you no longer permit him to do anything for his father or mother, thus making void the word of God* by your tradition that you have handed down. And many such things you do." (Mark 7:9–13)

The general principle that Jesus upholds here is that giving money (or, by implication, time and attention) to some kind of religious ministry activity does not excuse one from the obligation to care for one's parents. To do so would be "making void the word of God" (Mark 7:13).

4. Children Must Respect the Independence and Property Rights of Their Parents while the Parents Are Still Living. Scripture views positively the tradition of parents leaving an inheritance to their children and even grandchildren: "A good man leaves an inheritance to his children's children" (Prov. 13:22). Because children expect that they will inherit their parents' money, they can sometimes begin to think that part of it already belongs to them before the parents die. (Note the parable of the prodigal son in Luke 15:11–32, especially v. 12; and note the presumption of Absalom, who sought to take over his father David's throne while David was still alive, in 2 Samuel 15–18.)

But until the parents die or actually give some of the property to the child, it still belongs to the parents. The book of Proverbs warns against disrespecting the property rights of one's parents: "Whoever robs his father or his mother and says, 'That is no transgression,' is a companion to a man who destroys" (28:24).

5. The Blessings of Obedience to the Fifth Commandment. As noted above, the restatement of the Ten Commandments by Moses in Deuteronomy expands on the blessings that are promised for obedience to this commandment:

Honor your father and your mother, as the LORD your God commanded you, *that your days may be long, and that it may go well with you* in the land that the LORD your God is giving you. (Deut. 5:16)

Although this blessing of long and good life in the land of Israel was specific to the Mosaic covenant, in two different New Testament passages Paul also connects obedience to parents with blessings that will come to the children. In Ephesians, he directly quotes Deuteronomy 5 with the implication that the blessing—"that it may go well with you"—still applies to children in the new covenant age:

Children, obey your parents in the Lord, for this is right. "Honor your father and mother" (this is the first commandment with a promise), "*that it may go well with you* and that you may live long in the land." (Eph. 6:1–3)

Then, when Paul instructs children to obey their parents in his letter to the Colossians, he adds an even stronger motive, that of knowing that God himself is pleased with your obedience:

Children, obey your parents in everything, *for this pleases the Lord.* (Col. 3:20)

Do these passages mean that children who obey their parents and people who honor their parents in general will live longer on this earth than those who do not? This question requires a careful answer. I realize that the emphasis on rewards in the Old Testament was more earthly and material, while the emphasis on rewards in the New Testament is more heavenly and spiritual, for rather than the geographical land of Israel, "our citizenship is in heaven" (Phil. 3:20), and "here we have no lasting city, but we seek the city that is to come" (Heb. 13:14; see further discussion in chap. 8, p. 244). But I do not think that this shift in emphasis should cause us to totally dismiss the expectation that obedience to the fifth commandment will result in a longer and better life here on earth, at least as a general principle.

This is true partly because of the commonsense observation that obedient children have better success in education, learn better work habits and personal relationship skills, take better care of their health, and have higher integrity and stronger personal moral standards as adults[7] (at least in cases where parents teach these things to their children, as God intended).

---

[7] J. T. Piotrowski, M. A. Lapierre, D. L. Linebarger, "Investigating Correlates of Self-Regulation in Early Childhood with a Representative Sample of English Speaking American Families," *Journal of Children and Family Studies* 22, no. 3 (April 2013): 423–36, https://www.ncbi.nlm.nih.gov/pubmed/23525149. The authors write, "Children who possess less self-regulatory skill are at a disadvantage when compared to children who demonstrate greater skill at regulating their emotions, cognitions, and behavior. Children with these regulatory deficits have difficulty connecting with peers, generating relationships with teachers, negotiating their social world, and succeeding academically. . . . Parents who rely on nurturing parenting practices that reinforce the child's sense of autonomy while still maintaining a consistent parenting presence (i.e. authoritative parenting) have children who demonstrate strong self-regulatory skills."

According to D. H. Sailor, writing in *Supporting Children in Their Home, School, and Community*, "Parents who are nurturing and set, discuss, and enforce developmentally appropriate limits are the most successful in helping their children become autonomous, independent, self-controlled, self-confident, and cooperative. These children also are more likely to have high levels of competence and high self-esteem during middle childhood and adolescence. They also have internalized moral standards and their academic performance in high school is superior."[8]

Anthony Kane, a secular commentator, confirms this: "Learning obedience is an important part of child development." He states that through obedience, children "learn self-control and develop other positive character traits. . . . It is natural for a child to want to obey his parents. It is also necessary for his proper growth and development."[9]

But I think there is an additional spiritual factor of God's intentional blessing on the life of a child who obeys his or her parents. Paul implies as much when he says, "for this pleases the Lord" (Col. 3:20) and says, "that it may go well with you" (Eph. 6:3).

Should we teach our children, then, that God will bless them if they honor and obey their parents? Absolutely yes. Paul directly addresses children in both Ephesians 6 and Colossians 3, and he appeals to the motive of God's blessing in addressing them in both cases. Surely we should teach our children these passages that are specifically addressed to them! And when children seek to be obedient and to honor their parents in response to these verses, this will increase their faith and their expectation of God's blessing on their lives.

C. THE RESPONSIBILITIES OF PARENTS

1. Love. The Bible frequently assumes that parents will love their children, although it seldom directly commands them to do this. This is evident in passages such as God's words to Abraham, "Take your son, your only son Isaac, *whom you love*" (Gen. 22:2), and in David's deep grief even over his rebellious son Absalom, when Absalom died (see 2 Sam. 18:33). David compares God's love for us to a father's compassion for his children:

> As a father shows compassion to his children,
> so the Lord shows compassion to those who fear him. (Ps. 103:13)

Jesus took it as an accepted fact of life that fathers "know how to give good gifts to your children" (Luke 11:13). In addition, the deep love of a father for his straying son is seen in the father's response to the prodigal son (15:20, 22–24).

The following sections also illustrate ways in which the love of a parent is shown in discipline, patience and understanding, and wise instruction.

---

[8] D. H. Sailor, *Supporting Children in Their Home, School, and Community* (Boston: Allyn & Bacon, 2004), 158–59.

[9] Anthony Kane, MD, "The Seven Keys to Child Obedience," http://www.healthyplace.com/adhd/children-behavioral-issues/seven-keys-to-child-obedience/.

2. Discipline.

a. Parents Are Responsible for Having Obedient Children: Scripture is emphatic in teaching that parents, and especially fathers, are responsible for having their children under control, not defiant of parental authority but respectful and obedient. One of the qualifications for an elder is having obedient children, as Paul tells Timothy:[10]

> He must manage his own household well, *with all dignity keeping his children submissive,* for if someone does not know how to manage his own household, how will he care for God's church? (1 Tim. 3:4–5)

In another passage, Paul tells Titus that the conduct of a man's family is one of the qualifications for becoming an elder:

> [A man may serve as an elder if he] is above reproach, the husband of one wife, *and his children are believers*[11] *and not open to the charge of debauchery or insubordination.* (Titus 1:6)

On two occasions when I was a member of an elder board considering possible candidates to nominate to the board, out of obedience to these passages, we turned down an otherwise qualified nominee (a different person in each case) because it was quite evident to everyone in the church that his children were poorly behaved and lacked discipline. That was the only reason we turned the person down in both cases.

b. Various Forms of Discipline: Certainly discipline can take a variety of forms, depending on the circumstances and the age and personality of the child. God himself disciplines us in various ways appropriate to our personalities, circumstances, and maturity levels (see Heb. 12:5–11). A wise parent will seek to find effective methods of discipline that are appropriate for each child in each circumstance.

c. The Question of Spanking: While the discipline of a child must never be cruel or physically harmful to the child's body, several passages of Scripture emphasize that discipline must at times include inflicting pain on the child through some form of spanking (or what is called "smacking" in the United Kingdom today). These passages indicate that moral and spiritual benefit comes to a child who experiences physical discipline:[12]

---

[10] All of the qualifications for elders (except being able to teach) are character traits that should be true of all Christians.

[11] In a footnote, the ESV gives an alternative translation: "*are faithful.*" Both senses are possible meanings of the Greek text, and it is a question of deciding which interpretation is most appropriate in this context.

[12] For a more extensive treatment of these passages, see Andy Naselli, "Training Children for Their Good." *The Journal of Discipleship and Family Ministry* 3, no. 2 (2013): 48–64, http://andynaselli.com/wp-content/uploads/2013_training.pdf.

> *Whoever spares the rod hates his son,*
>> but he who loves him is diligent to discipline him. (Prov. 13:24)[13]

Personally, I can remember several instances in which I, with tears in my eyes, spanked one of our younger sons with a wooden spoon for particularly hard-hearted, willful disobedience. I did it because I did not "hate" my son (Prov. 13:24), but I loved him.

Other passages on this theme include the following:

> Folly is bound up in the heart of a child,
>> but *the rod of discipline* drives it far from him. (Prov. 22:15)

> Do not withhold discipline from a child;
>> if you strike him with a rod, he will not die.
> *If you strike him with the rod,*
>> *you will save his soul from Sheol.* (Prov. 23:13–14)

> *The rod and reproof give wisdom,*
>> but a child left to himself brings shame to his mother. . . .
> Discipline your son, and he will give you rest;
>> he will give delight to your heart. (Prov. 29:15–17)

There is nothing in these passages or their contexts to indicate that such instruction was intended only for the Jewish people living under the Mosaic covenant. Rather, as is the case with nearly the entire book of Proverbs, this is God's wise instruction for all human beings in all cultures in all societies.

The author of Hebrews recognizes the pain and the benefits that come from the discipline of human fathers and from God's discipline in our lives:

> We have had earthly fathers who disciplined us and we respected them. Shall we not much more be subject to the Father of spirits and live? . . . For the moment all discipline seems painful rather than pleasant, but later it yields the peaceful fruit of righteousness to those who have been trained by it. (Heb. 12:9, 11)

However, in many instances, physical discipline is not necessary, and only a word may be enough: "A *rebuke* goes deeper into a man of understanding than a hundred blows into a fool" (Prov. 17:10).

d. Opposition to Spanking in Modern Culture: Some parts of modern societies and some nations strongly oppose any form of physical discipline (what is sometimes called "corporal punishment") of children.[14]

---

[13] The word *rod* translates the Hebrew term *shēbeṭ*, here referring to a wooden stick of some sort.

[14] The rest of this section is adapted from Wayne Grudem, *Politics—According to the Bible: A Comprehensive Resource for Understanding Modern Political Issues in Light of Scripture* (Grand Rapids, MI:

In some European countries and elsewhere, laws now prohibit parents from spanking their children as part of the disciplinary process. Australia, Sweden, Finland, Norway, Austria, Cyprus, Denmark, Latvia, Croatia, Bulgaria, Germany, Israel, Iceland, Romania, Ukraine, and Hungary are among the countries that have outlawed corporal punishment in some form.[15] (In Sweden, in spite of such a law, it is interesting that assaults by adults against children between the ages of one and six increased fourfold between 1984 and 1994.)[16] Similar laws have been considered in parts of the United States as well—Massachusetts[17] and California,[18] for example—but they have not been adopted.

One anti-spanking crusader named Jordan Riak proposed "no-spanking zones" that would stigmatize parents.[19] He wrote in 1997:

> Whether any child, on any pretext, in any circumstance, should be subjected to physical battery, and whether such treatment is beneficial to the child, should have ceased long ago to be matters for serious debate. The fact is that the deliberate traumatization of a child by a caretaker is destructive to that child. . . . Some of our citizens cling to an anachronistic notion that children are chattels and that their owners have a right, or are even duty-bound, to control their property by violent means and may assign that right to others, such as teachers. The Proverbs of King Solomon have been cited, on occasion as their authority. . . . My hunch is that the fundamentalists' fondness for Old Testament authority is driven by a need for self-exculpation over their mistreatment of children.[20]

The laws already in place in the United States are sufficient to guard against genuine physical abuse of children and bring appropriate punishment when it occurs. But such laws should not be expanded to rule out the use of such physical discipline as spanking a child. A biblically based system of values understands that when spanking is administered wisely and with restraint, it is beneficial, not harmful, in the raising of children. Yet the Bible also cautions that parents should not be so demanding that they cause frustration and despair in their children: "Fathers, do not provoke your children, lest they become discouraged" (Col. 3:21).

From time to time the news media report various new scholarly studies claiming to

---

Zondervan, 2010), 256–60, with permission of the publisher.

[15] "The 42 Countries That Have Banned Corporal Punishment," *UN Tribune,* November 20, 2014 http://untribune.com/42-countries-banned-corporal-punishment/.

[16] "Kriminalistatistk vid SCB," 115 81 Stockholm, vol. 5 (1995): cited in John S. Lyons and Robert E. Lazelere, "Where Is Evidence That Non-Abusive Punishment Increases Aggression?" presented at the XXVI International Congress of Pyschology, Aug. 18, 1996, https://www.fisheaters.com/spanking.html.

[17] "Should Spanking Your Child Be Illegal?" *ABCNews.com,* Nov. 28, 2007, http://abcnews.go.com/GMA/story?id=3924024.

[18] Nancy Vogel, "A Spanking Ban: Are We Going to Get It?" *Los Angeles Times,* Jan. 20, 2007, http://articles.latimes.com/2007/jan/20/local/me-spanking20.

[19] See Edward Wong, "No-Spanking Zone Sought in Oakland," *Los Angeles Times,* Jan. 24, 1999, A10.

[20] Jordan Riak, "Spanking and Hitting Are Perilous," *The Brown University Child and Adolescent Behavior Letter* 13, no. 9 (September 1997): 1.

"prove" that spanking does no good or is psychologically harmful to children. But these studies seldom if ever distinguish wise, nonabusive spanking that causes temporary pain but no physical harm from more violent beatings that bring serious bruising or other physical harm to children. They also fail to distinguish wise, restrained parental spanking from unjustified rage and actual physical abuse coming from drunken or pathologically abusive parents. Thus, the studies are skewed and give distorted results.

Murray Straus of the University of New Hampshire is one of the most outspoken voices calling for the banishment of corporal punishment and has from time to time issued skewed and distorted studies to try to advance his agenda. Straus over the years has tried to link corporal punishment to lower IQs in children[21] and to antisocial behavior.[22]

In response to one of Straus's studies, even *Time* magazine, hardly an advocate for corporal punishment, wrote about the flawed methodology:

> The problem has to do with who was in the study. Straus and company culled their information from telephone interviews conducted by the U.S. Bureau of Labor Statistics beginning in 1979 with 807 mothers of children ages 6 to 9. They were then asked how many times they had spanked their children in the past week and what the kids' behavior was like—did they lie, cheat, act up in school? Then the bureau polled the same group two years later. Sure enough, the kids who had been spanked had become increasingly anti-social.
>
> But when you look a little closer at the findings, they start to seem a little murky. To begin with, observes Dr. Den Trumbull, a Montgomery, Alabama pediatrician . . . the mothers ranged in age from 14 to 21. That is hardly a slice of American motherhood. Moreover, those who spanked did so on average twice a week. These factors, says Trumbull, plus the fact that some of the kids were as old as nine, "are markers of a dysfunctional family in my mind, and in the minds of most psychologists and pediatricians."
>
> Trumbull also observed that limiting the study to 6 to 9 year olds skewed the results; by then the kids can understand the consequences of their actions. For them frequent physical punishment is likely to be humiliating and traumatic—and might well lead to worse behavior down the line.
>
> Trouble is, while spanking is down, child abuse is up. It appears that well-meaning professionals have been using the wrong whipping boy—and Straus' study offers little reason to change that assessment.[23]

[21] See "Want Smarter Kids? Don't Spank Them," Reuters, Aug. 3, 1999, and Lori Wright and Murray A. Straus., "Children Who Are Spanked Have Lower IQs, New Research Finds," University of New Hampshire, Sept. 25, 2009, http://scholars.unh.edu/news/205 and http://scholars.unh.edu/cgi/viewcontent.cgi?article=1204&context=news.
[22] Murray A. Straus, David B. Sugarman, Jean Giles-Sims, "Spanking by Parents and Subsequent Anti-Social Behavior of Children," *Archives of Pediatric and Adolescent Medicine* 151 (Aug. 1997): 761–67, https://jamanetwork.com/journals/jamapediatrics/article-abstract/518458.
[23] Michael D. Lemonick, "Spare the Rod? Maybe," *Time*, Aug. 25, 1997.

In 1993, a group of American pediatricians presented a review of all articles on corporal punishment to the American Academy of Pediatrics. Their results found that of the 132 studies that supposedly documented negative effects of corporal punishment on children, only 24 had any empirical data. All the others were either editorials, commentaries, opinions, or reviews. And of the 24 valid studies, 23 had ambiguous wording and broad definitions that skewed the results. They found that physical punishment was defined to include anything from mild spanking to beating a child with a hairbrush or electrical cord to pouring boiling water on the child. They concluded that the studies failed to "entirely answer the real scientific issue—does occasional spanking aid or harm the development of a child's ability to learn?"[24]

Christians should be suspicious of supposedly conclusive "expert studies" that result in telling parents that they should not do exactly what the Bible tells them to do.

Of course, opponents of spanking can always bring up extreme examples of abuse and of harsh distortion of biblical standards. Christians shouldn't advocate such actions either, but should instead oppose them. It must be kept in mind, however, that the *abuse* of something (such as spanking of children) does not prove that the action itself is wrong. Anything good can be abused or used wrongfully.

Gene Edward Veith, provost at Patrick Henry College and former executive director of the Cranach Institute at Concordia Theological Seminary, wrote in *World* magazine that not spanking children is actually a form of child abuse:

> Not only the ACLU but also many educators, child psychologists, and even parents subscribe to the "expressive" theory of mental health. According to this model, human beings, deep down, are basically good. They simply need to express their feelings they have inside. Obstacles to this expression—such as "society rules," "oppressive" authority figures, and "judgmental" belief systems—cause repression and thus mental unhappiness and twisted behavior. Under this worldview, any attempt to control or punish or suppress the feelings of a child is construed as cruel. And disciplining a child becomes next to impossible. . . . For all the attempts to discipline children through "positive reinforcement" and such non-painful methods as "time outs" and guilt trips, young people are learning that since adults will not exert force against them, they can pretty much ignore those in authority. . . . Allowing children to grow up without discipline—however kindly it appears on the surface—is child abuse, an expression of our culture's hatred for children.[25]

We should not be surprised that many non-Christians argue against spanking. Many of them do not think that there is a tendency toward evil in human hearts, including the

---

[24] David Larson, "Is Mild Spanking Abusive or Helpful for Young Children?" Physicians Research Forum Research Summary (1993).

[25] Gene Edward Veith, "Hating Our Children," *World,* June 12, 1999, https://world.wng.org/1999/06/hating _our_children.

hearts of children. But this is contrary to a Christian worldview, which holds that there is a tendency to evil (as well as a competing tendency to do good, by common grace) in every child's heart.[26] Therefore a non-Christian worldview is less likely to think that children should be disciplined for the wrong that they do. Moreover, many people's non-Christian worldviews do not hold that superior physical force should be necessary to restrain evil, but a Christian view understands that some of the evil in people's hearts is so irrational that it cannot be restrained by reasoning but only by force.[27] When applied to the discipline of children, the Christian worldview understands that there is sometimes a need for spanking, that spanking quickly overcomes willful or irrational wrongdoing in a way that hours of pleading and reasoning will not accomplish, and that it helps build a more righteous character in a child.

A deeper reason underlying the opposition to physical punishment of children may be, in at least some cases, opposition to the very idea of parental authority over children (because of a dislike of all authority) or opposition to the idea that parents can know better than children what is right and wrong (because of a belief that nobody can know right or wrong for anyone else). In a number of cases this opposition to all spanking may be strengthened by a deep spiritual influence (an evil influence) that seeks to undermine God's plan for the family and for the restraint of evil in children's lives.

3. Patience and Understanding. In addition to love and discipline, the Bible specifies that parents are responsible to show patience and understanding toward their children:

> Fathers, *do not provoke your children to anger*, but bring them up in the discipline and instruction of the Lord. (Eph. 6:4)

This means that discipline must not be overly harsh or overly demanding, which will frustrate children and provoke them to anger. On the other hand, children are also provoked to anger when they experience no discipline at all from their parents, especially from their fathers. The absence of discipline is not really an expression of love for one's children, and children instinctively sense this and will often respond to the absence of discipline by more and more outrageous behavior, almost as if they are begging for some form of discipline from their parents.

After surveying various parenting styles, Gwen Dewar observed: "The most substantial and significant predictor of poor self-regulation skills was having a parent who answered 'yes' to questions like 'I ignore my child's bad behavior,' and 'I give in to my child when he/she causes a commotion about something.'"[28]

---

[26] See Grudem, *Politics—According to the Bible*, 119–22.

[27] See ibid., 121–22.

[28] Gwen Dewar, "Kids with Permissive Parents Show Less Self-Control," BabyCenter.com, April 20, 2013, https://blogs.babycenter.com/mom_stories/preschoolers-with-permissive-parents-show-less-self-control/. See also Piotrowski et al., "Investigating Correlates of Self-Regulation," *Journal of Child and Family Studies* 22, no. 3 (April 2013): 423–36, http://europepmc.org/articles/PMC3602616.

4. Instruction. To bring children up "in the discipline and *instruction of the Lord*" (Eph. 6:4) includes teaching them about God and his ways. Much of the book of Proverbs consists of teachings from mothers and fathers to their children: "Hear, my son, your father's instruction, and forsake not your mother's teaching" (Prov. 1:8; see also Prov. 2:1; 3:1; 4:1; 5:1; 6:1; 7:1).

Moses gave directions to the people of Israel about training their children, and these directions set a wise pattern for all parents for all time:

> And these words that I command you today shall be on your heart. *You shall teach them diligently to your children*, and shall talk of them when you sit in your house, and when you walk by the way, and when you lie down, and when you rise. (Deut. 6:6–7)

Wise parenting is a joyful task, but is also remarkably challenging and sometimes very difficult. It requires much wisdom from God! (See the encouragement to ask God for wisdom in James 1:5–8.) Wise parenting means that parents must understand their children, including their children's unique and often different gifts and interests.

Parents must also remember that they are teaching their children by the example of their lives as much as by their words. The instructions of Paul and Peter to leaders in the early churches are also applicable to parents:

> Show yourself in all respects to be a *model* [Greek, *typos*, "model, example, pattern to imitate"] of good works, and in your teaching show integrity, dignity. (Titus 2:7)

> [Serve as] not domineering over those in your charge, but *being examples to the flock*. (1 Pet. 5:3)

What if parents make mistakes in raising their children? It is inevitable that we will all make mistakes, for we are imperfect human beings. "For we all stumble in many ways" (James 3:2). Looking back on my own life, I can recall times when I now think I was too strict with one or another of my children, and other times when I was too lenient with them. But if children know that their parents deeply love them, that will more than compensate for the occasional mistakes that we make (often not knowing that we were making mistakes at the time). Here the words of Peter are appropriate: "*Love* covers a multitude of sins" (1 Pet. 4:8).

Moreover, when parents and children are seeking after God, even the mistakes that parents make can turn out for the long-term benefit of the children, because Romans 8:28 remains true: "And we know that for those who love God *all things work together for good*, for those who are called according to his purpose."

It is a significant and weighty responsibility to transfer the truth about God and his Word and his way of life to future generations. Yet it is a responsibility that God entrusts to us throughout each generation until the Lord returns:

I will open my mouth in a parable;
　　I will utter dark sayings from of old,
things that we have heard and known,
　　that our fathers have told us.
We will not hide them from their children,
　　but tell to the coming generation
the glorious deeds of the LORD, and his might,
　　and the wonders that he has done.
He established a testimony in Jacob
　　and appointed a law in Israel,
which *he commanded our fathers*
　　to teach to their children,
that the next generation might know them,
　　the children yet unborn,
and arise and tell them to their children,
　　so that they should set their hope in God
and not forget the works of God,
　　but keep his commandments. (Ps. 78:2–7)

5. The Importance of Training Children. This entire issue of training children is a crucial one today. With societies drifting further and further from Christian standards of moral conduct, I expect that Christian families who have obedient, polite, well-disciplined, cheerful, happy, confident, and peaceful children will stand out more and more as different from the surrounding non-Christian culture. That culture is often characterized by rebellious, angry, undisciplined children, who at times can be very cruel to one another and present endless discipline problems in public schools.

D. SCHOOLING CHOICES: WHAT KIND OF SCHOOL IS BEST FOR CHILDREN?

In the United States today, as well as in many other countries, parents have various kinds of schools to choose from for the education of their children. These choices fall primarily into three categories:

1. Public school (or government-sponsored school)
2. Christian school
3. Homeschool

I will evaluate briefly the arguments offered in support of each kind of school.[29]

---

[29] Arguments in favor of each of these three kinds of schooling are also found in *Schooling Choices*, ed. H. Wayne House (Portland, OR: Multnomah, 1988).

1. Arguments for Sending Children to a Public School.

a. Positive Influence on Others: Christian children who go to a public school (I realize that in some countries this may be called a government-sponsored school) can have a positive influence on the school and especially on the other children. Here the teaching of Jesus provides the basis:

> *You are the salt of the earth*, but if salt has lost its taste, how shall its saltiness be restored? It is no longer good for anything except to be thrown out and trampled under people's feet. *You are the light of the world*. A city set on a hill cannot be hidden. Nor do people light a lamp and put it under a basket, but on a stand, and it gives light to all in the house. In the same way, let your light shine before others, so that they may see your good works and give glory to your Father who is in heaven. (Matt. 5:13–16)

In addition, Jesus prayed to his Father not that Christians would be taken *out* of the world but that they would be protected from the Evil One *in* the world:

> *I do not ask that you take them out of the world*, but that you keep them from the evil one. They are not of the world, just as I am not of the world. Sanctify them in the truth; your word is truth. As you sent me into the world, so I have sent them into the world. (John 17:15–18)

b. Better Educational Quality: Public schools sometimes provide higher-quality education than Christian schools or homeschooling, at least in some areas and some situations.

c. The Opportunity to Develop Stronger Faith and Stronger Moral Character: Biblical examples such as Joseph in Egypt (Genesis 39) and Daniel in Babylon (Daniel 1)[30] show that young people who are believers can endure opposition and hardship in a hostile environment and still grow to have strong moral character and strong faith.

d. Inadequacies of Christian Schools in Some Areas: Some areas have no Christian schools available, or the ones that exist do not have high academic standards. In addition, some Christian schools lack the necessary size to challenge excellent students, especially in high school, in areas such as band, orchestra, athletics, debate, advanced math and science, or advanced foreign languages. In addition, some parents may find that local Christian schools have teachers and administrators who are poor role models (they may be arbitrary, autocratic, or dictatorial), or they may find that the local

---

[30] Joseph was around 17 years old when he was sold into slavery in Egypt (see Gen. 37:2). Daniel "would likely have been about 14 or 15 years of age when he was taken into captivity and began his training," according to Stephen R. Miller, *Daniel*, NAC (Nashville: Broadman & Holman, 1994), 60, with reference to E. J. Young, *The Prophecy of Daniel* (Grand Rapids, MI: Eerdmans, 1949), 42.

Christian school seems overly repressive or legalistic, and the atmosphere might tempt students to rebel against Christianity itself.

e. Christian Teachers in Public Schools: In some geographical areas, a large number of public school teachers are Bible-believing Christians who have a strong influence on the atmosphere and the educational content in their schools.

f. Finances: Finally, many families are simply unable to afford the cost of sending children to a Christian school, though they would like to do this if they could.

2. Arguments for Sending Children to a Christian School.

a. All of a Child's Education Should Be Bible-Centered and God-Centered: The Bible explicitly teaches how children should be trained:

> Fathers, do not provoke your children to anger, but *bring them up in the discipline and instruction of the Lord*. (Eph. 6:4)

The contrast in this verse ("*do not* provoke your children, *but* bring them up in the discipline and instruction of the Lord") suggests that training that is not "of the Lord" will prove frustrating to students and perhaps even "provoke" them to anger.

It is true that all Christian parents can encourage God-centered training in the home and in the church, but school still has an immense influence on children's lives. While church training might account for three to five hours per week (3 percent to 5 percent of a child's waking hours), training in school accounts for 30 to 40 hours per week (30 percent to 40 percent of a child's waking hours)—nearly 10 times as much time as church.

If children receive "training and instruction" that excludes God's words for, say, six hours per day, five days a week, for 12 formative years, is this bringing them up "in the discipline and instruction of the Lord" (Eph. 6:4)?

b. Education Should Be Positive and Truthful: As far as the training of children is concerned, we read:

> Train up a child *in the way he should go*; even when he is old he will not depart from it. (Prov. 22:6)

I do not think any verse of Scripture encourages parents to give their children secular training that will "strengthen them." On the other hand, they may become more callous and desensitized to the sinful behavior of others around them.

c. Peer Influence Should Be Positive and Christlike: Scripture reminds us that children will tend to become more and more like their frequent companions:

Whoever walks with the wise becomes wise, but the companion of fools will suffer harm. (Prov. 13:20)

d. Every Teacher's Pattern of Life Should Be Worthy of Imitation: Children are naturally great imitators. A teacher they like will have a tremendous impact not only on their academic work, but also on their attitudes toward all aspects of life. Jesus said:

A disciple is not above his teacher, but everyone when he is fully trained will be like his teacher. (Luke 6:40)

This is an argument for a school that has Christian teachers whose pattern of life is worthy of imitation.

Someone may answer that there are excellent Christian teachers in public schools as well (as I mentioned above). I am thankful for their presence, and I know they do have a positive influence on students. On the other hand, in the United States at least, their ability to influence children in a specifically Christian direction, or even in a positive moral direction, is restricted by excessive government regulations and the intentional exclusion of Christian themes from many parts of the curriculum.

e. Only God-Centered Education Gives True Wisdom: The reason we send children to school is that they might increase in wisdom. But Scripture is clear that genuine wisdom comes only in the context of the fear of God and submission to Christ:

The fear of the LORD is the beginning of wisdom;
   all those who practice it have a good understanding.
   His praise endures forever! (Ps. 111:10)

The fear of the LORD is the beginning of wisdom,
   and the knowledge of the Holy One is insight. (Prov. 9:10)

[In] Christ . . . are hidden all the treasures of wisdom and knowledge. (Col. 2:2–3)

The question is whether we think the Bible still works in the real world of today. Does it give wise guidance for modern life? If so, does it not seem appropriate to train children from a perspective that respects the teachings of the Bible regarding all areas of study about the nature of the world and its history?[31]

---

[31] New York University professor of psychology Paul Vitz carried out an extensive examination of 90 widely used public school textbooks in reading, social studies and history. He discovered a nearly absolute omission of any positive mentions of Protestant history, Jewish and Christian contributions to historical events, conservative political views, private business activity, marriage, heroic roles for boys or men, or the value of motherhood or homemaking. See Paul C. Vitz, *Censorship: Evidence of Bias in Our Children's Textbooks* (Ann Arbor, MI: Servant, 1986). A wide-ranging analysis of the strongly anti-Christian pressures on children in

f. High Academic Standards: Many Christian schools today have exceptionally high academic standards, often equal to or surpassing the academic levels of public schools.

3. Arguments for Homeschooling.

a. The Bible Assumes That Parents Are Responsible to Train Their Children: The biblical passages that talk about training children are all directed to parents, not to teachers in schools. Examples include "You shall teach them diligently *to your children*" (Deut. 6:7) and "*Fathers* . . . bring them up in the discipline and instruction of the Lord" (Eph. 6:4).

Those who favor either public schools or Christian schools may respond that the parents are overseeing the process but are getting specialized help from those who are better trained in various subjects, and so the teachers are simply helping the parents with their task. Advocates for homeschooling respond that there is an advantage in having parents themselves do the training.

b. The Most Significant Learning Occurs in Companionship, and Parents Are the Best Companions for Young Children: This argument also finds support from those passages that speak about parents training their children, and from Jesus's statement that "everyone when he is fully trained will be like his teacher" (Luke 6:40).

c. A Child's Companions in a Public School or a Christian School May Not Be the Best Influence on the Child: Advocates for homeschooling point out that "bad company ruins good morals" (1 Cor. 15:33) and "the companion of fools will suffer harm" (Prov. 13:20). Some parents who favor homeschooling are concerned about the companions that a child will have even in a Christian school, and especially in a public school.

d. Training in Moral Standards and Personal Character Is at Least as Important as Academic Training: Homeschool advocates will say that parents are the best teachers regarding moral standards and personal character.

e. Homeschooled Children on Average Show Excellent Educational Achievement: One of the strongest arguments in favor of homeschooling is the remarkable academic record compiled by thousands of homeschooled children throughout the United States. A study done by Michael Cogan at the University of St. Thomas found that:

- The average ACT score for homeschooled students was 26.5, compared to 25.0 for public school students.
- The average ACT English score for homeschooled students was 27.8, compared to 24.5 for public school students.

---

today's culture is found in James C. Dobson and Gary Lee Bauer, *Children at Risk: The Battle for the Hearts and Minds of Our Kids* (Dallas: Word, 1990).

- The average ACT reading score for homeschooled students was 28.2, compared to 25.6 for public school students.
- Homeschooled students graduated from college at a higher rate than their peers—66.7 percent compared to 57.5 percent—and earned higher grade-point averages.[32]

While homeschooling parents recognize that not all parents are naturally good teachers, they respond that the training materials now available for parents to use are put together by highly trained experts and provide significant help for parents who might not have the training or skills to be teachers without such materials.

f. Many Opportunities Exist for Social Interaction with Other Children: While advocates for public schools or Christian schools emphasize the benefits that come to children from frequent social interactions in school, homeschooling parents have created many networks to provide social interactions for their children with other homeschooled children. In addition, a number of school districts in the United States allow homeschooled children to participate in some activities, such as sports teams, or even to take a selection of specialized classes in local public schools. Some Christian schools do the same.

g. Families Who Homeschool Find Great Joy and Family Interaction in the Process: This is probably one of the strongest reasons why many parents support homeschooling. They find that it is a positive experience for them and their children, and that it strengthens family bonds in ways that will last a lifetime.

4. What Is My Conclusion? My wife, Margaret, and I sent all three of our sons to a public high school (grades nine through 12), but there was really no option because there was no Christian school near where we lived. But when our children were younger, we helped to start a Christian school (Christian Heritage Academy, then in Northbrook and today in Northfield, IL) during their elementary school years. In fact, I was the first president of the board (1982–1984), and we were strong advocates for the benefits of Christian schools at that time and remain so today.

However, what is best for each child and for each family will vary according to the personality and needs of the child, the abilities and interests of the parents (including, certainly, their financial abilities), and the kinds of Christian schools and public schools where the family lives.

We did not choose the homeschooling option for any of our children, but we know of families for whom it has worked out very well.

In evaluating these three options, it is important to "compare apples to apples." It is not appropriate to compare a good public school to a bad example of a Christian school, or vice versa. It is best, when thinking of this issue as a theoretical question (as

---

[32] Michael Cogan, "Exploring Academic Outcomes of Homeschooled Students," University of St. Thomas, 2009, http://i.bnet.com/blogs/homeschool.pdf.

in an ethics class discussion), to compare the best examples of all three types of schooling. But then, of course, each family must make a decision each year according to the circumstances in which they live.

Finally, there is widespread concern about the tragic decline in educational achievement throughout the United States, particularly in the last 30 years. What can be done about this?

The most encouraging development, in my opinion, is the increasing prevalence of genuine options for *school choice* by means of government programs that provide parents with *tuition "vouchers"* that attach to the student and not to an individual school. Parents can use these vouchers (usually they are worth several thousand dollars per year per student) to enroll their children in any school, whether a public school, a charter school, a private school, or a Christian school. The use of such vouchers for religious schools was approved by the Supreme Court in a significant decision in 2002.[33]

Since 2002, many states have made remarkable gains in making school choice options available to parents (in spite of the vigorous opposition to these options by public school teachers' unions).

QUESTIONS FOR PERSONAL APPLICATION

1. After reading this chapter, can you think of any specific ways in which you might do a better job of honoring your father and your mother?
2. Did your parents teach you that you should obey them because "this pleases the Lord" (Col. 3:20)? When you were growing up, did you have a sense that it was pleasing to God for you to be obedient to your parents? If you have children yourself, have you taught them that it is pleasing to God when they are obedient to you?
3. How did your relationship with your parents change as you grew from childhood to adulthood? Looking back, are there things that you would do differently if you were able to?
4. Do you think it is wise for parents to spank their children within the constraints and circumstances discussed in this chapter?
5. If you have children, how do you teach them about God during the ordinary course of each day? How did your parents teach you about God?
6. What positive character traits (see p. 110) did you learn from your parents' example when you were growing up? If you have children, can you think of times when you have sought to act as a role model for your children with respect to certain character traits?

---

[33] The case was Zelman v. Simmons-Harris, 536 U.S. 639 (2002). In a related case, the Supreme Court also upheld the validity of an Arizona program that gives state tax credits to offset individual donations made to a charitable organization, the Arizona Christian School Tuition Organization: see Arizona Christian School Tuition Organization v. Winn, 563 U.S. 125 (2011). Both cases were decided by a 5–4 majority.

SPECIAL TERMS

children
homeschooling
honor
school choice
tuition vouchers

BIBLIOGRAPHY

Sections in Other Ethics Texts

(see complete bibliographical data, p. 64)

Frame, 575–92
McQuilkin and Copan, 333–42

Other Works

Dobson, James C., and Gary Lee Bauer. *Children at Risk: The Battle for the Hearts and Minds of Our Kids*. Dallas: Word, 1990.

Dobson, James C. *The New Dare to Discipline*. Wheaton, IL: Tyndale, 1992.

Francis, J. A. H. "Parenthood, Parenting." In *New Dictionary of Christian Ethics and Pastoral Theology*, edited by David J. Atkinson and David H. Field, 650–52. Leicester, UK: Inter-Varsity, and Downers Grove, IL: InterVarsity Press, 1995.

Fulgham, Nicole Baker. *Educating All God's Children: What Christians Can—and Should—Do to Improve Public Education for Low-Income Kids*. Grand Rapids, MI: Brazos, 2013.

House, H. Wayne, ed. *Schooling Choices*. Portland, OR: Multnomah, 1988.

Kimmel, Tim. *Grace-Based Parenting: Set Your Family Free*. Nashville: Thomas Nelson, 2004.

Lowrie, Roy W. *To Christian School Parents*. Whittier, CA: Association of Christian Schools International, 1982.

Vitz, Paul C. *Censorship: Evidence of Bias in Our Children's Textbooks*. Ann Arbor, MI: Servant Books, 1986.

Ware, Bruce A., and John Starke, eds. *One God in Three Persons: Unity of Essence, Distinction of Persons, Implications for Life*. Wheaton, IL: Crossway, 2015.

Wegner, Paul D., Catherine Wegner, and Kimberlee Herman. *Wise Parenting: Guidelines from the Book of Proverbs*. Grand Rapids, MI: Discovery House, 2009.

Wilson, Douglas, ed. *Repairing the Ruins: The Classical and Christian Challenge to Modern Education*. Moscow, ID: Canon Press, 2006.

SCRIPTURE MEMORY PASSAGE

Ephesians 6:1–2: Children, obey your parents in the Lord, for this is right. "Honor your father and mother" (this is the first commandment with a promise).

HYMN

"Children of the Heavenly Father"

Children of the Heavenly Father,
Safely in His bosom gather;
Nestling bird nor star in heaven
Such a refuge e'er was given.

God His own doth tend and nourish;
In His holy courts they flourish.
From all evil things He spares them;
In His mighty arms He bears them.

Neither life nor death shall ever
From the Lord His children sever;
Unto them His grace He showeth,
And their sorrows all He knoweth.

Though He giveth or He taketh,
God His children ne'er forsaketh;
His the loving purpose solely
To preserve them pure and holy.

Praise the Lord in joyful numbers;
Your Protector never slumbers.
At the will of your Defender,
Ev'ry foeman must surrender.

AUTHOR (SWEDISH): KAROLINA W. SANDELL-BERG, 1858

Chapter 15

EQUALITY AND LEADERSHIP IN MARRIAGE

How can husbands have a leadership role in marriage if men and women are equal in value before God?

How should a husband's headship and a wife's support of that headship work out in practice?

What are the arguments used by evangelical feminists today?

In the previous chapter we considered the relationship between parents and children in a family, particularly the authority that God has given to parents with regard to their children and the responsibility that children have to honor their fathers and mothers.[1]

In this chapter we will examine another aspect of God-ordained authority within family life, namely, the relationship between a husband and wife. We will find that the Bible teaches two important principles that must be taught together: the principle of equality in marriage and the principle of the husband's leadership responsibility in marriage.[2]

This idea that men and women are equal but that God ordained different roles for them in marriage is known as the "complementarian" position. By contrast, the view that men and women are equal and that there are no specific roles in marriage is known as the "egalitarian" position. In particular, complementarians hold that there is a unique

---

[1] The material in this chapter has been adapted from Wayne Grudem, *Evangelical Feminism and Biblical Truth: An Analysis of More Than 100 Disputed Questions* (Wheaton, IL: Crossway, 2012), 25–56, with permission of the publisher.

[2] On questions related to the definition of marriage, sexual intimacy in marriage, polygamy, and same-sex marriage, see chap. 28. I also discuss the question of singleness there.

leadership role for men in marriage (and in the church), while egalitarians deny this. (I sometimes use *evangelical feminist* to mean the same thing as *egalitarian*.)

Because the topic of this chapter has been extensively debated within the evangelical world (see bibliography at end of chapter), I have included fairly extensive interactions with different viewpoints.

A. MEN AND WOMEN ARE EQUAL IN VALUE AND DIGNITY

In the very first chapter of the Bible we read that both men and women are created "in the image of God." In fact, the first verse that tells us that God *created* human beings also tells us that both "male and female" are created in the image of God: :

> So God created man *in his own image,*
> > in the image of God he created him;
> > male and female he created them. (Gen. 1:27)

To be created in the image of God is an incredible privilege. It means that human beings are *like God* and *represent God.*[3] No other creatures in all of creation, not even the powerful angels, are said to be created in the image of God. It is a privilege given only to us men and women.[4]

Any discussion of manhood and womanhood in the Bible must start here. Every time we talk to another person, we should remember that that person is a creature of God who is *more like God than anything else in the universe,* and men and women share that status equally. Therefore, we should treat men and women with equal dignity and should think of both as having equal value. We *both* bear the image of God, and we have shared in that equality since the very first day that God created us. "In the image of God he created him; *male and female he created them*" (Gen. 1:27). Nowhere does the Bible say that men are created more in God's image than women, or vice versa.[5] Men and women share equally in the tremendous privilege of being made in the image of God.

---

[3] For further discussion, see Wayne Grudem, *Systematic Theology: An Introduction to Biblical Doctrine* (Leicester, UK: Inter-Varsity, and Grand Rapids, MI: Zondervan, 1994), 442–50.

[4] God created us so that our likeness to him would be seen in our moral judgment and actions; in our spiritual life and ability to relate to God, who is spirit; in our reasoning ability; in our use of language; in our awareness of the distant past and future; in our creativity; in the complexity and variety of our emotions; in the depth of our interpersonal relationships; in our equality and differences in marriage and other interpersonal relationships; in our rule over the rest of creation; and in other ways. All of these aspects are distorted by sin and therefore manifest themselves in ways that are *unlike* God and are displeasing to him, but all of these areas of our lives are also being progressively restored to greater Godlikeness through the salvation that is ours in Christ, and they will be completely restored in us when Christ returns. For a fuller discussion on what it means to be created in the image of God, see Bruce A. Ware, "Male and Female Complementarity and the Image of God," in *Biblical Foundations for Manhood and Womanhood*, ed. Wayne Grudem (Wheaton, IL: Crossway, 2002), 71–92.

[5] In 1 Cor. 11:7, Paul says, "For a man ought not to cover his head, since he is the image and glory of God, but woman is the glory of man." He is not denying here that the woman was created in the image of God, for

The Bible thus provides a clear correction for the errors of male dominance and male superiority that have come as the result of sin and that have been seen in nearly all cultures in the history of the world. Wherever men are thought to be better than women; wherever husbands act as selfish "dictators"; wherever wives are forbidden to have their own jobs outside the home, to vote, to own property, or to be educated; wherever women are treated as inferior; and wherever there is abuse or violence against women, such as rape, female infanticide, polygamy, or harems, the biblical truth of equality in the image of God is being denied. To all societies where these things occur, Christians must proclaim that the very first page of God's Word bears a fundamental and irrefutable witness against these evils.[6]

Yet we can say even more. If men and women are equally made in the image of God, then we are equally important and equally valuable *to God*. We have equal worth before him *for all eternity*, for this is how we were created. This truth should exclude all our feelings of pride or inferiority, and should exclude any idea that one sex is better or worse than the other. In contrast to many non-Christian cultures and religions, no one should feel proud or superior because he is a man, and no one should feel disappointed or inferior because she is a woman. If God thinks us to be equal in value, then that settles forever the question of personal worth, for God's evaluation is the true standard of personal value for all eternity.

Further evidence of our equality in bearing the image of God is seen in the New Testament church, where the Holy Spirit was given in new fullness to both men and women (Acts 2:17–18), where both men and women were baptized into membership in the body of Christ (v. 41),[7] and where both men and women received spiritual gifts for use in the life of the church (1 Cor. 12:7, 11; 1 Pet. 4:10). The apostle Paul reminds us that we are not to be divided into factions that think of themselves as superior and inferior (such as Jew and Greek, slave and free, or male and female), but rather that we should think of ourselves as united because we "are all one in Christ Jesus" (Gal. 3:28).

Whenever husbands and wives do not listen respectfully and thoughtfully to each other's viewpoints, do not esteem the wisdom that might be arrived at differently and

that is clearly affirmed in Gen. 1:27. Neither is he saying that the woman is the image of the man. Rather, Paul is simply saying that *in the relationship between man and woman*, man in particular reflects something of the excellence of the God who created him, and woman *in that relationship* reflects something of the excellence of the man from whom she was created. Yet Paul goes on almost immediately to say that men and women are interdependent (see vv. 11–12) and that we could not exist without each other. He does not say in this passage that man is more in the image of God than woman is, and we should not derive any such idea from this passage.

[6] A tragic example of male dominance continues to occur in India. Tehmina Arora, legal counsel for Alliance Defending Freedom in India, states: "In our country, 50,000 babies are aborted every month for one reason: they are girls instead of boys. India's skewed sex ratio shows that, as a nation, we have failed girls. They are either aborted, or once born, subject to various forms of violence." "India's Girls Need Love, Care, Right to Life," *ADFMedia.org*, March 7, 2016, http://www.adfmedia.org/News/PRDetail/?CID=89218.

[7] The fact that both men and women are baptized stands in contrast to the Old Testament, where the outward sign of inclusion in the community of God's people was circumcision, which, by its nature, was administered only to men. Because both men and women are baptized in the New Testament church, every baptism should remind us of our equality in the image of God.

expressed differently by the other person, or do not value the other person's different gifts and preferences as much as their own, they neglect this teaching on equality in the image of God.[8]

A healthy perspective on the way that equality manifests itself in marriage was summarized as part of a "Marriage and Family Statement" issued by Campus Crusade for Christ in July of 1999. After three paragraphs discussing the equality of and the differences between men and women, the statement says:

> In a marriage lived according to these truths, the love between husband and wife will show itself in listening to each other's viewpoints, valuing each other's gifts, wisdom, and desires, honoring one another in public and in private, and always seeking to bring benefit, not harm, to one another.[9]

Why do I list the equality of men and women in value and dignity before God as an important issue in the manhood-womanhood controversy? Not because we complementarians differ with egalitarians on this question, but because we differ at this point with sinful tendencies in our own hearts and with the oppressive male chauvinism and male dominance that has marred most cultures throughout history.

Anyone preaching or teaching on manhood and womanhood has to start here, where the Bible starts—not with our differences, but with our *equality* in the image of God.

There is yet another reason why I think this is a key issue, one that speaks especially to men. I personally think that one reason God allowed this controversy over manhood and womanhood to come into the church at this time is so that we men could correct some mistakes, change some wrongful traditions, and become more faithful to Scripture in treating our wives and all women with dignity and respect. The first step in correcting these mistakes is to be fully convinced in our hearts that women share equally with us in the value and dignity that belongs to being made in the image of God.

---

[8] I do not think I listened very well to my wife, Margaret, early in our marriage. I did not value her gifts and preferences as much as my own or the wisdom that she arrived at differently (often, it seemed, quickly and instinctively) and expressed differently from me. Later we made much progress in this area, but looking back, Margaret told me that early in our marriage she felt as though her voice was taken away and as though my ears were closed. I expect that there are other couples for whom God needs to open the husband's ears to listen and needs to restore the wife's voice to speak.

I realize that there is an opposite mistake in which the husband listens so much and the wife has so great a voice that she becomes the governing partner in the relationship. I am not advocating that mistake either, and in what follows I will argue for the necessity of a male leadership role in decision making within marriage.

[9] Policy statement announced and distributed to Campus Crusade staff members at a biannual staff conference on July 28, 1999, at Colorado State University, Fort Collins, Colorado. The statement was reported in a Religion News Service dispatch July 30, 1999; a Baptist Press story by Art Toalston on July 29, 1999 (www .baptistpress.com); and an article in *World* magazine on September 11, 1999, 32, and was also quoted in full in James Dobson's monthly newsletter, *Family News from Dr. James Dobson*, September 1999, 1–2. The statement is also reproduced and discussed in Dennis Rainey, *Ministering to Twenty-First Century Families: Eight Big Ideas for Church Leaders* (Nashville: Thomas Nelson, 2001), 39–56.

B. MEN AND WOMEN HAVE DIFFERENT ROLES IN MARRIAGE AS PART OF THE CREATED ORDER

In 1987, when I was part of the leadership of the organization known as the Council on Biblical Manhood and Womanhood, we wrote a statement of principles known as the "Danvers Statement."[10] This statement has been widely recognized as the primary definition of a complementarian view of biblical manhood and womanhood. Regarding the relationship between a husband and wife in marriage, the Danvers Statement includes the following affirmations:

1. Both Adam and Eve were created in God's image, equal before God as persons and distinct in their manhood and womanhood.
2. Distinctions in masculine and feminine roles are ordained by God as part of the created order, and should find an echo in every human heart.
3. Adam's headship in marriage was established by God before the fall, and was not a result of sin.

On June 14, 2000, the Southern Baptist Convention adopted a revision of its statement of faith, known as the Baptist Faith and Message. It includes this paragraph on the relationship between a husband and wife in marriage, which also expresses a complementarian position similar to that of the Danvers Statement:

> The husband and wife are of equal worth before God, since both are created in God's image. The marriage relationship models the way God relates to His people. A husband is to love his wife as Christ loved the church. He has the God-given responsibility *to provide for, to protect, and to lead his family*. A wife is to submit herself graciously to the servant leadership of her husband even as the church willingly submits to the headship of Christ. She, being in the image of God as is her husband and thus equal to him, has the God-given responsibility *to respect her husband and serve as his helper* in managing the household and nurturing the next generation.[11]

By contrast, egalitarians do not affirm such created differences. In fact, the statement

---

[10] The Danvers Statement was prepared by several evangelical leaders at a Council on Biblical Manhood and Womanhood (CBMW) meeting in Danvers, Massachusetts, in December 1987. It was first published in final form by CBMW in Wheaton, IL, in November 1988. See the appendix at the end of this chapter for the full text of this statement.

[11] The Baptist Faith and Message, http://www.sbc.net/bfm2000/bfm2000.asp, emphasis added. The Scripture passages added to this section on the family were: Gen. 1:26–28; 2:15–25; 3:1–20; Ex. 20:12; Deut. 6:4–9; Josh. 24:15; 1 Sam. 1:26–28; Pss. 51:5; 78:1–8; 127–128; 139:13–16; Prov. 1:8; 5:15–20; 6:20–22; 12:4; 13:24; 14:1; 17:6; 18:22; 22:6, 15; 23:13–14; 24:3; 29:15, 17; 31:10–31; Eccles. 4:9–12; 9:9; Mal. 2:14–16; Matt. 5:31–32; 18:2–5; 19:3–9; Mark 10:6–12; Rom. 1:18–32; 1 Cor. 7:1–16; Eph. 5:21–33; 6:1–4; Col. 3:18–21; 1 Tim. 5:8, 14; 2 Tim. 1:3–5; Titus 2:3–5; Heb. 13:4; 1 Pet. 3:1–7.

on "Men, Women and Biblical Equality" published by Christians for Biblical Equality (CBE) says:

> 1. The Bible teaches that both man and woman were created in God's image, had a direct relationship with God, and shared jointly the responsibilities of bearing and rearing children and having dominion over the created order (Gen. 1:26–28). . . .
>
> 5. The Bible teaches that the rulership of Adam over Eve resulted from the fall and was, therefore, *not a part of the original created order.* . . .
>
> 10. The Bible defines the function of leadership as the empowerment of others for service rather than as the exercise of power over them (Matt. 20:25–28, 23:8; Mark 10:42–45; John 13:13–17; Gal. 5:13; 1 Pet. 5:2–3).
>
> 11. The Bible teaches that husbands and wives are heirs together of the grace of life and that they are bound together in a relationship of mutual submission and responsibility (1 Cor. 7:3–5; Eph. 5:21; 1 Pet. 3:1–7; Gen. 21:12). The husband's function as "head" (*kephalē*) is to be understood as self-giving love and service within this relationship of mutual submission (Eph. 5:21–33; Col. 3:19; 1 Pet. 3:7).[12]

So which position is right? Does the Bible really teach that men and women had different roles from the beginning of creation? When we look carefully at Scripture, we can see at least 10 indications that God gave men and women distinct roles before the fall, and particularly that there was male headship in marriage before the fall.

C. TEN INDICATIONS OF MALE HEADSHIP IN MARRIAGE BEFORE THE FALL

1. The Order. Adam was created first, then Eve (note the sequence in Gen. 2:7, 18–23). We may not think of this as very important today, but it was important to the original readers of this text. The apostle Paul also sees it as important: he bases his argument for different roles in the assembled New Testament church on the fact that Adam was created prior to Eve. He says, "I do not permit a woman to teach or to exercise authority over a man. . . . For *Adam was formed first, then Eve*" (1 Tim. 2:12–13).

According to Scripture itself, then, the fact that Adam was created first and then Eve

---

[12] "Men, Women and Biblical Equality," https://www.cbeinternational.org/sites/default/files/english_3.pdf, emphasis added. The CBE statement regularly portrays a nonegalitarian position in pejorative language, using language such as "the rulership of Adam over Eve," and fails to even mention a third alternative, namely, loving, humble headship. For a discussion of repeated ambiguities in the CBE statement, see John Piper and Wayne Grudem, "Charity, Clarity, and Hope," in John Piper and Wayne Grudem, eds., *Recovering Biblical Manhood and Womanhood: A Response to Evangelical Feminism* (Wheaton, IL: Crossway, 1991), 403–22.

had implications not just for Adam and Eve, but also for the relationships between men and women throughout all of human history.[13]

2. The Representation. Adam, not Eve, had a special role in representing the human race.

Looking at the Genesis narrative, we find that Eve sinned first, then Adam sinned: "She took of its fruit and ate, and she also gave some to her husband who was with her, and he ate" (Gen. 3:6). Since Eve sinned first, we might expect that the New Testament would tell us that we inherit a sinful nature or that we are counted guilty because of Eve's sin. But this is not the case. The New Testament does not say that "*in Eve* all die," but rather, "For as *in Adam* all die, so also *in Christ* shall all be made alive" (1 Cor. 15:22).

This is further seen in the parallel between Adam and Christ, where Paul views Christ as the "last Adam":

> Thus it is written, "The first man Adam became a living being"; the last Adam became a life-giving spirit. . . . The first man was from the earth, a man of dust; the second man is from heaven. . . . Just as we have borne the image of the man of dust, we shall also bear the image of the man of heaven. (1 Cor. 15:45–49; see also Rom. 5:12–21, where another relationship between Adam and Christ is developed)

It is unmistakable that Adam had a leadership role in representing the entire human race, a leadership role that Eve did not have. Neither did Adam and Eve *together* represent the human race. *Adam alone* represented the race.

3. The Naming of Woman. When God made the first woman and "brought her to the man," the Bible tells us:

> Then the man said,
>
> "This at last is bone of my bones
>   and flesh of my flesh;
> she shall be called Woman,
>   because she was taken out of Man." (Gen. 2:23)

When Adam said, "she shall be called Woman," he was giving her a name. This is important because the original readers would have recognized that, in the context of Genesis 1–2, the person doing the "naming" of created things is always the person who has authority over those things.

Some egalitarians, such as Gilbert Bilezikian and Stanley Grenz, deny that Adam

---

[13] Ware adds yet another reason related to this temporal priority in creation, namely, that woman was created "from" or "out of" man. See his discussion in "Male and Female Complementarity and the Image of God," 82–84. It could be counted as an 11th reason along with the 10 I list.

gave a name to his wife in Genesis 2:23.[14] But this objection is hardly convincing when we see how Genesis 2:23 fits into the pattern of naming activities throughout these first two chapters of Genesis. We see this when we examine the places where the same verb (Hebrew, *qārā'*, "to call") is used in contexts of naming in Genesis 1–2:

> God *called* the light Day, and the darkness he *called* Night. (1:5)

> And God *called* the expanse Heaven. (1:8)

> God *called* the dry land Earth, and the waters that were gathered together he *called* Seas. (1:10)

> So out of the ground the LORD God had formed every beast of the field and every bird of the heavens and brought them to the man to see what he would *call* them. And whatever the man *called* every living creature, that was its name. (2:19)

> The man *gave names* to all livestock and to the birds of the heavens and to every beast of the field. (2:20)

In each of these verses prior to Genesis 2:23, the same Hebrew verb, *qārā'*, is used to indicate a naming activity. Just as God demonstrated his sovereignty over day, night,

---

[14] Gilbert Bilezikian says, "No mention of 'giving a name' is made in reference to the woman in verse 23. . . . The contrast between Genesis 2:23 and 3:20 bears out the fact that there was no act of naming in the first instance. When Eve actually receives her *name*, the text uses that very word, 'The man called his wife's *name* Eve.'" *Beyond Sex Roles: What the Bible Says about a Woman's Place in Church and Family* (Grand Rapids, MI: Baker, 1985), 259, 261.

Bilezikian apparently thinks that where *name* (the Hebrew noun *shēm*) is not used, no act of naming occurs. But he takes no account of the fact that *shēm* is not used in Gen. 1:5, 8, or 10 either, where God names the "Day," the "Night, "Heaven," "Earth," and "Seas." The idea of naming can be indicated by the verb *qārā'* ("to call") without the noun *shēm* being used, as it is in these verses.

Stanley Grenz says, "The usual Hebrew construction for the act of naming is not present in the Genesis 2:23 text. Phyllis Trible points out that in order to denote naming, the Hebrew verb 'call' must be followed by an actual name. . . . In the Genesis 2:23 text, however, no actual name is present, only the designation *woman*. . . . The narrator does not state that the man did in fact name his wife when God brought her to him. . . . It is not until after the Fall that Adam calls her Eve." *Women in the Church: A Biblical Theology of Women in Ministry* (Downers Grove, IL: InterVarsity Press, 1995), 163.

But Grenz (and Trible) are incorrect in this because they wrongly assume that *woman* (Hebrew, *'ishshāh*) is not a name. However, it is surely taken as a name here in Genesis, and Gen. 2:23 is parallel to the other naming verses in this context, especially Gen. 5:2, where it is said that God "blessed them and *named* [*qārā'*] them Man when [literally "on the day"] they were created." Grenz and Trible fail to account for the special nature of Genesis 1–2, where this same naming pattern is used of whole broad categories of the created order, and an individual personal name (such as Eve) would not yet be expected.

George W. Ramsey argues against Trible's claim, saying, "It is an error to argue that Genesis 2:23 is not an instance of name-giving. . . . The use of the noun *shēm* is not absolutely essential to the naming formula. *Qārā'* plus *lāmed* with an object indicates naming just as well as *qārā'* plus *shēm*." "Is Name-Giving an Act of Domination in Genesis 2:23 and Elsewhere?" *Catholic Biblical Quarterly* 50 (1988): 29. Ramsey points out similar examples, such as the naming of Ichabod in 1 Sam. 4:21, "And she named the child Ichabod," where the word *shēm* ("name") is not used, but the verb *qārā'* is used plus *lāmed* with an object, as in Gen. 2:23.

heaven, earth, and seas by assigning them names, so Adam demonstrated his authority over the animal kingdom by assigning every living creature its name. The original readers would have recognized this pattern and would have seen a continuation of it when Adam said, "she shall be *called* Woman."

In Genesis and the rest of the Old Testament, when someone gives a name to a person or thing, that name often indicates something of the character or quality of that person or thing. Thus, parents give names to their children (see Gen. 4:25, 26; 5:3, 29; 16:15; 19:37, 38; 21:3). And God changes the names of people when he wishes to indicate a change in their character or role (see Gen. 17:5, 15, where God changes Abram's name to Abraham and Sarai's name to Sarah). In each of these passages we have the same verb (*qārā'*) that is used in Genesis 2:23, and in each case the person who gives the name has authority over the person who receives the name. Therefore, when Adam gave to his wife the name "Woman," it indicated a kind of authority that God had given to Adam, a leadership function that Eve did not have with respect to her husband.[15]

Linda Belleville objects that naming in the Old Testament "was not an act of control or power."[16] But this misses the point. The point is not that there is some kind of magical power or control in the act of naming, but that the authority to give a name in itself assumes that the person giving the name *already has authority* over the person or thing receiving that name.[17]

---

[15] William J. Webb claims that when Adam calls Eve "Woman" (*'ishshāh*) in Gen. 2:23, it shows her role as an equal partner with Adam, because her name is similar to the name for man (*'ish*). *Slaves, Women and Homosexuals: Exploring the Hermeneutics of Cultural Analysis* (Downers Grove, IL: InterVarsity Press, 2001), 116. This argument is not convincing because the names for "man" and "woman" are similar, but they are not identical (*'ish* and *'ishshāh*), so they are somewhat the same and somewhat different.

The words also mean different things: *'ish* means "man" or "husband" (BDB, 35) and *'ishshāh* means "woman, wife, female" (BDB, 61), and though the words look similar, they are related to different roots; the BDB lexicon speaks of "the impossibility of deriving *'ish* and *'ishshāh* from the same root," 35.

For Webb to say that this name *only* indicates equality is reductionistic—it is taking part of the truth and making it the whole truth. The names signify *both* similarity *and* difference.

[16] Linda Belleville, "Women in Ministry: An Egalitarian Perspective," in *Two Views on Women in Ministry*, Counterpoints, series ed. Stanley N. Gundry, gen. ed. James R. Beck (Grand Rapids, MI: Zondervan, 2001), 143. Belleville refers to Anthony Thiselton, "Supposed Power of Words in the Biblical Writings," *Journal of Theological Studies*, n.s., vol. XXV, pt. 2 (1974): 283–99, and also to Ramsey, "Name-Giving" (see footnotes 14 and 17 for a discussion of Ramsey's article). Thiselton's article does not really address the question under discussion here regarding Gen. 2:23, however, because his concern is to show that name giving does not have some sort of automatic or magical power in the biblical writings. That, of course, is not what I am claiming, but rather that the *right* to give someone a name implies that the name giver has authority over that person or thing.

[17] Ramsey provides evidence that enables us to make a helpful qualification, however, between what we may term "private" and "public" names (this is my distinction, not his). Ramsey points out that Hagar gave a name to God in Gen. 16:13: "So she called the name of the LORD who spoke to her, 'You are a God of seeing.'" He rightly says, "It is difficult to imagine that the narrator intended us to understand that this woman . . . is exercising some sort of control over God." "Name Giving," 34. I agree, but what this verse demonstrates is simply a common human activity whereby people can make up all sorts of "private names" by which they refer to someone else, even someone great or famous (for example, someone who admires a current president of the United States might often refer to him as "our great president," while someone who opposes his policies might frequently refer to "that idiot in the White House"). Such private names do not change the

We should notice here that Adam did not give the personal name "Eve" to his wife until Genesis 3:20: "The man *called* [*qārā'*] his wife's name Eve, because she was the mother of all living." This is because in the creation story in Genesis 2, Adam was giving a broad category name to his wife, indicating the name that would be given to women generally; he was not giving a specific personal name designating the character of the individual person.[18]

4. The Naming of the Human Race. God named the human race "Man," not "Woman." Because the idea of naming is so important in the Old Testament, it is significant to notice what name God chose for the human race as a whole. We read:

> When God created man, he made him in the likeness of God. Male and female he created them, and he blessed them and *named them Man* when they were created. (Gen. 5:1–2)

The Hebrew word that is translated "Man" is *'ādām*. But this was by no means a gender-neutral term in the eyes of Hebrew readers, because in the four chapters prior to Genesis 5:2, *'ādām* is used many times to speak of a male human being in distinction from a female human being. In the following list, the italicized word *man* represents the Hebrew word *'ādām* in every case:

---

public, official, or widely used name of that person, and Ramsey is right to see that in a case such as this there is no indication of authority over the person named. Ramsey is wrong, however, to take this unusual example and from it derive a general conclusion that name giving does not indicate power or authority over the person or thing named.

The example of Hagar is not like the many other biblical examples of giving a public or official name to someone, a name commonly used by other people and by which the recipient of the name henceforth identifies himself or herself. In the Old Testament, that kind of bestowal of a public or official name is regularly done by those in authority over the person or thing named (as the many Genesis passages cited in my earlier paragraphs clearly demonstrate, as do the passages Ramsey cites [32], in which kings bestow names, and warriors who conquer territories bestow names). God gives public and official names frequently in Genesis, and parents also give such names, and they are able to do so because of their authority over the persons named.

Ramsey's citation of Gen. 26:17–21 as a counterexample is hardly persuasive, for in that very context there is significant evidence that the act of bestowing a name on a well is an act of asserting dominion over that well. Note Gen. 26:18: "And Isaac dug again the wells of water that had been dug in the days of Abraham his father, which the Philistines had stopped after the death of Abraham. And he gave them the names that his father had given them." The fact that Isaac named two wells Esek ("contention") and Sitnah ("enmity") before he left them for a third well (which he named!) shows that he was still asserting an inherent right to dominion over them, though he was temporarily relinquishing the exercise of that right for the sake of peace. Note that all of this contention over wells was carried out in the light of Gen. 26:3, where God had promised him, "To you and to your offspring I will give all these lands."

[18] Similarly, because God had Adam examine and name the entire animal kingdom (Gen. 2:19–20), it is likely that Adam gave names to one representative of each broad category or type of animal (such as dog, cat, deer, or lion, to use English equivalents). We hardly expect that he would have given individual, personal names (such as Rover, Tabby, Bambi, or Leo), because those names would not have applied to others of the same kind. This distinction is missed by Bilezikian, *Beyond Sex Roles*, 259–61, and Grenz, *Women in the Church*, 163, when they object that Adam did not name Eve until Gen. 3:20, after the fall. (See also Judy L. Brown, *Women Ministers According to Scripture* [Springfield, MO: Judy L. Brown, 1996], 31.) He did give her a specific personal name ("Eve") after the fall, but he also gave her the general category name "woman" before the fall. The one does not exclude the other, for the Bible reports both events.

And the rib that the LORD God had taken from the *man* he made into a woman and brought her to the *man*. (Gen. 2:22; note that it does not say that God made the rib into another *'ādām*, another "man," but that he made the rib into a "woman," which is a translation of a different Hebrew word.)

Then the *man* said, "This at last is bone of my bone and flesh of my flesh; she shall be called Woman." (Gen. 2:23)

And the *man* and his wife were both naked and were not ashamed. (Gen. 2:25)

And the *man* and his wife hid themselves from the presence of the LORD God. (Gen. 3:8)

But the LORD God called to the *man* and said to him, "Where are you?" (Gen. 3:9)

The *man* said, "The woman whom you gave to be with me, she gave me fruit of the tree, and I ate." (Gen. 3:12)

The *man* called his wife's name Eve. (Gen. 3:20)

When we come, then, to the naming of the human race in Genesis 5:2 (God "named them Man when they were created"), it was evident to the original readers that God was using a name that had clear male overtones or nuances.[19]

I am not saying that *'ādām* in the Hebrew Bible always refers to a male human being, for sometimes it has a broader sense and means something like "person." But in the early chapters of Genesis, the connection with the man in distinction from the woman is a very clear pattern. God gave the human race a name that, like the English word *man*, can mean a male human being or can refer to the human race in general.[20]

---

[19] In addition to the eight examples mentioned here, the word *'ādām* was used an additional five times as a proper name for Adam in distinction from Eve in the first four chapters of Genesis (3:17, 21; 4:1, 25; 5:1). However, there are actually more than 13 instances where the Hebrew word *'ādām* refers to a male human being, because prior to the creation of Eve there are 12 additional instances where references to "the man" speak only of a male person God has created (see Gen. 2:5, 7 [twice], 8, 15, 16, 18, 19 [twice], 20 [twice], 21). If we count these instances, there are 25 examples of *'ādām* used to refer to a male human being prior to Gen. 5:2. The male connotations of the word could not have been missed by the original readers.

[20] Linda Belleville denies that God's use of *'ādām* indicates male headship, because there were other male-oriented words available. She says, "'*ādām* is not a term that denotes gender. It . . . is properly translated with a generic term like *human* or *humankind*. When gender comes into play, the Hebrew terms *zākār* ('male') and *neqēbāh* ('female') are used. . . . That *'ādām* is a gender-inclusive term is clear from the repeated reference to *'ādām* as 'them' (Genesis 1:26–27; 5:2). The Septuagint's consistent choice of the generic term *anthrōpos* ('person,' 'human') to translate *'ādām* points to the same thing." *Women Leaders and the Church: Three Crucial Questions* (Grand Rapids, MI: Baker, 2000), 102.

Belleville here misses the point. The Hebrew word *'ādām* is not *exclusively* male-oriented (as *zākār* is), but can be used in four senses: (1) to refer to the human race as a whole, (2) to refer to a human being, (3) to refer to a man in distinction from a woman (especially in the early chapters of Genesis), and (4) as a proper

Does this make any difference? It does give a hint that God intended male leadership in choosing this name. It is significant that God did not call the human race "Woman" (I am speaking of Hebrew equivalents to these English words). Neither did he give the human race a name such as "humanity," which would have no male connotations and no connection with the man in distinction from the woman. Rather, he called the race "man." Raymond C. Ortlund rightly says, "God's naming of the race 'man' whispers male headship."[21]

When Genesis 5:2 reports this naming process, it refers to an event prior to sin and the fall:

> When God created man, he made him in the likeness of God. Male and female he created them, and he blessed them and named them Man *when they were created*. (Gen. 5:1–2)

And, in fact, the name is already indicated in Genesis 1:27: "So God created *man* in his own image, in the image of God he created him; male and female he created them."

If the name "man" in English (as in Hebrew) did not suggest male leadership or headship in the human race, there would be no objection to using *man* to refer to the human race today. But it is precisely the hint of male leadership in the word that has led some people to object to this use of *man* and to attempt to substitute other terms.[22] Yet it is that same hint of male leadership that makes this precisely the best translation of Genesis 1:27 and 5:2.

---

name for Adam (see BDB, 9). The Septuagint's term *anthrōpos* is therefore a useful translation of *'ādām*, because it can mean either person or man, depending on context. Belleville surprisingly gives readers only half the relevant evidence at this point, neglecting to mention that *anthrōpos* can also mean "a male person; *man*" (see BDAG, 81).

Belleville says nothing about the most significant evidence in these chapters: the male connotations that readers would pick up from the use of *'ādām* 25 times in the early chapters of Genesis to refer to Adam or to a male human being in distinction from a woman.

Aída Besancon Spencer, on the other hand, tries to deny the male nuance in *'ādām* by making it always collective, saying, "'The Adam' is a 'they.' . . . 'The Adam' is a 'male and female.' Thus 'the Adam' could be translated 'human' or 'humanity.'" She even goes so far as to speak of "Adam, the female." *Beyond the Curse: Women Called to Ministry* (Peabody, MA: Hendrickson, 1985), 21. But her argument will not work, because it is contradicted by many verses in Genesis 2–3, where *'ādām* has to refer to Adam alone, not Adam and Eve together (and it is never used of Eve alone). Spencer's attempt to squeeze all examples of the word into one meaning would yield absurd sentences like "And *the humanity* and his wife were both naked and were not ashamed" (Gen. 2:25) and "*The humanity* and his wife hid themselves from the presence of the LORD God" (3:8).

[21] Raymond C. Ortlund Jr., "Male-Female Equality and Male Headship," in Piper and Grudem, eds., *Recovering Biblical Manhood and Womanhood*, 98.

[22] Several gender-neutral Bible translations have changed the word *man*, which was standard in earlier English translations. *Humankind* is used in the New Revised Standard Version of Gen. 1:26–27. The New Living Translation uses *human beings*, as did the inclusive language Today's New International Version (TNIV) in 2001. The 2011 NIV changed it to *mankind*, which does still retain some male nuance. In Gen. 5:2, various gender-neutral substitutes replace the name *man*: *humankind* (NRSV), *human* (NLT), or *human beings* (TNIV, CEV, NCV). The 2011 NIV uses *mankind*.

5. The Primary Accountability. God spoke to Adam first after the fall.

After Adam and Eve sinned, they hid from the Lord among the trees of the garden. Then we read, "But the LORD God called to *the man* and said to *him*, 'Where are *you*?'" (Gen. 3:9).

In the Hebrew text, the expression "the man" and the pronouns "him" and "you" are all singular. Even though Eve had sinned first, God first summoned Adam to give account for what had happened in his family. Adam was the one primarily accountable.

An analogy to this accountability is seen in the life of a contemporary human family. When a parent comes into a room where several children have been misbehaving and have left the room in chaos, the parent will probably summon the oldest and say, "What happened here?" Though all are responsible for their behavior, the oldest child bears the primary responsibility. In a similar way, when God summoned Adam to give an account, it indicated a primary responsibility for Adam in the conduct of his family.

Likewise, God gave commands regarding the trees of the garden to Adam alone before the fall (Gen. 2:15–17), again indicating a primary responsibility that belonged to Adam.[23] By contrast, the Serpent spoke to Eve first (3:1), trying to tempt her to take responsibility for leading the family into sin and inverting the order that God had established at creation.

6. The Purpose. Eve was created as a helper for Adam, not Adam as a helper for Eve.

After God created Adam and gave him directions concerning his life in the garden of Eden, we read, "Then the LORD God said, 'It is not good that the man should be alone; I will make him a *helper* fit for him'" (Gen. 2:18).

It is true that the Hebrew word here translated as "helper" (*'ēzer*) is often used elsewhere in the Bible of God, who is our helper (see, for example, Ps. 33:20; 70:5; 115:9). But *helper* does not by itself decide what God intended the relationship to be between Adam and Eve. The activity of helping is so broad that it can be done by someone who has greater authority, someone who has equal authority, or someone who has lesser authority than the person being helped. For example, a father can help his son do his homework.[24] Or I can help my neighbor move his sofa. Or my son can help me clean

---

[23] Bilezikian claims that God approached Adam first not because there was any greater accountability for Adam as leader, but only because God had earlier spoken to Adam alone: "As the sole recipient of God's original order prohibiting consumption from the tree, God asked Adam to give an account of himself. That order had been given to Adam as a personal prohibition (2:17 is also in the second-person singular) when Eve was not yet formed. . . . God did not ask him any questions about Eve. Her turn would come." *Beyond Sex Roles*, 51.

I agree with Bilezikian that God had earlier commanded Adam alone regarding the forbidden tree, but that fact just reinforces the point, for God's actions in both cases imply a leadership role for Adam with respect to Eve. Just as God gave the command first to Adam alone, but Eve was also responsible to obey as soon as Adam told her of the command, so after the fall God spoke to Adam first and held him primarily accountable for disobeying the command he had received directly from God. This does not deny Eve's personal accountability (God also spoke to her), but it does assume Adam's leadership.

[24] I am taking this analogy from Ortlund, "Male-Female Equality," 104.

the garage. Yet the fact remains that *in each of these situations*, the person doing the helping puts himself in a subordinate role to the person who has primary responsibility for carrying out the activity. Even if a father helps his son with his homework, the primary responsibility for the homework remains his and not the father's. The father is just the helper. And even when God helps us, he still holds us primarily responsible for the activity, and therefore he holds us accountable for what we do.

But Genesis does not merely say that Eve was to function as Adam's helper in one or two specific events. Rather, it says that God made Eve to provide Adam with a helper, one who would function as his helper *by virtue of creation*.

> Then the LORD God said, "It is not good that the man should be alone; I will make him a helper fit for him." (2:18)

The Hebrew text can be translated literally as "I will make *for him* [Hebrew, *lô*] a helper fit for him." The apostle Paul understands this accurately, because he writes, "For indeed man was not created for the woman's sake, but woman for the man's sake" (1 Cor. 11:9, NASB). Eve's role, and the purpose that God had in mind when he created her, was that she would be "a helper . . . for him."

Yet in the same sentence God emphasized that she would not help him as one who was inferior to him. Rather, she was to be a helper "fit for him," and here the Hebrew word *kenegdô* means "a help corresponding to him," a help "equal and adequate to himself."[25] So Eve was created as a helper, but as a helper who was Adam's equal. She was created as one who differed from him, but who differed from him in ways that exactly complemented who Adam was.

7. The Conflict. The curse brought a distortion of previous roles, not the introduction of new roles. After Adam and Eve sinned, God spoke the following words of judgment to Eve:

> To the woman he said,
>
> "I will surely multiply your pain in childbearing;
>> in pain you shall bring forth children.
> *Your desire shall be contrary to your husband*,
>> but he shall rule over you." (Gen. 3:16)

The word translated as "desire" is an unusual Hebrew word, *teshûqāh*, which means "desire, urge, impulse" and can refer to a positive or negative impulse according to the context. Here it is used with the common preposition *'el*, which refers to motion toward something, and "where the motion or direction implied appears from the context to be of a hostile character," it has the sense "against."[26]

---

[25] This is the definition given in BDB, 617.

[26] BDB, 40; see also DCH, 4.265; NIDOTTE, 4:341–342. That the preposition *'el* can take the meaning "against" is clear, for example, from Gen. 4:8, which says, "Cain rose up *against* [*'el*] his brother Abel, and killed him."

In this context, the "desire" or impulse is best understood to be a negative one because the other components of God's pronouncement of a curse on Adam and Eve (3:16–19) are *all negative* (pain in childbearing, ill-effects on the ground, and their own eventual return to dust) and because a *positive* desire of Eve for Adam (for companionship or for sexual union) would not have been introduced as part of God's curse but would have existed before the fall. Therefore, the ESV translation, "Your desire shall be *contrary to* your husband," best expresses the sense of the verse.[27]

This understanding of Genesis 3:16 gains significant confirmation from the closely parallel expression in 4:7:

> Sin is crouching at the door. *Its desire is contrary to you*, but you must rule over it.

Here the sense is very clear. God pictures sin like a wild animal poised outside Cain's door, waiting to pounce on him and overpower him. In that sense, sin's "desire" or "instinctive urge" is "contrary to" him. This verse has a sequence of six Hebrew words that are identical or nearly identical to the wording in Genesis 3:16, which implies that the same idea—a negative or hostile desire—is in view in both verses.

Therefore, the sense of Genesis 3:16 is that, *as a judgment, God introduced conflict into the relationship between Adam and Eve* (her hostility toward him, his harsh rule over her), just as he introduced pain in childbearing to Eve (v. 16a) and pain in tilling the soil to Adam (vv. 17–19).[28]

Some have assumed that the "desire" in Genesis 3:16 refers to sexual desire.[29] Some Bible translations seem to support this idea by rendering this verse as, for example, "Yet your desire will be *for* your husband" (NASB). But this understanding is highly unlikely

---

[27] A similar sense is found in the translations of the NET Bible ("you will want to control your husband, but he will dominate you") and the New Living Translation ("you will desire to control your husband, but he will rule over you").

[28] The only other occurrence of *teshûqāh* in the entire Hebrew Old Testament (apart from Gen. 3:16 and 4:7) is in Song 7:10 (v. 11 in Hebrew): "I am my beloved's, and his *desire* is for me." In this context the word does not indicate a hostile or aggressive desire, but indicates the man's sexual desire for his wife. Therefore, Gen. 3:16 and 4:7 have the sense "desire, urge, impulse *contrary to*" and Song 7:10 has the sense "desire, urge, impulse *for*."

In any case, while the sense in Song 7:10 (11) is different, the context is different, and this example is removed in time and authorship from Gen. 3:16 and must be given lower importance in understanding the meaning of the word in Genesis. Surely the sense cannot be "sexual desire" in Gen. 4:7, and it seems very unlikely in the context of Gen. 3:16 as well.

Walter C. Kaiser Jr. argues that *teshûqāh* in Gen. 3:16 means "turning" and that the passage means that Eve's "turning" would be away from God and toward her husband. *Hard Sayings of the Old Testament* (Downers Grove, IL: InterVarsity Press, 1988), 34–35. The problem is that the text has no hint of any sense of "away from God," and Kaiser has to import that idea into the verse. In addition, the lexicons show no support for Kaiser's meaning for *teshûqāh* as a possibility (see BDB, HALOT, and NIDOTTE under *teshûqāh*). However, Kaiser rightly argues that the meaning "sexual desire" is contrary both to the context in Gen. 3:16 and to the rest of the Old Testament.

[29] See, for example, Belleville, *Women Leaders and the Church*, 106. She claims the use of *teshûqāh* in Song 7:10 (11), but she fails to discuss the difference in contexts.

because (1) the entire Bible views sexual desire within marriage as positive, not as evil or something that God imposed as a judgment; and (2) surely Adam and Eve had sexual desire for one another prior to their sin, for God had told them to "be fruitful and multiply" (Gen. 1:28), and certainly he would have given the desire that corresponded to the command. So "your desire" cannot refer to sexual desire. It is much more appropriate to the context of a curse to understand this as an aggressive desire *contrary to* her husband, one that would bring her into conflict with him.

Then God said that Adam "shall *rule* over you" (Gen. 3:16).[30] The Hebrew word here translated as "rule" is *māshal*, a common term in the Old Testament that regularly if not always refers to ruling by greater power, force, or strength. It is used of human military or political rulers, such as Joseph ruling over the land of Egypt (Gen. 45:26), the Philistines ruling over Israel (Judg. 14:4; 15:11), or Solomon ruling over all the kingdoms he had conquered (1 Kings 4:21). It is also used to speak of God ruling over the sea (Ps. 89:9) or over the earth generally (66:7). Sometimes it refers to oppressive rulers who cause the people under them to suffer (Neh. 9:37; Isa. 19:4). In any case, the word does not signify one who leads among equals, but rather one who rules by virtue of power and strength, and sometimes even rules harshly and selfishly.

Once we understand these two terms (for "desire" and "rule"), we can see much more clearly what was involved in the various aspects of the curse that God brought to Adam and Eve as punishment for their sins.

One aspect of the curse was the imposition of *pain on Adam's particular area of responsibility*, raising food from the ground:

> Cursed is the ground because of you;
>   in pain you shall eat of it all the days of your life;
> thorns and thistles it shall bring forth for you;
>   and you shall eat the plants of the field.
> By the sweat of your face
>   you shall eat bread,
> till you return to the ground. (Gen. 3:17–19)

Another aspect of the curse was the imposition of *pain on Eve's particular area of responsibility*, the bearing of children:

> I will surely multiply your pain in childbearing;
>   in pain you shall bring forth children (Gen. 3:16).

---

[30] Belleville says a "plausible" suggestion that "nicely fits the context" is "to read the pronoun *hû'* as *it* (neuter), rather than *he* (masculine). The wife's desire will be for her husband, and *it* (the desire) will rule her." *Women Leaders and the Church*, 107. Belleville shows no awareness that the word for "desire" (*teshûqāh*) is not masculine or neuter but feminine, and it would ordinarily require a feminine pronoun (*hî'*) for such a meaning. The pronoun *hû'* and the verb *yimshāl* ("he shall rule") are both masculine, and there is a corresponding masculine noun ("husband") that makes good sense in the immediate context. Belleville's suggestion simply does not match the Hebrew grammar of the verse.

And a third aspect of the curse was the introduction of *pain and conflict into the relationship* between Adam and Eve. Prior to their sin, they had lived in the garden of Eden in perfect harmony, yet with a leadership role belonging to Adam as the head of his family. But after the fall, God introduced conflict in that Eve would have an inward urging and impulse to oppose Adam, to resist his leadership (the verb *teshûqāh* + *'el*): "Your impulse, desire will be *contrary to* your husband." And Adam would respond with a rule over Eve that would come from his greater strength and aggressiveness, a rule that would be forceful and at times harsh (the verb *māshal*). We could paraphrase, "And he, because of his greater strength, will *rule* over you." There would be pain in tilling the ground, pain in bearing children, and pain and conflict in their relationship.

It is crucial at this point for us to realize that *we are never to try to increase or perpetuate the results of the curse.* We should never try to promote Genesis 3:16 as something good! In fact, the entire Bible after Genesis 3 is the story of God's working to overcome the effects of the curse that he imposed in his justice. Eventually God will bring in a new heaven and a new earth in which crops will come forth abundantly from the ground (Isa. 35:1–2; Amos 9:13; Rom. 8:20–21) and in which there will be no more pain or suffering (Rev. 21:4).

So we should *never* try to perpetuate the elements of the curse! We should not plant thorns and weeds in our gardens, but rather overcome them. We should do everything we can to alleviate the pain of childbirth for women. And we should do everything we can to undo the conflict that comes about through women desiring to oppose or even control their husbands, and husbands ruling harshly over them.

Therefore, Genesis 3:16 should never be used as a direct argument for male headship in marriage. But it does show us that the fall brought about a *distortion* of previous roles, not the introduction of new roles. The distortion was that Eve would now rebel against her husband's authority, while Adam would misuse that authority to rule forcefully and even harshly over Eve.[31]

8. The Restoration. When we come to the New Testament, salvation in Christ reaffirms the creation order. If the previous understanding of Genesis 3:16 is correct, as I believe it is, then what we would expect to find in the New Testament is a reversal of this curse. We would expect to find an *undoing* of the wife's hostile or aggressive impulses against her husband and the husband's response of harsh rule over his wife. In fact, that is exactly what we find. We read:

---

[31] The understanding of Gen. 3:16 as speaking of a hostile desire "contrary to" Eve's husband, or even a desire to rule over him, has gained significant support among Old Testament commentators. It was first suggested by Susan T. Foh, "What Is the Woman's Desire?" *WTJ* 37 (1975): 376–83. David Talley says the word is attested in Samaritan and Mishnaic Hebrew "with the meaning urge, craving, impulse," and says of Foh, "Her contention that the desire is a contention for leadership, a negative usage, seems probable for Genesis 3:16." NIDOTTE, 4:341, with reference to various commentators. Commentators who also understand "desire" in Gen. 3:16 to be a hostile one include C. John Collins, *Genesis 1–4* (Phillipsburg, NJ: P&R, 2006), 159–60, and Gordon J. Wenham, *Genesis 1–15*, WBC (Waco, TX: Word, 1987), 81–82. Bruce K. Waltke says, "Her desire will be to dominate." *Genesis: A Commentary* (Grand Rapids, MI: Zondervan, 2001), 94.

> Wives, *submit to your husbands*, as is fitting in the Lord. Husbands, *love your wives*, and *do not be harsh with them*. (Col. 3:18–19)

This command is an undoing of the impulse to oppose (Hebrew, *teshûqāh*) and the harsh rule (Hebrew, *māshal*) that God imposed at the curse. God reestablishes in the New Testament the beauty of the relationship between Adam and Eve that existed from the moment they were created. Eve was subject to Adam as the head of the family. Adam loved his wife and was not harsh with her in his leadership. That is the pattern that Paul commands husbands and wives to follow.[32]

9. The Mystery Revealed: The Relationship between Christ and the Church. From the beginning of creation, marriage was a picture of the relationship between Christ and the church. When the apostle Paul discusses marriage and wishes to speak of the relationship between a husband and wife, he does not look back to any sections of the Old Testament telling about the situation after sin came into the world. Rather, he looks all the way back to Genesis 2, prior to the fall, and uses that creation order to speak of marriage:

> "Therefore a man shall leave his father and mother and hold fast to his wife, and the two shall become one flesh." This mystery is profound, and I am saying that *it refers to Christ and the church.* (Eph. 5:31–32)

A "mystery" in Paul's writings is something that was understood only faintly if at all in the Old Testament, but that is made clearer in the New Testament. Here Paul makes clear the meaning of the "mystery" of marriage as God created it in the garden of Eden. Paul is saying that the "mystery" of Adam and Eve, the meaning that was not previously understood, is that marriage "refers to Christ and the church."

Although Adam and Eve did not know it, *their relationship represented the relationship between Christ and the church.* They were *created* to represent that relationship, and that is what *all marriages* are supposed to do. In that relationship, Adam represents Christ, while Eve represents the church, because Paul says, "The husband is the head of the wife *even as Christ is the head of the church*" (Eph. 5:23).

The relationship between Christ and the church is not culturally variable. It is the same for all generations. And it is not reversible. There is a leadership or headship role that belongs to Christ, a role that the church does not have. Similarly, in marriage as God created it to be, there is a leadership role for the husband that the wife does not have. This relationship was there from the beginning, in the beautiful marriage between Adam and Eve in the garden.

---

[32] There was a foreshadowing of these New Testament commands in several godly marriages recounted in the Old Testament and the honor given to women in passages such as Ruth, Esther, and Proverbs 31. But in the unfolding of God's plan of redemption, he waited until the New Testament to give the full and explicit directions for the marriage relationship that we find in Ephesians 5, Colossians 3, and 1 Peter 3.

10. The Parallel with the Trinity. The equality, differences, and unity between men and women reflect the equality, differences, and unity in the Trinity.

Though I list this here as the 10th argument why there were differences in roles between men and women from creation, I will discuss it in detail in a later section (see p. 413).

Here, then, are 10 arguments showing differences in the roles of men and women *before the fall*. Some arguments are not as forceful as others, though all have some force. Some of them whisper male headship, and some shout it clearly. But they form a cumulative case showing that Adam and Eve had distinct roles before the fall, and this was God's purpose when he created them. This is significant because it shows that male leadership in marriage is not a result of sin but was part of how God created man and woman at the beginning.

D. NEW TESTAMENT TEACHING ON THE HUSBAND'S LEADERSHIP ROLE

The New Testament reaffirms in several passages both the equality of men and women as created in the image of God (as discussed in the first section of this chapter) and a leadership role for the husband within marriage. The passages on a husband's leadership include:

> *Wives, submit to your own husbands, as to the Lord.* For the husband is the head of the wife even as Christ is the head of the church, his body, and is himself its Savior. Now as the church submits to Christ, so also wives should submit in everything to their husbands. *Husbands, love your wives, as Christ loved the church and gave himself up for her*, that he might sanctify her, having cleansed her by the washing of water with the word, so that he might present the church to himself in splendor, without spot or wrinkle or any such thing, that she might be holy and without blemish. In the same way husbands should love their wives as their own bodies. He who loves his wife loves himself. (Eph. 5:22–28)

The most common egalitarian objection to these verses is to say that the passage actually teaches "mutual submission," because the immediately preceding verse says all Christians should be "*submitting to one another* out of reverence for Christ" (Eph. 5:21).

However, that is not a persuasive objection, because *the following context specifies the kind of submission Paul has in mind.* He explains that wives are to be subject to their husbands (Eph. 5:22–23), children are to be subject to their parents (6:1), and bondservants are to be subject to their masters (6:5). These relationships are never reversed. He does not tell husbands to be subject to wives, parents to be subject to their children (thus nullifying all parental authority), or masters to be subject to their servants. In fact,

Paul does not tell husbands and wives generally to be subject to each other, nor does he tell wives to be subject to other women's husbands! He says, "Wives, submit to *your own husbands*, as to the Lord" (5:22).[33]

Therefore, what Paul has in mind is not a vague kind of "mutual submission" in which everybody is "considerate and thoughtful" to everybody else, but a specific kind of submission to an authority: the wife is subject to the authority of "her own husband." Similarly, parents and children aren't told to practice "mutual submission," but children are to be subject to ("obey") their parents (Eph. 6:1–3), and servants are told to be subject to ("obey") their masters (Eph. 6:5–8).[34]

Another egalitarian objection is that the term "head" (Greek, *kephalē*) in Ephesians 5:23, "the husband is the *head* of the wife," really means "source" rather than "authority over." But this would not make sense in the context of Ephesians 5, for husbands are not the "source" of their wives![35] And this is a claim with no persuasive evidence to support it, because, in ancient Greek literature, there are more than 50 examples in which one person is said to be the "head" of another person, and in every case the person who is said to be the "head" is in a position of authority over the other person. There are no exceptions.[36]

Other passages in the New Testament also affirm these distinct roles for husbands and wives within marriage:

> *Wives, submit to your husbands,* as is fitting in the Lord. *Husbands, love your wives,* and do not be harsh with them. (Col. 3:18–19)

> Older women likewise are to be reverent in behavior, not slanderers or slaves to much wine. They are to teach what is good, and so *train the young women*

---

[33] The Greek text has the adjective *idios*, meaning "your own."

[34] Daniel Doriani's study of the history of the interpretation of Eph. 5:21 demonstrated that a number of earlier writers thought that a kind of "mutual submission" was taught in the verse, but that such "submission" took very different forms for those *in authority* and for those *under authority*. They took it to mean that those in authority should govern wisely and with sacrificial concern for those under their authority. But Doriani found no author in the history of the church prior to the advent of feminism in the last half of the 20th century who thought that "be subject to one another" in Eph. 5:21 nullified the authority of the husband within marriage. It is precarious to claim that a New Testament verse means what no one in the history of the church has ever thought that it meant. See Daniel Doriani, "The Historical Novelty of Egalitarian Interpretations of Ephesians 5:21–22," in Grudem, ed., *Biblical Foundations for Manhood and Womanhood*, 203–19.

[35] Egalitarians answer that this is an allusion to the creation of Eve from Adam's rib, but Paul is not talking about Adam and Eve in this verse but about husbands and wives in general.

[36] I have quoted all of these examples in *Evangelical Feminism and Biblical Truth*, 544–51. See also my extended discussion of the meaning of *kephalē* in "The Meaning of *kephalē* ("head"): An Analysis of New Evidence, Real and Alleged," *JETS* 44, no. 1 (March 2001): 25–65. This *JETS* article is reprinted in *Evangelical Feminism and Biblical Truth*, 552–99 (including new material added in response to Anthony Thiselton, 592–96). My two earlier studies on *kephalē* were "Does *kephalē* ("head") Mean 'Source' or 'Authority Over' in Greek Literature? A Survey of 2,336 Examples," in *TrinJ*, n.s., 6 (1985): 38–59 (also published as an appendix in George W. Knight III, *The Role Relationship of Men and Women: New Testament Teaching*, rev. ed. [Chicago: Moody, 1985], 49–80); and "The Meaning of *kephalē* ("Head"): A Response to Recent Studies," *TrinJ*, n.s., 11 (1990): 3–72 (reprinted in Piper and Grudem, eds., *Recovering Biblical Manhood and Womanhood*, 425–68).

to love their husbands and children, to be self-controlled, pure, working at home, kind, *and submissive to their own husbands*, that the word of God may not be reviled. (Titus 2:3–5)

Likewise, *wives, be subject to your own husbands*, so that even if some do not obey the word, they may be won without a word by the conduct of their wives, when they see your respectful and pure conduct. Do not let your adorning be external—the braiding of hair and the putting on of gold jewelry, or the clothing you wear—but let your adorning be the hidden person of the heart with the imperishable beauty of a gentle and quiet spirit, which in God's sight is very precious. For this is how the holy women who hoped in God used to adorn themselves, *by submitting to their own husbands, as Sarah obeyed Abraham, calling him lord.* And you are her children, if you do good and do not fear anything that is frightening. Likewise, *husbands, live with your wives in an understanding way*, showing honor to the woman as the weaker vessel, since they are heirs with you of the grace of life, so that your prayers may not be hindered. (1 Pet. 3:1–7)[37]

E. AN ILLUSTRATION OF HOW THESE PRINCIPLES WORK IN PRACTICE

I would like to say something at this point about how male-female equality and male headship work out in actual practice. The situation I know best is my own marriage, so I will speak about it briefly.[38]

In our marriage, Margaret and I talk frequently and at length about many decisions. Sometimes these are large decisions (such as buying a house or a car), and sometimes they are small decisions (such as where we should go for a walk together). I often defer to her wishes, and she often defers to mine, because we love each other. In almost every case, each of us has some wisdom and insight that the other does not have, and we have learned to listen to each other and to place much trust in each other's judgment. Usually we reach agreement on the decision. Very seldom will I do something that she does not think to be wise. She prays, she loves God, and she is sensitive to the Lord's leading and direction, so I greatly respect her and the wisdom God gives her.

But in every decision, whether large or small, and whether we have reached agreement or not, the responsibility to make the decision still rests with me. (I am speaking here of decisions that involve both of us, not individual decisions we each make about

---

[37] I discuss other egalitarian objections to these verses at some length in *Evangelical Feminism and Biblical Truth*, 183–219, 329–61.

[38] Much additional material on the way husbands and wives should relate if they want to follow biblical teachings can be found on the website of the Council on Biblical Manhood and Womanhood, www.cbmw .org.

our personal spheres of responsibility.) I do not agree with those who say that male headship makes a difference only once in 10 years or so, when a husband and wife can't reach agreement. I think that male headship makes a difference in *every decision* that a couple makes every day of their married life. If there is genuine male headship in the marriage, there is a quiet, subtle acknowledgment that the focus of the decision-making process is the husband, not the wife. And even though there will often be much discussion, and there should be much mutual respect and consideration of each other, yet ultimately the responsibility to make the decision rests with the husband. And so in our marriage, the responsibility to make the decision rests with me.

This is not because I am wiser or a more gifted leader. It is because I am the husband, and God has given me that responsibility. In the face of cultural pressures to the contrary, I will not forsake this male headship; I will not deny it; and I will not be embarrassed by it.

This biblical pattern is God-given. It is very good. It brings peace and joy to our marriage, and both Margaret and I are thankful for it.

Yet there are dangers of distortion. Putting this biblical pattern into practice is a challenge, because we can err in one direction or the other. There are errors of passivity and errors of aggressiveness on either side of the biblical ideal. This can be seen in the following chart:

	Errors of Passivity	Biblical Ideal	Errors of Aggressiveness
Husband	Wimp	Loving, humble headship	Tyrant
Wife	Doormat	Joyful, intelligent submission	Usurper

Table 15.1. The Biblical Ideal and Errors Spouses Can Make.

The biblical ideal on the part of the husband, in the center column, is loving, humble headship, following Ephesians 5:25–33. The biblical ideal on the part of the wife is joyful, intelligent submission to and support of her husband's leadership, in accordance with Ephesians 5:22–24 and 31–33.

On the right side of the chart, the errors of aggressiveness are those that had their beginning, as we saw, in Genesis 3:16. The husband can become selfish, harsh, and domineering, acting like a "tyrant." This is not biblical headship, but a tragic distortion of it. A wife can also demonstrate errors of aggressiveness when she resists her husband's leadership, not supporting it but fighting against it and creating conflict every step of the way. She can become a "usurper," a tragic distortion of the biblical pattern of equality in the image of God.

On the left side of the chart are the opposite errors, the errors of passivity. A husband can abdicate his leadership and neglect his responsibilities. The children need to be disciplined, but he sits and watches TV and does nothing. The family is not going to church regularly, but he is passive and does nothing. The family keeps going further into debt, but he closes his eyes to it and does nothing. Some relative or friend is verbally harassing his wife, but he does nothing. This also is a tragic distortion of the biblical pattern. He has become a "wimp."

A wife can also commit errors of passivity. Rather than participating actively in family decisions, rather than contributing her wisdom and insight that is so much needed, her only response to every question is, "Yes, dear, whatever you say." She knows her husband and her children are doing wrong, but she says nothing. Her husband becomes verbally or physically abusive, but she never objects and never seeks church discipline or civil intervention to bring about an end to the abuse. She never expresses her preferences about friendships or family vacations, or her opinions about people or events. She thinks that what is required of her is to be "submissive" to her husband. But this also is a tragic distortion of biblical patterns. She has become a "doormat."

We all have different backgrounds, personalities, and temperaments. We also have different areas of life in which our sanctification is less complete. Some of us are more prone toward errors of aggressiveness, while others are more prone toward errors of passivity. We can even fall into errors of aggressiveness in our homes and errors of passivity when we visit our in-laws. Or it can be the other way around. In order to maintain a healthy, biblical balance, we need to keep reading God's Word each day and continue praying for God's help to obey his Word as best we can.

F. THE HUSBAND'S RESPONSIBILITY TO PROVIDE FOR AND PROTECT HIS WIFE AND FAMILY, AND THE WIFE'S RESPONSIBILITY TO CARE FOR THE HOME AND TO NURTURE CHILDREN

There are other differences in roles in addition to headship and submission. Two other aspects of a husband's headship in marriage are the responsibility to *provide for* and to *protect* his wife and family. A corresponding responsibility for the wife is to have primary responsibility to care for *home* and *children*. Each can help the other, but there remain primary responsibilities that are not shared equally.

These responsibilities are mentioned in both the Danvers Statement and the Southern Baptist Convention statement quoted above. I will not discuss these in detail at this point, but simply note that these additional aspects of differing roles are also established in Scripture.

Biblical support for the husband having the *primary* responsibility to provide for his family and the wife having *primary* responsibility to care for the household and children is found in Genesis 2:15, along with 2:18–23 and 3:16–19 (Eve is assumed to have the primary responsibility for childbearing, but Adam for tilling the ground to raise food, and pain is introduced into both of their areas of responsibility); Proverbs 31:10–31, especially verses 15, 21, 27; Isaiah 4:1 (shame at the tragic undoing of the normal order); 1 Timothy 5:8 (the Greek text does not specify "any man," but in the historical context that would have been the assumed referent except for unusual situations such as a household with no father); 1 Timothy 5:3–16 (widows, not widowers, are to be supported by the church); and Titus 2:5.

However, to say that the husband has the primary responsibility to provide for his family does not imply that it is wrong for a wife also to work at an income-producing job if she wants to and has opportunity to do so. In agricultural societies throughout history, including in biblical times, both women and men shared in many of the work responsibilities connected with farming (for example, see Ruth 2:22–23 and Prov. 31:13–31). But the primary responsibility to provide for the family still belongs to the husband. Similarly, it is entirely appropriate for the husband to help regularly, as he has opportunity, with care of the household and the children (see Prov. 1:8; 4:1; Eph. 6:4). But the primary responsibility for caring for the household and raising the children still belongs to the wife.[39]

Biblical support for the idea that the man has the *primary* responsibility to protect his family is found in Numbers 1:2–3 (only the men are "able to go to war"); Deuteronomy 3:18–19 (the men go to war while the women and children stay at home); Deuteronomy 20:7–8 and 24:5 (men go forth to war, not women, here and in many other Old Testament passages); Joshua 1:14; Judges 4:8–10 (Barak does not get the glory because he insisted that a woman accompany him into battle); Nehemiah 4:13–14 (the people are to fight for their brothers, homes, wives, and children, but it does not say they are to fight for their husbands); Jeremiah 50:37 (it is the disgrace of a nation when women become its warriors); Nahum 3:13 ("Behold, your troops are women in your midst" is a taunt of derision); Matthew 2:13–14 (Joseph is told to protect Mary and baby Jesus by taking them to Egypt); Ephesians 5:25 (a husband's love should extend even to a willingness to lay down his life for his wife, something many soldiers in battle have done throughout history to protect their families and homelands); and 1 Peter 3:7 (a

---

[39] Jewish psychoanalyst and clinical social worker Erica Komisar argued for the importance of mothers caring for children in her book *Being There: Why Prioritizing Motherhood in the First Three Years Matters* (New York: Penguin Random House, 2017). According to an interview in *The Wall Street Journal*, her book "draws on research in psychology, neuroscience and epigenetics" to argue that "mothers are biologically necessary for babies," not only for pregnancy and birth, but also for the development of children's ability to practice healthy emotional responses in social interactions throughout their lives.

She argues that "every time a mother comforts a baby in distress, she's actually regulating the baby's emotions from the outside in. After three years, the baby internalizes that ability to regulate their emotions, but not until then." For that reason mothers "need to be there as much as possible, both physically and emotionally, for children in the first 1000 days."

Komisar reports that in three decades of treating families who came to her practice, she has noticed an increase in children diagnosed with attention-deficit/hyperactivity disorder (ADHD), as well as more frequent aggression in little boys and depression in little girls, and other social disorders in which children were "having difficulty relating to other children, having difficulty with empathy." She then says, "The absence of mothers in children's lives on a daily basis was what I saw to be one of the triggers for these mental disorders." James Taranto, "The Politicization of Motherhood," *The Wall Street Journal*, Oct. 28–29, 2017, A11, https://www.wsj.com/articles/the-politicization-of-motherhood-1509144044.

wife is a "weaker vessel," and therefore the husband, as generally stronger, has a greater responsibility to use his strength to protect his wife).

In addition, there is the complete absence of evidence from the other side. Nowhere can we find Scripture passages encouraging women to be the primary means of support while their husbands care for the house and children. Nowhere can we find Scripture encouraging women to be the primary protectors of their husbands. Certainly women can help in these roles as time and circumstances allow (see Gen. 2:18–23), but they are not the ones primarily responsible for them.

Finally, there is the internal testimony from both men's and women's hearts. There is something in a man that says, "I don't want to be dependent on a woman to provide for me in the long term. I want to be the one responsible to provide for the family, the one my wife looks to and depends on for support." I have never met a man who is able to work and yet does not feel some measure of shame at the idea of being supported by his wife in the long term.

However, I recognize that in many families there may be a temporary reversal of roles due to involuntary unemployment or while the husband is getting further education, and in those circumstances these are entirely appropriate arrangements; yet the longer they go on, the more strain they put on a marriage. I also recognize that a husband's permanent disability or involuntary unemployment when he is earnestly seeking a job with adequate pay, or the absence of a husband in the home, can create a necessity for the wife to be the primary provider, but families in which that happens often testify to the unusual stress it brings and that they wish it did not have to be so.

On the other hand, there is something in a woman that says, "I want my husband to provide for me, to give me the security of knowing that we will have enough to buy groceries and pay the bills. It feels right to me to look to him and depend on him for that responsibility." I have never met a woman who did not want her husband to provide that sense of security for her.[40]

G. THE EQUALITY OF AND DIFFERENCES BETWEEN MEN AND WOMEN REFLECT BY ANALOGY THE EQUALITY AND DIFFERENCES IN THE TRINITY

In 1 Corinthians 11, Paul writes:

> But I want you to understand that the *head* of every man is Christ, the *head* of a wife is her husband, and the *head* of Christ is God. (v. 3)

In this verse, "head" (Greek, *kephalē*) refers to one who is in a position of authority

---

[40] For some further discussion, see John Piper, "A Vision of Biblical Complementarity," in Piper and Grudem, eds., *Recovering Biblical Manhood and Womanhood*, 31–59. See also Dorothy Patterson, "The High Calling of Wife and Mother in Biblical Perspective," ibid., 364–77.

over another, as this Greek word uniformly does whenever it is used in ancient literature to say that one person is "head of" another person or a group.[41] So Paul is here referring to a relationship of authority between God the Father and God the incarnate Son, and he is making a parallel between that Trinitarian relationship in the divine economy and the relationship between the husband and wife in marriage. This is an important analogy, one that must be drawn with care, but that at the very least shows that there can be *equality* and *differences* in relationships between persons at the same time. We can illustrate that in the following diagram, where the arrows indicate authority to exercise leadership with respect to the person to whom the arrow points:

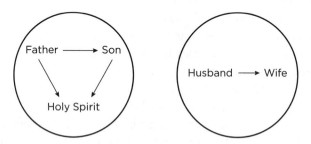

Figure 15.1. Authority in the Trinity and in Marriage. (Source: Wayne Grudem, *Evangelical Feminism and Biblical Truth: An Analysis of More Than 100 Disputed Questions* [Wheaton, IL: Crossway, 2004, 2012]. Adapted with permission.)

Just as the Father and Son are equal in their deity and in all their attributes, but distinguished in their person relations (as seen in their specific roles as God's plan unfolds), so a husband and wife are equal in dignity and value as image-bearers of God, but different in the roles God has given them. Just as God the Son is subject to the authority of God the Father, so God has planned that wives be subject to the authority of their husbands, which in no way minimizes their shared value.

Scripture frequently speaks of the Father-Son relationship within the Trinity, a relationship in which the Father "gave" his only Son (John 3:16); "sent" the Son into the world (3:17, 34; 4:34; 8:42; Gal. 4:4); "predestined" us to be conformed to the image of his Son (Rom. 8:29; cf. 1 Pet. 1:2); and "chose us" in the Son "before the foundation of the world" (Eph. 1:4). The Son obeys the commands of the Father who sent him (John 12:49) and says that he came to do "the will of him who sent me" (John 4:34; 6:38). All of these passages either imply or assume the equal deity of the Father and Son, yet they still teach a distinction of the persons in terms of roles.

And these relationships are never reversed. Never does Scripture say that the Son sends the Father into the world, that the Holy Spirit sends the Father or the Son into the world, or that the Father obeys the commands of the Son or the Holy Spirit. Never

---

[41] See discussion above, p. 408 and footnote 36.

does Scripture say that the Son predestined us to be conformed to the image of the Father. The role of predestining us, and sending and giving the Son, belongs to the Father only.

And the biblical evidence seems to indicate that these person relations are eternal, for the Father predestined us in the Son "*before* the foundation of the world" (Eph. 1:4), requiring that the Father has eternally been the Father and the Son has eternally been the Son. If the Father's love is seen in that he "gave his only Son" (John 3:16), then the Father had to be the Father and the Son had to be the Son before the Son came into the world. The Father did not give someone who was just another divine person in the Trinity, but he gave the One who was his only Son, the One who eternally had been his Son.

In addition, the names "Father" and "Son" have great significance for this question of their person properties. Within the Trinity, the eternally unbegotten Father has eternally been the Father, the eternally begotten Son has eternally been the Son, and the eternally proceeding Holy Spirit has eternally been the Holy Spirit. The names "Father" and "Son" in themselves signify personal distinctions within the Godhead and an eternal ordering reflected in an authority or leadership role for the One who is the Father, as every biblical author and every reader in the cultures of the biblical world would have recognized.

It was also this way in the creation of the world, where the Father initiated, commanded, and created "through" the Son (Heb. 1:2). The Son was the powerful Word of God who carried out the commands of the Father, for "all things were made through him" (John 1:3). All things were created by the Father working through the Son, for "there is one God, the Father, *from* whom are all things . . . and one Lord, Jesus Christ, *through* whom are all things" (1 Cor. 8:6). Nowhere does Scripture reverse this and say that the Son created "through" the Father.

The Son now sits at the Father's *right hand* (Rom. 8:34; Heb. 1:3, 13; 1 Pet. 3:22);[42] the Father does not sit at the Son's right hand. The Son receives from the Father the authority to pour forth the Holy Spirit in new covenant fullness (Matt. 28:18; Acts 2:33), makes intercession before the Father (Heb. 7:25), and receives revelation from the Father to give to the church (Rev. 1:1). The Father does not pray to the Son and does not receive revelation from the Son to give to the church.

Finally, for all eternity, the Son will be subject to the Father, for after the last enemy, death, is destroyed, the incarnate and triumphant "Son himself will also be subjected to him who put all things in subjection under him, that God may be all in all" (1 Cor. 15:28).[43]

We see from these passages then that *the idea of headship and submission within a*

---

[42] In both the Old Testament (Ps. 45:9; 110:1) and the New Testament (Matt. 20:21), the person sitting at the right hand of the king is subject to his authority.

[43] There has been some controversy about whether the Son has been eternally subject to the Father or whether this subjection is only for activities related to Christ's incarnation. Several discussions related to this issue are found in Dennis W. Jowers and H. Wayne House, eds., *The New Evangelical Subordinationism? Perspectives on the Equality of God the Father and God the Son* (Eugene, OR: Pickwick, 2012), and Bruce A. Ware and John Starke, eds., *One God in Three Persons: Unity of Essence, Distinction of Persons, Implications for Life* (Wheaton, IL: Crossway, 2015). (I contributed essays to each of these volumes, defending in more

personal filial relationship did not begin with some writings of the apostle Paul in the first century. Neither did it begin with a few patriarchal men in a patriarchal society in the Old Testament. Nor did the idea of headship and submission begin with Adam and Eve's fall into sin (Genesis 3). In fact, the idea of headship and submission did not even begin with the creation of Adam and Eve (Genesis 1–2). No, the idea of headship and submission within a personal relationship existed *before creation*, that is, uniquely within God. Now, as a result of creation, it exists analogously in human relationships.

Even if someone does not agree with my conclusion that the authority/submission relationship of the Father and the Son has existed *eternally*, there is still abundant biblical evidence that such a relationship has existed from the creation of the world, when the Father created through the Son, and continues even today, with the Son sitting at the right hand of the Father. Therefore, we can still see in the Trinity today an example of full equality in deity together with submission or roles, and this is still analogous to the husband-wife relationship in marriage.

The Father, Son, and Holy Spirit do not differ in any attributes, but only in how they relate to one another. And the outworking of that relationship is one of leadership and authority on the one hand and voluntary, willing, joyful submission to that authority on the other hand.

We can learn from this relationship among the persons of the Trinity that submission to a rightful authority is a noble virtue. It is a privilege. It is good and desirable. It is the virtue that the eternal Son of God has demonstrated *forever*. It is his glory, the glory of the Son as he relates to his Father.

In modern societies, we tend to think that if you are a person who has authority over another, that's a good thing, whereas if you are someone who has to submit to an authority, that's a bad thing. But that is the world's viewpoint, and it is not true. Submission to a rightful authority is a good, noble, and wonderful thing, because it is established by God himself for our good.

We can say then that there is a relationship of authority and submission between equals, with mutual giving of honor, that is part of the most fundamental and most glorious interpersonal relationship in the universe, that of the three persons in the Trinity, and that this kind of relationship also shows itself in God's creation of human relationships. Such a relationship allows for interpersonal differences without "better" or "worse," without "more important" and "less important."

When we begin to dislike the very idea of authority and submission—not distortions and abuses, but *the very idea*—we are tampering with something very deep. We are beginning to dislike God himself.

This teaching about the Trinity creates a problem for egalitarians. They try to force people to choose between equality and authority. They say, "If you have male headship, then you can't be equal. Or if you are equal, then you can't have male headship." And

detail the position I have advocated here, namely, that the Son is eternally subject to the Father, though fully equal in deity and in all attributes of deity.)

our complementarian response is that you *can* have both: just look at the Trinity. Within the being of God, there is both equality and authority.

In reply to this, egalitarians should say, "OK, we agree on this much. In God you *can* have equality and differences at the same time." In fact, some egalitarians have said this very thing.[44] But some prominent egalitarians have taken a different direction. Both Gilbert Bilezikian and Stanley Grenz have now written that they think there is "mutual submission" within the Trinity instead of ordered relations between the divine persons. They say that the Father also submits to the Son.[45] They make this affirmation even though no passage of Scripture affirms such a relationship, and even though an affirmation of ordered relations among the divine persons has always been the orthodox teaching of the church. This is a troubling and dangerous move. If we are to be biblical, we must preserve both equality *and* role differences in human relationships, which is analogous to the deep and beautiful relationships within the Godhead among Father, Son, and Holy Spirit.

H. THE EQUALITY OF AND DIFFERENCES BETWEEN MEN AND WOMEN ARE VERY GOOD

In today's hostile culture, we might be embarrassed to talk about God-given differences between men and women. We don't want to be attacked or laughed at by others. Perhaps we fear that someone will take offense if we talk clearly about such differences.

The fundamental statement of the excellence of our similarities and differences as men and women is found in Genesis 1:31: "And God saw everything that he had made, and behold, *it was very good*." Just four verses after the Bible tells us that God made us "male and female," it tells us that God looked at everything he had made, *including Adam and Eve created in his image*, and his evaluation of what he saw was that it was "very good." The way God created us as men and women, equal in his image and different in roles, is very good. And if it is very good, then we can make some other observations about the created order.

This created order is *fair*. Our egalitarian friends argue that it's "not fair" for men to

---

[44] See Craig Keener's "Is Subordination within the Trinity Really Heresy? A Study of John 5:18 in Context," *TrinJ*, n.s., 20 (1999): 39–51.

[45] For a fuller discussion of egalitarian thinking with regard to the doctrine of the Trinity, see Bruce A. Ware, "Tampering with the Trinity: Does the Son Submit to His Father?" in Grudem, ed., *Biblical Foundations for Manhood and Womanhood*, 233–53. See also my discussion of the egalitarian claim of mutual submission in the Trinity in *Evangelical Feminism and Biblical Truth*, 429–33; see also 405–29.

More recently, I have written two additional contributions to this discussion: Wayne Grudem, "Biblical Evidence for the Eternal Submission of the Son to the Father," in *The New Evangelical Subordinationism?*, 223–61, and Wayne Grudem, "Doctrinal Deviations in the Evangelical-Feminist Arguments about the Trinity," in *One God in Three Persons*, 17–45.

The primary statements by Bilezikian and Grenz are found in Bilezikian, "Hermeneutical Bungee-Jumping: Subordination in the Godhead," *JETS* 40, no. 1 (March 1997): 57–68, and Grenz, "Theological Foundations for Male-Female Relationships," *JETS* 41, no. 4 (December 1998): 615–30.

have a leadership role in the family simply because they are men. But if this difference is based on God's assignment of roles from the beginning, then it is fair. Does the Son say to the Father, "It's not fair for you to be in charge simply because you are the Father"? Does the Son say to the Father, "You've been in charge for fifteen billion years, and now it's my turn for the next fifteen billion"? Absolutely not! Rather, he fulfilled the psalm that said, "I delight to do your will, O my God; your law is within my heart" (Ps. 40:8; cf. Heb. 10:7). Of his relationship with the Father, he said, "I always do the things that are pleasing to him" (John 8:29) and "I have come down from heaven, not to do my own will but the will of him who sent me" (John 6:38). The order of relationships within the Trinity is fair. And the order of relationships established by God for marriage is fair.

This created order is also *best for us*, because it comes from an all-wise Creator. This order truly honors men and women. It does not lead to abuse, but guards against it, because both men and women are equal in value before God. It does not suppress women's gifts, wisdom, and insight, as people sometimes have done in the past, but encourages them.

This created order is also a *mystery*. I have been married to one very wonderful woman for 48 years. I cannot understand her. Just when I think I understand her, she surprises me again. Marriage is a challenge! And it's also very fun. But in our relationships with each other as men and women, there will always be elements of surprise, mystery, and difference that we cannot fully understand but simply enjoy.

This created order is also *beautiful*. God took delight in it and thought it was "very good." When it is functioning in the way that God intended, we will enjoy this relationship and delight in it, because there is a Godlike quality about it. And though some elements of modern societies have been pushing in the opposite direction for several decades, there is much evidence from "natural law"—from our observation of the world and our inner sense of right and wrong—that different roles within marriage are *right*. This is what we meant when we said in the Danvers Statement, "Distinctions in masculine and feminine roles are ordained by God . . . and should find an echo in every human heart" (Affirmation 2). God's created order for marriage is beautiful because it is God's way to bring amazing *unity* to people who are as *different* as men and women are.

The beauty of God's created order for marriage finds expression in our sexuality within marriage. "Therefore a man shall leave his father and his mother and hold fast to his wife, and they shall become one flesh" (Gen. 2:24). God designed our sexuality so that it reflects unity, differences, and beauty all at the same time. As husband and wife, we are most attracted to the parts of each other that are the most different. Our deepest unity—including a physical, emotional, and spiritual unity—comes at the point where we are most different. In our physical union, as God intended it, there is no dehumanization of women and no emasculation of men, but there is equality and honor for both the husband and the wife. And there is our deepest human joy and our deepest expression of unity.

This means that sexuality within marriage is precious to God. He designed it to show *equality*, *difference*, and *unity* all at the same time. It is a great mystery how this can be so, and it is also a great blessing and joy. Moreover, God has ordained that from the sexual union comes the most amazing, astounding event—the creation of new human beings in the image of God!

Within this most intimate of human relationships, we show equality, difference, unity, and much Godlikeness all at once. Glory be to God!

I. APPENDIX: THE DANVERS STATEMENT

In December 1987, the newly formed Council on Biblical Manhood and Womanhood met in Danvers, Massachusetts, to compose the Danvers Statement on Biblical Manhood and Womanhood. Prior to the listing of the actual affirmations that comprise the Danvers Statement, we have included a section detailing contemporary developments that serve as the rationale for these affirmations. We offer this statement to the evangelical world, knowing that it will stimulate healthy discussion, hoping that it will gain widespread assent.

Rationale

We have been moved in our purpose by the following contemporary developments, which we observe with deep concern:

1. The widespread uncertainty and confusion in our culture regarding the complementary differences between masculinity and femininity;
2. the tragic effects of this confusion in unraveling the fabric of marriage woven by God out of the beautiful and diverse strands of manhood and womanhood;
3. the increasing promotion given to feminist egalitarianism with accompanying distortions or neglect of the glad harmony portrayed in Scripture between the loving, humble leadership of redeemed husbands and the intelligent, willing support of that leadership by redeemed wives;
4. the widespread ambivalence regarding the values of motherhood, vocational homemaking, and the many ministries historically performed by women;
5. the growing claims of legitimacy for sexual relationships which have biblically and historically been considered illicit or perverse, and the increase in pornographic portrayal of human sexuality;
6. the upsurge of physical and emotional abuse in the family;
7. the emergence of roles for men and women in church leadership that do not conform to biblical teaching but backfire in the crippling of biblically faithful witness;

8. the increasing prevalence and acceptance of hermeneutical oddities devised to reinterpret apparently plain meanings of biblical texts;

9. the consequent threat to biblical authority as the clarity of Scripture is jeopardized and the accessibility of its meaning to ordinary people is withdrawn into the restricted realm of technical ingenuity;

10. and behind all this the apparent accommodation of some within the church to the spirit of the age at the expense of winsome, radical biblical authenticity which in the power of the Holy Spirit may reform rather than reflect our ailing culture.

Affirmations

Based on our understanding of biblical teachings, we affirm the following:

1. Both Adam and Eve were created in God's image, equal before God as persons and distinct in their manhood and womanhood (Gen. 1:26–27; 2:18).

2. Distinctions in masculine and feminine roles are ordained by God as part of the created order, and should find an echo in every human heart (Gen. 2:18, 21–24; 1 Cor. 11:7–9; 1 Tim. 2:12–14).

3. Adam's headship in marriage was established by God before the fall, and was not a result of sin (Gen. 2:16–18, 21–24; 3:1–13; 1 Cor. 11:7–9).

4. The fall introduced distortions into the relationships between men and women (Gen. 3:1–7, 12, 16).

   • In the home, the husband's loving, humble headship tends to be replaced by domination or passivity; the wife's intelligent, willing submission tends to be replaced by usurpation or servility.

   • In the church, sin inclines men toward a worldly love of power or an abdication of spiritual responsibility, and inclines women to resist limitations on their roles or to neglect the use of their gifts in appropriate ministries.

5. The Old Testament, as well as the New Testament, manifests the equally high value and dignity which God attached to the roles of both men and women (Gen. 1:26–27; 2:18; Gal. 3:28). Both Old and New Testaments also affirm the principle of male headship in the family and in the covenant community (Gen. 2:18; Eph. 5:21–33; Col. 3:18–19; 1 Tim. 2:11–15).

6. Redemption in Christ aims at removing the distortions introduced by the curse.

   • In the family, husbands should forsake harsh or selfish leadership and grow in love and care for their wives; wives should forsake resistance to their husbands' authority and grow in willing, joyful submission to their husbands' leadership (Eph. 5:21–33; Col. 3:18–19; Titus 2:3–5; 1 Pet. 3:1–7).

- In the church, redemption in Christ gives men and women an equal share in the blessings of salvation; nevertheless, some governing and teaching roles within the church are restricted to men (Gal. 3:28; 1 Cor. 11:2–16; 1 Tim. 2:11–15).

7. In all of life Christ is the supreme authority and guide for men and women, so that no earthly submission—domestic, religious, or civil—ever implies a mandate to follow a human authority into sin (Dan. 3:10–18; Acts 4:19–20; 5:27–29; 1 Pet. 3:1–2).

8. In both men and women a heartfelt sense of call to ministry should never be used to set aside biblical criteria for particular ministries (1 Tim. 2:11–15, 3:1–13; Titus 1:5–9). Rather, biblical teaching should remain the authority for testing our subjective discernment of God's will.

9. With half the world's population outside the reach of indigenous evangelism; with countless other lost people in those societies that have heard the gospel; with the stresses and miseries of sickness, malnutrition, homelessness, illiteracy, ignorance, aging, addiction, crime, incarceration, neuroses, and loneliness, no man or woman who feels a passion from God to make His grace known in word and deed need ever live without a fulfilling ministry for the glory of Christ and the good of this fallen world (1 Cor. 12:7–21).

10. We are convinced that a denial or neglect of these principles will lead to increasingly destructive consequences in our families, our churches, and the culture at large.

We grant permission and encourage interested persons to use, reproduce, and distribute the Danvers Statement.[46]

QUESTIONS FOR PERSONAL APPLICATION

1. Do you agree with the argument in this chapter that married women are equal to their husbands in importance before God and in their personhood, but that their husbands also have a leadership role in marriage that the wives do not have? If so, how do you feel about those two ideas? Are you glad that they are both found in the Bible? If not, why not?

---

[46] Reproduced from the website of the Council on Biblical Manhood and Womanhood, https://cbmw.org /uncategorized/the-danvers-statement/.

2. If you are not yet married but hope to marry someday, what do you hope that your marriage will look like in terms of equality and leadership in the relationship?

3. If you are married, are there any ways in which you hope your marriage relationship will change with respect to the questions of equality and leadership?

4. Do you think that you personally tend toward errors of passivity or errors of aggressiveness?

5. Do you believe in your heart that men and women are equal in value before God?

6. What character traits (see p. 110) are most helpful in a marriage?

7. What are some examples of good results that you would hope to see from a marriage lived according to the teachings of the Bible?

SPECIAL TERMS

Christians for Biblical Equality (CBE)
complementarian
Council on Biblical Manhood and Womanhood (CBMW)
Danvers Statement
egalitarian
evangelical feminist
head
mutual submission

BIBLIOGRAPHY

Sections in Other Ethics Texts

(see complete bibliographical data, p. 64)

Clark and Rakestraw, 2:293–338
Frame, 630–35
McQuilkin and Copan, 311–33

Other Works

Bilezikian, Gilbert G. *Beyond Sex Roles: What the Bible Says About a Woman's Place in Church and Family*. 2nd ed. Grand Rapids, MI: Baker, 1991. Egalitarian.

DeMoss, Nancy Leigh, ed. *Biblical Womanhood in the Home*. Foundations for the Family Series. Wheaton, IL: Crossway, 2002. Complementarian.

Gilder, George F. *Men and Marriage*. Gretna, LA: Pelican, 1986.

Grudem, Wayne, ed. *Biblical Foundations for Manhood and Womanhood*. Wheaton, IL: Crossway, 2002. Complementarian.

———. *Countering the Claims of Evangelical Feminism*. Sisters, OR: Multnomah, 2006. Complementarian. This is a 320-page condensation of my *Evangelical Feminism and Biblical Truth*.

———. *Evangelical Feminism: A New Path to Liberalism?* Wheaton, IL: Crossway, 2006. This book analyzes 25 arguments made by evangelical feminists and concludes that each argument undermines the authority of Scripture and leads in the direction of theological liberalism. Complementarian.

———. *Evangelical Feminism and Biblical Truth: An Analysis of More Than 100 Disputed Questions*. Wheaton, IL: Crossway, 2012. Complementarian. This 856-page book contains my most extensive interaction with egalitarian writers about disputed questions related to biblical manhood and womanhood.

Grudem, Wayne A., and Dennis Rainey, eds. *Pastoral Leadership for Manhood and Womanhood*. Wheaton, IL: Crossway, 2002.

James, Sharon. *God's Design for Women: Biblical Womanhood for Today*. Darlington, England: Evangelical Press, 2002. Complementarian.

Jones, Peter. *The God of Sex: How Spirituality Defines Your Sexuality*. Colorado Springs: Victor, 2006. Complementarian.

Jones, Rebecca. *Does Christianity Squash Women? A Christian Looks at Womanhood*. Nashville: Broadman & Holman, 2005. Complementarian.

Kassian, Mary A. *The Feminist Mistake: The Radical Impact of Feminism on Church and Culture*. Wheaton, IL: Crossway, 2005. Complementarian.

———. *Girls Gone Wise in a World Gone Wild*. Chicago: Moody, 2010. Complementarian.

———. *Women, Creation, and the Fall*. Westchester, IL: Crossway, 1990. Complementarian.

Knight, George W. *The Role Relationship of Men and Women: New Testament Teaching*. Rev. ed. Chicago: Moody, 1985. Complementarian.

Köstenberger, Andreas J., and David W. Jones. *God, Marriage and Family: Rebuilding the Biblical Foundation*. 2nd ed. Wheaton, IL: Crossway, 2010. Complementarian.

Köstenberger, Margaret Elizabeth. *Jesus and the Feminists: Who Do They Say That He Is?* Wheaton, IL: Crossway, 2008. Complementarian.

Lewis, Robert. *Real Family Values: Leading Your Family into the 21st Century with Clarity and Conviction*. Sisters, OR: Multnomah, 2000. Complementarian.

Lewis, Robert, and William Hendricks. *Rocking the Roles: Building a Win-Win Marriage*. Rev. ed. Colorado Springs: NavPress, 1999. Complementarian.

Olthuis, J. H. "Marriage." In *New Dictionary of Christian Ethics and Pastoral Theology*, edited by David J. Atkinson and David H. Field, 565–68. Leicester, UK: Inter-Varsity, and Downers Grove, IL: InterVarsity Press, 1995.

Pierce, Ronald W., and Rebecca Merrill Groothuis, gen. eds. *Discovering Biblical Equality: Complementarity without Hierarchy*. 2nd ed. Downers Grove, IL: InterVarsity Press, 2005. Egalitarian. This book is the most influential and most extensive defense of an egalitarian position, with essays by a number of evangelical scholars.

Piper, John, and Wayne Grudem, eds. *Recovering Biblical Manhood and Womanhood: A Response to Evangelical Feminism*. Wheaton, IL: Crossway, 1991. Complementarian. This is the most widely influential collection of academic essays defending a complementarian position.

Rainey, Dennis. *Building Strong Families*. Foundations for the Family Series. Wheaton, IL: Crossway, 2002. Complementarian.

Spencer, Aída Besançon. *Marriage at the Crossroads: Couples in Conversation about Discipleship, Gender Roles, Decision Making, and Intimacy*. Downers Grove, IL: InterVarsity Press, 2009. Contains interactions between representatives of egalitarian and complementarian viewpoints.

Stackhouse, John G. *Partners in Christ: A Conservative Case for Egalitarianism*. Downers Grove, IL: InterVarsity Press, 2015. Egalitarian.

Strachan, Owen, and Gavin Peacock. *Grand Design: Male and Female He Made Them*. Fearn, Ross-shire, Scotland: Christian Focus, 2016. Complementarian.

Waite, Linda J., and Maggie Gallagher. *The Case for Marriage: Why Married People Are Happier, Healthier, and Better Off Financially*. New York: Doubleday, 2000.

Webb, William J. *Slaves, Women and Homosexuals: Exploring the Hermeneutics of Cultural Analysis*. Downers Grove, IL: InterVarsity Press, 2001. Egalitarian.

Weber, Stu. *Tender Warrior: Every Man's Purpose, Every Woman's Dream, Every Child's Hope*. New ed. Sisters, OR: Multnomah, 2006. Complementarian.

SCRIPTURE MEMORY PASSAGE

Colossians 3:18–19: Wives, submit to your husbands, as is fitting in the Lord. Husbands, love your wives, and do not be harsh with them.

HYMN

"My Savior's Love"

I stand amazed in the presence
Of Jesus the Nazarene,
And wonder how He could love me,
A sinner condemned, unclean.

Refrain:
How marvelous! How wonderful!
And my song shall ever be:
How marvelous! How wonderful
Is my Savior's love for me!

For me it was in the garden
He prayed, "Not My will but Thine";
He had no tears for His own griefs
But sweat drops of blood for mine.

In pity angels beheld Him,
And came from the world of light
To comfort Him in the sorrows
He bore for my soul that night.

He took my sins and my sorrows,
He made them His very own;
He bore the burden to Calv'ry
And suffered and died alone.

When with the ransomed in glory
His face I at last shall see,
'Twill be my joy thru the ages
To sing of His love for me.

AUTHOR: CHARLES H. GABRIEL, 1856–1932

Chapter 16

CIVIL GOVERNMENT

Why did God establish civil government?

What should governments do?

Is it ever right to disobey the government or to try to change the government?

What is the right relationship between church and state?

Does the Bible support monarchies, or does it favor some sort of democracy?

In this section of the book we continue to discuss questions related to human authority. In the previous two chapters, we examined the authority of parents in the family ("Honor your father and your mother") and the authority of husbands in marriage. Now we come to the authority of civil government.[1]

What does the Bible teach us about civil government in general? Where did the idea of government come from? What should be the purpose of government? How should governments be chosen? What kind of government is best? What are the responsibilities of governmental rulers? These are the kinds of questions that I seek to answer in this chapter.

The first several sections show that God himself established civil government to bring multiple benefits to human societies. The sections after that show the limitations on governments and some specific values that governments should promote.

---

[1] This chapter has been adapted from Wayne Grudem, *Politics—According to the Bible: A Comprehensive Resource for Understanding Modern Political Issues in Light of Scripture* (Grand Rapids, MI: Zondervan, 2010), 77–115, with permission of the publisher.

A. GOVERNMENTS SHOULD PUNISH EVIL AND ENCOURAGE GOOD

1. The Old Testament Foundation.

a. Genesis 9:5–6: The first indication of God's establishment of civil government in human society happened when Noah and his family came out of the ark after the flood. At this point God said that he would require payment ("a reckoning") for the crime of murder, and that he would require this penalty to be carried out by other human beings:

> And for your lifeblood I will require a reckoning: from every beast I will require it and from man. From his fellow man *I will require a reckoning* for the life of man.
>
> Whoever sheds the blood of man,
>   by man shall his blood be shed,
> for God made man in his own image. (Gen. 9:5–6)

Here God indicated that the crime of murder (expressed by the biblical image of "shedding blood") would be repaid by the forfeiture of the criminal's own life: "by man shall his blood be shed" (see discussion of capital punishment in chap. 18, p. 505).

No further details are given here regarding civil government. But in speaking these words to Noah, God established the obligation for human beings to carry out the most severe punishment (the taking of a human life) in retribution for the most horrible crime (the murder of another human being). Once this principle was established, then the imposition of *lesser* penalties for *lesser* crimes was also validated, since a government that has the right to carry out the most severe punishment certainly has the right to carry out lesser punishments for lesser crimes as well. (For example, various kinds of punishments were established for the government of the people of Israel in the laws found in Exodus to Deuteronomy.)

This command that God gave to Noah is significant for our purposes in the 21st century because it was given long before the establishment of the people of Israel as descendants of Abraham (beginning in Genesis 12) or the establishment of Israel as a distinct nation (beginning with the exodus from Egypt in Ex. 12:33–42, the crossing of the Red Sea in Exodus 14, and the assembly of the nation at Mount Sinai in Exodus 19–20). The command to Noah in Genesis 9 was given *at the beginning of the reestablishment of human society* after God had destroyed all but Noah's family in the waters of the flood. Therefore, careful biblical interpretation would not limit the principles in Genesis 9:5–6 to the Old Testament only or to the nation of Israel only, for the context implies that these principles have relevance for the whole human race for all time.

b. Anarchy Is a Highly Destructive Evil: Another section of the Old Testament reinforces this need for government to restrain evil, for it shows that when there is no government or the government is so weak that it cannot enforce its laws, there are terribly destructive results. The stories in Judges 17–21 recount some of the most horrible sins recorded anywhere in the Bible. These passages teach us the dreadful results of *anarchy*, a situation that comes about when there is no effective government at all. This was the situation in Israel at that time, for "in those days there was no king in Israel. Everyone did what was right in his own eyes" (Judg. 17:6; cf. 18:1; 19:1; 21:25).

These tragic narratives in Judges show in gruesome detail why civil government is so badly needed among sinful human beings. Where there is no ruler, sinful people make up their own morality and soon begin to do terrible things to one another. If there is no governmental authority to stop evil people, evil simply increases.

c. Governments Should Enforce Justice and Defend the Weak: Another way to describe punishing evil and rewarding good is to speak of "enforcing justice," where "justice" means ruling according to the just standards of God's laws. If a king enforces justice, he brings punishment against those who have done wrong, and protects and rewards those who have done right. In this way, justice means that people receive what they deserve.[2]

The psalmist shows God speaking to earthly rulers about justice:

> How long will you judge unjustly
>   and show partiality to the wicked? . . .
> *Give justice to the weak and the fatherless*;
>   maintain the right of the afflicted and the destitute.
> Rescue the weak and the needy;
>   deliver them from the hand of the wicked. (Ps. 82:2–4)

This statement emphasizes that rulers (1) must judge with fairness and righteousness, that is, they must not "show partiality," but judge only according to the law and the facts in the case; (2) must pay special attention to defending "the weak and the fatherless" and, by implication, others who have little power to defend themselves; and (3) must use their power to stop "the wicked" from harming others, particularly those who are "weak" and "needy."

A similar passage in Daniel teaches the same thing. Daniel counseled King Nebuchadnezzar that God wanted him to practice "righteousness" and to show "mercy to the oppressed" (Dan. 4:27).

d. Governments Should Execute Swift Punishment as a Deterrent to Crime: A passage in Ecclesiastes reinforces the importance of civil punishment in restraining evil:

---

[2] Interestingly, the Roman Catholic Church defines justice in social institutions in a similar way: "Society ensures social justice when it provides the conditions that allow associations or individuals to obtain what is their due." *Catechism of the Catholic Church*, 2nd ed. (New York: Doubleday, 1997), para. 1928 (p. 521).

> Because the sentence against an evil deed is not executed speedily, the heart
> of the children of man is fully set to do evil. (Eccles. 8:11)

2. Similar New Testament Teaching.

a. Romans 13:1–7: The New Testament supplements and reinforces what we find in the Old Testament about the responsibility of the civil authority to punish evil. The longest passage comes from Paul:

> Let every person be subject to the governing authorities. For *there is no author-*
> *ity except from God, and those that exist have been instituted by God.* Therefore
> whoever resists the authorities resists what God has appointed, and those who
> resist will incur judgment. For rulers are not a terror to good conduct, but to
> bad. Would you have no fear of the one who is in authority? Then do what is
> good, and you will receive his approval, for *he is God's servant for your good.*
> But if you do wrong, be afraid, for he does not bear the sword in vain. For
> *he is the servant of God, an avenger who carries out God's wrath on the wrong-*
> *doer.* Therefore one must be in subjection, not only to avoid God's wrath but
> also for the sake of conscience. For because of this you also pay taxes, for the
> authorities are ministers of God, attending to this very thing. Pay to all what
> is owed to them: taxes to whom taxes are owed, revenue to whom revenue is
> owed, respect to whom respect is owed, honor to whom honor is owed.

This passage tells us several things about government:

1. God has appointed the authorities who have governmental power (Rom. 13:1–2). This idea is supported by Jesus's statement to Pilate: "You would have no authority over me at all unless it had been given you from above" (John 19:11).

2. Civil rulers are a "terror to . . . [bad] conduct" (Rom. 13:3), which means they restrain evil by the threat of punishment for wrongdoing. This is consistent with what is taught in Genesis 9:5–6.

3. Civil rulers give "approval" or praise (Greek, *epainos*, "approval, recognition, praise") to those who do what is good (Rom. 13:3). In addition, the ruler "is God's servant *for your good*" (v. 4). These verses indicate that government has a role in promoting the common good of a society. It not only should punish wrongdoing, but also should encourage and reward good conduct, behavior that contributes to the good of society.

One example of government supporting the common good is tax-supported playgrounds and parks where families can picnic and sports teams can practice and compete. This responsibility to promote what is good also provides a justification for giving tax-free status to churches on the understanding that churches generally are good for a society and promote the well-being of citizens. The same principle provides support for government promoting marriage through certain legal privileges and economic benefits.

4. Governmental officials serve God. Paul says that the ruler "is *God's servant* for your good" and that "he is *the servant of God*" (Rom. 13:4). He also says "the authorities are *ministers of God*" (v. 6).

This means that we should think of government officials as serving God when they punish evil and promote what is good, whether or not they realize it. This is a strong passage in support of the idea that we should view civil government as a gift from God, something that brings us great benefits. Although individual people and individual governments can do evil, *the institution of civil government* in itself is something very good, a benefit that flows to us from God's infinite wisdom and love.

5. Government officials are doing "good" as they carry out their work. Paul says the official is God's servant "for your *good*" (Rom. 13:4). This means that, in general, we should view the activities of government, when it rewards good and punishes evil, as something that is "good" according to God's Word. This is an additional reason to give thanks to God for civil government.

But this does not at all mean that we should think of everything that a ruler does as good! John the Baptist rebuked Herod "for all the *evil things* that Herod had done" (Luke 3:19). Daniel told Nebuchadnezzar, "Break off your *sins* by practicing righteousness" (Dan. 4:27). Old Testament history contains many stories of kings who "did what was evil in the sight of the LORD" (1 Kings 11:6). Therefore, we should say that governmental rulers do "good" when they carry out their responsibilities in a just and fair way, following God's principles for government.

6. Government authorities execute God's wrath on wrongdoers and thereby carry out a task of *retribution*. This is explicit in Paul's statement that the ruler "does not bear the sword in vain," but as "the servant of God" he functions as "an *avenger* who carries out God's wrath on the wrongdoer" (Rom. 13:4). The Greek word translated as "avenger" is *ekdikos*, meaning "agent of punishment."[3] This indicates that the purpose of civil punishment is *not only to prevent further wrongdoing*, but also *to carry out God's wrath on wrongdoing*, and that this will include bringing actual *punishment*—that is, some kind of pain or hardship to the wrongdoer, a punishment that is appropriate to the crime committed. That is why Paul can say that the government authority is "an avenger *who carries out God's wrath* on the wrongdoer."

This is significant especially in connection with Romans 12:19, which is only three verses before Paul's discussion of civil government beginning in Romans 13:1. (In the Greek text as Paul wrote it, there were no chapter or verse divisions, so this verse is very close to what we now refer to as Romans 13.) Paul says:

> Beloved, *never avenge yourselves*, but *leave it to the wrath of God*, for it is written, "Vengeance is mine, I will repay," says the Lord. (Rom. 12:19)

---

[3] This idea is reinforced by the other uses of this word (as in 1 Thess. 4:6) and the related verb *ekdikeō* ("inflict appropriate penalty for wrong done, punish, take vengeance for," as in Rev. 6:10; 19:2), as well as the related noun *ekdikēsis* ("vengeance, punishment," as in Acts 7:24; Rom. 12:19; 2 Thess. 1:8; Heb. 10:30).

Paul tells Christians not to take *personal vengeance* when wrong has been done to them; rather, they should allow the wrongdoer to be punished by "the wrath of God." Then, just a few sentences later (in Rom. 13:4), he explains that "God's wrath" against wrongdoers is carried out by civil government when it inflicts punishment on them. This means that it is often right for Christians to turn to the civil government to ask for justice to be done when they have suffered wrong at the hands of others. The civil government, in this life, is the means that God has established to carry out justice in such cases.

b. 1 Peter 2:13–14: Peter expresses a similar view of the role of government in his first epistle:

> Be subject for the Lord's sake to every human institution, whether it be to the emperor as supreme, or to governors as sent by him to punish those who do evil and to praise those who do good.

Peter, like Paul, begins with a command for his readers to "be subject" to human institutions such as the emperor or governors. He also says that these leaders are to restrain bad conduct and give praise and encouragement to good conduct, for they are "to *punish those who do evil* and to *praise those who do good*" (1 Pet. 2:14). The idea of the government being established by God is not made explicit, but it is hinted at when Peter says that Christians are to be subject "for the Lord's sake to every human institution" (v. 13). And Peter explicitly includes the idea of retribution against wrongdoers when he says that governors are sent "to *punish* those who do evil." (The word translated as "punish" is the Greek noun *ekdikēsis*, related to *ekdikos*, as we saw in Rom. 13:4.) The idea that they should "praise those who do good" gives additional support to the concept of government promoting the common good of a society.

c. What about "Turning the Other Cheek"? Some Christians today object to the idea that government should actually *punish* wrongdoers. They say government should instead try to correct the causes that lead people to commit crimes—blaming the society much more than the people who do the wrong. Such people who object to punishing wrongdoers often appeal to Jesus's words in Matthew 5:39:

> But I say to you, Do not resist the one who is evil. But if anyone slaps you on the right cheek, turn to him the other also.

Does this teaching prohibit even government from executing punishment on wrongdoers? No, not if it is rightly understood.

This "turn the other cheek" verse should be understood within its context. Jesus is not talking here about the *responsibilities of government*, but is giving principles for *individual personal conduct*. In addition, in this section of Matthew, Jesus is not giving absolute requirements that must be followed in every instance, but is rather giving specific, concrete *illustrations* of what personal conduct will often look like in the life of a Christian.[4]

To take another example, it would be disobedient to the rest of Scripture to obey in every situation the command that comes just three verses later: "Give to the one who begs from you, and do not refuse the one who would borrow from you" (Matt. 5:42). If that were an absolute requirement, then any one beggar could bankrupt any Christian simply by repeatedly asking for more and more! But the Bible *also* requires Christians to be good stewards of their resources (see Luke 16:10, "One who is faithful in a very little is also faithful in much"; 1 Cor. 4:2, "It is required of stewards that they be found faithful"; and the parable of the talents in Matt. 25:14–30).

For these reasons, therefore, Jesus's command for his followers to turn the other cheek is not a persuasive argument against governmental use of force or retributive punishment on wrongdoers, which are responsibilities of government that are explicitly taught in several other passages of Scripture.

d. There Would Be Civil Governments Even in a Sinless World: Is government required only because there is evil in the world? No, I do not think that conclusion follows. Even if there were no evil in the world, I think there would still be some need for government. Its role would include doing things that *promote the common good* of a society, such as (in modern societies at least) the building and regulation of roads, the establishment of standard weights and measures, the maintenance of public records, the enactment of laws for safety (such as speed limits and standards for building materials), the standardization of electrical power, and the establishment of a currency to be used as money for legal exchange within a nation. Such activities promote the common good. They "promote the general Welfare," as the first paragraph of the U.S. Constitution puts it.[5]

B. WHAT ABOUT THE DETAILED OLD TESTAMENT LAWS FOR THE GOVERNMENT OF ISRAEL?

If it is true that governments are responsible before God to punish evil and encourage good, then should we not look to the extensive laws that God gave to the nation of Israel in the Old Testament to find out in more detail how governments are to function?

We cannot do this directly, and we should do it only with much caution, because of the special place those laws occupy in the scope of the whole Bible. They belonged to the Mosaic covenant, and, as I argued in chapter 8, the Mosaic covenant has been terminated and replaced by the new covenant, which began at the point of Christ's death.

Neither did God give these laws to Israel as a pattern for all governments to imitate in every particular. This is true for several reasons:

---

[4] See also the discussion of the meaning of the word *slap* in this verse in chap. 20, p. 551.

[5] See http://constitutionus.com.

1. Israel as a Theocracy. Many of the laws were suited only to a theocracy. Israel was to be for God "a kingdom of priests and a holy nation" (Ex. 19:6). Thus, it was a theocracy ruled by God himself, and therefore *the laws of Israel governed the religious life of God's people* (such as their sacrifices, festivals, and worship of the one true God) as well as matters that ordinarily belong to civil governments in all ages of history.

2. God's End-Time Judgment Breaking In to Current History. A proper interpretation of Israel's laws requires an understanding of some unusual examples of God's judgment suddenly "breaking in" to human history.

Even before the establishment of Israel as a nation, there were some examples of God's judgment suddenly bringing swift retribution to extreme human sinfulness. The story of the flood and Noah's ark (Genesis 6–9) is one example of such judgment. The story of Sodom and Gomorrah (see 19:24–28), in which God destroyed these cities with sulfur and fire from heaven, is another.

The story of the destruction of the cities of Canaan by the people of Israel is still another example, a unique event carried out under God's direction (see Deut. 20:16–18; contrast vv. 10–15, where such a war of divine judgment was forbidden in other cases). This war for the conquest of Canaan and the destruction of the Canaanites was carried out at the specific command of God and was part of his plan for establishing his people in the land he had promised to them. It also foreshadowed God's ultimate final judgment on the whole earth.[6] But these examples of God's judgment "breaking in" to human history were either directly carried out by God (the flood, and the destruction of Sodom and Gomorrah) or were carried out by direct command of God (the conquest of Canaan). They should never provide a pattern for civil governments to imitate today. They were historically unique.

3. Extensive Application of the Death Penalty. A proper interpretation of the Old Testament laws also requires understanding of another unique aspect of those laws, namely, the imposition of the death penalty not only for murder (as in Gen. 9:5–6), but also for promoting a false religion (see Ex. 22:18, 20; Deut. 13:6–17), for rebellion against family authority (see Ex. 21:15, 17; Deut. 21:18–21), and for sexual sin (see Lev. 20:10–14).

These and other applications of the death penalty were part of Israel's identity as a "holy nation" (Ex. 19:6) before God, but that does not mean that nations today, which do not exist as theocracies or as "holy nations" before God, should ever attempt to follow these examples. In fact, the Old Testament historical narrative shows that such severe laws and penalties could not create a truly holy people, because the laws did not change people's hearts (see Jer. 31:31–33; Rom. 8:3–4; Gal. 3:21–24). Such severe penalties for religious infractions, family rebellion, and sexual sin should not be used as a pattern for governments today.

---

[6] See Meredith G. Kline, "The Intrusion and the Decalogue," *WTJ* 16, no. 1 (November 1953): 1–22.

4. The Ongoing Value of These Laws. If these distinctions are kept in mind, the laws that God gave to Israel can still provide useful information for understanding the purposes of government and the nature of good and bad government. In the rest of this chapter, I will seek to use that material thoughtfully with just such attention to the unique historical context in which it occurs. And we must remember that, by comparison with the laws and customs of the surrounding nations of the ancient Near East, the laws that God gave to Israel were an amazing model of how justice, fairness, compassion for the poor and oppressed, and genuine holiness of life can work out in daily life. In fact, Moses said to the people of Israel, "And what great nation is there, that has statutes and rules so righteous as all this law that I set before you today?" (Deut. 4:8).[7]

Although the specific provisions of the Mosaic Law in Exodus–Deuteronomy were intended to apply directly only to Israel at that time, some other sections of the Old Testament are not addressed specifically to the Jewish people but speak in general terms about governments and kings. For example, the book of Proverbs alone has 32 verses that mention a king. Psalms and Ecclesiastes add more. These verses give additional wisdom about civil government that we will use at specific points in the rest of this chapter.[8]

C. GOD IS SOVEREIGN OVER ALL NATIONS, AND ALL PEOPLE ARE ACCOUNTABLE TO HIM

Extensive sections of several of the Old Testament Prophetic Books are addressed not to Israel but to pagan nations. These prophecies show that God also holds *unbelieving nations* accountable for their actions (see Isaiah 13–23; Jeremiah 46–51; Ezekiel 25–32; Amos 1–2; Obadiah—written to Edom; Jonah—sent to Nineveh; Nahum—written to Nineveh; Habakkuk 2; Zephaniah 2).

A number of other passages teach God's sovereignty over the selection and establishment of governmental rulers, including rulers in secular nations. Through Moses, God said to Pharaoh, "For this purpose *I have raised you up*, to show you my power, so that my name may be proclaimed in all the earth" (Ex. 9:16).

God also predicted, through Isaiah, the establishment of Cyrus, king of Persia, about 150 years before his life:

> [The Lord] says of Cyrus, "He is my shepherd,
> and he shall fulfill all my purpose." . . .

---

[7] For further discussion see Christopher J. H. Wright, *Old Testament Ethics for the People of God* (Downers Grove, IL: InterVarsity Press, 2004); Walter C. Kaiser Jr., *Toward Old Testament Ethics* (Grand Rapids, MI: Zondervan, 1991); Gordon J. Wenham, *Story as Torah: Reading Old Testament Narrative Ethically* (Grand Rapids, MI: Baker, 2000).

[8] For a much more extensive discussion of how to apply biblical teachings to civil government, see Grudem, *Politics—According to the Bible*.

Thus says the LORD to his anointed, to Cyrus,
    whose right hand I have grasped,
to subdue nations before him. (Isa. 44:28–45:1)[9]

The idea of God's appointment of rulers is expressed in a general way by the psalmist:

For not from the east or from the west
    and not from the wilderness comes lifting up,
but it is God who executes judgment,
    putting down one and lifting up another. (Ps. 75:6–7)

Daniel also affirms this about God: "He removes kings and sets up kings" (Dan. 2:21) and "The Most High rules the kingdom of men and gives it to whom he will" (4:25; see also vv. 17, 32).

In the New Testament, Paul also teaches this principle:

Let every person be subject to the governing authorities. For there is no authority except from God, and *those that exist have been instituted by God.* (Rom. 13:1)

D. GOVERNMENTS SHOULD SERVE THE PEOPLE AND SEEK THE GOOD OF THE PEOPLE AND THE NATION

If the civil government is to be "God's servant for your good" (Rom. 13:4), then government exists for the *good of the people,* not for the *good of the king, the emperor, or the president.* In the Old Testament, Samuel illustrated this principle well during his service as judge. At the end of his judgeship, he said to the people of Israel:

"Here I am; testify against me before the LORD and before his anointed. Whose ox have I taken? Or whose donkey have I taken? Or whom have I defrauded? Whom have I oppressed? Or from whose hand have I taken a bribe to blind my eyes with it? Testify against me and I will restore it to you." They said, "You have not defrauded us or pressed us or taken anything from any man's hand." (1 Sam. 12:3–4)

In contrast to his own righteous conduct as judge, Samuel warned the people that a king would abuse his power and take from the people for the benefit of himself and his family:

---

[9] When Isaiah prophesied (about 740–681 BC), the Assyrian Empire was dominant in the ancient Near East. But Assyria was defeated by forces of the Babylonian empire in 612 BC. Then Babylon fell to the Persians in 539 BC. Cyrus became king of Persia in 538 BC. Therefore, Isaiah, under the inspiration of God, predicted Cyrus by name, a ruler who would come two empires and about 150 years after Isaiah prophesied.

These will be the ways of the king who will reign over you: he will *take* your sons and appoint them to his chariots and to be his horsemen and to run before his chariots . . . and some to plow his ground and to reap his harvest. . . . He will *take* your daughters to be perfumers and cooks and bakers. He will *take* the best of your fields and vineyards and olive orchards and give them to his servants. He will *take* the tenth of your grain and of your vineyards. . . . He will *take* your male servants and female servants. . . . He will *take* the tenth of your flocks, and you shall be his slaves. (1 Sam. 8:11–17)

This use of government power for the self-enrichment of the leader and his family members and friends betrays the fundamental purpose of government—to serve the people. It is repeatedly condemned in the Old Testament (see Deut. 16:19; Ps. 26:10; Prov. 15:27; 17:23; Isa. 33:15; Ezek. 22:12; Amos 5:12; Hab. 1:2–4).

Sadly, the more unchecked power a government has and the less public accountability it has to the people, the more likely a ruler is to forget to serve the people and to "take" more and more to himself, just as Samuel warned that the king would do.[10]

E. CITIZENS SHOULD BE SUBJECT TO THE GOVERNMENT AND OBEY ITS LAWS (EXCEPT IN CERTAIN CIRCUMSTANCES)

1. The General Obligation to Be Subject to the Civil Government. Because God has established the government to restrain evil and do good for the nation, citizens should, in general, be subject to the government and obey its laws. Paul writes:

Let every person be subject to the governing authorities. For there is no authority except from God, and those that exist have been instituted by God. Therefore whoever resists the authorities resists what God has appointed. (Rom. 13:1–2)

Similarly, Peter tells Christians, "*Be subject* for the Lord's sake to every human institution, whether it be to the emperor as supreme, or to governors as sent by him to punish those who do evil and to praise those who do good" (1 Pet. 2:13–14).

---

[10] One tragic example of such abuse of power was seen in the life of Omar Bongo, who ruled the African nation of Gabon for 41 years. When he died in 2009, the *Daily Telegraph* of London reported that Bongo "considered everything inside [Gabon] to be his personal property and elevated corruption to a method of government." Having taken for himself a large share of Gabon's oil wealth, he "owned 33 properties in Paris and Nice," plus he had an additional £86 million ($138 million) in accounts in New York—and "these discoveries were probably only the tip of the iceberg: Bongo's fortune certainly ran into the hundreds of millions of dollars and may have reached the billions." *The Daily Telegraph*, June 9, 2009, 29. Unfortunately, among countries where governments have no effective separation of powers, stories like this could be repeated many times.

These passages teach that people in general, and Christians in particular, have an obligation to obey the civil government.[11]

2. When Is It Right to Disobey the Civil Government? God does not hold people responsible to obey the civil government *when obedience would mean directly disobeying a command of God himself.* This principle is indicated by a number of passages in the narrative sections of the Bible.

One clear example comes from the early days of the Christian church. After Jesus had commanded the apostles to preach the gospel (see Matt. 28:19–20), the Jewish governing authority, the Sanhedrin, arrested some of them and ordered them "not to speak or teach at all in the name of Jesus" (Acts 4:18). But the apostles Peter and John answered, "We cannot but speak of what we have seen and heard" (v. 20), and later Peter proclaimed, "We must obey God rather than men" (5:29).

This is a clear affirmation of the principle that God requires his people to disobey the civil government if obedience would mean directly disobeying God.

Other passages also establish this. In Daniel 3:13–20, King Nebuchadnezzar commanded three Jewish men—Shadrach, Meshach, and Abednego—to bow down and worship a golden statue that he had erected. But they refused and said, "We will not serve your gods or worship the golden image that you have set up" (v. 18). God showed his approval of their actions by rescuing them from the burning fiery furnace (vv. 19–30).

When Pharaoh commanded the Egyptian midwives to put newborn Hebrew baby boys to death, they disobeyed, and God approved of their disobedience (Ex. 1:17, 21). When it was against the law for anyone to come into the presence of King Ahasuerus without being invited, Esther disobeyed the law, risking her life to save her people, the Jews (see Est. 4:16). Daniel likewise disobeyed a law that prohibited him from praying to God (see Dan. 6:10). In addition, when King Herod commanded the wise men to return and tell him where the newborn King of the Jews was to be found, they were warned

---

[11] What about speed limits? Does being subject to the government require Christians to follow the posted speed limit exactly when driving? For many years I thought that Romans 13 required me not to exceed the posted speed limit, and therefore I regularly held my speed to 30 mph, 45 mph, or 55 mph if that was what the sign said, with the result that probably 95 percent of other drivers would pass me going 5 to 10 mph faster. But I held my speed steady, even though it tried my patience.

Then one day a Christian lawyer told me that, in several cases, courts in the United States had upheld the principle that the speed limit people are required to obey is not the posted speed but "the speed that is customarily enforced." Where I live in Arizona, the speed limit that is "customarily enforced" is 10 or 11 mph above the posted speed (according to my personal observation and some media reports), although less tolerance might be given to erratic drivers or very young drivers. (Police practices in other states and other countries may differ.)

Therefore, my personal practice now, in general, is to drive with the flow of traffic and to stay under the limit that is customarily enforced. This I do with a clear conscience. However, this is a matter of making a wise application of Scripture to a specific situation, and Christians may differ about it. I have a good Christian friend (a professor at another seminary) who disagrees with me and believes he is conscience-bound to stay under the actual posted limit.

by an angel not to heed this command, so they disobeyed Herod and "departed to their own country by another way" (see Matt. 2:8, 12).

John Calvin put it this way:

> But in that obedience which we have shown to be due to the authority of rulers, we are always to make this exception . . . that such obedience is never to lead us away from obedience to him, to whose will the desires of all kings ought to be subject. . . . And how absurd would it be that in satisfying man you should incur the displeasure of him for whose sake you obey men themselves! The Lord, therefore is the King of Kings. . . . If they command anything against him, let it go unesteemed.[12]

3. Is It Ever Right to Attempt to Overthrow or Obtain Freedom from an Existing Government? Sometimes people raise the question of whether it was right for the early American colonies to declare their independence from Great Britain. Was the American Revolution not a failure to be subject to the governing authorities, and was it not therefore an act of disobedience to God's command in Romans 13?

Some Christian writers have argued for this position. For instance, John MacArthur says that rebelling against the British government and declaring independence was "contrary to the clear teachings and commands of Romans 13:1–7." Therefore, MacArthur says, "The United States was actually born out of a violation of New Testament principles, and any blessings that God has bestowed on America have come in spite of that disobedience by the Founding Fathers."[13]

At the time of the American Revolution, a number of Christians agreed with the position that MacArthur states here. Some left the American colonies and returned to England to be subject to the British crown rather than participate in the War of Independence.

But I disagree with this viewpoint. I am convinced, after studying the historical situation and the principles of Scripture, that the American Revolution was morally justified in the sight of God.

The reason that a number of colonists thought they were justified to rebel against the British monarchy is that *it is morally right for a lower government official to protect the citizens in his care from a higher official* who is committing crimes against these citizens.

This thinking in Protestant circles goes back as far as Calvin. In his *Institutes of the Christian Religion* (1559), he argued as follows:

> If there are now any magistrates of the people, appointed to restrain the willfulness of kings . . . if they wink at kings who violently fall upon and assault

---

[12] John Calvin, *Institutes of the Christian Religion*, ed. John T. McNeill, trans. Ford Lewis Battles, Library of Christian Classics, vols. 20–21 (Philadelphia: Westminster, 1960), 4.20.32 (1520).

[13] John MacArthur, *Why Government Can't Save You: An Alternative to Political Activism*, Bible for Life Series (Nashville: Word, 2000), 6–7.

the lowly common folk, I declare that . . . they dishonestly betray the freedom of the people, of which they know that they have been appointed protectors by God's ordinance.[14]

Other Lutheran and Reformed thinkers made similar statements. The right to rebel against tyrants is also found in the words of Roman Catholic philosopher Thomas Aquinas (c. 1225–1274) and many other Christian writers. According to Greg Forster, a scholar with expertise in the history of governmental theory, one common argument among Christian writers was that a tyrannical "government" is "not really a government at all but a criminal gang masquerading as a government, and is therefore not entitled to the obedience that governments (properly so called) can claim."[15] Another argument was that "the principle of the rule of law . . . implies the right to rebellion."[16]

Therefore, the leaders who founded the United States and declared its independence from Great Britain thought of themselves as doing something that was *morally right and even necessary, for they were protecting the citizens in their care from the evil attacks of King George III of England*, who had repeatedly acted as a "tyrant." The citizens of the colonies needed protection from King George just as much as they needed protection from a thief or murderer who would attack people from within the country, and just as much as they needed protection from a hostile army that would invade it from another country.

The Declaration of Independence, in fact, contains a long statement of grievances against England that made it "necessary for one people to dissolve the political bands which have connected them with another." The authors wrote that they had patiently endured much suffering, seeking other solutions:

> Prudence, indeed, will dictate that governments long established should not be changed for light and transient causes; and accordingly all experience hath shown that mankind are more disposed to suffer, while evils are sufferable, than to right themselves by abolishing the forms to which they are accustomed.

But then the Declaration's signers essentially said that they could suffer the abuses of the king no longer:

> But when a long train of abuses and usurpations, pursuing invariably the same object, evinces a design to reduce them under absolute despotism, it is their right, it is their duty, to throw off such government, and to provide new guards for their future security. . . . The history of the present King of Great Britain is a history of repeated injuries and usurpations, all having in direct

---

[14] Calvin, *Institutes*, 4.20.31 (1519).
[15] Greg Forster, personal email to me, Jan. 21, 2010.
[16] Ibid.

object the establishment of an absolute tyranny over these states. To prove this, let facts be submitted to a candid world.

What follows is a long and detailed list of the intolerable abuses of government power that the king of England had inflicted on the colonies. The king was a destructive criminal in the eyes of the colonial leaders, so they felt they had an obligation before God to protect their citizens from him.

Then the signers concluded the Declaration with the indication that they were not doing this as isolated individuals, but as "Representatives of the United States of America, in General Congress, assembled, appealing to the Supreme Judge of the world for the rectitude of our intentions."

Finally, these representatives of the various colonies declared:

> We . . . solemnly publish and declare that these united colonies are, and of right ought to be free and independent states; that they are absolved from all allegiance to the British Crown, and that all political connection between them and the state of Great Britain is and ought to be totally dissolved. . . . And for the support of this declaration, with a firm reliance on the protection of Divine Providence, we mutually pledge to each other our lives, our fortunes, and our sacred honor.[17]

Another argument for seeking to change or obtain freedom from an existing government is the general principle that *the Bible does not say it is always wrong to change an existing government.* For example, Christians who live in a democracy regularly vote to elect leaders, and sometimes they vote to elect different leaders from those currently in office. They are trying to change the government through an election. Could it ever be right to seek to change the government by other means (such as declaring one's independence, then defending that independent status against attack)?

I acknowledge that the Bible says that ruling officials have been "appointed" by God, but he certainly works through human actions to appoint *different* leaders at different times. The history of Israel shows how God worked again and again through many significant events to remove one king from office and establish another.

A third reason why it is sometimes right to attempt to change the existing government is that *the Bible gives some examples of God raising up leaders to deliver his people from the rule of tyrants,* such as Moses leading his people out of Egypt and out of the rule of Pharaoh (see Exodus 1–14). The book of Judges records many stories showing how foreign rulers oppressed the people of Israel, but then God delivered them through judges whom he had appointed: "The LORD raised up judges, who saved them out of the hand of those who plundered them" (Judg. 2:16).

---

[17] See the text of the Declaration of Independence, including the long list of grievances, in the appendix to this chapter, p. 477.

In the New Testament, the author of Hebrews speaks of some Old Testament heroes "who through faith *conquered kingdoms*" (Heb. 11:33), which means that by military action they overthrew governments and established other ruling powers.

Many of the Founding Fathers of the United States were aware of these biblical examples of tyrants being overthrown. In fact, Benjamin Franklin's remarkable proposal for a design of the Great Seal of the United States (which was not ultimately adopted) was this (the proposal still exists in Franklin's own handwriting):

> Moses standing on the Shore, and extending his Hand over the Sea, thereby causing the same to overwhelm Pharaoh who is sitting in an open Chariot, a Crown on his Head and a Sword in his Hand. Rays from a Pillar of Fire in the Clouds reaching to Moses, to express that he acts by Command of the Deity. Motto, Rebellion to Tyrants is Obedience to God.[18]

My conclusion is that the Declaration of Independence, like the American War of Independence, was morally justified and was actually necessary in order to free the people of the colonies from the tyranny under which they were suffering because of King George III of England.[19]

F. GOVERNMENTS SHOULD SAFEGUARD HUMAN LIBERTY

Liberty in a nation is of utmost importance because it allows people to have the freedom to choose to obey or disobey God, to serve him or not to serve him, according to their best judgment. The Bible consistently places a high value on individual human freedom and responsibility to choose one's actions. Beginning at the origin of the human race, when he put Adam and Eve in the garden of Eden, God gave people freedom of choice (see Gen. 2:16–17). Such freedom to choose is one of the highest manifestations of excellence in the human beings that God has created, and it is one of the ways in which mankind is more like God than any of the animals or plants that he has made.[20]

1. Biblical Arguments for Human Liberty. Several arguments from the Bible support the idea that governments should protect human liberty. The first consideration is the fact that *slavery and oppression are always viewed negatively in Scripture*, while *freedom is viewed positively*.

---

[18] Cited from www.greatseal.com/committees/firstcomm/.

[19] I should add that I am glad that today the United Kingdom is one of America's closest allies and friends. My wife, Margaret, and I spent four wonderful years living in the UK, and have returned for shorter visits on numerous occasions.

[20] In this chapter, I am specifically discussing political freedom or freedom from governmental constraint on one's actions. Regarding the relationship between human freedom of choice and God's sovereignty, see Wayne Grudem, *Systematic Theology: An Introduction to Biblical Doctrine* (Leicester, UK: Inter-Varsity, and Grand Rapids, MI: Zondervan, 1994), 315–54.

When God gave the Ten Commandments to the people of Israel, he began by saying, "I am the LORD your God, who brought you out of the land of Egypt, *out of the house of slavery*" (Ex. 20:2).

When the people of Israel turned against the Lord, he gave them into the hand of oppressors, who enslaved them and took away their freedom (see Deut. 28:28–29, 33; Judg. 2:16–23). Loss of freedom was a judgment, not a blessing.

That is why one blessing promised in the messianic prophecy in Isaiah 61 was that the coming deliverer would free the people from oppression by their enemies, for he would "proclaim liberty to the captives" (v. 1).

Individual liberty was also prized, for although people in Israel would sometimes sell themselves into slavery as a solution to severe poverty, the Jubilee year would come once every 50 years to set free those who had been thus enslaved:

> And you shall consecrate the fiftieth year, and *proclaim liberty throughout the land to all its inhabitants*. It shall be a jubilee for you, when each of you shall return to his property and each of you shall return to his clan. (Lev. 25:10)

Freedom of individual choice is viewed favorably again and again in Scripture. It is a component of full human personhood and is ultimately a reflection of God's own attribute of "will," his ability to approve and bring about various actions as he pleases. Therefore, we have not only God's testing of Adam and Eve in the garden of Eden, but also statements such as this:

> I have set before you life and death, blessing and curse. Therefore *choose* life, that you and your offspring may live. (Deut. 30:19)

> *Choose* this day whom you will serve. (Josh. 24:15)

> *Come to me*, all who labor and are heavy laden, and I will give you rest. (Matt. 11:28)

> The Spirit and the Bride say, "*Come*." And let the one who hears say, "*Come*." And let the one who is thirsty come; let the one who desires take the water of life without price. (Rev. 22:17)

From the beginning of Genesis to the last chapter of Revelation, God honors and protects human freedom and human choice. Liberty is an essential component of our humanity. Any government that significantly denies individual liberty exerts a terribly dehumanizing influence on its people.

2. Governments Should Protect Human Liberty. Therefore, God is pleased when governments *protect basic human liberties* and thereby allow people much freedom to decide how to use their time and their resources according to what they think is best. Such liberty in any nation will lead to an incredible diversity of choices in schooling, occupations, friendships and associations, religious beliefs, charitable activities, uses of money, uses of time, recreational activities, music, art, and thousands of other things.

Freedom in a society allows people to decide what they want to do from among many good uses of their time and resources. Many people will devote their free time to caring for family members or members of the community; helping to coach children's sports teams; doing volunteer work in churches or on mission trips; helping relief agencies; doing volunteer work at hospitals or schools; pouring time into starting and growing businesses; or pursuing hundreds upon hundreds of other worthwhile activities. A government that maximizes human freedom (while still punishing evildoers) will often find that its citizens do an amazing amount of good for others and for the world.

What human freedoms should be protected by civil government? The basic freedoms protected in the U.S. Constitution are freedom of religion, freedom of speech, freedom of the press, freedom of assembly, and freedom to petition the government (see the First Amendment to the Constitution). Other freedoms mentioned in the Bill of Rights are "the right of the people to keep and bear Arms" (Second Amendment), "the right of the people to be secure in their persons, houses, papers, and effects, against unreasonable searches and seizures" (Fourth Amendment), freedom from self-incrimination in court, and the right not to be "deprived of life, liberty, or property, without due process of law" (Fifth Amendment). Later, the Thirteenth Amendment in 1865 guaranteed freedom from "slavery" and "involuntary servitude."[21]

These requirements for the protection of human liberty imply that citizens and governments should agree to restrictions on human freedom only reluctantly and only where there is a significant need to do so. Totalitarian governments that control all aspects of life (as in several modern-day Muslim countries or in modern-day North Korea) are acting contrary to the Bible's emphasis on the high value of human liberty. In the United States, the slavery (or "involuntary servitude") that was allowed in some states until the Emancipation Proclamation of 1863 was another kind of wrongful denial of human liberty to those who were enslaved (see 1 Tim. 1:10 in the ESV, where "enslavers" are listed among various kinds of sinners before God).

In founding the United States, the authors of the Declaration of Independence understood the importance of liberty, for they affirmed at the outset not only that "all men are created equal" but also "that they are endowed by their Creator with certain unalienable Rights, that among these are Life, *Liberty*, and the pursuit of Happiness." The unalienable right to "liberty" was listed right next to the unalienable right to "life." The next sentence declared that it was the purpose of government to protect rights such as life and liberty: "That *to secure these rights*, Governments are instituted among Men, deriving their just powers from the consent of the governed." Protecting

---

[21] Quotations from the Constitution are cited from http://constitutionus.com. On the Thirteenth Amendment, see "The Abolition of Slavery," The Heritage Guide to the Constitution, http://www.heritage.org /constitution/#!/amendments/13/essays/166/abolition-of-slavery.

human liberty was seen as one of the most important and most basic of all the functions of government.[22]

3. How Much Restriction of Liberty Is Necessary? While liberty is to be highly valued, it cannot be an absolute right in light of other biblical teachings about the role of government. Of necessity, government sometimes infringes on people's "liberty" to do wrong, as when it prohibits murder and thus limits someone's "liberty" to take the life of another person. Governmental regulation of speed limits on highways necessarily limits a person's "liberty" to drive at whatever speed he wants—but most people think this is appropriate because of the need to protect the life and welfare of others.

What worries me is that in recent years political debates have shown almost no awareness of the huge value of liberty and the great loss that comes when it is restricted. Governments should restrict human liberty to the least extent necessary to carry out their legitimate functions, such as punishing evil and rewarding what is good. However, governments too often attempt to restrict human liberty in ways that are much more extensive and intrusive, not only prohibiting things that are clearly evil, but also things that are morally neutral or good simply because they are not favored by the government.

I do not have space here to discuss exactly how much government regulation is necessary or wise in multiple situations,[23] but it is important to note that *every incremental increase in governmental regulation of life is also an incremental removal of some measure of human liberty.* When small losses of liberty occur again and again over a period of years, people can become essentially slaves to a government without ever realizing what is happening.

For example, if a local government prohibits grocery stores from providing plastic bags (as San Francisco did in 2007), it forces me to use paper bags.[24] This deprives me of my liberty to choose which kind of bag I want. But I cannot carry nearly as many paper bags as plastic bags from the car to the house, because the paper bags break and tear more easily. Therefore, every trip to the grocery store will now require some additional trips between the car and the house, an incremental loss of human liberty for every citizen. The paper bags also take more storage room and don't work as well for certain other tasks, so there is another small loss of liberty.

Perhaps some people think this insignificant, and perhaps others think there is an environmental benefit that comes from avoiding plastic bags, making a plastic bag ban worth the price of depriving the citizens a small amount of liberty in this way. I do not. But my point is simply to note that my freedom to use my time as I wish has been eroded a bit by government action, and no one seems to notice that this has happened.

Government-compelled sorting of waste into various kinds of recyclable trash, to

---

[22] See the text of the Declaration of Independence in the appendix to this chapter, p. 477.

[23] See Grudem, *Politics—According to the Bible,* for more extensive discussions of several specific regulations.

[24] Charlie Goodyear, "S.F. First City to Ban Plastic Shopping Bags," *San Francisco Chronicle,* March 28, 2007, www.sfgate.com/cgi-bin/article.cgi?file=/c/a/2007/03/28/MNGDROT5QN1.DTL.

be put out on a separate day from other trash, is another erosion of liberty in people's use of time. (Is it worthwhile? Perhaps some is. I don't know for certain—the calculations are complex, especially because there are other alternatives, with good results.)[25] My only point is that at least the discussion must recognize that the cost of mandatory recycling is not only monetary, but that it also includes a *very real cost* in loss of human liberty, one small bit at a time.

By far the largest loss of liberty by government action is through taxation, for if I have to pay an additional $100 in taxes, then I (1) have lost the freedom to decide for myself how I want to spend that $100 and (2) have to work that much longer simply to have the same amount of money that I had to spend before I had to pay the tax. Therefore, every additional tax dollar collected from me takes away one more small amount of my freedom, as well as (often) one more small amount of my time, which is one more small amount of my life. These "small amounts" can become enormous, so that people in some countries work over half of their time just to pay taxes to the government! They have become like medieval serfs, bound not to the feudal lord but to the national government, living half their lives in servitude.[26] Taxes have robbed them of huge portions of their lives. Incremental loss of our human liberty is incremental loss of our lives.

G. GOVERNMENT CANNOT SAVE PEOPLE OR FUNDAMENTALLY CHANGE HUMAN HEARTS

1. Personal Salvation Is a Work of God, not Government. It is important to remember that there are tasks that government cannot do, tasks that God has entrusted to the church and to the Holy Spirit working through the Bible, which is the Word of God.

The civil government—even a very good one—cannot save people from their sins, for that can come about only through personal faith in Jesus Christ. "For by grace you have been saved through faith. And this is not your own doing; it is the gift of God, not a result of works, so that no one may boast" (Eph. 2:8–9). Only God can promise, "I will give you a new heart, and a new spirit I will put within you" (Ezek. 36:26). Only God can say, "I will put my laws into their minds, and write them on their hearts, and I will be their God, and they shall be my people" (Heb. 8:10).

Therefore, Christians should never place their ultimate hope in any government for changing human hearts or making a nation of sinful people into a nation of holy and righteous people before God. That is the work of God alone, and he carries it out through the church as it proclaims the gospel of Jesus Christ and as people personally put their trust in Christ and find that "If anyone is in Christ, he is a new creation. The old has passed away; behold, the new has come" (2 Cor. 5:17).

This is important for Christians who work to influence government. We must

---

[25] For discussion of various alternatives for waste disposal, see my *Politics—According to the Bible*, 346–48.

[26] For a classic description of how freedom is lost incrementally to government, see F. A. Hayek, *The Road to Serfdom*, Fiftieth Anniversary Ed. (Chicago: University of Chicago Press, 1994).

remember that *the primary need* of every society is the gospel of Jesus Christ, a gospel that is made known through the church, not through the government. Jesus is "the way, and the truth, and the life" (John 14:6). The Bible says that in Christ "are hidden all the treasures of wisdom and knowledge" (Col. 2:3). Through Jesus Christ alone people can truly know God and lead lives pleasing to God.

2. Inwardly Transformed People Are Necessary for a Transformed Society. Christians who seek to influence government must also remember that inwardly transformed people are needed if we are ever going to see a transformed society. Merely passing good laws and having good government will never be enough to change a society. The people of Israel in the Old Testament had good laws from God himself, but those laws did not keep people from going astray and eventually bringing God's judgment on themselves.

Therefore, we must constantly remember that *winning elections is not enough to change a nation.* Christians could (in theory, at least) gain enough influence to overturn the Supreme Court decision about abortion (Roe v. Wade), pass pro-life laws that protect the unborn, and pass defense-of-marriage laws, yet all of that would not stop people from having premarital sex, getting abortions somehow, or committing homosexual acts. There must be a change of people's hearts and minds.

Laws work best when they govern a people who have good moral character and moral convictions. If an entire society is corrupt, laws will be able to restrain only the most egregious examples of sin, leaving the rest untouched. As John Adams, one of the principal Founding Fathers, said, "Our Constitution was made only for a moral and righteous people. It is wholly inadequate for the governance of any other."[27]

Unless a country has transformed people, it is unlikely that it will be able to pass very good laws or elect very good leaders. No candidate can win elections campaigning on "moral values in government" if the population as a whole lacks those moral values. (Think of what elections would have been like in Sodom and Gomorrah!) Therefore, it is important that the church continue in its task of proclaiming the gospel of Jesus Christ to change people's hearts and minds one at a time. And once people become Christians, it is important to teach them about moral principles from the Bible, not only principles of conduct for their individual lives, but also principles concerning the roles and responsibilities of civil government.

Nevertheless, if we stopped at this point, we would only have part of the truth from the Bible.

3. Governments Significantly Influence People's Moral Convictions and Behavior, as Well as the Moral Fabric of a Nation. Despite their inability to save or transform people, governments *do* have an immense influence on the conduct of people in a society. The psalmist knew that there are "wicked rulers" who "frame injustice by statute"

---

[27] John Adams, *The Works of John Adams, Second President of the United States*, ed. Charles Francis Adams (Boston: Little, Brown, 1854), IX:229 (Oct. 11, 1798).

(Ps. 94:20)—that is, they pass laws to enable wrongdoing! Isaiah says, "Woe to those who decree *iniquitous decrees*, and the writers who keep writing oppression" (Isa. 10:1). Another psalm implies that evil rulers can influence people toward wrongdoing, because it says that if "the scepter of wickedness" (a symbol of authority held by wicked rulers) ever would "rest on the land allotted to the righteous," then there would be a much greater likelihood that the righteous would "stretch out their hands to do wrong" (Ps. 125:3). Sometimes governments can pass laws that authorize horribly evil deeds, as when Haman persuaded King Ahasuerus to sign a decree that all the people in the kingdom of Persia could "annihilate all Jews, young and old, women and children, in one day" and then "plunder their goods" (Est. 3:13).

This is one reason why Paul encouraged Christians to pray "for kings and all who are in high positions," so that Christian believers "may lead a peaceful and quiet life, godly and dignified in every way" (1 Tim. 2:2). Once again, the implication is that *good* rulers can influence a nation toward *good* conduct, while *evil* rulers can encourage and promote all sorts of *evil* conduct among their people.

In part, the influence of government comes by *personal example*. For many generations, schoolchildren were taught about the upright and heroic moral conduct of leaders such as George Washington and Abraham Lincoln, in order that they might imitate this conduct in their own lives. (I remember such teaching in my elementary school in Wisconsin.) By contrast, one reason the people of the United States—from both parties—felt such profound disappointment in President Bill Clinton's sexual misconduct in office was the poor example it set for adolescent children and, indeed, for all the rest of society.

Another reason that government influences conduct is that *laws have a teaching function*. If a government passes laws that say something is legal, many or perhaps most of the people in that society will also think that it is morally right. If the government says that something is illegal, many people will think that it is morally wrong. This is especially true for people who do not seek moral guidance from the Bible, but it can also be true for Christian believers.

The teaching function of law is one reason why there are still so many abortions in the United States, for example. Many people take the easy way out and reason that if the government allows something, society must think that it is morally right or at least morally permissible. So they decide to have abortions, perhaps even going against the quiet inward voice of their consciences. But if there were laws prohibiting people from taking the lives of unborn children, then many of these same people would find that their consciences agree with the law, and would support it and think that it is right.

To take another example, my own conversations in the state of Arizona (where I live) suggest to me that the large majority of evangelical Christians there think it perfectly natural and morally right for Christians to own guns for purposes of self-defense in cases of emergency. But I suspect that a similarly large majority of evangelical Christians in England (where I have stayed many times for study or for teaching) think it morally wrong for Christians to do this. I do not find this surprising, since the laws of England make it nearly impossible for private citizens to own guns, but the laws and customs in Arizona make it very easy for private citizens to do so. The laws have a teaching function, and they influence people's ideas of right and wrong.

The same considerations apply to people's attitudes about same-sex marriage, the proper grounds for divorce, the age at which it is appropriate for children to drink alcoholic beverages (compare laws in the United States with much more liberal laws in Europe), the place of secular religious speech in public activities, and so forth. Laws have a teaching function with respect to the general population.

In addition to this, what the government considers legal or illegal affects what is taught in schools to the children in any society. The Supreme Court's legalization of same-sex marriage in 2015 gave added incentive for schools to teach that homosexual conduct is to be considered normal and morally right, and to attempt to silence anyone who would express the view that homosexual conduct is morally wrong.[28] This influence on the children in a society will have a profound influence on their sense of moral right and wrong, and their future sexual conduct.

Therefore, the laws and policies of a government have enormous impact on the conduct of people in a society. Christians should care about this because (1) sin destroys people's lives, and Christians are commanded, "You shall love your neighbor as yourself" (Matt. 22:39), and (2) because the entire course of a nation is set by the moral conduct of its individual citizens, and "righteousness exalts a nation, but sin is a reproach to any people" (Prov. 14:34). While it is true, then, that government cannot save people or fundamentally change human hearts, whenever we say this, we must simultaneously affirm that government policies and laws do have an immense influence on a nation for good or for evil.

H. PRINCIPLES FOR A RIGHT RELATIONSHIP BETWEEN CHURCH AND STATE

In one dramatic encounter, Jesus's Jewish opponents tried to trap him with a question: "Is it lawful to pay taxes to Caesar, or not?" (Matt. 22:17). To say yes to Roman taxes ran the risk of appearing to support the hated Roman government. To say

[28] See Alex Grubbs, "California Soon to Be First State to Teach LGBT History in Public Schools," CNS News, July 20, 2016, https://www.cnsnews.com/news/article/alex-grubbs/california-soon-be-first-state-teach -lgbt-history-public-schools; Jessica Chasmar, "Las Vegas Schools Consider Teaching Kindergartners About Masturbation, Homosexuality," The Washington Times, Sept. 24, 2014, http://www.washingtontimes.com /news/2014/sep/24/las-vegas-schools-consider-teaching-kindergartners/; Todd Starnes, "Parents Furious over School's Plan to Teach Gender Spectrum, Fluidity," FoxNews.com, May 15, 2015, http://www.foxnews .com/opinion/2015/05/15/call-it-gender-fluidity-schools-to-teach-kids-there-s-no-such-thing-as-boys-or -girls.html; and Michael Alison Chandler, "In D.C. Schools, Gay-Tolerance Lessons Are Becoming Elementary," The Washington Post, Feb. 4, 2012, https://www.washingtonpost.com/local/education/in-dc-schools -gay-tolerance-lessons-are-becoming-elementary/2012/01/29/gIQA8YLFqQ_story.html.

no to Roman taxes would make Jesus sound like a dangerous revolutionary against Rome's power. Taking his opponents by surprise, Jesus said, "Show me the coin for the tax," and "they brought him a denarius" (v. 19). After that, here is how the teaching unfolded:

> And Jesus said to them, "Whose likeness and inscription is this?" They said, "Caesar's." Then he said to them, "Therefore render to Caesar the things that are Caesar's, and to God the things that are God's." (Matt. 22:20–21)

This is a remarkable statement because Jesus shows that there are to be *two different spheres of influence*, one for the government and one for the religious life of the people of God. Some things, such as taxes, belong to the civil government ("the things that are Caesar's"), and this implies that the church should not try to control these things. On the other hand, some things belong to people's religious life ("the things that are God's"), and this implies that the civil government should not try to control those things.

Jesus did not specify any list of things that belong to either category, but the mere distinction of these two categories had monumental significance for the history of the world. It signaled Jesus's endorsement of a different system from the one set up by the laws for the nation of Israel in the Old Testament era. In that time, Israel was a "theocracy" in that God was the ruler of the people, the laws were directly given to Israel by God (rather than being decided upon by the people or a human king), and *the whole nation* was considered "God's people." Therefore, everyone in the nation was expected to worship God, and the laws of Israel covered not only what we today would consider "secular matters," such as murder and theft, but also "religious matters," such as animal sacrifices and punishments for worshiping other gods (see Leviticus 21–23; Deut. 13:6–11).

In Jesus's statement about God and Caesar, he established the broad outlines of a new order in which "the things that are God's" are *not* to be under the control of the civil government (or "Caesar"). Such a system is far different from the Old Testament theocracy. Jesus's new teaching implies that all civil governments—even today—should give people freedom regarding the religious faith they choose to follow or not follow, the religious doctrines they hold, and how they worship God. "Caesar" should not control such things, for they are "the things that are God's."

This distinction leads us to several points of application:

1. The Church Should Not Govern "the Things That Are Caesar's." This principle means that *there should be no church control over the actions of civil government.* Here is a matter on which liberals and conservatives, both Democrats and Republicans, agree in the United States today.

One support for this idea is the fact that in the New Testament there is no indication that the elders in local churches had any responsibility in local, provincial, or empire-wide government. Officials in those governments were always distinct from the elders of the New Testament churches.

In fact, at one point in his ministry, Jesus himself refused to assume any governmental role. Someone came to him asking that he decide a dispute over an inheritance, and he refused:

> Someone in the crowd said to him, "Teacher, tell my brother to divide the inheritance with me." But he said to him, "Man, who made me a judge or an arbitrator over you?" (Luke 12:13–14)

Jesus refused to take authority in a realm of civil government that had not been assigned to him.

If the church should not govern the state, this implies that various popes in the Middle Ages were wrong to attempt to assert authority over kings and emperors, or even to claim a right to select the emperor. These things came about as a result of a failure to appreciate the distinction that Jesus made between "the things that are Caesar's" and "the things that are God's."

2. The Civil Government Should Not Govern "the Things That Are God's." This principle implies that every nation should allow freedom of religion, by which every person is free to follow whatever religion he or she chooses. The principle, it seems to me, is rightly protected in the First Amendment to the U.S. Constitution, which says, "Congress shall make no law respecting an establishment of religion, or prohibiting the free exercise thereof."[29]

Further support for the idea that government should not control the church (or synagogue or mosque) is found in the selection of church officers in the New Testament. The first apostles were chosen by Jesus, not by any Roman official (see Matt. 10:1–4). The early church, not any government official, chose "seven men of good repute" to oversee the distribution of food to the needy (Acts 6:3). Paul gave qualifications for elders and deacons, which would have been used by those within the church (see 1 Tim. 3:1–13; Titus 1:3–9). There was clearly no involvement by the civil government, either by local officials or by the Roman Empire, in any selection of officers in the early church.

This was because, in distinction from the nation of Israel in the Old Testament era, *the government of the church and the government of the state are different systems,* and the two governments have authority over different groups of people (with some overlap) for different purposes. The civil government should not rule the church or infringe on the church's right to govern itself.

3. The Civil Government Should Never Try to Compel Religion. Tragically, many Christians in earlier centuries made the mistake of thinking that civil government could compel people to follow the Christian faith. This view played a large role in the Thirty

---

[29] See http://constitutionus.com.

Years' War (1618–1648) that began as a conflict between Protestants and Roman Catholics over control of various territories, especially in Germany. There were many other "wars of religion" in Europe, particularly between Catholics and Protestants, in the 16th and 17th centuries. Also in the 16th century, the Reformed and Lutheran Protestants persecuted and killed thousands from the Anabaptist groups in Switzerland and Germany who sought to have churches for "believers only" and practiced baptism by immersion for those who made a personal profession of faith.

Over the course of time, more and more Christians realized that this "compel religion" view is inconsistent with the teachings of Jesus and inconsistent with the nature of faith itself (see discussion below). Today I am not aware of any major Christian group that still holds to the view that civil government should try to compel people to follow the Christian faith.[30]

But other religions still promote government enforcement of their views. This is seen in countries such as Saudi Arabia, which enforces laws compelling people to follow Islam and imposes severe penalties from the religious police on those who fail to comply. The law prohibits any public practice of any religion other than Islam and prohibits Saudis from converting to other religions. Islamic advocate Bilal Cleland writes at the pro-Islamic website *Islam for Today*, "Legislation contained in the Quran becomes the basic law of the state."[31]

The "compel religion" view is also used by violent groups around the world to justify persecution of Christians, such as the burning by Muslims of an entire Christian village in Pakistan, killing six Christians in early August 2009,[32] or the warfare waged by Islamic militant groups against Christians in Nigeria, Sudan, and other sub-Saharan African countries. Extremism and ongoing persecution against Christians by ISIS (Islamic State of Iraq and the Levant) is resulting in mass migration and internal displacement. The Yazidis in the region of Kurdistan have been almost entirely wiped out. In Iraq, the number of Christians dropped from 1.4 million in 2003 to below 200,000 in 2017; and in Syria, from 1.25 million in 2011 to as few as 500,000 in 2017.[33] In Iraq, as much as 81 percent of the Christian population has disappeared, either killed or forced to flee to the wilderness or to UN camps, where jihadists wait to terrorize them.[34]

The "compel religion" view has also led to the violent persecution of Christians

---

[30] There is a small fringe movement called theonomy or Christian Reconstructionism that advocates government enforcement of Old Testament laws today, but most or all recognized leaders in the evangelical movement in the United States have clearly distanced themselves from this position regarding civil laws. (See my critique of theonomy, beginning at p. 225.)

[31] Bilal Cleland, "Islamic Government," *Islam for Today*, www.islamfortoday.com/cleland04.htm.

[32] Ben Quinn, "Six Christians Burned Alive in Pakistan Riots," *The Guardian*, Aug. 2, 2009, www.guardian .co.uk/world/2009/aug/02/christians-burned-alive-pakistan.

[33] "Persecuted and Forgotten? A Report on Christians Oppressed for their Faith 2015–2017, Iraq—Country Profile and Incident Reports," Aid to the Church in Need, https://acnuk.org/wp-content/uploads/2017 /08/PF2017-Exec-Summ-WEB-VERSION.pdf.

[34] Kristiana Monk, "Kerry Urged to Accuse ISIS of Genocide against Christians," The Daily Signal, March 2, 2016, http://dailysignal.com/2016/03/02/kerry-urged-to-accuse-isis-of-genocide-against-christians/.

by some Hindu groups in India. Attorneys with Alliance Defending Freedom in India report more than 670 attacks on Christians across the country since January 2015.[35] In 1999, it was reported that 51 Christian churches and prayer halls were burned to the ground in the western state of Gujarat. An Australian missionary, Graham Staines, and his two young sons were burned to death in their jeep by a Hindu mob in Orissa state on the eastern coast of India.[36] In 2007, the Associated Press reported that Hindu extremists set fire to nearly a dozen churches.[37]

In addition, research conducted by Pew Research Center's Forum on Religion and Public Life revealed that Christians are being harassed in 130 countries. In 104 countries, the harassment is done by governments and organizations, and in 100 countries, by social groups and individuals.[38]

But it must be noted that other Muslims and other Hindus also favor democracy and allowing varying degrees of freedom of religion.

In the early years of the United States, support for freedom of religion increased both because of a need to form a united country with people from various religious backgrounds (such as Congregational, Anglican/Episcopalian, Presbyterian, Quaker, Baptist, Roman Catholic, and Jewish) and because many of the colonists had fled from religious persecution in their home countries. For example, the New England Pilgrims had fled from England, where they had faced fines and imprisonment for failing to attend services in the Church of England and for conducting their own church services.

In 1779, just three years after the Declaration of Independence, Thomas Jefferson drafted the Virginia Statute for Religious Freedom, which demonstrated the increasing support for religious freedom in the United States. Jefferson wrote:

> Be it therefore enacted by the General Assembly, that no man shall be compelled to frequent or support any religious worship, place, or ministry whatsoever, nor shall be enforced, restrained, molested, or burthened [burdened] in his body or goods, nor shall otherwise suffer on account of his religious opinions or belief; but that all men shall be free to profess, and by argument to maintain, their opinions in matters of religion, and that the same shall in no wise diminish, enlarge, or affect their civil capacities.[39]

---

[35] Information provided by Tehmina Arora, senior counsel, ADF India, in personal email to Craig Osten of ADF.

[36] Ramola Talwar Badam, "Christians, Hindus Clash in India," Associated Press, Oct. 30, 1999, www .washingtonpost.com/wp-srv/aponline/19991030/aponline111427_000.htm.

[37] Gabin Rabinowitz, "Hindus, Christians Clash in India," Associated Press, Dec. 27, 2007, www.foxnews .com/printer_friendly_wires/2007Dec27/0,4675,IndiaChurchesAttacked,00.html.

[38] Pew Research Center, The Pew Forum on Religion and Public Life, "Rising Restrictions on Religion—One-Third of the World's Population Experiences an Increase," August 2011, http://pewforum.org /Government/Rising-Restrictions-on-Religion.aspx.

[39] The Virginia Statute for Religious Freedom," drafted by Thomas Jefferson in 1779, passed by the Virginia General Assembly in 1786, http://www.vahistorical.org/collections-and-resources/virginia-history-explorer /thomas-jefferson.

Several teachings of the Bible show that civil governments should never try to compel people to follow any certain religion.

a. Jesus Distinguished the Realms of God and of Caesar: This is the foundational argument I made at the beginning of this section. A person's individual religious beliefs and practices certainly belong to "the things that are God's" (Matt. 22:21), and therefore this is an area where the civil government ("Caesar") should not intervene.

b. Jesus Refused to Try to Compel People to Believe in Him: Another incident in Jesus's life also shows how he opposed the idea that force should ever be used to try to persuade people to follow him, for he rebuked his disciples when they wanted instant punishment to come to people who rejected him:

> And he sent messengers ahead of him, who went and entered a village of the Samaritans, to make preparations for him. But the people did not receive him, because his face was set toward Jerusalem. And when his disciples James and John saw it, they said, "Lord, do you want us to tell fire to come down from heaven and consume them?" (Luke 9:52–54)

The disciples apparently thought they had an excellent way to convince people to come to hear Jesus in the next village. If fire came down from heaven and wiped out the Samaritan village that had rejected Jesus, then word would get around, and Jesus and the disciples would have 100 percent attendance in the next village. What a persuasive method to "compel religion"!

But Jesus would have nothing to do with this idea. The next verse says, "But he turned and rebuked them" (Luke 9:55). Jesus directly refused any attempt to try to force people to believe in him or follow him.

c. Genuine Faith Cannot Be Forced: The nature of genuine faith fits with Jesus's condemnation of any request for "fire from heaven" to compel people to follow him. The underlying reason is that *true faith in God must be voluntary.* If faith is to be genuine, it can never be compelled by force. This constitutes another reason why governments should never try to compel adherence to any particular religion.

A clear respect for people's individual will and voluntary decisions is seen throughout the ministry of Jesus and the apostles. They always *taught* people and *reasoned* with them, then *appealed* to them to make a personal decision to follow Jesus as the true Messiah (see Matt. 11:28–30; Acts 28:23; Rom. 10:9–10; Rev. 22:17).

Genuine religious belief cannot be compelled by force, whether by fire from heaven or by the civil government, and Christians should have no part in any attempt to use civil government power to *compel* people to support or follow Christianity or any other religion.

d. Practical Implications of Rejecting the "Compel Religion" View: What are the practical implications of rejecting the "compel religion" view? One implication is that governments should never attempt to force people to follow or believe in one specific religion, but should guarantee freedom of religion for followers of *all religions* within the nation.

Another implication is that Christians in every nation should support freedom of religion and oppose any attempt by government to compel any single religion. In fact, *complete freedom of religion* should be the first principle advocated and defended by Christians who seek to influence government.

Sometimes non-Christians express a fear that if Christians gain too much power in government, they will try to force Christianity on everyone. This is a common argument made by groups such as Americans United for Separation of Church and State, the Center for American Progress, and the Freedom from Religion Foundation. Some critics even suggest that right-wing Christians are trying to establish a theocracy in the United States by incremental means. Michelle Goldberg writes, "The Christian nation is both the goal of the religious right and its fundamental ideology, the justification for its attempt to overthrow the doctrine of separation of church and state. . . . Right now . . . is high tide for theocratic fervor."[40] To counter this kind of false accusation, it is important for Christians involved in politics to affirm again and again their commitment to complete religious freedom in America (and in every other country).

Another implication is that government should not favor or support any one specific religion or denomination. An "established church" does still exist in some countries, however. For example, in the United Kingdom today, the Church of England is still the state church;[41] in Scandinavian countries such as Norway and Sweden, the Lutheran Church is the state church;[42] and in many countries with a highly Roman Catholic populace, such as Spain, the Roman Catholic Church is the state-supported church. In Germany, church taxes are assessed on Catholic, Protestant, and Jewish wage earners, up to 8 percent or 9 percent of their total income. The state then disperses these funds to the churches to be used for social services.[43]

I recognize that some Christians in these countries argue that the benefits that come from having such state churches outweigh the negative effects, but I still cannot see sufficient warrant for it in the New Testament. I see no evidence that government tax money, rather than the donations of individual Christians, should be used to support the activities of a church. In addition, the historical pattern seems to be that direct government support weakens a church rather than strengthening it. (Notice the extremely low church attendance at state-sponsored Lutheran churches in Germany or Sweden, for example.)

---

[40] Michelle Goldberg, *Kingdom Coming: The Rise of Christian Nationalism* (New York: W. W. Norton, 2007), 27–28. See also Kevin Phillips, *American Theocracy: The Peril and Politics of Radical Religion, Oil, and Borrowed Money in the 21st Century* (New York: Viking, 2006).

[41] John L. Allen Jr., "In Europe, 'Church Taxes' Are Not Unusual," *National Catholic Reporter*, Jan. 29, 2009, available by subscription at: https://www.highbeam.com/doc/1G1-53744625.html.

[42] Ibid.

[43] Ibid.

4. Civil Government Should Support and Encourage Churches and Bona Fide Religious Groups in General. While the civil government should not rule over the church and should not compel or promote any one religion above another, it is an entirely separate question to ask whether government should give support to churches and to religion *in general*. One example of such support (though it is not direct support or funding) would be the granting of tax-exempt status to churches, so that churches would not pay taxes on their property or on the income and contributions they receive. Another example would be government support for chaplains in the military and in U.S. prisons.

These actions seem to me to be appropriate for government. They flow from the government's responsibility to "promote the general welfare" (in the words of the U.S. Constitution) or to promote the good of the nation as a whole (see above, p. 432). As long as the opportunity is available for *any religious group* to take advantage of these benefits, it does not seem that the government is inappropriately favoring one religion over another.

Sadly, some segments of American society have lost sight of the idea that churches are healthy for a society and therefore should be encouraged. An ominous trend is appearing in municipal zoning processes whereby it is increasingly difficult for churches to obtain approvals to build new facilities or buy buildings to use as houses of worship in many areas.[44]

5. The Most Difficult Church/State Questions Arise When People Disagree over What Belongs to Each Realm. Most of the really difficult questions regarding the relationship between church and state arise when there is a conflict over whether something is among "the things that are Caesar's" or "the things that are God's." In the ancient church, the civil government thought it was appropriate to require every person to bow to a statue of Caesar and swear allegiance to him as a god. Bowing to Caesar was something that was "Caesar's"! But the early Christians thought this practice forced them to commit idolatry, so they believed it was one of "the things that are God's." Many of the early Christians died for that conviction (which I think was the right conviction—that civil government has no rightful authority to command anyone to worship any person or supposed god).

In the United States, it seems to me that most of these God-versus-Caesar disputes in hard cases have been settled correctly. For instance, Jehovah's Witnesses have traditionally objected to blood transfusions, claiming that this is a *religious* belief. But the civil government, in a number of cases, has forcibly imposed blood transfusions to save

---

[44] The Alliance Defending Freedom (www.ADFMedia.org) has been involved in and won many of these zoning battles. See "New Hampshire Church Receives More Than $1.1 Million over Unconstitutional Zoning Restrictions," June 25, 2010, http://www.adfmedia.org/news/prdetail/4092; "Florida City's Discrimination against Church Costs Taxpayers Nearly $300,000," Oct. 15, 2015, http://www.adfmedia.org/News/PRDetail/9313; "Mich. Town Allows Church to Occupy Property in Wake of Lawsuit," Dec. 6, 2010, www.adfmedia.org/News/PRDetail/4457; and "Texas Town Hinders Church Ministry from Helping Parolees," April 28, 2008, http://www.adfmedia.org/News/PRDetail/1842.

the life of a young child over the objections of Jehovah's Witness parents, reasoning that the protection of a child's life is not a matter of worship or church activities, but is rightly the domain of civil government (and I agree).[45] In another case, practitioners of a Brazilian religion in New Mexico claimed that the use of hallucinogenic tea in worship services was part of their traditional religious practice.[46] The Supreme Court (rightly, it seems to me) allowed them to continue this practice as an element of their worship, but when a new religious group in California claimed that its recently invented religion required them to grow and use marijuana as part of their "worship," a federal district court (again rightly, I think) prohibited this, saying that there was no historic tradition establishing this as a genuine religious belief.[47]

In still another case, Sultanna Freeman, a Muslim woman in Orlando, Florida, claimed the right to be veiled except for a thin slit for her eyes when getting her driver's license photo. She claimed this to be a "sincerely held religious belief." The state made a reasonable effort to accommodate her, saying that she could be photographed in a private setting with only women present, but she was not satisfied with this solution. Finally, the Florida Circuit Court, on June 6, 2003, ruled that if she wanted a driver's license, the state did have a "compelling interest" in requiring her to have a photo taken without a veil.[48] Once again, I think the decision was correct, and that the requirement of an identifiable photo for a driver's license is not among "the things that are God's" but rather "the things that are Caesar's." Freedom of religion does not release people from the obligation to obey generally applicable laws—the ordinary and morally good laws that are required of all members of a society.

I. GOVERNMENTS SHOULD ESTABLISH A STRONG AND CLEAR SEPARATION OF POWERS

Because of the presence of sin in every human heart (see above, p. 445) and because of the corrupting influence of power, there should be a clear separation of powers at every level of civil government to prevent any one person or group from gaining too much power and then changing the government into a tyranny. The phrase "separation of powers" means that government power should be divided among several different groups or people, not concentrated in only one person or group.

Several parts of Scripture give support to the idea of separation of powers in a governing authority. The Old Testament narratives give many examples of kings who had unchecked power and abused it. Saul repeatedly put his own interests first rather than

---

[45] For example, see Catherine Philip, "Babies Seized after Jehovah's Witness Mother Refuses Blood for Sextuplets," *The Times*, Feb. 23, 2007, https://www.thetimes.co.uk/article/babies-seized-after-jehovahs-witness-mother-refuses-blood-for-sextuplets-0t8g5bfsbrl.

[46] Gonzales v. O Centro Espirita Beneficente Uniao Do Vegetal, 546 U.S. 418 (2006).

[47] Kiczenski v. Ashcroft, 2006 WL 463153, at *3 (E.D. Cal. Feb. 24, 2006).

[48] "U.S. Muslim Ordered to Lift Veil," BBC News, June 6, 2003, http://news.bbc.co.uk/1/hi/world/americas/2970514.stm.

those of the people. David misused his royal authority in his sin with Bathsheba (see 2 Samuel 11). Solomon wrongfully accumulated "700 wives, who were princesses, and 300 concubines. And his wives turned away his heart" (1 Kings 11:3). In addition, he had excessive silver and gold, even though that had been prohibited (1 Kings 10:14–22; Deut. 17:17). During the divided monarchy, most kings abused their power and did evil (see 1–2 Kings; 1–2 Chronicles). Many other examples of unchecked power throughout human history confirm the idea that when power is combined with sin in the human heart, it has a corrupting influence on people and is easily misused.

The prophet Samuel warned against just this thing, saying that a king would abuse his power and "take" and "take" again and again from the people (see 1 Sam. 8:11–17, quoted above, p. 436).

But what can prevent abuse of power by those in government? The best safeguard against the abuse of power is divided power, so that one person or group within a government provides "checks" on the use of power by another person or group. When power is divided among several people or groups, then different entities in different parts of government all struggle to be sure that no one part of government has too much power (because they tend to protect their own turf).

The Bible contains a number of positive examples of various kinds of divided power, reflecting the wisdom of God in protecting against the abuse of power by one person. In the Old Testament, the king had *some* checks on his power because of the existence of the offices of prophet and priest (even though the king often disregarded them).

In the New Testament, it is noteworthy that Jesus established not *one* apostle with authority over the church, but *12* apostles (see Matt. 10:1–4; Acts 1:15–26). Although Peter at first served as spokesman for the apostles (see Acts 2:14; 3:12; 15:7), James later seems to have assumed that role (see Acts 15:13; 21:18; Gal. 1:19; 2:9, 12). Moreover, the Jerusalem Council made its decision not on the authority of the apostles alone, but because it "seemed good to the apostles and the elders, *with the whole church*" (Acts 15:22). Every indication of the form of government that was followed by local churches in the New Testament shows that they were not governed by a single *elder* but by multiple *elders* (see Titus 1:5; James 5:14).

Separation of powers in a government can be accomplished in many ways, and different nations have adopted different structures. The example I know best is the United States, where the power of the national government is divided among three branches: the legislative (Congress), the executive (the president and everyone under his authority), and the judicial (the courts). The legislative power itself is divided between the House of Representatives (with members elected every two years), and the Senate (with members elected every six years). Legislation must be passed by both houses and signed by the president.

There are other ways that power is divided in the United States. Power is allocated in portions to the national government, to the 50 state governments, and to county and city governments, with each level retaining authority over some areas. The power of the army is under the authority of the president and a civilian secretary of defense (who is not a member of the armed forces but has authority over all of them). Funding for the military has to be approved by Congress. The power of the United States Army is itself limited, for the Army is prohibited by law from exercising civilian police functions within the United States. In addition, each state has a national guard not under the authority of the U.S. Army, the president, or any branch of the federal government, but under the governor of that state.

Local police forces are accountable only to the city or county governments for which they work. This means that no one could take over the United States simply by assuming control of the Army (as can happen in some nations), for the Army has no authority over the hundreds of thousands of local police forces that answer only to the citizens in their own cities and towns.

As a further safeguard against a tyranny imposed from the top, the Founding Fathers incorporated in the Second Amendment to the Constitution "the right of the people to keep and bear Arms."[49] An armed citizenry provides an additional level of defense against a potential tyrant and provides further separation of power in a nation. (Switzerland provides another example of this principle, with its requirement that all men in the nation be armed and trained in the use of firearms.)

Another kind of separation of power has to do with the dissemination of information. For this reason the First Amendment to the Constitution also prohibits "abridging the freedom of speech, or of the press; or the right of the people peaceably to assemble, and to petition the Government, for redress of grievances." This guarantees that there will be public knowledge of the workings of government and accountability to the people. It guarantees that opposition political parties cannot be outlawed or persecuted, but must be given rights and protected. In this way, freedom of speech, freedom of the press, and freedom of assembly are essential elements in protecting against governmental abuse of power.

J. THE RULE OF LAW MUST APPLY EVEN TO THE RULERS IN A NATION

In a nation with good government, the law rules over the rulers, not the rulers over the law. This principle was established in the nation of Israel and was reinforced by the requirement that a new king was to write a copy of the Mosaic Law for himself, so that he would understand it and remember to be subject to it:

> And when he sits on the throne of his kingdom, *he shall write for himself in a book a copy of this law*, approved by the Levitical priests. And it shall be with him, *and he shall read in it all the days of his life*, that he may learn to fear the

---

[49] See http://constitutionus.com.

LORD his God by keeping all the words of this law and these statutes, and doing them, that his heart may not be lifted up above his brothers, and that he may not turn aside from the commandment, either to the right hand or to the left, so that he may continue long in his kingdom, he and his children, in Israel. (Deut. 17:18–20)

In actual practice, the principle of the "rule of law" means that no king (or president or prime minister) has unchecked power. The king is not *above* the law, but is *subject* to the law—as was dramatically illustrated when Nathan the prophet rebuked King David for disobeying God's laws in his sin with Bathsheba (2 Samuel 12). Other kings were also rebuked by the prophets for disobeying the words of God, such as Saul (1 Sam. 13:13–14), Jeroboam (1 Kings 13–14), and Ahab (1 Kings 18:18). In the early church, even the apostle Peter was rebuked by Paul when he strayed from the principles of the Word of God and the teachings of Christ (see Gal. 2:11–12).

This principle that even rulers are not above the law is illustrated in the United States (and other countries) every time a sitting governor, senator, or representative is convicted in court for using his or her office for personal gain or for taking bribes to influence a decision.

The principle of the rule of law is violated, however, whenever any person or group in a society has unchecked power and therefore can disobey the law without fear of punishment. This is the case with dictators and their friends and family members in many smaller countries; with criminal mobs that repeatedly violate the law in Russia; with government-supported monopolies that have unchecked power (such as the telecommunications companies controlled by Carlos Slim in Mexico);[50] or with the "checkpoints" that notoriously extort payments from trucks attempting to travel highways in Cameroon and other African countries. The rule of law is also violated in countries where the government has a media monopoly and can publish lies or cover up government misconduct with no fear of consequence (as in the "trials" of many house-church leaders in China or the silencing of opposition journalists in Russia).

K. THE BIBLE GIVES INDIRECT BUT SIGNIFICANT SUPPORT TO THE IDEA THAT GOVERNMENT SHOULD BE CHOSEN BY THE PEOPLE (SOME KIND OF DEMOCRACY)

The Bible does not explicitly command or directly teach that governments should be chosen by a democratic[51] process; in fact, there are no biblical commands as to how God wants

---

[50] David Luhnow, "The Secrets of the World's Richest Man," *The Wall Street Journal*, Aug. 4, 2007, https://www.wsj.com/articles/SB118615255900587380.

[51] The word *democracy* can have either a broad or a narrow meaning. In a broad sense, *democracy* means "government by the people, exercised either directly or through elected representatives" (meaning 1 in *The*

governments to be chosen. There are actually many historical examples of *hereditary kings* throughout the Old Testament, and we also read about some Roman emperors and governors sent by them in the New Testament. These rulers are *recorded* in the Bible's history, but that does not mean their form of government is *endorsed* or *commanded*. There is no explicit teaching that other governments in other nations should take these forms.

If we look beyond these mere historical examples to biblical principles regarding government and the nature of human beings, a rather strong biblical argument can be made in support of the idea that *some form of government chosen by the people* is preferable to other kinds of government (at least during this present age, until the return of Christ). Several arguments consistent with biblical principles support this idea:

1. Equality in the Image of God. The first support for some kind of democracy is the concept of *the equality of all people in the image of God.* "So God created man *in his own image*, in the image of God he created him; male and female he created them" (Gen. 1:27; this applies also to the whole human race descended from Adam and Eve. Other passages of Scripture also affirm that all human beings are in the image of God: see Gen. 9:6; James 3:9). To be "in the image of God" means to be like God and to represent him on earth—the highest status given to anything God made.

But if *all people* share equally in the high privilege of being made in the image of God, then what reason can there be for any family to think that it has a special right to act as "royalty" or rule over others without their consent? Far from endorsing anything like a "divine right of kings," the foundational principle of equality in the image of God taught in the first chapter of the Bible argues against the idea of royalty.

This rejection of any hereditary right of any "royal family" to rule over others was the background that led to this statement in the second paragraph of the U.S. Declaration of Independence:

> We hold these truths to be self-evident, that *all men are created equal*, that they
> are endowed by their Creator with certain unalienable rights . . . [52]

American Heritage Dictionary [Boston: Houghton Mifflin, 1996], 497). In this sense, the United States is clearly a democracy: it is not a monarchy, an oligarchy, or a dictatorship, but is government "by the people . . . through elected representatives."

But sometimes people try to inform me, "The United States is a republic, not a democracy." There is some value in this claim, and I understand that people are trying to be more precise in describing the kind of government we have. But they also should understand that when they say this, they are using the word *democracy* in a more narrow sense, one in which it means a "simple majority rule," and they understand the word to refer only to a pure democracy, as in an ancient city-state, where all decisions were made by a vote of all the citizens. They understand the word *republic* to be the only proper term to describe a government by elected representatives who then make decisions for the government of all the people.

My response to these people is that, yes, the United States is a *republic*, but it is *also* a *democracy*, because I am not using the word *democracy* in the narrow sense of "pure democracy." I am simply using the word *democracy* to mean a system of government in which the leaders are elected by the people. That is the most common sense of the word today, and that is what it means in ordinary conversational and written English.

[52] See the text of the Declaration of Independence in the appendix to this chapter, p. 477. Emphasis added.

2. Accountability through Elections Guards against Abuse of Power. Another argument in favor of some form of democracy is that *accountability of rulers to the people* helps prevent a misuse of their power. As I argued above (see p. 456), a separation of powers in government tends to prevent abuse. Perhaps the most effective separation of powers is the separation between the power given to government and the power reserved for the people, which is evident in free elections. *The need to gain and maintain consent from those who are governed*, through elections at periodic intervals, is probably the single greatest protection against the abuse of power and the single greatest guarantee of accountability on the part of rulers. This is because elections provide a strong incentive to rulers to act for the benefit of the people, and thereby to act as "God's servant for your good" (Rom. 13:4), as Paul says governments should do. Rulers who become corrupt and abuse their power regularly abolish free elections, imprison or murder political opponents, intimidate voters, and rig elections so that they "win" because their cronies control the ballots, the counting of votes, and the media reports of the election results. (Rigged "elections" in Russia,[53] Zimbabwe,[54] and Venezuela[55] are notorious examples, as is the nullified election of Aung San Suu Kyi in Myanmar/Burma.[56])

How can we know if a country is actually functioning as a democracy? Former Soviet dissident Natan Sharansky, in his book *The Case for Democracy*, provides "the town square test" to determine whether a particular society is what he calls a "free society" (and thus a genuine democracy) or a "fear society":

> Can a person walk into the middle of the town square and express his or her views without fear of arrest, imprisonment, or physical harm? If he can, then that person is living in a free society, not a fear society.[57]

3. The People as a Whole Can Best Judge If Rulers Are Working for Their Good. The purpose of government also argues for democracy. *If government is to serve for the benefit of the people* (to be "God's servant for *your good*," Rom. 13:4), this means that the government does not exist ultimately for the good of the *king*, the good of the *emperor*,

---

[53] "'The election was not fair and failed to meet standards for democratic elections,' concluded the Organization for Security and Co-operation in Europe (OSCE) and the Council of Europe in a joint statement." "Russia's Election: How It Was Rigged," *The Economist*, Dec. 3, 2007, www.economist.com/world/europe/displaystory.cfm?story_id=10238268.

[54] Peta Thorneycraft, "Police 'Rigged Ballot' in Zimbabwe Election," *The Age*, April 12, 2008, www.theage.com.au/news/world/police-rigged-ballot-in-zimbabwe-election/2008/04/11/1207856835491.html.

[55] Christopher Toothaker, "Efforts to Dispel Claims of Vote-Rigging in Venezuela's Recall Vote Suffer a Setback," Associated Press, Aug. 19, 2004, http://staugustine.com/stories/081904/wor_2521920.shtml#.WXZdp63Mz64.

[56] Meghan Dunn, "UN Chief Urges Myanmar to Hold 'Fair' Election," CNN, July 14, 2009, www.cnn.com/2009/WORLD/asiapcf/07/13/myanmar.un.elections/index.html; and "Myanmar Junta Dismisses Suu Kyi Victory," Associated Press/*USA Today*, July 6, 2008, https://usatoday30.usatoday.com/news/world/2008-07-06-3081463627_x.htm.

[57] Natan Sharansky, *The Case for Democracy: The Power of Freedom to Overcome Tyranny and Terror* (New York: PublicAffairs, 2004), 40–41.

or the good of the *ruling council* (or their families and friends), but for the good of the people themselves.

The next question that follows is this: Who is best suited to decide what is best for the people? Shouldn't the people as a whole have the right to decide what kind of leaders best advance their good and the good of the nation? Of course, the people as a whole can make mistakes, just as any elite group of rulers could make mistakes about what is best for the people. But ultimately the people who are *supposed* to benefit from the rule of government should be the ones who can best decide what is *actually* for their benefit and what is not. (Rulers can delude themselves into thinking that their policies are "for the people's good," but it is hard to believe this if they have to rig elections, imprison political opponents, and silence dissent.)

4. Some Examples in Scripture Show the Value of Gaining Consent from the People Who Are Governed. A number of narrative examples in Scripture indicate that *government seems to work best with the consent of those who are governed*. Even though Moses had been appointed by God, he sought the public assent of the elders and the people of Israel (Ex. 4:29–31), as did Samuel when he stood before all the people in his role as judge (1 Sam. 7:5–6) and Saul after he had been anointed as king (1 Sam. 10:24).

When David became king over Judah, he gained the public consent of all the people: "The men of Judah came, and there they anointed David king over the house of Judah" (2 Sam. 2:4). When Zadok the priest anointed Solomon as king, then "All the people said, 'Long live King Solomon!'" (1 Kings 1:39; see also 12:1).

In the New Testament, the apostles asked for the help of the congregation in selecting leaders to oversee the distribution of food to the needy: "Therefore, brothers, *pick out from among you* seven men of good repute, full of the Spirit and of wisdom, whom we will appoint to this duty" (Acts 6:3).

By contrast, there are negative examples in Scripture of tyrants who did not gain the consent of the people but ruled harshly in opposition to the people's consent. "So the king [Rehoboam] did not listen to the people" (1 Kings 12:15), and as a result the 10 northern tribes rebelled against him: "And when all Israel saw that *the king did not listen to them*, the people answered the king, 'What portion do we have in David? . . . To your tents, O Israel!'" (v. 16). Israel was divided into the northern and southern kingdoms from that day onward.

In a similar way, the Old Testament contains several examples of oppressive rulers who subjected the people of Israel to slavery and who certainly did not rule by the consent of those over whom they ruled, whether this was Pharaoh as king in Egypt (Ex. 3:9–10), the Philistines, who ruled harshly over Israel during the time of the Judges (Judg. 14:4), or Nebuchadnezzar and other foreign kings who conquered and eventually carried the people off into exile (2 Kings 25:1–21). These events are all viewed negatively in the biblical narrative.

In the New Testament, under the Roman government, Herod the Great and his successors were also oppressive rulers, reigning without the consent of the Jewish people, and ruling harshly over them (see Matt. 2:16–17; Luke 13:1; Acts 12:1–2).

5. Conclusion: The Bible Gives Significant Support for the Idea of Government Chosen by the People. Therefore, substantial biblical arguments can be given in support of the idea of some form of government chosen by the people themselves (that is, in general terms, a democracy). Such a government seems to be preferable to all other forms of government, such as dictatorship, hereditary monarchy, or government by a hereditary or self-perpetuating aristocracy. (Several democracies today, such as the United Kingdom and Norway, have retained a monarchy that functions in a largely ceremonial and symbolic function, but they are democracies because the real governing power rests with the elected representatives of the people.)

There is, however, one King for whom the Bible gives unlimited approval, and that is Jesus Christ, who will one day return to the earth to reign as "King of kings and Lord of lords" (Rev. 19:16). There will be no injustice or abuse of power in his domain, for he will reign in perfect righteousness. The book of Daniel prophesies about his reign:

> And to him was given dominion
> and glory and a kingdom,
> that all peoples, nations, and languages
> should serve him;
> his dominion is an everlasting dominion,
> which shall not pass away,
> and his kingdom one
> that shall not be destroyed. (Dan. 7:14)

But until Christ returns to reign, some form of democracy seems to be the best form of government, based on the principles above.

6. The Early Development of Self-Government within the United States. In the early history of the United States, when the Pilgrims established the Mayflower Compact in 1620, and thereby established a form of self-government, they did so with a strong biblical knowledge influenced by many of the passages and principles of Scripture mentioned above. They also had vivid memories of oppression by the monarchy in England. As a result, the Mayflower Compact established a government *by the consent of the governed*, and this would set a pattern for the subsequent colonies and for the United States as a whole in later years. The Pilgrims declared that they were forming a "civil body politik" that would enact "laws" for the general good of the colony, and then they said that to that government "we promise all due submission and obedience."[58] This was a voluntary submission to a government that they themselves had created. It was not imposed on them from without by a king or some other conquering force. It was a government set up to function with the consent of the governed—a kind of democracy.

[58] For the wording of the Mayflower Compact, see www.historyplace.com/unitedstates/revolution/mayflower.htm. For primary source background on the Mayflower Compact, see http://mayflowerhistory.com/primary-sources-and-books/.

These same principles found fuller expression in the U.S. Declaration of Independence:

> We hold these truths to be self-evident, that all men are created equal, that they are endowed by their Creator with certain unalienable rights, that among these are life, liberty, and the pursuit of happiness. That to secure these rights, governments are instituted among men, *deriving their just powers from the consent of the governed.*[59]

Although there were some forms of democratic government in local areas in ancient and medieval history (such as ancient Athens), when the United States began as a representative democracy in 1776, it could be called the "American experiment," because there were at that time no other functioning national democracies in the world. But after the founding of the United States, and especially in the 20th century, the number of functioning national democracies grew remarkably. The World Forum on Democracy reports that in 1950 there were 22 democracies accounting for 31 percent of the world population, and a further 21 states with restricted democratic practices accounting for 11.9 percent of the globe's population. In 2015, electoral democracies represented 125 of the 196 existing countries.[60] Approximately 4.1 billion people live in electoral democracies, or 55.8 percent of the world's population.[61]

Therefore, when people today complain that they don't want to get involved in politics because they think that politicians are too corrupt (or arrogant, greedy, power-hungry, or other forms of "unspiritual"), I want to remind them that although democracy is messy, it still works quite well, and all the alternative forms of government are far worse. We should be thankful for those who are willing to be involved in it, often at great personal sacrifice.

L. NATIONS SHOULD VALUE PATRIOTISM

What should be the attitude of citizens toward the nation in which they live? Because any nation can have rulers who are evil, or basically good rulers who still do wrong things from time to time, a Christian view of government would never endorse a kind of *blind patriotism*, according to which a citizen would never criticize a country or its leaders. In fact, a *genuine patriotism*, which always seeks to promote the good of the nation, would honestly criticize the government and its leaders when they do things contrary to biblical moral standards.

---

[59] See the text of the Declaration of Independence in the appendix to this chapter, p. 477.

[60] "Freedom in the World: 2015," Freedom House, https://freedomhouse.org/sites/default/files/01152015_FIW_2015_final.pdf.

[61] The exact figure is 4,101,291,986 people out of the world population of 7,349,472,254 as of Aug. 11, 2016. See "Number of World Citizens Living under Different Regimes," Our World in Data, https://ourworldindata.org/grapher/world-pop-by-political-regime.

But is patriotism a virtue *at all*? My conclusion is that the Bible gives support to a genuine kind of patriotism in which citizens love, support, and defend their countries.

1. Biblical Reasons for Patriotism. Biblical support for the idea of patriotism begins with a recognition that *God has established nations on the earth.* Speaking in Athens, Paul said that God had "made from one man every *nation* of mankind to live on all the face of the earth, having determined allotted periods and the boundaries of their dwelling place" (Acts 17:26).

One example of this is found in God's promise to make the descendants of Abram (later Abraham) into a distinct nation:

> And I will make of you a great *nation*, and I will bless you and make your
> name great, so that you will be a blessing. (Gen. 12:2)

Later God said to Abraham, "In your offspring shall *all the nations* of the earth be blessed" (Gen. 22:18).

The ancient origin of many nations on earth is recorded in the Table of Nations descended from Noah, which concludes, "These are the clans of the sons of Noah, according to their genealogies, *in their nations*, and from these the nations spread abroad on the earth after the flood" (Gen. 10:32).

In the ongoing progress of history, Job says that God "*makes nations great*, and he destroys them; he enlarges nations, and leads them away" (Job 12:23).

The sense of what a "nation" was in the Bible is not different in any substantial way from what we mean by a nation today—a group of people living under the same government that is sovereign and independent in its relationship to other nations.

In the modern age, and for the purposes of this book, a nation is ordinarily a relatively large group of people living under an independent government, although today there are a few nations that aren't very large, such as Monaco and Luxembourg, and some nations are only partially independent from larger, more dominant nations.

The existence of many independent nations on the earth should be considered a blessing from God. One benefit of the existence of nations is that *they divide and disperse government power throughout the earth.* In this way they prevent the rule of any one worldwide dictatorship, which would be more horrible than any single evil government, both because it would affect everyone on earth and because there would be no nation that could challenge it. History has shown repeatedly that rulers with unchecked and unlimited power become more and more corrupt.

The signers of the U.S. Declaration of Independence realized that they were establishing a separate nation, as indicted in the first sentence:

> When, in the course of human events, it becomes necessary for one people
> to dissolve the political bands which have connected them with another, and

to assume among the powers of the earth, *the separate and equal station* to which the laws of nature and of nature's God entitle them, a decent respect to the opinions of mankind requires that they should declare the causes which impel them to the separation.[62]

The Bible also teaches Christians to obey and honor the leaders of the nation in which they live. Peter tells Christians to "honor the emperor" (1 Pet. 2:17), then adds:

Be subject for the Lord's sake to every human institution, whether it be to the emperor as supreme, or to governors . . . (vv. 13–14)

Paul likewise encourages not only obedience but also honor and appreciation for civil rulers when he writes, "Let every person be subject to the governing authorities" (Rom. 13:1). He adds that the ruler is "God's servant for your good" (v. 4). He concludes this section by implying that Christians should not only pay taxes, but also give respect and honor, at least in some measure, to rulers in civil government:

Pay to all what is owed to them: taxes to whom taxes are owed, revenue to whom revenue is owed, *respect to whom respect is owed, honor to whom honor is owed.* (v. 7)

These commands follow a pattern found in the Old Testament, as the following passages indicate:

My son, fear the Lord and the king,
    and do not join with those who do otherwise. (Prov. 24:21)

Even in your thoughts, do not curse the king,
    nor in your bedroom curse the rich. (Eccles. 10:20)

Thus says the Lord of Hosts, the God of Israel, to all the exiles whom I have sent into exile from Jerusalem to Babylon. . . . *Seek the welfare of the city where I have sent you into exile,* and pray to the Lord on its behalf, for in its welfare you will find your welfare. (Jer. 29:4–7)

God's establishment of individual nations, the benefits that come to the world from the existence of nations, and the biblical commands that imply that one should give appreciation and support to the government leaders where one lives all tend to support the idea of patriotism in a nation.

2. The Benefits of Patriotism in a Nation. With these factors in mind, I would define genuine patriotism more fully as including the following elements:

---

[62] See the text of the Declaration of Independence in the appendix to this chapter, p. 477.

1. A *sense of belonging* to a larger community of people, which provides one aspect of a person's sense of identity and his obligation to others
2. *Gratitude* for the benefits that a nation provides, such as the protection of life, liberty, and property; laws to deter wrongdoing and encourage good; the maintenance of a monetary system and economic markets; and a common language or languages
3. A *shared sense of pride in the achievements of other individuals* in the nation to which one "belongs" as fellow citizens of the same nation (including pride in athletic, scientific, economic, artistic, philanthropic, or other endeavors)
4. A *sense of pride for the good things that a nation has done*, something that is developed by a proper understanding of the nation's history and a sense of belonging to a group of people that includes previous generations within that nation
5. A *sense of security* with respect to the future because of an expectation that the larger group—that is, everyone in the nation—will work for the good of the nation and therefore will defend each person in the nation from attacks by violent evildoers, whether from within or outside its borders
6. A *sense of obligation to serve the nation* and do good for it in various ways, such as defending it from military attack or from unfair criticism by others; protecting the existence and character of the nation for future generations; and improving the nation in various ways where possible, even through helpful criticism of things that are done wrong within the nation
7. A *sense of obligation to live by and to transmit to newcomers and succeeding generations a shared sense of moral values and standards* that are widely valued by those within the nation. Such a sense of obligation to shared moral standards is more likely to happen within a nation than within the world as a whole, because a person can act as a moral agent and be evaluated by others within the context of an entire nation, but very seldom does anyone have enough prominence to act with respect to the entire world. Another reason is that values and standards can readily spread to most of the citizens of one nation (especially where most speak a common language), but the world is so large and diverse that it is difficult to find many moral values and standards that are shared throughout all nations, or any awareness in one nation of what values are held in other nations. Within an individual nation, if such moral values and national ideals are to be preserved and transmitted, it is usually necessary to share a common sense of the origins of the nation and its history.

By contrast, the opposite of patriotism is an attitude of dislike or even scorn or hatred for one's nation, accompanied by continual criticism of it. Rather than feeling gratitude for the benefits provided by the country and pride in the good things it has done, those opposed to patriotism will repeatedly emphasize any negative aspect of the country's actions, no matter how ancient or how minor compared with the whole of its history. They will not be proud of the nation or its history, and they will not be very willing to sacrifice for it or to serve it or defend it. Such antipatriotic attitudes will continually erode the ability of the nation to function effectively and will eventually tend to undermine the very existence of the nation itself. In such cases, a healthy but limited criticism of the wrongs of a nation becomes exaggerated to the point where reality is distorted and a person becomes basically opposed to the good of the nation in general.

To take a modern example, a patriotic citizen of Iran in 2017 might well say, "I love my country and its great traditions, ideals, and history, but I'm deeply saddened by the oppressive and evil nature of the current totalitarian government." A patriotic citizen of North Korea might say something similar. A patriotic citizen of Iraq under the regime of Saddam Hussein might have said similar things as well.

To take another example, a patriotic citizen of Germany might say, "I love my nation and I'm proud of its great historical achievements in science, literature, music, and many other areas of human thought, though I'm deeply grieved by the evils perpetrated under the leadership of Adolf Hitler, and I'm glad that we were finally liberated from his oppressive rule."

I give these examples to illustrate the fact that even citizens of countries with evil rulers can retain a genuine patriotism that is combined with sober and truthful criticism of current or past leaders. But such patriotism will still include the valuable components mentioned above, such as a sense of belonging to that particular nation, gratitude for the benefits it gives, shared pride in its achievements, a sense of security, a sense of obligation to serve and protect it (and hopefully to change any evil leadership), and a sense of obligation to follow and transmit shared values and ideals that represent the best of the country's history.

If such things can be true even in nations that have or have had bad governments, then certainly patriotism can be a value inculcated in all the other nations of the world as well. And a Christian view of government encourages and supports genuine patriotism within a nation.

M. CHRISTIANS SHOULD INFLUENCE GOVERNMENT FOR GOOD

1. Old Testament Support for Christian Influence on Government. The Bible shows several examples of believers in God who influenced secular governments, and it views their activities with approval. The first example is Joseph, who was the highest official after Pharaoh, king of Egypt, and had great influence in Pharaoh's decisions (see Gen. 41:37–45; 42:6; 45:8–9, 26). Later, Moses boldly stood before the Pharaoh and demanded freedom for the people of Israel, saying, "Thus says the LORD, 'Let my people go'" (Ex. 8:1).

The Jewish prophet Daniel exercised a strong influence on the secular government in Babylon. Daniel said to King Nebuchadnezzar:

> Therefore, O king, let my counsel be acceptable to you: *break off your sins* by *practicing righteousness*, and your iniquities by *showing mercy to the oppressed*, that there may perhaps be a lengthening of your prosperity. (Dan. 4:27)

Daniel's approach was bold and clear. It was the opposite of a modern multicultural approach, which might say something like this:

> O King Nebuchadnezzar, I am a Jewish prophet, but I would not presume to impose my Jewish moral standards on your Babylonian kingdom. Ask your astronomers and your soothsayers! They will guide you in your own traditions. Then follow your own heart! It would not be my place to speak to you about right and wrong.

No, Daniel boldly told the king, "*Break off your sins* by practicing righteousness, and your iniquities by showing mercy to the oppressed."

At that time Daniel was a high official in Nebuchadnezzar's court. He was "ruler over the whole province of Babylon" and "chief prefect over all the wise men of Babylon" (Dan. 2:48). He was regularly "at the king's court" (v. 49). Therefore, it seems that Daniel had a significant advisory role to the king. This leads to a reasonable assumption that, though it is not specified in the text, Daniel's summary statement about "sins," "iniquities," and "showing mercy to the oppressed" (Dan. 4:27) was followed by a longer conversation in which Daniel named specific policies and actions of the king that were either good or evil in the eyes of God.

The counsel that Jeremiah proclaimed to the Jewish exiles in Babylon also supports the idea of believers having influence on laws and government. Jeremiah told these exiles, "*Seek the welfare of the city* where I have sent you into exile, and pray to the LORD on its behalf, for in its welfare you will find your welfare" (Jer. 29:7). But if believers are to seek to bring good to such a pagan society, that must include seeking to bring good to its government, as Daniel did (as well as working in many other nongovernmental areas to bring good to individuals, families, schools, businesses, and other components of society). The true "welfare" of such a city will be advanced in significant measure through governmental laws and policies that are consistent with God's teaching in the Bible, not by those that are contrary to the Bible's teachings.

Other believers in God also had high positions of governmental influence in non-Jewish nations. Nehemiah was "cupbearer to the king" (Neh. 1:11), a position of high responsibility before King Artaxerxes of Persia.[63] Mordecai "was second in rank to King Ahasuerus" of Persia (Est. 10:3; see also 9:4). Queen Esther also had significant influence on the decisions of Ahasuerus (see Est. 5:1–8; 7:1–6; 8:3–13; 9:12–15, 29–32). And the psalmist said, "I will also speak of your testimonies before kings and shall not be put to shame" (Ps. 119:46).

In addition, there are several passages in the Old Testament prophets that address the sins of foreign nations around Israel: see Isaiah 13–23; Ezekiel 25–32; Amos 1–2; Obadiah (addressed to Edom); Jonah (sent to Nineveh); Nahum (addressed to Nineveh); Habakkuk 2; and Zephaniah 2. These prophets could speak to nations outside of Israel because the God who is revealed in the Bible is the God of *all peoples* and *all nations* of the earth.

Therefore, the moral standards of God as revealed in the Bible are the moral standards to which God will hold all people accountable. This includes more than the way people conduct themselves in their marriages and families, in their neighborhoods and schools, and in their jobs and businesses. It also concerns the way people conduct themselves *in government offices*. Believers have a responsibility to bear witness to the moral standards of the Bible by which God will hold all people accountable, including those in public office.

2. New Testament Support for Significant Christian Influence on Government. A New Testament example of influence on government is the life of John the Baptist. During his lifetime, the ruler of Galilee (from 4 BC to AD 39) was Herod Antipas, a "tetrarch" who had been appointed by the Roman emperor and was subject to the authority of the Roman Empire. Matthew's Gospel tells us that John the Baptist rebuked Herod for a specific personal sin in his life:

> For Herod had seized John and bound him and put him in prison for the sake of Herodias, his brother Philip's wife, because John had been saying to him, "It is not lawful for you to have her." (Matt. 14:3–4)

But Luke's Gospel adds more detail:

> [John the Baptist] preached good news to the people. But Herod the tetrarch, who had been reproved by him for Herodias, his brother's wife, *and for all the evil things that Herod had done*, added this to them all, that he locked up John in prison. (Luke 3:18–20)

Certainly "all the evil things that Herod had done" included wicked actions that he had carried out as a governing official of the Roman Empire. John the Baptist rebuked him *for all of them*. John boldly spoke to an official of the empire about the moral right

---

[63] "The position of cupbearer to the king was a high office and involved regular access to the king." *ESV Study Bible* (Wheaton, IL: Crossway, 2008), 825.

and wrong of his governmental policies. In doing this, John was following in the steps of Daniel and many Old Testament prophets. The New Testament portrays John the Baptist's actions as those of "a righteous and holy man" (Mark 6:20). He is an excellent example of a believer who had what I call "significant influence" on the policies of a government (though it cost him his life: see Mark 6:21–29).

Another example is the apostle Paul. While Paul was in prison in Caesarea, he stood trial before the Roman governor, Felix. Here is what happened:

> After some days Felix came with his wife Drusilla, who was Jewish, and he sent for Paul and heard him speak about faith in Christ Jesus. And *as he reasoned about righteousness and self-control and the coming judgment*, Felix was alarmed and said, "Go away for the present. When I get an opportunity I will summon you." (Acts 24:24–25)

While Luke does not give us any more details, the fact that Felix was "alarmed," and that Paul reasoned with him about "righteousness" and "the coming judgment," indicates that Paul was talking about moral standards of right and wrong, and about the ways in which Felix, as an official of the Roman Empire, had obligations to live up to the standards given by God. Paul no doubt told Felix that he would be accountable for his actions at "the coming judgment," and this likely was what caused Felix to be "alarmed." When Luke tells us that Paul "reasoned" with Felix about these things, the word (the present participle of the Greek verb *dialegomai*) indicates a back-and-forth conversation or discussion. It is not difficult to suppose that Felix asked Paul, "What about this decision that I made? What about this policy? What about this ruling?" It would be an artificial restriction on the meaning of the text to suppose that Paul spoke with Felix *only* about his "private" life and not about his actions as a Roman governor. Paul is thus another example of a believer attempting to exercise significant Christian influence on civil government.

Therefore, if Christians are wondering whether it is right to attempt to bring significant Christian influence to bear on civil governments and government leaders, we have encouragement from many positive examples in the narrative history of the Bible, including Joseph, Moses, Daniel, Jeremiah, Nehemiah, Mordecai, and Esther. We also have as examples the written prophecies of Isaiah, Ezekiel, Amos, Obadiah, Jonah, Nahum, Habakkuk, and Zephaniah. In the New Testament we have the courageous examples of John the Baptist and the apostle Paul. Such influences on governments are no minor examples in obscure portions of the Bible, but are found in Old Testament history from Genesis all the way to Esther (the last historical book), in the canonical writing prophets from Isaiah to Zephaniah, and in the New Testament in both the Gospels and Acts. And those are just the examples of God's servants bringing significant influence to pagan kings who gave no allegiance to the God of Israel or to Jesus in the New Testament times. If we add to this list the many stories of Old Testament prophets bringing counsel, encouragement, and rebuke to the good and evil kings of Israel, then we would include the histories of all the kings and the writings of all the prophets—nearly every book of the Old Testament. And we could add in several passages from Psalms and Proverbs that speak of good and evil rulers. Influencing government for good on the basis of the wisdom found in God's words is a theme that runs throughout the entire Bible.

3. Romans 13 and 1 Peter 2. In addition to these examples, *specific Bible passages that teach about government* present an argument for significant Christian influence. Why do we think God put Romans 13:1–7, 1 Peter 2:13–14, and related passages (as in Psalms and Proverbs) in the Bible? Are they there simply as a matter of intellectual curiosity for Christians who will read them privately but never use them to speak to government officials about how God understands their roles and responsibilities? Does God intend this material to be *concealed* from people in government and *kept secret* by Christians who read it and silently moan about "how far government has strayed from what God wants it to be"? Certainly God put such passages there not only to inform Christians about how *they* should relate to civil government, but also in order that *people with governmental responsibilities* might know what God himself expects from them.

This also pertains to other passages in the Bible that instruct us about God's moral standards, about the nature and purpose of human beings made in God's image, about God's purposes for the earth, and about principles concerning good and bad governments. All of these teachings are relevant for those who serve in governmental offices, and we should speak and teach about them when we have opportunity to do so.

4. Objections to Christian Influence on Government.

a. Objection: "You Can't Legislate Morality": When I argue that Christians should seek to have a significant influence for good on governments, some people are quick to raise the issue of "Prohibition," the period from 1920 to 1933 when a constitutional amendment outlawed the making or selling of alcoholic beverages in the United States.

The history is this: In 1919, the United States adopted the Eighteenth Amendment to the Constitution (effective Jan. 16, 1920), which prohibited "the manufacture, sale, or transportation of intoxicating liquors . . . for beverage purposes." But this law was widely disobeyed, and many people had their own breweries and distilleries. The law was impossible to enforce effectively. Finally, in 1933, the Twenty-First Amendment to the Constitution was passed, which said "the eighteenth article of amendment to the Constitution of the United States is hereby repealed" (however, it allowed states to regulate alcohol usage and sale according to their own laws).[64]

People explain that Prohibition was a failure, and from that they conclude, "You can't legislate morality." But I think the example of Prohibition proves something else entirely and actually supports my position.

What does this experience prove? It proves that it is impossible to enforce moral

---

[64] See http://constitutionus.com for the text of the Eighteenth and Twenty-First Amendments.

standards on a population *when those moral standards are more strict than the standards found in the Bible itself.* Although the Bible contains frequent warnings against drunkenness (see Eph. 5:18), it does not prohibit moderate use of alcoholic beverages, and the apostle Paul even tells his associate Timothy, "No longer drink only water, but use a little wine for the sake of your stomach and your frequent ailments" (1 Tim. 5:23). Therefore, the absolute prohibition on alcoholic beverages was a law that did not find an echo in the hearts of people generally, because it did not reflect the moral standards of God that he has written on all people's hearts (see Rom. 2:15).

I do not think, therefore, that Prohibition in the United States was an experiment in attempting to enforce biblical standards of conduct on the nation. I think it was an experiment that proved the impossibility of trying to enforce standards that go beyond what the Bible requires. And I think Prohibition was rightly repealed.

b. Objection: "All Government Is Evil and Demonic": Another objection to significant Christian influence on government comes from those who say that all use of government power is deeply infected by evil, demonic forces. The realm of government power is the realm of Satan and his forces, and therefore all governmental use of "power over" someone is worldly and not the way of life that Jesus taught. Jesus's method of overcoming evil is through the preaching of the gospel and the power of the Holy Spirit.

This view at first sounds rather spiritual, and therefore Christians are attracted to it. It provides a reason for Christians not to become involved in the messy, hard work of politics and government. But I do not find this view persuasive or consistent with biblical teaching.

(1) Support from Luke 4:6: This viewpoint was strongly promoted by Minnesota pastor Greg Boyd in his influential book *The Myth of a Christian Nation.*[65] Boyd's views in this book have had a large impact in the United States, especially on younger evangelical voters.[66]

Boyd says that all civil government is "demonic."[67] His primary evidence is Satan's statement to Jesus during Jesus's temptation in the wilderness:

> And the devil took him up and showed him all the kingdoms of the world in a moment of time, and said to him, "To you I will give all this authority and their glory, *for it has been delivered to me,* and I give it to whom I will. If you, then, will worship me, it will all be yours." (Luke 4:5–7)

Boyd emphasizes Satan's claim that all the authority of all the kingdoms of the world

---

[65] Gregory A. Boyd, *The Myth of a Christian Nation: How the Quest for Political Power Is Destroying the Church* (Grand Rapids, MI: Zondervan, 2005).

[66] For example, echoes of Boyd's writing can be seen at various places in Shane Claiborne and Chris Haw, *Jesus for President: Politics for Ordinary Radicals* (Grand Rapids, MI: Zondervan, 2008).

[67] Boyd, *The Myth of a Christian Nation,* 21.

"has been delivered to me," then says that Jesus "doesn't dispute the Devil's claim to own them. Apparently, the authority of all the kingdoms of the world has been given to Satan."

Boyd goes on to say, "Functionally, Satan is the acting CEO of all earthly governments."[68] This is indeed a thoroughgoing claim!

(2) The Mistake of Depending on Luke 4:6: Boyd is clearly wrong at this point. Jesus tells us how to evaluate Satan's claims, for he says,

> When he lies, he speaks out of his own character, for he is a liar and the father of lies. (John 8:44)

Jesus didn't need to respond to *every* false word Satan said, for his purpose was to resist the temptation itself, and this he did with the decisive words, "It is written, 'You shall worship the Lord your God, and him only shall you serve'" (Luke 4:8).

And so we have a choice: Do we believe *Satan's words* that he has the authority of all earthly kingdoms, or do we believe *Jesus's words* that Satan is a liar and the father of lies? The answer is easy: Satan wanted Jesus to believe a lie, just as he wanted Eve to believe a lie (Gen. 3:4), and he wants us to believe a lie as well, the lie that he is the ruler of earthly governments.

By contrast, there are passages in the Bible that tell us how we should think of civil governments. These passages do not agree with Satan's claim in Luke 4:6 or with Boyd's claim about Satan's authority over all earthly governments. Rather, these passages—where *God* is speaking, not Satan—portray civil government as a gift from God, something that is subject to God's rule and used by God for his purposes. Here are some of those passages:

> *The Most High rules the kingdom of men* and gives it to whom he will and sets over it the lowliest of men. (Dan. 4:17)

> Let every person be subject to the governing authorities. For *there is no authority except from God, and those that exist have been instituted by God.* . . . For rulers are not a terror to good conduct, but to bad. Would you have no fear of the one who is in authority? Then do what is good, and you will receive his approval, for *he is God's servant for your good.* . . . The *authorities are the ministers of God.* (Rom. 13:1–6)

Peter sees civil government as doing the *opposite* of what Satan does: civil governments are established by God "to *punish* those who do evil," but Satan *encourages* those who do evil! Civil governments are established by God "to *praise* those who do good" (1 Pet. 2:14), but Satan *discourages and attacks* those who do good.

The point is that Satan wants us to believe that all civil government is under his

---

[68] Ibid., 22.

control, but that is not taught anywhere in the Bible. The only verse in the whole Bible that says Satan has authority over all governments is spoken by the father of lies, and we should not believe it. Boyd is simply wrong in his defense of the view that "government is demonic."[69]

5. Christians Have Influenced Governments Positively throughout History. Historian Alvin Schmidt points out how the spread of Christianity and Christian influence on government was primarily responsible for the outlawing of infanticide, child abandonment, and abortion in the Roman Empire (in AD 374);[70] the abolition of the brutal battles to the death in which thousands of gladiators had died (in 404);[71] the ending of the cruel punishment of branding the faces of criminals (in 315);[72] the institution of prison reforms, such as the segregating of male and female prisoners (by 361);[73] the discontinuation of the practice of human sacrifice among the Irish, the Prussians, and the Lithuanians, as well as among the Aztec and Mayan Indians;[74] the outlawing of pedophilia;[75] the granting of property rights and other protections to women;[76] the banning of polygamy (which is still practiced in some Muslim nations today);[77] the prohibition of the burning alive of widows in India (in 1829);[78] the end of the painful and crippling practice of binding young women's feet in China (in 1912);[79] persuading government officials to begin a system of public schools in Germany (in the 16th century);[80] and advancing the idea of compulsory education of all children in a number of European countries.[81]

During the history of the church, Christians have had a decisive influence in opposing and often abolishing slavery in the Roman Empire, in Ireland, and in most of Europe (though Schmidt frankly notes that a minority of "erring" Christian teachers have supported slavery in various centuries).[82] In England, William Wilberforce, a

---

[69] For several additional arguments from Boyd, and my responses to those arguments, see my *Politics— According to the Bible*, 38–44.

[70] Alvin J. Schmidt, *How Christianity Changed the World* (Grand Rapids, MI: Zondervan, 2004; formerly published as *Under the Influence*, 2001), 51, 53, 59. See also D. James Kennedy and Jerry Newcombe, *What If Jesus Had Never Been Born?* (Nashville: Thomas Nelson, 1994).

[71] Ibid., 63.

[72] Ibid., 65.

[73] Ibid.

[74] Ibid., 65–66.

[75] Ibid., 87–88.

[76] Ibid., 111.

[77] Ibid., 115.

[78] Ibid., 116–17.

[79] Ibid., 119.

[80] Ibid., 179.

[81] Ibid., 179–80. Although this is not a matter of merely influencing laws, Schmidt also points out the immense influence of Christians on higher education: By the year 1932 there were 182 colleges and universities in the United States, and of that number, 92 percent had been founded by Christian denominations. Ibid., 190.

[82] Ibid., 274–76.

devout Christian, led the successful effort to abolish the slave trade and then slavery itself throughout the British Empire by 1840.[83]

In the United States, there were vocal defenders of slavery among Christians in the South, but they were vastly outnumbered by the many Christians who were ardent abolitionists, speaking, writing, and agitating constantly for the abolition of slavery. Schmidt notes that two-thirds of the American abolitionists in the mid-1830s were Christian clergymen,[84] and he gives numerous examples of the strong Christian commitment of several of the most influential of the anti-slavery crusaders, including Elijah Lovejoy (the first abolitionist martyr), Lyman Beecher, Edward Beecher, Harriet Beecher Stowe (author of *Uncle Tom's Cabin*), Charles Finney, Charles T. Torrey, Theodore Weld, William Lloyd Garrison, "and others too numerous to mention."[85] The American civil-rights movement that resulted in the outlawing of racial segregation and discrimination was led by Martin Luther King Jr., a Christian pastor, and supported by many Christian churches and groups.[86]

There was also strong influence from Christian ideas and influential Christians in the formulation of the Magna Carta in England (1215)[87] and of the Declaration of Independence (1776) and the Constitution (1787)[88] in the United States. These are three of the most significant documents in the history of governments on the earth, and all three show the marks of significant Christian influence on the foundational ideas about how governments should function. These foundations for British and American government did not come about as a result of the view that Christians should focus on evangelism and not get involved in politics.

Schmidt also argues that several specific components of modern views of government had strong Christian influence in their origin, such as the principles of individual human rights, individual freedom, the equality of individuals before the law, freedom of religion, and separation of church and state.[89]

As for the present time, Charles Colson's insightful book *God and Government*[90] reports dozens of encouraging narratives of courageous, real-life Christians who, in recent years, in causes large and small, have had significant impact for good on laws and governments around the world.

Therefore, I cannot agree with John MacArthur when he says, "God does not call the church to influence the culture by promoting legislation and court rulings that advance a scriptural point of view."[91] When I look over that list of changes in governments and

---

[83] Ibid., 276–78.

[84] Ibid., 279.

[85] Ibid., 279–90.

[86] Ibid., 287–89.

[87] Ibid., 251–52.

[88] Ibid., 253–58.

[89] Ibid., 258–70.

[90] Charles W. Colson, *God and Government: An Insider's View on the Boundaries between Faith and Politics* (Grand Rapids, MI: Zondervan, 2007; formerly published as *Kingdoms in Conflict*, 1987).

[91] MacArthur, *Why Government Can't Save You*, 130.

laws that Christians incited, I think God *did* call the church, and thousands of Christians within the church, to work to bring about these momentous improvements in human society throughout the world. Should we say that Christians who brought about these changes did *not* do so out of obedience to God? That these changes made *no difference* to God? This cannot be true.

MacArthur says, "Using temporal methods to promote legislative and judicial change . . . is not our calling—and has no eternal value."[92] I disagree. I believe those changes listed above were important to the God who declares, "Let justice roll down like waters, and righteousness like an ever-flowing stream" (Amos 5:24). God *cares* how people treat one another here on earth, and the changes in government listed above *do* have eternal value in God's sight.

If the Christian church had adopted the "do evangelism, not politics" view throughout its history, it would never have brought about these immeasurably valuable changes among the nations of the world. But these changes did happen, because Christians realized that if they could influence laws and governments for good, they would be obeying the command of their Lord, "Let your light shine before others, so that they *may see your good works* and give glory to your Father who is in heaven" (Matt. 5:16). They influenced governments for good because they knew that "we are his workmanship, created in Christ Jesus *for good works*, which God prepared beforehand, that we should walk in them" (Eph. 2:10).

N. APPENDIX: U.S. DECLARATION OF INDEPENDENCE

I have included the full text of the Declaration of Independence here because some people have never read it and others can remember only some fragments from the second paragraph. It is one of the most influential documents in the history of the world, and it takes only a few minutes to read. The Founding Fathers' faith in God is mentioned explicitly at the beginning and at the end.

In Congress July 4, 1776

The Unanimous Declaration of The Thirteen United States of America

When, in the course of human events, it becomes necessary for one people to dissolve the political bonds which have connected them with another, and to assume among the powers of the earth, the separate and equal station to which the laws of nature and of nature's God entitle them, a decent respect to the opinions of mankind requires that they should declare the causes which impel them to the separation.

We hold these truths to be self-evident, that all men are created equal, that they are

---

[92] Ibid., 15.

endowed by their Creator with certain unalienable rights, that among these are life, liberty and the pursuit of happiness. That to secure these rights, governments are instituted among men, deriving their just powers from the consent of the governed. That whenever any form of government becomes destructive to these ends, it is the right of the people to alter or to abolish it, and to institute new government, laying its foundation on such principles and organizing its powers in such form, as to them shall seem most likely to effect their safety and happiness. Prudence, indeed, will dictate that governments long established should not be changed for light and transient causes; and accordingly all experience hath shown that mankind are more disposed to suffer, while evils are sufferable, than to right themselves by abolishing the forms to which they are accustomed. But when a long train of abuses and usurpations, pursuing invariably the same object evinces a design to reduce them under absolute despotism, it is their right, it is their duty, to throw off such government, and to provide new guards for their future security.

Such has been the patient sufferance of these colonies; and such is now the necessity which constrains them to alter their former systems of government. The history of the present King of Great Britain is a history of repeated injuries and usurpations, all having in direct object the establishment of an absolute tyranny over these states. To prove this, let facts be submitted to a candid world.

He has refused his assent to laws, the most wholesome and necessary for the public good.

He has forbidden his governors to pass laws of immediate and pressing importance, unless suspended in their operation till his assent should be obtained; and when so suspended, he has utterly neglected to attend to them.

He has refused to pass other laws for the accommodation of large districts of people, unless those people would relinquish the right of representation in the legislature, a right inestimable to them and formidable to tyrants only.

He has called together legislative bodies at places unusual, uncomfortable, and distant from the depository of their public records, for the sole purpose of fatiguing them into compliance with his measures.

He has dissolved representative houses repeatedly, for opposing with manly firmness his invasions on the rights of the people.

He has refused for a long time, after such dissolutions, to cause others to be elected; whereby the legislative powers, incapable of annihilation, have returned to the people at large for their exercise; the state remaining in the meantime exposed to all the dangers of invasion from without, and convulsions within.

He has endeavored to prevent the population of these states; for that purpose obstructing the laws for naturalization of foreigners; refusing to pass others to encourage their migration hither, and raising the conditions of new appropriations of lands.

He has obstructed the administration of justice, by refusing his assent to laws for establishing judiciary powers.

He has made judges dependent on his will alone, for the tenure of their offices, and the amount and payment of their salaries.

He has erected a multitude of new offices, and sent hither swarms of officers to harass our people, and eat out their substance.

He has kept among us, in times of peace, standing armies without the consent of our legislatures.

He has affected to render the military independent of and superior to civil power.

He has combined with others to subject us to a jurisdiction foreign to our constitution, and unacknowledged by our laws; giving his assent to their acts of pretended legislation:

For quartering large bodies of armed troops among us:

For protecting them, by mock trial, from punishment for any murders which they should commit on the inhabitants of these states:

For cutting off our trade with all parts of the world:

For imposing taxes on us without our consent:

For depriving us in many cases, of the benefits of trial by jury:

For transporting us beyond seas to be tried for pretended offenses:

For abolishing the free system of English laws in a neighboring province, establishing therein an arbitrary government, and enlarging its boundaries so as to render it at once an example and fit instrument for introducing the same absolute rule in these colonies:

For taking away our charters, abolishing our most valuable laws, and altering fundamentally the forms of our governments:

For suspending our own legislatures, and declaring themselves invested with power to legislate for us in all cases whatsoever.

He has abdicated government here, by declaring us out of his protection and waging war against us.

He has plundered our seas, ravaged our coasts, burned our towns, and destroyed the lives of our people.

He is at this time transporting large armies of foreign mercenaries to complete the works of death, desolation and tyranny, already begun with circumstances of cruelty and perfidy scarcely paralleled in the most barbarous ages, and totally unworthy the head of a civilized nation.

He has constrained our fellow citizens taken captive on the high seas to bear arms against their country, to become the executioners of their friends and brethren, or to fall themselves by their hands.

He has excited domestic insurrections amongst us, and has endeavored to bring on the inhabitants of our frontiers, the merciless Indian savages, whose known rule of warfare, is undistinguished destruction of all ages, sexes and conditions.

In every stage of these oppressions we have petitioned for redress in the most humble terms: our repeated petitions have been answered only by repeated injury. A prince, whose character is thus marked by every act which may define a tyrant, is unfit to be the ruler of a free people.

Nor have we been wanting in attention to our British brethren. We have warned them from time to time of attempts by their legislature to extend an unwarrantable jurisdiction over us. We have reminded them of the circumstances of our emigration and settlement here. We have appealed to their native justice and magnanimity, and we have conjured them by the ties of our common kindred to disavow these usurpations, which, would inevitably interrupt our connections and correspondence. We must, therefore, acquiesce in the necessity, which denounces our separation, and hold them, as we hold the rest of mankind, enemies in war, in peace friends.

We, therefore, the representatives of the United States of America, in General Congress, assembled, appealing to the Supreme Judge of the world for the rectitude of our intentions, do, in the name, and by the authority of the good people of these colonies, solemnly publish and declare, that these united colonies are, and of right ought to be free and independent states; that they are absolved from all allegiance to the British Crown, and that all political connection between them and the state of Great Britain, is and ought to be totally dissolved; and that as free and independent states, they have full power to levy war, conclude peace, contract alliances, establish commerce, and to do all other acts and things which independent states may of right do. And for the support of this declaration, with a firm reliance on the protection of Divine Providence, we mutually pledge to each other our lives, our fortunes and our sacred honor.

[**Connecticut:**] Samuel Huntington, Roger Sherman, William Williams, Oliver Wolcott

[**Delaware:**] Thomas McKean, George Read, Caesar Rodney

[**Georgia:**] Button Gwinnett, Lyman Hall, George Walton

[**Maryland:**] Charles Carroll, Samuel Chase, William Paca, Thomas Stone

[**Massachusetts:**] John Adams, Samuel Adams, Elbridge Gerry, John Hancock, Robert Treat Paine

[**New Hampshire:**] Josiah Bartlett, Matthew Thornton, William Whipple

[**New Jersey:**] Abraham Clark, John Hart, Francis Hopkinson, Richard Stockton, John Witherspoon

[**New York:**] William Floyd, Francis Lewis, Philip Livingston, Lewis Morris

[**North Carolina:**] Joseph Hewes, William Hooper, John Penn

[**Pennsylvania:**] George Clymer, Benjamin Franklin, Robert Morris, John Morton, George Ross, Benjamin Rush, James Smith, George Taylor, James Wilson

[**Rhode Island:**] William Ellery, Stephen Hopkins

[**South Carolina:**] Thomas Heyward, Jr., Thomas Lynch, Jr., Arthur Middleton, Edward Rutledge

[**Virginia:**] Carter Braxton, Benjamin Harrison, Thomas Jefferson, Francis Lightfoot Lee, Richard Henry Lee, Thomas Nelson, Jr., George Wythe

QUESTIONS FOR PERSONAL APPLICATION

1. How did this chapter change your view of civil government? Have you previously thought of those who work for government as God's servants for your good (Rom. 13:4)?
2. Are you thankful to God for the civil government that you live under?
3. How does it make you feel when you hear that a government official is "an avenger who carries out God's wrath on the wrongdoer" (Rom. 13:4)?
4. Do you think you could in good conscience serve as a police officer or a soldier even if it meant you would have to use deadly force against an evildoer who was endangering others?
5. What character traits (see p. 110) are especially important for police officers and members of the armed forces?
6. If you were living in the American colonies in 1776, would you have supported the American War of Independence?
7. In what specific ways is the government of the country in which you are living accountable to the will of the people? How could it improve (if at all)? What can you do to help it stay accountable?
8. Have you ever been in a situation where you thought you had to disobey the government in order to obey God?
9. Are there any specific ways in which you think God is calling you personally to seek to influence your government for good?

SPECIAL TERMS

anarchy
freedom of religion
liberty
Mayflower Compact

patriotism
rule of law
separation of powers

BIBLIOGRAPHY

Sections in Other Ethics Texts

(see complete bibliographical data, p. 64)

Clark and Rakestraw, 2:423–50
Davis, 10–16, 215–33
Feinberg, John and Paul, 700–707
Frame, 602–21
Geisler, 220–25, 244–59
Hays, 317–46
Holmes, 109–12
McQuilkin and Copan, 555–60
Murray, 107–22
Rae, 252

Other Works

Balmer, Randall Herbert. *Thy Kingdom Come: How the Religious Right Distorts the Faith and Threatens America: An Evangelical's Lament.* New York: Basic Books, 2006.

Bandow, Doug. *Beyond Good Intentions: A Biblical View of Politics.* Turning Point Christian Worldview Series. Westchester, IL: Crossway, 1988.

Barton, David. *Original Intent: The Courts, the Constitution, and Religion.* 5th ed. Aledo, TX: WallBuilder Press, 2011.

Beckwith, Francis J. *Politics for Christians: Statecraft as Soulcraft.* Christian Worldview Integration Series. Downers Grove, IL: IVP Academic, 2012.

Boyd, Gregory A. *The Myth of a Christian Nation: How the Quest for Political Power Is Destroying the Church.* Grand Rapids, MI: Zondervan, 2005.

Budziszewski, J. *Written on the Heart: The Case for Natural Law.* Downers Grove, IL: InterVarsity Press, 1997.

Carson, D. A. *Christ and Culture Revisited.* Grand Rapids, MI: Eerdmans, 2008.

Chaplin, J. P. "Government." In *New Dictionary of Christian Ethics and Pastoral Theology,* edited by David J. Atkinson and David H. Field, 415–17. Leicester, UK: Inter-Varsity, and Downers Grove, IL: InterVarsity Press, 1995.

Chaput, Charles J. *Render unto Caesar: Serving the Nation by Living Our Catholic Beliefs in Political Life.* New York: Doubleday, 2008.

Claiborne, Shane, and Chris Haw. *Jesus for President: Politics for Ordinary Radicals.* Grand Rapids, MI: Zondervan, 2008.

Colson, Charles W. *God and Government: An Insider's View on the Boundaries between Faith and Politics.* Grand Rapids, MI: Zondervan, 2007.

D'Souza, Dinesh. *What's So Great about America.* New York: Penguin, 2003.

DeYoung, Kevin, and Greg Gilbert. *What Is the Mission of the Church? Making Sense of Social Justice, Shalom, and the Great Commission.* Wheaton, IL: Crossway, 2011.

Drew, Charles D. *A Public Faith: Bringing Personal Faith to Public Issues.* Colorado Springs: NavPress, 2000.

Forster, Greg. *The Contested Public Square: The Crisis of Christianity and Politics.* Downers Grove, IL: IVP Academic, 2008.

Frame, John M. *The Escondido Theology: A Reformed Response to Two Kingdom Theology.* Lakeland, FL: Whitefield Media Productions, 2011.

Garlow, James L. *Well Versed: Biblical Answers to Today's Tough Issues.* Washington, DC: Regnery Faith, 2016.

Gilder, George F. *The Israel Test.* Minneapolis: Richard Vigilante Books, 2009.

Goldberg, Michelle. *Kingdom Coming: The Rise of Christian Nationalism.* New York: W. W. Norton, 2007.

Grudem, Wayne. *Politics—According to the Bible: A Comprehensive Resource for Understanding Modern Political Issues in Light of Scripture.* Grand Rapids, MI: Zondervan, 2010.

Hamilton, Alexander, James Madison, and John Jay. *The Federalist Papers.* New York: Signet Classics, 2003.

Haugen, Gary A. *Good News about Injustice: A Witness of Courage in a Hurting World.* Downers Grove, IL: InterVarsity Press, 1999.

Hayek, F. A. *The Road to Serfdom.* Fiftieth Anniversary Ed. Chicago: University of Chicago Press, 1994.

Hewitt, Hugh. *The Fourth Way: The Conservative Playbook for a Lasting GOP Majority.* New York: Simon & Schuster, 2017.

———. *The Good and Faithful Servant: A Small Group Study on Politics and Government for Christians.* Arlington, VA: Townhall, 2009.

Hoffmeier, James K. *The Immigration Crisis: Immigrants, Aliens, and the Bible.* Wheaton, IL: Crossway, 2009.

Horner, Barry E. *Future Israel: Why Christian Anti-Judaism Must Be Challenged.* Nashville: B&H Academic, 2007.

Howard, Philip K. *The Death of Common Sense: How Law Is Suffocating America.* New York: Random House, 1994.

Hunter, James Davison. *To Change the World: The Irony, Tragedy, and Possibility of Christianity Today.* New York: Oxford University Press, 2010.

Jackson, Harry R., and Tony Perkins. *Personal Faith, Public Policy.* Lake Mary, FL: FrontLine, 2008.

Keller, Timothy. *Generous Justice: How God's Grace Makes Us Just.* New York: Dutton, 2010.

Kennedy, D. James, and Jerry Newcombe. *What If Jesus Had Never Been Born?* Nashville: Thomas Nelson, 1994.

Kidd, Thomas S. *God of Liberty: A Religious History of the American Revolution*. New York: Basic Books, 2010.

Kuyper, Abraham. *Guidance for Christian Engagement in Government: A Translation of Abraham Kuyper's Our Program*. Edited and translated by Harry Van Dyke. Grand Rapids, MI: Christian's Library Press, 2013.

Lillback, Peter A., and Jerry Newcombe. *George Washington's Sacred Fire*. Bryn Mawr, PA: Providence Forum, 2006.

Marshall, Peter, and David Manuel. *The Light and the Glory: 1492–1793*. Revised and expanded ed. Grand Rapids, MI: Revell, 2009.

MacArthur, John. *Why Government Can't Save You: An Alternative to Political Activism*. Bible for Life Series. Nashville: Word, 2000.

Minnery, Tom. *Why You Can't Stay Silent: A Biblical Mandate to Shape Our Culture*. Wheaton, IL: Tyndale, 2001.

Murray, Charles A. *American Exceptionalism: An Experiment in History*. Values and Capitalism. Washington, DC: AEI, 2013.

Neuhaus, Richard John. *The Naked Public Square: Religion and Democracy in America*. 2nd ed. Grand Rapids, MI: Eerdmans, 1986.

Niebuhr, H. Richard. *Christ and Culture*. New York: Harper & Bros., 1951.

Nyquist, J. Paul. *Is Justice Possible? The Elusive Pursuit of What Is Right*. Chicago: Moody, 2017.

Olson, Roger E. *How to Be Evangelical without Being Conservative*. Grand Rapids, MI: Zondervan, 2008.

Ovey, Michael, Wayne A. Grudem, Jonathan Chaplin, David McIlroy, and Timothy Laurence. *Good News for the Public Square: A Biblical Framework for Christian Engagement*. London: The Lawyers Christian Fellowship, 2014.

Prager, Dennis. *Still the Best Hope: Why the World Needs American Values to Triumph*. New York: Broadside, 2012.

Phillips, Kevin. *American Theocracy: The Peril and Politics of Radical Religion, Oil, and Borrowed Money in the 21st Century*. New York: Viking, 2006.

Robison, James, and Jay W. Richards. *Indivisible: Restoring Faith, Family, and Freedom before It's Too Late*. New York: FaithWords, 2012.

Schlafly, Phyllis, and George Neumayr. *No Higher Power: Obama's War on Religious Freedom*. Washington, DC: Regnery, 2012.

Schmidt, Alvin J. *How Christianity Changed the World*. Grand Rapids, MI: Zondervan, 2004.

Schutt, Michael P. *Redeeming Law: Christian Calling and the Legal Profession*. Downers Grove, IL: InterVarsity Press, 2007.

Schweikart, Larry. *48 Liberal Lies about American History (That You Probably Learned in School)*. New York: Sentinel, 2009.

Sears, Alan, and Craig Osten. *The ACLU vs America: Exposing the Agenda to Redefine Moral Values*. Nashville: Broadman & Holman, 2005.

Sharansky, Natan, and Ron Dermer. *The Case for Democracy: The Power of Freedom to Overcome Tyranny and Terror*. New York: PublicAffairs, 2004.

Sider, Ronald J. *Just Politics: A Guide for Christian Engagement*. 2nd ed. Grand Rapids, MI: Brazos, 2012.

Smith, Gary Scott, ed. *God and Politics: Four Views on the Reformation of Civil Government: Theonomy, Principled Pluralism, Christian America, National Confessionalism*. Phillipsburg, NJ: Presbyterian and Reformed, 1989.

Spencer, Nick, and Jonathan Chaplin, eds. *God and Government*. London: SPCK, 2009.

Stark, Rodney. *The Victory of Reason: How Christianity Led to Freedom, Capitalism, and Western Success*. New York: Random House, 2005.

Thomas, Cal, and Ed Dobson. *Blinded by Might: Why the Religious Right Can't Save America*. Grand Rapids, MI: Zondervan, 2000.

Tocqueville, Alexis de. *Democracy in America*. Edited by Richard D. Heffner. New York: Signet Classic, 2001.

Trewhella, Matthew J. *The Doctrine of the Lesser Magistrates: A Proper Resistance to Tyranny and a Repudiation of Unlimited Obedience to Civil Government*. North Charleston, SC: CreateSpace, 2013.

VanDrunen, David. *Living in God's Two Kingdoms: A Biblical Vision for Christianity and Culture*. Wheaton, IL: Crossway, 2010.

Vantassel, Stephen. *Dominion over Wildlife? An Environmental Theology of Human-Wildlife Relations*. Eugene, OR: Wipf & Stock. 2009.

Vaughan, Joel D. *The Rise and Fall of the Christian Coalition: The Inside Story*. Eugene, OR: Wipf & Stock, 2009.

Wallis, Jim. *God's Politics: Why the Right Gets It Wrong and the Left Doesn't Get It*. New York: HarperCollins, 2005.

Yoder, John Howard. *The Politics of Jesus: Vicit Agnus Noster*. Grand Rapids, MI: Eerdmans, 1972.

SCRIPTURE MEMORY PASSAGE

Romans 13:1–2: Let every person be subject to the governing authorities. For there is no authority except from God, and those that exist have been instituted by God. Therefore whoever resists the authorities resists what God has appointed, and those who resist will incur judgment.

HYMN

"America the Beautiful"

O beautiful for spacious skies,
For amber waves of grain,
For purple mountain majesties
Above the fruited plain!

America! America!
God shed His grace on thee,
And crown thy good with brotherhood
From sea to shining sea.

O beautiful for pilgrim feet,
Whose stern, impassioned stress
A thoroughfare for freedom beat
Across the wilderness!

America! America!
God mend thine ev'ry flaw,
Confirm thy soul in self-control,
Thy liberty in law.

O beautiful for heroes proved
In liberating strife,
Who more than self their country loved
And mercy more than life!

America! America!
May God thy gold refine,
Till all success be nobleness,
And ev'ry gain divine.

O beautiful for patriot dream
That sees, beyond the years,
Thine alabaster cities gleam
Undimmed by human tears!

America! America!
God shed His grace on thee,
And crown thy good with brotherhood
From sea to shining sea.

AUTHOR: KATHERINE LEE BATES, 1859–1929

ALTERNATIVE HYMN

"God Save the Queen" (for UK and British Commonwealth nations)

God save our gracious Queen,
Long live our noble Queen,

God save the Queen!
Send her victorious,
Happy and glorious,
Long to reign over us;
God save the Queen!

O Lord our God arise,
Scatter her enemies
And make them fall;
Confound their politics,
Frustrate their knavish tricks,
On Thee our hopes we fix,
God save us all!

Thy choicest gifts in store
On her be pleased to pour;
Long may she reign;
May she defend our laws,
And ever give us cause
To sing with heart and voice,
God save the Queen!

Not in this land alone,
But be God's mercies known,
From shore to shore!
Lord make the nations see,
That men should brothers be,
And form one family,
The wide world over.

From every latent foe,
From the assassin's blow,
God save the Queen!
O'er her Thine arm extend,
For Britain's sake defend,
Our mother, prince, and friend,
God save the Queen!

AUTHOR: UNKNOWN

Alternative: Other patriotic prayers set to music may be used for other countries.

Chapter

17

OTHER AUTHORITIES

How should Christians relate to people who have authority in the workplace, in the church, and in school?

In the previous three chapters, we considered the authority that God gives to parents, the leadership role that God entrusts to husbands, and the kind of authority that God gives to civil governments. In this chapter, we will consider three other roles to which God gives a measure of authority over others: (1) employers, (2) church elders, and (3) teachers.[1] These do not exhaust the list of authority relationships that exist among human beings. There are other areas of authority that I will not discuss here, such as authority within athletic teams, within voluntary civic associations, and within professional societies.

Paul did not specify what types of authorities he was talking about when he wrote this to Titus:

> Remind them *to be submissive to rulers and authorities*, to be obedient, to be ready for every good work, to speak evil of no one, to avoid quarreling, to be gentle, and to show perfect courtesy toward all people. (Titus 3:1–2)

While the primary type of "rulers and authorities" that Paul had in mind may have been the officials of the civil government, his words do not limit what he says only to that specific application. It seems appropriate to apply this general statement more broadly to include all legitimate authorities within human relationships.

A. EMPLOYERS AND EMPLOYEES

1. Masters and Bondservants Are the Closest New Testament Parallel to Employers and Employees Today. The most common employment situation in the Roman Empire

---

[1] The Westminster Larger Catechism affirms a broader application of the fifth commandment to others who have authority in different spheres of life: "By *father* and *mother*, in the fifth commandment, are meant, not only natural parents, but all superiors in age and gifts; and especially such as, by God's ordinance, are over us in place of authority, whether in family, church, or commonwealth" (Question 124).

in the first century AD was that of a "bondservant" (Greek, *doulos*, sometimes translated "servant" or "slave") who worked for his "master."

A bondservant had a higher status and greater economic security than a day laborer, who had to seek work each day in the marketplace (see Matt. 20:1–15). Bondservants could be entrusted with considerable responsibility and hold numerous jobs that involved significant freedom and responsibility.

In Greco-Roman households bondservants (also called "slaves" in much of the academic literature) served not only as cooks, cleaners, and personal attendants, but also as tutors of people of all ages, as physicians, as nurses, as close companions, and as managers of households. In the business world, bondservants not only were janitors and delivery boys, they also were managers of estates, shops, and ships, as well as salesmen and contracting agents. In the civil service, bondservants were used not only in street-paving and sewer-cleaning gangs, but also as administrators of funds and personnel, and as executives with decision-making powers.[2]

One example of the amount of freedom and responsibility that could be given to a bondservant is found in Jesus's parable of the talents:

> For it will be like a man going on a journey, who called his servants [Greek, *doulos*, plural] and entrusted to them his property. To one he gave *five talents*, to another *two*, to another *one*, to each according to his ability. Then he went away. (Matt. 25:14–15)

Since one talent was the equivalent of about 20 years' wages for a laborer, at a rate of $15 per hour this would amount to $600,000 per talent, meaning that the three servants received $3 million, $1.2 million, and $600,000 in today's money respectively. Then the master went away, leaving these servants or bondservants with great freedom to carry on business with the money he had entrusted to them.

Bondservants were "bound" by law to their employers for a certain period of time, but could often earn their freedom by about the time they were 30.[3] Therefore, there is some similarity to the status of many indentured servants who came as immigrants to America in the 17th and 18th centuries. Unlike American slavery, first-century bond-service was not based on racial categories. Although they did not have as many legal protections as Roman citizens or as those who had gained their freedom, bondservants did have a system of laws that protected them to some extent:

> It was, of course, recognized that those in slavery, as many as one-third of the population in the large cities such as Rome, Ephesus, Antioch, and Corinth,

---

[2] S. S. Bartchy, "Slavery," in *The International Standard Bible Encyclopedia*, rev. ed., ed. Geoffrey W. Bromiley (Grand Rapids, MI: Eerdmans, 1988), 4:544. A. A. Ruprecht agrees: see "Slave, Slavery," in *Dictionary of Paul and His Letters*, ed. Gerald F. Hawthorne, Ralph P. Martin, and Daniel G. Reid (Downers Grove, IL: InterVarsity Press, 1993), 881–83.

[3] Bartchy, "Slavery," 4:545.

were human beings if not "legal persons." As such they were protected by law against severe cruelty from their owners or others. . . . A slave's property was entirely under the control of the slave, who could seek to increase it for use in purchasing legal freedom and in establishing a comfortable life as a freed person.[4]

Scholars may debate exactly how evil first-century slavery was for a long time. No doubt there were many differences in a societal system that lasted so long and was so widely dispersed, and in such cases people can find data to support different views. What I am not willing to do is say that the first-century institution of the *doulos* (variously translated as "bondservant," "servant," or "slave") was inherently and pervasively so evil that the New Testament authors should have condemned it entirely, and their failure to do so shows that the New Testament's moral standards are inadequate. This would be to say that the New Testament actually teaches a defective moral standard, and I do not think that option is open for Christians who take the Bible as the flawless, pure Word of God.

It is also clear that a significant number of people voluntarily became bondservants because of the educational, economic, and social opportunities that it offered. Further information is provided in these notes from the *ESV Study Bible*:

> The Roman institution of being a "bondservant" (Gk. *doulos* . . .) was different from the institution of slavery in North America during the seventeenth through the nineteenth centuries. Slaves generally were permitted to work for pay and to save enough to buy their freedom (see Matthew 25:15 where the "servants" [again Gk. *doulos*] were entrusted with immense amounts of money and responsibility). The [New Testament] assumes that trafficking in human beings is a sin (1 Tim. 1:10; Rev. 18:11–13), and Paul urges Christian slaves who **can gain . . . freedom** to do so. . . . Paul does not condone the system of slavery but instead provides instructions to believing masters and slaves regarding their relationship to each other in the Lord, and how this should be lived out within the bounds of their social and legal culture. The result, as is often observed, is that slavery slowly died out in antiquity through the influence of Christianity. . . . There is no doubt that it would have been difficult for the institution of slavery to survive in the atmosphere of love created by the

---

[4] Ibid., 4:544. It should be noted that some scholars differ with Bartchy and portray ancient slavery more negatively. J. A. Harrill says that the subject of ancient slavery has been a matter of "fierce scholarly debate," and this is "more controversial a subject than any other in the study of ancient literature and society." "Slavery," in *Dictionary of New Testament Background*, ed. Craig A. Evans and Stanley E. Porter (Downers Grove, IL: InterVarsity Press, 2000), 1124. However, M. I. Finley, "Slavery," in the *Oxford Classical Dictionary*, 2nd ed., ed. N. G. L. Hammond and H. H. Scullard (Oxford: Clarendon, 1970), 994–96, substantially agrees with Bartchy's assessment. This is significant because Finley, a Cambridge professor of history, was apparently the greatest modern historian of ancient slavery; all studies of this topic mention his monumental study *Ancient Slavery and Modern Ideology* (New York: Viking, 1980) along with several related works.

letter [to Philemon], and in fact the elements of Paul's appeal found in this letter helped lay the foundation for the abolition of slavery.[5]

Therefore, although the parallels are not exact, the roles of master and bondservant in the first century provide the closest biblical analogy for the employer-employee relationship at the present time, and New Testament passages that speak to this issue provide helpful instructions for Christians today.[6]

2. Employees Should Be Subject to the Authority of Their Supervisors. Several New Testament passages instruct bondservants to be subject to their masters:

> *Bondservants are to be submissive to their own masters in everything;* they are to be well-pleasing, not argumentative, not pilfering, but showing all good faith, so that in everything they may adorn the doctrine of God our Savior. (Titus 2:9–10)

> *Servants, be subject to your masters with all respect,* not only to the good and gentle but also to the unjust. (1 Pet. 2:18)

In Ephesians and Colossians, Paul explicitly directs bondservants to "obey" their earthly masters—their supervisors in the workplace:

> *Bondservants, obey your earthly masters with fear and trembling,* with a sincere heart. (Eph. 6:5)

> *Bondservants, obey in everything those who are your earthly masters,* not by way of eye-service, as people-pleasers, but with sincerity of heart, fearing the Lord. (Col. 3:22)

But what if an employer today directs an employee to do something that is morally wrong or contrary to the civil law, such as telling the employee to lie to a customer or a supplier, or to falsify a financial report? In that case, the same principle applies that we discussed with respect to the authority of parents, husbands, and civil governments: Christians should disobey a human authority when that authority tells them to directly violate God's moral laws or do something in violation of a civil law.

However, it is a tragedy that multiple thousands of government regulations to which businesses are subject today, and the maddeningly broad and vague federal statutes,

---

[5] *ESV Study Bible* (Wheaton, IL: Crossway, 2008), 2201, 2273, 2353 (notes on 1 Cor. 7:21; Eph. 6:5; introduction to Philemon).

[6] Robertson McQuilkin and Paul Copan write: "Although the social context of Bible times was radically different from contemporary democratic society, the principles enunciated for slave-owner relationships are so humanitarian in their protection of the oppressed that they are easily transferable to labor-management relationships in the post-slavery era in which we live, an era brought about through the influence of New Testament teaching." *An Introduction to Biblical Ethics: Walking in the Way of Wisdom,* 3rd ed. (Downers Grove, IL: InterVarsity Press, 2014), 448.

often make it impossible for people to know what the law requires of them.[7] In such a context, even Christians who desire to be faithful in obeying their employers will find it difficult to know the right thing to do in each situation, and will need to pray for God's generous gift of wisdom (see James 1:5–6).

3. Employees Should Not Steal but Should Be Faithful in Everything. Today (just as in the first century) employees often have opportunities to steal small things without being noticed. But Paul told bondservants:

> [Be] well-pleasing, not argumentative, *not pilfering*, but showing all good faith. (Titus 2:9–10)

An employee who takes home merchandise without paying for it is pilfering. An employee who makes personal photocopies without permission and without paying is pilfering. A cashier who fails to charge a friend for all the merchandise that friend has brought to the counter is pilfering. An employee at an ice cream stand who gives free ice cream to some friends who drop by is pilfering. A contract employee who bills for time he or she did not actually work is pilfering. An employee who plays computer games at work when he or she is supposed to be working is pilfering.

Paul also tells bondservants not to be "argumentative," for an employee who is constantly arguing with his or her supervisor will create a tense, hostile, and extremely unpleasant workplace atmosphere.

The phrase "but showing all good faith" (Titus 2:10) probably indicates the trustworthy character of the Christian employee. A Christian is someone whom his employer can trust to show good faith (or to be "faithful, trustworthy," which is a legitimate sense for the Greek term *pistis* here). In addition, if employees are working "as for the Lord and not for men" (Col. 3:23; see next point), then they will not want to steal from Christ himself.

4. Employees Should Work Diligently, As If They Are Serving Christ. Paul explains a remarkable concept: Instead of thinking that they are working just to please their human masters, bondservants are to behave as if they are working for Christ himself, with the assurance that he will reward them for their work:

> Bondservants, obey your earthly masters with fear and trembling, with a sincere heart, *as you would Christ*, not by the way of eye-service, as people-pleasers, but *as bondservants of Christ*, doing the will of God from the heart, rendering service with a good will *as to the Lord and not to man*, knowing that whatever good anyone does, this *he will receive back from the Lord*, whether he is a bondservant or is free. (Eph. 6:5–8)

---

[7] See Harvey Silverglate, *Three Felonies a Day* (New York: Encounter, 2009, 2011).

Bondservants, obey in everything those who are your earthly masters, not by way of eye-service, as people-pleasers, but with sincerity of heart, *fearing the Lord*. Whatever you do, *work heartily, as for the Lord and not for men, knowing that from the Lord you will receive the inheritance as your reward. You are serving the Lord Christ*. For the wrongdoer will be paid back for the wrong he has done, and there is no partiality. Masters, treat your bondservants justly and fairly, knowing that you also have a Master in heaven. (Col. 3:22–4:1)

This is a powerful concept, and where it is practiced, it will absolutely transform a workplace. Employees will be diligent, hardworking, joyful (for they have the privilege of working for Christ!), faithful in the performance of their duties (for they know Christ will reward them), committed to a high quality of product or work output (for they are presenting the result to Christ), and completely honest in their dealings with others (for they are speaking in the hearing of Christ himself). Any employer would be glad to have employees like this.

This idea of working for Christ is a reminder of the intrinsic goodness of work. Scott Rae says:

Work has *intrinsic* value because God ordained it *prior* to the entrance of sin into the world. If you look at the Genesis account of creation closely, you will see that God commanded Adam and Eve to work in the garden *before* sin entered the picture (2:15). . . . Work is not a punishment on human beings for their sin. . . . God's original idea for work was that human beings would spend their lives in productive activity, with regular breaks for leisure, rest, and celebration of God's blessing (Ex. 20:8–11). . . . God is a worker, and human beings are workers by virtue of being made in God's image.[8]

5. What If Employees Are Treated Unjustly?

a. They Should Seek a Fair Resolution Where Possible: When Paul was about to be flogged in connection with a disturbance in Jerusalem that he did not create, he appealed to the centurion who was nearby, saying, "Is it lawful for you to flog a man who is a Roman citizen and uncondemned?" (Acts 22:25), and he was released.

In another situation, when Paul and Silas were unjustly thrown in prison in Philippi, and then were about to be secretly released so that the officials did not have to own up to their wrongdoing, Paul protested and demanded that the officials who had done wrong "come themselves and take us out" so that there would be a public vindication of Paul and Silas and their gospel message (Acts 16:37).

In a third situation, when Paul was concerned that a legal proceeding might turn against him, he exercised his right as a Roman citizen and said, "I appeal to Caesar" (Acts 25:11).

---

[8] Scott B. Rae, *Moral Choices: An Introduction to Ethics*, 3rd ed. (Grand Rapids, MI: Zondervan, 2009), 334–35.

These examples demonstrate the principle that when one is experiencing injustice, it is not wrong to appeal for justice to someone in a position of authority when one has the opportunity to do so.

By analogy, if an employee receives an inaccurate performance review, or if the promised compensation or working conditions are not provided, or if he feels wrongly treated in any other kind of situation, there is nothing at all wrong with asking the appropriate person in authority to review the situation and perhaps correct it. In some cases in a modern society, the actions of the employer violate federal or state regulations. There is nothing wrong with appealing to the governmental authority in such cases, "for he is God's servant for your good" (Rom. 13:4).

b. When a Fair Resolution Is Not Possible, Employees Should Trust Christ to Reward Them: In many employment situations, decisions are made that seem unfair to an employee, and there is no apparent human remedy or authority who can make them right (perhaps the employee fears that he might risk losing his job by pursuing the matter further).

Paul was aware that masters often treated their bondservants unfairly in first-century employment situations, and in those cases the bondservants had very little recourse but just to endure the suffering or hardship. Paul assured them that Christ would reward them and would one day settle all accounts. He told them that bondservants were to work heartily, "knowing that *from the Lord you will receive the inheritance as your reward*" (Col. 3:24). He also assured them that their dishonest masters would one day be punished: "For *the wrongdoer will be paid back for the wrong he has done*, and there is no partiality" (v. 25).

On the other hand, if the masters had cheated the bondservants so that they had not been rewarded fairly for their work, the Lord would reward them, for he said that bondservants should work "knowing that whatever good anyone does, this he will receive back from the Lord" (Eph. 6:8).

Peter goes beyond the encouragement to trust in Christ for future vindication and future reward. He also says that patient endurance of unjust suffering is pleasing to God and is "a gracious thing in the sight of God" (1 Pet. 2:20). Here is his entire statement to servants (Greek, *oiketēs*, a general term for household servants of various kinds) who were being mistreated:

> Servants, be subject to your masters with all respect, not only to the good and gentle *but also to the unjust*. For this is a gracious thing, when, mindful of God, one endures sorrows while *suffering unjustly*. For what credit is it if, when you sin and are beaten for it, you endure? But if *when you do good and suffer for it* you endure, this is a gracious thing in the sight of God. For to this you have been called, because Christ also suffered for you, leaving you an example, so that you might follow in his steps. (1 Pet. 2:18–21)

Peter's encouragement is different from that of Paul. Peter does not remind bondservants that God will one day settle all accounts fairly; rather, he says that if they suffer unjustly, they are imitating their Savior, Jesus Christ, who suffered unjustly and left an example for them to follow. Their consolation is that God sees and cares for them, and their patient endurance of suffering "is a gracious thing" in the sight of God—that is, it is something that finds God's grace or favor (Greek, *charis*). And this God is the One who is watching at all times and who will care for them and ultimately reward them (see 1 Pet. 5:10).

6. The Reason for Being a Faithful Employee Is to Commend the Gospel and to Honor Christ. Paul tells Titus that if bondservants are submissive to their masters, well-pleasing, not argumentative, not pilfering, but showing all good faith, the purpose is "so that in everything *they may adorn the doctrine* of God our Savior" (Titus 2:10). Faithful service as an employee will be a positive and even beautiful advertisement for the gospel of Christ, and will honor him.

If Christian employees understand this today, they will be faithful and productive employees, knowing that their work itself produces a beautiful aroma that surrounds the content of the gospel that they believe.

7. Employers Should Treat Their Employees Fairly. When the New Testament speaks to "masters," it also speaks to employers today, as well as to all supervisors, managers, and bosses in any kind of workplace. How are they to act? The New Testament churches included not only bondservants, but also masters who had a higher economic and social position. Paul's instructions were not as lengthy to masters, but they are very clear:

> Masters, *treat your bondservants justly and fairly*, knowing that you also have
> a Master in heaven. (Col. 4:1)

The reminder "that you also have a Master in heaven" was a subtle warning that any wrongdoing by masters would be known to the Lord and that he would call them to account for it on the last day. But it was also an encouragement that if they would act "justly and fairly," their heavenly Master would be pleased and would reward them in heaven.

Robertson McQuilkin and Paul Copan observe:

> The employer who pays less than a fair wage is stealing from the worker. The
> worker who carelessly arrives late and wastes time with small talk, inattentive
> work, long breaks, or daydreaming is a thief. And both sin against God, their
> true employer.[9]

Paul's instructions to masters in Ephesians are similar:

> Masters, do the same to them, and stop your threatening, knowing that he
> who is both their Master and yours is in heaven, and that there is no partiality
> with him. (6:9)

---

[9] McQuilkin and Copan, *An Introduction to Biblical Ethics*, 450–51.

The phrase "do the same to them" meant that masters were to act in the same way that Paul had told bondservants to act (vv. 5–8)—that is, working as serving the Lord and knowing that he would reward them for whatever good they did ("the same" is plural in Greek, *ta auta*, "the same things").

The encouragement to "stop your threatening" apparently meant that masters should stop even the threats of physical violence against slaves, which was the main means of disciplining bondservants and keeping them in order and submissive. Frank Thielman observes, "With this command, Paul has cut the thread that held the institution of slavery together."[10]

The requirement for masters to be just and fair in dealing with bondservants is undergirded by the fact that masters also are accountable to the Lord: "knowing that you also have a Master in heaven" (Col. 4:1). Masters may have a higher social and economic position than bondservants at the present time, but that will not gain them any privilege or status before the Lord when he judges all people fairly and impartially: "There is no partiality with him" (Eph. 6:9).

8. Employers Should Know That God Will Repay Their Good and Evil Deeds. While bosses and supervisors today (like masters in the first century) may think there is less accountability for them than for their employees, that is not true, because what Paul said to bondservants also has application to masters: "The wrongdoer will be paid back for the wrong he has done" (Col. 3:25). On the other hand, the same goes for any good that employers do: "Whatever good anyone does, this he will receive back from the Lord, whether he is a bondservant or is free" (Eph. 6:8).

Therefore, if bosses in the workplace today find that some employees are ungrateful and resentful even when they are treated generously and fairly, the bosses can bear in mind that Christ is pleased with the good they have done, and he will reward them.

B. CHURCH ELDERS AND CHURCH MEMBERS

1. Church Members Should Be Subject to the Authority of the Elders. Elders had authority over the people in their churches in the time of the New Testament. This is especially clear in Hebrews 13:17, which instructs Christians:

> *Obey your leaders and submit to them*, for they are keeping watch over your souls, as those who will have to give an account. Let them do this with joy and not with groaning, for that would be of no advantage to you.

This governing authority is also evident in the instruction that Peter gives to elders to shepherd the flock:

[10] Frank Thielman, *Ephesians*, BECNT (Grand Rapids, MI: Baker, 2010), 410. Rae says, "At a minimum, a Christian worldview requires that employees be treated with dignity and respect, consistent with being made in God's image." *Moral Choices*, 350.

So I exhort the elders among you, as a fellow elder and a witness of the sufferings of Christ, as well as a partaker in the glory that is going to be revealed: *shepherd the flock of God* that is among you, *exercising oversight*, not under compulsion, but willingly, as God would have you; not for shameful gain, but eagerly; not domineering over those in your charge, but being examples to the flock. (1 Pet. 5:1–3)

Peter goes on to encourage the others in the church to be subject to the elders: "Likewise, you who are younger, be subject to the elders" (1 Pet. 5:5).

Paul also indicates that elders have a governing role with regard to the churches, for he says that the elders who "*rule* well" should be considered worthy of "double honor" (1 Tim. 5:17). In addition, Paul says that an elder's record of leadership regarding his children provides information about whether he would be a good elder to oversee the activities of the church:

He must *manage his own household* well, with all dignity keeping his children submissive, for if someone does not know how to manage his own household, how will he care for God's church? (1 Tim. 3:4–5)

2. Church Members Should Honor the Elders of the Church. When Paul says that the elders who "rule well" should "be considered worthy of *double honor*, especially those who labor in preaching and teaching" (1 Tim. 5:17), he surely means that they should be well compensated for their work, for the next verse talks about the laborer deserving his wages (v. 18). But we should not think that "double honor" means only financial compensation, for "honor" is a broader category and would include such things as respect and giving the elder the benefit of the doubt when we don't know all the details or reasons behind various decisions that have been made.[11]

3. Elders Should Exercise Authority in the Church Willingly, Eagerly, and As Examples to Others. Peter is quite explicit in his counsel to elders regarding their conduct in the church. They are to exercise their task of shepherding "the flock of God" (that is, the church) "not under compulsion but willingly" (that is, not thinking that such shepherding is an onerous burden, but counting it a joyful privilege), "not for shameful gain, but eagerly" (that is, not merely as a job that they do only because they are getting paid, but something they desire to undertake), "not domineering over those in your charge, but being examples to the flock" (that is, not abusing their authority, but setting a pattern of faithful obedience to Christ).

C. TEACHERS AND STUDENTS

1. No Scripture Passage Speaks Directly to the Authority of Teachers. The role of teacher in a public or private educational setting today does not find a specific parallel

---

[11] For a discussion of the way in which elders should be selected, see Wayne Grudem, *Systematic Theology: An Introduction to Biblical Doctrine* (Leicester, UK: Inter-Varsity, and Grand Rapids, MI: Zondervan, 1994), 912–37.

in the New Testament. There is a statement from Jesus, however, that speaks to the influence of a teacher's life on his or her students:

> A disciple is not above his teacher, but everyone when he is fully trained will be like his teacher. (Luke 6:40)

The emphasis of the Bible is on the responsibility of parents for training their children (see Eph. 6:4; Col. 3:21; cf. Deut. 6:7). However, in modern societies (as sometimes in the ancient world) parents often delegate part of that responsibility to teachers who train their children (see Gal. 3:24–25, which speaks about the law as our "guardian" using the Greek term *paidagōgos*, "guardian, leader, guide, tutor, teacher").

But if parents entrust teachers with some of the responsibility of training their children, then teachers have some measure of authority that has been delegated to them by the parents. This means that teachers do have a legitimate authority within the realm of their activity in training children. This also means that the relationship of teachers and students is analogous to the relationship of parents and children. The relationship is also somewhat analogous to the relationship between employers and employees, since teachers give children tasks (academic assignments) that they are to carry out faithfully.

2. Similarities to Other Authority Relationships.

a. Students Should Be Submissive to the Authority of Their Teachers: Just as children should be obedient to parents (Eph. 6:1; Col. 3:20) and employees should be obedient to their supervisors (Eph. 6:5–7; Col. 3:22–24; Titus 2:9–10; 1 Pet. 2:18), so students should be submissive to their teachers.

Immense amounts of instructional time are wasted, and a significant diminution of teaching effectiveness occurs, simply because of the presence of undisciplined students in school classrooms in the United States today. Such conduct ultimately flouts the authority of God himself, who has entrusted parents and, by implication, teachers with their positions of authority.

b. Students Should Honor Their Teachers: Just as children should obey the fifth commandment, "Honor your father and your mother" (Ex. 20:12), so students should treat their teachers with honor and respect. Peter also tells servants to "be subject to your masters *with all respect*, not only to the good and gentle but also to the unjust" (1 Pet. 2:18).

c. Students Should Not Be Argumentative: While it is an essential part of the learning process for students to ask questions and reason back and forth with teachers as they investigate subjects, this should never degenerate into argumentativeness, just as Paul tells bondservants to be "well-pleasing, not argumentative" (Titus 2:9).

d. Students Should Work Heartily, As If They Are Serving the Lord: Just as Paul tells bondservants that they are to "work heartily, as for the Lord and not for men" (Col. 3:23). So students should also act in this way with regard to the work they do in their academic studies. This would also "adorn the doctrine of God our Savior" (Titus 2:10), and thus would be a good witness that would honor their Lord Jesus Christ.

QUESTIONS FOR PERSONAL APPLICATION

1. How do you feel about the New Testament teaching that you should be subject to your employer or (if you are in school) to your teacher? Do you like it? If not, why not?
2. Has a supervisor in your workplace ever told you to do something that was clearly morally wrong? How did you respond? How do you think you should have responded?
3. Can you honestly and joyfully seek to do good for your employer and your workplace each day?
4. Have you ever felt that you were treated unjustly in your workplace? How did you talk to God about this situation? Have you come to the place where you can trust God to bring a just resolution to this situation, even if not until the final judgment?
5. Do you think that your conduct in the workplace is honoring to Christ?
6. If you have supervisory authority in your workplace, how do you seek to treat your employees fairly? What is the most difficult part of your job?
7. Before reading this chapter, had you thought of yourself as being subject to the authority of the elders in your church? In what ways do you now think you are subject to them? Do you like this idea? If not, why?
8. If you are a teacher, do you feel that your students are appropriately respectful of you and your authority? What is the most difficult part of your job with respect to relating to your students? Is there anything you could do differently?
9. If you are a student, are there any ways in which you think you should be more respectful of your teachers (or your professors)?

SPECIAL TERMS

bondservant
doulos
elders

BIBLIOGRAPHY

Sections in Other Ethics Texts

(see complete bibliographical data, p. 64)

> Davis, 293–303
> Frame, 575–92
> McQuilkin and Copan, 449–50

Other Works

Barclay, William. *Educational Ideals in the Ancient World*. Grand Rapids, MI: Baker, 1974.

Buford, Bob. *Half Time: Changing Your Game Plan from Success to Significance*. Grand Rapids, MI: Zondervan, 1994.

Edersheim, Alfred. *Sketches of Jewish Social Life*. Peabody, MA: Hendrickson, 1998.

Estes, Daniel J. *Hear, My Son: Teaching and Learning in Proverbs 1–9*. Grand Rapids, MI: Eerdmans, 1997.

Miller, Darrow L., and Marit Newton. *LifeWork: A Biblical Theology for What You Do Every Day*. Seattle: YWAM, 2009.

Nelson, Tom. *Work Matters: Connecting Sunday Worship to Monday Work*. Wheaton, IL: Crossway, 2011.

Tidball, D. J. "Ministry." In *New Dictionary of Christian Ethics and Pastoral Theology*, edited by David J. Atkinson and David H. Field, 593–95. Leicester, UK: Inter-Varsity, and Downers Grove, IL: InterVarsity Press, 1995.

SCRIPTURE MEMORY PASSAGE

> **Colossians 3:22–25:** Bondservants, obey in everything those who are your earthly masters, not by way of eye-service, as people-pleasers, but with sincerity of heart, fearing the Lord. Whatever you do, work heartily, as for the Lord and not for men, knowing that from the Lord you will receive the inheritance as your reward. You are serving the Lord Christ. For the wrongdoer will be paid back for the wrong he has done, and there is no partiality.

HYMN

"Day by Day"

> Day by day and with each passing moment,
> Strength I find to meet my trials here;
> Trusting in my Father's wise bestowment,
> I've no cause for worry or for fear.

He whose heart is kind beyond all measure
Gives unto each day what He deems best
Lovingly, its part of pain and pleasure,
Mingling toil with peace and rest.

Ev'ry day the Lord Himself is near me
With a special mercy for each hour;
All my cares He fain would bear, and cheer me,
He whose name is Counselor and Pow'r.
The protection of His child and treasure
Is a charge that on Himself He laid;
"As thy days, thy strength shall be in measure,"
This the pledge to me He made.

Help me then in ev'ry tribulation
So to trust Thy promises, O Lord,
That I lose not faith's sweet consolation
Offered me with Thy holy word.
Help me, Lord, when toil and trouble meeting,
E'er to take, as from a father's hand,
One by one, the days, the moments fleeting,
Till I reach the promised land.

AUTHOR: LINA SANDELL BERG, 1832–1903

Part 4

PROTECTING HUMAN LIFE

"You shall not murder."

Chapter 18

CAPITAL PUNISHMENT

Is it ever right for the government to put a criminal to death?

The sixth commandment reads:

> You shall not murder. (Ex. 20:13)

A. THE MEANING OF THE COMMANDMENT

The Hebrew verb translated as "murder" is *rātsakh*, which means "murder, slay."[1] This verb is used in the Old Testament to refer to the unlawful taking of a human life, what we call "murder" (in a criminal sense) today. For example, this same verb is used in a different form to speak of a "murderer" in Numbers 35:16, 17, 18, 19. The verb is also used to speak of "causing human death through carelessness or negligence."[2] But *rātsakh* is *not* the ordinary word for judicial execution,[3] and it is never used to refer to killing in war.[4]

Therefore, the sixth commandment should not be used as an argument against

---

[1] BDB, 953. The HALOT definition is "to kill, murder, strike down, slay," 1283.

[2] ESV footnote to Ex. 20:13. Therefore, the word actually has a slightly broader sense than the English word *murder* today.

[3] The Hebrew word *mûth* and sometimes other expressions are used to speak about judicial execution (that is, capital punishment). Thus, Numbers 35:16 says, "The murderer [*rātsakh*] shall be put to death [*mûth*]." Out of 49 instances of *rātsakh* in the Old Testament, it is used only once for judicial execution, and that is in a law that is stated in a proverbial or axiomatic form, and that does not represent the ordinary use of the word elsewhere: "If anyone kills a person, the murderer [*rātsakh*] shall be put to death [*rātsakh*] on the evidence of witnesses. But no person shall be put to death [*mûth*] on the testimony of one witness" (Num. 35:30).

[4] This chapter is adapted from Wayne Grudem, *Politics—According to the Bible: A Comprehensive Resource for Understanding Modern Political Issues in Light of Scripture* (Grand Rapids, MI: Zondervan, 2010), 186–201, with permission of the publisher.

capital punishment, for that is not the sense in which the original readers would have understood it.[5]

Although this commandment is part of the Mosaic covenant, it is restated several times in the New Testament (see Rom. 1:29; 13:9; 1 Tim. 1:9; James 2:11; 4:2; 1 John 3:12, 15; Rev. 9:21; 16:6; 18:24; 21:8; 22:15; see also Jesus's teaching in Matt. 5:21–26; 15:19; 19:18). The New Testament authors frequently affirm the continuing moral validity of this commandment in the new covenant age.

God is the Creator and sustainer of human life, and human beings are the pinnacle of his creation, for only human beings are said to be created in the image of God. Therefore, God absolutely forbids human beings to murder one another.

Because the sixth commandment is concerned with the protection of life, I will consider the question of capital punishment in this chapter. One argument in favor of capital punishment for the crime of murder is that it protects human beings from those who might want to murder them, because the punishment is so great: if anyone murders someone else, he or she will be put to death. In this way, it is argued, capital punishment shows the extremely high value that should be attached to human life.

In the subsequent chapters I will also consider other issues related to questions of life and death, including war (chap. 19), self-defense (chap. 20), abortion (chap. 21), euthanasia (chap. 22), suicide (chap. 23), and aging and death (chap. 24). After that, I will consider three additional issues that do not concern life and death, but have to do with protecting the quality of human life: racial discrimination (chap. 25), health (chap. 26), and alcohol and drugs (chap. 27).

B. THE QUESTION OF CAPITAL PUNISHMENT

The question with regard to capital punishment (also called the death penalty or execution) is this: Should governments take the lives of people who are convicted of capital crimes?

Which crimes are these? The crimes for which capital punishment is specified as the penalty today usually include at least premeditated murder and treason. Other crimes that are sometimes thought to deserve capital punishment include an attempt to use a weapon of mass destruction, espionage that results in a country's citizens losing their lives, and crimes such as aggravated[6] rape, aggravated kidnapping, aircraft hijacking, or perjury that lead to a person's death.

But the primary question addressed in this chapter is whether governments should have the right to carry out capital punishment *at all*.

---

[5] The RSV and KJV are misleading when they translate Ex. 20:13 as "You shall not kill," which could be taken to mean all sorts of killing, a much broader sense than what is intended by the Hebrew verb. More recent translation teams have recognized this, for both the NRSV and the NKJV now translate this commandment "You shall not murder."

[6] An "aggravated" crime is one in which the intent or actual circumstances add significantly to the guilt of the criminal or the harm to the victim.

C. THE RELEVANT BIBLICAL TEACHING

1. Genesis 9:5–6. In the early history of the human race, God brought a massive flood on the earth, destroying all human beings except the eight who were rescued in the ark: Noah, his wife, his three sons, and their wives (Genesis 6–9).

When the flood ended, Noah and his family came out of the ark and started human society all over again. At that point God gave them instructions regarding the life they were about to begin. Among those instructions was the following passage, which, as we saw in chapter 16 (p. 427), provides the foundation for human government:

> And for your lifeblood I will require a reckoning: from every beast I will require it and from man. From his fellow man I will require a reckoning for the life of man.
>
> Whoever sheds the blood of man,
> by man shall his blood be shed,
> for God made man in his own image. (Gen. 9:5–6)

The word "sheds" in this statement translates the Hebrew verb *shāphak*, which in this passage means "to pour out in large amount, causing death." Therefore, "In this verse, 'shedding blood' refers to the violent, unjustified taking of human life (cf. Gen. 37:22; Num. 35:33; 1 Kings 2:31; Ezek. 22:4)."[7]

This commandment from God says that when someone murders another person, the murderer himself should be put to death. This execution of a murderer was not going to be carried out directly by God, but by a human agent: "by man shall his blood be shed." Yet this was not to be seen as human vengeance, but as carrying out God's own requirement of justice. God explains what he means when he says, "From his fellow man *I will require a reckoning* for the life of man" (Gen. 9:5).

The reason God gives for this is the immense value of human life: "*for* God made man in his own image" (v. 6). To be in the image of God is the highest status and privilege in all creation, and only human beings share in it (see Gen. 1:27). To be in God's image means that human beings are more like God than anything else on the earth, and it also means that they are God's representatives in this world (for they are like him and thus can best represent him). Therefore, to murder a human being is to murder someone who is more like God than any other creature on the earth. The murder of another human being is therefore a kind of attack against God himself, for it is an attack against his representative on the earth, an attack against the "image" of himself that he has left on the earth.

In order to give just punishment for such a serious crime, God decrees that the murderer will pay the ultimate price: he will forfeit his own life. The punishment will fit

---

[7] "Capital Punishment," in *ESV Study Bible* (Wheaton, IL: Crossway, 2008), 2552.

the crime: "Whoever sheds the blood of man, by man shall his blood be shed, for God made man in his own image" (Gen. 9:6).

This passage therefore lays the foundational principles for all human governmental authority. At the very beginning of human society, after the flood destroys the earth, God establishes that he will delegate to human beings the authority to carry out punishment on wrongdoers ("by man shall his blood be shed").

Therefore, the authority to execute punishment on wrongdoing was not simply invented by human beings on their own. Rather, it is an authority that has been delegated to human beings by God, and through this authority God carries out his righteous justice on wrongdoers, for he says this is the way in which he "will require a reckoning for the life of man" (Gen. 9:5). So the authority to punish wrongdoing (presumably through some form of government that would be established) is given by God to human beings.

Such authority to punish wrongdoing also implies that human governments will have to decide (1) what wrongdoing is worthy of punishment, (2) what punishment is appropriate for each wrongdoing, and (3) whether or not an individual is guilty of that wrongdoing.

This passage from Genesis 9 came long before the establishment of the nation of Israel (at the exodus from Egypt) or the giving of the laws of the Mosaic covenant (in Exodus, Leviticus, Numbers, and Deuteronomy). Therefore, the application of this passage is not limited to the nation of Israel for a specific period of time, but is for all people for all time.

The covenant God made with Noah after the flood is nowhere called the "old covenant," and it is nowhere said to be abolished or no longer in effect. The covenant God made with Noah applies to all human beings on the earth for all generations:

> When the bow is in the clouds, I will see it and remember the *everlasting covenant* between God and *every living creature* of all flesh that is on the earth. (Gen. 9:16)

We conclude from this passage that God gave to human government the authority to carry out capital punishment, and that this is the foundational authority of all governments on the earth.[8]

2. Romans 13:1–7. I discussed this passage in some detail in chapter 16, but two specific details deserve comment at this point. Here is the passage once again:

> Let every person be subject to the governing authorities. For there is no authority except from God, and those that exist have been instituted by God. Therefore whoever resists the authorities resists what God has appointed, and those who resist will incur judgment. For rulers are not a terror to good

---

[8] See chap. 18, p. 513, for a discussion of the view that Gen. 9:6 is a human proverb, not a command from God.

conduct, but to bad. Would you have no fear of the one who is in authority? Then do what is good, and you will receive his approval, for he is God's servant for your good. But if you do wrong, be afraid, for he does not bear the sword in vain. For *he is the servant of God, an avenger who carries out God's wrath on the wrongdoer.* Therefore one must be in subjection, not only to avoid God's wrath but also for the sake of conscience. For because of this you also pay taxes, for the authorities are ministers of God, attending to this very thing. Pay to all what is owed to them: taxes to whom taxes are owed, revenue to whom revenue is owed, respect to whom respect is owed, honor to whom honor is owed.

First, Paul says the agent of government is "the servant of God, an avenger [Greek, *ekdikos*, "one who carries out punishment"] who carries out God's wrath on the wrongdoer" (Rom. 13:4). This is consistent with the teaching of Genesis 9 that God requires a reckoning for wrongdoing and that this will be carried out through human agents.

Second, Paul says, the civil government "does not bear the sword in vain" (Rom. 13:4). The Greek word for "sword" is *macharia*, which is used in several other passages to speak of the instrument by which people are put to death. Here are some examples:

He killed James the brother of John with the *sword.* (Acts 12:2)

[The Philippian jailer] drew his *sword* and was about to kill himself, supposing that the prisoners had escaped. (Acts 16:27)

They were stoned, they were sawn in two, they were killed with the *sword.* (Heb. 11:37)

If anyone is to be slain with the *sword,* with the sword must he be slain. (Rev. 13:10)

A number of verses in the Septuagint (the Greek translation of the Old Testament) also use the word in this way, such as these:

You shall surely put the inhabitants of that city to the *sword,* devoting it to destruction. (Deut. 13:15)

And when the LORD your God gives it into your hand, you shall put all its males to the *sword.* (Deut. 20:13)

Therefore, the idea, suggested by some, that the sword here is simply a symbol of governmental authority is hardly persuasive.[9] When Paul says that civil government in

---

[9] David P. Gushee and Glen H. Stassen refer to (but do not quote) one 1976 article in a German academic journal as evidence that the mention of the "sword" in this passage "refers to the symbol of authority carried by the police who accompanied tax collectors." *Kingdom Ethics: Following Jesus in Contemporary Context,* 2nd

general is authorized to "bear the sword," he means that it has been given authority from God to use the sword for the purpose for which people used it in the first century, and that is to put people to death.

3. First Peter 2:13–14. The apostle Peter writes:

> Be subject for the Lord's sake to every human institution, whether it be to the emperor as supreme, or to governors as sent by him *to punish those who do evil* and to praise those who do good.

The expression translated "to punish" in verse 14 (*eis ekdikēsis*, literally "for the punishment") includes the same word that Paul uses for "vengeance" that belongs to God (Rom. 12:19). Paul also uses a word from the same root to say that the civil government is "*an avenger* [Greek, *ekdikos*] who carries out God's wrath" (Rom. 13:4). Both Romans 13 and 1 Peter 2 teach that government has a responsibility not only to deter crime, but also actually to bring God's punishment to the wrongdoer (in the sense of retribution for wrongdoing; see further discussion in chap. 16, p. 429). This is consistent with Genesis 9:5–6.

4. But Is It Right to Desire That Government Punish a Criminal? Sometimes Christians may think that if a loved one has been murdered, or if they themselves have been robbed, beaten, or severely injured by the actions of a drunk driver, they should merely forgive the person and never seek for the wrongdoer to be punished by the courts. But that is not the solution Paul gives in Romans 12:19. He does not say, "Beloved, never avenge yourselves, but simply forgive everyone who has done wrong to you." Rather, he tells his readers to give up any desire *to seek revenge themselves* and instead give it over to the civil government, for after he says, "Beloved, never avenge yourselves," he says, "*but leave it to the wrath of God.*" Then he goes on to explain that the civil government is "the servant of God, an avenger who carries out *God's wrath* on the wrongdoer" (Rom. 13:4).

In other words, people should not seek to take *personal revenge* when they have been wronged, but they should seek that *justice be done* through the workings of the civil

---

ed. (Grand Rapids, MI: Eerdmans, 2016), 223–24. They conclude that Paul's purpose was to urge Christians to pay taxes and not rebel against the government, and that this passage says nothing about the death penalty.

But their objection misses the point. Everyone agrees that Paul tells Christians to pay taxes in Rom. 13:6. That is one way he tells them to be subject to the government. But that is not until verse 6, while verses 1–5 are certainly not limited to the question of paying taxes. They speak about government authority in general and the need to be subject to "what God has appointed." Rom. 13:4 does not say, "But if you do not pay taxes, be afraid," but rather, "But *if you do wrong*, be afraid, for he does not bear the sword in vain." Paul is warning the Romans against all types of criminal activity. And he does not say that the governmental authority "is the servant of God, an avenger who carries out God's wrath on the tax evader," but "an avenger who carries out God's wrath *on the wrongdoer.*"

Gushee and Stassen incorrectly try to limit this general passage about governmental authority to one of the specific applications that Paul makes at the end of the passage. (And the fact that one academic article was published in a German journal 40 years ago is hardly sufficient to establish the consensus of evangelical New Testament scholarship regarding a passage.)

government. Letting the civil government carry out justice frees the believer to do good even to those who have wronged him. As Paul says, "If your enemy is hungry, feed him; if he is thirsty, give him something to drink" (Rom. 12:20). In that way the believer will "overcome evil with good" (v. 21), and that good comes not only through giving food and water but also through the justice system of the civil government, which is "God's servant for your good" (Rom. 13:4).[10]

But, someone might object, isn't it wrong for a Christian to *desire* vengeance? It depends on what kind of vengeance is desired. If we seek and desire to take *personal vengeance* (to harm the wrongdoer ourselves), then that is disobeying Romans 12 and 13. But if we desire that the government carry out *God's just vengeance* on the wrongdoer, then we are doing exactly what Paul says in 12:19 and are leaving vengeance "to the wrath of God." We are leaving it to the proper actions of government, which is "the servant of God" when it "carries out God's wrath on the wrongdoer" (13:4). It cannot be wrong for us to desire that God's justice be carried out in this manner, for it is another way in which God demonstrates the glory of his attribute of justice on the earth. (Jim Wallis fails to make this distinction between wrongful personal vengeance and a rightful desire for God's vengeance to come through government when he opposes capital punishment, saying it "just satisfies revenge."[11] No, it satisfies God's requirement of justice.)

Therefore, it does not seem to me to be wrong when Christians both (1) show personal kindness to and pray for the salvation and eternal forgiveness of those who have done them wrong, and (2) simultaneously pursue justice through the civil courts and desire that the wrongdoer be justly paid back for the wrong that he has done. In fact, I have spoken with more than one believer who has had a friend or loved one murdered, and who deeply longed for the courts to carry out punishment on the murderer. It seemed to me that this reflected a deep-seated sense of God's justice that he has put in our human hearts, a sense that was crying out for wrong to be punished and for justice to be done.

Another passage that confirms this understanding of vengeance is Revelation 6:9–10:

> When he opened the fifth seal, I saw under the altar the souls of those who had been slain for the word of God and for the witness they had borne. They cried out with a loud voice, "O Sovereign Lord, holy and true, *how long before you will judge and avenge* [Greek, *ekdikeō*, "punish, take vengeance"] *our blood on those who dwell on the earth*?"

The significant point about this passage is that these "souls" are completely free from sin, and this means that there is no trace of sinful desire left in their hearts. Yet they are

---

[10] There were no chapter or verse divisions in the earliest Greek manuscripts, and the connection between what we now know as the end of Romans 12 and the beginning of Romans 13 would have been even clearer to Paul's original readers.

[11] Jim Wallis, *God's Politics: Why the Right Gets It Wrong and the Left Doesn't Get It* (New York: HarperCollins, 2005), 303.

crying out for God to take vengeance on those who had murdered them, "on those who dwell on the earth" (v. 10).[12] Therefore, such a desire cannot be seen as morally wrong or as inconsistent with forgiving others and continually committing judgment into the hands of God, even as Jesus did when he was on the cross (see 1 Pet. 2:23; Luke 23:34). In fact, it is exactly this action of committing judgment into the hands of God that allows us to give up the desire to seek it for ourselves and that gives us freedom to continue to show acts of personal mercy to offenders in this life.

5. What Crimes Are Worthy of Capital Punishment? Are any crimes besides murder also worthy of capital punishment? The Bible does not give us explicit directions on that question, though some biblical principles can inform our reasoning process. The main question is whether other crimes are *sufficiently as horrible as murder in the degree of evil they involve* as to deserve capital punishment.

The final decision about which crimes deserve capital punishment should be made by each state or nation, ideally as the will of the people finds expression through the laws enacted by their elected representatives.

Christopher Wright points out a significant feature of Old Testament law: "No property offense in normal legal procedure was punishable by death."[13] That is, *people* could not be put to death for stealing *things*, but some kind of monetary retribution had to be made instead. This seems to be a wise principle that should prevent the death penalty from even being considered for crimes involving only property.

However, one reminder is in order: it is not legitimate to appeal to the *many kinds of crimes subject to the death penalty* in the laws in the Mosaic covenant (in Exodus, Leviticus, Numbers, and Deuteronomy) in order to say that those crimes should receive capital punishment today. Those laws were intended only *for the people of Israel at that particular time in history*. Many of those laws reflected the unique status of Israel as a people for God's own possession who were required to worship him and not to allow any hint of allegiance to other gods. There is no suggestion in the rest of the Bible that those particular uses of the death penalty in the Mosaic covenant should ever be applied by civil governments today, in the age of the new covenant. (See my discussion of theonomy beginning at p. 225; see also pp. 221, 433).

6. Conclusion. God gives to civil government the right and the responsibility to carry out capital punishment for certain crimes, at least for the crime of murder (which is specified in Gen. 9:6). Whether there should be other crimes subject to capital punishment is a question that each government in each society must decide through its normal political and governmental decision-making process.

---

[12] See also Gen. 4:10: "And the LORD said, 'What have you done? The voice of your brother's blood is crying to me from the ground.'"

[13] Christopher J. H. Wright, *Old Testament Ethics for the People of God* (Downers Grove, IL: InterVarsity Press, 2004), 308.

D. OBJECTIONS

1. Genesis 9:5–6. My argument to this point has claimed significant support for capital punishment from Genesis 9:5–6:

> And for your lifeblood I will require a reckoning: from every beast I will require it and from man. From his fellow man I will require a reckoning for the life of man. "Whoever sheds the blood of man, by man shall his blood be shed, for God made man in his own image."

Some object that this passage contains a "proverb" and not an actual command from God about how human beings should act. David Gushee and Glen Stassen say this about Genesis 9:6: "As it stands in Genesis, it does not command the death penalty but gives wise advice based on the likely consequence of your action: if you kill someone, you will end up being killed."[14]

But this interpretation is not persuasive, for three reasons:

1. When Genesis 9:5 is connected to verse 6, it shows that execution of the murderer is the way in which *God himself will carry out justice through his intermediary in human society.* God says, "From his fellow man *I will require a reckoning* for the life of man" (v. 5). But Gushee and Stassen say nothing about this verse.

2. The last clause of verse 6 *explains* the command. The death penalty is to be carried out for murder *because* man is in the image of God. This shows why the crime is so serious. But in Gushee and Stassen's view, this reason would make no sense. They understand this "proverb" to mean, in effect, "If you do something wrong (murder), another wrong will be done to you (another murder)." But how can our creation in God's image be a reason for such vengeful wrongdoing? This is like saying (on their view), "Violence (murder) will escalate among people because they are made in God's image." That line of thinking ends up saying that God's image is the reason why people do wrong!

On the other hand, on the interpretation I am advocating, this verse says, "Murder of another human being is so serious that capital punishment will be required, because that human being was made in God's image."

3. Later passages in the Old Testament show that God himself did institute the death penalty for the crime of murder (see Num. 35:16–34).

Because of these three reasons, Gushee and Stassen's interpretation is not persuasive.

2. Exodus 20:13. Some have argued that Exodus 20:13, "You shall not murder," prohibits the death penalty. They claim that not even a government should "murder" a criminal.

As I explained at the beginning of this chapter, that interpretation misunderstands the sense of the Hebrew verb *rātsakh*, which is here translated "murder." The term refers

---

[14] Gushee and Stassen, *Kingdom Ethics*, 222. Several of the objections I address in this section are raised by Gushee and Stassen in an extensive argument against the death penalty. Ibid., 215–33.

to the unlawful taking of a human life, not to all taking of human life. The original readers and hearers of Exodus 20:13 would not have understood this word to prohibit capital punishment, for which other words were usually used (see p. 505).

In addition, God himself commanded that the death penalty be carried out in the actual laws that he gave for the Mosaic covenant (see, for example, Num. 35:16–21, 30–34). It would not be consistent to think that in Exodus 20:13 God prohibited what he commanded in Numbers 35.

3. Matthew 5:38–39. This passage is sometimes cited as a prohibition of capital punishment. It says:

> You have heard that it was said, "An eye for an eye and a tooth for a tooth." But I say to you, Do not resist the one who is evil. But if anyone slaps you on the right cheek, turn to him the other also.

However, in this passage Jesus is speaking to *individual people* about how they should relate to other individuals. It is similar to Romans 12:19, where Paul prohibits personal vengeance. Jesus is not talking about the responsibility of governments or telling governments how they should act with regard to the punishment of crime. We need to pay attention to the context of passages so that we can accurately apply them to the situations they are addressing. Matthew 5 is addressing personal conduct, while Romans 13 explicitly addresses the responsibilities of governments.[15]

4. Matthew 22:39. Here Jesus says, "You shall love your neighbor as yourself." Does this command prohibit putting a murderer to death? Is it possible to love one's neighbor, in obedience to this command, and at the same time put him to death for murder? How can these actions be consistent? And shouldn't this command of Jesus take precedence over the Old Testament commands about executing the death penalty?

But this objection, if it pits Jesus's command against some Old Testament commands about the death penalty, clearly misunderstands the context from which Jesus took these words. Jesus is actually quoting from the Old Testament, from Leviticus 19:18, where God commanded the people:

> You shall not take vengeance or bear a grudge against the sons of your own people, but *you shall love your neighbor as yourself*. I am the LORD.

In that same context, God also commanded the death penalty for certain crimes (see Lev. 20:2, 10). Therefore, it must have been consistent for God to command love for one's neighbor and also to command the death penalty, for example, for people who put their own children to death in sacrificing to idols (Lev. 20:2). Love for one's neighbor does not nullify the requirement to carry out God's justice on wrongdoers.

---

[15] For further discussion of this passage, see chap. 20, p. 551.

5. Matthew 26:52. When Jesus was being arrested, Peter drew his sword and struck the servant of the high priest, thinking to defend Jesus against attack. But Jesus said to him:

> Put your sword back into its place. For all who take the sword will perish by the sword.

Does this verse argue against the death penalty?

Jesus's words to Peter should not be taken as a command to people serving as agents of a government. That interpretation would fail to take account of who Peter was and what his role was at that point. Jesus was not saying that no soldiers or police officers should ever have weapons; rather, he was telling Peter not to attempt to resist those who were arresting Jesus and would lead him to crucifixion. Jesus did not want to begin a civil uprising among his followers, and he certainly did not want Peter to be killed at that time for attempting to defend and protect him.

But it is also interesting that Jesus did not tell Peter to give his sword away or throw it away; rather, he said, "Put your sword back into its place" (Matt. 26:52). It was apparently right for Peter to continue carrying his sword, just not to use it to prevent Jesus's arrest and crucifixion.[16] In this context, therefore, "all who take the sword will perish by the sword" must mean that those who take up the sword *in an attempt to do the spiritual work of advancing the kingdom of God* will not succeed. If Jesus's followers attempted to overthrow the Roman government as a means of advancing the kingdom of God at that time, they would simply fail and perish by the sword.

6. John 8:2–11. The Old Testament commanded the death penalty for the crime of adultery (see Deut. 22:23–24), but in the New Testament story of the woman caught in adultery, Jesus first said to the woman's accusers, "Let him who is without sin among you be the first to throw a stone at her" (John 8:7), and then, when all the accusers had left, he said to the woman, "Neither do I condemn you; go, and from now on sin no more" (v. 11). Does this imply that Jesus did not want people to enforce the death penalty any longer?

There are several reasons why this passage should not be used as an argument against the death penalty. First, even if this text is used to argue against the death penalty *for adultery*, it is not a story about a murderer, so it cannot be applied to the use of the death penalty *for murder*, which was established in God's covenant with Noah long before the covenant with Moses.

Second, the historical context of this passage explains more about Jesus's answer. He did not allow himself to be drawn into a trap in which he would tell the Jewish leaders to carry out the death penalty, for the Roman government had prohibited anyone from carrying out the death penalty except the Romans themselves.[17]

---

[16] People commonly carried swords for self-defense against robbers or other kinds of violent attackers; see chap. 20, p. 556.

[17] The Jewish accusers of Jesus said to Pilate, "It is not lawful for us to put anyone to death" (John 18:31). For discussion of the extrabiblical historical evidence, see D. A. Carson, *The Gospel According to John*, Pillar New Testament Commentary (Grand Rapids, MI: Eerdmans, 1991), 591–92.

Third, the entire story contained in John 7:53–8:11 is a passage of doubtful origin, as is plain from the explanatory notes in any modern Bible translation. Although the passage is retained in many Bibles today, it is usually with double brackets or other marks showing that it almost certainly was not a part of the original manuscript of John's Gospel. Thus, the authority of this text itself is doubtful.

Therefore, on several levels the text does not provide a persuasive objection to the death penalty with respect to crimes such as murder.

7. "We Should Follow the Teachings of Jesus." Sometimes opponents of the death penalty say that we should follow the teachings of Jesus on this matter rather than other passages in the Bible, especially some Old Testament passages. Gushee and Stassen, for example, say, "One way to study the biblical teaching on the death penalty is to begin with Jesus Christ as Lord . . . and with the commitment to be followers of Jesus. . . . Then we ask first what Jesus taught on the death penalty as a response to murder."[18] They contrast this approach with using Genesis 9:6 as the key passage for understanding this issue.[19]

However, the primary biblical teaching about the responsibilities of civil government is found in passages such as Genesis 9, Romans 13, and 1 Peter 2 (see chap. 16 for other passages). *Jesus himself* did not give much explicit teaching about civil government. Therefore, when someone says, "We should follow the teaching of Jesus" regarding civil government, he or she has ruled out most of the relevant teaching in the Bible about civil government!

In another sense, however, the whole Bible comes with the authority of Jesus, and we should seek to follow all that it teaches on this topic. Jesus continually upheld the authority of the Old Testament as the Word of God, and he delegated his apostles to speak and write with his authority.[20] To follow the teaching of the whole Bible on any topic *is* to follow the teaching of Jesus on that topic.

Finally, as explained with regard to the passages from Matthew above, Gushee and Stassen incorrectly try to apply some of Jesus's teachings to the question of the death penalty as used by governments, a subject that these teachings were not intended to address.

8. "God Spared Some Murderers, Such as Cain and King David." The final biblical argument against the death penalty is that God's own actions show that murderers should not be put to death, because God himself spared Cain, who murdered his brother, Abel (Gen. 4:8–16), and also spared King David when David caused the death of Bathsheba's husband, Uriah (see 2 Sam. 12:13).[21]

---

[18] Gushee and Stassen, *Kingdom Ethics*, 218.

[19] Ibid., 221–23.

[20] See Grudem, *Systematic Theology: An Introduction to Biblical Doctrine* (Leicester, UK: Inter-Varsity, and Grand Rapids, MI: Zondervan, 1994), 54–89.

[21] Gushee and Stassen also mention Tamar (Genesis 38); see *Kingdom Ethics*, 221–22.

But this objection merely changes the subject from the responsibility of civil government to the freedom of God to pardon whomever he wishes. Of course, God can pardon some people until the day of final judgment. He is God! Likewise, he can execute immediate judgment on others according to his wise purposes. We see this with the fire that fell from heaven on Sodom and Gomorrah (Gen. 19:24–29); the flood (Genesis 6–9); and the sudden deaths of Nadab and Abihu (Lev. 10:1–2); Korah, Dathan, and Abiram (Num. 16:31–33); and Uzzah (2 Sam. 6:7).

But God is *not* telling us in these passages *what he wants civil governments to do!* He established that clearly in Genesis 9:5–6, Romans 13:1–7, 1 Peter 2:13–14, and elsewhere. Where God tells us what he wants governments to do, governments should follow those teachings.

It is characteristic of the opponents of capital punishment that they continue to appeal to passages that *do not* speak explicitly about the subject of civil government in order to use them to deny the teaching of those passages that *do* speak about civil government. This is hardly sound biblical interpretation.

9. "We Need to Apply a 'Whole-Life Ethic.'" Some opponents of the death penalty have said that Christians should apply a "whole-life ethic," in which they oppose all intentional taking of human life, including abortion, euthanasia, capital punishment, and war. (This view is sometimes called the "seamless garment" argument.) Wallis takes this position in his book *God's Politics*.[22] Joseph Cardinal Bernardin of Chicago was an advocate of this view, stating, "The spectrum of life cuts across the issues of genetics, abortion, capital punishment, modern warfare and the care of the terminally ill."[23] Pope John Paul II also advocated this position in his encyclical *Evangelium Vitae*, writing:

> This is the context in which to place the problem of the death penalty. On this matter there is a growing tendency, both in the Church and in civil society, to demand that it be applied in a very limited way or even that it be abolished completely. The problem must be viewed in the context of a system of penal justice ever more in line with human dignity and thus, in the end, with God's plan for man and society. The primary purpose of the punishment which society inflicts is "to redress the disorder caused by the offence." Public authority must redress the violation of personal and social rights by imposing on the offender an adequate punishment for the crime, as a condition for the offender to regain the exercise of his or her freedom. In this way authority also fulfills the purpose of defending public order and ensuring people's safety, while at the same time offering the offender an incentive and help to change his or her behaviour and be rehabilitated.

---

[22] Wallis, *God's Politics*, 300, 303–6. Wallis does not discuss any passages from the Bible in support of his view, but just his vague, general principle of a "consistent ethic of life."

[23] Joseph Cardinal Bernardin, *Consistent Ethic of Life* (Kansas City: Sheed and Ward, 1988), 7.

It is clear that, for these purposes to be achieved, the *nature and extent of the punishment* must be carefully evaluated and decided upon, and ought not go to the extreme of executing the offender except in cases of absolute necessity: in other words, when it would not be possible otherwise to defend society. Today however, as a result of steady improvements in the organization of the penal system, such cases are very rare, if not practically non-existent.[24]

In response, I must affirm that the proper approach to decide a biblical position on a topic is to take *the specific teaching of the Bible about that topic* rather than fleeing to a vague cloud of generalities (such as "whole life ethic") that can then be used to support most any position the proponent wants. As I argue in later chapters, the specific biblical texts pertaining to abortion and euthanasia teach against these things, but the specific texts that pertain to capital punishment support it.[25]

Rather than a "whole life ethic," Christians should adopt a "whole Bible ethic" and be faithful to the teaching of the entire Bible on this subject as well as on others.

10. Objections to the Death Penalty Based on Results and Fairness. Most arguments about capital punishment *apart from* the teachings of the Bible have to do with the results of using or abolishing the death penalty and its fairness. Those who argue against the death penalty say that (1) it does not deter crime; (2) innocent victims might be put to death; (3) violence by government provokes more violence in society; (4) it is unfairly administered, so that the poor and some ethnic minorities are much more likely to receive the death penalty; and (5) it historically has been used in cruel and oppressive ways, even by Christians.

By contrast, some advocacy groups have advanced persuasive arguments in favor of capital punishment based on the facts that (1) it does in fact deter violent crime; (2) adequate safeguards can be taken to prevent innocent people from being executed; (3) identifying both murder and capital punishment by the same word, "violence," fails to make a crucial distinction between taking the life of an innocent person and taking the life of a guilty person; (4) it can be fairly administered; and (5) while examples of abuse certainly can be found in history, a widespread human sense of justice acknowledges that the crime of premeditated murder can only be adequately punished through taking the life of the murderer.

I will examine these objections in more detail based on results and fairness in the following paragraphs.

a. Is the Death Penalty a Deterrent to Murder? When overall statistics are examined, there is *a fairly clear inverse relationship* between the number of executions of murderers and the number of murders in the United States. When the number of executions

---

[24] John Paul II, *Evangelium Vitae* ("The Gospel of Life"), March 25, 1995, para. 56, http://w2.vatican.va /content/john-paul-ii/en/encyclicals/documents/hf_jp-ii_enc_25031995_evangelium-vitae.html.

[25] I discuss abortion in chap. 21 and euthanasia in chap. 22.

goes down, the number of murders goes up, but when executions increase, murders drop. This is seen in the following chart summarizing the findings of two professors at Pepperdine University:[26]

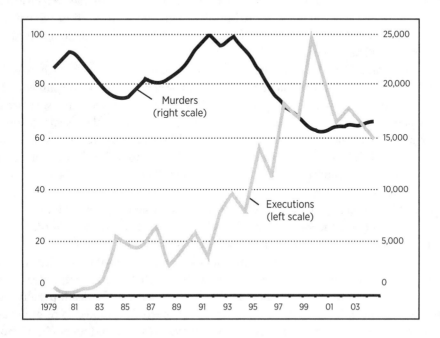

Figure 18.1. The Deterrence Effect: The Relationship between Executions and Murders, 1979–2004. (Source: Roy D. Adler and Michael Summers, based on Federal Bureau of Investigation statistics.)

Some studies have shown that for each murderer executed, as many as 14 to 18 additional murders are deterred.[27] David Muhlhausen, a research fellow at the Heritage Foundation, reports that in one study done in 2009, researchers found that adopting state laws making defendants in child murder cases subject to the death penalty resulted in an almost 20 percent reduction in rates of these crimes.[28]

This deterrence effect has been recognized even by researchers who oppose capital punishment. "I personally am opposed to the death penalty," says H. Naci Mocan, an

[26] Roy D. Adler and Michael Summers, "Capital Punishment Works," *The Wall Street Journal*, Nov. 2, 2007, http://online.wsj.com/article/SB119397079767680173.html.

[27] Testimony of David B. Muhlhausen, "The Death Penalty Deters Crime and Saves Lives," Heritage Foundation, Aug. 28, 2007, http://www.heritage.org/testimony/the-death-penalty-deters-crime-and-saves-lives, citing Paul R. Zimmerman, "State Executions, Deterrence, and the Incidence of Murder," *Journal of Applied Economics* 7, no. 1 (May 2004): 909–41.

[28] David B. Muhlhausen, "How the Death Penalty Saves Lives," *U.S. News and World Report*, Sept. 29, 2014, http://www.usnews.com/opinion/articles/2014/09/29/the-death-penalty-saves-lives-by-deterring-crime.

economist at Louisiana State University and an author of a study that found that each execution saves five lives. "But my research shows that there is a deterrent effect."[29]

Similarly, death penalty opponents Cass Sunstein of the University of Chicago and Adrian Vermeule of Harvard University write, "Capital punishment may well save lives." They add, "Those who object to capital punishment, and who do so in the name of protecting life, must come to terms with the possibility that the failure to inflict capital punishment will fail to protect life."[30]

These studies show the inadequacy of the arguments from authors such as Wallis, who claims it is part of a "consistent ethic of life" to be against capital punishment.[31] My response is to say that when we support capital punishment, we show that we place *the highest possible value on human life*, for when a life is wrongfully taken, society requires the greatest punishment—the forfeiture of the life of the murderer. The studies also show that Wallis is incorrect when he writes that "there is no real evidence that [capital punishment] deters murder; it just satisfies revenge."[32] (He offers no data to support this assertion.)

In addition, there is an argument from common sense: If a criminal knows he will possibly be put to death, will he be more likely or less likely to commit murder than if he knows he cannot be put to death? He will be less likely.[33]

The current legal system in the United States allows appeals of murder convictions to drag on for a decade or more, so we have not been able to see in recent years a reliable evaluation of the deterrent effect of the death penalty. If the death penalty were carried out more quickly when someone has clearly been determined to be guilty and reasonable appeals have been exhausted, the deterrent effect would no doubt be much greater than it is today. The Bible says, "Because the sentence against an evil deed is not executed speedily, the heart of the children of man is fully set to do evil" (Eccles. 8:11).

b. Are Innocent People Put to Death? With regard to the possibility of innocent victims being put to death, there has been (to my knowledge) *no known example* of an innocent person being executed in the United States since the resumption of the death penalty in 1976. A number of innocent death-row prisoners have been *released* due to

---

[29] H. Naci Mocan, quoted in Adam Liptak, "Does Death Penalty Save Lives? A New Debate," *The New York Times*, Nov. 18, 2007, www.nytimes.com/2007/11/18/us/18deter.html.

[30] Cass Sunstein and Adrian Vermeule, "Is Capital Punishment Morally Required? The Relevance of Life-Life Tradeoffs," *Stanford Law Review* 703 (2005): 58, quoted in Liptak, "Does Death Penalty Save Lives?"

[31] See Wallis, *God's Politics*, 300, 303.

[32] Ibid., 303.

[33] Dennis Prager offers an interesting thought experiment by the late sociologist Ernest van der Haag: Imagine what would happen if just one state passed a law that capital punishment would be carried out only for murders committed on Mondays, Wednesdays, and Fridays. Do you think that murders in that state would decrease on Mondays, Wednesdays, and Fridays? Of course they would. Prager writes: "The notion that parking tickets deter illegal parking but that death does not deter murder is truly irrational. It shows what happens when people put ideology over common sense." "A Response to Oregon's Governor on Capital Punishment," Townhall, Nov. 29, 2011, http://townhall.com/columnists/dennisprager/2011/11/29/a_response_to_oregons_governor_on_capital_punishment.

DNA testing,[34] but that does not prove that any people have wrongfully been executed. Of course, the death penalty should be carried out only when guilt is established with extremely high standards of proof, but that is done in many murder convictions.

What is the result of failing to carry out the death penalty in the case of premeditated murder? Life imprisonment is also a cruel kind of punishment and is extremely expensive. Moreover, giving a murderer life in prison or a long-term sentence may lead to his committing other murders in prison or after he escapes or is pardoned. For example, in 1981, Glen Stewart Godwin was sentenced to 25 years in prison for the stabbing death of a drug runner and pilot named Kim Robert LeValley. Godwin stabbed LeValley 26 times. He escaped from Folsom State Prison in California and fled to Mexico, where he began a new life as a drug dealer. He was arrested there and killed a member of a Mexican drug cartel while in prison. Soon afterward, he broke out of that prison and (as of 2016) has remained a refugee from justice.[35]

The fact remains that God gave the requirement for the death penalty in Genesis 9:6 at the beginning of human society after the flood, when methods of collecting evidence and the certainty of proof were far less reliable than they are today. Yet God still gave the command to fallible human beings, not requiring that they be omniscient to carry it out, but expecting only that they would act responsibly and seek to avoid further injustice as they obeyed. Among the people of Israel, a failure to carry out the death penalty when God had commanded it was to "pollute the land" and "defile" it before God, for justice had not been done (see Num. 35:32–34).

c. Does All Violence Lead to More Violence? The idea that "violence" by government (in capital punishment) leads to more violence is contrary to the teachings of Genesis 9:5–6, Romans 13:4, and 1 Peter 2:13–14. In fact, exactly the opposite is true: Capital punishment actually has a deterrent effect and saves many innocent lives, as several studies have shown (see discussion above).

d. Are There Racial or Economic Disparities in the Death Penalty? If capital punishment is unfairly or disproportionately carried out among certain segments of a population *when compared with the number of murders committed by that segment of the population*, then the necessary legal steps should be taken to correct that imbalance. But that is not an argument against the death penalty in general. It is merely an argument that demonstrates that it should be carried out fairly, among rich and poor alike, and among members of every ethnic group, when crimes worthy of capital punishment are

---

[34] One example is Nicholas James Yarris, who was exonerated by DNA evidence in 2003 for the rape and murder of a suburban Philadelphia woman, and was removed from death row. See Cindi Lash, "DNA Exonerates Death Row Inmate," *Pittsburgh Post-Gazette*, Dec. 10, 2003, www.post-gazette.com/localnews /20031210yarris1210p1.asp.

[35] Melissa Underwood, "Glen Stewart Godwin Wanted for Murder, Escape From Prison," Fox News, Jan. 28, 2008, www.foxnews.com/story/0,2933,326034,00.html, and Elisha Fieldstedt, "On the Lam: Seven Prison Escapees Who Never Were Found," NBCNews.com, June 8, 2015, http://www.nbcnews.com/storyline/new -york-prison-escape/lam-prison-escapees-who-were-never-found-could-still-be-n371901.

committed. There should be no discrimination based on a person's social status, economic class, or racial background.

Tragically, a 1983 study of Georgia's death penalty found that 22 percent of black defendants who killed white victims were sentenced to death, while 8 percent of white defendants who killed white victims were sentenced to death; and that 1 percent of black defendants who killed black victims were sentenced to death, compared to 3 percent of white defendants who killed black victims. So it does seem that the death penalty was disproportionately applied against black defendants in that state.[36]

e. Has the Death Penalty Been Abused in the Past? It is true that at times in history capital punishment has been used with horrible excess and for far lesser crimes than murder. There are tragic examples in the history of the church where people were put to death because of what the church considered to be the propagation of false doctrine. But these executions were *abuses* that should not be defended by anyone today; such abuses are not arguments against the rightful use of the death penalty.

E. THE IMPORTANCE OF THIS ISSUE

The issue of capital punishment is important for three reasons: (1) God, in both the Old Testament and the New Testament, teaches that governments should carry out this punishment at least for the crime of murder; (2) the death penalty acts as an important deterrent to the horrible crime of murder, especially in cases where the execution is carried out fairly, swiftly, and with adequate safeguards against punishing innocent people; and (3) the death penalty satisfies a deep human sense that just punishment is required when a murder has been committed.

QUESTIONS FOR PERSONAL APPLICATION

1. Has your view of capital punishment changed at all because of reading this chapter?
2. Have you ever been the victim of a crime? If so, did you want the criminal to be punished? How do you think you should have felt about this?
3. If you agree that the death penalty is morally right in the case of premeditated murder, do you think you could personally serve as a jury member and vote to approve the death penalty for a convicted murderer? How would you feel?
4. What character traits (see p. 110) should be prominent as you consider the question of capital punishment?

---

[36] "Race and the Death Penalty," Capital Punishment in Context, https://capitalpunishmentincontext.org /issues/race.

5. If your government were to adopt your view on capital punishment, what results would you hope to see in terms of giving glory to God and advancing the work of his kingdom on earth?

SPECIAL TERMS

capital punishment
murder
vengeance
whole-life ethic

BIBLIOGRAPHY

Sections in Other Ethics Texts

(see complete bibliographical data, p. 64)

Clark and Rakestraw, 2:451–88
Davis, 198–214
Feinberg, John and Paul, 227–66
Frame, 701–4
Geisler, 199–219
Gushee and Stassen, 217–33
Holmes, 95–103
Kaiser, 127–38
McQuilkin and Copan, 438–41
Murray, 107–22
Rae, 247–69

Other Works

Gleason, Ronald N. *The Death Penalty on Trial: Taking a Life for a Life Taken*. Ventura, CA: Nordskog, 2008.

House, H. Wayne, and John Howard Yoder, eds. *The Death Penalty Debate: Two Opposing Views of Capital Punishment*. Waco, TX: Word, 1991.

Lewis, C. S. "The Humanitarian Theory of Punishment." *The Twentieth Century: An Australian Quarterly Review* 3:3 (1949): 5–12.

Moreland, James Porter, and Norman L. Geisler. *The Life and Death Debate: Moral Issues of Our Time*. New York: Greenwood, 1990.

Owens, Erik C., John D. Carlson, and Eric P. Elshtain, eds. *Religion and the Death Penalty: A Call for Reckoning*. Grand Rapids, MI: Eerdmans, 2004.

Sider, Ronald J., ed. *The Early Church on Killing: A Comprehensive Sourcebook on War, Abortion, and Capital Punishment*. Grand Rapids, MI: Baker Academic, 2012.

Storms, Sam. "Can a Christian Support Capital Punishment?" In *Tough Topics 2: Biblical Answers to 25 Challenging Questions*, 255–67. Fearn, Ross-shire, Scotland: Christian Focus, 2015.

Van Ness, D. W. "Capital Punishment." In *New Dictionary of Christian Ethics and Pastoral Theology*, edited by David J. Atkinson and David H. Field, 214–15. Leicester, UK: Inter-Varsity, and Downers Grove, IL: InterVarsity Press, 1995.

Wallis, Jim. *God's Politics: Why the Right Gets It Wrong and the Left Doesn't Get It*. New York: HarperCollins, 2005.

Wright, Christopher J. H. *Old Testament Ethics for the People of God*. Downers Grove, IL: InterVarsity Press, 2004.

SCRIPTURE MEMORY PASSAGE

Romans 13:4: For he is God's servant for your good. But if you do wrong, be afraid, for he does not bear the sword in vain. For he is the servant of God, an avenger who carries out God's wrath on the wrongdoer.

HYMN

"O Quickly Come, Dread Judge of All"

(Can be sung to the tune of "Eternal Father, Strong to Save.")

O quickly come, dread Judge of all;
For, awful though thine advent be,
All shadows from the truth will fall,
And falsehood die, in sight of thee:
O quickly come; for doubt and fear
Like clouds dissolve when thou art near.

O quickly come, great King of all;
Reign all around us, and within;
Let sin no more our souls enthrall,
Let pain and sorrow die with sin:
O quickly come; for thou alone
Canst make thy scattered people one.

O quickly come, true Life of all;
For death is mighty all around;
On ev'ry home his shadows fall,

On ev'ry heart his mark is found:
O quickly come; for grief and pain
Can never cloud thy glorious reign.

O quickly come, sure Light of all;
For gloomy night broods o'er our way;
And weakly souls begin to fall
With weary watching for the day:
O quickly come; for round thy throne
No eye is blind, no night is known.

AUTHOR: LAWRENCE TUTTIETT, 1854

Chapter 19

WAR

How can we know if a war is a "just war"?
Is it right for a Christian to serve as a soldier?
What are the arguments in favor of a pacifist position?
Is it right for nations to have nuclear weapons?

War inevitably brings horrendous destruction to both sides in a conflict; therefore, this is one of the most difficult and most consequential topics in the study of ethics. It is appropriate to treat it in this section of chapters related to the protection of life, both because wars of defense are often fought to protect the lives of citizens in nations and because it is necessary to decide whether the sixth commandment prohibits Christians from participating in war.[1]

Princeton Seminary theologian Charles Hodge wrote in the 19th century about the horrors of war and the need for careful moral examination of the topic of war:

> It is conceded that war is one of the most dreadful evils that can be inflicted on a people; that it involves the destruction of property and life; that it demoralizes both the victors and the vanquished; that it visits thousands of non-combatants with all the miseries of poverty, widowhood, and orphanage; and that it tends to arrest the progress of society in everything that is good and desirable. . . . It is also conceded that the vast majority of the wars which have desolated the world have been unjustifiable in the sight of God and man. Nevertheless it does not follow from this that war in all cases is to be condemned.[2]

---

[1] This chapter has been adapted from Wayne Grudem, *Politics—According to the Bible: A Comprehensive Resource for Understanding Modern Political Issues in Light of Scripture* (Grand Rapids, MI: Zondervan, 2010), 388–94, 418–24, 433–35, with permission of the publisher.

[2] Charles Hodge, *Systematic Theology*, 3 vols. (1871–1873; repr., Grand Rapids, MI: Eerdmans, 1970), 3:365.

A. THE SIXTH COMMANDMENT DOES NOT PROHIBIT ALL PARTICIPATION IN WAR

As I explained in the previous chapter, the commandment "You shall not murder" (Ex. 20:13) uses a Hebrew verb (*rātsakh*) that refers to the unlawful taking of another human life (what we call "murder" in ordinary English today). The commandment also prohibits causing the death of another person through negligence or carelessness. But this verb *is never used to refer to killing in war*, so it is a misapplication of the sixth commandment to use it as an argument against all participation in war. The commandment is not speaking about killing in war, and the original Hebrew readers would have understood that it did not apply to soldiers who kill in combat (see chap. 18, p. 505).

In fact, at various times in the Old Testament, God himself commanded the people of Israel to go to war (see Deut. 20:1), and it would have been contradictory for him to command something and forbid it at the same time.

In the New Testament, soldiers are not condemned for serving in the Roman army, but John the Baptist tells them, "Be content with your wages" (Luke 3:14). Cornelius, a Roman centurion in charge of 100 soldiers, came to faith and was baptized as a believer in Jesus with no indication that there was anything morally wrong about his occupation (see Acts 10:1, 44–48; see also Luke 14:31).

However, that does not answer the question of whether it is a morally right for a Christian to participate in a war. That question will be the topic of much of the rest of this chapter.

B. GOVERNMENTS ARE RESPONSIBLE TO DEFEND THEIR NATIONS AGAINST ATTACKS BY OTHER NATIONS

As we saw in chapter 16 (see p. 427), one of the most basic responsibilities of government is to restrain evil and punish those who do evil. When a government does this, it defends the weak and defenseless, and deters further wrongdoing. The apostle Peter says the civil government is intended "*to punish those who do evil* and to praise those who do good" (1 Pet. 2:14). And Paul says that the government is authorized by God to "bear the sword" (Rom. 13:4) against evildoers so that it can be "a terror" to bad conduct (v. 3). It also "carries out God's wrath on the wrongdoer" (v. 4). According to Paul, when the ruler uses superior force—even deadly force—against evil, he is "God's servant for your good" (v. 4).

If a government is commanded by God to protect its citizens from a robber or thief who comes from *within* a country, then certainly it also has an obligation to protect its citizens against thousands of murderers or thieves who come as an army from somewhere *outside of* the nation. Therefore, a nation has a *moral obligation to defend itself* against foreign attackers who would come to kill, conquer, and subjugate the people in that nation.

John Calvin followed this line of reasoning when he wrote (in 1559) about the right of government to wage war:

> But kings and people must sometimes take up arms.... Indeed, if they rightly punish those robbers whose harmful acts have affected only a few, will they allow a whole country to be afflicted and devastated by robberies with impunity? For it makes no difference whether it be a king or the lowest of the common folk who invades a foreign country in which he has no right.... All such must, equally, be considered as robbers and punished accordingly. Therefore ... princes must be armed ... to defend by war the dominions entrusted to their safekeeping, if at any time they are under enemy attack.[3]

This reasoning was reflected in some early Protestant confessions of faith. For example, the Augsburg Confession (1530), widely followed by Lutherans, says:

> Christians may lawfully bear civil office ... engage in just war, act as soldiers. (Art. 16)

And the Westminster Confession of Faith (1646), followed by Presbyterian and other Reformed Christians, says:

> It is lawful for Christians to accept and execute the office of a magistrate, when called thereunto ... for that end, they may lawfully, now under the New Testament, *wage war, upon just and necessary occasion.* (23.2)

The moral obligation for a nation to defend itself is also seen in Old Testament narratives in which the nation of Israel repeatedly had to defend itself against attacks by peoples such as the Philistines, the Assyrians, and the Babylonians. When God blessed Israel, the Israelites defeated their enemies who were attacking them (see Judg. 2:16–18; 1 Samuel 17; 2 Sam. 5:17–25; and numerous other examples in the Old Testament narratives). But when the people disobeyed God and turned from him, he allowed other nations to defeat them as a manifestation of his judgment against them:

> They abandoned the LORD and served the Baals and the Ashtaroth. So the anger of the LORD was kindled against Israel, and he gave them over to plun-

---

[3] John Calvin, *Institutes of the Christian Religion*, ed. John T. McNeill, trans. Ford Lewis Battles, Library of Christian Classics, vols. 20–21 (Philadelphia: Westminster, 1960), 4.20.11 (1499). John Murray argues in a similar way: "By what kind of logic can it be maintained that the magistrate, who is invested with the power of the sword (Romans 13:4), may and must execute vengeance upon evildoers within his domain but must sheath the sword of resistance when evildoers from without invade his domain? . . . To plead pacifism or non-resistance under such conditions is to annul the New Testament teaching that the civil magistrate is sent by the Lord to punish and suppress evil doing and to maintain the order of justice, well-doing, and peace." *Principles of Conduct: Aspects of Biblical Ethics* (Grand Rapids, MI: Eerdmans, 1957), 115. (Murray himself lost an eye while serving in the British Army in World War I.)

derers, who plundered them. And he sold them into the hand of their surrounding enemies, so that they could no longer withstand their enemies. Whenever they marched out, the hand of the LORD was against them for harm, as the LORD had warned, and as the LORD had sworn to them. And they were in terrible distress. (Judg. 2:13–15)

This fulfilled God's promise through Moses in Deuteronomy 28. If the people obeyed God, he promised, "The LORD will cause your enemies who rise against you to be defeated before you. They shall come out against you one way and flee before you seven ways" (v. 7). But if they disobeyed, "The LORD will cause you to be defeated before your enemies. You shall go out one way against them and flee seven ways before them" (v. 25).

These promises were fulfilled multiple times in the history of Israel. They demonstrate that it is a good thing in God's sight—a special blessing—when a government has enough military power to defeat the enemies who would bring armies to attack it (that is, it is a good thing as long as a government has not become so corrupt and evil that God would be pleased to see it conquered).

C. HOW CAN WE KNOW IF A WAR IS A "JUST WAR"?

Of course, there are some wrong wars, such as those that are fought merely for conquest and plunder. How can we tell if a war is right or wrong?

During centuries of ethical discussions regarding the question of war, one very common viewpoint that developed, with much input from Christian scholars, is the "just war" tradition. That viewpoint argues that a war is morally right (or "just") when it meets certain criteria. It also argues that there are certain moral restrictions on the way that a war can be conducted.

It seems to me that this "just war" tradition, in general, is consistent with biblical teachings about the need for nations to defend themselves against their enemies. Here is a useful recent summary of the criteria for a just war, together with biblical references that are used to support these criteria. I think that these criteria, in general, are consistent with these biblical teachings:

> Over time, the just war ethic has developed a common set of criteria that can be used to decide if *going to war* in a specific situation is right. These include the following:
>
> 1. *Just cause* (Is the reason for going to war a morally right cause, such as defense of a nation? Cf. Rev. 19:11)
> 2. *Competent authority* (Has the war been declared not simply by a renegade band within a nation but by a recognized, competent authority within the nation? Cf. Rom. 13:1)

3. *Comparative justice* (Is it clear that the actions of the enemy are morally wrong, and the motives and actions of one's own nation in going to war are, in comparison, morally right? Cf. Rom. 13:3)

4. *Right intention* (Is the purpose of going to war to protect justice and righteousness rather than simply to rob and pillage and destroy another nation? Cf. Prov. 21:2)

5. *Last resort* (Have all other reasonable means of resolving the conflict been exhausted? Cf. Matt. 5:9; Rom. 12:18)

6. *Probability of success* (Is there a reasonable expectation that the war can be won? Cf. Luke 14:31)

7. *Proportionality of projected results* (Will the good results that come from a victory in a war be significantly greater than the harm and loss that will inevitably come with pursuing the war? Cf. Rom. 12:21; 13:4)

8. *Right spirit* (Is the war undertaken with great reluctance and sorrow at the harm that will come rather than simply with a "delight in war," as in Ps. 68:30?)

In addition to these criteria for deciding whether a specific war is "just," advocates of just war theory have also developed some *moral restrictions on how a just war should be fought*. These include the following:

1. *Proportionality in the use of force* (Can no greater destruction be caused than is needed to win the war? Cf. Deut. 20:10–12)

2. *Discrimination between combatants and noncombatants* (Insofar as it is feasible in the successful pursuit of a war, is adequate care being taken to prevent harm to noncombatants? Cf. Deut. 20:13–14, 19–20)

3. *Avoidance of evil means* (Will captured or defeated enemies be treated with justice and compassion, and are one's own soldiers being treated justly in captivity? Cf. Ps. 34:14)

4. *Good faith* (Is there a genuine desire for restoration of peace and eventually living in harmony with the attacking nation? Cf. Matt. 5:43–44; Rom. 12:18).[4]

In real life, some wars are clearly just wars, others are clearly unjust wars, and still others are more difficult to evaluate. When Adolf Hitler invaded and conquered one sovereign European nation after another, he was clearly carrying out an unjust war.

---

[4] "War," in *ESV Study Bible* (Wheaton, IL: Crossway, 2008), 2555, slightly edited. Sometimes the Latin phrase *jus ad bellum* ("justice toward war") is used to refer to the eight criteria for deciding whether going to war is just, and the phrase *jus in bello* ("justice in war") is used to refer to the four criteria for deciding whether conduct in fighting the war is just. On the question of the use of coercive means in the interrogation of prisoners, and why the term "torture" is used with such a wide variety of meanings that it often confuses the discussion, see Grudem, *Politics—According to the Bible*, 425–33.

When many European nations, including Great Britain, France, Belgium, the Netherlands, Yugoslavia, and other Allied nations such as Canada, South Africa, New Zealand, and Australia[5] fought to defend themselves against Hitler's aggression, they were clearly engaging in a just war to stop the Nazi armies. These wars of defense met all the criteria for a just war. But throughout history other wars have been more difficult to evaluate.

In some situations, several of the criteria for a just war may be clearly met, while decisions about other criteria may be unclear, and people may come to different conclusions. Often those conclusions depend on differing evaluations of the facts in the situation. There also may be times when a war very clearly meets most of the criteria, but not all of them, and yet the war seems necessary for the very survival of a nation. In such cases, a decision is more difficult, and Christians will need to pray for much wisdom from God regarding their individual decisions.

Can a preemptive war ever be justified? (A preemptive war is one in which nation A discovers overwhelming evidence that nation B is about to launch an attack against it, and so nation A attacks nation B first, not to conquer nation B but to prevent an attack.) When the actual facts of the situation clearly show that the preemptive strike is necessary to defend one's country, and the other criteria of a just war are met, then it seems to me that a preemptive war can be justified as fitting criterion 1, "Just cause."

D. SHOULD A CHRISTIAN PARTICIPATE IN A JUST WAR?

1. If a War Is Clearly Just. If a war is clearly a just war, then it is not a "morally wrong but necessary" task for a Christian to serve in a military capacity and fight in that war, nor is it merely something morally neutral. Rather, we should understand fighting in such a war as morally good, because the Christian who serves as a soldier falls into the category of the government official in Romans 13:4 who is "God's servant for your good." Therefore, as a Christian soldier fights to defeat an evil enemy force, it is right for him to view himself as "the servant of God, an avenger who carries out God's wrath on the wrongdoer" (v. 4).

When soldiers came to John the Baptist asking what they should do in response to his call to "bear fruits in keeping with repentance" (Luke 3:8), he did not tell them to quit the army or refuse to serve in combat for the Roman Empire, but he said simply this:

> Do not extort money from anyone by threats or by false accusation, and be content with your wages. (Luke 3:14)

Regarding this passage, Calvin writes:

---

[5] There were 26 nations overall that allied together to fight Hitler and the Nazis. See "Allied Powers," Britannica.com, https://www.britannica.com/topic/Allied-Powers-international-alliance#ref754272.

For if Christian doctrine (to use Augustine's words) condemned all wars, the soldiers asking counsel concerning salvation should rather have been advised to cast away their weapons and withdraw completely from military service. ... When he taught them to be content with their wages, he certainly did not forbid them to bear arms.[6]

Other passages from the Old Testament also understand God's people to be doing something morally good when they risk their lives by going forth to battle to defend their people against evil aggressors:

> He trains my hands for war,
>> so that my arms can bend a bow of bronze. (Ps. 18:34)

> Blessed be the LORD, my rock,
>> who trains my hands for war,
>> and my fingers for battle. (Ps. 144:1)

Before Israel's conquest of Canaan, the leading men of the tribes of Reuben and Gad came to Moses and asked that they be allowed to settle on the east side of the Jordan River rather than crossing over to the west side of the Jordan and entering the Promised Land. Moses allowed them to do this provided that they would first come with the army of Israel to defeat the Canaanites who were in the land. Moses even told them that it would be "sin" for them not to join in the battle to which God had called them:

> But Moses said to the people of Gad and to the people of Reuben, "Shall your brothers go to the war while you sit here? Why will you discourage the heart of the people of Israel from going over into the land that the LORD has given them? ... If you will do this, if you will take up arms to go before the LORD for the war, and every armed man of you will pass over the Jordan before the LORD, until he has driven out his enemies from before him ... then after that you shall return and be free of obligation to the LORD and to Israel, and this land shall be your possession before the LORD. *But if you will not do so, behold, you have sinned against the LORD, and be sure your sin will find you out.*" (Num. 32:6–7, 20–23)

However, if a Christian does fight in a war, it is important that he avoid using evil means to conduct the war (see above for a list of moral restrictions on how a war should be fought). And the attitude with which a Christian fights in war is important. As far as God enables him or her[7] to do so, the Christian should feel a deep sorrow over evil—and probably even godly anger against evil—as well as sorrow for the combatants on

---

[6] Calvin, *Institutes*, 4.20.12 (1500).

[7] I think it is morally right for Christian women also to participate in a war effort, but in noncombatant positions (see below, p. 543).

the other side, many of whom may have been forced to fight against their own will. A Christian should also participate in war with "goodness, faithfulness . . . self-control" (Gal. 5:22–23). I would even hope that Christians would fight with a heart of love for their enemies, even as David loved Absalom his son deeply while he sent out the army to fight against Absalom and defeat his wrongful insurrection (2 Samuel 18).[8]

One of the most eloquent and poignant expressions in all history of a Christian man resolutely leading a war he believed to be just, yet doing so with agonizing sadness and with trust in God's providence, is found in the Second Inaugural Address of Abraham Lincoln, delivered on March 4, 1865, after he had been leading the Union in the Civil War for four long years (and just six weeks before his assassination). I have reprinted this address as an appendix to this chapter (see page 545).

2. If a War Is Clearly Unjust. If a war is clearly unjust, then it is morally wrong for a Christian to participate in it. The principles discussed in chapter 16 about disobeying the civil government when it commands a believer to sin against God apply in this situation (see p. 437). This is a situation in which "we must obey God rather than men" (Acts 5:29).

If a Christian refuses to serve in a war, he (or she) may be forced to flee the country (see 1 Sam. 19:10–12; 2 Cor. 11:33) or face imprisonment or another penalty. But it is better to suffer for doing right than to give in and participate in doing wrong. "If when you do good and suffer for it you endure, this is a gracious thing in the sight of God" (1 Pet. 2:20).

In order to protect people from having to violate their consciences regarding war, I believe it is a good thing for countries to have laws allowing "conscientious objectors" to serve in nonmilitary capacities (such as medical care) rather than attempting to force them to participate in a war when they think it is morally wrong to do so.[9]

3. What If a War Is Not Clearly Just or Unjust? If a war is not clearly just or clearly unjust, the situation becomes more difficult, and it is important for Christians to seek God for wisdom to evaluate the situation rightly (see James 1:5–6). In open democratic societies, significant weight should be given to the decisions reached by elected representatives of the people after careful deliberation. Of course, Christians who hold to a just war position and Christians who hold to a pacifist position will likely also differ in their assessments of the relevant facts in any specific war, but when Christians who all hold to a just war position sincerely differ among themselves about how to evaluate a war, then the decision is particularly difficult.

---

[8] One of the most tragic verses in Scripture is 2 Sam. 18:33: "And the king was deeply moved and went up to the chamber over the gate and wept. And as he went, he said, 'O my son Absalom, my son, my son Absalom! Would I had died instead of you, O Absalom, my son, my son!'"

[9] However, I also recognize that conscientious-objector laws usually require the objector to have a moral conviction opposed to all wars, not just to a specific war. I'm not sure whether it is necessary for such a thought to be so restrictive. For a nation with an all-volunteer army, this difficulty is largely resolved.

E. PACIFISM

Although the just war view has been the most commonly held position throughout the history of the church, a minority view has been that of military pacifism.[10] The pacifist view holds that it is always wrong for *Christians* to use military force against others, and thus it is wrong for Christians to participate in military combat, even to defend their own nation. A related but somewhat different pacifist view holds that it is wrong for *anyone* to participate in military combat and that such "violence" is always morally wrong.

One influential recent advocate of pacifism is Jim Wallis, in his book *God's Politics*.[11] Similar arguments are also found in Shane Claiborne and Chris Haw's *Jesus for President*.[12] What follows here is a brief analysis of the key pacifist arguments as they apply to war.[13]

The arguments commonly used to support pacifism are that (1) Jesus commanded us to turn the other cheek (Matt. 5:39); (2) Jesus commanded us to love our neighbors as ourselves (Matt. 22:39); (3) engaging in military combat involves failure to trust God; (4) we should depend on international law rather than going to war; (5) the use of violence always leads to further violence, and pacifism should be adopted to stop that vicious cycle; and (6) more genuine Christian pacifism would have prevented previous wars.

1. Should We Just Turn the Other Cheek? In response to this pacifist argument, I would reply that the pacifist viewpoint wrongly applies Jesus's teaching about *individual conduct* in turning the other cheek (Matt. 5:39) to *civil government* (see discussion in chap. 18, p. 514), but the explicit teaching on civil government is that it should "bear the sword" to oppose evildoers and execute God's wrath on the wrongdoer (Rom. 13:4). In addi-

---

[10] Regarding pacifism in the early church, Hodge explains, "In the early ages of the Church there was a great disinclination to engage in military service, and the fathers at times justified this reluctance by calling the lawfulness of all wars into question. But the real sources of this opposition of Christians to entering the army, were that they thereby gave themselves up to the service of a power which persecuted their religion; and that idolatrous usages were inseparably connected with military duties. When the Roman Empire became Christian, and the cross was substituted for the eagle on the standards of the army, this opposition died away.... No historical Christian Church has pronounced all wars to be unlawful." *Systematic Theology*, 3.367.

[11] Jim Wallis, *God's Politics: Why the Right Gets It Wrong and the Left Doesn't Get It* (San New York: HarperCollins, 2005), especially 87–205.

[12] Shane Claiborne and Chris Haw, *Jesus for President: Politics for Ordinary Radicals* (Grand Rapids, MI: Zondervan, 2008), especially 199–224 and 338–47, but also at various other places in the book, most of which is structured as a loosely connected set of narratives rather than an organized, sequential, logical argument. Claiborne and Haw also list at least two widely used pacifist books in their recommended bibliography: Gregory A. Boyd, *The Myth of a Christian Nation: How the Quest for Political Power Is Destroying the Church* (Grand Rapids, MI: Zondervan, 2007), and John Howard Yoder, *The Politics of Jesus: Vicit Agnus Noster*, 2nd ed. (Grand Rapids, MI: Eerdmans, 1994).

[13] I have responded more extensively elsewhere to some additional arguments for pacifism, especially as they are related to the "all government is demonic" view advocated by Boyd; see my *Politics—According to the Bible*, 38–44.

tion, in Luke 22:36, Jesus actually commanded his followers to carry swords (which were used for self-defense and protection from robbers; see discussion in chap. 18, p. 515).

John Feinberg and Paul Feinberg express this distinction clearly:

> A fundamental problem with pacifist interpretations of Jesus's teachings is the failure to distinguish between private and public duties, personal duties, and duties of a state. As a private individual I may turn the other cheek when unjustly attacked. However, my responsibilities are quite different when I stand in the position of a guardian of a third party as a civil magistrate or parent. Because I am responsible for their lives and welfare, I must resist, even with force, unjust aggression against them. Moreover, loving my neighbor or enemy does not mean I must stand idly by as my child is kidnapped and murdered. I am to use whatever force is necessary to protect his or her life and safety. The state stands in this third-party relationship to its citizens. Texts that pacifists typically cite for nonresistance are verses that have to do with private or personal duties, not public duties.[14]

2. Does Love for Neighbor Require Pacifism? If we truly *love our neighbors* (as Jesus commanded in Matt. 22:39), then we will be willing even to go to war to protect them from evil aggressors who are attacking the nation. While the pacifist might ask, "How can you love your neighbor or even love your enemy and then kill him in war?" the answer has to be that *God commanded both* love for one's neighbor and going to war, for the command "You shall love your neighbor as yourself" is found in Leviticus 19:18 in the Old Testament, and Jesus quotes it from there. Therefore, it must be consistent for God to command *both* things, and one command should not be used to nullify the other.

One example of this is found in the tragic story of David sending out his army to defeat his rebellious son Absalom (2 Samuel 18). David had great love for Absalom, yet he was responsible to protect the office of king that God had entrusted to him. Therefore, with sorrow, and while still loving Absalom, David sent the army out against him.

3. Does Going to War Mean We Lack Faith? Christians have no right to tell others to "trust in God" for things that are different from what the Bible teaches, and Romans 13:1–4 teaches that God authorizes governments to use deadly force if necessary to oppose evil. Therefore, at this point the pacifist argument is telling people to disobey what Romans 13 says about government, and then to trust God to protect them anyway. This is like telling people they should not work to earn a living, but should "trust God" to provide their food anyway! A better approach is to obey what God says in Romans 13:1–4 about the use of government power to restrain evil, and then trust God to work

---

[14] John S. Feinberg and Paul D. Feinberg, *Ethics for a Brave New World*, 2nd ed. (Wheaton, IL: Crossway, 2010), 646.

through that government power to restrain evil, which is how he intends governments to function.

This is the problem I have with Jim Wallis when he criticizes the American reliance on military power to protect the nation from terrorists as "a foreign policy *based primarily on fear*."[15] He also attributes another wrong motive to Americans when he puts military responses to terrorist attacks in the category of "anger and vengeance," which lead a nation to "indiscriminately retaliate in ways that bring on even more loss of innocent life."[16]

By contrast, Romans 13 teaches that military action used to defend a nation is not a wrongful or sinful activity, *and neither is a desire to depend on military action (under God's guidance) a wrongful attitude*, because God has *authorized* nations to use such military power. Pacifists such as Wallis fail to realize that it is completely possible—as millions of Christians who have served in military forces have demonstrated—to *trust God* to enable them to use the military power he has put in their hands to successfully defend their countries. The solution is not pacifism, but *trusting God* to give success *while obeying him* by using the military defense that he has appointed.

John Jefferson Davis points out that the author of Hebrews holds up some of God's people who fought in wars as *examples* of faith:

> It is quite notable that a New Testament writer, the author of Hebrews, explicitly referred to the military exploits of the judges and David and saw their actions not as expressions of "hardness of heart," but rather as demonstrations of living *faith* in God. These men of God "through faith conquered kingdoms, enforced justice . . . became mighty in war, put foreign armies to flight" (Heb. 11:33–34). They are set before the New Testament church as *positive* examples of faith, and their faith in this case was exhibited in their military valor. God clearly approved their "putting foreign armies to flight" and their use of arms in the enforcement of justice. This Hebrews text clearly shows that from a New Testament perspective the use of armed force is not inconsistent with true faith in God, and that in the divine scale of values, the enforcement of justice has higher priority than nonviolence when these two values conflict.[17]

Davis goes on to hold up Jesus himself as an example of the need at times to use force to resist evil:

> In the cleansing of the temple (John 2:13–22), Christ himself drove out the moneychangers with a whip of cords. This incident alone shows the insuperable difficulties that surround an insistence on a literalistic understanding of

---

[15] Wallis, *God's Politics*, 88, emphasis added.

[16] Ibid., 92; see also 94.

[17] John Jefferson Davis, *Evangelical Ethics: Issues Facing the Church Today*, 4th ed. (Phillipsburg, NJ: P&R, 2015), 243.

the saying, "do not resist one who is evil." Christ did not remain passive in the face of evil; he acted forcibly to remove evil from his presence.

In the book of Revelation, John sees a heavenly vision of the risen Christ, who is mounted upon a horse, and who "in righteousness . . . judges and makes war" (19:11). John saw nothing morally offensive about portraying the activities of the risen Christ in martial terms.[18]

4. Is It Better to Depend on International Law and a World Court? Because of the teaching of Romans 13 that nations should protect their own citizens, I think pacifists such as Wallis are actually unbiblical when they say that nations should not act alone and use "unilateral action" to defend themselves, but should rather depend on a "world court to weigh facts and make judgments, with effective multi-national law enforcement."[19] Elsewhere, Wallis says we should depend on a much more powerful "international law" and "global police forces."[20] He says that only a world court with effective power "will be able to protect us."[21]

There are several objections to Wallis's argument:

First, it is mere wishful thinking. An effective worldwide government has never occurred in the entire history of the human race. (Even the Roman Empire at its largest extent did not reach to China, India, Sub-Saharan Africa, or North and South America.) It is foolishness to depend on something that has never existed to save us from a terrorist threat that we are facing at this very minute.

Second, if such a powerful world government ever did exist, it would likely be dominated by the votes of numerous small nations who are largely anti-American, because their governments are communist, totalitarian, or devoted to expanding the Muslim religion, and therefore opposed to the United States. It would be like the present makeup of the United Nations, with its frequent anti-American votes.

Third, depending on such a world government to keep peace in the world would require nations—including the United States—to give up their individual sovereignty. This would open the door to reducing the United States to a condition of servitude and domination by nations or leaders that seek its demise.

Far better than the pacifist position of trusting in a world court and a world police force is trusting in the Lord to use the means he has designated, which is the use of each nation's own military power, as I have argued above from Romans 13 and other passages.

5. Does Violence Always Lead to More Violence? It is simply untrue to say, as pacifists do, that violence always leads to more violence. The deadly force used by local police in restraining or killing a murderer brings that murderer's violence to an end. It is the same situation when armies are used to defend nations against aggressors. In fact, the

---

[18] Ibid., 244.
[19] Wallis, *God's Politics*, 106.
[20] Ibid., 164.
[21] Ibid., 106.

use of military power stopped Hitler from taking over all of Europe and ultimately all the world in World War II. It stopped the North Koreans from taking over South Korea in the Korean War. In the American Civil War, it stopped the Confederate armies from establishing a separate nation in which slavery would be preserved and protected.

The pacifist slogan "Violence always begets more violence" is misleading, because it uses the same word, *violence*, to refer to two very different things—the morally *good* use of deadly force to stop evildoers and the morally *wrong* use of force to carry out attacks on innocent people. A better slogan would be "Just governments should use superior force to stop criminal violence against innocent people" or simply "Superior force stops criminal violence."

6. Could More Pacifism Have Ended Slavery or Stopped Hitler? Near the end of the pacifist argument in Greg Boyd's book *The Myth of a Christian Nation*, he responds to the objection that war was necessary to end slavery in the United States (in the Civil War) and to stop Hitler's campaign to take over the world (in World War II). Didn't the use of military force bring about good in those cases?

Boyd argues that if Christians had been better pacifists, history would have been different: "Had professing Christians been remotely like Jesus in the first place, there would have been no slavery or war for us to wonder about what *would have happened* had Christians loved their enemies and turned the other cheek."[22] With regard to the U.S. Civil War, Boyd says, "A kingdom person should rather wonder what might have happened had more kingdom people been willing to live out the call of the radical kingdom."[23]

But this is just an elegant way of saying, "If history was different, it would prove my case." And that is another way of saying, "If the facts were different, they would prove my case." That is not a valid argument. It is appealing to wishful thinking rather than facts. Boyd is simply saying that if the world were different, the world would be different. But that proves nothing. History is what it is, and history shows that both the evil of American slavery and the evil of Hitler were stopped only by the power of superior military force. That is the task that God has assigned to governments that "bear the sword" (Rom. 13:4).

The logic of pacifism would lead ultimately to a total surrender to the most evil of governments, which would stop at nothing to use their power to oppress others. For all of these reasons, the pacifism of Wallis, Boyd, and others is not a persuasive position for Christians to adopt.

F. NUCLEAR WEAPONS

1. History of Nuclear Weapons. The only two nuclear weapons ever used in war were exploded by the United States over Hiroshima and Nagasaki, Japan—on August 6 and 9,

---

[22] Boyd, *The Myth of a Christian Nation*, 174.
[23] Ibid., 177.

1945, respectively. Both of these large cities had industrial and military significance for the Japanese war effort. Estimates are that from 90,000 to 150,000 people were killed in Hiroshima (out of 340,000) and about 80,000 people were killed in Nagasaki (out of 212,000).[24] (About half of those numbers were killed immediately, and half died afterward from burns, radiation, and other injuries.) In both cases, the bombs destroyed everything within a one-mile radius and caused fires as far as two miles from ground zero.

President Harry S. Truman's goal in authorizing the use of these bombs was to bring an end to World War II, and that was in fact the result. Six days after the second bomb was dropped, Japan announced its surrender to the Allied Powers.

While dropping these bombs caused the loss of approximately 200,000 Japanese lives, a commonly repeated estimate (from analysts who understand the U.S. and Japanese force strength at that time) is that if the war had gone on without the use of these bombs, the result would have been the loss of at least 500,000 American lives and possibly hundreds of thousands of Japanese lives.[25] In his 1955 autobiography, President Truman affirmed that the atomic bomb probably saved half a million U.S. lives, not to mention many Japanese lives. The Japanese had already shown in previous battles in the Pacific campaigns that they would not surrender.

Still, leftist critics claim that the number of 500,000 possible casualties was a "myth." In an article in the *New England Journal of History* in 2007, Michael Kort, professor of general studies at Boston University, answered those critics:

> Writing in *The Journal of Military History*, [military historian] D. M. Giangreco explained that in military hands these projections took three forms: Medical estimates, manpower estimates, and strategic estimates. He then demonstrated that there was substantial documentation for high-end casualty projections—which, to be sure, varied widely—from both military and civilian sources that reached upward of 500,000. Equally important, one estimate that reached Truman—from former president Herbert Hoover, who had high-level government contacts—led the president to convene an important meeting with the Joint Chiefs of Staff and top civilian advisers on June 18, 1945, to discuss the projected invasion of Japan. In short, as Giangreco stressed in a later article in the *Pacific Historical Review*, Truman both saw and was concerned about high-end casualty estimates prior to the scheduled invasion.[26]

What the precise number of casualties would have been is impossible to know, but it is clear that the use of the atomic bombs saved countless lives.

---

[24] C. Peter Chen, "Atomic Bombing of Hiroshima and Nagasaki," World War II Database, http://ww2db.com/battle_spec.php?battle_id=49.

[25] Jing Oh, "Hiroshima and Nagasaki: The Decision to Drop the Bomb," *The Michigan Journal of History* 1, no. 2 (2002): n.p., https://michiganjournalhistory.files.wordpress.com/2014/02/oh_jung.pdf.

[26] Michael Kort, "The Historiography of Hiroshima: The Rise and Fall of Revisionism," *New England Journal of History* 64, no. 1 (Fall 2007): 31–48, http://theamericanpresident.us/images/truman_bomb.pdf.

Since 1945, several other nations have acquired nuclear weapons, but no other nuclear weapon has since been used in war. What prevented their use, for example, during the period of the Cold War between the Soviet Union and the United States and its allies? What prevented the Soviets from launching nuclear attacks against the United States or Western Europe? It was primarily the fear of overwhelming retaliation by the United States, the United Kingdom, and France, which would have resulted in the horrifying destruction of the Soviet Union itself. In other words, it was *the possession of overwhelming numbers of nuclear weapons* by peace-loving nations that prevented their use by any aggressor nation. That system of deterrence has worked for nearly seven decades (since the Soviet Union developed nuclear weapons in 1949).

2. Which Nations Have Nuclear Weapons Today? According to the Federation of American Scientists, which tracks nuclear stockpiles, the United States has a total of 4,670 deployed and operational nuclear weapons as of 2016,[27] and current estimates are that Russia has 4,500.[28] According to the U.S. State Department, the United States has reduced its nuclear stockpile by 85 percent since 1967 (when it had 31,255 nuclear weapons) and 78 percent since the fall of the Berlin Wall in 1989 (when it had 22,217). From 1994 to 2014, the United States dismantled 9,952 nuclear warheads.[29] The reason for retaining such a large number is that in the event of a nuclear war, many weapons might be destroyed before they could be launched, others would fail, and others would not reach their targets. (The weapons depend on a three-part delivery system: bombers, missiles, and submarines.)

In addition to the United States and Russia (which now controls the nuclear arsenal of the former Soviet Union), the following nations also possess nuclear weapons: (3) the United Kingdom, (4) France, (5) China, (6) India, (7) Pakistan, and (8) North Korea. In addition, (9) Israel is widely thought to possess nuclear weapons but has never publicly confirmed this. Besides these nations, Iran is aggressively pursuing nuclear power and potentially nuclear weapons.[30] The terrorist group ISIS is also seeking nuclear weapons.[31] Moreover, when Israel destroyed Saddam Hussein's Osirak nuclear reactor on June 7, 1981, it temporarily destroyed Iraq's ability to develop nuclear weapons.[32]

---

[27] Hans M. Kristensen and Robert S. Norris, "United States nuclear forces, 2016," *Bulletin of the Atomic Scientists* 72, no. 2 (2016): 63–73, http://dx.doi.org/10.1080/00963402.2016.1145901.

[28] Hans M. Kristensen and Robert S. Norris, "Russia nuclear forces, 2016," *Bulletin of the Atomic Scientists* 72, no. 3 (2016): 125–34, http://www.tandfonline.com/doi/pdf/10.1080/00963402.2016.1170359.

[29] "Transparency in the U.S. Nuclear Weapons Stockpile," U.S. Department of State, April 29, 2014, https://2009-2017.state.gov/t/isn/npt/statements/241165.htm.

[30] Jason Matthews, "Make No Mistake, Iran Will Acquire Nuclear Weapons. Soon," Fox News, June 16, 2015, http://www.foxnews.com/opinion/2015/06/16/make-no-mistake-iran-will-acquire-nuclear-weapons-soon.html.

[31] Jenny Stanton, "ISIS claims it is 'infinitely' closer to buying a nuclear weapon from Pakistan and smuggling it into the US," *London Daily Mail*, May 22, 2015, http://www.dailymail.co.uk/news/article-3093244/ISIS-claims-infinitely-closer-buying-nuclear-weapon-Pakistan-smuggling-US.html.

[32] "1981: Israel Bombs Iraq Nuclear Reactor," BBC, June 7, 1981, http://news.bbc.co.uk/onthisday/hi/dates/stories/june/7/newsid_3014000/3014623.stm.

3. Can the World Successfully Abolish Nuclear Weapons? Many people today believe that the danger from nuclear weapons comes from the *mere presence* of so many of them in the world. For instance, Democratic Senator Diane Feinstein of California has said that nuclear weapons are "not a deterrent, but a grave and gathering threat to humanity."[33]

If people believe this, then it seems evident to them that reducing the number of nuclear weapons in the world would reduce the threat that any nation would ever launch a nuclear attack. Their goal, then, is complete nuclear disarmament around the world. Their hope is that the world will be able to get rid of all nuclear weapons once and for all.

Will worldwide nuclear disarmament ever be possible? The short answer is no.

The history of the world shows that once weapons are developed, they never disappear from the earth. Crossbows were declared illegal by the Second Lateran Council in 1139, but people kept using them anyway. After airplanes were invented, The Hague Convention banned aerial bombardment in 1899, but people continued to use planes to drop bombs.[34] The reason is that the earth will always have people whose hearts are evil and who will pursue the most destructive weapons they can obtain in order to carry out their evil purposes. "The heart is deceitful above all things, and desperately sick; who can understand it?" (Jer. 17:9).

Therefore, to hope that nuclear weapons can be abolished from the nations of the earth is merely wishful thinking, with no basis in reality. To say it is possible would be to say that it is possible to reverse the course of human history from the beginning of time with regard to the development of weapons. Such an expectation should not qualify as a rational defense policy for a nation.

Just after President Obama proclaimed to the United Nations his goal of a world without nuclear weapons, the editorial board of *The Wall Street Journal* rightly observed:

> In the bitter decades of the Cold War, we learned the hard way that the only countries that abide by disarmament treaties are those that want to be disarmed.[35]

4. How Can We Effectively Reduce the Risk of Using Nuclear Weapons? If it is not possible to rid the world of nuclear weapons, then the most important question is how we can guard against their use. There are two answers to this question: (1) deterrence by the credible threat of a superior nuclear force and (2) an antimissile defense system that will prevent nuclear weapons from reaching their targets.

---

[33] Dianne Feinstein, "Let's Commit to a Nuclear-Free World," *The Wall Street Journal*, Jan. 3, 2009, A9, https://www.wsj.com/articles/SB123094493785650643.

[34] "To Russia with Love: Degrading the U.S. Nuclear Arsenal," *The Wall Street Journal*, April 4, 2009, A10, https://www.wsj.com/articles/SB123879970564788365.

[35] "The Disarmament Illusion: Obama Pursues Arms Control Treaties; Iran Builds the Bomb," *The Wall Street Journal*, Sept. 26, 2009, A14, https://www.wsj.com/articles/SB10001424052970204488304574435001700218982.

Since it is the responsibility of governments to protect the people over whom God has placed them in authority (see discussion of Rom. 13:1–7 above, p. 429), it is necessary, in a world with nuclear weapons, for nations to be able to defend themselves in one or both of these ways, or else be able to depend on more powerful peaceful nations to defend them against such attacks. Since there is no stronger nation that protects the United States, and since many other nations depend on it for protection, the United States, in particular, has a weighty responsibility to maintain a clearly superior nuclear force that can defeat any potential attacker, and it must speak and act in such a way that the potential attacker is convinced the United States will overwhelmingly retaliate if a nuclear weapon is launched against it. To fail to do this would be to fail to protect the citizens of this nation effectively.

In addition, there are more than 30 other nations that depend on the United States for their protection from nuclear attack.[36] If the United States were to fail to maintain a sufficiently strong nuclear response capability, it would also be failing these allies that depend on our protection—and that might prompt them to decide they have to develop their own nuclear arsenals.

Also, because of the persistent threat of the use of nuclear weapons by an aggressor nation (whether Russia, North Korea, Iran, or perhaps even China), the United States has a clear responsibility to continue to develop and deploy an effective antimissile defense system that would shoot down an attacking missile before it could reach its target.

In fact, the antimissile defense system that the United States has now partially deployed in Alaska and California is a wonderful alternative to the horrible possibility of having to launch a nuclear attack in response to an attack against us. Instead of two nations blowing up each other's cities, antimissile defense systems will shoot down incoming missiles from an attacker before they reach their target, so that no nuclear weapons are exploded in the first place. (The nuclear payloads on the incoming missiles would ordinarily not detonate in such cases.) All Christians who love peace and believe in the protection of human life should rejoice greatly that military technology has advanced to the place where such systems are actually quite effective, as they have shown in many tests.

On January 26, 2002, it was reported that a ground-based interceptor missile fired from a Navy ship hit a dummy armed missile in space after it was fired over the Pacific.[37] In another test, conducted on September 1, 2006, a missile fired from a silo at Vandenberg Air Force Base in California shot down a missile launched from Kodiak Island in Alaska.[38] In a test of an airborne antimissile system on February 11, 2010:

---

[36]"Atomic Bombshells," *The Wall Street Journal*, Jan. 24–25, 2009, A10; Jack David, "No Reason," *The Wall Street Journal*, Feb. 21–22, 2009, A9.

[37]"Missile Shield Test Dubbed A Hit," Associated Press, Jan. 26, 2002, www.cbsnews.com/stories/2002/01/26/national/main325718.shtml.

[38]Amy Clark, "Interceptor Missile Passes Key Test," Associated Press, Sept. 1, 2006, https://www.cbsnews.com/news/interceptor-missile-passes-key-test/.

A flying Boeing 747 jumbo jet equipped with a massive laser gun shot down a Scud-like missile over the Pacific . . . , marking what analysts said was a major milestone in the development of the nation's missile-defense system. . . . The laser shot a heated, basketball-size beam that traveled 670 million mph to incinerate a missile moving 4,000 mph, the Pentagon said.[39]

Unfortunately, the testing of the airborne antimissile system was shut down in 2012 because of budget cuts.[40]

When President Reagan first proposed such antimissile defense systems, he was ridiculed by the political left and the media in the United States, which called it a "Star Wars" system and predicted that it would never work. But now such a system actually has been shown to work in tests time and again. Christians should eagerly and enthusiastically support such a defensive system.

These two means of defense against nuclear attacks (maintaining strong nuclear weapon capabilities and building a strong antimissile defense system) have another advantage as well: U.S. superiority to other nations in both areas discourages any potential enemies from trying to match our power or engage in an arms race with us.

By contrast, if the United States proceeds in a unilateral way to disarm itself further and further, it will simply encourage hostile nations into an immediate rush to begin to develop more nuclear weapons and delivery systems that they think might possibly lead to victory over the United States if they were able to attack. Thus, American *disarmament* would lead to an *arms race* on the part of other nations.

G. WOMEN IN COMBAT

Historically the position of the United States has been that women should never be sent into combat. Women could serve in other capacities in the armed forces, but not in roles where they were likely to engage in combat. However, that policy has undergone significant change in the past 40 years.

The first woman who joined the Navy specifically to be a pilot did so in 1981.[41] The first female fighter pilots were employed in Kosovo in 1993. In December 2015, U.S. Secretary of Defense Ashton Carter announced that all combat positions will be open to women, opening up more than 220,000 positions. Carter said at a news conference: "There will be no exceptions. They'll be allowed to drive tanks, fire mortars and lead

---

[39] W. J. Hennigan, "Airborne Laser Shoots Down Missile in Test, Pentagon Says" *Los Angeles Times,* Feb. 13, 2010, http://articles.latimes.com/2010/feb/13/business/la-fi-laser13-2010feb13.

[40] "US mothballs airborne laser missile defense weapon," Associated Press, Feb. 29, 2012, https://www.yahoo.com/news/us-mothballs-airborne-laser-missile-130251897.html. For a discussion of recent decisions by the U.S. government to cancel the deployment of additional antimissile defenses, see my *Politics—According to the Bible*, 423–24.

[41] "Women Fighter Pilots Flying Combat Missions over Afghanistan with Little or No Fanfare," Associated Press, Oct. 23, 2001, www.military.com/Content/MoreContent?file=FL_womenpilots_102301.

infantry soldiers into combat. They'll be able to serve as Army Rangers and Green Berets, Navy SEALs, Marine Corps infantry, Air Force parajumpers and everything else that was previously open only to men."[42]

I believe that the historical position of the United States was correct and that it is wrong to send women into combat. The biblical argument for this position is expressed well in the *ESV Study Bible* article "War":

> Most nations throughout history, and most Christians in every age, have held that fighting in combat is a responsibility that should fall only to men, and that it is contrary to the very idea of womanhood, and shameful for a nation, to have women risk their lives as combatants in a war. The assumption that only men and not women will fight in battle is also a frequent pattern in the historical narratives and is affirmed by leaders and prophets in the OT.[43]

Several passages include narrative examples showing that only men were to fight in battle:

> Take a census of all the congregation of the people of Israel . . . every male . . . all in Israel who are able to go to war. (Num. 1:2–3)

> All your *men of valor* shall cross over armed before your brothers, the people of Israel. Only *your wives*, your little ones, and your livestock . . . shall remain in the cities that I have given you. (Deut. 3:18–19)

> And is there *any man* who has betrothed a wife and has not taken her? Let him go back to his house, lest he die in the battle and another man take her. (Deut. 20:7)

> When a man is newly married, he shall not go out with the army or be liable for any other public duty. He shall be free at home one year to be happy with his wife whom he has taken. (Deut. 24:5)

> *Your wives*, your little ones, and your livestock shall remain in the land that Moses gave you beyond the Jordan, but *all the men of valor* among you shall pass over armed before your brothers and shall help them. (Josh. 1:14)

> I stationed the people by their clans, with their swords, their spears, and their bows. And I . . . said . . . "Do not be afraid of them. Remember the LORD, who is great and awesome, and *fight for your brothers, your sons, your daughters,*

---

[42] Matthew Rosenberg and Dave Philipps, "All Combat Roles Now Open to Women, Defense Secretary Says," *The New York Times*, Dec. 3, 2015, http://www.nytimes.com/2015/12/04/us/politics/combat-military-women-ash-carter.html.

[43] "War," 2555. The Scripture passages given in support are Num. 1:2–3; Deut. 3:18–19; 20:7–8; 24:5; Josh. 1:14; 23:10; Judg. 4:8–10; 9:54; 1 Sam. 4:9; Neh. 4:13–14; Jer. 50:37; Nah. 3:13.

your wives, and your homes." (Neh. 4:13–14; Nehemiah does not tell the people to fight for their husbands, for no wives were fighting.)

Other passages indicate that it was thought to be shameful to be killed by a woman in battle, and shameful for a nation to have women fighting in its armed forces:

> Then he called quickly to the young man his armor-bearer and said to him, "Draw your sword and kill me, lest they say of me, 'A woman killed him.'" And his young man thrust him through, and he died. (Judg. 9:54)

> A sword against her horses and against her chariots,
> and against all the foreign troops in her midst,
> *that they may become women!*
> A sword against all her treasures,
> that they may be plundered! (Jer. 50:37; cf. v. 30)

> Behold, *your troops*
> *are women* in your midst.
> The gates of your land
> are wide open to your enemies;
> fire has devoured your bars. (Nah. 3:13)

Some may object that these examples are from ancient history, when women were not physically as able to fight as men were. But that is not a persuasive objection because the Israelites, both men and women, were hard-working people who spent much of their lives outdoors. While women may not have been physically able to fight quite as effectively as men, they certainly could have contributed something to a battle effort, if it had been appropriate for them to do so. But God's Word continually shows that it was considered shameful for men to depend upon women to protect the nation in war. That is a task that was consistently entrusted to men.

H. APPENDIX: ABRAHAM LINCOLN'S SECOND INAUGURAL ADDRESS

Delivered at Washington, D.C., March 4, 1865

Fellow-countrymen: At this second appearing to take the oath of the presidential office, there is less occasion for an extended address than there was at the first. Then a statement, somewhat in detail, of a course to be pursued, seemed fitting and proper. Now, at the expiration of four years, during which public declarations have been constantly called forth on every point and phase of the great contest which still absorbs the attention and engrosses the energies of the nation, little that is new could be presented. The progress of our arms, upon which all else chiefly depends, is as well known to the public as to myself; and it is, I trust, reasonably satisfactory and encouraging to all. With high hope for the future, no prediction in regard to it is ventured.

On the occasion corresponding to this four years ago, all thoughts were anxiously directed to an impending civil war. All dreaded it—all sought to avert it. While the inaugural address was being delivered from this place, devoted altogether to saving the Union without war, insurgent agents were in the city seeking to destroy it without war— seeking to dissolve the Union, and divide effects, by negotiation. Both parties deprecated war; but one of them would make war rather than let the nation survive; and the other would accept war rather than let it perish. And the war came.

One-eighth of the whole population were colored slaves, not distributed generally over the Union, but localized in the Southern part of it. These slaves constituted a peculiar and powerful interest. All knew that this interest was, somehow, the cause of the war. To strengthen, perpetuate, and extend this interest was the object for which the insurgents would rend the Union, even by war; while the government claimed no right to do more than to restrict the territorial enlargement of it.

Neither party expected for the war the magnitude or the duration which it has already attained. Neither anticipated that the cause of the conflict might cease with, or even before, the conflict itself should cease. Each looked for an easier triumph, and a result less fundamental and astounding. Both read the same Bible, and pray to the same God; and each invokes his aid against the other. It may seem strange that any men should dare to ask a just God's assistance in wringing their bread from the sweat of other men's faces; but let us judge not, that we be not judged. The prayers of both could not be answered—that of neither has been answered fully.

The Almighty has his own purposes. "Woe unto the world because of offenses! for it must needs be that offenses come; but woe to that man by whom the offense cometh." If we shall suppose that American slavery is one of those offenses which, in the providence of God, must needs come, but which, having continued through his appointed time, he now wills to remove, and that he gives to both North and South this terrible war, as the woe due to those by whom the offense came, shall we discern therein any departure from those divine attributes which the believers in a living God always ascribe to him? Fondly do we hope—fervently do we pray—that this mighty scourge of war may speedily pass away. Yet, if God wills that it continue until all the wealth piled by the bondman's two hundred and fifty years of unrequited toil shall be sunk, and until every drop of blood drawn with the lash shall be paid by another drawn with the sword, as was said three thousand years ago, so still it must be said, "The judgments of the Lord are true and righteous altogether."

With malice toward none; with charity for all; with firmness in the right, as God gives us to see the right, let us strive on to finish the work we are in; to bind up the nation's wounds; to care for him who shall have borne the battle, and for his widow, and his orphan—to do all which may achieve and cherish a just and lasting peace among ourselves, and with all nations.

QUESTIONS FOR PERSONAL APPLICATION

1. Would you be willing to fight in a war to defend your nation against attack, even if it required killing soldiers who were attacking your country? Do you think that God would approve of what you were doing?
2. What character traits (see p. 110) would you especially seek to develop while serving as a soldier?
3. In the history of your nation, have there been some wars that you think were unjust wars, in which your nation did not have sufficient moral justification for going to war? What do you think you would do if your nation required you to serve in the armed forces during such a war?
4. What wars in the history of your nation do you think were just wars?
5. Do you think your nation currently has an adequate military force for national defense? How do you feel about that fact?
6. Do you think the United States (or your own country) should maintain nuclear weapons? In what situations (if any) do you think it would be morally right to use them?
7. If you are a woman, would you like to have the opportunity to serve in military combat situations, or do you think that is not a proper role for a woman? If you are a man, how would you feel about having women serve alongside you in combat situations?
8. How does the maintenance of a strong military force in a country give evidence of advancing the kingdom of God, if at all?

SPECIAL TERMS

just war
pacifism
preemptive war
unjust war

BIBLIOGRAPHY

Sections in Other Ethics Texts

(see complete bibliographical data, p. 64)

Clark and Rakestraw, 2:489–524
Davis, 234–57
Feinberg, John and Paul, 635–95
Frame, 704–6
Geisler, 220–43

Gushee and Stassen, 308–38

Hays, 317–46

Kaiser, 185–98

McQuilkin and Copan, 407–28

Rae, 302–28

Other Works

Attwood, D. J. E. "War." In *New Dictionary of Christian Ethics and Pastoral Theology*, edited by David J. Atkinson and David H. Field, 885–88. Leicester, UK: Inter-Varsity, and Downers Grove, IL: InterVarsity Press, 1995.

Boyd, Gregory A. *The Myth of a Christian Nation: How the Quest for Political Power Is Destroying the Church*. Grand Rapids, MI: Zondervan, 2005. Pacifist view.

Charles, J. Daryl. *Between Pacifism and Jihad: Just War and Christian Tradition*. Downers Grove, IL: InterVarsity Press, 2005.

Charles, J. Daryl, and Timothy J. Demy. *War, Peace, and Christianity: Questions and Answers from a Just-War Perspective*. Wheaton, IL: Crossway, 2010.

Claiborne, Shane, and Chris Haw. *Jesus for President: Politics for Ordinary Radicals*. Grand Rapids, MI: Zondervan, 2008. Pacifist view.

Clouse, Robert G., ed. *War: Four Christian Views*. Downers Grove, IL: InterVarsity Press, 1991

Cowles, C. S., ed. *Show Them No Mercy: 4 Views on God and Canaanite Genocide*. Grand Rapids, MI: Zondervan, 2003.

Gabriel, Brigitte. *Because They Hate: A Survivor of Islamic Terror Warns America*. New York: St. Martin's Griffin, 2008.

Harlow, J. Porter. *How Should We Treat Detainees? An Examination of "Enhanced Interrogation Techniques" under the Light of Scripture and the Just War Tradition*. Phillipsburg, NJ: P&R, 2016.

Holmes, Arthur F. "Just-War Theory." In *New Dictionary of Christian Ethics and Pastoral Theology*, 521–23.

———. *War and Christian Ethics: Classic and Contemporary Readings on the Morality of War*. 2nd ed. Grand Rapids, MI: Baker, 2005. Just war view.

Longman, Tremper, and Daniel G. Reid. *God Is a Warrior*. Grand Rapids, MI: Zondervan, 2010.

Wallis, Jim. *God's Politics: Why the Right Gets It Wrong and the Left Doesn't Get It*. New York: HarperCollins, 2005. Pacifist view.

Weigel, George. *Faith, Reason, and the War against Jihadism: A Call to Action*. New York: Doubleday, 2007.

Wright, Lawrence. *The Looming Tower: Al-Qaeda and the Road to 911*. New York: Vintage, 2007. Extensively researched history of the development of Islamic terrorism.

Yoder, John Howard. *The Politics of Jesus: Vicit Agnus Noster*. Grand Rapids, MI: Eerdmans, 1972. Pacifist view.

SCRIPTURE MEMORY PASSAGE

Revelation 19:11: Then I saw heaven opened, and behold, a white horse! The one sitting on it is called Faithful and True, and in righteousness he judges and makes war.

HYMN

"Eternal Father, Strong to Save"

Eternal Father, strong to save,
Whose arm doth bind the restless wave,
Who bidd'st the mighty ocean deep
Its own appointed limits keep:
O hear us when we cry to thee
For those in peril on the sea.

O Saviour, whose almighty word
The winds and waves submissive heard,
Who walkedst on the foaming deep
And calm amid its rage didst sleep:
O hear us when we cry to thee
For those in peril on the sea.

O Sacred Spirit, who didst brood
Upon the chaos dark and rude,
Who badd'st its angry tumult cease,
And gavest light and life and peace:
O hear us when we cry to thee
For those in peril on the sea.

O Trinity of love and pow'r,
Our brethren shield in danger's hour;
From rock and tempest, fire, and foe,
Protect them wheresoe'er they go;
And ever let there rise to thee
Glad hymns of praise from land and sea.

AUTHOR: WILLIAM WHITING, 1860

ALTERNATIVE HYMN

"Battle Hymn of the Republic"

Mine eyes have seen the glory of the coming of the Lord,
He is trampling out the vintage where the grapes of wrath are stored;
He hath loosed the fateful lightning of His terrible swift sword;
His truth is marching on.

Refrain:
Glory! Glory, hallelujah!
Glory! Glory, hallelujah!
Glory! Glory, hallelujah!
His truth is marching on.

I have seen Him in the watchfires of a hundred circling camps,
They have builded Him an altar in the evening dews and damps;
I can read His righteous sentence by the dim and flaring lamps;
His day is marching on.

He has sounded forth the trumpet that shall never sound retreat,
He is sifting out the hearts of men before His judgment seat;
O be swift, my soul, to answer Him! Be jubilant, my feet!
Our God is marching on.

In the beauty of the lilies Christ was born across the sea,
With a glory in His bosom that transfigures you and me;
As He died to make men holy, let us die to make men free,
While God is marching on.

AUTHOR: JULIA WARD HOWE, 1819–1910

Chapter 20

SELF-DEFENSE

Is it ever right for Christians to use physical force to defend themselves against physical attack?
Is it right to use a weapon if available?
Is it right for a Christian to own a gun?

Another topic related to the protection of life is self-defense. While the question of war has to do with the protection of life on a national scale, the possibility of physical attack also occurs on an individual, personal scale. This raises numerous questions related to self-defense. Is it ever right to defend ourselves from physical attacks or to attempt to use physical force to prevent or stop attacks on others? And if it is right to defend ourselves, is it also right to use some kind of weapon in self-defense?

A. BIBLICAL TEACHING

1. Jesus Did Not Prohibit Self-Defense. Sometimes people think that Jesus prohibited all self-defense when he told his disciples that they should turn the other cheek:

> You have heard that it was said, "An eye for an eye and a tooth for a tooth." But I say to you, do not resist the one who is evil. But *if anyone slaps you on the right cheek, turn to him the other also.* (Matt. 5:38–39)

But Jesus is not prohibiting self-defense here. He is prohibiting individuals from taking personal vengeance simply to "get even" with another person. The Greek verb translated as "slaps" is *rhapizō*, which refers to a sharp slap given in insult (a right-handed person would use the back of the hand to slap someone "on the right cheek").[1]

---

[1] In rabbinic literature there is a parallel to this expression: "If a man cuffed his fellow he must pay him a *sela....* If he slapped him he must pay him 200 *zuz*. If [he struck him] with the back of his hand he must pay

So the point is not to hit back when someone hits you as an insult. The idea of a violent attack to physically harm or even murder someone is not in view here.[2]

In the context of Matthew 5:38–39, several of Jesus's other statements give *examples* of how Christlike conduct will look, but they are *not absolute commands* to be obeyed in every situation. For example, Jesus's statement "Give to the one who begs from you, and do not refuse the one who would borrow from you" (Matt. 5:42, just three verses after the passage on turning the other cheek) cannot be obeyed in *every* situation, or a persistent beggar could bankrupt any Christian or any church just by asking.

John Piper comments on passages such as this in the Sermon on the Mount:

> The commands . . . are *not absolute prescriptions* with no exceptions but rather are pointed, *concrete illustrations* of how enemy love may and should often look in the life of a disciple. That these illustrations are *not always the way enemy love acts* is clear from Jesus's own behavior [Piper cites Jesus's cleansing of the temple] . . . and from the nature of love itself as that which aims at the best life for the beloved.[3]

2. Other Passages of Scripture Encourage Escaping from Danger. Elsewhere Scripture shows that it is right for Christians to try to avoid being harmed by a violent attacker. For example, when King Saul threw a spear at David, David dodged the spear and escaped:

> And Saul sought to pin David to the wall with the spear, *but he eluded Saul*, so that he struck the spear into the wall. And *David fled and escaped that night*. (1 Sam. 19:10)

David did not simply "turn the other cheek"—that is, he did not hand the spear back to Saul and say, "Try again!"

After this incident, the next several chapters of 1 Samuel show how Saul continually sought to kill David, but David repeatedly eluded Saul's grasp (see 1 Samuel 19–26). (Similarly, the Hebrew spies who came to Jericho were hidden by Rahab and then later escaped secretly out of the city; see Joshua 2.)

Likewise, when King Aretas attempted to capture him in Damascus, Paul escaped:

---

him 400 *zuz*." Mishnah, *Baba Kamma* 8.6; cited from *The Mishnah*, trans. Herbert Danby (Oxford: Oxford University Press, 1933), 343.

[2] John Murray writes, "When Jesus says, 'Resist not him that is evil,' we are not to suppose that he is inculcating passive non-resistance under all circumstances of attack upon our persons or property, and that when injured or insulted we are to invite more. . . . The form of statement is dictated by the necessity of showing the complete contrast in personal relations between the attitudes and reactions of the disciple of Christ and the attitudes and reactions of the person controlled by vengeful passion." *Principles of Conduct: Aspects of Biblical Ethics* (Grand Rapids, MI: Eerdmans, 1957), 175.

[3] John Piper, *Love Your Enemies: Jesus's Love Command in the Synoptic Gospels and the Early Christian Paraenesis*, Society for New Testament Studies Monograph Series, vol. 38 (Cambridge, UK: Cambridge University Press, 1979), 99.

At Damascus, the governor under King Aretas was guarding the city of Damascus in order to seize me, but I was let down in a basket through a window in the wall *and escaped his hands.* (2 Cor. 11:32–33)

Jesus also escaped from an angry crowd at Nazareth that was trying to throw him off a cliff:

And they rose up and drove him out of the town and brought him to the brow of the hill on which their town was built, so that they could throw him down the cliff. *But passing through their midst, he went away.* (Luke 4:29–30)

On another occasion Jesus hid himself in the temple and then escaped from hostile Jews who were seeking to harm him (see John 8:59; 10:39).

3. Some Passages Encourage the Use of Force in Self-Defense.

a. Self-Defense against an Animal: It is clearly right to use physical force or to use a weapon to defend oneself against an attack by a wild animal, such as a bear or a lion. David himself did this when he was tending sheep, and his statement that it was "the Lord" who delivered him from the lion and the bear indicates that these acts of self-defense were approved by God:

But David said to Saul, "Your servant used to keep sheep for his father. And when there came a lion, or a bear, and took a lamb from the flock, *I went after him and struck him* and delivered it out of his mouth. *And if he arose against me, I caught him by his beard and struck him and killed him.* Your servant has *struck down both lions and bears,* and this uncircumcised Philistine shall be like one of them, for he has defied the armies of the living God." And David said, "*The Lord who delivered me from the paw of the lion and from the paw of the bear* will deliver me from the hand of this Philistine." And Saul said to David, "Go, and the Lord be with you!" (1 Sam. 17:34–37)

It is significant that the apostle Peter writes that some unbelievers actually behave "like irrational animals, creatures of instinct" (2 Pet. 2:12). If it is morally right to defend oneself against an attacking lion, then would it also be morally right to fight to defend oneself against a violently drunk husband, or father, or neighbor? Or against an irrational, drug-crazed assailant in a parking lot at night?

b. Self-Defense in a Court of Law: The moral rightness of defending oneself in legal matters is clearly supported by several biblical examples dealing with a court of law. These do not involve the use of physical force, but they do lend support to the idea that some kinds of self-defense are morally good.

When Peter and John were accused of wrongdoing by the Jewish Sanhedrin, they spoke boldly in their own defense (see Acts 4:5–22). All the apostles who were arrested similarly defended themselves before the Sanhedrin (see Acts 5:27–42). Stephen did the same before his martyrdom (Acts 7).

The apostle Paul defended himself numerous times. He spoke in his own defense to the city authorities in Philippi (Acts 16:37), to the Roman tribune in Jerusalem (21:27–39), to a hostile Jewish mob in Jerusalem (22:1–21), to a Roman centurion in Jerusalem (22:25), before the Jewish Sanhedrin (23:1–10), again to the Roman tribune in Jerusalem (23:17–22), before the Roman governor Felix (24:10–21), before the Roman governor Festus (25:8–12), and before King Agrippa (26:1–29).

In addition, Paul defended himself and his ministry against numerous accusations in several of his epistles (see especially 2 Corinthians). Jesus also defended himself against verbal accusations frequently during his ministry (see discussion in chap. 12, p. 334).

c. Old Testament Passages on Self-Defense against Physical Attack: Although the laws of the Mosaic covenant prohibited murder (see Ex. 20:13), they did not prohibit striking and even killing a person who broke into one's house in the middle of the night, in darkness. Presumably in the dark of night, the homeowner would not know if his very life and the lives of his family members were in danger. But if the homeowner defended his home during the daytime, he was not allowed to go so far as to kill the intruder:

> If a thief is found breaking in and is struck so that he dies, there shall be no bloodguilt for him, but if the sun has risen on him, there shall be bloodguilt for him. (Ex. 22:2–3)

During daylight hours, there would more likely be witnesses, so the thief could be caught and punished.[4]

This law is found in the Mosaic covenant, and therefore it does not directly require our obedience under the new covenant (see chap. 8). But we can still gain wisdom from it (see 2 Tim. 3:17). The substance of this law does not concern matters unique to Israel, such as regulations for worship or details about Jewish rituals, sacrifices, and purity laws. Rather, the subject matter concerns the human situation generally. Therefore, we may conclude that it teaches us that God recognized then, and apparently would still recognize today, that there is a legitimate kind of self-defense with the use of force.

When Nehemiah was leading the people to rebuild the wall around Jerusalem, he made sure that every man working on the wall also had a sword to defend against enemies:

---

[4] Alan Cole explains: "To kill a thief digging through the mud-brick wall . . . is justifiable homicide, if done after dark. He may be an armed murderer, for all the householder knows. His death may even have been accidental, in the blundering fight in the darkness. But in the daylight, the householder has no excuse for killing: besides, he can identify the man." *Exodus: An Introduction and Commentary*, TOTC (London: Tyndale Press, 1973), 171.

Those who carried burdens were loaded in such a way that each labored on the work with one hand *and held his weapon with the other*. And each of the builders had his *sword strapped at his side* while he built. (Neh. 4:17–18)[5]

The book of Esther culminates in the story of God's miraculous intervention through Esther so that, by decree of King Ahasuerus, the Jewish people were allowed to fight to defend themselves:

Then he [Mordecai] sent the letters by mounted couriers riding on swift horses . . . saying that *the king allowed the Jews who were in every city to gather and defend their lives*, to destroy, to kill, and to annihilate any armed force of any people or province that might attack them, children and women included, and to plunder their goods. (Est. 8:10–11)

In this dramatic event in Jewish history, God delivered his people by allowing them to use physical force to fight back and defend themselves.

A passage in the book of Proverbs also has relevance here:

Like a muddied spring or a polluted fountain
   is a righteous man who gives way before the wicked. (Prov. 25:26)

Should a Christian just continually "give way" before a violent attack by a wicked person, not defending himself? This would be to act like a "polluted fountain"—the testimony of the Christian's life would be tarnished and diminished by acting in a cowardly way.

d. Old Testament Passages on Defending Others against Attack: Some passages in the Old Testament assumed that a righteous, godly citizen in Israel should fight back against a wicked person who attacked someone weaker, such as a young woman or child. Here is the law concerning a rape that occurred in the open country:

But if in the open country a man meets a young woman who is betrothed, and the man seizes her and lies with her, then only the man who lay with her shall die. But you shall do nothing to the young woman; she has committed no offense punishable by death . . . because he met her in the open country, and *though the betrothed young woman cried for help there was no one to rescue her*. (Deut. 22:25–27)

This passage assumes that anyone who heard the woman's screams should have rushed to her aid and fought off the attacker.

---

[5] Someone might object that these were soldiers who needed weapons because they were part of the army defending the nation of Israel. I agree, but the principle of God's people having weapons for defending themselves is still seen in this passage. There are many other passages in the Old Testament narratives in which God gives approval to the people of Israel defending themselves against attacks from other nations.

Although the following passage is specifically addressed to human rulers, the broader principle is still clear: It is right to defend the weak and fatherless, those who have no one else to defend them:

> Give justice to *the weak and the fatherless*;
>> maintain the right of the afflicted and the destitute.
> Rescue the weak and the needy;
>> *deliver them from the hand of the wicked.* (Ps. 82:3–4)

This passage and many others that talk about the "fatherless" in the Old Testament also indicate that ordinarily, among the people of Israel, the father in each family was responsible for defending his wife and children against any who would attempt to harm them. The "fatherless" needed special protection because they had no fathers to fulfill this protecting role.

e. Jesus's Teaching about Having a Sword: Near the end of his life, Jesus seemed to encourage his disciples to keep swords for self-defense:

> He said to them, "But now let the one who has a moneybag take it, and likewise a knapsack. And *let the one who has no sword sell his cloak and buy one.* For I tell you that this Scripture must be fulfilled in me: 'And he was numbered with the transgressors.' For what is written about me has its fulfillment." And they said, "*Look, Lord, here are two swords.*" And he said to them, "It is enough." (Luke 22:36–38)

People commonly carried swords at that time for protection against robbers, and apparently at least two of Jesus's disciples, who had been with him for three years, were carrying swords, and Jesus had not forbidden this. Although many interpreters understand Jesus to have been speaking about swords in a metaphorical way (meaning the disciples should be armed spiritually to fight spiritual enemies), this is not a persuasive interpretation, because in this context the *moneybag* and *knapsack* (see vv. 35–36) are both literal, and the *swords* that they showed him were literal swords. If Jesus meant a literal moneybag and a literal knapsack, then he must also have meant a literal sword. The fact that Jesus was going to be crucified meant an increasing danger of people attacking the disciples as well. When Jesus said, "It is enough," it was immediately in response to the disciples showing him "two swords," so "enough" is best understood to mean "enough swords."

In attempting to argue that this verse does *not* justify carrying a sword, some interpreters have said that Jesus meant, "It is enough of this talk about swords." But that makes little sense, for Jesus himself first brought up the topic of a sword, and the disciples had simply answered him by showing him swords and making a very brief comment. He would not have rebuked them ("Enough of this talk!") for merely answering him with one short sentence. When Jesus said, "It is enough," he meant that two swords were enough, and this was an expression of approval of what they had just said and done. There is no hint of a rebuke. But that means that *Jesus was encouraging his disciples to carry swords for self-defense*, and even to "buy one" if they did not have one.

Another argument that some people raise in favor of "swords" as a metaphor is that later in Luke 22 Jesus rebuked Peter for cutting off the right ear of the servant of the high priest (with a literal sword—see Luke 22:50; John 18:10). But Jesus rebuked Peter at that point because he did not want his disciples to attempt to stop his crucifixion or to try to start a military uprising against Rome, and he certainly did not want Peter to be killed at that time for attempting to protect him. This is also the meaning of Matthew 26:52: "All who take the sword will perish by the sword." Jesus meant that those who take up the sword *in an attempt to do the spiritual work of advancing the kingdom of God* will not succeed in that work, and if Jesus's followers attempted to overthrow the Roman government as a means of advancing the kingdom of God at that time, they would simply fail and perish by the sword. Jesus did not want Peter to try to advance the kingdom of God by force.[6]

But that does not mean that Jesus was prohibiting the use of a sword for self-defense or to defend another person against an attack by a murderer, rapist, or robber. In fact, despite rebuking Peter for striking the high priest's servant, Jesus did not tell Peter to throw away his sword, but allowed him to keep it, for he said, "Put your sword back into its place" (Matt. 26:52).

f. Two Additional Arguments in Favor of Self-Defense: Another argument in favor of self-defense is that God wants us to care for the health of our bodies, not to engage in actions that would harm them, for Paul says, "Your body is a temple of the Holy Spirit within you" (1 Cor. 6:19).

Yet another argument is that failing to oppose a violent attack will often lead to even more harm and wrongdoing. Therefore, acting in love *both* toward an attacker *and* toward oneself would include seeking to stop the attack before harm is done. "You shall love your neighbor as yourself" (Matt. 22:39).

4. Other Authors Writing about Self-Defense. The Westminster Larger Catechism says:

> [The sixth commandment forbids] all taking away the life of ourselves, or of others, except in case of public justice, lawful war, or *necessary defense*. (Question 136; the Scripture proof given is Ex. 22:2, the passage I quoted above about striking a thief who breaks into a house at night)

---

[6] Norman L. Geisler writes, "Since swords were forbidden by Jesus for spreading the gospel, what possible purpose lay behind Jesus's command for the disciples to sell their outer garments and buy a sword? If swords are excluded by Jesus on religious grounds, we may assume that they are included by Jesus on civil grounds. Thus swords are not valid weapons to fight spiritual battles, but they are legitimate tools for one's civil defense." *Christian Ethics: Contemporary Issues and Options*, 2nd ed. (Grand Rapids, MI: Baker, 2010), 230.

John Frame writes:

> Scripture does not say much about individual self-defense as such, though
> Exodus 22:2–3 sanctions the killing of someone who invades your home after
> dark. . . . If someone seeks to kill you, or a family member, and there is no
> help available, it is right for you to ward off the attack, by force if necessary.
> . . . The law of love limits our response even to a home invader. But it does
> not forbid us to defend our lives, our families, and our possessions by force,
> to the extent that it is necessary.[7]

Robertson McQuilkin and Paul Copan are in basic agreement with Frame, but they
also include a helpful distinction between defending oneself against a common criminal
and defending oneself from persecution for being a Christian:

> Physical resistance in self-defense seems to be validated in Scripture . . . but
> not commanded. . . . Another basic question for the Christian is whether the
> impending harm is crime-oriented or whether it is persecution for Christ's
> sake. One might choose nonresistance when suffering for Christ but choose
> to resist in a crime-oriented aggression for the sake of others or even for the
> sake of the aggressor himself.[8]

5. But Should Christians Not Expect Persecution? My friend John Piper eloquently
reminds us that the New Testament frequently tells Christians that we will experience persecution and that "we should expect and accept unjust mistreatment without
retaliation."[9] Piper quotes many verses, especially from 1 Peter, showing that we should
expect to suffer unjustly for being Christians:

> But even if you should suffer for righteousness' sake, you will be blessed.
> (1 Pet. 3:14)

> But rejoice insofar as you share Christ's sufferings, that you may also rejoice
> and be glad when his glory is revealed. (1 Pet. 4:13)

> Yet if anyone suffers as a Christian, let him not be ashamed, but let him glorify
> God in that name. (1 Pet. 4:16)

These verses and others remind us that we should expect to be persecuted as Christians, and that we should use such circumstances as an opportunity for Christian wit-

---

[7] John M. Frame, *The Doctrine of the Christian Life: A Theology of Lordship* (Phillipsburg, NJ: P&R, 2008),
692–93.

[8] Robertson McQuilkin and Paul Copan, *An Introduction to Biblical Ethics: Walking in the Way of Wisdom*,
3rd ed. (Downers Grove, IL: InterVarsity Press, 2014), 350.

[9] John Piper, "Should Christians Be Encouraged to Arm Themselves?" Desiring God, Dec. 22, 2015, http://
www.desiringgod.org/articles/should-christians-be-encouraged-to-arm-themselves.

ness (see Luke 21:13). Up to this point, I agree with my friend. When we are persecuted as Christians, Peter calls us to imitate Christ's own example:

> When he was reviled, he did not revile in return; when he suffered, he did not threaten, but continued entrusting himself to him who judges justly. (1 Pet. 2:23)

But what about a different situation, not a situation in which we are persecuted because we are Christians, but a criminal attack when we are confronted with an irrational, drunken, or drug-crazed evil assailant (or gang or mob) whose aggression has nothing to do with opposing our Christian convictions? In such situations, Piper agrees that "to call the police when threatened . . . seems right to do in view of Romans 13:1–4,"[10] but he is reluctant to affirm that an individual Christian should use force or a weapon in such a situation, even to defend his wife or children (he says that he would personally "counsel a Christian not to have a firearm available for such circumstances"[11]). He says he does not know what he would do before the situation arises "with all its innumerable variations of factors," but then he also adds, "I would be very slow to condemn a person who chose differently from me."[12]

While I agree with Piper's encouragement that Christians should expect persecution and that our dominant attitude when facing persecution should be trust in the Lord and faith that he will allow us to witness boldly for him, and while the depth of Piper's faith and his love for Christ are continually a wonderful example for me personally, I still differ with his ambivalence about the use of force for self-defense *in circumstances other than persecution* and about the use of force to protect others from violent harm by criminals. If it is morally right to call the police, who would use firearms to protect us in such circumstances, then it seems to me morally right to use a weapon, if necessary, before the police can arrive (not for vengeance, which Rom. 12:19 prohibits, but for self-defense). The Scripture passages quoted in the preceding pages seem to me to give sufficient justification for the use of force and use of a weapon in such situations.

B. HOW SHOULD WE TEACH OUR CHILDREN?

Certainly we should teach our children to be "peacemakers," for Jesus taught:

> Blessed are the peacemakers, for they shall be called sons of God. (Matt. 5:9)

In addition, we should teach our children not to be quick-tempered and to simply ignore a minor insult or a "slap" rather than striking back in anger and escalating a conflict, according to Jesus's teaching:

---

[10] Ibid.
[11] Ibid.
[12] Ibid.

> But *if anyone slaps you on the right cheek, turn to him the other also.* (Matt. 5:39)

However, there will be times when attempting to avoid a conflict is unsuccessful, and a bully simply escalates his attacks. If a parent or teacher will intervene, that is a preferable solution. But sometimes no teacher or parent is present, and the attack becomes more serious.

In such cases, the biblical passages above on self-defense convince me that children should be taught to fight back with courage and determination, not to seek vengeance, but to put a clear and decisive end to the attacks. The assailant must be made to recognize that he (or she) will pay a significant price if any more attacks occur, and often that will only happen if the victim fights back strongly and decisively (whether the victim actually wins or loses the encounter, the mere act of fighting back will often be enough to deter further attacks).

Otherwise, the failure to oppose physically harmful attacks with physical force will often lead to more harmful attacks and more wrong being done. "Like a muddied spring or a polluted fountain is a righteous man who gives way before the wicked" (Prov. 25:26).

In addition, Christian children who are taught not to defend themselves can often be harmed repeatedly and, because of that, can internalize deep feelings of injustice and despair. No parent should allow this to happen to his or her children.

Finally, children should also be taught to pray for and to forgive those who attack them. They can do this at the same time as fighting to defend themselves. Yes, they can even be taught to love their attackers and seek good for them in addition to fighting against them in self-defense:

> You have heard that it was said, "You shall love your neighbor and hate your enemy." But I say to you, Love your enemies and pray for those who persecute you, so that you may be sons of your Father who is in heaven. For he makes his sun rise on the evil and on the good, and sends rain on the just and on the unjust. (Matt. 5:43–45)

C. IS IT RIGHT FOR A PERSON TO USE A WEAPON FOR SELF-DEFENSE?

If it is morally right either to flee from physical danger or (depending on the circumstances) to fight to defend oneself or others from attack, then the use of a weapon would also seem to be morally right. Sometimes a person being attacked will simply use what is at hand, whether a club or some other heavy object, or perhaps a kitchen knife. The householder defending his family against an intruder by night in Exodus 22:2 (see above) would likely have used some kind of weapon, because striking a person with one's bare hands would not ordinarily cause death.

The passages about swords discussed above (Luke 22:36–38 and Matt. 26:52) give significant support for the idea that Jesus wanted his disciples to have an effective weapon to use in self-defense. Most of the time, merely carrying a sword would deter a criminal, who would not want to risk being harmed in an attack. The sword would also enable a person to defend someone else, such as a woman, a child, or an elderly person, who might be under attack from someone stronger.

Another reason for carrying a weapon such as a sword is that it could overcome great inequalities in size or strength between an attacker and a victim. One of Jesus's disciples might have been smaller or weaker than a potential assailant, but if he were reasonably skilled in the use of a sword, he still could provide an effective defense against an attacker.

A third reason why people carried swords was that although the Roman officials and local police were able to enforce the peace in general, there simply were not enough of them to be on the spot whenever a crime was being committed. The sword provided protection against violent crimes whenever a policeman or soldier was not in sight.

D. IS IT RIGHT TO USE A GUN FOR SELF-DEFENSE?

1. Arguments in Favor of the Use of a Gun for Self-Defense. If the Bible authorizes the idea of self-defense in general, and if Jesus encouraged his disciples to carry swords to protect themselves, then it seems to me that it is also morally right for a person to be able to use *other kinds of weapons* for self-defense. Today that would include the use of a gun (where the nation or state allows this) or other weapons, such as pepper spray, that would deter an attacker.

One significant reason why people will choose a gun as a weapon for self-defense is that a gun is a great equalizer that offsets huge differences in physical strength. With a gun, an 80-year-old woman, alone in her home at night, or a frail 70-year-old shopkeeper, working in a high-crime area, would have an effective means of defense against a 25-year-old, 280-pound male intruder. No other kind of weapon would give a person that ability.

In the vast majority of cases, merely brandishing a handgun will cause an attacker to flee (the literature cited at the end of this chapter contains references to hundreds of such stories), and in the next most common event, the attacker is wounded and disabled, but fully recovers and stands trial. The requirement to act in love toward our neighbors, including even an attacker, implies that the least amount of force required to stop the attack should be used, resulting in the least amount of physical harm to the attacker himself.

However, just as Christians who have money should not trust in their money but in the Lord (Ps. 62:10, and see chaps. 34–38), and just as Christians who live under good governments should still place their trust in the Lord for protection, not in their governments, so also Christians who decide to own a gun should still trust the Lord and not give in to the temptation of trusting their guns rather than the Lord.

2. Gun-Control Laws. In another book, I have discussed the question of the effectiveness of gun-control laws in the United States and other countries. I have also discussed the current legal situation in the United States with respect to the Second Amendment to the United States Constitution.[13]

3. Should an Individual Christian Own a Gun? This entire discussion does not address the question of whether individual Christians will decide that it is *wise* to own a gun themselves. There is room for Christians to differ about this question and for individuals to decide what is best in their own situations. Some Christians may live in areas where they think the need for any weapon of self-defense is so small that it is outweighed by the negative considerations of the cost and the potential danger of a gun being found and misused by a child or used in an accidental way. Others may live in areas where they think there is a significant possibility of a violent attack against themselves or their families by irrational assailants, and they think that owning a gun for self-defense is a wise decision. I think everyone would agree that if someone owns a gun, it is crucial to have proper training and somewhat regular practice of wise safety procedures and the proper use of the gun. But the question of whether to own a gun is a matter of individual preference and personal decision.

QUESTIONS FOR PERSONAL APPLICATION

1. If you happened upon someone brutally attacking a child or another person who was obviously smaller and weaker, and if words didn't stop

---

[13] See Wayne Grudem, *Politics—According to the Bible: A Comprehensive Resource for Understanding Modern Political Issues in Light of Scripture* (Grand Rapids, MI: Zondervan, 2010), 204–12. For example, despite a history of strict gun-control policies, Chicago is one of the nation's most violent and deadly cities. In 2012, there were over 500 gun-related deaths in Chicago. That is up over 10 percent from the rate in 2005. In contrast, Houston, a city close in size to Chicago and without strict gun-control laws, saw only 217 gun-related deaths in 2012. See Kristen Tate, "More Laws Do Not Mean Less Crime," Aug. 27, 2013, https://the libertarianchick.com/2013/07/05/more-laws-dont-mean-less-crime/, and Miya Shay, "Houston Leaders Say Crime Rate is Down," ABC13, Jan. 23, 2013, http://abc13.com/archive/8965115/. In 2016, the total soared to 762 gun-related deaths in Chicago; see Azadeh Ansari and Rosa Flores, "Chicago's 762 Homicides in 2016 Is Highest in 19 Years," CNN, Jan. 2, 2017, http://www.cnn.com/2017/01/01/us/chicago-murders-2016/.

In 1976, the Washington, DC, City Council passed a law that generally prohibited residents from possessing handguns. All firearms in private homes were required to be unloaded or be rendered inoperable. In 1976, the murder rate in Washington was approximately 28 per 100,000 residents. By 1990, the rate was 80 per 100,000. In 2008, the U.S. Supreme Court in District of Columbia v. Heller, 554 U.S. 570 (2008), struck down the law as unconstitutional. In 2014, six years after the law was struck down, the murder rate was approximately 15 homicides per 100,000 residents. See "A History of D.C. Gun Ban," *The Washington Post*, June 26, 2008, http://www.washingtonpost.com/wp-dyn/content/article/2007/07/17/AR2007071700689 .html, and "Uniform Crime Reporting Program, District of Columbia, 1960–2008," Federal Bureau of Investigation, Criminal Justice Investigative Services Division, This material can be found by using the table-building tool at https://www.ucrdatatool.gov/ and "2014 Crime in the United States," Federal Bureau of Investigation, Criminal Justice Information Services Division, Fall 2015, https://ucr.fbi.gov/crime-in-the -u.s/2014/crime-in-the-u.s.-2014/tables/table-5. Most of these articles can be accessed at http://www.just facts.com/guncontrol.asp.

the attack, would you try to use physical force to stop it? Would you use a club or other weapon if it was close at hand?

2. Were you taught as a child that you should try to defend yourself against physical attack or that you should not defend yourself? Do you think that teaching had good results in your life? Do you now wish that the teaching had been different?

3. Have you ever experienced any kind of persecution that was specifically directed against you because of your Christian faith? How did God enable you to deal with that situation?

4. Can you give a specific example of a time when you "turned the other cheek" and experienced God's favor and blessing as a result?

5. Do you think it is right for a Christian to own some kind of weapon for self-defense? If so, in what circumstances should it be used and not used?

6. What character traits (see p. 110) would be especially helpful in enabling you to make the right decisions about self-defense when an attack occurs and you need to make a decision instantly?

7. How do you hope that your position on self-defense will result in bringing glory to God and advancing the work of his kingdom on earth?

SPECIAL TERMS

self-defense

BIBLIOGRAPHY

Sections in Other Ethics Texts

(see complete bibliographical data, p. 64)

Frame, 690–93
Geisler, 230–35
Gushee and Stassen: see "Other Works" below
McQuilkin and Copan, 350
Rae, 304, 308, 314

Other Works

DeRouchie, Jason S. "Lethal Self-Defense," *Jason DeRouchie*, April 26, 2016, http://jason derouchie.com/derouchie-lethal-self-defense/.

Kleck, Gary, and Don B. Kates. *Armed: New Perspectives on Gun Control*. Amherst, NY: Prometheus, 2001.

Kopel, David B. *The Truth about Gun Control*. New York: Encounter Broadsides, 2013.

Lott, John R, Jr. *More Guns, Less Crime: Understanding Crime and Gun-Control Laws.* 2nd ed. Studies in Law and Economics. Chicago: University of Chicago Press, 2000.

———. *The War on Guns: Arming Yourself against Gun Control Lies.* Washington, DC: Regnery, 2016.

Piper, John. *Love Your Enemies: Jesus's Love Command in the Synoptic Gospels and in the Early Christian Paraenesis.* Wheaton, IL: Crossway, 2012.

———. "Should Christians Be Encouraged to Arm Themselves?" Desiring God, Dec. 22, 2015, http:// www.desiringgod.org/articles/should-christians-be-encouraged-to -arm-themselves.

Sprinkle, Preston, with Andrew Rillera. *Fight: A Christian Case for Nonviolence.* Colorado Springs: Cook, 2013.

Stassen, Glen H., and David P. Gushee, *Kingdom Ethics: Following Jesus in Contemporary Context,* 189–91. Downers Grove, IL: IVP Academic, 2003. Stassen and Gushee are opposed to allowing private gun ownership; this material is not in the 2016 2nd ed. of this book.

Van Wyk, Charl. *Shooting Back: The Right and Duty of Self-Defense.* Cape Town: Christian Liberty Books, 2001.

SCRIPTURE MEMORY PASSAGE

Proverbs 25:26: Like a muddied spring or a polluted fountain is a righteous man who gives way before the wicked.

HYMN

"A Mighty Fortress Is Our God"

A mighty fortress is our God, a bulwark never failing;
Our helper He amid the flood of mortal ills prevailing.
For still our ancient foe doth seek to work us woe;
His craft and pow'r are great, and, armed with cruel hate,
On earth is not his equal.

Did we in our own strength confide our striving would be losing,
Were not the right Man on our side, the Man of God's own choosing.
Dost ask who that may be? Christ Jesus it is He;
Lord Sabaoth His name, from age to age the same,
And He must win the battle.

And tho this world with devils filled, should threaten to undo us,
We will not fear, for God hath willed His truth to triumph thru us.
The prince of darkness grim, we tremble not for him;

His rage we can endure, for lo! his doom is sure,
One little word shall fell him.

That word above all earthly pow'rs, no thanks to them abideth;
The Spirit and the gifts are ours thru Him who with us sideth.
Let goods and kindred go, this mortal life also;
The body they may kill: God's truth abideth still
His kingdom is forever.

AUTHOR: MARTIN LUTHER, 1483–1546

Chapter 21

ABORTION

What does the Bible teach about the protection of an unborn child?

Is there scientific evidence that the unborn child is a distinct person?

What about abortion in the case of rape or to save the life of the mother?

Another important topic related to the protection of human life is abortion. In this chapter, I will discuss abortion in the sense of any action that intentionally causes the death and removal from the womb of an unborn child.[1]

A. BIBLICAL EVIDENCE FOR THE PERSONHOOD OF AN UNBORN CHILD

By far the most powerful argument against abortion is the consideration that the unborn child is a unique person. Several passages in the Bible indicate that an unborn child should be thought of and protected as a person from the moment of conception.

1. Luke 1:41–44. Before the birth of John the Baptist, when his mother, Elizabeth, was in about her sixth month of pregnancy, she was visited by her relative, Mary, who was to become the mother of Jesus. Luke reports:

---

[1] Much of the material in this chapter has been adapted from Wayne Grudem, *Politics—According to the Bible: A Comprehensive Resource for Understanding Modern Political Issues in Light of Scripture* (Grand Rapids, MI: Zondervan, 2010), 157–78, with permission of the publisher.

And when Elizabeth heard the greeting of Mary, the baby leaped in her womb. And Elizabeth was filled with the Holy Spirit, and she exclaimed with a loud cry, . . . "Behold, when the sound of your greeting came to my ears, *the baby in my womb leaped for joy.*" (Luke 1:41–44)

Under the influence of the Holy Spirit, Elizabeth called the unborn child in the sixth month of pregnancy a "baby" (Greek, *brephos*, "baby, infant"). This is the same Greek word that is used for a child *after* it is born, as when Jesus is called a "baby [*brephos*] lying in a manger" (Luke 2:16; see also Luke 18:15; 2 Tim. 3:15).

Elizabeth also said that the baby "leaped for joy," which attributes personal human activity to him. He was able to hear Mary's voice and somehow, even prior to birth, feel joyful about it. In 2004, researchers at the University of Florida found that unborn children can distinguish their mother's voices and distinguish music from noise.[2] Another study, reported in *Psychology Today* in 1998, confirmed that babies hear and respond to their mother's voice while still in the womb, and the mother's voice has a calming effect on them.[3] More recent research (2013) has shown that babies learn words and sounds in the womb, and retain memories of them after they are born.[4]

2. Psalm 51:5. In the Old Testament, King David sinned with Bathsheba and then was rebuked by Nathan the prophet. Afterward, David wrote Psalm 51, in which he pleads with God, "Have mercy on me, O God, according to your steadfast love" (v. 1). Amidst confessing his sin, he writes:

Behold, I was brought forth in iniquity,
   and *in sin did my mother conceive me.* (Ps. 51:5)

David thinks back to the time of his birth and says that he was "brought forth" from his mother's womb as a sinner. In fact, his sinfulness extended back even prior to his birth, for David, under the direction of the Holy Spirit, says, "In sin did my mother conceive me."

Up to this point in the psalm, David is not talking about his mother's sin in any of the preceding four verses, but is talking about the depth of *his own sinfulness* as a human being. Therefore, he must be talking about himself, not about his mother, in this verse as well. He is saying that from the moment of his conception he has had a sinful nature. This means that *he thinks of himself as having been a distinct human*

---

[2] University of Florida. "University of Florida Research Adds to Evidence That Unborn Children Hear 'Melody' of Speech," *Science Daily*, Jan. 23, 2004, www.sciencedaily.com/releases/2004/01/040123001433.htm.

[3] Janet L. Hopson, "Fetal Psychology," *Psychology Today*, Sept. 1, 1998 (last reviewed June 9, 2016), https://www.psychologytoday.com/articles/199809/fetal-psychology.

[4] Eino Partanen et al., "Learning-induced neural plasticity of speech processing before birth," *Proceedings of the National Academy of Sciences of the United States of America*, July 22, 2013, http://www.pnas.org/content/110/37/15145.full. Also see Beth Skwarecki, "Babies Learn to Recognize Words in the Womb," *Science*, Aug. 26, 2013, http://www.sciencemag.org/news/2013/08/babies-learn-recognize-words-womb.

being, a distinct person, from the moment of his conception. He was not merely part of his mother's body, but was distinct in his personhood from the time when he was conceived.

3. Psalm 139:13. David also thinks of himself as having been a person while he was growing in his mother's womb, for he says:

> You formed my inward parts;
>> you knitted *me* together in my mother's womb. (Ps. 139:13)

Here also he speaks of himself as a distinct person ("me") when he was in his mother's womb. The Hebrew word translated as "inward parts" is *kilyah*, literally "kidneys," but in contexts such as this it refers to the innermost parts of a person, including his deepest inward thoughts and emotions (see its uses in Pss. 16:7; 26:2; 73:21; Prov. 2:16; Jer.17:10).

4. Genesis 25:22–23. In an earlier example, Rebekah, the wife of Isaac, was pregnant with the twins who were to be named Jacob and Esau. We read:

> The children [Hebrew, *banîm*, plural of *ben*, "son"] struggled together within her, and she said, "If it is thus, why is this happening to me?" So she went to inquire of the LORD. And the LORD said to her,

> "Two nations are in your womb,
>> and two peoples from within you shall be divided;
> the one shall be stronger than the other,
>> the older shall serve the younger." (Gen. 25:22–23)

Once again, the unborn babies are viewed as "children" within their mother's womb. (The Hebrew word *ben* is the ordinary word used more than 4,900 times in the Old Testament for "son" or [in plural] "sons" or "children.") These twins are viewed as already struggling together. Before the point of birth they are thought of as distinct persons, and their future is predicted.

5. Exodus 21:22–25. For the question of abortion, perhaps the most significant passage of all is found in the specific laws God gave Moses for the people of Israel during the time of the Mosaic covenant. One particular law spoke of the penalties to be imposed if the life or health of a pregnant woman *or her unborn child* was endangered or harmed:

> When men strive together and hit a pregnant woman, so that her children come out, *but there is no harm*, the one who hit her shall surely be fined, as the woman's husband shall impose on him, and he shall pay as the judges determine. But *if there is harm*, then you shall pay life for life, eye for eye, tooth for

tooth, hand for hand, foot for foot, burn for burn, wound for wound, stripe for stripe. (Ex. 21:22–25)[5]

This law concerns a situation that arises when men are fighting and one of them accidentally hits a pregnant woman. Neither one of them intends to do this, but as they fight they are not careful enough to avoid hitting her. If that happens, there are two possibilities:

1. If this causes a premature birth but *there is no harm to the pregnant woman or her unborn child*, there is still a penalty: "The one who hit her shall surely be fined" (v. 22). The penalty is for carelessly endangering the life or health of the pregnant woman and her child. We have similar laws in modern society, such as when a person is fined for drunken driving, even though he hit no one with his car. He recklessly endangered human life and health, and he deserves a fine or other penalty.

2. But "*if there is harm*" to either the pregnant woman or *her child*, then the penalty is quite severe: "Life for life, eye for eye, tooth for tooth . . ." (vv. 23–24). This means that both the mother and the unborn child are given equal legal protection. The penalty for harming the unborn child is just as great as for harming the mother. Both are treated as persons who deserve the full protection of the law.[6]

This law is even more significant when seen in the context of other laws in the Mosaic covenant. Where the Mosaic Law addressed other cases of someone *accidentally* causing the death of another person, there was no requirement to give "life for life," no

---

[5] The phrase "so that her children come out" is a literal translation of the Hebrew text, which uses the plural of the common Hebrew word *yeled*, "child," and another very common word, *yātsā'*, which means "go out, come out." The plural "children" is probably the plural of indefiniteness, allowing for the *possibility* of more than one child. Other translations render this as "so that she gives birth prematurely," which is very similar in meaning (so NASB, from 1999 editions onward; similarly: NIV, TNIV, NET, HCSB, NLT, NKJV).

[6] Some translations have adopted an alternative sense of this passage. The NRSV translates it, "When people who are fighting injure a pregnant woman *so that there is a miscarriage, and yet no further harm follows* . . ." (RSV is similar, as was NASB before 1999). In this case, causing a miscarriage and the death of an unborn child results only in a fine. Therefore, some have argued, this passage treats the unborn child as *less worthy* of protection than others in society, for the penalty is less.

But the arguments for this translation are not persuasive. The primary argument is that this translation would make the law similar to a provision in the law code of Hammurabi (written about 1760 BC in ancient Babylon). But such a supposed parallel should not override the meanings of the actual words in the Hebrew text of Exodus. The moral and civil laws in the Bible often differed from those of the ancient cultures around Israel.

In addition, there are two Hebrew words for a "miscarriage" (*shākal*, used in Gen. 31:38; see also Ex. 23:26; Job 21:20; Hos. 9:14; and *nēphel*; see Job 3:16; Ps. 58:8; Eccles. 6:3), but neither is used here. The word that is used, *yātsā'*, is ordinarily used to refer to the live birth of a child (see Gen. 25:26; 38:29; Jer. 1:5).

Finally, even on this (incorrect) translation, a *fine* is imposed on the person who accidentally causes the death of the unborn child. This implies that *accidentally* causing such a death is still considered morally wrong. Therefore, *intentionally* causing the death of an unborn child would be much more wrong, even according to this translation.

capital punishment. Rather, the person who accidentally caused someone else's death was required to flee to one of the six "cities of refuge" until the death of the high priest (see Num. 35:9–15, 22–29). This was a kind of "house arrest," although the person had to stay only within a city rather than within a house for a limited period of time. It was a far lesser punishment than "life for life."

This means that God established for Israel a law code *that placed a higher value on protecting the life of a pregnant woman and her unborn child than the life of anyone else in Israelite society*. Far from treating the death of an unborn child as *less significant* than the death of others in society, this law treated the death of an unborn child or its mother as *more significant* and therefore worthy of more severe punishment. And the law did not make any distinction about the number of months the woman had been pregnant. Presumably it applied from a very early stage in pregnancy, whenever it could be known that the injury inflicted by the men who were fighting caused the death of the unborn child or children.

Moreover, this law applied to a case of *accidental* killing of an unborn child. But if *accidental* killing of an unborn child is so serious in God's eyes, then surely *intentional* killing of an unborn child must be an even worse crime.

6. Luke 1:35: The Incarnation. The angel Gabriel told Mary that she would bear a son, and that this would come about by the power of the Holy Spirit:

> And the angel answered her, "The Holy Spirit will come upon you, and the power of the Most High will overshadow you; therefore the child to be born will be called holy—the Son of God." (Luke 1:35)

Then Elizabeth called Mary "the mother of my Lord" (Luke 1:43) soon after Mary became pregnant. These verses are significant because they mean that the incarnation of Christ did not begin when he was a newborn baby, a small child, a teenager, or an adult man. Rather, the divine nature of God the Son was joined to the human nature of Jesus from the moment of his conception in Mary's womb. From that point on, Jesus Christ was a divine-human person, both God and man. This is significant for the discussion of abortion, because it means that Christ was a genuine human person long before his birth as a baby on the first Christmas.

John Jefferson Davis writes:

> In the New Testament, the incarnation of Jesus Christ is a profound testimony to God's affirmation of the sanctity of prenatal life. . . . His human history, like ours, began at *conception*. . . . The significant point is that God chose to begin the process of incarnation there, rather than at some other point, thus affirming the significance of that starting point for human life.[7]

---

[7] John Jefferson Davis, *Evangelical Ethics: Issues Facing the Church Today*, 4th ed. (Phillipsburg, NJ: P&R, 2015), 152, emphasis in original.

Scott Rae agrees:

> From the earliest points of life in the womb, Mary and Elizabeth realize that
> the incarnation has begun. This lends support to the notion that the incarna-
> tion began with Jesus's conception and that the Messiah took on human form
> in all of its stages, embryonic life included.[8]

7. Conclusion. The conclusion from all of these passages is that the Bible teaches that
we should think of the unborn child as a person from the moment of conception, and
therefore we should give to the unborn child legal protection at least equal to that of
others in the society.

8. A Note on Forgiveness. It is likely that many people reading this evidence from the
Bible, perhaps for the first time, have already had an abortion. Others reading this have
encouraged someone else to have an abortion. I cannot minimize or deny the moral
wrong involved in these actions, but I can point to the repeated offer of the Bible that
God will give forgiveness to those who repent of their sin and trust in Jesus Christ for
forgiveness: "If we confess our sins, he is faithful and just to forgive us our sins and to
cleanse us from all unrighteousness" (1 John 1:9). Although such sins, like all other sins,
deserve God's wrath, Jesus Christ took that wrath on himself as a substitute for all who
would believe in him: "He himself bore our sins in his body on the tree, that we might
die to sin and live to righteousness. By his wounds you have been healed" (1 Pet. 2:24).

B. SCIENTIFIC EVIDENCE FOR THE PERSONHOOD OF THE UNBORN CHILD

Alongside the biblical testimony about the personhood of the unborn child, scientific
evidence also indicates that each child in the womb should be considered a unique
human person. Dianne Irving, a biochemist and biologist who is a professor at Georgetown University, writes:

> To begin with, scientifically something very radical occurs between the pro-
> cesses of gametogenesis and fertilization—the change from a simple *part* of
> one human being (i.e., a sperm) and a simple *part* of another human being
> (i.e., an oocyte—usually referred to as an "ovum" or "egg"), which simply
> possess "human life," to a new, genetically unique, newly existing, individual,
> whole living human being (a single-cell embryonic human zygote). That is,
> upon fertilization, parts of human beings have actually been transformed
> into something very different from what they were before; they have been
> changed into a single, whole human being. During the process of fertilization,

---

[8] Scott B. Rae, *Moral Choices: An Introduction to Ethics*, 3rd ed. (Grand Rapids, MI: Zondervan, 2009), 130.

the sperm and the oocyte cease to exist as such, and a new human being is produced.

To understand this, it should be remembered that each kind of living organism has a specific number and quality of chromosomes that are characteristic for each member of a species. (The number can vary only slightly if the organism is to survive.) For example, the characteristic number of chromosomes for a member of the human species is 46 (plus or minus, e.g., in human beings with Down's or Turner's syndromes). Every somatic (or, body) cell in a human being has this characteristic number of chromosomes. Even the early germ cells contain 46 chromosomes; it is only their mature forms—the sex gametes, or sperms and oocytes—which will later contain only 23 chromosomes each. Sperms and oocytes are derived from primitive germ cells in the developing fetus by means of the process known as "gametogenesis." Because each germ cell normally has 46 chromosomes, the process of "fertilization" cannot take place until the total number of chromosomes in each germ cell is cut in half. This is necessary so that after their fusion at fertilization the characteristic number of chromosomes in a single individual member of the human species (46) can be maintained—otherwise we would end up with a monster of some sort.

To accurately see why a sperm or an oocyte are considered as only possessing human life, and not as living human beings themselves, one needs to look at the basic scientific facts involved in the processes of **gametogenesis** and of **fertilization**. It may help to keep in mind that the products of gametogenesis and fertilization are very different. The products of gametogenesis are mature sex gametes with only 23 instead of 46 chromosomes. The product of fertilization is a living human being with 46 chromosomes. Gametogenesis refers to the maturation of germ cells, resulting in gametes. Fertilization refers to the initiation of a new human being.[9]

In other words, the distinct genetic identity of the unborn child shows that he or she is far different (in every single cell of the child's body!) from any part of the mother's own body (for every cell of the mother's body contains the mother's DNA, not the child's).

C. OTHER ARGUMENTS AGAINST ABORTION

The biblical testimony and scientific evidence argue strongly that the unborn child is a person who should be protected by law, and that abortion therefore is wrong and should

---

[9] Dianne N. Irving, "When Do Human Beings Begin?" Catholic Education Resource Center, http://www.catholiceducation.org/en/controversy/abortion/when-do-human-beings-begin.html, emphasis in original. Irving is a former career-appointed bench research biochemist/biologist (National Institutes of Health, National Cancer Institute, Bethesda, MD), an MA and PhD philosopher (Georgetown University, Washington, DC), and professor of the history of philosophy and of medical ethics.

not be legal. However, not all people are convinced by these arguments. What are some other ways those who accept the personhood of the unborn can argue against abortion?

1. Treatment of a Baby after It Is Born. Arguments based on how we treat a child after it is born can have significant persuasive force. For example, would we think it right for our laws to allow a parent to kill a one-year-old child simply because the parent does not want the child or finds the child a difficult burden? If not, should we allow an unborn person to be killed?

2. Ultrasound Images. Modern ultrasound technology gives highly realistic images of the unborn child—images that look so much like a real human person that they have great persuasive force. So great is the resemblance to children after they are born that parents and grandparents often fasten these ultrasound images of unborn children on their refrigerators with magnets! Focus on the Family claims that 78 percent of women who see an ultrasound of their baby in the womb reject abortion.[10] The ministry's "Option Ultrasound" program has been credited with saving more than 350,000 lives from abortion as of 2016.[11]

Because of the powerful evidence of ultrasound images, many abortion advocates try to discourage pregnant women from seeing them. Nancy Keenan, president of the National Abortion Rights Action League Pro-Choice America in Washington, DC, said, "Politicians should not require a doctor to perform a medically unnecessary ultrasound, nor should they force a woman to view an ultrasound against her will."[12] Abortion advocate William Saletan, writing in *Slate* magazine, said, "Ultrasound has exposed the life in the womb to those of us who didn't want to see what abortion kills. The fetus is squirming, and so are we."[13]

3. The Loss of Millions of Valuable People. Another argument against abortion is the incalculable loss to the nation from the deaths of more than 1 million babies per year. Since the 1973 Supreme Court decision Roe v. Wade, nearly 60 million children have been put to death through abortion.[14] Some of those would now be 44 years old. Others would be 43, 42, and so on, down to approximately 1 million of them who would be in their first year of life.[15]

---

[10] See Adam Cohen, "The Next Abortion Battleground: Fetal Heartbeats," *Time*, Oct. 17, 2011, http://ideas .time.com/2011/10/17/the-next-abortion-battleground-fetal-heartbeats/.

[11] Leah Jessen, "How This Ultrasound Program Brought Life to 358,000 Babies," The Daily Signal, Jan. 7, 2016, http://dailysignal.com/2016/01/07/how-this-ultrasound-program-brought-life-to-358000-babies/.

[12] Quoted in Jennifer Parker, "Bill Would Mandate Ultrasound before Abortion," ABC News, March 16, 2007, http://abcnews.go.com/US/story?id=2958249&page=1&CMP=OTC-RSSFeeds0312.

[13] Quoted in ibid.

[14] As of October 28, 2016, the approximate number of abortions performed in the United States since Roe v. Wade is 59,489,251. See www.numberofabortions.com.

[15] The number of abortions is decreasing. As of 2015–2016, the number of abortion was approximately 926,000. See http://www.nrlc.org/uploads/factsheets/FS01AbortionintheUS.pdf. This is down from a peak of 1.6 million per year in 1990. From 1980 to 1992, the average was over 1.5 million per year.

Many of them by now would be scientists and doctors, engineers and business leaders, entrepreneurs, artists, electricians, poets, carpenters, musicians, farmers, sports figures, political leaders, and so forth. Many of them would be mothers taking care of their own children and fathers helping to raise their children. They would be contributing to society in all areas of life—but they never had the chance to be born. They never had the chance to contribute in a positive way to this world.

4. The Instinct of the Mother. A final potent argument is simply an appeal to the instinctive sense a pregnant woman has that what is growing in her womb is not a piece of tissue or merely a part of her body, but is in fact *a baby*. Such an instinct is given even to unbelievers by God himself, for the Bible tells us, with respect to Gentiles "who do not have the law," that "the work of the Law is *written on their hearts*, while their *conscience* also bears witness, and their conflicting thoughts accuse or even excuse them" (Rom. 2:14–15). This gives us some hope that arguments showing the personhood of the unborn child will eventually be persuasive to the majority of people in a society.

D. COUNTERING ARGUMENTS FOR ABORTION

Those who reject the biblical testimony and the scientific evidence that the unborn child should be treated as a person from the moment of conception present a number of arguments for the permissibility of abortion. In this section, I will summarize and respond to the most prominent of these arguments.

1. Unable to Interact with Others and Survive on Its Own. One objection is that the unborn child is unable to talk or interact with other people or perform moral actions. In addition, it is unable to survive without its mother.

But these factors do not mean that the unborn child is not a person. A newborn is still unable to talk or perform moral actions. This is also true for a person in a coma due to a serious accident. Moreover, a newborn infant is surely unable to survive without its mother. (Some people would say that most junior high students are unable to survive without their mothers!) Such an objection is not persuasive.

2. Birth Defects. Another objection concerns unborn children who are known to have birth defects. Should parents not have the right to abort such children, thus saving themselves much hardship and sparing the child from a life of suffering?

But would we think it right to put such a child to death *after* it is born?

If we have already established that the unborn child should be treated as a person from the moment of conception, then being born or not yet being born should make no difference in our assessment of the child's personhood. If we would not think it right to kill such a child after it is born, then we should not think it right to kill the child before it is born.

Moreover, prior to birth the diagnosis of "possible" or "probable" birth defects can be in error. Sometimes a child is born perfectly normal after such a diagnosis. Many birth defects are very small and have no significant impact on the child's life. And even when a birth defect is quite significant (for example, Down syndrome), the child can still lead a happy life and bring much joy and blessing to his or her own family and to many others.[16] In such cases Christians should be encouraged to trust in God's wise providence and his sovereign direction of their lives. The Lord said to Moses, "Who has made man's mouth? Who makes him mute, or deaf, or seeing, or blind? Is it not I, the LORD?" (Ex. 4:11). On one occasion, Jesus saw a man who had been blind from birth:

> His disciples asked him, "Rabbi, who sinned, this man or his parents, that he was born blind?" Jesus answered, "It was not that this man sinned, or his parents, but that the works of God might be displayed in him." (John 9:2–3)

Randy Alcorn quotes an example of a medical school professor who presented the following case study and asked students what they would do:

> The father had syphilis and the mother had tuberculosis. Of four previous children, the first was blind, the second died, the third was both deaf and dumb, and the fourth had tuberculosis. What would you advise the woman to do when she finds she is pregnant again?

> One student answered, "I would advise an abortion." Then the professor said, "Congratulations. . . . You have just killed Beethoven."[17]

3. Pregnancies Resulting from Rape or Incest. If a child has been conceived through rape or incest, we must recognize the genuine pain and hardship experienced by the mother, who is involuntarily pregnant, perhaps at a very young age. Christians who know of such situations should be ready to give encouragement and support in many ways.

But once again the question must be asked: Would we think it right to kill a baby conceived through rape or incest *after* it is born? Most people would say certainly not. Such a child does not lose its right to live because of the circumstances of its conception. Therefore, we should not think it right to kill the child *before* it is born either. The rape that occurred was not the fault of the child, and the child should not be put to death because of someone else's crime. "Fathers shall not be put to death because of their

---

[16] Robertson McQuilkin and Paul Copan raise a point that people often overlook: "Blessing and benefit come not only to the handicapped, but also to their caregivers, many of whom deepen in their compassion and even their courage while tending to the needs of others." *An Introduction to Biblical Ethics: Walking in the Way of Wisdom*, 3rd ed. (Downers Grove, IL: InterVarsity Press, 2014), 380.

[17] Randy Alcorn, *ProLife Answers to ProChoice Arguments* (Portland, OR: Multnomah, 1992), 175. By quoting this argument, I do not wish to imply that only the lives of famous composers are worth saving, but just the opposite: all human lives are worth saving both because we are created in the image of God and because we can never know in advance how much good a child will do in his or her lifetime, if allowed to live. Beethoven, who was born in circumstances that were far from ideal, is simply a vivid illustration of the second point. (See chap. 5, p. 139, on the importance of evaluating the results of our actions.)

children, nor shall children be put to death because of their fathers. Each one shall be put to death for his own sin" (Deut. 24:16; cf. Ezek. 18:20). In addition, pregnancies resulting from rape or incest are quite rare, accounting for at most 1 percent of all abortions,[18] but probably much less than that.

Alcorn points out that well-known gospel singer Ethel Waters was born as a result of a pregnancy that occurred when her mother was raped at age 12.[19] There are doubtless other people today who lead useful, productive, fulfilling lives even though their births were the result of the horrible crime of rape.[20] We should not justify taking the life of the unborn child in such cases.

4. Abortion to Save the Life of the Mother. According to the Centers for Disease Control, abortion carried out to save the life of the mother is extremely rare (less than 0.118 percent of all abortions).[21] A more recent study in the United Kingdom found that only 0.006 percent of all abortions there were to save the life of the mother.[22] Such a situation is different from the others we considered above, because here the choice is between the loss of one life (the baby's) and the loss of two lives (both the baby's and the mother's).

I cannot see a reason to say that abortion in this situation would be morally wrong, and in fact I believe it would be morally right for doctors to save the life that *can* be saved and take the life of the unborn child. This scenario is significantly different from the most abortion cases, because in this instance removing the unborn child from the mother's body (for example, from the fallopian tube in the case of an ectopic pregnancy) results from *directly intending to save the life of the mother*, not from *directly intending to take the child's life*. If the medical technology exists to save the child's life in such cases, then of course the child's life should also be saved. But if abortion is necessary to save the mother's life, this would seem to be the only situation in which abortion is morally justified.

Therefore, it seems right to me that all mainstream pro-life proposals for legal restrictions on abortion have included an exception to save the life of the mother.

But in politics, proponents of "abortion rights" too often lump together "life" and "health," and declare that they are willing to restrict abortion "except to save the *life or*

[18] According to the Alan Guttmacher Institute, the research arm of Planned Parenthood, less than 0.5 percent of abortions in 2004 were performed on victims of rape. See Lawrence B. Finer, Lori F. Frohwirth, Lindsay A. Dauphinee, Susheela Singh, and Ann M. Moore, "Reasons U.S. Women Have Abortions: Quantitative and Qualitative Perspectives," *Perspectives on Sexual and Reproductive Health* 37, no. 3 (2005): 114, https://www.guttmacher.org/sites/default/files/pdfs/journals/3711005.pdf.

[19] Alcorn, *ProLife Answers*, 179.

[20] An excellent student in one of my seminary classes confided to me privately that after he became an adult he learned from his parents that his legal father, who had brought him up from birth, was not his biological father, but had married the student's mother after she had been raped by another man. At the time the student told me this, he had already completed several years of fruitful ministry.

[21] Jeani Chang et al., "Pregnancy-Related Mortality Surveillance—United States, 1991–1999," Centers for Disease Control and Prevention, *Morbidity and Mortality Weekly Report*, Feb. 21, 2003, www.cdc.gov/mmwr/preview/mmwrhtml/ss5202a1.htm.

[22] According to The Parliamentary Under-Secretary of State, Department of Health (Earl Howe). See http://www.publications.parliament.uk/pa/ld201213/ldhansrd/text/120719w0001.htm.

health of the mother." Then in actual practice, "health" becomes defined so broadly in legal precedents that it also includes "mental health," including freedom from excessive distress; thus, "except to save the life *or health* of the mother" in practice means abortion is allowed whenever the mother wants to obtain one.

In fact, Doe v. Bolton, the companion case to Roe v. Wade, defined maternal "health" as "all factors—physical, emotional, psychological, familial, and the woman's age—relevant to the well-being of the patient." These factors are so vague and open-ended that almost any reason can be cited to allow an abortion in the second and third trimesters. Therefore, abortion is legal—and cannot be prohibited—in the fourth, fifth, sixth, seventh, eighth, or ninth month of pregnancy if any of the reasons is invoked.[23]

E. WHAT LAWS SHOULD GOVERNMENTS ENACT REGARDING ABORTION?

One of the fundamental responsibilities of a government is to *protect the lives* of the people it governs, for if government is to punish those who do evil and to prevent them from harming the innocent (see chap. 16, p. 428), then a government certainly must protect its people from the ultimate harm of being killed (see discussion of Gen. 9:5–6, p. 507). If unborn children are considered persons, then surely government should protect their lives.[24] In fact, it is *especially* the weak and helpless, those without other means of protection, who should be the objects of governmental protections:

> Give justice to the weak and fatherless; maintain the right of the afflicted and the destitute. Rescue the weak and needy; deliver them from the hand of the wicked. (Ps. 82:3–4)

Therefore, I would recommend the following governmental policies and laws regarding abortion:[25]

1. Governments should enact laws prohibiting abortions except to save the life of the mother.[26]
2. No government policies should promote or fund abortions.

---

[23] This Supreme Court case is Doe v. Bolton, 41 U.S. 179, 192 (1973); see http://caselaw.findlaw.com/us-supreme-court/410/179.html.

[24] As for penalties that would apply to those who break the law, that would be determined by the legislature in each state. (Prior to Roe v. Wade, most state penalties were against the doctor who performed the abortion rather than the woman who received the abortion.)

[25] Elsewhere I have discussed the current legal situation in the United States and the reasons for several specific recommendations concerning government laws about abortion. See Grudem, *Politics—According to the Bible*, 157–78. What follows in this section is a summary of that longer discussion.

[26] What if a "compromise" law were proposed that would prohibit abortions except to save the life of the mother or in cases of rape or incest? I think that Christians should support such legislation, since it would prohibit roughly 99 percent of the abortions that are occurring today. After such a law is passed, perhaps further modifications could be made to the law in the future, if public sentiment would support it. But even

3. No government policies should compel people to participate in abortions or to dispense drugs that cause abortions.

4. No government funding or support should be given to the process of creating human embryos for the purpose of destroying them in medical research.

However, we must also recognize that in the United States at the present time, the Congress *has no power* to pass a law prohibiting abortions at any stage of pregnancy. And the 50 state legislatures *have no power* to pass any law prohibiting abortion. (The prohibition on partial-birth abortion, which survived Supreme Court scrutiny, is the only exception.) This is because every law prohibiting abortion has been struck down by the Supreme Court as "unconstitutional" because the court says such laws violate the Constitution's guarantee of a right to abortion![27] And this is the decision of the court even though the Constitution itself says nothing about abortion.[28]

The blunt reality is that no laws prohibiting abortions can be enacted in the United States until the Supreme Court overturns Roe v. Wade. Therefore, Christians who genuinely seek significant changes in the abortion laws in the United States should support pro-life candidates for office, especially for the presidency and the Senate, because the president alone nominates Supreme Court justices, and the Senate must approve those nominations before a nominee can join the court.

F. OBJECTIONS TO LAWS RESTRICTING ABORTION

Here are some objections that people have raised against the idea of prohibiting abortions:

1. "These Laws Are a Wrongful Restriction of Freedom." Some people will argue that a law prohibiting abortions wrongfully restricts individual human freedom. Shouldn't the decision about whether to carry a baby to full term and give birth be made by the mother herself? How can it be right to say that the law should force a woman to endure a pregnancy and bear a child that she does not want? Isn't individual freedom a foundational principle of this country? Sometimes people will say, "I think that's a decision that should be up to the mother and her doctor, and the mother should be free to decide as she thinks best."

---

such a law would do a tremendous amount of good in protecting the lives of the vast majority of unborn children who today are being put to death.

[27] Under Roe and the companion case Doe v. Bolton, the Supreme Court allowed abortion for the mother's health, including emotional and psychological health, which effectively allows abortion at any time in the nine months of pregnancy (see discussion earlier in this chapter, p. 577).

[28] For an explanation of why Roe v. Wade was based on an illegitimate "interpretation" of the U.S. Constitution (it was actually a rewriting of part of the Constitution), see Grudem, *Politics—According to the Bible*, 133–34.

Individual freedom is of course important and should be protected. But the real question is not freedom in the abstract but what *appropriate restrictions* the law should place on individual freedom. Laws already restrict freedom in many ways that people accept. The law does not allow me the freedom to drive while intoxicated, to steal my neighbor's car, to beat up someone I don't like, or to fire a gun inside the city limits— and surely it does not allow parents to put their living children to death. So the question is not human freedom, but whether the law should allow people *freedom to take their child's life*. If the unborn child is considered a human person, the question is whether the government should allow people to commit murder against their own children. Certainly it should not.

2. "All Children Should Be Wanted Children." This is another popular phrase used by politicians who advocate for unrestricted abortion. The benefit of allowing abortions, some people say, is that it gives mothers the freedom not to bear children they really don't want, children that might grow up to be neglected, abused, and poorly cared for. Why not allow abortions so that only mothers who really *want* their children will have them?

But if we consider the unborn child to be a person, then this argument is merely another way of saying that people should be allowed to kill other people that they do not want to care for. In particular, parents should be able to kill the children that they do not want to care for.

Once a child is born, would we say that a parent who does not "want" to care for that child any longer should have the right to put him or her to death because "all children should be wanted children"? Surely not. This is a horrible thought, but it is simply the logical conclusion of the "all children should be wanted children" argument. This is really a morally bankrupt argument, one that so devalues human life that it values a mother's desire for convenience more highly than the right to life of a child made in the very image of God.

3. "I'm Personally against Abortion, but I Don't Support Laws against Abortion." This argument is made by a number of politicians who do not want to appear to be *supporting* the idea of killing unborn children, but who still are committed to protecting the *legal* right of women to have abortions if they choose. Presumably, if they were asked for advice by a pregnant woman, they would tell her that they would *personally recommend* that she not get an abortion. But the decision, of course, is still up to her.

This argument fails to understand the difference between personal moral persuasion and governmental laws. If we really believe that an action is taking innocent human lives, then we will not be content to depend on moral influence to stop it. This position would be similar to saying, "*I'm personally opposed to drunken driving, and I wouldn't personally recommend* drunken driving, but I don't support having laws against it, because I think *individual drivers should have the right to decide for themselves* whether to drive when drunk." The fact of the matter is that, apart from legal enforcement by the government, many people will foolishly decide to drive while intoxicated and will actually kill other people through their wrongful choices. Government is instituted by God to protect us from such wrongdoing by others.

This argument is, in fact, a subtle attempt at changing the subject. The subject under dispute is not *personal preferences* of individuals, but what *the laws of a government* should prohibit. Just as we would not say, "I'm personally opposed to murder, but I don't think there should be any laws against murder," so it seems naive and, I think, misleading to say, "I'm personally opposed to abortion, but I don't think that there should be laws against abortion."

4. "We Should Reduce the Causes of Abortion but Not Have Laws against Abortion." A similar position to "I'm personally against abortion, but I don't support laws against abortion" is that of Jim Wallis, expressed in his book *God's Politics*. Wallis says that "the abortion rate in America is much too high for a good and healthy society that respects both women and children," and he recommends "really targeting the problems of teen pregnancy and adoption reform, which are so critical to reducing abortion, while offering real support for women, especially low-income women, at greater risk for unwanted pregnancies."[29]

But this is just changing the subject. The subject under discussion is *laws* about abortion. The specific question is: *What should the laws about abortion be?* Should laws prohibit abortion (with certain exceptions) or not? Saying we should try to reduce teen pregnancy in order to stop abortion is like saying we should support Alcoholics Anonymous in order to stop drunken driving, or we should support job creation to stop stealing, or we should support anger-management clinics to stop murder. Those are helpful social programs, but they alone will not stop those crimes.

What Wallis refuses to say in *God's Politics* is that we should have *laws* that prohibit women from taking the lives of their unborn children. Our laws should protect human life. The main difference between conservatives and liberals on abortion is how they answer this question: *Should it be against the law to kill your unborn child?*

I believe it should be against the law (except to save the mother's life). Certainly we *also* should give support to low-income women who are pregnant, but both sides agree on this. The solution is "both-and"—both maternal support and laws. But Wallis will not say "both-and." When asked *what the laws should be*, he and others simply change the subject to maternal support. They will not support laws to prohibit abortion.

5. "Everyone Who Opposes Abortion Should Adopt a 'Consistent Ethic of Life.'" How can some evangelicals vote for proabortion candidates for the U.S. Senate or for president? One approach is to change the subject from discussing laws about abortion to saying we should give more support to women who are pregnant, and so reduce abor-

---

[29] Jim Wallis, *God's Politics: Why the Right Gets It Wrong and the Left Doesn't Get It* (New York: HarperCollins, 2005), 299–300.

tion (see discussion in the previous section). Another common approach is also exemplified by Wallis. He says that Christians should support "a consistent ethic of life," but *neither political party* is satisfactory in this area. He defines this ethic as including "the life issues" of "abortion, euthanasia, capital punishment, nuclear weapons, poverty, and racism." He calls these "critical components of a consistent ethic of life."[30] Then he says:

> The tragedy is that in America today, one can't vote for a consistent ethic of life. Republicans stress some of the life issues, Democrats some of the others, while both violate the seamless garment of life on several vital matters.[31]

In other words, no party practices "a consistent ethic of life" (according to Wallis) on all of these issues, and therefore people shouldn't think that they should vote for Republicans because of the abortion issue, because there are other "life" issues on which the Democratic position is better.

But Christians should understand what Wallis is doing here. He is changing the subject from laws prohibiting abortion to laws about a whole range of things, and he is claiming that a *truly Christian* prolife position would include such policies as opposition to capital punishment, opposition to nuclear weapons, and increased government help for the poor (as he explains elsewhere in his book *God's Politics*). The effect of this argument by Wallis is to downplay the importance of the abortion issue by saying that these are all "life" issues.

I agree that it is important to consider all the issues that politicians in both parties stand for before deciding how to vote. But it is hard to see how any issue could be more important than stopping the wrongful murder of more than 1 million innocent unborn children year after year. I think Wallis is wrong to diminish this issue by lumping it with a whole basket of other controversial and complicated questions.

In addition, many Christians sincerely disagree with Wallis about capital punishment, national defense, and solutions to poverty (see discussions elsewhere in this book). Wallis's phrase "a consistent ethic of life" is a misleading slogan that attempts to make people think that his pacifist views on capital punishment and war, his support for government redistribution of wealth, and his own solutions to racial discrimination are the truly "prolife" positions. This dilutes the argument about the biblical teaching against abortion by enlarging the discussion to include many other disputed issues. This sleight-of-hand argument should not blind us to the plain fact that every vote for every proabortion candidate for president or Congress undeniably has the effect of continuing to permit 1 million abortions per year in the United States.

6. "Christians Should Not Try to Impose Their Moral Standards on Other People."
People who make this objection would usually say that it's fine for Christians to think

---

[30] Ibid., 300–301.
[31] Ibid., 301.

that abortion is wrong *for themselves*, but they have no right to try to force that conviction on others who do not have a Christian viewpoint.

In response, it must be said that many of our laws are based on moral convictions that are held by the vast majority of the population. The laws against murder are based on the moral conviction that murder is wrong. The laws against stealing are based on the moral conviction that stealing is wrong. Laws against polygamy and incest are based on moral convictions that those practices are wrong. Laws against sexual harassment or adults having sex with minors are based on moral convictions that those actions are wrong. We could multiply examples by the thousands from all areas of the law.

Which moral standards support laws against abortions? There are two: (1) people should not be allowed to murder other people and (2) the unborn child should be considered a human person and therefore should be protected as a human person. No doubt almost everyone would agree on the first point. So the question really involves the second point, whether the unborn child should be considered a human person worthy of legal protection.

In our system of government, Christians cannot *impose* their moral convictions on anyone. But everyone in the nation is free to attempt to *persuade* others about the moral convictions that should be the basis for various laws. So instead of "Christians should not try to impose their moral standards on others," a more accurate way of phrasing this objection is "Christians should not try to persuade others that the unborn child is a human person who deserves the legal protections due to all human persons."

Of course, when the objection is stated that way, hardly anyone would agree with it. Surely our nation was founded on the freedom of citizens *to speak about their convictions and try to persuade others*, and thereby to try to influence laws. In fact, the First Amendment *guarantees* freedom of speech and freedom of the press, assuring us that people of all persuasions are free to argue and attempt to persuade others about what kinds of laws should be made.

Finally, Christians should not view their conviction about the personhood of the unborn child as "*our* moral conviction." We did not make it up out of our own minds, but found it written in the Bible. And the Bible presents it as not mere human opinion, but the moral standard of God himself, by which he holds all people in every nation accountable (see discussion above, chap. 16, p. 434).

It does seem right for Christians to attempt to persuade others that the moral standards found in the Bible are correct and should be used in human government. It was on the basis of this conviction that Paul could reason with the Roman governor Felix "about *righteousness* and self-control and the coming judgment" (Acts 24:25). It was on this basis that John the Baptist "reproved" Herod the Tetrarch "for all the *evil things* that Herod had done" (Luke 3:19). And it was on this basis that Daniel warned King Nebuchadnezzar of Babylon about his "sins" and "iniquities" (Dan. 4:27), and Jonah warned the entire city of Nineveh to repent (see Jonah 3:4; see also the discussion of Christian influence on government in chap. 16, p. 468).

G. THE IMPORTANCE OF THIS ISSUE

The Old Testament contains sober warnings to a nation that allowed people to put their children to death. In imitation of the practices of other nations, some of the people of Israel had begun "to burn their sons and their daughters in the fire" (Jer. 7:31), which referred to putting their live children into a fire to sacrifice them to Molech and other pagan gods. For allowing this practice to continue, God issued a severe warning of judgment through the prophet Jeremiah:

> For the sons of Judah have done evil in my sight, declares the LORD.... And they have built the high places of Topheth, which is in the Valley of the Son of Hinnom, *to burn their sons and their daughters in the fire*, which I did not command, nor did it come into my mind. Therefore, behold, the days are coming, declares the LORD, when it will no more be called Topheth, or the Valley of the Son of Hinnom, but the Valley of Slaughter; for they will bury in Topheth, because there is no room elsewhere. And the dead bodies of this people will be food for the birds of the air, and for the beasts of the earth, and none will frighten them away. And I will silence in the cities of Judah and in the streets of Jerusalem the voice of mirth and the voice of gladness, the voice of the bridegroom and the voice of the bride, *for the land shall become a waste.* (Jer. 7:30–34)

The troubling question with regard to the United States (and many other countries today) concerns the direction the nation has taken. It has willingly chosen to be represented and governed by elected officials who resolutely champion the right of a woman to take the life of her unborn child. What will God's evaluation of our nation be in light of such decisions? Or do we not think that God is still sovereign over the affairs of nations?

QUESTIONS FOR PERSONAL APPLICATION

1. How did this chapter affect your thinking about abortion?
2. If you have ever had an abortion or have encouraged someone else to have an abortion, have you asked God's forgiveness? Do you feel forgiven by him?
3. Is there anything that friends can do to help comfort someone who has had an abortion?
4. What are some practical ways in which Christians can help women who are dealing with an unwanted pregnancy?
5. Under what circumstances (if any) do you think abortion would be morally permissible?

6. Do you think that your government should have any laws prohibiting abortion? What do you think those laws should prohibit? What should they allow?

7. What character traits (see p. 110) would be helpful for women who are experiencing an unexpected or unwanted pregnancy? For their friends and loved ones who want to encourage them?

SPECIAL TERMS

abortion

BIBLIOGRAPHY

Sections in Other Ethics Texts

(see complete bibliographical data, p. 64)

Clark and Rakestraw, 2:21–56
Davis, 131–60
Feinberg, John and Paul, 63–155
Frame, 717–32
Geisler, 131–59
Gushee and Stassen, 418–28
Hays, 444–61
Kaiser, 105–16
McQuilkin and Copan, 363–82
Rae, 121–43

Other Works

Alcorn, Randy. *Does the Birth Control Pill Cause Abortion?* 7th ed. Gresham, OR: Eternal Perspective Ministries, 2004.

———. *ProLife Answers to ProChoice Arguments.* 2nd ed. Sisters, OR: Multnomah, 2000.

———. *Why Pro-Life? Caring for the Unborn and Their Mothers.* Revised and updated ed. Peabody, MA: Hendrickson, 2012.

Beckwith, Francis J. *Politically Correct Death: Answering the Arguments for Abortion Rights.* Grand Rapids, MI: Baker, 1993.

Best, Megan. *Fearfully and Wonderfully Made: Ethics and the Beginning of Human Life.* Kingsford, NSW, Australia: Matthias Media, 2012.

Cook, E. D. "Abortion." In *New Dictionary of Christian Ethics and Pastoral Theology,* edited by David J. Atkinson and David H. Field, 131–34. Leicester, UK: Inter-Varsity, and Downers Grove, IL: InterVarsity Press, 1995.

Ganz, Richard L., and C. Everett Koop, eds. *Thou Shalt Not Kill: The Christian Case against Abortion*. New Rochelle, NY: Arlington House, 1978.

George, Robert P., and Christopher Tollefsen. *Embryo: A Defense of Human Life*. New York: Doubleday, 2008.

Gorman, Michael J. *Abortion and the Early Church: Christian, Jewish and Pagan Attitudes in the Greco-Roman World*. Eugene, OR: Wipf & Stock, 1998.

Hekman, Randall J. *Justice for the Unborn: Why We Have "Legal" Abortion and How We Can Stop It*. Ann Arbor, MI: Servant, 1984.

Hensley, Jeff Lane, ed. *The Zero People: Essays on Life*. Ann Arbor, MI: Servant, 1983.

Klusendorf, Scott. *The Case for Life: Equipping Christians to Engage the Culture*. Wheaton, IL: Crossway, 2009.

Kreeft, Peter. *The Unaborted Socrates: A Dramatic Debate on the Issues Surrounding Abortion*. Downers Grove, IL: InterVarsity Press, 1983.

Olasky, Marvin N. *Abortion Rites: A Social History of Abortion in America*. Wheaton, IL: Crossway, 1992.

Piper, John. *Brothers, We Are Not Professionals: A Plea to Pastors for Radical Ministry*. In *The Collected Works of John Piper*, edited by David Mathis and Justin Taylor, vol. 3, 137–432. Wheaton, IL: Crossway, 2017. See "Brothers, Blow the Trumpet for the Unborn," 390–403.

———. "'Rescue Those Being Led Away to Death': A Defense of Trespassing Abortion Clinics When Life Is at Stake [1989]." In *The Collected Works of John Piper*, vol. 12, 339–45.

Platt, David. "Modern Holocaust: The Gospel and Abortion." In *Counter Culture: Following Christ in an Anti-Christian Age*, revised and updated ed., 59–80. Carol Stream, IL: Tyndale Momentum, 2017.

Taylor, Justin. "'Abortion Is about God': Piper's Passionate, Prophetic Pro-Life Preaching." In *For the Fame of God's Name: Essays in Honor of John Piper*, edited by Sam Storms and Justin Taylor, 328–50. Wheaton, IL: Crossway, 2010.

———. "Abortion: Why Silence and Inaction Are Not Options for Evangelicals." In *Don't Call It a Comeback: The Same Faith for a New Day*, edited by Kevin DeYoung, 179–90. Wheaton, IL: Crossway, 2011.

Tollefsen, Christopher O., Patrick Lee, and Robert P. George. "Marco Rubio Is Right: The Life of a New Human Being Begins at Conception." Public Discourse, Aug. 5, 2015, http://www.thepublicdiscourse.com/2015/08/15520/.

SCRIPTURE MEMORY PASSAGE

Luke 1:44: For behold, when the sound of your greeting came to my ears, the baby in my womb leaped for joy.

HYMN

"Does Jesus Care?"

Does Jesus care when my heart is pained
Too deeply for mirth and song;
As the burdens press, and the cares distress,
And the way grows weary and long?

Refrain:
O yes, He cares, I know He cares!
His heart is touched with my grief;
When the days are weary, the long nights dreary,
I know my Savior cares.

Does Jesus care when my way is dark
With a nameless dread and fear?
As the daylight fades into deep night shades,
Does He care enough to be near?

Does Jesus care when I've tried and failed
To resist some temptation strong;
When for my deep grief I find no relief,
Tho my tears flow all night long?

Does Jesus care when I've said goodbye
To the dearest on earth to me,
And my sad heart aches til it nearly breaks
Is it aught to Him? Does He see?

AUTHOR: FRANK E. GRAEFF, 1860–1919

Chapter 22

EUTHANASIA

*Is it wrong to put to death a person in great pain who has no
hope of recovery?*

*How can we know when to stop medical treatment near the
end of someone's life?*

*Should the law allow doctors to perform euthanasia
when a patient requests it?*

The word *euthanasia* is derived from the Greek words *eu* ("good") and *thanatos*
("death"), and therefore people sometimes understand it to mean "good death," a rather
misleading understanding of the term. Sometimes this procedure is popularly called
"mercy killing," another term that is misleading in portraying such an action in a positive way. *Euthanasia* is simply the act of intentionally ending the life of a person who is
elderly, terminally ill, or suffering from some incurable injury or disease.[1]

This issue often comes to focus in the case of terminally-ill patients who are experiencing chronic pain and therefore no longer want to live and may even wish to be
put to death. It also is a question in the case of people who have lost much or most of
their mental capacities because of a coma or severe dementia, or patients who appear
to have no reasonable human hope of recovery from a severe injury or illness. What is
the morally right thing to do in such cases?

A. BIBLICAL TEACHING

1. Exodus 20:13: The Sixth Commandment. The primary biblical teaching in this regard is found in the sixth commandment:

---

[1] This chapter has been adapted from Wayne Grudem, *Politics—According to the Bible: A Comprehensive
Resource for Understanding Modern Political Issues in Light of Scripture* (Grand Rapids, MI: Zondervan, 2010),
178–86, with permission of the publisher.

You shall not murder. (Ex. 20:13)

This commandment, which is affirmed in the New Testament in Matthew 19:18 and Romans 13:9, applies to all human beings created in the image of God. It does not say, "You shall not murder, except when a person is more than eighty or ninety years old," or, "You shall not murder, except when a very ill person wants to be murdered."

Just as the command against murder prohibits abortion in the very early stages of human life, so the command against murder also prohibits the intentional killing of a person in the final stages of human life.

As I explained in chapter 18 (p. 505), the word translated as "murder" in Exodus 20:13 refers to both premeditated murder (which is communicated by the English word *murder*) and also any accidental causing of a person's death through negligence or carelessness. The term is always applied to the murder of human beings, not of animals. Therefore, this biblical command prohibits taking the life of another person, even if that person is elderly, terminally ill, or in great pain.

2. Second Samuel 1:1–16: The Death of Saul. One other passage of special significance is 2 Samuel 1:1–16. King Saul had recently died in battle, in effect making David king. A few days after the battle in which Saul had died, a man came to David and claimed that he had found Saul gravely wounded and that Saul had begged the man to kill him, so the man had done so. In several ways this was an act of "euthanasia." Yet David's response was to order capital punishment for the man who had done this. Here is the story:

> After the death of Saul, when David had returned from striking down the Amalekites, David remained two days in Ziklag. And on the third day, behold, a man came from Saul's camp, with his clothes torn and dirt on his head. And when he came to David, he fell to the ground and paid homage. David said to him, "Where do you come from?" And he said to him, "I have escaped from the camp of Israel." And David said to him, "How did it go? Tell me." And he answered, "The people fled from the battle, and also many of the people have fallen and are dead, and Saul and his son Jonathan are also dead." Then David said to the young man who told him, "How do you know that Saul and his son Jonathan are dead?" And the young man who told him said, "By chance I happened to be on Mount Gilboa, *and there was Saul leaning on his spear, and behold, the chariots and the horsemen were close upon him.* And when he looked behind him, he saw me, and called to me. And I answered, 'Here I am.' And he said to me, 'Who are you?' I answered him, 'I am an Amalekite.' And he said to me, '*Stand beside me and kill me, for anguish has seized me,* and yet my life still lingers.' *So I stood beside him and killed him, because I was sure that he could not live after he had fallen.* And I took the crown that was on his head and the armlet that was on his arm, and I have brought them here to my lord."

Then David took hold of his clothes and tore them, and so did all the men who were with him. And they mourned and wept and fasted until evening for Saul and for Jonathan his son and for the people of the LORD and for the house of Israel, because they had fallen by the sword. And David said to the young man who told him, "Where do you come from?" And he answered, "I am the son of a sojourner, an Amalekite." David said to him, "How is it you were not afraid to put out your hand to destroy the LORD's anointed?" Then David called one of the young men and said, *"Go, execute him." And he struck him down so that he died*. And David said to him, "Your blood be on your head, for your own mouth has testified against you, saying, 'I have killed the LORD's anointed.'" (2 Sam. 1:1–16)

This narrative has several similarities to modern situations in which people sometimes say euthanasia is justified:

1. The patient (Saul) appeared to be terminally injured, with no reasonable human hope of recovery. (He had fallen on his own sword in an attempt to commit suicide: see 1 Sam. 31:4–5.)
2. The patient was in extreme pain, and if he did not die, he faced the prospect of even more suffering.
3. The patient clearly requested, even begged, that someone would put him to death.
4. This request was also a command from the head of government at that time, because Saul was still the king.

But David, who at that time is clearly portrayed as a man after God's "own heart" (1 Sam. 13:14; cf. Acts 13:22), declares that this man who had killed Saul is worthy of capital punishment. In other words, the person who carried out euthanasia is *guilty of murder*.

Three objections may be brought against this interpretation:

First, this story about the Amalekite messenger killing Saul is not mentioned in 1 Samuel 31:3–6, where Saul's death is first reported. Therefore the Amalekite messenger may be making up this story to convince David that he had killed Saul, who was David's enemy.

However, this idea does not nullify the force of this narrative, because even if the story is not true, *David accepts it as true and passes judgment on the man based on the story*. David condemns him based on his own confession of guilt. And thus the narrative of Scripture portrays the decision of this wise king, a man after God's own heart, as *an appropriate and morally right judgment* on the man who has carried out euthanasia.

In addition, the Amalekite messenger actually has the crown and the armlet that Saul had been wearing, and he knows that Saul had fallen on his own sword, so it is quite certain that the man was there in the vicinity of Saul when Saul was dying. Therefore, it is certainly possible that his story is entirely true and simply was not included in the summary of Saul's death in 1 Samuel 31. In fact, verse 4 of that chapter does not specify that Saul killed himself, but that he tried to do so: "Saul took his own sword and fell upon it." The next verse says that at some later point Saul's armor-bearer "saw that Saul was dead," but it allows for the Amalekite to end Saul's life before that. In any case, the events probably occurred very quickly in the heat of battle.

Second, this case is unique because Saul was king, and David refers to him as "the Lord's anointed" (2 Sam. 1:14). Therefore, it should not be used to establish a general principle that euthanasia is wrong, but only the specific application that assassination of a king is wrong.

However, this objection is not persuasive, because the wrongfulness of murder does not depend on the status or rank of the victim. Murder is wrong because God prohibits it (Ex. 20:13), and more specifically because it is the taking of the life of a person made in the image of God (see Gen. 9:5–6). A king does not possess a greater share of the image of God than others who do not happen to be king! All human beings share equally in the status of being "created in the image of God" (Gen. 1:27). Therefore, if it is wrong to kill a terminally ill king who requests it, then it is also wrong to kill anyone else who requests it.

Third, the sin of the Amalekite messenger was not murder, but rebellion against the king, who was "God's anointed."

However, this interpretation does not match the actual words of the text, for David does not put the man to death for rebellion, but for murder (2 Sam. 1:14, 16). And in fact, at the time this happened, the Amalekite was not rebelling against the king, but was actually obeying what the king commanded. The sin was murder, and David punishes it accordingly.

Therefore, this narrative gives significant confirmation of the rightness of applying "you shall not murder" to the question of euthanasia.

The conclusion is that both Exodus 20:13 and 2 Samuel 1:1–16 indicate that it is morally wrong to actively take the life of a terminally-ill person who is suffering and who asks to be put to death.

B. THE CRUCIAL DIFFERENCE BETWEEN KILLING AND LETTING DIE

A clear distinction must be made between "killing" and "letting die." *Killing* is actively doing something to a patient that hastens or causes his or her death. On the other hand, *letting die* is passively allowing someone to die from other causes, without interfering with that process.[2] In the first case, the cause of death is the action taken by another

---

[2] Sometimes actively killing a suffering person is called "active euthanasia" to distinguish it from letting someone die (which is sometimes called "passive euthanasia"). I have decided not to use these terms in this

person. In the second case, the cause of death is the disease, injury, or aging process that has already been occurring in the person who dies. While the Bible prohibits actively killing someone, in the case of letting someone die the moral decision is more complex.

Sometimes it is clearly wrong to let a person die. We *should* intervene and try to help a person recover, and *not* passively allow the person to die, when (1) there is a reasonable human hope of recovery and (2) we are able to help. This would be obeying Jesus's teaching "You shall love your neighbor as yourself" (Matt. 22:39) and his command "So whatever you wish that others would do to you, do also to them, for this is the Law and the Prophets" (Matt. 7:12). Moreover, in the parable of the good Samaritan, Jesus implicitly condemned the priest and the Levite who neglected to do what they could to help a badly injured man (see Luke 10:30–37).

On the other hand, in cases where (1) there is no reasonable human hope of recovery (sometimes called a situation of "futility"), and (2) it is the patient's wish to be allowed to die, and/or (3) we are unable to help (such as when a person is trapped in a burning car or when the expense of necessary medical treatments is more than we can bear), *then it may be right to allow the person to die.* This is morally distinct from actively murdering a person.

Allowing someone to die may include *not starting* a medical life-support system (such as an artificial respirator) or *stopping* a life-support system. Although many people in modern secular societies harbor a deep fear of death, Christians need not fear death. Sometimes in Scripture we see examples of people realizing that their death is near, and then they simply trust God and yield their lives into his hands (see Luke 2:29; 23:46; Acts 7:59; see also Gen. 49:33; 1 Cor. 15:55–57; Heb. 2:15).

My own personal decision may be helpful at this point. If a circumstance should arise where I am facing a terminal illness, and there is no reasonable human hope of recovery, and I am no longer conscious—no longer able to make my wishes known and probably no longer able even to consciously pray—in such a situation, would I want a large amount of effort and expense put forth to keep me from dying and therefore to keep me out of heaven? Certainly not.

The example of the apostle Paul is a good one at this point. He said he could see benefits in remaining alive and also great benefits in dying and going to be with Christ, but his affirmation of these two "good" alternatives leads us to conclude that he certainly would not have wanted to be somehow suspended between the two for weeks or even months. He wanted one or the other, either life or death:

> It is my eager expectation and hope that I will not be at all ashamed, but that with full courage now as always Christ will be honored in my body, *whether by life or by death.* For to me to live is Christ, and to die is gain. If I am to live in the flesh, that means fruitful labor for me. Yet which I shall choose I cannot

chapter because they wrongly make the two actions sound similar, blurring the crucial moral distinction between killing someone and letting someone die.

tell. I am hard pressed between the two. My desire is to depart and be with Christ, for that is far better. But to remain in the flesh is more necessary on your account. (Phil. 1:20–24)

It seems to me, however, that providing nutrition and hydration is different from an artificial life-support system. What if a patient is unconscious or so weak that he cannot feed himself? Should he be given a feeding tube to provide food and water (often called "nutrition and hydration")? My own conviction is that we *should* provide ongoing nutrition and hydration if we are able to do so. I believe this because it seems to me to be an ordinary expression of Christian mercy and compassion to prevent the patient from dying of thirst or starvation rather than dying from the disease or injury itself. By analogy, if the patient had been in a severe car accident and both arms had been broken, and he was therefore unable to feed himself, we would certainly want to provide nutrition and hydration. Therefore, I think we should also do this when the patient's inability to feed himself is caused not by broken arms but by being unconscious.

However, I recognize that at times the exact medical situation is more complex, and a decision about nutrition and hydration (especially nutrition) may be more difficult. On April 21, 2016, the Christian Medical & Dental Associations issued a thoughtful statement that takes into account more of these complexities.[3] The statement, printed as an appendix to this chapter, recommends that nutrition and hydration should be continued unless it is harmful to the patient or clearly contrary to the patient's expressed wishes.

In addition, modern medicine should be used to alleviate the pain and suffering of a terminally-ill patient (see Matt. 7:12; 22:39). In the vast majority of cases today, medicines, especially morphine or drugs known as opioids, are available that will protect people from ongoing, extreme suffering as they near death.[4] A recent study found that those with advanced cancer who receive early palliative care to help with physical and emotional issues have a better quality of life and do not experience as much suffering as those who do not receive such care.[5]

C. ARGUMENTS AGAINST EUTHANASIA FROM REASON AND EVIDENCE APART FROM THE BIBLE

In addition to the arguments given above from Exodus 20:13 ("You shall not murder") and 2 Samuel 1:1–16 (the death of Saul), four additional arguments can be made against euthanasia:

---

[3] "Artificially-Administered Nutrition and Hydration," Christian Medical & Dental Associations, https://cmda.org/resources/publication/artificially-administered-nutrition-and-hydration-ethics-statement.

[4] "Last Days of Life," National Institutes of Health, National Cancer Institute, www.cancer.gov/cancertopics/pdq/supportivecare/lasthours/Patient/page2#Keypoint7.

[5] "Study Confirms Benefits of Early Palliative Care for Advanced Cancer," National Institutes of Health, National Cancer Institute, Oct. 5, 2016, https://www.cancer.gov/news-events/cancer-currents-blog/2016/palliative-care-quality.

1. The Human Moral Instinct That Murder Is Wrong. Most people have a conviction that it is wrong to murder another human being. An argument can be made from this general conviction to the specific application that it is wrong to murder elderly or terminally ill people. Is murder not murder whether the victim is young or old, strong or weak, or in good health or suffering? None of these considerations should affect the moral status of the person as a human being.

2. The Slippery Slope from Euthanasia to an "Obligation" to Die. Concerns about a "slippery slope" in public policy have some persuasive force. If euthanasia is allowed for *some* patients who are suffering, then how can we prevent it from being applied to *more and more* patients who are suffering? And with the increasing cost of health care for elderly and extremely ill patients, there is likely to be growing pressure on people to ask that their lives be taken. Moreover, "nations that have allowed for physician-assisted suicide find that a society can quickly move from merely *allowing* 'the right to die' to the belief that there is 'an *obligation* to die' on the part of the elderly and the very ill people who are 'draining resources' from the society. In such situations it becomes likely that a number of elderly people will be put to death against their will."[6]

3. The Horror of Involuntary Euthanasia. The situation in the Netherlands has become particularly notorious—a large number of elderly people have been put to death against their will.[7] In 2012, 4,188 people were euthanized in the Netherlands through a mix of sedatives and a lethal dose of muscle relaxant.[8] Wesley Smith, an attorney for the International Anti-Euthanasia Task Force, has written that the number is actually much higher:

> The evidence of decades demonstrates that such involuntary euthanasia is rampant. Indeed, in its 1997 ruling refusing to create a constitutional right to assisted suicide (*Washington v. Glucksberg*) the United States Supreme Court quoted a 1991 Dutch government study finding that in 1990 doctors committed "more than 1000 cases of euthanasia without an explicit request" and "an additional 4,941 cases where physicians administered lethal morphine overdoses without the patients' explicit consent." That means in 1990, nearly 6,000 of approximately 130,000 people who died in the Netherlands that year were involuntarily euthanized—approximately 4 percent of all Dutch deaths. So much for "choice."[9]

---

[6] "The End of Life," in *ESV Study Bible* (Wheaton, IL: Crossway, 2008), 2543. (I was the primary author of this article, which was also modified and approved by at least three other editors.)

[7] A concise summary of the Netherlands' euthanasia law can be read at www.internationaltaskforce.org/hollaw.htm.

[8] Bruno Waterfield, "Number of Dutch Killed by Euthanasia Rises by 13 Percent," *The Telegraph*, Sept. 24, 2013, http://www.telegraph.co.uk/news/worldnews/europe/netherlands/10330823/Number-of-Dutch-killed-by-euthanasia-rises-by-13–per-cent.html.

[9] Wesley Smith, "We Ignore the Dutch Legalization of Euthanasia at Our Own Peril," Euthanasia.com, Dec. 17, 2000, http://www.euthanasia.com/nethcases.html.

Euthanasia advocate Philip Nitschke invented the so-called "peaceful pill" to induce suicide, and he also conducted "how to commit suicide" clinics. He said that his personal position is that "if we believe that there is a right to life, then we must accept that people have a right to dispose of that life whenever they want."[10] He continued:

> Many people I meet and argue with believe that human life is sacred. I do not. . . . If you believe that your body belongs to God and that to cut short a life is a crime against God, then you will clearly not agree with my thoughts on this issue. I do not mind people holding these beliefs and suffering as much as they wish as they die. For them, redemptive suffering may well pry open heaven's door that little bit wider, and if that is their belief they are welcome to it, but I strongly object to having those views shoved down my neck. I want my belief—that human life is not sacred—accorded the same respect.[11]

The slippery slope has also extended into infant euthanasia. In September 2005 the Dutch government announced its intention to expand its euthanasia policy to allow doctors to end the lives of infants with the parents' consent. Under the "Gronican Protocol," euthanasia is allowed when it is decided that a child is terminally ill with no prospect of recovery and suffering great pain.[12]

Christine Rosen, author of *Preaching Eugenics*, says:

> The Netherlands' embrace of euthanasia has been a gradual process aided by the growing acceptance (in a much more secular Europe) that some life is "unworthy of life." Indeed, Europe is doing just that. According to the Associated Press, 73 percent of French doctors have admitted to using drugs to end an infant's life, with between 2 and 4 percent of doctors in the United Kingdom, Italy, Spain, Germany, and Sweden confessing the same.[13]

Belgium has also passed a law allowing the euthanasia of children, and the first child was killed in September 2016.[14] Under Belgium's law, children of any age can ask to be euthanized if they are deemed to have a terminal illness.[15] Former Alliance Defending

---

[10] Quoted in Kathryn Jean Lopez, "Euthanasia Sets Sail: An interview with Philip Nitschke, the other 'Dr. Death,'" *National Review*, June 5, 2001, http://www.nationalreview.com/article/420133/euthanasia-sets-sail-kathryn-jean-lopez.

[11] Quoted in ibid.

[12] Wesley J. Smith, "From Holland to New Jersey," *National Review*, March 22, 2005, http://www.nationalreview.com/article/213965/pushing-infanticide-wesley-j-smith.

[13] Christine Rosen, *Preaching Eugenics: Religious Leaders and the American Eugenics Movement* (Oxford: Oxford University Press, 2004), cited in Kathryn Jean Lopez, "Mercy!" *National Review*, March 30, 2005, http://www.nationalreview.com/article/214029/mercy-kathryn-jean-lopez

[14] Yves Logghe, "First Child Dies by Legal Euthanasia in Belgium," CBS News, Sept. 19, 2016, http://www.cbsnews.com/news/child-dies-by-euthanasia-in-belgium-where-assistance-in-dying-is-legal/

[15] Charlotte McDonald-Gibson, "Belgium Extends Euthanasia Law to Kids," *Time*, Feb. 13, 2014, http://time.com/7565/belgium-euthanasia-law-children-assisted-suicide/.

Freedom (ADF) International attorney Roger Kiska, who led the legal fight against the law, said after its passage:

> No civilized society allows children to kill themselves. Far from a compassionate law, this law hands the equivalent of a loaded gun to a child with the astonishing belief that the child should be free to pull the trigger if he or she so chooses. Belgium's decision to allow this is grotesquely abhorrent and inhumane. As the legal analysis we provided to members of the Belgian Parliament explained, the law's underlying premise is that life is not worth living and that children are somehow mature enough to make such grave decisions about their own lives. On the contrary, this law exploits vulnerable children by handing to them a "freedom" that they are completely ill-equipped to bear.[16]

4. Examples of People Who Have Surprisingly Recovered. A final argument against euthanasia comes from personal narratives and testimonies from people who were apparently terminally ill or had life-threatening injuries but nevertheless recovered, as well as from elderly people who are still living happy, productive lives.

One example of this phenomenon is Jesse Ramirez of Mesa, Arizona. In May 2007, the 36-year-old Jesse was in a horrific automobile accident while he and his wife were engaged in an argument.[17] He suffered a broken neck and head trauma, and fell into a coma. Barely ten days after the accident, Jesse's food, water, and antibiotics were withdrawn at the request of his wife, who received only minor injuries in the accident. He was then transferred to hospice care, where he would have died, but Alliance Defending Freedom attorneys, at the behest of Jesse's sister, were successful in restoring food, water, and treatment. A few days later, Jesse came out of his coma. Although he went without food and water for six days, Jesse recovered and walked out of the hospital in October 2007, and continued his recovery at home.[18] In 2008 the state of Arizona passed "Jesse's Law," which closed a loophole in the decision-making process for patients who are physically unable to communicate their wishes regarding medical care.[19]

D. OBJECTIONS

There are three primary objections to the position opposing euthanasia that I have outlined above:

---

[16]"Belgium to Allow Children to Kill Themselves," Alliance Defending Freedom, Feb. 13, 2014, http://www.adfmedia.org/News/PRDetail/8847.

[17]Dennis Wagner, "Injured Man's Awakening Called 'Miracle,'" *USA Today*, June 27, 2007, https://usatoday30.usatoday.com/news/nation/2007-06-26-comatose_n.htm.

[18]Rick Dubek, "Comatose Mesa Man Walks Out of Hospital," AZCentral, Oct. 19, 2007, http://archive.azcentral.com/12news/news/articles/jesseramirezwalks10192007-CR.html.

[19]"ADF Commends Signing of 'Jesse's Law,'" Alliance Defending Freedom, June 25, 2008, http://www.adfmedia.org/News/PRDetail/1907.

1. "We Must Uphold the Value of Human Freedom." Proponents of euthanasia often emphasize the importance of human freedom, even the freedom of an individual to choose to end his or her own life.

But if it is morally wrong to actively murder another person, then the fact that a person would *choose* to be murdered does not nullify this moral conclusion. There are many cases in which someone might so despair of life that he or she would say, "I want to die." But should we then say that it is right to murder such a person? If murder is morally wrong, even the desire of the person who wants to be murdered cannot make it morally right, for it is still taking a human life. A person's right to life does not depend on the person himself wanting to live.

2. "Sometimes We Need to Alleviate Pain." Another objection is that some people are experiencing unbearable, unending pain, and they are often only a few months or years from death in any case.

However, pain and suffering are not sufficient reasons to overcome the moral prohibition against murder. A better solution is to alleviate the pain (which is almost always possible with modern medicine)[20] and do whatever else can be done to overcome the person's suffering.

3. "Medical Resources and Money Are Limited." A final argument is that money and medical resources are limited, and therefore we should put to death elderly or very ill people so that these resources are not wasted on them. This is not the question of allocating a scarce resource (say, a kidney transplant) to a younger or healthier person. Rather, it is the argument that older or very ill people *should not be using so much medical care at all.*

But this argument, phrased another way, essentially says that it is right to kill people whose care is costing us too much. This argument is simply a way of saying, "We don't have enough money to care for these elderly and terminally ill people." But is that a justification for taking another person's life? This would change the commandment "You shall not murder" into a different commandment: "You shall not murder unless you do so to spend your money on something else." This objection is hardly acceptable on moral grounds.

I must emphasize that this is not the discussion about "letting die," which may be the right decision with terminally-ill patients who have no reasonable human hope of recovery. In such cases, the wishes of the patient and the financial resources available to care for the patient become genuine considerations. But here we are not talking about letting die. We are talking about whether it is right to *actively kill* another person because we think society should spend less on caring for old, sick people and direct more of its spending to other medical purposes. We are talking about whether it is right to murder.

It is important to realize that all three of these objections are based on a viewpoint

---

[20] There are rare cases in which no significant relief from pain is possible with medication.

that is contrary to a Christian worldview. These three objections do not value human life as something sacred, something that uniquely carries the image of God in this world. And they do not give full weight to the moral force of God's command, "You shall not murder."

E. RECENT LEGAL TRENDS

Recent legal trends in at least some states in the United States seem to be moving in the direction of allowing more euthanasia. In most states, euthanasia is still prohibited and laws against murder apply to it. However, Oregon voters enacted the "Death with Dignity Act," what is called physician-assisted suicide, in 1994,[21] and this law was upheld by the U.S. Court of Appeals for the Ninth Circuit in 1997. The U.S. Supreme Court subsequently denied an appeal to the law. In a subsequent challenge contending that federal controlled-substances acts overrode the law, the U.S. Supreme Court ruled six to three in the law's favor in 2006.[22] In November 2008 the citizens of Washington state also legalized physician-assisted suicide.[23] In October 2015, Gov. Jerry Brown of California signed into law a bill that legalized assisted suicide in that state. The law went into effect on June 9, 2016.[24] Shortly thereafter, a health insurer refused to pay for chemotherapy for a woman suffering from terminal cancer, but agreed to pay for her less expensive suicide pills instead.[25] Assisted suicide is also legal in Vermont and Montana as well.[26]

On the other hand, in 1999, Jack Kevorkian, a physician in Michigan, was convicted for assisting a patient to commit suicide in an act that was displayed on television and that violated current Michigan law.[27]

F. THE IMPORTANCE OF THIS ISSUE

The direction a society takes on the question of euthanasia is a reflection of how highly it values human life and how highly it values God's command not to murder. In societies

---

[21] See http://www.oregon.gov/oha/PH/PROVIDERPARTNERRESOURCES/EVALUATIONRESEARCH/DEATHWITHDIGNITYACT/pages/index.aspx.

[22] Gonzales v. Oregon, 546 U.S. 243 (2006).

[23] "Washington State to Allow Assisted Suicide," Associated Press, March 2, 2009, https://usatoday30.usatoday.com/news/nation/2009-03-01-washington-assisted_N.htm.

[24] Lisa Aliferis, "California to Permit Medically Assisted Suicide as of June 9," National Public Radio, March 10, 2016, http://www.npr.org/sections/health-shots/2016/03/10/469970753/californias-law-on-medically-assisted-suicide-to-take-effect-june-9.

[25] Bradford Richardson, "Assisted-suicide law prompts insurance company to deny coverage to terminally ill California woman," *Washington Times*, Oct. 20, 2016, http://www.washingtontimes.com/news/2016/oct/20/assisted-suicide-law-prompts-insurance-company-den/.

[26] "'Death With Dignity' Laws By State," FindLaw, http://healthcare.findlaw.com/patient-rights/death-with-dignity-laws-by-state.html.

[27] "Kevorkian Gets 10 to 25 Years in Prison," CNN, April 13, 1999, www.cnn.com/US/9904/13/kevorkian.03/.

where physician-assisted suicide becomes legal, it sets the stage for a further erosion of the protection of human life. Some people will be thought "too old" to deserve medical treatment. Compassion and care for the elderly will diminish, and they will be more and more thought of as burdens to be cared for rather than valuable members of the society.

And unless we experience premature death, all of us reading this chapter will ourselves one day be those "elderly" people who need care and support from others.

G. APPENDIX: ARTIFICIALLY-ADMINISTERED NUTRITION AND HYDRATION

A statement of the Christian Medical & Dental Associations

A frequent ethical dilemma in contemporary medical practice is whether or not to employ artificial means to provide nutrition or hydration[28] in certain clinical situations. Legal precedents on this question do not always resolve the ethical dilemma or accord with Christian ethics. CMDA offers the following ethical guidelines to assist Christians in these difficult and often emotionally laden decisions. The following domains must be considered:

BIBLICAL

1. All human beings at every stage of life are made in God's image, and their inherent dignity must be treated with respect (Genesis 1:25–26). This applies in three ways:

   a. All persons or their surrogates should be given the opportunity to make their own medical decisions in as informed a manner as possible. Their unique values must be considered before the medical team gives their recommendations.

   b. The intentional taking of human life is wrong (Genesis 9:5–6; Exodus 20:13).

   c. Christians specifically (Matthew 25:35–40; James 2:15–17), and healthcare professionals in general, have a special obligation to protect the vulnerable.

2. Offering oral food and fluids for all people capable of being safely nourished or comforted by them, and assisting when necessary, is a moral requirement (Matthew 25:31–45).

3. All people are responsible to God for the care of their bodies, and healthcare professionals are responsible to God for the care of their patients. As

---

[28] ANH may be given enterically through a nasogastric (NG) tube. Alternatively, a percutaneous gastrostomy tube (PEG) may be inserted endoscopically so that a feeding tube is passed through the abdominal wall. Total parenteral nutrition (TPN) is administered through a large bore catheter inserted into a central vein in the chest. Hydration (water plus electrolytes) may be given with nutrition in any of these ways or alone through a peripheral intravenous catheter or, less commonly, through a catheter inserted subcutaneously.

Christians we understand that our bodies fundamentally belong to God; they are not our own (1 Corinthians 6:20).

4. We are to treat all people as we would want to be treated ourselves (Luke 6:31).

5. Technology should not be used only to prolong the dying process when death is imminent. There is "a time to die" (Ecclesiastes 3:2).

6. Death for a believer will lead to an eternal future in God's presence, where ultimate healing and fulfillment await (2 Corinthians 5:8; John 3:16, 6:40, 11:25–26, and 17:3).

7. Medical decisions must be made prayerfully and carefully. When faced with serious illness, patients may seek consultation with spiritual leaders, recognizing that God is the ultimate healer and source of wisdom (Exodus 15:26; James 1:5, 5:14).

8. Illness often provides a context in which the following biblical principles are in tension:

    a. God sovereignly uses the difficult experiences of life to accomplish his inscrutable purposes (Job; 1 Peter 4:19; Romans 8:28; 2 Corinthians 12:9).

    b. God desires his people to enjoy his gifts and to experience health and rest (Psalm 127:2; Matthew 11:28–29; Hebrews 4:11).

MEDICAL

1. Loving patient care should aim to minimize discomfort at the end of life. Dying without ANH need not be painful and in some situations can promote comfort.

    a. Nutrition: In the active stages of dying, as the body systems begin to shut down, the alimentary tract deteriorates to where it cannot process food, and forced feeding can cause discomfort and bloating. As a person can typically live for weeks without food, absence of nutrition in the short term does not equate with causing death.

    b. Hydration: In the otherwise healthy patient with reversible dehydration, deprivation of fluids causes symptoms of discomfort that may include thirst, fatigue, headache, rapid heart rate, agitation, and confusion. By contrast, most natural deaths occur with some degree of dehydration, which serves a purpose in preventing the discomfort of fluid overload. As the heart becomes weaker, if not for progressive dehydration, fluid would back up in the lungs, causing respiratory distress, or elsewhere in the body, causing excessive swelling of the tissues. In the dying patient, dehydration causes discomfort only if the lips and tongue are allowed to dry.

2. Complications of ANH.

    a. Tube feedings may increase the risk of pneumonia from aspiration of stomach contents.

b. Tube feedings and medications administered through the tube may cause diarrhea, increasing the possibility of developing skin breakdown or bedsores, and infections, especially in an already debilitated patient.

c. Patients with feeding tubes will, not infrequently, either willfully or in a state of confusion, pull at the feeding tube, causing damage to the skin at the insertion site or dislodging the tube. Prevention of harm may require otherwise unnecessary physical restraints or sedating medications.

d. The surgical procedure of inserting a percutaneous gastrostomy (feeding) tube can occasionally lead to bowel perforation or other serious complications.

e. Complications of TPN include those associated with the central venous catheter, such as blood vessel perforation or collapsed lung; local or blood stream infection; and complications associated with the feeding itself, such as fluid overload, electrolyte disturbances, labile blood glucose, liver dysfunction, or gall bladder disease.

3. Disease context.

a. Cancer: End-stage cancer often increases the metabolic requirements of the body beyond the nutrition attainable by oral means. When the cancer has progressed to this stage, the patient may experience considerable pain, and ANH may only prolong dying.

b. Severe neurologic impairment: This frequently has an indeterminate prognosis rendering decision making problematic. It requires a careful evaluation of the probability of improvement, the burdens and benefits of medical intervention, and a judgment of how much the patient can endure while awaiting the hoped-for improvement.

c. Dementia: If a patient survives to the late stages of dementia, the ability to swallow food and fluids by mouth may be impaired or lost. ANH has been shown in rigorous scientific studies to improve neither comfort nor the length of life and may, in fact, shorten it.

ETHICAL

1. There is no ethical distinction between withdrawing and withholding ANH. However, the psychological impact may be different if withdrawal or withholding is perceived to have been the cause of death.

2. If there is uncertainty about the wisdom of employing ANH, a time-limited trial may be considered.

3. Any medical intervention should be undertaken only after a careful assessment of the expected benefit versus the potential burden.

4. The decision whether to implement or withdraw ANH is based on a consideration of medical circumstances, values, and expertise, and involves the patient or designated surrogate in partnership with the healthcare team.

5. It is best that all stakeholders strive for consensus.

SOCIAL

1. Eating is a social function. Even for compromised patients unable to feed themselves, being fed by others provides some of the best opportunities they have for meaningful human contact and pleasure.

2 People suffering from advanced dementia frequently remain sentient and social.

CMDA endorses ethical guidelines in four categories:

1. **Strong indications**: Situations where the use of ANH is strongly indicated and it would be unethical for a medical team to decline to recommend it or deny its implementation. Examples of these situations would be:

    a. A patient with inability to take oral fluids and nutrition for anatomic or functional reasons with a high probability of reversing in a timely manner.

    b. A patient who is in a stable condition with a disease that is not deemed to be progressive or terminal and the patient or surrogate desires life prolongation (e.g., an individual born unable to swallow but who is otherwise viable, or the victim of trauma or cancer who has had curative surgery but cannot take oral feedings).

    c. A patient with a newly-diagnosed but not imminently fatal severe brain impairment in the absence of other life-threatening comorbidities.

    d. Gastrointestinal tract failure or the medical need for total bowel rest may justify the use of TPN in some contexts not otherwise terminal.

    e. An otherwise terminal patient who requests short-term ANH, fully informed of the risk being taken, to allow him or her to experience an important life event.

2. **Allowable indications**: Situations where the use of ANH is morally neutral and the patient or surrogate should be encouraged to make the best decision possible after the medical team has provided as much education as necessary. Examples of these situations would be:

    a. A patient with severe, progressive neurologic impairment who otherwise desires that life be prolonged (e.g., end-stage amyotrophic lateral sclerosis).

b. Conditions that would not be terminal if ANH were provided but, in the opinion of either the patient or surrogate, there is uncertainty whether the anticipated benefits versus burdens justify the intervention.

3 **Not recommended but allowable:** Situations where the use of ANH may not be recommended in all instances but, depending on the clinical context, would be morally licit, assuming the patient or surrogate has been informed of the benefits and potential complications and requests that it be initiated or continued. Examples of these situations would be:

a. A patient who has a disease state, such as a major neurologic disability, where, after several months of support and observation, the prognosis for recovery of consciousness or communication remains poor or indeterminate. In cases where ANH is withdrawn or withheld, oral fluids should still be offered to the patient who expresses thirst.

b. A patient whose surrogate requests overruling the patient's advance directive and medical team's recommendation against ANH because of the particular or changing clinical context.

c. Placement of a PEG in a patient who is able but compromised in the ability to take oral feeding as a convenient substitute for the sometimes time-consuming process of oral feeding, for ease of medication administration, or to satisfy eligibility criteria for transfer from an acute-care setting to an appropriate level of short-term nursing care, long-term care, or a rehabilitation facility. ANH decisions in such cases should consider the potential benefits versus risks and burdens of available feeding options, the capacity of caregivers to administer feedings, and prudent stewardship of medical and financial resources, always in regard to the best interest of the patient.

4. **Unallowable indications:** Situations where it is unethical to employ ANH. Examples of these situations would include:

a. Using ANH in a patient against the patient's or surrogate's expressed wishes, either extemporaneously or as indicated in an advance directive and agreed to by the surrogate. There may be particular medical contexts in which a surrogate may overrule an advance directive that requests ANH on the basis of substituted judgment if the surrogate knows the patient would not want it in the present context.

b. Compelling a medical professional to be involved in the insertion of a feeding tube or access for TPN in violation of his or her conscience. In this situation the requesting medical professional must be willing to transfer the care of the patient to another who will provide the service. (See CMDA statement on Healthcare Right of Conscience.)

    c. Using ANH in a situation where it is biologically futile, as in a patient declared to be brain dead. An exception would be the brain dead pregnant patient in which the purpose of ANH is to preserve viable fetal life; ANH in this circumstance is not futile for the life in the womb.

    d. Using ANH in an attempt to delay the death of an imminently dying patient (except in the context in 1.e. above).

CMDA recognizes that ANH is a controversial issue with indistinct moral boundaries. Disagreements should be handled in the spirit of Christian love, showing respect to all.

Unanimously approved by the House of Representatives
April 21, 2016
Ridgecrest, North Carolina[29]

QUESTIONS FOR PERSONAL APPLICATION

1. How has this chapter affected the way you think about euthanasia?
2. If the time should come when you are experiencing a terminal illness and you have no reasonable human hope of recovery, what kinds of medical treatments would you want done for you for the purpose of prolonging your life? For the purpose of alleviating your pain?
3. Have you talked with members of your immediate family about your wishes regarding end-of-life care? Have you put these wishes in a written document that will be legally recognized, such as (in the United States) a "medical power of attorney" document? (See further discussion in chap. 24, p. 631.)
4. What character traits (see p. 110) would be especially helpful for people going through a terminal illness? For the members of their families who are close to them?

SPECIAL TERMS

assisted suicide
euthanasia
killing
letting die
nutrition and hydration
slippery slope

---

[29] Reproduced from the website of the Christian Medical & Dental Associations, https://www.cmda.org /resources/publication/artificially-administered-nutrition-and-hydration-ethics-statement.

BIBLIOGRAPHY

Sections in Other Ethics Texts

(see complete bibliographical data, p. 64)

Clark and Rakestraw, 2:95–138
Davis, 161–97
Feinberg, John and Paul, 157–226
Frame, 734–38
Geisler, 160–79
Gushee and Stassen, 434–41
Kaiser, 139–50
McQuilkin and Copan, 387–93
Rae, 212–46

Other Works

Cameron, N. M. de S. "Euthanasia." In *New Dictionary of Christian Ethics and Pastoral Theology*, edited by David J. Atkinson and David H. Field, 357–59. Leicester, UK: Inter-Varsity, and Downers Grove, IL: InterVarsity Press, 1995.

Frame, John M. *Medical Ethics: Principles, Persons, and Problems.* Christian Perspectives. Phillipsburg, NJ: Presbyterian and Reformed, 1988.

Kilner, John Frederic. *Life on the Line: Ethics, Aging, Ending Patients' Lives, and Allocating Vital Resources.* Grand Rapids, MI: Eerdmans, 1992.

———, ed. *Why the Church Needs Bioethics: A Guide to Wise Engagement with Life's Challenges.* Grand Rapids, MI: Zondervan, 2011.

Kilner, John Frederic, Arlene B. Miller, and Edmund D. Pellegrino, eds. *Dignity and Dying: A Christian Appraisal.* Horizons in Bioethics Series. Carlisle, UK: Paternoster, 1996.

Kilner, John Frederic, and C. Ben Mitchell. *Does God Need Our Help? Cloning, Assisted Suicide, and Other Challenges in Bioethics.* Vital Questions. Wheaton, IL: Tyndale, 2003.

Mitchell, C. Ben. *Biotechnology and the Human Good.* Washington, DC: Georgetown University Press, 2007.

Mitchell, C. Ben, and D. Joy Riley. *Christian Bioethics: A Guide for Pastors, Health Care Professionals, and Families.* B&H Studies in Christian Ethics. Nashville: B&H Academic, 2014.

Tada, Joni Eareckson. *When Is It Right to Die? A Comforting and Surprising Look at Death and Dying*, updated ed. Grand Rapids, MI: Zondervan, 2018.

VanDrunen, David. *Bioethics and the Christian Life: A Guide to Making Difficult Decisions.* Wheaton, IL: Crossway, 2009.

SCRIPTURE MEMORY PASSAGE

Exodus 20:13: You shall not murder.

HYMN

"Great Is Thy Faithfulness"

Great is Thy faithfulness, O God my Father!
There is no shadow of turning with Thee;
Thou changest not, Thy compassions, they fail not:
As Thou hast been Thou forever wilt be.

Refrain:
Great is Thy faithfulness! Great is Thy faithfulness!
Morning by morning new mercies I see;
All I have needed Thy hand hath provided
Great is Thy faithfulness, Lord unto me!

Summer and winter, and springtime and harvest,
Sun, moon and stars in their courses above,
Join with all nature in manifold witness
To Thy great faithfulness, mercy and love.

Pardon for sin and a peace that endureth,
Thine own dear presence to cheer and to guide,
Strength for today and bright hope for tomorrow
Blessings all mine, with ten thousand beside![30]

AUTHOR: THOMAS O. CHISHOLM, 1866–1960

Chapter 23

SUICIDE

Can a person who commits suicide be forgiven?

The topic of suicide is an extremely painful one even to mention, and especially to discuss, for those who have lost a family member or friend who took his or her own life. Therefore, any discussion of the topic must be approached with thoughtfulness and compassion, and with the recognition that the memory of a suicide from many years ago may still be extremely painful and difficult. Nevertheless, in dealing with moral questions connected to the protection of life, it is necessary to consider the topic of suicide.

According to the American Foundation for Suicide Prevention, citing statistics from the Centers for Disease Control and Prevention, suicide is the tenth-leading cause of death in the United States. In 2014 (the latest year for which statistics are available), 42,773 Americans died by suicide. The age-adjusted suicide rate was 12.93 per 100,000 individuals in 2014, compared with 10.5 per 100,000 in 1999. On average, there are 117 suicides per day, and men die by suicide three and one-half times as often as women, but females attempt suicide three times as often as males. Suicide costs the United States $44 billion annually in medical and work-related losses.[1]

Since 2000, the suicide rate among white males in the United States has risen from approximately 12.0 per 100,000 to 14.7 per 100,000 in 2014, and constitutes the highest rate of suicide among adults. However, there has also been a sharp rise in suicides involving middle-aged and young women. The rate for middle-aged women rose 63 percent, from 6 to 9.8 per 100,000, from 1999 to 2014. Over the same period, the number of suicides increased among all racial groups except black males.[2]

---

[1] "Suicide Statistics," American Foundation for Suicide Prevention, citing data from the Centers for Disease Control and Prevention Data & Statistics Fatal Injury Report for 2015, https://afsp.org/about-suicide/suicide-statistics/. Also see https://www.nationalcouncildocs.net/wp-content/uploads/2015/10/2015-National-Facts-and-Figures.pdf.

[2] Carina Storrs, "U.S. Suicide Rates Up, Especially among Women, But Down for Black Males," CNN, April 22, 2016, http://www.cnn.com/2016/04/22/health/suicide-rates-rise/.

According to the World Health Organization (WHO),[3] an estimated 804,000 people committed suicide in 2012, for a global age-standardized suicide rate of 11.4 per 100,000. Over the past 45 years, according to WHO, global suicide rates have risen by 60 percent. WHO also estimates that, on average, one person dies by suicide every 40 seconds somewhere in the world.[4]

A. THE BIBLE'S TEACHING ABOUT MURDER ALSO PROHIBITS SUICIDE

When God speaks in the Ten Commandments and says, "You shall not murder" (Ex. 20:13; repeated in Rom. 13:9 and elsewhere), he uses the Hebrew verb *rātsakh*, which refers to what we today would call "murder," and also can refer to causing the death of another person through negligence or carelessness (see discussion of *rātsakh* above, p. 505). But if it applies to murdering *another* person, then it seems evident that it would also apply to murdering ourselves. Therefore, "You shall not murder" is also a prohibition that means, "You shall not murder yourself."[5]

An earlier passage that long predates the Mosaic covenant affirms this moral principle:

> And for your lifeblood I will require a reckoning: from every beast I will require it and from man. From his fellow man I will require a reckoning for the life of man.
>
> Whoever sheds the blood of man,
>   by man shall his blood be shed,
> for God made man in his own image. (Gen. 9:5–6)

To "shed the blood of man" is an Old Testament expression for willfully taking the life of another person, and for that crime God here imposes the most severe of all human penalties, the taking of the life of the murderer (see discussion above, p. 507). While that is not possible in the case of a suicide, for the murderer is already dead, the principle that God views this as a serious moral wrong remains. It is significant that this passage is at the very foundation of human society following the flood, and therefore we can rightly understand it as applying to the entire human race.

Taking these two passages together, we can conclude that suicide is morally wrong

---

[3] "Global Health Observatory Data, Suicide Rates (per 100,000 population)," World Health Organization, http://www.who.int/gho/mental_health/suicide_rates/en/.

[4] "International Suicide Statistics," Suicide.org, citing data from the World Health Organization, www.suicide.org/international-suicide-statistics.html.

[5] The Westminster Larger Catechism interprets this commandment as explicitly prohibiting suicide. It asks, "What are the sins forbidden in the sixth commandment?" and the first words in the answer are these: "The sins forbidden in the sixth commandment are, *all taking away the life of ourselves*, or of others, except in case of public justice, lawful war, or necessary defense" (Question 136).

in the eyes of God and violates his commands against willful taking of innocent human life (murder). It is not only wrong to murder another human being, it is also wrong to murder yourself.

B. SCRIPTURE NEVER VIEWS SUICIDE POSITIVELY

The narrative examples of suicide in the Bible show that it is often the last act of despair of a person who has turned against God and his purposes. For example:

1. Saul. After King Saul "rejected the word of the LORD," the prophet Samuel told him, "The LORD has rejected you from being king over Israel" (1 Sam. 15:26). Saul then exhibited increasingly irrational and hostile behavior toward David, repeatedly seeking to kill David (see 1 Samuel 18–28). Instead of experiencing victory over the Philistine armies as a result of God's protection, Saul was defeated by the Philistines and was about to suffer a humiliating death at their hands. Therefore, Saul fell on his own sword, taking his own life:[6]

> The battle pressed hard against Saul, and the archers found him, and he was badly wounded by the archers. Then Saul said to his armor-bearer, "Draw your sword, and thrust me through with it, lest these uncircumcised come and thrust me through, and mistreat me." But his armor-bearer would not, for he feared greatly. Therefore *Saul took his own sword and fell upon it*. And when his armor-bearer saw that Saul was dead, he also fell upon his sword and died with him. (1 Sam. 31:3–5)

2. Ahithophel. David's trusted adviser Ahithophel deserted him and joined Absalom's wrongful rebellion (see 2 Sam. 15:12, 31). But Absalom did not follow Ahithophel's counsel, and Ahithophel soon realized that Absalom's cause was lost and he would be defeated. Therefore, in despair at choosing the losing side and realizing that he had wrongfully betrayed King David, Ahithophel committed suicide:

> When Ahithophel saw that his counsel was not followed, he saddled his donkey and went off home to his own city. *He set his house in order and hanged himself*, and he died and was buried in the tomb of his father. (2 Sam. 17:23)

3. Judas. When Judas experienced bitter regret that he had betrayed Jesus, he took his own life:

> Then when Judas, his betrayer, saw that Jesus was condemned, he changed his mind and brought back the thirty pieces of silver to the chief priests and the

---

[6] There is a supplemental narrative in 2 Sam. 1:1–16, in which an Amalekite soldier claims that he killed Saul at Saul's request. Whether that is accurate or a self-serving embellishment of the facts, Saul at least attempted suicide and was the primary cause of his own death. See discussion at p. 589.

elders, saying, "I have sinned by betraying innocent blood." They said, "What is that to us? See to it yourself." And throwing down the pieces of silver into the temple, he departed, *and he went and hanged himself.* (Matt. 27:3–5; see also the suicide of Zimri in 1 Kings 16:18–19, as well as the prevention of the suicide of the Philippian jailer in Acts 16:28)

The cumulative force of these passages, along with many biblical passages that serve to honor and protect human life, lead John Jefferson Davis to say, "The biblical attitude toward human life is so affirmative that an explicit condemnation of suicide is unnecessary; its evil is self-evident."[7]

4. Samson's Death Should Not Be Considered Suicide. Samson effectively brought about his own death, but he did it as a last act of self-sacrifice for the sake of his people:

Then Samson called to the LORD and said, "O Lord GOD, please remember me and please strengthen me only this once, O God, that I may be avenged on the Philistines for my two eyes." And Samson grasped the two middle pillars on which the house rested, and he leaned his weight against them, his right hand on the one and his left hand on the other. *And Samson said, "Let me die with the Philistines." Then he bowed with all his strength, and the house fell upon the lords and upon all the people who were in it.* So the dead whom he killed at his death were more than those whom he had killed during his life. (Judg. 16:28–30)

By his sacrifice he brought a giant defeat to the Philistine enemies and a great encouragement to the people of Israel. Thus, Samson's death was similar to that of soldiers in combat who heroically give their lives to save the lives of others. In spite of his earlier shameful conduct, Samson became an example of the teaching of Jesus, "Greater love has no one than this, that someone lay down his life for his friends" (John 15:13). In addition, in sacrificing his life to defeat the Philistines who were oppressing Israel, he in some ways foreshadowed the death of Christ himself.[8]

C. THE GOAL OF SATAN IS TO DESTROY HUMAN BEINGS MADE IN THE IMAGE OF GOD

Scripture tells us that human beings alone out of all of God's creation are given the high status of being made in the "image" and "likeness" of God (see Gen. 1:27; 9:6;

---

[7] John Jefferson Davis, *Evangelical Ethics: Issues Facing the Church Today*, 4th ed. (Phillipsburg, NJ: P&R, 2015), 193.

[8] Robertson McQuilkin and Paul Copan write, "Self-sacrificially laying down one's life for another is not sinful suicide. If it were, God himself would be the guiltiest. No one took Christ's life from him. He laid it down of his own volition (Jn 10:18)." *An Introduction to Biblical Ethics: Walking in the Way of Wisdom*, 3rd ed. (Downers Grove, IL: InterVarsity Press, 2014), 386.

James 3:9). We, then, are the pinnacle of God's creation. Therefore, God requires the strongest punishment for anyone who destroys that image by murdering a human being (see Gen. 9:5–6).

But Satan hates God and hates human beings who are made in the image of God. His goal is to destroy us:

> You are of your father the devil, and your will is to do your father's desires. *He was a murderer from the beginning*, and does not stand in the truth, because there is no truth in him. When he lies, he speaks out of his own character, for he is a liar and the father of lies. (John 8:44)

Therefore, Satan will try to persuade people to commit suicide. For this reason, when people tell me that they "hear voices" telling them to kill themselves, I suspect that in some cases this may be the result of a demonic influence attacking them and seeking to cause them to harm themselves or even take their own lives.[9] (However, in other cases the supposed voices may be amplified self-critical accusations from the person's own mind.)

By contrast, the Holy Spirit dwells within Christians and wants them to glorify God in their bodies, not to destroy their bodies:

> Or do you not know that *your body is a temple of the Holy Spirit within you*, whom you have from God? You are not your own, for you were bought with a price. *So glorify God in your body.* (1 Cor. 6:19–20)[10]

Although a person's circumstances may seem extremely difficult at times, God promises that there is always a solution that is available without giving in to the temptation to sin:

> No temptation has overtaken you that is not common to man. God is faithful, and he will not let you be tempted beyond your ability, but with the temptation he will also provide the way of escape, that you may be able to endure it. (1 Cor. 10:13)

With respect to this verse, John Frame writes, "God never forsakes his children. He never leads them to a situation where sinful self-destruction is the only option (1 Cor. 10:13)."[11]

---

[9] For a discussion of demonic influence in people's lives and a biblical treatment of how Christians should respond, see Wayne Grudem, *Systematic Theology: An Introduction to Biblical Doctrine* (Leicester, UK: Inter-Varsity, and Grand Rapids, MI: Zondervan, 1994), 412–36.

[10] In the context of 1 Corinthians 6, Paul says "your body is a temple of the Holy Spirit" to argue against sexual immorality. But the same principle would also apply to other actions by which we misuse or mistreat our bodies and thereby dishonor this "temple," and it would certainly apply to the destruction of our bodies by suicide.

[11] John M. Frame, *The Doctrine of the Christian Life: A Theology of Lordship* (Phillipsburg, NJ: P&R, 2008), 738.

D. SUICIDE INJURES OTHER PEOPLE DEEPLY

When someone commits suicide, that person's family members and friends experience a deep grief that can remain intense for many years. They can experience great sorrow and pain, intensified by the fact that there is no hope for changing the outcome or (often) for finding in this lifetime any further explanations for the suicide.

Therefore, the person who commits suicide is acting in contradiction to Jesus's command "You shall love your neighbor as yourself" (Matt. 22:39). Someone who takes his or her life is even acting contrary to a rightful love of himself or herself.

Another harmful result from suicide is that sometimes other people follow the person's example and commit suicide as well. This is especially true with highly publicized celebrity suicides,[12] but it can happen within anyone's social network. Therefore, one suicide can lead to the destruction of several other lives and multiply grief and sorrow among many other families and networks of friends.

E. CAN PEOPLE WHO COMMIT SUICIDE BE FORGIVEN?

1. Yes, Certainly, If They Were Believers in Christ. While it is true that taking one's own life is a sin against God, we will all remain sinners in need of forgiveness until the time of our deaths.

> If we say we have no sin, we deceive ourselves, and the truth is not in us. (1 John 1:8)

Therefore, the question is not whether someone was a sinner at the moment he or she died (for we all will still be sinners when we die), but whether that person had truly trusted in Christ for forgiveness of sins.

If the person had believed the gospel and genuinely trusted in Christ, then the familiar passages having to do with Christ's death for our sins and the gift of salvation are very appropriate here, assuring us that even the sin of suicide can be forgiven:

> For the wages of sin is death, but the free gift of God is eternal life in Christ Jesus our Lord. (Rom. 6:23)

> For I delivered to you as of first importance what I also received: that *Christ died for our sins* in accordance with the Scriptures. (1 Cor. 15:3)

> And this is the will of him who sent me, that I should lose nothing of all that he has given me, but raise it up on the last day. For this is the will of my Father,

---

[12] See Margot Sanger-Katz, "The Science behind Suicide Contagion," *The New York Times*, Aug. 13, 2014, http://www.nytimes.com/2014/08/14/upshot/the-science-behind-suicide-contagion.html.

that everyone who looks on the Son and believes in him should have eternal life, and I will raise him up on the last day. (John 6:39–40)

For I am sure that neither death nor life, nor angels nor rulers, nor things present nor things to come, nor powers, nor height nor depth, nor anything else in all creation, will be able to separate us from the love of God in Christ Jesus our Lord. (Rom. 8:38–39)

2. Roman Catholic Teaching. Sometimes there is confusion about the teaching of the Roman Catholic Church on this issue. This is perhaps due to earlier Roman Catholic teaching that would not grant a funeral Mass or church burial to someone who had committed suicide.[13] However, the current *Catechism of the Catholic Church* teaches the following:

We should not despair of the eternal salvation of persons who have taken their own lives. By ways known to him alone, God can provide the opportunity for salutary repentance. The Church prays for persons who have taken their own lives.[14]

F. HOW TO RESPOND IF SOMEONE ASKS, "IF I COMMIT SUICIDE, WILL I GO TO HEAVEN?"

Such a question must be taken very seriously. You do not want to say anything that would encourage someone to commit suicide or would appear to give permission for it.

It is important to ask about what circumstances have led the person to ask this question. Sometimes intense feelings of sadness, regret, frustration, confusion, and hopelessness prompt people to contemplate and even attempt suicide. In other cases, there may be a desire for revenge or a desire to escape from shame or intense pain.

After listening sympathetically and praying for God to give you insight into the cause of this question, it is important to seek to somehow turn the person's despair into at least a glimmer of hope.

If the person professes to be a Christian believer, often the words of God in Scripture will themselves bring hope to the person's heart in a way that no merely human words can do. Psalm 42 can be very useful for reading aloud. And the following familiar passages may be helpful:

---

[13] A change to canon law in 1983 permitted funeral rites, including Mass and burial in consecrated grounds, for those who die by suicide, as suicide was removed from the list of reasons why a funeral Mass or Catholic burial would be denied. See "Code of Canon Law," The Holy See, Chap. II, http://www.vatican.va/archive/ENG1104/__P4C.HTM.

[14] *Catechism of the Catholic Church*, 2nd ed. (New York: Doubleday, 1997), para. 2283 (609), http://www.vatican.va/archive/ENG0015/__P7Z.HTM.

Do not be anxious about anything, but in everything by prayer and supplication with thanksgiving let your requests be made known to God. And the peace of God, which surpasses all understanding, will guard your hearts and your minds in Christ Jesus. (Phil. 4:6–7)

No temptation has overtaken you that is not common to man. God is faithful, and he will not let you be tempted beyond your ability, but with the temptation he will also provide the way of escape, that you may be able to endure it. (1 Cor. 10:13; this verse should encourage the person that God will always give hope for a way out of very difficult circumstances)

And we know that for those who love God all things work together for good, for those who are called according to his purpose. (Rom. 8:28)

If the person does not profess to be a Christian believer or if you doubt that the person has come to genuine faith, then it is important to seek and to pray for an opportunity to present the good news of the forgiveness of sins and the offer of salvation in Jesus Christ, for the gospel is especially powerful in circumstances such as this.

However, all of this counsel must be presented with great sensitivity, and only when it seems that the person is at least somewhat ready to hear it. Attempting to force cheerfulness on a person in despair can make the situation worse if it is done in an insensitive way:

Whoever sings songs to a heavy heart
    is like one who takes off a garment on a cold day,
    and like vinegar on soda. (Prov. 25:20)

Finally, in addition to giving help and counsel yourself, if there is any indication that the person is continuing to contemplate suicide, it would be wise to seek the help of a trained counselor (or, in especially urgent cases, to seek intervention by calling emergency care at 911 in the United States or a suicide-prevention hotline, such as the National Suicide Prevention Lifeline, 1-800-273-8255).

QUESTIONS FOR PERSONAL APPLICATION

1. How has this chapter changed the way you understand suicide?
2. Are there any practical ways in which Christians can comfort and encourage those who have lost a loved one to suicide?
3. Do you know of any friends or relatives who you think might be tempted to commit suicide? What might you do to help them make a different decision?

SPECIAL TERMS

None

BIBLIOGRAPHY

Sections in Other Ethics Texts

(see complete bibliographical data, p. 64)

Feinberg, John and Paul, 187–88, 205–7
Frame, 738–39
Geisler, 43, 172–73
Kaiser, 139–50
McQuilkin and Copan, 384–87

Other Works

Blocher, Henri. *Suicide*. Translated by Roger Van Dyk. Downers Grove, IL: InterVarsity Press, 1972.

Chamberlain, Paul C. *Final Wishes: A Cautionary Tale on Death, Dignity & Physician-Assisted Suicide*. Downers Grove, IL: InterVarsity Press, 2000.

Demy, Timothy J., and Gary Stewart. *Suicide: A Christian Response*. Grand Rapids, MI: Kregel, 1998.

Dyck, Arthur J. *Life's Worth: The Case against Assisted Suicide*. Grand Rapids, MI: Eerdmans, 2002.

Harris, B. "Suicide." In *New Dictionary of Christian Ethics and Pastoral Theology*, edited by David J. Atkinson and David H. Field, 825–26. Leicester, UK: Inter-Varsity, and Downers Grove, IL: InterVarsity Press, 1995.

Moreland, James Porter, and Norman L. Geisler. *The Life and Death Debate: Moral Issues of Our Time*. New York: Greenwood Press, 1990.

Moreland, James Porter, and Scott B. Rae. *Body & Soul: Human Nature & the Crisis in Ethics*. Downers Grove, IL: InterVarsity Press, 2000.

Stewart, Gary P., William R. Cutrer, Timothy J. Demy, Dónal P. O'Mathúna, Paige C. Cunningham, John F. Kilner, and Linda K. Bevington. *Basic Questions on Suicide and Euthanasia: Are They Ever Right?* BioBasics Series. Grand Rapids, MI: Kregel, 1998.

Tada, Joni Eareckson. *When Is It Right to Die? A Comforting and Surprising Look at Death and Dying*, updated ed. Grand Rapids, MI: Zondervan, 2018.

Wennberg, Robert N. *Terminal Choices: Euthanasia, Suicide, and the Right to Die*. Grand Rapids, MI: Eerdmans, 1990.

SCRIPTURE MEMORY PASSAGE

Philippians 4:6–7: Do not be anxious about anything, but in everything by prayer and supplication with thanksgiving let your requests be made known to God. And the peace of God, which surpasses all understanding, will guard your hearts and your minds in Christ Jesus.

HYMN

"What a Friend We Have in Jesus"

What a Friend we have in Jesus, all our sins and griefs to bear!
What a privilege to carry ev'rything to God in prayer!
O what peace we often forfeit, O what needless pain we bear,
All because we do not carry ev'rything to God in prayer!

Have we trials and temptations? Is there trouble anywhere?
We should never be discouraged, take it to the Lord in prayer.
Can we find a friend so faithful who will all our sorrows share?
Jesus knows our ev'ry weakness, take it to the Lord in prayer.

Are we weak and heavy laden, cumbered with a load of care?
Precious Savior, still our refuge, take it to the Lord in prayer;
Do thy friends despise, forsake thee? Take it to the Lord in prayer!
In His arms He'll take and shield thee; thou wilt find a solace there.

AUTHOR: JOSEPH SCRIVEN, 1819–1886

Chapter 24

AGING AND DEATH

What are the blessings that come with aging?
Is it right for Christians to spend money on hair dye or cosmetic surgery?
Why is it important to have a will and other end-of-life documents?
What about cremation?

The gradual process of aging provides frequent reminders that we are going to die. Therefore, it is appropriate to consider the topics of aging and death in this section, which is concerned about issues related to the protection of life.

As we grow older, it is inevitable that our bodies will grow weaker. This is true even for champion athletes—no athlete has ever failed to retire from the most competitive skill levels of professional sports. In the midst of our lives, we begin to experience increasingly frequent reminders that death eventually is coming. Modern Western culture seeks to avoid thinking about aging and death, and some people put immense amounts of money and time into attempts to hide the signs of aging and to appear younger than they really are.

How should Christians approach this phase of life? The perspective of Christians regarding aging and death should be far different from that of the secular culture in which we live. We do not have to fear death as unbelievers do, because Jesus came to earth to triumph over Satan and "deliver all those *who through fear of death* were subject to lifelong slavery" (Heb. 2:15).

A. UNDERSTANDING AGING AND DEATH

1. Aging and Death Are the Result of Sin. Human beings experience aging and death because of Adam's sin:

Sin came into the world through one man, *and death through sin*, and so death spread to all men because all sinned. (Rom. 5:12)

For as by a man came death, by a man has come also the resurrection of the dead. For *as in Adam all die*, so also in Christ shall all be made alive. (1 Cor. 15:21–22)

God warned Adam that he would impose the penalty of death in the case of disobedience:

But of the tree of the knowledge of good and evil you shall not eat, for in the day that you eat of it *you shall surely die*. (Gen. 2:17)

When Adam and Eve ate from the tree, God, in his justice, pronounced this curse upon them:

By the sweat of your face
    you shall eat bread,
till you return to the ground,
    for out of it you were taken;
for you are dust,
    and to dust you shall return. (Gen. 3:19)

However, the penalty of death was not imposed instantly when Adam and Eve sinned. Instead, they experienced it gradually as they began to age and eventually grew old and died (Gen. 5:5).

2. Death Is Not a Punishment for Christians. Paul affirms that there is "no condemnation for those who are in Christ Jesus" (Rom. 8:1). All the penalty for our sins has been paid. Therefore, even though Christians still die, we should not view the death of Christians as a punishment from God or as a penalty for our sins.[1] The penalty of death no longer applies to us—neither in terms of physical death nor of spiritual death (separation from God). So there must be another reason why Christians die.[2]

3. Aging and Death Are the Final Outcome of Living in a Fallen World. In his great wisdom, God decided that he would not apply to us the benefits of Christ's redemptive

---

[1] Paul saw the death of some Corinthian Christians who had been abusing the Lord's Supper (1 Cor. 11:30) as a disciplining or chastening process, not a condemnation. He says, "When we are judged by the Lord, we are disciplined so that we may not be condemned along with the world" (1 Cor. 11:32). (In this discussion I am using the word *punishment* to mean retribution from God that is intended to do us harm, and *discipline* to mean hardship through which God intends to do us good.)

[2] The material from here to the end of this section has been adapted from Wayne Grudem, *Systematic Theology: An Introduction to Biblical Doctrine* (Leicester, UK: Inter-Varsity, and Grand Rapids, MI: Zondervan, 1994), 810–13, with permission of the publishers.

work all at once. Rather, he chose to apply the benefits of salvation to us gradually over time. Similarly, he chose not to remove all evil from the world immediately, but to wait until the final judgment and the establishment of the new heaven and new earth. In short, we still live in a fallen world and our experience of salvation is still incomplete. Death will be the last aspect of the fallen world to be removed. Paul says:

> Then comes the end, when he delivers the kingdom to God the Father after destroying every rule and every authority and power. For he must reign until he has put all his enemies under his feet. *The last enemy to be destroyed is death.* (1 Cor. 15:24–26)

When Christ returns:

> Then shall come to pass the saying that is written:
>
> "Death is swallowed up in victory.
> O death, where is your victory?
>   O death, where is your sting?" (1 Cor. 15:54–55)

So death remains a reality in the lives of Christians. Although death does not come to us as a *penalty* for our individual sins (for that has been paid by Christ), it does come to us as a *result of living in a fallen world*, where the effects of sin have not all been removed.

Likewise, we experience other results of the fall that harm our bodies and reveal the presence of death in the world. Christians, like non-Christians, experience aging, illnesses, injuries, and natural disasters. God often answers prayers to deliver Christians (and also non-Christians) from some of these effects of the fall for a time (thereby revealing the nature of his coming kingdom), but Christians eventually experience all of these things to some measure, and, until Christ returns, all of us will grow old and die. The "last enemy" has not yet been destroyed. And God has chosen to allow us to experience death before we gain all the benefits of salvation that have been earned for us.

4. God Uses the Experiences of Aging and Death to Complete Our Sanctification. As we discussed above, Christians never have to pay any penalty for sin, for that has all been taken by Christ (Rom. 8:1). Therefore, when we do experience pain and suffering in this life, we should never think it is because God is *punishing* us (for our harm). Sometimes suffering is simply a *result of living in a sinful, fallen world*, but sometimes God is *disciplining* us (for our good) through suffering, and sometimes he is allowing us to experience hardship as an *opportunity to express our faith in him and find our joy in him* (see James 1:2–3; 1 Pet. 1:6–9). In all cases, Romans 8:28 assures us that "for those who love God all things work together for good, for those who are called according to his purpose."

The challenge that Jesus gives to the church in Smyrna could be given to every believer: "*Be faithful unto death*, and I will give you the crown of life" (Rev. 2:10). Paul says his goal in life is that he may become like Christ: "[I desire] that I may know him and the power of his resurrection, and may share his sufferings, *becoming like him in his death*" (Phil. 3:10). He thought about the way in which Jesus died, and he made it his goal to exemplify the same characteristics in his life when it came time for him to die—that in whatever circumstances he found himself, he, like Christ, would continue obeying God, trusting God, forgiving others, and caring for the needs of those around him, thus bringing glory to God even in his death. Therefore, when in prison, without knowing whether he would die there or come out alive, he could still say, "It is my eager expectation and hope that I will not be at all ashamed, but that with full courage now as always *Christ will be honored* in my body, whether by life *or by death*" (Phil. 1:20).

This understanding of aging and death should be a great encouragement to us. It should take away from us the fear of growing old and dying that haunts the minds of unbelievers (cf. Heb. 2:15). Nevertheless, although God will bring good to us through this process, we must still remember that aging and death are not natural; they are not right; and, because of sin, they mar the perfect creation that God originally made. Death is an enemy, something that Christ will finally destroy (1 Cor. 15:26).

5. Our Experience of Death Completes Our Union with Christ. Another reason why God allows us to experience death, rather than taking us immediately to heaven when we become Christians is that through death we imitate Christ in what he did and thereby experience closer union with him. Paul can say that we are fellow heirs with Christ "provided we *suffer with him* in order that we may also be glorified with him" (Rom. 8:17). And Peter tells his readers not to be surprised at the fiery testing that comes on them, but encourages them, "Rejoice insofar as *you share Christ's sufferings*, that you may also rejoice and be glad when his glory is revealed" (1 Pet. 4:13). Union with Christ in suffering includes union with him in death (see Phil. 3:10). Peter writes, "Christ also suffered for you, leaving you an example, so that you might follow in his steps" (1 Pet. 2:21).

6. Obeying God Is More Important Than Preserving Our Own Lives. If God uses the experience of death to deepen our trust in him and to strengthen our obedience to him, then it is important that we remember that the world's goal of preserving one's physical life at all costs is not the highest goal for a Christian—obedience to God and faithfulness to him in every circumstance are far more important. Paul could say, "I am ready not only to be imprisoned but even to die in Jerusalem for the name of the Lord Jesus" (Acts 21:13; cf. 25:11). He told the Ephesian elders, "I do not account my life of any value nor as precious to myself, if only I may finish my course and the ministry that I received from the Lord Jesus, to testify to the gospel of the grace of God" (20:24). It was this conviction—that obedience to God is far more important than the preservation of life—that gave Paul courage to go back into the city of Lystra after he had just been stoned and left for dead (Acts 14:20), and then to return there again shortly thereafter (vv. 21–22). He endured many sufferings and dangers (2 Cor. 11:23–27), often risking his life, in order to obey Christ fully. Therefore, he could say at the end of his life, with a note of great triumph, "The time of my departure has come. *I have fought the good fight,* I have finished the race, I have kept the faith" (2 Tim. 4:6–7).

This conviction empowered Old Testament saints to accept martyrdom rather than sin: "Some were tortured, refusing to accept release, so that they might rise again to a better life" (literally, "might obtain a better resurrection," Heb. 11:35). It also gave Peter and the other apostles courage, when they faced the threat of death, to say, "We must obey God rather than men" (Acts 5:29). We also read that there will be rejoicing in heaven when the faithful saints have conquered the Devil "by the blood of the Lamb and by the word of their testimony, for *they loved not their lives even unto death*" (Rev. 12:11).

The persuasion that we may honor the Lord even in our death, and that faithfulness to him is far more important than preserving our lives, has given courage and motivation to martyrs throughout the history of the church. When faced with a choice of preserving their lives and sinning, or giving up their lives and being faithful, they chose to give up their lives—"*They loved not their lives even unto death.*" Even if we live in countries where there is now little persecution and little likelihood of martyrdom, it would still be good for us to fix this truth in our minds, for if we are willing to die for faithfulness to God, we will find it easier to give up everything else for the sake of Christ as well.

B. SOME BLESSINGS THAT COME WITH AGING

As difficult as the aging process can be, it also provides some opportunities that should be seen as blessings in the Christian life:

1. An Opportunity for Greater Trust in Christ for Effectiveness in Ministry and in the Ordinary Conduct of Life. The apostle Paul experienced some kind of weakness or affliction that God did not remove, because he writes about a "thorn . . . in the flesh" (2 Cor. 12:7). He does not give any further explanation of it, but he says that he asked God three times to remove it (v. 8). Instead of removing this "thorn," God answered Paul: "My grace is sufficient for you, for *my power is made perfect in weakness*" (v. 9a). Paul concluded:

> Therefore I will boast all the more gladly of my weaknesses, so that the power of Christ may rest upon me. For the sake of Christ, then, I am content with weaknesses, insults, hardships, persecutions, and calamities. For when I am weak, then I am strong. (2 Cor. 12:9b–10)

The aging process, as it causes our bodies to become weaker, provides a similar kind of opportunity for us today to discover how Christ's "power is made perfect in weakness." This means that advanced years for a Christian might mean the exciting discovery of a more and more powerful work of God through his or her ministry to others, with great fruitfulness in the work of the kingdom of God.

2. An Opportunity for Greater Growth in Holiness of Life, Spiritual Maturity, and Prayer. Paul faced numerous difficulties and hardships, including some measure of increasing weakness of his body, for he said, "Our outer self is wasting away" (2 Cor. 4:16; see also 2 Tim. 4:6–7, written later in his life). Yet he was not discouraged, but wrote this remarkable statement:

> So we do not lose heart. *Though our outer self is wasting away, our inner self is being renewed day by day.* For this light momentary affliction is preparing for us an eternal weight of glory beyond all comparison, as we look not to the things that are seen but to the things that are unseen. For the things that are seen are transient, but the things that are unseen are eternal. (2 Cor. 4:16–18)

Such inner renewal would have had many positive effects in Paul's spiritual life, and should bring benefits in our lives as well. As "our inner self is being renewed day by day," we can look forward to increased growth in personal holiness and in closeness to God in prayer.

Therefore, as we think of the prospect of growing older, we should be encouraged in the hope that our lives will be like "the path of the righteous" that is "like the light of dawn, which shines brighter and brighter until full day" (Prov. 4:18).

3. An Opportunity to Believe That God Will Reveal a Proper Response to Every Difficult Situation. As I explained in chapter 7, Christians in general should have confidence that God will never put them in a situation in which all their potential choices are sinful and they must pick "the lesser sin." Rather, God is faithful in his ordering of our circumstances each day, so that even in difficult situations, we will always have a "way of escape" (1 Cor. 10:13) by which we can respond in a way that is pleasing to God.

The aging process provides its own special set of circumstances that give us opportunities to trust in God in the midst of new and unforeseen hardships that must be dealt with in appropriate ways. Once again, the proper response in each such situation is to settle in our minds that *God has a right solution for this circumstance,* and then to ask him for wisdom (see James 1:5–6) to understand the solution.

The weakening of our bodies also provides an opportunity to ask God that the blessing that Moses bestowed on the tribe of Asher may also be true of us: "As your days, so shall your strength be" (Deut. 33:25). We should ask that we would continue to have enough strength to fulfill our changing responsibilities each day until we die.

4. An Opportunity to Be Grateful for the Dignity That Belongs to Physical Signs of Aging. As our bodies grow older, they will show numerous physical signs of aging—loss of strength, gray hair (or loss of hair), more wrinkles, and so forth. But the author of Proverbs saw some dignity in these things:

> The glory of young men is their strength, *but the splendor of old men is their gray hair.* (20:29)

The *ESV Study Bible* note on this verse contains an astute observation:

> **Gray hair** (cf. 16:31) is a concrete example of a general truth: many of the physical evidences of old age have a dignity and splendor of their own, often representing experience, maturity, wisdom, and holiness.[3]

C. SOME DIFFICULTIES OF AGING

1. Aging Still Brings Difficulties, and Death Is Still an Enemy. I would not be treating the biblical text fairly if I left the impression that Scripture views aging and death as unmitigated blessings. It does not. Yes, God can and does bring to us many of the blessings mentioned above during the process of aging, and this is a result of his wonderful grace. But the fact remains that death is an enemy that has not yet been destroyed, and it will only be destroyed at the last trumpet, when Christ returns: "The last enemy to be destroyed is death" (1 Cor. 15:26).

Paul understands that we experience pain in this life while we long to have our resurrection bodies, for he says that "we ourselves, who have the firstfruits of the Spirit, *groan inwardly as we wait eagerly for* adoption as sons, *the redemption of our bodies*" (Rom. 8:23). He compares our present earthly bodies to "tents" in which we desire to put on our renewed bodies: "For in this tent we groan, longing to put on our heavenly dwelling" (2 Cor. 5:2).

Therefore, while God does promise many blessings that we can seek and expect to receive from him in the process of aging, yet as we grow older we will increasingly long for those perfect resurrection bodies that Christ will give to us when he returns, bodies that will exhibit an amazing contrast with our current weak bodies. For Paul says our old and weak bodies that will die and be buried are like seeds that are planted in the ground and that then produce amazing plants as a result of "dying":

> So is it with the resurrection of the dead. What is sown is perishable; what is raised is imperishable. It is sown in dishonor; it is raised in glory. It is sown in weakness; it is raised in power. (1 Cor. 15:42–43)

2. Should Christians Use Hair Dye, Dental Braces, and Cosmetic Surgery to Hide the Effects of Aging? Since aging and death were imposed by God as a curse after the sin of Adam and Eve, the loss of physical attractiveness that people experience as they grow older should also be considered a result of the fall. And just as it is right to try to alleviate other results of the fall (for example, we seek to alleviate pain in childbearing and seek to remove thorns and thistles from our agricultural fields, reversing Gen. 3:16, 18), so it is right to attempt to alleviate *at least some* of the physical unattractiveness that has come as a result of the fall and that increases as we grow older.

---

[3] *ESV Study Bible* (Wheaton, IL: Crossway, 2008), 1170.

God has put within us an instinct to delight in beauty rather than ugliness, and while the physical beauty of a rebellious sinner can be a deceptive danger (see Prov. 6:25; 11:22), there are several biblical examples of godly delight in the physical beauty of God's righteous people (see Est. 2:7; Job 42:15; Ps. 45:2, 11; Song 1:15–16). In addition, God's temple and his city are beautiful (Pss. 48:2; 50:2; 96:6), and God himself is magnificent in his beauty (see Ps. 27:4; Isa. 33:17). Therefore, it is not inherently wrong for human beings to desire beauty or to desire to be attractive, handsome, or beautiful in appearance.

In addition, earthly physical beauty brings a measure of joy to us because we sense in it a hint of the exceptionally beautiful kingdom of God when it is fully manifested, when we will receive perfect resurrection bodies that are remarkable in their physical beauty because they will be "raised in glory" (1 Cor. 15:43). When the New Jerusalem comes down out of heaven from God, it will be exceedingly beautiful, "prepared as a bride adorned for her husband" (Rev. 21:2). The city will have beauty that cannot be fully described in this age, but that will resemble and surpass the beauty of precious jewels (see vv. 10–27). Moreover, Paul's command for us to think on "whatever is lovely" (Phil. 4:8; Greek, *prosphilēs*, "pleasing, agreeable, lovely") certainly includes things of physical beauty.

However, there is a danger of placing excessive emphasis on physical beauty in this age, for things are not always what they seem outwardly, and "charm is deceitful, *and beauty is vain*" (Prov. 31:30). Therefore, while there is value and goodness in physical beauty, it should not be the main focus of our efforts to be attractive to others, which should instead be the excellence of our character and the good works that we do for the Lord and for others:

> Do not let your adorning be external—the braiding of hair and the putting on of gold jewelry, or the clothing you wear—but let your adorning be *the hidden person of the heart with the imperishable beauty of a gentle and quiet spirit*, which in God's sight is very precious. For this is how the holy women who hoped in God used to adorn themselves, by submitting to their own husbands, as Sarah obeyed Abraham, calling him lord. And you are her children, if you do good and do not fear anything that is frightening. (1 Pet. 3:3–6; see also 1 Tim. 2:9–10)

If this caution is heeded, and if people do not place excessive emphasis on physical beauty or wastefully spend too much money pursuing it, then it seems to me that some efforts to improve physical attractiveness are morally good (but often optional) choices.[4]

For example, getting a haircut, combing or brushing one's hair, and shaving (for men)

---

[4] People might imagine that a concern with outward physical beauty is only a feature of modern society, but items such as nose rings and earrings were known even in primitive societies many centuries ago (see, for example, Gen. 24:47; Ezek. 16:12).

are ways of altering the "natural" appearance of our bodies, but they seem to me to be good and wise things to do. Similarly, if a person can afford it without neglecting or distorting other stewardship responsibilities, and if he or she wishes to do so, taking similar actions to improve the person's physical appearance seems to me a morally good thing.

This also applies to other "cosmetic" actions. If a person can afford it and wishes to do so, I think it can be a morally good (though optional) choice to use dye to color one's hair[5] or to get braces to straighten a person's crooked teeth. In Arizona, where I live, with its year-round intense sunshine, it is common for people to visit a dermatologist periodically for the removal of skin blemishes by instantly freezing them with liquid nitrogen—partially to prevent skin cancer, but partially also for cosmetic reasons.

At least some kinds of cosmetic surgery seem to me to fall into this same general category, although the matter of financial expense can quickly become more significant here. In addition, the person contemplating cosmetic surgery must honestly evaluate his or her heart motives in light of 1 Peter 3:3–6 (quoted above). There is certainly nothing wrong with a moderate effort to improve one's physical appearance, but the pursuit of a "perfect" body or a continual desire to disguise one's actual age can easily become an idol, turning our hearts away from God and the things he wants us to focus on.[6]

In conclusion, I see no moral objections to these and other similar procedures so *long as* these expenses do not represent an excessive focus on physical beauty to the exclusion of spiritual beauty (see 1 Pet. 3:3–6), and so long as the person is able to afford such expenditures while remaining faithful to other budgetary responsibilities of good stewardship. The principle of the sufficiency of Scripture should apply here: we should not pass judgment on or prohibit what Scripture does not itself prohibit. In this matter, the principle that Paul applied to disputes over foods and days of the week is relevant:

> Why do you pass judgment on your brother? Or you, why do you despise your brother? For we will all stand before the judgment seat of God. (Rom. 14:10)

D. HOW SHOULD WE THINK AND FEEL ABOUT OUR OWN DEATH AND THE DEATHS OF OTHERS?

1. We Should Not Be Fearful about Our Own Death. According to the New Testament, we should view our own death not with fear but with joy at the prospect of going to

---

[5] However, the dignity that attaches to "gray hair" should also be considered; see my comment above about Prov. 16:31.

[6] In the area where I live in Arizona, there are many plastic surgeons, leading me to conclude that plastic surgery for cosmetic purposes is common. While I have no overall moral objection to plastic surgery (any more than I have an objection to dental braces for crooked teeth), it strikes me as sad when I see someone whose evidently artificial face gives the appearance of multiple plastic surgeries carried out in a futile attempt to look 40 instead of 70. What is the purpose? Actions taken to improve one's appearance need at least to be distinguished from actions taken to disguise one's age, and the question of whether this is a wise use of one's money also needs to be honestly addressed in each specific situation.

be with Christ. Paul says, "We would rather be away from the body and at home with the Lord" (2 Cor. 5:8).[7] When he was in prison, facing the possibility of execution, he could say:

> For to me to live is Christ, and *to die is gain*. If I am to live in the flesh, that means fruitful labor for me. Yet which I shall choose I cannot tell. I am hard pressed between the two. *My desire is to depart and be with Christ*, for that is far better. (Phil. 1:21–23)

Likewise, the apostle John wrote:

> And I heard a voice from heaven saying, "Write this: Blessed are the dead who die in the Lord from now on." "Blessed indeed," says the Spirit, "that they may rest from their labors, for their deeds follow them!" (Rev. 14:13)

Believers need have no fear of death, therefore, for Scripture assures us that not even "death" will "separate us from the love of God in Christ Jesus our Lord" (Rom. 8:38–39; cf. Ps. 23:4). In fact, Jesus died to "deliver all those who through fear of death were subject to lifelong slavery" (Heb. 2:15).[8] This verse reminds us that a clear testimony to our lack of fear of death will provide a strong witness for Christians in a world that tries to avoid talking about death and has no answer for it.

2. It Is Right for Us to Experience Both Grief and Joy When Loved Ones Die. Sometimes Christians might wonder if weeping and expressing sorrow when friends or relatives die shows a lack of faith. Should we just to try to be strong and restrain our emotions?

Jesus himself provided an answer by his sorrow when he came to the home of Mary and Martha, whose brother, Jesus's friend Lazarus, had recently died. We read, "Jesus wept" (John 11:35). He felt sorrow at the pain that Lazarus had experienced and sorrow at the loss of fellowship with Lazarus that Mary and Martha—and he himself—were experiencing. No doubt he also felt deep grief at the fact that death existed at all in God's creation and among God's own people. He expressed his sorrow so openly that the Jewish people who were watching exclaimed, "See how he loved him!" (v. 36).

There are other examples in Scripture as well. After Stephen had been stoned for his faithful witness to Christ, "Devout men buried Stephen and made *great lamentation* over him" (Acts 8:2). These devout Christians had no doubt that Stephen was in heaven with Jesus. They had seen how, just before he died, Stephen "gazed into heaven and saw the glory of God, and Jesus standing at the right hand of God" (7:55). And then he had exclaimed:

---

[7] The material from here to the end of this section has been adapted from Grudem, *Systematic Theology*, 813–16, with permission of the publishers.

[8] Louis Berkhof is certainly correct to say that the burial of Jesus "did not merely serve to prove that Jesus was really dead, but also to remove the terrors of the grave for the redeemed and to sanctify the grave for them." *Systematic Theology*, 4th ed. (Grand Rapids, MI: Eerdmans, 1941), 340.

> Behold, I see the heavens opened, and the Son of Man standing at the right hand of God. (Acts 7:56)

As Stephen was dying, he cried out, "Lord Jesus, receive my spirit" (Acts 7:59).

These faithful Christians did not doubt that *Stephen was at that moment in the presence of Jesus* in heaven, and rejoicing. But they still "made great lamentation over him" (Acts 8:2). They visibly and publicly expressed their grief at what Stephen had suffered and at the fact that they would have wonderful fellowship with him no longer.

Paul did not tell the Thessalonian Christians not to grieve *at all* over those who had died, but he wrote to them "that you may *not grieve as others do who have no hope*" (1 Thess. 4:13).[9] The Thessalonians were not to grieve in the same way, with the same bitter despair, as unbelievers, "those who have no hope." This indicates that the sorrow that we feel at the death of believers should also be mingled with hope and joy. Paul assured them that Christ "died for us so that whether we are awake or asleep we might live with him" (5:10), and thereby he encouraged them that those who have died have gone to be with the Lord. That is why Scripture says, "*Blessed are the dead who die in the Lord from now on* . . . that they may rest from their labors" (Rev. 14:13). Scripture even tells us, "Precious in the sight of the LORD is the death of his saints" (Ps. 116:15).

Therefore, though we have sorrow when Christian friends and relatives die, we also can say with Scripture, "O death, where is your victory? O death, where is your sting? . . . Thanks be to God, who gives us the victory through our Lord Jesus Christ" (1 Cor. 15:55–57). Our mourning should be mixed with worship of God and thanksgiving for the life of the loved one who has died.

The examples of David and Job teach us that worship is especially important at such times. When David's child died, he stopped praying that the child would recover and worshiped God: "Then David arose from the earth and washed and anointed himself and changed his clothes. And he went into the house of the LORD *and worshiped*" (2 Sam. 12:20).

Job did the same when he heard of the death of his 10 children:

> Then Job arose and tore his robe and shaved his head and fell on the ground *and worshiped*. And he said, "Naked I came from my mother's womb, and naked shall I return. The LORD gave, and the LORD has taken away; blessed be the name of the LORD." (Job 1:20–21)

3. Sorrow at the Death of Unbelievers. When unbelievers die, the sorrow we feel is not mingled with the joy of assurance that they have gone to be with the Lord. This sorrow, especially regarding those to whom we have been close, is very deep and real. Paul himself, when thinking about some of his Jewish brothers who had rejected Christ, and no doubt thinking about their eternal destiny, said, "I am speaking the truth in Christ—

---

[9] See Acts 20:37–38 and Phil. 2:27 for further examples of rightful sorrow in this life.

I am not lying; my conscience bears me witness in the Holy Spirit—that *I have great sorrow and unceasing anguish in my heart.* For I could wish that I myself were accursed and cut off from Christ for the sake of my brothers, my kinsmen according to the flesh" (Rom. 9:1–3).

Yet it also must be said that we often do not have absolute certainty that a person has persisted in refusal to trust in Christ all the way to the point of death. The awareness of one's impending death often will bring about genuine heart searching on the part of a dying person. Sometimes he or she will recall words of Scripture or words of Christian testimony that were heard long ago, and the dying person may come to genuine repentance and faith. Certainly we cannot have any assurance that this has happened unless there is explicit evidence, but it is also good to realize that in many cases we have only probable but not absolute knowledge that those whom we have known as unbelievers have persisted in their unbelief until they died. In some cases we simply do not know.

However, after a non-Christian has died, it would be wrong to give any indication to others that we think that person has gone to heaven. This would simply give misleading information and false assurance, and diminish the urgency of the need for those who are still alive to trust in Christ. It is better, as we have opportunity, to focus on the fact that the sorrow we feel at the loss of someone whom we love should cause us to reflect on our own lives and destinies as well. In fact, when we are able to talk as a friend to the loved ones of an unbeliever who has died, the Lord will often open up opportunities for us to speak with them about the gospel.

In such circumstances it is often very helpful to speak with genuine thankfulness about the good qualities that we noticed and were encouraged by in the life of the person who has died.[10] For example, even though Saul had become an evil king and had pursued David and tried to kill him many times, once Saul had died, David spoke publicly about the good things Saul had done:

> Your glory, O Israel, is slain on your high places!
>> How the mighty have fallen! . . .
> Saul and Jonathan . . .
> they were swifter than eagles;
>> they were stronger than lions.
> You daughters of Israel, weep over Saul,
>> who clothed you luxuriously in scarlet,
>> who put ornaments of gold on your apparel.
> How the mighty have fallen
>> in the midst of battle! (2 Sam. 1:19–25)[11]

---

[10] It is right to thank God for the benefits of common grace in the lives of unbelievers; see the discussion of common grace in Grudem, *Systematic Theology*, 657–68.

[11] Speaking about the life of a person who has died requires honesty and mature judgment, however, for if we are called upon to perform a funeral service for someone whose life has been widely known as evil and destructive, we do not want to give people the impression that what a person does in this life makes no

E. PREPARING FOR DEATH

1. The Importance of Having a Will and Preparing End-of-Life Medical Directives.
When Paul was in a Roman prison (Phil. 1:13), he did not know whether the imprisonment would end in his release or his death. But whatever happened, Paul hoped to be able to act in a way that would honor Christ—in his life, and also at the time of his death:

> As it is my eager expectation and hope that I will not be at all ashamed, but that with full courage now as always *Christ will be honored in my body, whether by life or by death.* (Phil. 1:20)

Following Paul's pattern, it should be the goal of every Christian to be able, by God's grace, to die in a way that honors Christ, and so to "do all to the glory of God" (1 Cor. 10:31).

Another principle from Scripture that is relevant here is the Golden Rule:

> So whatever you wish that others would do to you, do also to them, for this is the Law and the Prophets. (Matt. 7:12)

If you would want your loved ones to have prepared a will and an advance directive regarding medical care for themselves (to give directions in case you had to make end-of-life decisions for their health care), then Jesus's statement tells you that *you should also have these documents prepared ahead of time to save your loved ones from much unnecessary difficulty.*

Two important legal documents that will help a person die in a way that honors Christ are a will (or a similar legal document regarding the disposition of one's assets) and an advance medical directive (a document giving instructions about end-of-life care).

a. The Importance of a Will: The benefits of having a will (or similar legal document, such as a trust) are numerous. It will make the processing of your estate far simpler and faster after you die. It will possibly save your loved ones the additional legal expenses they will incur if you die without a will. It will give you the opportunity to decide how your assets should be divided (including any gifts that you want to make to your church or other charities) rather than having the assets divided automatically according to a formula devised by the state in which you live.[12]

---

difference, or that we are ignorant of the noticeably bad qualities of such a person, or we will lose credibility with those who hear us. As an example of the inevitable reaction of people to the death of someone clearly evil, such as Adolf Hitler, note Prov. 11:10: "When the wicked perish there are shouts of gladness."

[12] There are excellent helps available for deciding how to allocate one's assets, including Ron Blue, *Splitting Heirs: Giving Your Money and Things to Your Children without Ruining Their Lives* (Chicago: Northfield Publishing, 2004). Although this book has much excellent counsel, especially for parents, Blue explains that there are sometimes good reasons to divide one's assets unequally among one's children. I agree with this in

In addition, couples with underage children should clearly make known their wishes regarding who will gain custody of the children if both parents should suddenly die.

In light of these advantages, it is tragic that in 2014 an estimated 51 percent of American adults between the ages of 55 and 64 did not have wills. Sixty-two percent of those between the ages of 45 and 54 did not have wills either. Overall, 64 percent of Americans did not have wills.[13]

According to Legalzoom.com, many people avoid making wills because:

1. They just don't get around to it.
2. They are not comfortable sharing personal details with strangers.
3. They are not ready to make important life decisions.
4. They are unaware of the consequences of not having a will.
5. They are avoiding dealing with family issues.
6. There is a disagreement between spouses about having a will.
7. They think it takes too much effort.
8. They are unsure where to start.
9. Young people believe they do not need wills.
10. They believe only wealthy people need wills.[14]

According to FindLaw.com, the top 10 reasons for having a will are:

1. You decide how your estate will be distributed. A will is a legally binding document that lets you determine how you would like your estate to be handled upon your death. If you die without a will, there is no guarantee that your intended desires will be carried out. Having a will helps minimize any family fights about your estate that may arise, and also determines the "who, what, and when" of your estate.
2. You decide who will take care of your minor children. A will allows you to make an informed decision about who should take care of your minor children. Absent a will, the court will take it upon itself to choose among family members or a state-appointed guardian. Having a will allows you to appoint the person you want to raise your children or, better, make sure it is not someone you do not want to raise your children.
3. To avoid a lengthy probate process. Contrary to common belief, all estates must go through the probate process, with or without a will. Having a will, however, speeds up the probate process and informs the court how

principle, but parents should also be aware that any significantly unequal distribution of assets carries with it the potential for leaving a legacy of bitterness and resentment for many years after the parents have died.

[13] Richard Eisenberg, "Americans' Ostrich Approach to Estate Planning," *Forbes*, April 9, 2014, http://www .forbes.com/sites/nextavenue/2014/04/09/americans-ostrich-approach-to-estate-planning/#3e48d437f07b.

[14] Heleigh Bostwick, "Don't Have a Will? 10 Common But Misguided Excuses," LegalZoom, https://www .legalzoom.com/articles/dont-have-a-will-10-common-but-misguided-excuses.

you'd like your estate divided. Probate courts serve the purpose of "administering your estate," and when you die without a will (known as dying "intestate"), the court will decide how to divide your estate without your input, which can also cause long, unnecessary delays.

4. To minimize estate taxes. Another reason to have a will is because it allows you to minimize your estate taxes. The value of what you give away to family members or charity will reduce the value of your estate when it's time to pay estate taxes.

5. You decide who will wind up the affairs of your estate. Executors make sure all your affairs are in order, including paying off bills, canceling your credit cards, and notifying the bank and other business establishments. Because executors play the biggest role in the administration of your estate, you'll want to be sure to appoint someone who is honest, trustworthy, and organized (which may or may not be a family member).

6. You can disinherit individuals who would otherwise stand to inherit. Most people do not realize they can disinherit individuals out of their wills. Yes, you may wish to disinherit individuals who may otherwise inherit your estate if you die without a will. Because wills specifically outline how you would like your estate distributed, absent a will your estate may end up in the wrong hands or in the hands of someone you did not intend (such as an ex-spouse with whom you had a bitter divorce).

7. To make gifts and donations. The ability to make gifts is a good reason to have a will because it allows your legacy to live on and reflect your personal values and interests. In addition, gifts up to $13,000 are excluded from estate tax, so you're also increasing the value of your estate for your heirs and beneficiaries to enjoy.

8. To avoid greater legal challenges. If you die without a will, part or all of your estate may pass to someone you did not intend. For example, one case involved the estate of a deceased son who was awarded over $1 million from a wrongful death lawsuit. When the son died, the son's father—who had not been a part of his son's life for over thirty-two years—stood to inherit the entire estate, leaving close relatives and siblings out of the picture!

9. You can change your mind if your life circumstances change. A good reason for having a will is that you can change it at any time while you're still alive. Life changes, such as births, deaths, and divorce, can create situations where changing your will is necessary.

10. Tomorrow is not promised. Procrastination and the unwillingness to accept death as part of life are common reasons for not having a will. Sometimes the realization that wills are necessary comes too late—such as when an unexpected death or disability occurs. To avoid the added stress

on families during an already emotional time, it may be wise to meet with an estate-planning lawyer to help you draw up a basic estate plan at the minimum, before it's too late.[15]

One other reason people might avoid preparing a will is that they do not think they are about to die. However, "No man has power to retain the spirit, or power over the day of death" (Eccles. 8:8), and "Man does not know his time" (9:12). In the parable Jesus told of the rich fool, he thought he could "eat, drink, be merry" because he had "ample goods laid up for many years" (Luke 12:19). But Jesus said:

> God said to him, "Fool! This night your soul is required of you, and the things you have prepared, whose will they be?" (Luke 12:20)

We cannot know the day of our death, and it is right to make appropriate preparations while we are able to do so.

The supposed cost of preparing a legal document may also be a deterrent. However, online resources are available at a very nominal cost for a simple will.[16] Families with more complex situations would be wise to use the services of a lawyer who specializes in estate planning.

b. The Importance of an Advance Medical Directive: An *advance medical directive* (or similar document in other countries) can save family members much agony and painful disagreement over what you would want regarding care at the end of your life. It also can save you much suffering, because it can prevent you from being kept alive for days or weeks by artificial means when you are longing to die but can no longer make your wishes known. It also can save your family much needless expense, preventing them from spending thousands of dollars keeping you alive when you do not want to be kept alive—but they have no written documentation by which they can know this for certain.

However, it is difficult to be able to specify in advance what to do in all the complex medical situations that might happen in a terminal illness or as a result of a serious accident. Therefore, it is also wise to sign a *durable medical power of attorney* document that designates who is authorized to make medical decisions on your behalf if you are unconscious and unable to make decisions for yourself. John Jefferson Davis explains:

> In a society prone to see legislation and litigation as the solutions to personal and social problems, the "durable power of attorney" concept is much to be preferred to the "living will." The "durable power of attorney" places the emphasis on a relationship of trust and understanding between patient, family,

---

[15] "Top Ten Reasons to Have a Will," FindLaw, http://estate.findlaw.com/wills/top-ten-reasons-to-have-a-will.html/. (The estate tax exlusion amount mentioned in point 7 can be changed by Congress.)

[16] One Christian organization that assists low- and middle-income families to prepare a very simple will and other important end-of-life documents for a very minimal cost is Legacy Wise; see http://www.legacywise.org/.

and physician, and such a climate is crucial for preserving the proper interests of both the patient and the medical profession.[17]

Therefore, the biblical principles of doing unto others as you would have them do to you and of seeking to die in a way that honors Christ provide strong arguments for preparing an advance medical directive stating your precise wishes regarding your end-of-life care, especially in situations where there is no reasonable hope of recovery and extraordinary and highly expensive means would be necessary just to prolong the process of dying. (See further discussion on euthanasia in chapter 22, p. 587.)

F. IS CREMATION AN ACCEPTABLE ALTERNATIVE TO BURIAL?

In many developed economies, the traditional process of burying someone's body in a coffin has become more and more costly, and in many places finding appropriate ground for a cemetery burial is also quite difficult and costly. For these reasons, many people have begun to use cremation as an alternative way of paying final respects to a loved one who has died. In terms of financial stewardship, this often seems to many people to be a wise solution.

The Bible does not give any explicit commands about how we should treat a person's body after death. However, there are several narrative examples of a person's body being treated with dignity and respect up to and including the time of burial. Some "valiant men" in Israel risked their lives to rescue the bodies of Saul and his sons from the Philistines and to give them a decent burial (1 Sam. 31:11–13). The old prophet who lived in Bethel traveled and found the body of the man of God who had been killed by a lion (and whose body was being guarded by the lion!), and took the body and gave him a decent burial (1 Kings 13:24–31).

In the New Testament, the disciples of John the Baptist rescued his dead body and gave it a proper burial (Mark 6:29). And the body of Jesus himself was respectfully cared for and buried in a new tomb by his disciples (see John 19:38–42; also Luke 23:55–56). Before his death, Jesus gave strong words of approval to a woman who anointed him with very expensive ointment in the last week of his life. Jesus said, "She has done a beautiful thing to me. . . . She has anointed my body beforehand for burial" (Mark 14:6–8). These examples show a pattern of treating a dead person's body with dignity and respect.

However, there are many ways, varying from culture to culture, to show respect for a person who has died and to honor his or her memory.

Therefore, I cannot say that cremation is inappropriate or wrong (though it would

[17] John Jefferson Davis, *Evangelical Ethics: Issues Facing the Church Today*, 4th ed. (Phillipsburg, NJ: P&R, 2015), 189–90.

not be my personal preference; see below). Our bodies are eventually going to disintegrate anyway (except for the bones), and cremation vastly accelerates that process.

However, when a believer dies, no matter if he or she is buried or cremated, it is important not to imply that you think there will be no resurrection of *the very same body* that was buried or cremated. When Jesus rose from the dead, his very same body was raised up, and ours will be too. When Christ returns, our very bodies that have been buried or cremated (or what is left of them) will be raised from the dead and transformed to a state of perfect health, great physical attractiveness,[18] and eternal life (see 1 Cor. 15:23, 42–44, 51–52; Phil. 3:21; 1 Thess. 4:16).

My personal preference would be to be buried in a traditional way with my body in a simple casket that is placed in the ground. Paul said:

> What is sown is perishable; what is raised is imperishable. . . . For the trumpet will sound, *and the dead will be raised imperishable*, and we shall be changed. (1 Cor. 15:42, 52)

Traditional burial of one's body in a casket has the advantage of giving a more visible expression to our hope of the resurrection of the body—from that very spot in the ground—when Christ returns. Yet it is also important to avoid another mistake: spending excessive money on a coffin, perhaps out of a futile hope that a person's body will not decay very fast, perhaps to try to assuage guilt or remorse at not having treated a deceased person very well in the latter years of his or her life, or for some other reason. This is an unwise stewardship of one's money.

John Piper addresses both of these concerns in a persuasive article in which he argues for burial, not cremation. He concludes:

> I am encouraging churches to cultivate a Christian counter-culture where people expect simple, less expensive funerals and burials, and where we all pitch in so that a Christian burial is not a financial hardship on anyone. And because of the Biblical pointers and the additional reasons above, I am arguing that God-centered, gospel-rooted burial is preferable to cremation. *Preferable*. Not *commanded*, but rich with Christian truth that will become a clearer and clearer witness as our society becomes less and less Christian.[19]

For those who have been cremated, however, Christ will gather their ashes from wherever they have been scattered, and from them he will create a new resurrection body that will never grow weak or old again, and will never die. Christians who decide to use the process of cremation for their loved ones can take care in the funeral

---

[18] For a discussion of the physical attractiveness of the resurrection bodies of all Christians when we are raised "in glory" (1 Cor. 15:43), see Grudem, *Systematic Theology*, 831–32.

[19] John Piper, "Burying versus Burning," *World*, July 8, 2017, https://world.wng.org/content/burying_vs_burning.

ceremony to make clear that they are still hoping for the future resurrection of the body from the ashes.

QUESTIONS FOR PERSONAL APPLICATION

1. Have you reached an age where you are beginning to notice some physical decline due to aging? Honestly, how do you feel about this?
2. Read 2 Corinthians 4:16–18. How does this affect your attitude about your aging (whether you are now noticing its effects or that point is still far in the future)?
3. How has this chapter affected your view of your aging and eventual death?
4. Do you think that you show appropriate respect and gratitude for the dignity and wisdom represented by the signs of aging (such as gray hair and wrinkles)?
5. Do you value faithfulness to God more than preserving your life?
6. Do you have a will, an advance medical directive, and a medical power of attorney document? If not, why not?
7. Do you fear death? If so, what do you think might be helpful in overcoming that fear?
8. What do you think about cremation?
9. What character traits (see p. 110) would be most helpful to you as you approach the time of your death?

SPECIAL TERMS

advance medical directive
medical power of attorney
will

BIBLIOGRAPHY

Sections in Other Ethics Texts

(see complete bibliographical data, p. 64)

Frame, 732–37

Other Works

Blue, Ron. *Splitting Heirs: Giving Your Money and Things to Your Children without Ruining Their Lives.* Chicago: Northfield Publishing, 2004.

Dunlop, John. *Finding Grace in the Face of Dementia.* Wheaton, IL: Crossway, 2017.

Graham, Billy. *Nearing Home: Thoughts on Life, Faith and Finishing Well*. Nashville: Thomas Nelson, 2011.

Morey, Robert A. *Death and the Afterlife*. Minneapolis: Bethany House, 1984.

Moss, M. J. "Ageing." In *New Dictionary of Christian Ethics and Pastoral Theology*, edited by David J. Atkinson and David H. Field, 148–49. Leicester, UK: Inter-Varsity, and Downers Grove, IL: InterVarsity Press, 1995.

Kilner, John F. "Aged, Aging." In *Dictionary of Scripture and Ethics*, edited by Joel B. Green, 50–52. Grand Rapids, MI: Baker, 2011.

———. *Life on the Line: Ethics, Aging, Ending Patients' Lives, and Allocating Vital Resources*. Grand Rapids, MI: Eerdmans, 1992.

Packer, J. I. *Finishing Our Course with Joy: Guidance from God for Engaging with Our Aging*. Wheaton, IL: Crossway, 2014.

Piper, John. "Getting Old to the Glory of God [2008]." In *The Collected Works of John Piper*, edited by David Mathis and Justin Taylor, vol. 13, 313–24. Wheaton, IL: Crossway, 2017.

———. *Rethinking Retirement: Finishing Life for the Glory of Christ*. Wheaton, IL: Crossway, 2008.

Sweeting, Donald W., and George Sweeting. *How to Finish the Christian Life: Following Jesus in the Second Half*. Chicago: Moody Publishers, 2012.

Vere, D. W. "Death and Dying." In *New Dictionary of Christian Ethics and Pastoral Theology*, 284–85.

SCRIPTURE MEMORY PASSAGE

2 Corinthians 4:16–17: So we do not lose heart. Though our outer self is wasting away, our inner self is being renewed day by day. For this light momentary affliction is preparing for us an eternal weight of glory beyond all comparison.

HYMN

"My Jesus I Love Thee"

My Jesus, I love thee, I know thou art mine;
For thee all the follies of sin I resign.
My gracious Redeemer, my Savior art thou;
If ever I loved thee, my Jesus 'tis now.

I love thee because thou hast first loved me,
And purchased my pardon on Calvary's tree.
I love thee for wearing the thorns on thy brow;
If ever I loved thee, my Jesus, 'tis now.

I'll love thee in life, I will love thee in death;
And praise thee as long as thou lendest me breath;
And say, when the death-dew lies cold on my brow:
If ever I loved thee, my Jesus, 'tis now.

In mansions of glory and endless delight,
I'll ever adore thee in heaven so bright;
I'll sing with the glittering crown on my brow:
If ever I loved thee, my Jesus, 'tis now.

AUTHOR: WILLIAM R. FEATHERSTONE, 1864

Chapter 25

RACIAL DISCRIMINATION

Why is it wrong to discriminate against others on the basis of racial differences?

Does the Bible say anything about interracial marriage?

What was wrong with the arguments of people who tried to defend racial discrimination from the Bible?

This section of the book (Part 4) concerns the protection of human life, and therefore all the chapters are related in a broad sense to the sixth commandment, "You shall not murder" (Ex. 20:13). First we considered several topics directly related to life and death (chaps. 18–24). Now, in the last three chapters of this section, we turn to three topics not directly concerned with life and death, but with people's well-being in this life: racial discrimination (chap. 25), health (chap. 26), and then a specific health issue, alcohol and drugs (chap. 27).[1]

Discrimination against people because of their racial or ethnic backgrounds has been common in many societies throughout history. This was certainly true in the time of Jesus and the apostles. Jesus's parable of the good Samaritan who cared for a wounded Jewish man (Luke 10:30–37) was shocking to his hearers because "Jews have no dealings with Samaritans" (John 4:9). The teaching of the apostle Paul about racial relationships in the church would have appeared revolutionary to many new Christians: "Here there is not Greek and Jew, circumcised and uncircumcised, barbarian, Scythian, slave, free; but Christ is all, and in all" (Col. 3:11). Then as now, outside of the Christian

---

[1] Much of this chapter is adapted from the article "Racial Discrimination" in the *ESV Study Bible* (Wheaton, IL: Crossway, 2008), 2557–58, with permission of the publisher. (I was the primary author of this article.)

church, racial and ethnic separation and discrimination were all too common among the nations of the world.

My goal in this chapter will be to show that, from beginning to end, the Bible provides no basis for favoring or discriminating against any groups of people on the basis of their backgrounds, but rather views all human beings as worthy of honor and respect, because all alike are made in the image of God.

Perceptions of racial discrimination remain a serious concern in the United States. A June 2016 study by the Pew Research Center found that an overwhelming majority of blacks (88 percent) say the United States needs to continue making changes for blacks to have equal rights with whites, but 43 percent are skeptical that such changes will ever occur. According to the study, blacks are more likely than whites to say black people are treated less fairly in the workplace (a difference of 42 percentage points), when applying for a loan or mortgage (41 points), in dealings with the police (34 points), in the courts (32 points), in stores or restaurants (28 points), and when voting in elections (23 points). By a margin of at least 20 percentage points, blacks are also more likely than whites to say racial discrimination (70 percent vs. 36 percent), lower quality schools (75 percent vs. 53 percent), and lack of jobs (66 percent vs. 45 percent) are major reasons that blacks may have a harder time getting ahead than whites.[2]

Sadly, perceptions of racial discrimination have worsened over the past several years. In 2016, Gallup published an extensive report of its polls on perceptions of racial discrimination and race relations during the previous 12 years. In 2004, 74 percent of non-Hispanic whites and 68 percent of blacks said race relations were "very good" or "somewhat good." By 2016, only 55 percent of non-Hispanic whites and 49 percent of blacks said race relations were "very good" or "somewhat good." In 2004, only 8 percent of blacks felt that race relations were "very bad." That percentage soared to 21 percent in 2016. In 2005, 30 percent of blacks were "very dissatisfied" with how they were being treated. That percentage rose to 42 percent in 2016.[3]

The report also showed that in 2003, 52 percent of blacks felt new civil-rights laws were needed to address racial discrimination. That percentage rose to 69 percent in 2015.[4] Among Hispanics over the same period, the percentage rose from 44 percent saying new civil-rights laws were needed to 52 percent.[5]

According to the 2016 Pew Research study on race in America, about half of Hispanics in the United States (52 percent) now say they have experienced discrimination or have been treated unfairly because of their race or ethnicity. The study found that among Hispanics ages 18 to 29, 65 percent say they have experienced discrimination or

---

[2] "On Views of Race and Inequality, Blacks and Whites Are Worlds Apart," Pew Research Center, June 27, 2016, http://www.pewsocialtrends.org/2016/06/27/on-views-of-race-and-inequality-blacks-and-whites-are-worlds-apart/.

[3] "Race Relations," Gallup, http://www.gallup.com/poll/1687/Race-Relations.aspx.

[4] Ibid.

[5] Ibid.

unfair treatment because of their race or ethnicity. By comparison, only 35 percent of Hispanics 50 and older say the same—a gap of 30 percentage points.[6]

But there have been areas of improvement. In 1965, for instance, whites were 63.2 percentage points more likely to be registered to vote than blacks. But by 2004, black voters were 3.8 percentage points *more* likely to be registered to vote than whites.[7] In addition, in contrast to America before the mid-1960s, racial discrimination is now explicitly prohibited by law in university admissions, in corporate employment and promotion practices, in public accommodations such as restaurants and hotels, and in other areas of life.

Since 1965, blacks have been gaining in every economic area, but not at the same rate as whites. According to the Pew Research Center, median family income (in inflation-adjusted dollars) is up from $22,000 in 1963 to more than $40,000 today, but still just two-thirds of the median for all Americans.[8] Black unemployment remains twice the level of white unemployment, similar to where it was in 1972.[9]

A 2014 survey by CBS News found that most Americans think the Civil Rights Act of 1964 has improved things for blacks in the United States, including 84 percent of whites and 83 percent of blacks.[10] It is fair to conclude that there has been some progress, and compared to 50 years ago, things are much better for racial minorities in America. But clearly problems still remain.

Racial discrimination is not just an American problem. A 2003 European Union study found that 22 percent of respondents said they had experienced discrimination because of their race, nearly twice as much as the second most cited reason, which was learning difficulties or mental illness.[11] Another study, done four years later, found that perceptions of racial discrimination had increased, with 49 percent feeling it had become more widespread.[12] A 2013 report found that 56 percent of respondents thought ethnic origin remained the most widely perceived ground for discrimination in the EU.[13]

---

[6] Jens Manuel Krogstad and Gustavo Lopez, "Roughly Half of Hispanics Have Experienced Discrimination," Pew Research Center, June 29, 2016, http://www.pewresearch.org/fact-tank/2016/06/29/roughly-half-of-hispanics-have-experienced-discrimination/.

[7] "Yes, Race Relations Have Improved Since 1965," *National Review*, June 26, 2013, http://www.national review.com/article/352038/yes-race-relations-have-improved-1965-editors.

[8] Richard Wolf, "Equality Still Elusive 50 Years after Civil Rights Act," *USA Today*, April 1, 2014, http://www .usatoday.com/story/news/nation/2014/01/19/civil-rights-act-progress/4641967/.

[9] Ibid.

[10] Sarah Dutton, Jennifer De Pinto, Anthony Salvanto, and Fred Backus, "As Civil Rights Act Turns 50, Most Americans Appreciate Its Importance," CBS News, April 9, 2014, http://www.cbsnews.com/news/as -civil-rights-act-turns-50-most-americans-appreciate-its-importance/.

[11] "Discrimination in Europe," 2003, http://ec.europa.eu/public_opinion/archives/ebs/ebs_168_exec.sum _en.pdf.

[12] "Discrimination in the European Union," 2007, http://ec.europa.eu/public_opinion/archives/ebs/ebs _263_en.pdf.

[13] "Racism and Discrimination in Employment in Europe," 2013, 10, http://cms.horus.be/files/99935 /MediaArchive/publications/shadow%20report%202012-13/shadowReport_final.pdf.

A. ALL PEOPLE ON EARTH ARE
DESCENDED FROM ADAM AND EVE

The first three chapters of Genesis, along with the other chapters in Genesis, are presented as truthful historical narratives about the origin of the human race.[14] These early chapters provide the historical basis for understanding the essential unity of all human beings, because they show that all people on earth are descended from Adam and Eve. This is evident, first, at the beginning of the human race, when God created Adam and Eve as the first human beings on the earth:

> Then God said, "Let us make man in our image, after our likeness." . . .
>
> So God created man in his own image,
>   in the image of God he created him;
> male and female he created them. (Gen. 1:26–27)

In the next chapter, we read that "the man called his wife's name Eve, because *she was the mother of all living*" (Gen. 2:20).

Then, after the flood (Genesis 6–8), Noah and his wife, together with his three sons and their wives, came out of the ark:

> The sons of Noah who went forth from the ark were Shem, Ham, and Japheth. . . . These three were the sons of Noah, and *from these the people of the whole earth were dispersed*. (Gen. 9:18–19)

Paul explicitly affirms that all people on earth have descended from Adam, for in speaking to the philosophers in Athens, he says:

> And he *made from one man every nation of mankind* to live on all the face of the earth, having determined allotted periods and the boundaries of their dwelling place. (Acts 17:26)[15]

The doctrinal importance of all human beings descending from Adam is that it shows the physical unity of the human race. Therefore, it shows that just as Adam could be the representative of all people, so Christ can be the representative of all who believe.[16] As Paul explains:

---

[14] For a detailed discussion of the reasons why Genesis 1–3 should be taken as truthful historical narrative, including an affirmation of their reliability by Jesus and 10 different New Testament books, see Wayne Grudem, "Theistic Evolution Undermines Twelve Creation Events and Several Crucial Christian Doctrines," in *Theistic Evolution: A Scientific, Philosophical, and Theological Critique*, ed. J. P. Moreland, Stephen C. Meyer, Christopher Shaw, Ann K. Gauger, and Wayne Grudem (Wheaton, IL: Crossway, 2017), 783–837.

[15] In Paul's understanding, this one man is Adam (for Paul repeatedly calls Adam the "one man" in referring to the beginning of the human race in Rom. 5:12, 14, 15, 16, 17, 19).

[16] For further discussion, see Guy Waters, "Theistic Evolution Is Incompatible with the Teachings of the New Testament," in Moreland et al., eds., *Theistic Evolution*, 879–926.

For as by the one man's disobedience the many were made sinners, so by the one man's obedience the many will be made righteous. (Rom. 5:19)

For as by a man came death, by a man has come also the resurrection of the dead. *For as in Adam all die, so also in Christ shall all be made alive.* (1 Cor. 15:21–22)

B. ALL HUMAN BEINGS SHARE EQUALLY IN BEING CREATED "IN THE IMAGE OF GOD"

Since "God created man *in his own image* . . . male and female he created them" (Gen. 1:28), and since "Adam . . . fathered a son in his own likeness, *after his image*" (5:3), Scripture expects us to understand that all human beings share in the status of being "in the image of God"—that is, representing God on the earth and being more like God than any other creature on the earth.[17] This point is reinforced when God tells Noah that he will require human beings to execute punishment on murderers:

Whoever sheds the blood of man,
    by man shall his blood be shed,
for God made man in his own image. (Gen. 9:6)

This affirmation that all people are still made in the image of God is the general principle that shows the deep moral evil of the murder of any human being.

In the New Testament, James affirms a similar idea when he speaks of people "who are made in the likeness of God" (James 3:9; note that Gen. 1:26 speaks of man being created in both the "image" and the "likeness" of God).

Since all human beings are descended from Adam and Eve, and since they all are in the image of God, Scripture rules out any ideas of racial superiority or inferiority in God's sight. We should treat all human beings with dignity and respect: "Honor *everyone*" (1 Pet. 2:17); "Show perfect courtesy toward *all people*" (Titus 3:2).

James also cautions us not to show "partiality," favoring one type of person or another (in context, he is speaking about rich and poor, but the principle applies to other kinds of partiality as well). He writes, "My brothers, *show no partiality* as you hold the faith in our Lord Jesus Christ, the Lord of glory" (James 2:1; see also v. 9). John Frame explains:

James also opposes partiality (James 2:4; 3:17). Partiality is the biblical term for prejudice. It involves treating someone badly, not because the person deserves it, but because of an irrational preference.[18]

---

[17] See discussion in chap. 10, p. 281. See also the discussion of the image of God in Wayne Grudem, *Systematic Theology: An Introduction to Biblical Doctrine* (Leicester, UK: Inter-Varsity, and Grand Rapids, MI: Zondervan, 1994), 442–50.

[18] John M. Frame, *The Doctrine of the Christian Life: A Theology of Lordship* (Phillipsburg, NJ: P&R, 2008), 663.

C. PEOPLE FROM EVERY RACIAL BACKGROUND WILL BE UNITED IN HEAVEN

If we skip to the end of the Bible, we see the same emphasis on racial and ethnic unity, because the innumerable multitude of people worshiping before God's throne in heaven includes people from every tribe and nation of the earth:

> After this I looked, and behold, a great multitude that no one could number, *from every nation, from all tribes and peoples and languages,* standing before the throne and before the Lamb, clothed in white robes, with palm branches in their hands, and crying out with a loud voice, "Salvation belongs to our God who sits on the throne, and to the Lamb!" (Rev. 7:9–10)

D. GENETIC EVIDENCE FOR THE UNITY OF THE HUMAN RACE

The *ESV Study Bible* summarizes current scientific evidence regarding the unity of the human race:

> Recent genetic studies from the Human Genome Project give interesting confirmation to the very large degree of genetic similarity shared by all human beings and the extremely small degree of genetic dissimilarity distinguishing one group from another. The best contemporary science shows that the human genome sequence is almost (99.9 percent) exactly the same in all people.[19]

Then follows this statement from the Human Genome Project:

> DNA studies do not indicate that separate classifiable sub-species (races) exist within modern humans. While different genes or physical traits such as skin and hair color can be identified between individuals, no consistent patterns of genes across the human genome exist to distinguish one race from another. There is also no genetic basis for divisions of human ethnicity. People who have lived in the same geographic region for many generations have some alleles [possible forms in which a gene for a specific trait can occur] in common, but no allele will be found in all members of one population and in no members of any other.[20]

In addition, some recent genetic studies give substantial scientific plausibility to the idea that all human beings have descended from one human couple in the early history of the human race.[21]

---

[19] "Racial Discrimination," 2557.

[20] "Minorities, Race, and Genomics," Human Genome Project Information Archive 1990–2003, http://web .ornl.gov/sci/techresources/Human_Genome/elsi/minorities.shtml, cited in ibid., 2557–58.

[21] See information on Adam and Eve in Moreland et al., eds., *Theistic Evolution*, chaps. 27–29, pp. 783–926.

Why do people with different racial characteristics originate from different regions of the world? Beginning with Adam and Eve, the human race has always included genetic variations of eye color, height, and facial appearance, as well as variations of skin and hair color that are now associated with different racial groups. At some early point in the history of the human race, when people began migrating to various parts of the earth, some variations within the human gene pool became *geographically isolated* from other variations, so that people living in what is now northern Europe came to look more like each other. People living in what is now Africa began to look more like each other, and the same was true for people living in Asia or in North America. The result was that groups of people in different parts of the world came to have different skin colors and other characteristics that we today associate with racial differences.

One interesting implication of this has to do with genetic inheritance of skin color. Modern genetic studies tell us that when a lighter-skinned person has a child with a darker-skinned person, the child's skin will be no darker than that of the darkest parent. This means that, if the hereditary transfer of skin color has operated in the same way from the beginning of human history, then the current variety in skin color must have existed from the very beginning. This suggests that Adam and Eve's many children (see Gen. 5:4) likely had different skin colors, and that Adam and Eve possibly had different skin colors as well.

E. EXAMPLES OF INTERRACIAL MARRIAGE VIEWED POSITIVELY IN THE BIBLE

In light of the biblical teaching about the unity of the human race, it is not surprising that some marriages between people of different racial or ethnic backgrounds are viewed positively in the Bible, and even play an important part in biblical history.

For example, when Joseph was in Egypt, he took an Egyptian wife:

> Before the year of famine came, two sons were born to Joseph. Asenath, the daughter of Potiphera priest of On, bore them to him. Joseph called the name of the firstborn Manasseh. "For," he said, "God has made me forget all my hardship and all my father's house." The name of the second he called Ephraim, "For God has made me fruitful in the land of my affliction." (Gen. 41:50–52)

Joseph was of Semitic origin (a descendant of Abraham), while his wife, Asenath, was an Egyptian from North Africa. And yet these children became the forefathers of the tribes of Ephraim and Manasseh, two of the largest of the 12 tribes of Israel (see Gen. 41:51–52).

Later we read that Moses had married an Ethiopian woman:

> Miriam and Aaron spoke against Moses because of the Cushite woman whom he had married, for he had married a Cushite woman. And they said, "Has the LORD indeed spoken only through Moses? Has he not spoken through us also?" And the LORD heard it. (Num. 12:1–2)

The "Cushite" (Hebrew, *kushî*) people were from the region of Africa that is now Ethiopia and Sudan. The Hebrew term is the same as the one used in Jeremiah 13:23: "Can the *Ethiopian*[22] change his skin or the leopard his spots?" Therefore, in this passage Miriam and Aaron are criticizing Moses, a Jewish man, for marrying an African woman with much darker skin. But God brings immediate judgment on Miriam and Aaron for this complaint:

> And suddenly the LORD said to Moses and to Aaron and Miriam, "Come out, you three, to the tent of meeting." And the three of them came out. And the LORD came down in a pillar of cloud and stood at the entrance of the tent and called Aaron and Miriam, and they both came forward. And he said, "Hear my words: If there is a prophet among you, I the LORD make myself known to him in a vision; I speak with him in a dream. Not so with my servant Moses. He is faithful in all my house. With him I speak mouth to mouth, clearly, and not in riddles, and he beholds the form of the LORD. Why then were you not afraid to speak against my servant Moses?" And the anger of the LORD was kindled against them, and he departed. When the cloud removed from over the tent, *behold, Miriam was leprous, like snow.* And Aaron turned toward Miriam, and behold, she was leprous. (Num. 12:4–10)[23]

John Piper says about this passage:

> God says not a critical word against Moses for marrying a black Cushite woman. But when Miriam criticizes God's chosen leader for this marriage, God strikes her skin with white leprosy. If you ever thought black was a biblical symbol for uncleanness, be careful how you use such an idea; a white uncleanness could come upon you.[24]

Further evidence of God's concern for interracial harmony is seen in the fact that there are some non-Jewish ancestors in the line of Jesus, for his ancestry included Rahab, who was a Canaanite from Jericho (see Josh. 6:25; Matt. 1:5), and Ruth, who was a Moabite (see Ruth 1:4, 22; 2:2, 6, 21; 4:5, 10; Matt. 1:5).

At first someone might think that Old Testament laws against marrying foreign women would provide an argument against interracial marriage. It is true that in the Mosaic covenant, there were some laws preventing the Jewish people from intermarrying with people of other nations, such as:

> You shall not intermarry with them, giving your daughters to their sons or taking their daughters for your sons, for they would turn away your sons

---

[22] Hebrew, *kûshî*, a variant spelling of the same word.

[23] Moses then prayed to the Lord, and Miriam was healed within seven days (Num. 12:11–15).

[24] John Piper, *Bloodlines: Race, Cross, and the Christian* (Wheaton, IL: Crossway, 2011), 212.

from following me, to serve other gods. Then the anger of the Lord would be kindled against you, and he would destroy you quickly. (Deut. 7:3–4; see also Ezra 10:11)

But the context of these passages shows that the purpose for these laws was to prevent the Jewish people from marrying people *of other religions*. The specific reason is given in Deuteronomy 7:4: "*For they would turn away your sons from following me, to serve other gods.*" And the passages in Ezra about marrying foreign wives also show that the concern was with *marrying people of false religions* who would turn the Jewish people away from serving the Lord (see Ezra 9:1–2, 11, 14). The New Testament counterpart to these laws against marrying foreigners is a prohibition against marrying unbelievers. It has nothing to do with race or national origin. Therefore, a widow "is free to be married to whom she wishes, *only in the Lord*" (1 Cor. 7:39; see also 2 Cor. 6:14).

F. WHAT WAS THE CURSE OF HAM (OR CANAAN)?

Sometime after the flood, Noah became drunk and fell asleep, lying naked in his tent (Gen. 9:21). One of Noah's sons named Ham saw his father in this disreputable state and apparently ridiculed Noah to his brothers, Shem and Japheth, who then treated their father respectfully and covered Noah's nakedness:

Then Shem and Japheth took a garment, laid it on both their shoulders, and walked backward and covered the nakedness of their father. Their faces were turned backward, and they did not see their father's nakedness. (Gen. 9:23)

When Noah "awoke from his wine" and learned what had happened, he cursed not Ham but Canaan, one of Ham's sons:

He said, "*Cursed be Canaan*; a servant of servants shall he be to his brothers." (Gen. 9:25)

Some people have shamefully used this passage to attempt to justify racial discrimination and even the enslavement of people of African origin, with the claim that the result of this curse was dark-colored skin.[25] However, the Bible itself shows that it was *not* the descendants of Canaan but the descendants of the *other children* of Ham who populated northern Africa:

The sons of Ham: *Cush* [Ethiopia, Sudan], *Egypt, Put* [Libya],[26] and Canaan. (Gen. 10:6)

---

[25] For a detailed history of interpreters who promoted this viewpoint in previous centuries, see Edwin Yamauchi, "The Curse of Ham," *Criswell Theological Review* n.s. 6, no. 2 (Spring 2009): 45–60.

[26] See Gordon J. Wenham, *Genesis 1–15*, WBC (Waco, TX: Word, 1987), 221, for notes on the identification of both Cush and Put.

The descendants of Canaan did not migrate to Africa, but lived in the land of Palestine in the regions of Sidon, Gaza, Sodom, and Gomorrah:

> Canaan fathered Sidon his firstborn and Heth, and the *Jebusites, the Amorites, the Girgashites, the Hivites, the Arkites, the Sinites, the Arvadites, the Zemarites, and the Hamathites.* Afterward the *clans of the Canaanites* dispersed. And the *territory of the Canaanites* extended from Sidon in the direction of Gerar as far as Gaza, and in the direction of Sodom, Gomorrah, Admah, and Zeboiim, as far as Lasha. (Gen. 10:15–19)

Later in biblical history, we see that these were the tribes of Canaanites that were destroyed by the people of Israel when they conquered the Promised Land (notice many of the same names of tribal groups):

> When the LORD your God brings you into the land that you are entering to take possession of it, and clears away many nations before you, the Hittites, the Girgashites, the Amorites, the Canaanites, the Perizzites, the Hivites, and the Jebusites, seven nations more numerous and mightier than you, and when the LORD your God gives them over to you, and you defeat them, then you must devote them to complete destruction. You shall make no covenant with them and show no mercy to them. (Deut. 7:1–2)

But not all the Canaanites were killed, and those that remained were subjected to servanthood during the time of Solomon:

> All the people who were left of the Amorites, the Hittites, the Perizzites, the Hivites, and the Jebusites, who were not of the people of Israel—their descendants who were left after them in the land, whom the people of Israel were unable to devote to destruction—these Solomon drafted to be slaves, and so they are to this day. But of the people of Israel Solomon made no slaves. They were the soldiers, they were his officials, his commanders, his captains, his chariot commanders and his horsemen. (1 Kings 9:20–22)

Therefore, *the curse on the descendants of Canaan was fulfilled* in the destruction of the Canaanite people by the nation of Israel when they conquered the Promised Land and later when they subjected the Canaanite peoples to servitude.[27] This curse had nothing to do with racial superiority, with skin color, or even with people of African descent.

---

[27] Derek Kidner says, "It is likely . . . that the subjugation of the Canaanites to Israel fulfilled the oracle sufficiently (cf. Josh. 9:23; 1 Kings 9:21)." *Genesis*, TOTC (Chicago: InterVarsity Press, 1967), 104. Similarly, see Wenham, *Genesis 1–15*, 201–2.

G. HOW SHOULD WE RELATE TO PEOPLE FROM DIFFERENT RACIAL BACKGROUNDS?

The New Testament gives us guidance on the question of relating to people of different racial backgrounds. We see from the New Testament that there was racial strife between Jews and Samaritans during the time of Jesus, for "Jews have no dealings with Samaritans" (John 4:9). But Jesus talked openly and freely with the woman at the well in Samaria (see 4:1–42). And he also told the parable of the good Samaritan (Luke 10:25–37), in part to teach that the Jews should consider a Samaritan to be a "neighbor," the proper object of the command "You shall love your neighbor as yourself" (see vv. 27, 29).

At the end of his earthly ministry, Jesus told his disciples to "make disciples of *all nations*" (Matt. 28:19), and Paul implies that there should be no racial discrimination within the church when he writes, "There is neither Jew nor Greek . . . for you are all one in Christ Jesus" (Gal. 3:28).

A highly significant passage on racial unity in the church is found in Paul's letter to the Ephesians:

> For this reason I, Paul, a prisoner for Christ Jesus on behalf of you Gentiles—assuming that you have heard of the stewardship of God's grace that was given to me for you, how the *mystery was made known to me by revelation*, as I have written briefly. When you read this, you can perceive my insight into the mystery of Christ, which was not made known to the sons of men in other generations as it has now been revealed to his holy apostles and prophets by the Spirit. This *mystery is that the Gentiles are fellow heirs*, members of the same body, and partakers of the promise in Christ Jesus through the gospel.
>
> *Of this gospel I was made a minister* according to the gift of God's grace, which was given me by the working of his power. To me, though I am the very least of all the saints, *this grace was given, to preach to the Gentiles the unsearchable riches of Christ*, and to bring to light for everyone what is the plan of the mystery hidden for ages in God, who created all things, *so that through the church the manifold wisdom of God might now be made known to the rulers and authorities in the heavenly places*. (3:1–10)

Here Paul talks about a magnificent "mystery" that was only partially hinted at in the Old Testament, but which God had revealed "to his holy apostles and prophets" (Eph. 3:5) in the New Testament. This mystery was "that the Gentiles are fellow heirs" (v. 6)—that they were included on an equal basis in the church! (It would have been shocking to first-century Jews to think that non-Jews were included among God's people on an equal footing.)

But as Paul preached the gospel to the Gentiles, and as people from different racial and ethnic backgrounds were brought into the church, something dramatic happened in the invisible realm of spiritual activity: the "rulers and authorities in the heavenly places" (that is, the angelic and demonic spiritual forces that are invisible to us at this time) began to see and understand the amazing wisdom and complexity of God's eternal plan for the church. They began to see the outworking of "the manifold wisdom of God." (Here "manifold" translates the Greek word *polypoikilos*, "having many facets, diversified, very many-sided.")

Paul was saying here that when people from diverse racial and ethnic backgrounds are able to love one another and work together in the church, *this is remarkably different from the tendency throughout history for people of different backgrounds* to live in animosity and sometimes even war against one another. But God brings it about because in Christ he has "broken down in his flesh the dividing wall of hostility" (Eph. 2:14). Angels see this and rejoice, while demons witness it and are infuriated.

This remarkable truth has significant implications for the Christian church. As I wrote elsewhere:

> If the Christian church is faithful to God's wise plan, it will be always in the forefront in breaking down racial and social barriers in societies around the world, and will thus be a visible manifestation of God's amazingly wise plan to bring great unity out of great diversity and thereby to cause all creation to honor him.[28]

Finally, the picture of worship before God's throne in heaven (Rev. 7:9–10) is an amazing image of racial unity:

> After this I looked, and behold, a great multitude that no one could number, *from every nation, from all tribes and peoples and languages,* standing before the throne and before the Lamb, clothed in white robes, with palm branches in their hands, and crying out with a loud voice, "Salvation belongs to our God who sits on the throne, and to the Lamb!"

This biblical picture does not necessarily mean that ethnically homogeneous churches are displeasing to God, at least for a generation or two because of language differences. (It is common in the Phoenix area, where I live, to see Hispanic churches, Korean churches, and Chinese churches, for example.) This is because people will feel most comfortable worshiping and fellowshipping with others who speak the same language.[29] But it does mean that churches should recognize that such ethnic separateness is not the ideal that Paul holds out in Ephesians, where he declares that a multiethnic church proclaims "the manifold wisdom of God" to "the rulers and authorities in the

---

[28] Grudem, *Systematic Theology*, 194.

[29] To take another example, I remember that my grandmother in Minneapolis kept her Swedish hymnal until she died.

heavenly places" (3:10). And certainly, once the language barrier can be overcome, churches should welcome and never exclude or demonstrate hostility toward others from different ethnic or racial backgrounds.

In other words, it is God's purpose that his churches become living examples of racial unity and harmony, welcoming and including people from all racial and ethnic backgrounds to full and equal fellowship in the body of Christ.[30]

H. THE QUESTION OF IMMIGRATION LAWS

Because people of many races and ethnicities may want to immigrate into a country, it is appropriate to say something at this point about racial discrimination and the question of whether countries should allow immigration by people from all kinds of racial and ethnic backgrounds.

Certainly the Bible's teaching about the equality of all human beings in the image of God (see above) should lead us to conclude that there should be no discrimination against people of any specific racial or ethnic group when deciding who should be allowed into a country. In addition, I would encourage churches to welcome new immigrants from other countries into their churches, since this will promote the kind of interracial congregations that, according to the apostle Paul, will glorify God by showing his amazing wisdom in the breaking down, in Christ, of barriers that would otherwise separate rather than unite human beings (see discussion in previous section).[31]

The question of the specific policies that should be adopted with respect to immigration is a political matter that I discuss at length in another book.[32] And in yet another book, I and my coauthor present historical data showing that when a country excludes certain groups and keeps them from entering that country, it inevitably hinders that country's economic development. But countries that encourage immigration by skilled and highly motivated people from other nations generally realize significant economic benefits from such a policy.[33]

---

[30] Some readers may wonder why I do not say this is an issue of "social justice." I discuss my decision not to use the expression "social justice" in chap. 37, p. 961.

[31] I hope that all readers would agree with this sentence insofar as it applies to immigrants who have entered a country *legally*. Regarding the more difficult and complex question of how to relate to those who have entered a country *illegally*, see my discussion in Wayne Grudem, *Politics—According to the Bible: A Comprehensive Resource for Understanding Modern Political Issues in Light of Scripture* (Grand Rapids, MI: Zondervan, 2010), 470–83.

[32] My viewpoint is that the United States is a land of immense opportunity and vast open spaces, and we should continue to welcome large numbers of *legal* immigrants, as we have done throughout our history. However, the process of admitting such immigrants should allow in only those we are reasonably confident will be of benefit to the nation, will seek to uphold its laws and its positive cultural values, and will not seek to harm it. In addition, it is necessary that our borders be made much more secure to stop the large influx of *illegal* immigrants. For many other details, see ibid.

[33] See Wayne Grudem and Barry Asmus, *The Poverty of Nations: A Sustainable Solution* (Wheaton, IL: Crossway, 2013), 294–97, 356–58.

QUESTIONS FOR PERSONAL APPLICATION

1. Have you ever experienced discrimination because of your race? How did you deal with this? Were there any ways in which your Christian faith helped you in that situation?

2. Have you ever discriminated against someone else because of his or her racial background? Looking back, how could you have acted differently?

3. Can you give any examples of situations in which you experienced healthy interracial unity, whether in your workplace, in your school (if you are a student), in sports activities, in your neighborhood, or in your church?

4. Can you describe what you think the absence of racial discrimination would look like in each of the settings mentioned in the previous question?

5. What are some things you can do to overcome racial discrimination in situations in which it still exists? What can your church do?

6. What character traits (see p. 110) would be especially helpful to lead people to have right attitudes and choose right actions regarding racial discrimination?

SPECIAL TERMS

racial discrimination

BIBLIOGRAPHY

Sections in Other Ethics Texts

(see complete bibliographical data, p. 64)

Clark and Rakestraw, 2:261–92
Davis, 291–324
Frame, 666–78
Gushee and Stassen, 396–416
Hays, 407–43
Holmes, 83–94
Kaiser, 31–42
McQuilkin and Copan, 238–39, 355–62

Other Works

Anyabwile, Thabiti. "The Glory and Supremacy of Jesus Christ in Ethnic Distinctions and over Ethnic Identities." In *For the Fame of God's Name: Essays in Honor of John Piper*, edited by Sam Storms and Justin Taylor, 293–307. Wheaton, IL: Crossway, 2010.

Bray, Gerald. "Racial and Ethnic Equality." In *God Is Love: A Biblical and Systematic Theology*, 336–40. Wheaton, IL: Crossway, 2012.

Carson, D. A. "Hard Case One: Racism." In *Love in Hard Places*, 87–108. Wheaton, IL: Crossway, 2002.

Cheung-Judge, L. M.-Y. "Discrimination." In *New Dictionary of Christian Ethics and Pastoral Theology*, edited by David J. Atkinson and David H. Field, 312–14. Leicester, UK: Inter-Varsity, and Downers Grove, IL: InterVarsity Press, 1995.

DeYoung, Kevin. "10 Reasons Racism Is Offensive to God." *DeYoung, Restless, and Reformed*, June 25, 2015, http://www.thegospelcoalition.org/blogs/kevindeyoung/2015/06/25/10-reasons-racism-is-offensive-to-god/.

D'Souza, Dinesh. *The End of Racism: Principles for a Multiracial Society*. New York: Free Press Paperbacks, 1996.

Emerson, Michael O., and Christian Smith. *Divided by Faith: Evangelical Religion and the Problem of Race in America*. Oxford: Oxford University Press, 2000.

Evans, Tony. *Oneness Embraced*. Chicago: Moody, 2011.

Hamilton, James M., Jr. "Does the Bible Condone Slavery and Sexism?" In *In Defense of the Bible: A Comprehensive Apologetic for the Authority of Scripture*, edited by Steven B. Cowan and Terry L. Wilder, 335–48. Nashville: Broadman & Holman, 2013.

Hays, J. Daniel. *From Every People and Nation: A Biblical Theology of Race*. New Studies in Biblical Theology 14. Downers Grove, IL: InterVarsity Press, 2003.

Hoffmeier, James K. *The Immigration Crisis: Immigrants, Aliens, and the Bible*. Wheaton, IL: Crossway, 2009.

Loritts, Bryan, ed. *Letters to a Birmingham Jail: A Response to the Words and Dreams of Martin Luther King, Jr.* Chicago: Moody Publishers, 2014.

McKissic, William Dwight, and Anthony T. Evans. *Beyond Roots II: If Anybody Ask You Who I Am: A Deeper Look at Blacks in the Bible*. Wenonah, NJ: Renaissance Productions, 1994.

Piper, John. *Bloodlines: Race, Cross, and the Christian*. Wheaton, IL: Crossway, 2011.

Perkins, John M. *Dream with Me*. Ada, MI: Baker Books, 2017.

Platt, David. "Unity in Diversity: The Gospel and Ethnicity." In *Counter Culture: Following Christ in an Anti-Christian Age*, revised and updated ed., 189–216. Carol Stream, IL: Tyndale Momentum, 2017.

Priest, Robert J., and Alvaro L. Nieves, eds. *This Side of Heaven: Race, Ethnicity, and Christian Faith*. New York: Oxford University Press, 2007.

Sharp, Douglas R. *No Partiality: The Idolatry of Race & the New Humanity*. Downers Grove, IL: InterVarsity Press, 2002.

Sowell, Thomas. *Intellectuals and Race*. New York: Basic Books, 2013.

Steele, Shelby. *Shame: How America's Past Sins Have Polarized Our Country*. New York: Basic Books, 2015.

———. *White Guilt: How Blacks and Whites Together Destroyed the Promise of the Civil Rights Era*. New York: Harper Perennial, 2007.

Thernstrom, Abigail M., and Stephan Thernstrom. *No Excuses: Closing the Racial Gap in Learning*. New York: Simon & Schuster, 2003.

Williams, Jarvis J. *One New Man: The Cross and Racial Reconciliation in Pauline Theology*. Nashville: B&H Academic, 2010.

SCRIPTURE MEMORY PASSAGE

Revelation 7:9–10: After this I looked, and behold, a great multitude that no one could number, from every nation, from all tribes and peoples and languages, standing before the throne and before the Lamb, clothed in white robes, with palm branches in their hands, and crying out with a loud voice, "Salvation belongs to our God who sits on the throne, and to the Lamb!"

HYMN

"The Church's One Foundation"

The church's one Foundation is Jesus Christ her Lord;
She is his new creation by water and by Word:
From heav'n he came and sought her to be his holy bride;
With his own blood he bought her, and for her life he died.

Elect from ev'ry nation, yet one o'er all the earth,
Her charter of salvation one Lord, one faith, one birth;
One holy Name she blesses, partakes one holy food,
And to one hope she presses, with ev'ry grace endued.

Though with a scornful wonder men see her sore oppressed,
By schisms rent asunder, by heresies distressed,
Yet saints their watch are keeping, their cry goes up, "How long?"
And soon the night of weeping shall be the morn of song.

The church shall never perish! Her dear Lord to defend,
To guide, sustain and cherish, is with her to the end;
Though there be those that hate her, and false sons in her pale,
Against a foe or traitor she ever shall prevail.

'Mid toil and tribulation, and tumult of her war
She waits the consummation of peace for evermore;
Till with the vision glorious her longing eyes are blest,
And the great church victorious shall be the church at rest.

Yet she on earth hath union with God the Three in One,
And mystic sweet communion with those whose rest is won:
O happy ones and holy! Lord, give us grace that we,
Like them, the meek and lowly, on high may dwell with thee.

AUTHOR: SAMUEL J. STONE, 1866

Chapter 26

HEALTH

Why does God want us to care for our physical bodies?
What should we think about sleep, vaccinations,
organic foods, tattoos, and circumcision?

Sometimes people mistakenly assume that only "spiritual" realities are morally good and that physical realities, including our physical bodies, are inherently evil. But the Bible from beginning to end presents a positive view of *the moral goodness of our physical bodies*, yet this is tempered by the realization that our bodies have also been affected by the fall and by ongoing sin. The Bible also makes clear that we are to care for our bodies. Therefore, in this chapter, we will consider a number of ethical questions related to the care of our physical bodies.

A. OUR PHYSICAL BODIES ARE NOT EVIL BUT ARE GOOD GIFTS FROM GOD

1. Creation. When God created the first human physical bodies, they were "very good." We know this because they were included in God's culminating assessment on the sixth day of creation: "And God saw *everything* that he had made, and behold, it was *very good*" (Gen. 1:31).

God took particular care in the creation of the physical bodies of the first man and woman, as is evident from the detailed biblical description of God's activity in this process. Whereas the other parts of creation had been formed simply by God commanding "Let there be light" (Gen. 1:3), "Let the earth sprout vegetation" (v. 11), or "Let the earth bring forth living creatures according to their kinds" (v. 24), when we come to the creation of Adam and Eve we read:

> Then the LORD God *formed the man of dust from the ground* and breathed into his nostrils the breath of life, and the man became a living creature. (Gen. 2:7)

Here the Hebrew word translated as "formed" is *yātsar*, a verb elsewhere used of a potter who "forms" clay into a pot (Isa. 29:16) or of people who "fashion" idols (44:9–10). Regarding the creation of Eve, we read:

> And the rib that the LORD God had taken from the man *he made into a woman* and brought her to the man. (Gen. 2:22)

The Hebrew word translated as "made" is *bānāh*, which usually means "to build," and is used of Cain building a city (Gen. 4:17), Noah building an altar (8:20), or people building houses (Deut. 8:12; 20:5).

Both of these verses in Genesis 2 speak of God's detailed personal attention in forming the physical bodies of man and woman. Certainly Adam and Eve's bodies were included in the delight that God felt when he "saw everything that he had made," and "behold, it was *very good*" (Gen. 1:31).

Therefore, the fundamental biblical perspective on our physical bodies is that they are good. They are not evil in themselves, as was taught by the ancient heresy of Gnosticism, the Manichaean religion from which Augustine escaped, and other ancient or modern theories that deny the inherent goodness of material things. Neither are our bodies merely morally neutral. God created the material universe, including our physical bodies, and declared that it was all "very good."

2. The Fall. God told Adam that if he ate from the tree of the knowledge of good and evil, "you shall surely die" (Gen. 2:17). God did not execute that punishment immediately after Adam and Eve sinned, but the *aging that led to death* slowly began to take effect in their bodies. After the fall, God said, "You are dust, and to dust you shall return" (3:19). So Paul can say in the New Testament:

> Therefore, just as sin came into the world through one man, *and death through sin*, . . . so death spread to all men because all sinned. (Rom. 5:12)

Throughout our lifetimes on earth, therefore, we should not try to avoid acknowledging the imperfections and weaknesses of our physical bodies. The recognition that our bodies are wearing down should not cause Christians to despair, but should cause us to long for our perfectly healthy "resurrection bodies" that will never be sick or weak, will never grow old, and will never die. Paul says, "We ourselves, who have the firstfruits of the Spirit, groan inwardly as *we wait eagerly for* adoption as sons, *the redemption of our bodies*" (Rom. 8:23).

3. Death. Except for those who are alive when Christ returns (1 Thess. 4:17), everyone who lives in this present age will experience physical death. "It is appointed for man to die once" (Heb. 9:27). God will not finally put an end to physical death until the time when Christ returns, for "the last enemy to be destroyed is death" (1 Cor. 15:26).

Therefore, even though our bodies were originally created as "very good," in this age they are all subject not only to aging, weakness, and illness, but also to eventual death.

4. Future Bodily Resurrection. Death is not the end of the story for our physical bodies! God has promised that he will one day raise these same bodies and restore them to perfect health and strength at "the last trumpet," when death is conquered:

> Behold! I tell you a mystery. We shall not all sleep, but we shall all be changed, in a moment, in the twinkling of an eye, at the last trumpet. For *the trumpet will sound, and the dead will be raised imperishable, and we shall be changed.* For this perishable body must put on the imperishable, and *this mortal body must put on immortality.* When the perishable puts on the imperishable, and the mortal puts on immortality, then shall come to pass the saying that is written:
>
>> "Death is swallowed up in victory."
>> "O death, where is your victory?
>> O death, where is your sting?" (1 Cor. 15:51–55)

These resurrection bodies will be amazingly attractive, strong, and fully healthy, never subject to illness or aging again (see 1 Cor. 15:42–44).[1]

5. Therefore, Our Physical Bodies Are Important to God. God has made our bodies, and they are awe-inspiring in their intricate complexity:

> For you formed my inward parts;
>> you knitted me together in my mother's womb.
> *I praise you, for I am fearfully and wonderfully made.*
> Wonderful are your works;
>> my soul knows it very well. (Ps. 139:13–14)

God will someday fulfill his original purpose for our bodies and make them to be perfect once again, and in our perfected resurrection bodies we will glorify him forever. Therefore, we should not despise or neglect our physical bodies, but care for them and be thankful to God for them, imperfect though they are.

B. WE SHOULD TAKE REASONABLE CARE OF OUR PHYSICAL BODIES

1. Our Bodies Belong to God and Are the "Temples" of the Holy Spirit. In contrast to the Old Testament era, when God dwelt among his people in the tabernacle in the wil-

---

[1] For further discussion of the nature of our resurrection bodies, see Wayne Grudem, *Systematic Theology: An Introduction to Biblical Doctrine* (Leicester, UK: Inter-Varsity, and Grand Rapids, MI: Zondervan, 1994), 828–39.

derness and then in the temple in Jerusalem, and in contrast to the surrounding pagan cultures of that era, where Greek and Roman "gods" supposedly lived in the temples that proliferated in every major city, Paul said that, as Christians, *our bodies* are now temples of the Holy Spirit:

> Or do you not know that *your body is a temple of the Holy Spirit within you*, whom you have from God? You are not your own, for you were bought with a price. So glorify God in your body. (1 Cor. 6:19–20)

In the Old Testament, God gave the Jewish people detailed instructions about caring for the tabernacle and later for the temple, where God dwelt in the midst of his people. Even the pagan Greeks and Romans took special care of the temples in which their supposed "gods" dwelt. But rather than telling the Corinthian Christians to care for such physical temples, Paul encouraged them to be careful how they treated their own bodies, because the Holy Spirit dwelt within them.

In fact, our physical bodies are *the means by which we serve God* in this life. Every kind of ministry activity that people do today involves some use of their physical bodies. When we sing praise to God, we use our voices. When we do evangelism, we use our voices to share the good news, our minds to think, and our ears to listen to the other person's responses. When we pray, we use our physical voices, or if we pray silently, we at least use our brain cells. Bible teaching uses a person's voice (and hopefully his brain). Ministries of mercy often involve carrying food to those in need or physically going to a hospital room to visit someone who is sick. Parents use the strength of their physical bodies to care for their children, and people who work in secular jobs use their bodies as they "work heartily, as for the Lord and not for men" (Col. 3:23).

I do not think there is any kind of ministry or service for the Lord that we do in this life that does not in some way involve our physical bodies. And in all of these activities, the Holy Spirit chooses to work *through our physical bodies* to bring about positive results in the world.

When we read Paul's comments about his own ministry, we see a hint of the immense amount of physical energy and effort that he brought to the task of Christian ministry:

> Therefore be alert, remembering that for three years *I did not cease night or day* to admonish every one with tears. (Acts 20:31)

> For this I toil, struggling with *all his energy* that he *powerfully works* within me. (Col. 1:29)

Because our physical bodies are the means by which the Holy Spirit ministers through us in this life, our physical health is important. So we should take reasonable care of our bodies in order to make them effective instruments for the Holy Spirit to work through in this life. The strength of our bodies is something that we can present to God as an offering to be used in service to him:

> I appeal to you therefore, brothers, by the mercies of God, to *present your bodies as a living sacrifice, holy and acceptable to God*, which is your spiritual worship. (Rom. 12:1)

In another place, Paul says he wants us to present our "members" (by which he seems to mean the members of our physical bodies) to God to serve him:

> Do not present your members to sin as instruments for unrighteousness, but present yourselves to God as those who have been brought from death to life, and *your members to God as instruments for righteousness*. (Rom. 6:13)

2. Physical Weakness or Illness Reduces the Amount of Time and Energy That We Are Able to Give to Any Ministry. I realize that God often works in powerful and even miraculous ways in spite of physical weakness or illness (I discuss this in section D below, p. 670). However, in the ordinary course of life and ministry, when we become physically weak or seriously ill, we are not able to do as much kingdom and ministry work.

As I write this chapter, I am 68 years old. I am aware that when I travel somewhere to speak, I tire more quickly than I did 10 or 15 years ago, and it takes me more days to recover my strength when I return home. As far as I know, my health is excellent for my age,[2] but I do not have the energy to work the long hours, day after day, that I previously had. The same exact route through our neighborhood that I previously could run in 26 or 27 minutes now takes me 29 minutes. When I go to the gym, I find that I cannot lift as much weight as I could five years ago. This is simply a factor of age, and it is foolish to try to deny it.

Of course, even Christians who are quite old and infirm, often living in nursing homes or with their adult children, still can have very effective worldwide ministries through prayer. But they are limited in any other kind of ministries that they can do (beyond the valuable testimony of their words and actions to influence those around them, and any ministry they may have through letters and other written materials).

3. It Is Better to Be Healthy Than Not Healthy. All other things being equal, it is better to be healthy than not healthy, and to be physically strong rather than physically weak. The curse of Genesis 3:19—"For you are dust, and to dust you shall return"—is not good for us. It is not something we should try to accelerate or rejoice in, for it is part of God's judgment on sin.

Because it is better to be healthy than not healthy (all other things being equal), John tells his readers, "I pray that all may go well with you and *that you may be in good health*, as it goes well with your soul" (3 John 2).

Another argument indicating that physical health is better than sickness (if we have the ability to choose) is that our bodies will be physically healthy and strong in the age

---

[2] That is, I am in good health with the exception of some symptoms connected to the early stages of Parkinson's disease; see http://www.desiringgod.org/articles/i-have-parkinson-s-and-i-am-at-peace.

to come: "It is sown in weakness, it is raised in power" (1 Cor. 15:43). God's final intention for us is not that we would live in weakness and sickness forever, but in health and strength, showing that these are inherently better qualities to desire and seek.

Yet another argument showing the goodness of physical health, where possible, is that people who are sick normally take medicine or seek help from a doctor when they are able to do so. By seeking to be well, they indicate that they believe that being well is better than being sick.

C. EVALUATING SPECIFIC FACTORS THAT INFLUENCE PHYSICAL HEALTH

1. Commonsense Health Habits. It is easy for people who are young and in good health to think, "It doesn't matter much whether I try to care for my health or not, because I feel great anyway." But if our bodies are important to God, and if we can serve him more effectively and extensively in healthy bodies, then such carelessness may not be wise.

We should recognize that it is pleasing to God and that it is consistent with his purposes for us in this life for us to give attention to commonsense health habits, such as getting regular exercise, eating a proper diet, getting enough sleep, wearing a seat belt while driving, washing our hands before eating, and not ordinarily taking physically reckless or foolish risks. In addition, if a flu shot each year substantially reduces your risk of getting the flu and being disabled for several days, then it is certainly wise to get one.

I also have concluded that there is some general medical benefit from regularly taking multivitamin supplements, at least in a reasonable amount, for people who can afford to do so. For example, a study reported in the *Journal of Steroid Biochemistry and Molecular Biology* found increased bone density and reduced fractures in post-menopausal women who took calcium and vitamin D.[3] The Physicians' Health Study II, published by Harvard Health Publications in 2014, looked at the effect of long-term multivitamin use by healthy men on various aspects of their health. It found that men who took multivitamins were 8 percent less likely to be diagnosed with cancer and had a lower risk of developing cataracts. However, the subjects of the study did not experience any protections from heart attacks, strokes, or other forms of cardiovascular disease.[4]

The fact is that most people, at most stages of life, have the ability to make a significant difference in their own health and physical well-being. By their choices of lifestyle and health habits, they can affect the number of years they are able to live and carry out effective work in God's kingdom.

---

[3] J. Christopher Gallagher M.D. and Sri Harsha Tella, M.D., "Prevention and Treatment of Postmenopausal Osteoporosis," *The Journal of Steroid Biochemistry and Molecular Biology* 142 (July 2014): 155–70, https://www.ncbi.nlm.nih.gov/pmc/articles/PMC4187361/.

[4] "Do Multivitamins Make You Healthier?" Harvard Health Publications, Harvard Medical School, March 2014, http://www.health.harvard.edu/mens-health/do-multivitamins-make-you-healthier.

2. Physical Exercise. Paul recognizes that bodily training is "of some value." It is not as valuable as training in godliness, but it is still worthwhile:

> While *bodily training is of some value*, godliness is of value in every way, as it holds promise for the present life and also for the life to come. (1 Tim. 4:8)

Paul also apparently exercised some kinds of self-discipline with respect to his own physical body, for he explains the Christian life using an athletic metaphor (but says he is doing this not for earthly honor but for an "imperishable" heavenly reward):

> Every athlete exercises *self-control in all things*. They do it to receive a perishable wreath, but we an *imperishable*. So I do not run aimlessly; I do not box as one beating the air. But *I discipline my body and keep it under control*, lest after preaching to others I myself should be disqualified. (1 Cor. 9:25–26)

Modern medical research continues to demonstrate multiple benefits that come from regular physical exercise. According to the Mayo Clinic, there are seven major benefits of regular exercise:

- Exercise controls weight because you burn more calories.
- Exercise combats health conditions and diseases such as heart disease by boosting good cholesterol (HDL).
- Exercise improves mood by stimulating brain chemicals that make you feel happier or more relaxed.
- Exercise boosts energy by increasing the flow of oxygen and nutrients to your tissues.
- Exercise promotes better sleep by helping you fall asleep faster.
- Exercise improves your sex life by improving energy levels.
- Exercise helps build social bonds with friends and family members as you engage in shared activities.[5]

Maintaining regular exercise requires more self-discipline than it did in previous centuries, because people in economically developed societies today can drive a car instead of walking, use a washing machine instead of washing clothes by hand, work at a desk or computer instead of in the fields, and adjust the thermostat instead of chopping wood or shoveling coal for a fire. It is easy to become passive and sedentary, but our bodies—and our ministries—suffer as a result.

3. Sleep. Recent studies suggest that many Americans do not get enough sleep. A 2010 study conducted by the Centers for Disease Control and Prevention found that 41 mil-

---

[5] "Exercise: 7 Benefits of Regular Physical Activity," The Mayo Clinic, http://www.mayoclinic.org/healthy -lifestyle/fitness/in-depth/exercise/art-20048389.

lion American workers are sleep deficient.[6] In 2013, Gallup reported that 40 percent of Americans get less than the minimally recommended seven hours of sleep per night.[7]

But the Bible views sleep as important and as a gift from God. In fact, not getting enough sleep can be an indication of anxiety and lack of trust in God for the successful outcome of one's efforts:

> It is in vain that you rise up early
>> and go late to rest,
> eating the bread of anxious toil;
>> *for he gives to his beloved sleep*. (Ps. 127:2)

An effective day of productive work leads to a good night's sleep, according to the book of Ecclesiastes: "*Sweet is the sleep of a laborer*, whether he eats little or much, but the full stomach of the rich will not let him sleep" (5:12).

I have found in my own life and in conversations with many people that getting enough sleep is important to an effective prayer life. Paul tells the Ephesian Christians that they should be "praying at all times in the Spirit, with all prayer and supplication. *To that end, keep alert* with all perseverance" (Eph. 6:18). But it is hard to "keep alert" when one keeps falling asleep. Lack of sleep can lead to a spiritual dullness and diminishing of one's ability to pray or worship effectively.[8]

On the other hand, there is a possibility of excessive sleep. Too much sleep is a sign of laziness, which will lead to poverty:

> I passed by the field of a sluggard . . .
> and behold, it was all overgrown with thorns. . . .
> A little sleep, a little slumber,
>> a little folding of the hands to rest,
> and poverty will come upon you like a robber,
>> and want like an armed man. (Prov. 24:30–34)

The "sluggard" in Proverbs is one who loves sleep too much. When it is time to wake up he simply rolls over and rolls back again and goes back to sleep:

---

[6] "Short Sleep Duration among Workers—United States, 2010," Centers for Disease Control and Prevention, *Morbidity and Mortality Weekly Report* 61, no. 16 (April 27, 2012): 281–85, http://www.cdc.gov/mmwr /preview/mmwrhtml/mm6116a2.htm.

[7] Jeffrey M. Jones, "In U.S., 40% Get Less Than Recommended Amount of Sleep," Gallup, Dec. 19, 2013, http://www.gallup.com/poll/166553/less-recommended-amount-sleep.aspx.

[8] When I was teaching at Trinity Evangelical Divinity School in Deerfield, Illinois, one of the chapel speakers was a veteran district superintendent from the Evangelical Free Church of America, the denomination that owned the seminary. In the course of his chapel talk, he mentioned that he had been a district superintendent overseeing the work of dozens of pastors for more than 20 years. He said that every time a pastor came to him and said he had decided to give up the ministry because he was discouraged, he told the pastor, "Go home and get enough sleep for the next month and then come back and talk to me again." He said that in every case, the pastor came back a month later and decided to continue in ministry.

> As a door turns on its hinges,
> so does a sluggard on his bed. (Prov. 26:14)

Individual people vary in the amount of sleep they need in order to function effectively. Some people can function well with only six hours of sleep per night, while others seem to need about eight hours to be fully rested. While allowing for individual variability, research has shown that for most people seven hours of sleep is probably the optimal level.[9] And a few people (about 1 percent to 3 percent of the population) have been known to need only four or five hours of sleep a night. Some of the successful people who have averaged four to five hours of sleep include President Donald Trump, former Presidents Clinton and Obama, Jay Leno, Condoleeza Rice, Martha Stewart, Marissa Mayer (CEO of Yahoo), Margaret Thatcher, Thomas Edison, and Benjamin Franklin.[10] The optimal amount of sleep is something each person must ascertain for himself or herself.

This issue is important, because prolonged lack of sufficient sleep can have serious health consequences. The effects include:

- Fatigue, lethargy, and lack of motivation; concentration and memory problems
- Moodiness and irritability
- Reduced creativity and problem-solving skills; difficulty making decisions
- Inability to cope with stress
- Reduced immunity; frequent colds and infections; weight gain
- Impaired motor skills and increased risk of accidents
- Increased risk of diabetes, heart disease, and other health problems[11]

It is important also that we think of sleep as a gift from the Lord: "He gives to his beloved sleep" (Ps. 127:2).[12]

4. Vaccinations. Recently, a troubling anti-vaccination trend has spread among young parents. Based on information found on the Internet or heard from friends, a number of them are deciding not to allow their children to get the routine vaccinations that the medical profession recommends for disease prevention in early childhood.

---

[9] Sumathi Reddy, "Why Seven Hours of Sleep Might Be Better Than Eight," *The Wall Street Journal*, July 21, 2014, http://www.wsj.com/articles/sleep-experts-close-in-on-the-optimal-nights-sleep-1405984970.

[10] Carolyn Cutrone and Max Nisen, "19 Successful People Who Barely Sleep," *Business Insider*, Sept. 18, 2012, http://www.businessinsider.com/successful-people-who-barely-sleep-2012-9.

[11] "Sleep Needs: What to Do If You're Not Getting Enough Sleep," HelpGuide.org, http://www.helpguide.org/articles/sleep/how-much-sleep-do-you-need.htm.

[12] John Piper writes, "For me, adequate sleep is not just a matter of staying healthy. It's a matter of staying in the ministry." *Brothers, We Are Not Professionals: A Plea to Pastors for Radical Ministry*, 2nd ed. (Nashville: Broadman & Holman, 2013), 189. See also Joe Carter, "How to Love God by Getting More Sleep," The Gospel Coalition, Dec. 15, 2015, http:// www.thegospelcoalition.org/article/how-to-love-god-by-getting-more-sleep; Adrian Reynolds, *And So to Bed . . . : A Biblical View of Sleep* (Fearn, Ross-shire, Scotland: Christian Focus, 2014).

This anti-vaccination trend seems to me to be gravely mistaken. Much of it was prompted by a 1988 report published in a British medical journal, *The Lancet*, claiming a link between vaccinations and autism. But *The Lancet* later retracted the story because it had been widely proven to be fraudulent, and the medical license of the author, a British surgeon named Andrew Wakefield, was taken away.[13]

Children who are not vaccinated against whooping cough (pertussis), for example, are 24 times more likely to catch the disease. Because of falling vaccination rates, California in 2010 experienced an outbreak of whooping cough greater than any since 1947—and 10 children died from it. Whereas the U.S. Centers for Disease Control and Prevention declared that the United States was measles-free in 2000, in 2014 667 cases of measles occurred,[14] and in 2015 there were 189 cases, including a multi-state outbreak of 113 cases linked to Disneyland in California.[15]

The diseases that are preventable by a simple series of vaccinations (chicken pox, diphtheria, hepatitis A, hepatitis B, Hib, HPV, influenza, measles, meningococcal disease, mumps, pneumococcal disease, polio, rotavirus, rubella, shingles, tetanus, and whooping cough)[16] are serious, sometimes very debilitating, and even potentially fatal diseases that modern medicine has been able to almost entirely eradicate—if parents will have their children vaccinated.

Extensive and repeated medical tests have shown that the risk of complications or diseases as a result of early childhood vaccinations is insignificant, and there is an almost infinitely small chance of harm. For example, studies have found that after receiving the first shot of the measles/mumps/rubella (MMR) vaccination, a child has a roughly 1 in 3,000 chance of developing a fever that leads to a seizure,[17] whereas the chance of harm from the diseases is far greater.

The idea that these vaccines are not "natural" is not persuasive from a biblical standpoint. That is because what is "natural" in the world as it exists has not only been created by God, but has also experienced the result of the curse that God imposed on the ground:

And to Adam he said,

"Because you have listened to the voice of your wife
    and have eaten of the tree
of which I commanded you,
    'You shall not eat of it,'

[13] Paul A. Offit, "The Anti-Vaccination Epidemic," *The Wall Street Journal*, Sept. 24, 2014, A21, https://www.wsj.com/articles/paul-a-offit-the-anti-vaccination-epidemic-1411598408.

[14] Vincent Iannelli, "Measles Outbreaks in the United States," VeryWell, Aug. 15, 2017, https://www.verywell.com/measles-outbreaks-2633845.

[15] Ibid.

[16] "Recommended Vaccines by Disease," Centers for Disease Control and Prevention, https://www.cdc.gov/vaccines/vpd/vaccines-diseases.html.

[17] Dina Fine Maron, "Fact or Fiction? Vaccines Are Dangerous," *Scientific American*, March 6, 2015, https://www.scientificamerican.com/article/fact-or-fiction-vaccines-are-dangerous/.

> *cursed is the ground because of you;*
> in pain you shall eat of it all the days of your life." (Gen. 3:17)

Therefore, disease and death are part of the "natural" order of things in the world after the sin of Adam and Eve. The command to "subdue" the earth (Gen. 1:28) implies God's expectation that Adam and Eve would develop the earth's resources to make them less harmful and more useful to the human race.

Therefore, vaccines are also part of "nature," because they are made from products developed from nature. The whole world belongs to God, including all the ingredients for vaccines that he placed in the earth. And he has given men and women the wisdom to develop vaccines for human beings made in his image. It all belongs to God and it is all from him: "The earth is the Lord's and the fullness thereof, the world and those who dwell therein" (Ps. 24:1).

For parents to fail to vaccinate their children, and therefore to vastly increase the risk that they will catch some seriously painful and harmful disease—which they might spread to other children and adults—is a blatant failure to obey the command "You shall love your neighbor as yourself" (Matt. 22:39), even with respect to their own children.

5. "Organic" Foods. Paul knew that there were disputes among Christians about which foods were right to eat, so he wrote to the Roman Christians about this, telling them that they had much freedom in deciding what to eat and not to eat, but that they should not pass judgment on each other over such questions:

> One person believes he may eat anything, while the weak person eats only vegetables. Let not the one who eats despise the one who abstains, and let not the one who abstains pass judgment on the one who eats, for God has welcomed him. (Rom. 14:2–3)

It seems to me that the same principle applies today to the question of eating organic foods.

If some people think that foods labeled "organic" are healthier, and if they can afford them (for they are often more expensive), then they are free to eat them, but not to condemn others who do not choose to spend their money in that way.

As for the question of whether organic foods actually are healthier, it is simply a question of getting proper data and rightly assessing it. I do not think that any biblical principles are at stake. It is simply a fact-oriented question.

However, I do think it is incorrect for people to assume that foods found in a "natural" state, unaffected by fertilizers, pesticides, herbicides, or genetic modifications, are more spiritual, more Christian, or more pleasing to God than foods that have been modified with modern agricultural research tools and methods. I do not think that these innovations of modern agriculture are wrong because I do not think that what grows in an "unimproved" form in nature is necessarily the best way for that plant, vegetable, or fruit to exist. The way foods grow in nature might well be affected by the fall and by the curse that God put on the earth:

> Cursed is the ground because of you;
> in pain you shall eat of it all the days of your life;
> thorns and thistles it shall bring forth for you;
> and you shall eat the plants of the field. (Gen 3:17–18)

In addition to "thorns and thistles," some of the difficult and painful things that occur in nature are insects that eat crops and plant diseases that infect crops. When herbicides are sprayed on fields, they overcome the "thorns and thistles" that are part of the curse and that can hinder the growth of crops. This process of killing weeds is therefore a *morally good thing* for farmers to do in their fields, and there is no moral benefit to clearing weeds by hand as opposed to spraying them with a chemical that is designed to kill them.

If "the earth is the LORD's and the fullness thereof, the world and those who dwell therein" (Ps. 24:1), then the material to make a herbicide is also the Lord's, and the intelligence in the scientist who discovers the herbicide is also a gift from God. Therefore, we should use such things with thanksgiving.

The command to Adam and Eve to "fill the earth and subdue it" (Gen. 1:28) implied that agricultural development would be a necessary activity, and it would be even more needed after the curse on the earth that came as a result of sin.

Therefore, the issue of organic foods turns on the questions of whether they *taste better*, are *affordable*, and have any significant measurable *health benefits*. These are questions for individuals to decide for themselves and their families.

My own personal inclination in this area is not to spend extra money on organic foods unless they clearly taste better or are fresher. I am willing to eat whatever fruits and vegetables are sold in the grocery store, being thankful to God for all of it. I am happy to apply 1 Timothy 4:4–5 to all of the fresh produce that is available to me:

> For everything created by God is good, and *nothing is to be rejected if it is received with thanksgiving*, for it is made holy by the word of God and prayer.

6. Tattoos. Sometimes people read a statement about tattoos in the Old Testament and wonder if it applies today:

> You shall not make any cuts on your body for the dead *or tattoo yourselves*: I am the LORD. (Lev. 19:28)

a. Leviticus 19:28 Is Part of the Mosaic Covenant and No Longer Binding: As I argued earlier (see p. 210), the Mosaic covenant has been terminated with the death of Christ, and we are now under the new covenant. Therefore, this law from the Mosaic covenant is not directly binding on us today.[18]

But the remaining question is whether the prohibition on tattoos still reflects wisdom for godly living, wisdom that we would do well to follow today, or whether it is a prohibition particular to the circumstances of the old covenant.

b. This Command Probably Refers to Canaanite Religious Practices: This same sentence in Leviticus also prohibits making "any cuts on your body for the dead," which has nothing to do with Jewish religious commands and must therefore reflect a prohibition against Canaanite religious practices connected to the deaths of friends or relatives. Therefore, it is likely that the tattoos in question relate to Canaanite religious practices as well. But this is not certain. R. K. Harrison says, "The shaving of the hair on the temples and beard (27), or the incising of patterns on the skin, formed part of pagan mourning practices and as such were prohibited. The disfiguring of the skin, which probably included some emblems of pagan deities, dishonored the divine image in a person."[19] Jay Sklar writes, "Tattoos today—at least in Western cultures—do not have the same pagan associations as they did in ancient Israel, so believers are no longer prohibited from getting them."[20] Gordon J. Wenham, however, sees an additional, deeper reason for this command: "Man is not to disfigure the divine likeness implanted in him by scarring his body. The external appearance of the people should reflect their internal status as the chosen and holy people of God (Deut. 14:1–2)."[21]

c. This Verse Is Part of the Mosaic Covenant's Physical Purity Laws: Even if Leviticus 19:28 were shown to be unrelated to pagan religious practice, the prohibition against tattoos should still be seen as part of the physical purity laws that were unique to the Mosaic covenant, such as the prohibition against cutting one's hair or one's beard (v. 27), the prohibition against eating from a fruit tree until the fifth year (vv. 23–25), or the prohibitions against hybrid cattle, planting two kinds of seed in a field, or wearing garments made of two kinds of material (v. 19). These laws all emphasized outward physical purity, a purity of appearance, that is no longer binding on people in the new covenant. There seems to be no reason to see any abiding moral principles reflected in these commands. Therefore, there is no biblical prohibition against tattoos for people who are no longer living under the Mosaic covenant.

d. Is It Wise to Get a Tattoo? Beyond the question of whether there is a direct biblical prohibition against tattoos is the question of whether it is wise to get a tattoo.[22]

---

[18] Note how the previous verse, if followed today, would also prohibit haircuts and shaving: "You shall not round off the hair on your temples or mar the edges of your beard" (Lev. 19:27).

[19] R. K. Harrison, *Leviticus*, TOTC (Downers Grove, IL: InterVarsity Press, 1980), 201.

[20] Jay Sklar, *Leviticus*, TOTC (Downers Grove, IL: InterVarsity Press, 2014), 250.

[21] Gordon J. Wenham, *The Book of Leviticus*, NICOT (Grand Rapids, MI: Eerdmans, 1979), 272.

[22] Andrew David Naselli and J. D. Crowley conclude that tattoos are not "inherently sinful" but may be unwise because of how other people might understand them: see *Conscience: What It Is, How to Train*

It is similar to buying a piece of clothing that you can never take off for the rest of your life, even if you no longer like it. Tattoos are extremely difficult and very expensive to remove, with the total cost potentially reaching $10,000, depending on the number of sessions needed,[23] and the removal process requires several treatments that are very painful.[24] Tattoos that are visible are a barrier to employment or are prohibited for jobs in many companies. A survey done by Salary.com found that 76 percent of respondents felt tattoos and piercings hurt an applicant's chances of being hired during a job interview. More than one-third—39 percent—felt that employees with tattoos and piercings reflected poorly on their employers. Finally, 42 percent felt that tattoos are always inappropriate at work.[25] Another study from Scotland's University of St. Andrews showed that managers thought visibly tattooed workers could be perceived as "abhorrent, repugnant, unsavory, and untidy" by customers.[26] Anyone considering getting a tattoo should at least be aware of these common perceptions.

7. Self-Mutilation. Sometimes people intentionally hurt their bodies by cutting them or wounding them in other ways. This is different from getting a tattoo, because the goal in getting a tattoo is to enhance a person's bodily appearance (whether it does that or not is a matter of disagreement and personal taste). But with self-mutilation, the intention is to *hurt* one's body and *harm* its appearance.

Paul's teaching about our bodies is appropriate here. As we have seen previously, he says that "your body is a temple of the Holy Spirit within you, whom you have from God" (1 Cor. 6:19). We Christians have the Holy Spirit living within us, so we should not dishonor our bodies.

In addition, it is Satan's purpose to destroy human beings made in the image of God. Jesus says, "He was a murderer from the beginning" (John 8:44). He is like the thief who "comes only to steal and to kill *and destroy*" (John 10:10). Therefore, along with a person's own sinful desires and self-hatred, another factor motivating self-mutilation might be a demonic influence urging a person to hurt himself or herself.

The question of what motivates this behavior is very important, and will require wisdom and spiritual discernment to understand. In many cases, the help of a wise and mature Christian counselor will be needed, along with much prayer, in order to effectively address this problem.

It, and Loving Those Who Differ (Wheaton, IL: Crossway, 2016), 73–75.

[23]"How Much Does Tattoo Removal Cost?" CostHelper, http://health.costhelper.com/tattoo-removal .html.

[24]Courtney Rubin, "How to Get Rid of a Tattoo You've Outgrown," *The New York Times*, Feb. 23, 2016, http://www.nytimes.com/2016/02/25/fashion/tattoo-regret-a-painful-if-improved-reversal-awaits.html? _r=0.

[25]Aaron Gouveia, "Survey: Tattoos Hurt Your Chances of Getting a Job," Salary.com, http://www.salary .com/tattoos-hurt-chances-getting-job/slide/2/.

[26]Cited in Alex Mierjeski, "Can Tattoos Lead to Job Discrimination," ATTN:, Aug. 23, 2015, https://www .attn.com/stories/2845/tattoos-workplace-discrimination.

8. Circumcision.

a. Circumcision Is No Longer Commanded by God in the New Covenant: Long before the time of Moses, God instituted the ceremony of circumcision for all of the male descendants of Abraham:

> This is my covenant, which you shall keep, between me and you and your offspring after you: *Every male among you shall be circumcised.* (Gen. 17:10)

This requirement was repeated in the Mosaic Law regarding newborn baby boys: "And on the eighth day the flesh of his foreskin shall be circumcised" (Lev. 12:3).

But even at the time of Moses there was a realization that the outward, physical act of circumcision was intended by God to symbolize an inward "circumcision of the heart" by which people ceased to be stubborn and resistant to God's will, and willingly followed it instead. Moses told the people of Israel, "*Circumcise therefore the foreskin of your heart,* and be no longer stubborn" (Deut. 10:16).

By the time of the new covenant, Paul taught that the true people of God were not those who have physical circumcision, but those whose hearts are circumcised and who are submissive to God in their lives:

> For no one is a Jew who is merely one outwardly, nor is circumcision outward and physical. But a Jew is one inwardly, and *circumcision is a matter of the heart,* by the Spirit, not by the letter. His praise is not from man but from God. (Rom. 2:28–29)

Paul especially was careful to emphasize that circumcision is no longer required for believers in the new covenant:

> For neither circumcision counts for anything nor uncircumcision, but keeping the commandments of God. (1 Cor. 7:19)

Several other passages make clear that circumcision is no longer a requirement under the new covenant (see Gal. 2:3; 5:2–6, 11; Phil. 3:2–3; Col. 2:11, Titus 1:10; and the long narrative of the Jerusalem Council in Acts 15:1–29).

b. Is Circumcision Beneficial from a Health Standpoint? Even though circumcision is not required under the new covenant, is it wise because of the health benefits it confers? The answer to this question appears to be yes. For example, researchers Brian Morris, professor emeritus at the School of Medical Sciences at the University of Sydney, and Thomas Wiswell found that uncircumcised newborns face a 50-50 chance of contracting urinary-tract infections, while circumcised infants have only a 33 percent risk. The researchers found that the benefits of circumcision outweighed the risks by 100 to 1, as half of all uncircumcised men will need treatment for a condition related to foreskin retention.[27] In addition, circumcision has been found to lead to a reduced risk of some sexually transmitted diseases and protection against penile cancer.[28]

Therefore, many parents will decide to have their infant boys circumcised in order to provide this health benefit for the rest of their lives.

c. We Know That Circumcision Is Not Harmful, because God Commanded It: It should not be argued that circumcision will harm a baby boy or that the pain that accompanies circumcision will be harmful, because God would never have commanded all males among his people to experience something that brought physical harm or damaged them in some way.

d. Should Parents Let the Child Choose Later? Some parents might argue that it is better to allow the boy to grow to adulthood and then decide whether he wants to be circumcised. But it seems to me this is a case in which parents have a responsibility to make a wise decision regarding what is best for their son. Allowing a child to decide about this is somewhat like allowing a child to choose what food he will eat and what vaccinations he will get—he is not old enough to make a wise decision at the time the choice has to be made. If he waits until adulthood, the experience of circumcision will be more painful and difficult. A 2013 study in the *Journal of Urology* found that men who were circumcised suffered moderate to severe pain during recovery, losing at least a week's work and experiencing limitations on heavy physical activity for 11 days.[29]

e. Are Anti-Circumcision Advocates Wrongly Idealizing Our "Natural State"? Those who oppose circumcision might argue that it is better to leave the human body in its "natural state." But this argument does not take account of the fact that since the fall, our bodies are subject to sickness and eventually to death (Gen. 2:17; 3:19). Many times people's bodies need glasses to correct the "natural state" of their vision or braces to correct the "natural state" of their teeth. Therefore, it would not be surprising if God required for his people, the Jews, in the old covenant a "correction" of the natural state in which boys were born in order to protect them from infection and disease later in life.

9. Spiritual Influences on Physical Health. Our physical health is affected not only by food, exercise, sleep, and proper medicine to cure diseases, but also by our spiritual health.

On the one hand, living in obedience before God is said to be good for our health:

---

[27] B. Morris, S. Bailis, and T. Wiswell, "Circumcision Rates in the United States: Rising or Falling? What Effect Might the New Affirmative Pediatric Policy Statement Have?" *Mayo Clinic Proceedings*, 2014, cited in Chris Weller, "Circumcision Benefits Exceed Risks 100 to 1, 'Equivalent to Childhood Vaccination,'" *Medical Daily*, April 2, 2014, http://www.medicaldaily.com/circumcision-benefits-exceed-risks-100-1-equivalent-childhood-vaccination-273992.

[28] "Circumcision Basics," WebMD, http://www.webmd.com/sexual-conditions/guide/circumcision.

[29] B. P. Rai, A. Qureshi, N. Kadi, R. Donat, "How Painful is Adult Circumcision? A Prospective, Observational Cohort Study," *Journal of Urology* 189 (June 2013): 2237–42, https://www.ncbi.nlm.nih.gov/pubmed/23276514.

> Be not wise in your own eyes;
>> fear the LORD, and turn away from evil.
>> *It will be healing to your flesh*
>> *and refreshment to your bones.* (Prov. 3:7–8)

> A tranquil heart gives life to the flesh,
>> but envy makes the bones rot. (Prov. 14:30)

> *A joyful heart is good medicine,*
>> but a crushed spirit dries up the bones. (Prov. 17:22)

On the other hand, unconfessed sin and the realization of moral guilt before God can eat away at our health:

> *For when I kept silent, my bones wasted away*
>> through my groaning all day long.
> For day and night your hand was heavy upon me;
>> my strength was dried up as by the heat of summer. *Selah*
> I acknowledged my sin to you,
>> and I did not cover my iniquity;
> I said, "I will confess my transgressions to the LORD,"
>> and you forgave the iniquity of my sin. *Selah.* (Ps. 32:3–5)

These passages make us realize the importance of keeping our relationship with God healthy, and confessing and forsaking known sin when it comes to our attention. It also reminds us that living in obedience to God will ordinarily have a positive influence on our health.

D. GOD CAN AND OFTEN DOES WORK THROUGH US IN SPITE OF WEAKNESS OR ILLNESS

The preceding material on the importance of physical health and the need to take reasonable care of our bodies must be balanced with another factor that is also taught in Scripture: God can work in surprising and powerful ways through our weaknesses and in spite of our weaknesses. This is important because in this life we will all experience some measure of sickness or physical disability, and we will all eventually become weak and die (unless Christ returns first).

The apostle Paul was acutely aware of this, and particularly in 2 Corinthians he writes about his weakness and how God manifested his power through it:

> But we have this treasure in jars of clay, *to show that the surpassing power belongs to God and not to us.* We are afflicted in every way, but not crushed; perplexed, but not driven to despair; persecuted, but not forsaken; struck

down, but not destroyed; always carrying in the body the death of Jesus, *so that the life of Jesus may also be manifested in our bodies.* For we who live are always being given over to death for Jesus's sake, so that the life of Jesus also may be manifested in our mortal flesh. (4:7–11)

A few verses later he continues explaining that he is not discouraged by his physical sufferings:

So we do not lose heart. *Though our outer self is wasting away,* our inner self is being renewed day by day. For *this light momentary affliction* is preparing for us an eternal weight of glory beyond all comparison, as we look not to the things that are seen but to the things that are unseen. For the things that are seen are transient, but the things that are unseen are eternal. (2 Cor. 4:16–18)

Paul even prayed that God would remove from him something he called a "thorn . . . in the flesh, a messenger of Satan" (2 Cor. 12:7).[30] Paul repeatedly asked the Lord to take it away: "Three times I pleaded with the Lord about this, that it should leave me" (v. 8).

In spite of Paul's earnest prayers, the Lord did not remove his "thorn in the flesh," but explained his secret purpose behind it:

But he said to me, "My grace is sufficient for you, for *my power is made perfect in weakness.*" Therefore I will boast all the more gladly of my weaknesses, so that the power of Christ may rest upon me. For the sake of Christ, then, I am content with weaknesses, insults, hardships, persecutions, and calamities. *For when I am weak, then I am strong.* (2 Cor. 12:9–10)

Paul's proclamation of the gospel throughout the Gentile world was monumentally successful, in spite of his affliction and weakness. But that just showed that the power behind his preaching was God, not Paul's own strength.

In the Old Testament, Psalm 119 contains some striking verses on the spiritual benefits that came to the psalmist through his suffering:

Before I was afflicted I went astray,
    but now I keep your word. . . .
It is good for me that I was afflicted,
    that I might learn your statutes. (Ps. 119:67, 71)[31]

---

[30] Commentators are uncertain about the nature of this "thorn in the flesh." Some think it was a physical affliction, some think it was harassment by a demon ("a messenger of Satan"), and some think it was the repeated hostile opposition of Jewish opponents that Paul faced in city after city. My own conclusion, after reading arguments on various sides, is that we do not have enough evidence to decide conclusively what this thorn in the flesh was. But that uncertainty is beneficial for us because it allows us to make wider application of this passage to all sorts of difficulties and hardships that we face in this lifetime.

[31] New Testament passages about the spiritual benefits that come through trials and suffering are also applicable here: see James 1:2–4; 1 Pet. 1:6–7.

When we couple these verses with the earlier material about the importance of physical health and caring for our bodies, our conclusion should be that it is right to seek to protect and nurture our physical health insofar as we are able to do so while caring for other responsibilities of life. However, when physical affliction or disability occurs in our lives, we should not be discouraged but continue to trust God to work through us in spite of our weaknesses, for in them God's power can be made more evident in our lives and ministries.

E. IS IT RIGHT TO SACRIFICE PHYSICAL HEALTH FOR THE SAKE OF MINISTRY?

1. Paul Sometimes Sacrificed His Physical Health in Order to Spread the Gospel. Paul was willing at times to prioritize the spreading of the gospel ahead of his physical health and bodily well-being. Consider this remarkable paragraph:

> Three times I was beaten with rods. Once I was stoned. Three times I was shipwrecked; a night and a day I was adrift at sea; on frequent journeys, in danger from rivers, danger from robbers, danger from my own people, danger from Gentiles, danger in the city, danger in the wilderness, danger at sea, danger from false brothers; in toil and hardship, through many a sleepless night, in hunger and thirst, often without food, in cold and exposure. (2 Cor. 11:25–27)

Such persistence in relentlessly traveling from city to city to spread the gospel, in spite of the toll that it must have taken on Paul's physical body, stands in marked contrast to our modern culture and its ideal (perhaps its "idol") of protecting our physical health as one of our highest goals. Paul's experience shows that effective ministry for Christ often will cost something in terms of our physical health. In fact, Peter tells us that Christ endured physical sufferings as an example for us: "Christ also suffered for you, leaving you an example, so that you might follow in his steps" (1 Pet. 2:21).

Furthermore, Christ's example tells us that we at times might even have to lay down our lives for others in order to be obedient to him and his calling: "Greater love has no one than this, that someone lay down his life for his friends" (John 15:13). In the book of Revelation, we see those who conquered Satan "by the blood of the Lamb and by the word of their testimony," and they were able to do this because "they loved not their lives even unto death" (Rev. 12:11).

2. Wisdom Is Required in Deciding between Caring for Physical Health and Sacrificing It for Ministry Purposes. It is sometimes difficult to know how to decide between the need to care for one's body as a temple of the Holy Spirit (that is, not acting foolishly in harming one's body) and sacrificing one's physical well-being for the sake of the advancement of God's kingdom (that is, not being selfish). This is a matter for mature wisdom, and we also must recognize that the right choice may vary from person to person and from circumstance to circumstance.

Seeking the counsel of friends is important in such circumstances: "In an abundance of counselors there is safety" (Prov. 11:14). The Holy Spirit will often guide us in this area as well, especially as we pray and seek his leading.

QUESTIONS FOR PERSONAL APPLICATION

1. Do you think of your physical body is something that is basically "good" because it has been created by God?
2. How do you feel about the fact that you will exist in a physical body (one that is made perfect) forever?
3. Do you normally get enough sleep? Why or why not? To what extent is this affected by your trust in God?
4. Do you think that you get too little exercise or that you spend too much time on exercise and personal fitness? After reading this chapter, do you intend to make any changes in this area of your life? Why might it be difficult?
5. What is your conviction about tattoos? About circumcision for male children?
6. Are you aware of any ways in which your spiritual health is having an impact on your physical health?
7. Can you think of some ways in which God has worked through you in spite of physical weakness?
8. What character traits (see p. 110) are strengthened by regularly taking care of your physical health? What character traits will be especially helpful in encouraging you to care wisely for your health?

SPECIAL TERMS

BIBLIOGRAPHY

Sections in Other Ethics Texts

(see complete bibliographical data, p. 64)

Frame, 739–43

Other Works

Brand, Paul, and Philip Yancey. *Fearfully and Wonderfully Made*. Grand Rapids, MI: Zondervan, 1980.
———. *In His Image: The Sequel to Fearfully & Wonderfully Made*. Grand Rapids, MI: Zondervan, 1984.

Cook, E. D. "Health and Health Care." In *New Dictionary of Christian Ethics and Pastoral Theology*, edited by David J. Atkinson and David H. Field, 435–37. Leicester, UK: Inter-Varsity, and Downers Grove, IL: InterVarsity Press, 1995.

Cutillo, Bob. *Pursuing Health in an Anxious Age*. Wheaton, IL: Crossway, 2016.

Jones, David W., and Russell S. Woodbridge. *Health, Wealth and Happiness: Has the Prosperity Gospel Overshadowed the Gospel of Christ?* Grand Rapids, MI: Kregel, 2011.

Murray, David. *Reset: Living a Grace-Paced Life in a Burnout Culture*. Wheaton, IL: Crossway, 2017.

Reynolds, Adrian. *And So to Bed . . . : A Biblical View of Sleep*. Fearn, Ross-shire, Scotland: Christian Focus, 2014.

Saunders, Peter. *The Human Journey: Thinking Biblically about Health*. London: Christian Medical Fellowship, 2014.

SCRIPTURE MEMORY PASSAGE

1 Corinthians 6:19–20: Or do you not know that your body is a temple of the Holy Spirit within you, whom you have from God? You are not your own, for you were bought with a price. So glorify God in your body.

HYMN

"Cleanse Me"

Search me, O God, and know my heart today;
Try me, O Savior, know my thoughts I pray.
See if there be some wicked way in me;
Cleanse me from ev'ry sin and set me free.

I praise Thee, Lord, for cleansing me from sin;
Fulfill Thy Word and make me pure within.
Fill me with fire where once I burned with shame;
Grant my desire to magnify Thy name.

Lord, take my life and make it wholly Thine;
Fill my poor heart with Thy great love divine.
Take all my will, my passion, self and pride;
I now surrender, Lord in me abide.

O Holy Ghost, revival comes from Thee;
Send a revival, start the work in me.
Thy Word declares Thou wilt supply our need;
For blessings now, O Lord, I humbly plead.

AUTHOR: J. EDWIN ORR, 1912–

Chapter 27

ALCOHOL AND DRUGS

What are the dangers of alcoholic beverages?

Is it wrong to use alcohol in moderation?

What are the dangers related to the legalization of marijuana?

This chapter treats two specific topics that are broadly related to the question of health, namely, alcoholic beverages and drugs. Most of the chapter will be devoted to alcoholic beverages, and then at the end of the chapter I will discuss the extent to which the same principles can be applied to drug use.[1]

The question of the use of alcoholic beverages has been hotly disputed. For example, in the United States in the late 19th and early 20th centuries, public awareness of the destructive consequences of drunkenness became so strong that the U.S. Constitution was actually amended to prohibit "the manufacture, sale, or transportation of intoxicating liquors . . . for beverage purposes."[2]

This political development was remarkable because of the extreme difficulty of amending the Constitution. The process requires a two-thirds vote of both houses of Congress and then ratification by three-fourths of the states (at that time, 36 of the 48 states). But public support for the Eighteenth Amendment was so strong that in 1917 it was passed in the Senate by a vote of 65 to 20 and in the House by 282 to 128, with more than two-thirds of both Democrats and Republicans voting in favor of it.[3] Then it was submitted to the states. The first state to ratify it was Mississippi on January 7, 1918, and on January 16, 1919, Nebraska became the 36th state to ratify it.[4] The amendment

---

[1] See below, p. 688, for a definition of the kinds of drugs I am concerned with in this chapter.

[2] United States Constitution, Amendment 18, ratified Jan. 16, 1919. See http://constitutionus.com for the text of the amendment. (I also mentioned this briefly at p. 472.)

[3] "The States and the Prohibition Amendment," *CQ Researcher*, http://library.cqpress.com/cqresearcher/document.php?id=cqresrre1931022500.

[4] Ibid.

specified that it would go into effect one year after ratification, and therefore it took effect January 16, 1920, and remained in effect for more than 13 years.[5]

This amendment was widely referred to by the single word *Prohibition*. It did not prohibit the private *use* of alcoholic beverages, but banned their *transportation and sale*, which made it more difficult for people to obtain them. There was widespread disobedience to the law while it was in effect.

Public opposition to Prohibition increased throughout its 13 years. Finally, the Eighteenth Amendment was repealed by the ratification of the Twenty-First Amendment on December 5, 1933.[6]

Alcohol is presently illegal in many Muslim-majority countries, as well as some regions of India.[7] On the other side, 19 countries have no age restrictions on consuming alcohol.[8]

A. CONTEMPORARY INFORMATION ABOUT THE DESTRUCTIVE RESULTS OF ALCOHOL ABUSE

The abuse of alcohol is one of the greatest evils in the world today, one that leads to many destructive consequences:

1. Family members (especially women and children) suffer the consequences of alcohol-induced violence. According to a 2012 study, more than 10 percent of U.S. children live with a parent with alcohol problems.[9] Of married couples who get into physical altercations, some 60 percent to 70 percent abuse alcohol.[10]

2. Many innocent victims are killed by drunk drivers. In 2014, alcohol-impaired driving fatalities accounted for 9,967 deaths (31 percent of overall driving fatalities).[11]

3. People lose their jobs and destroy their careers. Studies have documented that

[5] The law that was passed by Congress specifying details of the enforcement of this prohibition was known as the Volstead Act, passed through an override of President Woodrow Wilson's veto on October 28, 1919.

[6] See "The States and the Prohibition Amendment." See also http://constitutionus.com for the text of the Twenty-First Amendment.

[7] "14 Countries Where Drinking Alcohol Is Illegal," WorldAtlas, http://www.worldatlas.com/articles/14–countries-where-drinking-alcohol-is-illegal.html. The countries prohibiting alcohol are Bangladesh, Brunei, Iran, Iraq, India (certain states), Libya, Kuwait, Maldives, Pakistan, Saudi Arabia, Sudan, Somalia, United Arab Emirates, and Yemen.

[8] "Minimum Drinking Age (MLDA) in 190 Countries," ProCon.org, http://drinkingage.procon.org/view.resource.php?resourceID=004294. The countries with no age restrictions on consuming alcohol are Benin, Bolivia, Burkina Faso, Burundi, Cambodia, Cameroon, China, Gabon, Guinea-Bissau, Indonesia, Kosovo, Laos, Mali, Rwanda, Sao Tome and Principe, Sierra Leone, Solomon Islands, Timor-Leste, and Togo.

[9] "More than 7 Million Children Live with a Parent with Alcohol Problem," Center for Behavioral Health Statistics and Quality, *Data Spotlight*, Feb. 16, 2012, http://media.samhsa.gov/data/spotlight/Spot061ChildrenOfAlcoholics2012.pdf.

[10] "Alcoholism and Family/Marital Problems," American Addiction Centers, http://americanaddictioncenters.org/alcoholism-treatment/family-marital-problems/.

[11] "2014 Crash Data Key Findings," U.S. Department of Transportation, National Highway Traffic Safety Administration, November 2015, http://www-nrd.nhtsa.dot.gov/Pubs/812219.pdf.

heavy alcohol use increases absenteeism, as well as "presenteeism," the act of showing up at work sick, decreasing productivity.[12]

4. People have a much higher likelihood of liver disease, pneumonia, cancer of the esophagus, internal bleeding, and suicide. Nearly 88,000 people (approximately 62,000 men and 26,000 women) die from alcohol-related causes annually, making alcohol the fourth leading preventable cause of death in the United States.[13]

5. Many experience serious mental disabilities, some of which are irreversible even when alcohol consumption is stopped. According to Laurence Westreich, a clinical associate professor in the Division of Alcoholism and Drug Abuse at New York University, more than 20 percent of those with mental illness also suffer from alcohol abuse or dependence.[14] The National Bureau of Economic Research found that there is a definite connection between mental illness and the use of addictive substances. According to the bureau, individuals with an existing mental illness consume roughly 38 percent of all alcohol, as well as 44 percent of all cocaine and 40 percent of all cigarettes. Furthermore, people who have experienced mental illness consume about 69 percent of all alcohol, as well as 84 percent of all cocaine and 68 percent of all cigarettes.[15]

6. Some estimates say that people shorten their life expectancy by 10 to 12 years with alcohol abuse.[16]

7. In 2014, 24.7 percent of people ages 18 or older reported that they had engaged in binge drinking in the past month, while 6.7 percent reported that they had engaged in heavy drinking in the past month.[17] In the United States, nearly 14 million adults, or one in every 13 adults, abuse alcohol or have an alcoholism problem.[18] According to the World Health Organization in 2011, about 140 million people throughout the world suffered from alcohol-related disorders.[19]

---

[12] Carmel Lobello, "How Drinking Too Much Sabotages Your Finances," *The Week*, Nov. 4, 2013, http://the week.com/articles/457336/how-drinking-much-sabotages-finances.

[13] "Alcohol and Public Health: Alcohol-Related Disease impact (ARDI)," Centers for Disease Control and Prevention, https://nccd.cdc.gov/DPH_ARDI/default/default.aspx, and M. Stahre, J. Roeber, D. Kanny, et al., "Contribution of excessive alcohol consumption to deaths and years of potential life lost in the United States," *Preventing Chronic Disease* 11 (2014): E109.

[14] "Alcohol and Mental Illness," Primary Psychiatry, Jan. 1, 2005, http://primarypsychiatry.com/alcohol -and-mental-illness/.

[15] Marie Bussing-Birks, "Mental Illness and Substance Abuse," National Bureau of Economic Research, Dec. 13, 2016, http://www.nber.org/digest/apr02/w8699.html.

[16] "Alcohol Use Disorder," *The New York Times*, March 8, 2013, http://www.nytimes.com/health/guides /disease/alcoholism/possible-complications.html.

[17] "Results from the 2014 National Survey on Drug Use and Health: Detailed Tables," Substance Abuse and Mental Health Services Administration, Table 2.46B: "Alcohol use, binge alcohol use, and heavy alcohol use in the past month among persons aged 18 or older, by demographic characteristics: Percentages, 2013 and 2014," http://www.samhsa.gov/data/sites/default/files/NSDUH-DetTabs2014/NSDUH-DetTabs2014 .htm#tab2–46b.

[18] Lizmarie Maldonado, "Drug Addiction Statistics—Alcoholism Statistics and Data Sources," Project-Know, http://www.projectknow.com/research/drug-addiction-statistics-alcoholism-statistics/.

[19] "Global Status Report on Alcohol and Health," World Health Organization, 2011, http://www.who.int /substance_abuse/publications/global_alcohol_report/msbgsruprofiles.pdf.

B. THE BIBLE CLEARLY FORBIDS DRUNKENNESS

Several New Testament passages specify the moral evil of becoming drunk:

> I am writing to you not to associate with anyone who bears the name of brother if he is . . . [a] *drunkard*. (1 Cor. 5:11)

> And *do not get drunk with wine*, for that is debauchery. (Eph. 5:18)

In addition, Paul includes "drunkards" among those who will not "inherit the kingdom of God" (1 Cor. 6:10). Elsewhere he says that "drunkenness" is among those activities of which "those who do such things will not inherit the kingdom of God" (Gal. 5:21; see also Luke 21:34; Rom. 13:13; 1 Pet. 4:3). In listing the qualifications for an elder in the church, Paul says that he must not be "a drunkard" (1 Tim. 3:3; also Titus 1:7), and a deacon must not be "addicted to much wine" (1 Tim. 3:8).

Some Old Testament passages also warn against drunkenness. Two prominent stories show that people who get drunk lose good judgment and moral restraint, as happened with Noah, who shamefully "became drunk and lay uncovered in his tent" (Gen. 9:21), and with Lot, who twice became drunk and, without realizing what he was doing, committed incest with his daughters (Gen. 19:30–36).

The author of Proverbs counsels:

> Be not among *drunkards*
> > or among gluttonous eaters of meat,
> *for the drunkard and the glutton will come to poverty,*
> > and slumber will clothe them with rags. (Prov. 23:20–21)

A longer passage describes with vivid poetic imagery the consequences of drunkenness:

> Who has woe? Who has sorrow?
> > Who has strife? Who has complaining?
> Who has wounds without cause?
> > Who has redness of eyes?
> Those who tarry long over wine;
> > those who go to try mixed wine.
> Do not look at wine when it is red,
> > when it sparkles in the cup
> > and goes down smoothly.
> In the end it bites like a serpent
> > and stings like an adder.
> Your eyes will see strange things,
> > and your heart utter perverse things.

You will be like one who lies down in the midst of the sea,
    like one who lies on the top of a mast.
"They struck me," you will say, "but I was not hurt;
    they beat me, but I did not feel it.
When shall I awake?
    I must have another drink." (Prov. 23:29–35)

But how should we define being drunk? Individual people vary widely in the amount of alcohol they are able to drink without becoming drunk, but some passages in Scripture emphasize the loss of good judgment and moral restraint (see Gen. 9:21; 19:30–36; Prov. 31:4–5) or being "led astray" by alcohol (Prov. 20:1). Paul says that being drunk "is debauchery" (Eph. 5:18; the Greek word, *asōtia*, refers to "reckless abandon, debauchery, dissipation, profligacy," and the related adjective is used in Luke 15:13 of the prodigal son who "squandered his property in *reckless living*").

Therefore, a definition of drunkenness would specify that a person is drunk when he or she:

- has lost good judgment;
- is not thinking clearly;
- has lost some moral restraint;
- acts in a way that brings reproach on the person's own reputation or the reputation of the gospel; or
- has lost good physical coordination (as in the inability to drive a car safely).

C. THE BIBLE CONTAINS STRONG WARNINGS ABOUT THE DANGERS OF ALCOHOL

1. Scripture Warns against Being Deceived by Alcoholic Beverages. The book of Proverbs frequently cautions about the deceptive nature of alcohol:

Wine is a mocker, strong drink a brawler,
    and *whoever is led astray by it* is not wise. (Prov. 20:1)

Whoever loves pleasure will be a poor man;
    he who loves wine and oil will not be rich. (Prov. 21:17)

Governmental leaders have a special responsibility in this regard. They must be particularly careful of clouding their judgment through the use of alcohol, and thereby making wrong decisions:

It is not for kings, O Lemuel,
    it is not for kings to drink wine,
    or for rulers to take strong drink,

> lest they drink and forget what has been decreed
> and pervert the rights of all the afflicted. (Prov. 31:4–5; see also
> Eccles. 10:17; Jer. 13:13)

Under the Mosaic covenant, certain groups of people were actually prohibited from all use of wine or "strong drink," such as Aaron and his sons, who were priests (Lev. 10:8–9), and people who took a Nazirite vow (Num. 6:1–4; see also Luke 1:15 regarding John the Baptist).

2. Scripture Also Warns against Making Another Person "Stumble." An important passage on this topic is 1 Corinthians 8:1–13. Though it does not specifically discuss alcoholic beverages, but rather food offered to idols, there are still some helpful principles in the passage that we can apply to the question of alcoholic beverages.

The city of Corinth was full of temples to various Greek and Roman gods, which Paul identified as "idols" (1 Cor. 8:1). Many of the Corinthian Christians had previously participated in the worship of these idols in their various temples (see 1 Cor. 12:2). But then the question arose whether it was right to eat food that had previously been offered to idols and then was sold in the meat market at Corinth.

Paul responded to this question with these instructions:

> Eat whatever is sold in the meat market without raising any question on the ground of conscience. For "the earth is the Lord's, and the fullness thereof." (1 Cor. 10:25–26)

In other words, the Corinthians were free to eat such meat without worrying that it had been tainted by its previous dedication to an idol in a temple. (However, Paul specified that they should refrain if an unbeliever explicitly stated that it had been offered to an idol, for then it would appear as though the Christians were agreeing with the offering of such food to idols and the spiritual efficacy connected with it; see 1 Cor. 10:28–29.)

Yet there was another complicating factor: though the Corinthians were ordinarily free to eat such food, realizing there was no spiritual harm connected with it, not all the Christians in Corinth shared this conviction or understood this principle. For them, it was morally wrong to eat food offered to idols, and thus it violated the conviction of their consciences.

Therefore, Paul warned the Corinthian Christians to be careful in how they used their freedom to eat such food that had been offered to idols. In itself, the practice was harmless, but *if it set an example that led other Christians to act contrary to the convictions of their consciences*, then it was wrong. Therefore, Paul said, "Take care that this right of yours does not somehow *become a stumbling block* to the weak" (1 Cor. 8:9). Then he explained:

> For if anyone sees you who have knowledge eating in an idol's temple, will he not be encouraged, if his conscience is weak, to eat food offered to idols? And

so by your knowledge this weak person is destroyed, the brother for whom Christ died. (1 Cor. 8:10–11)

The sin involved here is encouraging a Christian to sin against his conscience by eating food offered to idols, *even though he believes it is wrong* to do so (see also 1 Cor. 8:7).[20]

Paul's conclusion was that he would be very careful not to *publicly* eat food offered to idols in a place or a time that would encourage Christians to do so even though they themselves believed it was wrong:

Therefore, *if food makes my brother stumble*, I will never eat meat, lest I make my brother stumble. (1 Cor. 8:13)[21]

We can apply this teaching to the question of alcoholic beverages. Christian believers who have no moral objection to drinking alcoholic beverages should still be careful that they not drink them in a way that might encourage younger Christians (or others who think drinking alcoholic beverages is wrong) to drink also and thereby to violate their consciences. This would be to cause them to "stumble" in the way Paul means in 1 Corinthians 8:13.

But it is also important to keep in mind that the verse does not say, "If food makes another person become upset with me or irritated with me . . ." It is talking only about the question of encouraging people who think that eating meat offered to idols is wrong to eat it anyway and thereby to violate their consciences. The verse does not mean that a person has to refrain from all use of alcohol when in the company of others who disagree about this question.

Romans 14 contains a similar teaching about observing special days or refraining from eating certain foods, such as meat. But here Paul adds that Christians should not judge one another on questions of food:

As for the one who is weak in faith, welcome him, but not to quarrel over opinions. One person believes he may eat anything, while the weak person eats only vegetables. *Let not the one who eats despise the one who abstains, and let not the one who abstains pass judgment on the one who eats*, for God has welcomed him. Who are you to pass judgment on the servant of another? It is before his own master that he stands or falls. And he will be upheld, for the Lord is able to make him stand. . . . Therefore let us not pass judgment on one another any longer, but rather decide never to put a stumbling block or hindrance in the way of a brother. (vv. 1–4, 13)

---

[20] See a longer discussion of this question in Andrew David Naselli and J. D. Crowley, *Conscience: What It Is, How to Train It, and Loving Those Who Differ* (Wheaton, IL: Crossway, 2016), 109–10.

[21] The word translated as "makes . . . stumble" (Greek, *skandalizō*, "to cause to sin, cause to stumble") is elsewhere translated as "cause to sin" (see Matt. 5:29, 30; 18:6, 8, 9).

Taken together, the passages in 1 Corinthians 8 and Romans 14 encourage Christians to allow freedom for individual convictions on this matter and to be content to let each person individually be accountable before God for how he or she answers this question.

D. OTHER PASSAGES IN SCRIPTURE VIEW ALCOHOLIC BEVERAGES MORE POSITIVELY

We should recognize that the warnings against drunkenness in Scripture (see passages above) reveal a tacit assumption that there is a right use of alcohol that does not lead to drunkenness. If it had been God's intention to prohibit all use of alcoholic beverages in all circumstances, the Bible would explicitly prohibit it rather than prohibiting only drunkenness.

In contrast to the Bible's repeated and strong prohibitions against *drunkenness* and the frequent warnings about the *dangers* of alcoholic beverages, a number of other biblical passages see these beverages as part of God's good creation, for which people should give thanks:

> You cause the grass to grow for the livestock
> and plants for man to cultivate,
> that he may bring forth food from the earth
> and *wine to gladden the heart of man*,
> oil to make his face shine
> and bread to strengthen man's heart. (Ps. 104:14–15)

This psalm says that one of the reasons God causes "plants for man to cultivate" on the earth is so that people may bring forth "wine to gladden the heart of man" as one of the good products of the earth, similar to oil and bread. A related verse is found in Ecclesiastes: "Go, eat your bread with joy, and *drink your wine with a merry heart*, for God has already approved what you do" (9:7).

Proverbs says:

> Honor the LORD with your wealth
> and with the firstfruits of all your produce;
> then your barns will be filled with plenty,
> and *your vats will be bursting with wine*. (Prov. 3:9–10)

These "vats" may have contained unfermented grape juice for the first day or two, but in the climate of the Middle East, without modern refrigeration, it quickly turned to wine.

Sometimes wine is seen as part of a joyful celebration in the presence of God, as when Melchizedek "brought out bread and wine" and blessed Abraham after his victory over the kings who had captured Lot (Gen. 14:18–20), or when the people of Israel were to "eat the tithe of your grain, of *your wine* and of your oil, and the firstborn of your herd and flock" in the presence of the Lord at a place he had commanded (see Deut. 14:22–26).

In the New Testament, Jesus celebrated the Passover with the use of a cup of wine (see Matt. 26:27–29), and John's Gospel records that Jesus's first miracle was turning water to wine in six large jars, each holding "twenty or thirty gallons" and filled with water "up to the brim" (John 2:6–7). This wine was so good that the master of the feast thought the bridegroom had saved "the good wine" until the end (v. 10). The point is that Jesus "manifested his glory" by miraculously creating excellent wine at a wedding feast (v. 11).

When Paul names some things about which Christians should "not pass judgment on one another" (Rom. 14:13), he explicitly names wine:

> *Everything is indeed clean*, but it is wrong for anyone to make another stumble by what he eats. It is good not to eat meat *or drink wine* or do anything that causes your brother to stumble. (Rom. 14:20–21)

Paul elsewhere says that one of the "teachings of demons" is to "forbid marriage" and also to "require abstinence from foods that God created to be received with thanksgiving" (1 Tim. 4:1–3). Though he does not specify wine in this passage, the principle still applies, and Paul's reasoning in the following passages is relevant to the question of wine as well as food:

> For *everything created by God is good*, and *nothing is to be rejected* if it is received with thanksgiving, for it is made holy by the word of God and prayer. (1 Tim. 4:4–5; see also Col. 2:20–23)

In one passage Paul explicitly tells Timothy to drink wine, and implies that there is some health benefit from it:

> No longer drink only water, but use a little wine for the sake of your stomach and your frequent ailments. (1 Tim. 5:23)

According to the Mayo Clinic, red wine seems to have heart-healthy benefits, because it contains antioxidants, such as flavonoids or a substance called resveratrol, which are good for the heart. Resveratrol helps prevent damage to blood vessels, reduces bad cholesterol (LDL), and prevents blood clots. Other antioxidants in red wine called polyphenols may also protect the lining of blood vessels in the heart. However, the Mayo Clinic says that additional research needs to be done to verify these benefits.[22] John Hopkins University has found that red wine also helps protect against strokes.[23]

---

[22] "Red Wine and Resveratrol: Good for Your Heart?" The Mayo Clinic, Nov. 12, 2016, http://www.mayo clinic.org/diseases-conditions/heart-disease/in-depth/red-wine/art-20048281.

[23] "How Red Wine May Shield Brain from Stroke Damage," John Hopkins Medicine, April 21, 2010, http://www.hopkinsmedicine.org/news/media/releases/How_Red_Wine_May_Shield_Brain_From_Stroke _Damage.

But Paul's words of caution about not causing others to stumble by what we do are a reminder that not everything that is morally right in itself is wise or helpful in every situation. Paul also says, "'All things are lawful,' but not all things are helpful" (1 Cor. 10:23).

E. SPECIFIC APPLICATION TO INDIVIDUALS AND CHURCHES

Based on the biblical principles outlined above, in this section I will give my own personal judgments on specific issues related to alcoholic beverages, while remembering Paul's reminder that there are some matters on which people can simply agree to disagree, matters in which there is room for personal differences of opinion. In this area, we should not judge one another, as Paul explains (with my additional applications in brackets):

> Let not the one who eats [or drinks!] despise the one who abstains, and let not the one who abstains pass judgment on the one who eats [or drinks!], for God has welcomed him. (Rom. 14:3)

1. Should Christians Practice Total Abstinence from Alcoholic Beverages? This is a personal question, and the answer will vary from individual to individual. It will depend in part on knowing one's self, one's personal history, one's family history, and one's cultural context.

Many people who have come to realize that they are alcoholics[24] find that they must practice total abstinence in order to avoid being drunk again. One of these people is former President George W. Bush, who quit drinking at the age of 40 and has not touched a drop of alcohol since 1986.[25] Others practice total abstinence because they have seen alcohol addiction destroy some member of their family.[26] Many people in positions of Christian leadership (such as many pastors) practice total abstinence because they do not want their example to lead others astray into harmful patterns of conduct.

But many other Christians drink alcoholic beverages in moderation and have never

[24] Those who have suffered from alcoholism and have overcome the addiction continue to regard themselves as alcoholics. They realize that drinking just one drop of alcohol can lead them down the road back to alcoholism. Therefore, they must engage in total abstinence.

[25] Kathleen Koch, "Bush Opens Up on Struggle with Alcohol Abuse," CNN, Dec. 11, 2008, http://edition.cnn.com/2008/POLITICS/12/11/bush.alcohol/.

[26] As I am writing this footnote (November 2016), President-elect Donald Trump falls in that category. He has said that he does not drink alcohol because it ruined the life of his older brother, Freddy. Freddy died from alcoholism at the age of 43 in 1981. In an interview with *The New York Times*, Trump said that he learned from watching his brother how bad choices may "drag down those who seemed destined to rise," and Freddy's suffering led him to avoid ever trying alcohol or cigarettes. Jason Horowitz, "For Donald Trump, Lessons from a Brother's Suffering," *The New York Times*, Jan. 2, 2016, http://www.nytimes.com/2016/01/03/us/politics/for-donald-trump-lessons-from-a-brothers-suffering.html.

been drunk or even close to drunk. Because the Bible does not prohibit all use of alcoholic beverages, my view is that they have the freedom to do this.

2. Should Churches Require Total Abstinence from Alcoholic Beverages? In the past, many churches required people to make a pledge of total abstinence in order to join the church, or else expected total abstinence for church officers. In my childhood, my family attended a Baptist church where the "Church Covenant" was pasted inside the back cover of the church hymnal, and it included a promise to abstain from the "sale and use of intoxicating drinks as a beverage" (if I remember the wording correctly). Anyone who wanted to become a member of the church had to agree to abide by that promise.

But I would not favor or support such a requirement. It is requiring a standard of conduct stricter than the Bible itself. Neither Jesus (John 2:6–11) nor Paul (1 Tim. 5:23) could have joined such a church. Such a requirement will cause the church to gain a reputation in the community as "the church where people can't drink," and thus it will become known for requiring a moral standard that does not naturally find an echo in the hearts of non-Christians (as the moral standards of God in Scripture ordinarily will do; see Rom. 2:14–15). In this way, such a requirement can become a wrongfully legalistic prohibition that actually prevents people from coming to the church and being saved.

3. What Is the Best Witness to Society? Someone might argue that a practice of total abstinence is the best witness to a society where alcoholism is immensely harmful. However, that assumes that the best form of witness is a kind of lifestyle that is stricter than what God requires in his Word.

On the other hand, a good argument can be made that the best witness to society is responsible and moderate use of alcohol, so that a Christian would not become drunk at a neighborhood party, but would also be an example of moderation in this regard. This seems to me to be closer to Paul's example of becoming "all things to all people, that by all means I might save some" (1 Cor. 9:22).

F. OBJECTIONS TO THE MODERATE USE OF ALCOHOL

In this section I will state some common objections to a moderate use of alcohol by Christians, and give my response to each one.

1. Objection: "Alcoholic Beverages in Biblical Times Were Watered Down and Therefore Not As Intoxicating." Robertson McQuilkin uses this as one of his arguments in support of total abstinence for Christians today:

> I believe total abstinence is the most biblical position in twentieth-century America. The principle is one of giving up my rights for the welfare of others

(Rom. 14; 1 Cor. 8, 10) in a situation that is radically different from Bible times. In the biblical culture where water was scarce and often polluted, wine was the simplest way of purifying drinking water and was the common mealtime beverage. It was mixed with water, up to two hundred parts water to one part wine. In fact, it was considered barbaric to drink wine that was only half-and-half. Because of the common use of high-alcohol-content beverages today, we have problems the people of Bible days could not have imagined. [McQuilkin then gives sobering data on alcohol-related traffic fatalities, marital violence, murders, rapes, thefts, suicides, and industrial injuries.][27]

In response, the following may be said:

First, McQuilkin's claim that water in biblical culture was "often polluted" and needed to be purified with wine is unsubstantiated. Several biblical narratives speak of drawing fresh water directly from wells (see Gen. 24:11; 29:2; 2 Sam. 23:15; John 4:6), and such water ordinarily would have been pure enough to drink safely.

Second, ancient sources that speak about wine *sometimes* being mixed with water[28] cannot prove that it was *always* mixed with water or that wine was not intoxicating in the ancient world, because the Bible talks about people being drunk with wine. The stories of the drunkenness of Noah and Lot (see Gen. 9:21; 19:30–36), the warnings against intoxication (Prov. 23:20–21), and the warnings against being a drunkard (1 Cor. 5:11; Gal. 5:21; 1 Tim. 3:2–3; Titus 1:7) show that, even if wine was at times diluted, at many other times it was concentrated enough to make people drunk. Paul does not say "and do not get drunk with water diluted with a tiny speck of wine," but "do not get drunk with wine, for that is debauchery" (Eph. 5:18). And presumably the excellent wine Jesus miraculously created at the wedding in Cana of Galilee was drawn directly from the stone jar and brought undiluted to the master of the feast (see John 2:8–10).

Sometimes such mixed wine was seen *not* as a normal part of life but as a sign of poverty and judgment. Isaiah's lament about the corruption and decay of Jerusalem includes this statement:

> Your silver has become dross,
> *your best wine mixed with water.* (Isa. 1:22)

2. Objection: "Total Abstinence Is the Only Sure Guarantee of Not Becoming an Alcoholic." This objection is also raised by McQuilkin in *An Introduction to Biblical Ethics.* He writes:

---

[27] Robertson McQuilkin, *An Introduction to Biblical Ethics*, 2nd ed. (Wheaton, IL: Tyndale, 1995), 97–98; the same paragraph is found in the book's 3rd edition, by McQuilkin and Paul Copan (Downers Grove, IL: InterVarsity Press, 2014), 137.

[28] Robert H. Stein, "Wine Drinking in New Testament Times," *Christianity Today* 20 (June, 1975), 9, cited in McQuilkin, 620n6.

The only certain way to avoid alcohol- or drug-influenced thinking, speaking, and behavior and to avoid addiction is not to take the first drink or the first dose of a drug. Though others may not reach the same conclusions from these data, I conclude that the production, sale, and use of beverage alcohol and addictive or mind-altering nonprescribed drugs are incompatible with biblical principles.[29]

In response, first, I will argue below that I agree with this argument with respect to many kinds of "addictive or mind-altering nonprescribed drugs," for which I can see a strong biblical argument for never taking the first dose. But I put alcoholic beverages in a different category because of the biblical evidence that I cited above.

Second, I recognize that many people have felt the validity of McQuilkin's kind of argument and have decided that total abstinence is the best policy for themselves. I respect and support the right of individual Christians to decide that total abstinence is the best approach for themselves, for various reasons. Christians should not put pressure on people who hold such a position to try to persuade them to change it.

Third, the most recent edition of McQuilkin's book, coauthored by Paul Copan, contains an additional three paragraphs that are labeled as "Copan's Perspective." While Copan shows respect for McQuilkin's position, he says, "I hesitate in urging total abstinence since the Scriptures themselves suggest the festive, social, celebratory place of alcoholic drinks as a gift from God." Therefore, he argues that the biblical witness does not allow him to advocate total abstinence, but argues against "any misuse of alcohol."[30]

Fourth, the Bible does not counsel Christians in general to be stricter than what Scripture requires just to be "safe" from violating the Scriptures.[31] The overly strict nature of such a requirement for all people can be seen if we ask what such a procedure would look like in order to avoid other sins. For example, how can you guarantee that you will never shoot somebody accidentally with a gun? Never buy a gun and never go hunting. How can you guarantee that you will never declare bankruptcy? Never start a business. These are excessively strict rules that Christians would not want to enforce on themselves or others.

Fifth, it is not true that total abstinence is the only certain way to avoid becoming drunk. Another certain way is to practice moderation and restraint at all times. Millions of Christians have done this throughout their lives.

3. Objection: "Drinking Even One Glass of Wine Kills Millions of Brain Cells." I have not found this objection in academic literature, but it is sometimes repeated by students

---

[29] McQuilkin, *An Introduction to Biblical Ethics*, 2nd ed., 98; also in 3rd ed., 137, with the added sentence, "I am, indeed, 'my brother's keeper,' and I may, by my example, prove a stumbling block."

[30] McQuilkin and Copan, *An Introduction to Biblical Ethics*, 3rd ed., 137–38.

[31] This is similar to rabbinic teaching in first-century Judaism that "put a fence around the law," with more strict provisions than the law of God required.

in my classes (who have heard it in popular sermons or presentations). But God was fully aware of the effect of alcohol on the human brain when he inspired the biblical writers to portray a moderate use of alcohol in a positive way in Scripture itself. And from a medical standpoint, this claim is simply not true. Roberta J. Pentney, a former researcher at the State University of New York at Buffalo, found that while consumption of alcohol disrupts brain function in adults by damaging message-carrying dendrites on neurons in the cerebellum, a structure involved in learning and motor coordination, it does not kill off entire brain cells.[32] In fact, besides warding off strokes, wine consumption has also been tied to decreased likelihood of Alzheimer's and Parkinson's disease. In short, "The research indicates that adults who drink in moderation are not in danger of losing brain cells."[33]

4. Objection: "When Churches Require Total Abstinence, There Is No Harm Done, and It Might Do Much Good by Stopping People from Becoming Alcoholics." In response, I think harm *is* done when we keep people away from the church by standards that are stricter than Scripture (proclaiming, in effect, that to be a Christian you have to give up all use of alcohol).

In the first century, Paul recognized the harm that came from the "circumcision party," which was requiring something stricter than Scripture and thereby "upsetting whole families" by teaching "what they ought not to teach" (Titus 1:10–11). Paul also rebuked the Colossians for submitting to an overly strict asceticism that proclaimed, "Do not handle, Do not taste, Do not touch" (Col. 2:21). And he warned Timothy to beware of teachings that required more strict abstinence than God's Word required (see 1 Tim. 4:1–5). The Christian life is hard enough without our adding man-made rules to what God has already given us.

The broader issue here is not alcoholic beverages in themselves but whether we believe the moral standards of Scripture are God's best rules for our lives (this is the doctrine of the sufficiency of Scripture again; see chap. 3, p. 97). In every generation there is a temptation to depart from the sufficiency of Scripture with new kinds of legalism that God does not require. Therefore, we must avoid two errors: the error of disobeying Scripture and the error of adding to Scripture more than God requires.

G. THE USE OF ILLICIT RECREATIONAL DRUGS

1. Categories of Drugs. The term *drug* in English can be applied to a wide variety of substances, so it is important to define at the outset what I am discussing.

I am not discussing chemical substances used for *medicinal* purposes (what are com-

---

[32] Anahad O'Connor: "The Claim: Alcohol Kills Brain Cells," *The New York Times*, Nov. 23, 2004, http://www.nytimes.com/2004/11/23/health/the-claim-alcohol-kills-brain-cells.html.

[33] "Wine experts less vulnerable to Alzheimer's, study says," Fox News, Sept. 8, 2016, http://www.foxnews.com/health/2016/09/08/wine-experts-less-vulnerable-to-alzheimers-study-says.html.

monly called pharmaceutical drugs). Rather, I am talking about "recreational drugs"—drugs that are used not for medicinal purposes but because people think they will enjoy the mental and emotional effects the drugs cause.

Neither am I discussing drugs that are *legally permitted* because governments in various countries have determined that the danger of abuse or harmful results is not significant enough to justify their prohibition. For example, sometimes people will say that coffee, tea, and Coca-Cola are "drugs" because the caffeine they contain is a "stimulant" that gives people increased alertness, and that alcohol is a "depressant" because it makes people feel relaxed. But in general, most governments have not prohibited the use of these substances. That is why I have used the category "illicit drugs," where the word *illicit* means "illegal" or "not legally permitted."

Within the category of illicit recreational drugs, there are three groups: (1) stimulants (drugs that increase alertness or improve athletic performance); (2) depressants (drugs that relax people); and (3) hallucinogenic drugs (drugs that give people a "perception of . . . experiences without an external stimulus and with a compelling sense of their reality";[34] that is, drugs that cause people to think they are seeing, hearing, or touching objects when they are not).

2. The Need for Christians to Obey the Law. Because we are talking about "illicit" drugs, their use is prohibited by state or federal law. For that reason alone, Christians should avoid using them, according to Romans 13:1: "Let every person be subject to the governing authorities."

3. The Requirement to Avoid Drunkenness. Many illicit recreational drugs cause effects similar to drunkenness, and therefore the biblical commands against being drunk also apply to the use of such drugs. If their use distorts a person's good judgment, causes the loss of some measure of moral restraint, causes the loss of good physical coordination, or brings reproach on a person's reputation or on the gospel, then the passages against "drunkenness" also forbid becoming "drunk" by means of these drugs. The command "Do not get drunk with wine" (Eph. 5:18) also can be rightly applied in the sense of "Do not get drunk with marijuana (or cocaine, heroin, or similar drugs)." (See also 1 Cor. 5:11; 6:9–11; Gal. 5:21; 1 Tim. 3:2, 8; Titus 1:7.)

4. The Requirement to Maintain Sober-Mindedness and Self-Control. Other Scripture passages encourage us to remain sober: "Be . . . sober-minded for the sake of your prayers" (1 Pet. 4:7; see also 1 Thess. 5:6–8). Still others hold up self-control as a moral virtue for Christians to cultivate (see Gal. 5:23, where it is part of the fruit of the Spirit; also 1 Pet. 4:7; 2 Pet. 1:6). Whenever the use of an illicit recreational drug results in a significant loss of self-control, its use is prohibited by these verses.

---

[34] Taken from the definition of *hallucination* in *American Heritage Dictionary* (Boston: Houghton Mifflin, 2006), 792.

5. The Requirement to Avoid What the Bible Calls "Sorcery." We should not imagine that recreational drugs are a modern invention. Several passages in Scripture mention "sorcery" among lists of sins against God, and the practice of sorcery in the ancient world often included the use of mind-altering drugs:

> Now the works of the flesh are evident: sexual immorality, impurity, sensuality, idolatry, *sorcery* [Greek, *pharmakeia*]. . . . Those who do such things will not inherit the kingdom of God. (Gal. 5:19–21)

> Nor did they repent of their murders or their *sorceries* [Greek, *pharmakon*, plural] or their sexual immorality or their thefts. (Rev. 9:21)

> But as for the cowardly, the faithless, the detestable, as for murderers, the sexually immoral, *sorcerers* [Greek, *pharmakos*, plural], idolaters, and all liars, their portion will be in the lake that burns with fire and sulfur, which is the second death. (Rev. 21:8; see also Rev. 18:23; 22:15)

The three related Greek terms used in these passages (from the stem *pharmak-*) can be used in either a positive or negative sense. In a positive sense, these terms sometimes refer to the use of medicinal drugs to cure people (as in our English words *pharmacist* or *pharmacy*). But all three of these biblical passages refer to an activity that is morally evil. Therefore, these passages must be using the terms in a negative sense. *Pharmakon* (Rev. 9:21) means "a drug used as a controlling medium, *magic potion, charm*"[35]—which would certainly include drugs taken for hallucinogenic purposes, and probably also strong stimulants and depressants (though the ancient world would not have distinguished those exact categories). The noun *pharmakeia* (Gal. 5:20; Rev. 18:23) refers to "sorcery, magic,"[36] and would have involved the use of mind-altering drugs. The term *pharmakos* (Rev. 21:8; 22:15) refers to "one who does extraordinary things through occult means, sorcerer, magician."[37] The occult practices prohibited in these passages would have included both the use of drugs as magical potions and other practices, such as attempting to cast magic spells upon people. Another lexicon says that *pharmakeia* and *pharmakon* refer to "the use of magic, often involving drugs and the casting of spells upon people."[38]

The conclusion is that, while these terms are not limited to the use of drugs for mind-altering purposes, their meaning certainly *includes* such practices, along with other occult practices in the ancient world. Therefore, these passages about "sorcery" provide additional biblical testimony against the use of illicit recreational drugs.

---

[35] BDAG, 1050.

[36] Ibid., 1049.

[37] Ibid., 1050.

[38] J. P. Louw and Eugene Albert Nida, *Greek-English Lexicon of the New Testament* (New York: United Bible Societies, 1988), 53.100, 1:545). The Liddell-Scott *Greek-English Lexicon* says *pharmakeia* refers to "the use of any kind of drugs, potions, or spells," and the related verb *pharmakeuō* means to "drug a person, give him a poisonous or stupefying drug" (LSJ, 1917).

6. The Harmful Results to Society from the Legalizing of Marijuana. In the United States, by the end of 2016, eight states had legalized the recreational use of marijuana,[39] although it was still against federal law.[40] (But the Justice Department under the Obama administration had not attempted to enforce the federal laws regarding marijuana for several years in states that had legalized its recreational use.[41])

For societies considering any changes to laws concerning marijuana, it is important to recognize the negative consequences of the use of marijuana:

a. The Likelihood of Addiction: Marijuana is addictive. According to the National Institute on Drug Abuse, up to 30 percent of marijuana users may have marijuana-use disorder to some degree.[42] Among people who start using marijuana before the age of 18, such a disorder is four to seven times more likely than among those who begin using it as adults.[43] According to researchers at Yale University, it is frequently a "gateway drug" leading users to other, even more addicting and harmful drugs, including such prescription drugs as opioids.[44]

b. The Loss of Drive to Achieve: Marijuana and other depressants frequently cause an increase in laziness and lethargy, resulting in a lack of drive to be productive members of society. According to researchers at Northwestern University, casual marijuana use is linked to brain abnormalities. One of the researchers said: "Drugs of abuse can cause more dopamine release than natural rewards like food, sex and social interaction. In those you also get a burst of dopamine but not as much as in many drugs of abuse. That is why drugs take on so much salience, and everything else loses its importance."[45]

c. A Decrease in IQ: Frequent use of marijuana by adolescents can cause a decrease in IQ that is often permanent. Researchers at Duke University found that marijuana lowered IQ by as much as eight points for heavy, lifelong users who started in adolescence.[46]

---

[39] "State Marijuana Laws in 2016 Map," Governing, http://www.governing.com/gov-data/state-marijuana -laws-map-medical-recreational.html. The states are Alaska, California, Colorado, Maine, Massachusetts, Nevada, Oregon, and Washington.

[40] Kevin Johnson and Raju Chebium, "Justice Dept. Won't Challenge State Marijuana Laws," *USA Today*, Aug. 29, 2013, http://www.usatoday.com/story/news/nation/2013/08/29/justice-medical-marijuana-laws /2727605/.

[41] Ibid.

[42] "Is Marijuana Addictive?" National Institute on Drug Abuse, April 2017, https://www.drugabuse.gov /publications/research-reports/marijuana/marijuana-addictive.

[43] Ibid.

[44] Amanda Cuda, "Yale Study: Marijuana May Really Be a Gateway Drug," *Connecticut Post*, Aug. 21, 2012, http://www.ctpost.com/local/article/Yale-study-Marijuana-may-really-be-gateway-drug-3805532.php.

[45] Marla Paul, "Casual Marijuana Use Linked to Brain Abnormalities," Northwestern Now, April 16, 2014, https://news.northwestern.edu/stories/2014/04/casual-marijuana-use-linked-to-brain-abnormalities-in -students.

[46] "Pot Does Lower IQ, Study Finds," Fox News, Jan. 15, 2013, http://www.foxnews.com/health/2013/01 /15/does-pot-really-lower-iq.html.

d. Traffic Accidents and Fatalities: Because marijuana causes a loss of good judgment, moral restraint, physical coordination, and response time, widespread use often leads to an increase in traffic accidents and fatalities. In Washington state, traffic accidents surged after recreational use of marijuana was legalized. In 2014, the AAA Foundation for Traffic Safety found that in 462 fatal crashes, 85 of the involved drivers tested positive for marijuana.[47]

e. Crime: Both because of the loss of good judgment and moral restraint, and because of the need to finance an addictive drug habit, the widespread use of marijuana regularly leads to a significant increase in crime in the areas where its use is prevalent.[48]

Some advocates of legalizing marijuana claim that prisons in the United States are filled with people incarcerated for minor drug offenses, and this is a misuse of prison space and law-enforcement time and money. However, such claims appear to have little basis in actual fact. Ernie Martinez, Denver-based at-large director for the National Narcotics Officers Association Coalition, said, "It's this myth that won't go away and gets repeated by people who should know better. Unfortunately, no one reads public records. But the truth is there—and it looks a lot different than the story pushed by marijuana-legalization advocates and amplified in news media."[49]

In 2004, according to the Bureau of Justice Statistics:

- One-tenth of 1 percent of people in state prisons were serving sentences for first-time marijuana possession. Those people also may have concurrent sentencing for other offenses.
- Three-tenths of 1 percent of people in state prisons were serving time for marijuana possession with prior criminal offenses. They, too, may have concurrent sentencing for other offenses.
- 1.4 percent of people in state corrections were imprisoned for offenses involving only marijuana-related crimes.[50]

Likewise, in 2011, according to the U.S. Sentencing Commission:

- There were 216,362 inmates in the federal system. Among them were 6,961 marijuana offenders, only 103 of whom were imprisoned for simple possession—the result of plea bargains in which prisoners pleaded down to possession in exchange for lesser sentences.

---

[47] Andrea Noble, "Marijuana-Related Fatal Car Accidents Surge in Washington State after Legalization," *Washington Times*, May 10, 2016, http://www.washingtontimes.com/news/2016/may/10/marijuana-related -fatal-car-accidents-surge-washin/.

[48] Rob Hotakainen, "Marijuana is Drug Most Often Linked to Crime," McClatchy, May 23, 2013, http:// www.mcclatchydc.com/news/politics-government/article24749413.html.

[49] "Legalization Didn't Unclog Prisons," *Washington Examiner*, March 31, 2015, http://www.washington examiner.com/legalization-didnt-unclog-prisons/article/2562326.

[50] Ibid.

- The federal government convicted only 48 marijuana offenders who possessed less than 5,000 grams of marijuana. The average amount possessed was 3,800 grams—the equivalent of about 9,000 joints, or marijuana cigarettes.[51]

Therefore, while many prisoners have been convicted of drug-related offenses previously in their lives, the actual offenses for which people are serving time in prison are much more serious crimes, such as drug trafficking.[52]

7. The Question of Medical Marijuana. Christians should have no objection to using a substance found in nature for genuine medicinal purposes, though in such cases the substance should be regulated by law, available only by a doctor's prescription, manufactured by pharmaceutical companies according to Food and Drug Administration standards, and sold in pharmacies along with other medicines.

The problem with "medical marijuana" is the frequency of abuse. Some doctors see no harm in widespread use of marijuana, so they will write thousands of prescriptions for people who claim any kind of chronic pain, even though the doctors and patients know that the purpose for the marijuana is recreational use. Such flagrant abuse then makes the general public more resistant to considering or authorizing any genuine medicinal use for marijuana.

8. The Abuse of Prescription Drugs. Christians should not oppose but should be thankful to God for the availability of several strong painkillers that have been developed by modern medical research. A large group of such painkillers are called opioids, a category that includes drugs such as morphine,[53] hydrocodone, and oxycodone.

However, there is a fine line between the *wise use* of such opioids and their *abuse*. If such drugs are taken for the legitimate medical purpose of relieving pain, this should be seen as a wise use. But if a patient begins to use such medicines primarily for the purpose of feeling "high" rather than for pain relief, or if a patient becomes addicted to such medications, then a wise use has crossed over the line and become abuse.[54] Christian doctors and Christian patients alike need to pray for God's wisdom in such situations (see James 1:5–6).

QUESTIONS FOR PERSONAL APPLICATION

1. What is your personal conviction regarding the use of alcoholic beverages? What is your personal practice?

---

[51] Ibid.

[52] Ibid.

[53] Morphine is derived from opium, the painkilling and mind-altering effects of which have been known for thousands of years.

[54] I realize also that in some cases, especially concerning patients with unremitting acute pain in end-of-life situations, long-term use of unusually strong painkillers may be justified.

2. If you have ever been drunk in the past, were there any negative consequences? Are you ever tempted to get drunk again? What are some practical things that can help you resist that temptation?

3. If your own personal practice is total abstinence from alcoholic beverages, what positive results do you see coming from that? If your own practice is use of alcohol in moderation, what positive results do you see coming from that?

4. What character traits (see p. 110) would be helpful in avoiding the temptation to be drunk or to misuse drugs?

5. Would you say that your own experience of a personal relationship with Christ brings you more joy than people might find in drunkenness or in the use of illicit drugs? (See Ps. 4:7: "You have put more joy in my heart than they have when their grain and wine abound.")

SPECIAL TERMS

drunkenness
illicit drugs
Prohibition
sorcery (in the Bible)
stumbling block
total abstinence
Volstead Act

BIBLIOGRAPHY

Sections in Other Ethics Texts

(see complete bibliographical data, p. 64)

Frame, 740–42
Geisler, 359–73
Kaiser, 163–72
McQuilkin and Copan, 116–18

Other Works

Batchelor, Ollie. *Use and Misuse: A Christian Perspective on Drugs.* Leicester, UK: InterVarsity, 1999.

Breeden, Tom, and Mark L. Ward Jr. *Can I Smoke Pot? Marijuana in Light of Scripture.* Adelphi, MD: Cruciform, 2016.

Bustanoby, Andre. *The Wrath of Grapes: Drinking and the Church Divided*. Grand Rapids, MI: Baker, 1987.

Gentry, Kenneth L. *The Christian and Alcoholic Beverages: A Biblical Perspective*. Grand Rapids, MI: Baker, 1986.

———. *God Gave Wine: What the Bible Says about Alcohol*. Lincoln, CA: Oakdown, 2001. This is a revised treatment of the preceding title.

Masters, Peter. *Should Christians Drink? The Case for Total Abstinence*. London: Sword & Trowel; Metropolitan Tabernacle, 2011.

Minirth, Frank B., Paul D. Meier, and Stephen Arterburn. *Miracle Drugs*. Nashville: Thomas Nelson, 1995.

Morey, Robert A. *The Bible and Drug Abuse*. Grand Rapids, MI: Baker, 1973.

Vale, J. A. "Drugs." In *New Dictionary of Christian Ethics and Pastoral Theology*, edited by David J. Atkinson and David H. Field, 320–22. Leicester, UK: Inter-Varsity, and Downers Grove, IL: InterVarsity Press, 1995.

Vere, D. W. "Alcoholism." In *New Dictionary of Christian Ethics and Pastoral Theology*, 152–53.

———. "Dependence." In *New Dictionary of Christian Ethics and Pastoral Theology*, 298–99.

Wilder-Smith, A. E. *The Drug Users: The Psychopharmacology of Turning On*. Wheaton, IL: Harold Shaw, 1970.

SCRIPTURE MEMORY PASSAGE

Ephesians 5:18: And do not get drunk with wine, for that is debauchery, but be filled with the Spirit.

HYMN

"Just As I Am"

Just as I am, without one plea
But that thy blood was shed for me,
And that thou bidd'st me come to thee,
O Lamb of God, I come, I come.

Just as I am, and waiting not
To rid my soul of one dark blot,
To thee, whose blood can cleanse each spot,
O Lamb of God, I come, I come.

Just as I am, though tossed about
With many a conflict, many a doubt,

Fightings and fears within, without,
O Lamb of God, I come, I come.

Just as I am, poor, wretched, blind;
Sight, riches, healing of the mind,
Yea, all I need, in thee to find,
O Lamb of God, I come, I come.

Just as I am! Thou wilt receive,
Wilt welcome, pardon, cleanse, relieve;
Because thy promise I believe,
O Lamb of God, I come, I come.

Just as I am! Thy love unknown
Has broken ev'ry barrier down;
Now, to be thine, yea, thine alone,
O Lamb of God, I come, I come.

AUTHOR: CHARLOTTE ELLIOT, 1836

Part 5

PROTECTING MARRIAGE

"You shall not commit adultery."

Chapter 28

MARRIAGE

What are the essential elements for a marriage to occur?
Why does Scripture place a high value on sexual intimacy
within marriage, but prohibit it outside of marriage?
Should the Bible's definition of marriage apply to all cultures
and all societies?
What safeguards can help protect a marriage against adultery?
Is it wrong for a couple to live together prior to marriage?
What does the Bible say about singleness?

The seventh commandment reads:

> You shall not commit adultery. (Ex. 20:14)

The English word *adultery* means "voluntary sexual intercourse between a married person and a partner other than the lawful spouse."[1] That definition is suitable to the meaning of the Hebrew word *nā'ap*, which is used in this verse, as is clear from other passages that talk about adultery in terms of sexual intercourse with someone who is married to someone else.

One such passage is Leviticus 20:10: "If a man *commits adultery* with the wife of his neighbor, both the adulterer and the adulteress shall surely be put to death."

Similarly, Proverbs 6:32 says, "*He who commits adultery* lacks sense; he who does it destroys himself," and the context shows that it is talking about "He who goes in to his neighbor's wife" (v. 29a). This verse warns, "None who touches her will go unpunished" (v. 29b).

---

[1] *American Heritage Dictionary*, 4th ed. (Boston: Houghton Mifflin, 2006), 24.

The moral evil of adultery is also affirmed in some narrative passages. For example, when the wife of Potiphar, the captain of the guard in Egypt, enticed Joseph to have sex with her, he replied, "How . . . can I do this great wickedness *and sin against God*?" (Gen. 39:9). But King David was not as righteous, for he sinned gravely by committing adultery with Bathsheba, the wife of Uriah the Hittite (2 Samuel 11).

The commandment against adultery is reaffirmed several times in the New Testament (see Matt. 19:18; Rom. 2:22; 13:9; James 2:11), and therefore is clearly morally binding in the new covenant age as well. Jesus teaches about its deeper application to the attitudes of our hearts, saying, "Everyone who looks at a woman with lustful intent has already committed adultery with her in his heart" (Matt. 5:28). But God had already indicated the deeper application of this commandment when he said in the tenth commandment, "You shall not covet your neighbor's wife" (Ex. 20:17).

The purpose of this commandment is to protect marriage, and therefore in this chapter we will consider the Bible's teaching on marriage in some detail.[2] Then in the subsequent chapters in this part of the book we will deal with other specific questions related to marriage: birth control (chap. 29), modern reproductive technology (chap. 30), pornography (chap. 31), divorce and remarriage (chap. 32), and homosexuality (chap. 33).

A. WHAT IS MARRIAGE?

1. Definition of Marriage. Marriage has been understood as "the legal union of a man and woman as husband and wife"[3] in all cultures and societies throughout all of human history. No society in all of recorded history ever permitted same-sex marriage before the 21st century.[4] But beginning with the Netherlands in 2001,[5] a number of countries have recognized same-sex marriage, including the United States in the Supreme Court decision Obergefell v. Hodges on June 26, 2015.

As I will argue below, the historic definition of marriage as a union of a man and a woman is consistent with biblical teaching, and that is the understanding of marriage that I will use in the remainder of this chapter.[6]

---

[2] However, I discussed the question of leadership and partnership in marriage in chap. 15, so I will not revisit that discussion in this chapter.

[3] *American Heritage Dictionary*, 1073.

[4] Supreme Court of the United States, Obergefell v. Hodges, 576 U.S. __ (2015), https://www.supreme court.gov/opinions/14pdf/14-556_3204.pdf, dissent by Chief Justice John Roberts, joined by Justice Antonin Scalia and Justice Clarence Thomas. In the text of their dissent, they called attention to the fact that the lawyers *arguing in favor of same-sex marriage* conceded "that they are not aware of any society that permitted same-sex marriage before 2001" (4).

[5] Adam Taylor, "What Was the First Country to Legalize Gay Marriage?" *The Washington Post*, June 25, 2016, https://www.washingtonpost.com/news/worldviews/wp/2015/06/26/what-was-the-first-country-to -legalize-gay-marriage/?utm_term=.c1dcc9ef7ff9.

[6] A number of societies historically have recognized polygamy as a valid form of marriage, but in the case of polygamy the marriage is still between a man and a woman, except that the man can be married to more

2. Fuller Definition of Marriage from Scripture. In Scripture, marriage is seen as a lifelong relationship between a man and a woman that is established by a solemn covenant before God. The prophet Malachi speaks of marriage as a "covenant" to which God is a witness:

> But you say, "Why does he not [accept your offerings]?" Because the LORD was witness between you and the wife of your youth, to whom you have been faithless, though she is your companion and *your wife by covenant.* (Mal. 2:14)

In this passage, a "covenant" is a solemn agreement establishing a marriage relationship between a man and a woman. In this agreement, the man and woman promise each other that they will be faithful to this marriage for a lifetime, and they call God to witness their promise and to hold them accountable for being faithful to it.

Traditional marriage ceremonies have regularly included the recognition of both (1) the public nature of the marriage (at least requiring legal registration of the marriage in a publicly accessible record), so that the society will know that this man and woman are husband and wife, and (2) God's presence as a witness to the wedding vows.

Both of these elements are found, for example, in a recently published update of a "traditional" wedding ceremony by veteran pastor R. Kent Hughes. This wording draws on centuries of Christian tradition (and especially on the traditional service found in the Episcopalian Book of Common Prayer):

> We have come together here *in the sight of God* and *in the presence of this congregation* to join together this man and this woman in holy matrimony, which is an honorable state of life, instituted in the beginning by God himself, signifying to us the spiritual union that is between Christ and the church.[7]

3. Marriage Changes a Person's Status before God and before Society. It does so not only because of the husband's and wife's solemn vows of mutual faithfulness in the presence of God and their asking God to hold them to account regarding these vows, but also because God himself acts during the wedding ceremony. In the context of discussing the nature of marriage, Jesus says, "What therefore *God has joined together*, let not man separate" (Matt. 19:6). In other words, when a marriage occurs, *it is not merely a human ceremony*. Rather, something deeply spiritual happens. God himself joins the couple together in a spiritual union as husband and wife—their union is something that "God has joined together."

In addition, marriage changes a person's status before society. God's Word makes it clear that, from the very start of the human race, he intended each unique marriage to

---

than one woman at a time. Polygamous marriages were never understood to include homosexual unions. (For further discussion of polygamy, see below, p. 718.)

[7] R. Kent Hughes with Douglas O'Donnell, *The Pastor's Book: A Comprehensive and Practical Guide to Pastoral Ministry* (Wheaton, IL: Crossway, 2015), 141.

be the beginning of a new societal unit, a new household, a new family distinct from the families of the parents of the bride and groom. This is clear in Genesis 2: "Therefore a man shall *leave his father and his mother* and *hold fast to his wife*, and they shall become one flesh" (v. 24). The phrase "a man shall leave his father and his mother" pictures a man departing from the household of which he was a part, and it implies that a new household is being established. The phrase "hold fast to his wife" indicates that this new relationship between a man and his wife is the basis of the new household that has been established.

Society recognizes that marriage changes a man's and a woman's roles in society. It happens not only in movies, but sometimes also in real life, that a wedding is called off at the last minute, even after the guests have arrived, because the bride or groom decides not to show up! The wedding does not take place, and the man and woman remain single. This indicates a common belief in society that all the preliminaries do not constitute a marriage, and until the public ceremony occurs, the couple is not actually husband and wife.

But after the wedding ceremony occurs, everybody thinks of them as husband and wife. They are no longer single people, no longer eligible to date other people. And in addition (in the United States and in many other societies), their legal status has changed. If one spouse dies, the remaining spouse has inheritance rights that no one else has. If one spouse becomes ill, the other spouse has authority and responsibility to care for the one who is sick. If children are born to them, they have responsibility and authority for raising the children.

4. Some Kind of Public Awareness Is Necessary for a Marriage. Because marriage changes the way a society regards a man and woman, weddings mentioned in Scripture were often accompanied by a public celebration. When the time came for Jacob to marry Rachel, "Laban gathered together all the people of the place and made a feast" (Gen. 29:22), though he tricked Jacob and brought to him Leah instead of Rachel (v. 23)! When Isaac married Rebekah, the sparse narrative simply says that "Isaac brought her into the tent of Sarah his mother and took Rebekah, and she became his wife, and he loved her" (24:67). But this narrative shows that Isaac's taking of Rebekah to be his wife happened in the midst of the social community in which they lived, so the marriage was publicly known.

Similarly, in the New Testament, the wedding at Cana in Galilee was a large public event (John 2:1–11).

In modern societies, this need for public awareness of a marriage is reflected in the requirement that a couple have a marriage license issued by the local government authority, and then have the marriage validated by someone recognized as having the authority to perform weddings, such as a judge, a justice of the peace, or a member of the clergy. (Even the captain of a ship at sea can officiate in such a ceremony.)

These customs reflect the common understanding in society that there must be a public awareness of some sort for a marriage to occur, so that the society will be able to think of the man and woman as a married couple and to begin to relate to them as a married couple, not as unmarried individuals, both for legal and social purposes.

5. Sexual Intercourse Alone Does Not Constitute a Marriage. In the Old Testament era, if an unmarried couple had sexual intercourse, the Mosaic Law required them to get married. But if the woman's father refused to give permission, then they were not married, but the man was compelled to pay a fine:

> If a man seduces a virgin who is not betrothed and lies with her, he shall give the bride-price for her and make her his wife. If her father utterly refuses to give her to him, he shall pay money equal to the bride-price for virgins. (Ex. 22:16–17; see also Deut. 22:28–29)[8]

In the New Testament, when Jesus spoke with the woman at the well in Samaria, he surprised her by telling her details about her life: "You have had five husbands, and the one you now have is not your husband" (John 4:18). She was living with a man but she was not married to him because no wedding ceremony had taken place. Therefore, Jesus said to her that the man was not her husband. Sexual intercourse alone did not constitute a marriage.

6. Sexual Union Is an Essential Component of Marriage (with Rare Exceptions). Jesus connected the physical union of a husband and wife in marriage to their being joined together in marriage by God. He made this connection in the context of a challenge from the Pharisees about divorce:

> And Pharisees came up to him and tested him by asking, "Is it lawful to divorce one's wife for any cause?" He answered, "Have you not read that he who created them from the beginning made them male and female, and said, 'Therefore a man shall leave his father and his mother and hold fast to his wife, and the two shall become one flesh'? *So they are no longer two but one flesh.* What therefore God has joined together, let not man separate." (Matt. 19:3–6)

In the expression "so they are no longer two but one flesh," the word *so* represents the Greek word *hōste*, "for this reason, therefore, so."[9] Because of their sexual union, "they are no longer two," but they are "one flesh." This unity was an essential component of marriage from the very beginning of the human race. In addition, when husband and wife come together in this "one flesh" unity, they are a couple whom "God has joined

---

[8] I have used these passages from the Mosaic covenant to show that sexual intercourse alone did not constitute a marriage in the Mosaic covenant. However, since the Mosaic covenant has been terminated with the establishment of the new covenant in Christ (see chap. 8), we should not understand this legal requirement to be one that we must seek to implement in public laws or in church discipline or counseling situations today.

On the other hand, these passages remind us that God has never considered sexual intercourse to be an inconsequential, casual event. It involves not only a physical union, but also a deep emotional and spiritual bonding that is only appropriate within the secure bounds of a lifelong, committed, faithful marriage relationship.

[9] BDAG, 1107.

together" (v. 6). The sexual union of the husband and wife was thought to be essential to their marriage bond.

On this same theme, Paul tells husbands and wives that they should maintain a pattern of regular sexual intimacy within their marriage (see 1 Cor. 7:3), and this likely reflects an understanding of the importance of sexual union to the marriage bond similar to that seen in Genesis 2.

For this reason, if a man and woman have a marriage ceremony but then do not have sexual intercourse following the ceremony, their marriage is spoken of as not "consummated." In some traditions and societies, this can provide grounds for nullifying the marriage (in Roman Catholic tradition, it provides grounds for the church or the pope to annul the marriage).[10]

In British law, a marriage can be annulled if it is seen to be defective or "voidable," with one of the conditions being nonconsummation.[11] In the United States, annulment laws vary by state, but annulments can be received for nonconsummation or lack of physical capacity (impotence or other reasons) to fully engage in sexual relations in several states, as well as the District of Columbia.[12]

On the other hand, there are unusual cases in which a marriage occurs and a couple is physically unable to have sexual intercourse (because of advanced age or because of a physical disability, for example). In such cases, there is still a deep spiritual and emotional unity, and a public promise before God and society, so there is no reason to consider the marriage invalid.

7. Marriage Pictures the Relationship between Christ and the Church. When the apostle Paul discusses marriage and wishes to speak of the relationship between husband and wife, he does not look back to any sections of the Old Testament telling about marriage after sin came into the world. Rather, he looks all the way back to Genesis 2, prior to the fall, and he uses that creation pattern to speak of marriage:

> "Therefore a man shall leave his father and mother and hold fast to his wife,
> and the two shall become one flesh." This mystery is profound, and I am say-
> ing that it refers to Christ and the church. (Eph. 5:31–32)

---

[10] According to the Roman Catholic Code of Canon Law, "For a just cause, the Roman Pontiff can dissolve a non-consummated marriage between baptized persons or between a baptized party and a non-baptized party at the request of both parties or of one of them, even if the other party is unwilling." Art. 1, Can. 1142, http://www.vatican.va/archive/ENG1104/__P44.HTM.

[11] "Annul a Marriage," United Kingdom government website, https://www.gov.uk/how-to-annul-marriage /when-you-can-annul-a-marriage.

[12] The states are Alaska, California, Colorado, Connecticut, Delaware, Idaho, Illinois, Iowa, Kentucky, Michigan, Minnesota, Montana, North Carolina, North Dakota, Ohio, South Carolina, South Dakota, Texas, Vermont, West Virginia, Wisconsin, and Wyoming. See "Annulment and Prohibited Marriage Laws—Information on the Law about Annulment and Prohibited Marriage—Prohibited Marriage," Law Library— American Law and Legal Information, http://law.jrank.org/pages/11834/Annulment-Prohibited-Marriage -Prohibited-Marriage.html#ixzz4SM5LNXBf.

In Paul's writings, a "mystery" is something that was understood only faintly if at all in the Old Testament, but which is now made clearer in the New Testament era. Here Paul makes clear the meaning of the "mystery" of marriage as God created it in the garden of Eden. He is saying that the "mystery" of Adam and Eve (the meaning that was not previously understood) is that marriage "refers to Christ and the church."

Although Adam and Eve did not understand this, their relationship represented the relationship between Christ and the church. They were *created* to represent that relationship, and that is what Paul says *all marriages* are supposed to do. In a marriage, just as Adam represented Christ and Eve represented the church, so for all time, in all marriages, husbands should represent Christ and wives should represent the church, "for the husband is the head of the wife even as Christ is the head of the church" (Eph. 5:23).[13]

8. Christians Should Marry Only Other Christians. In the Old Testament, God frequently prohibited the Jewish people from marrying people of other nations who worshiped other gods:

> You shall not intermarry with them [the Canaanites], giving your daughters to
> their sons or taking their daughters for your sons, for they would turn away
> your sons from following me, to serve other gods. Then the anger of the LORD
> would be kindled against you, and he would destroy you quickly. (Deut. 7:3–4;
> see also Ex. 34:16; Josh. 23:12–13; Ezra 9:14)

The most tragic example of violating this command was King Solomon, who married many foreign wives, and "when Solomon was old *his wives turned away his heart after other gods*, and his heart was not wholly true to the LORD his God" (1 Kings 11:4).

In the New Testament, there is a similar concern that genuine Christian believers *not marry unbelievers*. This becomes explicit when Paul is speaking about a woman whose husband dies. He says:

> A wife is bound to her husband as long as he lives. But if her husband dies,
> she is free to be married to whom she wishes, *only in the Lord*. (1 Cor. 7:39)

When Paul says "only in the Lord," he means she may marry only someone who is "in Christ," that is, a believer.[14] Although Paul speaks here of the specific case of widows, the principle is consistent with God's expectations for his people in the Old Testament, and there is no reason to think that it should not apply to all marriages today as well.

In addition, there is the more general teaching that Christians are not to be "unequally yoked" with unbelievers:

---

[13] See the discussion of leadership and partnership in marriage in chap. 15, p. 389.

[14] Paul frequently uses the expression "in Christ" to speak of Christian believers. In 1 Corinthians alone, he uses this expression in 1:2, 30; 3:1; 4:10, 15, 17; 15:18, 22; 16:24.

Do not be unequally yoked with unbelievers. For what partnership has righteousness with lawlessness? Or what fellowship has light with darkness? What accord has Christ with Belial? Or what portion does a believer share with an unbeliever? What agreement has the temple of God with idols? For we are the temple of the living God. (2 Cor. 6:14–16)

In a society familiar with agricultural life, the image of two animals yoked together side by side to pull a plow would have been familiar. The animals would ordinarily have been equally matched, or nearly so.[15] Essential to the image is the idea that where one ox goes, the other ox has to go as well. Whatever work one ox is doing, the other has to work at it as well. In other words, the animals have significant influence over each other's lives, and each one also limits the amount of freedom the other has.

Even though Paul does not specifically mention marriage in this passage, the metaphor surely applies to marriage (although it would also have application to other human relationships that similarly require a person to be significantly influenced in conduct of life by another person). This passage therefore would prohibit a Christian from marrying a non-Christian.

B. THE GOODNESS OF SEXUAL INTIMACY WITHIN MARRIAGE

1. Sex within Marriage Was Created by God as Fundamentally Good. When God made the first man and woman, he created them with sexual differences and expected that, through sexual intercourse, they would have offspring who would eventually fill the earth:

So God created man in his own image,
    in the image of God he created him;
    male and female he created them.

And God blessed them. And God said to them, "*Be fruitful and multiply* and fill the earth and subdue it, and have dominion over the fish of the sea and over the birds of the heavens and over every living thing that moves on the earth." . . . And God saw everything that he had made, *and behold, it was very good*. And there was evening and there was morning, the sixth day. (Gen. 1:27–28, 31)

Therefore, before there was any sin in the world, at the very beginning of the human race, sexual intercourse between Adam and Eve was something God commanded as part of the "very good" creation.

---

[15] In the Mosaic covenant, God prohibited the people of Israel from plowing with two unequally matched animals: "You shall not plow with an ox and a donkey together" (Deut. 22:10).

Adam and Eve also would have had a strong sexual desire for one another. This is because God would have implanted within their hearts a desire consistent with God's command for them to "be fruitful and multiply." Also, they would have had some instinctive, spontaneous sense of longing to reunite in a "one flesh" relationship (see Gen. 2:24) what God had separated when he took a rib from Adam's side and made it into a woman:

> And the rib that the Lord God had taken from the man he made into a woman and brought her to the man. Then the man said,
>
> "*This at last is bone of my bones*
>   *and flesh of my flesh;*
> she shall be called Woman,
>   because she was taken out of Man." (Gen. 2:22–23)

Both Adam and Eve would have recognized that they were originally one body (Adam's), and sexual intercourse would have restored some sense of that original unity, while still retaining their individual personal distinctiveness.

In the creation narrative, sex is always seen within the context of marriage, implying that it has belonged within marriage from the very beginning. This is clear from Genesis 2:24:

> Therefore a man shall leave his father and his mother and *hold fast to his wife*,
> and they shall become one flesh.

The phrase "hold fast to *his wife*" implies that it is within the context of marriage that they "become one flesh."

2. Sexual Unity and Relational Unity. The sexual union between Adam and Eve occurred within the context of a deep relational unity between them: "And the man and his wife were both naked and were not ashamed" (Gen. 2:25). This implies a complete openness with one another, a lack of any desire to hide from one another. The sexual union between Adam and Eve was an appropriate reflection of their deep interpersonal unity.

Even after the fall, the biblical language used for sex within marriage implies a deep interpersonal involvement with one another. For example:

> Now Adam *knew* Eve his wife, and she conceived and bore Cain, saying,
> "I have gotten a man with the help of the Lord." (Gen. 4:1)

The Hebrew word translated as "knew" is *yāda‘*, which is the common Hebrew word for knowing or understanding something, but it is also used several times in the Old Testament to speak of sexual intercourse (see also Gen. 4:17, 25; 24:16; Num. 31:17; 1 Kings 1:4).

3. Sin Brought Disruption to the Relational and Sexual Intimacy in Marriage. After Adam and Eve ate the forbidden fruit in the garden of Eden, "then the eyes of both were opened, and they knew that they were naked. And they sewed fig leaves together and made themselves loincloths" (Gen. 3:7).

The fig leaves covered their sexual organs, showing that they were suddenly not as intimate in their relationship. They were no longer "naked and . . . not ashamed" (Gen. 2:25). When they concealed their sexual organs from each other, it implied that there was also a mental and emotional barrier to their relationship, and it suggested some reluctance or hesitancy regarding their sexual union. Sin had marred to some extent both their physical and relational intimacy and the beauty of that intimacy that they had shared prior to their sin.

4. However, Sex within Marriage Is Still Seen as Good after the Fall. The entrance of sin into the world did not destroy the goodness of sex within marriage, for it is still viewed as positive and even delightful in later passages of Scripture. This is certainly true in the Song of Solomon, an entire book of Scripture devoted to the beauty of physical intimacy within marriage. And it is also evident from passages such as this section of Proverbs, which commends the idea of enjoyment and delight in sex within marriage:

> Drink water from your own cistern,
>   flowing water from your own well.
> Should your springs be scattered abroad,
>   streams of water in the streets?
> Let them be for yourself alone,
>   and not for strangers with you.
> Let your fountain be blessed,
>   and rejoice in the wife of your youth,
>   a lovely deer, a graceful doe.
> Let her breasts fill you at all times with delight;
>   be intoxicated always in her love. (Prov. 5:15–19)

In this passage, "water" is an image of sexual fulfillment and enjoyment in marriage, and in this context the father is counseling the son to maintain sexual faithfulness within his marriage for his entire life.

This passage also tells the husband regarding his wife that he should "be intoxicated always in her love" (Prov. 5:19). The Hebrew verb translated as "intoxicated," *shāgah*, is elsewhere used at times of those who are led astray with too much to drink (see Prov. 20:1; Isa. 28:7). And the expressions "at all times" and "always" in this same verse imply that sexual intimacy should be a joyful experience for a married couple even into old age.

5. Married Couples Have the Greatest Sexual Fulfillment. In distinction from the picture that is often painted in popular culture today, the greatest joy and fulfillment in sex are experienced not by unmarried single adults who have sex together, but rather by faithful married couples, and especially faithful married couples with a strong religious commitment in their personal lives.

A University of Chicago study found that religious people who are married have the best sex lives. They engage in sex more frequently, find it more satisfying and fun, and have the longest-lived sex lives. The study found that conservative evangelical Protestant women reported the most satisfying sex and the most orgasms. Thirty-two percent said they achieve orgasm every time they make love. Mainline Protestants and Catholics were only five points behind, while those with no religious affiliation were at 22 percent.[16]

Another recent study done by the Harvard University T. H. Chan School of Public Health found that regular church attendance is associated with greater marital stability—in particular, a 30 percent to 50 percent lower likelihood of divorce.[17]

These conclusions are opposite to the stereotypes, caricatures, and deceptive temptations that are often presented to people in the world today by television, movies, novels, and much modern music. But these conclusions are surely consistent with a biblical worldview, from which we would expect that obedience to God's moral commands would bring us the greatest joy in this life.

6. Sex Is an Important Part of an Ongoing Healthy Marriage Relationship. The apostle Paul counsels Christians in Corinth in a very specific way about sex within marriage:

> But because of the temptation to sexual immorality, each man should have his own wife and each woman her own husband. *The husband should give to his wife her conjugal rights, and likewise the wife to her husband.* For the wife does not have authority over her own body, but the husband does. Likewise the husband does not have authority over his own body, but the wife does. Do not deprive one another, except perhaps by agreement for a limited time, that you may devote yourselves to prayer; but then come together again, so that Satan may not tempt you because of your lack of self-control. (1 Cor. 7:2–5)

In this passage, the expression "conjugal rights" means the sexual rights that belong to marriage, that is, the right of spouses to have sexual intercourse with one another. Here God's Word is teaching that continuing to have sexual relations within marriage

---

[16] Walt Larimore, "Poll Shows Sex within Marriage Is More Fulfilling," iMom, http://www.imom.com /poll-shows-sex-within-marriage-is-more-fulfilling/#.WEr28uYrKUk, citing Edward O. Laumann, John H. Gagnon, Robert T. Michael, and Stuart Michaels, *The Social Organization of Sexuality: Sexual Practices in the United States* (Chicago: University of Chicago Press, 1994).

[17] The report says, "A number of studies have found similar results: namely, that those who attend religious services are about 30 to 50 percent less likely to divorce than those who do not." Tyler J. VanderWeele, "Religious Service Attendance, Marriage, and Health," Harvard School of Public Health, Nov. 29, 2016, https:// family-studies.org/religious-service-attendance-marriage-and-health/. Additional evidence for the increased stability of marriages with regular church attendance is found in Shaunti Feldhahn, *The Good News about Marriage: Debunking Discouraging Myths about Marriage and Divorce* (Colorado Springs: Multnomah, 2014); see my summary of her findings in chap. 32, p. 800.

is an important part of a healthy relationship. When Paul says, "so that Satan may not tempt you because of your lack of self-control" (v. 5), he indicates that Satan wants to tempt us to stray in our hearts and actions, and this implies that he does not want us to have the physical joy of sexual union within marriage, and suggests that he will oppose it however he can.

Therefore, for married couples, continuing to have sex with one another is one way of doing battle against Satan's plans and is one protection that God has provided for us against temptation. Sexual intimacy within marriage tends to keep our desires focused within our own marriages and tends to give us strong desires for our own spouses. This is the opposite of coveting *another person's* wife or husband, as is prohibited in the tenth commandment (see Ex. 20:17).

However, sometimes physical disability within a marriage will hinder or prevent frequent sexual intercourse. In such circumstances, married couples are still required by God's Word to remain faithful to each other, and they should seek, if possible, some solution to the difficulty that would enable them to respect the principles taught in 1 Corinthians 7:2–5. It is also important to remember in this situation, as in every situation, that 1 Corinthians 10:13 remains true: "God is faithful, and he will not let you be tempted beyond your ability, but with the temptation he will also provide the way of escape, that you may be able to endure it." In such cases, both husband and wife, individually and together, should seek God's help and direction in finding an appropriate solution or way of coping with a difficult situation.

C. GOD'S DEFINITION OF MARRIAGE IS MORALLY BINDING ON ALL PEOPLE IN ALL SOCIETIES FOR ALL OF HUMAN HISTORY

1. God's Definition of Marriage Was Not for the Jewish People Only, but Was Intended to Apply to All People in All Societies for All Time.[18] As we have seen, a number of laws in the Old Testament were intended only for the Jewish people for a particular time in their history. These included the laws about the sacrifices of animals and about clean and unclean foods. These laws—which God gave to the people after their exodus from Egypt (Exodus 1–15), and which are recorded in Exodus 20–40 and in Leviticus, Numbers, and Deuteronomy—belonged specifically to the Mosaic covenant.

But the foundational biblical teaching about marriage comes from *the beginning of the human race*, the time when Adam and Eve were created. It comes even before there was any evil or sin in the world (which came with the fall, recorded in Genesis 3). That

---

[18] This section and the next are adapted from Wayne Grudem, *Politics—According to the Bible: A Comprehensive Resource for Understanding Modern Political Issues in Light of Scripture* (Grand Rapids, MI: Zondervan, 2010), 215–17, with permission of the publisher. For a more extensive discussion of specific laws and policies concerning marriage, see 221–44 in that book.

is why Jesus says that these truths about marriage come "from the beginning" (Matt. 19:4). They belong to the essence of God's creation of us as male and female.

Therefore, God intends the understanding of marriage as the lifelong union between one man and one woman to be the correct definition of marriage for all people on the earth, for all cultures and societies, and for all periods of history until the beginning of the new heaven and new earth.[19]

This is why it was just for God to bring judgment, for example, on the non-Jewish cities of Sodom and Gomorrah because of their widespread practice of homosexual conduct (see Gen. 19:1–28, especially v. 5; also Jude 7). He had also brought judgment against Pharaoh, king of Egypt, for taking Sarai, Abram's wife (see Gen. 12:17–20). The book of Proverbs, which contains much wisdom not just for the people of Israel in the Old Testament era but for the conduct of life generally, gives frequent warnings against adultery (see 2:16–19; 5:1–23; 6:20–35; 7:4–27; 23:27–28).

In the New Testament era, John the Baptist rebuked Herod Antipas—an Idumean, not part of the people of Israel—for committing incest by taking his brother's wife (Mark 6:17–18). And Paul could say that Gentiles, *who did not have the Jewish laws*, were still guilty of violating God's moral standards regarding sexual conduct (see Rom. 1:26–27; 1 Cor. 5:9–11, 13; 6:9; cf. 1 Pet. 4:3–5). In the book of Revelation, the great city called "Babylon," the center of earthly rebellion against God, is judged for many sins, and among them is "sexual immorality" (Rev. 18:3, 9). In addition, those left outside the heavenly city include "the sexually immoral" (Rev. 21:8).

So from Genesis to Revelation, from the beginning of the Bible to the end, God has established moral standards regarding the nature and conduct of marriage. Moreover, he indicates repeatedly that he will hold *all people on the earth* accountable if they choose to disobey those standards.

A very clear example of this is seen in Leviticus 18, which states that the Canaanites were morally responsible before God for many kinds of sexual sin (specified in vv. 6–23): "For the people of the land, who were before you, did all of these abominations, so that the land became unclean" (v. 27). God held them accountable for violating his standards regarding marriage despite the fact that they did not have the written laws of Israel and were not part of the Jewish people. However, God's moral standards were written on their hearts, and their consciences bore witness to those standards, and therefore God rightly held them accountable (see Rom. 2:14–15).

These passages indicate that *the definition of marriage as established by God in the Bible* (a lifelong union between one man and one woman) *should be the standard adopted by all governments*. And this standard for marriage should apply to all people, not merely to Christians or those who personally happen to agree with the Bible's standards.

---

[19] In Matt. 22:30, Jesus indicates that a significant change will occur after the final resurrection of believers: "For in the resurrection *they neither marry nor are given in marriage*, but are like angels in heaven." But that evident change does not affect the legal or moral definition of marriage in this age.

2. Marriage between a Man and a Woman Is the Most Fundamental Institution in Any Society. Following immediately after his creation of man and woman, God established marriage (Genesis 1–2) before any other institution of human society. It came before any establishment of cities, nations, courts of law, or any human laws. It certainly preceded any national, state, or city government. It came before the establishment of any schools, businesses, churches, and other nonprofit organizations. It came before the establishment of *any other institution* in any human society. And it is foundational to the establishment of any society.

Societies have long recognized the crucial importance of some kind of normalization of a dependable, ongoing, faithful marriage relationship between men and women. I am not aware of any exceptions to the generalization that every human nation on earth, every society of any size or permanence at all, has recognized and protected the institution of heterosexual marriage.[20] (Though some have recognized polygamy as a form of marriage, it was still heterosexual marriage.)

J. D. Unwin, a British anthropologist, reached this conclusion after investigating assertions made by Sigmund Freud. He discovered that Freud's call for the liberation of sexual behavior had grave consequences for society. Unwin was able to chronicle the historical decline of 86 different cultures, and he found that "strict marital monogamy" was so central to social energy and growth that no society flourished for more than three generations without it. Unwin wrote, "In human records there is no instance of a society retaining its energy after a complete new generation has inherited a tradition which does not insist on prenuptial and postnuptial continence" (that is, abstinence from sex outside of marriage).[21]

D. ADULTERY

At the beginning of this chapter, I quoted and briefly explained the seventh commandment, "You shall not commit adultery" (Ex. 20:14). In this section I will explain more specifically why God so strictly prohibits adultery, and in later sections I will discuss other kinds of sexual relationships that are contrary to God's moral standards.

1. Adultery Is Prohibited in Scripture.

a. Scripture Repeatedly Affirms That Adultery Is Wrong: The seventh commandment, "You shall not commit adultery" (Ex. 20:14), is affirmed several times in the New Testament (see Matt. 15:19; 19:18; Luke 18:20; Rom. 2:22; 13:9; James 2:11; 2 Pet. 2:14), showing that it still applies in the new covenant age.

---

[20] See my discussion of the definition of marriage above, p. 700.

[21] Joseph Daniel Unwin, *Sex and Culture* (London: Oxford University Press, 1934); *Sexual Regulations and Cultural* Behavior (London: Oxford University Press, 1935); and *Hopousia: Or the Sexual and Economic Foundations of a New* Society (London: George Allen and Unwin, 1940), cited in Daniel R. Heimbach, "Deconstructing the Family," *The Religion and Society Report* 22, no. 7 (October/November 2005).

b. Adultery Wrongly Intrudes Another Person into the "One Flesh" Relationship of Marriage. Scripture emphasizes that within marriage, "a man shall . . . hold fast to his wife, and they shall become one flesh" (Gen. 2:24; also Eph. 5:31), but adultery means that three people are involved in the "one flesh" relationship, contrary to God's intention for unity and exclusiveness within the marriage.

c. Adultery Wrongly Pictures Unfaithfulness in the Relationship between Christ and the Church. Paul teaches that the relationship between a husband and wife is a profound "mystery" that "refers to Christ and the church" (Eph. 5:32). Therefore, if a husband commits adultery, he is portraying Christ as being unfaithful to his people, abandoning them, and not keeping his covenant with them (see also Mal. 2:14). If a wife commits adultery, it is a picture of the church worshiping another god and being unfaithful to Christ. Both portrayals are deeply dishonoring to Christ.

d. Adultery Destroys Trust within a Marriage. Adultery is a most serious violation of a person's marriage promise to be faithful for his or her whole life. If one spouse violates that promise, the other spouse will rightly wonder whether the adulterous spouse can ever be trusted again. And if trust is destroyed within a marriage, all other aspects of the relationship become much more difficult.

e. Adultery Often Results in New Children Being Born or Aborted. As was the case with David and Bathsheba (2 Samuel 11), an adulterous relationship often leads to the birth of a child, but only one of the spouses in the marriage is a biological parent to this child. This child likely cannot be raised by both the father and the mother of the child, but only by one of them (usually the mother). At other times, such a pregnancy will lead to an abortion, taking the innocent child's life.

f. Adultery Frequently Destroys a Person's Entire Life. The warnings against adultery in Proverbs are harsh, blunt, and vivid in their portrayal of terrible destruction: one warning against adultery portrays a man grasping hot, burning coals and clutching them to his chest:

> Can a man carry fire next to his chest
>   and his clothes not be burned?
> Or can one walk on hot coals
>   and his feet not be scorched?
> So is he who goes in to his neighbor's wife;
>   none who touches her will go unpunished. . . .
> He who commits adultery lacks sense;
>   *he who does it destroys himself.*
> He will get wounds and dishonor,
>   and his disgrace will not be wiped away. (Prov. 6:27–33)

Another vivid image compares a man who commits adultery to an animal that ignorantly walks to its violent and sudden death:

> With much seductive speech she persuades him;
>> with her smooth talk she compels him.
> All at once he follows her,
>> *as an ox goes to the slaughter,*
> or as a stag is caught fast
>> till an arrow pierces its liver;
> as a bird rushes into a snare;
>> he does not know that *it will cost him his life.* (Prov. 7:21–23)

Just prior to these two warnings there is a longer one that portrays the allurement of a woman who tempts a man to commit adultery:

> *For the lips of a forbidden woman drip honey,*
>> and *her speech is smoother than oil,*
> but in the end she is bitter as wormwood,
>> sharp as a two-edged sword.
> Her feet go down to death;
>> her steps follow the path to Sheol;
> she does not ponder the path of life;
>> her ways wander, and she does not know it.
> And now, O sons, listen to me,
>> and do not depart from the words of my mouth.
> *Keep your way far from her,*
>> and do not go near the door of her house,
> lest you give your honor to others
>> and your years to the merciless,
> lest strangers take their fill of your strength,
>> and your labors go to the house of a foreigner,
> and *at the end of your life you groan,*
>> when *your flesh and body are consumed.* (Prov. 5:3–11)

These passages provide a challenge to parents: Are we willing to give such vivid warnings (perhaps even these verses) to our children today? If parents had inculcated such warnings in their children for the last two or three generations, the moral fabric of our society would look much different than it does today.[22]

---

[22] These warnings from Scripture are confirmed year after year in the tragic news stories of high-profile leaders whose careers and families are destroyed by adulterous relationships. Especially tragic are the stories of numerous Christian leaders who have committed adultery and destroyed their ministries as a result.

2. Safeguards against Adultery. People who have committed adultery often tell similar stories of how it began with a seemingly "innocent" friendship that then progressed into more frequent times together, until eventually more and more boundaries were crossed and adultery finally occurred.

Some passages of Scripture warn people to *avoid situations* that might lead to adultery or that would give even the appearance of inappropriate behavior. For example, when speaking about "a forbidden woman" (Prov. 5:3), the counsel of a father to a son in Proverbs 5:8 is "keep your way far from her" and "do not go near the door of her house." In other words, don't spend time in the company of someone for whom you begin to feel a sexual attraction toward an immoral relationship. Don't even decide to go near to where she is, and so give more opportunity for temptation. Joseph, when he was pursued by Potiphar's wife, "left his garment in her hand and fled and got out of the house" (Gen. 39:12).

In the New Testament, Paul says, "Make no provision for the flesh, to gratify its desires" (Rom. 13:14), and "Give no opportunity to the devil" (Eph. 4:27). This again implies that people should avoid situations in which they would likely be tempted to inappropriate behavior.

Some commonsense safeguards that some people have followed include taking care not to be alone with a person of the opposite sex,[23] keeping one's office door open or having a window in the door (as do all offices at Phoenix Seminary, where I teach), and, if traveling for business with a coworker of the opposite sex, taking care not to get seats together on the airplane and not to have rooms on the same floor in the hotel.

One prominent Christian ministry known to me has a policy that discourages staff members of the opposite sex from traveling alone together on business, either locally or out of town. If this cannot be avoided, or if a third party cannot be added to the trip, then the two employees must use public ground transportation (such as buses or trains) or separate nonpublic ground transportation (such as rental cars), and all meetings must be in public areas. One-on-one meetings outside of the office are strongly discouraged. If they cannot be avoided, each person must notify his or her spouse (if applicable) and manager about the location, date, and time the meeting will be held. One-on-one meetings between members of the opposite sex at the office also must be held in a visible area.

Another safeguard is to beware of danger signs in one's own heart. "Keep your heart with all vigilance, for from it flow the springs of life" (Prov. 4:23). If we are honest with ourselves, we can recognize when we feel an unusual attraction to a person of the opposite sex to whom we are not married, or when we desire to find excuses to meet

---

[23] Vice President Mike Pence "never eats alone with a woman other than his wife," according to a *Washington Post* story on March 28, 2017. The revelation of this practice received scathing criticism from the liberal press, but it seems a wise policy to me. See https://www.washingtonpost.com/politics/karen-pence -is-the-vice-presidents-prayer-warrior-gut-check-and-shield/2017/03/28/3d7a26ce-0a01-11e7-8884 -96e6a6713f4b_story.html?utm_term=.afa2e1e497ce.

that person or be with that person in various situations, or when we desire to prolong conversations beyond what is necessary, and so forth. When such feelings arise in one's heart, it is probably wise to intentionally distance oneself from the relationship.

3. Scripture Sets an Even Higher Standard: Do Not Desire to Commit Adultery. Such safeguards as I discussed in the previous section are entirely consistent with the tenth commandment, which goes beyond the command not to commit adultery and speaks about our hearts: "*You shall not covet your neighbor's wife*" (Ex. 20:17). As I noted in an earlier chapter (see p. 138), God requires of us not only purity of actions, but also purity of thoughts and attitudes in our hearts. And this commandment specifically directs us to seek after purity in our hearts. Though none of us in this lifetime will ever be perfect in what our hearts desire, we can still hope to grow in purity of heart throughout our lives. We also can take comfort in the forgiveness that Christ promises us when our hearts go astray (see 1 John 1:9).

The book of Proverbs has a similar command regarding a person's attitude toward someone who is not his wife: "Do not desire her beauty *in your heart*" (Prov. 6:25).

When our hearts are more perfectly conformed to these commandments, those of us who are married will find a deeper love for our own wives or husbands, and a deepened desire for maintaining a healthy sexual relationship within our own marriages. Purity of heart in this regard will also lead increasingly to a genuine sense of revulsion at the thought of embracing anyone other than one's own spouse in a sexually affectionate manner.

Jesus understood the deeper intention of the seventh commandment, that it was meant to prohibit adulterous desires as well as the physical act of adultery. He taught:

> You have heard that it was said, "You shall not commit adultery." But I say to you that everyone who *looks at a woman with lustful intent* has already committed adultery with her in his heart. (Matt. 5:27–28)

The Greek phrase that is translated "with lustful intent" is *pros to epithymēsai autēn*, literally "for the purpose of lusting for her." This means that a man who is looking at a woman (or a picture of a woman) should ask himself, "*Why* am I looking at her?" If the honest answer is that you are looking at her for the purpose of arousing lustful thoughts toward her or thinking about having sex with her, then Jesus says you have "already committed adultery with her" in your heart. And you need to turn from this sin and ask God's forgiveness.

The wisdom of God is seen in these scriptural teachings, because they reflect a common theme in Scripture—wrongful actions begin in the heart. The following passages emphasize that:

> *Keep your heart* with all vigilance,
>   for from it flow the springs of life. (Prov. 4:23)

For from within, *out of the heart of man*, come evil thoughts, sexual immorality, theft, murder, adultery. (Mark 7:21)

But each person is tempted when he is lured and enticed by *his own desire*. Then desire when it has conceived gives birth to sin, and sin when it is fully grown brings forth death. (James 1:14–15)

Some people reading this, especially non-Christians or younger Christians, may think that such teachings are simply impossible to follow. But the testimony of millions of Christians throughout history has been that these teachings are not impossible to obey as a regular habit of life, even if we all fail in maintaining purity of heart in one area or another from time to time, and even if our hearts will never be completely pure until the day we die and go into the Lord's presence.

If we believe that Scripture is true, then we must believe its teachings that people who have been regenerated (or "born again," John 3:3, 7; 1 Pet. 1:3, 23) have a new inward power, from the work of the Holy Spirit, to overcome temptation and to live lives of increasing moral purity. Paul says, "You also must consider yourselves dead to sin and alive to God in Christ Jesus" (Rom. 6:11), and, by the power of the Holy Spirit within us, we "walk not according to the flesh but according to the Spirit" (Rom. 8:4). He also says that "if by the Spirit you put to death the deeds of the body, you will live" (Rom. 8:13). The path of growth in personal holiness of life is an upward path on which God *expects* us to continue and *enables* us to continue, step by step throughout our earthly lives. Even the apostle Paul knew that he was not "already perfect," but he said, "Forgetting what lies behind and straining forward to what lies ahead, I press on toward the goal for the prize of the upward call of God in Christ Jesus" (Phil. 3:12–14; see also Prov. 4:18).

In addition, Scripture promises that the joy we can experience in close fellowship with God is far greater than any supposed earthly pleasure that we think might come from disobeying God:

In your presence there is fullness of joy;
at your right hand are pleasures forevermore. (Ps. 16:11)

If you keep my commandments, you will abide in my love, just as I have kept my Father's commandments and abide in his love. These things I have spoken to you, that my joy may be in you, and that your joy may be full. (John 15:10–11)

Though you have not seen him, you love him. Though you do not now see him, you believe in him and rejoice with joy that is inexpressible and filled with glory. (1 Pet. 1:8)

Finally, we should keep in mind the repeated emphasis of Scripture that God's blessing on our lives and ministries depends in significant measure on our maintaining purity of heart before him:

For the eyes of the LORD run to and fro throughout the whole earth, to give strong support to those whose *heart is blameless* toward him. (2 Chron. 16:9)

Why should you be intoxicated, my son, with a forbidden woman
 and embrace the bosom of an adulteress?
For a man's ways are before the eyes of the LORD,
 and he ponders all his paths. (Prov. 5:20–21)

Therefore, *if anyone cleanses himself from what is dishonorable*, he will be a vessel for honorable use, set apart as holy, useful to the master of the house, ready for every good work. So *flee youthful passions* and *pursue righteousness*, faith, love, and peace, along with those who call on the Lord *from a pure heart*. (2 Tim. 2:21–22)

E. WHY DID GOD ALLOW POLYGAMY IN THE OLD TESTAMENT?

There are a number of examples of polygamy in the Old Testament. Does having more than one wife reflect God's pattern for marriage?

The answer is that God *temporarily allowed* polygamy to occur without giving explicit commands against it, even though it did not conform to his original purpose for marriage as indicated in Genesis 1–2. But we get some hints from the narrative passages that polygamy was not in line with God's purpose, because in every example where a man has more than one wife, the situation leads to significant difficulty in the marriage relationship, and readers are left to draw their own conclusions from this fact.

A helpful summary of the biblical material on polygamy is found in the *ESV Study Bible*:

Why did God allow polygamy in the Old Testament? Nowhere in the Bible did God ever command polygamy or tell anyone to marry more than one wife. Rather, God temporarily allowed polygamy to occur (he did not give any general prohibition against it) without giving it any explicit moral approval. Nevertheless, in the OT narratives, whenever a man has two or more wives, it seems to lead to trouble (see Genesis 16; 29–31; 1 Samuel 1; 1 Kings 11; note also the prohibition in Deut. 17:17). In addition, polygamy is horribly dehumanizing for women, for it does not treat them as equal in value to their husbands, and therefore it does not recognize that they share fully in the high status of being created "in the image of God" (Gen. 1:27), and of being worthy of honor as "heirs with you of the grace of life" (1 Pet. 3:7). The requirement "husband of one wife" (1 Tim. 3:2) would exclude polygamists from being elders (evidence for polygamy among Jews in the first century is found in Josephus, *Antiquities* 17.14; Mishnah, *Yebamoth* 4.11; *Ketuboth* 10.1,

4, 5; *Sanhedrin* 2.4; *Kerithoth* 3.7; *Kiddushin* 2.7; *Bechoroth* 8.4; and Justin Martyr, *Dialogue with Trypho*, chapter 134; for polygamy among non-Jews see 2 Macc. 4:30; Josephus, *Antiquities* 17.19; Tertullian, *Apology* 46). This has practical application today in missionary contexts in cultures where polygamy is still practiced: the Bible would not encourage a husband to divorce any of his multiple wives, which would leave them without support and protection. But it would not allow a man with multiple wives to be an elder. This restriction would provide a pattern that would generally lead to the abolition of polygamy in a church in a generation or two.[24]

F. SEXUAL PRACTICES PROHIBITED IN SCRIPTURE

1. Incest. A long section in the Mosaic Law, Leviticus 18:6–18, prohibits various specific kinds of incest. It begins by saying, "None of you shall approach any one of his close relatives to uncover nakedness" (Lev. 18:6), and commentators generally agree that "to uncover nakedness" in this context is a euphemism for having sexual relations with a person.[25] Then the subsequent verses prohibit sexual intercourse (and by implication marriage) with one's mother (v. 7), stepmother (v. 8), sister or stepsister (v. 9), granddaughter (v. 10), aunt (vv. 12–14), daughter-in-law (v. 15), sister-in-law (v. 16), or stepdaughter or step-granddaughter (v. 17). One's daughter is not explicitly mentioned, since sex with one's own daughter would have been uniformly prohibited both in Israel and in the surrounding cultures.[26] In addition, sex with one's stepdaughter and step-granddaughter are prohibited (v. 17), and so surely having sex with one's own daughter would be even more clearly prohibited. (See also Ezek. 22:11.)

The prohibition against marrying one's stepmother is repeated in Deuteronomy: "A man shall not take his father's wife, so that he does not uncover his father's nakedness" (Deut. 22:30).

There is no reason to think that these laws are limited to the nation of Israel or the Mosaic covenant only. They are matters that pertain to human conduct generally, and we should understand them as a helpful guide to the kind of life that pleases God in the area of human sexuality.

Paul actually rebukes the Corinthian church for failing to discipline a man who was living in an incestuous relationship with his stepmother:

> It is actually reported that there is sexual immorality among you, and of a kind that is not tolerated even among pagans, for a man has his father's wife.

---

[24] "Marriage and Sexual Morality," *ESV Study Bible* (Wheaton, IL: Crossway, 2008), 2544. (I was the primary author of this article, though it was modified by other editors.)

[25] Some translations even render the phrase explicitly as "to have sexual intercourse" (NET), "to have sexual relations" (NIV), "have sexual relations with" (NLT), or "for sexual intercourse" (CSB).

[26] See *ESV Study Bible*, 240 (note on Lev. 18:6–18).

> And you are arrogant! Ought you not rather to mourn? Let him who has done
> this be removed from among you. (1 Cor. 5:1–2)

This statement indicates that Paul is astounded to think that the Corinthians do
not understand that incest is morally wrong. This provides specific confirmation that,
at least in this particular, the Old Testament laws about incest reflect the abiding moral
standards of God. Therefore, it seems appropriate to conclude that the other standards
about incest are also applicable today.

2. Homosexual Conduct. I will treat the topic of homosexuality in a separate chapter
(see chap. 33, p. 843). At this point it is sufficient to note that both the Old Testament
(Lev. 18:22; 20:13) and the New Testament (Rom. 1:26–27; 1 Cor. 6:9–11; 1 Tim. 1:9–10)
prohibit homosexual conduct.

3. Having Sex before Marriage. The Old Testament clearly prohibited sexual intercourse between two unmarried people. For example, here is a law concerning a couple
who were discovered to have had sexual intercourse:

> If a man seduces a virgin who is not betrothed and lies with her, he shall give
> the bride-price for her and make her his wife. If her father utterly refuses to
> give her to him, he shall pay money equal to the bride-price for virgins. (Ex.
> 22:16–17)

The requirement that they get married indicates the impropriety of sex outside of
marriage. They needed to get married so that any further sexual relations would occur
within the proper context of marriage. The degree of intimacy involved was such that
it belonged only within marriage. If the woman's father refused to allow the marriage,
the man still had to pay a substantial fine, indicating again that what they had done was
wrong. (The Hebrew word translated as "seduces" in this verse, *pātāh*, indicates that
this was not a forcible rape, but that consent was given to some degree; it was different
from the situation of forcible rape addressed in Deut. 22:25–27, for example.) A similar
law requiring the marriage of a couple who had sex is found in Deuteronomy 22:28–29.

The requirement that a woman remain a virgin until her marriage is seen explicitly
in a long passage in Deuteronomy 22:13–21. If a man accused his new wife of not being
a virgin, "then the father of the young woman and her mother shall take and bring out
the evidence of her virginity to the elders of the city in the gate" (v. 15; apparently the
"evidence of her virginity" was a cloth stained with blood from her broken hymen on
her wedding night). Then the man who brought the false accusation would be flogged
as punishment (v. 18).

On the other hand, "if the thing is true, that evidence of virginity was not found
in the young woman," then "the men of her city shall stone her to death with stones,
because she has done an outrageous thing in Israel by whoring in her father's house"
(Deut. 22:20–21). Her sexual activity outside of marriage was punishable by death. (See

also the story of Tamar's pregnancy and the initial assumption by Judah that she was guilty of a crime worthy of death, Gen. 38:24.)

Once again, we must bear in mind that these laws are part of the Mosaic covenant, which has been terminated, and we should not think that the *specific punishments* required under the government of Israel at that time should be required by civil governments today (see discussion of Old Testament laws in chap. 8, especially p. 225). However, there is no reason to think that the *moral standard* against sexual intercourse outside of marriage was something applicable to the Jewish people only or to the Mosaic covenant only, for these are matters that concern human life in general.

The New Testament also shows that sexual intercourse between two unmarried people is considered sin according to God's moral standards. This is seen in several passages that prohibit "sexual immorality," such as:

> Flee from *sexual immorality*. Every other sin a person commits is outside the body, but the sexually immoral person sins against his own body. (1 Cor. 6:18)

The Greek word translated as "sexual immorality" is *porneia*, a widely inclusive term that refers to any kind of "unlawful sexual intercourse, *prostitution, unchastity, fornication*."[27]

The fact that *porneia* refers to sex between people who are not married is seen in a statement from Jesus's Jewish opponents when they say, "We were not born of *sexual immorality* [*porneia*]. We have one father—even God" (John 8:41). It is clear that they mean they were not born out of wedlock, as a result of sex between unmarried persons.

This meaning of *porneia* is also made explicit when Paul writes to the Corinthians about sexual ethics:

> But because of the temptation to *sexual immorality*, each man should have his own wife and each woman her own husband. (1 Cor. 7:2)

Here Paul says that the solution to overcome the "temptation to sexual immorality" is for a man and a woman to get married. Then he adds:

> But if they cannot exercise self-control, they should marry. For it is better to marry than to burn with passion. (1 Cor. 7:9)

Once again, to avoid the temptation to have sex prior to marriage, Paul tells couples that "they should marry." The assumption again is that sex prior to marriage is sin.

---

[27] BDAG, 854. The term *porneia* does not refer specifically to "adultery" (designated by a different Greek term, *moicheia*). "Adultery" (*moicheia*) is distinguished from "sexual immorality" (*porneia*) in Matt. 15:19 and Mark 7:21. However, in the Apocrypha, one passage refers to a woman who "committed adultery by sexual immorality" (*en porneia emoicheuthē*, Sirach 23:23), showing that *porneia* was the broader term, one that included all kinds of sexually immoral conduct, and *moicheia* was the narrower term, specifically referring to sexually immoral conduct by a married person. (In 1 Cor. 5:1, *porneia* is used to refer to incest, also showing that it is the broader term.)

Therefore, the first-century readers of the New Testament would certainly have understood the passages that prohibit "sexual immorality" to be forbidding all sexual intercourse between unmarried persons. The problem for modern English readers is that the phrase "sexual immorality" can seem somewhat vague and abstract, and it is easy for readers to overlook the fact that the Greek expression was used most often to refer to sexual intercourse between unmarried people.

In English, the word *fornication* means sex between unmarried persons, and in the King James Version, *porneia* was regularly translated as "fornication," so that 1 Corinthians 6:18 says, "flee fornication." When *porneia* was translated as "fornication," it was clear to readers that all of the passages that mention "fornication" were explicitly prohibiting sex between unmarried people.

But in all modern versions today, the word "fornication" (which some may find archaic or obsolete) has disappeared, and the more abstract, more general expression "sexual immorality" is commonly used. I agree that "sexual immorality" is the most accurate translation in English today.[28] But the disadvantage of the translation "sexual immorality" is that modern readers do not as readily realize that *it primarily refers to sex between two unmarried people*—and that it includes not only casual sex between people not committed to each other, but also to sex between a man and a woman who are committed to each other but not yet married.

This understanding of *porneia* means that a number of very clear verses in the New Testament explicitly prohibit a man and woman from having sex together before they are married. Here are some of the verses:

> Those who sinned earlier . . . have not repented of the impurity, *sexual immorality*, and sensuality that they have practiced. (2 Cor. 12:21)

> Now the works of the flesh are evident: *sexual immorality*, impurity, sensuality. (Gal. 5:19)

> But *sexual immorality* and all impurity or covetousness must not even be named among you, as is proper among saints. (Eph. 5:3)

> Put to death therefore what is earthly in you: *sexual immorality*, impurity, passion, evil desire, and covetousness, which is idolatry. (Col. 3:5)

> For this is the will of God, your sanctification: that you abstain from *sexual immorality*. (1 Thess. 4:3)

Finally, Paul uses marriage imagery to talk about his concern for the Corinthians. He says:

---

[28] The expression "sexual immorality" rightly indicates that the word *porneia* refers to all kinds of sexual conduct that were considered morally wrong at the time of the New Testament, including incest (as in 1 Cor. 5:1) and adultery (see Rev. 17:2; presumably the kings were married).

> For I feel a divine jealousy for you, since I betrothed you to one husband, to present you as a pure virgin to Christ. (2 Cor. 11:2)

When he says, "I betrothed you to one husband," he refers to the Jewish custom of "betrothal," a legally binding agreement to be married at some future time. Paul uses the imagery of presenting the Corinthian church to Christ at his second coming "as a pure virgin," that is, as a church that was faithful to Christ alone. But the image of a "pure virgin" (Greek, *parthenon hagnēn*) implies once again the expectation that in order to be considered morally pure, a bride would come as a "virgin" to her husband.

There is abundant evidence that couples who refrain from sex prior to their marriage have a significantly happier and more fulfilling sex life once they are married than those who have intercourse prior to marriage, confirming again that obedience to God's commands leads to human well-being. Numerous studies suggest that adults who waited to have sex until they were married experienced higher levels of satisfaction compared to those who engaged in sexual relations before marriage. According to the American Psychological Association's *Journal of Family Psychology*, a study of 2,035 married couples found that those who waited for sex until marriage rated their relationship stability 22 percent higher, their relationship satisfaction 20 percent higher, the sexual quality of their relationship 15 percent better, and communication 12 percent better than couples who engaged in sex before marriage.[29]

In addition, the National Health and Social Life Survey, the most comprehensive study of sex in America, indicated that a "monogamous sexual partnership embedded in a formal marriage evidently produces the greatest satisfaction and pleasure."[30]

G. PHYSICAL INTIMACY PRIOR TO MARRIAGE

However, it is important to ask another question. While Scripture is clear that sexual intercourse prior to marriage is morally wrong in God's sight and ultimately harmful to a relationship, is there any further guidance that can be given regarding the degree of physical affection and intimacy that is appropriate between a man and a woman prior to marriage? There are longer Christian resources that seek to provide wise guidance in this area,[31] but I can add a brief comment at this point.

If a man and a woman are already in a romantic relationship with one another,

---

[29] "Couples who delay having sex get benefits later, study suggests," *Science Daily*, Dec. 29, 2010, https://www.sciencedaily.com/releases/2010/12/101222112102.htm.

[30] Bradley Wilcox, "A Scientific Review of Abstinence and Abstinence-Based Programs," February 2008, https://d1li5256ypm7oi.cloudfront.net/ampartnership/2015/05/AScientificReviewofAbstinenceandAbstinencePrograms.pdf.

[31] See, for example, Focus on the Family's website for young adults, Boundless.org, which has several excellent articles and resources. Go to http://www.boundless.org/relationships/Sexuality#P=0 for a complete listing. Helpful books include: Henry Cloud and John Townsend, *Boundaries in Dating: How Healthy Choices Grow Healthy Relationships* (Grand Rapids, MI: Zondervan, 2000) and Andy Stanley, *The New Rules for Sex and Dating* (Grand Rapids, MI: Zondervan, 2014).

God has designed our human bodies in such a way that, if one of them physically touches or stimulates the sexual organs of the other, that action will arouse a desire for further stimulation and ultimately awaken a strong desire to engage in sexual intercourse immediately. That means that the physical stimulation is more than an innocent expression of affection; it is an intentional awakening of the desire to have sex prior to marriage, something that Scripture explicitly forbids. Therefore, though it may be difficult, couples need to be cautious about the intensity of physical intimacy they allow for themselves prior to marriage. If the purpose of their actions is primarily to arouse strong physical desires that cannot rightly be fulfilled prior to marriage, then they have gone too far. And because I believe that God has given men a leadership role with respect to marriage (see chap. 15, p. 407), I would challenge men to show leadership, responsibility, and respect in this area. In other words, in a dating relationship prior to marriage, the man should bear the primary responsibility for drawing boundaries on the extent of the couple's physical expressions of affection and intimacy.

Commenting on Jesus's teaching in Matthew 5:28, Westminster Seminary professor John Murray wrote the following in 1957 (I realize that his expressions sound a bit outdated today, but there is still wisdom in the paragraph):

> The line of demarcation between virtue and vice is not a chasm but a razor's edge. Sex desire is not wrong and Jesus does not say so. To cast any aspersion on sex desire is to impugn the integrity of the Creator and of his creation. Furthermore, it is not wrong to desire to satisfy sex desire and impulse in the way God has ordained. Indeed, sex desire is one of the considerations which induce men and women to marry. The Scripture fully recognizes the propriety of that motive and commends marriage as the honorable and necessary outlet for sex impulse. What is wrong is the earliest and most rudimentary desire to satisfy the impulse to the sex act outside the estate of matrimony. It is not wrong to desire the sex act with the person who may be contemplated as a spouse if and when the estate of matrimony will have been entered upon with him or her. But the desire for the sex act outside that divinely instituted and strictly guarded sanctuary which God has reserved for the man and his wife alone is wrong; and it is from this fountain of desire that proceed all the evils by which the sanctity of sex is desecrated.[32]

H. MASTURBATION

Christian writers differ about the question of whether masturbation is always sinful. I have presented two viewpoints in the following section.

---

[32] John Murray, *Principles of Conduct: Aspects of Biblical Ethics* (Grand Rapids, MI: Eerdmans, 1957), 56.

1. First View: Masturbation Is Always Wrong (Written by Jason DeRouchie).[33] Sexual intimacy within marriage is a beautiful gift from God. It is an outlet for play and passion, and it nurtures closeness with one's spouse, supplying a unique context for giving and receiving love.

Many medical professionals treat masturbation as a natural part of human development, and some church leaders have attempted to supply practical and theological reasons to masturbate. However, I do not believe this approach pleases God, and I have seen the devastation that such a practice brings to both singles and married people alike. My focus here is to clarify biblically why engaging in such activity outside the marriage bed is sinful and should therefore be avoided.

Jesus said, "If your right hand causes you to sin, cut it off" (Matt. 5:30). We cannot stand against sexual temptation in our own strength. But *with God's help*, all things are possible (Mark 9:23; 10:27). Jesus "bore our sins in his body on the tree, that we might die to sin and live to righteousness" (1 Pet. 2:24).

This is our plea and our confidence in the new covenant light of Christ: we can overcome with God's help (Deut. 30:6; Jer. 32:40; Ezek. 36:27)! In Christ, we become new creations. From this perspective, consider the following thoughts about the practice of masturbation in the life of one who is in Christ:

a. God Purposed That All Righteous Forms of Sexual Expression Be for the Marriage Bed: Sexual expression manifest in orgasm is a good gift of God (1 Tim. 4:2–5) that men and women are to enjoy only in the context of marital intimacy (Gen. 2:23; Song 8:4–6; 1 Cor. 7:2–5; Heb. 13:4). When people reach orgasm outside the covenant-confirming act of lovemaking in marriage, the act expresses a lack of self-control and becomes solely self-seeking, divorced from its purpose of creating intimacy.

b. Sexual Intimacy between a Husband and Wife Points to the Love between Christ and His Church: The most ultimate reason sexual expression manifest in orgasm is to be enjoyed only in the context of marriage is because God gives the sexual drive that leads to sexual expression to picture the intimate "one-flesh" nature of covenant love between Christ and his church (Eph. 5:31–32).

---

[33] This section was written at my request by an advocate of this view, Jason S. DeRouchie, professor of Old Testament and biblical theology at Bethlehem College and Seminary in Minneapolis, Minnesota. For a more developed version of his argument, see "If Your Right Hand Causes You to Sin: Ten Biblical Reflections on Masturbation," Desiring God, Dec. 3, 2016, https://www.desiringgod.org/articles/if-your-right-hand-causes -you-to-sin.

This view is also held by Norman Geisler, *Christian Ethics: Contemporary Issues and Options*, 2nd ed. (Grand Rapids, MI: Baker, 2010), 275–76, and Daniel R. Heimbach, *True Sexual Morality: Recovering Biblical Standards for a Culture in Crisis* (Wheaton, IL: Crossway, 2004), 222–23.

The *Catechism of the Catholic Church*, 2nd ed. (New York: Doubleday, 1997) also states that "masturbation is an intrinsically and gravely disordered action." However, it goes on to say that certain factors "can lessen, if not even reduce to a minimum, moral culpability." Para. 2352. See also http://www.vatican.va/archive /ENG0015/__P85.HTM. No supporting evidence from Scripture is cited in this section of the catechism.

c. Masturbation outside the Marriage Bed Does Not Glorify God because Evil Desire Always Fuels It: Any desire that we exert at a wrong time or for a wrong object is evil, and God focuses the proper time and object of sexual desire in marriage. As such, *evil* desire fuels all sexual expression outside the marriage bed, including masturbation, so we must treat all such acts as sinful and as deserving of hell (Matt. 5:29–30; Mark 7:20–23; 1 Cor. 6:9–10; Gal. 5:17, 19–21; Eph. 5:5; Col. 3:5–6).

In light of these realities, I believe that anyone who masturbates outside the marriage bed sins and insults God's glory in Christ. As men and women of God, therefore, may we not engage in it. Instead, may we look to our Lord for help and seek to honor him with our bodies by allowing our only outlet for sexual desire to be the covenant-nurturing intimacy of marital lovemaking (Job 31:1). The one who calls us to holiness is faithful, and he will surely bring it about (1 Thess. 5:23–24).

2. Second View: Masturbation Is Not Always Wrong. An alternative viewpoint is held by some other evangelical writers, and this is the position that seems to me most persuasive.[34]

a. Not Explicitly Forbidden by Scripture: The first thing to say about masturbation is that Scripture nowhere speaks about it (except possibly Lev. 15:16, which is not a prohibition). And the principle of the sufficiency of Scripture (see chap. 3, p. 97) tells us that we are not to forbid what Scripture does not itself forbid. This would be adding to the commands of Scripture, something that God does not allow us to do.

b. The Harm Caused by Adding to the Moral Requirements of Scripture: Christian leaders must treat this subject cautiously, being careful not to make pronouncements where Scripture does not do so. Otherwise, they can encourage much false guilt and a needless sense of alienation from God by requiring of people a pattern of conduct that God himself does not require and for which, therefore, he will not empower obedience.

A 2008 study from the *Archives of Sexual Behavior* reported that 73 percent of men and 36.8 percent of women in Great Britain had engaged in masturbation in the four weeks before the study was conducted.[35] Psychologist James Dobson says, "Between 95

---

[34] For the view that masturbation is not always wrong, see James Dobson, *Bringing Up Boys* (Wheaton, IL: Tyndale, 2001), 78–80; Richard Foster, "Sexuality and Singleness," in *Readings in Christian Ethics, vol. 2: Issues and Applications*, ed. David K. Clark and Robert Vincent Rakestraw (Grand Rapids, MI: Baker, 1996), 161–64; Scott B. Rae, *Moral Choices: An Introduction to Ethics*, 3rd ed. (Grand Rapids, MI: Zondervan, 2009), 289–90; J. H. Olthuis, "Masturbation," in *New Dictionary of Christian Ethics and Pastoral Theology*, ed. David J. Atkinson and David H. Field (Leicester, UK: Inter-Varsity, and Downers Grove, IL: InterVarsity Press, 1995), 574–75. J. Robertson McQuilkin and Paul Copan are ambivalent: "While we recognize that we cannot make an absolute case for forbidding the practice, it seems clear to us that one cannot make a solid case for condoning it." *An Introduction to Biblical Ethics: Walking in the Way of Wisdom*, 3rd ed. (Downers Grove, IL: InterVarsity Press, 2014), 261. All of these authors warn against dangers, including wrongful lust, obsessiveness, and allowing masturbation to become a substitute for sexual intimacy in marriage.

[35] Makeda Gerressu, Catherine H. Mercer, Cynthia A. Graham, Kaye Wellings, and Anne M. Johnson, "Prevalence of Masturbation and Associated Factors in a British National Probability Survey," *Archives of Sexual Behavior* 37, no 2 (2008): 266–78, http://link.springer.com/article/10.1007%2Fs10508–006–9123–6.

and 98 percent of all boys engage in this practice—and the rest have been known to lie. It is as close to being a universal behavior as is likely to occur."[36]

If this is conduct that God does not completely forbid, it is not surprising that human attempts to exercise self-discipline and refrain from masturbation would often be frustrating to people. (This practice does not fall in the same category as refraining from murder, adultery, stealing, taking God's name in vain, or lying, for example, because most Christians and many non-Christians can and do refrain from these sins for their entire lives.)

Dobson warns against the spiritual danger of placing a moral burden on people that (in his view) Scripture does not support:

> Boys and girls who labor under divine condemnation can gradually become convinced that even God couldn't love them. They promise a thousand times with great sincerity never again to commit this "despicable" act. Then a week or two passes, or perhaps several months. Eventually, the hormonal pressure accumulates until nearly every waking moment reverberates with sexual desire. Finally, in a moment (and I do mean a *moment*) of weakness, it happens again. What then, dear friend? Tell me what a young person says to God after he or she has just broken the one thousandth solemn promise to Him? I am convinced that some teenagers have thrown over their faith because of their inability to please God on this point.[37]

Dobson's statement highlights the spiritually harmful results of the false guilt that can follow if Christian leaders add moral requirements that are not taught in Scripture, and in my opinion that is the likely result of teaching that masturbation is always wrong. But what harmful results come from teaching that it is not *always* wrong, but is wrong *only when* accompanied by wrongful lust, obsessiveness, or allowing it to become a substitute for sexual intimacy in marriage? When we consider the things Scripture clearly prohibits (taking God's name in vain, dishonoring parents, murder, adultery, stealing, lying, drunkenness, slander, and so forth), we can readily see the harm that results from these actions, but it is less clear how masturbation can be said to *always* bring harmful results.

c. However, Looking at a Woman Lustfully Is Forbidden by Scripture: Even if Scripture does not directly condemn masturbation, there is a danger that it can be accompanied by other sins, such as wrongful lust. Jesus said, "Everyone who looks at a woman with lustful intent has already committed adultery with her in his heart" (Matt. 5:28). Therefore, if a man looks at a woman (or a picture of a woman or a mental image of a woman) for the purpose of being sexually aroused, he is sinning. He has committed adultery with her in his heart. Therefore, if masturbation is accompanied by a mental desire for

---

[36] Dobson, *Bringing Up Boys*, 78.
[37] Ibid.

engaging in immoral activity, the mental desire is wrong, even if the act of masturbation is not itself morally wrong. (The same considerations would apply to the situation of a woman looking lustfully at a picture of a man or a mental image of a man.) (See further discussion in chap. 31 on pornography, p. 784.)

d. Husbands and Wives Should Not Neglect to Have Sexual Intercourse Together: Scripture does not indicate how frequently couples should have sex together, and in fact the frequency will vary from couple to couple and according to circumstances, personal preferences, physical health, and age. But Paul is very clear that maintaining sexual intimacy is important:

> The husband should give to his wife her conjugal rights, and likewise the wife to her husband. . . . Do not deprive one another, except perhaps by agreement for a limited time, that you may devote yourselves to prayer; but then come together again, so that Satan may not tempt you because of your lack of self-control. (1 Cor. 7:3–5; see longer quotation and discussion above, p. 709)

In this passage, Paul's solution to sexual tension is sexual intercourse, not masturbation that replaces regular intercourse. Therefore, married couples must not fall into a pattern in which masturbation replaces sexual intercourse together. On the other hand, we must return to the principle that masturbation is not forbidden, nor does Paul forbid it in this passage. What he does teach is that married couples should not neglect regular sexual intercourse (so long as they are physically able to do so and it would not be prohibitively painful or physically damaging to one partner or the other).

I. SINGLENESS

1. The New Testament Highly Values Singleness. Author Barry Danylak rightly points out:

> Of the three great monotheistic religions of modern time, Judaism, Christianity and Islam, only Christianity affirms singleness as a distinctive calling and gift within the community of God's people.[38]

Danylak argues that this is not accidental but is directly connected to the unique claims of the New Testament about the people of God (which I will explain more fully below).

The value of singleness is affirmed first by the remarkably prominent example of singleness in the life of Jesus himself, who had no home or family of his own (see Luke 9:58). He considered those who followed him to be his spiritual family (Matt. 12:48–50).

---

[38] Barry Danylak, *A Biblical Theology of Singleness* (Cambridge, UK: Grove Books, 2007), 3; see also Barry Danylak, *Redeeming Singleness* (Wheaton, IL: Crossway, 2010), 16–17.

The other example is the apostle Paul, who wrote 13 of the 27 books of the New Testament and whose missionary journeys occupy the entire second half of the book of Acts, chaps. 13–28). Paul was unmarried, at least during the time of his apostolic ministry. Explaining the rights that he could have exercised but did not, he says, "Do we not have the right to take along a believing wife, as do the other apostles and the brothers of the Lord and Cephas?" (1 Cor. 9:5). In commending singleness as having many benefits for ministry, he says, "I wish that all were as I myself am. But each has his own gift from God, one of one kind and one of another" (7:7). In other words, Paul sees a great benefit that would come if all Christians were single as he is—but then he quickly adds that he realizes that not all have this gift from God.

Later in 1 Corinthians 7 he says:

> I think that in view of the present distress it is good for a person to remain as he is. Are you free from a wife? Do not seek a wife. (vv. 26–27)[39]

> I want you to be free from anxieties. The unmarried man is anxious about the things of the Lord, how to please the Lord. But the married man is anxious about worldly things, how to please his wife, and his interests are divided. And the unmarried or betrothed woman is anxious about the things of the Lord, how to be holy in body and spirit. But the married woman is anxious about worldly things, how to please her husband. (vv. 32–34)

> So then he who marries his betrothed does well, and he who refrains from marriage will do even better. (v. 38)

2. There Is Spiritual Value in Having Single People in a Church. Danylak rightly notes that when a church has both single and married people in it, that is a reminder that we live in a "time between the times"—that is, we are still part of this present age, and people do get married and bear physical children, but we are also part of the age to come, and single people vividly remind us that the true family of God is spiritual, and the single people in our churches who belong to the same spiritual family show that the age to come has already begun in our lives.[40]

Danylak adds:

> [The presence and ministry of single people] is a visible reminder that the kingdom of God points to a reality which stands beyond worldly preoccupations

---

[39] Some commentators think Paul's instructions in this section of 1 Corinthians 7 are not intended as general instructions for all Christians for all time but rather are due to a specific crisis (perhaps the food shortage due to a famine in Greece in AD 51–52), because he says these instructions are "in view of the present distress." Other commentators understand "the present distress" to refer to the entire period of time until Christ returns (see v. 31).

[40] Danylak says it this way: "The presence of both single and married people in the church together signifies the fact that the church lives between the ages." *Biblical Theology of Singleness*, 27.

of marriage, family, and career. . . . Singles . . . serve as tangible reminders to the larger church of its anticipated future inheritance in the new creation.[41]

By "our anticipated future inheritance" he means the fact that we look forward to "an inheritance that is imperishable, undefiled, and unfading, kept in heaven for you" (1 Pet. 1:4).

In other words, single people in the church remind us that we will all be single in the age to come, and the joyful fellowship and companionship that single people and married people can have in this age provides a reminder and a foretaste of the age to come as well.

3. The New Testament Emphasizes the Church as a Spiritual Family That Is Greater Than One's Physical Family. Danylak also mentions:

> Those who are single may experience two different but related voids. The first is the absence of intimacy and companionship resulting from living without a marriage partner. . . . A second is the absence of physical offspring.[42]

The New Testament answer to the need for intimacy and companionship, notes Danylak, is fulfilled in the relationship of brothers and sisters in a new spiritual family. Thus, Jesus could say, "Whoever does the will of my Father in heaven is *my brother and sister and mother*" (Matt. 12:50).

The New Testament Epistles frequently view the church as a family. For example, the New Testament authors refer to fellow believers in the church as "brothers" (or "brothers and sisters") 127 times in the Epistles,[43] and Paul tells Timothy to relate to the church as he would to a family:

> Do not rebuke an older man but encourage him as you would a *father*, younger men as *brothers*, older women as *mothers*, younger women as *sisters*, in all purity. (1 Tim. 5:1–2)

This means that if a church is functioning properly, the single adults within the church will feel welcomed and included as members of the family, and they will be experiencing the kind of intimate communication and companionship that is commonly found in healthy physical families. In this way the need for intimacy and companionship can be fulfilled in the fellowship of the church.

4. In the New Testament, the People of God Multiply through Spiritual Birth. What about the other void that Danylak mentions single people often feel—the absence of physical offspring?

---

[41] Ibid., 28.

[42] Ibid., 3–4.

[43] I excluded 1 Cor. 9:5 and Heb. 7:5 from this count, as the references to "brothers" in these verses seem to have physical relatives in view.

Danylak points out a contrast between the Old Testament and the New Testament. In the Old Testament, beginning with Abraham and continuing through his descendants Isaac and Jacob, and then through Jacob's 12 sons (who became the heads of the 12 tribes of Israel), God's promise to give Abraham a multitude of descendants and make of him "a great nation" (Gen. 12:2; see also 15:5; 17:4–6) was primarily fulfilled through physical offspring—children, grandchildren, great-grandchildren, and so on for many generations who became the nation of Israel. But in the new covenant, Paul makes clear that "not all who are descended from Israel belong to Israel. . . . It is *not the children of the flesh* who are the children of God, but the children of the promise are counted as offspring" (Rom. 9:6–8), and he also says that "in Christ Jesus you are all sons of God, through faith" (Gal. 3:26).

Therefore, the Old Testament method of God expanding his people by physical propagation of children has been replaced by the spiritual process of people being born again (see John 3:1–8).

This awareness of the spiritual family of God enables Paul to call the Corinthian church "my beloved children" (1 Cor. 4:14), and he tells them, "I became your father in Christ Jesus through the gospel" (v. 15). He calls the Galatian Christians "my little children" (Gal. 4:19), and he tells the Thessalonian Christians that when he was among them, he acted like a mother with "her own children" (1 Thess. 2:7) or "like a father with his children" (v. 11). He calls Timothy "my true child in the faith" (1 Tim. 1:2; see also 1 Cor. 4:17) and calls Titus "my true child in a common faith" (Titus 1:4). He refers to "my child, Onesimus, whose father I became in my imprisonment" (Philem. 10). Finally, the apostle John refers to his readers as "my little children" (1 John 2:1; see also 3 John 4).

These passages indicate that the family of God here on earth grows not merely through parents having physical children, but through people becoming spiritual children and members of God's family by believing the gospel. (Of course, we hope and pray that the *physical* children of believers also become *spiritual* children of God and members of his family.)

This means that single people in the church can be encouraged to bear spiritual children through the work of evangelism and prayer, and also to nurture and train spiritual children through discipleship ministries, encouragement, wise counsel, and simply helping other believers in many ways.

5. Marriage Is Not Necessary for Full Humanity or for a Truly Fulfilling Life. Jesus and Paul are examples of people who were fully human and who had amazingly fulfilling lives in obedience to God regarding their callings on earth. But neither Jesus nor Paul was married.

In addition, every individual person on earth will be single for some part of his or her life. People are not born married, but remain single for a time until marriage. Then, at the other end of life, one spouse generally dies before the other, and the remaining spouse is again single.

In addition, all believers will someday live forever in the new heaven and new earth, where there is no marriage, for "in the resurrection they neither marry nor are given in marriage, but are like angels in heaven" (Matt. 22:30). Yet in that age to come we will certainly be fully human, and in fact we will experience much more of the excellence of our humanity as created in the image of God than we do in this age. We will have truly fulfilling lives as unmarried people, living forever in the presence of God among our spiritual brothers and sisters. (Therefore, this section of the book on "singleness" does not concern only those people who are currently unmarried; in some measure, it concerns all of us, married and unmarried people alike.)

6. Singleness Allows Greater Time to Be Given to Christian Ministry. Paul emphasizes the benefits of being free from the distractions of marriage and family when he says that "the unmarried man is anxious about the things of the Lord, how to please the Lord," and "the unmarried . . . woman is anxious about the things of the Lord, how to be holy in body and spirit" (1 Cor. 7:32, 34). This is different from the situation of the married man, who is "anxious about worldly things, how to please his wife," and the married woman, who is "anxious about worldly things, how to please her husband" (vv. 33–34).

Numerous other Christian workers throughout the history of the church have carried out their ministries in ways that would not have been possible if they had been married. Some examples include David Brainerd,[44] Mary Slessor,[45] Amy Carmichael,[46] John R. W. Stott,[47] Nancy Leigh DeMoss (she married in 2015 and is now Nancy DeMoss Wolgemuth),[48] and others.[49]

7. Jesus Promises a Great Reward for Those Who Are Faithful in Their Lives of Singleness. Jesus speaks about those who have left their families for his sake:

> Jesus said, "Truly, I say to you, there is no one who has left house or brothers or sisters or mother or father or children or lands, for my sake and for the gospel, who will not receive a hundredfold now in this time, houses and brothers and sisters and mothers and children and lands, with persecutions, and in the age to come eternal life." (Mark 10:29–30)

---

[44] "David Brainerd Historical Marker," ExplorePAHistory.com, http://explorepahistory.com/hmarker.php ?markerId=1-A-20C. Brainerd was engaged to be married to Jerusha Edwards, the daughter of the famous Great Awakening preacher Jonathan Edwards, but he died at the age of 29.

[45] Lex Loizides, "Mary Slessor the 'Mother of All Peoples,'" *Church History Review*, Feb. 26, 2011, https:// lexloiz.wordpress.com/2011/02/26/mary-slessor-the-mother-of-all-peoples/.

[46] Susan Verstraete, "The Reluctant Mother: Amy Carmichael," Christian Communicators Worldwide, http://www.ccwtoday.org/article/the-reluctant-mother-amy-carmichael/.

[47] John R. W. Stott and Al Hsu, "John Stott on Singleness," *Christianity Today*, Aug. 17, 2011, http://www .christianitytoday.com/ct/2011/augustweb-only/johnstottsingleness.html.

[48] Hannah Anderson, "Nancy Leigh DeMoss' Big Adventure," CT Pastors, May 2015 http://www.christianity today.com/pastors/2015/may-web-exclusives/nancy-leigh-demoss-big-adventure.html.

[49] Another famous Christian leader who remained single for her entire life was Henrietta Mears, who founded the modern Sunday school. See "Henrietta C. Mears: 1890–1963," The Women of Faith Series, http://secretplaceseries.com/Support/Testimonies/H_Mears1.html.

Certainly this also applies to those who have forsaken marriage for the sake of service to God and faithfulness to him. It would also include unmarried women who have declined opportunities to marry a non-Christian in order to be faithful to Scripture (1 Cor. 7:29; 2 Cor. 6:14), but then have remained unmarried for their entire lives. Surely they have given up the privilege of a family for Jesus's sake "and for the gospel" (Mark 10:29). Here Jesus promises that they will "receive a hundredfold now in this time" (v. 30), which must mean in the fellowship of the church, the family of God, and in fellowship with God himself.

In the parallel account in Matthew's Gospel, the reward is not specified as "in this life," but may be more future-oriented: "And everyone who has left houses or brothers or sisters or father or mother or children or lands, for my name's sake, will receive a hundredfold and will inherit eternal life" (Matt. 19:29). This statement follows immediately after the verse in which Jesus talks about "the new world" where "the Son of Man will sit on his glorious throne" (v. 28).

8. God Is Sovereign over Who Gets Married and Who Doesn't.[50] With regard to singleness and marriage, John Piper wisely says, "God rules in these affairs, and we will be the happier when we bow before His inscrutable ways and confess, '. . . no good thing does He withhold from those whose walk is blameless' (Ps. 84:11)."[51]

Those who wish to get married and have not been able to do so surely experience a test of their faith, whether they can believe that through difficult circumstances that they did not choose, God will still bring good to them and Romans 8:28 will still prove true: "And we know that for those who love God *all things work together for good*, for those who are called according to his purpose."

Even if prolonged singleness is seen as a type of suffering and a trial, Peter says that when a person's faith in God remains strong, it is more precious than gold in God's sight:

> Now for a little while, if necessary, you have been grieved by various trials, so that *the tested genuineness of your faith*—more precious than gold that perishes though it is tested by fire—may be found to result in praise and glory and honor at the revelation of Jesus Christ. Though you have not seen him, you love him. Though you do not now see him, you believe in him and rejoice with joy that is inexpressible and filled with glory. (1 Pet. 1:6–8)

God is indeed sovereign over all of our affairs, and he is invisibly working his good plan for all of his people, for the advancement of his kingdom on earth, and for his glory in all of our lives.

---

[50] I have taken this section heading verbatim from the excellent foreword by John Piper, "For Single Men and Women (and the Rest of Us)," in *Recovering Biblical Manhood and Womanhood: A Response to Evangelical Feminism*, ed. John Piper and Wayne Grudem (Wheaton, IL: Crossway, 1991), xxv.

[51] Ibid.

9. Practical Implications for Church Life. The spiritual realities mentioned in the previous sections should cause us to wonder if evangelical churches today place enough emphasis on the value of singleness as a legitimate and honored calling in the Christian life. In past centuries, the pendulum swung so far in the direction of the affirmation of celibacy that many generations of people believed that the highest spiritual calling was to be a priest, a monk, or a nun living in celibate service to God throughout a lifetime. But now one wonders if the pendulum has not swung back too far in the other direction, with an overemphasis on ministry to married couples, to the neglect of the value and importance of celibate single ministry.

Churches certainly need to emphasize the importance of involving singles in home fellowship groups and in other kinds of frequent social interactions in which interpersonal intimacy, companionship, and trust can flourish and be enjoyed. In addition, churches need to be sure to encourage and affirm the value of the great heritage that a person can leave behind when he or she has been able, through evangelism or discipleship, or simply through a quiet ministry of helping and encouragement, to lead to the birth of and nurturing of many spiritual children throughout the course of a lifetime.

10. What about Single Christians Who Long to Be Married but Have Not Found a Marriage Partner? Finally, while I affirm the high value of singleness for those whom God calls to such a life, I am also concerned about the large number of single men and women in evangelical churches who long to be married and who do not sense a calling from God to remain single.

I received the following email from a woman in such a situation:

> Increasing numbers of Christian women like me in their 30s, 40s, and beyond cannot find a way to marriage, despite our best efforts and constant prayers. . . . Marriage has fallen on hard times in our modern society. . . . But while many unmarried non-Christians have opted to cohabitate or are deliberately choosing to remain single and childless to pursue personal interests, the vast majority of single Christians greatly desire to marry and form families.
>
> The evangelical church seems completely unprepared for the rise in undesired lifelong singleness among its members—and sometimes totally unconcerned. . . . It is extremely difficult for most people to live a life of celibacy when they are designed by God for intimate companionship. What is a single Christian expected to do about sexual desires when they cannot marry? How can they avoid falling into sin?
>
> Though the church is a spiritual family, and friends are blessings from the Lord, living life outside of a physical family is unbearably lonely. . . . Sometimes I feel as if I'm nothing. Is it really God's intention for scores of people to live their life completely alone? Doesn't Genesis 2:18 and Ecclesiastes 4:9–12 speak against this? . . . Although I work to support myself (and I'm grateful to God for the ability to do so) I don't draw identity from

my career. I always thought my identity would be that of wife and mother, something I have looked forward to since I was a young girl. When you're a childless single woman, especially in the church, it's hard to know who or what you are or to feel that you have any value. . . . I cared for both of my parents until they died. Who will care for me when I'm too old to care for myself?

We don't attribute the increase in divorce to the will of God because we know God hates divorce. We don't attribute the rise of abortions to God either. Yet both of these things are happening in our society. How can we assume then that singleness in increasing numbers is God's will? Couldn't the fact that many of us can't get married be a problem? And if it is a problem, isn't there something the church can do to help?

Unmarried women like me, however, who love the Lord dearly but struggle greatly with unfulfilled sexual desires, loneliness, lack of identity, and concerns about the future, feel like invisible members of the church. The focus is typically on those who are married or those who are still young and marriageable, and older singles are left to carry their unique burdens alone. As a fellow child of God lovingly saved by His grace, I plead with you to look more deeply into this issue.

In Christ,
[name]

What this woman says in this email makes me think that her situation falls in the category of the "various trials" that Peter talks about (see 1 Pet. 1:6; also James 1:2 and section 8 above on God's sovereignty). I think of her unwanted lifelong singleness as a kind of painful suffering that is experienced by many thousands of Christians today who long to be married but are not. And just as churches seek to alleviate other kinds of suffering that people experience, so I think that churches should be proactive in providing ways for single men and women to be more fully integrated into the social interactions of the church.

In addition, this email calls attention to a problem parallel to the failure of churches to emphasize the *importance and goodness of singleness*—the failure of churches to promote the *importance and goodness of marriage*. The author rightly says, "Marriage has fallen on hard times in our modern society." In the United States in the last 50 years, there has been an alarming drop in the percentage of adults who are married. In 1960, 72.2 percent of people over 18 were married, but by 2012 that had dropped to 50.5 percent—a remarkable change in the status of over 20 percent of the adult population.[52]

[52] Richard Fry, "New census data show more Americans are tying the knot, but mostly it's the college-educated," Pew Research Center, Feb. 6, 2014, http://www.pewresearch.org/fact-tank/2014/02/06/new-census-data-show-more-americans-are-tying-the-knot-but-mostly-its-the-college-educated/.

Apparently there are many more people, and especially many more men, who simply are not interested in getting married, at least not very soon.

Several reasons lie behind this loss of interest in marriage in modern culture generally. First, the abandonment of biblical moral standards means that many women are willing to have sex with their boyfriends without first getting married, but this removes what is probably the primary incentive for men to commit to marriage—sexual desire. Paul wrote, "But if they cannot exercise self-control, they should marry. For it is better to marry than to burn with passion" (1 Cor. 7:9). But this implies a culture in which women generally refuse to have sex until after they are married, which is far different from today's culture. Second, the widespread use of pornography, primarily but not exclusively by men, is a deceptive and addicting substitute for seeking sexual fulfillment within marriage. Third, modern secular society neglects or even denigrates marriage as something far less desirable than a self-centered life of having sex without commitment and finding fulfillment in career, hobbies, sports, and travel. (For example, few movies or TV programs portray long-term, stable, happy marriages.) Unfortunately, many single Christians in their 20s and 30s, influenced by this secular culture, also view marriage with suspicion and are reluctant to make such a lifelong commitment.

The Bible's perspective is far different. Scripture views marriage very positively, from the marriage of Adam and Eve in the garden of Eden (Genesis 2) to the marriage of Christ and his bride, the church, at the end of the book of Revelation (19:6–9). The author of Hebrews writes, "*Let marriage be held in honor among all*" (13:4). This positive biblical view of marriage needs to be promoted in our churches, not only among adults in their 20s and 30s, but also among children and teenagers, many of whom will be surprised and will rejoice to learn of the Bible's teaching about the great beauty and joy of marriage.[53]

My earlier discussion of a husband's leadership responsibility in marriage (see ch. 15, p. 407) has implications here as well. Single men in particular need to overcome their fear of commitment, seek the Lord's guidance and blessing, and take the initiative in developing relationships that might lead to marriage. Then—without too much delay!—men should also take the initiative in proposing marriage to the women they love. In a church where marriage is "held in honor among all," this will happen frequently and with much joy.

J. CIVIL GOVERNMENTS SHOULD DEFINE MARRIAGE FOR ALL CITIZENS

1. Defining and Regulating Marriage Fits the Purposes of Government, according to the Bible. Among the most important purposes of civil government, according to

---

[53] See p. 800 for information showing that the divorce rate is far lower than commonly assumed, and far lower still among couples who attend church regularly.

the Bible, are (1) to restrain evil, (2) to bring good to society, and (3) to bring order to society. (See the discussion of these purposes in chap. 16, p. 427.) On all three of these grounds, a Christian should conclude that it is right for government to define and regulate marriage.[54]

First, marriage *restrains evil* by promoting sexual faithfulness between men and women, by establishing a legally binding commitment for parents to care for their children, by establishing a legally binding commitment for spouses to be financially responsible for and to care for one another, and by providing a legal protection to keep women from being exploited by men who might otherwise enjoy a sexual relationship for a time and then abandon a woman and any children she may have borne from that union.

Second, marriage *brings good* to society in multiple ways. It promotes social stability,[55] economic well-being,[56] educational and economic benefits for children,[57] the transmission of moral and cultural values to the next generation, and a stable social unit for interactions within society.[58] (These benefits are explained more fully in section K below.)

Third, the establishment of marriage *brings order* to society so that the general public will know who is married and who is not. Marital status should be a matter of public record, so the society as a whole can honor and protect individual marriages in various ways and can know who is responsible for the care, protection, and training of children and for the care of spouses who have medical, financial, or other needs.

Thus, defining and regulating marriage gives stability and order to society. Marriage is an extremely important social good that government should encourage and protect.

2. Governments Should Define and Establish Marriage because No Other Institution Can Do So for an Entire Society. Only a civil government is able to define what constitutes a marriage for a whole nation or society. No churches or denominations could do this, because they speak only for their own members. Likewise, no voluntary societies could do this, because they do not include all the people in the society.

If no definition of marriage is given to an entire society, then chaos and much oppression of women and children will result. Stanley Kurtz of the Hudson Institute writes:

---

[54] This section is adapted from Grudem, *Politics—According to the Bible*, 221–25, with permission of the publisher.

[55] James S. Coleman, "Social Capital in the Creation of Human Capital," *American Journal of Sociology* 94 (1988): S109–S113, http://courseweb.ischool.illinois.edu/~katewill/for-china/readings/coleman%20 1988%20social%20capital.pdf.

[56] Mary Parke, "Are Married Parents Really Better for Children? What Research Says about the Effects of Family Structure on Child Well-Being," Center for Law and Social Policy, May 2003, 7, www.clasp.org /resources-and-publications/states/0086.pdf.

[57] Ibid., 2–3; see also Robert I. Lerman, "Marriage and the Economic Well-Being of Families with Children: A Review of the Literature," July 2002, https://aspe.hhs.gov/system/files/pdf/73481/LitReview.pdf, and *Why Marriage Matters: Twenty-One Conclusions from the Social Sciences* (New York: Institute, 2002), http://americanvalues.org/catalog/pdfs/WhyMarriageMatters1.pdf.

[58] Coleman, "Social Capital in the Creation of Human Capital," S109–S113.

In setting up the institution of marriage, society offers special support and encouragement to the men and women who together make children. Because marriage is deeply implicated in the interests of children, it is a matter of public concern. Children are helpless. They depend upon adults. Over and above their parents, children depend upon society to create institutions that keep them from chaos. Children cannot articulate their needs. Children cannot vote. Yet children *are* society. They are us, and they are our future. That is why society has the right to give special support and encouragement to an institution that is necessary to the well-being of children—even if that means special benefits for some, and not for others. The dependence intrinsic to human childhood is why unadulterated libertarianism can never work.[59]

Without a governmentally established standard of what constitutes marriage, the result will be a proliferation of children born in relationships of incest and polygamy, as well as in many temporary relationships without commitment, resulting in many children being born with no one having a legal obligation to care for them.

Marriage researcher and advocate Maggie Gallagher says:

The purpose of marriage law is inherently normative, to create and to force others to recognize a certain kind of union: permanent, faithful, co-residential, and sexual couplings.[60]

The consensus from nations all over the world from all of history is that the society as a whole, through its governing authorities, needs to define and regulate marriage for all its citizens. Even Aristotle said that the first duty of wise legislators is to define and regulate marriage. He wrote:

Since the legislator should begin by considering how the frames of the children whom he is rearing may be as good as possible, his first care will be about marriage—at what age should his citizens marry, and who are fit to marry?[61]

Some people may argue that governments today no longer need to define marriage at all, but this is just saying that we can now hope to act contrary to the entire course of all

---

[59] Stanley Kurtz, "Deathblow to Marriage: Gay Marriage Has Real Implications," Feb. 5, 2004, http://www.nationalreview.com/article/209401/deathblow-marriage.

[60] Maggie Gallagher, "(How) Will Gay Marriage Weaken Marriage as a Social Institution: A Reply to Andrew Koppelman," *University of St. Thomas Law Review* 2, no. 1 (Fall 2004): 43, http://maggiegallagher.com/2011/09/how-will-gay-marriage-weaken-marriage-as-a-social-institution-a-reply-to-andrew-koppelman/.

[61] Aristotle, *Politics*, 10.7.16, in *The Politics of Aristotle*, trans. Benjamin Jowett (Oxford: Clarendon Press, 1885), 238.

societies in world history for all time.[62] Such a prospect does not encourage optimism for success.

K. BENEFITS OF MARRIAGE BETWEEN ONE MAN AND ONE WOMAN

We should not be surprised that marriage established according to God's principles in Scripture generally brings many benefits to society.

1. Marriage between One Man and One Woman Brings Many Benefits to Children. One large set of societal benefits consists of the advantages that come to children who grow up in homes where the father and mother are married to each other (a heterosexual marriage):

1. Children who live with their own two married parents have significantly higher educational achievement.[63]

2. Children who live with their own two married parents are much more likely to enjoy a better economic standard in their adult lives and are much less likely to end up in poverty.[64]

3. Children who live with their own two married parents have much better physical and emotional health.[65]

4. Children who live with their own two married parents are far less likely to commit crimes,[66] are less likely to engage in alcohol and substance abuse,[67]

---

[62] Even if anarchy regarding marriage were to prevail for a short period in a society, such a situation would be inherently unstable and would soon result in some standardization of marriage or the dissolution of the society.

[63] Parke, "Are Married Parents Really Better for Children?" 2–3.

[64] Robert I. Lerman, "How Do Marriage, Cohabitation, and Single Parenthood Affect the Material Hardships of Families with Children?" July 2002, and Robert I. Lerman, "Married and Unmarried Parenthood and Economic Well-Being: A Dynamic Analysis of a Recent Cohort," July 2002, https://aspe.hhs.gov/system/files/pdf/73496/parenthood.pdf.

[65] Frank F. Furstenburg Jr. and Andrew J. Cherlin, *Divided Families: What Happens to Children When Parents Part* (Cambridge, MA: Harvard University Press, 1991), 56; and Paul R. Amato, "Children's Adjustment to Divorce: Theories, Hypothesis, and Empirical Support," *Journal of Marriage and the Family* 23 (1993); cited in Lynn Wardle, "Is Preference for Marriage in Law Justified?" *World Family Policy Forum 1999* http://www.law.byu.edu/wfpc/forum/1999/wardle.pdf.

[66] Cynthia Harper and Sarah McClanahan, "Father Absence and Youth Incarceration," *Journal of Research on Adolescence* 14 (2004): 369–97, http://onlinelibrary.wiley.com/doi/10.1111/j.1532-7795.2004.00079.x/abstract.

[67] "Family Matters: Substance Abuse and the American Family," The National Center on Addiction and Substance Abuse at Columbia University, March 2005, 17, https://www.centeronaddiction.org/sites/default/files/Family-matters-substance-abuse-and-the-american-family_0.pdf ; and Robert L. Flewelling and Karl E. Bauman, "Family Structure as a Predictor of Initial Substance Abuse and Sexual Intercourse in Adolescence," *Journal of Marriage and the Family* 52 (1990): 171–81. Abstract available at http://www.jstor.org/stable/352848?seq=1#page_scan_tab_contents.

and are more likely to live according to higher standards of integrity and moral principles.[68]

5. Children who live with their own two married parents are less likely to experience physical abuse and are more likely to live in homes that provide support, protection, and stability for them.[69]

6. Children who live with their own two married parents are more likely to establish stable families in the next generation.[70]

2. Marriage between One Man and One Woman Brings Many Benefits to the Married Couple. Another set of societal benefits that come from marriage consists of the advantages that marriage generally brings to the husband and wife:

1. Marriage provides a guarantee of lifelong companionship and care far better than any other human relationship or institution.[71]

2. Marriage leads to a higher economic standard and diminished likelihood of ending up in poverty for men and women.[72]

3. Marriage provides women with protection against domestic violence and abandonment far better than any other human relationship or institution.[73]

4. Marriage encourages men to socially beneficial pursuits far better than any other human relationship or institution.[74]

5. Men and women in general have an innate instinct that values sexual faithfulness in intimate relationships, and marriage provides a societal

---

[68] Furstenburg and Cherlin, *Divided Families*, and Amato, "Children's Adjustment to Divorce"; cited in Wardle, "Is Preference for Marriage in Law Justified?" http://www.law.byu.edu/wfpc/forum/1999/wardle.pdf.

[69] Patrick F. Fagan, "The Child Abuse Crisis: The Disintegration of Marriage, Family, and the American Community," Heritage Foundation, *Backgrounder #115*, May 15, 1997, http://www.heritage.org/marriage-and-family/report/the-child-abuse-crisis-the-disintegration-marriage-family-and-the, and E. Thompson, T. L. Hanson, and S. S. McLanahan, "Family Structure and Child Well-Being: Economic Resources versus Parental Behaviors," *Social Forces* 73: 221–42; cited in Jeffry H. Larson, "The Verdict on Cohabitation vs. Marriage," http://scholarsarchive.byu.edu/cgi/viewcontent.cgi?article=1027&context=marriage andfamilies.

[70] Patrick F. Fagan, "How Broken Families Rob Children of Their Chances for Future Prosperity," Heritage Foundation, *Backgrounder #1283*, June 11, 1999, http://www.heritage.org/marriage-and-family/report/how-broken-families-rob-children-their-chances-future-prosperity.

[71] Linda J. Waite and Maggie Gallagher, *The Case for Marriage: Why Married People are Happier, Healthier, and Better Off Financially* (New York: Doubleday, 2000), cited in Larson, "The Verdict on Cohabitation vs. Marriage."

[72] David J. Eggebeen and Daniel T. Lichter, "Race, Family Structure, and Changing Poverty Among American Children," *American Social Review* 56: 801, 806, cited in Wardle, "Is Preference for Marriage in Law Justified?"

[73] Patrick F. Fagan and Kirk A. Johnson, "Marriage: The Safest Place for Women and Children," Heritage Foundation, *Backgrounder #1535*, April 10, 2002, http://www.heritage.org/marriage-and-family/report/marriage-still-the-safest-place-women-and-children.

[74] Linda Waite, "Does Marriage Matter?" *Demographics* 32 (1995): 483, cited in Wardle, "Is Preference for Marriage in Law Justified?"

encouragement of such faithfulness far better than any other relationship or institution.[75]

6. Marriage provides greater protection against sexually transmitted diseases than any other relationship or institution.[76]

7. The biological design of men's and women's bodies argues that sexual intimacy is designed to be enjoyed between only one man and one woman.

For all of these reasons, marriage is the basic building block of any stable society, and it is essential to the continuation of a healthy, stable society. All of these reasons argue that it is right that governments *encourage* and *reward* marriage between one man and one woman. This institution gives immeasurable benefits to a society that no other relationship or institution can provide. Therefore, society has a high interest in protecting and encouraging marriage through its laws.

QUESTIONS FOR PERSONAL APPLICATION

1. How did this chapter change your understanding of marriage, if at all?

2. If you are married, how does it affect you to think of your own marriage as a picture of the relationship between Christ and the church?

3. If you are not married, much of the material in this chapter was not directly relevant to your present life experience. But were there any parts of the chapter that were beneficial to your Christian life?

4. If you are married, is sexual intimacy functioning in the way God intends it to do in your marriage? Why or why not? Does your sexual relationship with your spouse reflect your overall personal relationship with each other?

5. In the non-Christian parts of the culture in which you live, what are some of the harmful consequences that come from violating God's moral standards for marriage?

6. If you are married, make a list of 30 harmful consequences that would happen if you were to commit adultery. List ten specific things you can do to guard yourself against committing adultery.

7. How pure in God's eyes are the desires of your heart in this area? Over the past few years, have you noticed any growth in Christian maturity with respect to the desires of your heart?

8. If you are single, what are some of the benefits of singleness in your own experience?

---

[75] Robert T. Michael, John H. Gagnon, Edward O. Laumann, and Gina Kolata, *Sex in America: A Definitive Survey* (Boston: Little Brown, 1994), 105, cited in "What's Happening to Marriage?" *State of Our Unions 2009*, Rutgers University National Marriage Project, http://stateofourunions.org/2009/SOOU2009.pdf.

[76] Fagan and Johnson, "Marriage: The Safest Place for Women and Children."

9. If you are single, do you feel welcomed and affirmed in your church, and are there opportunities for you to use your spiritual gifts for the benefit of others?

SPECIAL TERMS

adultery
cohabitation
fornication
marriage
sexual immorality

BIBLIOGRAPHY

Sections in Other Ethics Texts

(see complete bibliographical data, p. 64)

Clark and Rakestraw, 2:139–76
Feinberg, John and Paul, 589–94
Frame, 748–55
Geisler, 299–303
Gushee and Stassen, 270–87
Holmes, 113–21
Jones, 153–76
Kaiser, 67–90
McQuilkin and Copan, 219–41
Murray, 27–30, 45–81
Rae, 271–79

Other Works

Anderson, Ryan T. *Truth Overruled: The Future of Marriage and Religious Freedom*. New York: Regnery, 2015.

Andreades, Sam A. *enGendered: God's Gift of Gender Difference in Relationship*. Wooster, OH: Weaver, 2015.

Ash, Christopher. *Married for God: Making Your Marriage the Best It Can Be*. Wheaton, IL: Crossway, 2016.

Balswick, Judith K., and Jack O. Balswick. *Authentic Human Sexuality: An Integrated Christian Approach*. Downers Grove, IL: InterVarsity Press, 1999.

Burk, Denny. *What Is the Meaning of Sex?* Wheaton, IL: Crossway, 2013.

Chandler, Matt. *Mingling of Souls: Love, Marriage, Redemption, and Sex in the Song of Solomon*. Colorado Springs: Cook, 2015.

Cutrer, William, and Sandra Glahn. *Sexual Intimacy in Marriage*. Grand Rapids, MI: Kregel, 1998.

Danylak, Barry. *A Biblical Theology of Singleness*. Cambridge, UK: Grove Books, 2007.

DeMoss, Nancy Leigh, ed. *Biblical Womanhood in the Home*. Foundations for the Family Series. Wheaton, IL: Crossway, 2002.

DeYoung, Kevin. "Saints and Sexual Immorality." In *The Hole in Our Holiness: Filling the Gap between Gospel Passion and the Pursuit of Godliness*, 107–22. Wheaton, IL: Crossway, 2012.

Dobson, James C. *Marriage under Fire: Why We Must Win This War*. Sisters, OR: Multnomah, 2004.

Driscoll, Mark, and Grace Driscoll. *Real Marriage: The Truth about Sex, Friendship and Life Together*. Nashville: Thomas Nelson, 2012.

Eggerichs, Emerson. *Love and Respect: The Love She Most Desires, the Respect He Desperately Needs*. Nashville: Integrity, 2004

Feldhahn, Shaunti. *The Good News about Marriage: Debunking Discouraging Myths about Marriage and Divorce*. Colorado Springs: Multnomah, 2014.

———. *The Surprising Secrets of Highly Happy Marriages: The Little Things That Make a Big Difference*. Colorado Springs: Multnomah, 2013.

Furstenberg, Frank F., Jr., and Andrew J. Cherlin. *Divided Families: What Happens to Children When Parents Part*. Cambridge, MA: Harvard University Press, 1991.

Gilder, George F. *Men and Marriage*. Gretna, LA: Pelican, 1986.

Girgis, Sherif, Ryan T. Anderson, and Robert P. George. *What Is Marriage? Man and Woman*. New York: Encounter Books, 2012.

Green, Rob. *Tying the Knot: A Premarital Guide to a Strong and Lasting Marriage*. Greensboro, NC: New Growth, 2016.

Grudem, Wayne, ed. *Biblical Foundations for Manhood and Womanhood*. Wheaton, IL: Crossway, 2002.

———. *Countering the Claims of Evangelical Feminism*. Sisters, OR: Multnomah, 2006. This is a 320-page condensation of my *Evangelical Feminism and Biblical Truth*.

———. *Evangelical Feminism and Biblical Truth: An Analysis of More Than 100 Disputed Questions*. Wheaton, IL: Crossway, 2012.

Grudem, Wayne, and Dennis Rainey, eds. *Pastoral Leadership for Manhood and Womanhood*. Wheaton, IL: Crossway, 2002.

Harley, Willard F. *His Needs, Her Needs: Building an Affair-Proof Marriage*. Grand Rapids, MI: Revell, 1994.

Haugen, Gary A. *Good News about Injustice: A Witness of Courage in a Hurting World*. Downers Grove, IL: InterVarsity Press, 1999.

Heimbach, Daniel R. *True Sexual Morality: Recovering Biblical Standards for a Culture in Crisis*. Wheaton, IL: Crossway, 2004.

Heitritter, Lynn, and Jeanette Vought. *Helping Victims of Sexual Abuse*. Minneapolis: Bethany House, 1989.

Hiestand, Gerald, and Jay Thomas. *Sex, Dating, and Relationships: A Fresh Approach*. Wheaton, IL: Crossway, 2012.

James, Sharon. *God's Design for Women: Biblical Womanhood for Today*. Darlington, England: Evangelical Press, 2002.

Jones, Peter. *The God of Sex: How Spirituality Defines Your Sexuality*. Colorado Springs: Victor, 2006.

Kassian, Mary A. *Women, Creation, and the Fall*. Westchester, IL: Crossway, 1990.

Keller, Timothy, with Kathy Keller. *The Meaning of Marriage: Facing the Complexities of Commitment with the Wisdom of God*. New York: Dutton, 2011.

Köstenberger, Andreas J., and David W. Jones. *God, Marriage, and Family: Rebuilding the Biblical Foundation*. 2nd ed. Wheaton, IL: Crossway, 2010.

Lewis, Robert. *Real Family Values: Leading Your Family into the 21st Century with Clarity and Conviction*. Sisters, OR: Multnomah, 2000.

Lewis, Robert, and William Hendricks. *Rocking the Roles: Building a Win-Win Marriage*. Rev. ed. Colorado Springs: NavPress, 1999.

Mahaney, C. J., and Carolyn Mahaney. *Sex, Romance, and the Glory of God: What Every Christian Husband Needs to Know*. Wheaton, IL: Crossway, 2004.

Mohler, R. Albert, Jr. *We Cannot Be Silent: Speaking Truth to a Culture Redefining Sex, Marriage, and the Very Meaning of Right and Wrong*. Nashville: Thomas Nelson, 2015.

Olthuis, J. H. "Marriage." In *New Dictionary of Christian Ethics and Pastoral Theology*, edited by David J. Atkinson and David H. Field, 565–68. Leicester, UK: Inter-Varsity, and Downers Grove, IL: InterVarsity Press, 1995.

Ortlund, Ray. *Marriage and the Mystery of the Gospel*. Short Studies in Biblical Theology. Wheaton, IL: Crossway, 2016

Piper, John. *This Momentary Marriage: A Parable of Permanence*. Wheaton, IL: Crossway, 2009.

Piper, John, and Justin Taylor, eds. *Sex and the Supremacy of Christ*. Wheaton, IL: Crossway, 2005.

Piper, John, and Wayne Grudem, eds. *Recovering Biblical Manhood and Womanhood: A Response to Evangelical Feminism*. Wheaton, IL: Crossway, 1991.

Platt, David. *Counter Culture: Following Christ in an Anti-Christian Age*, revised and updated ed. Carol Stream, IL: Tyndale Momentum, 2017.

Rainey, Dennis. *A Call to Family Reformation: Restoring the Soul of America One Home at a Time*. Little Rock, AR: FamilyLife, 1996.

———. *Preparing for Marriage Devotions for Couples: Discover God's Plan for a Lifetime of Love*. Minneapolis: Bethany House, 2013.

———. *Stepping Up: A Call to Courageous Manhood*. Little Rock, AR: FamilyLife, 2011.

Ricucci, Gary, and Betsy Ricucci. *Love That Lasts: When Marriage Meets Grace*. Wheaton, IL: Crossway, 2006.

Tripp, Paul David. *What Did You Expect? Redeeming the Realities of Marriage*. Wheaton, IL: Crossway, 2010.

Uhlmann, Steve and Barbara. *Plastic Promises: Discovering What Our Marriage Was Made Of*. Scottsdale, AZ: Love Like Jesus, 2016.

Waite, Linda J., and Maggie Gallagher. *The Case for Marriage: Why Married People Are Happier, Healthier, and Better Off Financially*. New York: Doubleday, 2000.

Weber, Stu. *Tender Warrior: Every Man's Purpose, Every Woman's Dream, Every Child's Hope*. New ed. Sisters, OR: Multnomah, 2006.

Wheat, Ed, and Gaye Wheat. *Intended for Pleasure: Sex Technique and Sexual Fulfillment in Christian Marriage*. 4th ed. Grand Rapids, MI: Revell, 2010.

SCRIPTURE MEMORY PASSAGE

Ephesians 5:31–32: "Therefore a man shall leave his father and mother and hold fast to his wife, and the two shall become one flesh." This mystery is profound, and I am saying that it refers to Christ and the church.

HYMN

"O Perfect Love"

O perfect Love, all human thought transcending,
Lowly we kneel in prayer before Thy throne,
That theirs may be the love which knows no ending,
Whom Thou forevermore dost join in one.

O perfect Life, be Thou their full assurance
Of tender charity and steadfast faith,
Of patient hope and quiet, brave endurance,
With childlike trust that fears no pain nor death.

Grant them the joy which brightens earthly sorrow,
Grant them the peace which calms all earthly strife,
And to life's day the glorious unknown morrow
That dawns upon eternal love and life.

DOROTHY B. GURNEY, 1858–1932

Chapter 29

BIRTH CONTROL

Should we think that birth control is morally acceptable?
If so, are there types of birth control that are morally wrong?
What birth-control methods are morally acceptable?

The topic of birth control is related to the broad subject of marriage because every married couple must face the question of birth control today, and modern society presents a wide variety of viewpoints. On the one hand, many in modern society find no moral problem with birth control, and use condoms and/or birth-control pills commonly in order to have sex while avoiding the fear of unwanted pregnancy. On the other hand, the Roman Catholic Church considers all forms of birth control to be morally wrong except periodically abstaining from intercourse during a woman's fertile period each month (which is a "natural" as opposed to "artificial" form of birth control).

The *Catechism of the Catholic Church* says:

> Unity, indissolubility, and *openness to fertility* are essential to marriage. . . . The refusal of fertility turns married life away from its "supreme gift," the child.[1]

> It is necessary that each and every marriage act remain ordered *per se* to the procreation of human life.[2]

> Every action which . . . proposes to render procreation impossible is intrinsically evil.[3]

---

[1] *Catechism of the Catholic Church*, 2nd ed. (New York: Doubleday, 1997), para. 1664 (463), emphasis added.
[2] Ibid., para. 2366 (628).
[3] Ibid., para. 2370 (629).

Sacred Scripture and the Church's traditional practice see in *large families* a sign of God's blessing and the parents' generosity.[4]

Among evangelical Protestants, a few support essentially the Roman Catholic position and oppose all forms of "artificial" birth control, but most believe that birth control is a personal decision for each family and that couples should be free to decide how many children they will have.

What does the Bible actually teach about birth control? That is the subject of this chapter.

Because of the subject matter, almost all of this chapter pertains to couples who are married and who are still able to have children. I discussed the topic of singleness in chapter 28 and will address the difficult question of infertility in chapter 30 (along with the topic of adoption).

A. SCRIPTURE VIEWS CHILDREN NOT AS A BURDEN BUT AS A GREAT BLESSING

Some in contemporary society view children mostly as a burden, a huge expense, and an inconvenience that interferes with the happiness of a married couple. From time to time there are news stories that make the task of raising children seem frightfully expensive! In 2013, the U.S. Department of Agriculture estimated that the cost of raising a child from birth to high school graduation was $245,340. In more expensive areas, such as the Northeast United States, that figure reaches $455,000.

That does not include the costs for the college years, which were conservatively estimated by the College Board for 2016–2017 to be $20,090 (in-state) per year for tuition and housing at four-year public colleges and universities, and $45,370 for four-year private colleges and universities.[5]

But the Bible does not view raising children as a burden or as something that is financially or emotionally impossible to do. It consistently views children as a blessing from God. This positive perspective begins at the earliest point of human history, for the first command that God ever gave to human beings was a mandate to bear children:

> And God blessed them. And God said to them, "*Be fruitful and multiply* and fill the earth and subdue it, and have dominion over the fish of the sea and over the birds of the heavens and over every living thing that moves on the earth." (Gen. 1:28)

To "multiply" implies having more than two children, because a couple with only two children will simply replace themselves on the earth, without multiplying the population.[6]

---

[4] Ibid., para. 2373 (630), emphasis in original.

[5] "Expenditures on Children by Families 2015," United States Department of Agriculture, revised March 2017, 20, https://www.cnpp.usda.gov/sites/default/files/crc2015_March2017_0.pdf. The exact figures are $9,650 per year for in-state public college and university tuition, plus $10,440 for room and board; for private colleges and universities, it is $33,480 for tuition, plus $11,890 for room and board.

[6] See below, p. 750, on the question of overpopulation today.

Other passages in the Old Testament continue promoting a positive view of children, even after Adam and Eve sinned:

> Behold, *children are a heritage from the Lord,*
>   *the fruit of the womb a reward.*
> Like arrows in the hand of a warrior
>   are the children of one's youth.
> Blessed is the man
>   who fills his quiver with them!
> He shall not be put to shame
>   when he speaks with his enemies in the gate. (Ps. 127:3–5)

> Your wife will be *like a fruitful vine*
>   within your house;
> your children will be like olive shoots
>   around your table.
> Behold, *thus shall the man be blessed*
>   who fears the Lord. (Ps. 128:3–4)

Did he not make them one, with a portion of the Spirit in their union? *And what was the one God seeking? Godly offspring.* So guard yourselves in your spirit, and let none of you be faithless to the wife of your youth. (Mal. 2:15)

In the New Testament, Jesus demonstrated a remarkably positive attitude toward children:

> Then children were brought to him that he might lay his hands on them and pray. The disciples rebuked the people, but Jesus said, "Let the little children come to me and do not hinder them, for to such belongs the kingdom of heaven." And he laid his hands on them and went away. (Matt. 19:13–15)

In addition, Paul's directions to Timothy about how he should teach churches included this statement about widows:

> So I would have younger widows marry, *bear children*, manage their households, and give the adversary no occasion for slander. (1 Tim. 5:14)

These passages indicate that the first question couples should ask themselves when considering birth control is this: *Do we agree in our hearts with the Bible's positive view of children as a blessing from God*, or do we agree with a modern secular view that children are an inconvenience and a burden?

These questions are important because the Bible is unquestionably prochild in its perspective. The scriptural emphasis on children as a blessing leads me to think that married couples should, in almost all cases, plan to have children sometime in their marriages.[7] In fact, my personal encouragement to most young couples would be to plan to have several children and to enjoy their large families for their entire lifetimes. (I have seldom if ever met couples who told me, "We had too many children.")

Having several children is also a way of expanding the church. Although I argued in the previous chapter that God's kingdom on earth in the new covenant age is primarily expanded by having spiritual children (people who are born again), not simply through physical procreation (see p. 730), it remains true that the pattern we see in Scripture is that the children of believers ordinarily become believers themselves.[8] Therefore, having several children is also a way for couples to expand the population of God's people in the world, people who will ultimately glorify him for all eternity.

These biblical truths remind us that our primary emphasis in any discussion of birth control should be on the wonderful privilege, joy, and blessing of having children, in many cases having several of them. Children will usually continue to be a blessing and a joy to parents throughout their lives.

However, Scripture also recognizes that sometimes children can be a cause of great sorrow for their parents. Absalom was a source of tremendous grief to David, from his rebellious attempt to usurp David's throne to his death at the hands of David's general Joab (2 Samuel 13–18). The parable of the prodigal son (Luke 15:11–32) tells of a son who must have caused immense grief to his father. And some verses from Proverbs show an awareness of similar tragedies with rebellious children:

> A wise son makes a glad father,
> > but *a foolish son* is a sorrow to his mother. (Prov. 10:1)

> *A foolish son* is a grief to his father
> > and bitterness to her who bore him. (Prov. 17:25; see also 19:13; 29:3;
> > > Deut. 21:18–21)

Nevertheless, these verses show the exceptions rather than the general case, and the overall perspective of Scripture remains very positive toward children. In addition, we may hope that the prophetic promise of Malachi would yet find a partial or even greater fulfillment in our own lifetimes, so that before the day when the Lord comes in judgment, prodigal sons and daughters will be reconciled with their parents:

> Behold, I will send you Elijah the prophet before the great and awesome day of
> the LORD comes. And he will turn *the hearts of fathers to their children* and *the*

---

[7] The rare exceptions would be cases in which the wife has a medical condition, such as a disability that would make pregnancy prohibitively dangerous, or in which couples are past childbearing age when they marry.

[8] See Wayne Grudem, *Systematic Theology: An Introduction to Biblical Doctrine* (Leicester, UK: Inter-Varsity, and Grand Rapids, MI: Zondervan, 1994), 500.

hearts of children to their fathers, lest I come and strike the land with a decree of utter destruction. (Mal. 4:5–6)

B. OBJECTION: "THE WORLD ALREADY HAS TOO MANY PEOPLE"

One objection that may be brought against this positive biblical perspective on having children is the idea that the world already has too many people. Someone might argue that in the time of the Bible, there were not very many people on earth and the encouragement to have more children made sense, but today the world already has so many people that there is a danger of overpopulation.

Two answers may be given to this objection. First, the command to "be fruitful and multiply and fill the earth" (Gen. 1:28) expressed God's purpose that Adam and Eve would fill the earth *with God-glorifying people*, people who would honor, serve, and worship God. It is commonly true that children of believers also become believers, and therefore it is still a morally good activity for Christians to have children and thus fill the earth with more God-glorifying people. While there are some exceptions, the vast majority of the children of believers, in general, do much more good than harm to the world during their lifetimes.

The other answer is that the world is far from being overpopulated. The pattern throughout all nations of the world is that, as prosperity increases, people have fewer and fewer children. This is acutely evident now in several countries, most notably Canada, Germany, Hungary, Italy, Japan, Russia, and South Korea, where people have had so few children in recent decades that the population is stable or declining, with fertility rates down to as little as 1.5 children per woman.[9] As of December 2016, according to the U.S. Census Bureau, the population of the world was 7.36 billion.[10] In 2004, the United Nations Department of Economic and Social Affairs Population Division published a paper stating that it expects population to stabilize at about 9.22 billion sometime around 2075.[11] Other models, done later than 2004, show world population stabilizing at 10.1 billion by 2100 because of declining fertility rates.[12] I've discussed the stabilization of world population at greater length in another book,[13] and I also address it in chapter 41 of this book (see p. 1110).

In fact, many of the most densely populated areas of the world are also the most

---

[9] Joseph Chamie, "Global Population of 10 Billion by 2100?—Not So Fast," YaleGlobal Oct. 26, 2011, http://yaleglobal.yale.edu/content/global-population-10-billion-2100-not-so-fast. Chamie is the former director the UN Population Division.

[10] U.S. and World Population Clock, U.S. Census Bureau, http://www.census.gov/popclock/.

[11] "World Population to 2300," United Nations Department of Economic and Social Affairs Population Division, 2004, http://www.un.org/esa/population/publications/longrange2/WorldPop2300final.pdf.

[12] Chamie, "Global Population of 10 Billion by 2100?—Not So Fast."

[13] See Wayne Grudem, *Politics—According to the Bible: A Comprehensive Resource for Understanding Modern Political Issues in Light of Scripture* (Grand Rapids, MI: Zondervan, 2010), 333–36.

prosperous, such as The Netherlands, the United Kingdom, Germany, and Japan. The population density of Massachusetts today (871 people per square mile) is far greater than the population density of China (375 people per square mile) and not greatly less than the population density of India (1,169 people per square mile)[14] but Massachusetts is, in general, a much more pleasant place to live, with a higher standard of living. The difference is increased prosperity, which enables people to have better living conditions.

Neither is it true that the billions of people on the earth are rapidly depleting the earth's resources, so that we will soon have widespread shortages of various essential resources. I discuss this more fully in chapter 41 of this book, as well as in another place,[15] so I will simply say here that an infinitely wise God created for us an earth that was "very good" (Gen. 1:31) and "he formed it to be inhabited!" (Isa. 45:18).

C. BIRTH CONTROL FOR A LIMITED TIME IS MORALLY PERMISSIBLE

While I believe that, in almost all circumstances, married couples should plan to have children sometime, this does not mean they have a moral obligation to have as many children as they are physically capable of having. The existence of modern birth-control methods gives many options for deciding when to have children and how many.

For example, a newly married couple might decide not to have children for the first few years of their marriage, perhaps until their educational process is complete or until they have more financial stability. In such a case, deciding to postpone having children may be a wise and morally good choice.

After a couple has had some children, one or both spouses will often have a sense that "we should not have any more children," perhaps because "we cannot do a good job of raising more children." This can be a morally good and wise decision, because deciding to have more children means taking on another weighty responsibility, and God wants us to be faithful in that responsibility:

> But if anyone does not provide for his relatives, and especially for *members of his household*, he has denied the faith and is worse than an unbeliever. (1 Tim. 5:8)

The specific context of this verse is dealing with the provision of support for widows, but the expression "members of his household" would certainly include one's own children too. Regarding this passage, I think John Feinberg and Paul Feinberg are correct when they say that to provide for "members of his household" a person should provide for "financial, physical, emotional, and spiritual needs."[16] Therefore, it is appropriate

---

[14] See chap. 41, p. 1110, for these and other statistics on population density.

[15] Grudem, *Politics—According to the Bible*, 320–86.

[16] John S. Feinberg and Paul D. Feinberg, *Ethics for a Brave New World*, 2nd ed. (Wheaton, IL: Crossway, 2010), 305.

for couples to consider whether they are reasonably able to do that with more children than they already have.

In addition, Jesus gives a principle that pertains to undertaking obligations generally, and it can appropriately apply to the question of having more children:

> For which of you, desiring to build a tower, does not first sit down and count the cost, whether he has enough to complete it? (Luke 14:28)

The application to birth control is that it seems wise for couples to realistically "count the cost" and see whether they have enough physical and emotional resources, and reasonable expectation of financial resources as well, to raise more children.

However, it also must be said that many modern families with four, five, or even more children often find that the Lord gives them the strength and resources needed for raising their children well "in the discipline and instruction of the Lord" (Eph. 6:4).

The broader consideration here is that all of life consists in deciding not to do some good things in order to be able to do some other good things. There are many more good things in the world to do than we can possibly achieve even in many lifetimes.

Later in this chapter I will consider the arguments for an alternative perspective, namely, that birth control is always wrong for Christian couples (see p. 754).

D. MORALLY ACCEPTABLE AND MORALLY UNACCEPTABLE METHODS OF BIRTH CONTROL

Various methods of birth control prevent the husband's sperm from fertilizing the wife's ovum (egg), and thus they do not destroy any new human life. Therefore, they are *morally acceptable* means of birth control. According to the Life Issues Institute, this would include the use of a condom, a diaphragm, a sponge, a spermicide, and most birth-control pills.[17] The older "rhythm" method, now superseded by natural family planning (NFP), also falls in this category.[18] In addition, if a couple has reached a decision not to have any more children for their lifetimes, a vasectomy (for the man) or a tubal ligation (for the woman, commonly called having one's "tubes tied") would also be morally acceptable.

On the other hand, some methods of birth control allow conception to occur and then cause the death of the newly conceived child. As I argued in the earlier chapter on abortion (see chap. 21, p. 566), Scripture indicates that we should consider the unborn child to be a human person from the moment of conception (Ps. 51:5; see further

---

[17] "Abortifacients: An Overview," Life Issues Institute, Inc., Sept. 29, 2014, http://www.lifeissues.org/2014/09/abortifacients-overview/.

[18] Information on natural family planning can be found at National Family Planning International, http://nfpandmore.org/; the U.S. Department of Health and Human Services, https://www.hhs.gov/opa/pregnancy-prevention/non-hormonal-methods/natural-family-planning/index.html; and WebMd: http://www.webmd.com/sex/birth-control/features/today-natural-family-planning#1. The Roman Catholic Church, in particular, has a number of resources on natural family planning.

discussion below, p. 765). This is also evident from the fact that when the husband's sperm fertilizes the wife's ovum (egg), a new living creature with its own distinct DNA begins to form as cells divide and multiply. Birth-control methods that would cause the death of this newly conceived child (methods known as abortifacients) include the morning-after pills (RU-486 and ellaOne).[19]

The intrauterine device (IUD) should also be considered an abortifacient. This medical device allows a woman's egg to be fertilized by a man's sperm, but prevents the resulting embryo from being implanted in the mother's womb. According to Donna Harrison, a board-certified obstetrician-gynecologist, preventing an embryo from implanting effectively kills the embryo, and thus is an abortion.[20] Therefore, such a means of birth control is not morally acceptable on biblical grounds. (See also the discussion of modern reproductive technology in the next chapter.)

E. HUSBANDS SHOULD BE CAREFUL NOT TO DENY TO THEIR WIVES FOR TOO LONG THE PRIVILEGE AND JOY OF HAVING CHILDREN

While I believe that using birth control for a limited time is morally permissible for couples, it is also important for husbands to realize that their wives frequently will have a deep, intense longing to bear children that their husbands may not be aware of. It was not Jacob who said to Rachel, but Rachel who said to Jacob in despair of her infertility, "Give me children, or I shall die!" (Gen. 30:1).

One example of the insensitivity husbands can show toward their wives in this area is the reaction of Elkanah to the sorrow felt by his wife Hannah when she had no children:

> And Elkanah, her husband, said to her, "Hannah, why do you weep? And why do you not eat? And why is your heart sad? *Am I not more to you than ten sons?*" (1 Sam. 1:8)

But Hannah felt this sorrow deeply, for "she was deeply distressed and prayed to the Lord and wept bitterly" (1 Sam. 1:10).

Psalm 113 emphasizes the joy that comes to a previously barren woman when God enables her to bear children:

> He gives the barren woman a home,
> *making her the joyous mother of children.*
> Praise the Lord! (Ps. 113:9; see also Isa. 54:1)

---

[19] "Abortifacients: An Overview"; see also James Trussell, Elizabeth G. Raymond, and Kelly Cleland, "Emergency Contraception: A Last Chance to Prevent Unintended Pregnancy," Princeton University, Office of Population Research, November 2016, http://ec.princeton.edu/questions/ec-review.pdf.

[20] Donna Harrison, "Contraception That Kills," *National Review*, July 8, 2014, http://www.nationalreview.com/article/382172/contraception-kills-donna-harrison.

By contrast, when Abram (later Abraham) was distressed over his childlessness, his focus was not on his personal longing to bear and raise a child, but on his lack of an heir:

> And Abram said, "Behold, you have given me no offspring, *and a member of my household will be my heir.*" (Gen. 15:3)

F. AN ALTERNATIVE VIEWPOINT: ALL BIRTH CONTROL IS WRONG (OR ALL "ARTIFICIAL" BIRTH CONTROL IS WRONG)

In recent decades a "natural family planning" movement has gained influence among evangelical Christians. Such Christians oppose birth control (or most methods of birth control). They support their view with at least the following three arguments:

1. Children are a blessing; therefore, we should have many children.
2. We should trust God to decide how many children we should have.
3. Birth control is unnatural.

I will respond to these three arguments in the following sections.

1. Children Are a Blessing; Therefore, We Should Have Many Children. Mary Pride is an influential evangelical opponent of birth control. She makes the following argument:

> The two methods Christians use to plan their families—(1) spacing and (2) limiting family size—both have one thing in common: *they make a cut off point on how many blessings a family is willing to accept.* Can anyone find one single Bible verse that says Christians should refuse God's blessings? Children are an *unqualified* blessing, according to the Bible.[21]

My response to this argument is that it is based on reasoning that is mistaken and unbiblical. The reasoning, at its base, is this: if something is good or a blessing, we should seek to maximize it.

The problem with this reasoning is that there are many good things in life, many blessings from God, and we cannot possibly maximize all of them. Sleep is a good thing (Ps. 127:2), but God does not require us to get as much sleep as we possibly can (see the warning against sleeping too much in Prov. 6:10–11). Food is a good thing and a blessing from God, but it would be wrong to eat all that we can possibly eat. Work is also a blessing from God (Eccles. 2:24; 3:13; 5:18), but that does not mean we are required to work as much as we possibly can. The same could be said of physical exercise, giving to the poor, evangelism, worship, or Bible study.

---

[21] Mary Pride, *The Way Home: Beyond Feminism, Back to Reality* (Westchester, IL: Crossway, 1985), 76, emphasis in original.

Instead of the false principle "If something is good, you should seek to maximize it," God requires us to pray and exercise mature wisdom in seeking to know how to allocate the limited time we have among the various good activities available to us in this life.

Such mistaken reasoning as Pride offers is not limited to opponents of birth control. Often in Christian circles one hears exhortations of the type: "Since activity XYZ is good, you should do more of activity XYZ," where activity XYZ is teaching children in Sunday school, ministering to the poor, taking part in evangelistic campaigns—or having more children. But this exhortation fails to take into account God's individual callings on different people. God may be calling a person to focus more on activity ABC or activity DEF instead of activity XYZ.

Paul's direction is better:

> Only let each person lead *the life that the Lord has assigned to him*, and to which God has called him. This is my rule in all the churches. (1 Cor. 7:17)

"The life that the Lord has assigned" to each person is best determined by prayerful, wise consideration of one's own gifts and callings from God, and that might not include a calling for a married couple to raise as many children as they can physically conceive. Allowing people to have freedom to follow their own individual callings from God means that people will make many different decisions about which good activities to emphasize. Some will have many children, while others will have fewer children and will devote more time to different ministries and other worthwhile activities. Allowing for such freedom respects the diversity of callings within the church. "There are many parts, yet one body" (1 Cor. 12:20).

2. We Should Trust God to Decide How Many Children We Should Have. Pride also makes this argument:

> There *is* an alternative to scheming and plotting how many babies to have and when to have them. It can be summed up in three little words: trust and obey. If God is willing to plan my family for me . . . then why should I muddle up his plan with my ideas?[22]

This argument against birth control fails to recognize that God's sovereignty does not normally override the ordinary functioning of the natural world that he has created. We do not say to a farmer, "Trust God's sovereignty regarding how many weeds will grow in your field." If he did nothing to overcome the weeds, they would soon overgrow his field.

To take another example, my neighbors have a grapefruit tree that produces delicious grapefruits every year—so many that they cheerfully give them to the neighbors. But they don't allow the grapefruits that fall from the tree to remain there and disperse their seeds on the ground, so that many more grapefruit trees eventually sprout! An

---

[22] Pride, *The Way Home*, 77.

advocate of "natural grapefruit tree planning" might tell them to "trust God to decide how many grapefruit trees you will have," but the result would be that they would soon have more grapefruit trees than they could ever care for. It is far wiser for them to exercise some grapefruit "birth control" and gather up the grapefruits that fall to the ground.

The important concept to remember here is that *God does not usually, in his sovereignty, override the natural, ordinary consequences of human actions.* If a couple decides that they will have sex often and "trust God" to decide how many children they will have, the answer is that God has already decided (through the way he has ordered the natural world and our physical bodies) that they will have many children (assuming the couple is in good reproductive health). To say they are *trusting God* for how many children they will have is something like throwing wildflower seeds on their backyard once a week for a year and then saying, "We are trusting God to decide how many flowers will grow in our backyard." If seeds are repeatedly tossed on fertile ground, flowers will bloom.

The broader principle is that God wants us to trust him *regarding his commands and his promises that he has given to us in Scripture.* But there is nothing in Scripture that tells us to avoid using birth control and then to trust him for how many children we will have. We are not authorized to trust him for things he has not promised or commanded.

Daniel Doriani wisely analyzes the appeal to trusting in God's sovereignty that is made by Christians who oppose birth control:

> The "no birth control" movement says family planning usurps God's sovereignty by banning children who might have existed. This misunderstands the way God works with human agents and other "secondary means," such as the weather. If I say family planning interferes with God's sovereignty, I might as well argue that I should not plan my vocation or my next meal or where I live lest I interfere with God's plan. This concept of God's sovereignty could justify every kind of laziness and inaction, including refusal of medical care. It also assumes what is to be proved, that God wants the couple to have more children and wants them to cooperate through "unprotected" intercourse. But perhaps God has not planned more children for the couple and wants them to cooperate by using birth control! Ignorance of God's will never excuses us from the honest work of discerning and planning.[23]

3. Birth Control Is Unnatural. This argument is often the unstated assumption behind many objections to birth control: since sex without birth control is "natural," and since this "natural" process often leads to more babies, having more babies is morally right (or is God's will for us).

In response to this argument, we must reply that God does not command us simply

---

[23] Daniel Doriani, "Birth Dearth or Bring on the Babies? Biblical Perspectives on Family-Planning," *Journal of Biblical Counseling* 12, no. 1 (Fall 1993): 33. The entire article (24–35) contains many helpful insights regarding Christian arguments about birth control.

to follow what is "natural," but rather to follow his commands in Scripture. (Here we differ with the Roman Catholic view that places much greater emphasis on what they perceive as "natural law.")

The Bible often directs us on a course that differs from the course of nature. With respect to sexual intercourse itself, God does not command us to do what is "natural"; rather, he commands us to limit sex to a married relationship rather than following our "natural instincts," which would sometimes lead us to have sex with a number of different people, even outside of marriage.

It is important to keep in mind that God changed the order of the natural world at the time of the fall, and this means that our highest ideal is not simply to let "untouched nature" take its course. After Adam and Eve sinned, God said, "Cursed is the ground because of you; in pain you shall eat of it all of the days of your life; thorns and thistles it shall bring forth for you" (Gen. 3:17–18). Suddenly, life in the natural world became more difficult and painful.

When we couple this alteration that God imposed on the natural world with God's command to "subdue" the earth (Gen. 1:28), it is right to conclude that we should often take active steps to change or even overcome the course of untouched nature. This applies not only to the plants of the field, but also to our physical bodies, for which we often need medicines to remedy some disability or illness.

We modify nature in many ways. We prune fruit trees; we thin carrots; we clear out trees in order to plant crops; we kill weeds; and we put up barriers to exclude wild animals. In all of these ways we are interfering with the course of nature in order to more effectively obey God.

This is especially relevant to the question of childbirth, because after Adam and Eve sinned, God changed the effects that childbirth would have on a woman's body:

To the woman he said,

> "*I will surely multiply your pain in childbearing*;
>   in pain you shall bring forth children." (Gen. 3:16)

This indicates that childbirth is much more painful and probably much more taxing on a woman's body than it would have been prior to the fall.

So if Adam and Eve had not sinned, and if there had been no curse placed upon the woman with regard to childbearing, it is possible that Eve, in her unfallen body, could have easily borne 15, 20, or more children, at a rate of one per year, while feeling no pain and suffering, and experiencing no lasting wear and tear on her body. But this was no longer the case after the curse was imposed. What is now "natural" will not always be what is best.

In addition, it is possible that Genesis 3:16 also indicates an increase in the frequency of a woman's fertility, more than her body is suited to bear in her fallen state. The King James Version (and the New King James Version) provides an alternative translation:

I will greatly multiply thy sorrow *and thy conception.* (KJV)

I will greatly multiply your sorrow *and your conception.* (NKJV)

This translation is a grammatically legitimate and entirely literal translation of the Hebrew term *wehēronēk,* "and your conception." Based on this translation, it is possible that, prior to the fall, Eve's period of fertility would have occurred less frequently, perhaps once every year or two years. And this would have meant that sexual intercourse for almost the entire year would not have been for the purpose of procreation, but for the purpose of mutual enjoyment and companionship.[24]

Related to the idea that we should follow what is "natural" is the idea that procreation is the main purpose (or perhaps even the only legitimate purpose) for sexual intercourse. But surely that idea is not found in Scripture. Sexual intercourse also gives realization to the "one flesh" union that is the essence of marriage (see Gen. 2:24; Eph. 5:31). And sexual intimacy in marriage is also given by God for the purpose of mutual pleasure and deep companionship (see Prov. 5:18–19; Song of Solomon; see also the discussion in the previous chapter, p. 706). Because procreation is not the only purpose for sexual intercourse, sex within marriage is also a good thing during a woman's nonfertile times each month, as well as after she experiences menopause.

As for the claim that procreation is the primary purpose of sexual intercourse, it is difficult to know how any criteria could be found that would prove this. If God creates something with multiple purposes, who are we to determine that one purpose is primary and others are secondary?

In conclusion, these three arguments against birth control are not persuasive.

G. HOW CAN A COUPLE KNOW HOW MANY CHILDREN TO HAVE?

If children are a blessing, and if it is good to have children, and if birth control is acceptable for at least some periods of time in a marriage, then how can a couple decide how many children they should have?

Scripture does not give us one answer that fits every married couple. In such a case, we should be gracious and allow people to have a wide variety of different answers because of their different individual callings from God.

---

[24] However, in defense of most other translations, including the ESV, the vast majority of translation committees have understood the Hebrew expression to be an example of *hendiadys,* the use of two words joined by "and" to express a single idea, in this case not just "pain and childbearing" but "pain in childbearing," a single idea. This is also a grammatically legitimate translation, and translation committees have tended to favor it, probably because of a conviction that the overwhelming prochild perspective of Scripture would not easily be compatible with the idea that increased fertility was a part of the curse.

Yet I do not want to dismiss the possibility of the KJV translation too quickly. One veteran missionary who had worked with women in poor countries for several decades told me, for example, that she had frequently seen the devastating physical effects on poor women of 15 or 20 sequential years of childbirth.

In general, couples should pray for God's wisdom, which may become increasingly clear to them over several months or years:

> *If any of you lacks wisdom, let him ask God,* who gives generously to all without reproach, and it will be given him. But let him ask in faith, with no doubting, for the one who doubts is like a wave of the sea that is driven and tossed by the wind. (James 1:5–6)

If they are comfortable doing so, couples might also decide to seek the counsel of others, through whom God will often give us wisdom

The conclusions I have argued for in this chapter imply that a couple's fundamental perspective in this decision should be that children are a blessing from the Lord, and that having children is a good thing and pleasing to God (Gen. 1:28; Ps. 127:3–5; 128:3–4; Mal. 2:15; 1 Tim. 5:14). But it is also right for them to "count the cost" (Luke 14:28) of undertaking such a weighty responsibility. If they deeply desire to have more children, then it is likely that God is calling them to do this, and they should willingly trust him to provide for their needs and enable them to provide for their family (1 Tim. 5:8), so long as they are not making a reckless, foolish decision that is in essence demanding miraculous provision from God. But if one or both of them is strongly opposed to having more children, and if that opposition is based on biblical, godly desires, then that opposition should be weighed heavily in the decision-making process, and use of birth control would seem appropriate.

In between those two situations, a couple may feel unsure or ambivalent about having more children, and in that case they will probably decide not to actively try to prevent pregnancy, to thank God that he often grants us the blessing of children, and then to wait and see if God in his sovereignty will provide them with more children.

However, there are two errors that should clearly be avoided: (1) basing a decision on fear, selfishness, and the unsanctified expectations of a non-Christian culture, and thus failing to obey God's calling; and (2) basing a decision on a reckless, irresponsible sort of "faith" that is not from God but is only a projection of a person's wrongful motives.

The kind of attitude Christians have toward others who have few or many children is also important. In this regard, as with getting married or not getting married, "each has his own gift from God, one of one kind and one of another" (1 Cor. 7:7), and Christians should respect and honor the different decisions that other families have made in this regard: "Who are you to pass judgment on the servant of another? It is before his own master that he stands or falls" (Rom. 14:4; see also v. 10).

QUESTIONS FOR PERSONAL APPLICATION

1. Do you tend to view children more as a burden or as a positive blessing?
2. Consider the possibility that you will have several children (say, five, six, or more). If that happened, do you think they would bring mostly

positive or mostly negative consequences to the world in the future? Does the idea of having that many children cause you to fear that you might not be able to afford it or that you might not be able to be a good enough parent? How do you think God would view this possibility?

3. What do you think would be the ideal number of children for you to have?

4. What character traits (see p. 110) will help to influence you to have the right attitudes and make the right decisions regarding birth control?

SPECIAL TERMS

abortifacient
IUD
natural family planning (NFP)
rhythm method
RU-486

BIBLIOGRAPHY

Sections in Other Ethics Texts

(see complete bibliographical data, p. 64)

Davis, 17–58
Feinberg, John and Paul, 286–306
Frame, 782–87
Geisler, 396–405
Gushee and Stassen, 431–34
McQuilkin and Copan, 333–34
Murray, 45–81
Rae, 286–89

Other Works

Best, Megan. *Fearfully and Wonderfully Made: Ethics and the Beginning of Human Life.* Kingsford, NSW, Australia: Matthias Media, 2012.

Biebel, David B., ed. *The Sterilization Option: A Guide for Christians.* Grand Rapids, MI: Baker, 1995.

Cutrer, William R., and Sandra L. Glahn. *The Contraception Guidebook: Options, Risks, and Answers for Christian Couples.* Grand Rapids, MI: Zondervan, 2005.

Doriani, Daniel. "Birth Dearth or Bring on the Babies? Biblical Perspectives on Family-Planning." *Journal of Biblical Counseling* 12, no. 1 (1993), 24–35.

Fletcher, D. B. "Birth Control." In *New Dictionary of Christian Ethics and Pastoral Theology*, edited by David J. Atkinson and David H. Field, 193–95. Leicester, UK: InterVarsity, and Downers Grove, IL: InterVarsity Press, 1995.

Köstenberger, Andreas J. "To Have or Not to Have Children: Special Issues Related to the Family, Part 1." In *God, Marriage, and Family: Rebuilding the Biblical Foundation*. 2nd ed., 117–37, 334–40. Wheaton, IL: Crossway, 2010

Pride, Mary. *The Way Home: Beyond Feminism, Back to Reality*. Westchester, IL: Crossway, 1985. Against birth control.

Wheat, Ed, and Gaye Wheat. *Intended for Pleasure: Sex Technique and Sexual Fulfillment in Christian Marriage*. 4th ed., 162–94. Grand Rapids, MI: Revell, 2010.

SCRIPTURE MEMORY PASSAGE

Psalm 127:3: Behold, children are a heritage from the LORD, the fruit of the womb a reward.

HYMN

"All the Way My Savior Leads Me"

All the way my Savior leads me—What have I to ask beside?
Can I doubt His tender mercy, who thru life has been my Guide?
Heav'nly peace, divinest comfort, here by faith in Him to dwell!
For I know, whate'er befall me, Jesus doeth all things well.

All the way my Savior leads me—Cheers each winding path I tread,
Gives me grace for ev'ry trial, feeds me with the living bread.
Tho my weary steps may falter and my soul athirst may be,
Gushing from the Rock before me, lo! a spring of joy I see.

All the way my Savior leads me—O the fullness of His love!
Perfect rest to me is promised in my Father's house above.
When my spirit, clothed immortal, wings its flight to realms of day,
This my song thru endless ages: Jesus led me all the way.

FANNY J. CROSBY, 1820–1915

Chapter 30

INFERTILITY, REPRODUCTIVE TECHNOLOGY, AND ADOPTION

How do biblical principles help us evaluate modern reproductive technologies, particularly artificial insemination, in vitro fertilization, embryo adoption, and surrogate motherhood? Why does the Bible view adoption so positively?

A. INFERTILITY

Infertility is the inability of a couple to conceive and bear children due to a lack of normal function in either the man's or the woman's reproductive system. Modern medical developments provide several solutions for infertility, and it is appropriate to consider these in this section of the book dealing with topics related to marriage. At the end of this chapter, I will also consider a related issue, adoption.

1. Infertility in the Old and New Testaments. Infertility has been a source of deep sorrow for both men and women, but especially for women, for all of human history, as we see from some of the early chapters of the Bible. Sarah (Sarai) was unable to bear children to Abraham (Gen. 11:30; 16:1) for most of her life, until she miraculously bore Isaac in her old age (see Gen. 21:1–7). Jacob's wife Rachel was unable to bear children for a long time after her marriage to Jacob (Gen. 29:31), as was Samson's mother, the wife of Manoah (Judg. 13:2). Hannah, the mother of Samuel, cried out to the Lord in deep sorrow because of her infertility (1 Sam. 1:2–18). In the New Testament, Zechariah and Elizabeth "had no child, because Elizabeth was barren, and both were advanced in years" (Luke 1:7), but, again through God's miraculous intervention, Elizabeth eventually gave birth to John the Baptist (vv. 57–66). These narrative examples show that *overcoming infertility is something that pleases God*, and is often a manifestation of his special blessing on a couple.

In addition, there are some general passages that show God's great blessing when "he gives the barren woman a home, making her the joyous mother of children. Praise the Lord!" (Ps. 113:9; see also Ex. 23:26; Deut. 7:14; Isa. 54:1; Gal. 4:27). These passages are entirely consistent with the perspective that I presented in the previous chapter, that the broad teaching of the Bible is that children are a great blessing from God: "Behold, children are a heritage from the Lord, the fruit of the womb a reward" (Ps. 127:3; see also Gen. 1:28; Ps. 128:3–4; Mal. 2:15; 1 Tim 5:14; see also chap. 29, p. 747).

Because of the consistent force of these biblical passages, it is right to consider infertility as something that we should seek to overcome with the confidence that God is pleased with such efforts. Infertility should not be something about which we are indifferent, such as the color of our hair or eyes, but rather something we see as a condition that is another result of the fall, one of the diseases and disabilities that entered the human race after Adam and Eve sinned. Infertility was not part of God's good creation as he originally made it or intended it to function.

2. A Feeling of Grief in Childlessness. God in his wisdom shows compassion and awareness of the deep grief of childlessness in several passages, such as the stories of Rachel (Gen. 30:1) and Hannah (1 Sam. 1:5–10).

The deep grief that is felt by childless couples must not be minimized or dismissed lightly by others, especially pastors and counselors, but also friends. Because only women are able to bear and nurse children, this grief can be especially acute for wives due to a sense of loss at not being able to have a jointly conceived child, at not having the experience of pregnancy, at not going through the birth and breastfeeding of a child, and at not being able to serve as a mother for her own children.

3. Faith in the Midst of Sorrow. Sometimes a childless couple will wonder if their situation is a result of God's displeasure or discipline, and this will make it difficult for them to believe that God has good purposes for them and for their lives. But the example of Zechariah and Elizabeth in the beginning of Luke's Gospel shows that infertility can happen even to a godly, morally exemplary couple, because Zechariah and Elizabeth "were both righteous before God" (Luke 1:6; this is a reminder that their infertility was not a result of their individual sin), yet they were still unable to have children:

> In the days of Herod, king of Judea, there was a priest named Zechariah, of the division of Abijah. And he had a wife from the daughters of Aaron, and her name was Elizabeth. *And they were both righteous before God, walking*

blamelessly in all the commandments and statutes of the Lord. But they had no child, because Elizabeth was barren, and both were advanced in years. (Luke 1:5–7)

It is important to recognize that the inability to have children is a difficult trial, a kind of suffering that many couples endure privately and silently. In such situations, Scripture passages that deal with trials and suffering in the Christian life are often helpful in encouraging people's faith:

> In this [your salvation] you rejoice, though now for a little while, if necessary, *you have been grieved by various trials*, so that the tested genuineness of your faith—more precious than gold that perishes though it is tested by fire—may be found to result in praise and glory and honor at the revelation of Jesus Christ. Though you have not seen him, you love him. Though you do not now see him, you believe in him and rejoice with joy that is inexpressible and filled with glory, obtaining the outcome of your faith, the salvation of your souls. (1 Pet. 1:6–9; see also James 1:2–4)

Here Peter encourages believers going through trials to continue in faith, which is very precious to God, and which will result in great reward. In addition, he encourages suffering believers to love Christ and believe in him, for that relationship with him will fill them with joy.

It will also be an encouragement for infertile couples to recall that neither Jesus nor Paul had physical children, but both found great fulfillment in the ministries that God had entrusted to them. They had many spiritual children, who came into the kingdom of God and were nurtured by their ministries.

As I mentioned in the previous two chapters, the New Testament several times puts a positive emphasis on spiritual children who are the result of a person's ministry. Paul tells the Corinthian church, "I became your father in Christ Jesus through the gospel" (1 Cor. 4:15). He calls the Galatian Christians "my little children" (Gal. 4:19). He calls Timothy "my true child in the faith" (1 Tim. 1:2) and similarly calls Titus "my true child in a common faith" (Titus 1:4). And Peter refers to Mark, who often traveled with him, as "Mark, my son" (1 Pet. 5:13).

B. THREE MORAL PRINCIPLES TO CONSIDER IN RELATION TO REPRODUCTIVE TECHNOLOGY

1. Modern Medicine in General Is Morally Good. Modern medicine (and medicine in the ancient world, for that matter) can be used to overcome many diseases and disabilities today. We should view this as a good thing, and as something for which we can give thanks to God.

God put resources in the earth for us to discover and develop, including resources that are useful for medicinal purposes, and he gave us the wisdom and the desire to do this. The warrant for this is found in God's command to Adam and Eve to "subdue" the earth (Gen. 1:28), and it is reinforced by the fact that all of the medicines we have today are made from resources found in the earth, and "*the earth is the LORD's* and the fullness thereof, the world and those who dwell therein" (Ps. 24:1).

Jesus's ministry of healing also indicated that God is pleased when we try to help people overcome diseases and disabilities:

> Now when the sun was setting, all those who had any who were sick with various diseases brought them to him, and *he laid his hands on every one of them and healed them.* (Luke 4:40)

This was a common pattern in Jesus's earthly ministry, and the inclusive nature of the expression "*all* those who had *any* who were sick with *various* diseases" allows us to suppose that Jesus also healed the infertility of many women (and men) who had previously been unable to conceive and bear children.

Therefore, it seems morally right to support and welcome advances in medicine that today can bring health to people with various diseases and disabilities, including infertility.

2. We Should Treat the Unborn Child as a Human Person from the Moment of Conception. The earlier chapter on abortion (chap. 21) argued at some length that various passages in Scripture lead us to consider the unborn child as a human person from the moment of conception. In thinking back on the beginning of his existence as a sinner, David mentioned his sinfulness even at the moment of his conception: "I was brought forth in iniquity, and *in sin did my mother conceive me*" (Ps. 51:5; see discussion, p. 567). In addition, David said to God, "You knitted me together in my mother's womb" (39:13). In the old covenant, if an unborn child died, even because of an accidental injury, the one who caused the unborn child to die was subject to capital punishment (see Ex. 21:22–25: "You shall pay life for life"). Jacob and Esau were viewed as two unique children who would become two nations struggling within Rebekah's womb (Gen. 25:22–23). And Elizabeth, in the sixth month of her pregnancy, said, "The baby in my womb leaped for joy"—surely a human action (Luke 1:44). (See above, p. 566, for further discussion of these passages.)

These passages are relevant for the question of reproductive technologies, because they mean that we should not condone any such technology that will certainly lead to the death of even one unborn child who was conceived when the man's sperm fertilized the woman's egg, the cells began to divide, and the human embryo began to grow into a little baby.

3. God Intends That a Child Should Be Conceived by and Born to a Man and Woman Who Are Married to Each Other. I affirm this third principle with somewhat more hesitation than the first two because this principle is not derived from any direct command of Scripture, but rather from a pattern of biblical narratives and probable implications from biblical moral commands about some related topics.

Many ethical questions related to reproductive technology have to do with the medical possibility of a woman becoming pregnant and bearing a child *even when the child's biological father is not that woman's husband*. But the entire scope of the biblical narratives and biblical moral standards views this situation as contrary to God's intended plan for the birth of a child.[1]

At the beginning of creation God said to Adam and Eve (who were husband and wife), "Be fruitful and multiply and fill the earth" (Gen. 1:28). This verse by itself does not say that no other means of producing children would be pleasing to God, but it is the foundational pattern for marriage in the entire Bible, and it is the first instance of the command to be fruitful. (Scripture calls Adam and Eve "the man and his wife" in Gen. 2:25, and uses the relationship between Adam and Eve as the pattern for marriage generally in v. 24.)

God's repeated commands against adultery (Ex. 20:14; Lev. 20:10; Deut. 5:18; Prov. 6:32; Matt. 15:19; Rom. 13:9; James 2:11; 2 Pet. 2:14) also support this idea. One reason that sexual intercourse should occur only within the context of marriage is that this guarantees that children will only be born to a man and a woman who are married to each other.

Another piece of evidence supporting this conclusion is found in the detailed laws in Exodus:

> If a man seduces a virgin who is not betrothed and lies with her, he shall give the bride-price for her and make her his wife. (Ex. 22:16; the rare exception is seen in v. 17, but the general principle is that marriage should occur; see also Deut. 22:28–29)

Here again, the specific provision of the law guaranteed that if a man and a woman had sexual intercourse, they would be married, once again guaranteeing that a child would be born in the context of a man and a woman who are married to each other.

Jesus's teachings against divorce gave further protection that guaranteed that children would be born within marriage. The general principle is, "What therefore God has joined together, let not man separate" (Matt. 19:6). The only exceptions (where divorce is allowed) are cases in which the marriage has been so seriously defiled by adultery or by long-term desertion that cannot be reconciled, but those are intended to be rare situations (see chap. 32), and in such cases the conception of further children would not occur in any case.

The prohibitions against "sexual immorality" (in older translations "fornication,"

---

[1] However, the situation of the virgin birth of Jesus to his mother Mary is an event that was unique in the entire history of the human race because, in the wise providence of God, Jesus had no biological human father.

Greek, *porneia*) also seek to ensure that sexual intercourse occurs only within the context of marriage. This would guarantee that children would be conceived only within the context of marriage (see 1 Cor. 6:18; 2 Cor. 12:21; Gal. 5:19; Eph. 5:3; Col. 3:5; 1 Thess. 4:3; see also discussion in chap. 28, p. 706).

Finally, there is no indication anywhere in Scripture that God ever considered it morally right for a child to be conceived by a man and a woman who were not married to each other.

This broad pattern of scriptural teaching, then, leads me to conclude that a child should be conceived by and born to a man and a woman who are married to each other, and in no other situation or relationship.

C. SOME MODERN REPRODUCTIVE TECHNOLOGIES ARE MORALLY ACCEPTABLE

The general category for various medical methods to help people have children is "assisted reproductive technology" (abbreviated ART). In this section I will consider some specific kinds of modern assisted reproductive technology in light of the three moral principles above. However, a word of caution is in order. Medical technology in this area is developing at a remarkable speed, and it is impossible to predict what new procedures might be available in the next several years. Other evangelical ethicists have analyzed reproductive technologies in more detail than I am able to do in this chapter,[2] and I hope that they and others like them will continue such detailed studies.

However, I also hope that the individual topics that I discuss in this chapter will provide a pattern of ethical reasoning that readers will find useful in evaluating future techniques and procedures.

The three conclusions from the previous section may be summarized as follows:

1. Modern medicine in general is morally good.
2. We should treat the unborn child as a human person from the moment of conception.
3. God intends that a child should be conceived by and born to a man and woman who are married to each other.

These three principles give us a useful perspective from which we can conclude that some kinds of modern reproductive technology are morally acceptable and other kinds are not.

---

[2] In the bibliography at the end of this chapter, see especially the works by John S. Feinberg and Paul D. Feinberg, John M. Frame, John Kilner, C. Ben Mitchell, Scott B. Rae, and David VanDrunen. The website of the Center for Bioethics and Human Dignity at Trinity International University also has extensive resources on many detailed questions in bioethics: https://cbhd.org/. I also recommend the bioethics statement on this subject produced by the Christian Medical and Dental Associations; see https://www.cmda.org/resources/publication/assisted-reproductive-technology-ethics-statement.

1. Artificial Insemination by Husband (AIH). The process of artificial insemination by husband does not violate any of the biblical principles named above. It simply enables a wife to become pregnant by her husband's sperm when, for some reason, it is physically unlikely or impossible for this to happen through ordinary sexual intercourse. The husband's sperm is first collected and then injected into the wife's cervix or uterus using a needleless syringe or other medical device. The child is conceived by and born to a man and a woman who are married to each other. No unborn human person (or embryo) is destroyed in the process. And the wonderful result is that infertility is overcome for this couple.

2. In Vitro Fertilization without Destruction of Embryos. In vitro fertilization (abbreviated IVF) is the process of joining together a woman's egg (ovum) and a husband's sperm in a laboratory rather than inside a woman's body. (The Latin phrase *in vitro* means "in glass.")

Evangelical Christians differ on the moral acceptability of this procedure, as I will indicate below (some respected evangelical writers argue that in vitro fertilization is always morally unacceptable). My own position is that, in principle, there should be no moral objection to in vitro fertilization according to scriptural standards, as long as no human embryos are destroyed in the process, because it is once again simply enabling an infertile husband and wife to have children and thereby overcoming their infertility by means of modern medicine. Someone might object that this is not the "natural" process of conception through sexual intercourse that God intended, but such an argument must assume a definition of "natural" that arbitrarily excludes modern medical means from what we consider part of nature. Is not the laboratory equipment that is used for in vitro fertilization also made from resources that God planted in the earth? Are not the medical researchers and medical technicians, with all their wisdom and skill, part of God's creation also?

To cite another analogy, consider a woman who uses a modern thermometer to take her body temperature every day in order to find out the best time to have intercourse so that she will be able to conceive a child. Is this an "unnatural" process because she uses a modern medical thermometer in order to know when she is ovulating? Surely not. The thermometer is made from part of the natural world that God created. Similarly, consider a husband who uses Viagra or a similar modern medicine to overcome erectile dysfunction so that he and his wife can have intercourse and conceive a baby. Is that process to be rejected as "unnatural" because he is using modern medicine to overcome his medical problem? Surely not. The Viagra is made from materials that God placed in the natural world, and so it is also part of nature considered in a broad sense.

Therefore, there seems to be no valid reason to reject in vitro fertilization on the ground that it is not part of the natural process that God established for the conception of children. The essential considerations in this issue are all satisfied: modern medicine is used to overcome a disability, no unborn children's lives are destroyed, and the child is conceived by and born to a man and a woman who are married to each other.

However, in vitro fertilization is often carried out in a way that destroys multiple human embryos, and therefore wrongly results in the destruction of human life. This happens because, in order to increase the probability of pregnancy, more of the wife's eggs may be fertilized in laboratory equipment than are actually implanted in her womb.[3]

In most cases, couples going through in vitro fertilization where multiple embryos are created can indicate one of the following options for the handling of any remaining embryos:

1. Freezing (cryopreservation) of unimplanted embryos for use by the couple in any future treatment cycles.
2. Anonymously donating the embryos for use by other infertile couples. (See the section on "Embryo Adoption" below.)
3. Allowing the embryos to develop in the laboratory until they perish, at which time they are discarded, which is usually within six to eight days of collection.[4]

The fertilization of multiple eggs is not necessary, however. Technological development of in vitro fertilization has reached the point where, if the couple wishes to fertilize only one egg or two and then have them both implanted in the mother's womb, that can be done. In fact, one 2012 British study found that women should never have more than two eggs implanted. "Previous research—before more modern techniques for IVF—still showed that implanting three [embryos] increased the likelihood of successful live birth rate, compared with the transfer of two or one," said the lead researcher, Debbie Lawlor of the University of Bristol. "Our research shows this is no longer the case."[5] In such cases, where no embryos are destroyed, I think that in vitro fertilization is morally acceptable.

John Feinberg and Paul Feinberg disagree with my position here and argue that IVF is morally unacceptable, even when only one egg is fertilized, because the success rate is so low in such cases. They write:

> We believe the embryo is human and a person from conception onward. . . .
> Our views on the embryo's status lead to our greatest moral objection to IVF,
> namely, its waste and loss of embryonic life. . . . If the success rate of IVF had
> risen to 95 percent or even 80–85 percent, we would be more sympathetic to
> it, but . . . IVF technology is currently nowhere near such success rates. We

---

[3] "In-Vitro Fertilization and Embryo Transfer: Overview for IVF Patients," Georgia Reproductive Services, http://www.ivf.com/overview.html.

[4] Ibid. See also "In Vitro Fertilization (IVF)," The Mayo Clinic, http://www.mayoclinic.org/tests-procedures /in-vitro-fertilization/details/how-you-prepare/ppc-20206941.

[5] Cited in Catharine Pearson, "IVF Study Shows Two Eggs are Good, 3 Too Many," *Huffington Post*, Jan. 18, 2012, http://www.huffingtonpost.com/2012/01/12/ivf-study-shows-2–eggs-ar_n_1202020.html.

find the loss of so much human life morally unacceptable. . . . Success rates [are] at best only about 17 percent when one embryo is used. . . . Too many human lives are lost to think this is morally acceptable.[6]

I have much respect for the Feinbergs' book, which I used as my primary textbook for teaching Christian ethics for many years. I agree with their conclusions far more often than I disagree. In addition, both John and Paul Feinberg were valued colleagues of mine when I taught at Trinity Evangelical Divinity School. I find their objection at this point to be significant and I take it seriously, but in the end I am not persuaded by it.

My response is that fertilizing only one egg or two at a time, and implanting these with the hope that they will survive, is far different from the common practice of in vitro fertilization, where several eggs are fertilized and then most of them are intentionally destroyed. In that case, there is a willful destruction of human lives. But with the fertilization of only one or two eggs at a time, the intent of the doctor and the husband and wife is that all of the fertilized eggs will live and come to normal birth. Therefore, I still think that this kind of in vitro fertilization is morally acceptable.[7]

This does not mean that couples have an obligation to try in vitro fertilization, only that it is a morally acceptable thing to do. Many couples may reason that the process is too expensive for them to afford. On average, the cost of a basic IVF cycle in the United States ranges from about $12,000 to $15,000. Another less-complicated process called "Mini-IVF" is approximately $5000 to $7000.[8]

Others may reason that the likelihood of success for the procedure is so slim that they do not want to embark on such a difficult process. According to the Society of Assisted Reproductive Technologies (SART) in 2014, the live birth rate per IVF cycle with their own eggs is 54.4 percent among women younger than 35; 42.0 percent for those aged 35 to 37; and 26.6 percent for those aged 38 to 40. The success rate drops to 13.3 percent in those older than 40, and success in women older than 44 is rare, approximately 3.9 percent.[9]

---

[6] John S. Feinberg and Paul D. Feinberg, *Ethics for a Brave New World*, 2nd ed. (Wheaton, IL: Crossway, 2010), 424–25. British author John Ling also objects to IVF: see John R. Ling, *Bioethical Issues: Understanding and Responding to the Culture of Death*, revised & updated ed. (Leominster, UK: Day One Publications, 2014). He summarizes his objections here: http://www.johnling.co.uk/thirtyyears.htm.

[7] Two other objections that may be brought up against IVF are (1) that advances in IVF technology are often developed by researchers who intentionally destroy hundreds of embryos, and (2) that IVF separates conception from the "one-flesh" sexual union (Gen. 2:24) in which God intended it to occur. I recognize that some readers will find these objections persuasive, but I do not because (1) I do not think we are responsible to avoid using all modern technologies developed by sinful human beings at various times and places around the world, and (2) no command of Scripture says that the conception of a child by a husband and wife must only occur through such a "one-flesh" union. I want to be careful both to teach all the ethical standards that Scripture teaches and also not to prohibit what Scripture does not forbid.

[8] "IVF Costs—In Vitro Fertilization Costs," Internet Health Resources, Infertility Resources, https://www.ihr.com/infertility/ivf/ivf-in-vitro-fertilization-cost.html.

[9] "Final Cumulative Outcome Per Egg Retrieval Cycle," Society of Assisted Reproductive Technologies, 2014, https://www.sartcorsonline.com/rptCSR_PublicMultYear.aspx?ClinicPKID=0.

A Swedish study found that a woman who had just one embryo implanted in her womb had nearly as great a chance of getting pregnant as a woman who had two or more embryos implanted. Transferring only one embryo also reduced the chances of twins being born with low birth weight and the accompanying complications.[10]

Another consideration is that a couple may decide that embarking on another pregnancy carries increased risks for the mother's health that are too significant for them to think they should try IVF. In such cases also, the *medical possibility* and the *moral acceptability* of trying in vitro fertilization do not mean that there is any obligation on them to use this procedure if they do not want to do so.

3. Embryo Adoption. Often during the process of in vitro fertilization, more of a woman's eggs are fertilized in the laboratory than are implanted in her womb. As noted above, instead of destroying these embryos, some couples decide to freeze them, in case they decide to have more children later or for other reasons. As of 2015, it is estimated that there are more than one million frozen embryos in storage in the United States alone.[11] Many of them will never be claimed or used by the original parents. What should be done with these embryos?

One possibility is that other couples might adopt the embryos, have them implanted in the wife's womb, and allow them to grow and be born as normal children. Sometimes these children are called "snowflake children."[12]

While we should not encourage or give approval to the process of creating embryos that will not be used in the first place, once these embryos have been created, they seem to be in a situation very similar to that of orphans. They are very, very young children who have not yet been born and whose parents are no longer taking care of them.

In this case, the Bible's encouragement that we should care for orphans seems applicable:

> Religion that is pure and undefiled before God the Father is this: *to visit orphans and widows in their affliction,* and to keep oneself unstained from the world. (James 1:27; see also Hos. 14:3)[13]

---

[10] "Good Results with Only One Egg in In-Vitro Fertilization," *Science Daily*, Dec. 14, 2004, https://www.sciencedaily.com/releases/2004/12/041203091047.htm.

[11] John Burger, "Frozen Embryo Population in the U.S. Hits 1 Million," *Aleteia*, June 18, 2015, http://aleteia.org/2015/06/18/frozen-embryo-population-in-the-us-hits-1-million-mark/.

[12] The term "snowflake children" refers to the children that result from the adoption of frozen embryos left over from in vitro fertilization. These embryos are transferred to infertile couples via *embryo adoption.* After adoption, the child has legal parents other than the man and woman whose sperm and egg originally conceived the embryo. The legal process of taking ownership of an embryo differs from that of traditional adoption. For more information, see https://www.nightlight.org/snowflakes-embryo-adoption-donation/embryo-adoption/.

[13] Several Old Testament passages about "the fatherless" also show God's care for children who are unable to care for or protect themselves. See Ex. 22:22; Deut. 10:18; 24:17, 19–21; 26:12–13; 27:19; Pss. 10:14, 18; 68:5; 82:3; 146:9; Isa. 1:17; Jer. 7:6; 22:3; Zech. 7:10.

If we consider these frozen embryos as "orphans" who have been abandoned by their parents, then it clearly seems morally right for couples to adopt them, bring them to birth, and raise them in their own families as their own adopted children. In fact, God may bring much blessing to those who adopt and raise these embryos as children.[14]

Someone may wonder if there is damage to the physical or mental development of these children as a result of their existing in a frozen state over a period of time, sometimes for several years. But the surprising evidence shows that such snowflake children will often grow to be healthy and normal, and some are even now nearing adulthood. For example, Hannah Strege, the first adopted frozen embryo, born on December 31, 1998, is not only perfectly healthy, but has traveled to Washington, DC, several times to testify before Congress as part of an effort to stop the killing of frozen embryos for stem cell research.[15] Another girl, Marley Jade, born to a Denver couple on June 3, 2016, had been frozen for more than 17 years. Little Marley is perfectly healthy.[16]

Someone may object that adopting such an embryo and bringing it to birth as a normal child violates our earlier principle that God intends a child to be conceived by and born to a man and woman who are married to each other. But in these cases the child has already been conceived and already exists. Even if the child will not be born to the parents who *conceived it,* that child will be *born to a man and a woman who are married to each other,* and this is a far better result than being destroyed as an embryo.

But should a single or divorced woman be allowed by herself to adopt such a frozen embryo and bring him or her to birth and raise him or her as a child? This is a difficult question, and there is room for Christians to differ on the answer. While some might argue that this should not be permitted because being raised in a single-parent household is much more difficult for children (see below, p. 801), it seems to me that, from the child's perspective, it is still much better to grow up in a single-parent household than to die as a discarded embryo or to exist perpetually as a frozen embryo for decades to come. If the society decides through the political process that it is acceptable for single parents to adopt children once the children are born (and many societies have concluded that it is right),[17] then there seems to be no reason to prohibit a single mother from adopting an unborn child and bringing him or her to birth.

---

[14] Feinberg and Feinberg also agree that adopting these frozen embryos and using them to produce babies is morally right; see *Ethics for a Brave New World,* 430–32.

[15] Marilyn Synek, "A Person Is a Person No Matter How Small (Or Frozen)," *National Right to Life News Today,* Jan. 8, 2015, http://www.nationalrighttolifenews.org/news/2015/01/a-person-is-a-person-no-matter-how-small-or-frozen/#.WGPmqo-cGUk.

[16] Sara McGinnis, "Meet the Baby Girl Who Spent Over 17 Years as a Frozen Embryo," BabyCenter, Oct. 17, 2016, http://blogs.babycenter.com/mom_stories/embryo-adoption-10172016-infertility-snowflakes/.

[17] In the United States, single-parent adoption is legal in all 50 states. Some states have restrictions based on age, sexual orientation, criminal record, and state residency. See "Can Single Parents Adopt a Child?" Considering Adoption, https://consideringadoption.com/adopting/types-of-adoption/can-single-parents-adopt-a-child. It is estimated that 5 percent to 10 percent of all adoptions are done by singles. See "Single Parent Adoption," Adoption Services, http://www.adoptionservices.org/adoption_special/adoption_single.htm. Other countries that permit adoptions by single parents from other countries (with restrictions) are Haiti,

4. Prefertilization Genetic Screening for Genetic Diseases. It is now possible to genetically screen a husband prior to fertilization of a woman's egg in in vitro fertilization or prior to artificial insemination by the husband. Such screening can determine if certain genetically determined diseases will be passed on from the father to the children. Since the male sperm by itself is not yet a human person, I see no moral objection to this procedure in itself, if used to prevent the conception of a child who would likely have a serious genetically transmitted disease (such screening can now test for cystic fibrosis, heart malformation, hemophilia, Huntington's disease, and sexually transmitted diseases such as syphilis, gonorrhea, and chlamydia).[18]

However, the same procedure could also be used not just to prevent diseases, but to allow the parents to choose among various types of perfectly healthy children. For example, prior to fertilization, a couple might decide that they want to have a baby boy, and therefore only use sperm that contain a Y chromosome. Or they might decide that they want to have a baby girl, and therefore decide to use sperm that contain no Y chromosome. Future types of selection might include the possibility of choosing the minimum height to which a child will grow, color of eyes or hair, or even IQ level. Would this be right?

While such genetic screening processes do not involve new human life being put to death (because fertilization has not occurred), I would seriously question the motives of couples who would seek to make such selections. These are not cases of attempting to prevent diseases that are a result of the fall and of sin and death coming into the world, but rather are choices among the wonderful diversity and variety of human persons that would have resulted from God's creation at the beginning, even with no sin or death in the world. Especially regarding the matter of sex selection, does the preference for a boy or a girl reflect some underlying prejudice that girls are better than boys or boys are better than girls? This would be contrary to God's creation of both men and women as wonderful bearers of his image (see chap. 15, p. 390).[19]

D. OTHER MODERN REPRODUCTIVE TECHNOLOGIES ARE MORALLY UNACCEPTABLE

The same three moral principles listed above lead us to conclude that other reproductive technologies are morally unacceptable.

Russia, China, Ethiopia, Guatemala, Vietnam, and Kazakhstan. See "Single Parent International Adoption," Single Parent Center, Dec. 16, 2016. http://www.singleparentcenter.net/single-parent-international-adoption/.

[18] "New guidelines for screening of sperm, egg and embryo donors in the UK," British Fertility Society, Jan. 9, 2009, https://britishfertilitysociety.org.uk/press-release/new-guidelines-for-screening-of-sperm-egg-and-embryo-donors-in-the-uk/#sthash.sBcCn5RJ.dpuf.

[19] See Paige Comstock Cunningham, "Baby-Making Pt. 2: The Fractured Fulfillment of Huxley's Brave New World," The Center for Bioethics & Human Dignity, Feb. 10, 2012, https://cbhd.org/content/baby-making-pt-2the-fractured-fulfillment-huxleys-brave-new-world. Cunningham sees parallels between the eugenics movement of the early 20th century and the recent increase in genetic screening for sex selection or other characteristics as parents seek to have "perfect" babies.

1. In Vitro Fertilization with Selective Reduction. In many uses of in vitro fertilization, numerous eggs are fertilized, then the doctor chooses the one or possibly two embryos that look most likely to survive. The doctor implants those embryos in the woman's womb and then destroys the others. But this is the destruction of human life, and should not be considered morally acceptable.

This process is often accompanied by preimplantation genetic diagnosis (PGD).[20] This is the most commonly used genetic screening for disease in the embryo, and is done around five to seven days after fertilization. One cell (or sometimes two) is removed from the embryo "conceived" by in vitro fertilization prior to implanting the embryo into the mother. Since this cell is like all others in the child's body, it contains the entire genetic complement of that individual, a combination of both the mother's and father's genomes (one of each gene from each parent).

Just as any living person (child or adult) can be genetically tested using a cell from that person (typically done through a swab from the mouth, collecting saliva that contains cells), so this cell from the embryo can be tested prior to the embryo's implantation in the mother's womb (thus the name of the procedure). Therefore, a decision can be made whether or not to implant the embryo based on its genetic makeup.

But this procedure leads to the destruction of the embryos that are not implanted, which is the destruction of human life, and therefore not morally acceptable. In addition, this procedure can easily be adapted to promote a form of eugenics, the belief that only those who are "desirable" should be allowed to live. Similarities to the theories of the American eugenics movement of the early twentieth century cause serious concern.

Similar to in vitro fertilization with selective reduction is IVF with multifetal pregnancy reduction. In this case, several fertilized eggs are implanted in a woman's womb, and after a certain period of time, the one or two unborn children that look the strongest and healthiest are allowed to survive, while the others are destroyed. This too is a form of abortion, and is not morally acceptable.

2. Artificial Insemination by Donor (AID). Artificial insemination with the sperm of a man who is not the husband is called artificial insemination by donor (abbreviated AID). While some ethicists believe this is morally acceptable in certain cases,[21] it does not seem so to me. It oversteps the boundaries of the pattern of laws that God established in Scripture, which always sought to guarantee that a child would be conceived by and born to a man and a woman who are married to each other (see discussion above, p. 765). But in this case the child is conceived by a man and a woman who are not married to each other. While people might differ as to whether this technically constitutes adultery, it certainly is a transgression of the normal means by which God planned for children to be conceived and born.

---

[20] I am grateful to Dr. Jacque Chadwick for her initial draft of these two paragraphs, and for helpful counsel at several other points in this entire chapter.

[21] See Feinberg and Feinberg, *Ethics for a Brave New World*, 405–6.

In addition, there are some possible emotional complexities that, while not providing a direct scriptural argument against AID, still alert us to the danger of introducing significant stress into a marriage. If a woman receives artificial insemination from a man who is not her husband, she will go through the intensely personal and life-changing experience of carrying a child through pregnancy to birth without the deep satisfaction of knowing that the child inside her was conceived with her husband. It is not unreasonable to think that the mother will wonder what kind of man the (perhaps anonymous) sperm donor is, and if she ever might be able to meet him. Such emotional complexities will not be healthy for the marriage relationship. (I do not claim that such emotional temptations prove that this arrangement is morally unacceptable, but I simply mention here that AID can put more strain than is expected on a marriage relationship.)

The use of AID by a woman who has no husband is clearly morally unacceptable. This would include a single woman being impregnated from a sperm bank, thus violating God's intent that children should be conceived by and born to a man and a woman who are married to each other. The moral laws that God gave in Scripture were designed to prevent unmarried women from conceiving children with men to whom they were not married, and thereby intentionally bearing children who would not have fathers to help raise them.[22]

Similarly, the use of AID by a woman in a lesbian relationship in order to bear a child is a violation of the principle that a child should be conceived by and born to a man and a woman who are married to each other, not two women who are living together (see chap. 33 for a discussion of homosexuality).

3. Surrogate Motherhood. Sometimes a married woman who is physically unable to carry and bear children herself will reach an agreement with another woman, who agrees to be impregnated with the original couple's embryo and carry the child to term. This could involve in vitro fertilization, using both the egg and the sperm of the married couple, or it could involve artificial insemination by donor, using the husband's sperm but the surrogate mother's egg.

This arrangement also seems to me to violate God's intention that children should be conceived by and born to a man and a woman who are married to each other. In this case the child would not be born to the woman who is part of the married couple, but to the surrogate mother.[23]

---

[22] This is a different situation from a single man or woman adopting a child who has already been born or even adopting a frozen embryo; see above, p. 771.

[23] Feinberg and Feinberg think that surrogate motherhood involving in vitro fertilization using the original couple's sperm and egg is morally acceptable in certain limited situations; see *Ethics for a Brave New World*, 442–43. They raise a very interesting but highly unusual possibility—early in a pregnancy the mother unexpectedly dies, and a friend or relative is willing to carry the baby to term so that the baby does not also die. They say that in such a case, "We think surrogacy would be moral" (443). I agree with them in this highly unusual case, for it would be similar to the case of adopting a frozen embryo, which I discussed above. But this does not provide an argument for the legitimacy of surrogacy in other situations, for in this highly

In addition, the likely emotional components of this arrangement must be given serious consideration. It is likely that the personal intimacy involved in carrying and bearing a child will be so deep that the process of surrogate motherhood runs the danger of putting a nearly intolerable strain on the marriage. The husband and wife are including a third person into their marriage relationship, at least in some senses. The husband may find himself with an increasing emotional attachment to the woman who is bearing his child. The surrogate mother will likely feel a similar emotional attachment to the man whose child she is bearing. And the deep bond that inevitably develops between a woman and the child she bears will be disrupted and broken only with much heartache, and possibly even legal battles.

The most famous surrogacy case was perhaps the battle over "Baby M" in the mid-1980s. A surrogate (Mary Beth Whitehead) agreed to carry a child for Elizabeth and William Stern, using her own egg and artificial insemination with his sperm. But she then reneged on the agreement to give the Sterns the child. The New Jersey Supreme Court ruled that a mother could not be forced to surrender her child, and in 1988 declared Ms. Whitehead the legal mother. Because of that precedent, almost all surrogacy agreements are now gestational—using not the egg of the surrogate mother but the egg of the intended mother, or an anonymous egg from a donor.[24]

In 2012, the New Jersey Supreme Court tackled another surrogacy case in which a husband and wife obtained an egg from an anonymous donor and made an agreement with a surrogate mother to carry it for them. They had the surrogate renounce all legal rights to the child and had a judge preemptively put their names on the birth certificate. A hospital worker questioned this arrangement—a child born to one woman, but intended for another—and called the state bureau of vital statistics. The bureau called the attorney general's office, which sued to overturn the judge's order about the birth certificate. A lower court agreed with the attorney general and stripped the mother's name from the birth certificate. The New Jersey Supreme Court deadlocked on the issue. The court's split basically left the child legally motherless.[25]

There is one event in Scripture that bears several similarities to the modern practice of surrogate motherhood: Abram (later Abraham) conceived a child with Hagar, the Egyptian maidservant of his wife, Sarai (later Sarah). Almost immediately it led to marital conflict, and much strife followed:

> Now Sarai, Abram's wife, had borne him no children. She had a female Egyptian servant whose name was Hagar. And Sarai said to Abram, "Behold now, the LORD has prevented me from bearing children. *Go in to my servant; it may*

---

unusual case there was no intention to involve surrogate motherhood at the time of the initial conception of the child.

[24] Kate Zernike, "Court's Split Decision Provides Little Clarity on Surrogacy," *The New York Times*, Oct. 24, 2012, http://www.nytimes.com/2012/10/25/nyregion/in-surrogacy-case-nj-supreme-court-is-deadlocked-over-whom-to-call-mom.html.

[25] Ibid.

be that I shall obtain children by her." And Abram listened to the voice of Sarai. So, after Abram had lived ten years in the land of Canaan, Sarai, Abram's wife, took Hagar the Egyptian, her servant, and gave her to Abram her husband as a wife. *And he went in to Hagar, and she conceived.* And when she saw that she had conceived, she looked with contempt on her mistress. And Sarai said to Abram, "May the wrong done to me be on you! I gave my servant to your embrace, and when she saw that she had conceived, she looked on me with contempt. May the LORD judge between you and me!" (Gen. 16:1–5)

This case is not exactly like modern surrogate motherhood, for sexual intercourse was involved, and the child was born only from Abram's sperm, not from Abram's sperm and Sarai's egg. But deep interpersonal tension and conflict is evident from this narrative. A perceptive interpreter of Scripture will observe this resultant conflict (and the conflict that lasts even to this day between the Jewish people, who are descended from Abram and Sarai, and the Arab people, who are descended from Abram and Hagar) and rightly conclude that in this text God intends to warn us that such a means of bringing children into the world is likely to lead to much trouble.

Infertility is a cause of deep sorrow, distress, and grief for many couples, and we must recognize that and show understanding and compassion for those who experience this grief. But this deep grief should not be counted as a valid reason to overstep the moral boundaries that God has set in his Word concerning the conception and bearing of children.

4. Cloning. It is not currently possible for infertile couples to gain a child by cloning. But should this ever become possible, would it be morally acceptable?

Modern scientific advances have now made it possible to clone plants. For instance, a wood-products company can plant an entire field with cloned trees, so that every tree has the same shape of branches in the same place on the tree, and every tree grows to an identical height.[26] Cloning has also been used to preserve vanishing varieties of trees.[27] I see no moral objection to this process, and it can make agricultural land more productive and result in better quality crops (or trees). This seems to me to be a legitimate part of subduing the earth, according to Genesis 1:28.

Another possibility is the cloning not of plants but of animals. According to the National Human Genome Research Institute, the following animals have been cloned:

[26] According to the Department of Primary Industries and Resources of South Australia, a clone is one of a group of offspring that are identical. Each individual has the same genes as the original plant from which the clone was made. Clones can be created using cuttings, but more commonly it is done in a laboratory using tissue culture. The original seed embryo can yield up to 100,000 plantlets. The advantage of growing forests from clones is that the trees will be more uniform in height and diameter, with the same wood properties. See "How Pine Forests are Managed," http://www.pir.sa.gov.au/__data/assets/pdf_file/0005/79835/Forestry _Matters_-_Fact_sheet_-_How_pine_forests_are_managed.pdf.

[27] Denisa R. Superville, "Historic trees get a second shot at life with cloning efforts," Phys.org, June 6, 2013, http://phys.org/news/2013-06-historic-trees-shot-life-cloning.html.

cow, sheep, cat, deer, dog, horse, mule, ox, rabbit, and rat. A rhesus monkey has been cloned by embryo splitting.[28]

I am uncertain how we should evaluate the cloning of animals from a moral standpoint. It might be possible to make a distinction between higher forms of animals, such as mammals (perhaps those that appeared to have "the breath of life" in them, see Gen. 1:30), and lower, less complex animals. Higher forms of animals (such as dogs, cats, horses, and chimpanzees) often seem to have something akin to a human personality, and it is common for domestic animals to develop a genuine kind of friendship with their human companions. It remains to be seen whether higher forms of animal life can actually be cloned successfully, so that they survive more than a short period of time. The first cloned animal, a sheep named Dolly, was born in 1996. Dolly died prematurely at the age of six from joint and lung problems associated with old age. However, four clones from her same line have turned nine and are doing just fine.[29] Two years after Dolly was born, researchers in Japan cloned eight calves from a single cow, but only four survived.[30]

But regarding the cloning of human beings, I think Christians should have significant moral objections. Scientists might think that they can create the *exact duplicate* of a world champion athlete or a scientist with an incredibly high IQ, but it will simply not be the same person in any case. All of the life circumstances and experiences that a person goes through from childhood to adulthood could never be the same. Sometimes people become stronger by overcoming hardships, but would people want cloned duplicates of themselves to experience such hardships?

In addition, the process of producing a human being from cloning (if it could ever be done) is significantly different from God's intention that the wonderful diversity and variety of the human race be protected with children being born from a mixture of genetic information from both the father and the mother. This does not happen in cloning. God, in his wisdom, makes us all different as individuals, not as clones of one another, and in this way protects the uniqueness and value of each human being.

Moreover, there is a significant question as to whether a cloned human being, even if *physically* and *genetically* identical to the person from whose cells the cloning originated, would really be a human person at all. How would we know if this person even had a soul? Would God be forced by the cloning process to impart a human soul to someone who just happened to have a physical human body?

Scripture repeatedly speaks of our soul (or spirit) as something distinct from our physical bodies. When Rachel died, "*her soul was departing* (for she was dying)" (Gen. 35:18), and when Elijah prayed for a dead child to come back to life, he prayed that the

---

[28] "Cloning," National Human Genome Research Institute, https://www.genome.gov/25020028/#al-7.

[29] Rachel Feltman, "Dolly the Sheep Died Young—But Her Clones Seem Perfectly Healthy As They Turn 9," *The Washington Post*, July 26, 2016, https://www.washingtonpost.com/news/speaking-of-science/wp/2016/07/26/dolly-the-sheep-died-young-but-her-clones-seem-perfectly-healthy-as-they-turn-9/.

[30] "Cloning."

child's "soul" would come into him again (1 Kings 17:21 RSV, KJV, NKJV[31]). Elsewhere the Old Testament speaks of death as a time when "the *spirit* returns to God who gave it" (Eccles. 12:7; see also Luke 23:46; John 19:30; Acts 7:59). And Scripture warns us that the origin of the connection between a person's body and spirit is mysterious, something that God does not reveal to us: "As you do not know the way the spirit comes to the bones in the womb of a woman with child, so you do not know the work of God who makes everything" (Eccles. 11:5).

But if our modern society begins to create physical human bodies without the sanction or blessing of God himself in the process, what will we in fact be creating? Could a human being without a soul even live at all? Or if so, would it have any conscience, any sense of right and wrong? These are deeply troubling questions.

Finally, the process of producing a cloned human being, even if it is possible, would once again violate the principle that God intends children to be conceived by and born to a man and woman who are married to each other, for a person who is cloned from one specific human being another would not be created from a father and a mother who are married to each other. I conclude that cloning of human beings is morally unacceptable.

E. ADOPTION

Adoption is often a wonderful option for childless couples, if it is their desire to be parents and something they believe God is calling them to do. Adoption is also a wonderful reflection of God's own actions in adopting us to be his children (see John 1:12; Rom. 8:14–17; Gal. 4:5; Eph. 1:5).[32] And adoption is a very practical way to care for "orphans," which is something that James says is part of "religion that is pure and undefiled before God the Father" (James 1:27). For these reasons, not only many childless couples but also many Christian couples who already have some naturally born children have decided that God is calling them to adopt one or more additional children. Russell Moore's 2009 book *Adopted for Life*[33] has had wide influence in promoting adoption among evangelical families.

Because Scripture views adoption in such a positive way, and because the adoption process is often difficult and expensive, some churches have established or work closely with programs that will provide financial, legal, and other support to couples as they go through the adoption process. For example, Bethlehem Baptist Church in Minneapolis partners with the "LYDIA Fund," which provides financial help for qualified Christian

---

[31] Several translations render the Hebrew word *nephesh* as "life" in this verse (see ESV, NIV, NASB). The word can mean either "soul" or "life," depending on context (HALOT, 1.712–13; BDB, 659).

[32] See Wayne Grudem, *Systematic Theology: An Introduction to Biblical Doctrine* (Leicester, UK: InterVarsity, and Grand Rapids, MI: Zondervan, 1994), 736–45.

[33] Russell D. Moore, *Adopted for Life: The Priority of Adoption of Christian Families and Churches* (Wheaton, IL: Crossway, 2009).

parents to adopt children from orphanages around the world.[34] Focus on the Family offers a number of resources to help parents seeking to adopt children.[35] And Bethany Christian Services is another organization that provides a wide range of assistance to couples seeking to adopt,[36] as do numerous other state and local adoption ministries.

QUESTIONS FOR PERSONAL APPLICATION

1. If you are unable to have children because of some kind of infertility, how fully would you say you are trusting God to bring good out of this situation, in the sense of Romans 8:28? To what extent has God given your heart peace about this matter?
2. Considering the various kinds of modern reproductive technology discussed in this chapter, which of them would you be comfortable using in your own marriage if you faced a situation of infertility? Which of them would you not think appropriate for you, or not morally acceptable?
3. What do you think about the idea of embryo adoption? Do you think churches should promote this idea more actively?
4. Do you think it would be morally right for scientists to attempt to clone a human being? Do you think there should be laws prohibiting this?
5. Do you know friends or relatives who have adopted one or more children? Would you say their overall experience has been positive or negative? If it has been a positive experience, what factors contributed to this?
6. What character traits (see p. 110) are especially important in considering the questions of infertility, modern reproductive technologies, and adoption?

SPECIAL TERMS

artificial insemination by donor (AID)
artificial insemination by husband (AIH)
cloning
cryopreservation
embryo adoption
infertility
in vitro fertilization
prefertilization genetic screening
snowflake children
surrogate motherhood

[34] See https://bethlehem.church/adoption/.
[35] See http://www.focusonthefamily.com/parenting/adoptive-families/.
[36] See https://www.bethany.org/adoption.

BIBLIOGRAPHY

Sections in Other Ethics Texts

(see complete bibliographical data, p. 64)

Clark and Rakestraw, 2:57–94
Davis, 59–89
Feinberg, John and Paul, 387–459
Frame, 787–95
Geisler, 180–98
Gushee and Stassen, 428–31
Kaiser, 151–62
McQuilkin and Copan, 396–99
Rae, 155–81

Other Works

Batura, Paul J., Eric Metaxas, and Larry King. *Chosen for Greatness: How Adoption Changes the World*. Washington, DC: Regnery Faith, 2016.

Best, Megan. *Fearfully and Wonderfully Made: Ethics and the Beginning of Human Life*. Kingsford, NSW, Australia: Matthias Media, 2012.

Brinton, Sara, and Amanda Bennett. *In Defense of the Fatherless: Redeeming International Adoption & Orphan Care*. Fearn, Ross-shire, Scotland: Christian Focus, 2015.

Cook, E. David. "Reproductive Technologies." In *Dictionary of Scripture and Ethics*, edited by Joel B. Green, 669–71. Grand Rapids, MI: Baker, 2011.

Fletcher, D. B. "Reproductive Technologies." In *New Dictionary of Christian Ethics and Pastoral Theology*, edited by David J. Atkinson and David H. Field, 733–34. Leicester, UK: Inter-Varsity, and Downers Grove, IL: InterVarsity Press, 1995.

Hui, Edwin C. *At the Beginning of Life: Dilemmas in Theological Bioethics*. Downers Grove, IL: InterVarsity Press, 2002.

Kilner, John F. *Dignity and Destiny: Humanity in the Image of God*. Grand Rapids, MI: Eerdmans, 2015.

———, ed. *Why the Church Needs Bioethics: A Guide to Wise Engagement with Life's Challenges*. Grand Rapids, MI: Zondervan, 2011.

Kilner, John Frederic, and C. Ben Mitchell. *Does God Need Our Help? Cloning, Assisted Suicide, and Other Challenges in Bioethics*. Vital Questions. Wheaton, IL: Tyndale, 2003.

Meilaender, Gilbert. *Not by Nature but by Grace: Forming Families through Adoption*. Notre Dame, IN: University of Notre Dame Press, 2016.

Mitchell, C. Ben. *Biotechnology and the Human Good*. Washington, DC: Georgetown University Press, 2007.

Mitchell, C. Ben, and D. Joy Riley. *Christian Bioethics: A Guide for Pastors, Health Care Professionals, and Families.* B&H Studies in Christian Ethics. Nashville: B&H Academic, 2014.

Moore, Russell D. *Adopted for Life: The Priority of Adoption for Christian Families and Churches.* Wheaton, IL: Crossway, 2009.

———. *Adoption: What Joseph of Nazareth Can Teach Us about This Countercultural Choice.* Wheaton, IL: Crossway, 2015.

Moore, Russell, Andrew T. Walker, and Randy Stinson. *The Gospel & Adoption.* Nashville: B&H Publishing, 2017.

Rae, Scott B. *Brave New Families: Biblical Ethics and Reproductive Technologies.* Grand Rapids, MI: Baker, 1996.

———. *Outside the Womb: Moral Guidance for Assisted Reproduction.* Chicago: Moody, 2011.

VanDrunen, David. *Bioethics and the Christian Life: A Guide to Making Difficult Decisions.* Wheaton, IL: Crossway, 2009.

SCRIPTURE MEMORY PASSAGE

1 Peter 1:6–7: In this you rejoice, though now for a little while, if necessary, you have been grieved by various trials, so that the tested genuineness of your faith—more precious than gold that perishes though it is tested by fire—may be found to result in praise and glory and honor at the revelation of Jesus Christ.

HYMN

"It Is Well with My Soul"

When peace, like a river, attendeth my way,
When sorrows like sea billows roll
Whatever my lot, Thou hast taught me to say,
"It is well, it is well with my soul."

Refrain:
It is well
With my soul,
It is well, it is well
With my soul.

Tho Satan should buffet, tho trials should come,
Let this blest assurance control,
That Christ hath regarded my helpless estate,
And hath shed His own blood for my soul.

My sin—O the bliss of this glorious tho't
My sin, not in part, but the whole,
Is nailed to the cross, and I bear it no more:
Praise the Lord, praise the Lord, O my soul!

And, Lord, haste the day when my faith shall be sight,
The clouds be rolled back as a scroll:
The trump shall resound and the Lord shall descend,
"Even so" it is well with my soul.

HORATIO G. SPAFFORD, 1828–1888

Chapter 31

PORNOGRAPHY

Why is viewing pornography wrong?
What are the harmful results?

A. BIBLICAL TEACHING

The issue of pornography must be analyzed within the broader framework of the Bible's teaching on marriage, as discussed in chapter 28. God protects the sanctity of marriage through the seventh commandment, "You shall not commit adultery" (Ex. 20:14), and through other biblical teachings related to that commandment. This commandment clearly and directly prohibits a *married person* from having sex with anyone other than his or her own husband or wife.

As I further explained in chapter 28, the moral teachings of the Bible also prohibit sex between *unmarried people*. This is clear not only from the laws of Moses that penalized such conduct (see Ex. 22:16–17; Deut. 22:13–21), but also from the teachings of Jesus, who pointed out sin in the life of the woman at the well in Samaria by saying to her, "You have had five husbands, and the one you now have is not your husband" (John 4:18; Jesus implies that it is wrong for her to live with a man outside of marriage). Other verses that translate the Greek word *porneia* as "sexual immorality" (such as Matt. 15:19; Gal. 5:19; Eph. 5:3) also show that sexual intercourse outside of marriage is sin (see the discussion in chap. 28, p. 712).

The Bible also talks about our desires. The consistent teaching of Scripture is that God is concerned not merely with human *actions*, but also with the attitudes of our hearts (see p. 138). That is clear from the last of the Ten Commandments:

> You shall not covet your neighbor's house; *you shall not covet your neighbor's wife*, or his male servant, or his female servant, or his ox, or his donkey, or anything that is your neighbor's. (Ex. 20:17)

The command not to "covet" means not to have a desire to take what belongs to someone else as your own. The command not to covet "your neighbor's wife" therefore is a command not to *desire* to have her as your own or to have intercourse with her. This is made explicit, for example, in Proverbs 6:25, referring to an adulteress: "Do not desire her beauty in your heart."

Jesus brought out the intent of these Old Testament laws of sexual purity in his teaching in the Sermon on the Mount:

> You have heard that it was said, "You shall not commit adultery." But I say to you that everyone who looks at a woman with lustful intent has already committed adultery with her in his heart. (Matt. 5:27–28)

The conclusion from these passages is that God's moral standards require that people avoid longing for sexual intercourse with someone apart from being married to that person (a relationship in which the Bible views sexual attraction and intimacy as a wholesome and wonderful gift from God).

With regard to pornography, the question is whether it is wrong to look at pictures or read written materials that arouse sexual desires that are contrary to God's moral standards, or, to put the question in terms of the words of Jesus, whether it is wrong to look at a *picture* of a woman "with lustful intent" (Matt. 5:28).[1]

In fact, one of the prophets in the Old Testament shows an example of the relationship between looking at visual images and lusting after what one sees, and then committing sinful actions. Speaking of the city of Jerusalem in a parable of a woman called Oholibah, Ezekiel says the following:

> But she carried her whoring further. She *saw* men portrayed on the wall, the images of the Chaldeans portrayed in vermilion, wearing belts on their waists, with flowing turbans on their heads, all of them having the appearance of officers, a likeness of Babylonians whose native land was Chaldea. When she saw them, she *lusted* after them and *sent* messengers to them in Chaldea. And the Babylonians came to her into the bed of love, and they *defiled* her with their whoring lust. And after she was defiled by them, she turned from them in disgust. (Ezek. 23:14–17)

Here Ezekiel traces a progression of sexual sin. Oholibah saw, then she lusted, then she sent for those who were pictured, and finally she committed adultery with them.

Other passages from the Old Testament encourage a general habit of purity regarding what we look at with our eyes:

---

[1] The Greek text translated as "with lustful intent" is *pros to epithymēsai autēn*, where the construction *pros* + infinitive indicates the purpose of looking, giving the sense "everyone who looks at a woman *for the purpose of lusting after her*." Jesus thus addresses the purposes in a man's heart.

> I will walk with integrity of heart
>> within my house;
> *I will not set before my eyes*
>> *anything that is worthless.* (Ps. 101:2–3)[2]

When Job protested his innocence before God, one of his claims was that he had guarded his eyes so as not to look at a young woman in a way that was displeasing to God:

> I have made a covenant with my eyes;
>> *how then could I gaze at a virgin?*
> What would be my portion from God above
>> and my heritage from the Almighty on high? (Job 31:1–2)

The moral question about pornography, then, is whether it is right to create, to distribute, to acquire, and to view photographs and videos (or to read or listen to written and audio material) *for the primary purpose of arousing in a person sexual desires that are contrary to God's moral standards,* that is, sexual desires for someone other than the person's spouse. Once the question is phrased in this way, it should be evident that creating and using pornography is itself morally wrong, because *the purpose of creating and using pornography* is to arouse sinful desires in a person's mind and heart, desires that are displeasing to God. Such actions cannot be considered morally acceptable.

B. THE HARMFUL EFFECTS OF PORNOGRAPHY

1. Spiritual Harm. There is certainly spiritual harm that comes from viewing pornography, because the lustful desires it arouses are considered by Jesus to be adultery in a person's heart (Matt. 5:28). And the awareness of this sin will bring a sense of distance from God: "If I had cherished iniquity in my heart, the LORD would not have listened" (Ps. 66:18).

The apostle John recognizes that a guilty conscience will be a hindrance to our prayers:

> Beloved, *if our heart does not condemn us, we have confidence before God*; and whatever we ask we receive from him, because we keep his commandments and do what pleases him. (1 John 3:21–22)

Certainly we should ask God for forgiveness whenever we sin (see 1 John 1:9), but damage has still been done to our spiritual lives. This is why Peter counsels Christians "to abstain from the passions of the flesh, which *wage war* against your soul" (1 Pet. 2:11;

---

[2] "Worthless" here translates the Hebrew word *beliyya'al,* "uselessness, wickedness" (HALOT, 133–34).

the warfare imagery implies that our souls can be damaged if we allow ourselves to be immersed in sinful "passions").

In addition, pornography is spiritually deceptive because its initial attractiveness will never satisfy and will never lead to the deep spiritual joy and happiness that can only come in close fellowship with God himself. David spoke of this joy when he wrote, "In your presence there is fullness of joy; at your right hand are pleasures forevermore" (Ps. 16:11). Because pornography can never provide deep, lasting joy, it can snare and entrap people into pursuing more and more vile materials, until it destroys their lives (see sect. 4 below on the possibility of addiction).

2. Harm to Marriages and Other Relationships. Another significant impact of pornography is that it attracts a person's affections and desires away from his or her spouse and in a direction outside of one's marriage. A man who uses pornography is robbing his wife of emotional affection that should be hers. He is turning his heart away from her and from desiring her affection. This will hinder his sexual relationship within marriage and will create harmful memories that will last for a long time, probably interfering with his marriage for several years to come. (Although it is less common for women to view pornography, if they do, similar destructive results can be expected.)

When a man uses pornography, his wife (or girlfriend, or other women acquainted with him) will often have an instinctive sense of some impurity or moral uncleanness in the man even if she does not discover any facts about what he is doing.

Beyond this instinctive sense, she might observe a change in his behavioral patterns. His interest in sex with his wife might decline because of his pornography use.[3] Expressions of anger when asked about pornography usage are another sign that he is using it.[4] Other factors that often provide a wife with clues that may indicate that her husband is using pornography include emotional distance, increased secrecy, excessive Internet use, antisocial behavior, and increased criticism of his wife's appearance.[5] Not surprisingly, a recent study by the American Sociological Association found that once one spouse begins to use pornography, the chance that the marriage will end in divorce increases.[6]

3. Distorted Views of and Attitudes toward Sex. An abundance of evidence from sociological studies also shows the harmful effects of pornography on those who view it and

---

[3] Juli Slattery, "The Impact of Pornography on Marital Sex," Focus on the Family, http://www.focuson thefamily.com/marriage/sex-and-intimacy/when-your-husband-isnt-interested-in-sex/the-impact-of -pornography-on-marital-sex.

[4] "Spouse May Be Involved with Pornography," Focus on the Family, http://family.custhelp.com/app /answers/detail/a_id/25856/~/i-suspect-that-my-spouse-is-viewing-pornography.-what-should-i-do%3F.

[5] Matt Fradd, "10 Signs of Porn Addiction: Do These Describe Your Husband?" Covenant Eyes, Aug. 21, 2015, http://www.covenanteyes.com/2015/08/21/10-signs-of-porn-addiction-do-these-describe-your -husband/#.

[6] "Beginning pornography use associated with increase in probability of divorce," *Science Daily*, Aug. 22, 2016, https://www.sciencedaily.com/releases/2016/08/160822083354.htm. See also http://www.asanet.org /sites/default/files/pr_am_2016_perry_news_release_final.pdf.

then on those who are subsequently harmed by these people. The harmful results may be summarized in the following points taken from an extensively documented research paper by psychologist Patrick Fagan of the Marriage and Religion Research Institute, a project of the Family Research Council:

> Pornography hurts adults, children, couples, families, and society. Among adolescents, pornography hinders the development of a healthy sexuality, and among adults, it distorts sexual attitudes and social realities. In families, pornography use leads to marital dissatisfaction, infidelity, separation, and divorce. Society at large is not immune to the effect of pornography. Child sex-offenders, for example, are often involved not only in the viewing, but also in the distribution, of pornography.[7]

Pornography greatly impacts teens' perception of sex. The report states:

> Pornography viewing among teenagers disorients them during that developmental phase when they have to learn how to handle their sexuality and when they are most vulnerable to uncertainty about their sexual beliefs and moral values. A study of 2,343 adolescents found that sexually explicit Internet material significantly increased their uncertainties about sexuality. The study also showed that increased exposure to sexually explicit Internet material increased favorable attitudes toward sexual exploration with others outside of marriage and decreased marital commitment to the other spouse. Another study by Todd G. Morrison, professor of psychology at the University of Saskatchewan, and colleagues found that adolescents exposed to high levels of pornography had lower levels of sexual self-esteem. A significant relationship also exists between frequent pornography use and feelings of loneliness, including major depression. Finally, viewing pornography can engender feelings of shame: In a study of high school students, the majority of those who had viewed pornography felt some degree of shame for viewing it. However, 36 percent of males and 26 percent of females said they were never ashamed of viewing pornography, giving some idea of the level of desensitization already reached in society.
>
> High adolescent consumption of pornography also affects behavior. Male pornography use is linked to significantly increased sexual intercourse with nonromantic friends, and is likely a correlate of the so-called "hook-up" culture. Exposure to pornographic sexual content can be a significant factor in teenage pregnancy. A three year longitudinal study of teenagers found that frequent exposure to televised sexual content was related to a substantially

---

[7] Patrick F. Fagan, "The Effects of Pornography in Individuals, Marriages, Families, and Communities," https://www.scribd.com/document/23477007/The-Effects-of-Pornography, 3. Fagan is senior fellow at and director of the Center for Marriage and Religion Research at the Family Research Council, Washington, DC.

greater likelihood of teenage pregnancy within the succeeding three years. This same study also found that the likelihood of teenage pregnancy was two times greater when the quantity of that sexual content exposure, within the viewing episodes, was high rather than low. . . .

Pornography leads to distorted perceptions of social reality: an exaggerated perception of the level of sexual activity in the general population, an inflated estimate "of the incidence of premarital and extramarital sexual activity, as well as increased assessment of male and female promiscuity," "an overestimation of almost all sexual activities performed by sexually active adults," and an overestimation of the general prevalence of perversions such as group sex, bestiality, and sadomasochistic activity. Thus the beliefs being formed in the mind of the viewer of pornography are far removed from reality. A case could be made that repeated viewing of pornography induces a mental illness in matters sexual. These distortions result in an acceptance of three beliefs: (1) sexual relationships are recreational in nature, (2) men are generally sexually driven, and (3) women are sex objects or commodities.[8]

4. The Significant Possibility of Addiction. Fagan's report goes on to deal with the issue of pornography and addiction. He writes:

Pornography and "cybersex" are highly addictive and can lead to sexually compulsive behaviors (that decrease a person's capacity to perform other major tasks in life). Over 90 percent of therapists surveyed in one study believed that a person could become addicted to "cybersex." In an American survey, 57 percent of frequent viewers used online sexual activity to deal with stress. A 2006 Swedish study of regular Internet pornography users found that about six percent were compulsive users and that these compulsives also used much more non-Internet pornography as well. Addictive pornography use leads to lower self-esteem and a weakened ability to carry out a meaningful social and work life. A survey of pornography addicts found that they disliked the "out of control" feeling and the time consumption that their pornography use engendered. All of the sexual compulsives reported they had felt distressed and experienced impairment in an important aspect of their lives as a result of their addiction. Almost half of the sexual compulsives said their behavior had significant negative results in their social lives, and a quarter reported negative effects on their job. In another survey, sexual compulsives and sexual addicts were 23 times more likely than those without a problem to state that discovering online sexual material was the worst thing that had ever happened in their life. No wonder then that severe clinical

[8] Ibid., 5–6, 12–13. Phrases within quotation marks in this paragraph are quotations from other academic studies that are documented in footnotes in Fagan's paper.

depression was reported twice as frequently among Internet pornography users compared to non-users.[9]

In fact, Victor Cline, an expert on sexual addiction, found that there is a four-step progression among many who consume pornography:

1. *Addiction*: Pornography provides a powerful sexual stimulant or aphrodisiac effect, followed by sexual release, most often through masturbation.
2. *Escalation*: Over time addicts require more explicit and deviant material to meet their sexual "needs."
3. *Desensitization*: What was first perceived as gross, shocking and disturbing in time becomes common and acceptable.
4. *Acting out sexually*: There is an increasing tendency to act out behaviors viewed in pornography.[10]

One study found that more than 30 million Americans are thought to suffer from a sexual addiction in the United States,[11] which, given the current U.S. population of around 326,000,000, would mean approximately 9.2 percent of all Americans have some form of sexual addiction—a spiritual and moral cancer that is relentlesssly working to destroy the nation.

5. Harm to Communities. Land-use studies by the National Law Center for Children and Families show evidence of a correlation between "adult businesses" (pornography shops) and crime.[12] For example, "in Phoenix neighborhoods where adult businesses were located, the number of sex offenses was 506 percent greater than in areas without such businesses. The number of property crimes was 43 percent greater, and the number of violent crimes, 4 percent greater."[13]

Mary Anne Layden, director of education for the University of Pennsylvania Health System, points out, "I have been treating sexual violence victims and perpetrators for 13 years. I have not treated a single case of sexual violence that did not involve pornography."[14]

---

[9] Ibid., 16.

[10] Victor B. Cline, "Pornography's Effects on Adults and Children," https://www.scribd.com/doc/20282510/Dr-Victor-Cline-Pornography-s-Effects-on-Adults-and-Children, 3–5.

[11] Roxanne Dryden-Edwards, "Sexual Addiction," Medicine Net, http://www.medicinenet.com/sexual_addiction/article.htm#sexual_addiction_facts.

[12] For more information, go to http://www.nationallawcenter.org/. This organization provides training seminars to equip and train prosecutors, investigators, and law-enforcement officers to stop sexual predators. It also helps provide technology to assist communities in dealing with issues involving adult businesses and criminal activity.

[13] "Library Protection Plan: A Guide to Help Concerned Citizens Persuade Public Libraries to Protect Children from Internet Pornography," National Coalition for the Protection of Children and Families, 7, http://www.plan2succeed.org/library_protection.pdf.

[14] Ibid. Also available at Haven Bradford Gow, "Child Sex Abuse: America's Dirty Secret," MS Voices for Children, March 2000, cited in "A Guide to What One Person Can Do About Pornography," American Family Association, 10, http://www.macbma.net/uploads/6/5/7/9/657914/what_can_one_person_do.pdf.

6. Child Pornography. Finally, with regard to child pornography, its production is illegal. Material digitally doctored to look like child pornography was also illegal, until a Supreme Court decision in April 2002 found the "virtual" child-porn law unconstitutional.[15] The amount of harm inflicted on victims of child pornography is tragic. Cline writes:

> It is mainly pedophiles who create true child pornography using children. And they do this for their own use as well as to exchange or sell the materials they produce. When this occurs, the children are doubly abused: at the time the films or videos or pictures are made, and then when others observe their victimization in the years to come and get turned on sexually by observing the children being sexually used. Child pornography invariably produces great shame and guilt in the children involved, especially as they get older and more fully comprehend the enormity of their abuse and know that there is a permanent record of their degradation out there, circulating around for people to see—maybe future friends or their own children when grown up.[16]

7. Selfishness Replaces Love. Alan Sears, president and CEO of the Alliance Defending Freedom and former director of then-Attorney General Edwin Meese III's Commission on Pornography, adds:

> The sexual union within marriage, between one man and one woman, is meant by the Creator to be an act of supreme love, giving and unity. It's a picture, if you will, of supreme selflessness. Virtually all advocates of secular sexual behavior center on an "it's all about me" philosophy rather than mutual love and care for the other partner. . . . In years of public speaking since that time, I have repeatedly referred to pornography as the "true hate literature" of our age, because of its hatred and exploitation of the human person, regardless of size, shape, color or gender. It reduces human beings to valueless commodities to be ogled at and disposed of like used tissue.[17]

C. OBJECTIONS AND RATIONALIZATIONS

With all kinds of sins, it is possible for people who commit them to minimize or rationalize their behavior, attempting to persuade themselves that what they are doing is not really sin or not really that bad. Some examples of rationalization for the sin of pornography use would include the following:

---

[15] Ashcroft v. Free Speech Coalition, (00–795) 535 U.S. 234 (2002). See https://www.law.cornell.edu/sup ct/html/00-795.ZS.html.

[16] Cline, "Pornography's Effects on Adults and Children," 12.

[17] "Pornography: The Degrading Behemoth (Part 1)," Catholic Online, July 29, 2004, https://www.catholic .org/featured/headline.php?ID=1193.

1. "It's Not a Real Woman, It's Just a Picture." My response is that it is a picture image of a *real woman*. If you are looking at the picture "with lustful intent" (Matt. 5:28), that is, for the purpose of being sexually aroused, then Jesus says you are already committing adultery with that woman in your heart. In addition, modern pornographic images show far more intimate details than Jewish men ever saw in the time of Jesus, when they were looking at women wearing long Middle Eastern robes, and therefore it is likely that the intensity of lustful desire directed at modern pornography is also much greater.

2. "Well, I'm Just Curious; I'm Not Really Lusting." But the question is, are you sexually aroused by what you are looking at? If so, then you are looking "with lustful intent" (Matt. 5:28) and committing adultery in your heart.

3. "The Stuff I Look at Isn't That Bad—It's Just "Soft Porn," Not Hard-Core Stuff." Once again, the question is, if you are honest about what is in your heart, what is your purpose for looking at it? If your purpose is to enjoy the sexual arousal that it gives you, then you are looking "with lustful intent" (Matt. 5:28), and Jesus says this is sin against God.

D. SHOULD GOVERNMENTS MAKE LAWS RESTRICTING PORNOGRAPHY?

The fact that something is morally wrong according to the Bible does not by itself mean that governments should have laws against it. For instance, there are no laws against private drunkenness, laziness, or foolish and wasteful uses of money. To take another example, for the entire history of the United States, either there were *no laws* against fornication (in the sense of private sexual intercourse between consenting unrelated, unmarried adults of the opposite sex) or else those laws were almost *never enforced* (see p. 229, n. 31). Apparently both governmental officials and the people who elect them feel instinctively that such laws would constitute too great an intrusion into the private lives of individuals. For similar reasons, I do not think Christians should advocate laws against *looking at* pornographic material, no matter how a person might obtain it.

But the question of *creating* such material and *distributing* it to others is a different question. In that case a person is creating material that (from a biblical point of view) has a harmful effect on the moral standards of the society, and specifically on the people who use the pornography and those to whom they relate in intimate ways.

Therefore, since pornography makes people more likely to commit violence against women or children, or more likely to commit rape, a strong argument can be made for enacting or maintaining laws against the production, distribution, and sale of pornographic materials.

E. SHOULD PORNOGRAPHERS BE PROSECUTED?

The First Amendment to the United States Constitution, which protects freedom of the press (among other freedoms), was primarily intended to protect *political* speech. This means that not all kinds of speech are protected. Slander, libel, and incitement to riot are not protected, for example, and neither is consumer fraud or mail fraud, and courts have rightly recognized this. The courts have also recognized that the First Amendment cannot rightly be used to claim protection for obscene material. But what is meant by "obscene"?

In the 1957 Supreme Court decision Roth v. United States, the standard established by the court was "whether to the average person, applying contemporary community standards, the dominant theme of the material taken as whole appeals to the prurient interest." (The word *prurient* means "inordinately interested in matters of sex."[18]) Then, in the 1973 case Miller v. California, the Supreme Court decided that a work is not considered obscene unless it "lacks serious literary, artistic, political, and scientific value."[19]

These cases still provide a standard that can be used effectively in prosecutions of pornographers, provided that juries are allowed to give a commonsense meaning to the word *serious*, so that the word is not robbed of its force by misleading jury instructions or undue deference to testimony by so-called "experts" brought in by lawyers defending pornographers.[20] In addition, from a practical standpoint, most of the problems in the country concerning pornography could be addressed if prosecutors would decide to bring charges only against the production and distribution of *visual images* (photographs and videos) and not try to prosecute publications that contain only words, where standards are more blurry and some literary merit is easier to claim.

Former federal prosecutor Alan Sears claims that "obscenity laws, though far from perfect, are more definite than many other criminal laws successfully and regularly used in the criminal justice system."[21] He notes that the Attorney General's Commission on Pornography, for which he served as director, provided a useful definition of pornography as "sexually explicit material designed primarily for arousal."[22]

Sears also says:

> Pornography includes several classes of material: obscenity, material harmful to minors, child pornography, indecency, and lawful but nonetheless pornographic depictions. . . .

[18] *American Heritage Dictionary of the English Language*, 4th ed. (Boston: Houghton Mifflin, 2006), 1413.
[19] Miller v. California, 413 U.S. 15.
[20] See United States v. Kilbride, No. 07–10528, and United States v. Schaeffer, No. 07–10534, United States Court of Appeals for the 9th Circuit (2008).
[21] Alan E. Sears, "The Legal Case for Restricting Pornography," in *Pornography: Research Advances and Policy Considerations*, ed. Dolf Zillman and Jennings Bryant (Hillsdale, NJ: Lawrence Erlbaum Associates, 1989), 327.
[22] "Pornography: The Degrading Behemoth."

Depending on the type of material, its offensiveness ranges from the "merely immoral"—which depicts women and other persons as a subspecies of humans to be used, to be abused and to amuse—to what I have always called "crime scene photographs," actual depictions of unlawful sexual behavior for profit or exploitation.

I call those who produce material that is unlawful part of a "criminal enterprise," not an "industry."

So, pornography is shamefully large in its scope and, depending on how broadly it is defined, it is a multibillion-dollar enterprise. As large and pervasive as it may be, however, it is not too large to be reined in and dramatically limited in any community with the will to do so.[23]

Therefore, the ongoing problem with pornography in the United States is not that laws are inadequate but that prosecutors are not sufficiently willing to bring charges against those who produce and distribute pornography.

One specific example of the lack of prosecution concerns Internet pornography, which has a corrosive effect on society. An *ABA Journal* article on this topic concludes, "The real reason Internet obscenity has not been tackled stems from the fact that law enforcement seems not to have the time, resources or inclination to pursue it."[24]

F. PRACTICAL STEPS TO PROTECT AGAINST PORNOGRAPHY

At the level of the individual family or household, some practical steps can be taken to protect against pornography. For example, people can install filters on their computers that screen out offensive material. Parents can also require that children always use computers in rooms and settings where the computer screen is visible to others in the family.[25] A recently developed plug-in device called the Circle can be used by parents to regulate every computer and every phone in the home with device-specific filters that block various kinds of materials and even regulate the hours that each device can access the Internet.[26]

---

[23] Ibid.

[24] Jason Krause, "The End of the Net Porn Wars," *ABA Journal*, Feb. 1, 2008, www.abajournal.com /magazine/article/the_end_of_the_net_porn_wars.

[25] To take a personal example, my home office is reached by a hallway leading from the kitchen and family room, but I continually leave my door open and work with my back to the door so that my computer screen is instantly visible to Margaret long before I even know that she is standing in the hallway. This provides a helpful kind of constant accountability to her for my computer use. But my greatest sense of accountability is still to the Lord: "The eyes of the LORD are in every place, keeping watch on the evil and the good" (Prov. 15:3).

[26] For a detailed discussion of the Circle, see Tony Reinke, "Walk the Worldwide Garden: Protecting Your Home in the Digital Age," Desiring God, May 14, 2016, https://www.desiringgod.org/articles/walk -the-worldwide-garden. See also Tim Challies, "Ask Me Anything," challies.com, May 28, 2017, https://www .challies.com/feedback/ask-me-anything-7.

Similarly, Christians can promote the use of filters for local library computers that are available for use by children, and can advocate the placement of computers in relatively public spaces. They can also be effective in organizing community pressure to drive out stores that sell a lot of pornography.

Other ways to help rid a community of the spread and influence of pornography can be found at the website of the National Center on Sexual Exploitation: http://endsexualexploitation.org/.

G. FREEDOM FROM PORNOGRAPHY IS POSSIBLE

Finally, many Christian counseling ministries report significant success in helping people to gain freedom from addiction to pornography. It should not be surprising that such programs are often effective in helping born-again Christians, for Scripture promises that "sin will have no dominion over you, since you are not under law but under grace" (Rom. 6:14).

Some reputable ministries that specialize in helping people overcome addiction to pornography include the following: Pure Hope (http://purehope.net); Pure Intimacy (http://www.pureintimacy.org); and Seven Places (http://sevenplaces.org).

QUESTIONS FOR PERSONAL APPLICATION

1. If you have ever viewed pornography in the past, what were some of the negative results that came from that experience?
2. Have you tended to make excuses or rationalizations regarding looking at pornography? How has this chapter changed your viewpoint about pornography?
3. Do you often feel a temptation to look at pornography? If so, what steps might you take to overcome the temptation?
4. If you were to spend some time looking at pornography now, what harmful consequences would come to your relationships with family and friends? To your marriage (if you are married)? To your relationship with God? To your personal spiritual health? To your job? To your future ministry effectiveness and fruitfulness?
5. Think about the effect of different kinds of movies on your own heart and your relationship with God. Which kinds of movies are not right for you to watch?
6. Have you ever known someone who was addicted to pornography? How would you characterize the emotional and relational health of that person's life? Would you trust this person?
7. Because of the widespread prevalence of pornography in modern society, I think it is necessary to ask the following question: If you are being honest,

are you addicted to pornography? Are you willing to admit that you need help from others, that this is not a battle you can win on your own?

8. What character traits (see p. 110) are especially helpful as Christians seek to act with maturity and integrity with regard to pornography?

SPECIAL TERMS

BIBLIOGRAPHY

Sections in Other Ethics Texts

(see complete bibliographical data, p. 64)

Frame, 766–68, 775–76
Geisler, 381–95
Kaiser, 55–66
McQuilkin and Copan, 254 62

Other Works

Alcorn, Randy. *The Purity Principle*. Sisters, OR: Multnomah, 2003.

———. *Sexual Temptation: Establishing Guardrails and Winning the Battle*. 3rd ed. Sandy, OR: Eternal Perspective Ministries, 2011.

Arterburn, Stephen, and Fred Stoeker. *Every Man's Battle: Winning the War on Sexual Temptation One Victory at a Time*. Edited by Mike Yorkey. 1st ed. Colorado Springs: WaterBrook Press, 2000.

Chester, Tim. *Closing the Window: Steps to Living Porn Free*. Downers Grove, IL: Inter-Varsity Press, 2010.

Court, J. H. "Pornography." In *New Dictionary of Christian Ethics and Pastoral Theology*, edited by David J. Atkinson and David H. Field, 675–77. Leicester, UK: Inter-Varsity, and Downers Grove, IL: InterVarsity Press, 1995.

Eberstadt, Mary, and Mary Anne Layden. *The Social Costs of Pornography: A Statement of Findings and Recommendations*. Princeton, NJ: Witherspoon Institute, 2010.

Hall, Laurie. *An Affair of the Mind: One Woman's Courageous Battle to Salvage Her Family from the Devastation of Pornography*. Colorado Springs: Focus on the Family, 1996.

Harris, Joshua. *Sex Is Not the Problem (Lust Is): Sexual Purity in a Lust-Saturated World*. Sisters, OR: Multnomah, 2003.

Hart, Archibald D. *The Sexual Man: Masculinity without Guilt*. Dallas: Thomas Nelson, 1995.

Haugen, Gary A. *Good News about Injustice: A Witness of Courage in a Hurting World*. Downers Grove, IL: InterVarsity Press, 1999.

Kastleman, Mark B. *The Drug of the New Millennium: The Science of How Internet Pornography Radically Alters the Human Brain and Body*. Orem, UT: Granite Publishing, 2001.

Keller, Timothy. *Counterfeit Gods: The Empty Promises of Money, Sex, and Power, and the Only Hope That Matters*. New York: Dutton, 2009.

Lambert, Heath. *Finally Free: Fighting for Purity with the Power of Grace*. Grand Rapids, MI: Zondervan, 2013.

McLawhorn, Richard. *Summary of the Final Report of the Attorney General's Commission on Pornography*. Cincinnati: National Coalition Against Pornography, 1986.

Naselli, Andrew David. "Seven Reasons You Should Not Indulge in Pornography." *Themelios* 41 (2016): 473–83.

———. "When You Indulge in Pornography, You Participate in Sex Slavery." *Journal for Biblical Manhood and Womanhood* 20, no. 2 (2015): 23–29.

Piper, John. "Faith in Future Grace vs. Lust." In *Future Grace: The Purifying Power of the Promises of God*, 2nd ed., 329–38. Colorado Springs: Multnomah, 2012.

Platt, David. "A War on Women: The Gospel and Sex Slavery." In *Counter Culture: Following Christ in an Anti-Christian Age*, revised and updated ed., 109–32. Carol Stream, IL: Tyndale Momentum, 2017.

Struthers, William M. *Wired for Intimacy: How Pornography Hijacks the Male Brain*. Downers Grove, IL: InterVarsity Press, 2009.

Tripp, Paul David. *Sex and Money: Pleasures That Leave You Empty and Grace That Satisfies*. Wheaton, IL: Crossway, 2013.

White, John. *Eros Defiled: The Christian and Sexual Sin*. Downers Grove, IL: InterVarsity Press, 1977.

SCRIPTURE MEMORY PASSAGE

Matthew 5:27–28: You have heard that it was said, "You shall not commit adultery." But I say to you that everyone who looks at a woman with lustful intent has already committed adultery with her in his heart.

HYMN

"Turn Your Eyes upon Jesus"

O soul, are you weary and troubled?
No light in the darkness you see?
There's light for a look at the Savior,
And life more abundant and free!

Refrain:
Turn your eyes upon Jesus,
Look full in His wonderful face,
And the things of earth will grow strangely dim
In the light of His glory and grace.

Thru death into life everlasting,
He passed, and we follow Him there;
Over us sin no more hath dominion
For more than conq'rors we are!

His word shall not fail you—He promised;
Believe Him, and all will be well:
Then go to a world that is dying,
His perfect salvation to tell!

HELEN H. LEMMEL, 1864–1961

Chapter 32

DIVORCE AND REMARRIAGE

According to the Bible, what are the legitimate grounds for divorce, if any?

Is divorce morally acceptable in a case of physical abuse? Neglect?

If a divorce is granted for biblically legitimate reasons, is remarriage always allowed?

Can a divorced person become a church officer?

What reasons are given for the "no remarriage" view?

In marriage, a man and woman commit to live with each other as husband and wife for life. In order for them to keep this commitment, *both parties* have to remain in the marriage. But when one party decides to leave the marriage, either to be with another partner or simply to end the existing relationship, it becomes impossible for the remaining spouse to faithfully fulfill his or her commitment (a husband, for example, cannot *live with* and *act as a husband to* a wife who is living with another man). Therefore, the question of divorce arises. It is important to consider this question in this section of the book, which deals with ethical issues connected to marriage.[1]

Under what circumstances, if any, is it morally right to obtain a divorce and thereby dissolve a marriage? And if divorce occurs, is it morally right for a divorced person to marry someone else? These and other questions will be addressed in this chapter.

[1] Some portions of this chapter have been adapted from the essay "Divorce and Remarriage" in the *ESV Study Bible* (Wheaton, IL: Crossway, 2008), 2545–47, with permission of the publisher. (I was the primary author of this article.)

A. DIVORCE AND ITS CONSEQUENCES

1. The Divorce Rate Is Higher, but Not As High as Is Sometimes Said. Divorce has now become more common than it was in previous generations. In the early part of the twentieth century, the divorce rate in the United States was approximately 0.9 per 1,000 total population.[2] Throughout the twentieth century the divorce rate slowly increased, then rose rapidly in the 1970s and 1980s as many states passed no-fault divorce laws.[3] The divorce rate peaked in the early 1980s at approximately 5.0 per 1,000 total population (approximately 1.2 million divorces).[4] After 1985, the divorce rate gradually declined, so that in 2014 there were approximately 813,862 divorces or annulments in America, or 3.2 per 1,000 total population.[5] But the number of divorces per 1000 population has gone down primarily because many couples are now living together instead of getting married and more people are remaining single. (There were approximately 10.6 marriages per 1000 people in the early 1980s, but only 6.8 marriages per 1000 people in 2009–2012.[6])

However, it is not true that 50 percent of marriages end in divorce today (a statistic that is sometimes repeated in popular media reports). After extensive statistical analysis, social researcher Shaunti Feldhahn reported in 2014, "According to one of the most recent Census Bureau surveys, 72 percent of people who have ever been married are still married to their first spouse"—and the remaining 28 percent are not all divorced persons, because the total also includes those who have been widowed through the death of a spouse, a category that accounts for perhaps as many as 8 percent.[7] That suggests that "somewhere around 20 to 25 percent of first marriages end in divorce."[8] Feldhahn concludes, "Imagine the difference to our collective consciousness if we say 'Most marriages last a lifetime' rather than 'half of marriages end in divorce.'"[9]

The divorce rate is even lower for those who attend church regularly. Feldhahn says:

> Weekly church attendance alone lowers the divorce rate significantly—
> roughly 25 to 50 percent, depending on the study. The popular belief that the

---

[2] "Marriages and Divorces, 1900–2012," Information Please, citing information from the U.S. Centers for Disease Control and Prevention, National Center for Health Statistics, http://www.infoplease.com/ipa /A0005044.html.

[3] No-fault divorce laws allow for a divorce to be granted without any requirement to show that one party to the marriage has committed some wrongdoing (such as adultery, desertion, or cruelty) that makes the marriage unworkable. In a no-fault divorce proceeding, one of the parties simply has to show that the marriage is no longer viable and is beyond repair (for example, because of "irreconcilable differences") without having to prove that the other party is responsible. Specific requirements vary from state to state.

[4] "Marriages and Divorces, 1900–2012."

[5] Centers for Disease Control and Prevention, National Center for Health Statistics, National Marriage and Divorce Trends, https://www.cdc.gov/nchs/nvss/marriage_divorce_tables.htm. Note: The CDC's statistics exclude data for California, Georgia, Hawaii, Indiana, and Minnesota.

[6] "Marriages and Divorces, 1900–2012."

[7] Shaunti Feldhahn, *The Good News about Marriage: Debunking Discouraging Myths about Marriage and Divorce* (Colorado Springs: Multnomah, 2014), 21–22.

[8] Ibid., 22.

[9] Ibid., 25.

rate of divorce is the same inside and outside the church is based on a deeply entrenched *misunderstanding* about the results of several George Barna surveys over the past decades. A misunderstanding that, Mr. Barna told me, he would love to correct in the public's mind.[10]

Speaking personally, I have long been skeptical of the claims that 50 percent of marriages end in divorce and that the divorce rate among evangelical Christians is the same as in the general society. I have been skeptical because such claims seemed to be wildly inaccurate in terms of the people we have known. Margaret and I have come to know many hundreds and probably thousands of actual married couples over our 48 years of marriage. We have lived in six different states and two countries (we spent over four years in the UK); we have been active members of nine different churches; and I have taught for 40 years in three different educational institutions with hundreds of students, and the number of divorces that we are aware of is absolutely tiny, certainly less than 5 percent of the married couples we have known and probably closer to 1 percent.

Marriage counselors Jan and David Stoop report similar anecdotal evidence:

> One couple, who work together in a marriage ministry involving many couples, shared in their response to our questionnaire that they had found only one couple in 1500 who pray together on a regular basis ever gets divorced.[11]

Feldhahn includes other encouraging statistics about marriage, tabulating sociological research from multiple sources. She reports, "The median number of those who say they are in happy marriages is around 90 percent," and, after discounting for some statistical variability, she concludes, "The actual percentage of happy marriages could be a bit lower or higher, but 80 percent seems like a very safe—in some ways, even conservative—number."[12]

However, it is still the case that millions of couples in the United States and other countries, including Christian couples, get divorced every year. And therefore it is important that we understand the teaching of God's Word on this issue, and that we understand more fully the consequences of divorce as well.

2. The Tragic Consequences of Divorce. Because divorce is more common today than in previous generations, some people might assume that it is less harmful in people's lives than it used to be. But the most thorough long-term study of the consequences of divorce does not confirm that assumption. The study was headed by Judith Wallerstein,

---

[10] Ibid., 66.

[11] Jan Stoop and David Stoop, *When Couples Pray Together: Creating Intimacy and Spiritual Wholeness* (Ann Arbor, MI: Servant, 2000), 31.

[12] Feldhahn, *The Good News about Marriage*, 51.

founder and executive director of the Center for the Family in Transition in Corte Madera, California. The results of this study have been published in a number of books stretching over many years.[13]

The results of Wallerstein's study are heartbreaking, and I can only mention a few points. She and her colleagues interviewed 60 families (120 parents with 131 children) who were going through divorces in 1971. They then interviewed the same people at intervals of one year, five years, and 10 years after the divorces in order to ascertain the results on people's lives. No other study of this magnitude has ever been done on the long-term consequences of divorce.[14]

Here are some of the notable conclusions from the study:

> Men and women tell us very clearly at the 10-year mark that the stress of being a single parent never lightens and that the fear of being alone never ceases. (*Second Chances*, p. 10)

> Incredibly, one-half of the women and one-third of the men are still intensely angry at their former spouses despite the passage of 10 years. Because their feelings have not changed, anger has become an ongoing, and sometimes dominant, presence in their children's lives as well. (p. 29)

> In only one in seven of the former couples did the former wife and husband experience stable second marriages. (p. 41)

> Some men and women seem to be held together by marriage; it brings order and security to their lives, and the structure itself provides their *raison d'être* and their highest level of adult adjustment. For both men and women, marriage in middle or later life has an additional and very important function: it provides an internal buffer against the anxieties of aging, of being old and alone, and of facing the inevitability of death. It also provides external supports to cope with the increasing disabilities and infirmities of old age. When the structure is removed, they are left feeling extremely vulnerable, and the external symptoms of physical deterioration are symbolic of the internal conflict and emotional distress. (p. 53)

---

[13] The material that I cite below is taken from the study published 10 years after divorces had occurred: Judith Wallerstein and Sandra Blakeslee, *Second Chances: Men, Women, and Children a Decade after Divorce* (New York: Ticknor and Fields, 1989). Supplemental material that does not contradict but largely affirms the earlier study is found in Judith Wallerstein, Julia Lewis, and Sandra Blakeslee, *The Unexpected Legacy of Divorce: The 25 Year Landmark Study* (New York: Hyperion, 2000).

[14] Wallerstein explains that the researchers chose a homogeneous population group for their study, where the majority of the men were highly educated professionals or who were owners or in management positions in businesses, and 75 percent of the women had at least some college education. Half of the families belonged to churches or synagogues. Wallerstein says, "This, then, is divorce under the best of circumstances." Wallerstein and Blakeslee, *Second Chances*, xv.

People like to think that because there are so many divorced families, adults and children will find divorce easier or even easy. But neither parents nor children find comfort in numbers. Divorce is not a more "normal" experience simply because so many people have been touched by it. Our findings revealed that all children suffer from divorce, no matter how many of their friends have gone through it. . . . Each and every child cries out, "Why me?" (p. 303)

Children of all ages feel intensely rejected when their parents divorce. . . . Some keep their anger hidden for years out of fear of upsetting parents or for fear of retribution and punishment; others show it. (p. 12)

Children feel intense loneliness. . . . Even when children are encouraged not to take sides, they often feel that they must. However, when they do take sides to feel more protected, they also feel despair because they are betraying one parent over the other. If they do not take sides, they feel isolated and disloyal to both parents. There is no solution to their dilemma. (p. 13)

[After 10 and sometimes 15 years,] even though they no longer have any illusions that their parents could ever remarry their sense of loss and wistful yearning persists, and their emotions run deep and strong. They feel less protected, less cared for, less comforted. . . . These children share vivid, gut-wrenching memories of their parents' separation. (p. 23)

[Nearly one-third of the children] between the ages of 19 and 29 have little or no ambition 10 years after their parents' divorce. They are drifting through life with no set goals, limited educations, and a sense of helplessness. . . . They don't make long-term plans and are aiming below the intellectual and educational achievements of their fathers and mothers. (pp. 148–149)

One of the great tragedies of divorce is that many fathers have absolutely no idea that their children feel rejected. . . . Without the continued support of their fathers, these boys lack self-confidence and pride in their own masculinity. . . . [The girls] too feel hurt, unsure of their femininity, and insecure in their relationships with men. . . . Many young people, especially boys, cannot express the anger they feel toward the parent who is rejecting them. (pp. 150–151)

I am not quoting this material to say that such destructive consequences are inevitable, for statistics and probabilities do not imply certain results for any one individual. In addition, Christians who go through divorce and Christians who provide support to those going through divorce have the additional factor of the power of the Holy Spirit to heal people's lives. Sometimes long-standing anger or fear can be changed by the Holy Spirit's transforming power working within people in answer to prayer. And well-functioning churches can often provide the effective "family" that will make up in some measure for what is lost in divorce. Still, these sobering findings help us understand why God established a wonderful moral standard of lifelong marriage between one man and one woman as the pattern for marriages in the human race (see the next section).

One verse that is commonly understood to reveal God's own sorrow regarding the painful consequences of divorce is found in the last book of the Old Testament. According to several translations, Malachi says this:

> "For I hate divorce," says the LORD, the God of Israel, "and him who covers his garment with wrong," says the LORD of hosts. (Mal. 2:16 NASB)[15]

If this is the correct translation, it does not mean that God considers all divorces to be morally wrong (for other passages of Scripture must be considered), but only that God is deeply grieved to see the painful consequences that flow from divorces.

Whatever view one takes of Malachi 2:16, interpreters who have differing views of this verse still agree that the consistent emphasis of both the Old and New Testaments is on the importance of preserving marriage and avoiding divorce in all but a few very narrowly defined circumstances.

B. GOD'S ORIGINAL PLAN IS FOR LIFELONG, MONOGAMOUS MARRIAGE

God's original plan for the human race, as indicated in his creation of Adam and Eve as husband and wife (Gen. 1:27–28; 2:22–25), is lifelong, monogamous marriage. Jesus affirmed this in responding to a question about divorce:

> And Pharisees came up to him and tested him by asking, "Is it lawful to divorce one's wife for any cause?" He answered, "Have you not read that he who created them from the beginning made them male and female [from Gen. 1:27], and said, 'Therefore a man shall leave his father and his mother and hold fast to his wife, and the two shall become one flesh' [from Gen. 2:24]? So they are no longer two but one flesh. *What therefore God has joined together, let not man separate.*" (Matt. 19:3–6)

In this reply Jesus rebukes and corrects a first-century practice of easy divorce for trivial reasons. For example, the Mishnah said:

> The school of Shammai say: A man may not divorce his wife unless he has found unchastity in her. . . . And the school of Hillel say . . . [he may

---

[15] The RSV, NRSV, NET, NIV 1984, and NLT all translate this as God saying, "I hate divorce." The ESV translates this sentence as "For the man who does not love his wife but divorces her, says the LORD, the God of Israel, covers his garment with violence, says the LORD of hosts." See the appendix to this chapter (p. 836) for a discussion of the translation issues involved in this difficult verse.

divorce her] even if she spoiled a dish for him. . . . Rabbi Akiba says, [he may divorce her] even if he found another fairer than she . . ." (Mishnah, *Gittin* 9:10)[16]

Rather than entering into this debate among rabbis, Jesus affirms God's original plan for marriage and shows that it is still his ideal for all marriages.

The Old Testament prophet Malachi views marriage as a "covenant" between a husband and wife. Furthermore, God is a witness to this covenant, and he will hold people accountable for it: "The LORD was witness between you and the wife of your youth, to whom you have been faithless, *though she is your companion and your wife by covenant*" (Mal. 2:14). Therefore, marriage is an especially serious commitment (1) between husband and wife, (2) to the society in which they live, and (3) before God himself (whether or not he is explicitly acknowledged in the marriage ceremony).[17]

It is important to begin this chapter about divorce with a clear affirmation that God's original intention is that a husband and wife remain married to each other for their entire lives, or, as the traditional marriage ceremony puts it, "so long as you both shall live." Although the following discussion will show that God allowed divorce as a remedy in some cases where marriages were irreparably damaged, Scripture still shows that God's ideal is lifelong, monogamous marriage, and that the first question to be asked of any couple contemplating divorce should be, "Is it possible that this marriage can be restored and preserved?"

C. IN THE OLD TESTAMENT, DIVORCE WAS ALLOWED IN CERTAIN CASES

The only Old Testament law concerning divorce is found in Deuteronomy 24:

When a man takes a wife and marries her, if then she finds no favor in his eyes because he has found some indecency in her, *and he writes her a certificate of divorce* and puts it in her hand and sends her out of his house, and she departs out of his house, *and if she goes and becomes another man's wife*, and the latter man hates her and writes her a certificate of divorce and puts it in her hand and sends her out of his house, or if the latter man dies, who took her to be his wife, then *her former husband, who sent her away, may not take her again to be his wife*, after she has been defiled, for that is an abomination before the LORD. And you shall not bring sin upon the land that the LORD your God is giving you for an inheritance. (vv. 1–4)

---

[16] The Mishnah was put in written form in the late second century or early third century AD, but it reflects earlier oral tradition, including much from before the time of Christ. With respect to this particular quotation, both Hillel (died AD 10) and Shammai (50 BC–AD 30) lived prior to Jesus's earthly ministry.

[17] See additional discussion of the solemnity of marriage in chap. 28, p. 701.

This is not the kind of law that says something like "A person may obtain a divorce for such-and-such a reason." There is no law exactly like that anywhere in the Old Testament. Rather, this passage *assumes* that some divorces would take place between a husband and wife "because he has found some indecency in her" (v. 1), but the text does not specify exactly what that "indecency" is.[18] This text only specifies that a woman may not return to her first husband in the following circumstance:

1. if he divorces her because he finds "some indecency" in her, *and*
2. if she marries another man, *and*
3. if that second husband dies or divorces her;
4. then her first husband may not remarry her.

We can notice, however, that the passage assumes that, after the divorce, the woman had a right to marry someone else, and that second marriage was not considered to be adultery but to be a legitimate marriage: She "becomes another man's wife" (Deut. 24:2).[19]

Other passages in the Old Testament also assumed that divorces were occurring among the Jewish people, indicating that, even if God did not command divorce in any specific circumstances, he tolerated it and to some degree regulated it, at least in some cases:

They [the priests] shall not marry a prostitute or a woman who has been defiled, neither shall they marry *a woman divorced from her husband*, for the priest is holy to his God. (Lev. 21:7; the verse assumes that those who were not priests could marry "a woman divorced from her husband")[20]

But if a priest's daughter is widowed *or divorced* and has no child and returns to her father's house, as in her youth, she may eat of her father's food. (Lev. 22:13)

But any vow of a widow *or of a divorced woman*, anything by which she has bound herself, shall stand against her. (Num. 30:9)

[If a man accuses his wife of not being a virgin when they got married, and if her parents bring proof of her virginity to the elders, then] *he may not divorce*

---

[18] Other translations speak of "some indecency" (NASB, RSV), "something indecent" (NIV, CSB), "something offensive" (NET), "something improper" (HCSB), or "some uncleanness" (KJV, NKJV). The Hebrew expression *'erwat dābār*, "the nakedness/ shamefulness of a thing," is quite vague, and John Murray wisely says, "It is exceedingly difficult if not precarious to be certain as to what the 'unseemly thing' really was." *Divorce* (Philadelphia: Presbyterian and Reformed, 1961), 9.

[19] Murray writes, "One thing is certain, that the second marriage was not placed in the category of adultery. . . . The woman and her second husband were not put to death as the Pentateuch required in the case of adultery." Ibid., 14–15.

[20] See a similar restriction in Ezek. 44:22.

her all his days. (Deut. 22:19; the verse assumes that divorce was a possibility in other marriages; see also v. 29)

She saw that for all the adulteries of that faithless one, Israel, *I had sent her away with a decree of divorce.* Yet her treacherous sister Judah did not fear, but she too went and played the whore. (Jer. 3:8; in this verse, God portrays himself as a husband who "sent away"—that is, divorced—his unfaithful wife because of all her "adulteries"—that is, her worship of other gods)

But these Old Testament passages do not give us much guidance regarding ethical standards for divorce in the new covenant age because (1) they assume that divorces would occur without giving us specific details about how to know when divorce is morally justified and (2) they all belong to the Mosaic covenant, which is no longer in effect in the new covenant age in which we now live (see discussion in chap. 8, p. 210).

D. IN THE NEW TESTAMENT, DIVORCE IS ALLOWED IN TWO CASES

Christian interpreters have held different views about divorce and remarriage for several centuries, and every scriptural passage about divorce has been extensively debated among commentators. In this section I will give an overview of my understanding of the relevant New Testament passages, and then later in the chapter I will interact with alternative interpretations.

1. Jesus Allowed for Divorce and Remarriage on Account of Adultery.

a. Matthew 19:3–9: We can now examine in more detail Matthew 19:3–9, which (along with its parallel in Mark 10:2–12) is the longest passage in the Bible dealing with the topic of divorce. I will discuss this longer passage first and then examine Matthew 5:32, which is the shorter passage about divorce in Matthew. As we will see, Jesus was establishing a far stricter requirement regarding divorce than the standard taught by many rabbis of his day.

Earlier in this chapter, I quoted the first four verses of Matthew 19:3–9, but here is the passage in its entirety:

And Pharisees came up to him and tested him by asking, "Is it lawful to divorce one's wife for any cause?" He answered, "Have you not read that he who created them from the beginning made them male and female, and said, 'Therefore a man shall leave his father and his mother and hold fast to his wife, and the two shall become one flesh'? So they are no longer two but one flesh. What therefore God has joined together, let not man separate." They said to him, "Why then did Moses command one to give a certificate of divorce and to send her away?" He said to them, "*Because of your hardness of heart Moses allowed you to divorce your wives, but from the beginning it was not so*. And I say to you: whoever divorces his wife, except for sexual immorality, and marries another, commits adultery."

Jesus's statement "Because of your hardness of heart . . ." should not be understood to mean that only "hard-hearted" people *initiate* divorces, but rather, "because your hard-hearted rebellion against God led to serious defilement of marriages." The presence of sin in the community meant that some marriages would be deeply harmed by hard-hearted spouses, and therefore Moses "allowed" the *other* spouse to obtain a divorce. God was providing a partial remedy for the harm that a hard-hearted husband or wife could do to the other person in the marriage.

In the final verse of this passage, Jesus provides significant guidance about divorce in the new covenant age:

> And I say to you: whoever divorces his wife, except for sexual immorality, *and marries another*, commits adultery. (Matt. 19:9)

The first thing to notice is that Jesus decisively terminates all other grounds by which people were divorcing their wives because of liberal Jewish interpretations of Deuteronomy 24:1–4. The only legitimate reason to initiate a divorce is "sexual immorality" committed by one's spouse. Jesus is certainly not approving easy divorces. According to this passage, he is prohibiting divorces for reasons other than adultery. He is directly contradicting the viewpoints promoted by followers of the rabbinic school of Hillel and the followers of Akiba, because "the school of Hillel say . . . [he may divorce her] even if she spoiled a dish for him. . . . Rabbi Akiba says, [he may divorce her] even if he found another fairer than she . . ." (Mishnah, *Gittin* 9:10).

The implication of Jesus's statement is that divorce for reasons other than adultery does not actually dissolve a marriage in the eyes of God. This is clear because Jesus says that a man who divorces his wife "except for sexual immorality, and marries another, *commits adultery*" (Matt. 19:9). But "adultery" (Greek, *moichaomai*) can only be committed by a married person. This means that Jesus is saying that a man who wrongly divorces his wife has not received a legitimate divorce and is in fact still married to his original wife at the time he initiates the second marriage.[21]

Jesus's disciples apparently were shocked at the strictness of his teaching in comparison to that of many of the rabbis of that day, for they said to him in the following verse, "If such is the case of a man with his wife, it is better not to marry" (Matt. 19:10). They jumped to the conclusion that it would be safer never to get married than to be stuck in an unhappy marriage for one's whole life. But Jesus corrected their misunderstanding,

---

[21] If marriage is a solemn covenant made in the presence of God (see chap. 28, p. 701), then God's decision about whether a husband and wife are still married or not is highly significant.

explaining that the calling and the ability not to be married was itself something that was only "given" by God to certain people. The conversation went like this:

> The disciples said to him, "If such is the case of a man with his wife, it is better not to marry." But he said to them, "Not everyone can receive this saying [that is, the saying that "it is better not to marry"], *but only those to whom it is given.* For there are eunuchs who have been so from birth, and there are eunuchs who have been made eunuchs by men, and there are eunuchs who have made themselves eunuchs for the sake of the kingdom of heaven. Let the one who is able to receive this receive it." (Matt. 19:10–12)

But when Jesus allowed *divorce* because of adultery, this was also a break with the Old Testament law, under which the penalty for adultery was death (see Lev. 20:10; Deut. 22:22; cf. John 8:4–5). Although it is unlikely that first-century Jewish people, living under the Roman government more than 1,400 years after the time of Moses, were actually carrying out the death penalty for adultery,[22] the law was still there in Leviticus and Deuteronomy. But in the new covenant age, according to Jesus's teaching, the penalty for adultery would no longer be death but the "sending away" involved in divorce (or perhaps even forgiveness and the restoration of the marriage, for Jesus *allows* divorce for adultery but he does not *command* it).

We must emphasize that when Jesus says that "whoever divorces his wife, *except for sexual immorality*, and marries another, commits adultery" (Matt. 19:9), he implies the converse: divorce and remarriage on the ground of sexual immorality are *not* prohibited and do *not* constitute adultery.

Here is an example of a similar "except for" statement from my work as a seminary professor: Suppose that I say this to my class:

> Whoever hands in a term paper after Tuesday at 9 a.m., *except for students who have received a deadline extension from me*, will receive a reduction of one letter grade per day.

This statement implies that a student who hands in a late paper but has received a deadline extension *will not* receive a reduction of one letter grade per day. In the same way, Jesus's statement "except for sexual immorality" implies that a man who divorces his wife because of sexual immorality and marries another person does *not* commit adultery.

This statement from Jesus is also significant for the question of remarriage. When Jesus says, "and marries another," he implies that *both divorce and remarriage are allowed* in the case of sexual immorality, and that someone who divorces because his spouse has

---

[22] As I mentioned in chap. 18 (see p. 515), the Roman Empire did not allow anyone except its own officials to carry out the death penalty. This is why the Jewish accusers of Jesus said to Pilate, "It is not lawful for us to put anyone to death" (John 18:31). For discussion of the extrabiblical historical evidence, see D. A. Carson, *The Gospel According to John*, PNTC (Grand Rapids, MI: Eerdmans, 1991), 591–92.

committed adultery may marry someone else without committing sin. This is evident because if we remove "and marries another," the saying does not make any sense:

> And I say to you: *whoever divorces his wife*, except for sexual immorality, . . . *commits adultery.*

But that would not be true, because some husbands will divorce their wives and then they will not remarry or live with any other woman. They will remain single and chaste. In that case, they would not be committing adultery with anyone, and Jesus's words would not make sense. Therefore, the phrase "and marries another" must be present for the verse to make sense. And that means that "whoever divorces his wife . . . *and marries another*" because of sexual immorality is not committing adultery in that second marriage.

As for the meaning of the exception clause, the expression "sexual immorality" in Jesus's statement translates the Greek term *porneia*, which was a broad term that included all kinds of sexually immoral conduct (see discussion in chap. 28, p. 720; see also BDAG, 854). It certainly included adultery,[23] as well as prostitution, incest, homosexuality, and bestiality.[24]

In conclusion, if "sexual immorality" occurs, then Jesus says that divorce is allowed. But he does not say that divorce is required. Even in such cases, forgiveness and reconciliation should always be the first option.

b. Divorce in the First Century Always Included the Right to Remarry: In Greek, Roman, and Jewish cultures in the first century, wherever divorce was allowed, the right to remarry was always assumed to accompany it. Regarding the Jewish culture, the Mishnah says:

> The essential formula in the bill of divorce is, "lo, thou art free to marry any man." (Mishnah, *Gittin* 9:3)[25]

---

[23] The term *porneia* is used to refer to adultery in Rev. 17:2 as well as in the *Apocrypha* (Sir. 23:23) and in the early Christian writing *Shepherd of Hermas* (Mandate 4.1.5).

[24] But *porneia* would *not* include, in ordinary usage, committing "adultery" in one's heart by looking at a woman with lustful intent, as someone might wish to argue from Matt. 5:28, any more than becoming angry with someone would mean that you have "murdered" the person according to Matt. 5:21–22 and you should be subject to capital punishment! In ordinary Greek usage, *porneia* referred only to physical actions of sexual immorality, and Jesus recognized that, because he had to add "in his heart" to show that he was speaking about a different kind of adultery, not the physical act, in Matt. 5:28.

I should add, however, that it seems to me possible that the kinds of sexual sin implied by the term *porneia* could also include, in today's world, such extensive sexual defilement of a marriage as is committed by a husband who repeatedly visits strip clubs or indulges an ongoing addiction to pornography. Each situation is different, and if such an actual situation comes up involving someone in a church, my recommendation would be that the church elder board should accept the difficult responsibility of evaluating the case and seeking to make a wise decision.

[25] David Instone-Brewer says the divorce formula that said, "You are allowed to marry any man you wish" (or close equivalent), can be traced as far back as the fifth century BC in Jewish documents, and as far back

In Greek culture, "a man could divorce his wife by sending her back to her father, who could then give her in marriage to a second husband."[26] And in Roman culture, "Although the virtue and good fortune of a woman who in her lifetime had only one husband was valued . . . , remarriage was acceptable and necessary."[27]

This does not necessarily mean that Jesus had to agree with any of the surrounding cultures on this issue, but it does mean that if Jesus intended to teach that divorce was sometimes allowed but remarriage was never allowed, he would have had to make it exceptionally clear in his teaching. Otherwise his hearers, as well as readers of the Gospels throughout the Roman Empire, would naturally have assumed that where divorce is allowed, the right to remarry someone else is also allowed.

c. Matthew 5:32: In this verse, Jesus affirms essentially the same teaching as in Matthew 19:

> But I say to you that everyone who divorces his wife, *except on the ground of sexual immorality*, makes her commit adultery, and whoever marries a divorced woman commits adultery.

Jesus says that the husband who wrongfully divorces his wife "makes her commit adultery." In that society it was assumed that a divorced woman would need to marry someone else for financial support and protection, and yet Jesus still says this new marriage begins with "adultery" because there was not a proper reason for her divorce (sexual immorality). But Jesus places most of the blame on the original husband who wrongly divorced her, saying that he thereby "makes her commit adultery."[28]

The exception that we saw in Matthew 19 is also present in this passage: "except on the ground of sexual immorality." Here again, Jesus is teaching that divorce is allowed in the case of sexual immorality. He is simply teaching that divorce for other, less serious reasons, is not acceptable.

In the last sentence of the passage, "whoever marries a divorced woman" should be

---

as the 14th century BC in Babylonian marriage certificates and law codes. *Divorce and Remarriage in the Bible: The Social and Literary Context* (Grand Rapids, MI: Eerdmans, 2002), 29.

[26]"Marriage Law," in *Oxford Classical Dictionary*, 3rd ed., ed. Simon Hornblower and Antony Spawforth (Oxford: Oxford University Press, 1996), 928.

[27]Ibid.

[28]An alternative translation is, "anyone who divorces his wife, except for sexual immorality, *makes her the victim of adultery*" (Matt. 5:32 NIV). However, I found no other English version that translates it this way, and such a translation does not seem necessary. The Greek verb is *moicheuthēnai*, an aorist passive infinitive of the verb *moicheuō*, for which BDAG (p. 657) gives the meaning "to commit adultery," and under that meaning says the passive voice can be used in the case of a woman, as in Sirach 23:23 ("through her fornication she has *committed adultery* and brought forth children by another man," NRSV); Philo, *On the Decalogue*, 124; Josephus, *Antiquities of the Jews*, 7.131; and John 8:4. In addition, the Liddell-Scott *Greek-English Lexicon* cites Aristotle, *Historia Animalium* 586.a.3, as another example of a passive form of *moicheuō* used with an active sense to speak of "the woman in Sicily who *committed adultery* (*moicheutheisa*) with the Ethiopian" (LSJ, 1141). Neither BDAG nor LSJ give "to be the victim of adultery" as a possible meaning for the passive voice of the verb.

taken together with the preceding words in this sentence. Understood in this context, this last clause does not directly contradict the previous part of the verse (and Matt. 19:9), where Jesus allows the legitimacy of divorce because of adultery. Rather, this clause is continuing the same topic that he is discussing in the earlier part of the verse, and so it means "and whoever marries *such a wrongly divorced woman as I have just spoken about . . .*"

d. Mark 10:11–12 and Luke 16:18:

> And he said to them, "*Whoever divorces his wife and marries another commits adultery against her*, and if she divorces her husband and marries another, she commits adultery." (Mark 10:11–12)

> *Everyone who divorces his wife and marries another commits adultery*, and he who marries a woman divorced from her husband commits adultery. (Luke 16:18)

In these statements about divorce in Mark and Luke, Jesus does not include the exception clause "except for sexual immorality." The most likely reason is that there was no dispute or disagreement among Jews, or in Greek or Roman culture, that adultery was a legitimate ground for divorce, and Jesus is not addressing that issue. The disputes among the Jews of that time were rather about how many *other* grounds of divorce were legitimate (such as spoiling a meal!).

The primary force of Jesus's statements in these verses is to nullify the practice of divorce for trivial reasons that many Jewish interpreters were defending from Deuteronomy 24. In both Mark and Luke, Jesus decisively nullifies those practices. This does not invalidate the more extensive teaching given in Matthew, because the exception for adultery is assumed but not stated explicitly in Mark and Luke.

It is common in ordinary speech to fail to make pedantic qualifications to a statement when both the speaker and the hearers assume that the qualifications apply and do not need to be stated. For example, suppose a teenage girl in Arizona said to her father, "Dad, can I drive 100 mph on Highway 101?" Her father would probably reply, "No—anybody who drives 100 mph on Highway 101 will be arrested." He does not need to add, "unless you are a policeman in pursuit of a criminal," because everyone assumes that to be true.

Another example is Jesus's statement that "everyone who looks at a woman with lustful intent has already committed adultery with her in his heart" (Matt. 5:28). But there is an unexpressed exception that is assumed: "everyone who looks at a woman *except for his wife.*"[29]

Similarly, in a context where there was no controversy about the legitimacy of divorce because of adultery, there was no need to specifically state that exception.

---

[29] This exception was pointed out to me by Andy Naselli.

2. Paul Adds Desertion as a Second Reason for Divorce. Paul gives a second legitimate reason for divorce in 1 Corinthians 7:10–15:

> To the married I give this charge (not I, but the Lord): the wife should not separate from her husband (but if she does, she should remain unmarried or else be reconciled to her husband), and the husband should not divorce his wife. To the rest I say (I, not the Lord) that if any brother has a wife who is an unbeliever, and she consents to live with him, he should not divorce her. If any woman has a husband who is an unbeliever, and he consents to live with her, she should not divorce him. For the unbelieving husband is made holy because of his wife, and the unbelieving wife is made holy because of her husband. Otherwise your children would be unclean, but as it is, they are holy. *But if the unbelieving partner separates, let it be so. In such cases the brother or sister is not enslaved.* God has called you to peace.

In the first two verses (vv. 10–11), Paul teaches that husbands and wives should stay together, and if for some reason they separate for a time, they should not marry someone else, but should seek to be reconciled to each other and come to live together once again.

When Paul says "not I, but the Lord," and then later says, "I, not the Lord," he is distinguishing a matter on which he has a record of Jesus's own teaching about marriage (1 Cor. 7:10–11) from a matter about which Jesus did not leave any specific teaching (vv. 12–15).[30] In churches such as the one in Corinth, Paul was facing a new situation that Jesus had not addressed—that of a Christian and non-Christian married to each other. (In the context in which Jesus was speaking, Jewish people only married other Jews, and both husband and wife therefore were part of the Jewish religious community.)

When a believer has an unbelieving spouse, Paul says that they should remain married if the unbeliever is willing to do so (1 Cor. 7:12–14).[31] Then he adds:

> But *if the unbelieving partner separates, let it be so.* In such cases the brother or sister is not enslaved. God has called you to peace. (1 Cor. 7:15)

The most likely interpretation of this verse is that it implies the freedom to obtain a legal divorce and the freedom to marry someone else. The spouse who has been

---

[30] See further discussion in Wayne Grudem, *Systematic Theology: An Introduction to Biblical Doctrine* (Leicester, UK: Inter-Varsity, and Grand Rapids, MI: Zondervan, 1994), 76–77.

[31] This direction to remain married to an unbelieving wife or husband stands in contrast to the situation in Ezra 10, in which the exiles who had returned from Babylon to Jerusalem agreed to "put away" (or to "cause to go out"; Hiphil verb stem of *yātsā'*) their foreign wives (Ezra 10:3). However, the *ESV Study Bible* notes that in the statement "We have broken faith with our God and have *married* foreign women from the peoples of the land" (Ezra 10:2), the word translated as "married" (Hiphil of *yāshab*, "to dwell") is not the usual one, but means literally "we have given a home," and that these words "may imply that these illicit relationships were not marriages in the full sense." *ESV Study Bible* (Wheaton, IL: Crossway, 2008), 819.

abandoned "is not enslaved" to any obligation to maintain the marriage. When an unbelieving spouse has deserted the marriage, God releases the believing spouse from the "enslavement" of the twin unending stresses of (1) a lifelong vain hope of reconciling with an unbeliever who has left and (2) a lifelong prohibition against enjoying the good blessings of marriage again.

Would this passage apply to desertion by someone who professes to be a Christian? In such cases, a question arises as to whether the person is genuinely a believer or has simply made a false profession of faith. Each situation will be different, and a Christian involved in such a difficult circumstance should seek wise counsel from the leaders of his or her church. Where possible, the steps of church discipline outlined in Matthew 18:15–17 should be followed in an attempt to bring reconciliation to the marriage. If that process results in the final step of excommunication from the church, then it would seem appropriate to treat the deserting spouse as an unbeliever ("let him be to you as a Gentile and a tax collector," Matt. 18:17). But it must be emphasized that if reconciliation of the marriage can at all be brought about, that should always be the first goal.

3. Two Legitimate Grounds for Divorce. When we combine the teaching of Jesus with the teaching of Paul on this subject, it seems that there are two legitimate grounds for divorce: (1) adultery and (2) desertion by an unbeliever when all reasonable attempts at reconciliation have failed (including desertion by a professing Christian who has refused all the steps of church discipline and has come to be treated as an unbeliever).

The position that I have briefly summarized here—that both divorce and remarriage are allowed when a person's spouse has committed adultery or has irreparably deserted the marriage—is the most common position that has been held among Protestants since the Reformation. This is the position set forth, for example, in the Westminster Confession of Faith (1646):

> In the case of adultery after marriage, it is lawful for the innocent party to sue out a divorce: and, after the divorce, to marry another, as if the offending party were dead. . . . Nothing but *adultery*, or such *willful desertion* as can no way be remedied by the church or civil magistrate, is cause sufficient of dissolving the bond of marriage. (24.5, 6)

This is the position defended in the extensive exegetical argument by John Murray[32] and in the careful and detailed but less technical discussions by Jay Adams[33] and Thomas

---

[32] Murray, *Divorce*. This entire book consists of a detailed exegetical study of the biblical passages related to divorce. D. A. Carson also gives an extended defense of the view that, in Matthew 19:3–12, Jesus allows both divorce and remarriage in the case of adultery: see D. A. Carson, "Matthew," in *The Expositor's Bible Commentary: Matthew & Mark (Revised Edition)*, vol. 9 in EBC, ed. Tremper Longman III and David E. Garland (Grand Rapids, MI: Zondervan, 2010), 465–74.

[33] Jay Adams, *Marriage, Divorce, and Remarriage in the Bible* (Grand Rapids, MI: Zondervan, 1980).

Edgar.[34] It is also the position advocated in ethics texts by John Jefferson Davis,[35] John Feinberg and Paul Feinberg,[36] and Robertson McQuilkin and Paul Copan.[37]

E. ARE THERE ANY ADDITIONAL LEGITIMATE GROUNDS FOR DIVORCE?

In addition to the two grounds of sexual immorality and desertion by an unbeliever, are there any other legitimate biblical grounds for divorce?

1. Divorce Because of Physical Abuse? Some have argued that repeated instances of physical abuse should be an additional legitimate ground for divorce, for at least three reasons: (1) the abuser has "separated" from the marriage—not *physically* left the home, but separated *relationally*, and so 1 Corinthians 7:15 (see above) would apply; (2) while the abuse is not technically "adultery" in the sense of *porneia* ("sexual immorality") in Matthew 19:9, it is another kind of immoral conduct that also destroys the marriage covenant or the "one flesh" relationship (Gen. 2:24) that is essential to a marriage; (3) by specifying two conditions that so deeply damaged a marriage that divorce is allowed, Jesus and Paul imply that there might be other conditions (such as repeated violent physical abuse) that would damage the marriage so deeply as to justify divorce in those cases as well; and (4) physical abuse is such a serious violation of a husband's responsibility to care for and protect his wife that it breaks the marriage covenant (see Ex. 21:10–11).

A strong motive behind these arguments is the recognition that physical abuse of a wife by her husband (or, in some cases, physical abuse of a husband by his wife) is deeply evil and severely damages the marriage relationship. The recognition of this evil then prompts an instinctive sense among Christians that *something* must be done to protect the abused partner from suffering further abuse. Is not divorce the most obvious and cleanest remedy for such a situation?

Some authors for whom I have the highest respect have argued that physical abuse (and perhaps other serious offenses that severely damage the marriage relationship) also constitutes a sufficient ground for divorce. For example, John Frame agrees that divorce and remarriage are permissible because of adultery or irreparable desertion by an unbeliever, but he also would allow divorce when an unbelieving spouse can no longer make "a credible claim to be upholding his marriage vows," whether because of

---

[34] Thomas Edgar, "Divorce & Remarriage for Adultery or Desertion," in *Divorce and Remarriage: Four Christian Views*, ed. H. Wayne House (Downers Grove, IL: InterVarsity Press, 1990), 151–96.

[35] John Jefferson Davis, *Evangelical Ethics: Issues Facing the Church Today*, 4th ed. (Phillipsburg, NJ: P&R, 2015), 90–105.

[36] John S. Feinberg and Paul D. Feinberg, *Ethics for a Brave New World*, 2nd ed. (Wheaton, IL: Crossway, 2010), 583–633.

[37] Robertson McQuilkin and Paul Copan, *An Introduction to Biblical Ethics: Walking in the Way of Wisdom*, 3rd ed. (Downers Grove, IL: InterVarsity Press, 2014), 234–48.

"physical or verbal abuse, emotional entanglements with people other than the spouse, failure to provide, literal desertion, and so on." But he also specifies that "the church should recognize divorces in these cases only when all available remedies have failed."[38]

I recognize the force of this type of reasoning, and in the case of physical abuse I strongly agree that *something*—perhaps *several things*—must be done quickly to prevent the abused spouse from having to endure further suffering.[39] As soon as church leaders become aware of a situation of physical abuse, they should act to bring the abuse to an immediate halt, often by encouraging the abused spouse to separate and move to another, perhaps undisclosed, living location (for the eventual purpose of bringing restoration of the marriage along with the complete cessation of the abuse). In addition, other actions may need to be taken, and these will vary from case to case. These actions may include church discipline, confrontation and counseling, police intervention, a court order, and other kinds of intervention by church members, family members, and friends.[40] As I argued in chapter 20, when a person is facing the likelihood of physical assault, self-defense or fleeing from the danger are both morally right actions. In some cases, filing a complaint with local police and pressing charges may also be appropriate, because violently attacking one's spouse and doing physical harm is a criminal act and subject to legal penalties. Using every available means, the abuse must be stopped and the abused spouse must be protected.

However, I am not persuaded by the preceding arguments attempting to show that we should consider physical abuse to be another ground for divorce, according to biblical teaching. My response to the arguments on the other side are these:

1. In 1 Corinthians 7:15, when Paul says, "if the unbelieving partner *separates*," the Greek verb *chōrizō* ("to separate, depart, leave") in this context would not have suggested to Paul's original readers a relational alienation

---

[38] John M. Frame, *The Doctrine of the Christian Life: A Theology of Lordship* (Phillipsburg, NJ: P&R, 2008), 781. David Clyde Jones also thinks that physical abuse so violates the marriage covenant that it is a sufficient ground, as well as adultery and desertion, for divorce. *Biblical Christian Ethics* (Grand Rapids, MI: Baker, 1994), 177–204.

[39] For specific solutions, see Chris Moles, *The Heart of Domestic Abuse: Gospel Solutions for Men Who Use Control and Violence in the Home* (Bemidji, MN: Focus, 2015). See also Jason Meyer, "A Complementarian Manifesto against Domestic Abuse," The Gospel Coalition, Dec. 2, 2015, http://www.thegospelcoalition.org /article/a-complementarian-manifesto-against-domestic-abuse. For compassionate and wise help in bringing healing to victims of abuse, see Steven R. Tracy, *Mending the Soul: Understanding and Healing Abuse* (Grand Rapids, MI: Zondervan, 2005).

[40] I am aware of at least two situations in which a woman told my wife, Margaret, and me that in the past she had been physically abused by her husband and that she had gone to her pastor for help, but he had minimized the problem and sent her away. This was a tragic and inexcusable shirking of responsibility on the part of those pastors.

But we are also aware of at least one situation where several people in our church (including my wife and teenage son) helped an abused wife move out of her house in the middle of the day when her husband was at work, after which church discipline was initiated, eventually leading to repentance and reconciliation. More than 10 years after that the marriage was still healthy.

but a physical separation (the same verb is used in verse 10 to say, "the wife should not *separate* from her husband").[41]

2. While *porneia* in Matthew 19:9 referred to a broad range of sexual intercourse outside the bounds of marriage under the term "sexual immorality," it was not used to refer to other kinds of immorality that were not sexual in nature, such as physical abuse.

3. Although Paul, with his apostolic authority, was able to add an additional ground for divorce, that fact does not give us, as people who do not have such apostolic authority to write new words of Scripture, the freedom to add any additional grounds for divorce on our own initiative nearly 2,000 years later. In addition, Paul was giving his apostolic judgment *regarding a new situation* that Jesus did not teach about (a Christian married to a non-Christian). But abuse within marriage is not a new situation that has only arisen in the 21st century. Given the sinful hearts of human beings, surely physical abuse within marriage was occurring at the time of Jesus's earthly ministry as well, yet neither Jesus nor Paul taught that abuse provided a legitimate ground for divorce.

4. The argument that physical abuse breaks the marriage covenant introduces a new category into the discussion, the category of breaking a covenant. But neither Jesus nor Paul used that category in teaching about divorce, so I do not think it is legitimate to affirm that "breaking the marriage covenant" is a biblical standard to use in deciding when divorce is legitimate, and then to begin to list various kinds of sin that might fall in this broad category. Such reasoning would likely open the door to a multiplication of sins that "break the marriage covenant" so that not just physical abuse but many other sins will be counted as valid grounds for divorce.

Still, I sympathize with the deep concern of those who argue that divorce should be allowed for ongoing physical abuse, for they understand the destructive evil in such a situation, and it seems easy to conclude that divorce is the best solution. I too feel emotionally attracted to this solution, and I recognize that my own rejection of the solution might be wrong. But I simply cannot see a legitimate way to justify it from the teachings of Scripture, and in this matter, as in all other ethical matters, God's words in Scripture must remain my ultimate guide and standard.

My reluctance in this matter stems in large measure from the strong wording in Jesus's teaching, in which he seems so clearly to be excluding other grounds for divorce:

---

[41] Other verses where *chōrizō* describes physical separation include Acts 1:4; 18:1, 2; Philem. 15. Jesus also used it to speak of ending a marriage (Matt. 19:6; Mark 10:9).

> But I say to you that *everyone who divorces his wife, except on the ground of sexual immorality*, makes her commit adultery, and whoever marries a divorced woman commits adultery. (Matt. 5:32)

> And I say to you: *whoever divorces his wife, except for sexual immorality*, and marries another, commits adultery. (Matt. 19:9)

Yet I must emphasize again that, when a pastor or other church leader becomes aware of an abusive situation, the church should quickly act to institute all necessary measures to protect the abused spouse so that the abuse will immediately be brought to an end.

Finally, we should recognize that among couples who live together, abuse is more than twice as common among those who don't get married compared to married couples who did not live together before marriage. According to a 2015 study by the American College of Pediatricians, citing research done by C. T. Kenney and S. S. McLanahan, the rate of abuse for married couples who remained married was 15.5 percent (a tragically high number). But for cohabiting couples who did not eventually marry, the percentage was 35.3 percent. Cohabiting couples who eventually got married had a rate of 21.9 percent.[42]

2. Divorce Because of Material Neglect or Emotional Neglect? David Instone-Brewer argues that, in addition to adultery and desertion by an unbeliever, the New Testament also allows divorce for material neglect or emotional neglect. Here is his summary of his position:

> I agree with the two traditional grounds of adultery and desertion by an unbeliever, and two other OT grounds that are alluded to by Paul and Church tradition. These two are emotional neglect and material neglect and are alluded to in 1 Corinthians 7:3–5, 32–34. These two grounds were derived from Exodus 21:10–11, which states that a husband must give a wife food, clothing, and love.[43]

Instone-Brewer bases much of his argument on an Old Testament law concerning slaves. In a context of laws concerning a man who has taken a slave woman as his wife, and then takes a second wife, we read:

> If he takes another wife to himself, he shall not diminish her food, her clothing, or her marital rights. And if he does not do these three things for her, she shall go out for nothing, without payment of money. (Ex. 21:10–11)

---

[42] "Cohabitation: Effects of Cohabitation on the Men and Women Involved Part 1 of 2," American College of Pediatricians, March 2015, http://www.acpeds.org/the-college-speaks/position-statements/societal-issues/cohabitation-part-1-of-2, citing C. T. Kenney and S. S. McLanahan, "Why are cohabiting relationships more violent than marriages?" *Demography* 43, no. 1 (February 2006): 127–40.

[43] Instone-Brewer, *Divorce and Remarriage in the Bible*, 275. He has presented the same argument in a more popular book as well, *Divorce and Remarriage in the Church: Biblical Solutions for Pastoral Realities* (Downers Grove, IL: InterVarsity Press, 2003).

Instone-Brewer then quotes later rabbinic interpretations that referred to or alluded to this passage when discussing the responsibilities of a husband and wife within marriage. He says that the three categories of "food . . . clothing . . . marital rights"[44] could be summarized as material and emotional support.[45]

He goes on to argue that even the strict rabbinic interpreters, the followers of Shammai, agreed that *failure to provide material or emotional support was a sufficient ground for divorce.*[46] Therefore, the rabbinic quotation that we cited earlier in this chapter is significant:

> The school of Shammai say: A man may not divorce his wife unless he has found unchastity[47] in her. . . . And the school of Hillel say . . . [he may divorce her] even if she spoiled a dish for him. . . . Rabbi Akiba says, [he may divorce her] even if he found another fairer than she." (Mishnah, *Gittin* 9:10)

Instone-Brewer argues as follows:

1. All Jewish interpreters at the time of Christ accepted neglect of the three categories of Exodus 21:10–11 (food, clothing, marital rights) as legitimate grounds for divorce (pp. 100–109).
2. Therefore, the followers of Shammai (the "Shammites") accepted the three grounds of Exodus 21:10–11, and these were included in their understanding of "unchastity" (or "some indecency") in Deuteronomy 24:1 (p. 111).
3. Jesus was quoting Deuteronomy 24:1 when he prohibited divorce "except for sexual immorality" (*mē epi porneia*, Matt. 19:9) and "except on the ground of sexual immorality" (*parektos logou porneias*, Matt. 5:32) (pp. 158–59, 185–87).
4. Jesus nowhere denied the three grounds for divorce in Exodus 21:10–11, and "If Jesus said nothing about a universally accepted belief, then it is assumed by most scholars that this indicated his agreement with it" (p. 185).
5. Therefore, Jesus must have agreed with the strict Shammite view, that divorce was allowed both for adultery and also for neglect of the three obligations in Exodus 21:10–11 (pp. 159, 167, 184).
6. In summary, Jesus allowed divorce not only because of adultery but also because of failure to provide food, clothing, and marital rights (which may be summarized as material or emotional neglect).

---

[44] The phrase "marital rights" was commonly understood to refer to sexual relations within marriage.

[45] Instone-Brewer, *Divorce and Remarriage in the Bible*, 100–107.

[46] Ibid., 111–12.

[47] The Hebrew wording of the Mishnah here is *debar 'erwat*, "a matter of indecency," which simply borrows two words from Deut. 24:1 (*'erwat dābār*, "some indecency") but reverses the word order.

In response, while I wish to affirm my appreciation for Instone-Brewer as a gracious friend who has helped me on numerous occasions with research at Tyndale House in Cambridge, England, and also as a meticulous scholar with vast knowledge of the ancient world, I still must confess that I do not find his argument on this matter to be persuasive, for several reasons:

1. While he provides evidence that many Jewish interpreters referred to Exodus 21:10–11 to teach about *the responsibilities of a husband and wife in marriage*, I could not find evidence on pages 100–109 of Instone-Brewer's book that *all* Jewish interpreters agreed that the neglect of food, clothing, or marital rights was *grounds for divorce*.

2. I could find no evidence in his discussion on pages 100–109 that specifically demonstrated that the followers of Shammai held that neglect of food, clothing, or marital rights was grounds for divorce, or that the Shammites believed that "something indecent" in Deuteronomy 24:1 included neglect of food, clothing, or marital rights.

3. The argument that Jesus is quoting Deuteronomy 24:1 when he speaks of "sexual immorality" in Matthew 5:32 and 19:9 is not persuasive. The Septuagint does not use *porneia* to translate *'erwat dābār* ("some indecency"), but *aschēmon pragma* ("an indecent or shameful thing"), and this suggests that the Greek-speaking Jews at the time of Christ would not have heard the term *porneia* as a reference to Deuteronomy 24:1. In addition, the word *porneia* was used to refer to various kinds of sexual intercourse outside of the legitimate bounds of marriage (including adultery), but adultery at the time when Deuteronomy 24:1 was written would have required the death penalty, not divorce (Lev. 20:10; Deut. 22:22). Therefore, it is highly unlikely that Jesus's hearers would have thought he was referring to Deuteronomy 24:1 when he said "except for sexual immorality."[48]

4. It is not enough to say that Jesus did not deny the three grounds for divorce found in Exodus 21:10–11, and therefore he must have agreed with them. Instone-Brewer admits that this is an argument "from silence" (p. 184), but I think it is even weaker than an argument from silence. It is an argument *contrary to* what Jesus explicitly says.

In the context of answering a question from the Pharisees, "Is it lawful to divorce one's wife *for any cause*?" (Matt. 19:3), after Jesus says, "Because of your hardness of heart Moses *allowed* you to divorce your wives, but from the beginning it was not so" (v. 8), we expect Jesus to teach a more strict view of divorce than the very lenient interpretations of Deuteronomy 24 that were promoted by the rabbis. He gives no hint indicating that he is endorsing various views of divorce promoted by different Jewish teachers.

In that context, Jesus explicitly excludes all other grounds for divorce, for he explicitly says:

---

[48] Earlier in this chapter I argued that Jesus, in Matt. 19:9, was *rejecting* the highly permissive grounds for divorce found in some rabbinic interpretations of Deut. 24:1. But his *allowance* for divorce for "sexual immorality" (*porneia*) was not based on Deut. 24:1 because sexual immorality at the time of Moses would have resulted in the death penalty, not in a divorce.

> Whoever divorces his wife, except for sexual immorality, and marries another, commits adultery. (Matt. 19:9)

The construction, "Whoever . . . except for" explicitly rules out all of the grounds for divorce other than adultery. It is not just that Jesus failed to explicitly deny that divorce was valid for failure to provide food, clothing, or marital rights. He also failed to explicitly deny that divorce was valid for a wife spoiling a meal or because a man found another woman whom he thought more beautiful than his present wife. He did not need to deny any of these explicitly because he was denying them all at once when he said, "*Whoever* divorces his wife, except for sexual immorality . . ."

5. Therefore, I do not find that Instone-Brewer has provided convincing evidence that Jesus allowed divorce for neglect of the three obligations in Exodus 21:10–11 (failure to provide food, clothing, or marital rights). Jesus did not teach that divorce was allowed for material or emotional neglect.[49] In the light of contrary evidence about what Jesus clearly *did* teach, an argument based on what Jesus did *not* say has dubious validity.

6. Finally, it is important to step back and remember how far removed Instone-Brewer's argument is from the direct teaching of the New Testament. His argument is based on Exodus 21:10–11, but that is part of the Mosaic covenant, which is no longer in force for the new covenant age (see chap. 8). In addition, that passage is not about marriage and divorce in general, but about the rights of a slave woman who has been taken as a man's wife. And the argument is based not on the direct teaching of the passage but on later Jewish application of the passage to the question of divorce, and not just on any Jewish application of the passage, but on the supposed application by the strict followers of Shammai, for which there is no specific documented evidence. And then it is based not on Jesus's explicit affirmation of this supposed view of the Shammites regarding Exodus 21:10–11, but on the fact that Jesus did not explicitly deny this view in his teaching.

Therefore, this position seems to me to be based on something that Jesus did not say about a view of the Shammites that is not documented about a passage that is talking about slavery laws and not about marriage and divorce in general, a passage that is found in the laws of the Mosaic covenant, which is no longer in force. Therefore, this position does not have nearly enough evidence to be persuasive.

3. Divorce Because the Marriage Can't Be Repaired? Should a divorce be granted when a husband and wife have been strongly alienated from each other for many months or years, and their entrenched hostility against each other has not responded to repeated

---

[49] I should add that Instone-Brewer's book is an immensely valuable resource for information about divorce and remarriage in ancient Jewish, Greek, and Roman writings, and also (pp. 268–99) for an extensive categorization of a variety of ancient and modern positions on divorce, with detailed documentation for authors who hold each position. In addition, from beginning to end the book gives evidence of genuine and wise pastoral care for people who are experiencing or have experienced divorce in their own lives.

attempts at counseling and reconciliation? In such a situation, people who know the couple might say that the marriage is beyond repair.

Craig Blomberg apparently advocated this position for severely damaged marriages. He wrote:

> Perhaps the best way of describing when divorce and remarriage are permitted, then, is to say simply that it is when an individual, in agreement with a supportive Christian community of which that individual has been an intimate part, believes that he or she has no other choice or option in trying to avoid some greater evil. All known attempts at reconciliation have been exhausted.[50]

Blomberg's article demonstrates admirable compassion for people in painful marital situations and for those who already have been divorced. I sympathize with his desire to bring a solution to a deeply dysfunctional situation. Nevertheless, as with the case of physical abuse, I simply do not see sufficient justification for Blomberg's position in Scripture itself.

4. Divorce Because of Incompatibility? Many divorces today are granted not because of adultery, desertion, physical abuse, or material or emotional neglect, but because of some kind of "incompatibility"—the husband and wife are not getting along, and no longer want to be married to each other. According to a report by the National Fatherhood Initiative, one survey indicated that the most common reasons for divorce were as follows:

1. Lack of commitment: cited by 73 percent, who said they wished their ex-spouses had "worked harder" to stay married.
2. Arguing: cited by 56 percent.
3. Infidelity: cited by 55 percent.
4. Marrying too young: according to the report, the Centers for Disease Control and Prevention states that nearly 50 percent of teenage marriages fail in the first 15 years.
5. Unrealistic expectations: cited by 45 percent.
6. Lack of "equality": cited by 44 percent.
7. Lack of preparation: cited by 41 percent.

---

[50] Craig Blomberg, "Marriage, Divorce, Remarriage, and Celibacy: An Exegesis of Matthew 19:3–12," *TrinJ*, n.s., 11 (1990): 193.

Larry Richards also believes that Scripture allows for divorce when a husband and wife decide that "the marriage is really over and it is time to divorce." He argues, "No ecclesiastical court has ever been granted the biblical right to determine who can and cannot divorce," and he would allow for divorce because of hard-heartedness as displayed by "mental and physical abuse, sexual abuse, repeated adulteries, and emotional and spiritual abandonment of the relationship." "Divorce & Remarriage under a Variety of Circumstances," in *Divorce and Remarriage: Four Christian Views*, 242.

8. Abuse: cited by 29 percent.[51]

In Europe, the most common reasons cited for divorce by couples are fairly similar, but also include some additional factors, such as substance abuse (50 percent), health problems, (27.8 percent), and religious differences (33.3 percent).[52]

It should be clear from the previous discussion, however, that God considers marriage to be a solemn, lifelong commitment, and only the most serious kinds of destructive misconduct (adultery or desertion) are counted as valid grounds for divorce in the teaching of the New Testament.

F. QUESTIONS ABOUT SPECIFIC SITUATIONS

1. People Who Have Been Divorced for Unbiblical Reasons. What should be done if someone has been divorced for reasons other than those given in the Bible and then has married someone else? Jesus says that in such a case the person has committed "adultery," so the marriage began with adultery:

> And I say to you: whoever divorces his wife, except for sexual immorality, and marries another, commits adultery. (Matt. 19:9)

But after such a couple has been married, if they decide they want to follow the teachings of Scripture, what should they do now?

When Jesus says, "and marries another" in that same verse, he implies that the second marriage is in fact a true marriage. Jesus does not say, "and *lives outside of marriage* with another" (which was possible),[53] but "and *marries* another." Therefore, once a second marriage has occurred, it would be further sin to break it up, for it would be destroying another marriage.

This means that the second marriage should not be thought of as a man and a woman living in continual adultery, *for they are now married to each other*, not to anyone else. Yes, Jesus teaches that the marriage began with adultery, but his words also indicate that these two people are now married.[54] The responsibility of the husband and wife in

---

[51] "With This Ring, A National Survey on Marriage," The National Fatherhood Initiative, 2005, 32, http://wyofams.org/index_htm_files/NationalMarriageSurvey.pdf. Many of the divorced couples surveyed noted several reasons that led to their divorce, so the percentages here add up to more than 100 percent.

[52] Shelby B. Scott, Galena K. Rhoades, Scott M. Stanley, Elizabeth S. Allen, and Howard J. Markman, "Reasons for Divorce and Recollections of Premarital Intervention: Implications for Improving Relationship Education," *Couple and Family Psychology* 2, no. 2 (June 2013): 131–45, https://www.ncbi.nlm.nih.gov/pmc/articles/PMC4012696/.

[53] See the story of the woman at the well in John 4, to whom Jesus says, "You have had five husbands, and the one you now have is not your husband" (v. 18).

[54] Here are two analogies that may help people to understand how marriage could *begin* with adultery but, once it has begun, should not be seen as two people living in adultery:

1. Some people think that the American War of Independence (1776–1783) was not a just war, but was a morally wrongful rebellion against Great Britain (I do not agree with this viewpoint; see chap. 16). But such people would not argue that Americans today are still living in a state of sinful rebellion against the British

such a case is to ask God for his forgiveness for their previous sin, and also for his blessing on their current marriage. Then they should strive to make the current marriage a good and lasting one.

2. Can Divorced People Ever Become Church Officers? When Paul lists the qualifications for elders, he includes this statement:

> Therefore an overseer must be above reproach, *the husband of one wife*, soberminded, self-controlled, respectable, hospitable, able to teach . . . (1 Tim. 3:2)

Similarly, he writes this to Titus about choosing elders:

> This is why I left you in Crete, so that you might put what remained into order, and appoint elders in every town as I directed you—if anyone is above reproach, *the husband of one wife*, and his children are believers and not open to the charge of debauchery or insubordination. (Titus 1:5–6)

This is also a requirement for deacons:

> Let deacons each be *the husband of one wife*, managing their children and their own households well. (1 Tim. 3:12)

a. The Qualifications All Refer to a Man's Present Life and Character: Sometimes people think that these requirements refer to a man who has not been married more than once, and therefore that it excludes from the offices of elder and deacon all men who have been divorced for whatever reason and then remarried, and also all whose wives have died and who have remarried.

A better understanding of this passage is that it refers to the *present status* of a man, either to his *character* of being faithful to his wife or else to the fact that he is not a polygamist—he does not have more than one wife *at the present time*. In either of these interpretations, the verse does not prohibit all divorced men from being elders or deacons.

In favor of the view that these passages mean a man should be "the husband of one wife" *at the present time* is the fact that *all of the other qualifications* for being an elder or deacon in these contexts refer to a man's *present character*, not his entire past life. This

government. Once the government of the United States was established, it became a separate country, and it is now morally right for it to continue as a separate country.

2. Suppose some parents have an unusually bright daughter and, when they move to a new city, they lie about her birthdate so she can start first grade. She does very well in school, both academically and socially, but then, before the next school year begins, they feel convicted about their wrongdoing and confess it to the principal. Should the school make her attend first grade all over again? No, that would be useless. Her firstgrade education began with a lie, but it was still a genuine first-grade education and should be considered legitimate. Her schooling began with a sinful act, but there is no sin involved in counting her as a legitimate student for all her subsequent years of schooling.

becomes evident when we examine the full list of qualifications for elder in 1 Timothy 3 (I have put in italics the other qualifications that do not necessarily refer to a man's entire previous lifetime, especially those who do not become Christians until sometime during their adult lives):

> The saying is trustworthy: If anyone aspires to the office of overseer, he desires a noble task. Therefore an overseer must be *above reproach*, the husband of one wife, *sober-minded, self-controlled, respectable, hospitable, able to teach, not a drunkard, not violent but gentle, not quarrelsome, not a lover of money*. He must *manage his own household well*, with all dignity *keeping his children submissive*, for if someone does not know how to manage his own household, how will he care for God's church? He must *not be a recent convert*, or he may become puffed up with conceit and fall into the condemnation of the devil. Moreover, he must be *well thought of by outsiders*, so that he may not fall into disgrace, into a snare of the devil. (1 Tim. 3:1–7)

All the other qualifications that Paul lists refer to a man's *present status*, not his entire past life. For example, Paul does not mean "one who has *never been* violent," but "one who is *not now* violent, but gentle." He does not mean "one who has *never been* a lover of money," but "one who is *not now* a lover of money." He does not mean "one who has been above reproach *for his whole life*," but "one who is *now* above reproach." If we made these qualifications apply to a person's entire past life, then we would exclude from office almost everyone who becomes a Christian as an adult, for it is doubtful that any non-Christian could meet these qualifications.

b. It Is No Character Flaw if a Man's Wife Dies and Then He Marries Again: Another argument in support of this position is that Paul clearly encourages *widows* to marry again: "So I would have younger widows marry" (1 Tim. 5:14). Therefore, there would seem to be no moral shortcoming or character flaw simply because a man marries again after his wife dies (see also 1 Cor. 7:39, encouraging remarriage). Therefore, there is no legitimate reason for excluding such a man from becoming an elder or deacon if he is otherwise qualified.

c. These Passages Probably Prohibit a Polygamist from Being an Elder or Deacon: A better interpretation is that Paul is prohibiting a polygamist (a man who *presently* has more than one wife) from being an elder or deacon. Several reasons support this view: (1) Paul could have said "having been married only once," but he did not.[55] (2) We would

---

[55] The Greek expression translated as "having been married only once" is *hapax gegamēmenos*, using the word "once" (*hapax*) and a perfect participle of *gameō*, "to marry," giving the sense, "having been married once and continuing in the state resulting from that marriage." (Such a construction with *hapax* plus a perfect participle is found, for example, in Heb. 10:2, and a similar construction is found in Heb. 9:26. Related expressions with aorist verbs are found in Heb. 6:4; 9:28; and Jude 3.)

have to prevent remarried widowers from being elders or deacons if we take the phrase to mean "having been married only once." But the qualifications for church officers are all based on a man's moral and spiritual character, and there is nothing in Scripture to suggest that a man who remarries after his wife dies has lower moral or spiritual qualifications.[56] (3) Polygamy was possible in the first century. Although it was not common, it was practiced, especially among the Jews. The Jewish historian Josephus says, "For it is an ancestral custom of ours to have several wives at the same time."[57] Rabbinic legislation also regulated inheritance customs and other aspects of polygamy.[58]

Therefore, it is reasonable to understand "the husband of one wife" (Titus 1:6) to prohibit a polygamist from holding the office of elder or deacon.[59] The passages then say nothing about divorce and remarriage with respect to qualifications for church office.

If this is the correct understanding of the phrase, then it has significant practical application in missionary contexts even today in cultures where polygamy is still practiced. The Bible would not encourage a husband to divorce any of his multiple wives, which would leave them without support and protection. But it would not allow a man with multiple wives to be an elder or deacon. This restriction would provide a pattern that, if followed, would generally lead to the abolition of polygamy in a church in a generation or two.

d. Another Possibility Is That These Passages Mean a Man Must Be "Faithful to His Wife":

An alternative view of these passages claims that the expression *mias gunaikos andra*, "husband of one wife," means "having the character of a one-woman man"; that is, "faithful to his wife." In support of this view is the fact that a similar phrase is used in 1 Timothy 5:9 for qualifications for widows (Greek, *henos andros gunē*; "one-man woman," i.e., "wife of one husband"):

> Let a widow be enrolled if she is not less than sixty years of age, *having been the wife of one husband.*

Paul also could have expressed the idea of having been married only once by using a perfect participle of *ginomai* to say "having been a husband of one wife" (*gegonōs mias gunaikos anēr*).

[56] Some interpreters in the early church did try to exclude remarried widowers from church office (see, for example, *Apostolic Constitutions* 2.2; 6.17 [third or fourth century AD], and *Apostolic Canons* 17 [fourth or fifth century AD]), but these statements reflect not a biblical perspective but a false asceticism that held that celibacy in general was superior to marriage. (These texts can be found in ANF 7:396, 457, and 501.) However, Chrysostom (d. AD 407) understood 1 Tim. 3:2 to prohibit polygamy, not second marriages after death or divorce (see his *Homily X* on 1 Tim. 3:1–4 in NPNF[1] 13:438).

[57] Josephus, *Antiquities* 17.14; in 17.19 he lists the nine women who were married to King Herod at the same time. An English translation can be found in Josephus, *Jewish Antiquities*, vol. 8, trans. Ralph Marcus (Cambridge, MA: Harvard University Press, and London: Heinemann, 1969), 379 and 381.

[58] See Mishnah, *Yebamoth* 4:11; *Ketuboth* 10:1, 4, 5; *Sanhedrin* 2:4; *Kerithoth* 3:7; *Kiddushin* 2:7; *Bechoroth* 8:4 (the Mishnah reflects much oral tradition going back to the first century or earlier). Other evidence on Jewish polygamy is found in Justin Martyr, *Dialogue with Trypho*, chap. 134, ANF 1:266–67. Evidence for polygamy among non-Jews is not as extensive but is indicated in Herodotus (d. 420 BC) 1.135; 4.155; 2 Macc. 4:30 (about 170 BC); Tertullian, *Apology* 46 in ANF 3:50–51.

[59] This is also the view of Davis, *Evangelical Ethics*, 103.

In this verse, "wife of one husband" seems to refer to the trait of faithfulness, for a prohibition of remarriage after the death of a spouse would be in contradiction to Paul's advice in 1 Timothy 5:14, "I would have younger widows marry." In addition, it would not make sense for "wife of one husband" to mean a woman could not be married to more than one man at the same time (polyandry), for that was unknown in Jewish or Greco-Roman cultures. Therefore, it is argued that verse 9 must mean "having been faithful to her husband." The commentators who favor the view that 3:2 means "faithful to his wife" all seem to be swayed by this parallel expression in 5:9.[60]

But I do not find this supposed parallel to be very persuasive, because the context is different, the reason for the requirement is different, and the tense of the Greek verbs used in the longer sentence is different in each case. (Commentators do not generally take account of these differences.) In addition, there is a common Greek word meaning "faithful" (the adjective *pistos*), a word that Paul uses several times in 1 Timothy, and he easily could have used this word in 1 Timothy 3:2 if he had wanted to say "faithful to his wife." But he did not.

It is natural that "having been the wife of one husband" (1 Tim. 5:9) would refer to the entire *past life* of a widow, because Paul is talking about requirements for receiving financial support from the church: a woman who had been married to more than one husband would have had more extended family members who could provide support for her. And all of the requirements for widows to receive financial support in 1 Timothy 5:9–10 have to do with their entire *past lives*, not their present lives and characters, as is the case in the requirements for elders and deacons in chapter 3.[61] This is why many English translations render the requirement for a widow in 1 Timothy 5:9 as "*having been* the wife of one husband" (ESV, NASB, RSV, KJV, all referring to past life (similarly, NIV says "has been"; NLT says "was faithful"), but translate the requirement for elders in 1 Timothy 3:2 as "an overseer must *be* . . . the husband of one wife" (referring to present life).

But I appreciate the weight of the arguments for the "faithful to his wife" interpretation also. And whether someone holds to the "not a polygamist" interpretation or the "faithful to his wife" interpretation, it is clear that Paul is not speaking about all second marriages. He is not prohibiting from church leadership a man whose wife has died and

---

[60] The majority of modern commentators seem to favor the explanation that says "husband of one wife" means "having the character of a one-woman man," that is, a man who is faithful to his wife. See George Knight III, *Commentary on the Pastoral Epistles*, NIGTC (Grand Rapids, MI: Eerdmans, 1992), 157–59; also I. Howard Marshall, *The Pastoral Epistles*, ICC (Edinburgh: T&T Clark, 1999), 250–51. The most extensive discussion of different options for "husband of one wife" is found in William Mounce, *Pastoral Epistles*, WBC (Nashville: Thomas Nelson, 2000), 170–73.

[61] This contextual focus on a widow's past life makes the translation "having been the wife of one husband" appropriate, and this is even more true if we understand the force of the perfect participle *gegonuia* in 1 Tim. 5:9 to carry over from the previous phrase. In any case, all the qualifications for enrolling widows in 1 Tim. 5:9–10 speak of past history in their lives. But in 1 Tim. 3:2 and Titus 1:6, the sense is different, because present-tense forms of *eimi* ("to be") are used: "an overseer must *be* above reproach, the husband of one wife . . ." (1 Tim. 3:2).

who has remarried, or a man who has been divorced and who has remarried (these cases should be evaluated on an individual basis).

e. Do the Qualifications for Leadership Require That Elders and Deacons Must Be Married? When Paul says that an elder or deacon must be the "husband of one wife," it is unlikely that he means that every elder or deacon must be married, for two reasons:

1. Both Jesus and Paul (1 Cor. 7:7–8; 9:5) were single, and it is unlikely that Paul would have given a requirement for eldership that not even he or Jesus himself could fulfill.

2. Paul also gives requirements about children, saying that an elder must be someone whose "*children* are believers" (Titus 1:6) and "he must manage his own household well, with all dignity keeping his *children* submissive" (1 Tim. 3:4). He says that deacons must be "managing their *children* and their own households well" (1 Tim. 3:12). It is unlikely that Paul is requiring that elders must have two or more children (the nouns are plural, implying more than one). Rather, it seems that Paul is speaking about the most common kind of situation, a married man with children, and the sense of the passage is, "*If he has children*, the children should be believers and submissive to their parents."

Similarly, the "husband of one wife" passages should be understood to mean, "*If he is married*, he should have only one wife" (or "he should be faithful to his wife"). That would be the most common situation for an elder or deacon, and Paul is speaking about the ordinary cases, giving a picture of the typical approved overseer or deacon as a faithful husband and father, and not absolutely requiring marriage or children.

3. Should Laws about Divorce Reflect Biblical Standards? It is appropriate to comment briefly on a question about civil laws. Should Christians seek to influence laws so that they reflect biblical standards regarding marriage and divorce?

Since marriage is not an institution only for Christians, but is an institution established by God at creation (Gen. 1:27–28; 2:24–25), God intended it to apply to all people, believers and unbelievers alike, and he intended it to be beneficial both to individual husbands and wives, and to society in general (see discussion in chap. 28, p. 710).

Therefore, the standards expressed in Scripture regarding divorce and remarriage are the standards that are ultimately best for all people, according to the purpose of our Creator. It seems to me, therefore, that the church, where it has opportunity, should give personal encouragement to non-Christians as well as Christians to abide by God's high moral standards regarding divorce and remarriage, and should encourage legislative proposals that would provide more legal support for the solemnity of marriage and its intended lifelong commitment; assistance for troubled marriages; more protection for spouses who sincerely seek to repair their marriages; and provisions for temporary separation and permanent divorce when it is clear that no other solution is possible.

In addition, in societies and cultures where rampant divorce for all sorts of reasons has been occurring for decades, individual Christians as well as churches should also seek to support and minister to women and men and children who have been hurt by divorces in the past.

G. EVALUATION OF MORE RESTRICTIVE VIEWS REGARDING DIVORCE AND REMARRIAGE

While the position on divorce and remarriage that I have supported in this chapter has been the most common one among conservative Protestants since the Reformation, and while I have discussed the views of other authors who have *less restrictive* positions (they allow additional grounds for divorce), we also must analyze at this point the positions of some other authors who hold *more restrictive* views of divorce and remarriage. There are two categories of more restrictive views: (1) no divorce and no remarriage, and (2) divorce but no remarriage.

1. No Divorce and No Remarriage. J. Carl Laney argues that the Bible never approves of divorce and, if a divorce occurs, remarriage to someone else is never permitted. He says, "I believe Scripture teaches that marriage was designed by God to be permanent unto death, and that divorce and remarriage constitute the sin of adultery."[62]

Laney emphasizes Jesus's teaching on the permanence of marriage in Matthew 19:4–6 (p. 32), and especially Jesus's statement, "What therefore God has joined together, let not man separate" (v. 6). In answer to the question of the Pharisees, "Is it lawful to divorce one's wife for any cause?" (v. 3), Laney says that Jesus's answer "indicates, 'There is no valid reason at all' for divorce" (p. 33).[63]

What then shall we make of the phrase "except for sexual immorality" in Matthew 19:9?

> And I say to you: whoever divorces his wife, *except for sexual immorality* [Greek, *porneia*], and marries another, commits adultery.

Laney says that *porneia* in this verse refers to incest, and this means that Jesus was allowing divorce in the case of a marriage to a close relative, as defined in Leviticus 18:6–18. Laney writes, "The exception clause in Matthew 19:9 simply states that Christ's prohibition against divorce (Mt 19:6) does not apply in the case of an

---

[62] J. Carl Laney, "No Divorce and No Remarriage," in *Divorce and Remarriage: Four Christian Views*, 16. This chapter is a summary of Laney's earlier book, *The Divorce Myth: A Biblical Examination of Divorce and Remarriage* (Minneapolis, MN: Bethany House, 1981).

[63] I might add at this point that "no divorce" is also the historic position of the Roman Catholic Church. See *Catechism of the Catholic Church*, 2nd ed. (New York: Doubleday, 1997), para. 1650, 2382–86. "A rectified and consummated marriage cannot be dissolved by any human power or for any reason other than death" (para. 2382). "Divorce is a grave offense against the natural law. . . . Contracting a new union, even if it is recognized by civil law, adds to the gravity of the rupture: the remarried spouse is then in a situation of public and permanent adultery" (para. 2384). As for those who have been divorced and then married someone else, "they cannot receive Eucharistic communion as long as this situation persists" (para. 1650).

However, the catechism also includes another statement that seems to allow for divorce in several specific circumstances: "If civil divorce remains the only possible way of ensuring certain legal rights, the care of the children, or the protection of inheritance, it can be tolerated and does not constitute a moral offense" (para. 2383). I do not understand how this statement is consistent with the other statements I quoted that strictly prohibit divorce.

illegal, incestuous marriage" (p. 35). He points out that *porneia* refers to incest in 1 Corinthians 5:1.

I do not find Laney's argument persuasive. The term *porneia* is quite common (75 instances in the New Testament and Septuagint combined, 25 in the New Testament alone) and can be used to refer to any kind of "unlawful sexual intercourse."[64] Laney himself agrees that the term "basically refers to unlawful sexual activity, including prostitution, unchastity and fornication. *Porneia* is a general term which can be interpreted in various ways" (p. 34).

Therefore, it is highly unlikely that Matthew or the Greek-speaking readers of Matthew's Gospel would have ever understood "sexual immorality" (*porneia*) to be restricted to the kinds of incest described in Leviticus 18:6–18, especially when the term *porneia* does not even occur in the Septuagint translation of that passage. There is no clearly restrictive wording in these passages, such as "except for sexual immorality *with members of one's own family*," that would signal readers that Jesus is using the word in a highly restrictive sense here. The fact that *porneia* is used in one verse to refer to incest (1 Cor. 5:1) does not nullify the evidence from many other passages in both the Old Testament and New Testament showing that the word refers to a wide range of immoral sexual activity, so that is the sense we should give it in Matthew 19:9 as well.

David Instone-Brewer points out:

> [Understanding *porneia* to mean "incest" in Matthew 19:9] would not make good sense in the context of Jesus's teaching. Jesus was criticizing those who use a divorce certificate too freely. . . . In the case of incest, however, there is no need for a divorce certificate because the marriage would be considered invalid from the start. The rabbis did not consider that any marriage had taken place.[65]

My conclusion is that the "no divorce and no remarriage" view cannot adequately account for the precise wording found in Matthew 19:9 and 1 Corinthians 7:15, where divorce is allowed for adultery and for desertion.

2. Divorce but No Remarriage. In 1990, William Heth argued that even though divorces sometimes will occur, remarriage to another person is never justified. Heth later changed his position,[66] as I explain later (p. 834), but his 1990 argument still remains

---

[64] BDAG, 854.

[65] *Divorce and Remarriage in the Bible*, 158. Instone-Brewer also argues that more recent analysis of the linguistic evidence from Qumran, to which Joseph Fitzmyer appealed and to which Laney also appeals, shows that *porneia* should not be understood to apply strictly to incest (pp. 157–58).

[66] See William Heth, "Jesus on Divorce: How My Mind Has Changed," *Southern Baptist Journal of Theology* 6, no. 1 (Spring 2002): 4–29. But Heth's co-author, Gordon Wenham, continued to hold the divorce but no remarriage view; see Wenham, "Does the New Testament Approve Remarriage after Divorce?" *Southern Baptist Journal of Theology* 6, no. 1 (Spring 2002), 30–45. Wenham emphasizes that this was apparently the unanimous view of the church in the second century AD, and doubts that they all could have misread

a widely accessible, articulate defense of this position, and it is still profitable to understand it and interact with it.

A crucial point in Heth's earlier argument was his explanation of Matthew 19:9: "And I say to you: whoever divorces his wife, except for sexual immorality, and marries another, commits adultery."

Heth claimed that the phrase "except for sexual immorality" only applied to the first part of the sentence ("whoever divorces his wife"), but not to the second part of the sentence ("and marries another"). He wrote:

> Matthew 19:9 contains two conditional statements, one that is qualified and one that is unqualified or absolute: (1) A man may not divorce his wife unless she is guilty of adultery, and (2) Whoever marries another woman after divorcing his wife commits adultery. Or to paraphrase the idea another way: "Divorcing for reasons other than marital unfaithfulness is forbidden, and remarriage after every divorce is adulterous."[67]

However, I do not find Heth's explanation to be a plausible understanding of Matthew 19:9. This is because he fails to account for the fact that there is one subject ("whoever," or *hos an* in Greek) for all three verbs:

whoever *divorces . . . and marries . . . commits adultery.*

the New Testament texts and forgotten apostolic teaching so quickly (p. 41). See also Wenham and Heth, *Jesus and Divorce: Towards an Evangelical Understanding of New Testament Teaching,* 2nd ed. (Carlisle, UK: Paternoster, 2002).

[67] William Heth, "Divorce, but No Remarriage," in *Divorce and Remarriage: Four Christian Views,* 104. This chapter is a summary of Heth's longer argument in William Heth and Gordon J. Wenham, *Jesus and Divorce: The Problem with the Evangelical Consensus* (Nashville: Thomas Nelson, 1984).

Another thoughtful and carefully reasoned defense of the "no remarriage" position is found in a paper by John Piper, "Divorce & Remarriage: A Position Paper," Desiring God, July 21, 1986, http://www.desiringgod .org/articles/divorce-remarriage-a-position-paper. Piper's arguments are, as one might expect, exceptionally clear and forceful. He places much weight on what he sees as the clear prohibition of remarriage in several other New Testament passages and on the possible alternative explanations for Matt. 19:9. Although I count John as a valued lifelong friend, and although I agree with nearly everything he teaches, I respectfully disagree with him on this topic.

Piper also notes that the official position of the church he pastored at the time, adopted by its Council of Deacons in 1989, differs with his own "no remarriage" position. The church's position includes these statements: "(3) Divorce may be permitted when a spouse deserts the relationship, commits adultery, or is dangerously abusive (1 Cor. 7:15; Matthew 19:9; 1 Cor. 7:11). . . . (4) The remarriage of the aggrieving, divorced spouse may be viewed as severing the former marriage so that the unmarried spouse whose behavior did not biblically justify being divorced, may be free to remarry a believer (Matthew 19:9). . . . (5) After serious efforts have been made toward reconciliation the aggrieved partners referred to in guideline #3 may, together with the leadership of the church, come to regard their marriages as irreparably broken. In such cases remarriage may be a legitimate step, if taken with serious reckoning that this cuts off all possibility of a reconciliation that God may yet be willing to produce." See "A Statement on Divorce & Remarriage in the Life of Bethlehem Baptist Church," Desiring God, May 2, 1989, http://www.desiringgod.org/articles/a-statement-on-divorce -remarriage-in-the-life-of-bethlehem-baptist-church. Piper also discusses the divorce passages in *What Jesus Demands from the World* (Wheaton, IL: Crossway, 2006), 301–22.

But Heth's explanation wrongly introduces two different subjects, and this illegitimately turns the verse into two separate statements, as his explanation shows:

1. *A man* may not divorce his wife unless she is guilty of adultery, and
2. *Whoever* marries another woman after divorcing his wife commits adultery.[68]

This is not what Jesus said. He did not make two separate statements on two different subjects, but made one statement about "whoever":

> And I say to you: *whoever divorces* his wife, except for sexual immorality, *and marries* another, *commits adultery*. (Matt. 19:9)

In order to do justice to this verse, it is best to conclude, as I did earlier, that Jesus is saying that a man who divorces his wife because of sexual immorality and marries another woman does not commit adultery. In other words, Jesus permits remarriage in this case.

Another difficulty with Heth's earlier understanding is that, on his explanation, Matthew 19:9 does not make sense. As we noted earlier, if we remove the clause "and marries another," then the verse says, "Whoever divorces his wife, except for sexual immorality, . . . commits adultery." But this is not true, because divorce itself does not constitute adultery. Some people will divorce and not have sex with or marry anybody else. In order to answer such an objection, Heth claims that "divorce is tantamount to committing adultery,"[69] and he appeals to Matthew 5:27–32, but there Jesus does not say that divorce *is* adultery but that someone who wrongly divorces his wife "makes her commit adultery." Nowhere does the Bible say that divorce itself is adultery.

A different explanation of "except for sexual immorality" in Matthew 19:9 is sometimes given by those who support the "no remarriage" position. They argue that *porneia*, as used in Matthew 19:9, does not refer to adultery committed by a married woman but to *fornication by an engaged woman* that is discovered prior to her marriage.[70]

I agree that *porneia*, which refers to a wide range of unlawful sexual activity, was sometimes used to refer to sexual intercourse prior to marriage (see John 8:41). But it was also used to refer to other kinds of sexual immorality, such as incest (1 Cor. 5:1) and adultery (Rev. 17:2; and, from both Jewish and Christian literature near the time of the New Testament, see Sirach 23:23; *Shepherd of Hermas*, Mandate 4.1.5). The most decisive argument against this view is the context of Matthew 19:9, for when the conversation begins, the Pharisees do not ask Jesus about divorce during a betrothal (or engagement)

---

[68] Heth, "Divorce, but No Remarriage," 104. The same understanding of Matt. 19:9 (the exception clause applies to "whoever divorces" but not to "and marries another") is supported by Andrew Cornes, *Divorce and Remarriage: Biblical Principle and Pastoral Practice*, 2nd ed. (Fearn, Ross-shire, UK: Mentor, 2002), 216–19.

[69] Heth, "Divorce, but No Remarriage," 104.

[70] Heth mentions this view as a "good possibility"; ibid., 126n66. Piper also favors this interpretation in his "Position Paper," sect. 11.

period, but about divorces in general: "And Pharisees came up to him and tested him by asking, 'Is it lawful to divorce one's wife for any cause?'" (Matt. 19:3). Nothing in the context would support limiting the discussion to fornication discovered during the engagement period, nor can it be supported by the common uses of *porneia*, for it refers to a wide variety of sexually immoral acts.

Heth also appeals to Mark 10:11–12 and Luke 16:18,[71] which do not include the exception clause found in Matthew 5:32 and 19:9. I agree that these passages in Mark and Luke do not include an exception for sexual immorality, and if we did not have the verses in Matthew, we might conclude that Jesus did not allow any grounds for divorce. But we do have the verses in Matthew, and they explicitly allow for divorce in the case of sexual immorality. A reasonable explanation is that Mark and Luke did not include Jesus's statement of this exception because there was no dispute about it and everyone agreed that it was a legitimate ground for divorce.

Another argument Heth uses is that "when Paul does specifically discuss the 'right' to remarry he always mentions the matter of the death of one of the spouses in the same context (1 Cor. 7:39; see also Rom. 7:2–3)."[72] But in these statements Paul is talking about marriage in general and the topic of divorce is not in view in either context, so his failure to mention any grounds for divorce in these passages is not a decisive argument.

It is important to note that, in order to be consistent, Heth argues that remarriage is never allowed, not even when the other spouse has married someone else. What is the abandoned spouse to do in such a case? Heth says the abandoned spouse has to remain single for the rest of his or her life:

> If Jesus calls remarriage adultery, and if reconciliation is seemingly impossible, then the path of God's highest blessing must lie in the direction of pursuing a single life.[73]

I appreciate that this is consistent with Heth's understanding of Scripture in his chapter, but it will strike many interpreters as unreasonable. For example, if James and Susan are married, and if James divorces Susan and marries Alice, he is no longer married to Susan. Therefore, Susan is no longer married, but is single (in fact, Heth says she should pursue a "single life"). And if she is single, then there is no reason why she could not marry someone else.

There is another reason why I am not persuaded by the "no remarriage" view, and that is the argument that this position is so unlike the emphasis of the entire New Testament on the healing and restoration of those who have been hurt by the effects of sin and evil in the world. Jesus frequently healed all who were brought to him with any affliction, as we see in verses such as this:

---

[71] Heth, "Divorce, but No Remarriage," 107–8.
[72] Ibid., 109.
[73] Ibid., 115.

That evening they brought to him many who were oppressed by demons, and he cast out the spirits with a word and *healed all who were sick*. (Matt. 8:16)

He also said:

The thief comes only to steal and kill and destroy. I came that they may have life and have it abundantly. (John 10:10)

And the Old Testament said:

No good thing does he withhold
from those who walk uprightly. (Ps. 84:11)

Also, the Bible views marriage as a *blessing* from God, something good and wonderful for us to enjoy during this lifetime (see Gen. 1:31; Prov. 18:22). And marriage presents to the world a beautiful picture of the relationship between Christ and the church (see Eph. 5:31–32).

Therefore, it just does not seem to me to be consistent with the way God acts with his children in the new covenant age to say, for those who have already suffered greatly because a spouse has abandoned them or has committed adultery with someone else, and have suffered even more when that spouse married another person, and who still long to be married, that God would require these suffering victims, *who are no longer married to anyone*, to avoid marrying again for their entire lifetimes. For those who long to marry again, such a prohibition would prolong their hardship and suffering, and it would do so unnecessarily. I simply do not believe that God acts this way with his children in this age.

I recognize that this is a "big-picture" argument that depends on how one sees the New Testament (or the entire Bible) as a whole. I am aware of many passages that speak of the blessings that come to those who endure suffering in this life, and I am sure that those who disagree with me on this topic could quote those passages back to me, and could also quote 1 Corinthians 7 on the value of singleness (for those who are called to such a life and have a gift of celibacy). I realize that in the nature of the Christian life, we will all experience some measure of suffering in this lifetime, for some suffering cannot be avoided. But being prohibited from marriage for the rest of one's lifetime, even for those who do not have the gift of celibacy and who long to be married, is a kind of suffering that *can* be avoided if churches will allow them to remarry. Jesus tells us to pray, "deliver us from evil" (Matt. 6:13), and surely we should pray that those who have been victims of unwanted divorces would be delivered from their suffering at least to the extent that new marriages would bring healing and blessing to their lives.

Significantly, as I mentioned above, Heth himself later changed his position in a 2002 article entitled "Jesus on Divorce: How My Mind Has Changed."[74] He wrote, "It

---

[74] Heth, "Jesus on Divorce: How My Mind Has Changed," 4–29.

seems most probable that the exception clause in Matthew points to divorce with just cause, a valid divorce that would permit remarriage, and Jesus limits that just cause to *porneia*."[75]

Heth also now thinks that 1 Corinthians 7:15 ("But if the unbelieving partner separates, let it be so. In such cases the brother or sister is not enslaved") allows for divorce and remarriage in the case of irreconcilable desertion. He says he was persuaded by Craig Keener's argument that in this verse Paul "distinctly frees the innocent party to remarry" and that "If Paul meant that remarriage was not permitted, he said precisely the opposite of what he meant."[76]

H. PRACTICAL COUNSEL REGARDING PEOPLE WHO HAVE EXPERIENCED PAINFUL DIVORCES

Probably every church today has people who have experienced painful divorces—perhaps some children who still are deeply grieved because their mothers and fathers dissolved their marriages many years ago, or perhaps adults who did not want a divorce at all but whose spouses filed for divorce anyway. As the Wallerstein study mentioned earlier in this chapter demonstrated, such people can experience deep pain and sorrow, and the feeling of being deserted and betrayed, many years later—though they will seldom mention it to anyone.

It is important that pastors and other church members be aware that such situations are not uncommon today. At some place and time in the life of the church, it is important to provide a setting in which people feel sufficiently safe to discuss these feelings and then have opportunity to pray with one or two others at some length, until the Holy Spirit gives them the ability to genuinely forgive the ones who caused their hurt and brings genuine comfort and peace to the grieving individuals' hearts and minds.

Christians who have been through divorces also have a wonderful encouragement to realize that Jesus understands our sufferings and is willing to walk beside us in them:

> For we do not have a high priest who is unable to sympathize with our weaknesses, but one who in every respect has been tempted as we are, yet without sin. Let us then with confidence draw near to the throne of grace, that we may receive mercy and find grace to help in time of need. (Heb. 4:15–16)

Although Jesus was never married, and so he never experienced divorce specifically, he certainly knew what it was to be betrayed and abandoned by friends who were close to him, particularly Judas, who had been with him for three remarkable years (see

---

[75] Ibid., 20.

[76] Ibid., 13, quoting Craig Keener, *And Marries Another: Divorce and Remarriage in the Teaching of the New Testament* (Peabody, MA: Hendrickson, 1991), 61.

Matt. 26:14, 25, 47; see also Matt. 26:56: "all the disciples left him and fled"). Christians can pray directly to Jesus, knowing that he understands desertion more deeply than any human friend ever will.

It is also important for Christians who have experienced divorces not to let the rest of their lives be ruled by this pain from the past. For children who have suffered deeply from divorces, Peter's words have special relevance, showing that Christ's sacrifice purchased freedom for us even from any wrongful patterns of life that we experienced from our parents:

> You were *ransomed from the futile ways inherited from your forefathers*, not with perishable things such as silver or gold, but with the precious blood of Christ, like that of a lamb without blemish or spot. (1 Pet. 1:18–19)

And for adults who have been abandoned by a previous wife or husband, the promise of God's comfort in 2 Corinthians should also bring great encouragement:

> Blessed be the God and Father of our Lord Jesus Christ, the Father of mercies and God of all comfort, who comforts us in all our affliction, so that we may be able to comfort those who are in any affliction, with the comfort with which we ourselves are comforted by God. For as we share abundantly in Christ's sufferings, so through Christ we share abundantly in comfort too. (2 Cor. 1:3–5)

Finally, it is important for churches to establish programs or ministry practices that teach about and encourage strong marriages, and that also will provide counseling and help for couples who are going through difficult times in their marriages.[77]

And for every married person reading this chapter, even those who wrongfully were divorced in the past and have now married someone else, God's purpose for you from this point onward is to ask him for forgiveness for wrongs done in the past and then to seek God's blessing *on your present marriage*. He does not want you now to get another divorce, but to stay married. Therefore, no matter what circumstances led up to this present marriage, if you are married, *you are now married to the right person*, and God wants you to make that marriage a good one for the rest of your life.

I. APPENDIX: THE TRANSLATION OF MALACHI 2:16

There are three main translation options for Malachi 2:16:

1. Several translations have the Lord saying, "I hate divorce," as in the NASB:

---

[77] FamilyLife, a Christian ministry led by my longtime friend Dennis Rainey, is an outstanding, biblically sound organization that has a variety of excellent programs to encourage and strengthen marriages. See http://www.familylife.com. (Margaret and I were previously members of the Speaker Team for FamilyLife marriage conferences.)

"For *I hate divorce*," says the LORD, the God of Israel, "and him who covers his garment with wrong," says the LORD of hosts. "So take heed to your spirit, that you do not deal treacherously." (Mal. 2:16, NASB)

The RSV, NRSV, NIV 1984, NLT, and NET also have the Lord saying, "I hate divorce."

2. Other translations, such as the NIV 2011, understand the subject of "hates" to be the husband, and they translate this sentence this way:

"*The man who hates and divorces his wife*," says the LORD, the God of Israel, "does violence to the one he should protect," says the LORD Almighty. (Mal. 2:16, NIV)

The ESV translation is similar, but it understands "hates" to mean failing to love one's wife:

For *the man who does not love his wife but divorces her*, says the LORD, the God of Israel, covers his garment with violence, says the LORD of hosts. (Mal. 2:16, ESV)

The Christian Standard Bible is also similar: "'If he hates and divorces *his wife*,' says the LORD God of Israel, 'he covers his garment with injustice,' says the LORD of Armies" (Mal. 2:16, CSB).

3. A third alternative is to translate the verb as "he hates," but to understand "the LORD" to be the subject, not the husband. This is the alternative translation found in the marginal note of the ESV:

Or "The LORD, the God of Israel, says that *he hates divorce*." (Mal. 2:16, ESV mg.)

The NKJV also translates it this way: "For the LORD God of Israel says that *He hates divorce*." The KJV is similar: "For the LORD, the God of Israel, saith that he hateth putting away: for *one* covereth violence with his garment, saith the LORD of hosts."

Is there a best solution among these three options? The Hebrew of this verse is notoriously difficult to understand. No solution is without difficulties. Here are the three main solutions, with the arguments in favor of each:

1. Several translations have God saying, "I hate divorce" (NASB, RSV, NRSV, NET, NIV 1984, and NLT). To render the Hebrew text this way, the translators have to understand the verb *sānē'* as a participle, "hating" (ordinarily this would be spelled *sonē'*), and assume that the pronoun "I" is understood, giving the sense, "For I hate [am hating] divorce, says the LORD" (Zech. 9:12 is cited as a parallel in Hebrew). On this view, as well as view 3, some slight change has to be made to the third-person singular verb *wekissāh*, "and he covers," in the next clause, altering it to say something like "and the one who covers" or "and covering."

2. The ESV understands the first clause in a sense similar to the Septuagint, taking

the Hebrew to represent an "if-then" statement, because the first word (Hebrew, *kî*) can mean either "for" or "if." This gives the sense, "If he [that is, a man] hates and divorces, says the LORD God of Israel, he covers his garment with violence." Reasons in support of this sense are: (1) It understands the subject of "hates" as a divorcing husband, which is consistent with the use of "hate" in marriage contexts elsewhere, where the hatred in question is invariably the husband's (Gen. 29:31; Deut. 21:15–17; 22:13, 16; 24:3; Judg. 15:2; Prov. 30:23). In some of these cases, "hate" has the sense "cease to love," and this is how the ESV translates the verb. (2) This translation requires no slight change of the Hebrew text. (3) The alternative translations "I hate divorce" or "the LORD . . . says that he hates divorce" sound like a complete condemnation of divorce, but such a blanket condemnation of divorce in Malachi 2:16 would contradict the qualified permission, at least as a response to sexuality infidelity, that is implied by Deuteronomy 22:19, 29; 24:1–4; Jeremiah 3 (God's figurative divorce of Israel); Matthew 5:32; 19:8–9; and 1 Corinthians 7:15. (4) The subject of the second verb must be a sinful human being, for it cannot mean, "For the LORD says that he hates divorce *and he covers his garment with violence.*" Therefore, other translations have to change the finite third-person verb "and he covers" (Hebrew, *wekissāh*) to a participle, giving the sense "and *covering* one's garment with violence."

3. An ESV footnote gives this alternative sense: "The LORD, the God of Israel, says that he hates divorce, and him who covers. . . ." Supporting reasons are: (1) "The LORD" is the only person explicitly named in the verse, and it is natural to understand him as the one about whom the verse says, "he hates." (2) Several other examples of this exact grammatical construction in Hebrew (perfect verb plus infinitive with no conjunction or preposition between them) show that the infinitive should be taken as the direct object of the first verb, giving the sense, "he hates [perfect verb] divorce [infinitive]" (cf. Num. 10:31; Deut. 2:7; Pss. 77:10 [English v. 9]; 139:2; Isa. 56:11). But there are no examples of this combination in the Hebrew Old Testament that would support the sense of "and" in "he hates *and* divorces." What is needed for view 2 is some example of a finite verb X (such as "he hates") followed immediately by an infinitive Y (such as "divorce") where it means "X and Y," but no examples have been found. (3) All of the other 60 Old Testament instances of a finite form of this same verb *sānē'* ("hate") have an object expressed (the person or thing hated). Therefore, this verb must require a direct object here as well, and this supports the sense "he hates divorce" (with "divorce" as the direct object), but not the sense "he hates and divorces" (with no expressed object for "hate"). (4) In other contexts that mention sin, where "the Lord" is mentioned along with the word *hates* (Hebrew, *sānē'*), the Lord is often the subject (e.g., Isa. 1:14; 61:8; Jer. 44:4; Zech. 8:17; Mal. 1:3). (5) This verse then gives a clear reason for Malachi 2:15: Let no one be faithless to his wife (v. 15) *for* (Hebrew, *kî*) the Lord hates divorce (v. 16).

The decision is not an easy one, but the translation of the ESV footnote (and KJV and NKJV), represented by view 3, seems somewhat preferable to me for the reasons given above: "The LORD, the God of Israel, says that he hates divorce . . ."

In any case, the Bible's teaching on divorce is not changed by any of these translations, because all of them signify that divorce for reasons not specified elsewhere in Scripture is condemned by the Lord as a serious sin. On interpretations 1 and 3, what the Lord "hates" is probably only the kind of "faithless" sending away of one's wife mentioned in the context (see vv. 13, 15); or the verse may be speaking to God's hatred of the destructiveness and pain that is always involved with divorce.

QUESTIONS FOR PERSONAL APPLICATION

1. Were you surprised by the information in this chapter about how many marriages are happy and about how few Christian marriages end in divorce? What was the source of your previous ideas regarding how many marriages succeed?

2. Were you surprised to read about the long-term consequences of divorce? How did this material affect your thinking about divorce?

3. After reading the discussion in this chapter, how many legitimate grounds do you think there are for divorce, according to the New Testament? In such cases, do you think that remarriage to another person is morally acceptable?

4. What character traits (see p. 110) would be most helpful in protecting a marriage so that it does not end in divorce? Which ones would be most important in dealing with the consequences of an unwanted divorce?

5. Read Exodus 20:17. Do you ever "covet your neighbor's wife" (or husband)? Are you willing right now to bring that desire into the presence of God, ask his forgiveness, and ask for his help in changing that desire in your heart into a positive desire for your own wife or husband?

6. If you are married, what are some practical things you can do now to strengthen your marriage and help to protect it from ending in divorce?

SPECIAL TERMS

BIBLIOGRAPHY

Sections in Other Ethics Texts

(see complete bibliographical data, p. 64)

Clark and Rakestraw, 2:225–60
Davis, 90–105
Feinberg, John and Paul, 583–633
Frame, 769–81

Geisler, 303–13

Gushee and Stassen, 270–87

Hays, 347–78

Jones, 177–204

Kaiser, 91–104

McQuilkin and Copan, 241–48

Other Works

Adams, Jay E. *Marriage, Divorce, and Remarriage in the Bible*. Grand Rapids, MI: Zondervan, 1980.

Atkinson, D. J. "Remarriage." In *New Dictionary of Christian Ethics and Pastoral Theology*, edited by David J. Atkinson and David H. Field, 729–30. Leicester, UK: InterVarsity, and Downers Grove, IL: InterVarsity Press, 1995.

Cornes, Andrew. *Divorce and Remarriage: Biblical Principle and Pastoral Practice*. 2nd ed. Fearn, Ross-shire, Scotland: Mentor, 2002.

Feldhahn, Shaunti. *The Good News about Marriage: Debunking Discouraging Myths about Marriage and Divorce*. Colorado Springs: Multnomah, 2014.

Hawthorne, Gerald F. "Marriage and Divorce, Adultery and Incest." In *Dictionary of Paul and His Letters*, edited by Gerald F. Hawthorne, Ralph P. Martin, and Daniel G. Reid, 594–600. Downers Grove, IL: InterVarsity Press, 1993.

Heth, William A., and Gordon J. Wenham. *Jesus and Divorce: The Problem with the Evangelical Consensus*. Nashville: Thomas Nelson, 1984.

House, H. Wayne, ed. *Divorce and Remarriage: Four Christian Views*. Downers Grove, IL: InterVarsity Press, 1990.

Instone-Brewer, David. *Divorce and Remarriage in the Bible: The Social and Literary Context*. Grand Rapids, MI: Eerdmans, 2002.

———. *Divorce and Remarriage in the Church: Biblical Solutions for Pastoral Realities*. Downers Grove, IL: InterVarsity Press, 2003.

Keener, Craig S. *And Marries Another: Divorce and Remarriage in the Teaching of the New Testament*. Peabody, MA: Hendrickson, 1991.

Köstenberger, Andreas J., with David W. Jones. *God, Marriage, and Family: Rebuilding the Biblical Foundation*. 2nd ed. Wheaton, IL: Crossway, 2010, 223–38, 363–69, 275–88, 373–77.

Laney, J. Carl. *The Divorce Myth: A Biblical Examination of Divorce and Remarriage*. Minneapolis: Bethany House, 1981.

MacArthur, John. *The Divorce Dilemma: God's Last Word on Lasting Commitment*. Family Focal Point. Leominster, England: Day One, 2009.

Moles, Chris. *The Heart of Domestic Abuse: Gospel Solutions for Men Who Use Control and Violence in the Home*. Bemidji, MN: Focus, 2015.

Murray, John. *Divorce*. Philadelphia: Presbyterian & Reformed, 1961.

Newheiser, Jim. *Marriage, Divorce, and Remarriage: Critical Questions and Answers.* Phillipsburg, NJ: P&R, 2017.

Small, Dwight Hervey. *Remarriage and God's Renewing Grace: A Positive Biblical Ethic for Divorced Christians.* Grand Rapids, MI: Baker, 1986.

Storms, Sam. "What Did Jesus Teach about Divorce and Remarriage? What Did Paul Teach about Divorce and Remarriage?" In *Tough Topics 2: Biblical Answers to 25 Challenging Questions,* 209–35. Fearn, Ross-shire, Scotland: Christian Focus, 2015.

Strauss, Mark L., ed. *Remarriage after Divorce in Today's Church: Three Views.* Counterpoints. Grand Rapids, MI: Zondervan, 2006.

Tracy, Steven R. *Mending the Soul: Understanding and Healing Abuse.* Grand Rapids, MI: Zondervan, 2005.

Wallerstein, Judith S., Julia Lewis, and Sandra Blakeslee. *The Unexpected Legacy of Divorce: A 25 Year Landmark Study.* New York: Hyperion, 2000.

Wallerstein, Judith S., and Sandra Blakeslee. *Second Chances: Men, Women, and Children a Decade after Divorce.* New York: Ticknor & Fields, 1989.

Wenham, Gordon J. "Divorce." In *New Dictionary of Christian Ethics and Pastoral Theology,* 315–17.

Wenham, Gordon J., and William A. Heth. *Jesus and Divorce: Towards an Evangelical Understanding of New Testament Teaching.* 2nd ed. Carlisle, UK: Paternoster, 2002.

SCRIPTURE MEMORY PASSAGE

Matthew 19:9: And I say to you: whoever divorces his wife, except for sexual immorality, and marries another, commits adultery.

HYMN

"Like a River Glorious"

Like a river glorious is God's perfect peace,
Over all victorious in its bright increase;
Perfect, yet it floweth fuller ev'ry day,
Perfect, yet it groweth deeper all the way.

Refrain:
Stayed upon Jehovah,
Hearts are fully blest
Finding, as He promised,
Perfect peace and rest.

Hidden in the hollow of His blessed hand,
Never foe can follow, never traitor stand;

Not a surge of worry, not a shade of care,
Not a blast of hurry touch the spirit there.

Ev'ry joy or trial falleth from above,
Traced upon our dial by the Sun of Love;
We may trust Him fully all for us to do—
They who trust Him wholly, find Him wholly true.

FRANCES R. HAVERGAL, 1836–1879

ALTERNATIVE HYMN

"I Need Thee Every Hour"

I need Thee ev'ry hour,
Most gracious Lord;
No tender voice like Thine
Can peace afford.

Refrain:
I need Thee, O I need Thee,
Ev'ry hour I need Thee!
O bless me now, my Savior
I come to Thee!

I need Thee ev'ry hour,
Stay Thou nearby;
Temptations lose their pow'r
When Thou art nigh.

I need Thee ev'ry hour,
In joy or pain;
Come quickly and abide,
Or life is vain.

I need Thee ev'ry hour,
Most Holy One;
O make me Thine indeed,
Thou blessed Son!

ANNIE S. HAWKS, 1835–1918

Chapter 33

HOMOSEXUALITY AND TRANSGENDERISM

Do the biblical passages about homosexuality still apply today?
How should we analyze recent arguments claiming that the
Bible can be interpreted to allow for faithful homosexual
relationships?
Is homosexual desire wrong?
Can people be "born gay"?
How should we evaluate the claims of certain people that they
are "transgender"?
Can sex-change surgery change a man into
a woman, or a woman into a man?

What does the Bible teach about homosexuality? Does it even speak to the modern concepts of committed same-sex relationships and same-sex marriage? It is appropriate to discuss these questions in this unit of the book, which treats various aspects of human sexuality.[1]

To my knowledge, no evangelical Christian pastors or Bible scholars in previous generations ever claimed that the Bible gives moral approval to any kind of homosexual

---

[1] Several sections of this chapter are adapted from the article "Homosexuality" in the *ESV Study Bible* (Wheaton, IL: Crossway, 2008), 2547–50, with permission of the publisher. (I was the primary author of this article, but it also benefited greatly from additions and wording changes suggested by Robert Gagnon, Daniel Heimbach, and Justin Taylor.)

conduct.[2] The unanimous consensus of centuries of Christian teaching on such a major moral issue cannot be dismissed lightly. Even today, most of the widely used textbooks on Christian ethics written by evangelicals continue to hold the same position that the church has held throughout its history, namely, that homosexual conduct is morally wrong in God's sight, according to the uniform teaching of Scripture, and that people engaged in homosexual activity should be treated with love and compassion by those in the church, but not in a way that would signal approval for their homosexual conduct.[3]

On the other hand, some authors who may be considered part of evangelicalism (construed more broadly) have given cautious or qualified affirmation to some types of homosexual relationships. In the first edition of *Kingdom Ethics*, Glen Stassen and David Gushee affirmed a traditional Christian position, stating that "homosexual conduct is one form of sexual expression that falls outside the will of God."[4] But in the second edition, Gushee advocates what he calls "an evangelical revisionist view," which he defines as follows: "It is morally permissible in God's sight for gay and lesbian people to enter covenantal-marital same-sex relationships (not casual or promiscuous relationships)."[5]

Judith and Jack Balswick, both professors at Fuller Seminary, say that the male-female pattern found in the Genesis account of creation "persuades us to uphold the heterosexual union as God's intended design for marriages."[6] However, they conclude their discussion of homosexuality with this somewhat ambiguous paragraph:

> We acknowledge that some gay Christians may choose to commit themselves
> to a lifelong, monogamous homosexual union, believing that this is God's

---

[2] See S. Donald Fortson and Rollin G. Grams, *Unchanging Witness: The Consistent Christian Teaching on Homosexuality in Scripture and Tradition* (Nashville: B&H Academic, 2016).

[3] See John Jefferson Davis, *Evangelical Ethics: Issues Facing the Church Today*, 4th ed. (Phillipsburg, NJ: P&R, 2015), 106–30; John S. Feinberg and Paul D. Feinberg, *Ethics for a Brave New World*, 2nd ed. (Wheaton, IL: Crossway, 2010), 307–85; John M. Frame, *The Doctrine of the Christian Life: A Theology of Lordship* (Phillipsburg, NJ: P&R, 2008), 757–63; Norman L. Geisler, *Christian Ethics: Contemporary Issues and Options*, 2nd ed. (Grand Rapids, MI: Baker, 2010), 280–98; Robertson McQuilkin and Paul Copan, *An Introduction to Biblical Ethics: Walking in the Way of Wisdom*, 3rd ed. (Downers Grove, IL: InterVarsity Press, 2014), 285–310; Scott B. Rae, *Moral Choices: An Introduction to Ethics*, 3rd ed. (Grand Rapids, MI: Zondervan, 2009), 279–86. See also Richard B. Hays, *The Moral Vision of the New Testament: Community, Cross, New Creation: A Contemporary Introduction to New Testament Ethics* (San Francisco: HarperSanFrancisco, 1996), 379–406.

[4] Glen H. Stassen and David P. Gushee, *Kingdom Ethics: Following Jesus in Contemporary Context* (Downers Grove, IL: InterVarsity Press, 2003), 311.

[5] David P. Gushee and Glen H. Stassen, *Kingdom Ethics: Following Jesus in Contemporary Context*, 2nd ed. (Grand Rapids, MI: Eerdmans, 2016), 266. In a footnote, Gushee explains that he completed this section of the second edition after Stassen had died. Then he adds, "I must disclose that while my late co-author Glen Stassen definitely agreed that the second edition needed considerable revision in this particular section, he became too ill to engage my latest thinking. He did take pride in being the faculty sponsor of the gay student support group at Fuller Seminary." Ibid., 267n1.

On Sept. 15, 2017, Gushee published a book announcing that he had left evangelicalism; see David P. Gushee, *Still Christian: Following Jesus out of American Evangelicalism* (Louisville: Westminster John Knox, 2017).

[6] Judith K. Balswick and Jack O. Balswick, *Authentic Human Sexuality: An Integrated Christian Approach*, 2nd ed. (Downers Grove, IL: InterVarsity Press, 2008), 135.

best for them. They believe that this reflects an authentic sexuality that is congruent for them and their view of Scripture. Even though we hold to the model of a heterosexual, lifelong, monogamous union, our compassion brings us to support all Christians who pursue God's direction for their lives. A suffering Jesus knows the way and longs to meet those who seek him.[7]

Tony Campolo, a well-known sociology professor and popular speaker in evangelical circles, announced in 2015, "I am finally ready to call for the full acceptance of Christian gay couples into the Church."[8] And in the UK, prominent evangelical pastor Steve Chalke "announced his belief that monogamous same-sex relationships are not sinful and that churches should support them in the February 2013 issue of *Christianity* magazine."[9]

However, such advocacy of the moral legitimacy of committed same-sex relationships is still very rare among evangelical leaders. To understand why, it is necessary to examine in some detail the relevant biblical passages.

A. GOD'S ORIGINAL DESIGN

According to God's original design, human sexual conduct was to occur within the context of marriage between one man and one woman. The first chapter of the Bible says:

> So God created man *in his own image,*
>   in the image of God he created him;
>   male and female he created them. (Gen. 1:27)

Differentiation of the human race into two complementary sexes ("male and female") is the first fact mentioned in connection with being "in the image of God."

In Genesis 2, which describes in more detail the process summarized in 1:27, we learn that God said, "It is not good that the man should be alone; I will make him a helper fit for him" (2:18). Genesis then applies the example of Adam and Eve to all marriages:

> Therefore *a man* shall leave his father and his mother and hold fast to *his wife,*
>   and they shall become *one flesh.* (Gen. 2:24)

This "one flesh" sexual union was thus established as the pattern for marriage generally, and this explains why Jesus cites Genesis 1:27 and 2:24 as the normative pattern that God expects all marriages to follow (see Matt. 19:4–6; Mark 10:6–8).

Paul, as a good disciple of Jesus, likewise strongly echoes Genesis 1:27 and 2:24 in

---

[7] Ibid., 136.

[8] Tony Campolo, "For the Record," Tony Campolo blog, June 8, 2015, http://tonycampolo.org/for-the-record-tony-campolo-releases-a-new-statement/.

[9] Sarah, Eekhoff Zylstra, "Major Ministry Kicked Out of Evangelical Alliance UK over Homosexuality Stance," *Christianity Today*, May 5, 2014, http://www.christianitytoday.com/gleanings/2014/may/major-ministry-kicked-out-evangelical-alliance-chalke-oasis.html.

his two primary texts on homosexual practice, Romans 1:23–27 and 1 Corinthians 6:9. Jesus and Paul both assume the logic of sexual intercourse implied in Genesis: a sexual bond requires two (and only two) different sexual halves ("a man" and "his wife") being brought together into a sexual whole ("one flesh").

The importance of this male-female sexual bond is further emphasized in the way the author of Genesis reasons from the story of the creation of Eve from Adam's side to the sexual union within marriage:

> And the rib that the LORD God had taken from the man he made into a woman and brought her to the man. Then the man said, "This at last is bone of my bones and flesh of my flesh; she shall be called Woman, because she was taken out of Man." *Therefore* a man shall leave his father and his mother and hold fast to his wife, and they shall become one flesh. (Gen. 2:22–24)

The word *therefore* connects the making of Eve from a part of Adam's body with the "one flesh" sexual union between a man and a woman in marriage: it is the reunion of the two constituent parts of a sexual whole. It is not another man who is the missing part or sexual complement of a man, but rather a woman.

B. HOMOSEXUAL CONDUCT IS ONE OF SEVERAL KINDS OF SEXUAL RELATIONS PROHIBITED IN SCRIPTURE

Later passages in the Bible uphold the pattern for marriage established in Genesis 1–2 and prohibit any other kind of sexual intercourse outside of the marriage relationship between one man and one woman. For example, having sex with an opposite-sex person other than your husband or wife is forbidden by the command "You shall not commit adultery" (Ex. 20:14; reaffirmed by Jesus in Matt. 19:18; cf. Rom. 13:9; James 2:11). And sex between two unmarried people (what was called "fornication" in older Bible translations) is prohibited in passages such as Exodus 22:16–17; Deuteronomy 22:13–21, 28–29; 1 Corinthians 6:18; 2 Corinthians 11:2; 12:21; Galatians 5:19; Ephesians 5:3; Colossians 3:5; 1 Thessalonians 4:3.[10]

Other specific kinds of sexual intercourse outside of marriage are also prohibited, such as prostitution (1 Cor. 6:15–18), incest (Lev. 20:11–21; 1 Cor. 5:1–2), and bestiality (Lev. 18:23; 20:15–16). In addition, several passages of Scripture prohibit homosexual intercourse, and I will discuss these in the material that follows.

In this chapter, I will interact at several points with Matthew Vines's book *God and the Gay Christian: The Biblical Case in Support of Same-Sex Relationships*.[11] This

---

[10] See chap. 28, p. 720, for discussion of these passages in relation to cohabitation prior to marriage.

[11] Matthew Vines, *God and the Gay Christian: The Biblical Case in Support of Same-Sex Relationships* (New York: Convergent, 2014). For a book-length response to Vines, see R. Albert Mohler Jr., ed., *God and the Gay*

is a thoughtful, extensively researched, and carefully reasoned defense of committed same-sex relationships that has been widely influential in the evangelical world, and it depends on and makes frequent reference to many of the earlier, more technical academic works that have attempted to defend the legitimacy of committed homosexual relationships through alternative interpretations of key passages of Scripture.[12] (For the sake of simplicity, I have included page references to Vines's book in the text rather than in footnotes.)

1. Genesis 19. The first Old Testament text that pertains to the question of homosexuality is the Sodom and Gomorrah narrative in Genesis 19:

> The two angels came to Sodom in the evening, and Lot was sitting in the gate of Sodom. When Lot saw them, he rose to meet them and bowed himself with his face to the earth and said, "My lords, please turn aside to your servant's house and spend the night and wash your feet. Then you may rise up early and go on your way." . . .
>
> But before they lay down, the men of the city, the men of Sodom, both young and old, all the people to the last man, surrounded the house. And they called to Lot, "Where are the men who came to you tonight? *Bring them out to us, that we may know them.*" Lot went out to the men at the entrance, shut the door after him, and said, "I beg you, my brothers, do not act so wickedly." . . . Then they pressed hard against the man Lot, and drew near to break the door down. But the men reached out their hands and brought Lot into the house with them and shut the door. And they struck with blindness the men who were at the entrance of the house, both small and great, so that they wore themselves out groping for the door. Then the men said to Lot, "Have you anyone else here? Sons-in-law, sons, daughters, or anyone you have in the city, bring them out of the place. For we are about to destroy this place, because the outcry against its people has become great before the LORD, and the LORD has sent us to destroy it." . . .
>
> As morning dawned, the angels urged Lot, saying, "Up! Take your wife and your two daughters who are here, lest you be swept away in the punishment of the city." But he lingered. So the men seized him and his wife and his two daughters by the hand, the LORD being merciful to him, and they brought him out and set him outside the city. . . .

Christian? A Response to Matthew Vines, Conversant (Louisville: SBTS Press, 2014). This ebook contains chapters by Mohler, James Hamilton, Denny Burk, Owen Strachan, and Heath Lambert.

[12] Vines depends extensively on the more technical academic arguments in James V. Brownson, *Bible, Gender, Sexuality: Reframing the Church's Debate on Same-Sex Relationships* (Grand Rapids, MI: Eerdmans, 2013). Brownson is a New Testament professor at Western Theological Seminary in Holland, Michigan, which is a denominational seminary for the Reformed Church in America. For an extensive critical review of Brownson's book, see Preston Sprinkle, "Romans 1 and Homosexuality: A Critical Review of James Brownson's *Bible, Gender, Sexuality*," *Bulletin for Biblical Research* 24, no. 4 (2014): 515–28.

> Then the LORD rained on Sodom and Gomorrah sulfur and fire from the LORD out of heaven. And he overthrew those cities, and all the valley, and all the inhabitants of the cities, and what grew on the ground. . . .
>
> And Abraham went early in the morning to the place where he had stood before the LORD. And he looked down toward Sodom and Gomorrah and toward all the land of the valley, and he looked and, behold, the smoke of the land went up like the smoke of a furnace. So it was that, when God destroyed the cities of the valley, God remembered Abraham and sent Lot out of the midst of the overthrow when he overthrew the cities in which Lot had lived. (Gen 19:1–29)

Vines claims that the Sodom and Gomorrah episode does not point to God's judgment on homosexual practice, but only on *coercive* homosexual practice. He says that "the sin of Sodom had far more to do with a lack of hospitality and a bent toward violence than with any sexual designs the men had on Lot's visitors." Vines says that "it was a threatened gang rape" and adds that "in the ancient world, for a man to be raped was considered the ultimate degradation" (p. 65).

But it is not persuasive to claim that God's judgment came on Sodom only because of a lack of hospitality and a threatened gang rape. Rampant homosexuality must have spread throughout the city of Sodom long before the two angelic visitors came to it, because men who have no prior life pattern of homosexual conduct do not spontaneously decide to gather about the door of a house and demand that two male visitors should come out so that the men might "know them":

> The men of Sodom, both young and old, *all the people to the last man*, surrounded the house. And they called to Lot, "Where are the men who came to you tonight? *Bring them out to us, that we may know them.*" (Gen. 19:4–5)

When the men of the city said they wanted to "know" the visitors (who were angels), they were using the word *know* in the common Old Testament sense of having sexual intercourse (see Gen. 4:1, 17, 25; also the similar passage in Judg. 19:22). Lot, who knew the men of the city personally, understood perfectly well what they wanted and called their intended action "wicked" (Gen. 19:7). Therefore, this attempted violence against the visitors was not a one-time, incidental sin unrelated to God's judgment, but should be understood as a particularly reprehensible manifestation of a pervasive pattern of homosexuality that was commonplace throughout the city. These were men who habitually engaged in homosexual conduct, and it manifested itself in their behavior that night.

We know the Lord's judgment on Sodom did not come only on account of the men's attempts to force themselves on the angel visitors inside Lot's house because the Lord's conversation with Abraham in Genesis 18 shows that God was coming in judgment *because of the Sodomites' prior conduct* long before the angels visited the city. God told

Abraham that he was visiting Sodom "because the outcry against Sodom and Gomorrah is great and their sin is very grave" (Gen. 18:20). Eventually the Lord told Abraham, "For the sake of ten [righteous people] I will not destroy it" (v. 32), but he did not find even 10 righteous people in Sodom.

It is sometimes argued that the guilt of Sodom and Gomorrah was due not to homosexuality but to *other sins*, because these are mentioned by other Old Testament authors. Vines makes this argument and mentions the sins of "oppressing marginalized groups, murder, and theft," as well as "adultery, idolatry, and power abuses," as specified in Isaiah 1:4, 10; 13:19; Jeremiah 23:14; Lamentations 4:6; Amos 4:1–11; and Zephaniah 2:8–11. Finally, he quotes Ezekiel 16:49–50 and adds that "sexuality goes unmentioned, both in the Ezekiel passage and in every other Old Testament reference to Sodom following Genesis 19" (pp. 63–64).

This list of Old Testament passages given by Vines is misleading, because most of them do not mention any specific sins of Sodom at all, but simply say that God will judge other groups of people in the same way he judged Sodom. For example, "Moab shall become like Sodom, and the Ammonites like Gomorrah, a land possessed by nettles and salt pits, and a waste forever" (Zeph. 2:9). Similarly, in Isaiah 1:4, 10; 13:19; Lamentations 4:6; and Amos 4:1–11, no specific sins of Sodom are mentioned, so these passages hardly support Vines's argument.

The passage in Jeremiah does list specific sins:

> But in the prophets of Jerusalem
>   I have seen a horrible thing:
> they commit *adultery* and walk in *lies*;
>   they *strengthen the hands of evildoers*,
>   so that no one turns from his evil;
> all of them have become like Sodom to me,
>   and its inhabitants like Gomorrah. (Jer. 23:14)

It is not surprising that Jeremiah mentioned *other* sins in saying that *the prophets in Jerusalem* were as hateful in God's sight as the people of Sodom, because it is likely that homosexuality was not being practiced by these Jerusalem prophets. But Sodom was still a good point of comparison for Jeremiah to mention, because seldom does any deeply depraved society commit only one kind of sin. Sodom was no doubt given over to every kind of evil practice, which was why God rained down such immediate and total judgment upon it.

What about the Ezekiel passage that Vines mentions?

> Behold, this was the guilt of your sister Sodom: she and her daughters had *pride*, excess of food, and prosperous ease, but *did not aid the poor and needy*. They were *haughty* and did an *abomination* before me. So I removed them, when I saw it. (Ezek. 16:49–50)

This passage shows that pride and selfishness were other sins in Sodom, and Ezekiel chose to highlight those sins, but homosexuality is not absent from these verses, because the last sin mentioned, and the one that comes immediately before God says, "So I removed them," is that they "did an *abomination* before me." The word *abomination* translates the Hebrew term *tôʿēbāh*, which is the same term used to say that it is an "abomination" before God for a male to "lie with a male as with a woman" in Leviticus 18:22 and 20:13. This linguistic parallel with the Mosaic laws prohibiting homosexual conduct, together with an awareness of the well-known narrative about the attempt at homosexual rape in Genesis 19, would have certainly brought to the minds of Ezekiel's hearers and readers the sin of homosexuality when they encountered the expression "did an *abomination*" in Ezekiel 16:50.

Finally, Jude 7 understands the sin of Sodom to be homosexuality (see discussion in the treatment of Jude 7 below).

2–3. Leviticus 18:22 and 20:13.

> You shall not lie with a male as with a woman; it is an abomination. (Lev. 18:22; "abomination" translates the Hebrew word *tôʿēbāh*, which is used to refer to actions that are extremely displeasing to God)

> If a man lies with a male as with a woman, both of them have committed an abomination. (Lev. 20:13; again, "abomination" translates the Hebrew word *tôʿēbāh*)

Vines objects that these verses are part of the Mosaic Law, and the Mosaic covenant has now come to an end. Therefore, just as we no longer obey prohibitions on eating pork or wearing clothing made of two kinds of material, we no longer have to obey other laws in the Mosaic Law, and that fact calls into question the contemporary validity of these laws about homosexual conduct (pp. 78–81).

Then Vines admits that some Old Testament laws remain valid today, such as "prohibitions of murder, adultery, and idolatry, for instance" (p. 82). Does that mean that laws about sexual morality do still apply today? In response, Vines points out that even in the area of sexual ethics, several aspects of Old Testament law are not considered binding today, such as the prohibition of sex during a woman's menstrual period (Lev. 18:19; 20:18), the requirement of levirate marriage (Deut. 25:5–6), and the allowance of polygamy (Deut. 21:15–17) (pp. 83–84).

In response, while I agree that the laws of the Mosaic covenant are no longer directly binding on people today, we still have to decide, in the case of individual laws, whether they reflect the wisdom of God regarding actions that are pleasing or displeasing to him for all ages and all societies (see discussion in chap. 8, p. 234). Such a decision can only be made through consideration of the specific content of the law in question, the context in which it occurs, and especially the way in which the same topic is treated in the New Testament.

With respect to the prohibitions of homosexual conduct in Leviticus, there are several reasons why we should consider them to reflect God's wisdom about the kind of conduct that displeases him for all time: (1) Leviticus 18:22 and 20:13 occur in contexts that prohibit several other kinds of sexual conduct that are permanently immoral, such as adultery, incest, and bestiality: see Leviticus 18:1–23 and 20:10–16.[13] (2) There are no details in Leviticus 20:13 that suggest that this standard of conduct is unique to the particular circumstances of the Mosaic covenant that have been terminated (such as the details concerning sacrifices and festivals, for example; see discussion in chap. 8, p. 215). (3) The prohibitions against homosexual conduct are reaffirmed in several New Testament passages (see below). (4) These passages in Leviticus are part of a consistent pattern of moral teaching throughout the entire Bible that views all kinds of sexual intercourse outside of the creation pattern of marriage between a man and a woman as morally wrong. (5) These passages also reflect a moral standard that is seen in the narrative passage about the destruction of Sodom and Gomorrah (Genesis 19), which occurred long before the Mosaic covenant and the Mosaic Law that begins in Exodus 19–20.

Finally, Vines objects that these verses in Leviticus did not prohibit homosexual conduct because it was inherently immoral, but because it violated the patriarchal assumptions common in that culture, in which it was "degrading for a man to be treated like a woman," because in that ancient culture women "were thought to have *less value*" (pp. 88, 91; emphasis in original). Therefore, these Old Testament prohibitions against homosexual conduct "reflect the inferior value that was commonly accorded to women in ancient times" (p. 93). But since we no longer think of women as having inferior value, this moral standard does not apply to us today (see p. 93).

My response to this claim is to say that Vines is inventing an explanation that is based on no evidence whatsoever in the text of Leviticus 18:22 or 20:13. These verses do not say, "You shall not lie with a male as with a woman *because that would be treating one of the men as a creature of inferior value.*" They just say, "You shall not lie with a male as with a woman." Rather than inventing a reason that is not specified *anywhere* in the text of Scripture,[14] it is far better to conclude that God prohibits homosexual conduct because it violates the moral standard found throughout the Bible from Genesis to Revelation that sexual intercourse should only be between a man and a woman, and only within the bounds of marriage.

Therefore, in spite of the objections raised by Vines and others, it seems best to conclude that the prohibitions against homosexual conduct found in Leviticus 18:22

---

[13] However, I think that the prohibition against intercourse during a woman's menstrual period probably belongs to a set of laws unique to the Mosaic covenant, like other laws that specified uncleanness for coming in contact with blood.

[14] In fact, on this very page (p. 91), Vines himself quotes a book edited by John Piper and me in which we say that "Women are indeed *fully equal* to men in personhood, in importance, and in status before God." *Recovering Biblical Manhood and Womanhood: A Response to Evangelical Feminism* (Wheaton, IL: Crossway, 1991), xv.

and 20:13, while not directly binding on us as part of the Mosaic covenant, still reflect a standard of moral conduct that is revealed by God for all cultures and all periods of history.

4. Romans 1:26–27. Paul speaks of homosexual conduct in the midst of a long catalog of sins of human beings "who by their unrighteousness suppress the truth" (Rom. 1:18):

> For this reason God gave them up to dishonorable passions. For their women exchanged natural relations for those that are *contrary to nature*; and the men likewise gave up natural relations with women and were consumed with passion for one another, men committing shameless acts with men and receiving in themselves the due penalty for their error. (Rom. 1:26–27)

The phrase "contrary to nature" in verse 26 means that homosexual conduct does not represent what God intended when he made men and women with physical bodies that have a "natural" way of interacting with each other and "natural" desires for each other.

This same verse also shows that Paul regards homosexual *desires* ("passions," from the Greek word *pathos*, plural) as "dishonorable." This is because such desires are contrary to God's purpose and intention that sexual intercourse should be restricted to marriage. Also, these desires treat a person's biological sex as only half of what it is. The logic of a *heterosexual* bond is that of bringing together the two (and only two) *different and complementary sexual halves* into a sexual whole ("they shall become one flesh," Gen. 2:24). But by contrast, the logic of a *homosexual* bond is that another person of the *same* sex complements and fills what is lacking in that same sex, implying that each participant is only half of his or her own sex: two half males making a full male or two half females making a full female. In other words, the logic of sexual intercourse requires a sexual complement, which is self-devaluing of one's own gender in a same-sex bond inasmuch as one sees the need to complement structurally one's own sex with someone of the same sex.

Vines objects that in this passage Paul is not talking about committed same-sex relationships such as those that exist today (pp. 99, 113) because Paul was only condemning sins by people who were "capable of making the opposite, virtuous choice" (p. 103). But Paul could not have meant his statements to apply to people with same-sex orientation today, because "gay people cannot choose to follow opposite-sex attractions, because they have no opposite-sex attractions to follow—nor can they manufacture them" (p. 103). Vines says that "what Paul was describing is *fundamentally different from what we are discussing*" (p. 103; emphasis in original).

According to Vines, it is important to recognize the way the ancient world viewed homosexual conduct. "The most common forms of same-sex behavior in the Greco-Roman world were pederasty, prostitution, and sex between masters and their slaves. . . . The overwhelming majority of visible same-sex behavior fit easily into a paradigm of excess" (p. 104). He concludes, "Paul wasn't condemning the expression of same-sex orientation as opposed to the expression of an opposite-sex orientation. He was condemning *excess* as opposed to *moderation*" (p. 105; emphasis in original).

My response is that Vines is making the passage say exactly the opposite of what it actually does say. Paul does not say that "women could not get enough sex with male partners so they *added* additional sex with same-sex partners," and he does not say that "men could not get enough sex with women so they *added* sex with men," but rather that women *gave up* sex with men and turned to women instead, and men *gave up* sex with women and turned to men instead:

> For their women *exchanged* natural relations for those that are contrary to nature; and the men likewise *gave up* natural relations with women and were consumed with passion for one another, men committing shameless acts with men . . . (Rom. 1:26–27)

Vines claims that "Paul wasn't condemning the expression of a same-sex *orientation*" (p. 105; emphasis added), but that is exactly what Paul is condemning in this passage, because he talks about wrongful sexual desires when he says that "God gave them up to *dishonorable passions*" (Rom. 1:26), which he further explains when he says that men were "consumed with passion for one another" (v. 27).

The type of argument Vines makes here is not new. Among defenders of homosexual conduct, one common claim is that the biblical passages concerning homosexuality prohibit *only certain kinds of homosexual conduct*, such as homosexual prostitution or pedophilia (homosexual conduct involving children), or uncommitted, unfaithful homosexual conduct. (This is sometimes called the "exploitation argument": the Bible prohibits only exploitative forms of homosexuality.)

But where is the evidence that the relevant passages should have this kind of restricted application? If we reexamine Romans 1:26–27, we find that there is no legitimate evidence in the *actual wording*, the *context*, or *evidence from the ancient world* to prove that the passages were referring to anything less than all kinds of homosexual conduct by all kinds of people.

In addition, two other biblical counterarguments against the "exploitation argument" may be briefly mentioned:

1. In Romans 1:23–27, Paul is clearly echoing Genesis 1 when he speaks of "birds and animals and creeping things" (v. 23), says that people "worshiped and served the *creature* rather than the *Creator*" (v. 25), and then, when he talks about "women" and "men" in verses 26–27, uses the less common Greek terms *thēlys* for "women" and *arsēn* for "men," terms that are also used in the Septuagint in Genesis 1:27, which says, "*male* [*arsēn*] and female [*thēlys*] he created them." But this means that Paul's argument in Romans 1:26–27 is reflecting a conviction that any kind of sexual intercourse that does not reflect the male-female complementarity that God created in Genesis 1:27–28 is a

violation of God's will for all mankind from the moment of creation, irrespective of whether such a relationship is loving or committed.

2. Paul's absolute indictment against all forms of homosexuality is underscored by his mention of lesbian intercourse in Romans 1:26 ("their women exchanged natural relations for those that are contrary to nature"), since this form of intercourse in the ancient world was not typically characterized by sex with adolescents, slaves, or prostitutes.

The argument about whether ancient cultures disapproved of all homosexual conduct or only exploitative and oppressive homosexual conduct (as Vines claims on pp. 103–5) does not really affect our understanding of the biblical passages, because New Testament writers such as Paul had no hesitation in disagreeing with the moral standards of the surrounding society (see 1 Cor. 10:20; Eph. 4:17; 1 Thess. 4:5).

While Vines argues that "contrary to nature" in Romans 1:26 refers to violations of "customary gender roles in a patriarchal context" (p. 109), and therefore essentially means "contrary to cultural expectations," Robert Gagnon, after an extensive study of the Greek expression *para physin* ("contrary to nature") and similar expressions in ancient Jewish literature,[15] concludes that for "Jewish authors writing within a century or two of Jesus's birth," the phrase "contrary to nature" referred to same-sex intercourse, and the phrase "in accordance with nature" referred to opposite-sex intercourse for two primary reasons: (1) "the unique capacity for procreation of heterosexual intercourse" and (2) "the anatomical complementarity or fixedness of the male and female sex organs and the gender-transgressing feminization of the receptive homosexual partner."[16] Given this background of emphatic and unanimous Jewish condemnation of homosexual practice, Gagnon writes:

> The notion that first century Jews, such as Jesus and Paul, would have given general approval to a homosexual lifestyle if they had only been shown adequate examples of mutually caring and non-explicated same-sex relationships is fantastic. . . . Because the anatomical, sexual, and procreative complementarity of male and female unions, in contrast with those between female and female or male and male, would have remained indisputable.[17]

Turning to Paul's statement in Romans 1:26–27 that the heterosexual conduct that people "gave up" is "natural" (or "in accordance with nature") while homosexual conduct is "contrary to nature," Gagnon concludes that "Paul is referring to the anatomical and procreative complementarity of male and female," or, "put in more crude terms, Paul in effect argues that even pagans who have no access to the book of Leviticus should know that same-sex eroticism is 'contrary to nature' because the primary sex organs fit

---

[15] Robert A. J. Gagnon, *The Bible and Homosexual Practice: Texts and Hermeneutics* (Nashville: Abingdon, 2001), 159–83.

[16] Ibid., 180–81.

[17] Ibid., 182.

male to female, not female to female or male to male."[18] He adds that "Paul was thinking of 'nature' not as 'the way things are usually done' (i.e., cultural convention) but rather as 'the material shape of the created order,'" and he notes that this is consistent with Paul's numerous references to God's original creation in Romans 1:18–32.[19]

This evidence is also relevant for another kind of objection that is brought against Romans 1:26–27. Although Vines does not hold this position, others have claimed that the phrase "contrary to nature" (Greek, *para physin*) in Romans 1:26–27 shows that Paul is only talking about people who "naturally" feel desires toward a person of the opposite sex. Therefore, it would not apply to people who "naturally" feel homosexual desires. For them, this argument says, homosexual conduct is not contrary to *their nature*.

But this objection is reading into the text a restriction that has no basis in the actual words that Paul wrote. Here again are the verses in question:

> For their women exchanged *natural* relations for those that are *contrary to nature*; and the men likewise gave up *natural* relations with women and were consumed with passion for one another. (Rom. 1:26–27)

Paul does not say "contrary to *their* nature," but "contrary to nature" (Greek, *para physin*), a phrase that, as Gagnon showed, is used several times in literature outside the Bible to speak of all kinds of homosexual conduct as something contrary to the natural order of the world. Here are some examples:

Long before the time of the New Testament, the Greek philosopher Plato (c. 429–347 BC) wrote:

> When male unites with female for procreation, the pleasure experienced is held to be due to nature, but contrary to nature [Greek, *para physin*, the same phrase used in Rom. 1:26] when male mates with male or female with female, and . . . those . . . guilty of such enormities were impelled by their slavery to pleasure.[20]

The Jewish historian Josephus (AD 37–c. 100) wrote that the people of Elis and Thebes, in their homosexual conduct, practiced an "unnatural [*para physin*, the same expression found in Rom. 1:26] vice," and in that context, he referred to "the practice of sodomy" (homosexual conduct) as "the monstrous and unnatural [*para physin* again] pleasures in which they . . . indulged."[21]

The Greek historian Plutarch (c. AD 50–c. 120) referred to homosexual conduct between men as "contrary to nature" (*para physin*) and "indecent."[22]

---

[18] Ibid., 254.

[19] Ibid., 256–57.

[20] Plato, *Laws*, 1.636C. (In quoting these examples from Greek literature outside the Bible, I am not endorsing the opinions of homosexuality that were held by Plato or others, but only giving examples to show that the phrase *para physin* was commonly understood to apply to all kinds of homosexual intercourse.)

[21] Josephus, *Against Apion*, 2.273–75.

[22] Plutarch, *Moralia*, *Dialogue on Love*, 751.D–E.

These quotations show that when the New Testament writers condemned homosexual conduct, they were using the same terminology that was commonly used in other Greek literature to condemn all homosexual conduct as "contrary to nature" and morally wrong. The words of the New Testament do not allow these prohibitions to be limited, as homosexual advocates claim, to a narrowly defined particular type of homosexual conduct.

In conclusion, Vines and other advocates for the moral legitimacy of homosexual orientation and conduct attempt to show that Paul is not talking about modern, committed same-sex relationships but rather about exploitative or oppressive homosexual conduct, or conduct that is simply a manifestation of excess sexual passion. But these arguments are not persuasive. Paul makes none of these qualifications in Romans 1:26–27, but condemns all homosexual intercourse in general as contrary to God's created order, and also says that even the desires for such homosexual activity (what is today called sexual orientation) are "dishonorable passions."

5. 1 Corinthians 6:9. Paul elsewhere mentions homosexual conduct in a long list of sins:

> Or do you not know that the unrighteous will not inherit the kingdom of God? Do not be deceived: neither the sexually immoral, nor idolaters, nor adulterers, *nor men who practice homosexuality*, nor thieves, nor the greedy, nor drunkards, nor revilers, nor swindlers will inherit the kingdom of God. And such were some of you. But you were washed, you were sanctified, you were justified in the name of the Lord Jesus Christ and by the Spirit of our God. (1 Cor. 6:9–11)

The phrase "nor men who practice homosexuality" translates the Greek phrase *oute malakoi oute arsenokoitai*, meaning "nor *malakoi* nor *arsenokoitai*." But what do these two Greek terms mean? The first one is the plural of *malakos*, which means "soft" or "effeminate," and was commonly used in the Greco-Roman world to refer to the "passive" partner in homosexual acts.[23] The second term is the plural of *arsenokoitēs*, a combination of the Greek words *arsēn* ("man") and *koitē* (here meaning "sexual intercourse"). The term *arsenokoitēs* was apparently coined by Paul from the Septuagint (Greek translation) of Leviticus 20:13,[24] and means (in plural) "men who have intercourse with men."[25]

---

[23] See BDAG, 613.

[24] Lev. 20:13 says, "If a man lies with a male as with a woman," and the Septuagint has *meta arsenos koitēn gunaikos*, "with a man in the manner of sexual intercourse of a woman," using the words *arsēn* ("man") and *koitē* ("sexual intercourse"), which means that Paul's use of the compound word *arsenokoitēs* is most likely an allusion to Lev. 20:13.

For two extensive studies of the usage and background of the term *arsenokoitēs*, see Gagnon, *The Bible and Homosexual Practice*, 312–39, and James B. DeYoung, *Homosexuality: Contemporary Claims Examined in Light of the Bible and Other Ancient Literature and Law* (Grand Rapids, MI: Kregel, 2000), 175–203. Both Gagnon (p. 315) and DeYoung (p. 195) conclude that Paul coined this word from the Septuagint wording of Lev. 18:22 and 20:13.

[25] See BDAG, 135. The footnote at 1 Cor. 6:9 in the ESV explains the Greek wording behind the ESV expression "men who practice homosexuality" in the following way: "The two Greek terms translated by this phrase refer to the passive and active partners in consensual homosexual acts."

Vines objects that these terms do not denote committed same-sex relationships, but *malakoi* refers to "those who lack self-control," and the word "encompasses an entire disposition toward immoderation" (p. 122). As for *arsenokotēs*, Vines says "it most often referred to economic exploitation, not same-sex behavior," and he mentions that it is sometimes used in lists of sins that include stealing and other kinds of economic sins (p. 124). He concludes that the word "describes some kind of sexual *and* economic exploitation" (p. 125; emphasis in original). In any case, he says, even if these two words did refer to both male partners in same-sex relationships, the context "would still differ significantly from our context today," because "same-sex behavior in the first century was not understood to be the expression of an exclusive sexual orientation. It was understood as excess" (p. 126).

However, these assertions stand in direct conflict with Gagnon's conclusions from his far more extensive study of both *malakos* and *arsenokotēs* in ancient Greek literature.[26] After quoting and analyzing numerous examples of both terms, Gagnon concludes,

> It is self-evident, then, that the combination of terms, *malakoi* and *arsenokoitai*, are correctly understood in our contemporary context when they are applied to every conceivable type of same-sex intercourse.[27]

Vines's claim that *arsenokotēs* refers to some kind of economic exploitation, just because other sins mentioned in lists where it appears include stealing and other acts of economic injustice, is not persuasive either, because it is commonplace in lists of sins to include various kinds of sins, as is evident even in this passage under discussion (1 Cor. 6:9–11), which also mentions idolaters, thieves, the greedy, drunkards, revilers, and swindlers. Words in a list can obviously differ from one another in meaning. (This is also very evident in the next passage that we discuss, 1 Tim. 1:10.) The question is what this word means, not what other words mean.

6. 1 Timothy 1:10. In this verse, Paul uses the same word as in 1 Corinthians 6:9, *arsenokotēs*, in a list of vices derived from "the law" (here, the Ten Commandments), which means that this verse also should be interpreted as an absolute prohibition of male-male intercourse, in keeping with Leviticus 18:22 and 20:13.

> Now we know that the law is good, if one uses it lawfully, understanding this, that the law is not laid down for the just but for the lawless and disobedient, for the ungodly and sinners, for the unholy and profane, for those who strike their fathers and mothers, for murderers, the sexually immoral, *men who practice homosexuality*, enslavers, liars, perjurers, and whatever else is contrary to sound doctrine, in accordance with the gospel of the glory of the blessed God with which I have been entrusted. (1 Tim. 1:8–11)

---

[26] See Gagnon, *The Bible and Homosexual Practice*, 303–39.
[27] Ibid., 330.

The same arguments about the meaning of *arsenokoitēs* apply here. It refers to all kinds of male homosexual intercourse.

7. Jude 7. Jude makes this comment about the judgment on Sodom and Gomorrah (Genesis 19):

> Sodom and Gomorrah and the surrounding cities, which likewise indulged in sexual immorality *and pursued unnatural desire*, serve as an example by undergoing a punishment of eternal fire. (Jude 7)

The Greek phrase translated by "pursued unnatural desire" is *apelthousai opisō sarkos heteras*, literally, "went after other flesh," meaning that it was "other" or different from the heterosexual immorality with women that Jude refers to earlier in the sentence by saying they had "indulged in *sexual immorality*."[28] In other words, the people of Sodom and Gomorrah committed sin both through heterosexual adultery and through homosexual conduct.

In conclusion, at least seven passages show that Scripture consistently views all types of homosexual conduct as contrary to God's moral will.

C. WHAT ABOUT HOMOSEXUAL DESIRES?

Does the Bible address the question of homosexual attitudes and desires? As I have mentioned in several previous chapters in this book, God ultimately requires moral perfection, not only in human actions, but also in attitudes of the heart, in all areas of our lives. Therefore, the Bible prohibits not only adultery but also the *desire* for adultery (Ex. 20:14, 17; cf. Matt. 5:28); not only theft but also *coveting* (Ex. 20:15, 17). This is because "the LORD sees not as man sees: man looks on the outward appearance, but the LORD looks on the heart" (1 Sam. 16:7).

Therefore, Scripture teaches that any desire to break God's commandments is also wrong in God's sight. "Blessed are the pure in heart, for they shall see God" (Matt. 5:8). While an impulse to do what God expressly forbids is (by definition) an impulse contrary to God's will, the Bible also recognizes that Christians will be "tempted" by their "own desire" (James 1:14), so it encourages Christians in such circumstances to "remain steadfast" (v. 11) and to "be doers of the word" (v. 22). This implies not actively entertaining the wrongful impulse (cf. Matt. 5:28) and not dwelling on it so that it "gives birth to sin" (James 1:15).

So it is not surprising that not only homosexual conduct but also homosexual desires are viewed as contrary to God's will. Homosexual desires are regarded as "dishon-

---

[28] Extrabiblical Jewish literature similarly interpreted the sin of Sodom as homosexuality; see Josephus, *Antiquities*, 1.200–201; Philo, *On Abraham*, 134–36; *Testament of Naphtali*, 3.4. See the further discussion of this passage, with additional references to extrabiblical Jewish literature, in Thomas R. Schreiner, *1, 2 Peter, Jude*, NAC 37 (Nashville: Broadman & Holman, 2003), 451–53.

orable passions" (Rom. 1:26), and Paul says that homosexual partners are "consumed with passion for one another" (v. 27), giving an image of a powerful but destructive inward craving.

This is not to say that homosexual *desire* is as harmful as homosexual *conduct*. Though all sin is wrong and brings legal guilt before God (cf. James 2:10–11), a distinction between wrongful desires and wrongful actions can be made with regard to many areas of life. Hatred of another person is wrong in God's sight, but murdering the person is far more harmful. Coveting a neighbor's farm animals is wrong, but actually stealing them is much more harmful. And lustful desires for adultery are wrong, but actually committing adultery is far more harmful. Similarly, homosexual desires are wrong in God's sight, but actually committing homosexual acts is far more harmful.[29]

Vines claims that the Bible does not talk about sexual desires for same-sex rather than opposite-sex people, what he calls same-sex "orientation." He writes:

> The bottom line is this: The Bible doesn't directly address the issue of same-sex *orientation*—or the expression of that orientation. (p. 130; emphasis in original)

But two arguments show that claim to be incorrect: (1) the explicit mention of "dishonorable passions" in Romans 1:26 and (2) the consistent teaching of Scripture regarding all sin, that God requires not only purity of action but also purity of heart (see discussion in chap. 4, p. 138).

D. THE BIBLE'S SOLUTION FOR HOMOSEXUALITY

As with every other sin, the Bible's solution for homosexuality is trusting in Christ for the forgiveness of sin, the imputation of righteousness, and the power to change. After talking about the "sexually immoral . . . adulterers . . . men who practice homosexuality . . . thieves . . . [and] drunkards" (1 Cor. 6:9–10), Paul tells the Corinthian Christians, "*And such were some of you*" (v. 11). Then he adds, "But you were washed, you were *sanctified*, you were justified in the name of the Lord Jesus Christ and by the Spirit of our God" (v. 11; cf. Rom. 6:23; Phil. 2:13; 1 John 1:9). This implies that some former homosexuals in the church at Corinth had left their previous homosexual lifestyle and, by the power of the Holy Spirit, were seeking to live lives of sexual purity, whether in celibacy or in faithful heterosexual marriages.

It is important that the Christian community always show love and compassion toward those engaged in homosexual conduct, and also extend friendship toward them where opportunities arise, though not in a way that signals approval of homosexual

---

[29] On the moral status of same-sex attraction, see Denny Burk and Heath Lambert, *Transforming Homosexuality: What the Bible Says about Sexual Orientation and Change* (Phillipsburg, NJ: P&R, 2015). See also the Nashville Statement, p. 881.

practice. It is also important to extend hope for change, since many homosexuals will say that they long to establish a different pattern of life.[30]

There are many testimonies of former homosexuals who now attest not only to a heterosexual, married lifestyle, but also to sexual desires that are now predominately heterosexual. Alan Sears and Craig Osten report several of these stories, such as the following:

> [Long before leaving her lesbian lifestyle] she knew deep down about the sinfulness of her lesbian behavior and *wanted to escape*, but she felt nothing but anger and condemnation from individuals who called themselves Christians. The anger she felt repelled her from Christianity for many years. Despite this, God continued to work on her heart and eventually brought her to him.[31]

However, the conclusion of a number of studies and a frequent theme in personal testimonies is that long-term change from a homosexual lifestyle seldom occurs without a program of help and encouragement from others, often including the love and care of compassionate Christians and ministries devoted to helping those who engage in homosexual behavior.[32]

E. OBJECTIONS

A number of objections are regularly raised against the biblical view that homosexuality is morally wrong. These include the following:

1. "Some People Are 'Born Gay' and Are Unable to Change." One objection is that some people are "born gay," that is, that many homosexuals do not choose their sexual orientation but it is part of their genetic makeup from the time of birth, and so ho-

---

[30] Erik Eckholm reports on interviews with several men who are part of an ex-gay movement in "'Ex-Gay' Men Fight Back Against View That Homosexuality Can't Be Changed," *The New York Times*, Oct. 31, 2012, http://www.nytimes.com/2012/11/01/us/ex-gay-men-fight-view-that-homosexuality-cant-be-changed.html.

[31] Alan Sears and Craig Osten, *The Homosexual Agenda: Exposing the Principal Threat to Religious Freedom Today*, rev. and updated ed. (Nashville: Broadman & Holman, 2003), 8. The introduction to this book includes several personal testimonies of how individuals engaging in homosexual behavior were able to leave that lifestyle with help from Christian friends and/or Christian organizations.

[32] Ministries that help people struggling with homosexuality include: Courage (http://couragerc.net); Desert Hope (http://deserthope.com); Desert Stream Ministries (www.desertstream.org); Genesis Counseling (http://www.genesiscounseling.org); Harvest USA (http://www.harvestusa.org); Healing for the Soul (http://healingforthesoul.org); Mastering Life Ministries (http://www.masteringlife.org); Pure Intimacy (http://www.pureintimacy.org); Regeneration (http://regenerationministries.org); Restored Hope Network (http://www.restoredhopenetwork.com); and Where Grace Abounds (http://wheregraceabounds.org). See also the resources at the Focus on the Family website: http://www.focusonthefamily.com/social issues/sexuality/leaving-homosexuality/resources-for-men-and-women-with-unwanted-homosexuality.

See also the discussion of what such "change" means in Mark A. Yarhouse, *Homosexuality and the Christian: A Guide for Parents, Pastors, and Friends* (Minneapolis: Bethany House, 2010), 81–98.

mosexuals can never change, and therefore, for them, homosexual behavior cannot be wrong.

Vines writes:

> Sexual orientation is not a choice and it is highly resistant to change. . . . Same-sex attraction is completely natural to me. It's not something I chose or something I can change. (pp. 28–29)

We must respond to such a claim with compassion and sympathy for the earnestness of his statement. But we must also recognize that this is not the way the Bible talks about any patterns of behavior or any heart desires that are contrary to God's moral will. As noted above, when Paul was talking about "men who practice homosexuality" (1 Cor. 6:9), he said to the Corinthian church, "And such *were* some of you" (v. 11), indicating that the church at Corinth had some former homosexuals who were no longer engaging in homosexual conduct. This is significant evidence that, according to the Bible, it is possible for homosexuals at least to change their actions and become former homosexuals.

In addition, several other passages in the New Testament provide hope that it is possible for people to change, not only in their pattern of sinful actions, but also in the desires of their hearts. Here are some of those passages:

> Let not sin therefore reign in your mortal body, to make you obey its passions. Do not present your members to sin as instruments for unrighteousness, but present yourselves to God as those who have been brought from death to life, and your members to God as instruments for righteousness. For *sin will have no dominion over you*, since you are not under law but under grace. (Rom. 6:12–14)[33]

> But thanks be to God, that you who were once slaves of sin have become *obedient from the heart* to the standard of teaching to which you were committed. (Rom. 6:17)

> Therefore, if anyone is in Christ, he is a new creation. The old has passed away; behold, the new has come. (2 Cor. 5:17)

> Since we have these promises, beloved, let us cleanse ourselves from every defilement of body and spirit, bringing holiness to completion in the fear of God. (2 Cor. 7:1)

> It is God who works in you, both *to will* and to work for his good pleasure. (Phil. 2:13)

---

[33] See discussion of this passage and related verses at p. 145.

> As he who called you is holy, you also be holy in all your conduct, since it is written, "You shall be holy, for I am holy." (1 Pet. 1:15–16)

> If we confess our sins, he is faithful and just to forgive us our sins *and to cleanse us from all unrighteousness.* (1 John 1:9)

And in the Old Testament, David prayed:

> Create in me a clean heart, O God,
>   and renew a right spirit within me. (Ps. 51:10)

This does not mean that homosexual desires will automatically or necessarily be eradicated for those who come to Christ. Becoming a Christian does not mean that people will no longer experience intense sinful urges (sexual or otherwise). But genuine faith does produce the fruit of obedience and real, substantive change, and Paul indicates that this is precisely what happened with some who had practiced homosexuality in Corinth.

The objection from advocates for committed same-sex relationships is that there is no evidence that people's "orientation" (that is, desire for same-sex affection and intercourse) can ever change. Vines says that the evidence from "ex-gay" organizations shows that they "did not claim to be changing anyone's sexual *orientation.* . . . None of the evidence seemed to show God was changing the people's sexual orientation" (p. 10; emphasis in original; see also pp. 28, 40, 130).

But a balanced examination of the literature on this topic shows quite a different picture. Jeffrey Satinover, a psychiatrist who is a graduate of MIT, Harvard, and the University of Texas, and who has lectured at both Yale and Harvard, tells how the ruling academic climate on homosexual studies has changed so much that the professional psychiatric literature operates under a kind of "censorship," so that most studies that show evidence of success in treatment programs that help homosexuals overcome homosexual conduct and orientation cannot even be published.[34] Still, Satinover points to many earlier studies in which "the composite of these results gives an overall success rate of over 50 percent—where success is defined as 'considerable' to 'complete' change. . . . *All the existing evidence suggests strongly that homosexuality is quite changeable.*"[35]

An interesting example of research about homosexuals who have changed, and also an example of the immense pressure brought against researchers who claim that this has happened, is seen in the story of psychiatrist Robert Spitzer and his repudiation of

---

[34] See Jeffrey Satinover, *Homosexuality and the Politics of Truth* (Grand Rapids, MI: Baker, 1996), 168–78. This is an excellent book explaining the medical harm and addictive nature of homosexual conduct, and also the ability of homosexuals to change.

[35] Ibid., 186, emphasis in original. Satinover, who is himself Jewish, documents the particularly effective ministry of Christian programs that include healing prayer for homosexuals who wish to escape from their lives of homosexuality (pp. 196–209).

his earlier research. I mention the story here so that readers can evaluate its implications for themselves.

In 2001, Spitzer, a highly respected professor of psychiatry at Columbia University, published a study demonstrating that numerous gay men and lesbians had changed not only their behavior but also their pattern of sexual desires. This was especially significant because in the early 1970s Spitzer had led the efforts to have homosexuality removed from the American Psychiatric Association's (APA) list of mental illnesses. But in 2001 he presented a paper at the APA's convention claiming that homosexuals can change. He said his research "shows some people can change from gay to straight, and we ought to acknowledge that."[36]

Spitzer reported that he had conducted 45-minute telephone interviews with 200 people. He interviewed 143 men, whose average age was 42, and 57 women, whose average age was 44. All claimed they had changed their orientation from homosexual to heterosexual. Each person answered 114 closed-ended questions about their sexual feelings and behavior before and after their efforts to change. The majority interviewed said they had used more than one strategy to change their orientation. About half said the most helpful step was work with a psychologist or a pastoral counselor. About a third said a support group helped, and a few mentioned such aids as books and mentoring by a heterosexual. Spitzer came to the conclusion that 66 percent of the men and 44 percent of the women reported functioning well heterosexually after therapy.[37]

In spite of his prestigious standing in the field of psychiatry, Spitzer was immediately attacked. David Elliot, a spokesman for the National Gay and Lesbian Task Force in Washington, attacked his sample of interviewees, saying, "The sample is terrible, totally tainted, totally unrepresentative of the gay and lesbian community."[38] Then, in 2012, three years before his death and after more than a decade of attacks from the homosexual community (including one that cited the Nuremburg Code of Ethics to denounce his study as not only flawed but "morally wrong"), Spitzer recanted and apologized for his study.[39] But his brief letter of apology did not say that he had misrepresented any of the answers given to him in his interviews, but only that "there was no way to determine if the subject's accounts of change were valid" and "not self-deception or outright lying."[40]

---

[36] Malcolm Ritter, "Study: Some Gays Can Go Straight," *The Washington Post,* May 9, 2001, http://www.washingtonpost.com/wp-srv/aponline/20010509/aponline013921_000.htm.

[37] Robert Spitzer, "Can Some Gay Men and Lesbians Change Their Sexual Orientation? 200 Participants Reporting a Change from Homosexual to Heterosexual Orientation," *Archives of Sexual Behavior* 32, no. 3 (2003): 403–17 (the specific details I cited are from pp. 406–7 and 411), https://www.stolaf.edu/people/huff/classes/Psych130F2010/LabDocuments/Spitzer.pdf.

[38] Cited in Ritter, "Study: Some Gays Can Go Straight."

[39] Benedict Carey, "Psychiatry Giant Sorry for Backing Gay 'Cure,'" *The New York Times,* May 18, 2012, http://www.nytimes.com/2012/05/19/health/dr-robert-l-spitzer-noted-psychiatrist-apologizes-for-study-on-gay-cure.html.

[40] Cited in John M. Becker, "Exclusive: Dr. Robert Spitzer Apologizes to Gay Community for Infamous 'Ex-Gay' Study," Truth Wins Out, April 25, 2012, http://www.truthwinsout.org/news/2012/04/24542/.

My conclusion is that it still remains significant that Spitzer's 2001 study summarized the personal testimonies of so many people who *claimed* that they had experienced long-lasting change not only from homosexual conduct but also homosexual orientation. The only way to deny this, apparently, is to say that people who make such claims cannot be believed because they are self-deceived or lying.

Similar evidence of the ability of many homosexuals to change has come from other, more recent studies and reports of programs. One study by psychologists Stanton L. Jones of Wheaton College and Mark A. Yarhouse of Regent University and published in the *Journal of Sex and Marital Therapy* assessed 98 individuals over six to seven years after therapy occurred. It found that 23 percent reported success in changing to heterosexual orientation and functioning, while an additional 30 percent reported no longer identifying as homosexual and remaining sexually chaste.[41] The researchers were immediately attacked by CNN, which claimed that the authors were biased because of their affiliation with religious institutions.

Interestingly, in its criticism of the study, CNN quoted several academics who stated that they were aware that sexual behavior can change during one's lifetime, but they still disagreed with the results of the study. CNN quoted Eli Coleman, professor and director of human sexuality at the University of Minnesota Medical School: "I don't think we have anything really new here. We have known for some time that some people are able to shift their behavior and their perception of their sexual identity through these attempts at conversion." But he went on to claim, in direct contradiction to the results of the study, "You can get behavioral changes, but that's not orientation change. You can get short-term behavioral change. It's not sustained."[42]

2. "Scientific Evidence Shows That Some People are Homosexuals by Genetic Makeup." Some argue that science supports the argument that homosexuality is determined by one's biological makeup from before the time of birth. In fact, studies have shown some indirect, congenital influences on homosexual development that may increase the *likelihood* of homosexual development. There are certain hereditary factors that give people a greater likelihood of developing all sorts of sinful behavior patterns (such as frequent wrongful anger, violence, adultery, alcoholism, and so forth), so it would not be surprising to find that some people, from certain hereditary backgrounds, have a greater likelihood of developing homosexual desires and conduct.

However, this is far different from proving congenital *determinism* of homosexuality, that is, that some people are genetically incapable of making any other choice than to entertain homosexual desires and engage in homosexual conduct. Especially significant

---

[41] Kathleen Gilbert, "Major Study: Changing Sexual Orientation Is Possible," LifeSite News, Sept. 29, 2011, https://www.lifesitenews.com/news/major-study-changing-sexual-orientation-is-possible. The full study is available in Stanton L. Jones and Mark A. Yarhouse, *Ex-Gays? A Longitudinal Study of Religiously Mediated Change in Sexual Orientation* (Downers Grove, IL: IVP Academic, 2007).

[42] Cited in Madison Park, "Study Supporting Gay Conversion Challenged," CNN, Oct. 4, 2011, http://thechart.blogs.cnn.com/2011/10/04/study-supporting-gay-conversion-challenged/.

are studies of identical twins, one of whom has become a homosexual while the other has not, even though they have identical genetic makeups. For example, in 2015 researchers at the University of California studied 37 sets of identical male twins. In each pair, one of the twins was homosexual. They found that in only 20 percent of the sets were *both* twins homosexual—though they were genetically identical.[43]

Twenty-five years ago, J. Michael Bailey and Richard C. Pillard examined identical and fraternal twin brothers and adopted brothers in an effort to establish a genetic link to homosexuality. Fifty-two percent of the identical twins were reportedly homosexual, while only 22 percent of fraternal twins fell into the same category. The authors noted that since identical twins have identical genetic material, the fact that nearly half of the identical twins were *hetero*sexual effectively refutes the idea that homosexuality has a genetic basis.[44]

Finally, the moral teachings of God's Word, not people's inward desires, must be our final standard of right and wrong. It is important to recognize that (1) virtually all behavior is, at some level, biologically influenced and (2) no command of God depends for its validity on humans first losing all desire to violate the command in question.

3. "Some Environmental Factors Dispose Some People toward Homosexuality." This is not exactly an objection to the view I have advocated, but is a factor that should be taken into account. Some studies have shown that some environmental factors increase the *likelihood* (but not the necessity) of homosexual behavior. Two of the most significant, particularly for male homosexuals, are the physical or emotional absence of a caring father during a boy's childhood years and sexual abuse sometime during childhood or adolescence. The University of California research cited above indicates this, and it is confirmed by numerous personal testimonies.

For example, Mike Haley, a former homosexual who later joined the staff of Focus on the Family, recounted how he was raised by a father who called him "worthless" when it became evident that he was not going to become a "macho" athlete. He became a victim of sexual abuse from ages 11 to 18, and then entered into a homosexual lifestyle, eventually becoming a male prostitute. After living as a homosexual for 12 years, through the influence of a friend who shared Christ's love with him, Mike left his homosexual life, and later married and became the father of two sons.[45]

To take another example, Teresa Britton traced her struggle with lesbianism to her father's alcoholism and physical abuse. She would say to herself, "I will never, ever let

---

[43] Sarah Knapton, "Homosexuality 'May Be Triggered by Environment after Birth,'" *The Telegraph*, Oct. 8, 2015, http://www.telegraph.co.uk/science/2016/03/15/homosexuality-may-be-triggered-by-environment-after-birth/.

[44] J. Michael Bailey and Richard C. Pillard, "A Genetic Study of Male Sexual Orientation," *Archives of General Psychiatry* 48 (1991): 1089–96.

[45] Mike Haley, "How One Man Found Freedom in Christ," https://www.focusonthefamily.ca/content/how-one-man-found-freedom-in-christ; see also http://exgayisok.wixsite.com/mhaley.

a man treat me like that. If that's what a man is all about, why would I want to be with one?" She also renounced homosexuality after seeing the love of Christ exhibited by other Christians.[46] There are many such testimonies.

4. "Many Homosexual Relationships Today Are Beneficial, Not Harmful." Finally, there is an objection from experience: Some homosexual couples have faithful, fulfilling relationships, so why should these be thought immoral?

But experience should not be used as a higher standard for moral right and wrong than the teaching of the Bible.

In addition, there is also negative evidence from experience, because several studies indicate that, particularly among male homosexuals, long-term one-partner relationships are uncommon, and the widespread pattern is many sexual partners, often numbering many hundreds over the years.

The damaging consequences of homosexual conduct are rarely mentioned in the mainstream press. However, Satinover reports some of the medical harm that is typically associated with male homosexual practice:

- A twenty-five- to thirty-year decrease in life expectancy
- Chronic, potentially fatal liver disease—infectious hepatitis
- Inevitably fatal immune disease, including associated cancers
- Frequently fatal rectal cancer
- Multiple bowel and other infectious diseases
- A much higher than usual incidence of suicide[47]

What is the reason for these medical conditions? Satinover explains that many are due to the common homosexual practice of anal intercourse:

We are designed with a nearly impenetrable barrier between the bloodstream and the extraordinarily toxic and infectious contents of the bowel. Anal intercourse creates a breach in this barrier for the receptive partner, whether or not the insertive partner is wearing a condom. As a result, homosexual men are disproportionately vulnerable to a host of serious and sometimes fatal infections caused by the entry of feces into the bloodstream. These include hepatitis B and the cluster of otherwise rare conditions.[48]

---

[46] Eileen E. Flynn, "Former Lesbian Discusses Life-Changing Experience," *Austin-American Statesman*, Feb. 16, 2003, cited in Sears and Osten, *The Homosexual Agenda*, 8.

[47] Satinover, *Homosexuality and the Politics of Truth*, 51.

[48] Ibid., 67. See also Anne Rompalo, "Sexually Transmitted Causes of Gastrointestinal Symptoms in Homosexual Men," *Medical Clinics of North America* 74, no. 6 (November 1990): 1633–45, preview of article available at http://www.sciencedirect.com/sdfe/pdf/download/eid/1-s2.0-S0025712516304990/first-page-pdf; "Safer Sex STD Prevention for Gay and Bi-Men," LGBT Health Channel, Aug. 1, 2001, www.gayhealthchannel.com/stdmsm/.

A 2010 study indicated that the rate of new human immunodeficiency virus (HIV) diagnoses among actively homosexual men was more than 44 times that of other men and more than 40 times that of women.

Satinover also points out a significant contrast in the sexual behaviors of heterosexual and homosexual people. Among heterosexuals, sexual faithfulness was relatively high: "90 percent of heterosexual women and more than 75 percent of heterosexual men have never engaged in extramarital sex." But among homosexual men the picture is far different:

> A 1981 study revealed that only 2 percent of homosexuals were monogamous or semi-monogamous—generously defined as ten or fewer lifetime partners. ...A 1978 study found that 43 percent of male homosexuals estimated having sex with five hundred or more different partners. . . . Seventy-nine percent said that more than half of these partners were strangers.[49]

More recent studies showed somewhat different numbers but also confirmed a general pattern among male homosexual couples (but not among lesbian couples) of attaching significantly less importance to sexual "faithfulness" to one's partner. A 2010 study by researchers at San Francisco State University found that homosexual men do not place much value on monogamy. The "Gay Couples Study" surveyed 556 homosexual male couples over three years and found that about 50 percent of the men surveyed had sex outside their relationships, with the knowledge and approval of their partners. Colleen Hoff, the study's principal investigator, said, "With straight people, it is called affairs and cheating, but with gay people it does not have such negative connotations."[50] (It should be noted that this study does not necessarily contradict the earlier studies cited by Satinover, because those studies concerned male homosexuals in general, while this latter study surveyed only "couples" in committed relationships.)

Another study of data from 2000 found the percentage of heterosexual men who reported having sex with someone other than their wife was 10 percent, while 14 percent of married heterosexual women reported having sex with someone other than their husband. By contrast, among gay men, the percentage who reported having sex with people other than their partners was 59 percent; for lesbians it was 8 percent.[51]

In addition, the rate of primary and secondary syphilis among actively homosexual men was more than 46 times that of other men and more than 71 times that of women. Centers for Disease Control and Prevention, "CDC Analysis Provides New Look at Disproportionate Impact of HIV and Syphilis among U.S. Gay and Bisexual Men," March 10, 2010, https://www.cdc.gov/stdconference/2010/msmpressrelease.pdf.

[49] Satinover, *Homosexuality and the Politics of Truth*, 55. Satinover points out, however, that "Lesbian sexual practices are less risky than gay male practices; and lesbians are not nearly so promiscuous as gay men." Ibid., 52.

[50] Cited in Scott James, "Many Successful Gay Marriages Share an Open Secret," *The New York Times*, Jan. 28, 2010, http://www.nytimes.com/2010/01/29/us/29sfmetro.html. The full study can be read at: https://www.ncbi.nlm.nih.gov/pmc/articles/PMC2906147/.

[51] Sharon Jayson, "Gay-Straight Couples More Monogamous in the Past," *USA Today*, Sept. 9, 2011, http://usatoday30.usatoday.com/news/health/wellness/marriage/story/2011–09–05/Gay-straight-couples-more-monogamous-than-in-the-past/50267258/1.

F. IS IT RIGHT TO ATTEND OR PARTICIPATE IN A SAME-SEX WEDDING CEREMONY?

Same-sex marriage is now recognized in several countries, including the United States (since 2015). This means that many Christians will find themselves invited to a same-sex wedding ceremony in which one or both of the partners are friends or family members. Should Christians attend such a ceremony?

The main question is whether attending such a wedding ceremony gives a public signal of approval of the wedding. It seems to me that it does. By attending the wedding, I am saying, by my presence, something like this: "I'm thankful for this marriage, I am supporting it by my presence, and I'm seeking God's blessing on it." But I do not think that a Christian who is subject to the moral standards of Scripture can say these things in good conscience with regard to a same-sex wedding. Therefore, I do not think it is right for a Christian to attend a same-sex wedding ceremony.

This question comes up even more forcefully when Christians who own businesses are asked to contribute their artistic skills to help in the celebration of a same-sex wedding. Should a Christian photographer agree to take the wedding pictures? Should a Christian florist agree to assemble the flower arrangements? Should a Christian baker agree to bake and decorate the wedding cake? Should a Christian who owns a private chapel that is used for weddings allow a same-sex wedding ceremony there?

In the past several years, several Christians in such professions have respectfully declined to contribute their artistic skills to enhance same-sex wedding ceremonies. I believe this was the morally right decision for them—in fact, I think it was a morally *necessary* decision if they wanted to avoid being forced to publicly endorse something they think is morally wrong. But in several court cases, Christians in such situations have lost and been subjected to fines of many thousands of dollars, often with the result that their businesses have been destroyed and they have lost their means of livelihood.

Here are some examples of cases that, as I write, have been defended or are being defended by the Christian legal defense organization Alliance Defending Freedom (ADF):

1. Richland, Washington, florist Barronelle Stutzman, as of March 2017, could lose her business and all of her personal assets for politely declining to create floral arrangements for a long-time customer and friend's same-sex wedding. The Washington Supreme Court ruled unanimously against her right of conscience to decline using her talent for such a ceremony. ADF has appealed her case to the U.S. Supreme Court.[52]
2. Denver-area baker Jack Phillips declined to create a wedding cake for an event celebrating a same-sex marriage. The Colorado Court of Ap-

---

[52] See analysis by Denny Burk, "A Florist Loses Religious Freedom, and Much More," CNN, Feb. 20, 2015, http://www.cnn.com/2015/02/20/living/stutzman-florist-gay/index.html.

peals has affirmed a Colorado Civil Rights Commission ruling ordering Phillips and his staff to create cakes for same-sex celebrations, as well as undergo "re-education" and file quarterly "compliance" reports for the next two years. ADF has also appealed that case to the U.S. Supreme Court.

3. Lexington, Kentucky, T-shirt designer Blaine Adamson, a Christian, declined to design and print T-shirts for a "gay pride" event. The Lexington Human Rights Commission ruled against Blaine. ADF appealed the case in court, which reversed the decision and affirmed Blaine's right of conscience. The case is now under appeal.

4. Albuquerque, New Mexico, photographer Elaine Huguenin was ordered to pay nearly $7,000 in attorneys' fees to a lesbian couple for respectfully declining to use her talent to commemorate a same-sex commitment ceremony. She lost at the New Mexico Supreme Court, with one of the justices writing that it was her "price of citizenship" to be forced to violate her personal religious beliefs regarding marriage as the union between one man and one woman. Huguenin, her husband, and her children received several death threats, and she ultimately closed her business.[53]

The agenda behind the movement to punish Christians severely if they refuse to contribute their artistic talents to same-sex wedding ceremonies is ominous. It seems to me to be an attempt to use the power of government to compel everyone in society to give moral approval to homosexual conduct. Therefore, it is an attempt to compel Christians to violate their consciences and sin against God. This kind of campaign, which is pushed by homosexual advocacy groups, strikes at the very foundation of freedom of religion, which is the very first fundamental right protected in the Bill of Rights in the United States Constitution: "Congress shall make no law respecting an establishment of religion, *or prohibiting the free exercise thereof*."[54] But such court decisions against Christians clearly prohibit them from freely exercising their religion and following their deeply held religious beliefs. This is a threat of massive proportions.

Such cases are currently working their way through the court system in the United States, and they will ultimately be settled by the Supreme Court.[55] We may hope and pray that the Supreme Court will rule that national and state governments in the United States may not prohibit people from "free exercise" of religion.

---

[53] Information on these cases was provided to me in a personal email on April 1, 2017, from Osten, co-author of *The Homosexual Agenda* and senior director, research and grant writing, for the ADF. For more information on these cases, see http://www.adflegal.org/issues/religious-freedom/conscience.

[54] See http://constitutionus.com.

[55] The landmark case Masterpiece Cakeshop v. Colorado Civil Rights Commission was argued before the Supreme Court on Dec. 5, 2017. No decision had been when this book went to press.

G. GOVERNMENTAL LAWS AND POLICIES REGARDING SAME-SEX MARRIAGE

Although several countries, including the United States, have now recognized same-sex marriage,[56] these decisions are not consistent with biblical teachings. This is because one role of civil government is to "praise those who do good" (1 Pet. 2:14), but homosexual relationships cannot be classified as morally "good" in light of the biblical teachings discussed above.

It is important to recognize that government recognition of a relationship as a "marriage" carries with it the *endorsement* and *encouragement* of that relationship by a society. Couples who are legally married enjoy many protections and benefits (legal, financial, and interpersonal) that society has granted in order to encourage marriage and signal that the institution of marriage brings benefits to society as a whole.

So the question is really whether a society, through its laws, should give approval and encouragement to homosexual relationships, which both the Bible and most cultures throughout history have considered to be morally wrong rather than "good," and which also bring significant harmful consequences. My own view is that governments should remain "neutral" regarding homosexual conduct—not promoting it, as with recognition of same-sex marriage, but also not prohibiting it, as so-called "sodomy laws" previously did in the United States.[57]

Governmental recognition of same-sex marriage implies other legal consequences, such as requirements to allow homosexual couples to adopt and raise children, but this robs many children of the opportunity to be raised in a home with both a father and a mother, which is by far the best environment for them (see chap. 28, p. 739). In addition, there is a real danger that freedom of religion and freedom of speech could be threatened, because government recognition of same-sex marriage might also lead to governmental prohibitions against criticizing homosexual conduct.

---

[56] Recognition of same-sex marriage in the United States was affirmed June 26, 2015, by a 5-4 vote of the United States Supreme Court in the case Obergefell v. Hodges. Justice Anthony Kennedy joined with the four liberal justices on the court (Ruth Bader Ginsburg, Stephen Breyer, Sonia Sotomayor, and Elena Kagan) to give a fifth vote, while justices Antonin Scalia, Clarence Thomas, and Samuel Alito, as well as Chief Justice John Roberts, issued strong dissenting opinions.

Prior to this decision, individual states were reaching different conclusions about this question, and constitutional amendments limiting marriage to one man and one woman had actually been passed in 30 of the 50 states, but these amendments were all overruled by the U.S. Supreme Court decision.

As of September 2017, the following countries have legalized same-sex marriage: Argentina, Belgium, Brazil, Canada, Columbia, Denmark, England/Wales, Finland, France, Germany, Greenland, Iceland, Ireland, Luxembourg, Malta, The Netherlands, New Zealand, Norway, Portugal, Scotland, South Africa, Spain, Sweden, the United States, and Uruguay. See http://www.pewforum.org/2015/06/26/gay-marriage-around-the-world-2013/.

[57] See further recommendations about laws in Wayne Grudem, *Politics—According to the Bible: A Comprehensive Resource for Understanding Modern Political Issues in Light of Scripture* (Grand Rapids, MI: Zondervan, 2010), 233–38. (See also p. 229, n. 31)

Further discussion of the legal and political issues involved can be found in my book *Politics—According to the Bible*.[58]

H. CONCLUSION ON HOMOSEXUALITY

Homosexual conduct of all kinds is consistently viewed as sin in the Bible, and recent interpretations of the Bible that have been raised as objections to that view do not give a satisfactory explanation of the words or the contexts of the relevant passages. Sexual intimacy is to be confined to marriage, and marriage is to be only between one man and one woman, following the pattern established by God in creation. The church should always act with love and compassion toward homosexuals, yet never affirm homosexual conduct as morally right. The gospel of Jesus Christ offers the "good news" of forgiveness of sins and real hope for a transformed life to homosexuals, just as it does for all sinners.

I. THE TRANSGENDER QUESTION: CAN PEOPLE CHOOSE THEIR GENDER?

Some people today claim to be "transgender"—that is, they think of themselves (or "identify") as having a gender that is different from their biological sex. Someone who is biologically a male may claim to identify as a female, and someone who is biologically a female may claim to identify as a male. These claims are based on an assumption that "gender" is something that people can choose, not something that is determined by the biological sex of their bodies. In the material that follows, I attempt to provide a biblical perspective on this question.

1. God Created Only Two Sexes, Male and Female. At the very beginning of creation, God made men and women equal in value and personhood but distinct in their sexuality:

> So God created man *in his own image,*
>> in the image of God he created him;
>> male and female he created them. (Gen. 1:27)

While men and women are similar in many ways, we are also different in many ways. There are about 37.2 trillion cells in the human body,[59] and these cells (except for red blood cells)[60] are different in men and women, because men have an X chromosome

---

[58] See Grudem, *Politics—According to the Bible*, 221–38.

[59] Nicholas Bakalar, "37.2 Trillion: Galaxies or Human Cells," *The New York Times*, June 19, 2015, https://www.nytimes.com/2015/06/23/science/37-2-trillion-galaxies-or-human-cells.html; see also Rose Eveleth, "There Are 37.2 Trillion Cells in Your Body," *Smithsonian*, Oct. 24, 2013, http://www.smithsonianmag.com/smart-news/there-are-372-trillion-cells-in-your-body-4941473/.

[60] Red blood cells do not have a nucleus and therefore do not have XX or XY chromosomes. Red blood cells constitute about one-fourth of the cells in a normal human body. See "Blood Basics," American Society of Hematology, http://www.hematology.org/Patients/Basics/; Ananya Mandal, "What Are Genes?" News Medi-

and a Y chromosome in each cell, while women have two X chromosomes in each cell. In other words, if we count all the cells except for (an estimated) 10 trillion red blood cells, at the cellular level, there are still over 27 *trillion* biological differences between men and women.

There are other physical differences. Men and women differ in the "wiring" of their brains—the arrangement of various connections between different parts of the brain, resulting in differences in the way men and women process information. Neuropsychiatrist Louann Brizendine of the University of California, San Francisco, writes:

> Scientists have discovered an astonishing array of structural, chemical, genetic, hormonal, and functional brain differences between men and women. . . . The female and male brains process stimuli, hear, see, "sense," and gauge what others are feeling in different ways.[61]

Other interesting differences (using *averages* for men and women) include:

- An average man is taller and heavier than an average woman.
- Girls, on average, enter into puberty approximately two years before boys.
- Men have larger hearts and lungs, and their higher levels of testosterone cause them to produce greater amounts of red blood cells.
- Men have better distance vision and depth perception. Women have better night vision and better visual memory.
- Women are more sensitive to sound than men.
- Men, on average, are over 30 percent stronger than women, especially in the upper body.
- Female fertility decreases after age 35, ending with menopause, but men are capable of fathering children even when very old.
- Men's skin has more collagen and sebum, which makes it thicker and oilier than women's skin.
- Women generally have a greater body fat percentage than men.[62]

2. God Intends That a Person's Gender Identity Should Be Determined by That Person's Biological Sex. There is no hint anywhere in Scripture that a biological woman should "identify" as a man or attempt to act in ways that are perceived as appropriate only for men. And there is no hint anywhere in Scripture that a biological man should "identify" as a woman or attempt to act in ways that are perceived as appropriate only for women. Instead, there are multiple passages *that assume that someone is either a man*

---

cal, http://www.news-medical.net/life-sciences/What-are-Genes.aspx; and "Red Blood Cell Count—Types," Symptoms, http://www.symptoms.in/red-blood-cell-count.html.

[61] Louann Brizendine, *The Female Brain* (New York: Morgan Road Books, 2006), 4.

[62] Heidi Miller, "Difference Between Male and Female Structures (Mental and Physical)," SteadyHealth, March 19, 2007, http://www.steadyhealth.com/articles/difference-between-male-and-female-structures -mental-and-physical?show_all=1.

or woman, and that society regularly will be able to know the difference between them. Here are some of the passages:

> If a woman conceives and bears a *male child*, then she shall be unclean seven days. . . . But if she bears a *female child*, then she shall be unclean two weeks. (Lev. 12:2–5)

> You shall not lie with a *male* as with a *woman*; it is an abomination. (Lev. 18:22)

> If a man lies with a *male* as with a *woman*, both of them have committed an abomination; they shall surely be put to death; their blood is upon them. (Lev. 20:13)

> If anyone makes a special vow to the Lord involving the valuation of persons, then the valuation of a *male* from twenty years old up to sixty years old shall be fifty shekels of silver, according to the shekel of the sanctuary. If the person is a *female*, the valuation shall be thirty shekels. (Lev. 27:2; the difference probably reflected the common price for slaves and the expected value of their labor)

> If a man dies and has no *son*, then you shall transfer his inheritance to his *daughter*. And if he has no daughter, then you shall give his inheritance to his brothers. (Num. 27:8–9)

> If a *man* vows a vow to the Lord, or swears an oath to bind himself by a pledge. . . . If a *woman* vows a vow to the Lord and binds herself by a pledge . . . (Num. 30:2–3)

> [With reference to a conquered city in warfare:] And when the Lord your God gives it into your hand, you shall put all its *males* to the sword, but the *women* and the little ones, the livestock, and everything else in the city, all its spoil, you shall take as plunder for yourselves. (Deut. 20:13)

> A *woman* shall not wear a *man's* garment, nor shall a *man* put on a *woman's* cloak, for whoever does these things is an abomination to the Lord your God. (Deut. 22:5)

> For their *women* exchanged natural relations for those that are contrary to nature; and the *men* likewise gave up natural relations with *women* and were consumed with passion for one another, men committing shameless acts with men and receiving in themselves the due penalty for their error. (Rom. 1:26–27)

Every *man* who prays or prophesies with his head covered dishonors his head, but every *wife* who prays or prophesies with her head uncovered dishonors her head. . . . For a *man* ought not to cover his head, since he is the image and glory of God, but *woman* is the glory of man. For *man* was not made from *woman*, but woman from man. Neither was *man* created for *woman*, but woman for man. That is why a wife ought to have a symbol of authority on her head, because of the angels. Nevertheless, in the Lord woman is not independent of man nor man of woman. (1 Cor. 11:2–11)

I desire then that in every place the *men* should pray, lifting holy hands without anger or quarreling; likewise also that *women* should adorn themselves in respectable apparel, with modesty and self-control, not with braided hair and gold or pearls or costly attire, but with what is proper for women who profess godliness—with good works. Let a *woman* learn quietly with all submissiveness. I do not permit a *woman* to teach or to exercise authority over a man; rather, she is to remain quiet. (1 Tim. 2:8–12)

Do not rebuke an *older man* but encourage him as you would a father, *younger men* as brothers, *older women* as mothers, *younger women* as sisters, in all purity. (1 Tim. 5:1–2)

Older men are to be sober-minded, dignified, self-controlled, sound in faith, in love, and in steadfastness. *Older women* likewise are to be reverent in behavior, not slanderers or slaves to much wine. They are to teach what is good, and so train the *young women* to love their husbands and children, to be self-controlled, pure, working at home, kind, and submissive to their own husbands, that the word of God may not be reviled. Likewise, urge the *younger men* to be self-controlled. (Titus 2:2–6)

While Christians today may ponder the meaning of these passages and may disagree over their proper application in the new covenant age, the only point I'm seeking to establish here is that Scripture *repeatedly distinguishes between men and women*, assumes that people will always be able to tell the difference between them, and assumes that in several ways men and women will act differently, in ways appropriate to their sex. In all of these passages, it is assumed that a person's biological sex determines how the person should act—that is, in ways appropriate to each person's sex, whether male or female. Every person's sense of his or her own "gender identity" should be the same as that person's biological sex.[63]

---

[63] I do not discuss here the various kinds of disorders of sex development that are collectively referred to as "intersex." Such cases involve various ambiguities in physical markers of sexuality, and therefore they differ from transgenderism, which concerns psychological ambiguities in a person's feelings and preferences. For a biblically based analysis of intersex, see Denny Burk, *What Is the Meaning of Sex?* (Wheaton, IL: Crossway,

3. Deuteronomy 22:5: A Passage of Special Importance in the Transgender Debate.
One passage in the Mosaic Law has particular relevance to this discussion:

> A woman shall not wear a man's garment, nor shall a man put on a woman's cloak, for whoever does these things is an abomination to the LORD your God. (Deut. 22:5)

Old Testament professor Jason DeRouchie published an especially perceptive analysis of this verse and its relevance for transgender questions today, and my discussion here depends significantly on his work.[64]

DeRouchie recognizes that this law is found in the Mosaic Law, and that we are no longer under the Mosaic covenant. He says, "While Christians are not legally bound to the Mosaic law, we do not throw out the law itself," and he carefully analyzes the meaning of this commandment in the light of Christ's redemptive work and our position in the new covenant age. The Mosaic law still has theological significance and we can still learn from it "about God and his ways."

With this background, DeRouchie says that "on the surface, the prohibition relates to what the APA terms 'gender expression'—'the way a person acts to communicate gender within a given culture' through things like dress." Then he says:

> At a deeper level, however, the law assumes a more fundamental rule—that there are only two biological sexes—male and female—and that what is gender normative in God's world is that one's biological sex should govern both one's gender identity and expression. Before divine wrath is poured out, this text provides a kind corrective to gender confusion and transgender identity.[65]

Because the Hebrew term translated "man" in Deuteronomy 22:5 is not 'ish, which can often mean "husband," but rather *geber*, which means "man" or "strong man" but never means "husband," DeRouchie concludes:

> From God's perspective, maleness and femaleness bears implications beyond the home or gathered worshiping community. It also impacts daily life in society. . . . Within Israelite culture, then, there were certain styles of dress, ornaments, or items that distinguished men and women. As such, two things

---

2013), 157–83. Burk concludes, I think rightly, that the decision of whether to treat an intersex child as male or female should be determined by the child's chromosomal pattern, whether XX or XY, wherever that is possible to determine.

[64] Jason DeRouchie, "Confronting the Transgender Storm: New Covenant Reflections from Deuteronomy 22:5," *Journal for Biblical Manhood and Womanhood* 21, no. 1 (May 25, 2016), http://cbmw.org/topics/transgenderism/jbmw-21-1-confronting-the-transgender-storm-new-covenant-reflections-from-deuteronomy-225/. Another perceptive article on this passage, which discusses and rejects several alternative interpretations, is P. J. Harland, "Menswear and Womenswear: A Study of Deuteronomy 22:5," *Expository Times* 110, no. 3 (1998): 73–76.

[65] DeRouchie, "Confronting the Transgender Storm."

appear to be at stake in this law: (1) everyone needed to let their gender expression align with their biological sex, and (2) everyone needed to guard against gender confusion, wherein others could wrongly perceive a man to be a woman and a woman to be a man based on dress.[66]

With respect to the last phrase of Deuteronomy 22:5, "for whoever does these things is an abomination to the LORD your God," DeRouchie concludes that blurring the distinctions between men and women in society undermines the ability of men and women to rightly reflect the nature of God: "what makes transgenderism abominable is that it maligns humanity's ability to reflect, resemble, and represent God rightly in this world."[67] Why is this? It is because both Old and New Testaments picture the relationship between God and his people as a relationship between a husband and his bride, an analogy in which the man represents God and the woman represents God's people. The God-given differences between men and women are necessary for that reflection of God's glory to be seen in human activity.

> Gender identity and gender expression is about God's glory and about maintaining the God-created distinctions on earth that in turn point to the ultimate distinction between God and his bride. Just as husbands and wives in the human household and men and women in the collective household of God bear distinct roles and, by this, uniquely display God's image, so too the creator and Lord of all things is rightly magnified in the lives of males and females when our gender identity and gender expression align perfectly with our God-ordained biological sex. Those born boys are to live and thrive as boys, and those born girls are to live and thrive as girls.[68]

Finally, by way of practical application, DeRouchie says:

> As believers, we should be among those who celebrate men being masculine and women being feminine, both in the way we act and in the way we dress.[69]

---

[66] Ibid.

[67] Ibid.

[68] Ibid.

[69] Ibid. However, DeRouchie recognizes that clothing styles for men and women change over time, so that some forms of dress that previously were worn only by men or by women are no longer viewed as gender-specific: "in our present culture ladies can wear slacks . . . and even ties with none questioning their femaleness. . . . Guys too could have ear rings or long hair with none questioning their maleness." Ibid. I agree with his assessment of current cultural opinions of these things, but his comments about the appropriateness of distinctly masculine and distinctly feminine clothing gave me new appreciation for the widespread, instinctive suspicion of long hair for men that millions of parents felt in the 1960s, when, to the parents, long hair made their sons "look like girls."
This article also helped me understand why, after 48 years of marriage, I still feel uncomfortable if for some reason an occasion arises when I have to carry Margaret's purse even for a short time in a public place. In the United States in 2017, men don't carry purses—that is something that belongs to femininity and womanhood. Someone might ask, "Does it threaten your manhood to carry a purse?" My response is yes,

4. What about Sex-Reassignment Surgery? For people who claim to be transgendered, some surgical procedures are available to alter their sexual organs and sometimes other physical characteristics, such as breast size and facial hair. Such surgeries are far more invasive and long-lasting than such activities as a woman wearing a man's garment or a man putting on a woman's cloak, which are prohibited in Deuteronomy 22:5, and they attack more deeply the God-given manhood of a man and the God-given womanhood of a woman.

And yet, such surgeries cannot change a man into a woman or change a woman into a man. A biological male, after such surgery, still has about 27 trillion male cells in his body with XY chromosomes, and a biological female, after such surgery, still has about 27 trillion female cells in her body with XX chromosomes. A biological male still has billions of typically male neurological connections in his brain, and a biological female still has billions of typically female neurological connections in her brain. Both before and after such surgery, a biological man is still a man and a biological woman is still a woman.

Paul McHugh, former psychiatrist in chief at Johns Hopkins Hospital, published a substantial objection to transgender surgery in *The Wall Street Journal* in 2014.[70] McHugh writes that transgenderism is "a mental disorder that deserves understanding, treatment and prevention." He adds that "the idea of sex misalignment is simply mistaken—it does not correspond with physical reality. . . . It can lead to grim psychological outcomes."[71]

McHugh compares people who claim to be transgender to "those who suffer from anorexia and bulimia nervosa, where the assumption that departs from physical reality is the belief by the dangerously thin that they are overweight." He then says:

> For the transgendered, this argument holds that one's feeling of "gender" is a conscious, subjective sense that, being in one's mind, cannot be questioned by others. The individual often seeks not just society's tolerance of this "personal truth" but affirmation of it. . . . Psychiatrists obviously must challenge the solipsistic concept that what is in the mind cannot be questioned.[72]

He goes on to give some deeply troubling statistics about the results of sex-reassignment surgery, including a study by the Karolinska Institute in Sweden that

---

to a certain extent it undermines my sense of manhood. It feels uncomfortable to me because it appears that I am giving a signal that I would rather be a woman than a man, a signal that I'm uncomfortable in my manhood. And so I will carry it (if necessary) while holding it in a manner that doesn't resemble the way a woman normally holds a purse! It seems to me that such a human instinct to preserve some measure of distinctiveness in male and female clothing is a healthy one.

[70] Paul McHugh, "Transgender Surgery Isn't the Solution: A Drastic Physical Change Doesn't Address Underlying Psycho-Social Troubles," *The Wall Street Journal*, June 12, 2014, updated May 13, 2016, https://www.wsj.com/articles/paul-mchugh-transgender-surgery-isnt-the-solution-1402615120.

[71] Ibid.

[72] Ibid.

followed 324 people for up to 30 years after they had sex-reassignment surgery. This study showed that "beginning about 10 years after having the surgery, the transgendered began to experience increasing mental difficulties," and their suicide rate was nearly 20 times greater than the comparable nontransgender population.[73]

As for children with transgender feelings, McHugh reports, "When children who reported transgender feelings were tracked without medical or surgical treatment at both Vanderbilt University and London's Portman Clinic, 70%-80% of them spontaneously lost those feelings." He disagrees with doctors who administer puberty-delaying hormones to young children, "even though the drugs stunt the children's growth and risk causing sterility."

He concludes:

> "Sex change" is biologically impossible. People who undergo sex-reassignment surgery do not change from men to women or vice versa. Rather, they become feminized men or masculinized women. Claiming that this is a civil-rights matter and encouraging surgical intervention is in reality to collaborate with and promote a mental disorder.[74]

In another, longer study that McHugh coauthored with Lawrence Mayer, they write:

> The hypothesis that gender identity is an innate, fixed property of human beings that is independent of biological sex—that a person might be "a man trapped in a woman's body" or "a woman trapped in a man's body"—is not supported by scientific evidence.[75]

5. Bathrooms, Locker Rooms, and Sports Teams. Recently a number of American governmental bodies at both the national and state/local levels have authorized or required schools to allow transgender children to use restrooms and locker rooms other than the ones that correspond to their biological sex, so that girls who are biologically female but claim to "identify as male" must be allowed into boys' restrooms and locker rooms, and boys who are biologically male but claim to "identify as female" must be allowed into girls' restrooms and locker rooms.

If parents object that such children could be allowed to use separate individual restrooms, transgender advocates reply that this is bullying and discrimination because

[73] Ibid.
[74] Ibid.
[75] Lawrence Mayer and Paul McHugh, "Sexuality and Gender: Findings from the Biological, Psychological, and Social Science," *The New Atlantis* 50 (2016): 8, http://www.thenewatlantis.com/publications/preface-sexuality-and-gender. The entire report is 143 pages long. The "Editor's Note" with this special issue states that the report is written by "Dr. Lawrence S. Mayer, an epidemiologist trained in psychiatry, and Dr. Paul R. McHugh, arguably the most important American psychiatrist of the last half-century." Ibid., 4.
See also Paul McHugh, "Surgical Sex: Why We Stopped Doing Sex Change Operations," *First Things*, November 2004, 34–38, https://www.firstthings.com/article/2004/11/surgical-sex.

it does not allow these transgender children to use the same restrooms or locker rooms as other children in the gender with which they identify. Alliance Defending Freedom (ADF) is working on several legal cases involving parents and children who have had no choice but to sue their local school districts in order to maintain opposite-sex restrooms, showers, and locker rooms.

In one case, a high school student and his parents sued the Boyertown Area School District in Pennsylvania for intentionally violating his right to bodily privacy after he was exposed involuntarily to an undressed female student while he was changing in his school's boys' locker room.

The school district had secretly opened its schools' sex-specific restrooms and locker rooms to students of the opposite sex, without notice to students or parents. When the student, identified in the lawsuit as "Joel Doe," was standing in his underwear about to put on his gym clothes, he suddenly noticed that a female student, also in a state of undress, was in the locker room.

When "Joel Doe" brought a complaint to school officials, they informed him that they now allow students who subjectively identify themselves as the opposite sex to choose whichever locker room they wish to use. He asked officials to protect his privacy, but they instead told him twice that he must "tolerate" it and make changing with students of the opposite sex as "natural" as he can.[76]

In another ADF case in Minnesota, a biologically male student who identifies as a female was allowed to enter the girls' locker room under the district's policy. According to the complaint in the case, he went on to dance in the locker room "in a sexually explicit manner—'twerking,' 'grinding' and dancing like he was on a 'stripper pole' to songs with explicit lyrics, including 'Milkshake' by Kelis. On another occasion, a female student saw the male student lift his dress to reveal his underwear while 'grinding' to the music."[77]

On sports teams, children who are biologically boys but who claim to "identify as girls" have been allowed to participate as members of girls' sports teams, and, because some (biological) boys will be larger and stronger than any girls in that sport, they have begun to beat all the girls they compete against.[78]

In Texas, a 17-year-old female taking testosterone in an attempt to become male won the Texas girls' wrestling title after wrestling an undefeated season against girls.[79] In March 2017, a New Zealand transgender weightlifter who had formerly participated in

[76] "Student Sues Pennsylvania School District for Sexual Harassment, Violation of Personal Privacy," Alliance Defending Freedom, March 21, 2017, http://www.adfmedia.org/News/PRDetail/?CID=93267. The case is Doe v. Boyertown Area School District.

[77] "Families Sue Feds, Minnesota School District for Violating Student Privacy," Alliance Defending Freedom, Sept. 8, 2016, http://www.adfmedia.org/News/PRDetail/?CID=91352.

[78] See Joy Pullmann, "Boys Will Keep Winning Girls' Sports Trophies Until We Are Willing to Re-Assert Sex Distinctions," *The Federalist*, April 11, 2017, http://thefederalist.com/2017/04/11/boys-will-keep-winning-girls-sports-trophies-willing-re-assert-sex-distinctions/.

[79] Kristie Rieken, "Transgender Boy Wins Controversial Girls State Wrestling Title in Texas," *Chicago Tribune*, Feb. 25, 2017, http://www.chicagotribune.com/sports/highschool/ct-transgender-wrestler-texas-20170225-story.html.

the male division before "transitioning" to female dominated the international competition in "her" debut on the women's circuit, setting four world records in the process.[80] In Alaska, a biologically male student competed as a female and captured all-state honors in girls' track and field. One of the parents of the girls competing against the transgender athlete said his wins were "not fair and it is not right for our female athletes."[81]

Such mistaken government policies are simply wrong because they are attempting to compel people to affirm a blatant lie. A child who is biologically male is a boy, not a girl, no matter how many thousand times he proclaims that he is a girl. A child who is biologically female is a girl, not a boy, no matter how many thousand times she proclaims that she is a boy. For a society to affirm such outright lies is (to use McHugh's analogy mentioned above) similar to a society telling a severely underweight, anorexic girl who is near to starvation that what she sincerely believes about herself is true, that she is really too fat.

In addition, these governmental policies sow seeds of gender confusion among the boys and girls whose restrooms are invaded by members of the opposite sex, and who are forced by school policy to undress in the presence of members of the opposite sex. Such policies thus attempt to reinforce the lie that a person's gender is something one can choose, not something determined by biological reality. In addition, such policies tend to undermine the God-given instinct of modesty regarding the exposure of the private parts of boys and girls, of men and women. "Our unpresentable parts are treated with greater modesty, which our more presentable parts do not require" (1 Cor. 12:23–24).

6. Pronouns: Shall We Call a Boy *She* and a Girl *He*? One further aspect of the transgender movement is the apparent determination by much mainstream media to refer to biological males and females with pronouns that do not correspond to the truth of who they are but reflect the "gender" that they have chosen for themselves. Thus, a transgender "woman" who is biologically a man will be referred to in media reports with the pronouns *she* and *her*, because that is what he prefers. For example, Bruce Jenner, the famous Olympic athlete (gold-medal winner in the decathlon in 1976), who now claims to be transgender and identifies himself as Caitlyn Jenner, will be referred to with the pronouns *she* and *her*.

This is something I do not think Christians should do, and something that I, in good conscience, cannot do. This is the pressure of society attempting to force me to affirm a lie, to affirm that Jenner is actually now a woman. But this is false. He is a man, he has

---

[80] Bradford Richardson, "Transgender Weightlifter Breaks Record in Women's Competition," *The Washington Times*, March 21, 2017, http://www.washingtontimes.com/news/2017/mar/21/transgender-weightlifter-breaks-womens-record/.

[81] Douglas Ernst, "Transgender Students' All-State Honors in Girls' Track and Field Ignites Backlash," *The Washington Times*, June 6, 2016, http://www.washingtontimes.com/news/2016/jun/6/nattaphon-wangyot-transgender-student-riles-critic/.

always been a man, and he will always be a man. Therefore, I will always refer to him with the pronouns *he* and *him*.

J. APPENDIX 1: THE NASHVILLE STATEMENT

Several evangelical organizations have recently sought to formulate wise policy statements about homosexuality and transgenderism. Because every church and Christian organization will likely be asked about their position on these issues in the next few years, I decided to include as appendixes in this chapter two recent, biblically faithful sets of guidelines that churches and parachurch organizations might find useful in formulating their own policies.

The first is the Nashville Statement, published by the Council on Biblical Manhood and Womanhood. The statement was finalized at a meeting of evangelical pastors, leaders, and scholars in Nashville, Tennessee, on Aug. 25, 2017. I was part of the drafting committee and also one of the more than 180 initial signers. Many thousands of others have subsequently signed it.[82]

Nashville Statement
A Coalition for Biblical Sexuality

"*Know that the* Lord *Himself is God;*
It is He who has made us, and not we ourselves . . ."
Psalm 100:3

Preamble
Evangelical Christians at the dawn of the 21st century find themselves living in a period of historic transition. As Western culture has become increasingly post-Christian, it has embarked upon a massive revision of what it means to be a human being. By and large the spirit of our age no longer discerns or delights in the beauty of God's design for human life. Many deny that God created human beings for his glory, and that his good purposes for us include our personal and physical design as male and female. It is common to think that human identity as male and female is not part of God's beautiful plan, but is, rather, an expression of an individual's autonomous preferences. The pathway to full and lasting joy through God's good design for his creatures is thus replaced by the path of shortsighted alternatives that, sooner or later, ruin human life and dishonor God.

This secular spirit of our age presents a great challenge to the Christian church. Will the church of the Lord Jesus Christ lose her biblical conviction, clarity, and courage, and blend into the spirit of the age? Or will she hold fast to the word of life, draw courage

---

[82] See https://cbmw.org/nashville-statement.

from Jesus, and unashamedly proclaim his way as the way of life? Will she maintain her clear, counter-cultural witness to a world that seems bent on ruin?

We are persuaded that faithfulness in our generation means declaring once again the true story of the world and of our place in it—particularly as male and female. Christian Scripture teaches that there is but one God who alone is Creator and Lord of all. To him alone, every person owes gladhearted thanksgiving, heart-felt praise, and total allegiance. This is the path not only of glorifying God, but of knowing ourselves. To forget our Creator is to forget who we are, for he made us for himself. And we cannot know ourselves truly without truly knowing him who made us. We did not make ourselves. We are not our own. Our true identity, as male and female persons, is given by God. It is not only foolish, but hopeless, to try to make ourselves what God did not create us to be.

We believe that God's design for his creation and his way of salvation serve to bring him the greatest glory and bring us the greatest good. God's good plan provides us with the greatest freedom. Jesus said he came that we might have life and have it in overflowing measure. He is for us and not against us. Therefore, in the hope of serving Christ's church and witnessing publicly to the good purposes of God for human sexuality revealed in Christian Scripture, we offer the following affirmations and denials.

Article 1
WE AFFIRM that God has designed marriage to be a covenantal, sexual, procreative, lifelong union of one man and one woman, as husband and wife, and is meant to signify the covenant love between Christ and his bride the church.

WE DENY that God has designed marriage to be a homosexual, polygamous, or polyamorous relationship. We also deny that marriage is a mere human contract rather than a covenant made before God.

Article 2
WE AFFIRM that God's revealed will for all people is chastity outside of marriage and fidelity within marriage.

WE DENY that any affections, desires, or commitments ever justify sexual intercourse before or outside marriage; nor do they justify any form of sexual immorality.

Article 3
WE AFFIRM that God created Adam and Eve, the first human beings, in his own image, equal before God as persons, and distinct as male and female.

WE DENY that the divinely ordained differences between male and female render them unequal in dignity or worth.

Article 4

WE AFFIRM that divinely ordained differences between male and female reflect God's original creation design and are meant for human good and human flourishing.

WE DENY that such differences are a result of the Fall or are a tragedy to be overcome.

Article 5

WE AFFIRM that the differences between male and female reproductive structures are integral to God's design for self-conception as male or female.

WE DENY that physical anomalies or psychological conditions nullify the God-appointed link between biological sex and self-conception as male or female.

Article 6

WE AFFIRM that those born with a physical disorder of sex development are created in the image of God and have dignity and worth equal to all other image-bearers. They are acknowledged by our Lord Jesus in his words about "eunuchs who were born that way from their mother's womb." With all others they are welcome as faithful followers of Jesus Christ and should embrace their biological sex insofar as it may be known.

WE DENY that ambiguities related to a person's biological sex render one incapable of living a fruitful life in joyful obedience to Christ.

Article 7

WE AFFIRM that self-conception as male or female should be defined by God's holy purposes in creation and redemption as revealed in Scripture.

WE DENY that adopting a homosexual or transgender self-conception is consistent with God's holy purposes in creation and redemption.

Article 8

WE AFFIRM that people who experience sexual attraction for the same sex may live a rich and fruitful life pleasing to God through faith in Jesus Christ, as they, like all Christians, walk in purity of life.

WE DENY that sexual attraction for the same sex is part of the natural goodness of God's original creation, or that it puts a person outside the hope of the gospel.

Article 9

WE AFFIRM that sin distorts sexual desires by directing them away from the marriage covenant and toward sexual immorality— a distortion that includes both heterosexual and homosexual immorality.

WE DENY that an enduring pattern of desire for sexual immorality justifies sexually immoral behavior.

Article 10

WE AFFIRM that it is sinful to approve of homosexual immorality or transgenderism and that such approval constitutes an essential departure from Christian faithfulness and witness.

WE DENY that the approval of homosexual immorality or transgenderism is a matter of moral indifference about which otherwise faithful Christians should agree to disagree.

Article 11

WE AFFIRM our duty to speak the truth in love at all times, including when we speak to or about one another as male or female.

WE DENY any obligation to speak in such ways that dishonor God's design of his image-bearers as male and female.

Article 12

WE AFFIRM that the grace of God in Christ gives both merciful pardon and transforming power, and that this pardon and power enable a follower of Jesus to put to death sinful desires and to walk in a manner worthy of the Lord.

WE DENY that the grace of God in Christ is insufficient to forgive all sexual sins and to give power for holiness to every believer who feels drawn into sexual sin.

Article 13

WE AFFIRM that the grace of God in Christ enables sinners to forsake transgender self-conceptions and by divine forbearance to accept the God-ordained link between one's biological sex and one's self-conception as male or female.

WE DENY that the grace of God in Christ sanctions self-conceptions that are at odds with God's revealed will.

Article 14

WE AFFIRM that Christ Jesus has come into the world to save sinners and that through Christ's death and resurrection forgiveness of sins and eternal life are available to every person who repents of sin and trusts in Christ alone as Savior, Lord, and supreme treasure.

WE DENY that the Lord's arm is too short to save or that any sinner is beyond his reach.

K. APPENDIX 2: RESOLUTION OF THE SOUTHERN BAPTIST CONVENTION ON TRANSGENDER IDENTITY

At its annual denominational meeting in 2014, the Southern Baptist Convention, the largest Protestant denomination in the United States, approved a clear, wise, biblically based resolution on transgender identity, which could serve as a model for other churches and denominations. The resolution was coauthored by Boyce College professor Denny Burk and Ethics and Religious Liberty Commission policy director Andrew Walker.[83]

"On Transgender Identity"

Resolution of the Southern Baptist Convention, June 10–11, 2014, in Baltimore, Maryland

WHEREAS, All persons are created in God's image and are made to glorify Him (Genesis 1:27; Isaiah 43:7); and

WHEREAS, God's design was the creation of two distinct and complementary sexes, male and female (Genesis 1:27; Matthew 19:4; Mark 10:6) which designate the fundamental distinction that God has embedded in the very biology of the human race; and

WHEREAS, Distinctions in masculine and feminine roles as ordained by God are part of the created order and should find expression in every human heart (Genesis 2:18, 21–24; 1 Corinthians 11:7–9; Ephesians 5:22–33; 1 Timothy 2:12–14); and

WHEREAS, The Fall of man into sin and God's subsequent curse have introduced brokenness and futility into God's good creation (Genesis 3:1–24; Romans 8:20); and

WHEREAS, According to a 2011 survey, about 700,000 Americans perceive their gender identity to be at variance with the physical reality of their biological birth sex; and

WHEREAS, Transgenderism differs from hermaphroditism or intersexualism in that the sex of the individual is not biologically ambiguous but psychologically ambiguous; and

WHEREAS, The American Psychiatric Association removed this condition (aka, "gender identity disorder") from its list of disorders in 2013, substituting "gender identity disorder" with "gender dysphoria"; and

---

[83] See "On Transgender Identity," The Southern Baptist Convention, http://www.sbc.net/resolutions/2250 /on-transgender-identity.

WHEREAS, The American Psychiatric Association includes among its treatment options for gender dysphoria cross-sex hormone therapy, gender reassignment surgery, and social and legal transition to the desired gender; and

WHEREAS, News reports indicate that parents are allowing their children to undergo these therapies; and

WHEREAS, Many LGBT activists have sought to normalize the transgender experience and to define gender according to one's self-perception apart from biological anatomy; and

WHEREAS, The separation of one's gender identity from the physical reality of biological birth sex poses the harmful effect of engendering an understanding of sexuality and personhood that is fluid; and

WHEREAS, Some public schools are encouraging parents and teachers to affirm the feelings of children whose self-perception of their own gender is at variance with their biological sex; and

WHEREAS, Some public schools are allowing access to restrooms and locker rooms according to children's self-perception of gender and not according to their biological sex; and

WHEREAS, The state of New Jersey prohibits licensed counselors from any attempt to change a child's "gender expression"; and

WHEREAS, These cultural currents run counter to the biblical teaching as summarized in The Baptist Faith and Message, Article III, that "Man is the special creation of God, made in His own image. He created them male and female as the crowning work of His creation. The gift of gender is thus part of the goodness of God's creation"; now, therefore, be it

RESOLVED, That the messengers to the Southern Baptist Convention meeting in Baltimore, Maryland, June 10–11, 2014, affirm God's good design that gender identity is determined by biological sex and not by one's self-perception—a perception which is often influenced by fallen human nature in ways contrary to God's design (Ephesians 4:17–18); and be it further

RESOLVED, That we grieve the reality of human fallenness which can result in such biological manifestations as intersexuality or psychological manifestations as gender identity confusion and point all to the hope of the redemption of our bodies in Christ (Romans 8:23); and be it further

RESOLVED, That we extend love and compassion to those whose sexual self-understanding is shaped by a distressing conflict between their biological sex and their gender identity; and be it further

RESOLVED, That we invite all transgender persons to trust in Christ and to experience renewal in the Gospel (1 Timothy 1:15–16); and be it further

RESOLVED, That we love our transgender neighbors, seek their good always, welcome them to our churches and, as they repent and believe in Christ, receive them into church membership (2 Corinthians 5:18–20; Galatians 5:14); and be it further

RESOLVED, That we regard our transgender neighbors as image-bearers of Almighty God and therefore condemn acts of abuse or bullying committed against them; and be it further

RESOLVED, That we oppose efforts to alter one's bodily identity (e.g., cross-sex hormone therapy, gender reassignment surgery) to refashion it to conform with one's perceived gender identity; and be it further

RESOLVED, That we continue to oppose steadfastly all efforts by any governing official or body to validate transgender identity as morally praiseworthy (Isaiah 5:20); and be it further

RESOLVED, That we oppose all cultural efforts to validate claims to transgender identity; and be it finally

RESOLVED, That our love for the Gospel and urgency for the Great Commission must include declaring the whole counsel of God, proclaiming what Scripture teaches about God's design for us as male and female persons created in His image and for His glory (Matthew 28:19–20; Acts 20:27; Romans 11:36).

QUESTIONS FOR PERSONAL APPLICATION

1. Did God create you as a man or as a woman? Are you happy about who you are as a man or a woman?
2. Do you relate in exactly the same way to men as you do to women, or do you sense that there is an instinctive difference in how you relate?
3. How has your thinking about homosexuality changed as a result of reading this chapter (if at all)?
4. If you were invited to a same-sex wedding ceremony for a relative or close friend, would you attend? Why or why not?
5. Do you have any close friends or extended family members who are living in a homosexual lifestyle? How do you relate to them as a Christian? How do you think God wants you to relate to them? How do you think Jesus would relate to them?
6. What character traits (see p. 110) are especially helpful in dealing with homosexual desires in your own life or in relating to friends who are living in a homosexual lifestyle?

SPECIAL TERMS

transgender identity

BIBLIOGRAPHY

Sections in Other Ethics Texts

(see complete bibliographical data, p. 64)

Clark and Rakestraw, 2:177–224
Davis, 106–30
Feinberg, John and Paul, 307–85
Frame, 757–61
Geisler, 280–98
Gushee and Stassen, 264–68
Hays, 379–406
Kaiser, 117–26
McQuilkin and Copan, 285–310
Rae, 279–86

Other Works

Allberry, Sam. *Is God Anti-Gay?* Questions Christians Ask. Purcellville, VA: The Good Book Co., 2013.

Balswick, Judith K., and Jack O. Balswick. *Authentic Human Sexuality: An Integrated Christian Approach.* 2nd ed. Downers Grove, IL: IVP Academic, 2008.

Branch, J. Alan. *Born This Way? Homosexuality, Science, and the Scriptures.* Wooster, OH: Weaver Book Co., 2016.

Burk, Denny. "Training Our Kids in a Transgender World." In *Designed for Joy: How the Gospel Impacts Men and Women, Identity and Practice*, edited by Jonathan Parnell and Owen Strachan, 89–98. Wheaton, IL: Crossway, 2015.

———. *What Is the Meaning of Sex?* Wheaton, IL: Crossway, 2013.

Burk, Denny, and Heath Lambert. *Transforming Homosexuality: What the Bible Says about Sexual Orientation and Change.* Phillipsburg, NJ: P&R, 2015.

Burtoft, Larry. *Setting the Record Straight: What Research Really Says about the Social Consequences of Homosexuality.* Colorado Springs: Focus on the Family, 1994.

Butterfield, Rosaria Champagne. *The Secret Thoughts of an Unlikely Convert: An English Professor's Journey into Christian Faith.* Pittsburgh: Crown & Covenant, 2012.

Carlson, Jodi. *The Truth Comes Out: The Roots and Causes of Male Homosexuality.* Colorado Springs: Focus on the Family, 2002.

Carson, D. A. *The Intolerance of Tolerance.* Grand Rapids, MI: Eerdmans, 2012.

Citlau, Ron. *Hope for the Same-Sex Attracted: Biblical Direction for Friends, Family Members, and Those Struggling with Homosexuality*. Minneapolis: Bethany House, 2017.

Dallas, Joe. *Speaking of Homosexuality: Discussing the Issues with Kindness and Clarity*. Grand Rapids, MI: Baker, 2016.

DeRouchie, Jason S. "Confronting the Transgender Storm: New Covenant Reflections on Deuteronomy 22:5." *Journal for Biblical Manhood and Womanhood* 21, no. 1 (2016): 58–69.

DeYoung, James B. *Homosexuality: Contemporary Claims Examined in Light of the Bible and Other Ancient Literature and Law*. Grand Rapids, MI: Kregel Academic & Professional, 2000.

DeYoung, Kevin. "40 Questions for Christians Now Waving Rainbow Flags." *DeYoung, Restless, and Reformed*, July 1, 2015, http://www.thegospelcoalition.org/blogs/kevin deyoung/2015/07/01/40-questions-for-christians-now-waving-rainbow-flags/.

———. *What Does the Bible Really Teach about Homosexuality?* Wheaton, IL: Crossway, 2015.

Field, D. H. "Homosexuality." In *New Dictionary of Christian Ethics and Pastoral Theology*, edited by David J. Atkinson and David H. Field, 450–54. Leicester, UK: InterVarsity, and Downers Grove, IL: InterVarsity Press, 1995.

Fortson III, S. Donald, and Rollin G. Grams. *Unchanging Witness: The Consistent Christian Teaching on Homosexuality in Scripture and Tradition*. Nashville: B&H Academic, 2016.

Gagnon, Robert A. J. *The Bible and Homosexual Practice: Texts and Hermeneutics*. Nashville: Abingdon, 2001.

Gagnon, Robert A. J., and Dan O. Via. *Homosexuality and the Bible: Two Views*. Minneapolis: Fortress, 2004.

Girgis, Sherif, Robert P. George, and Ryan T. Anderson. *What Is Marriage? Man and Woman: A Defense*. New York: Encounter, 2012.

Grenz, Stanley J. *Welcoming but Not Affirming: An Evangelical Response to Homosexuality*. Louisville: Westminster John Knox, 1998.

Grisanti, Michael A. "Cultural and Medical Myths about Homosexuality." *The Master's Seminary Journal* 19 (2008): 175–202.

Guthrie, George H. "Changing Our Mind." The Gospel Coalition, Jan. 9, 2015, http://www.thegospelcoalition.org/article/changing-our-mind.

Heimbach, Daniel R. *Why Not Same-Sex Marriage: A Manual for Defending Marriage against Radical Deconstruction*. Sisters, OR: Trusted Books, 2014.

Hill, Wesley. *Washed and Waiting: Reflections on Christian Faithfulness and Homosexuality*. Updated and expanded ed. Grand Rapids, MI: Zondervan, 2016.

Hubbard, Peter. *Love into Light: The Gospel, the Homosexual, and the Church*. Greenville, SC: Ambassador International, 2013.

Jones, Peter. *The God of Sex: How Spirituality Defines Your Sexuality*. Colorado Springs: Victor, 2006.

Jones, Peter. *One or Two: Seeing a World of Difference, Romans 1 for the Twenty-First Century*. Escondido, CA: Main Entry Editions, 2010.

Jones, Stanton L., and Mark A. Yarhouse. *Homosexuality: The Use of Scientific Research in the Church's Moral Debate*. Downers Grove, IL: InterVarsity Press, 2000.

———. *Ex-Gays?: A Longitudinal Study of Religiously Mediated Change in Sexual Orientation*. Downers Grove, IL: IVP Academic, 2007.

Keller, Timothy. "The Bible and Same-Sex Relationships: A Review Article." The Gospel Coalition, June 5, 2015, http:// www.thegospelcoalition.org/article/the-bible-and -same-sex-relationships-a-review-article.

Köstenberger, Andreas J. "Abandoning Natural Relations: The Biblical Verdict on Homosexuality." In *God, Marriage, and Family: Rebuilding the Biblical Foundation*. 2nd ed., 199–222. Wheaton, IL: Crossway, 2010.

Köstenberger, Andreas J., and Margaret E. Köstenberger. *God's Design for Man and Woman: A Biblical-Theological Survey*. Wheaton, IL: Crossway, 2014.

Lovelace, Richard F. *Homosexuality and the Church*. Old Tappan, NJ: Revell, 1978.

MacArthur, John F. "God's Word on Homosexuality: The Truth about Sin and the Reality of Forgiveness." *The Master's Seminary Journal* 19 (2008): 153–74.

McDowell, Sean, and John Stonestreet. *Same-Sex Marriage: A Thoughtful Approach to God's Design for Marriage*. Grand Rapids, MI: Baker, 2014.

Mohler, R. Albert, Jr., ed. *God and the Gay Christian? A Response to Matthew Vines*. Conversant. Louisville: SBTS Press, 2014. (This ebook includes chapters by Mohler, James M. Hamilton, Denny Burk, Owen Strachan, and Heath Lambert.)

———. *We Cannot Be Silent: Speaking Truth to a Culture Redefining Sex, Marriage, and the Very Meaning of Right and Wrong*. Nashville: Thomas Nelson, 2015.

Nicolosi, Joseph, and Linda Ames Nicolosi. *A Parent's Guide to Preventing Homosexuality*. Downers Grove, IL: InterVarsity Press, 2002.

Phelan, James, Neil Whitehead, and Philip Sutton. "What Research Shows: NARTH's Response to the APA Claims on Homosexuality." *Journal of Human Sexuality* 1 (2009): 5–121.

Piper, John. "'Let Marriage Be Held in Honor'—Thinking Biblically about So-Called Same-Sex Marriage." *Journal for Biblical Manhood and Womanhood* 17, no. 2 (2012): 36–40.

Protecting Your Ministry from Sexual Orientation Gender Identity Lawsuits. Scottsdale, AZ: Alliance Defending Freedom, 2015.

Roberts, Vaughn. *Transgender*. Talking Points. Purcellville, VA: The Good Book Co., 2016.

Satinover, Jeffrey. *Homosexuality and the Politics of Truth*. Grand Rapids, MI: Baker, 1996.

Schmidt, Thomas E. *Straight and Narrow? Compassion and Clarity in the Homosexuality Debate*. Downers Grove, IL: InterVarsity Press, 1995.

Sears, Alan, and Craig Osten. *The Homosexual Agenda: Exposing the Principal Threat to Religious Freedom Today*. Rev. and updated ed. Nashville: Broadman & Holman, 2003.

Shaw, Ed. *Same-Sex Attraction and the Church: The Surprising Plausibility of the Celibate Life*. Downers Grove, IL: InterVarsity Press, 2015.

Siker, Jeffrey S. *Homosexuality in the Church: Both Sides of the Debate*. Louisville: Westminster John Knox, 1994.

Sprigg, Peter, and Timothy Dailey. *Getting It Straight: What the Research Shows about Homosexuality*. Washington: Family Research Council, 2004.

Sprigg, Peter. *The Top Ten Myths about Homosexuality*. Washington: Family Research Council, 2010.

———. *The Top Ten Harms of Same Sex "Marriage."* Washington: Family Research Council, 2011.

Sprinkle, Preston. *People to Be Loved: Why Homosexuality Is Not Just an Issue*. Grand Rapids, MI: Zondervan, 2015.

———. "Romans 1 and Homosexuality: A Critical Review of James Brownson's *Bible, Gender, and Sexuality*." *Bulletin for Biblical Research* 24 (2014): 515–28.

———, ed. *Two Views on Homosexuality, the Bible, and the Church*. Counterpoints. Grand Rapids, MI: Zondervan, 2016.

Vines, Matthew. *God and the Gay Christian: The Biblical Case in Support of Same-Sex Relationships*. New York: Convergent, 2014.

Wink, Walter, ed. *Homosexuality and Christian Faith: Questions of Conscience for the Churches*. Minneapolis: Fortress, 1999.

Winter, Bruce W. "Roman Homosexual Activity and the Elite (1 Corinthians 6:9)." In *After Paul Left Corinth: The Influence of Secular Ethics and Social Change*, 110–20. Grand Rapids, MI: Eerdmans, 2001.

Yuan, Christopher, and Angela Yuan. *Out of a Far Country: A Gay Son's Journey to God*. Colorado Springs: Waterbrook, 2011.

SCRIPTURE MEMORY PASSAGE

Romans 1:26–27: For this reason God gave them up to dishonorable passions. For their women exchanged natural relations for those that are contrary to nature; and the men likewise gave up natural relations with women and were consumed with passion for one another, men committing shameless acts with men and receiving in themselves the due penalty for their error.

HYMN

"Be Still My Soul"

Be still, my soul: the Lord is on thy side;
Bear patiently the cross of grief or pain;
Leave to thy God to order and provide;
In ev'ry change he faithful will remain.

Be still, my soul: thy best, thy heav'nly friend
Through thorny ways leads to a joyful end.

Be still, my soul: thy God doth undertake
To guide the future as he has the past.
Thy hope, thy confidence let nothing shake;
All now mysterious shall be bright at last.
Be still, my soul: the waves and winds still know
His voice who ruled them while he dwelt below.

Be still, my soul: when dearest friends depart,
And all is darkened in the vale of tears,
Then shalt thou better know his love, his heart,
Who comes to soothe thy sorrow and thy fears.
Be still, my soul: thy Jesus can repay
From his own fullness all he takes away.

Be still, my soul: the hour is hast'ning on
When we shall be forever with the Lord,
When disappointment, grief, and fear are gone,
Sorrow forgot, love's purest joys restored.
Be still, my soul: when change and tears are past,
All safe and blessed we shall meet at last.

AUTHOR: KATHARINA VON SCHLEGEL, BORN 1697

Part 6

PROTECTING PROPERTY

"You shall not steal."

CHAPTER 34

PROPERTY: THE GOODNESS AND NECESSITY OF PRIVATE OWNERSHIP OF PROPERTY

Why does God enable human beings to own property?
Is this a good thing?
Does God approve of increased human flourishing on the earth?
What are the dangers of the "health-and-wealth gospel"?

The eighth commandment reads:

> "You shall not steal." (Ex. 20:15)

A. THE MEANING OF THE COMMANDMENT

The eighth commandment tells us not to "steal." The Hebrew verb *gānab* ("to steal") is used to refer to Rachel stealing her father's household gods (Gen. 31:19); to the stealing of silver or gold from someone's house (44:8); to the stealing of an ox or a sheep (Ex. 22:1); and even to the stealing of a human being by kidnapping (Ex. 21:16). It means taking something that does not belong to you.

This command clearly applies to Christians in the new covenant age because it is affirmed several times in the New Testament:

You shall not steal. (Rom. 13:9)

Thieves . . . will [not] inherit the kingdom of God. (1 Cor. 6:10)

Let the thief no longer steal. (Eph. 4:28; see also Rom. 2:21; 1 Cor. 5:11; Titus 2:10; Heb. 10:34; James 5:4; Rev. 9:21)

B. A COMMANDMENT NOT TO STEAL IMPLIES PRIVATE OWNERSHIP OF PROPERTY

The command "you shall not steal" assumes that *there is something to steal*—something that belongs to someone else and not to you. You should not steal someone else's ox or donkey—or his car, his cell phone, or his computer—because it belongs to him and not to you. Therefore, the eighth commandment assumes private ownership of property.[1]

1. Support for Private Ownership of Property Elsewhere in the Old Testament. Other passages in the Old Testament show that God was concerned to protect the private ownership of property. Property was to be owned by individuals, not by the government or by society as a whole. For instance, God told the people of Israel that when the Year of Jubilee came, "it shall be a jubilee for you, when *each of you shall return to his property* and each of you shall return to his clan" (Lev. 25:10).

The Mosaic covenant included many other laws that defined punishments for stealing and appropriate restitution for damage to another person's farm animals or agricultural fields (see, for example, Ex. 21:28–36; 22:1–15; Deut. 22:1–4; 23:24–25). Another person's animals and fields belonged to him, not to anyone else, and the Jewish people were to honor such property rights.[2]

Another commandment guaranteed that property boundaries would be protected: "You shall not move your neighbor's landmark, which the men of old have set, in the inheritance that you will hold in the land that the LORD your God is giving you to possess" (Deut. 19:14). To move the landmark was to move the boundaries of the land, and thus to steal land that belonged to one's neighbor (cf. Prov. 22:28; 23:10).

The Old Testament also shows an awareness that governments could wrongly use their immense power to disregard property rights and steal what they should not. At the urging of wicked Queen Jezebel, King Ahab wrongfully stole Naboth's vineyard and had Naboth killed in the process (1 Kings 21). And, as I mentioned earlier (p. 435), the

---

[1] Portions of this section have been adapted from Wayne Grudem and Barry Asmus, *The Poverty of Nations: A Sustainable Solution* (Wheaton, IL: Crossway, 2013), 141–43, with permission of the publisher. Other parts of this chapter have been taken from Wayne Grudem, "The Eighth Commandment as the Moral Foundation for Property Rights, Human Flourishing, and Careers in Business," *Themelios* 41 (2016): 76–87, with permission of the publisher.

[2] This paragraph and the next have been adapted from Wayne Grudem, *Politics—According to the Bible: A Comprehensive Resource for Understanding Modern Political Issues in Light of Scripture* (Grand Rapids, MI: Zondervan, 2010), 262, with permission of the publisher.

prophet Samuel had warned of the evils of such a king, who would "take" and "take" and "take":

> So Samuel told all the words of the LORD to the people who were asking for a king from him. He said, "These will be the ways of the king who will reign over you: he will *take* your sons and appoint them to his chariots and to be his horsemen and to run before his chariots. And he will appoint for himself commanders of thousands and commanders of fifties, and some to plow his ground and to reap his harvest, and to make his implements of war and the equipment of his chariots. He will *take* your daughters to be perfumers and cooks and bakers. He will *take* the best of your fields and vineyards and olive orchards and give them to his servants. He will *take* the tenth of your grain and of your vineyards and give it to his officers and to his servants. He will *take* your male servants and female servants and the best of your young men and your donkeys, and put them to his work. He will *take* the tenth of your flocks, and you shall be his slaves. And in that day you will cry out because of your king, whom you have chosen for yourselves, but the LORD will not answer you in that day." (1 Sam. 8:10–18)[3]

2. Private Ownership of Property in the New Testament. Several New Testament passages show that individuals had the right of ownership of money and possessions, and were expected to use those possessions wisely. The New Testament contains many encouragements to generosity, but there is no hint of disapproval of a system in which *property is owned not by the government or by society in general, but by individual people* who are responsible for wisely deciding how to use it. Here are a few such passages:

> [Let] the one who contributes . . . [do so] in generosity. (Rom. 12:8)

> On the first day of every week, each of you is to put something aside and store it up, as he may prosper, so that there will be no collecting when I come. (1 Cor. 16:2)

> Each one must give as he has decided in his heart, not reluctantly or under compulsion, for God loves a cheerful giver. (2 Cor. 9:7)

> Let the thief no longer steal, but rather let him labor, doing honest work with his own hands, so that he may have something to share with anyone in need. (Eph. 4:28)

> As for the rich in this present age, charge them not to be haughty, nor to set their hopes on the uncertainty of riches, but on God, who richly provides us

---

[3] By contrast, King David was a good example because he insisted on purchasing a threshing floor from Araunah when he could have received it as a gift (see 2 Sam. 24:23–24).

with everything to enjoy. They are to do good, to be rich in good works, to be generous and ready to share. (1 Tim. 6:17–18)

You joyfully accepted the plundering of your property, since you knew that you yourselves had a better possession and an abiding one. (Heb. 10:34)

Keep your life free from love of money, and be content with what you have, for he has said, "I will never leave you nor forsake you." (Heb. 13:5)

Behold, the wages of the laborers who mowed your fields, which you kept back by fraud, are crying out against you, and the cries of the harvesters have reached the ears of the Lord of hosts. (James 5:4; here the rebuke for a misuse of property still implies that God holds dishonest rich people accountable for their stewardship of their wealth)

But if anyone has the world's goods and sees his brother in need, yet closes his heart against him, how does God's love abide in him? (1 John 3:17)

Sometimes people claim that Christians practiced a form of "early communism" because the book of Acts says that believers had all things in common. It is important to look at the passages carefully:

And all who believed were together and had all things in common. And they were selling their possessions and belongings and distributing the proceeds to all, as any had need. And day by day, attending the temple together and breaking bread in their homes, they received their food with glad and generous hearts. (Acts 2:44–46)

Now the full number of those who believed were of one heart and soul, and no one said that any of the things that belonged to him was his own, but they had everything in common. And with great power the apostles were giving their testimony to the resurrection of the Lord Jesus, and great grace was upon them all. There was not a needy person among them, for as many as were owners of lands or houses sold them and brought the proceeds of what was sold and laid it at the apostles' feet, and it was distributed to each as any had need. (Acts 4:32–35)

These texts certainly show an amazing level of trust in God, generosity, and love for one another, all as a result of a remarkable outpouring of the Holy Spirit's power in a time of great revival. But it is a great mistake to call this "early communism," for (1) the giving was voluntary and was not compelled by government, and (2) people still had personal possessions, because they still met in "their homes" (Acts 2:46). Many other Christians still owned homes later, such as Mary, the mother of John Mark (12:12),

Jason (17:5), Titius Justus (18:7), many Christians in Ephesus (20:20), Philip the evangelist (21:8), Mnason of Cyprus (21:16, in Jerusalem), Priscilla and Aquila (Rom. 16:5; 1 Cor. 16:19), Nympha (Col. 4:15), Philemon (Philem. 2), and other Christians in general to whom John wrote (2 John 10).

One other proof that the early church did not practice a kind of "early communism" is that (3) immediately after the description of such amazing generosity in Acts 4, there is the story of Ananias and Sapphira, who lied about the sale price of some land. But Peter told them there was no need to do this:

> While it remained unsold, did it not remain your own? And after it was sold, was it not at your disposal? Why is it that you have contrived this deed in your heart? You have not lied to men but to God. (Acts 5:4)

It is significant that this story occurs immediately after the passage that says "they had everything in common" (Acts 4:32). It reminds us that all of the generosity we see in Acts 4 was voluntary and was not intended to nullify the ideas of individual ownership or inequality of possessions. When Peter says, "While it remained unsold, did it not remain your own?" (5:4), he reaffirms the idea of private property. Thus, he keeps us from the mistaken idea that the church was establishing a new requirement that Christians must give up all private property or that all Christians must have equal possessions.

3. Communism Seeks to Abolish Private Property. Karl Marx said, "The theory of the Communists may be summed up in the single sentence: abolition of private property."[4] Communist countries such as North Korea, Cuba, and the former Soviet Union have prohibited all private ownership of property, such as land and buildings. In doing this, these governments have trapped their people in a depressing cycle of brutal poverty.

For example, North Korea, one of the very poorest countries in the world with a per-capita income of $1,800,[5] is a particularly glaring example of the effects of communism, because it stands in stark contrast to South Korea, a free-market economy that allows private ownership of property. The result is that, according to the CIA World Factbook, South Korea over the past four decades has demonstrated incredible economic growth and global integration to become a high-tech industrialized economy. In the 1960s, its per capita income was comparable with levels in the poorer countries of Africa and Asia. But by 2004, South Korea had joined the trillion-dollar club of world economies, and in 2016, its per capita income was $36,511,[6] or 20 times that of North Korea. This comparison is

---

[4] Karl Marx, *Communist Manifesto* (New York: International Publishers, 1948), 23.

[5] The CIA World Factbook estimates a per capita income of $1,800 for North Korea for 2014, but also notes that this is based on an extrapolation from an earlier estimate, and North Korea does not publish reliable national economic data. It is clearly among the poorest nations of the world, and "a large portion of the population continues to suffer from prolonged malnutrition and poor living conditions." Central Intelligence Agency, The World Factbook, https://www.cia.gov/library/publications/the-world-factbook/geos/kn.html.

[6] "2017 Index of Economic Freedom," The Heritage Foundation, http://www.heritage.org/index/country/southkorea.

especially significant because North and South Korea were one country until 1948, and its people share the same cultural background, language, and history. The difference is that one country suffers from the oppressive effects of communism and the other country benefits from the economic growth that is due to a free-market economic system.

A similar difference can be seen in a comparison of China and Taiwan. In 1949, the government officials of the Republic of China fled to Taiwan to continue their government there after they lost to the Communists in the Chinese Civil War. Mainland China became a communist nation, while Taiwan established a free-market economy. Both populations shared a similar cultural and ethnic background and a similar language, but under communist rule, the people of China remained trapped in abject poverty for decades. Beginning in 1978, Deng Xiaoping instituted widespread free-market reforms in many areas of the economy, so that China was no longer a truly communist economic system, and rapid economic growth followed. Even so, decades of growth lost to communism could not be made up quickly, and economic freedoms are still limited. Therefore, a widespread difference remains: Taiwan has a per capita income of $46,800, making the Chinese who live in Taiwan more than three times as wealthy as those who live in China, with a per capita income of $14,100.[7]

Such an abolition of private property as occurs under communism is horribly dehumanizing because it greatly minimizes people's freedom to make wise choices regarding the stewardship of their resources and prevents human economic and cultural flourishing as God intended it to occur. It should not be surprising to us that a nullification of the system of private ownership of property that is found in both the Old and New Testaments is deeply harmful to people's lives.

4. The Importance of the Eighth Commandment. If the eighth commandment implies private ownership of property, then its focus is different from that of the other nine commandments. The eighth commandment covers an entire range of human activity that is not addressed by the other commandments.

> Commandments one through four (Ex. 20:3–11) focus primarily on our relationship to God and the duties we owe to him. (The fourth commandment does require us to labor, but it does not specify what we should labor for.)
> Commandment five protects family ("Honor your father and your mother," Ex. 20:12).
> Commandment six protects life ("You shall not murder," Ex. 20:13).
> Commandment seven protects marriage ("You shall not commit adultery," Ex. 20:14).
> Commandment nine protects truth ("You shall not bear false witness against your neighbor," Ex. 20:16).
> Commandment ten requires purity of heart ("You shall not covet your neighbor's house; you shall not covet your neighbor's wife . . . or anything that

---

[7] Ibid., http://www.heritage.org/index/country/taiwan and http://www.heritage.org/index/country/china.

is your neighbor's," Ex. 20:17). By implication, the tenth commandment also requires purity of heart regarding all the other commandments, but it adds no unique area of life as an additional focus that was not already treated in the previous commandments.

Therefore, the eighth commandment is unique. It protects property and possessions. By implication, we are right to think it also protects another person's time, talents, and opportunities—everything over which people have been given stewardship. We are not to steal someone else's property, time, talents, or opportunities.

Without the eighth commandment, therefore, the Ten Commandments would not cover in summary form all aspects of our moral life. We would have God's instructions protecting worship, family, life, marriage, and truth. But where would the Ten Commandments tell us *what we should do* with our possessions, our time, our talents, and our opportunities? Yes, the first four commandments would instruct us in the worship of God, but beyond such worship, would we be expected to *achieve* anything beyond mere subsistence living? Would we be expected just to act as the animal kingdom does: eating, sleeping, bearing offspring, and dying, with no other achievements to show the excellence of the human race created in the image of God?

But the eighth commandment implies that we have property to care for. Therefore, it is this commandment that sets us apart from the animal kingdom as property owners and those who have been given stewardship of possessions. In that way, the eighth commandment relates to most of our work activity for most of our earthly lifetimes.

C. PROPERTY IS A STEWARDSHIP THAT WE HAVE FROM GOD

1. We Are Accountable to God for How We Use "Our" Property. If God himself has commanded, "You shall not steal," and if in that commandment God himself establishes a system of private property, then it follows that we are accountable to him for how we use that property. This is certainly the Bible's perspective: our ownership of property is not absolute, but we are *stewards* who will have to give an account of our stewardship. This is because, ultimately, everything belongs to God: "The earth is the LORD's and the fullness thereof, the world and all those who dwell therein" (Ps. 24:1; see also Gen. 1:1; Lev. 25:23; Ps. 50:10–12; Hag. 2:8).

In practical terms, once I realize that God commands others not to steal my land, my ox, or my donkey—or my car or my laptop—then I understand that I have an individual responsibility for how those things are used. I have been entrusted with those things by the God who created the universe, and I must act as a faithful "steward" to manage what he has entrusted to me. What Paul says about his stewardship of the ministry of the gospel can also be applied in a broader sense to everything that God entrusts to us: "It is required of stewards that they be found faithful" (1 Cor. 4:2).

This idea of stewardship applies to much more than merely physical possessions and land. God has also entrusted us with time, talents, and opportunities, and we are equally accountable to him for how we use these things (see 1 Cor. 4:2 in the previous paragraph regarding Paul's stewardship of his ministry).

2. Greater or Lesser Stewardship Responsibilities. Nowhere does Scripture assume that everyone will have equal stewardship responsibilities. We read in the Old Testament, "The LORD makes poor and makes rich; he brings low and he exalts" (1 Sam. 2:7). And in the Wisdom Literature we read, "The rich and the poor meet together; the LORD is the Maker of them all" (Prov. 22:2). This verse does not simply mean that God *created* all human beings, for the specific contrast between "the rich" and "the poor" implies that God, in his sovereignty, has ordained or become the "maker" of their individual circumstances and conditions.

In the New Testament, Jesus teaches that the operation of the kingdom of heaven is like a man who entrusted his property to his servants:

> To one he gave five talents, to another two, to another one, to each according to his ability. Then he went away. (Matt. 25:15)

The servants received differing amounts of money, over which they were to exercise stewardship, but they were all responsible for being faithful with what they had received (see Matt. 25:16–30). Even those who had received smaller stewardships were commended when the master returned:

> His master said to him, "Well done, good and faithful servant. You have been faithful over a little; I will set you over much. Enter into the joy of your master." (Matt. 25:21)

This reward was consistent with the principle that Jesus teaches in Luke's Gospel: "One who is faithful in a very little is also faithful in much, and one who is dishonest in a very little is also dishonest in much" (16:10).

In fact, those who receive large stewardships will be held to a higher standard of expectation:

> Everyone to whom much was given, of him much will be required, and from him to whom they entrusted much, they will demand the more. (Luke 12:48)

This principle applies not only to stewardship of material possessions, but also to stewardship of leadership positions and teaching responsibilities in the church, for James says, "Not many of you should become teachers, my brothers, for you know that we who teach will be judged with greater strictness" (James 3:1).[8]

---

[8] Even among angels, who have no sin, there are varying levels of stewardship, because Scripture sometimes speaks not only about angels but also about archangels (see "the archangel Michael" in Jude 9; see also 1 Thess. 4:16).

Therefore, while we must remember that many passages in Scripture encourage us to care for the poor (see discussion below, p. 910; see also Ex. 23:11; Lev. 19:10; Ps. 41:1; Prov. 14:21; 19:17; 21:20; 28:27; Matt. 19:21; Rom. 15:26; Gal. 2:10; 1 John 3:17; and many other verses), yet there is no expectation in Scripture that God will bring about complete equality of stewardship or equality of possessions among his people either in this life or the age to come.[9]

D. BENEFITS THAT COME FROM PRIVATE OWNERSHIP OF PROPERTY

When we ask why God in his wisdom established a system of private ownership of property among human beings (in distinction from, for example, the animal kingdom), several benefits of private property become evident to us.

1. A Continual Opportunity for Glorifying God. We can use our property (and other stewardship responsibilities) wisely or foolishly. If we use our property wisely, we reflect God's wisdom, his creativity, and his sovereignty over creation (compared to our derived sovereignty over a small portion of his creation), as well as his love for others, truthfulness, and several other attributes. In acting as wise stewards, we act as "imitators of God" (Eph. 5:1), and thereby we bring him glory.

This means that we should not think that the desire to own things over which we exercise stewardship is an evil desire in itself. It is a God-given desire to imitate in a very faint way his sovereignty over creation. This imitation of God's sovereignty is implied in the command to Adam and Eve that they should "fill the earth and subdue it" and "have dominion" over the creatures (Gen. 1:28).

Such a desire to have a measure of stewardship (a faint reflection of sovereignty) over creation is seen even in young children, who enjoy having small toys that are their own, and often enjoy having a pet that they are responsible to care for. Although such a desire to have things that are their own can be distorted and manifest itself in failure to care for others and in wanting more than they should rightfully have, it should not automatically be called "greed," for the desire to exercise stewardship in itself is a uniquely human property that God implanted in our hearts at the beginning of creation.

---

[9] 2 Cor. 8:14 is best translated "that there may be fairness" (so ESV; NRSV has "fair balance"), not "that there may be equality" (RSV; similarly, NIV, NASB). The Greek term used here is *isotēs*, which can mean either "equality" or "fairness," depending on the context (see BDAG, 481), but the only other place it occurs in the New Testament is Col. 4:1, where the word is translated "fairly"; "Masters, treat your bondservants justly and *fairly*." In addition, an analysis of the situation of believers in Macedonia, Achaia (Corinth), and Jerusalem, which Paul is writing about, will show that in this context he is not seeking to bring about complete economic equality among the Christians of these diverse regions of the ancient world (he didn't ask the wealthy Corinthian church to contribute to the poor churches in Macedonia), but is simply seeking a fair sharing of the burden of caring for the extremely poor Christians in Jerusalem.

2. A Continual Opportunity for Giving Thanks to God. If God is the One "who richly provides us with everything to enjoy" (1 Tim. 6:17), then we should continually have hearts of thanksgiving to him. "Bless the Lord, O my soul, and forget not all his benefits" (Ps. 103:2). This refrain occurs several times in Scripture: "Give thanks to the Lord, for he is good, for his steadfast love endures forever" (Ps. 136:1).

3. A Continual Source of Joy. When we view the things that God has entrusted to us as gifts from him that he wants us to enjoy with thanksgiving, then we can rightly set our hearts on God "who richly provides us with everything to enjoy" (1 Tim. 6:17). He does not say that God "provides us with everything to feel guilty about." Neither does he say that God provides us with things in order to tempt us to enjoy the things *rather than enjoying God himself*. Instead, God's purpose in entrusting things to us is that we should enjoy them. He richly provides us with everything *to enjoy*.[10]

A simple example from ordinary life can illustrate this. When my grandson Will was two years old, we went to a toy store together, and I bought him a small wooden train set. It had no batteries, no electric wires, and not even any paint on the parts. It was just plain wooden tracks and some wooden train cars.

The next day, Will's father told me that Will had spent the entire afternoon happily playing with his wooden train set. Was I sad that he was enjoying the train set instead of me, his grandpa? No, I was happy because he was enjoying the train set, which was what I had intended. And I have no doubt that a number of times throughout the afternoon he remembered that I had bought it for him. I was the (grand)father who had provided him with "everything to enjoy." So it is with God's gifts to us. He wants us to enjoy them, with thanksgiving.

4. A Continual Test for Our Hearts. Though the possessions that God entrusts to us are good in themselves, they also provide a continual test of what is in our hearts. King David wisely warns, "If riches increase, set not your heart on them" (Ps. 62:10). We must not allow our hearts to be drawn away from God, but we should continually have this attitude:

> Whom have I in heaven but you?
>> And there is nothing on earth that I desire besides you.
> My flesh and my heart may fail,
>> but God is the strength of my heart and my portion forever.
>> (Ps. 73:25–26)

In this passage, when the psalmist says that God is "my portion forever," the reader would naturally think of the portion of land or possessions that had been allotted to

---

[10] A refreshing and eye-opening discussion of how we can rightly enjoy all of creation as a manifestation of God's own character and glory is found in Joe Rigney, *The Things of Earth: Treasuring God by Enjoying His Gifts* (Wheaton, IL: Crossway, 2015).

him. What is his "portion" that will be given to him? But the psalmist's perspective is that his "portion," above everything else, is God himself.

This is why Paul warns "the rich in this present age" not to "set their hopes on the uncertainty of riches, but on God, who richly provides us with everything to enjoy" (1 Tim. 6:17).

In addition, the ownership of property tests our hearts regarding care for the needs of others, for John writes:

> But if anyone has the world's goods and sees his brother in need, yet closes his heart against him, how does God's love abide in him? (1 John 3:17)

E. STEWARDSHIP PROVIDES THE BASIS FOR HUMAN ACHIEVEMENT AND FLOURISHING ON THE EARTH

1. The Expectation of Human Achievement. There is another implication to this idea of stewardship of private property. If God *entrusts* us with property as stewards, then he expects us to do something worthwhile with it, something that he finds valuable.

This was evident from the very beginning, when God placed Adam and Eve on the earth. He said:

> Let us make man in our image, after our likeness. And *let them have dominion* over the fish of the sea and over the birds of the heavens and over the livestock and *over all the earth* and over every creeping thing that creeps on the earth.
>
> So God created man in his own image,
>   in the image of God he created him;
>   male and female he created them.
>
>   And God blessed them. And God said to them, "Be fruitful and multiply and fill the earth *and subdue it*, and have dominion . . . over every living thing that moves on the earth." (Gen. 1:26–28)

The Hebrew word translated as "subdue" (*kābash*) means to make the earth useful for human beings' benefit and enjoyment. God was entrusting Adam and Eve, and by implication the entire human race, with stewardship over the earth. God wanted them to create useful products from the earth for their benefit and enjoyment—at first, perhaps, simple structures in which to live and store food; later, various forms of transportation, such as carts and wagons; then eventually modern homes, office buildings, and factories, as well as cars and airplanes—the entire range of useful products that could be made from the earth. In this way, God gave to human beings the ability to *create value* in the world that did not exist before.

Here is a simple example: not far from my home there is a shop called LensCrafters that sells eyeglasses. When I went into the shop, I handed my new glasses prescription to a clerk, and she handed it to a laboratory technician. I watched while the technician selected a small, concave plastic disk and put it in a machine. Then he entered some numbers into the machine. When he pushed a button, the machine started up, and soon the right lens for my glasses popped out of the other end.

Now the plastic disk by itself, before it entered the machine, had very little value. Perhaps the raw plastic was worth a few cents (in terms of the material itself, before it had been formed into a concave disk). But when the plastic came out the other end of the machine, it was a specialized bifocal lens worth about $100! By feeding the plastic disk through the machine, the technician had *created* $100 of new value that had never existed in the world before that moment.

This is the same process by which a woman in a poor village can buy a length of cloth for $3 and use it to sew a shirt that she will sell in the market for $13. She has *created* $10 worth of new value that did not exist in the world before. When this process is completed hundreds of thousands of times for hundreds of thousands of products, human achievement in the realm of material productivity continually increases.

Stewardship of the earth in obedience to God implies this kind of productivity. Stewardship of resources implies God's expectation of *human achievement and human flourishing* .

Therefore, the eighth commandment gives (1) the *opportunity for human achievement* (by entrusting property to us), (2) the *expectation of human achievement* (by making us accountable stewards), and (3) the *expectation of human enjoyment* of products made from the earth, with thanksgiving to God.

2. More Than Material Productivity. Certainly, human flourishing includes more than material inventions. It also includes art, music, literature, and the complex and wonderful relationships we find in the home, church, and community. But as we participate in those activities, we still utilize products produced from the earth—food to sustain life, construction materials to build houses and buildings, furnaces and air conditioners to make the buildings comfortable, cars and airplanes with which to travel and enjoy fellowship with friends and family, and a communications network to let us stay in touch with them at times when we cannot be together face to face.

3. The Human Desire to Understand and Create Products from the Earth. Because God gave to human beings the command to subdue the earth, it is reasonable to conclude that he also placed in our hearts a desire to fulfill that command. In fact, we see abundant evidence from the conduct of the human race throughout history that human beings have an innate desire to understand the earth and to create useful things from it.

We should not dismiss this innate human drive for material productivity and flourishing as greedy materialism or sin. It can be *distorted* by selfishness and sin, but the drive to create, produce, and enjoy useful products ultimately comes from a morally good God-given instinct that he placed within the human race before there was any sin in the world, when he commanded Adam and Eve to fill the earth, subdue it, and have dominion over all of it.

4. Ownership of Property Motivates Human Achievement. Ownership of property brings another benefit. It motivates people to create, invent, and produce because they have hope of keeping and enjoying what they earn. This means that the system of personal ownership of property that is affirmed throughout Scripture is essential for human flourishing, because without the ability to own and enjoy something of the fruit of his labor, a person will have little motivation to create and produce.

In 1776, Scottish professor of moral philosophy Adam Smith explained why the hope of enjoying the fruits of one's labor inspires people to be productive and lifts entire nations out of poverty:

> That security which the laws in Great Britain give to every man that he shall enjoy the fruits of his own labour, is alone sufficient to make any country flourish. . . . The natural effort of every individual to better his own condition, when suffered [allowed] to exert itself with freedom and security, is so powerful a principle, that it is alone, and without any assistance . . . capable of carrying on the society to wealth and prosperity.[11]

Plants and animals show a measure of God's glory by merely surviving and repeating the same activities for thousands of years, while human beings glorify God by *achieving* much more than mere survival. We glorify God by understanding and ruling over the creation, then by producing more and more wonderful goods from it for our enjoyment, with thanksgiving to the God who "richly provides us with everything to enjoy" (1 Tim. 6:17).

F. WISDOM IS REQUIRED FOR US TO RIGHTLY USE AND ENJOY PROPERTY

1. The Danger of Materialism. While the ownership of property is a good gift from God, the Bible also gives clear warnings against loving material things too much. Paul warns that an elder must be "not a lover of money" (1 Tim. 3:3). Other passages speak clearly of this sin:

> No one can serve two masters, for either he will hate the one and love the other, or he will be devoted to the one and despise the other. *You cannot serve God and money.* (Matt. 6:24)

> But those who desire to be rich fall into temptation, into a snare, into many senseless and harmful desires that plunge people into ruin and destruction. For *the love of money is a root of all kinds of evils.* It is through this craving that some have wandered away from the faith and pierced themselves with many pangs. (1 Tim. 6:9–10)

---

[11] Adam Smith, *An Inquiry into the Nature and Causes of the Wealth of Nations*, ed. Edwin Cannan (New York, Modern Library, 1994; first published 1776), Book IV, chap. 5, 581.

> Keep your life free from *love of money*, and be content with what you have, for he has said, "I will never leave you nor forsake you." (Heb. 13:5)

Whether or not someone is led astray by "love of money" is primarily an issue of the heart. Other people can often see outward indications of a love of money (How else would churches know when a candidate for elder is a "lover of money"?), so we must guard our hearts daily in personal fellowship with God. "If riches increase, set not your heart on them" (Ps. 62:10).

However, John also points out that our response to others who are in need is an indication of what is in our hearts: "But if anyone has the world's goods and sees his brother in need, yet closes his heart against him, how does God's love abide in him?" (1 John 3:17).

2. The Error of the "Health-and-Wealth Gospel." Related to the danger of materialism is the danger of the "health-and-wealth gospel" (also called the "prosperity gospel"), a kind of teaching that says that if you have enough faith, and if you just give enough money, then God will make you prosperous and protect you from sickness. This teaching claims that it is God's will for every believer in this lifetime to have good health and material prosperity, and our role is simply to believe it (to have enough faith) and to make a "positive confession" of that faith with our spoken words.

Kenneth Copeland, one of the most prominent leaders in this movement, writes:

> Jesus bore the curse of the law in our behalf. . . . Consequently, there is no reason for you to live under the curse of the law, no reason for you to live in poverty of any kind. . . . Since God's covenant has been established and prosperity is a provision of this covenant, you need to realize that prosperity belongs to you *now!* . . . You *must* realize that it is God's will for you to prosper (see 3 John 2). This is available to you, and frankly, it would be stupid of you not to partake of it! . . . *You must realize that prosperity is the will of God for you.*[12]

I disagree with this emphasis on material prosperity for the following reasons:

a. There Are No New Testament Promises of Wealth for Believers: No verse in the New Testament promises that God will make believers wealthy. Instead, we find promises that God will provide for his people's *needs*:

> And God is able to make all grace abound to you, so that having all *sufficiency* in all things at all times, you may abound in every good work. (2 Cor. 9:8; note that this verse promises "sufficiency," not prosperity or riches)

---

[12] Kenneth Copeland, *The Laws of Prosperity* (Fort Worth, TX: Kenneth Copeland Publications, 1974), 43–45; emphasis in original except for the last sentence, which is boldface in the original. (The same wording is found in the 2013 Kindle edition of this book, published by Harrison House, beginning at Kindle location 579.)

Regarding Copeland's understanding of 3 John 2, see my discussion below (p. 911).

And my God will supply *every need* of yours according to his riches in glory in Christ Jesus. (Phil. 4:19)

It is true that the Old Testament promises, "Your barns will be filled with plenty, and your vats will be bursting with wine" (Prov. 3:10), but we find no promises like this in the New Testament. This is because the New Testament places a relatively greater emphasis on *spiritual* blessings than the Old Testament, and a relatively lesser emphasis on *material* blessings (though both kinds of blessings are present to some degree in both testaments).

Copeland provides a possible answer to this objection when he quotes Galatians 3, showing that Christians in the new covenant have inherited the blessings of the covenant that God made with Abraham. Here are the verses he quotes:

Christ redeemed us from the curse of the law by becoming a curse for us—for it is written, "Cursed is everyone who is hanged on a tree"—so that in Christ Jesus *the blessing of Abraham* might come to the Gentiles, so that we might receive the promised Spirit through faith. (Gal. 3:13–14)

And if you are Christ's, then you are Abraham's offspring, heirs according to promise. (Gal. 3:29)

But this answer is not convincing, because Paul does not conclude from the covenant with Abraham that we Christians are going to be wealthy. Rather, he concludes that we receive the gift of the Holy Spirit as a result of the "blessing of Abraham," for he says this is "so that we might receive the promised Spirit through faith" (Gal. 3:14). And he clearly emphasizes that we, like Abraham, receive the gift of justification by faith, "just as Abraham 'believed God, and it was counted to him as righteousness'" (Gal. 3:6; see also Rom. 4:1–25).

Another objection might come from these words of Jesus:

Give, and it will be given to you. Good measure, pressed down, shaken together, running over, will be put into your lap. For with the measure you use it will be measured back to you. (Luke 6:38)

Clearly this verse teaches that God will reward our generous giving, but the verse does not promise that we will become wealthy in terms of earthly possessions. It does affirm that, when we give generously to his work, he will generously supply our needs in return—a teaching that evangelical churches today probably need to emphasize more.

b. Unlike Miracles of Healing, There Are No New Testament Miracles That Make People Wealthy: Jesus frequently performed miracles of physical healing (see Luke 4:40 and many other verses in the Gospels), and this gives us warrant to believe it is right for us today to ask God for physical healing as well (see James 5:14–15). By contrast, there are no examples of piles of gold coins suddenly appearing when Jesus ministers to people or when the apostles pray for people. When Jesus fed the five thousand with five loaves and two fish (Matt. 14:13–21), he met people's immediate needs but did not send them home with bags full of money or even food for the next day. There was one miraculous provision of money when Jesus told Peter to catch a fish and then take the coin out of its mouth (Matt. 17:27), but this was just enough to pay the tax that was due at the moment, not the beginning of a collection of piles of extra money. The theme in the New Testament is *sufficiency*; there is no promise of prosperity.

c. The New Testament Portrays Several Poor People as Examples of Faith: While the prosperity-gospel message tells people, "It is God's will for you to prosper . . . and frankly, it would be stupid of you not to partake of it,"[13] the New Testament has a different message. It contains several examples of people who were *obedient to God and rich in faith*, but still were financially very *poor*.

The first example is Jesus himself, who was poor ("the Son of Man has nowhere to lay his head," Matt. 8:20; cf. 2 Cor. 8:9). Jesus himself commended the poor widow who had only "two small copper coins" to put into the offering box (Luke 21:1–4). In addition, Paul praised the generosity of the Macedonian Christians, who gave freely out of "their extreme poverty" (2 Cor. 8:2). And Paul himself, though he had great faith, was not wealthy, because he said, "To the present hour we hunger and thirst, we are poorly dressed and buffeted and homeless" (1 Cor. 4:11), and he spoke of traveling from city to city on his missionary journeys "through many a sleepless night, in hunger and thirst, often without food, in cold and exposure" (2 Cor. 11:27).

James wrote more generally to all Christians in the first century:

> Has not God chosen those who are *poor in the world* to be *rich in faith* and heirs of the kingdom, which he has promised to those who love him? (James 2:5)

These verses sound very different from the emphasis in prosperity-gospel preaching, where financially wealthy people are held up as examples of faith in God and faithful obedience to him. In fact, some leaders in the prosperity-gospel movement have visibly opulent lifestyles, flagrantly showing off their wealth (much of which has come from the sacrificial donations of very poor people). But many people, both believers and unbelievers, instinctively object to this. It seems so different from the pattern set by Jesus and his followers in the New Testament.

d. The New Testament Does Not Teach Us to Seek Prosperity but Warns Us of Its Dangers: While prosperity gospel advocates teach people to seek God for prosperity, to believe that God will give it to them, and to confess in their words that God will give (or even that God has given!) it to them, the New Testament authors do not speak this way. Consider this warning from Paul:

---

[13] Copeland, *The Laws of Prosperity*, 44.

But if we have food and clothing, with these we will be content. But *those who desire to be rich fall into temptation*, into a snare, into many senseless and harmful desires that plunge people into ruin and destruction. For the love of money is a root of all kinds of evils. It is through this craving that some have wandered away from the faith and pierced themselves with many pangs. But as for you, O man of God, flee these things. (1 Tim. 6:8–11)

Other passages contain similar warnings:

Again I tell you, it is easier for a camel to go through the eye of a needle than for a rich person to enter the kingdom of God. (Matt. 19:24)

But woe to you who are rich, for you have received your consolation. (Luke 6:24)

But God said to him [the rich fool who decided to tear down his barns and build bigger ones], "Fool! This night your soul is required of you, and the things you have prepared, whose will they be?" So is the one who lays up treasure for himself and is not rich toward God. (Luke 12:20–21; see also 16:19–31)

Are not the rich the ones who oppress you, and the ones who drag you into court? Are they not the ones who blaspheme the honorable name by which you were called? (James 2:6–7)

Come now, you rich, weep and howl for the miseries that are coming upon you. Your riches have rotted and your garments are moth-eaten. Your gold and silver have corroded, and their corrosion will be evidence against you and will eat your flesh like fire. You have laid up treasure in the last days. (James 5:1–3)

This is not to say that the New Testament always views prosperity as evil, for it does not, as I argued earlier in this chapter. The New Testament authors recognize that God will grant prosperity to some Christians in this age, and they give warnings about the temptations of wealth and some instruction about its proper use. But the balanced emphasis in the New Testament is not reflected in the prosperity-gospel message that it is God's will to make every Christian wealthy, and Christians simply need to believe this and claim it.

Someone might object that 3 John 2 seems to encourage us to pray for material prosperity. In the King James Version, this verse uses the verb "prosper":

Beloved, I wish above all things *that thou mayest prosper* and be in health, even as thy soul prospereth. (3 John 2 KJV)

"Prosper" is also found in three other translations (NKJV, NASB, and CSB). However, all other major translations, including the ESV, use the expression "go well" rather than "prosper":

Beloved, I pray *that all may go well with you* and that you may be in good health, as it goes well with your soul. (3 John 2)

The Greek verb is *euodoō*, which means "have things turn out well, prosper, succeed."[14] It can be used to speak of monetary prosperity, as in, "On the first day of every week, each of you is to put something aside and store it up, as he may *prosper*" (1 Cor. 16:2), but it can also be used to speak more generally of a plan that succeeds or turns out well, as in, "always in my prayers, asking that somehow by God's will I may now at last *succeed* in coming to you" (Rom. 1:10). It also applies to spiritual well-being, as in the second half of 3 John 2, "as it *goes well* with your soul."[15]

We may conclude from this verse that it is right for us to pray for both spiritual and physical health for other people, and that things in general would "go well" for them. It is right to pray that a person's business activities would succeed or that someone would be rewarded fairly or promoted for his or her work in the business world or elsewhere. (This is similar to the kinds of things that Christians normally pray for one another today.) But the verse does not directly encourage us to pray for people *to become rich*, for it does not use terms that would more explicitly imply material prosperity, such as the verb *plouteō*, "to be rich" (see 1 Tim. 6:9), or the adjective *plousios*, "rich" (as in Matt. 19:23, 24; 27:57; Luke 16:19; 1 Tim. 6:17).

e. Many Extremely Poor Christians Today Have Strong Faith: Steve Corbett and Brian Fikkert tell how a visit to a slum in Kenya emphasized to them that many Christians today have remarkably strong faith in God but remain trapped in poverty:

At its core, the health and wealth gospel teaches that God rewards increasing levels of faith with greater amounts of wealth. When stated this way, the health and wealth gospel is easy to reject on a host of biblical grounds. Take the case of Job, for example. He had enormous faith and lived a godly life, but he went from riches to poverty *because* he was righteous and God wanted to prove this to Satan....

The poor could be poor due to injustices committed against them.... [During a visit to the massive Kibera slum of Nairobi, Kenya,] I was ... amazed to see people ... who were simultaneously so spiritually strong and so devastatingly poor. Right down there in the bowels of hell was this Kenyan church, filled with spiritual giants who were struggling just to eat every day. This shocked me. At some level I had implicitly assumed that my economic superiority goes hand in hand with my spiritual superiority. This is none other than the lie of the health and wealth gospel: spiritual maturity leads to financial prosperity.[16]

---

[14] BDAG, 410.

[15] Other examples in the Septuagint show *euodoō* used to speak of plans "going well" or "succeeding," as in Gen. 24:12, 21; 39:3; Isa. 54:17.

[16] Steve Corbett and Brian Fikkert, *When Helping Hurts: How to Alleviate Poverty without Hurting the Poor ... and Yourself* (Chicago: Moody, 2009), 69–70.

f. The Prosperity Gospel Overcorrects What It Sees as Lack of Faith in Evangelical Churches: It must be admitted that many evangelical churches in prosperous nations today are weak in faith, and to some extent the prosperity-gospel movement can be seen as an "overcorrection" that promotes a mistaken hyperfaith rather than genuine biblical faith. We can see this in the following chart:

	Modern Lack of Faith	Biblical Faith	Hyperfaith (the Overcorrection of the Prosperity-Gospel Movement)*
Prayer	Fatalism: God seldom or never will answer our prayers.	We can trust God to be faithful to his promises in Scripture (John 15:7), but prayer is still *asking* God, not *demanding* things from him.	We can work up faith by our own efforts at positive confession and visualization, and God must give us what we request.
Prosperity	Only poverty is a sign of spiritual maturity and strong faith.	Spiritually mature people might experience poverty, adequacy, or prosperity (Phil. 4:12–13).	Only prosperity is a sign of spiritual maturity and strong faith.
Words that we speak	Words often affirm doubt and skepticism.	Our words should affirm truthfully what our eyes perceive (Eph. 4:25).	Our words should affirm that we already have the healing or the prosperity that we prayed for even though our eyes perceive this to be false.
Giving to the Lord's work	In practice, people give only a little, thinking they can't afford to give any more.	We should give generously, in proportion to how God has blessed us (1 Cor. 16:2).	We should give far beyond what we can afford, even giving what we need for food and shelter.
Consequences of giving	Whether we give or not, it has no effect on our financial status.	If we give faithfully, God will provide for our needs (2 Cor. 9:6–11).	If we give beyond our ability, God will make us prosperous.
What God will do	We should not assume that God will do anything to help our financial situation.	God will provide for our needs if we trust him (Phil. 4:19).	God is obligated by his Word to give us health and prosperity.

* Of course, not everyone in the prosperity-gospel movement will affirm all of these "hyperfaith" beliefs, but I have tried to represent fairly what many people have perceived as the excesses and mistakes seen frequently in this movement.

Table 34.1. The "Overcorrection" of the Prosperity Gospel Movement

g. The Need for a Balanced Evaluation of the Health-and-Wealth Gospel Movement:
It is not my purpose here to give an overall evaluation of the health-and-wealth gospel movement. Other books have already done that, some of them supporting their negative assessments with extensive quotations from the teachings of prosperity-gospel leaders.[17] These books effectively document the advocacy of a number of unbiblical doctrines and several troubling examples of collecting money through manipulative promises of wealth proclaimed in mass rallies, particularly among desperate people in poor countries. These books also criticize the opulent lifestyles of several prosperity-gospel preachers whose ministries are supported through the sacrificial giving of many relatively poor people. Because the prosperity-gospel movement is promoted by hundreds of pastors and evangelists in numerous countries, and is governed by no denominational structure or parachurch organization, I have no doubt that these criticisms rightly apply to many in this movement.

However, a balanced assessment is necessary. On the positive side, it seems to me that many of the prominent prosperity-gospel preachers are not non-Christians but rather Christians with some unbiblical (and harmful) teachings and emphases. These leaders repeatedly advocate belief in the Bible as the inerrant word of God, belief in the atoning sacrifice of Christ as the only payment for our sins, and the need for personal salvation through faith alone in Christ alone.[18] Many thousands of people have come to genuine faith in Christ through their ministries. Many of their followers have deep and genuine personal prayer lives and strong personal faith. Their worship services are regularly filled with heartfelt praise to Jesus, and many of the leaders teach the need for living daily in full obedience to God's moral commands in Scripture. Many of them have started substantial ministries that care for poor and needy people around the globe. In addition, it is fair to recognize that few if any leaders in the movement have the kind of advanced theological training that might have prevented them from making a number of unguarded and speculative comments about certain biblical teachings.

The most balanced evaluation of this movement, in my judgment, is found in an extensively researched book, *Faith, Health and Prosperity*, edited by Andrew Perriman.[19] The book is the report of a commission established by the Evangelical Alliance in the

---

[17] See David W. Jones and Russell S. Woodbridge, *Health, Wealth and Happiness: Has the Prosperity Gospel Overshadowed the Gospel of Christ?* (Grand Rapids, MI: Kregel, 2011); Hank Hanegraaff, *Christianity in Crisis* (Eugene, OR: Harvest House, 1993). Another thoughtful critique from the standpoint of someone who was on the inside of the prosperity-gospel movement for nearly 20 years is Don Enevoldsen, *The Wealth of the Wicked: The Truth about the Prosperity Message* (Los Angeles: ReWrite, 2012). Enevoldsen dedicates his book "To all my friends who did exactly what prosperity preachers told them to do—and lost everything" (p. 1).

[18] I agree with Douglas Moo, who wrote, "Most of the proponents of this movement do not seek to downplay the significance of spiritual salvation. What they believe about the basic doctrines of the faith is well within the parameters of orthodoxy. If, indeed, theirs is 'another gospel,' it is so not because any basic doctrines have been subtracted, but because certain questionable doctrines have been added," Douglas Moo, "Divine Healing in the Health and Wealth Gospel," *TrinJ* 9, n.s., no. 2 (1988): 191.

[19] Andrew Perriman, ed., *Faith, Health and Prosperity: A Report on Word of Faith and Positive Confession Theologies by ACUTE (The Evangelical Alliance Commission on Unity and Truth among Evangelicals)* (Carlisle, UK: Paternoster, 2003).

United Kingdom. While this book contains multiple thoughtful critiques in its 316 pages,[20] it also notes with appreciation that some "Word of Faith leaders have also shown signs of a willingness to listen to their detractors," and it documents some public retractions of previous teachings that have been made by Kenneth Copeland, John Avanzini, and F. K. C. Price.[21] It also mentions that "much of the extremism and many of the more esoteric teachings are quite naturally filtered out at the grassroots level."[22]

While the book contains many criticisms of the prosperity-gospel movement, it also adds at the end that "there are some important lessons that evangelicalism might learn through dialogue and through exposure to the life of Word of Faith churches," and notes especially these five items: "1. The priority given to the Word of God. . . . 2. Belief in a powerful God. . . . 3. A thoroughgoing optimism. . . . 4. The subordination of Mammon to the kingdom of God. . . . 5. A theology of godly prosperity" (in contrast to the teaching of some evangelicals that only poverty, never prosperity, can be spiritual, and that the only good use of money is giving it away).[23]

With regard to material prosperity in general, while I strongly disagree with the distinctive teachings of the prosperity gospel for the reasons given above, it should be clear from the earlier part of this chapter that I do not claim that material prosperity is always viewed negatively in the New Testament. In fact, I have written elsewhere that when national governments obey biblical teachings in their laws, the conduct of government officials, and their economic system, and when their cultures largely follow biblical values, this will lead to increasing prosperity in those nations as a whole.[24]

But some poverty will always remain in this lifetime, even among Christians, because poverty is still the result of many factors. *Individual poor people* may be spiritually mature and still materially poor because of injustices committed against them, because of personal tragedies or misfortunes, or because of the destructive systems, laws, and policies in the nations in which they live.

Therefore, I conclude that it is contrary to Scripture to say that if you are a faithful Christian God will make you rich. Often he will not.

3. The Error of False Asceticism. While Paul warned against materialism, he also warned against the opposite error—a false asceticism, a kind of teaching that constantly opposes and criticizes the enjoyment of material things that God has placed in this world:

> If with Christ you died to the elemental spirits of the world, why, as if you were still alive in the world, do you submit to regulations—"*Do not handle, Do not*

---

[20] However, its concluding evaluations are found on pp. 195–235.

[21] Perriman, *Faith, Health and Prosperity*, 215. Also, at the end of his life, Kenneth Hagin published a strongly worded critique of the excesses of the prosperity-gospel movement in his book *The Midas Touch: A Balanced Approach to Biblical Prosperity* (Tulsa, OK: Kenneth Hagin Ministries, 2000).

[22] Perriman, *Faith, Health and Prosperity*, 216.

[23] Ibid., 217–222.

[24] See Grudem and Asmus, *The Poverty of Nations*.

taste, Do not touch" (referring to things that all perish as they are used)—according to human precepts and teachings? These have indeed an appearance of wisdom in promoting *self-made religion and asceticism* and severity to the body, but they are of *no value* in stopping the indulgence of the flesh. (Col. 2:20–23)

Paul also explained that he personally had learned how to live in circumstances of both poverty and of prosperity:

I know how to be brought low, and *I know how to abound*. In any and every circumstance, I have learned the secret of *facing plenty* and hunger, abundance and need. I can do all things through him who strengthens me. (Phil. 4:12–13)

Materialism is primarily a matter of the heart, and so is false asceticism. It is important for believers to be on guard against speaking harsh criticisms of others (or even of themselves) for enjoyment of material prosperity. God's Word asks us to avoid both the error of materialism and the error of asceticism, and charting the right course for our hearts in this area requires daily prayer and meditation on Scripture, and regular fellowship with other believers who will speak honestly with us about these matters.

4. There Are Several Different Good and Wise Uses of Possessions. There is much more to wise stewardship than avoiding materialism, avoiding the health-and-wealth gospel, and avoiding false asceticism. Even if we avoid these things, we still need wisdom from God in the rightful use and enjoyment of property.

Among the good and wise uses of our possessions, we should include an allocation of some amount of spending on ourselves (for food, clothing, shelter, and other things), some amount of giving to the work of the church and to those in need, some amount of saving for the future, and some amount of investing to increase our resources and productivity. I will explain these and other uses of our possessions in chapter 37.

QUESTIONS FOR PERSONAL APPLICATION

1. What kind of property do you own (clothing, a phone, a bicycle, a computer, a car, a house)? Does any of it reflect your distinctive personality? How often do you think of it as a gift from God?
2. How does your job enable you to create value for other people? (If you are not now working at a job, answer in terms of a job you hope to have in the future.)
3. In what ways does your stewardship of your property give glory to God and advance the work of the kingdom of God on earth?
4. Do you find that you can both enjoy your property and also enjoy your relationship with Christ even more? Or has your property turned your heart away from love for God and Christ?

5. Look again at Table 34.1 above (p. 913). Do you think that you tend to make the mistake of "modern lack of faith" or the mistake of "hyperfaith" in the prosperity-gospel movement? Or would you say that you fall in the center column of "biblical faith" in the day-to-day attitude of your heart?

6. Is your life "free from love of money," and are you "content with what you have" because you know that God has promised, "I will never leave you nor forsake you" (Heb. 13:5)? Is it possible to combine that attitude of heart with seeking to work hard at your job and thereby earn more money?

7. What do you think are the most harmful results of the prosperity-gospel movement? Is there anything you think you can learn from the teachings of this movement?

8. Do you sometimes fall into the error of false asceticism?

9. What character traits (see p. 110) would most strongly influence you to act, think, and feel in ways that are pleasing to God with respect to your ownership of property?

SPECIAL TERMS

asceticism
communism
health-and-wealth gospel
human flourishing
property
prosperity gospel
stealing
stewardship

BIBLIOGRAPHY

Sections in Other Ethics Texts

(see complete bibliographical data, p. 64)

Frame, 796–98
Gushee and Stassen, 375–77
Kaiser, 199–210
McQuilkin and Copan, 447–48

Other Works

Blomberg, Craig L. *Christians in an Age of Wealth: A Biblical Theology of Stewardship*. Biblical Theology for Life. Grand Rapids, MI: Zondervan, 2013.

Chan, Francis, with Danae Yankoski. *Crazy Love: Overwhelmed by a Relentless God.* Colorado Springs: Cook, 2008.

Copeland, Kenneth. *The Blessing of the Lord: Makes Rich and He Adds No Sorrow with It.* Fort Worth, TX: Kenneth Copeland Publications, 2011.

———. *The Laws of Prosperity.* Fort Worth, TX: Kenneth Copeland Publications, 1974.

Corbett, Steve, and Brian Fikkert. *When Helping Hurts: How to Alleviate Poverty without Hurting the Poor . . . and Yourself.* Chicago: Moody, 2009.

Enevoldsen, Don. *The Wealth of the Wicked: The Truth about the Prosperity Message.* Los Angeles: ReWrite, 2012.

Farah, Charles. *From the Pinnacle of the Temple: Faith or Presumption.* Plainfield, NJ: Logos International, 1979.

Forster, G. S. "Property." In *New Dictionary of Christian Ethics and Pastoral Theology,* edited by David J. Atkinson and David H. Field, 696–97. Leicester, UK: Inter-Varsity, and Downers Grove, IL: InterVarsity Press, 1995.

Grudem, Wayne, and Barry Asmus. *The Poverty of Nations: A Sustainable Solution.* Wheaton, IL: Crossway, 2013.

Hagin, Kenneth E. *The Midas Touch: A Balanced Approach to Biblical Prosperity.* Tulsa, OK: Kenneth Hagin Ministries, 2000.

Hanegraaff, Hank. *Christianity in Crisis.* Eugene, OR: Harvest House Publishers, 1993.

King, Paul L. *Only Believe: Examining the Origin and Development of Classic and Contemporary Word of Faith Theologies.* Tulsa, OK: Word & Spirit, 2008.

Jones, David W., and Russell S. Woodbridge. *Health, Wealth and Happiness: Has the Prosperity Gospel Overshadowed the Gospel of Christ?* Grand Rapids, MI: Kregel, 2011.

Perriman, Andrew, ed. *Faith, Health and Prosperity: A Report on Word of Faith and Positive Confession Theologies by ACUTE (The Evangelical Alliance Commission on Unity and Truth among Evangelicals).* Carlisle, UK: Paternoster, 2003.

Piper, John. *Don't Waste Your Life.* Wheaton, IL: Crossway, 2003.

Platt, David. *Radical: Taking Back Your Faith from the American Dream.* Colorado Springs: Multnomah, 2010.

Read, Leonard. *I, Pencil: My Family Tree as Told to Leonard E. Read.* Irving on the Hudson, NY: Foundation for Economic Education, 2006.

Richards, Jay W. *Money, Greed, and God: Why Capitalism Is the Solution and Not the Problem.* New York: HarperOne, 2009.

Rigney, Joe. *The Things of Earth: Treasuring God by Enjoying His Gifts.* Wheaton, IL: Crossway, 2015.

Schaeffer, Franky, ed. *Is Capitalism Christian? Toward a Christian Perspective on Economics.* Westchester, IL: Crossway, 1985.

Schlossberg, Herbert, Vinay Samuel, and Ronald J. Sider, eds. *Christianity and Economics in the Post-Cold War Era: The Oxford Declaration and Beyond.* Grand Rapids, MI: Eerdmans, 1994.

Schluter, Michael, and John Ashcroft, eds. *Jubilee Manifesto: A Framework, Agenda and Strategy for Christian Social Reform*. Leicester, UK: Inter-Varsity, 2005.

Schneider, John R. *Godly Materialism: Rethinking Money and Possessions*. Downers Grove, IL: InterVarsity Press, 1994.

Sirico, Robert A. *Defending the Free Market: The Moral Case for a Free Economy*. Washington: Regnery, 2012.

Smith, Adam. *An Inquiry into the Nature and Causes of the Wealth of Nations*. Edited by Edwin Cannan. New York: Modern Library, 1994.

Sowell, Thomas. *A Conflict of Visions*. New York: Quill, 1987.

———. *Basic Economics: A Common Sense Guide to the Economy*. New York: Basic Books, 2007.

Sproul, R. C. *Biblical Economics: A Commonsense Guide to Our Daily Bread*. Bristol, TN: Draught Horse, 2002.

Weber, Max. *The Protestant Ethic and the Spirit of Capitalism*. Los Angeles: Roxbury, 1996.

Wittmer, Michael. *Becoming Worldly Saints: Can You Serve Jesus and Still Enjoy Your Life?* Grand Rapids, MI: Zondervan, 2015.

Wuthnow, Robert, ed. *Rethinking Materialism: Perspectives on the Spiritual Dimension of Economic Behavior*. Grand Rapids, MI: Eerdmans, 1995.

SCRIPTURE MEMORY PASSAGE

Ephesians 4:28: Let the thief no longer steal, but rather let him labor, doing honest work with his own hands, so that he may have something to share with anyone in need.

HYMN

"More Love to Thee, O Christ"

More love to Thee, O Christ,
More love to Thee!
Hear Thou the prayer I make
On bended knee;
This is my earnest plea:

Refrain:
More love, O Christ, to Thee,
More love to Thee,
More love to Thee!

Once earthly joy I craved,
Sought peace and rest;

Now Thee alone I seek—
Give what is best;
This all my prayer shall be:

Let sorrow do its work,
Send grief and pain;
Sweet are Thy messengers,
Sweet their refrain,
When they can sing with me:

Then shall my latest breath
Whisper Thy praise;
This be the parting cry
My heart shall raise;
This still its prayer shall be:

ELIZABETH PRENTISS, 1818–1878

Chapter 35

WORK, REST, VACATIONS, AND RETIREMENT

Why did God give us productive work to do?

Is work today a blessing or curse?

Does God approve of longer vacations?

What about retirement?

In this section of the book I am discussing ethical issues related to the protection of property, which is something implied by the eighth commandment, "You shall not steal" (Ex. 20:15). In this chapter I will deal with human work, which is the means by which property is produced and improved. I will also discuss topics related to rest from work, including vacations and retirement.

A. WORK IN ITSELF IS GOOD AND PLEASING TO GOD

Although many people seek to avoid work or to work as little as possible, the Bible presents, in general, a positive view of work. It views work in itself as a good thing and as pleasing to God.

We see this first because, before there was any sin in the world, God gave Adam and Eve work to do: "Be fruitful and multiply and fill the earth and *subdue* it, and *have dominion . . .*" (Gen. 1:28). Furthermore, before there was sin in the world, "the LORD God took the man and put him in the garden of Eden *to work it* and keep it" (2:15). Work is not simply a painful part of the fallen human condition, but is part of what God intended for us in his "very good" creation. In fact, the first thing God does in the Bible is work, for the entirety of Genesis 1 describes God's work of creation, suggesting to us that our work is a faint imitation of God's own activity of creative work (see John 5:17).

Other passages in the Old Testament also view work in a positive way. The fourth commandment not only says, "Remember the Sabbath day, to keep it holy," but also adds, "Six *days you shall labor*, and do all your work" (Ex. 20:8–9). With this statement, God placed a requirement for productive work into the Ten Commandments, and he explained it by telling how our work was to imitate his own work: "For in six days the LORD made heaven and earth, the sea, and all that is in them" (Ex. 20:11).

Passages in the Old Testament Wisdom Literature also place a high value on work:

> *In all toil there is profit,*
>> but mere talk tends only to poverty. (Prov. 14:23)

> Whoever *works* his land will have plenty of bread,
>> but he who follows worthless pursuits will have plenty of poverty. (Prov. 28:19)

The New Testament reaffirms this emphasis on the goodness of work in several places. Paul's practice of working as a tentmaker (Acts 18:3) as he went from city to city on his missionary journeys gave an example to believers that they should work hard and support themselves. He reminded the elders of the church at Ephesus of the example that he had set in his ministry among them:

> You yourselves know that *these hands ministered to my necessities* and to those who were with me. In all things I have shown you that *by working hard in this way* we must help the weak and remember the words of the Lord Jesus, how he himself said, "It is more blessed to give than to receive." (Acts 20:34–35)

Paul also wrote to the Ephesians:

> Let the thief no longer steal, but rather *let him labor, doing honest work with his own hands*, so that he may have something to share with anyone in need. (Eph. 4:28)

And in both of his letters to the Thessalonian church he wrote about the importance of people supporting themselves by working:

> . . . and to aspire to live quietly, and to mind your own affairs, and *to work with your hands*, as we instructed you, so that you may walk properly before outsiders and be dependent on no one. (1 Thess. 4:11–12)

> Now we command you, brothers, in the name of our Lord Jesus Christ, that you *keep away from any brother who is walking in idleness* and not in accord with the tradition that you received from us. For you yourselves know how

you ought to imitate us, because we were not idle when we were with you, nor did we eat anyone's bread without paying for it, but *with toil and labor we worked night and day*, that we might not be a burden to any of you. It was not because we do not have that right, but *to give you in ourselves an example to imitate*. For even when we were with you, we would give you this command: *If anyone is not willing to work, let him not eat.* For we hear that some among you walk in idleness, not busy at work, but busybodies. Now such persons we command and encourage in the Lord Jesus Christ to *do their work* quietly and to earn their own living. (2 Thess. 3:6–12)

It is also helpful to remember that when we do productive work we are producing something that brings benefit to others (whether it is making a physical product that they can buy or providing a service such as teaching a class or repairing an automobile). But if our work actually results in a benefit to other people, then we should understand our work as one way of showing love to others. Doing productive work is one way to obey the commandment "You shall love your neighbor as yourself" (Matt. 22:39).

B. UNPAID WORK

Much work receives no monetary compensation, but it is valuable nonetheless.

1. Homemaker (Caring for Home and Children). Several passages in Scripture teach that the work of a homemaker is of the utmost importance, even though such work does not receive economic payment in the marketplace:

An excellent wife who can find?
> She is far more precious than jewels. . . .
She seeks wool and flax,
> and works with willing hands.
She is like the ships of the merchant;
> she brings her food from afar.
She rises while it is yet night
> and provides food for her household
> and portions for her maidens. . . .
She opens her hand to the poor
> and reaches out her hands to the needy. . . .
She makes bed coverings for herself;
> her clothing is fine linen and purple. . . .
She opens her mouth with wisdom,
> and the teaching of kindness is on her tongue.
She looks well to the ways of her household
> and does not eat the bread of idleness. (Prov. 31:10–27)

The New Testament also commends the work of a woman who cares for her household and her family, and also for others. Paul writes that an exemplary godly woman is one who has "a reputation for good works . . . [and] has brought up children, has shown hospitality, has washed the feet of the saints, has cared for the afflicted, and has *devoted herself to every good work*" (1 Tim. 5:10).

Paul also tells Titus that older women in the church should:

> train the young women to love their husbands and children, to be self-controlled, pure, *working at home*, kind, and submissive to their own husbands, that the word of God may not be reviled. (Titus 2:4–5)

These passages do not require that all women remain at home instead of working at jobs outside the home, for the "excellent wife" of Proverbs 31 engages in real-estate transactions: "she considers a field and buys it" (Prov. 31:16). She also sells things in the marketplace because "she perceives that her merchandise is profitable" (v. 18), and "she makes linen garments and sells them; she delivers sashes to the merchant" (v. 24). But she does not do these things *instead of* caring for her home and children, but *in addition to* caring for her home and children, because it is still true that "she looks well to the ways of her household and does not eat the bread of idleness" (v. 27). It seems right to conclude from these passages that, in a family, the wife has primary responsibility for caring for the household and the children (see p. 411), and, in addition to those responsibilities, some wives may choose to have paid jobs outside their homes as well.

2. Volunteer Work in the Church and Other Organizations. Another vast area of unpaid work is volunteer work that people do in the church or other charitable organizations. Peter reminds Christians that they all have gifts that they can use for the benefit of others: "As each has received a gift, use it to serve one another, as good stewards of God's varied grace" (1 Pet. 4:10). Churches and thousands of other volunteer organizations bring immense benefit to every society, and they do this primarily through the unpaid work that is contributed by those who support them.

Retired people often find great fulfillment in contributing voluntary work to the church and to other charitable organizations. I have also met a number of retired people who continue to give their time for short-term mission trips, and others find it fulfilling to help younger people start new businesses. In addition, many retired people find they are able to give more time to caring for grandchildren or people in nursing homes or hospitals.

3. School. Children and young adults usually spend most of their days in school or in doing homework in preparation for school. This is not paid work, but it trains them to be productive workers later, as well as (we hope) virtuous people and good citizens.

Because most Western societies today are highly complex, with advanced technology and vast areas of specialization, receiving training to be productive workers will often take much longer than it did in previous generations in societies that were primarily agricultural.

In every case, those who are in school from childhood onward should think of their academic study as the main way in which they are to "work" in obedience to God for this segment of their lives. Even Jesus, when he was 12 years old, was found by his parents "in the temple, sitting among the teachers, listening to them and asking them questions" (Luke 2:46). Jesus must have spent many hours in study during his childhood, for we read that "Jesus *increased in wisdom* and in stature and in favor with God and man" (Luke 2:52).

C. THE "SLUGGARD" IN PROVERBS EXEMPLIFIES THE FOOLISHNESS OF LAZY PEOPLE

Several sobering and even humorous passages in Proverbs describe the lazy person, often calling him a "sluggard." Here are some examples:

> How long will you lie there, O *sluggard*?
>   When will you arise from your sleep?
> A little sleep, a little slumber,
>   a little folding of the hands to rest,
> and poverty will come upon you like a robber,
>   and want like an armed man. (6:9–11)

> The soul of the *sluggard* craves and gets nothing,
>   while the soul of the diligent is richly supplied. (13:4)

> Whoever is slack in his work
>   is a brother to him who destroys. (18:9)

> Slothfulness casts into a deep sleep,
>   and an idle person will suffer hunger. (19:15)

> The sluggard does not plow in the autumn;
>   he will seek at harvest and have nothing. (20:4)

> The desire of the sluggard kills him,
>   for his hands refuse to labor. (21:25)

> The sluggard says, "There is a lion in the road!
>   There is a lion in the streets!"
> As a door turns on its hinges,
>   so does a sluggard on his bed.
> The sluggard buries his hand in the dish;
>   it wears him out to bring it back to his mouth.

> The sluggard is wiser in his own eyes
> than seven men who can answer sensibly. (26:13–16)

These passages depict a person who rejects the Bible's positive picture of productive work, with numerous negative results.

D. WHY DID GOD GIVE US PRODUCTIVE WORK TO DO?

1. The Satisfaction That Comes from Productive Work and "Earned Success." God created human beings in such a way that we gain deep joy and satisfaction from doing meaningful, productive work. Economist Arthur Brooks, former professor at Syracuse University and now president of the American Enterprise Institute, summarizes academic research showing that, surprisingly, the most satisfying economic activity for human beings is not earning great amounts of money but rather what he calls "earned success"—that is, having a specific responsibility and then doing good work to fulfill that responsibility, in whatever career or field of life one chooses. Brooks says, "The secret to human flourishing is not money but earned success in life."[1] He further explains:

> Earned success means the ability to create value honestly—not by winning the lottery, not by inheriting a fortune, not by picking up a welfare check. It doesn't even mean making money itself. Earned success is the creation of value in our lives or in the lives of others.[2]

It seems to me that this idea of "earned success" echoes the biblical theme that we experience a deep satisfaction from God's recognition that we have been faithful servants and have accomplished the work that he gave us to do. This ultimately will be affirmed when God says to us, "Well done, good and faithful servant. You have been faithful over a little; I will set you over much. Enter into the joy of your master" (Matt. 25:21; see also 2 Tim. 4:7; 1 Pet. 1:7).

2. The Privilege of Creating Something New. When we work to make things (whether we are building a house or a car, or simply making a loaf of bread), we create something that did not exist in the world before we made it. This is a faint imitation of God's own creative activity. It also reflects other attributes of God, such as his wisdom, knowledge, strength, and patience. God gives us the privilege of imitating him in various ways, for Scripture tells us, "Be imitators of God, as beloved children" (Eph. 5:1).

Of course, all of nature manifests God's glory. For example, the amazing complexity

---

[1] Arthur C. Brooks, *The Battle: How the Fight between Free Enterprise and Big Government Will Shape America's Future* (New York: Basic Books, 2010), 71. (See chap. 37, p. 968, for an example of earned success.)
[2] Ibid., 75.

of the plant and animal kingdoms, and the ways in which they work together, certainly bear witness to God's glory. And animals certainly do some useful work (horses and oxen help to plow fields, and dogs are good at herding sheep or serving as watchdogs or guide dogs).

But the creativity exhibited by human beings is of a different kind altogether from anything displayed by animals. Only human beings create, invent, and innovate. No animal has ever used intelligent thought to create a new product that others would value and buy for their use. Our ability to do creative work therefore shows an important aspect of the excellence of human nature as created by God in his image.

3. The Privilege of Creating Value. It is not just that we create products. It is that these products have *value* to ourselves and others. Whether we bake a loaf of bread or assemble a new computer, these things have greater value than the raw materials themselves possessed. Therefore, in doing productive work, we add to the total value of the useful things that exist in the world for the benefit of mankind.

4. The Privilege of Supporting Ourselves. Paul told the Thessalonian Christians to "work with your hands . . . so that you may *live properly* before outsiders and *be dependent on no one*" (1 Thess. 4:11–12).

Our natural human sense of dignity is reinforced when we are able to support ourselves and no longer depend on our parents or others. In other words, productive work gives people a new sense of self-respect, and it also glorifies God by giving a faint imitation of God's own attribute of independence.

This is why involuntary unemployment (in the case of people who are laid off and can't find another job, or who can't work because of illness or injury) is such a great challenge and difficulty. Not having productive work soon brings frustration due to not being able to do what God made human beings to do, that is, to be engaged in useful, productive work and thereby support themselves.

5. Individuality. God created human beings with vast differences in skills, preferences, and inclinations for the types of work we enjoy and want focus on. This diversity among human beings is a gift that leads us to specialize in different kinds of work (it leads to a division of labor), and it makes the human race thousands of times more productive than if we all had to produce everything we needed for ourselves (as do animals, when they all have to find their own food). Therefore, because of specialization, we are able to fulfill God's command to "subdue" the earth (Gen. 1:28) and make useful products from it in a much more extensive way than we otherwise could.

Individual specialization in work is vastly more important than most people recognize. It is the key to greater economic productivity in any society or nation. Adam Smith in 1776 gave a now-famous example of a pin factory where people were manufacturing a very simple product, pins. He showed that when everyone acted as a specialist, more pins were produced than if each person made the final product from start to finish.

(Making pins might appear to us to be a trivial example, but before staplers—invented and patented only in 1866—people often used pins to fasten papers together in businesses. Most people also made their own clothing at home, using pins in the process, so pins were a crucial part of an economy.)

Here is Smith's famous description of the division of labor in a pin factory.

> To take an example, therefore, from a very trifling manufacture; but one in which the division of labour has been very often taken notice of, the trade of the pin-maker; a workman not educated to this business (which the division of labour has rendered a distinct trade), nor acquainted with the use of the machinery employed in it (to the invention of which the same division of labour has probably given occasion), could scarce, perhaps, with his utmost industry, make one pin in a day, and certainly could not make 20.
>
> But in the way in which this business is now carried on, not only the whole work is a peculiar trade, but it is divided into a number of branches, of which the greater part are likewise peculiar trades. One man draws out the wire, another straights it, a third cuts it, a fourth points it, a fifth grinds it at the top for receiving the head; to make the head requires two or three distinct operations; to put it on, is a peculiar business, to whiten the pins is another; it is even a trade by itself to put them into the paper; and the important business of making a pin is, in this manner, divided into about 18 distinct operations, which, in some manufactories, are all performed by distinct hands, though in others the same man will sometimes perform two or three of them.
>
> I have seen a small manufactory of this kind where 10 men only were employed, and where some of them consequently performed two or three distinct operations. But though they were very poor, and therefore but indifferently accommodated with the necessary machinery, they could, when they exerted themselves, make among them about 12 pounds of pins in a day.
>
> There are in a pound upwards of four thousand pins of a middling size. Those 10 persons, therefore, could make among them upwards of forty-eight thousand pins in a day. Each person, therefore, making a tenth part of forty-eight thousand pins, might be considered as making four thousand eight hundred pins in a day. But if they had all wrought separately and independently, and without any of them having been educated to this peculiar business, they certainly could not each of them have made 20, perhaps not one pin in a day; that is, certainly, not the two hundred and fortieth, perhaps not the four thousand eight hundredth part of what they are at present capable of performing, in consequence of a proper division and combination of their different operations. In every other art and manufacture, the

effects of the division of labour are similar to what they are in this very trifling one.[3]

E. WORK BECAME MORE DIFFICULT AND INCLUDED PAIN AFTER THE FALL

Although God had given work to Adam and Eve when they were first created, after they sinned he introduced changes into the created order that made their work more difficult. When God pronounced judgment on Adam, he said this:

And to Adam he said,

"Because you have listened to the voice of your wife
    and have eaten of the tree
of which I commanded you,
    'You shall not eat of it,'
cursed is the ground because of you;
    in pain you shall eat of it all the days of your life;
thorns and thistles it shall bring forth for you;
    and you shall eat the plants of the field.
By the sweat of your face
    you shall eat bread,
till you return to the ground,
    for out of it you were taken;
for you are dust,
    and to dust you shall return." (Gen. 3:17–19)

God's curse on the ground meant that it would yield useful food for human beings only as the result of difficult labor. The "thorns and thistles" would cause pain and would tend to choke out plants that produced useful food. Adam and Eve would still be able to eat food and they would not die, but that food would come "by the sweat of your face," that is, with difficult toil.

Therefore, Moses could later characterize human life as simply "toil and trouble":

The years of our life are seventy,
    or even by reason of strength eighty;
yet *their span is but toil and trouble;*
    they are soon gone, and we fly away. (Ps. 90:10)

[3] Adam Smith, *An Inquiry into the Nature and Causes of the Wealth of Nations*, ed. Edwin Cannan (1776; repr., New York: Modern Library, 1994), Book I, chap. 1; 4–5.

In addition, even in Paul's proclamation of the gospel, he recalled that he had often worked "in toil and hardship, through many a sleepless night, in hunger and thirst, often without food, in cold and exposure" (2 Cor. 11:27). Even the work of gospel ministry includes a significant share of pain and difficulty.

F. YET WE CAN STILL FIND JOY IN WORK

Although God introduced an element of pain and unpleasantness into work in Genesis 3, yet because of common grace it is still possible to find joy in our work. In fact, several Old Testament passages view the ability to enjoy our work as a blessing from God in itself:

> The LORD your God will bless you in all your produce and in all the work of your hands, so that you will be altogether *joyful*. (Deut. 16:15)

> The LORD will open to you his good treasury, the heavens, to give the rain to your land in its season and *to bless all the work of your hands*. And you shall lend to many nations, but you shall not borrow. (Deut. 28:12)

> Let the favor of the LORD our God be upon us,
>   and establish the work of our hands upon us;
>   yes, establish the work of our hands! (Ps. 90:17)

> My heart found *pleasure in all my toil*, and this was my reward for all my toil. (Eccles. 2:10)

> There is nothing better for a person than that he should eat and drink and *find enjoyment in his toil*. This also, I saw, is from the hand of God, for apart from him who can eat or who can have enjoyment? (Eccles. 2:24–25)

> Everyone also to whom God has given wealth and possessions and power to enjoy them, and to accept his lot and *rejoice in his toil*—this is the gift of God. For he will not much remember the days of his life because God keeps him occupied with joy in his heart. (Eccles. 5:19–20)

In the New Testament we do not see as much emphasis on joy in work, except the author of Hebrews encourages leaders in the church to carry out their responsibilities "*with joy* and not with groaning" (Heb. 13:17; and note the caution against "grumbling" in Phil. 2:14). But the earlier passages quoted above from Ecclesiastes about joy in work contain nothing that would lead us to think they apply only to Israel under the old covenant. We should rather understand them as applying to the situation of human work in general.

In addition, even though God imposed pain in connection with work at the statement of the curse in Genesis 3, the rest of Scripture shows God patiently and steadily working to bring about redemption for his people from the curses of the fall, and that means that we should never seek to perpetuate, but to alleviate wherever possible, the painful aspects of work today.

This idea is contrary to the Hindu belief that people deserve to suffer in this life due to their behavior in a previous life. In the Hindu caste system, a group of people called the Dalits occupy the lowest rung in the system. They supposedly did evil in a previous life and thus are denied employment opportunities, treated without regard to human dignity, and are doomed to a life of poverty and despair, with little hope of ever escaping the system that oppresses them unless they renounce the Hindu faith. If they do renounce that faith, they then often become the target of violent persecution, especially if they become Christians.[4]

The importance of minimizing the painful and often dangerous aspects of work is also contrary to a kind of Islamic fatalism, in which "Allah wills" is too frequently used as an explanation for serious and even fatal industrial accidents. "Fatalism is constantly used as an excuse for human neglect and errors," says Turkish writer Mustafa Akyol, adding that this "is a global Muslim problem."[5]

G. WE SHOULD WORK TO PLEASE THE LORD IN EVERY OCCUPATION

Paul presented a wonderful perspective on work to the Christians in Colossae, many of whom were working for secular employers in secular jobs. Yet he encouraged them that they could work for the Lord in whatever occupation they had:

> Bondservants, obey in everything those who are your earthly masters, not by way of eye-service, as people-pleasers, but with sincerity of heart, fearing the Lord. *Whatever you do, work heartily, as for the Lord and not for men*, knowing that from the Lord you will receive the inheritance as your reward. You are serving the Lord Christ. For the wrongdoer will be paid back for the wrong he has done, and there is no partiality. (Col 3:22–25; see also a similar passage in Eph. 6:5–8)

H. GOD CALLS DIFFERENT PEOPLE TO A WIDE VARIETY OF DIFFERENT JOBS OR "VOCATIONS"

Like believers in the early church, most Christians today work not in full-time church ministry but in more "secular" occupations, often working for employers who are

---

[4] Verified by Tehmina Arora, senior counsel of Alliance Defending Freedom-India, in several personal phone conversations and emails in 2016 and earlier with Craig Osten, senior director of research and grant writing with Alliance Defending Freedom.

[5] Mustafa Akyol, "Islam's Tragic Fatalism," *The New York Times*, Sept. 23, 2015, http://www.nytimes.com /2015/09/24/opinion/islams-tragic-fatalism.html. Akyol is the author of *Islam without Extremes: A Muslim Case for Liberty* (New York: W. W. Norton, 2013).

unbelievers. Most of the Epistles were written to churches where Christians were a small minority in an overwhelmingly pagan or secular society. Yet even in that context Paul could say that the people were in jobs that God had "called" them to:

> Only let each person lead the life that the Lord has assigned to him, and to which God has *called* him. This is my rule in all the churches. (1 Cor. 7:17; see also v. 24)

In this specific context Paul is speaking about being a slave or being a free person, but his principle certainly has wider application. Whatever occupation a person is in, for that time at least, that is the situation to which "God has called him." (Our English word *vocation* comes from the Latin term *voco/vocare*, a verb that means "to call, summon.") When we realize that God has "called" our friends in the church to the occupations in which they work, it will be much easier for us to encourage them, pray for them in their jobs, and honor them for the work that they are doing out of obedience to the Lord and his calling.

However, Paul recognizes that people can also have opportunities to follow God's leading to other employment situations, because in this very passage he tells those who are slaves, "but if you can gain your freedom, avail yourself of the opportunity" (1 Cor. 7:21). Therefore, it is possible both to be called by God to a specific occupation or job, and then at a later time to be similarly called by him to another job or occupation.

I. WORK ALSO PRESENTS MANY TEMPTATIONS TO SIN

Although Scripture views work as fundamentally good, and although God calls us to work in various occupations, we still live in a fallen world, and work carries with it a number of temptations to sin.

1. Being Argumentative, Disagreeable, or Even Stealing from an Employer. Paul knew that Christians needed to be warned about falling into destructive patterns of behavior at their work, perhaps imitating the sullen or rebellious attitudes among non-Christian employees among whom they worked, and perhaps even stealing ("pilfering") from their employers:

> Bondservants are to be submissive to their own masters in everything; *they are to be well-pleasing, not argumentative, not pilfering*, but showing all good faith, so that in everything they may adorn the doctrine of God our Savior. (Titus 2:9–10)

2. Laziness and Carelessness in Work. The book of Proverbs warns, "Whoever is slack in his work is a brother to him who destroys" (Prov. 18:9), showing that laziness and carelessness bring harmful results in the job one is doing. In contrast to this attitude, Paul writes to Christians, "Whatever you do, *work heartily, as for the Lord and not for men*" (Col. 3:23).

3. Overworking. The opposite error to laziness is working too much, becoming a "workaholic." In the Old Testament, in order to prevent people from working all the time, God commanded them not to work one day a week: "Remember the Sabbath day, to keep it holy.... On it you shall not do any work" (Ex. 20:8–10). The Sabbath day was a reminder that God did not require people to work all the time, but gave them periods of joyful rest.

A word of caution in this regard is found in the Psalms:

> *It is in vain that you rise up early*
> >*and go late to rest,*
> *eating the bread of anxious toil;*
> >*for he gives to his beloved sleep.* (127:2)

This does not mean that there should never be times of intense work activity, with long hours and long days of hard work in certain periods of time. But it does mean that we should be warned against making such intense work a regular, continual pattern of our lives, to the extent that we neglect our health, our family responsibilities, our time in church, our private time with the Lord in Scripture reading and prayer, and our time in fellowship with Christian friends.

Just as individuals differ in the kinds of skills they possess, in their interests and preferences, and in many other ways, so also individual people differ quite widely in the amount of work they are able to sustain and still maintain a healthy balance regarding other areas of responsibility in their lives.

4. Self-Reliance. Although the Bible repeatedly commands us to work, it also warns us against trusting ultimately in our own abilities for the success of our work. Jesus gave us a pattern of prayer that reminds us that we need to trust God for his provision: "Give us this day our daily bread" (Matt. 6:11).

This teaching from Jesus builds on an idea that was present in the Old Testament. For instance, Moses gave this caution to the people of Israel:

> Beware lest you say in your heart, "My power and the might of my hand have gotten me this wealth." *You shall remember the LORD your God, for it is he who gives you power to get wealth*, that he may confirm his covenant that he swore to your fathers, as it is this day. (Deut. 8:17–18)

A similar caution is found in this psalm by Solomon:

> *Unless the LORD builds the house,*
> >*those who build it labor in vain.*

> Unless the LORD watches over the city,
>> the watchman stays awake in vain. (Ps. 127:1)

J. WE SHOULD TAKE REGULAR TIMES OF REST FROM OUR WORK

As we discussed earlier, the privilege of productive work is a reminder that we can, in a small way, be like God in our creation of useful products with our work. But God did not make us to be like machines that can function 24 hours a day with no need for rest. Instead, God made us with a need for regular periods of rest and sleep. This reminds us that, while we may imitate God in a faint way in our work, we are certainly not God, for "he does not faint or grow weary" (Isa. 40:28). God alone never needs rest or sleep, for "he who keeps you will not slumber. Behold, he who keeps Israel will neither slumber nor sleep" (Ps. 121:3–4).[6]

Therefore, God gave the people of Israel a regular pattern of six days of work and a seventh day, the Sabbath day, in which they would rest (see Ex. 20:8–11). And God commended the goodness of sleep after a day of work: "Sweet is the sleep of a laborer, whether he eats little or much" (Eccles. 5:12). Therefore, sleep is a gift from God: "He gives to his beloved *sleep*" (Ps. 127:2).

The ability to rest and to sleep sometimes is a matter of being willing to trust God and turn over to him the urgent desire to be successful in the work we are doing. We are not to eat "the bread of anxious toil" (Ps. 127:2).

By contrast, Scripture says that "the wicked" are often unable to rest and be at peace:

> But the wicked are like the tossing sea;
>> for it cannot be quiet,
>> and its waters toss up mire and dirt.
> *"There is no peace," says my God, "for the wicked."* (Isa. 57:20–21)

K. LONGER VACATIONS

Although we are no longer under the old covenant, we can gain some wisdom from observing that God required not only that his people rest from their work one day in seven, but also that they take some longer periods of rest from their work. Every year, they celebrated the Feast of Booths, which lasted seven days (see Lev. 23:34–43), and every seventh year was a Sabbath year, "a Sabbath of solemn rest for the land . . . [when] you shall not sow your field or prune your vineyard, . . . [but] the Sabbath of the land

---

[6] God's rest at the end of the six days of creation (Gen. 2:2) was not from fatigue but signified a completion of his work of creation, along with a delight in the creation that he had made.

shall provide food for you" (25:4–6; see also the instructions about the Jubilee year every 50 years in vv. 8–12).[7]

Therefore, it seems that it is wise from time to time to take longer vacations from work, perhaps a week or two at a time, if possible. (Scripture gives no specific guidance about how long those vacations should be or how often we should take them, and people's decisions in this regard will vary widely according to their situation in life, time of life, financial situation, and the amount of vacation their employers allow. But the principle of taking occasional longer times away from work seems to be a wise one.)

L. RETIREMENT

In modern American society and also in many other nations there is an assumption that the "ideal life" for people is to work until about age 65 (or earlier in Europe) and then retire, and then not work productively for the rest of their lives. This assumption has no basis in Scripture that I can find.

God put us on the earth to work productively and to carry out work that brings benefit to others. Paul wrote that Christians should "do their work quietly and earn their own living" (2 Thess. 3:12), and he did not indicate that there were Christians beyond a certain age who should not be working at all!

Certainly, as people grow older, their physical ability to do work will diminish, and it is normal therefore for people to begin to work fewer hours and perhaps fewer days when they find themselves physically unable to work as much as they did before.

In addition, if people have worked for many years and saved enough money so they do not need to earn any more income, then they can wisely spend some time each week in volunteer work helping other people or helping the work of the church, or in other useful activities. In this way, they may engage in mostly unpaid work, but it will still be a kind of work. There should be joy and a sense of fulfillment in continuing to do some productive work throughout one's life. To make this possible, entire societies, and particularly churches, should provide as many opportunities as possible for people to continue in productive work, both paid and unpaid, as they age.

There are many examples of people who made significant contributions after age 65. Moses led the people of Israel out of Egypt when he was 80 (see Ex. 7:7)! Ronald Reagan became president at age 69, and he began his second term when he was 73.[8] As I write this chapter, Donald Trump has recently won election as president of the United States at age 70.[9]

---

[7] Even Jesus himself, together with his apostles, attempted to take a longer period of time away from ministry, for at one point we read, "And he said to them, 'Come away by yourselves to a desolate place and rest a while.' . . . And they went away in the boat to a desolate place by themselves" (Mark 6:31–32). However, the crowds followed them and Jesus continued to heal (vv. 53–56).

[8] Ronald Reagan was born Feb. 6, 1911, and was 69 at the time of his election in 1980; see http://www.biography.com/people/ronald-reagan-9453198.

[9] Donald Trump was born June 14, 1946; see https://www.biography.com/people/donald-trump-9511238.

Other examples of people over the age of 65 who are active and continue to contribute to society in 2016 include former President Jimmy Carter, who is 92;[10] diplomat and former Secretary of State Henry Kissinger, 93;[11] Queen Elizabeth II, at 90;[12] actor and director Clint Eastwood, 87;[13] famous investor Warren Buffet, 86;[14] and James Dobson, of Family Talk and formerly of Focus on the Family, 81.[15]

Looking back at the past, others who did remarkable work after the age of 65 included John Glenn, who was a U.S. senator until he was 77 and who traveled in space at the same age,[16] and Sir Winston Churchill, who served as British prime minister at 76.[17] Many other examples could be given.

Especially destructive in a society is the idea that older workers who are still productive should retire to "make room" for younger workers to take their jobs. This wrong-headed idea is based on the incorrect assumption that there is a fixed number of jobs in a country, whereas in fact a larger number of workers in the labor force will be able to find jobs in new businesses and in expanding capacities of old businesses (if high government regulations and taxes do not prevent it), so that the total productivity of society will be increased by adding productive workers. This "make room for younger workers" notion wrongly assumes that workers are people who "take jobs" rather than what they really are—valuable parts of the entire labor force who are working productively for the benefit of society.

In addition, when companies or nations adopt mandatory retirement ages that force people out of work when they are still healthy, wise, skilled, mature workers, it significantly harms the productivity of society and results in significant frustration for those who are prohibited from working anymore at a point when they are still highly productive in their jobs. For this reason, it is good when businesses are willing to hire older people for part-time work, because many such people don't want to work as many hours as they formerly did but still need some additional income.

QUESTIONS FOR PERSONAL APPLICATION

1. What kind of work do you do? What do you enjoy about your work? What do you find difficult or unpleasant about your work?
2. Do you regularly think of yourself as pleasing God while you work?

---

[10] Jimmy Carter was born Oct. 1, 1924; see http://www.biography.com/people/jimmy-carter-9240013#!.

[11] Henry Kissinger was born May 17, 1923; see http://www.biography.com/people/henry-kissinger-9366016.

[12] Queen Elizabeth II was born April 21, 1926; see https://www.biography.com/people/queen-elizabeth-ii-9286165.

[13] Clint Eastwood was born May 31, 1930; see http://www.imdb.com/name/nm0000142/.

[14] Warren Buffett was born Aug. 30, 1930; see http://www.biography.com/people/warren-buffett-9230729.

[15] James Dobson was born April 21, 1936; see http://www.imdb.com/name/nm1538867/.

[16] Senator John Glenn was born July 18, 1921. He went into space at the age of 77 on Oct. 29, 1998. See http://www.biography.com/people/john-glenn-9313269.

[17] Sir Winston Churchill was born Nov. 30, 1874. He became prime minister of Great Britain for the second time in October 1951. See http://www.biography.com/people/winston-churchill-9248164#world-war-ii.

3. Do you think you are in a job that God has called you to? Do you think he is calling you to seek a different job in the future?

4. What temptations to sin are you most subject to in your work?

5. Do you enjoy times of rest from work and times of vacation, or do they make you feel vaguely guilty? Do you get enough times of rest from work?

6. What do you think about the idea of retirement? Do you plan to retire someday, and if so, how do you plan to spend your time then?

7. What character traits (see p. 110) would be most helpful in encouraging you to think, act, and feel rightly with respect to work and rest?

SPECIAL TERMS

earned success
sluggard
workaholic

BIBLIOGRAPHY

Sections in Other Ethics Texts

(see complete bibliographical data, p. 64)

> Frame, 540–54
> McQuilkin and Copan, 205–16, 458–61
> Murray, 35–44, 82–106

Other Works

Allison, Gregg R. "Why Are You Here? Heavenly Work vs. Earthly Work." *The Southern Baptist Journal of Theology* 19, no. 2 (2015): 69–80.

Baab, Lynne. *Sabbath Keeping: Finding Freedoms in the Rhythms of Rest.* Downers Grove, IL: InterVarsity Press, 2005.

Colson, Chuck, and Jack Eckerd. *Why America Doesn't Work: How the Decline of the Work Ethic Is Hurting Your Family and Future—and What You Can Do about It.* Dallas: Word, 1991.

Crouch, Andy. *Culture Making: Recovering Our Creative Calling.* Downers Grove, IL: InterVarsity Press, 2008

Field, D. H. "Sabbath." In *New Dictionary of Christian Ethics and Pastoral Theology*, edited by David J. Atkinson and David H. Field, 754–55. Leicester, UK: Inter-Varsity, and Downers Grove, IL: InterVarsity Press, 1995.

Grudem, Wayne. *Business for the Glory of God: The Bible's Teaching on the Moral Goodness of Business.* Wheaton, IL: Crossway, 2003.

Hamilton, James M., Jr. *Work and Our Labor in the Lord*. Short Studies in Biblical Theology. Wheaton, IL: Crossway, 2017.

Hughes, R. Kent. *Disciplines of a Godly Man*. 2nd ed. Wheaton, IL: Crossway, 2001.

Keller, Timothy. *Every Good Endeavor: Connecting Your Work to God's Work*. New York: Dutton, 2012.

Laansma, John C. "Rest." In *New Dictionary of Biblical Theology*, edited by T. Desmond Alexander and Brian S. Rosner, 729–32. Downers Grove, IL: InterVarsity Press, 2000.

Nelson, Tom. *Work Matters: Connecting Sunday Faith to Monday Work*. Wheaton, IL: Crossway, 2011.

Marshall, P. A. "Work." In *New Dictionary of Christian Ethics and Pastoral Theology*, 899–901.

Miller, Darrow L., and Marit Newton. *Lifework: A Biblical Theology for What You Do Every Day*. Seattle: YWAM, 2009.

Packer, J. I. *Finishing Our Course with Joy: Guidance from God for Engaging with Our Aging*. Wheaton, IL: Crossway, 2014.

———. Packer, J. I. "Leisure and Life-Style: Leisure, Pleasure, and Treasure." In *God and Culture: Essays in Honor of Carl F. H. Henry*, edited by D. A. Carson and John D. Woodbridge. Grand Rapids, MI: Eerdmans, 1993.

Piper, John. "Don't Waste Your Life." In *The Collected Works of John Piper*, edited by David Mathis and Justin Taylor, vol. 5, 385–534. Wheaton, IL: Crossway, 2017.

———. *Rethinking Retirement: Finishing Life for the Glory of Christ*. Wheaton, IL: Crossway, 2008.

Ryken, Leland. *Redeeming the Time: A Christian Approach to Work and Leisure*. Grand Rapids, MI: Baker, 1995.

Traeger, Sebastian. *The Gospel at Work: How Working for King Jesus Gives Purpose and Meaning to Our Jobs*. Grand Rapids, MI: Zondervan, 2013.

Veith, Gene Edward. *God at Work: Your Christian Vocation in All of Life*. Focal Point Series. Wheaton, IL: Crossway, 2002.

Whelchel, Hugh. *How Then Should We Work? Rediscovering the Biblical Doctrine of Work*. Bloomington, IN: WestBow, 2012.

Wittmer, Michael E. *Heaven Is a Place on Earth: Why Everything You Do Matters to God*. Grand Rapids, MI: Zondervan, 2004.

SCRIPTURE MEMORY PASSAGE

Proverbs 14:23: In all toil there is profit, but mere talk tends only to poverty.

HYMN

"Work, for the Night Is Coming"

Work, for the night is coming, work thru the morning hours;
Work while the dew is sparkling, work 'mid springing flow'rs.

Work when the day grows brighter, work in the glowing sun;
Work, for the night is coming, when man's work is done.

Work, for the night is coming, work thru the sunny noon;
Fill brightest hours with labor—rest comes sure and soon.
Give ev'ry flying minute something to keep in store;
Work, for the night is coming, when man works no more.

Work, for the night is coming, under the sunset skies:
While their bright tints are glowing, work, for daylight flies.
Work till the last beam fadeth, fadeth to shine no more;
Work, while the night is dark'ning, when man's work is o'er.

ANNIE L. COGHILL, 1836–1907

Chapter 36

INCREASING PROSPERITY: IS MORE PROSPERITY A GOOD THING?

Is poverty more pleasing to God than prosperity?

Did God intend human beings to continue inventing and developing new and better products?

How can we guard against materialism?

Why has the influence of the Bible led to increased material prosperity in many nations?

In the previous two chapters I argued that God established private ownership of property among human beings and wants us to exercise faithful stewardship of what we own (chap. 34), and that he wants us to work faithfully in producing goods from the earth for our benefit (chap. 35). But what will happen to the goods that we produce? Some of them we will consume (such as the food we grow), but some of them will last for a long time (such as the houses and factories that we construct, the cars and trucks that we manufacture, the books that we write, the musical instruments that we make, and thousands of other things).[1]

Therefore, people who work faithfully and steward their property carefully will often

---

[1] Portions of this chapter are adapted from Wayne Grudem and Barry Asmus, *The Poverty of Nations: A Sustainable Solution* (Wheaton, IL: Crossway, 2013), with permission of the publisher.

come to own an increasing amount of possessions. Eventually entire societies and whole nations will grow more and more prosperous. But *is it a morally good thing to continually increase people's material prosperity?* (For purposes of this chapter, I will define prosperity as the accumulation and enjoyment of significantly more material wealth than previous generations.) The question of the moral right or wrong of increasing prosperity is the topic of this chapter.

A. IS POVERTY MORE PLEASING TO GOD THAN PROSPERITY?

Over the last five centuries, and especially over the last 100 years, many nations of the world have experienced an astounding increase in material prosperity that is unlike anything seen before in the history of the world. It is easy to forget that, for thousands of years, no one in the world had automobiles; telephones; radios; televisions; computers; running water; indoor plumbing; electrical lighting; thermostatically controlled home furnaces and air conditioners; antibiotics; grocery stores offering thousands of different food items including fresh fruits and vegetables every day of the year; access to travel anywhere in the world by automobile, train, or airplane; and an almost infinite variety of choices for clothing and other kinds of consumer goods.

Economist J. Bradford DeLong of the University of California-Berkeley published an estimate of the total annual economic value of goods and services produced in the world throughout the history of the human race.[2] His estimates show both the gross world product (the value of all goods produced in the whole world) and also the value of goods produced per person each year. Here are some of his estimates:

Year	Gross World Product Per Year (in billions of U.S. dollars)*	Gross World Product Per Person (in U.S. dollars)
2000 BC	3.02	112
1000 BC	6.35	127
AD 1	18.50	109
500	19.92	102
1000	35.31	133
1500	58.67	138
1600	77.01	141

---

[2] J. Bradford DeLong, "Estimating World GDP, One Million B.C.–Present," http://holtz.org/Library/Social%20 Science/Economics/Estimating%20World%20GDP%20by%20DeLong/Estimating%20World%20GDP.htm.

Year	Gross World Product Per Year (in billions of U.S. dollars)*	Gross World Product Per Person (in U.S. dollars)
1700	99.80	164
1800	175.24	195
1850	359.90	300
1900	1,102.96	679
1920	1,733.67	956
1940	3,001.36	1,356
1960	6,855.25	2,270
1970	12,137.94	3,282
1980	18,818.46	4,231
1990	27,539.57	5,204
2000	41,016.69	6,539

* DeLong's figures are purchasing power parity (PPP) estimates that are standardized according to their value in 1990 U.S. dollars.

Table 36.1. Gross World Product, 2000 BC to AD 2000

According to this estimate, by the year 2000 human beings were producing, on average, a level of economic prosperity that was about 60 times greater per person than what was produced at the time of Christ (comparing $109 to $6,539).[3] This increase in gross world product per person has continued since 2000.[4] Although every nation of the world has experienced a measure of economic development, some nations have attained much higher levels of prosperity than others. The long-term trend of economic growth continues in most countries.[5]

[3] Sadly, millions of people have not received much economic benefit from this world increase in prosperity, because many nations of the world remain trapped in poverty. But the path to economic development that has been followed by wealthy nations, combined with biblical teachings and sound economic analysis, shows that there are workable solutions to poverty in all nations of the world. Economist Barry Asmus and I coauthored a book devoted to solutions to world poverty based on biblical principles: see Wayne Grudem and Barry Asmus, *The Poverty of Nations: A Sustainable Solution* (Wheaton, IL: Crossway, 2013). See also chap. 37 (p. 958) on economic issues related to wealth and poverty.

[4] Gross world product per capita (PPP) was $15,700 in 2015, according to the World Factbook of the Central Intelligence Agency (https://www.cia.gov/library/publications/the-world-factbook/geos/xx.html), but this number is not standardized to 1990 U.S. dollars, so it is not comparable to the numbers in DeLong's study. If I adjusted $15,700 for inflation, it would equal $8,658 in 1990 U.S. dollars.

[5] For a fascinating 4.5-minute video tracing the economic and health development of every nation of the world over the last 200 years, see the visualization produced by Swedish professor Hans Rosling, "200 Years That Changed the World," Gapminder, http://www.gapminder.org/videos/200-years-that-changed-the-world/.

Is this incredible economic development a good thing? Should we thank God for it? Or should we view it as the evil result of ungodly materialism and greed? Doesn't ever-increasing prosperity seem to be in tension with the teachings of Jesus, who said, "Blessed are you who are poor, for yours is the kingdom of God" (Luke 6:20)? And even if such economic development has been good up to this point, isn't it time that the wealthy nations of the world finally said, "Enough!" and decided to be content with what they now have?

I will argue in this chapter that this ongoing historic development of material prosperity is fundamentally a good thing that God intended for the human race, something that will most likely continue indefinitely (until Christ returns and even beyond that time), and something for which we should thank God. But I will also warn that prosperity carries with it significant temptations to sin.

B. MATERIAL PROSPERITY IS A MATTER OF SECONDARY IMPORTANCE, AND IT CARRIES DANGERS

Before considering what ethical evaluation we should attach to increasing economic prosperity, it is important to consider this topic in the light of the teaching of the Bible about what is most important in life. Scripture gives frequent warnings that a person's relationship with God is far more important than material prosperity, and that the pursuit of material wealth can, in fact, very easily take first place in one's life rather than a relationship with God.

Jesus was quite blunt: "No servant can serve two masters, for either he will hate the one and love the other, or he will be devoted to the one and despise the other. *You cannot serve God and money*" (Luke 16:13). He also said, "What does it profit a man if he gains the whole world and loses or forfeits himself?" (9:25). And he told a parable about a rich man who decided to build bigger barns for all of his wealth: "But God said to him, 'Fool! This night your soul is required of you, and the things you have prepared, whose will they be?'" Then Jesus added, "So is the one who lays up treasure for himself and is not rich toward God" (12:20–21). He also said in this context, "One's life does not consist in the abundance of his possessions" (v. 15). And he emphasized how easy it is for wealthy people to fail to recognize their need for God: "Again I tell you, it is easier for a camel to go through the eye of a needle than for a rich person to enter the kingdom of God" (Matt. 19:24).

This is why the Bible warns that those who obtain some measure of financial prosperity in this life should set their hearts on God, not on their wealth:

> As for the rich in this present age, charge them not to be haughty, *nor to set their hopes on the uncertainty of riches, but on God,* who richly provides us with everything to enjoy. They are to do good, to be rich in good works, to be generous and

ready to share, thus storing up treasure for themselves as a good foundation for the future, so that they may take hold of that which is truly life. (1 Tim. 6:17–19)

Relationships with family members, friends, and other people are also more important than material prosperity. The fifth commandment says, "Honor your father and your mother" (Ex. 20:12). Here God establishes and protects the importance of maintaining strong relationships that include honor and respect within a family. Other Bible passages give instructions on how to maintain healthy marriages and how parents should care for and discipline their children (see Eph. 5:22–6:4; Col. 3:18–21). In addition, Jesus said that the second greatest commandment is "You shall love your neighbor as yourself" (Matt. 22:39). Therefore, relationships with other people, and particularly relationships with one's family members, are of great importance to God. Without such relationships, what benefit is there in amassing more and more personal wealth?

This is why greater economic productivity, while a good thing in itself, also brings significant temptations. The pursuit of greater prosperity can easily become a person's ultimate good, and then greed, selfishness, bitterness, and frustration will increasingly characterize his or her life. Family relationships and friendships will be destroyed in the quest for ever more material prosperity. But this relentless quest for wealth can never satisfy, for by itself it will leave a person isolated from others, with no one with whom to enjoy his prosperity, and alienated from God.

However, it is certainly possible for an individual or even an entire society to increase in material prosperity *while also maintaining a positive emphasis on healthy relationships with God and with other people.* There are many individuals in wealthy countries who are notable exceptions to Western patterns of ungodly materialism and excessive individualism, and their strong love for God and strong family lives testify to the fact that it is possible even for wealthier persons with highly productive jobs also to give significant attention to personal faith and to family and friends. They have not forgotten the words of Jesus, "You cannot serve God and money" (Luke 16:13).

C. THE BIBLE PRESENTS A POSITIVE VIEW OF INCREASING ECONOMIC PROSPERITY

As I explained in chapter 34, the Bible contains significant teachings that encourage human beings to create things of value from the resources of the earth. The idea of creating profitable and useful products from the earth began with God's command to Adam and Eve: "Be fruitful and multiply and fill the earth and *subdue it,* and have dominion over the fish of the sea and over the birds of the heavens and over every living thing that moves on the earth" (Gen. 1:28), a command implying that Adam and Eve were to make the resources of the earth useful for their own benefit and enjoyment (see chap. 34, p. 904).

This means that God intended Adam and Eve to explore the earth and learn to create products from the abundant resources that he had put in it. It was God's purpose for Adam and Eve, as they followed this command, to discover and develop agricultural products; to domesticate animals; and then create housing, works of craftsmanship and beauty, and eventually buildings, means of transportation, and inventions of various kinds.[6] This is the process that ultimately resulted in the creation of computers and cell phones, modern houses and office buildings, and automobiles and airplanes. All of this is what God wanted Adam and Eve and their offspring to produce when he told them to "subdue" the earth.

The idea that Adam and Eve would make useful products from the earth is also implied by the verse that says that God "took the man and put him in the garden of Eden *to work it* and keep it" (Gen. 2:15). As Adam worked in the garden, and Eve alongside him, they would discover and develop useful products from the earth.

This ability to create is unique to the human race (as I explained in chap. 34, p. 905) and is part of what it means that God made us "in his own image" (Gen. 1:27). He created us to be like him and to imitate him in many ways. That is why Paul can say, "Be imitators of God, as beloved children" (Eph. 5:1). God is pleased when he sees us imitating his creativity by creating goods and services from the resources of the earth.

Therefore, God's ideal for us is not that we live in caves and barely survive on a subsistence diet of nuts and berries, but rather that we discover and develop the abundant resources that he has placed in the earth for our benefit and enjoyment. Paul says that God is the One "who richly provides us with everything to enjoy" (1 Tim. 6:17).

Another reason God is pleased when we create goods and services is seen in Jesus's command "You shall love your neighbor as yourself" (Matt. 22:39). The woman who creates a shirt that someone wears and treasures, the man who creates a pair of shoes that someone wears and enjoys, and the teacher who genuinely helps her children learn can do all this with an attitude of love for their neighbors—that is, seeking to bring benefit to other people. In this way, creating goods and services for others is one way of obeying Jesus's command to love our neighbor as ourselves.

One example from the Old Testament is the description of an "excellent wife" in Proverbs 31:10–31: This woman is productive, for "she seeks wool and flax, and works with willing hands" (v. 13). She produces valuable products: "She makes linen garments and sells them; she delivers sashes to the merchant" (v. 24). She produces agricultural products from the earth, because "with the fruit of her hands she plants a vineyard" (v. 16). She sells products in the marketplace, because "she perceives that her merchandise is profitable" (v. 18).[7] Through all this creative economic activity, this woman increases the total economic output of Israel in each given year.

Jesus also gave us an example of such productivity, for he worked about 15 years as a "carpenter" (Mark 6:3). The apostle Paul supported himself by working as a tentmaker

---

[6] Darrow L. Miller and Stan Guthrie, *Discipling Nations: The Power of Truth to Transform Cultures* (Seattle: YWAM, 1998), 221–37, has an excellent discussion of the wonder of human creativity as a key part of responsible stewardship in obedience to God.

[7] The CSB translates this verse as, "She sees that *her profits are good*"; this is also a legitimate translation, because the Hebrew term *saḥar* can refer to profit or gain from merchandise.

(Acts 18:3; 2 Thess. 3:7–10). Peter and some of the other disciples worked as fisherman (Matt. 4:18); they did not actually "create" fish (only God can do that), but they caught them from the sea and brought them to a market, where they were sold as useful food products for others to eat.

Paul also told the early Christians that they should work with their hands, implying that he wanted them to continually create goods and services that were of value to other people:

> Let the thief no longer steal, but rather *let him labor, doing honest work with his own hands*, so that he may have something to share with anyone in need. (Eph. 4:28)

> Aspire to live quietly, and to mind your own affairs, *and to work with your hands*, as we instructed you. (1 Thess. 4:11)

> For even when we were with you, we would give you this command: *If anyone is not willing to work, let him not eat.* (2 Thess. 3:10)

In the new heaven and new earth, it seems that the nations of the world will continue to produce goods and services for others, perhaps products that are unique to each nation. This would follow a well-established historical pattern whereby the kings of various nations would send abundant products as tribute or as gifts to other nations (see 2 Chron. 9:9, 10, 24, 28). It is said of the New Jerusalem: "the kings of the earth will bring their glory into it. . . . They will bring into it the glory and honor of the nations" (Rev. 21:24–26).

D. GOD GAVE HUMAN BEINGS AN INNATE DESIRE TO CREATE MORE AND BETTER ECONOMIC GOODS

As I indicated in chapter 34 (p. 906), God gave human beings not only a command to "subdue" the earth (Gen. 1:28), but also an innate *desire* to fulfill that command.[8] This is the reason why human beings have a deep, instinctive drive to create useful products from the earth. This drive is amazingly powerful, and it is *unlimited*. Rabbits and squirrels, birds and deer are content to live in the same kinds of homes and eat the same kinds of food for thousands of generations. But human beings are different—we have an innate desire to explore, to discover, to understand, to invent, to create, to produce, and then to *enjoy* the products that can be made from the earth. This drive to subdue the earth has never been satisfied throughout the entire history of mankind. This is because God created us not merely to *survive* on the earth but to *flourish*.

God has created us with very *limited needs* for our physical survival (if we have a

---

[8] Parts of this section have been taken from Wayne Grudem, "The Eighth Commandment as the Moral Foundation for Property Rights, Human Flourishing, and Careers in Business," *Themelios* 41 (2016): 76–87, with permission of the publisher.

minimal amount of food, clothing, and shelter, we can survive on a desert island or in a horrible prison camp). But he has also created us with *unlimited wants for new and improved products.*

To take a simple example, think of cell phones. For many thousands of years, human beings did not know that they wanted cell phones, because such things did not exist. But now that they exist and are affordable, everybody seems to want one. They are both useful and enjoyable. Paul says that God "richly provides us with *everything* to enjoy" (1 Tim. 6:17), and I think "everything" today includes cell phones.

The same thing can be said about electric light bulbs, plastic water bottles, gas furnaces, air conditioners, automobiles, computers, and airplane travel. For thousands of years, human beings did not know that they wanted these things, because nobody knew they could be made. But human achievement continues to progress, and thereby human beings give more and more evidence of the glory of our creation in the image of God. With such inventions we demonstrate creativity, wisdom, knowledge, skill in use of resources, care for others who are distant (through the use of a telephone or email system), and many other Godlike qualities. We should enjoy these inventions and give thanks to God for them. This is part of God's purpose for us on the earth.

E. WARNINGS ABOUT THE TEMPTATIONS OF MATERIALISM MUST BE TAKEN SERIOUSLY, BUT THEY SHOULD NOT CAUSE US TO ABANDON THE BLESSINGS OF INCREASED PROSPERITY

Every situation of life carries unique temptations, and that is certainly the case with material prosperity. If people increase in material prosperity, they must beware that it should never become their highest goal, nor should they begin to think that material prosperity can provide lasting happiness or rewarding fellowship with God. This is taught repeatedly in the Bible:

> He who loves money will not be satisfied with money, nor he who loves wealth with his income; this also is vanity. (Eccles. 5:10)

> For what will it profit a man if he gains the whole world and forfeits his soul? Or what shall a man give in return for his soul? (Matt. 16:26)

> You cannot serve God and money. (Luke 16:13)

The abundant productivity of modern wealthy economies provides strong temptations to greed, materialism, and insensitivity to the needs of others. God warned the people of Israel through Moses that when he blessed them with material prosperity, there would be greater temptations to be proud and to forget about God and his commands (see Deut. 8:11–18, quoted below).

Another temptation is to fall prey to the deceptive message of the so-called "prosperity gospel" preachers who declare that if you have enough faith, God will make you wealthy. As I explained in chapter 34 (see p. 908), I strongly disagree with this viewpoint. Jesus was poor and Paul was poor, and Peter said, "I have no silver and gold, but what I do have I give to you" when he healed the man lame from birth (Acts 3:6). And James said, "Has not God chosen those who are *poor in the world* to be *rich in faith* and heirs of the kingdom, which he has promised to those who love him?" (James 2:5). Therefore, I must emphasize that it is contrary to Scripture to say that if you are a faithful Christian God will make you rich. Often he will not.

Yet another temptation is to fall into a trap of continual coveting, never being satisfied with what one has. While it is not wrong for people to work hard and attempt to be successful in their occupations (this will often result in increased individual prosperity), Scripture also tells us in several places that we are not to long to be rich but to be content with what we have:

> But godliness *with contentment* is great gain, for we brought nothing into the world, and we cannot take anything out of the world. But if we have food and clothing, with these we will be *content*. But *those who desire to be rich fall into temptation*, into a snare, into many senseless and harmful desires that plunge people into ruin and destruction. For the love of money is a root of all kinds of evils. It is through this craving that some have wandered away from the faith and pierced themselves with many pangs. (1 Tim. 6:6–10)

> Keep your life free from love of money, and *be content with what you have*, for he has said, "I will never leave you nor forsake you." (Heb. 13:5; see also Luke 3:14; Phil. 4:11)

There are also other temptations that come with modern prosperity. The increased labor mobility that comes with prosperity carries with it temptations to neglect or break important ties of family and community interaction, and to live isolated lives in which it is easier to violate long-established moral standards. The lure of ever-higher salaries can lead to a workaholic mentality that distorts every other part of life. The abundance of material things can make people feel self-sufficient, insensitive to their need for God. And the temptations of wealth can turn people's hearts from God. The apostle Paul said, "Those who desire to be rich fall into temptation, into a snare, into many senseless and harmful desires that plunge people into ruin and destruction" (1 Tim. 6:9; cf. Luke 16:13). Increasing wealth can easily lead to wasteful, excessive spending on luxuries and gaudy trinkets while neglecting the desperate needs of those in poverty. The apostle James was unsparing in his condemnation of the self-indulgent rich:

> Come now, you rich, weep and howl for the miseries that are coming upon you. Your riches have rotted and your garments are moth-eaten. Your gold

and silver have corroded, and their corrosion will be evidence against you and will eat your flesh like fire. You have laid up treasure in the last days. . . . You have lived on the earth in luxury and in self-indulgence. You have fattened your hearts in a day of slaughter. (James 5:1–5)

In addition, when a wealthy society provides freedom of opportunity for people, some people choose to use that freedom badly, in ways that harm others and dishonor God.

However, it is important to remember that these evils are not *caused* by increased prosperity, but are *temptations* that come along with the prosperity, and we need to guard against them. They are best countered not by returning to poverty (which is not God's intention for human beings), but by strong moral examples and teachings that show how people can resist these temptations. This is something that churches are especially well-equipped to do.

Regarding the temptations that come with the blessings of prosperity, God did not tell the people of Israel that they should seek to return to poverty, but warned them to guard their hearts:

Take care lest you forget the LORD your God by not keeping his commandments and his rules and his statutes, which I command you today, lest, when you have eaten and are full and have built good houses and live in them, and when your herds and flocks multiply and your silver and gold is multiplied and all that you have is multiplied, then your heart be lifted up, and you forget the LORD your God, who brought you out of the land of Egypt, out of the house of slavery, who led you through the great and terrifying wilderness, with its fiery serpents and scorpions and thirsty ground where there was no water, who brought you water out of the flinty rock, who fed you in the wilderness with manna that your fathers did not know, that he might humble you and test you, to do you good in the end. Beware lest you say in your heart, "My power and the might of my hand have gotten me this wealth." *You shall remember the LORD your God*, for it is he who gives you power to get wealth. (Deut. 8:11–18)

If all this is true, then why do we need more "stuff"? Because increased productivity and prosperity are not in themselves evil. They are morally good, and they provide another way we can glorify God.

Plants and animals show a measure of God's glory by merely surviving and repeating the same activities for thousands of years, while human beings glorify God by *achieving* much more than mere survival. We glorify him by understanding and ruling over the creation, and then producing more and more wonderful goods from it for our enjoyment, with thanksgiving to God. "Everything created by God is good, and nothing is to be rejected if it is received with thanksgiving, for it is made holy by the word of God and prayer" (1 Tim. 4:4). The commandment "You shall not steal" (Ex. 20:15), together with the entire Bible's teachings on stewardship, implies that God created us not merely to survive but to achieve much and to flourish on the earth.

God gives us these various stewardship responsibilities so that through them we have unlimited potential for glorifying him through discovery, creation, production, distribution, and use of potentially limitless material and intellectual resources. All these are good things (though they can be distorted and misused by sin) and it is right for us to pursue them, with gratitude to our wise Creator for making such an excellent, resourceful earth and giving us the wisdom to develop its resources and flourish as we live on it.

Many Christians in wealthy nations today have discovered with joy that they have an incredible opportunity to use their wealth with great effectiveness in advancing the work of the kingdom of God in thousands of ways in hundreds of nations throughout the earth. In addition, wealthy non-Christians, by God's common grace, can and do provide financial support to help people throughout the world through a variety of philanthropic activities advancing education, medical care, agricultural productivity, and other beneficial projects. In these ways, the wealth in today's prosperous nations can be used and is being used to do much good in the world.

F. POVERTY CAN ONLY BE SOLVED BY INCREASED PROSPERITY, NOT BY ATTEMPTING TO COMPEL EQUALITY

As I will argue more extensively in chapter 37,[9] the challenging problems of persistent poverty in poor nations can never be solved by government policies that attempt to penalize the rich merely because they are rich in order to reduce economic "inequality" in a nation. This is because the problem is not that some people in a nation are wealthy. The problem is that many people in that nation are poor, and the only solution to this poverty will come through increased economic productivity—the production of more goods and services of value—in the entire nation. In other words, poverty can be solved only when nations adopt *productive* economic systems.

When a society does this, it moves from poverty to increased prosperity, providing immense advantages to the poor, the powerless, and the dispossessed in that society. Daron Acemoglu and James A. Robinson remind us of the incredible differences in the lives of people in rich countries and very poor ones:

> In rich countries, individuals are healthier, live longer, and are much better educated. They also have access to a range of amenities and options in life, from vacations to career paths, that people in poor countries can only dream of. People in rich countries also drive on roads without potholes, and enjoy toilets, electricity, and running water in their houses. They also typically have governments that do not arbitrarily arrest or harass them; on the contrary, the governments provide services, including education, health care, roads, and law

---

[9] See also Grudem and Asmus, *The Poverty of Nations.*

and order. Notable, too, is the fact that the citizens vote in elections and have some voice in the political direction their countries take. The great differences in world inequality are evident to everyone, even to those in poor countries.[10]

We dare not abandon the hope of the poor for increased prosperity because of an excessive, paralyzing fear of increased materialism.

G. THE INFLUENCE OF THE BIBLE HAS HISTORICALLY BROUGHT INCREASING PROSPERITY TO NATIONS

Historically, in the nations of the world where the Bible has been the main influence on people's moral values, poverty is less common. People in these nations have more income, which enables them to be healthier and better educated, take better care of the environment, and have more choices as to where they work, where they live, and where they travel.

Several studies have shown the positive effect of biblical beliefs on economic development. For example, Lawrence Harrison of Tufts University analyzed 117 nations that (1) had over a million people and (2) had one clear "majority religion" (that is, where over half of the population identified with a major world religion).

Harrison found a clear relationship between the dominant religious background of a nation and how rich or poor the average person was in each country. Here are the results from Harrison's study:[11]

Dominant Religious Background in the Nation	Gross Domestic Product (GDP) Per Capita
Protestant	$29,784
Jewish	$19,320
Roman Catholic	$9,358
Orthodox	$7,045
Confucian	$6,691
Buddhist	$4,813
Islamic	$3,142

Table 36.2. A Nation's Religious Background and Its Prosperity

---

[10] Daron Acemoglu and James A. Robinson, *Why Nations Fail: The Origins of Power, Prosperity and Poverty* (New York: Crown, 2012), 40–41.

[11] Lawrence E. Harrison, *The Central Liberal Truth: How Politics Can Change a Culture and Save It from Itself* (Oxford: Oxford University Press, 2006), 88–89.

In this chart, the top four categories are Protestant, Jewish, Roman Catholic, and Orthodox. Those religious groups all have historically taken their teachings from the Bible.

Then why are there some differences among Bible-based groups? In the past, Protestant and Jewish groups placed more emphasis on individual people reading the teachings of the Bible for themselves rather than just being taught by a pastor or priest. (But Roman Catholic leaders and some Orthodox leaders today also encourage people to read the Bible for themselves.) This was important, because people who valued individual Bible reading placed more emphasis on teaching both boys and girls to read, and as a result, year after year, more people in those countries were able to read. This enabled widespread education, which in turn enabled people to have more complex jobs, invent more, and earn more income.

Other studies have reached similar conclusions. Professor David Landes of Harvard, an expert on the history of economic development around the world, concluded that the Protestant emphasis on the Bible's teachings made all the difference in the increasing prosperity of Northern Europe and North America from 1770 to the present time. Landes says, "The heart of the matter lay indeed in the making of a new kind of man—rational, ordered, diligent, productive. These virtues, while not new, were hardly commonplace. Protestantism generalized them among its adherents."[12]

Of course, the teachings of the Bible also had some influence in countries where Jewish, Roman Catholic, and Orthodox beliefs were common. This made them different from Confucian, Buddhist, Islamic, and Hindu countries.

What were the beliefs taught in the Bible that made such a difference in these nations? These beliefs included the promotion of several life habits that contribute to economic development:

1. Being able to read (Ps. 1:2)
2. Pursuing one's job as a calling from God because one is working "as for the Lord and not for men" (Col. 3:23)
3. Being honest and diligent at work (Prov. 10:4; 18:9)
4. Treating employees fairly (Col. 4:1)
5. Being thrifty with money, which people have as a stewardship entrusted to them from God (Matt. 25:14–30)
6. Not being greedy or swindlers (Lev. 19:13; Prov. 16:11; 20:10; 1 Cor. 6:10)
7. Using time well, or "making the best use of the time" (Eph. 5:16)
8. Viewing the creation and production of goods from the earth as a calling from God (Gen. 1:28)
9. Using resources joyfully and with thanksgiving, because the Bible teaches that God "richly provides us with everything to enjoy" (1 Tim. 6:17)

[12] David S. Landes, *The Wealth and Poverty of Nations: Why Some Are So Rich and Some So Poor* (New York: W. W. Norton, 1999), 177.

10. Investigating nature rationally and not being superstitious, because God made an orderly world that reflects his wisdom, and therefore it is subject to rational investigation (Ps. 104:24)
11. Remembering that all people are accountable to God for their actions: "The eyes of the LORD are in every place, keeping watch on the evil and the good" (Prov. 15:3; also 1 Pet. 4:5)

These beliefs led to diligent, creative workers, and to continuing investigation and creation of new products from the resources of the earth.

Finally, two more biblical values are crucially important to economic growth. It is important to discuss these two values in more detail:

12. Not lying (Ex. 20:16)
13. Not stealing (Ex. 20:15)

Truthfulness (not lying) is important because most business transactions depend on trust. A businessperson has to trust that a supplier will deliver a product on the date that he specified, and that the product will have the agreed quality and specifications. The supplier has to trust that the buyer will pay for the product when he promised to do so. When buyers and sellers are in the habit of telling the truth and keeping their word, business transactions run smoothly and the economy functions efficiently. When a business is building a highly complex product (such as an airplane or automobile), there can be hundreds or even thousands of suppliers and workers on which the company depends in order to make a quality product in a timely manner. The issue of trust is influenced by the Bible, because Harrison's study also found significantly higher levels of trust and lower levels of corruption in countries most influenced by the Bible.[13]

But if a culture tolerates lying and breaking one's word, then the entire economic system begins to break down. Products are not delivered on time. Needed parts come in the wrong sizes or do not meet quality standards. Invoices and accounting reports are falsified so that companies no longer have an accurate picture of their inventories or costs of goods. Additional time-wasting procedures have to be built in to check and double-check the accuracy of every report. Economic productivity begins a rapid downward spiral. Therefore, it is not surprising that economic development expert William Easterly of New York University reports that cultures with high levels of trust have higher per capita incomes, and cultures with lower levels of trust have significantly lower per capita incomes.[14]

The Bible opposes such a breakdown in trust in a culture by upholding a high standard of truthfulness in speech. It says, "You shall not bear false witness against your neighbor" (Ex. 20:16) and "Do not lie to one another" (Col. 3:9). A society that honors these commands will value and expect truthfulness.

---

[13] Harrison, *The Central Liberal Truth*, 93.

[14] William Easterly, *The White Man's Burden: Why the West's Efforts to Aid the Rest Have Done So Much Ill and So Little Good* (New York: Penguin, 2006), 79–81.

A belief that it is wrong to steal is also crucially important. The idea of not stealing assumes the moral goodness of people owning property that is their own. Not only does the Bible command, "You shall not *steal*" (Ex. 20:15), but it also prohibits even the *desire* to steal, for it says, "You shall not *covet* your neighbor's house; you shall not *covet* your neighbor's wife, or his male servant, or his female servant, or his ox, or his donkey, or anything that is your neighbor's" (v. 17).

But in countries where stealing is just accepted and people's property is not respected, this tends to destroy incentives for people to work harder and earn more. This is because what a person earns or buys might suddenly be taken away from him by someone else who thinks he "needs" it more. A culture of stealing also tends to prevent anyone from lending money to others—there is no certainty of being repaid. In addition, it discourages employment because an employer cannot trust an employee to deal honestly with any funds that are entrusted to him. Therefore, the employer has to perform many routine transactions and errands himself, when his time could better be spent in more productive activities. All of these problems hinder the economic growth of a nation. A strong cultural conviction that stealing is morally wrong is crucial to the economic growth of a country.

It should not be surprising, therefore, that in nations that have been more strongly influenced by the Bible and have held to the positive values discussed above, greater economic growth in nation after nation has been the result. History shows that nations that follow biblical moral standards do much better than nations that do not, especially in terms of reducing poverty and increasing prosperity for people in the nation.

For a more extensive discussion of issues of wealth and poverty, see chapter 37.

QUESTIONS FOR PERSONAL APPLICATION

1. Do you think the increase in material prosperity in the world in the last 200 years has been mostly a good thing or mostly a harmful thing? Do you think it is what God intended for human beings on the earth?
2. Do you think that human beings in wealthy nations now have enough, and they should stop seeking to produce even more prosperity each year? What do you think God would have people in wealthy nations do going forward?
3. Jesus tells us to pray, "Your kingdom come, your will be done, on earth as it is in heaven" (Matt. 6:10). In your own city and in your own neighborhood, what would it look like, in terms of material prosperity, for God's kingdom to come into more full realization and God's will to be done more fully, "as it is in heaven"?
4. Have you found your personal relationship with God to be more healthy in times of greater financial scarcity or in times of greater financial prosperity? How do you think the apostle Paul dealt with such situations (see Phil. 4:12)?

5. What character traits (see p. 110) are especially helpful in encouraging entire societies and nations to move from poverty toward greater prosperity?

6. What character traits (see p. 110) are especially helpful in enabling people to avoid the temptations that always come with increasing prosperity?

SPECIAL TERMS

gross world product
prosperity

BIBLIOGRAPHY

Sections in Other Ethics Texts

(see complete bibliographical data, p. 64)

Frame, 590–92
McQuilkin and Copan, 471–79
Rae, 331–33

Other Works

Acemoglu, Daron, and James A. Robinson. *Why Nations Fail: The Origins of Power, Prosperity, and Poverty*. New York: Crown, 2012.

Alcorn, Randy. *Managing God's Money: A Biblical Guide*. Carol Stream, IL: Tyndale, 2011

———. *Money, Possessions, and Eternity*. 2nd ed. Wheaton, IL: Tyndale, 2003.

———. *The Treasure Principle: Unlocking the Secret of Joyful Giving*. Lifechange Books. Sisters, OR: Multnomah, 2001.

Beisner, E. Calvin. *Prosperity and Poverty : The Compassionate Use of Resources in A World of Scarcity*. Westchester, IL: Crossway Books, 1988.

Blomberg, Craig L. *Neither Poverty nor Riches: A Biblical Theology of Possessions*. New Studies in Biblical Theology 7. Downers Grove, IL: InterVarsity Press, 1999.

Blomberg, Craig L. *Christians in an Age of Wealth: A Biblical Theology of Stewardship*. Biblical Theology for Life. Grand Rapids, MI: Zondervan, 2013.

Forster, G. S. "Property." In *New Dictionary of Christian Ethics and Pastoral Theology*, edited by David J. Atkinson and David H. Field, 696–97. Leicester, UK: Inter-Varsity, and Downers Grove, IL: InterVarsity Press, 1995.

Grudem, Wayne. *Business for the Glory of God: The Bible's Teaching on the Moral Goodness of Business*. Wheaton, IL: Crossway, 2003.

Grudem, Wayne, and Barry Asmus. *The Poverty of Nations: A Sustainable Solution.* Wheaton, IL: Crossway, 2013.

Harrison, Lawrence E. *The Central Liberal Truth: How Politics Can Change a Culture and Save It from Itself.* Oxford: Oxford University Press, 2006.

Kotter, David. "Greed vs. Self-Interest: A Case Study of How Economists Can Help Theologians Serve the Church." *The Southern Baptist Journal of Theology* 19, no. 2 (2015): 17–47.

Landes, David S. *The Wealth and Poverty of Nations: Why Some Are So Rich and Some So Poor.* New York: W. W. Norton, 1999.

Mahaney, C. J., ed. *Worldliness: Resisting the Seduction of a Fallen World.* Wheaton, IL: Crossway, 2008.

Miller, Darrow L., and Stan Guthrie. *Discipling Nations: The Power of Truth to Transform Cultures.* 2nd ed. Seattle: YWAM Publishing, 2001.

Piper, John. *Desiring God: Meditations of a Christian Hedonist.* Colorado Springs: Multnomah, 2011.

Richards, Jay W. *Money, Greed, and God: Why Capitalism Is the Solution and Not the Problem.* New York: HarperOne, 2009.

Rigney, Joe. *The Things of Earth: Treasuring God by Enjoying His Gifts.* Wheaton, IL: Crossway, 2015.

Schneider, John R. *Godly Materialism: Rethinking Money and Possessions.* Downers Grove, IL: InterVarsity Press, 1994.

Sowell, Thomas. *Basic Economics: A Common Sense Guide to the Economy.* 4th ed. New York: Basic Books, 2011.

Verbrugge, Verlyn D., and Keith R. Krell. *Paul and Money: A Biblical and Theological Analysis of the Apostle's Teachings and Practices.* Grand Rapids, MI: Zondervan, 2015.

Whitney, Donald S. *Spiritual Disciplines for the Christian Life.* 2nd ed. Colorado Springs: NavPress, 2014.

SCRIPTURE MEMORY PASSAGE

1 Timothy 6:17–19: As for the rich in this present age, charge them not to be haughty, nor to set their hopes on the uncertainty of riches, but on God, who richly provides us with everything to enjoy. They are to do good, to be rich in good works, to be generous and ready to share, thus storing up treasure for themselves as a good foundation for the future, so that they may take hold of that which is truly life.

HYMN

"When I Survey the Wondrous Cross"

When I survey the wondrous cross
On which the Prince of Glory died,

My richest gain I count but loss,
And pour contempt on all my pride.

Forbid it, Lord, that I should boast,
Save in the death of Christ my God:
All the vain things that charm me most,
I sacrifice them to his blood.

See, from his head, his hands, his feet,
Sorrow and love flow mingled down:
Did e'er such love and sorrow meet,
Or thorns compose so rich a crown?

His dying crimson, like a robe,
Spread o'er his body on the tree;
Then am I dead to all the globe,
And all the globe is dead to me.

Were the whole realm of nature mine,
That were a present far too small;
Love so amazing, so divine,
Demands my soul, my life, my all.

AUTHOR: ISAAC WATTS, 1707

Chapter 37

POVERTY AND WEALTH

Is all monetary inequality morally wrong?
How can we best help the poor?
How can poor nations overcome poverty?
Are Western affluence and lack of generosity the
main reasons why poverty continues today?

In chapter 36, I argued that part of God's plan for human beings on the earth is that we will continually increase in material prosperity as we work faithfully and seek to be good stewards of the property that he entrusts to us, but also that prosperity brings multiple temptations that we must guard against.

However, both individual people and nations grow in material prosperity at different rates over the long term. Some people accumulate much wealth, while others struggle just to have enough money to live on. Some nations have become wealthy while others have remained poor. To put it briefly, prosperity does not come to everyone at once or in equal amounts. Some become rich while others remain poor.

Therefore, it is important to consider the question of poverty and wealth, which is a major concern in Scripture and the topic of this chapter.

A. SOME INEQUALITY IS INEVITABLE

Before considering the question of poverty, it will be helpful to clarify the general notion of inequality. It may seem surprising to us to think that some inequalities of possessions in themselves can be good and pleasing to God. But it should not be surprising. There is no sin or evil in heaven, and yet there will be varying degrees of reward in heaven and various kinds of stewardships that God entrusts to different people. When we stand before Jesus to give account of our lives, he will say to one person, "You shall have authority over ten cities," and to another, "You are to be over five cities" (Luke 19:17, 19).[1]

Therefore, there will be inequalities of stewardship and responsibility in the age to come. This means that the idea of some inequalities of stewardship in itself must be given by God and therefore must be good.

In a similar teaching, Paul is speaking not to unbelievers but to the Corinthian Christians when he says, "For *we must all appear before the judgment seat of Christ*, so that each one may receive *what is due for what he has done in the body*, whether good or evil" (2 Cor. 5:10). This implies degrees of reward for what we do in this life.

Many other passages teach or imply degrees of reward for believers at the final judgment.[2] Even among the angels, there are differing levels of authority and stewardship established by God (1 Thess. 4:16 and Jude 9 mention an "archangel"), and we cannot say that such a system is wrong or sinful in itself.

Inequalities are actually necessary in a world that requires a great variety of tasks to be done. Some tasks require stewardship of large amounts of resources (such as ownership of a steel mill or a company that manufactures airplanes), and some tasks require stewardship of small amounts of resources. In addition, God has given some people greater abilities than others in art, music, or athletics; mathematics or science; leadership or business; buying and selling; and so forth. If reward for one's labor is given fairly and is based on the value of what a person produces, then those with larger abilities in such areas will naturally gain larger rewards. Since people are different in abilities and in the effort they put forth, I don't think there could be a fair system of rewards for work unless the system had different rewards for different people. Fairness of reward requires such differences.

In fact, it has never been God's goal to produce equality of possessions among people, and it will never be God's goal to do so. In the Year of Jubilee (see Leviticus 25), agricultural land returned to its previous owners and debts were canceled, but there was no equalizing of money, jewels, cattle, or sheep, and houses inside walled cities did not revert to the previous owners (see v. 30).

Some people have seen an argument for equal possessions in 2 Corinthians 8, but there Paul did not say that God's goal was equality. For example, he did not tell the wealthy Corinthians to send money to the poor Macedonians mentioned in verses 1–5, but only that they should contribute their fair share in helping the famine-stricken Christians in Jerusalem:

---

[1] This section has been adapted from Wayne Grudem, *Business for the Glory of God: The Bible's Teaching on the Moral Goodness of Business* (Wheaton, IL: Crossway: 2003), chap. 7, with permission of the publisher. Material in later sections is adapted from Wayne Grudem and Barry Asmus, *The Poverty of Nations: A Sustainable Solution* (Wheaton, IL: Crossway, 2013), with permission of the publisher.

[2] See especially 1 Cor. 3:12–15; also Dan. 12:2; Matt. 6:20–21; 19:21; Luke 6:22–23; 12:18–21, 32, 42–48; 14:13–14; 1 Cor. 3:8; 9:18; 13:3; 15:19, 29–32, 58; Gal. 6:9–10; Eph. 6:7–8; Phil. 4:17; Col. 3:23–24; 1 Tim. 6:18; Heb. 10:34, 35; 11:10, 14–16, 26, 35; 1 Pet. 1:4; 2 John 8; Rev. 11:18; 22:12; see also Matt. 5:46; 6:2–6, 16–18, 24; Luke 6:35. For more discussion on different levels of reward in heaven, see Wayne Grudem, *Systematic Theology: An Introduction to Biblical Doctrine* (Leicester, UK: Inter-Varsity, and Grand Rapids, MI: Zondervan, 1994), 1144–45.

As a matter of *fairness* your abundance at the present time should supply their need, so that their abundance may supply your need, that there may be *fairness*. (2 Cor. 8:13–14; the Greek word *isotēs* also means "fairness" in Col. 4:1, where it cannot mean "equality")

Neither does the book of Acts teach an "early communism" when it says that believers "had all things in common" (Acts 2:44). As I argued more fully in chapter 34 (see p. 898), this situation was far different from communism, because (1) the sharing was voluntary, and not compelled by a government, and (2) people still had personal possessions and owned property, because they still met in "their homes" (Acts 2:46), and many other Christians after this time still owned homes (see Acts 12:12; 17:5; 18:7; 20:20; 21:8; 21:16; Rom. 16:4–5; 1 Cor. 16:19; Col. 4:15; Philem. 2; 2 John 10). In addition, (3) Peter even told Ananias and Sapphira that they did not have to feel any obligation to sell their property and give away the money: "While it remained unsold, did it not remain your own? And after it was sold, was it not at your disposal?" (Acts 5:4).

Later in the New Testament, when Paul gives specific instructions to those who are wealthy, he does not tell them to give up all their possessions, but simply to be generous and to set their hearts on God, not on their wealth:

> As for *the rich in this present age*, charge them not to be haughty, nor to set their hopes on the uncertainty of riches, but on God, who richly provides us with everything to enjoy. They are to do good, to be rich in good works, to be generous and ready to share, thus storing up treasure for themselves as a good foundation for the future, so that they may take hold of that which is truly life. (1 Tim. 6:17–19)

So we should not think of all inequalities of possessions as wrong or evil. In fact, inequality in possessions provides many opportunities for glorifying God.

If God gives us a small stewardship with regard to material possessions or opportunities and abilities, then we can glorify him by being content in him, trusting in him for our needs, expecting reward from him, and being faithful to our commitments. In fact, those who are poor will often give more sacrificially than those who are rich. Jesus saw a poor widow put a penny in the offering, and he told his disciples:

> Truly, I say to you, this poor widow has put in more than all those who are contributing to the offering box. For they all contributed out of their abundance, but she out of her poverty has put in everything she had, all she had to live on. (Mark 12:43–44)

And James tells us:

> Has not God chosen those who are *poor in the world* to be *rich in faith* and heirs of the kingdom which he has promised to those who love him? (James 2:5)

Thus, the Bible does not teach a "health-and-wealth gospel" (the idea that if you have enough faith God will make you healthy and wealthy in this life), as I argued earlier (see p. 908). In this present age, there are inequalities of gifts and abilities, and there are also evil, oppressive systems in the world, and because of these things many of God's most righteous people will not be rich in this life.

As for those who have large resources, they also are to be content in God and trust in him, not in their riches, and both James and Paul suggest that they face greater temptations (see 1 Tim. 6:9–10; James 2:6–7; 5:1–6). Those who are rich have more opportunities and also more obligations to give generously to the poor (1 Tim. 6:17–19) and to the work of the church (Luke 12:48; 1 Cor. 4:2; 14:12).

Inequalities in possessions, opportunities, and abilities provide many temptations to sin. There are temptations for the wealthy or those who have other kinds of large stewardships to be proud, to be selfish, to think too highly of themselves, and not to trust God. On the other hand, those to whom God has entrusted less wealth face temptations to coveting, to jealousy, and to not valuing the position and calling in life to which God has called them, at least for the present time.

But such temptations that accompany wealth and poverty, and the wrongful actions of the rich and the poor that sometimes follow, must not cause us to think that inequality in itself is evil, or that all inequalities are wrong, or that God's goal is total equality of possessions. Inequalities in possessions, opportunities, and abilities will be part of our life in heaven forever, and they are in themselves good and pleasing to God, and provide many opportunities for glorifying him.

However, I must be very clear about another distinction. The fact that not all inequality is wrong does not nullify another frequent theme in Scripture, that *poverty* is not pleasing to God but is a condition that Scripture commands us to seek to eradicate. While the Bible does not teach us to overcome all inequality, it does teach us to seek to overcome poverty. But our focus must be on overcoming poverty, not on overcoming inequality. I will discuss possible solutions to poverty in much of the remainder of this chapter.

B. POVERTY: HOW BEST TO HELP THE POOR?

1. The Question of "Social Justice." In connection with this discussion of solutions to poverty, some readers may expect me to argue that governments (or societies) should practice "social justice." While I certainly believe that individuals, governments, and societies should act in ways that are "just" (for the Bible contains frequent references to "justice"), I have not generally used the phrase "social justice" in this book, for four reasons:

1. The phrase "social justice" is not found in the Bible, and therefore people can define it in many different ways. This means that it is important to

understand precisely *what the phrase means* before we can think clearly about which Bible passages, if any, apply to this issue.

2. In actual usage, the phrase "social justice" means several different things to different people, and too often this has allowed it to be used as a vague, ill-defined term that can attract initial support for some political positions that people would not otherwise favor if they understood what was being promoted by the use of that term. (After all, who would ever want to oppose "justice"?)

3. The phrase "social justice" is sometimes used to advocate political or economic policies that I personally do not support. For example, David Gushee and Glen Stassen devote an entire chapter to "justice,"[3] which they also refer to as "social justice" (pp. 137, 146). But they explain this justice as "an end to unjust economic structures, unjust domination, unjust violence, and unjust exclusion from community" (p. 147). What do they mean by "unjust" in these references? Other sections of the book show that, for them, "unjust domination" includes the complementarian view of men's and women's roles in the church (as opposed to their evangelical feminist view, pp. 143, 242); "unjust violence" includes participation in warfare, even wars of defense (as opposed to their pacifist position, pp. 308–38); and "unjust economic structures" seems to include modern free-market economies (economic systems that, in their view, need *more* government regulation in order to guarantee more fair distribution of goods, pp. 359–78). But if those policies are what people mean by "social justice," then it would be unwise for me to use the phrase, for this would make it easy for people to misunderstand me and think I was affirming feminism, pacifism, and quasi-socialism, policies with which I disagree.[4]

4. The phrase "social justice" can wrongly encourage a victim mentality and resentment toward the entire society or nation. This is because, rather than precisely specifying illegal or immoral activity by individual X, Y, or Z, the adjective *social* focuses blame on "society" as a whole, thus promoting a conviction that society in general is "unjust," and therefore society as a whole must be forced (through use of government power) to better the circumstances of any people who feel that life has not gone well for them.[5]

---

[3] David P. Gushee and Glen H. Stassen, *Kingdom Ethics: Following Jesus in Contemporary Context*, 2nd ed. (Grand Rapids, MI: Eerdmans, 2016), 126–48.

[4] Interestingly, I did not find the expression "social justice" in the indexes for the ethics texts by John S. Feinberg and Paul D. Feinberg, John M. Frame, Norman L. Geisler, Richard B. Hays, David Clyde Jones, Walter C. Kaiser Jr., Robertson McQuilkin and Paul Copan, or Scott B. Rae. John Jefferson Davis mentions the phrase on p. 223 but does not discuss it. (See full bibliographic information on these texts in chap. 1, p. 64.)

[5] I should add, however, that I have coauthored an entire book on biblically based, sustainable solutions to poverty in entire nations: see Grudem and Asmus, *The Poverty of Nations*.

2. We Should Help the Poor. Why should Christians want to help the poor? The Bible gives us two kinds of reasons.

First, there are the *general commands* of Scripture. Jesus said, "You shall love your neighbor as yourself" (Matt. 22:39). If we love someone who is poor, we will want to help that poor person.

Jesus also said, "Let your light shine before others, so that they may see your good works and give glory to your Father who is in heaven" (Matt. 5:16). If we want to let the "light" of our conduct shine before others, we certainly should give help to those in need. In fact, the apostle Paul says that God has called us to live lives that are characterized by "good works": "For we are his workmanship, created in Christ Jesus *for good works*, which God prepared beforehand, that we should walk in them" (Eph. 2:10). Certainly one of the good works that God wants us to do is helping those who are in need.

Second, we should want to help the poor because there are numerous *specific commands* in Scripture that tell us to do so.[6] Here are some of them:

> Only, they asked us to *remember the poor*, the very thing I was eager to do. (Gal. 2:10)

> But if anyone has the world's goods and *sees his brother in need*, yet closes his heart against him, how does God's love abide in him? (1 John 3:17)

> If among you, one of your brothers should become poor, in any of the towns within your land that the LORD your God is giving you, you shall not harden your heart or shut your hand against your poor brother, but *you shall open your hand to him* and lend him sufficient for his need, whatever it may be. (Deut. 15:7–8)

> For there will never cease to be poor in the land. Therefore I command you, "You shall open wide your hand to your brother, *to the needy and to the poor*, in your land." (Deut. 15:11)

> Blessed is the one who *considers the poor*!
>   In the day of trouble the LORD delivers him. (Ps. 41:1)

> Whoever oppresses *a poor man* insults his Maker,
>   but he who is generous to the needy honors him. (Prov. 14:31)

In some nations of the world, laws and entrenched special interests can be "structural" forces that make it impossible for individual people to rise out of poverty. The

---

[6] A very helpful discussion of biblical teachings about the need to care for the poor is found in Steve Corbett and Brian Fikkert, *When Helping Hurts: How to Alleviate Poverty without Hurting the Poor . . . and Yourself* (Chicago: Moody, 2009), 31–49. See also Craig L. Blomberg, *Neither Poverty nor Riches: A Biblical Theology of Material Possessions* (Grand Rapids, MI: Eerdmans, 1999).

laws and the court systems function so that the powerful elites keep all the power and retain all the wealth for themselves. Somehow these powerful groups must be persuaded (or compelled by law) to give up some of their power and privilege, and their tight hold on the wealth of the nation. (But note that this must be done because the laws have been unjust and criminal actions by the powerful have gone unpunished. It is not to be done simply because some people are rich and others are poor, but because some people have acted in immoral and illegal ways that have oppressed the poor and defenseless.)

In such cases, God's words through Isaiah are appropriate:

> Is not this the fast that I choose:
>> to loose the bonds of wickedness,
>> to undo the straps of the yoke,
> to let the oppressed go free,
>> and to break every yoke? (Isa. 58:6)

If genuine solutions to structural causes of poverty can be implemented, this will provide for poor people in many nations a means by which the "bonds of wickedness" and the "yoke" of oppression will be broken, and in that way the Lord himself will be glorified. If the Bible commands us to love and care for individual poor people that cross our paths, should not our love for them lead us to be even more eager to seek *to change oppressive laws and policies* in an entire nation when we have the opportunity, and thereby to help many thousands and or even millions of poor people all at once?

Love for the poor as fellow human beings created in the image of God should pour from our hearts when we realize the tragic situation faced by many in poverty. Steve Corbett and Brian Fikkert point out that, while North Americans tend to think of poverty in terms of "a lack of material things such as food, money, clean water, medicine, housing, etc.," this is not how the poor themselves evaluate their situation:

> While poor people mention having a lack of material things, they tend to describe their condition in far more psychological and social terms than our North American audiences. Poor people typically talk in terms of shame, inferiority, powerlessness, humiliation, fear, hopelessness, depression, social isolation, and voicelessness.[7]

> Low-income people daily face a struggle to survive that creates feelings of helplessness, anxiety, suffocation, and desperation that are simply unparalleled in the lives of the rest of humanity.[8]

When we understand these aspects of poverty, including a "lack of freedom to be

---

[7] Corbett and Fikkert, *When Helping Hurts*, 52–53.
[8] Ibid., 70.

able to make meaningful choices—to have an ability to affect one's situation,"[9] our hearts should be genuinely moved to try to seek solutions to these problems.

3. Immediate Short-Term Relief: Direct Aid to Individual Poor People and Communities.

a. Help from Individuals and Christian Organizations: James warns us that words alone are not enough to help the poor, but actions are also necessary:

> If a brother or sister is poorly clothed and lacking in daily food, and one of you says to them, "Go in peace, be warmed and filled," without giving them the things needed for the body, what good is that? So also faith by itself, if it does not have works, is dead. (James 2:15–17)

A similar theme is found in John's first epistle:

> But if anyone has the world's goods and sees his brother in need, yet closes his heart against him, how does God's love abide in him? (1 John 3:17)

This was certainly the pattern followed by the early church, for "there was not a needy person among them" (Acts 4:34).

Therefore, it is right for Christians regularly to give food, shelter, and other necessities to those who are poor and cannot afford these things. Many charitable organizations, churches, and governments around the world regularly help poor individuals and communities in this way, often very effectively. Examples of such work include programs to dig wells, provide medical and dental clinics, and build schools, as well as support for evangelism and Bible teaching in several nations.

Microfinance projects have also been successful in helping individuals in many countries, and we can be thankful for thousands of other development projects that have brought access to clean water and sanitation systems, improved crop yields, promoted educational advancement, and made progress toward the eradication of diseases in many nations.

Many Christian organizations have accumulated years of experience and wisdom for helping individual poor people and communities. In addition, several Christian authors have provided excellent Christian perspectives on helping the poor.[10]

---

[9] Ibid., 71, quoting economist Amartya Sen.

[10] Corbett and Fikkert, *When Helping Hurts*, explains how to help the whole person while humbly learning and respecting local wisdom. Darrow L. Miller and Stan Guthrie, *Discipling Nations: The Power of Truth to Transform Cultures* (Seattle: YWAM, 1998), gives an extensive and insightful explanation of a Christian worldview particularly as it affects economic questions.

Another insightful book, based on experiences in many poor countries, is Udo Middelmann, *Christianity versus Fatalistic Religions in the War against Poverty* (Colorado Springs: Paternoster, 2007). Middelmann rightly claims that any long-term solution to poverty must include a cultural transformation to key elements of a Christian worldview, including a positive view of growth in economic productivity and a hopeful perspective

b. Help from Government Welfare Programs: I have sometimes heard Christians propose that *civil governments* should not be involved in helping the poor, because there is a pattern of *churches* doing that in the New Testament. My response is that, yes, churches did help the poor, especially poor Christians, at the time of the New Testament, and they have done so throughout history, but there is *no* teaching of Scripture that prohibits civil governments from doing this as well. In a number of countries today, evangelical Christians constitute only a few tenths of 1 percent of the population, and it simply would not be possible for such tiny groups of people to care for all the poor people in those nations.

From a biblical perspective on government, it seems to me that if a government official is "God's servant *for your good*" (Rom. 13:4), then surely we could agree that a government aid program is doing "good" for people when it prevents them from starving or from dying because of lack of clothing or shelter—and it would certainly not be "good" for a society to allow such tragedies to happen.

Therefore, I think there is some need for government-supported welfare programs *to help cases of urgent need* (for example, to provide a "safety net" to keep people from going hungry or without clothing or shelter). In addition, I think it is appropriate for government to use tax money to provide enough funding so that everyone is able *to gain enough skills and education to earn a living*. Therefore, I think it is right for both governments and churches to contribute to helping the poor with regard to food, clothing, shelter, and some level of education.[11] Those convictions are based on the purpose of government *to promote the general well-being of the society*.[12]

c. Short-Term Help Is Not Enough: But in spite of these various kinds of short-term direct aid to individuals and communities, *longer-term solutions are still needed*. At the individual level, one long-term solution would be providing job training and job opportunities to the poor, so that eventually they can support themselves and no longer be among the poor. Christian churches could be especially effective in this task. I discuss the biblical support for that solution in the next section. Then in the section after that, I discuss still another crucial factor to consider, namely, the effect of laws, economic policies, and cultural values on *an entire nation*, leading the nation either in the direction of prolonged poverty or sustained economic growth and development.

4. For Individuals, the Permanent Solution to Poverty Is Productive Work.

a. The Bible Does Not Encourage Any Able-Bodied Person to Continually Live off Donations from Others: Dependence on donations from others (whether from

---

on the possibilities for change in one's life situation. After years of experience, he writes, "Most proposals for aid show a tragic ignorance of the basic economics of poverty and wealth as well as an unawareness of the influence of antihuman cultural and religious practices. In fact, the latter factors are often deliberately ignored" (p. 194).

[11] A local government official once said to me privately, "Wayne, if it weren't for the work of churches directly helping people in our area, we would never be able to keep up with the needs that are there."

[12] Certainly helping with such needs would fall under one of the main purposes of government as defined in the beginning of the U.S. Constitution: "to promote the general welfare." See http://constitutionus.com.

friends, churches, or government) is not God's ideal for able-bodied human beings on the earth. As we have seen, God's purpose from the beginning has been for people to work and create goods and services, not simply to receive donations (Gen. 1:28; 2:15).[13]

In the history of Israel, when God promised multiple economic blessings to his people, it was clear that these blessings would not come to inactive Israelites simply living off donations from other people; instead, they would be blessed when their work brought fruitful results:

> For the LORD your God is bringing you into a good land, a land of brooks of water, of fountains and springs, flowing out in the valleys and hills, a land of wheat and barley, of vines and fig trees and pomegranates, a land of olive trees and honey, a land in which you will eat bread without scarcity, in which you will lack nothing, a land whose stones are iron, and out of whose hills you can dig copper. And you shall eat and be full, and you shall bless the LORD your God for the good land he has given you. (Deut. 8:7–10)

The Israelites would have to harvest the wheat and the barley; they would have to tend and pick the vines and the fig trees; they would have to bake the bread; and they would have to dig copper out of the ground to make tools and implements. God's blessing would come through *productive work that created new goods and services*. It would not come by dependence on donations.

Far from being the continual recipients of donations from other countries, the people of Israel were to have enough surplus to be lenders: "You shall lend to many nations, but you shall not borrow" (Deut. 15:6; cf. 28:11–12).

Even the poor people in Israel were not to become dependent on donations from others, for they had to *work* to "glean" their food from what was left behind in the fields after the first harvesting (see Lev. 19:9, 22; Deut. 24:19–22; Ruth 2:2, 7).

Another provision for the poor in Israel was that others were to lend to them without charging interest (see Ex. 22:25; Lev. 25:37; Deut. 23:19; Prov. 28:8; Neh. 5:7–10). But the fact that God spoke of a *loan* (even one without interest) assumed that it would be repaid, not that the recipient would depend on donations year after year.[14]

Still another solution for poverty was the provision that a poor person could become an indentured servant to a wealthier person for a specified period of time,

---

[13] One exception is older widows, who, according to 1 Tim. 5:3–16, were supported by the church, apparently because they no longer were physically able to work and support themselves due to their advanced age. I agree that "elders who rule well" are to be supported by the church (1 Tim. 5:17–18; cf. 1 Cor. 9:14), but they are being *paid* for their work; they are not living off merely gratuitous donations from others.

[14] However, see Deut. 15:1–3 for debt payments that were temporarily suspended every seven years. For a discussion of this passage, see E. Calvin Beisner, *Prosperity and Poverty: The Compassionate Use of Resources in a World of Scarcity* (Westchester, IL: Crossway, 1988), 58–62, arguing that the release from payments was temporary, for that year only, and not a permanent cancellation, as in the Year of Jubilee.

after which his debts would be considered repaid and he would obtain his freedom (Lev. 25:39–43; Deut. 15:12–18; compare the story of Jacob serving Laban in Gen. 29:18–27). Indentured servants automatically had their debts cancelled in the seventh year of their servitude (see Deut. 15:12–15) or in the Year of Jubilee (Lev. 25:28, 40).

The important point is this: *there is no thought in the Bible that poor people would become permanent recipients of gifts of money, year after year*, or would become dependent on such gifts. The only exceptions were people who were completely unable to work due to permanent disabilities, such as a blind beggar (Mark 10:46; Luke 18:35) or a lame beggar (Acts 3:2–10).[15]

In the New Testament, Paul rebuked those who were "idle" (1 Thess. 5:14; 2 Thess. 3:7), stipulating, "If anyone is not willing to work, let him not eat" (v. 10).

The Bible's expectations that people must work to earn their living should not be seen as harsh or unkind. The fact that God gave Adam and Eve work to do before there was sin in the world (see Gen. 1:28; 2:15) indicates that we should see work as a *blessing*, a valuable gift from God. Although God has now added a dimension of pain and difficulty to our work because of the sin of Adam (see Gen. 3:17–19), the ability to work and create useful goods and services is still seen throughout the rest of the Bible as a positive gift and as something that God commands his people for their good (see Ex. 20:9; Eph. 4:28).

b. "Earned Success" Gives More Human Dignity and Fulfillment Than Gifts of Money:

As I explained in the chapter on work and rest (see chap. 35, p. 921), Arthur C. Brooks, president of the American Enterprise Institute, argues that the primary economic factor that makes people happy is not money but what he calls "earned success," that is, having a specific responsibility and then doing good work to fulfill that responsibility. Brooks writes, "The secret to human flourishing is not money but earned success in life."[16]

One example of this involved a recent student of mine at Phoenix Seminary. He was an outstanding student, getting straight As in his classes. He worked for me for two years and was highly responsible in every task. He had a stable marriage, and I expect him to do very well in his career.

When I got to know him, I found that several years earlier his life was going entirely downhill. He had a history of crime and substance abuse, and had spent time in jail for drug dealing. But after he got out of jail, he got a job at a Wendy's fast-food restaurant. One day his manager told him, "You're doing a good job of keeping the french fries hot."

He remembers that remark as a turning point in his life. Suddenly he realized that

---

[15] Modern technology even allows many physically disabled people to provide for themselves through information-processing work or intellectual creativity. One example is Stephen Hawking, a renowned physicist who is almost completely paralyzed and communicates by means of speech-generating technology.

[16] Arthur C. Brooks, *The Battle: How the Fight between Free Enterprise and Big Government Will Shape America's Future* (New York: Basic Books, 2010), 71.

he was able to do something well. He had experienced a touch of the joy of "earned success." He began to think that if he worked hard he might eventually become a shift manager, or even the manager of the restaurant itself. It was not money that gave him this happiness and sense of satisfaction, but rather earned success.

It is not surprising that God created us with the ability to develop goods and services, and commanded us to work in order to do this. And it is not surprising that he also created us so that we would have a great sense of happiness when we follow his plan, work to create goods and services, and then achieve earned success.

c. Private Businesses, not the Government, Must Be the Primary Means of Providing Individual Poor People with Productive Jobs: Earlier in this section, I affirmed the importance and the moral goodness of government acting as a "safety net" to provide people at least with food, clothing, and shelter.[17] However, we also must remember that such government handouts, while necessary in the short term, *will never provide a long-term solution to the problem of poverty*. These handouts simply have to be repeated month after month and year after year, and the recipients remain poor. And such gifts from the government can also create a wrongful kind of dependency. The only long-term solution to poverty comes when people have enough skills and discipline to get *economically productive jobs* and keep them.

The government itself cannot provide most people with economically productive jobs (except for some government-funded jobs such as police, firefighters, military personnel, highway maintenance workers, and teachers in the educational system). By far the largest number of *economically productive jobs*—jobs that actually contribute something new of value to a society—are found in the private sector, in the business world. A bakery employee bakes new loaves of bread each day and creates that amount of new wealth in the society. Someone working in an automobile factory creates new automobiles and thus adds economic wealth to the society. In the service industries, a plumber repairs a leaky faucet and thereby adds the value of one working faucet to the society. A landscaper trims trees and bushes, adding the aesthetic value of beautiful trees and bushes to the society. In this way, *every successful business gives people economically productive jobs* for which they are paid, and in that way it contributes value to the society. The poor person who goes to work at such a job is paid according to that added value, and thus begins to climb out of poverty.

This is what should happen, for God intends people to be economically productive. God actually created us with a need for food to survive, at least in part because this provides an incentive to regular work: "A worker's appetite works for him; his mouth urges him on" (Prov. 16:26).

Therefore, for those who desire to help the poor and overcome the problem of poverty, their *primary goal* should *not* be to increase and prolong government handouts of

---

[17] I also included education to provide skills that will lead to productive jobs, another important part of the solution.

money to those who are poor. Rather, it should be to provide incentives and appropriate conditions for privately owned businesses to grow and thrive, and thus provide the jobs that will be the only long-term solution to poverty and the only way for the poor to gain the dignity and self-respect that comes from supporting themselves.

d. Biblical Support for Human Freedom in Economic Systems: I agree that there is a proper role for government in restraining crime and punishing criminal wrongdoing (see the discussion of Rom. 13:1–7 in chap. 16, p. 429). Therefore, human "freedom" is not an absolute value, for people should not have freedom to commit fraud, violate contracts, use deceptive advertising, or steal from others.

But the value of promoting a free-market economic system and promoting human freedom in economic transactions finds significant support from various strands of teaching in Scripture:[18]

1. *The teaching about private property in the Bible.* Property is seen as belonging not to the government or to society as a whole but to individuals (see Ex. 20:15; Lev. 25:10; Deut. 19:14; 1 Sam. 8:10–18; 1 Kings 21; and the discussion of property in chap. 34).

2. *The biblical concept of personal stewardship responsibility to God for the property we have* (see Ps. 24:1 and the teaching on stewardship in chaps. 34 and 38). This stewardship can be exercised only when individuals are free to choose how to use their property.

3. *The biblical teaching that all human beings are created in the image of God* (Gen. 1:26–27; 9:6; James 3:9), and therefore should have equal rights before the law. The opposing view is that a small group of rulers has superior rights to dictate everyone else's economic decisions.

4. *The biblical teaching of a limited role for government.* Government is to punish wrongdoers, reward those who do good, and maintain order in society. There is no biblical teaching that government has the right to manage the economic decisions of a nation (see Rom. 13:1–6 and 1 Pet. 2:13–14 on the responsibilities of the state, and chap. 16).

5. *The absence of any clear biblical support for the idea that government should control the economy of a nation and should not allow economic freedom.* In fact, government does not need any special warrant to leave people alone and leave the economy alone (except for punishing criminal activity).

But I do not want government leaders to think they somehow have to "create" a free market. If government stays out of the way and simply prevents people from wrongfully harming one another, economic freedom just happens. In that sense, freedom already

---

[18] See Grudem and Asmus, *The Poverty of Nations*, 188–90, on the importance of promoting human freedom of choice for moral actions; also chap. 6 in that book on the moral advantages of a free-market system.

exists wherever people begin to enter into voluntary exchanges with one another, which is everywhere in human society. Governments do not have to create free markets. But governments do have to protect free markets in various ways, as I have explained in more detail elsewhere.[19]

e. Governments That Seek to Help the Poor Should Encourage and Not Punish Businesses: It is important, therefore, that government not hinder the development and profitability of businesses, but rather encourage them. Such encouragement should include a free-market (not a socialist) economic system with a functioning price system that will guide the allocation of resources, a stable system of money, and a legal system that effectively punishes crime, that enforces contracts, patent laws, and copyrights, and that documents and protects private ownership of property. It should also include a fair court system that is not partial to the rich or the poor, or to the powerful or the weak. Relatively low levels of taxation, an effective educational system, and a trustworthy banking system are also needed. When such factors are implemented by governments, then businesses can grow and thrive, providing the jobs that alone will lift people permanently out of poverty.[20]

And it is not only governments that should encourage businesses. Other influences on culture are also important. Because businesses are necessary to provide jobs and produce goods and services that lift people out of poverty, it is harmful for a nation when its dominant educational systems and entertainment media routinely exhibit hostility toward businesses in general and only portray typical business executives as villainous rather than virtuous. Yes, corrupt business practices should be exposed, but socially beneficial business behavior should also be celebrated.

Because businesses need to compete with one another to produce better goods at lower prices, the competitive free market *continually rewards those who improve their productivity and the quality of their products*. Thus, economically beneficial activity is encouraged and rewarded in a free-market economy.

Unfortunately, too many Christians in contemporary society are suspicious of economic competition. They think it is somehow "unspiritual" or "unchristian." I do not agree with that at all. Competition is simply a system that encourages people to strive for excellence in their work. Even people who say they dislike competition still encourage it by shopping for a product at the lowest price they can find or by buying the best quality product. For instance, people will buy the best strawberries and tomatoes they can find at a local farmer's market. In doing this, they are encouraging the more efficient, more effective farmer who produces a higher quality of product. People who read *Consumer Reports* to find the best brand of computer, washing machine, or bicycle are also encouraging competition, because they are

---

[19] See Grudem and Asmus, *The Poverty of Nations*, chaps. 7–8.

[20] More explanation of these factors in an effective free-market system is found in Grudem and Asmus, *The Poverty of Nations*, especially chaps. 4 and 5.

looking for a higher quality product that is a "best buy," that is, one produced at a more economical price. Therefore, even those who say they dislike competition continually support it by their shopping habits! If Christians are going to be good stewards of their money, they have to act in ways that support healthy economic competition.

But the competition of the free market that continually improves products and prices is far different from what government does, because government activities ordinarily face no competition. Whatever the government does, it is the only government in power at that time, and therefore it has a monopoly, both on the ability to collect taxes and on the ability to require people to buy its goods. (The U.S. Postal Service is a government monopoly, for example, for the delivery of first-class mail.) Because government does not have to compete for customers, government in general is a poor creator of wealth in an economy. In fact, it is difficult to think of many goods or services that a government might produce that could not be produced better by private companies.[21]

5. For Entire Nations, the Permanent Solution to Poverty Is Increasing Gross Domestic Product.

a. Solutions That Affect Entire Nations: The previous section discussed solutions to poverty for individuals. But in many cases, entire nations remain trapped in poverty. When we look at the world as a whole, *the primary factor that determines whether a person is rich or poor is what country that person lives in*. The vast majority of people in poor countries (such as Bangladesh, Pakistan, Cuba, Haiti, the Democratic Republic of the Congo, or Sierra Leone) are very poor by the standards of the rest of the world. But the vast majority of people in modern wealthy countries (such as Switzerland, Norway, Germany, the United Kingdom, Australia, Canada, or the United States) are quite wealthy by the standards of the rest of the world. The comparison between living in a rich country and living in a poor country is especially striking when we compare two countries close to each other, such as North Korea (where people live in horrendous poverty and many starve) and South Korea (today one of the 50 wealthiest countries in the world by per capita income).

Therefore, it is important to understand what factors make a country rich or poor. The best answer is a combination of factors that have to do with (1) a nation's economic system, (2) its government and freedoms, and (3) its cultural values. Economist Barry Asmus and I discuss 79 factors that lead to poverty or prosperity in nations in our book *The Poverty of Nations*,[22] and the following material will give a brief overview of our conclusions.

---

[21] I realize of course that some services and products needed by the entire society are best provided by government, such as the judicial system, law enforcement by police, national defense, and roads and highways. These are not ordinary consumer goods and services.

[22] Grudem and Asmus, *The Poverty of Nations*, 369–73.

b. No Simple Solution: The solution to poverty in poor nations is not a simple "quick fix," one that says, "Just do this one thing and poverty will go away." The solution is a complex one made up of many diverse factors.

The solution to poverty at a whole-nation level is complex because economic systems are complex. That is because economic systems are the result of millions of human beings making millions of choices every day. Who can ever expect to understand all of this?

In fact, writer Jay Richards explains why economics can be thought of as more complex than any other field of study:

> In biology . . . we enter a higher order of complexity than in physics and chemistry. We are now dealing with organisms, which resist simple mathematical explanations. . . . From biology we move to the human sciences. Here the effects of intelligent agents appear everywhere. So it's no surprise that it's harder to use math to model human behavior than it is to use it to model, say, the movement of a ball rolling down a hill. By the time we reach economics, we are dealing not only with human agents, but with the complexity of the market exchanges of millions or billions of intelligent agents. As we go from physics at one end to economics at the other, we are moving up a "nested hierarchy" of complexity, in which higher orders constrain but cannot be reduced to lower orders.[23]

Therefore, it should not be surprising that *the solution to poverty must be complex, because multiple factors affect human decision making.* Some of those factors are purely economic, but others have to do with laws, cultural values, moral convictions, long-term habits and traditions, and even spiritual values. Everything plays a part, so everything must be considered.

c. The Right Goal: In order to solve the problem of poverty in a poor nation, it is important to have the correct goal in mind. To discover this goal, we must first understand two economic concepts that determine whether a country is rich or poor: *per capita income* and *gross domestic product* (GDP).[24] Once those concepts are understood, it becomes

---

[23] Jay W. Richards, *Money, Greed, and God: Why Capitalism Is the Solution and Not the Problem* (New York: HarperOne, 2009), 222–23. Richards uses this observation to argue for God's design in the amazing operation of the free market, because, he says, nowhere along the scale of increasing complexity do we find "evidence of order emerging from chaos." Ibid. Richards's book as a whole is an outstanding overview of a biblical understanding of economics.

[24] I am speaking only of economic wealth and poverty here. As I stated in chap. 36 (p. 943), relational and spiritual wealth is more valuable than economic prosperity. And there are other kinds of wealth, such as moral wealth, the wealth of wisdom, and cultural and artistic wealth, that are not the focus of this section. I must reaffirm that I believe that a person's relationship with God takes priority over everything else: "You shall love the Lord your God with all your heart and with all your soul and with all your mind" (Matt. 22:37).

Still, our material well-being is important to us and also to God, and I understand growth in material prosperity to be the best and, in fact, the only real solution for world poverty. My goal in this section is to help nations increase their economic wealth as one means of obedience to God.

evident that if we want to solve poverty, the single correct goal is that a nation continually produces more goods and services per person each year.

(1) Per Capita Income: The standard measurement of whether a country is rich or poor (in economic terms) is called "per capita income" ("per capita" means "per person"). Per capita income is calculated by dividing the total market value of everything produced in a nation in a year by the number of people in the nation. If we sort countries by per capita income, we get an idea of the differences in economic conditions between rich and poor countries.

Here are some examples of per capita income for 2015 in various nations. In the "high-income" category we can include nations with more than $20,000 per year per capita income.[25]

> Norway, $68,600
> Switzerland, $58,600
> United States, $56,100
> Australia, $47,600
> Germany, $47,000
> Taiwan, $46,800
> Canada, $45,600
> France, $41,500
> UK, $41,500
> Japan, $38,100
> South Korea, $36,600
> Israel, $34,100
> Poland, $26,500
> Chile, $23,500

In the "high-middle-income" category are nations with per capita income of $8,000–$20,000 per year:[26]

> Mexico, $18,400
> Botswana, $16,400
> Brazil, $15,600
> China, $14,300
> Peru, $12,500

---

[25] These numbers are based on purchasing power parity (PPP) rather than official currency-exchange rates. Data for specific countries were taken from the World Factbook, Central Intelligence Agency, https://www.cia.gov/library/publications/the-world-factbook/rankorder/2004rank.html.

[26] The income ranges for "high income," "high-middle income," "low-middle income," and "low income" are somewhat arbitrary, but I have used these income ranges because they are consistent with the ones that Barry Asmus and I used in *The Poverty of Nations*, and they formed the basis for the color-coded world map on the cover of that book.

Albania, $11,300
Jamaica, $8,800
Ukraine, $8,000

The next category is "low-middle income," which includes countries with per capita income of $3,000–$8,000 per year:

Philippines, $7,300
India, $6,200
Honduras, $5,100
Pakistan, $4,900
Kenya, $3,200

Finally, the "low-income" category includes countries with less than $3,000 per capita income per year:

Tanzania, $2,900
Nepal, $2,500
Uganda, $2,000
Zimbabwe, $2,000
Afghanistan, $1,900
Ethiopia, $1,800
North Korea, $1,800
Haiti, $1,800
Congo (Democratic Republic), $800
Somalia, $400

These are *average* income figures, which included a small number of high-income people within each country, whose income numbers pulled the averages up. That means that *more than half of the people* in these countries were *below* these average levels of income.

Per capita income does not tell us everything we need to know about a nation. For instance, it does not measure important things that are not sold in the market, such as leisure time, religious faith, or strong families. But per capita income is the best commonly used numerical measure of whether a country is rich or poor in an economic sense.

Per capita income also does not tell us about the *distribution* of income—whether a large number of people share in the wealth of the nation or whether it is concentrated in the hands of a wealthy few. Increasing per capita income is not an adequate solution if only a few wealthy people benefit. Therefore, it is important that countries take steps to prevent a small, wealthy elite from controlling all the wealth and power in a nation, as happens too often in poor countries today.[27]

---

[27] For specific policies and values that enable a genuinely free market to function and thereby permanently open opportunities for *any* poor person to rise from poverty to an adequate income or even to prosperity,

But increasing per capita income is still very important, for as long as it remains low, the country remains poor. And higher per capita income is strongly correlated with some undeniably important factors, such as longer life expectancy, lower incidence of disease, higher literacy, and a healthier environment (for example, clean air and water, and effective sanitation).[28]

If a country wants to move up the scale from "low-income" to "middle-income" to "high-income," what must it do? *It must increase the total amount of goods and services that it produces*, which means there will be more to go around. This will affect per capita income, because per capita income is calculated by dividing the total market value of everything produced in a nation in a year by the number of people in the nation.

To understand what is needed in more detail, it is also necessary to understand the concept of gross domestic product.

(2) Gross Domestic Product (GDP): The standard economic measurement of what a nation's economy produces is called the gross domestic product. It is "the market value of all final goods and services produced within a country in a given period of time."[29] The period of time ordinarily used is one year.

This definition includes "goods and services." "Goods" include all the shoes, clothing, vegetables, bicycles, books, newspapers, cars, and every other material thing that is produced and then sold in the market. "Services" include things such as classes taught by teachers, examinations given by doctors, car repairs made by mechanics, and the work of paid house cleaners.

"Market value" indicates that goods and services counted in GDP are sold legally in markets. A loaf of bread baked and eaten at home is not counted in GDP because it is not sold in a market. But loaves of bread baked in a home and then sold in public are counted, because they have been sold in a market and a monetary value can be attached to them.

The size of a nation's GDP is the main factor that determines its wealth or poverty. This is because per capita income is calculated by dividing the GDP by the total population. If the population does not change much from year to year but the GDP grows, the per capita income goes up.[30]

For example, in 2014, Zambia had a GDP of $61 billion (I will round it down to

---

see Grudem and Asmus, *The Poverty of Nations*, esp. chap. 4, sect. D; chap. 5, sects. B, F, and G; chap. 6, sects. B and C; all of chaps. 7 and 8; and chap. 9, values 4, 5, 8, 9, 14, 15, 18, 21–24, and 29.

[28] See, for example, the strong correlation between per capita income and life expectancy in Stephen Moore, *Who's the Fairest of Them All? The Truth about Opportunity, Taxes, and Wealth in America* (New York: Encounter Books, 2012), 57.

[29] N. Gregory Mankiw, *Principles of Economics* (Orlando, FL: Dryden Press, 1998), 480.

[30] More specifically, as long at GDP grows faster than the population, the per capita income will go up.

$60 billion for ease of calculation) with a population of 15 million people.[31] If we divide $60 billion by 15 million, that gives a per capita income of $4,000 per year. This places Zambia near the lower end of the "low-middle" category among the nations of the world.

But if Zambia could somehow *double* its GDP from $60 billion to $120 billion and still have a population of 15 million people, suddenly *its per capita income would double* to about $8,000 ($120 billion divided by 15 million), which would place it in the "high-middle" income category among the nations of the world. The "average" person in Zambia would be twice as wealthy as before. Increasing a nation's GDP is what moves it along the path from poverty to greater prosperity.

(3) What Increases a Country's GDP? The most important question, then, is this: What will increase a country's GDP?

The answer is complex, involving dozens of factors, all of them contributing to or hindering the growth of GDP (see list below, p. 984). But I can briefly say here that GDP is increased when a nation continually creates more goods and services that have enough value to be sold in the marketplace. Therefore, the focus of efforts to overcome poverty must be on increasing the production of goods and services.

The correct goal for a poor nation, then, is *to continually produce more goods and services each year*. If a nation is going to succeed in overcoming poverty, it must be willing to examine its official policies, laws, economic structures, and cultural values and traditions to see whether they promote or restrain increases in the production of goods and services.

d. Wrong Goals: As Barry Asmus, my coauthor for *The Poverty of Nations*, and I have spoken to various audiences about solutions to poverty, we have heard many people propose other goals for eliminating poverty, goals that do not focus on increasing a country's GDP. But these approaches will not provide any sustainable solutions to a nation's poverty. We refer to these as "wrong goals" and discuss each of them at some length, but I will mention them briefly here:[32]

(1) More Aid: Some people argue that wealthy countries need to give massive amounts of additional aid money to jump-start the economies of poor nations. Unfortunately, aid has not proven helpful in increasing GDP in the long run. In fact, no poor nation in history has grown wealthy by depending on donations from other nations.[33]

---

[31] Statistics for Zambia taken from Terry Miller and Anthony B. Kim, eds., *2016 Index of Economic Freedom* (Washington: Heritage Foundation, and New York: Dow Jones Co., 2016), 455.

[32] For more detailed discussion of these wrong goals, see Grudem and Asmus, *The Poverty of Nations*, chap. 2 (pp. 65–106).

[33] The Marshall Plan (1948–1952), which was instrumental in rebuilding Western Europe after World War II, is sometimes cited as an example of how foreign aid can build an economy. But the Marshall Plan was not economic development of a poor country. Germany had been a wealthy nation with a developed economic infrastructure, legal traditions and systems, and immense human capital (skilled workers) before

An Oxford-trained African economist, Dambisa Moyo of Zambia, argues that foreign aid is actually the main cause of continuing poverty in Africa. She explains that aid has prevented Africa from moving toward economic growth:

> But has more than US$1 trillion in development assistance over the last several decades made African people better off? No. In fact across the globe recipients of this aid are worse off; much worse off. Aid has helped make the poor poorer and the growth slower. . . . The notion that aid can alleviate systemic poverty, and has done so, is a myth. Millions in Africa are poorer today because of aid; misery and poverty have not ended but have increased. Aid has been, and continues to be, an unmitigated political, economic and humanitarian disaster for most parts of the developing world.[34]

Moyo goes on to explain that she is not opposed to "humanitarian or emergency aid," which helps people affected by catastrophes, and neither is she opposed to "charity-based" aid, which is disbursed by charitable organizations (presumably religious groups and humanitarian agencies). But she is opposed to "aid payments made directly to governments," either through government-to-government transfers or through agencies such as the World Bank.[35]

Why is aid so harmful? Moyo explains that foreign aid props up corrupt governments—providing them with freely usable cash:

> These corrupt governments interfere with the rule of law, the establishment of transparent civil institutions and the protection of civil liberties, making both domestic and foreign investment in poor countries unattractive. Greater opacity and fewer investments reduce economic growth, which leads to fewer job opportunities and increasing poverty levels. In response to growing poverty, donors give more aid, which continues the downward spiral of poverty. This is the vicious cycle of aid. The cycle that chokes off desperately needed investment, instills a culture of dependency, and facilitates rampant and systematic corruption. . . . [It] perpetuates underdevelopment and guarantees economic failure in the poorest aid-dependent countries.[36]

Moyo adds, "Aid supports rent-seeking—that is the use of governmental authority to take and make money without greater production of wealth."[37] She quotes Rwandan

it was destroyed by the war. It needed only a massive infusion of cash to repair the destruction and get back to its previous wealthy condition. See this explanation in more detail in Dambisa Moyo, *Dead Aid: Why Aid Is Not Working and How There Is a Better Way for Africa* (New York: Farrar, Straus & Giroux, 2009), 35–37.

[34] Ibid., xix.
[35] Ibid., 7.
[36] Ibid., 49.
[37] Ibid., 52.

President Paul Kagame, who explains, "Much of this aid was spent on creating and sustaining client regimes of one type or another, with minimal regard to developmental outcomes on our continent."[38]

Why, then, do Western governments continue to give aid to poor countries? Moyo calculates that in the world today there are around 500,000 people who work for aid agencies, and "they are all in the business of aid . . . 7 days a week, 52 weeks a year, and decade after decade. Their livelihood depends on aid, just as those of the officials who take it. For most developmental organizations, successful lending is measured almost entirely by the size of the donor's lending portfolio."[39]

(2) More Equal Distribution of Wealth: Others say that the solution to poverty is using the power of government to redistribute wealth from the rich to the poor. They argue that greater economic equality is a matter of simple justice that governments should enforce. I certainly agree with the goal of helping the poor share in more of the wealth of a nation, and Asmus and I discuss ways this can happen through fair, open, market-based solutions in several sections of *The Poverty of Nations*.[40] The goal of our entire book is finding truly workable, sustainable ways to overcome poverty. However, some nations have tried to bring about more economic equality in economically harmful ways, not through opening up free markets but through brute use of government power. Making equality a more important goal than overall economic growth is a mistake for a government, because merely distributing the same amount of wealth in different ways does not change the total amount of wealth a nation produces each year, which is the only way that any nation has grown from poverty to prosperity.

Economic freedom and government-forced economic equality are opposing goals, and when government forces economic equality (for example, through heavy taxes on the rich), it can actually diminish economic incentives and harm the GDP. This can be seen in the history of every nation ruled by Communism, whether the Soviet Union, Cuba, North Korea, or China before it implemented many free-market reforms. Economist Milton Friedman rightly said, "A society that puts equality before freedom will get neither. A society that puts freedom before equality will get a high degree of both."[41] A nation must *produce* wealth before it can redistribute or enjoy it. The goal must be to increase a nation's GDP.

---

[38] Cited in ibid., 27.

[39] Ibid., 54.

[40] See, for example, the sections on making it easy for even poor people to obtain clearly documented property rights (pp. 152–54), on overcoming the oppression when a few wealthy families control all the wealth and power (pp. 75–77, 297–307), on protecting genuine opportunities and ease of entry in free markets (pp. 263–72), on the importance of widespread education and literacy (pp. 253–56, 291–92), on the importance of wealthy and powerful people also being equally subject to the rule of law (pp. 154–55, 225–30, 239–41), and many other sections.

[41] Milton Friedman, "Created Equal," part five in the "Free to Choose" video lecture series, http://www.free tochoose.tv/program.php?id=ftc1980_5&series=ftc80.

(3) Discovery of Natural Resources: Some believe that poor nations need to discover new natural resources, perhaps oil, precious metals, or rare earths. This solution has some merit, because when minerals are "produced" from the ground, their value directly increases GDP. But this is too narrow a focus, both because some nations have few resources (therefore this solution does not help them) and because some nations with almost no natural resources (Japan, Singapore, Taiwan, Switzerland) have become very wealthy. By contrast, many poor nations in Africa and Latin America have immense natural resources, but they remain poor. In addition, long-term prosperity in a nation cannot be preserved by resource wealth alone. Many economists consider natural resources a disguised curse, because bitter contests and even armed conflicts break out over gaining control of the government in order to gain control of the money that comes from resource wealth. But this hurts conditions for building the institutions that produce long-term growth. The goal must be to increase a nation's GDP.

(4) Debt Forgiveness: Others say that rich nations need to forgive the impossibly high debts that have been incurred by poor nations, because the costs of repaying these loans are a crippling burden. Unfortunately, this suggestion is similar to the proposal that more aid be given to poor countries, because it simply changes a loan into a gift, which is more aid (but aid given in two steps—first the loan, then the forgiveness). Debt forgiveness is at best a means to an end, not the end itself. It helps only if a nation produces more goods and services in the long run. The goal must be to increase a nation's GDP.

(5) Better Terms of Trade: Still others advocate negotiating more favorable prices for international trade between rich and poor nations. This would increase the value of a country's exports (total exports are added to GDP, since a country produced these things) and decrease the cost of its imports (imports are subtracted from GDP, since a nation did not produce these things but bought them from abroad). Therefore, if some sellers or buyers in a nation can negotiate more favorable terms of trade in dealing with many thousands of buyers and sellers on a world market, I agree that would bring some benefit.[42]

But no single poor nation is likely on its own to exert much of an effect on world prices of its goods. Focusing one's hope and effort on something that one probably cannot change is not a wise strategy. The goal must be to focus on something that a nation can certainly change: producing more goods and services, and so increasing its GDP.

(6) Restraining Multinational Corporations: Others believe that the solution is to break up or somehow restrain the power of large multinational corporations that are

---

[42] In addition, I object to most tariffs and quotas imposed on products that poor countries seek to export to richer countries. I also oppose the practice of rich nations providing above-market subsidies for some agricultural goods and then "dumping" them on world markets, depressing world prices for those goods (see discussion of dumping in chap. 40, p. 1083).

suspected of taking unfair advantage of poor nations. But those who focus on multinational corporations seldom evaluate their actual overall impact on a nation's production of goods and services.[43] The goal should not be to hurt *productive* firms or make them less powerful (however, if they are doing illegal or immoral activities, those must be stopped, and any local government officials who allowed these activities must be held accountable). The goal must be to make every person and every company within the nation more productive, and thus increase a nation's GDP.

(7) Fair-Trade Coffee: Others seem to think that the solution is to persuade Starbucks customers and other coffee drinkers to buy "fair-trade" coffee, and then to expand fair-trade agreements to other products and other companies. This is a form of the "better terms of trade" approach, and most economists believe that the fair-trade movement mainly benefits a small number of producers while it harms others, and very little of the higher retail price actually reaches the farmers themselves. (See my longer discussion of fair-trade coffee in chap. 40, p. 1080.) In any case, I doubt that this movement can succeed in persuading more than a small portion of the overall world market to pay more than the world price of a commodity (essentially making a charitable contribution every time they buy that commodity), while the world price continues to be determined by the continual interplay of supply and demand, factors that are continually reset each hour and each day by millions of individual decisions made by millions of individual people around the world. The effect of any such fair-trade charitable contribution for a specific commodity is extremely limited in scope with respect to the entire world economy, so this practice does not have a really significant impact on a nation's overall production of goods and services.

While some of these proposals provide some limited help and others are actually harmful, none of them provides an overall, sustainable solution to poverty. That comes only through increasing a nation's GDP.

e. The Amazing Process of Creating Value That Did Not Exist Before: When I talk about producing more goods and services, I am referring to an amazing process by which human beings are able to better their own economic situation by creating valuable things that did not exist before. When they do this, they add not only to their own wealth but also to the wealth of their nation. They do this not by taking something of value from someone else (which would not increase total GDP), but by *creating* new products or services that no one ever had because they previously did not exist.

(1) Examples of the Creation of Products of Value: To take a simple example, think of the example I discussed in chapter 34 (p. 906), that of a woman in a poor country who has a piece of cloth that cost her $3. If she uses that cloth to sew a shirt that she sells for $13, then she has created a new product of value. She has made a shirt that did not exist

---

[43] See Grudem and Asmus, *The Poverty of Nations*, 99–106.

in the world before she made it. She has made the piece of cloth $10 more valuable than it was when she bought it.

She has also contributed something to the total value of everything that her nation will produce in that year (the GDP). If the total value of everything produced in her nation that year was $2,000,000,000 before she made the shirt, then after she made the shirt the total value of everything produced was $2,000,000,010.[44] She moved her nation $10 along the path toward prosperity.

This amazing process of increasing GDP by creating products of value is at the heart of the means by which nations can grow from poverty to increased prosperity. If this creative process can be expanded to thousands of people making thousands of kinds of products, then the total value of everything in the nation increases day after day. If a nation can increase the value of what it produces each year, GDP will grow, and the nation will become more prosperous each year. This is the process that brings nations from poverty to prosperity.

The $10 profit that the woman earned when she sold the shirt is a measure of the value that she added to the economy. The buyer of the shirt voluntarily decided that the shirt was worth $13 to him. Therefore (in economic terms), it is worth $13. But the cloth only cost the woman $3. Her $10 profit is important because it shows that *new value has actually been created*. It is important to note here that her profit is not immoral but is a measure of *morally positive value* that has been added to the nation.

When a baker uses $3 worth of flour and other ingredients to make a loaf of bread that he sells for $4, he has suddenly added $1 to the GDP. When a shoemaker uses pieces of leather that cost him $5 to make a pair of shoes that he sells for $30, he has added $25 to the GDP.

Another example is a farmer who grows a crop of beans worth $400. When the ground had no crops, it was producing nothing of value. By cultivating the ground, the farmer "creates" (with the help of God, who directs the weather) $400 worth of beans that did not exist in the world before he grew them and harvested them. He increases the prosperity of the nation by $400 (minus the cost of the seed, fertilizer, irrigation, and so forth). And if, with better seeds, fertilizer, and irrigation, he grows $800 worth of beans the next year, then he doubles his contribution to the nation's GDP.

More complex processes can turn simple materials into very expensive items. To cite another example I mentioned earlier, think of eyeglasses. The original value of the raw plastic in the lenses might be about 3 cents and the original value of the metal in the frame might be about 5 cents. But a pair of eyeglasses can cost $200 or more in the United States today. How can 8 cents worth of materials end up with a value of $200? It is because skillful human beings create a product of value from the resources of the earth, and so the GDP grows.

It is crucial to keep this creative process in mind in trying to solve the problem of

---

[44] After she uses the cloth to make a shirt, the cloth (which cost her $3) is no longer a "final good" that can be counted in the GDP, so the GDP increases by $13 − $3 = $10.

poverty in poor nations. A nation will expand its GDP not by taking products from other nations but by creating more goods and services within the nation itself. This is the only permanent solution to poverty in poor nations.

(2) Transfers of Goods from One Person to Another Do Not Increase GDP: When a man who has two shirts gives a shirt worth $13 to a man who has none, this is a good deed that genuinely helps the poor man (see Luke 3:11). But it does nothing to increase the GDP. No new product is created, so no new $13 of value is added to the nation's GDP. The shirt is just moved from one person to another.

(3) Printing Money Does Not Increase GDP: Increasing a nation's production of goods and services is also different from simply printing money, because money itself is not a "product of value." People cannot eat money, wear it, ride on it, drive it, or plant it. They cannot put it over their heads to protect them from the sun and the rain. They can use money to buy other things, of course, but this is because money is a medium of exchange. It is not a product of value in itself.[45]

To understand this difference between printing money and creating goods and services, think back to our example of the woman who used a $3 piece of cloth to sew a shirt worth $13. She increased the GDP of the nation by $10, from, say, $2,000,000,000 to $2,000,000,010.

Now imagine that the government of that poor country suddenly prints an additional $3,000,000,000 of paper money (assuming dollars are the currency of that nation). Now what is the total value of all the products and services in that country? It is still only $2,000,000,010. There is more paper money in the nation, but there are no more shirts, shoes, beans, or houses, no more products of value that people can sell or buy and use for themselves. Printing money does not increase the GDP or improve the wealth of a nation. That must be done through producing more goods and services.[46]

Here is another example. Imagine that 200 people from a sinking ship find themselves stranded on a fertile but uninhabited island and have to support themselves. They organize themselves, and after a few days some people are building houses, some are catching fish, some are planting vegetables, some are picking cotton to make into cloth to make clothing, and so forth. They are all producing useful goods and services, so they are increasing the total "GDP" of the island, but they are still cut off from the outside world.

Now imagine that someone salvages a copier and a generator from the crippled

---

[45] I am oversimplifying here to make the point. In another sense, money is a "product of value" because it gives to the society a commonly recognized medium of exchange (which saves time over bartering), acts as a store of value, and provides a commonly recognized measure of value and unit of accounting.

[46] I realize that printing that much more money will cause inflation and the prices of everything will increase within that nation. But in terms of the actual goods and services available for people to use, nothing more of value has been created by printing that money.

ship, prints $100,000 worth of "Lost Island Dollars," then gives $500 of that money to each person so that people can buy and sell their goods and services more easily. Does printing that money make the people of the island any more prosperous? No. It does not give anyone more food, clothing, or shelter. It does not produce any more goods and services. It does not increase the island's GDP.

Of course, the money makes commerce easier than just bartering, and that adds value to the society because it saves people's time and enables them to become more productive, but printing money in itself does not make the island more prosperous in terms of the goods and services the people have.

(4) How Can a Nation Create More Goods and Services? If we keep our focus on the goal of continually producing *more* goods and services, then the question becomes, how can a nation *increase* the total value of the products and services that it produces? For example, how can the woman produce more shirts per week? And how can she produce higher-quality shirts that people value more and therefore pay more to purchase? Many factors contribute to such an increase (such as having a sewing machine, having easy access to markets, having expert training, having a microloan to buy more materials and better equipment, having confidence that she can keep and use her profits, and so forth). Asmus and I discuss these factors in detail in *The Poverty of Nations*. For now, the important point is to maintain our focus on this single goal: nations can move from poverty to prosperity only by continually creating more goods and services.

f. 79 Factors That Will Lead Nations from Poverty to Prosperity: I have briefly discussed several *wrong* solutions to the problem of poverty at the level of an entire nation. At this point I will now list, without giving additional explanation, the many components that belong to what I believe to be the *right* solution. These factors together will provide a genuinely workable solution to poverty in a nation, and these factors are also consistent with biblical teachings. For discussion of each point, see the related section in the book *The Poverty of Nations*, as indicated below. Of course, no nation can change all 79 of these factors at once, but genuine improvement in any individual factor will make a positive contribution to overall economic growth in the nation.

These 79 factors can actually be simplified into three broad principles:

1. A free-market economic system with rule of law and low taxes (section A below)
2. A government that works for the good of the people as a whole rather than the good of the rulers and their friends and relatives (sections B and C below)
3. Cultural values that reflect biblical moral teachings (section D below)

A Composite List of Factors That Will Enable a Nation to Overcome Poverty

A summary of the solution to poverty advocated in
The Poverty of Nations: A Sustainable Solution,
by Wayne Grudem and Barry Asmus
(Wheaton, IL: Crossway, 2013).
Numbers in parentheses refer to page numbers in this book.

A. The Nation's Economic System (details in chap. 4)

1. The nation has a free-market economy. (pp. 131–221)
2. The nation has widespread private ownership of property. (pp. 141–54)
3. The nation has an easy and quick process for people to gain documented, legally binding ownership of property. (pp. 149–54)
4. The nation maintains a stable currency. (pp. 155–58)
5. The nation has relatively low tax rates. (pp. 158–62)
6. The nation is annually improving its score on an international index of economic freedom. (p. 162)

B. The Nation's Government (details in chap. 7)

1. Every person in the nation is equally accountable to the laws (including wealthy and powerful people). (pp. 225–26)
2. The nation's courts show no favoritism or bias, but enforce justice impartially. (p. 227)
3. Bribery and corruption are rare in government offices, and they are quickly punished when discovered. (pp. 227–29)
4. The nation's government has adequate power to maintain governmental stability and to prevent crime. (pp. 229–30)
5. There are adequate limits on the powers of the nation's government so that personal freedoms are protected. (pp. 230–33)
6. The powers of the government are clearly separated between national, regional, and local levels, and between different branches at each level. (pp. 234–36)
7. The government is accountable to the people through regular, fair, open elections, and through freedom of the press and free access to information about government activities. (pp. 236–39)
8. The government adequately protects citizens against crime. (pp. 239–41)

9. The government adequately protects citizens against epidemics of disease. (pp. 241–42)

10. The nation's legal system adequately protects people and businesses against violations of contracts. (pp. 242–43)

11. The nation's legal system adequately protects people and businesses against violations of patents and copyrights. (pp. 243–46)

12. The government effectively protects the nation against foreign invasion. (pp. 246–48)

13. The government avoids useless wars of conquest against other nations. (pp. 248–50)

14. The nation's laws protect the country against destruction of its environment. (pp. 250–52)

15. The nation requires universal education of children up to a level where people are able to earn a living and contribute positively to society. (pp. 253–56)

16. The nation's laws protect and give some economic incentives to stable family structures. (pp. 256–57)

17. The nation's laws protect freedom of religion for all religious groups and give some benefits to religions generally. (p. 258)

C. The Nation's Freedoms (details in chap. 8)

1. Everyone in the nation has freedom to own property. (p. 263)

2. Everyone in the nation has freedom to buy and sell goods and services, so that there are no protected monopolies. (pp. 263–64)

3. Everyone in the nation has freedom to travel and transport goods anywhere within the nation. (pp. 264–67)

4. Everyone in the nation has freedom to relocate anywhere within the nation. (pp. 267)

5. Everyone in the nation has freedom to trade with other countries without dealing with restrictive quotas or tariffs. (pp. 267–269)

6. Everyone in the nation has freedom to start and register a business quickly and inexpensively. (pp. 269–271)

7. Everyone in the nation has freedom from expensive and burdensome government regulations. (pp. 271–72)

8. Everyone in the nation has freedom from demands for bribes. (pp. 272–75)

9. Everyone in the nation has freedom to work in whatever job he or she chooses. (pp. 275–77)

10. Every worker in the nation has freedom to be rewarded for his or her work at a level that motivates good job performance. (pp. 277–78)

11. Every employer has freedom to hire and fire employees based on job performance and changing business cycles. (pp. 278–79)

12. Every employer in the nation has freedom to hire and promote employees based on merit, regardless of family connections or personal relationships. (pp. 279–80)

13. Everyone in the nation has freedom to use the earth's resources wisely, and particularly to utilize any type of energy resource. (pp. 280–84)

14. Everyone in the nation has freedom to change and adopt newer, more effective means of work and production. (pp. 284–85)

15. Everyone in the nation has freedom to access useful knowledge, inventions, and technological developments. (pp. 285–91)

16. Everyone in the nation has freedom to be educated. (pp. 291–92)

17. Every woman in the nation has the same educational, economic, and political freedoms as men. (pp. 292–93)

18. Everyone in the nation, from every national, religious, racial, and ethnic origin, has the same educational, economic, and political freedoms as those from other backgrounds. (pp. 294–97)

19. Everyone in the nation has freedom to move upward in social and economic status. (pp. 297–300)

20. Everyone in the nation has freedom to become wealthy by legal means. (pp. 301–7)

21. Everyone in the nation has freedom to practice any religion (p. 307)

D. The Nation's Values (details in chap. 9)

1. The society in general believes that there is a God who will hold all people accountable for their actions. (pp. 318–19)

2. The society in general believes that God approves of several character traits related to work and productivity. (pp. 319–22)

3. The society in general values truthfulness. (pp. 322–24)

4. The society in general respects private ownership of property. (pp. 324–26)

5. The society in general gives honor to several other moral values. (pp. 326–29)

6. The society in general believes that there are both good and evil in every human heart. (pp. 329–30)

7. The society in general believes that individuals are responsible for their actions. (pp. 330–31)

8. The society in general highly values individual freedom. (pp. 331–32)

9. The society in general opposes discrimination against people on the basis of race, gender, or religion. (p. 332)

10. The society in general honors marriage between one man and one woman. (pp. 333–34)

11. The society in general values permanency of marriage and has a low divorce rate. (pp. 334–35)

12. The society in general believes that human beings are more important than all other creatures on the earth. (pp. 335–36)

13. The society in general believes that the earth is here for the use and benefit of human beings. (pp. 336–37)

14. The society in general believes that economic development is a good thing and shows the excellence of the earth. (pp. 337–38)

15. The society in general believes that the earth's resources will never be exhausted. (pp. 339–40)

16. The society in general believes that the earth is orderly and subject to rational investigation. (pp. 340–41)

17. The society in general believes that the earth is a place of opportunity. (p. 341)

18. The society in general believes that time is linear and therefore there is hope for improvement in the lives of human beings and nations. (pp. 341–42)

19. The society in general believes that time is a valuable resource and should be used wisely. (pp. 342–43)

20. The society in general manifests a widespread desire to improve on life, to do better, to innovate, and to become more productive. (pp. 343–44)

21. The society in general is open to change, and people therefore work to solve problems and make things better. (pp. 344–45)

22. The society in general gives honor to productive work. (pp. 345–48)

23. The society in general gives honor to economically productive people, companies, inventions, and careers. (pp. 348–50)

24. The society's business owners and workers in general view their companies primarily as means of providing customers with things

of value, for which they will then be paid according to that value. (pp. 350–51)

25. The society in general places a high value on savings in contrast to spending. (p. 351)

26. The society in general believes that mutual gains come from voluntary exchanges, and therefore a business deal is "good" if it brings benefits to both buyer and seller. (pp. 351–53)

27. The society in general values knowledge from any source and makes it widely available. (pp. 353–54)

28. The society in general values a highly trained workforce. (pp. 354–55)

29. The society in general assumes that there must be a rational basis for knowledge and recognized channels for spreading and testing knowledge. (pp. 355–56)

30. The society in general demonstrates a humble willingness to learn from other people, other nations, and members of other religions. (pp. 356–57)

31. The society in general believes that the purpose of government is to serve the nation and bring benefit to the people as a whole. (pp. 358–59)

32. The society in general believes that government should punish evil and promote good. (p. 359)

33. The society in general values patriotism and reinforces a shared sense of national identity and purpose. (pp. 359–64)

34. The society in general counts family, friends, and joy in life as more important than material wealth. (pp. 364–66)

35. The society in general counts spiritual well-being and a relationship with God as more important than material wealth. (pp. 366–67)

g. Material Poverty Is a Secondary Issue, While Spiritual Poverty Is a Primary Issue: Finally, it is important to remember the Bible's clear emphasis that a person's relationship to God is far more important than material prosperity, and that the pursuit of material wealth can, in fact, very easily take first place in one's life.

Jesus said, "No servant can serve two masters, for either he will hate the one and love the other, or he will be devoted to the one and despise the other. You cannot serve God and money" (Luke 16:13). He also said, "One's life does not consist in the abundance of his possessions" (12:15).

Christian writers Corbett and Fikkert wisely warn that the wrong attitude toward material possessions can easily affect Western Christians and harm our efforts to help the poor if we do not include a spiritual component in the ministry that we do. They point out that economically rich Christians in the West often have a "poverty of being," a "god-complex," and a merely "material definition of poverty" that can cause them to do more harm than good when trying to help the poor.[47]

Corbett and Fikkert also warn that in order for us to help the poor most effectively, both we and they need a proper worldview and right relationships with God, with ourselves, with others, and with the rest of creation.[48] They say, "We are very prone to putting our trust in ourselves and in technology to improve our lives, forgetting that it is God who is the Creator and Sustainer of us and of the laws that make the technology work."[49]

This is why the Bible warns that those who obtain some measure of financial prosperity in this life should not set their hearts and hopes on their wealth, but on God:

> As for the rich in this present age, charge them not to be haughty, *nor to set their hopes on the uncertainty of riches, but on God*, who richly provides us with everything to enjoy. They are to do good, to be rich in good works, to be generous and ready to share, thus storing up treasure for themselves as a good foundation for the future, so that they may take hold of that which is truly life. (1 Tim. 6:17–19)

Therefore, my hope for the poor nations of the world is that they will begin to grow in material prosperity but also not decline in relational or spiritual prosperity. I deeply hope that material prosperity does not come at the cost of the loss of interpersonal relationships, the loss of love for family, and alienation from God. I certainly do not want to encourage a society that worships and serves money, and then is destroyed by that greed and idolatry.[50] I hope, rather, that all nations of the world, while they pursue growth in economic prosperity, will continue to value relationships with family members and friends more than they value wealth, and that they will be nations that, in general, truly worship and serve God, not money.

C. WEALTH: HOW MUCH IS TOO MUCH?

1. Warnings but No Condemnation of Much Wealth. Is there such a thing as having too much wealth? There is no specific teaching that a large amount of wealth is wrong

---

[47] Corbett and Fikkert, *When Helping Hurts*, 65–67.

[48] Ibid., 84–89, discusses these relationships in detail.

[49] Ibid., 95.

[50] Paul Mills puts a very high priority on the influence of economic policy on relationships: "The ultimate goal of economic policy ought to be enriching the quality of relationships within a society." "The Economy," in *Jubilee Manifesto: A Framework, Agenda and Strategy for Christian Social Reform*, ed. Michael Schluter and John Ashcroft (Leicester, UK: Inter-Varsity, 2005), 217.

in itself. But there are some narrative examples that give us warnings, such as the story of the rich young ruler (Matt. 19:16–22) who talked with Jesus, but then "he went away sorrowful, *for he had great possessions*" (v. 22).

In the Old Testament, God told the people of Israel that when they had a king ruling over them, "*he shall not acquire many wives* for himself, lest his heart turn away, *nor shall he acquire for himself excessive silver and gold*" (Deut. 17:17), but these two commands were flagrantly violated by Solomon: "He had 700 wives, who were princesses, and 300 concubines. And his wives turned away his heart. For when Solomon was old his wives turned away his heart after other gods, and his heart was not wholly true to the LORD his God, as was the heart of David his father" (1 Kings 11:3–4; Solomon also accumulated huge amounts of gold and other riches, 1 Kings 10:14–22).

In addition, the New Testament gives a strong warning against spending too much on oneself and living in self-indulgent luxury:

> Come now, you rich, weep and howl for the miseries that are coming upon you.... Your gold and silver have corroded, and their corrosion will be evidence against you and will eat your flesh like fire. You have *laid up treasure* in the last days.... *You have lived on the earth in luxury and in self-indulgence.* You have fattened your hearts in a day of slaughter. (James 5:1–5)

James does not imply here that *all* those who are rich are evil, for in this same chapter he speaks of the fraud and murder committed by these particular rich people to whom he is referring (James 5:4, 6). Also, Paul does not say that the rich are to give away all their wealth, but that they are "to do good, to be rich in good works, to be generous and ready to share" (v. 18).

Yet James clearly warns against a kind of "luxury and ... self-indulgence" that is wrong, that shows little or no concern for others, and that does not take seriously the stewardship obligations that God bestows along with great wealth. It seems that those who are wealthy can too easily slip beyond a level of spending on themselves that is appropriate to their place in life and spend excessively and ostentatiously on themselves while neglecting to give generously to others.

2. Governments Must Punish Those Who Have Gained Wealth by Illegal and Immoral Activities. But what if people live in a country where nearly all the rich people have gained their wealth *through immoral means*, such as drug dealing, theft, or political corruption? In such cases, the society somehow needs to find enough strength to punish those criminals for the evil things they have done—not punishing them for the *wealth* itself, but for the wrongful *means* they used to gain that wealth. Then it needs to open up and protect genuine opportunities for anyone to become rich by legal, morally right means. If the only rich people in a nation are known to have become wealthy through bribery, theft, or corruption, then no honest people will believe there is any hope for them to increase their own wealth.[51]

Countries can stifle economic growth by a corrupt political and legal system that allows wealth to be concentrated in the hands of a few specially privileged and powerful families while the vast majority of people are trapped in poverty. In Russia and in other Slavic countries, "serfdom persisted in its worst form" long after the Industrial Revolution began in Northern Europe. According to David Landes, "So much wealth" was held "in the hands of a spendthrift nobility," but the poor peasants had so little they could not even have provided sufficient demand for the purchase of ordinary consumer goods if such goods had been produced.[52] Russia under the czars had "a privileged, self-indulgent aristocracy contemptuously resisting modernization."[53]

Many newly independent countries in Latin America had similar problems, with a very few wealthy people at the top and masses trapped in poverty: "At the top, a small group of rascals, well taught by their earlier colonial masters, looted freely. Below, the masses squatted and scraped."[54] Landes sums up what happens in these situations, to the detriment of both rich and poor:

> Where society is divided between a privileged few landowners and a large mass of poor, dependent, perhaps un-free laborers—in effect, between a school for laziness (or self-indulgence) over against a slough of despond— what the incentive [sic] to change and improve? At the top, a lofty indifference; below, the resignation of despair.[55]

In every case where vast wealth is held by a privileged few and everyone else is trapped in poverty, the economic system should not be called a "free-market" system because the free market is not allowed to operate. Certain wealthy people are above the law. Crimes can be committed and contracts broken without fear of punishment. Monopolies are tolerated or even enforced by government. Obtaining a license to run a business or obtaining documented ownership of property is so difficult that it is essentially impossible for ordinary people.

These are not the failures of the free market, but the failures of a government to protect the free market and allow everyone to compete fairly in it. Where a government allows the free market to operate, ordinary human ingenuity and ambition provide more and more competition and diversity in the marketplace. More and more people find that they can rapidly advance to higher levels of income and status in society simply

---

[51] I wish to thank Jeff Michler for emphasizing to me the importance of this section for many poor countries where wealthy criminals too often go unpunished.

[52] David S. Landes, *The Wealth and Poverty of Nations: Why Some Are So Rich and Some So Poor* (New York: W. W. Norton, 1999), 251.

[53] Ibid., 268.

[54] Ibid., 313.

[55] Ibid., 296.

by hard work and skill in what they do. The free market, if it is truly allowed to function, provides such social and economic freedom to move upward in generation after generation.

3. Governments That Want Their Economies to Become More Productive Must Allow Freedom for Anyone to Become Wealthy by Legal Means. If any poor country is going to grow from poverty toward increasing prosperity, and if any wealthy country is going to continue to grow its economy, the governments of these countries must protect (1) the freedom for *anyone* in the society to move to a higher income level and (2) the freedom for *anyone* to accumulate and retain even large amounts of wealth, so long as they do so by legal means and activities. This is the opposite of the situation in which the wealth of a nation is concentrated in the hands of a few privileged families and no one else has the opportunity to become wealthy. Instead, I am speaking of a society that promotes opportunity for anyone who works hard and has skill to increase his economic status as much as he is able.

Once again, government leaders must keep in mind the one thing that will lift their nation from poverty toward increasing prosperity: continually producing more goods and services of value. If that is going to happen, every person in the nation must somehow be *motivated* to contribute what he or she can to the increase in productive economic activity.

What most effectively motivates people to make their best contributions toward a more productive economy? They are best motivated by *the hope of earning more and bettering their positions in life*, as well as those of their families. Nothing else provides the needed motivation—not appeals to patriotism, not challenges to love their fellow man, not calls to do more to help the poor, not envy of the rich, and certainly not forced labor in systems of slavery or totalitarianism. Nothing motivates a person nearly as well as his own self-interest; that is, the hope of earning more money and bettering his own condition.

But if people are going to be motivated by the hope of earning more money, they must be able to see *actual evidence* that this is possible. They must be able to look around and identify examples of ordinary people (such as an uncle, a cousin, or a neighbor) who started out poor and then became rich or at least moderately well-off. People must be able to see that a measure of financial success is possible with good work habits, honesty, thrift, and perseverance.[56]

However, if people know that they live in a country where *no ordinary person* is able to improve his family's economic condition—such as a communist country, where wages are set by the government—then no one tries. Likewise, if people live in a country where powerful government officials and a few wealthy families have kept all the wealth

---

[56] Thomas J. Stanley and William D. Danko, *The Millionaire Next Door: The Surprising Secrets of America's Wealthy* (New York: Pocket Books, 1996), is filled with such examples, as well as numerous studies of the surprisingly frugal and unassuming lifestyles of most American millionaires.

for themselves for generations (as in some Latin American countries), and where the poor really have no opportunity to work hard and succeed economically, then again they do not try.

The need for people to see examples of others who have gone from poverty to wealth means that it is very destructive for a society to continually vilify "the rich," to portray them as evil and to promote envy and hatred toward them. (The idea that wealth comes from the exploitation of others rather than from creating new value is a Marxist idea, not a Christian viewpoint.) Such class-warfare rhetoric tends to discourage poorer people from trying to succeed in business and become wealthy through hard work and perseverance. (After all, who wants to be hated by everyone else?) If a society focuses on envy or hatred of the rich, it significantly hinders its economic productivity.

Every time a nation moves from poverty toward increasing prosperity, some people will do better economically than others. People have different gifts and skills, different degrees of ambition, different work habits, and different levels of intelligence in various areas. Many people will become moderately prosperous because they do quite a good job of providing useful products of value for the economy. The government—and the customs of the society—must allow them to keep the fruits of their labor, because this is what motivates them to continue to make valuable contributions to the economy. In fact, in free societies, most of the people who become moderately wealthy have quite "ordinary" occupations, such as owning a bakery, a grocery store, an auto-repair shop, or a home-building business. By these ordinary jobs they clearly improve the economic situation of their families compared with the previous generations.

There also will be a very few people who will become spectacularly successful. Often they are people who invent products or new ways to mass-produce products. In the history of the United States, these have been the people who figured out how to build an assembly line to mass-produce automobiles for ordinary families (Henry Ford), how to build a vast network of railroads (Cornelius Vanderbilt), how to build a vast oil refining and distribution system for the whole nation (John D. Rockefeller, founder of Standard Oil), or how to build huge steel mills (Andrew Carnegie, founder of U.S. Steel). They included those who developed home computers and a new generation of cell phones (Steve Jobs, founder of Apple), a computer operating system that is used in every country of the world (Bill Gates, founder of Microsoft), and an Internet marketing firm that delivers thousands of products quickly to any home (Jeff Bezos, founder of Amazon).

The important point for the United States' economic development is not that each of these business leaders made multiple millions of dollars. It is that each of them *contributed a vast amount of economic productivity to his nation* and, in many cases, to the entire world. These people and others like them enabled the United States to continually produce more products and services of value beyond anything that could be imagined from the efforts of one person. They succeeded, and the economy of their country grew significantly as a result of their efforts.

This kind of thing happens only in a nation that allows people unlimited opportunities to earn money with the hope of keeping large amounts of it. The people who can earn such millions of dollars are very rare, but they provide immense economic productivity for the society as a whole.

If a nation allows the freedom for anyone to accumulate much wealth in this way, it encourages multitudes of people to try. Some fail, many do moderately well, and only a very few become truly wealthy. But the millions who do moderately well form the backbone of a healthy economy, and those who become extremely wealthy provide significant benefit to that economy.

If the opportunity to work hard, succeed, and become wealthy is removed by government policies (such as extremely high rates of taxation on "the rich," or arbitrary and biased trials and imprisonments of high-profile wealthy people, as in Russia or China), then hardly anyone will even try to become wealthy by building a productive business, and this will keep the entire nation from much of the economic growth that it could have experienced.

Therefore, if a nation is going to grow from poverty toward increasing prosperity, it must not confiscate wealth through punitive taxes on the rich, through high inheritance taxes, through unjust court decisions against the rich, or through social ostracism or moral condemnations of prosperity.

4. The Importance of Economic Mobility. The ability for anyone to become wealthy (discussed in the previous section) can be quantified by attempting to determine how many of the wealthy people in a country began their lives in poor or middle-income circumstances. If there is a high level of economic mobility in a country, it provides a great incentive for economic growth. To take one example, economic mobility in the United States is still a significant part of its economy today: "Eighty percent of America's millionaires are first-generation rich," report Thomas Stanley and William Danko.[57] Moreover, most of them did not inherit their wealth—fewer than 20 percent of millionaires inherited 10 percent or more of their wealth, and fewer than 25 percent of them ever received a gift of $10,000 or more from parents or other relatives.[58] Many of "the poor" do not, for the most part, remain poor generation after generation, or even year after year, but many advance to higher economic levels. Neither do "the rich" necessarily stay rich year after year and generation after generation.[59]

5. The Importance of Honoring Economically Productive People. Cultural attitudes toward economic productivity are an important factor in overcoming poverty in any nation. If a society wants to move out of poverty toward greater economic prosperity, it will place a high importance on honoring economically productive people, companies, inventions, and careers.

---

[57] Ibid., 3.

[58] Ibid., 16.

[59] See further discussion of economic mobility in Grudem and Asmus, *The Poverty of Nations*, 297–307; see also the graph on income mobility opposite p. 193.

Each society uses various means to honor certain people, companies, inventions, and careers. For example, the "hero stories" that children are told can hold up one kind of person or another, or one kind of career or another, as either a good example to imitate or a bad example to avoid. Movies and television shows in a culture do the same thing, and so does popular music. The moral instruction that children are given in schools and churches provides another way of honoring various people and careers. The literature that is popular in a society can play the same role. Teachers in schools can have a huge impact on the kinds of people, companies, inventions, and careers that students think to be honorable, and the kinds of literature and historical studies that children read in schools also have a significant impact. In addition, the speeches given by governmental leaders and political campaigners have an effect on the kinds of people and careers that are honored in the society.

If a country is going to move from poverty toward greater prosperity, its culture should honor economically productive people who develop different segments of the economy. It should honor entrepreneurs who build small or large companies that provide jobs for many people and produce valuable goods or services to people in the society. It should honor inventors and innovators, and the things they create. Finally, the culture should honor careers that produce goods and services with economic value.

By contrast, a society that is trapped in poverty will place little or no value on people, companies, inventions, and careers that create and produce goods and services. Through movies, music, literature, political speeches, and instruction in schools and churches, the society will honor those who get something for nothing, whether through luck, by getting paid without working very hard, by making a lot of money while producing little of value, or by depending on government handouts. It might even honor, through its literature, films, and television programming, those who live by theft and extortion. Such a society will view economically productive people with disdain, guilt, shame, or envy.

On a broader scale, when people in such a society speak of their hope for economic progress in the nation, they will focus mostly on getting grants from the government or aid from other nations. The hope for progress also may be focused on attempts to redistribute income from the rich to the poor in a society rather than on opportunities for the poor to earn money and become wealthy themselves.

Several passages in the Bible give honor to those who are economically productive. Jesus's parable of the talents, for example, honors the servant whose five talents made five talents more and the servant whose two talents made two talents more (see Matt. 25:20–23).

In the Old Testament, the blessings God promised to the people of Israel, if they were obedient, included abundant agricultural productivity (see Deut. 28:1–14). In Proverbs 31, the ideal wife is portrayed as one whose merchandise is "profitable" (v. 18). By contrast, the disreputable "sluggard" in Proverbs is one who is lazy and produces very little of value (6:9; 13:4; 20:4).

In accordance with this biblical pattern, economic history points to the influence of the "Protestant Ethic" in Northern Europe, one part of which was the honor given to those who were economically productive and successful in the business world.[60]

By contrast, during the 18th and 19th centuries, when Europe and North America were making rapid economic progress, cultural values in India placed a high premium on perpetuating the old tradition of hard manual labor for most of the lower castes. As a result, no one placed much value on innovations that would have made labor easier or would have introduced machines to replace human and animal effort.[61]

A productive society that honors economically productive people, companies, inventions, and careers will not focus on the question "How much more does person A have than person B?" (for such a question produces envy and resentment). Rather, it will focus on the questions "How much has person A contributed to the economic well-being of society?" and "Has person A earned his money by legal means?" The emphasis in a productive society will be on productivity, not equality.

D. APPENDIX: AN ANALYSIS OF RON SIDER'S *RICH CHRISTIANS IN AN AGE OF HUNGER*

The most influential book in the evangelical world in the last 50 years regarding the topic of wealth and poverty has probably been Ron Sider's *Rich Christians in an Age of Hunger.*[62] The book contains several commendable aspects, which I will mention first. But the most basic claims in the book, it seems to me, are seriously incorrect, regarding both Sider's analysis of the *problem* of poverty and his proposals for a *solution*.

1. Helpful Emphases in Sider. The strongest part of Sider's book is his call for Christians to have genuine compassion for the poor and to meet cases of urgent need around the world. His analysis of biblical teachings in his section on "God and the Poor" (pp. 41–63) contains much insightful analysis of the frequent biblical teachings that God wants us to care for the poor. He rightly says, "But even if the rich did not cause any part of global poverty, we would still be responsible to help those in need" (p. 134).

In addition, Sider appropriately warns of the danger of riches (pp. 93–97) and clearly emphasizes that material affluence will not bring people true joy and fulfillment (pp. 23–24).

Sider also helpfully affirms the benefits of a free-market economic system (what he calls a "market economy"), and he rightly affirms that "communism's state ownership and central planning did not work. . . . Market economies, on the other hand, have produced enormous wealth. . . . The evidence is overwhelming. Market economies are more

---

[60] See Landes, *The Wealth and Poverty of Nations*, 175–78; see also, on Britain, 234–35.

[61] See ibid., 225–30.

[62] Ron Sider, *Rich Christians in an Age of Hunger: Moving from Affluence to Generosity*, 5th ed. (Nashville: Thomas Nelson, 2005). This book was first published in 1977. The cover of the 2005 edition says that the book was named "One of the Top 100 Religious Books of the Century" by *Christianity Today*.

successful than centrally owned and centrally planned economies at creating economic growth" (p. 136). He later adds, "The most obvious structural solution to hunger is rapid economic development in poorer nations" (p. 223). Sider rightly calls for the removal of most trade barriers (pp. 143–46, 241) and agricultural subsidies (pp. 146–47). Finally, he understands that the lack of access to land ownership in many poor countries is a major factor in trapping people in poverty, and that wealthy elites within poor nations maintain their stranglehold on ownership of private property through close connections with corrupt or at least indifferent government officials in those countries (pp. 125–27).

2. Sider's Incorrect Analysis of the Problem as "Affluence." The subtitle of Sider's book summarizes the overall perspective that he presents. The main title is *Rich Christians in an Age of Hunger*, but the subtitle is "*Moving from Affluence to Generosity.*" That subtitle indicates that he thinks the *primary problem* is too much affluence in the world. However, in reality the primary problem is too much poverty. The problem is not that rich people have too much money but rather that poor people have too little.

The subtitle also summarizes Sider's overall approach to solving the problem as "generosity." In other words, to solve the problem of poverty, rich Christians in the world must move "from affluence" (they should stop being so rich) "to generosity" (they should give away more). But if the real solution to poverty is not continually receiving gifts from rich people or governments but rather increased productivity on the part of poor people, so that they have productive jobs that reward them with steady income, then focusing on "generosity" also fails to get at the heart of the problem.

An analogy may be seen in the area of health and sickness.[63] Someone might say, "There is too large a gap between the healthy people and the sick people in the world today. We need to reduce this inequality in health. We should have more healthy people getting sick so there is not so much inequality." That would be a foolish suggestion, because the problem is not the gap between healthy people and sick people. The problem is that there are too many sick people. And the solution is to seek measures to make the sick people well. Similarly, the only final and long-term solution to poverty is finding measures by which poor people in poor nations can become more productive and produce their own prosperity.

a. Sider Incorrectly Portrays Increased Prosperity and the "Market Economy" as Mostly Unfair and Harmful to Individuals, Families, the Environment, and Culture: Although Sider does in passing affirm the benefits of economic development and an essentially free-market economy (see above), what he gives with his right hand he takes away with his left. After a brief affirmation of the benefits of these things (pp. 135–38), he devotes 40 pages (pp. 138–79) to describing in great detail the *damage* that comes from economic growth, increased prosperity, and a free-market economic system (what he calls a market economy; see pp. 138–39).

---

[63] I first read this illustration in the excellent book by Jay Richards, *Money, Greed, and God*, 110.

He says, "Today's market economies also have fundamental weaknesses. When measured by biblical standards, glaring injustices exist." He describes 14 of these weaknesses:

1. He says the poor are largely left out of economic development because "at least a quarter of the world's people lack the capital to participate in any major way in the global market economy" (p. 138). He calls for "redistribution" to solve this problem (p. 138).

2. He says it is "very disturbing" that "the gap between rich and poor is increasing again in very wealthy countries" (p. 139). While he admits that "over time, with proper government measures, the poor usually benefit" (p. 139) from economic growth in a nation (he mentions South Korea, Taiwan, Singapore, Hong Kong, China, Indonesia, Malaysia, and Thailand as nations where the poor "are vastly better off economically" than they used to be, p. 139), he immediately adds that "without corrective action, today's global markets appear to create unjust dangerous extremes between rich and poor. . . . Centralized wealth equals concentrated power. And that . . . is dangerous" (p. 140).

3. Sider says that "pervasive cultural decline seems to follow the expansion of the market," including "sweeping materialism" and "ever-more seductive advertising," especially on television (pp. 140–41). And then this growing materialism "destroys social relationships" (p. 142).

4. As a result of economic growth and the global market economy, "our rivers and lakes are polluted, the ozone layer is depleted, and global warming has already begun. . . . Companies seldom count pollution costs in their profit and loss statements. . . . The market rewards polluters who pass their costs to neighbors—those who live downstream from where they dump polluted water into the river" (p. 142).

5. International trade is largely unfair because of "restrictive tariffs and import quotas" that "keep out many of the goods produced in the less developed countries" (p. 144).

6. Many poor nations cannot repay their international debts. For example, in Tanzania, "the government spent $155 million in 1993–94 on debt repayments. This was more than the combined budget for clean water and health" (p. 147). In addition, "poor nations' debt payments have also deprived children of basic education" (p. 147).

7. Sider says that "economic life today, especially in industrialized societies, is producing . . . severe environmental pollution. . . . We are destroying our air, forests, lands, and water so rapidly that we face disastrous problems" (p. 149). The environmental impact of modern economic development includes global warming (pp. 150–52), destruction of the oceans

(152–54), deforestation (154–58), and the degradation of agricultural land (158–60).

8. Rich nations selfishly eat the food that is exported from the poor nations who really need it (pp. 160–64). "Developing nations with large numbers of malnourished and even starving people nevertheless have exported substantial amounts of food to wealthy nations" (p. 160).

9. Multinational corporations have far too much power and contribute to corruption in poor countries (pp. 164–69).

10. Many poor countries have latent discrimination against women (pp. 169–71).

11. In many poor nations there is continuing racism and ethnic hostility (pp. 171–72).

12. War "results from a complex web of structural evils and certainly produces poverty and death" (pp. 172–74).

13. Bribery is frequent in poor countries (p. 175).

14. The United States has supported evil dictators in the past (pp. 175–76).

Sider's response to all of these evils is to tell Christians in wealthy countries that "we are participants in structures that also contribute to the suffering and death of millions of people" (p. 178). Sider tells how United Brands, an American company that imports fruit, paid bribes to government officials in Honduras so they would lower an export tax on their bananas (p. 175). Sider concludes that "the story of the bananas shows how all of us are involved in unjust international economic structures" (p. 177; Sider fails to mention that such a payment of bribes to foreign officials is a violation of U.S. law).

He concludes that we need to repent of our involvement in unjust economic structures (apparently the free-market system, about which he has been listing evil consequences for 40 pages). He says:

> What should be our response? For biblical Christians, the only correct response to sin is repentance. We have become entangled, to some degree unconsciously, in a complex web of institutionalized sin. . . . Biblical repentance involves conversion. It involves a whole new lifestyle. The One who stands ready to forgive us for our sinful involvement in economic injustice offers us his grace to begin living a generous new lifestyle that empowers the poor and oppressed. . . . If God's Word is true, then all of us who dwell in affluent nations are trapped in sin. We have profited from systematic injustice. . . . We are guilty of sin against God and neighbor. (p. 177)

The reader is left with the clear impression that increasing economic prosperity and the free-market economic system that brings it about are *mostly harmful* for individuals and nations. Those who participate in these things and benefit from them need to repent.

b. Sider Incorrectly Portrays the Problem as Inequality Rather Than Poverty: Sider claims that the increasing "gap between the rich and the poor" is harmful because "centralized wealth equals concentrated power" (pp. 139–40).

However, Sider apparently fails to recognize that any *government* action to take some wealth from those who earn the highest incomes would result in more power for the government, which is already the most powerful factor in any society, far more powerful than any individual wealthy person. Therefore, any increase in taxation on the rich for the purpose of reducing their "concentrated power" would just add to the already immensely concentrated power of the government. And while Sider deplores the "vast political power" of wealthy people (p. 140), he fails to mention that wealthy donors, overall, give about the same amount of support to Democrats as well as Republicans in the United States.

In fact, as individual nations develop economically, and as world economic development advances, the "gap" between rich and poor in terms of absolute number of dollars *will inevitably continue to grow*, even though the poor will continue to grow more and more prosperous. What has in fact happened in the last century, and what will most likely continue to happen into the future, is that the poor will become richer and the rich will become richer at an even faster rate.

This is simply a mathematical reality. For example, if an economy grows 20 percent in a year, a 20 percent increase for someone who earns $500,000 is necessarily going to be larger *in dollars* than a 20 percent increase for someone who earns $50,000 a year, and that in turn will be larger than a 20 percent increase for someone with a part-time job who earns $5,000 a year. But they will all be better off—it's just that the higher-income person will be even farther ahead. This will happen year after year, whether the annual growth is 2 percent, 5 percent, 10 percent, or 20 percent. The only way to prevent this perpetually increasing "inequality" is by the government forcibly confiscating most of the gains made by an upper-income worker. But that concentrates even more power in the hands of the government, and it removes incentives for the most productive members of a society to keep on working and producing, which hinders economic growth.

Therefore, the problem with continual attacks on inequality is that they actually result in hindering overall economic growth and productivity, thus reducing the total growth in GDP. Unfortunately, if GDP growth is hindered, this will certainly affect the poor and hinder rather than help them in overcoming poverty.[64]

c. Sider Incorrectly Portrays the Use and Enjoyment of the Earth's Resources as Mostly Harmful: Sider argues that the earth's resources are so limited that we need to restrain our use of them. He says, "Due to overconsumption, small numbers of affluent people strain the earth's limited resources far more than much larger numbers of poor people" (p. 30). Elsewhere he says, "The earth's resources are limited" (p. 240).

---

[64] John M. Frame rightly observes, "We don't have a biblical mandate, in my judgment, to 'narrow the gap between rich and poor,' as an end in itself. We do, however, have a mandate to feed hungry people." *The Doctrine of the Christian Life: A Theology of Lordship* (Phillipsburg, NJ: P&R, 2008), 822n11.

I have argued extensively elsewhere that God has given us an earth with abundant natural resources, and has also given us the ingenuity to use them wisely, so that we have sufficient resources in terms of clean air, water, forests, coal, oil, and natural gas to last for many hundreds of years to come.[65]

Because he mistakenly assumes the imminent scarcity of natural resources, Sider incorrectly focuses on how much rich nations *consume* rather than on how much they *produce*. He says, "North Americans use vastly more energy per year per person than South Americans" (p. 29; see also pp. 30–31). But Sider fails to mention that North Americans also *produce* vastly more energy per year per person than South Americans. South America also has vast resources of coal, oil, natural gas, and the potential for nuclear power production. North Americans do not *steal* those resources from South America, but develop them from the abundant storehouses of energy supplies that God has placed in North America or purchase them from other countries that want to sell.

Sider's criticism is not harmless. When he deplores the wise use of the earth's resources and people believe him, this hinders human economic progress, and therefore hinders helping the poor. It also reduces human freedom.

For example, Sider says, "We can organize our lives so that it is easier and more desirable to walk, bike, carpool and use public transportation more and personal vehicles less" (p. 251). Well, I once tried this. For a little over a year, I rode a bicycle 30 minutes to teach at Phoenix Seminary when it was located only six miles from my home. However, I found that it so often limited my freedom to travel from the seminary to other meetings or appointments that I eventually gave up the bicycle and began to drive. That used more of the earth's boundless supply of oil, but *it also increased my productivity* in the long run because of greater freedom in my schedule. (Sider's argument for riding a bicycle is not the physical health benefits that would come from it but rather that it would use fewer of the earth's resources. That is a persuasive argument only if there is a significant danger of running out of the world's supply of oil, which I simply do not think to be the case.)

Sider encourages us to "buy recycled paper products" because it will "help reduce the destruction of rain forests overseas" (p. 253). But the paper that I buy comes not from overseas rain forests but from tree farms in the United States and Canada, where the trees that are harvested are replaced by planting new trees every year. And recycled paper products cost something like 30 percent more (for legal pads at Staples, for example). So this seems to me to be a needless and wasteful suggestion. (Sider has similar recommendations on reducing the use of resources on pp. 246–55.)

d. Sider Places Disproportionate Blame on the Free Economic Choices of Wealthy Nations and Fails to Adequately Blame Corrupt Rulers within Poor Nations: In his long section of material on the harmful effects of increased prosperity and a free-market economy (pp. 138–179), Sider occasionally mentions the harm that comes from corrupt

---

[65] See Wayne Grudem, *Politics—According to the Bible: A Comprehensive Resource for Understanding Modern Political Issues in Light of Scripture* (Grand Rapids, MI: Zondervan, 2010), 320–61.

leaders in poor nations, but he places most of the blame for these abuses on *wealthy nations* rather than on the corrupt rulers in those poor countries. Of the 14 specific "weaknesses" in free-market economies that Sider names (see the list in section (a) above), the following are primarily problems that can be solved only by a reformation of government within a poor nation itself (I mention here only the items that fall in that category): (1) When the poor are left out of participation in the economic system, solutions must come from changes in laws, policies, and government corruption. (4) Pollution must be regulated by laws within the country. (6) Debt repayments are necessary only because the money that the poor nation borrowed was misused by corrupt leaders and much of it ended up in their private bank accounts. That money must be recovered so that debts can be repaid. (7) Destruction of the environment can only be controlled by laws within the poor nation, just as antipollution regulations have stopped most pollution within nearly all wealthy nations today. As for (9) the excessive power exercised by multinational corporations, (10) discrimination against women, (11) racism, (12) war, and (13) bribery, these also can be stopped only by reformation of the government within the poor nation itself. (However, many wealthy nations have rightly outlawed the payment of bribes by companies with headquarters located within their jurisdictions.)

3. Sider's Incorrect Analysis of the Solution to Poverty as "Generosity." Just as Sider incorrectly sees the main problem as "affluence" rather than poverty, he also incorrectly sees the primary solution as "generosity" rather than a poor nation producing more goods and services.

a. Sider Incorrectly Sees the Primary Solution as "Generosity" by Rich Countries Rather Than Increased Production by Poor Countries: Sider speaks of the need for "trying to share the world's resources more justly" (p. 20) without mentioning that many of the world's poorest countries in Africa, Asia, and Latin America have immense natural resources. He says, "There is more than enough food to feed everyone if it is shared fairly" (p. 35) without mentioning that there is more than enough land to produce adequate food, or to make other products that can be sold so that food can be imported, in all or nearly all the poor countries of the world.

But if the only long-term solution to poverty in poor nations is that those nations begin to produce their own prosperity, then Sider's emphasis wrongly encourages poor nations to think they have to depend on increased generosity from wealthy nations before they can escape from poverty. Placing the primary emphasis on the need for more generosity from wealthy nations diminishes the attention that should be focused on the only real solution: correcting the corrupt governments and laws, the oppressive economic systems, and the harmful cultural values that continue to trap poor nations in poverty.[66]

---

[66] See the extensive evidence for this claim throughout many chapters in Grudem and Asmus, *The Poverty of Nations*.

b. Sider Incorrectly Advocates More Government Control Rather Than More Economic Freedom: While abundant economic evidence indicates that *economic freedom*, not government control, is what leads to increased prosperity and overcomes poverty in poor nations,[67] Sider frequently advocates policies that would increase government control and thereby hinder economic productivity in poor nations. He says that "Christians must insist on redistribution—through both private voluntary efforts and effective government programs" (p. 230). He also says, "Only if redistribution occurs—through private and/or public measures—will the poorest obtain the capital to earn a decent living in the global market" (p. 138). He advocates international enforcement mechanisms for fair labor standards (pp. 243–44; such "enforcement" would require international governmental power of some kind). He advocates more foreign aid to poor nations (p. 32–34), but, as I argued above (see p. 977), this foreign aid has multiple harmful effects, entrenching corrupt leaders in power, enriching their personal bank accounts, and often fomenting civil war to gain control of the country's treasury (which oversees the receipt and distribution of foreign aid payments).

c. Sider Fails to Adequately Emphasize the Need for Poor Countries to Replace Their Corrupt Rulers: Again and again Sider emphasizes the need for wealthy people and nations to share more of their wealth with poor nations (pp. 1–37, 41–63, 183–203), but he makes only a very occasional and parenthetical mention of the primary cause of poverty in poor nations: the corrupt rulers and unjust laws and economic policies that currently oppress citizens in all of the poor countries of the world today.

In addition, when Sider warns against wealthy people having too much power, he fails to mention the greater danger, that of government leaders in poor countries having too much power that they use for their personal benefit.

When he does mention the evil of rulers in foreign countries, he characterizes them either as "wealthy elites" (p. 224) or as evil dictators, and then he focuses blame not on those rulers themselves but on the support that the United States allegedly provided to keep those rulers in power (see p. 224).

d. Sider Incorrectly Advocates More Governmental Foreign Aid Rather Than Less: Sider advocates more foreign aid and argues that the United States is the least generous of major Western donors to poor countries (pp. 32–34), but he bases this only on percentage of GNP[68] given in "official development assistance"—in other words, given by government programs—and he fails to mention that U.S. *private* charitable giving as a percentage of GDP

---

[67] See, for example, Terry Miller and Anthony B. Kim, *2016 Index of Economic Freedom* (Washington: Heritage Foundation, and New York: Dow Jones Co., 2016).

[68] GNP (gross national product) is an economic measurement similar to (but not the same as) GDP, but now less commonly used.

is much larger than that of other developed countries.[69] And Sider also seems unaware of the extensive criticisms of "official" (that is, governmental) foreign aid from economic experts who have extensively documented its failures and the damage it has caused.[70]

In contrast to Sider's attempt to characterize Americans as stingy, the *Almanac of American Philanthropy* reported that for 2011–2014 (the most recent years for which data was available to me), *private charitable giving* by individuals in the United States, as a percentage of the nation's GDP, showed that "Americans are about twice as generous in their private giving as . . . the Canadians, and 3–15 *times* as charitable as the residents of other developed nations," as the following chart from that report shows:[71]

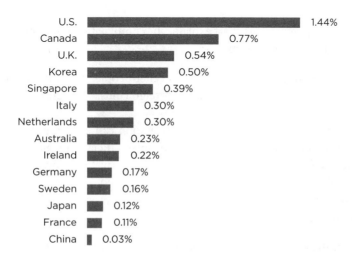

Figure 37.1. Charitable Giving by Country (as a Percentage of Gross Domestic Product). (Source: Karl Zinsmeister, *The Almanac of American Philanthropy* [Washington: Philanthropy Roundtable, 2016]. Used with permission.)

Of course, not all charitable giving goes to needy people in poor countries, but when we isolate that portion of personal charitable giving that goes to helping the poor in other nations, the United States also gives far more than any other country:[72]

---

[69] Melanie Grayce West, "Charitable Giving in the U.S. Continues to Rise," *The Wall Street Journal*, June 16, 2015, http://www.wsj.com/articles/charitable-giving-in-u-s-continues-to-rise-1434427261.

[70] See the discussion of foreign aid above, p. 977, and Grudem and Asmus, *The Poverty of Nations*, 65–75. See also Moyo, *Dead Aid*; William Easterly, *The White Man's Burden: Why the West's Efforts to Aid the Rest Have Done So Much Ill and So Little Good* (New York: Penguin, 2006); Abhijit Vinayak Banerjee et al., *Making Aid Work* (Cambridge, MA: The MIT Press, 2007).

[71] Karl Zinsmeister, *The Almanac of American Philanthropy* (Washington, DC: Philanthropy Roundtable, 2016), last page (online pages are not numbered), http://www.philanthropyroundtable.org/almanac/statistics/, italics original.

[72] Ibid. It is important in understanding this chart to recognize that the GDP of the United States is about four times as large as the GDP of Japan and about six times as large as the GDP of the United Kingdom, and this explains part of the difference in the actual amounts given.

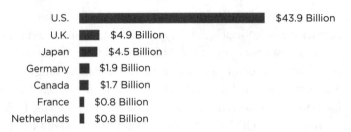

U.S.	$43.9 Billion
U.K.	$4.9 Billion
Japan	$4.5 Billion
Germany	$1.9 Billion
Canada	$1.7 Billion
France	$0.8 Billion
Netherlands	$0.8 Billion

Figure 37.2. Charitable Giving by Country (Private Donations). (Source: Karl Zinsmeister, *The Almanac of American Philanthropy* [Washington: Philanthropy Roundtable, 2016]. Used with permission.)

The text accompanying this chart explains the complexities of measurement of various sources of help for poor countries:

> Americans are much more willing than other peoples to voluntarily donate money to help the poor and stricken in foreign lands. The figures here depict private charitable giving in various forms.
>
> Of course there are other ways that a nation can give to less developed countries in addition to private philanthropy—official government aid, remittances to families back home by immigrants, private business investment, etc. . . . When you add up all of these sources of aid, the U.S. comes out far ahead of any other nation, sending $365 billion overseas annually to developing countries.

The report then goes on to explain other sources of aid for poor countries as well:

> Another very large source of economic assistance to the overseas poor, which we have chosen not to depict here but which has been painstakingly estimated in the Hudson Institute report from which this data is taken, is remittances sent back home by U.S. immigrants from poor lands. These amount to over a hundred billion dollars every year, and are more important to family welfare, health, and education in many underdeveloped countries than either private or governmental charity.
>
> Anyone trying to understand the financial flows that aid the poor overseas must also consider one final element: private investment in developing countries. More than $179 billion of U.S. capital was committed to projects in poor nations in 2014, with for-profit aspirations. This job- and growth-creating money is probably the most important form of all of international sharing.[73]

Sider also urges forgiveness of foreign debt that is owed by poor nations (pp. 147–49;

---

[73] Ibid., next-to-last page.

also 244–46), but that is simply more foreign aid given in a two-step process: first the loan, then forgiveness of the loan.

In summary, Sider mistakenly advocates more generosity on the part of wealthy nations as the primary solution to world poverty. While more generosity would certainly do more to help cases of urgent need, Sider fails to focus on the only genuine solution to poverty in poor nations, namely, that poor nations begin to produce more of their own prosperity.[74]

4. Harmful Results of Sider's Analysis.

a. False Guilt: The first harmful result from Sider's analysis will be a sense of false guilt on the part of people in wealthy countries who buy bananas (see p. 177) or any products produced in poor countries and brought to wealthy countries through international trade agreements. While Sider's call for greater generosity and sharing on the part of wealthy Christians is commendable and is a strength of his book, the overall force of his argument is to persuade Christians in wealthy countries that they should repent of their wealth, live a much simpler lifestyle, and feel guilt about participating in the economic benefits of increased prosperity. I did not find in the entire book any affirmation of the goodness of enjoyment of the use of the world's resources or enjoyment of the products of economic development in wealthy countries today.

But if the overall emphasis simply increases the guilt that wealthy people feel, even among those who are already quite generous in giving of their time and money, and if this feeling of guilt is for things that are not in themselves morally wrong or for things (such as living in a wealthy country with a free-market system) for which people are not directly responsible, then this is not a healthy spiritual result.

b. Increased Hostility toward Economic Development: Another negative result of Sider's book will be a net increase in hostility toward economic development in wealthy nations and hostility toward any free-market economic system that makes development possible. Sider's book will increase people's suspicion of and even hostility toward corporations, toward the use of the earth's resources, and toward growth in economic prosperity itself.

But if these things are (as I believe) basically good (though they can be used in evil ways), then Sider's book will have, in the long term, the net result of hindering the very economic development that is the only genuine solution to world poverty.

Therefore, it seems to me that, while Sider's book will have the beneficial effect of increasing the generosity of wealthy Christians in meeting the short-term urgent needs of people in poor nations, the overall effect of the book will be to hinder economic productivity and thus ultimately to hinder rather than help the people in poor nations who are seeking to climb out of poverty.[75]

---

[74] See extensive support for this claim in Grudem and Asmus, *The Poverty of Nations*, chaps. 1–4.

[75] A more balanced view is found in David Platt, *Radical: Taking Back Your Faith from the American Dream* (Colorado Springs: Multnomah, 2010). He challenges readers to ask if they are really maximizing their

QUESTIONS FOR PERSONAL APPLICATION

1. Do you think that all financial inequality is wrong? In an ideal world, do you think everyone should have the same amount of money?

2. Do you agree with James when he says, "Has not God chosen those who are poor in the world to be *rich in faith* and heirs of the kingdom, which he has promised to those who love him? (James 2:5). Have you ever been "poor in the world" and "rich in faith" at the same time?

3. If you are relatively wealthy by the world's standards, what temptations to wrongful attitudes are you aware of in your own life? If you are relatively poor by the world's standards, what temptations to wrongful attitudes are you aware of in your own life?

4. Have you ever experienced what this chapter calls "earned success"? What effect did it have in your life?

5. Do you think that you have the same kind of love for the poor that Jesus exhibited in his earthly ministry?

6. Do you think that there is some amount of wealth that is "too much" for a Christian to have? How would you deal with this matter if you suddenly discovered an invention or designed a website that made you millions of dollars?

7. Did this chapter change your thinking on the causes and solutions for poverty in poor nations?

8. Have you ever created products of value that added to your nation's GDP?

9. Is your general attitude toward business an attitude of suspicion or one of appreciation? Do you think well of highly successful people in the business world?

10. What character traits (see p. 110) are especially helpful in enabling people to think and act rightly in matters of poverty and wealth?

SPECIAL TERMS

debt forgiveness
fair-trade coffee
gross domestic product (GDP)
inequality
per capita income
social justice

---

impact for the kingdom of God and warns that the comforts of prosperous America can deafen our ears to the needs of the world (see p. 64). My conclusion after reading *Radical* twice is that it is a very good, much needed book. However, I still wonder if Platt has a blind spot regarding the moral good of increased material prosperity, which I think is God's purpose, in economic terms, for all people and all nations on the earth.

BIBLIOGRAPHY

Sections in Other Ethics Texts

(see complete bibliographical data, p. 64)

> Clark and Rakestraw, 2:339–80
> Frame, 808–29
> Gushee and Stassen, 359–75
> Kaiser, 19–30, 199–210
> McQuilkin and Copan, 474–79, 484–91
> Rae, 332–33, 338–42

Other Works

Alcorn, Randy. *Money, Possessions, and Eternity*. Carol Stream, IL: Tyndale, 2003.

Baker, David L. *Tight Fists or Open Hands? Wealth and Poverty in Old Testament Law*. Grand Rapids: Eerdmans, 2009.

Banerjee, Abhijit Vinayak. *Making Aid Work*. Cambridge, MA: The MIT Press, 2007.

Beisner, E. Calvin. *Prosperity and Poverty: The Compassionate Use of Resources in a World of Scarcity*. 1988. Repr., Eugene, OR: Wipf & Stock, 2001.

Blomberg, Craig L. *Christians in an Age of Wealth: A Biblical Theology of Stewardship*. Biblical Theology for Life. Grand Rapids, MI: Zondervan, 2013.

———. *Neither Poverty Nor Riches: A Biblical Theology of Material Possessions*. Grand Rapids, MI: Eerdmans, 1999.

Bradley, Anne, and Art Lindsley, eds. *For the Least of These: A Biblical Answer to Poverty*. Bloomington, IN: WestBow, 2014.

Brooks, Arthur C. *The Battle: How the Fight between Free Enterprise and Big Government Will Shape America's Future*. New York: Basic Books, 2010.

Bunting, I. D. "Poverty." In *New Dictionary of Christian Ethics and Pastoral Theology*, edited by David J. Atkinson and David H. Field, 677–79. Leicester, UK: Inter-Varsity, and Downers Grove, IL: InterVarsity Press, 1995.

Chester, Tim. *Good News to the Poor: Social Involvement and the Gospel*. Wheaton, IL: Crossway, 2013.

Corbett, Steve, and Brian Fikkert. *Helping without Hurting in Church Benevolence: A Practical Guide to Walking with Low-Income People*. Chicago: Moody, 2015.

———. *When Helping Hurts: How to Alleviate Poverty without Hurting the Poor . . . and Yourself*. Chicago: Moody, 2009.

DeYoung, Kevin, and Greg Gilbert. *What Is the Mission of the Church? Making Sense of Social Justice, Shalom, and the Great Commission*. Wheaton, IL: Crossway, 2011.

Easterly, William. *The White Man's Burden: Why the West's Efforts to Aid the Rest Have Done So Much Ill and So Little Good*. New York: Penguin, 2006.

Edwards, Jonathan. "The Duty of Charity to the Poor." In *Works of Jonathan Edwards: Vol. 17, Sermons and Discourses, 1730–1733*, edited by Mark Valeri, 369–405. New Haven, CT: Yale University Press, 1999.

Fikkert, Brian, and Russell Mask. *From Dependence to Dignity: How to Alleviate Poverty through Church-Centered Microfinance.* Grand Rapids, MI: Zondervan, 2015.

Grudem, Wayne, and Barry Asmus. *The Poverty of Nations: A Sustainable Solution.* Wheaton, IL: Crossway, 2013.

Hansen, Collin. *Blind Spots: Becoming a Courageous, Compassionate, and Commissioned Church.* Cultural Renewal. Wheaton, IL: Crossway, 2015.

Haugen, Gary A., and Victor Boutros. *The Locust Effect: Why the End of Poverty Requires the End of Violence.* Oxford: Oxford University Press, 2014.

Henry, Carl F. H. *The Uneasy Conscience of Modern Fundamentalism.* Grand Rapids, MI: Eerdmans, 2003.

Hillyer, P. N. "Stewardship." In *New Dictionary of Christian Ethics and Pastoral Theology*, 814–15.

Hubbard, R. Glenn, and William R. Duggan. *The Aid Trap: Hard Truths about Ending Poverty.* New York: Columbia Business School Publishing, 2009.

Jones, David W. *Reforming the Morality of Usury: A Study of Differences That Separated the Protestant Reformers.* Dallas: University Press of America, 2004.

Jones, David W., and Russell S. Woodbridge. *Health, Wealth and Happiness: Has the Prosperity Gospel Overshadowed the Gospel of Christ?* Grand Rapids, MI: Kregel, 2011.

Keller, Timothy. *Center Church: Doing Balanced, Gospel-Centered Ministry in Your City.* Grand Rapids, MI: Zondervan, 2012.

———. *Generous Justice: How God's Grace Makes Us Just.* New York: Dutton, 2010.

———. *Ministries of Mercy: The Call of the Jericho Road.* 3rd ed. Phillipsburg, NJ: P&R, 2015.

Landes, David S. *The Wealth and Poverty of Nations: Why Some Are So Rich and Some So Poor.* New York: W. W. Norton, 1999.

Litfin, Duane. *Word Versus Deed: Resetting the Scales to a Biblical Balance.* Wheaton, IL: Crossway, 2012.

Lupton, Robert D. *Toxic Charity: How Churches and Charities Hurt Those They Help (And How to Reverse It).* New York: HarperOne, 2011.

Mangalwadi, Vishal. *Truth and Transformation: A Manifesto for Ailing Nations.* Seattle: YWAM, 2009.

Maranz, David E. *African Friends and Money Matters: Observations from Africa.* 2nd ed. Dallas: SIL International, 2015.

McCloskey, Deirdre N. *Bourgeois Dignity: Why Economics Can't Explain the Modern World.* Chicago: University of Chicago Press, 2010.

McConnell, Mez, and Mike McKinley. *Church in Hard Places: How the Local Church Brings Life to the Poor and Needy.* 9Marks. Wheaton, IL: Crossway, 2016.

Middelmann, Udo W. *Christianity versus Fatalistic Religions in the War against Poverty.* Colorado Springs: Paternoster, 2007.

Miller, Darrow L., and Stan Guthrie. *Discipling Nations: The Power of Truth to Transform Cultures.* 2nd ed. Seattle: YWAM, 2001.

Moore, Stephen. *Who's the Fairest of Them All? The Truth about Opportunity, Taxes, and Wealth in America.* New York, London: Encounter Books, 2012.

Moyo, Dambisa. *Dead Aid: Why Aid Is Not Working and How There Is a Better Way for Africa.* New York: Farrar, Straus & Giroux, 2009.

Novak, Michael. *The Spirit of Democratic Capitalism.* Lanham, MD: Madison Books, 1991.

Nyquist, J. Paul. *Is Justice Possible? The Elusive Pursuit of What Is Right.* Chicago: Moody, 2017.

Olasky, Marvin N. *Compassionate Conservatism: What It Is, What It Does, and How It Can Transform America.* New York: Free Press, 2000.

———. *The Tragedy of American Compassion.* Washington, DC: Regnery Gateway, 1995.

Platt, David. *Counter Culture: Following Christ in an Anti-Christian Age.* 2nd ed. Carol Stream, IL: Tyndale, 2017.

———. *Radical: Taking Back Your Faith from the American Dream.* Colorado Springs: Multnomah, 2010.

Richards, Jay W. *Money, Greed, and God: Why Capitalism Is the Solution and Not the Problem.* New York: HarperOne, 2009.

Ryken, Philip G., and Noah J. Toly. *What Is Mercy Ministry?* Basics of the Faith. Phillipsburg, NJ: P&R, 2013.

Schneider, John R. *The Good of Affluence: Seeking God in a Culture of Wealth.* Grand Rapids, MI: Eerdmans, 2002.

Sider, Ronald J. *Rich Christians in an Age of Hunger: Moving from Affluence to Generosity.* 5th ed. Nashville: Thomas Nelson, 2005.

Smith, Warren Cole, and John Stonestreet. *Restoring All Things: God's Audacious Plan to Change the World through Everyday People.* Grand Rapids, MI: Baker, 2015.

Stanley, Thomas J., and William D. Danko. *The Millionaire Next Door: The Surprising Secrets of America's Wealthy.* New York: Pocket Books, 1996.

Strom, Bruce D. *Gospel Justice: Joining Together to Provide Help and Hope for Those Oppressed by Legal Injustice.* Chicago: Moody, 2013.

Wilkinson, Richard G., and Kate Pickett. *The Spirit Level: Why Greater Equality Makes Societies Stronger.* New York: Bloomsbury, 2011.

Winter, Bruce W. *Seek the Welfare of the City: Christians as Benefactors and Citizens.* First-Century Christians in the Graeco-Roman World. Grand Rapids, MI: Eerdmans, 1994.

SCRIPTURE MEMORY PASSAGE

1 John 3:17: But if anyone has the world's goods and sees his brother in need, yet closes his heart against him, how does God's love abide in him?

HYMN

"If Thou But Suffer God to Guide Thee"

If thou but suffer God to guide thee,
And hope in him through all thy ways,
He'll give thee strength, whate'er betide thee,
And bear thee through the evil days:
Who trusts in God's unchanging love
Builds on the rock that naught can move.

What can these anxious cares avail thee,
These never-ceasing moans and sighs?
What can it help, if thou bewail thee
O'er each dark moment as it flies?
Our cross and trials do but press
The heavier for our bitterness.

Only be still, and wait his leisure
In cheerful hope, with heart content
To take whate'er thy Father's pleasure
And all-deserving love hath sent;
Nor doubt our inmost wants are known
To him who chose us for his own.

All are alike before the highest;
'Tis easy to our God, we know,
To raise thee up though low thou liest,
To make the rich man poor and low;
True wonders still by him are wrought
Who setteth up and brings to naught.

Sing, pray, and keep his ways unswerving,
So do thine own part faithfully,
And trust his Word, though undeserving,
Thou yet shalt find it true for thee;
God never yet forsook at need
The soul that trusted him indeed.

AUTHOR: GEORG NEUMARK, 1641

Chapter 38

PERSONAL FINANCIAL STEWARDSHIP

How much of our income should we give to the Lord's work?

What blessings come to us as a result of generous giving?

Is it right to leave an inheritance to our children?

How much should we save for the future?

How much should we spend on ourselves?

Is gambling morally wrong?

When a pastor announces a sermon on "stewardship," most people assume that he will be preaching about giving and that he will exhort them to give more money to the work of the church. I agree that generous giving is a significant part of wise stewardship, but it also includes much more than giving.

In this chapter, we will discuss stewardship under three major categories:

A. Wise giving: How much should we give away, and where should we give it?
B. Wise saving: How much should we save for the future, and where should we put our savings?
C. Wise spending: How much should we spend on ourselves?

In chapter 34, when I discussed private ownership of property, I briefly mentioned the concept of personal stewardship: if God entrusts us with ownership of property, then he expects us to use it wisely and faithfully in service to him. This chapter develops that idea of stewardship in much more detail.

A. WISE GIVING

1. Both the Old and New Testaments Teach That God's People Should Give Away Some of What They Earn. In the Old Testament, God required the people of Israel to give a "tithe" (that is, one-tenth) of their crops each year:

> You shall tithe all the yield of your seed that comes from the field year by year. (Deut. 14:22)

It was assumed that such tithing also applied to domesticated animals, for we read in Leviticus:

> *And every tithe of herds and flocks, every tenth animal* of all that pass under the herdsman's staff, *shall be holy to the LORD.* (27:32; cf. Deut. 14:23)

In this law the Lord claimed as his own 10 percent of the agricultural produce that he provided for his people. That amount was not their own; it was "holy to the LORD." These tithes were to be given for the support of the Levites, who attended to the needs of the tabernacle/temple and the sacrificial system (see Num. 18:21–24; Deut. 26:12–14; Neh. 10:37–38; 13:5, 12), and they also were used to support "the sojourner, the fatherless, and the widow" (Deut. 26:13; see also 14:28–29)—in other words, the poor among the people of Israel, those who were least able to support themselves. In addition, part of each person's tithe was offered in sacrifice and then eaten at the annual journey to God's temple, where additional sacrifices would be made (see 14:22–26).

Some interpreters have claimed that the different instructions regarding tithes in Leviticus 27:30–32, Numbers 18:21–28, and Deuteronomy 12:5–19; 14:22–28; and 26:12–14 refer to different tithes, with the result that the people of Israel were expected to give perhaps 20 percent or even 30 percent of their income in tithes. Evangelical scholars are divided on this issue.[1]

However, even if we do not decide how many tithes God required of the Israelites, it is clear that God expected them to give more than just 10 percent of their income, because there were numerous other sacrifices that he commanded from them (see Leviticus 1–7), as well as "freewill offerings" that the people made (see Lev. 22:18–23). Therefore, we can safely summarize this material by saying that the Lord expected the people of Israel to give "10 percent plus something" of their increase every year.

In the New Testament, no specific percentage of giving is required for Christians in the new covenant. (Jesus's words to the scribes and the Pharisees in Matt. 23:23 and Luke 11:42 were addressed to people still living under the old covenant law.) However, Paul

[1] For an overview of the arguments, see *Perspectives on Tithing: 4 Views*, ed. David A. Croteau (Nashville: B&H Academic, 2011). See also the additional works by Croteau in the bibliography for this chapter. For the idea that there was only one tithe, see J. A. Thompson, *Deuteronomy: An Introduction and Commentary*, TOTC (Leicester, UK: Inter-Varsity, 1974), 180–85.

clearly expected every Christian to put aside something to give to the needs of others and to the Lord's work:

> Now concerning the collection for the saints: as I directed the churches of Galatia, so you also are to do. On the first day of every week, each of you is to *put something aside* and store it up, as he may prosper, so that there will be no collecting when I come. (1 Cor. 16:1–2)

> Each one must *give* as he has decided in his heart, not reluctantly or under compulsion, for God loves a cheerful giver. (2 Cor. 9:7)

2. Where Should People Give? It is certainly right to give to the work of *the local church and its extended ministries,* for Paul wrote to the Philippian church that "the gifts you sent" were "a sacrifice acceptable and pleasing to God" (Phil. 4:18). Their gifts helped Paul's ministry and resulted in "fruit that increases to your credit" (v. 17).

In addition, Paul directly encouraged giving to support those who work in leading and teaching the church:

> Let the elders who rule well be considered worthy of double honor, especially those who labor in preaching and teaching. For the Scripture says, "You shall not muzzle an ox when it treads out the grain," and, "The laborer deserves his wages." (1 Tim. 5:17–18)

Elsewhere, he told the Corinthian Christians that they should "strive to excel in building up the church" (1 Cor. 14:12), and surely that applies to the giving that Christians do to support the work of the church.

The Old Testament pattern of giving tithes to Levites who carried out the ministry of the temple and the sacrificial system (see Num. 18:21–24; Deut. 14:28–29; Neh. 10:37–38; 13:5, 12) is an Old Testament a parallel to the idea that some of our giving should be directed to supporting the ministry of the local church.

Sometimes people wonder if it is right to give some of their money to support the work of *parachurch organizations* in addition to supporting their local churches. Such organizations include mission agencies; Christian schools, colleges, and seminaries; campus ministries; Christian radio and television stations and publication houses; and other kinds of specialized ministries. Certainly it is also right to support these organizations, since they are advancing the overall work of the kingdom of God throughout the world, and, though they may not be part of one specific local church or denomination, they are part of the worldwide body of Christ, and therefore worthy of our support.

Another significant emphasis in Scripture is that we should give to *the needs of the poor.* This is evident in the Old Testament, where some of the tithes of the people of Israel were to be given to "the sojourner, the fatherless, and the widow" (Deut. 14:29; 26:12–14). This is also evident from other passages of the Old Testament that did not explicitly mention a "tithe" but commanded the people of Israel to give generously to those in need (see Deut. 15:7–11; 24:19–22; Ps. 41:1).

In the New Testament, Paul spent two entire chapters (2 Corinthians 8–9) encouraging the Corinthian church to give generously to the needs of the poor in Jerusalem.

3. Trust in God Enables People to Give. When the Christians at Philippi sent gifts to Paul, he wrote and thanked them by saying, "I am well supplied, having received from Epaphroditus the gifts you sent" (Phil. 4:18). Then he assured them that these gifts were "a sacrifice acceptable and pleasing to God," and he added this promise:

> And *my God shall supply every need of yours* according to his riches in glory in Christ Jesus. (v. 19)

It would have been natural for the Philippian Christians to think, "We have sent generous gifts to the apostle Paul, but now what about our own financial needs? Who will provide for us?" Paul's answer was that God himself would provide for their needs. He would "supply *every need* of yours." They could feel free to give generously because, if they did, God would take care of them as well.

Paul made a similar affirmation in 2 Corinthians:

> Each one must give as he has decided in his heart, not reluctantly or under compulsion, for God loves a cheerful giver. And God is able to make all grace abound to you, so that *having all sufficiency in all things at all times*, you may abound in every good work. (9:7–8)

Just as Paul could assure the Philippians that God would supply their needs, he could tell the Corinthians that as they gave cheerfully to the needs of poor Christians in Jerusalem, God would cause his "grace" to abound to them and that they would have "all sufficiency in all things at all times." In other words, they could trust God to take care of their needs.

These statements from Paul echo a similar theme taught by Jesus:

> *Give, and it will be given to you.* Good measure, pressed down, shaken together, running over, will be put into your lap. For with the measure you use it will be measured back to you. (Luke 6:38)

The Old Testament contains several similar promises that God would provide for the needs of those who gave generously to him:

> Honor the LORD with your wealth
>   and with the firstfruits of all your produce;
> then your barns will be filled with plenty,
>   and your vats will be bursting with wine. (Prov. 3:9–10)

> Bring the full tithe into the storehouse, that there may be food in my house. And thereby put me to the test, says the LORD of hosts, if I will not open the windows of heaven for you and pour down for you a blessing until there is no more need. (Mal. 3:10; see also Hag. 2:15–19)

But these passages must not be misunderstood. Nothing in the Bible teaches that we should give money *in order to earn a right relationship with God*. That comes by faith alone (see Eph. 2:8–9). But after we have been forgiven and have come into a right relationship with God through Christ, *then* generous giving will be one result that flows out of our trust in God and desire to please him in our daily lives.

4. God Promises Several Blessings for Those Who Give. When we give to support the work of the Lord and to care for the needs of others, God promises several blessings. First, God himself will be pleased. Paul said that the gifts that the Philippians sent to him were "a fragrant offering, *a sacrifice acceptable and pleasing to God*" (Phil. 4:18). Another verse that emphasizes this idea says simply, "God loves a cheerful giver" (2 Cor. 9:7). And the author of Hebrews says:

> Do not neglect to do good and to share what you have, for *such sacrifices are pleasing to God*. (13:16)

This language indicates a conscious analogy with the sacrificial system in the Old Testament. Just as the Old Testament says God was pleased when the people of Israel offered their animals and crops as sacrifices on a physical altar, so these New Testament verses view our gifts as "sacrifices" of another kind that are pleasing to God. Therefore, when we put money in the offering plate, or write a check to support a certain ministry, or spend time volunteering at a homeless shelter, we should remember that God is watching our actions, and he recognizes the sacrifice of time or money that we are making, and he is pleased.

A second blessing that results from our giving is that God himself will provide for our needs, as explained in the previous section (see Luke 6:38; Phil. 4:17–19; 2 Cor. 9:7–8, 11, and similar Old Testament passages such as Prov. 3:9 and Mal. 3:10–11).

A third blessing is that our giving will advance the work of God's kingdom on earth. When Paul thanked the Philippians for sending gifts to him, he said, "Not that I seek the gift, but *I seek the fruit that increases to your credit*" (Phil. 4:17). In other words, the gifts from the Philippians enabled Paul to continue his ministry more effectively. As a result of his missionary work, there would be increased advancement in the work of God's kingdom, what Paul called "fruit" in his work. And he said that the fruit would increase "to your credit"—that is, the gifts from the Philippian church would directly increase Paul's fruitful ministry for the kingdom, and God would remember that the gifts from Philippi were a crucial part of that ministry increase.

In fact, those who give more generously to the work of God's kingdom on earth will see more abundant results, because Paul writes this:

> The point is this: whoever sows sparingly will also reap sparingly, and whoever sows bountifully will also reap bountifully. (2 Cor. 9:6)

In addition, Paul seems to indicate that when people give generously, God will continue to provide for their needs in such a way that they will be able to continue giving generously in the future:

> You will be enriched in every way to be generous in every way, which through us will produce thanksgiving to God. (2 Cor. 9:11)

This is similar to a verse from Proverbs:

> One gives freely, yet grows all the richer;
>   another withholds what he should give, and only suffers want. (11:24)

A fourth blessing that comes from our giving is the joy of being able to help others directly. Jesus himself taught, "It is more blessed to give than to receive" (Acts 20:35). Paul wrote that the gifts that the Corinthians were sending to the poor Christians in Jerusalem were a ministry that was "supplying the needs of the saints" (2 Cor. 9:12). In fact, as a result of the abundant generosity seen in the early church in Jerusalem in Acts 4, "there was not a needy person among them," for people who sold lands or houses brought the proceeds "and laid it at the apostles' feet, and it was distributed to each as any had need" (vv. 34–35).

A fifth blessing that God promises for those who give is increased heavenly reward. Jesus taught this:

> Do not lay up for yourselves treasures on earth, where moth and rust destroy and where thieves break in and steal, but *lay up for yourselves treasures in heaven*, where neither moth nor rust destroys and where thieves do not break in and steal. For where your treasure is, there your heart will be also. (Matt. 6:19–21)

Paul expressed a similar idea:

> They are to do good, to be *rich in good works, to be generous* and ready to share, *thus storing up treasure for themselves as a good foundation for the future*, so that they may take hold of that which is truly life. (1 Tim. 6:18–19)

However, these blessings will come only if our hearts are right before God in our giving. If we persist in outright patterns of sinful rebellion against God in other areas of our lives, we should not expect these blessings. Amos rebuked the people of Israel "who oppressed the poor, who crushed the needy" (Amos 4:1), even though they were people who "bring your sacrifices every morning, your tithes every three days . . . for so you love to do, O people of Israel!" (vv. 4–5).

5. The Error of the "Prosperity Gospel." Some Christian writers and speakers have wrongfully promoted a "prosperity gospel" (also called a "health-and-wealth gospel"), claiming that the Bible teaches that if God's people are faithful and give generously, then God will reward their faith with material wealth. In short, if they truly trust God, they will become rich! This teaching is certainly a mistake.

I responded to that viewpoint in chapter 34 (p. 908), but is appropriate to mention it again at this point. While the New Testament promises that God will provide for his people's *needs* (2 Cor. 9:8; Phil. 4:19), it offers no promises that God will always make believers *wealthy* when they trust in him.

6. How Should We Give?

a. Cheerfully: It is not surprising that when we give in the way that God wants us to, our giving will be accompanied by joy, because Jesus himself taught that "it is more blessed to give than to receive" (Acts 20:35). This is consistent with what Paul says:

> Each one must give as he has decided in his heart, not reluctantly or under compulsion, for *God loves a cheerful giver.* (2 Cor. 9:7)

This provides an opportunity for us to consider what is in our hearts as we give. Are we giving reluctantly, almost grudgingly, simply because we know that God requires it? This is not the kind of giving that God requires, because Paul says it should be done "not reluctantly or under compulsion." But if we realize that giving is a privilege that God has given us, that he enables us through giving to participate in the advancement of his kingdom, that he is pleased with our gifts, and that our gifts are a form of worship, then giving should bring joy to our hearts. That is why "God loves a cheerful giver."

b. Regularly: Apparently Paul taught all his churches to establish a regular pattern of giving, because when he wrote to Corinth about "the collection for the saints," he said that they should imitate what he told other churches in Galatia:

> As I directed the churches of Galatia, so you also are to do. *On the first day of every week*, each of you is to put something aside and store it up, as he may prosper, so that there will be no collecting when I come. (1 Cor. 16:1–2)

Many modern banks allow customers to set up regular payments to be sent automatically wherever they wish, and this means that Christians can easily establish a regular pattern of contributions to their churches and to other charitable organizations. There is some loss of personal participation in the process of giving each week or each month by this method, but there is a significant gain in the regularity and predictability of the giving. Of course, not all of our giving needs to be done in this way.

c. Generously: See the discussion below on generous giving, in the section on how much we should give (p. 1021).

d. Proportionately: Those who earn more are able to give more, and Paul explicitly said that "each one of you is to put something aside and store it up, *as he may prosper*" (1 Cor. 16:2). If God enables us to earn more income, our giving should increase as well.

On the other hand, some people are not able to give very much, and Paul reassures them that God sees their heart desire to give even if they can give only a small amount:

> For if the readiness is there, *it is acceptable according to what a person has*, not according to what he does not have. (2 Cor. 8:12)

e. While You Are Still Living: There are several examples of wealthy people who left much of their estate to a charitable foundation that continued to give away their money many years after they died, but the foundation later began to give to causes that the original donor never would have favored.

For example, the Ford Foundation was created in 1936 by Henry Ford and his son Edsel Ford with the mission that their resources were to be used "for scientific, educational and charitable purposes, all for the public welfare."[2] Henry Ford, in particular, was known for his political conservatism. However, after both men passed away, Edsel's son, Henry Ford II, took over, and the Ford Foundation became one of the leading funders of politically liberal groups around the world, for causes such as "reproductive justice."[3] One of the foundation's executives, Anthony Romero, became the head of the American Civil Liberties Union in 2001.[4]

Another example is the John D. and Catherine D. MacArthur Foundation. MacArthur was a political free-market conservative. After he died of cancer in 1978, the board members started dispensing the foundation's funds to various politically liberal causes that he never would have supported, such as the Center for Reproductive Rights (which promotes abortion rights) and the American Civil Liberties Union.[5]

In order to avoid this kind of situation, financial advisers will often recommend that people attempt to give away as much of their money as they can before they die. In fact, one Christian financial adviser uses this slogan:

---

[2] "The Ford Foundation," *Discover the Networks*, http://www.discoverthenetworks.org/funderprofile.asp?fndid=5176.

[3] Joseph Smith, "The Left Wing Money Machine," *American Thinker*, Aug. 9, 2012, http://www.americanthinker.com/articles/2012/08/the_left_wing_money_machine.html.

[4] "Anthony D. Romero Is New ACLU Executive Director; First Latino to Head Premier Civil Liberties Group," American Civil Liberties Union, May 1, 2001, https://www.aclu.org/news/anthony-d-romero-new-aclu-executive-director-first-latino-head-premier-civil-liberties-group.

[5] The John D. and Catherine T. MacArthur Foundation, *Discover the Networks*, http://www.discoverthenetworks.org/funderProfile.asp?fndid=5223.

Do your givin' while you're livin'
so you're knowin' where it's goin'.[6]

I cannot say this is an absolute biblical requirement, because I cannot point to a specific biblical teaching that would support this idea except the general principle "It is required of stewards that they be found faithful" (1 Cor. 4:2). However, it seems like a generally wise principle because leaving our money to be given away by others who might not exercise the same kind of wise stewardship that we would exercise does not seem to be acting as a faithful steward.

7. How Much Should We Give? As I explained above (see p. 1014), the Old Testament required the Israelites to give a regular tithe of 10 percent plus a number of other sacrifices and freewill offerings. So the expectation was at least "10 percent plus something."

In the New Testament there is no command to Christians in the new covenant to give 10 percent of their income. But it certainly seems like a wise guideline, a level of giving that is significant and yet not excessively burdensome for people.

In the history of the church, there are multiplied thousands of individuals who have faithfully tithed 10 percent of their income throughout their lives and who testify that they have seen countless examples of God's faithfulness in providing for their needs and have experienced the joy of participating in the privilege of giving to the Lord's work regularly throughout their lives.

One of my earliest childhood memories is of receiving a weekly allowance of 50 cents and being taught by my parents to put five cents in the offering at church on Sunday, which I faithfully did, imitating the lifelong habit of my father, who frequently spoke of regularly tithing from the first day he began to earn money as a young man.

Margaret and I eventually came to the point where we were able to give more than 10 percent of our income, and for many years now we have decided at the beginning of the year what percentage of our income we will give to the Lord's work. After that, I do not consider that amount of the money I earn to be "my own," but consider it to be the Lord's.

For many years, whenever I have received a substantial book royalty check in the mail (the amount of which is impossible to know in advance), my heart would not be at peace until I wrote a check for the percentage of that payment that we were giving to the Lord's work that year, then walked a half block from my house and put it in the outgoing mailbox. To this day, whenever I do that, this passage goes through my mind as soon as I have dropped the check in the mail:

> When you have finished paying all the tithe of your produce . . . then you shall say before the LORD your God, "*I have removed the sacred portion out of my house . . .*" (Deut. 26:12–13)

---

[6] Ron Blue, *Splitting Heirs: Giving Your Money and Things to Your Children without Ruining Their Lives* (Chicago: Northfield Publishing, 2004), 99. This entire book is filled with much practical, biblically based wisdom about how to allocate the distribution of one's assets after death.

And there is joy in my heart.

Several verses in the New Testament affirm that our giving should be generous:

[Let] the one who contributes [do so] *in generosity*. (Rom. 12:8)

The point is this: whoever sows sparingly will also reap sparingly, and *whoever sows bountifully will also reap bountifully*. (2 Cor. 9:6)

You will be enriched in every way *to be generous in every way*, which through us will produce thanksgiving to God. (2 Cor. 9:11)

[Those who are rich] are to do good, *to be rich in good works, to be generous and ready to share*. (1 Tim. 6:18; see also Acts 2:46; 10:2)

Several verses in the Old Testament Wisdom Literature also commended generosity among God's people:

The wicked borrows but does not pay back,
　　but the righteous *is generous* and gives. (Ps. 37:21; see also v. 26)

It is well with the man *who deals generously* and lends;
　　who conducts his affairs with justice. (Ps. 112:5)

Whoever despises his neighbor is a sinner,
　　but *blessed is he who is generous to the poor*. (Prov. 14:21)

Whoever oppresses a poor man insults his Maker,
　　but *he who is generous to the needy* honors him. (Prov. 14:31)

Whoever is generous to the poor lends to the LORD,
　　and he will repay him for his deed. (Prov. 19:17)

But those verses about generosity do not specify any specific percentage, and that will certainly vary from person to person and from situation to situation. This brings us back to Paul's counsel: "Each one must give as he has decided in his heart, not reluctantly or under compulsion" (2 Cor. 9:7).

Therefore, my conclusion about how much we should give is that *the New Testament does not specify any certain amount* such as 10 percent, but a tithe certainly seems like a wise guideline, at least when someone is beginning to give to the Lord's work.

On the other hand, I do not think the New Testament requires everyone to give all that they have, or to give to the point where they are living close to poverty, for the New Testament standard is generosity, not "give until you are poor."

Some passages do emphasize the benefits of *sacrificial giving*. This was certainly the point of Jesus's teaching when he saw a poor widow who put two small copper coins in the offering box. Jesus said that "this poor widow has put in more than all of them," because the wealthy people contributed out of their abundance, "but she *out of her poverty* put in all she had to live on" (Luke 21:1–4). Paul also commended the sacrificial giving of Christians in Macedonia, "for in a severe test of affliction, their abundance of joy and *their extreme poverty* have overflowed in a wealth of generosity on their part" (2 Cor. 8:2). He said that they even gave "beyond their means, of their own accord" (v. 3). Yet we must also recognize that these passages were written with reference to a poor widow and to very poor Christians in Macedonia, people for whom giving was genuinely a sacrifice.

Should these passages on sacrificial giving by very poor people also apply to wealthy Christians? Others might differ with me about this, but I do not think the Bible requires wealthy Christians to give away nearly all of their income, to the point where they are giving "sacrificially" in a way that is similar to the sacrificial giving of the poor widow in Luke 21 or of the extremely poor Macedonians. The New Testament counsel to those who are wealthy is not that they should give "all that they have" (like the poor widow) or nearly all, but that they should be "rich in good works" and "generous," according to Paul's command for "the rich in this present age":

> They are to do good, to be *rich in good works*, to be *generous* and ready to share, thus storing up treasure for themselves as a good foundation for the future, so that they may take hold of that which is truly life. (1 Tim. 6:18–19)

The ability to enjoy the fruits of our labor is a large factor in motivating people to work hard at building businesses or in striving to excel in highly specialized professions such as law or medicine. If we tell these people that God expects them to give away *nearly all* of what they earn, we will remove a significant motivation for them to work, and I think that will be contrary to the expectation of God, "who richly provides us with everything to enjoy" (1 Tim. 6:17). In the case of wealthy people who are already giving generously, I want to allow for the possibility that the Holy Spirit will lead different people to different conclusions about the actual percentage of their assets they will give away and the degree of personal sacrifice to which God is calling them.

8. Giving When We Die. Although I mentioned above the wisdom of giving most of your charitable contributions while you are still alive (so that you know where they are going), most people will still have some financial assets when they die. Therefore, a separate question is how to wisely dispose of your assets that remain at the time of your death.

a. The Old Testament Viewed Leaving an Inheritance to One's Family as a Normal Practice: In the Old Testament, the Lord gave the following law to Moses:

> And you shall speak to the people of Israel, saying, "If a man dies and has no son, then you shall transfer his inheritance to his daughter. And if he has no daughter, then you shall give his inheritance to his brothers. And if he

has no brothers, then you shall give his inheritance to his father's brothers. And if his father has no brothers, then you shall give his inheritance to the nearest kinsman of his clan, and he shall possess it. And it shall be for the people of Israel a statute and rule, as the LORD commanded Moses." (Num. 27:8–11)

These details of the law guaranteed that the property of a family would remain within that family as nearly as possible (and the conversation between God and Abram in Gen. 15:1–3 indicates that this custom of leaving one's property to an heir connected to one's family predated the existence of the nation of Israel).

b. The Old Testament Viewed Leaving an Inheritance to One's Family as a Good Thing: There is no hint in the Old Testament that it was morally wrong to leave an inheritance to one's children. In fact, such a practice is viewed in a positive way:

> *A good man leaves an inheritance to his children's children,*
>> but the sinner's wealth is laid up for the righteous. (Prov. 13:22)

> House and wealth are inherited from fathers,
>> but a prudent wife is from the LORD. (Prov. 19:14)

By contrast, if a man died with nothing to leave to his heirs, it was viewed as a tragedy:

> There is a grievous evil that I have seen under the sun: riches were kept by their owner to his hurt, and those riches were lost in a bad venture. And he is father of a son, but he has nothing in his hand. (Eccles. 5:13–14)

c. The Economic and Political Benefits of Passing Down Property in a Family throughout Succeeding Generations: It commonly happens in ordinary life that people do not die in absolute poverty but still own some possessions when they die. This was true in ancient societies as well as today. This is not surprising, because in the ordinary course of life, people will often accumulate a house and perhaps some other property, such as land, livestock, jewelry, or some amount of money. But then they die, leaving some accumulation of wealth behind.

Sometimes members of the next generation will squander all of that inheritance, but very often they will not spend all of it but continue to accumulate more assets throughout their lifetimes. And in this way, in many nations, there is a gradual accumulation of more wealth in families and in nations over successive generations.

The question is, *what should be done with that wealth as it accumulates?* One possible solution is for the government to take some or all of the property that people have when they die (a so-called "death tax"). But this is not without harmful consequences, because the result is to place more power in the hands of the government, which is already the most powerful force in any society. In addition, this policy is contrary to the basic principle in Scripture that, in general, most property should be owned by individuals in a society, not by the government (see discussion in chap. 34, p. 896).

Allowing families to retain property that is passed down from one generation to another avoids the accumulation of more power in the hands of the government. As long as private ownership of wealth and property is legally available to the vast majority of people throughout a society (and not selfishly confined to a few powerful families by restrictive laws and corrupt government in a country), then passing a family's property down through generations guarantees that there will be widespread ownership of private property in that society or nation. This is a necessary condition for sustained economic growth in any nation.[7]

d. In the Old Testament, Governments Did Not Have the Right to Take Property Owned by Individual Families: A dramatic narrative in the life of King Ahab illustrated the evil of a king who sought to seize property that did not belong to him:

> Now Naboth the Jezreelite had a vineyard in Jezreel, beside the palace of Ahab king of Samaria. And after this Ahab said to Naboth, "Give me your vineyard, that I may have it for a vegetable garden, because it is near my house, and I will give you a better vineyard for it; or, if it seems good to you, I will give you its value in money." But Naboth said to Ahab, "The Lord forbid that I should give you the inheritance of my fathers." (1 Kings 21:1–3)

In the story that follows, Ahab and his wife, Jezebel, plotted to falsely accuse Naboth and then have him put to death so that Ahab could seize Naboth's vineyard (see 1 Kings 21:5–16). But God pronounced judgment on Ahab and Jezebel through the prophet Elijah (see vv. 17–24).

In addition, in Ezekiel's vision of a future restoration of Israel in which God's righteous laws are to reign, there is the following stipulation:

> *The prince shall not take any of the inheritance of the people, thrusting them out of their property.* He shall give his sons their inheritance out of his own property, so that none of my people shall be scattered from his property. (Ezek. 46:18)

e. The New Testament Contains Little Explicit Teaching about Monetary Inheritance: There are no direct statements in the New Testament that give detailed instructions about God's principles for inheritance. However, as I argued earlier, the New Testament gives significant support for the importance of private ownership of property (see chap. 34, p. 897) and a government role limited to punishing evil, rewarding and

---

[7] See discussion of the economic importance of private ownership of property in Wayne Grudem and Barry Asmus, *The Poverty of Nations: A Sustainable Solution* (Wheaton, IL: Crossway, 2013), 141–54.

encouraging good, and maintaining order (see chap. 16, p. 427). These principles lend indirect support to the idea that it is morally right for people to be able to pass on property to their heirs, or to whomever they wish, when they die, because the property still belongs to them and does not belong to the government or to "society," nor does government have any inherent right to take it simply because people die.

In the one passage where Jesus addressed the question of inheritance, a person in the crowd asked him to settle a family dispute over what different brothers would inherit. But Jesus refused to take the role of earthly divider of inheritances, and instead turned people's attention to greater heavenly wealth:

> Someone in the crowd said to him, "Teacher, tell my brother to divide the inheritance with me." But he said to him, "Man, who made me a judge or arbitrator over you?" And he said to them, "Take care, and be on your guard against all covetousness, for *one's life does not consist in the abundance of his possessions*." (Luke 12:13–15)

In the following verses, Jesus then told the parable of a rich fool who died suddenly and had to give an account of himself to God. Jesus concluded:

> But God said to him, "Fool! This night your soul is required of you, and the things you have prepared, whose will they be?" So is the one who lays up treasure for himself and is not rich toward God. (Luke 12:20–21)

Jesus also emphasized the much greater importance of heavenly inheritance:

> Blessed are the meek, for *they shall inherit the earth*. (Matt 5:5)

> Then the King will say to those on his right, "Come, you who are blessed by my Father, *inherit the kingdom* prepared for you from the foundation of the world." (Matt. 25:34)

We find this same emphasis in the New Testament Epistles:

> [I pray that] the eyes of your hearts [may be] enlightened, that you may know what is the hope to which he has called you, what are the riches of *his glorious inheritance in the saints*. (Eph. 1:18)

> [It is] from the Lord *you will receive the inheritance as your reward*. You are serving the Lord Christ. (Col. 3:24)

> Blessed be the God and Father of our Lord Jesus Christ! According to his great mercy, he has caused us to be born again to a living hope through the resurrection of Jesus Christ from the dead, *to an inheritance* that is imperishable, undefiled, and unfading, kept in heaven for you. (1 Pet. 1:3–4)

These passages should encourage Christians to remember that the spiritual legacy they leave to their children, the relationship with Jesus Christ that they pass on to succeeding generations, is a far greater treasure than any earthly wealth.

On the other hand, the Old Testament passages quoted above show the moral goodness of leaving an inheritance to one's family, and therefore they seem to speak to the human situation generally, making them applicable beyond the specific context of the nation of Israel at that time. Therefore, it seems to me that laws and economic systems that allow people to leave an inheritance to their families (or to others if they wish) are still appropriate.

f. Practical Wisdom Regarding Giving an Inheritance to Children: The well-known parable of the prodigal son shows the mistake of giving an inheritance to a young man too soon, for in the parable "he squandered his property in reckless living" (Luke 15:13). This is a specific example of a general principle in Proverbs:

> An inheritance gained hastily in the beginning
> will not be blessed in the end. (Prov. 20:21)

In a classic study of wealthy families in the United States, Thomas Stanley and William Danko include many warnings against wealthy parents giving their children too much too soon, so that the children become "daddy dependent." Here are some of their key findings:

> In general, the more dollars adult children receive, the fewer they accumulate, while those who are given fewer dollars accumulate more.[8]

> Paying for an education is the equivalent to teaching your children how to fish. . . . Conversely, what is the effect of cash gifts that are knowingly earmarked for consumption and the propping up of a certain lifestyle? We find that the giving of such gifts is the single most significant factor that explains lack of productivity among the adult children of the affluent. . . . Cash gifts earmarked for consumption dampen one's initiative and productivity. They become habit forming. These gifts must then be extended throughout most of the recipient's life.[9]

> If you are wealthy and want your children to become happy and independent adults, minimize discussions and behavior that center on the topic of receiving other people's money.[10]

---

[8] Thomas J. Stanley and William D. Danko, *The Millionaire Next Door: The Surprising Secrets of America's Wealthy* (New York: Pocket Books, 1996), 143.

[9] Ibid., 148–49. However, Stanley and Danko add that earmarking gifts that a child will use to start or enhance a business generally does not have this negative effect, but is similar to paying for an education.

[10] Ibid., 195. See also additional counsel on this matter on 203–9.

In a similar category is a statement from longtime psychologist and family advocate James Dobson, who says that large trust funds are usually destructive to those who inherit them. In his book *Solid Answers*, Dobson wrote:

> In a word, I'm convinced that it is very dangerous to give large amounts of money to kids who haven't earned it. A sociological study published some time ago called *Rich Kids* validated the concerns I have observed. The authors of that study concluded that large trust funds are usually destructive to those that inherit them. The case studies they cited were convincing.[11]

> It's also been my observation that *nothing* will divide siblings more quickly than money. Giving them a large inheritance increases the probability of tension and disharmony within a family. Your sons and daughters will fight over control of your businesses, and they'll resent those who are designated as decision makers. Some of them will lose their motivation to be responsible and will experiment with various addictive behaviors—from gambling to alcoholism. There are exceptions to these negative consequences, of course, and some people do handle wealth and power gracefully. But it is a difficult assignment at best and one that requires the greatest maturity and self-control.[12]

g. How Much Should People Give to Their Heirs? If we begin with the principle that property belongs to individuals, not to the government, then it follows that individuals should have the right to decide how to dispose of their property when they die. Although there were specific rules for a family inheritance in the Old Testament laws for Israel, such laws are not repeated or affirmed in the New Testament. And even in the Old Testament one statement in Proverbs that seems to have a broader application speaks of leaving an inheritance not just to children but to "children's children" (Prov. 13:22).

I conclude that for the New Testament age, the Bible's teachings give some endorsement to the idea that leaving an inheritance to one's family members is a good thing, but not the only good thing that we can do with the resources we have at death. For example, another good thing to do with our resources is to give them to the Lord's work or to those in need (see discussion above).

The question then becomes one of wise stewardship of our possessions. Laws about inheritance vary from country to country. However, in the United States and other countries where wills are allowed, it is simply foolish stewardship not to have a will or similar estate-planning document (such as a trust) that specifies how one's assets are to be disposed at the time of death. If a person dies without a will, the government will step in and apply a formula to determine the distribution of possessions. When that

---

[11] James Dobson, *Solid Answers: America's Foremost Family Counselor Responds to Tough Questions Facing Today's Families* (Wheaton, IL: Tyndale, 1997), 430, citing John Sedgwick, *Rich Kids: America's Young Heirs and Heiresses, How They Love and Hate Their Money* (New York: William Morrow and Co., 1985).

[12] Ibid., 431.

happens, the person who dies has failed to exercise any kind of stewardship at all and has left the decision to the impersonal mechanisms of government.

A will is especially important for any parents who have children under the age of 18, because the will can specify whom the parents wish to have legal custody of their children if they should die, but if parents die suddenly without a will, the state will decide who has legal custody of the children (see chap. 24, p. 628, for more information about the importance of a will and other legal documents that will take effect at one's death).

Most Christians, in exercising wisdom about the distribution of their property after death, will decide to give some percentage or some specific amount to their church and to various other ministries. Then they will give the rest to their children and to other relatives and friends.

One widely followed Christian financial adviser, Ron Blue, argues that there is no compelling reason why people have to leave their assets to their children in equal amounts.[13] Particularly in cases where some children are living recklessly irresponsible and destructive lives and others are living in ways that honor God and further the work of his kingdom, it would be wise stewardship to leave unequal amounts to one's children.

However, there is a significant downside to such a decision also. If a child is cut out of his parents' will completely (or in some significant measure), this can leave a legacy of bitterness and resentment toward the parents that may last for decades beyond the parents' deaths and may become a barrier rather than an incentive to the child's leading a more responsible life. In any case, the decision to leave unequal amounts to one's children is not a trivial action but an extremely weighty one that will have consequences that last for many years. Especially if the decision is motivated by anger or a desire to hurt the disfavored child after one dies, the decision will often bring more negative results and more dishonor to God's kingdom.

B. WISE SAVING

Up to this point we have been talking about one wise use of money and possessions: *giving* them away. But *saving* for the future is another wise use of the money we receive.

1. It Is Right to Save for a Time When We Cannot Support Ourselves. Only a few people in modern Western societies continue to work and earn income until the day they die. Because of increasing age, physical weakness, prolonged sickness, or loss of a job, most people will experience a time in life when they are unable to work enough to provide for their own needs. Therefore, it is wise to save regularly for such a time, in order to continue to "be dependent on no one" (1 Thess. 4:12). If people choose not to save for such a future time, they are basically deciding to impose a burden on their children or relatives, or on society, in the future. (I do not think it is a persuasive answer

---

[13] See Blue, *Splitting Heirs*, especially 72–92.

for such people to say, "I am trusting God to take care of me," and then to refuse to save if they are able to do so, because it is likely that the way God intends to care for them in the future is through their regular saving at the present time.)

Some people may object and say that they enjoy their work and will always continue to work as long as they live, but we do not know what our future physical capabilities will be. Assuming that we will always be able to work enough to support ourselves seems to me to be forcing a test on God, contrary to Jesus's words in Matthew 4:7: "You shall not put the Lord your God to the test."

2. It Is Right to Save in Order to Provide for Unforeseen Emergencies. Even before old age, sometimes unforeseen emergencies arise, such as a prolonged illness, a serious injury, theft, or sudden loss of a home or car through a natural disaster, a fire, or an accident. Or unforeseen expenses can come from a lawsuit, sudden large medical expenses for a child or other family member, or for other reasons. It is wise for people to accumulate some savings in order to be able to provide for the needs that arise in these emergency situations. James encourages us to realize that we cannot know the future:

> Come now, you who say, "Today or tomorrow we will go into such and such a town and spend a ycar there and trade and make a profit"—yet *you do not know what tomorrow will bring.* What is your life? For you are a mist that appears for a little time and then vanishes. Instead you ought to say, "If the Lord wills, we will live and do this or that." (James 4:13–15)

Therefore, it seems wise for people to begin a regular pattern of accumulation of savings from the time when they first begin to earn an income. If they save wisely, the amount they set aside will gradually increase over time. (See the discussion below on saving too much or too little.)

3. It Is Right to Save by Purchasing a Reasonable Amount of Insurance. To purchase an insurance policy on one's health, one's car or house, and one's life is a form of saving. The idea of an insurance fund is that many hundreds of people put a little bit of their savings into a large fund, and even though only a few of the people will draw money from that fund, everybody benefits from the financial security that the fund provides.

Because we don't know the future, and because suffering and evil still exist in this world, it seems that purchasing some amount of insurance is another wise way to protect against large or catastrophic expenses in the future.

4. It Is Right to Save in Order to Purchase Things That Are More Expensive Than We Can Presently Afford. Sometimes a child will save for a long time to purchase a bicycle or to go to a summer camp. In a similar way, adults will often save in order to be able to purchase a house, start a business, pay for college expenses or a wedding for their children, or perhaps take a special vacation. I do not think that such saving is a violation of Jesus's command "Do not lay up for yourselves treasures on earth" (Matt. 6:19), so long as the hoped-for future purchase is in itself a morally good thing. The passage from Scripture that seems more applicable to this situation is this one:

> Wealth gained hastily will dwindle,
> but *whoever gathers little by little* will increase it. (Prov. 13:11)

5. Some Kinds of Savings Also Do Good for Others. There are some kinds of savings that, perhaps surprisingly, enable our money to do some good for other people even while we are saving it for our own use in the future.

For example, if we put $1,000 we have saved in a *bank*, then the bank is able to lend some of that money to someone else who may be trying to start a business or build a house. In that way, we are not only saving for ourselves but also enabling our money to do good for others.

In a similar way, if we purchase a *bond* from a city government or from a private company, then we not only get interest on the bond but we also allow the city or the company to use our money for other good projects. And if we save the money by buying *stocks* in a company, we are investing in that company and enabling it to accomplish its purpose of producing goods and providing jobs for people.

6. The Temptations That Come with Saving. As people accumulate savings, the money that is set aside can be a source of temptation and can increasingly tie their hearts to earthly things rather than to God and to their life in heaven. Several passages in the New Testament warn against this temptation:

> *Do not lay up for yourselves treasures on earth,* where moth and rust destroy and where thieves break in and steal, *but lay up for yourselves treasures in heaven,* where neither moth nor rust destroys and where thieves do not break in and steal. *For where your treasure is, there your heart will be also.* (Matt. 6:19–21)

> But if we have food and clothing, with these we will be content. But *those who desire to be rich fall into temptation,* into a snare, into many senseless and harmful desires that plunge people into ruin and destruction. For *the love of money is a root of all kinds of evils.* It is through this craving that some have wandered away from the faith and pierced themselves with many pangs. (1 Tim. 6:8–10)

> *Keep your life free from love of money,* and be content with what you have, for he has said, "I will never leave you nor forsake you." (Heb. 13:5)

The Old Testament also has warnings against becoming enamored with one's wealth:

> *Take care lest you forget the LORD your God* by not keeping his commandments and his rules and his statutes, which I command you today, lest, when

you have eaten and are full and have built good houses and live in them, and *when your herds and flocks multiply and your silver and gold is multiplied* and all that you have is multiplied, *then your heart be lifted up, and you forget the* LORD *your God*, who brought you out of the land of Egypt, out of the house of slavery. (Deut. 8:11–14)

Put no trust in extortion;
    set no vain hopes on robbery;
    if riches increase, set not your heart on them. (Ps. 62:10)

He who loves money will not be satisfied with money, nor he who loves wealth with his income; this also is vanity. (Eccles. 5:10)

These passages do not specify any certain amount of money that is wrong to save or that will certainly cause us to give in to temptation, but they provide a strong warning against allowing the love of money to capture our hearts, something that can happen whether a person's savings are small or great.

7. It Is Possible to Save Too Much and It Is Possible to Save Too Little. The passages quoted in the previous section show that people can become overly concerned about saving for the future and inappropriately fearful. This will lead them to hoard large amounts of savings and to trust in their riches rather than in God.

It is also possible to save too little. This happens if someone is acting foolishly and not being reasonably prepared for the future. Sometimes this takes the form of accumulating greater and greater debt rather than saving for the future, but accumulating debt is, in a sense, spending one's future life before it happens. (See further discussion of borrowing in chap. 39.)

How much then should a person save? As with the question of how much a person should give away, the answer will vary widely according to each person's situation in life, earning capacity, and reasonably expected expenses.[14] However, there are several Christian ministries that provide financial counseling programs to help individuals and families in making such decisions.[15]

8. We Are Responsible to God for Our Decisions about Saving. As was the case in our discussion of giving, so it is in this discussion of saving: the Bible does not tell us what

---

[14] One guideline that many people have found useful is "give 10 percent, save 10 percent, and live on the rest." This is an easy, simple formula, and for many people these will be reasonable amounts, at least as a guideline to begin with, while future adjustments can be made as circumstances change.

[15] Here are four Christian ministries that help people with financial planning: Crown Financial Ministries, which was founded by the late Larry Burkett as Christian Financial Concepts: http://www.crown.org/; Master Your Money, founded by Ron Blue: http://masteryourmoney.com/home.html; Managing God's Money: http://www.managinggodsmoney.com/; and Dave Ramsey: www.daveramsey.com. All provide wise counsel to people who have no savings and find themselves burdened with a large amount of debt. They provide practical advice on how to get out of debt and to start building savings.

amount or what percentage of our income is right to save. That will vary widely from person to person and from situation to situation. However, it remains true that we are entrusted with our possessions as stewards, and "it is required of stewards that they be found faithful" (1 Cor. 4:2). We must give account of our stewardship to God:

> For we must all appear before the judgment seat of Christ, so that each one may receive what is due for what he has done in the body, whether good or evil. (2 Cor. 5:10)

Therefore, it is important that we seek God's wisdom and trust him to give us wisdom in our decisions about how much to save. This promise certainly applies:

> If any of you lacks wisdom, let him ask God, who gives generously to all without reproach, and it will be given him. (James 1:5)

9. Various Ways to Save. There are different ways in which we can save money, all of which are morally acceptable at least to some extent, and none of which in themselves are morally wrong. In fact, most investment advisers teach that it is wise to save in a variety of different ways so that one has "diversified" savings,[16] probably including all four of the following categories.

a. Mattress (Keeping Cash at Home): The proverbial simplest way of saving money is to "put it under your mattress," or to accumulate cash in some other hidden place at home or in a safe deposit box at a bank.

The rate of return on this kind of saving is exactly 0 percent. And the benefit that comes to others from this money that is concealed privately is exactly nothing. This is similar to the action of the wicked servant who told the master, "I went and hid your talent in the ground" (Matt. 25:25). However, there is nothing inherently wrong with saving money in this way, and it does have the benefit of keeping the money immediately available. In countries where the banking system is unstable or unreliable, people may also think that storing cash in a concealed place provides more security.

Buying and storing gold or silver coins (or other precious metals) has the same effect on others (no benefit), and the rate of return is uncertain because the prices of gold and silver fluctuate. The advantage is that the coins or metals retain their value even in the event of rampant inflation or some other disruption in a nation's banks or economic system.

b. Bank: Putting money in a bank is another possibility. The rate of return depends on the current interest rate, which historically has ranged generally between 2 percent and 5 percent (but more recently has been much closer to 0 percent, which unfortunately

---

[16] Some support for the idea of diversified savings can be found in Eccles. 11:2: "Give a portion to seven, or even to eight, for you know not what disaster may happen on earth."

discourages saving). The present benefit to others from saving money this way is significant because the bank is able to lend the money to others and thus bring additional benefit to society.

In most modern countries, the risk of storing money in a bank is very small, and deposits are usually guaranteed up to a certain amount by the government itself.

c. Bonds: Buying a bond is essentially lending money to a business or to a government agency. If I buy a bond for $1,000 from the city of Phoenix, Arizona, at a 4 percent interest rate, then the city of Phoenix promises me that it will pay me $40 per year (4 percent interest), plus it will give me my $1,000 back when the term of the bond is up.

In this way, the bond gives me a stable rate of return, and the money can do good by helping the city with its activities (such as building a road or a bridge). In addition, the value of the bond itself might increase if interest rates for bonds are lower in the future (for instance, if people can only get bonds that pay 3 percent, they might be willing to pay more than $1,000 to buy my bond, which is getting 4 percent).

The risk is quite small, especially in stable countries with an established rule of law. If the business or government agency from which you bought the bond loses money, it still owes you the $1,000 back at the date specified.

d. Stocks:

(1) What Are Stocks? A stock is different from a bond, in that buying a bond is a way of *lending money to a company* (money that you will get back), while buying stock is a way of *buying a part of a company* itself. If a company issues 1 million shares of stock and you buy one share, you have just purchased one one-millionth ownership of that company. If the company prospers, the value of the company will increase and your stock will be worth more. If the company fails, you might find that your stock is worth little or nothing.

The rate of return for stock ownership is highly unpredictable, just as the success or failure of individual businesses is unpredictable. However, over the long term (for example, over 10 years or more) stocks have historically shown a pattern of steady increase in value (though with many down periods as well). During the 10 years that ended on September 30, 2014, the stocks in the Standard & Poor's 500—a stock index that measures the performance of the 500 largest U.S. companies—registered an average annual total return of 8.11 percent.[17] According to Oppenheimer Asset Management Investment Strategy, which also used figures from the S&P 500, if you hold on to stock for 20 years, the maximum average one-year return is 14.4 percent.[18] For the entire 20th century, the stock market averaged yearly returns of 10.4 percent per year. According to

[17] Thomas Kenny, "Stocks vs. Bonds: The Long-Term Performance Data," The Balance, Nov. 6, 2016, https://www.thebalance.com/stocks-vs-bonds-the-long-term-performance-data-416861.

[18] Adam Shell, "Holding Stocks for 20 Years Can Turn Bad Returns to Good," *USA Today*, June 8, 2011, http://usatoday30.usatoday.com/money/perfi/stocks/2011-06-08-stocks-long-term-investing_n.htm.

one financial adviser, if you invested $1,000 in 1900, that investment would have been worth $19.8 million in 1999.[19]

It is not surprising that, in general, stocks would increase in value over time. If we think back to preindustrial times in the United States (or in Western Europe, Japan, or China), we realize that all developing countries have moved from having almost *no companies of value* to having many thousands of companies with factories, office buildings, and transportation and communication networks that have *immense value*. Over a long period of time, the total value of the companies in each nation tends to increase, and thus the value of those companies (as reflected in the value of their stocks) also tends to increase. This reflects mankind's increasing progress in subduing the earth as God intends us to do (see Gen. 1:28).

Investing in stocks also brings benefits to other people because it provides companies with the financial resources they need to build their businesses, become productive, provide jobs for people who work for them, and produce goods and services for people in the society. Therefore, buying stock in a company (so long as the company succeeds) does bring benefit to other people, as well as some rate of return for the owner of the stock.

Buying stock in a company is not entirely a modern idea. Even in the ancient Roman Empire, people would buy "shares" in larger companies, and would get a return on their investment if the company prospered.[20]

(2) Risks in Buying Stocks: But the risk in buying stocks is larger. If you buy a $30 share of stock in a company that fails, your $30 share of stock might be worth only three cents, and so you have lost your entire investment. Because the short-term return on stocks is unpredictable, many financial advisers will say it is not wise to invest money in stocks if you will likely need the money in the next few years. Investing in the stock market is especially dangerous for people who have little experience or technical knowledge, and who invest their money on a "hot tip" that a friend has told them or on some "instinct."

However, I do not agree with people who say investing in stocks is "gambling" (this categorization carries with it the hint that buying any stocks is unwise or even morally wrong). The risk involved with stocks is significantly less than that of gambling. For example, the probability of losing all the money you invest in a lottery ticket is often greater than 99 percent. It has been estimated that the chance of obtaining a winning lottery ticket for a relatively small lottery prize such as $5,000 is one in ten thousand or 0.01 percent.[21] For large lottery prizes, the chances are far less.

---

[19] Tom DeGrace, "The Historical Rate of Return for the Stock Market Since 1900," Stock Picks System, July 30, 2014, http://www.stockpickssystem.com/historical-rate-of-return/.

[20] See Jules Toutain, *The Economic Life of the Ancient World* (London: Routledge & Kegan Paul, 1930), 246–49.

[21] Courtney Taylor, "What Are the Odds of Winning the Lottery?" ThoughtCo., June 7, 2017, http://statistics.about.com/od/Applications/a/What-Are-The-Odds-Of-Winning-The-Lottery.htm.

But the probability of losing your entire investment in a widely diversified group of stocks is far less than 1 percent. Financial adviser Robert Farrington, who helps young adults with investing decisions, has written: "In the worst stock market crash during the Great Depression, the stock market lost 89 percent of its value. In the most recent stock market crash in 2008–2009, the stock market lost 54 percent of its value from market top to market bottom. While both of these are huge drops, it's important to remember . . . in both cases the stock market didn't go to $0. Meaning if you invested in the total market, you wouldn't have lost everything."[22]

Buying a lottery ticket is clearly gambling. Buying stock is not gambling, but is putting money in an investment that carries some degree of risk.

One common way to minimize risk and daily worry about stock investment is to buy what is called an "index fund," a stock fund that includes a small bit of every stock in a given stock index. In that way, if some stocks decline, others will increase. Over time such index funds seem to have provided a healthy return.

Another method that some people use to minimize risk and daily worry about stocks is to pay a commission to an investment-management firm that will decide for you which stocks and bonds to buy and sell. (For example, a firm might charge you 1 percent of your savings per year in return for their wise management of your savings.) Many people who work for large companies have retirement savings accounts that are managed by a pension department in that company, which is similar to trusting other professionals to manage one's savings.

Both of these ways of minimizing risk also protect us against the pitfall of spending so much time "managing our investments" that it begins to consume our lives and hearts. This can turn our attention away from productive work or ministry, and turn our hearts away from God.

(3) What about "Ethical Investing"? Sometimes Christians advocate "ethical investing," which means investing only in companies that produce products for which one has no moral objection.[23] For instance, an "ethical investing" stock fund might decide not to invest in tobacco companies because of concerns about the harm done by cigarette smoking.

I have no objection in principle to investing or not investing in companies based on someone's personal ethical convictions, but Christians should first examine the philosophy of any so-called "ethical investment" fund in some detail. This is because for some of them, to be "ethical" might mean, for example, not investing in companies that have

---

[22] Robert P. Farrington, "You Won't Lose All Your Money Investing (If You Take This Advice)," The College Investor, July 11, 2015, http://thecollegeinvestor.com/16569/you-wont-lose-all-your-money-investing-if-you-take-this-advice/.

[23] The Biblically Responsible Investing Institute (http://www.briinstitute.com/index.htm) is one organization that provides Christians with information on over 2,000 corporations and whether they support or promote certain kinds of activities that would be of concern to many Christians (such as abortion, pornography, homosexuality, and gambling).

ties to producers of military products or that have ties to Israel, and many Christians would not want to support antimilitary and anti-Israel investment restrictions.

C. WISE SPENDING

In the first two sections of this chapter, we discussed *giving* and *saving* as two wise uses of money. The third wise use is *spending* the money.

1. We Must Spend Something to Provide for Ourselves Food, Clothing, Shelter, and Other Things. Paul told the Thessalonian Christians to "work with your hands, as we instructed you, so that you may walk properly before outsiders and be dependent on no one" (1 Thess. 4:11–12). When people work, they earn wages, and in that way they gain money to spend on necessities for their lives. This is a morally good process, and it is implied in Paul's instructions to "be dependent on no one." He also tells Timothy that a person should "provide for . . . members of his household" (1 Tim. 5:8).

2. Spending Turns Money into Goods and Services That We Should Use and Enjoy with Thanksgiving to God. Jesus evidently enjoyed eating and drinking with friends and others, because people accused him of excessive indulgence in these things:

> The Son of Man came eating and drinking, and they say, "Look at him! *A glutton and a drunkard*, a friend of tax collectors and sinners!" Yet wisdom is justified by her deeds. (Matt. 11:19)[24]

When Jesus said, "Wisdom is justified by her deeds," he apparently meant that the wisdom of his conduct was evident from the good deeds that he did throughout his earthly ministry, no doubt including the good that he did in conversation with others at meals.

Paul also faced criticism from people who taught an excessive kind of asceticism, a rejection of material blessings such as marriage and food:

> Now the Spirit expressly says that in later times some will depart from the faith by devoting themselves to deceitful spirits and *teachings of demons*, through the insincerity of liars whose consciences are seared, who *forbid marriage* and *require abstinence from foods that God created to be received with thanksgiving* by those who believe and know the truth. For everything created by God is good, and nothing is to be rejected if it is received with thanksgiving, for it is made holy by the word of God and prayer. (1 Tim. 4:1–5)

Paul emphasized that God is pleased when we enjoy the products of the earth that he has provided for us, for God "*richly provides us with everything to enjoy*" (1 Tim. 6:17).

---

[24] Although some enemies accused Jesus of being a "drunkard," this was no doubt a false accusation. For Jesus to have become drunk would have been to sin against biblical teachings (see chap. 27, p. 678).

In fact, one verse in Ecclesiastes says that it is God who gives us power to enjoy our wealth and possessions:

> Everyone also to whom God has given wealth and possessions and power to enjoy them, and to accept his lot and rejoice in his toil—this is the gift of God. (Eccles. 5:19)

3. It Is Possible to Spend Too Much, and It Is Possible to Spend Too Little. Those who spend too much indulge in foolish, extravagant spending on themselves while giving relatively little to others and saving too little for the future. This was the case of the prodigal son in Jesus's parable, who "squandered his property in reckless living" (Luke 15:13).

James also rebukes wealthy people who engage in gluttonous self-indulgence:

> *You have lived on the earth in luxury and in self-indulgence.* You have fattened your hearts in a day of slaughter. (James 5:5)

On the other hand, it is possible for people to spend too little on themselves and their families. People can become miserly, stingy, and even fearful, perhaps hoarding their wealth (saving too much) or perhaps simply being greedy (failing to give to the needs of others). (The character Ebenezer Scrooge in Charles Dickens's story *A Christmas Carol* is a classic example.) Such people fail to use the good resources of the earth with thanksgiving to God. They have no power to enjoy the wealth and possessions that God has given them:

> There is an evil that I have seen under the sun, and it lies heavy on mankind: a man to whom God gives wealth, possessions, and honor, so that he lacks nothing of all that he desires, *yet God does not give him power to enjoy them,* but a stranger enjoys them. This is vanity; it is a grievous evil. (Eccles. 6:1–2; see also 1 Tim. 4:1–5, quoted above)

4. How Much Should You Spend? As with giving and saving, the Bible does not state a specific percentage or amount we should spend on ourselves or our families. But one simple way to approach this issue is for a person first to decide how much to give away and how much to save. Then the remainder can be spent with enjoyment and thanksgiving to God. If a person ends up spending less than the expected amount in a month or a year, then the excess can be put to more giving or more saving, or designated for some future expense. It seems to me that God gives us much freedom here with regard to how much we give, how much we save, and how much we spend. But we are still accountable to him for all our decisions.

Finally, it is unwise to spend more than you have and then to go into debt. This is an increasingly serious problem in the United States and several other countries today. I treat the question of debt in chapter 39. The simple rule for staying out of debt is "Spend less than you earn."

D. GAMBLING

I am not aware of any specific Bible verses that directly prohibit gambling.[25] However, in most cases, gambling is an unwise use of a person's money. If people place their hope of economic advancement in winning the lottery rather than developing job skills, working hard, and saving money, they are acting foolishly and will experience economic loss—perhaps significant loss—as a result. In addition, there is the danger of becoming addicted to gambling, something that happens to a certain percentage of people. Gambling addicts lose their rational judgment and end up thousands of dollars in debt, destroying their lives and the lives of those around them for years to come.

Therefore, while I cannot find a biblical basis for absolutely insisting that it is wrong to participate in a charity raffle (understanding that you are essentially giving money to the charity rather than giving it in the hope of winning something) or in an office pool that is betting on a sports event (in which you might participate for the social value of being part of a group activity in the workplace), my personal practice for many years has been to avoid gambling (except for purchasing an occasional raffle ticket to help a charity), and thereby to avoid the foolish expense and the danger of addiction that can come with it.

In addition, my own judgment is that large commercial gambling outlets such as casinos and state-sponsored lotteries bring much more harm to a society than the benefits they generate (as explained below). Therefore, I personally would vote against allowing a lottery in a state or allowing Indian casinos or commercial business casinos to operate in a state. I have also decided personally to avoid any gambling at a commercial gambling outlet, because I do not want to give visible support or lend legitimacy to something I think is socially so harmful.

But I admit that this is a judgment call based on observing the consequences of gambling, not an issue that I would put in the category of a clear moral right and wrong (as I would with abortion, for example, or stealing or lying).

Supporters of gambling argue that it brings benefits to society. It allows people to be free to enjoy the entertainment value that comes from spending money at casinos, buying lottery tickets, betting on horse racing, and so forth. Informal gambling through raffles is also a popular way of raising money for charities when they sell tickets to raise money for certain events. And supporters of gambling claim that it provides jobs and tax revenue to states where gambling is allowed, and that this tax revenue is often used for improving the educational systems in those states.

However, serious societal objections can be brought against gambling, or at least against commercial gambling as a business. A number of studies have shown that commercial gambling brings negative effects to a society, and these must be seriously considered.

First, it is socially harmful because a large percentage of gamblers come from the

---

[25] This section has been adapted from my book *Politics—According to the Bible: A Comprehensive Resource for Understanding Modern Political Issues in Light of Scripture* (Grand Rapids, MI: Zondervan, 2010), 550–51, with permission of the publisher.

poorer segments of the population, who make unwise financial decisions and trap themselves deeper and deeper in debt. According to the National Gambling Impact Commission, in 1999, people with annual incomes of less than $10,000 spent almost three times as much on gambling as those with incomes of more than $50,000.[26] A study in the *American Indian Law Journal* found that growing tribal gaming revenues result in even worse poverty. The study looked at two dozen tribes in the Pacific Northwest between 2000 and 2010. During that time, casinos owned by those tribes doubled their total annual take in real terms, to $2.7 billion. Yet the tribes' mean poverty rate rose from 25 percent to 29 percent.[27]

Second, as noted above, the existence of gambling businesses leads some to become addicted to gambling, destroying marriages, families, and any hope for career advancement. In this way it increases societal breakdown. According to the National Council on Problem Gambling, gambling addiction costs society at least $6 billion per year.[28] The California Council on Problem Gambling reports that according to a 2006 California Prevalence Survey, problem gamblers are three to three and a half times more likely to be arrested or spend time in jail, and are two to seven times more likely to smoke, binge drink, and take illegal drugs than the general population.[29]

Third, studies have shown that where gambling businesses are established, crime rates increase. One study, done by researchers at Baylor University, the University of Georgia, and the University of Illinois, found that 8 percent of crimes in counties that had casinos were attributable to the presence of the casinos, costing residents, on average, $65 per year.[30] Another study, done by University of Maryland researchers on Indian casinos, found that auto theft, larceny, and bankruptcy increased by 10 percent in communities that allowed gambling.[31]

Finally, even if gambling provides some revenue to states, it essentially does so by functioning as a heavy "tax" on some of the poorest people in the state, those who can least afford to pay it but who gamble because of a misplaced hope of winning a large amount of cash. According to the National Center for Policy Analysis, citing research

---

[26] Mark Lange, "The Gambling Scam on America's Poor," *The Christian Science Monitor*, May 2, 2007, http://www.csmonitor.com/2007/0502/p09s01-coop.html.

[27] "Of Slots and Sloth: How Cash from Casinos Makes Native Americans Poorer," *The Economist*, Jan. 15, 2015, http://www.economist.com/news/united-states/21639547-how-cash-casinos-makes-native-americans-poorer-slots-and-sloth.

[28] "Don't Let Betting on the Super Bowl Take Control: The National Council on Problem Gambling Offers Help and Hope to Gambling Addicts," National Council on Problem Gambling, Jan. 31, 2013, http://www.ncpgambling.org/files/Press/Super%20Bowl%20XLVII%20Release%202013.pdf.

[29] "Problem Gamblers: Impacts on the Community," California Council on Problem Gambling, http://www.calpg.org/impacts-on-the-community/, citing "2006 California Gambling Prevalence Study: Final Report," August 2006, http://www.calpg.org/wp-content/uploads/2012/06/2006-California-Prevalence-Study.pdf.

[30] Dylan Matthews, "Studies: Casinos Bring Jobs, But Also Crime, Bankruptcy, and Even Suicide," *Washington Post*, Oct. 30, 2012, https://www.washingtonpost.com/news/wonk/wp/2012/10/30/studies-casinos-bring-jobs-but-also-crime-bankruptcy-and-even-suicide/.

[31] Ibid.

by the National Gambling Impact Study Commission at Duke University, households earning $10,000 spend twice as much on gambling as households earning $90,000. This translates to the lowest-earning households spending about 10.8 percent of income on gambling, versus 0.7 percent of income for the highest earners.[32] Therefore, gambling is a socially undesirable form of raising revenue for state governments.

Lotteries are especially tempting for states to adopt because they are seen as a harmless way of generating revenue. But the advertising for lotteries is remarkably misleading, because it does not state fairly and clearly, in terms most buyers can understand, the remarkably small odds of winning any significant jackpot.

QUESTIONS FOR PERSONAL APPLICATION

1. Do you enjoy giving money to your church or to Christian ministries, or do you do it more out of a sense of obligation? Or both?

2. How much does trusting in God to provide for your needs affect your pattern of giving?

3. If your annual income were to double suddenly, what percentage of your income do you think you would give away? Where would you give it?

4. Are there any specific blessings that have come into your life as a result of generous giving in the past?

5. Have there been any times when you did not give an amount that you thought the Lord wanted you to give, and then your financial circumstances became even more difficult?

6. What percentage of your income do you spend? What percentage do you save? What percentage do you give away? Did this chapter convince you that you should alter the amount of money that you allocate to any of those categories?

7. When you think about your future financial needs, especially at a time when you may be too old to work very much, would you say you are trusting mostly in the money you have saved or will save, mostly in the Lord, mostly in your children, or some combination of those?

8. What character traits (see p. 110) are most important for making wise choices and having right attitudes regarding personal stewardship?

SPECIAL TERMS

bonds
ethical investing

---

[32] "Taxing the Poor," National Center for Policy Analysis, June 22, 2007, http://www.ncpa.org/pub/st300?pg=5.

parachurch organization
stewardship
stocks
tithe

BIBLIOGRAPHY

Sections in Other Ethics Texts

(see complete bibliographical data, p. 64)

Frame, 796–807
Geisler, 377
Kaiser, 43–55
McQuilkin and Copan, 471–79
Rae, 335–38

Other Works

Alcorn, Randy C. *Money, Possessions, and Eternity*. Wheaton, IL: Tyndale, 2003.

Blomberg, Craig L. *Christians in an Age of Wealth: A Biblical Theology of Stewardship*. Biblical Theology for Life. Grand Rapids, MI: Zondervan, 2013.

Blue, Ron. *Splitting Heirs: Giving Your Money and Things to Your Children without Ruining Their Lives*. Chicago: Northfield Publishing, 2004.

Blue, Ron, and Jodie Berndt. *Generous Living: Finding Contentment through Giving*. Grand Rapids, MI: Zondervan, 1997.

Burkett, Larry. *Debt-Free Living: Eliminating Debt in a New Economy*. Revised and expanded ed. Chicago: Moody, 2010.

———. *Your Finances in Changing Times*. The Christian Financial Concepts Series. Chicago: Moody, 1982.

Crosson, Russ, and Kelly Talamo. *The Truth about Money Lies: Help for Making Wise Financial Decisions*. Eugene, OR: Harvest House, 2012.

Croteau, David A. "A Biblical and Theological Analysis of Tithing: Toward a Theology of Giving in the New Covenant Era." PhD diss., Southeastern Baptist Theological Seminary, 2005.

———, ed. *Perspectives on Tithing: Four Views*. Nashville: B&H Academic, 2011.

———. *Tithing after the Cross: A Refutation of the Top Arguments for Tithing and New Paradigm for Giving*. Areopagus Critical Christian Issues 7. Gonzalez, FL: Energion, 2013.

———. *You Mean I Don't Have to Tithe? A Deconstruction of Tithing and a Reconstruction of Post-Tithe Giving*. McMaster Theological Studies. Eugene, OR: Pickwick, 2010.

Dayton, Howard. *Your Money: Frustration or Freedom?* Wheaton, IL: Tyndale, 1979.

Getz, Gene A. *Rich in Every Way: Everything God Says about Money and Possessions*. West Monroe, LA: Howard, 2004.

Green, David. *Giving It All Away . . . And Getting It All Back Again: The Way of Living Generously*. Grand Rapids, MI: Zondervan, 2017.

Hillyer, P. N. "Stewardship." In *New Dictionary of Christian Ethics and Pastoral Theology*, edited by David J. Atkinson and David H. Field, 814–15. Leicester, UK: Inter-Varsity, and Downers Grove, IL: InterVarsity Press, 1995.

Ramsey, Dave. *The Total Money Makeover: A Proven Plan for Financial Fitness*. Nashville: Thomas Nelson, 2003.

Schreiner, Thomas R. "7 Reasons Christians Are Not Required to Tithe." The Gospel Coalition, March 28, 2017, https:// www.thegospelcoalition.org/article/7-reasons -christians-not-required-to-tithe.

Stanley, Thomas J., and William D. Danko. *The Millionaire Next Door: The Surprising Secrets of America's Wealthy*. New York: Pocket Books, 1996.

Storms, Sam. *Tough Topics: Biblical Answers to 25 Challenging Questions*. Wheaton, IL: Crossway, 2013.

Verbrugge, Verlyn D. *Paul & Money: A Biblical and Theological Analysis of the Apostle's Teachings and Practices*. Grand Rapids, MI: Zondervan, 2015.

SCRIPTURE MEMORY PASSAGE

2 Corinthians 9:6–8: The point is this: whoever sows sparingly will also reap sparingly, and whoever sows bountifully will also reap bountifully. Each one must give as he has decided in his heart, not reluctantly or under compulsion, for God loves a cheerful giver. And God is able to make all grace abound to you, so that having all sufficiency in all things at all times, you may abound in every good work.

HYMN

"Take My Life and Let It Be"

Take my life and let it be
Consecrated, Lord, to Thee;
Take my hands and let them move
At the impulse of Thy love,
At the impulse of Thy love.

Take my feet and let them be
Swift and beautiful for Thee;
Take my voice and let me sing

Always, only, for my King,
Always only for my King.

Take my lips and let them be
Filled with messages for Thee;
Take my silver and my gold
Not a mite would I withhold,
Not a mite would I withhold.

Take my love—my God, I pour
At Thy feet its treasure store;
Take myself and I will be
Ever, only, all for Thee,
Ever, only, all for Thee.

FRANCES R. HAVERGAL, 1836–1879

Chapter 39

BORROWING, LENDING, AND THE QUESTION OF DEBT

Why is the ability of human beings to borrow and lend a good gift from God?

Does the Bible teach us that it is always wrong to charge interest on a loan?

When is it right to go into debt, and what are the dangers of it?

If we understand the eighth commandment, "You shall not steal" (Ex. 20:15), to imply the need for wise stewardship of all that God entrusts to us, then it is appropriate to treat the question of borrowing and lending at this point. Can borrowing and lending be part of faithful stewardship?

Many Christians today use credit cards (and therefore borrow money temporarily from the credit card company) or take out a loan to purchase a car or a home, or to start a business. But is that inconsistent with the command "Owe no one anything" (Rom. 13:8)?

In addition, Christians often deposit money in bank accounts (and earn interest on it) or purchase certificates of deposit or bonds (which earn interest from the company, organization, or government that sells the certificate of deposit or bond). But then they sometimes wonder about verses such as Psalm 15:5, which says that a righteous person "does not put out his money at interest."

Therefore, it is important to understand the biblical teachings on borrowing, lending, and the idea of debt in general.

A. BORROWING AND LENDING ARE REMARKABLY BENEFICIAL HUMAN ACTIVITIES

1. Borrowing and Lending Are Sometimes Viewed Positively in Scripture. While there are warnings in Scripture against harmful kinds of borrowing and lending (see below), not all borrowing and lending is prohibited, and sometimes borrowing and lending are viewed positively. For example, we read in the Old Testament:

> When you make your neighbor a loan of any sort, you shall not go into his house to collect his pledge. (Deut. 24:10)

The phrase "when you make your neighbor a loan" assumed that people would lend things to and borrow things from one another. The process was regulated, but it was not prohibited.

In fact, some verses commend the person who lends:

> It is well with the man who deals generously *and lends*;
> > who conducts his affairs with justice. (Ps. 112:5; see also 2 Kings 4:3; Ps. 37:26)

In the New Testament, Jesus assumes the moral rightness of putting money in a bank and receiving interest on it in both the parable of the talents and the parable of the 10 minas:

> You ought to have invested my money with the bankers, and at my coming I should have received what was my own *with interest*. (Matt. 25:27)

> Why then did you not put my money in the bank, and at my coming I might have collected it *with interest*? (Luke 19:23)[1]

Therefore, the warnings against the wrongful use of borrowing and lending should not make us think that these actions are wrong in themselves. In fact, upon reflection, we will realize that they are wonderfully beneficial human activities.

While Romans 13:8 says, "Owe no one anything, except to love each other," I do not think this prohibits all borrowing, and an examination of the context will make this clear:

> Pay to all what is *owed* to them: taxes to whom taxes are *owed*, revenue to whom revenue is *owed*, respect to whom respect is *owed*, honor to whom

---

[1] Someone might object that this is just a parable, and the servant who buried the money in the ground characterizes the "nobleman" (Luke 19:12) as a "severe man" (vv. 21–22), suggesting that Jesus does not intend us to approve of the nobleman's positive evaluation of earning interest at the bank. But this objection is not persuasive because (1) the nobleman in the parable represents Jesus himself, and he is never unjust, and (2) the lazy servant has probably misjudged the nobleman's character.

honor is *owed. Owe no one anything*, except to love each other, for the one who loves another has fulfilled the law. (Rom. 13:7–8)

Paul's point here is to direct Christians in Rome to pay whatever is rightfully expected of them, including taxes, but also including honor and respect. This teaching does not prohibit all borrowing, *so long as the debt is repaid at the time it is promised*. The point is that we should pay *what* we owe *when* we owe it, and the command "Owe no one anything" is simply a summary of the preceding verses and means that we should pay our debts when they are due.

Therefore, if I have a mortgage on my house, I should make the payments when they are "owed"; that is, I should make the payments on time, as I have agreed to do. In that sense of "owe," the command "Pay to all what is owed to them" means paying back the loan on the dates specified, even if those dates include multiple payments over many years. In that sense, I do not "owe" the entire balance of the mortgage to the lender until the date we agreed on when I took out the loan. Therefore, if I make the agreed-upon payments on time, I am completely obedient to Romans 13:8. I "owe no one anything" because I have no past-due payments on my mortgage.

2. Borrowing and Lending Multiply the Usefulness of the Wealth of a Society. The process of borrowing and lending multiplies the available wealth in the world more times than it is possible to calculate.

Here is a simple illustration of this principle: my local library may have only one copy of a reference book, but 300 people might use it in a year, thus giving my community approximately as much value as 300 copies of that book if each person had to buy one.

Another example: I own a car in Arizona, but because of the process of borrowing and lending, I can fly into any city in the United States (or almost any city in the world) and have the use of a rental car for a day without having to own a car in that city. The existence of the wonderful mechanism of borrowing and lending thus gives me approximately as much value as owning thousands of cars, one in each city that I may want to fly to in the whole world! And it does the same for every other person in society. The same is true for hotel rooms, apartments, lake cabins, boats, formal clothing for weddings, trucks and trailers for moving things, and thousands of other goods that can be rented for a time.

The same kinds of benefits occur with borrowing and lending money. When I borrow money to buy a house or start a business, I enjoy the usefulness of that money (just as I enjoy the usefulness of a rental car) for a period of time without actually having to own the money myself. Just as I pay a fee for the rental car while I use it, so I pay a "rental fee" for the money while I use it (this rental fee is called interest). Borrowing the money and using it for a time is far easier than obtaining all the money myself before I can gain the use of it.

The process of borrowing and lending money also means that more people can use the money, just as more people can use a rental car. To take a simplified example, let's say a banker has $90,000 in his bank vault doing no good for anybody; it is just sitting there. But you want to buy a house for $100,000, and you only have $10,000. It would take you many years to save $100,000 to buy that house. But the banker lends you the $90,000, and suddenly that money is doing some good—it enables you to buy and live in the house. (And you pay the banker 6 percent interest on the use of the money, or $5,400 per year, which makes the banker happy as well.)

The story does not stop there, however. You pay the $100,000 to the builder of the house. Let's say the builder in turn puts $80,000 of that money back into the very same bank for a while. The banker now sees that $80,000 sitting in his bank vault, doing nothing worthwhile, so he lends part of it (say $70,000) to Person B, who uses it to buy an $80,000 house. Once again, the builder of that house puts the same money back in the very same bank, let's say $60,000 this time. So the banker then lends out $50,000 of this money to Person C, and by this time the formerly "useless" money that was sitting in the bank vault has been used three times to enable three separate people to buy houses. And the process goes on and on. Thus, borrowing and lending multiply the usefulness of money many times over (and it is a technical task for economists to calculate just how many times it multiplies, given various interest rates and other factors in the economy).

This process is not just "smoke and mirrors" with no reality behind it. You really are making use of the $90,000 and you really are living in your own house, just as you really are using the rental car when you visit another city. The difference is that you can't both use the rental car and return it to be rented by someone else at the same time, but you can do that with money.

What is true of buying a house is also true of starting a business. Very few people have enough money on hand to buy the equipment and supplies needed to start a new business. But when people can borrow the money, they can get their businesses running and then pay back the loans from the money they earn. Such loans to start small businesses ("microloans" for "microenterprises") are starting to have an amazing impact among the poor in many countries of the world. Through the amazing process of borrowing and lending, the usefulness of money is multiplied, and even very poor people are able to start profitable businesses and work their way out of poverty.

The point is that if we could not borrow and lend money, but had to operate only on a cash basis, the world would have a vastly lower standard of living, not only in the richest nations, but also in the poorest nations as well. The existence of borrowing and lending means that the total available amount of goods and services in the world has been multiplied many times over.

In this way, borrowing and lending multiply phenomenally our God-given enjoyment of the material creation, as well as our potential for being thankful to God for all these things and glorifying him through our use of them.

3. Borrowing and Lending Are Uniquely Human Activities That Give Opportunities to Imitate God in Ways the Rest of Creation Cannot Do. When we ponder what borrowing and lending really are, we realize that this process is another wonderful gift that God has given to us as human beings. It is another activity that is unique among human beings, for animals don't borrow, lend, or pay interest, nor could they even understand the process.

What is lending and what is borrowing? A little reflection will show that they are not entirely simple activities but can occur with great variation in specific details. In itself, *lending is the temporary transfer of the use of property, but not of the ownership of property, to another person*. This wonderful process gives the lender an infinite variety of choices between keeping an item and giving it away:

1. Control: I can lend you my car and come with you while you run your errand, or lend it with the provision that you will not drive it to another state, or lend it to you without restrictions.
2. Duration: I can lend you my car for an hour, for a day, for a week, or for a year.
3. Amount: I can lend you a small item (such as my pocketknife) or a large item (such as my car or house), and there are all sorts of choices in between.
4. Risk: There is a very small risk in letting my wife borrow my car keys or my jacket, but there is a very large risk in letting a total stranger borrow my car, and there are all sorts of choices in between.
5. Cost: I can lend you my car for free, I can charge a very small or very large rental fee, or anything in between.

Conversely, borrowing is gaining the temporary use of property but not the ownership of that property. Borrowing also gives a borrower a similarly large variety of choices between no use of an item and owning the item.

In borrowing and lending, we can reflect many of God's attributes. We can demonstrate trustworthiness, faithful stewardship, honesty, wisdom, and thanksgiving. We can ponder and even act on a reasonable expectation of what will happen several months or even years in the future, show love and mercy, and express thankfulness to God.

B. OLD TESTAMENT PROHIBITIONS AGAINST CHARGING INTEREST WERE LIMITED TO CERTAIN KINDS OF SITUATIONS

Some passages in the Old Testament prohibit charging interest on a loan. The righteous person is said to be one who "does not put out his money at interest and does not take a bribe against the innocent" (Ps. 15:5), and this reflects an expectation of obedience to this Mosaic law: "You shall not charge interest on loans to your brother, interest on money, interest on food, interest on anything that is lent for interest" (Deut. 23:19).

Verses like these raise the question of whether it is wrong to work in the banking business, which charges interest on loans, or perhaps even wrong to put my money in a bank that pays interest on that money—in doing this, am I not charging interest to the bank, and isn't that disobeying these verses in the Old Testament?

First, it is important to remember that the laws against charging interest are part of the Mosaic covenant, which is no longer in force today (see chap. 8). Therefore, such laws are no longer binding on us. But we can still ask what was the purpose for these laws at the time of the Mosaic covenant, and what we might learn from them today.

Most commentators seem to agree that these passages have in view a situation of lending to the poor, who are forced to borrow out of necessity so that they can have enough to eat or to plant crops for the following year. This is made clear in at least the following two passages:

> If you lend money to any of my people with you *who is poor*, you shall not be like a moneylender to him, and you shall not exact interest from him. (Ex. 22:25)

> *If your brother becomes poor* and *cannot maintain himself with you*, you shall support him as though he were a stranger and a sojourner, and he shall live with you. Take no interest from him or profit, but fear your God, that your brother may live beside you. You shall not lend him your money at interest, nor give him your food for profit. (Lev. 25:35–37)

These passages that prohibit lending with interest when the poor need to borrow out of necessity suggest that this situation is also in view in other passages that prohibit lending money with interest but do not mention the poor. This situation was probably in view in passages such as these:

> You shall not charge interest on loans to your brother, interest on money, interest on food, interest on anything that is lent for interest. You may charge a foreigner interest, but you may not charge your brother interest, that the Lord your God may bless you in all that you undertake in the land that you are entering to take possession of it. (Deut. 23:19–20)[2]

> I took counsel with myself, and I brought charges against the nobles and the officials. I said to them, "You are exacting interest, each from his brother." (Neh. 5:7)

The situation in Nehemiah 5 was one of great famine, where people were being

---

[2] "Loans were generally made to alleviate poverty, as is made clear by the parallel legislation to these verses." Peter Craigie, *The Book of Deuteronomy*, NICOT, 2nd ed. (Grand Rapids, MI: Eerdmans, 1976), 302, with reference in the footnote to Ex. 22:25; Lev. 25:35–36. Craigie also refers to more extensive academic studies supporting this statement.

forced into slavery (see vv. 1–5). Once again, this reinforces the idea that it is wrong to charge interest from the poor when they need to borrow money for food in order to live.

In Deuteronomy 23:20, God told the people, "*You may charge a foreigner interest, but you may not charge your brother interest.*" That was probably because lending to a foreigner would carry more risk (the foreigner might suddenly return to his homeland without repaying the debt). Such lending could be done for business purposes, since most travelling merchants would be foreigners. But this passage also shows that not all charging of interest was considered wrong, and that the prohibition against charging interest was limited to specific situations. John Frame rightly concludes that the passages that prohibited charging interest "pertain to charitable loans, not commercial or housing loans."[3]

Similar considerations apply to other prohibitions against charging interest in other parts of the Old Testament: they likely have in mind the situation of taking advantage of poor people who needed to borrow in order to live or to have enough seed to plant for next year's crops (see Neh. 5:10; Ps. 15:5; Prov. 28:8; Ezek. 18:5–8, 13, 17; 22:12). For example, Proverbs 28:8 says, "Whoever multiplies his wealth by interest and profit gathers it for him who is generous to the poor," and the ESV footnote after the word *profit* explains, "That is, profit that comes from charging interest to the poor." The NIV translates the verse "whoever increases wealth by taking interest or profit from the poor . . . ," while other translations specify "exorbitant interest" (NRSV) or "excessive interest" (CSB).

There is no prohibition against charging interest in the New Testament. One passage that might at first be understood this way is this one:

> And if you lend to those from whom you expect to receive, what credit is that to you? Even sinners lend to sinners, to get back the same amount. But love your enemies, and do good, and *lend, expecting nothing in return*, and your reward will be great, and you will be sons of the Most High, for he is kind to the ungrateful and the evil. (Luke 6:34–35)

In this passage Jesus cannot be prohibiting us from lending to those from whom we expect to receive, any more than verse 32 prohibits loving those who love us ("If you love *those who love you*, what benefit is that to you?"). Jesus means that we should *also* love our enemies who do not love us, and that we should *also* lend to those (the poor) from whom we expect nothing in return. But lending to people from whom we expect to get our money back with interest (such as wealthy people or banks) is also permitted.

C. CHANGING VIEWS OF CHARGING INTEREST IN CHURCH HISTORY

For the first several centuries of the church, interpreters largely agreed that all charging of interest was wrong. (Charging of interest was commonly called "usury," the word

---

[3] John M. Frame, *The Doctrine of the Christian Life: A Theology of Lordship* (Phillipsburg, NJ: P&R, 2008), 818.

used for "interest" in the King James Version.) After the Protestant Reformation, more and more interpreters adopted the viewpoint advocated above, namely, that Old Testament prohibitions against charging interest were intended to prevent anyone from taking advantage of the poor, and should not be understood to prohibit all charging of interest.

Robert Clouse summarizes the historical development as follows:

> In the patristic age usury was condemned by most of the Church Fathers. . . . At the Third Lateran Council (1179) usury was condemned, although Jews were allowed to engage in the practice by the Fourth Lateran Council (1215). . . . Although some 16th-century Protestant reformers like Luther, Zwingli, and Latimer condemned the practice, others such as Calvin and Beza justified it by distinguishing between consumption loans and those for production. . . . Laws were passed in Geneva that allowed for a moderate rate of interest. Later (1571) England and Germany along with other continental lands followed suit, although in France interest was not legalized until 1789.[4]

John Calvin wrote as follows on the prohibition against charging interest in Exodus 22:25:

> But if we would form an equitable judgment, reason does not suffer us to admit that all usury is to be condemned without exception. . . . If any rich and moneyed man, wishing to buy a piece of land, should borrow some part of the sum required of another, may not he who lends the money receive some part of the revenues of the farm until the principal shall be repaid? Many such cases daily occur in which, as far as equity is concerned, usury is no worse than purchase. . . . But those who think differently, may object, that we must abide by God's judgment, when he generally prohibits all usury to his people. I reply, that the question is only as to the poor, and consequently, if we have to do with the rich, that usury is freely permitted; because the Lawgiver, in alluding to one thing, seems not to condemn another, concerning which he is silent. . . . Usury is not now unlawful, except insofar as it contravenes equity and brotherly union.[5]

Widely respected Puritan pastor and ethicist Richard Baxter expressed a similar view in his 1673 *Christian Directory*:

> Now I prove that such usury [lending to people who make a profit] is not forbidden by God. 1. It is not forbidden us by the law of Moses: (1.) Because

---

[4] Robert Clouse, "Usury," *New International Dictionary of the Christian Church*, ed. J. D. Douglas (Grand Rapids, MI: Zondervan, 1974), 1006.

[5] John Calvin, *Commentaries on the Four Last Books of Moses*, trans. Charles Bingham (1852; repr., Grand Rapids, MI: Baker, 2005), 3:131–32.

Moses's law never did forbid it. . . . It is only lending to the needy, and not lending to drive on any enriching trades, which is meant where usury is forbidden. . . . And it is expressly allowed to be used to strangers . . . to whom nothing unjust or uncharitable might be done. . . . And there were more merchants of strangers that traded with them in foreign commodities, than of Jews that fetched them home: so that the prohibition of usury is in the law itself restrained only to their lending to the poor. . . . (2.) And if it had been forbidden in Moses's law only, it would not extend to Christians now; because the law of Moses, as such, is not in force.[6]

D. RIGHT AND WRONG REASONS FOR BORROWING AND LENDING

1. Reasons for Borrowing. If a person borrows simply to make temporary use of an asset that he does not need to purchase (such as renting a car in another city or renting a specialized tool from a local rental shop), this is certainly wise stewardship. Borrowing for education or to start a business is also appropriate, provided that there is a reasonable expectation that the loan can be paid off through increased earning capacity or increased profit in the business later. It is also appropriate to borrow in order to enjoy the use of an asset that appreciates in value (such as a house) while gradually buying it over a period of time (mortgages on houses often extend for 15 or 30 years, for example). In addition, borrowing can meet sudden unexpected needs that might arise from a personal accident, a severe illness, or a similar circumstance.

However, Scripture commands us, "You shall not covet" (Ex. 20:17), and "Be content with what you have" (Heb. 13:5), and therefore it would be wrong to borrow money (or run up a credit card debt) simply to allow wrongful coveting to be fulfilled at once, even though you have no reasonable expectation of paying off the debt anytime soon.[7] (See below on the dangers of excessive debt.)

2. Reasons for Lending. It is appropriate to lend money or other assets to someone out of a desire to show mercy to those in need or out of love for our neighbor or family member.

Jesus's positive references to investing money with a bank and receiving interest (see Matt. 25:27; Luke 19:23) also imply that another proper reason for lending is simply the desire to make a profit from lending something to someone else—whether it is renting

---

[6] Richard Baxter, *A Christian Directory* (1673; repr., Morgan, PA: Soli Deo Gloria, 1996), 838.

[7] More practical advice about borrowing can be found in Larry Burkett, *Debt-Free Living: Eliminating Debt in a New Economy*, revised and updated ed. (Chicago: Moody, 2010), and Mary Hunt, *Debt-Proof Living: How to Get Out of Debt & Stay That Way*, revised ed. (Grand Rapids, MI: Revell, 2014). Many churches today offer practical classes in personal financial management. Also see chap. 38, p. 1032, note 15, for a list of reputable Christian financial counseling ministries that help Christians get out of debt and stay out.

a car or an apartment to someone, or lending money to someone and collecting interest on it.

However, it would be wrong to lend to someone simply out of a desire to profit from that person's misfortune or poverty, or out of greed rather than rightful self-interest.

3. The Dangers of Borrowing. Borrowing, though a good activity in itself, also carries dangers. For example:

> If a man borrows anything of his neighbor, and it is injured or dies, the owner
> not being with it, he shall make full restitution. (Ex. 22:14)

Therefore, while borrowing allows a person to use something temporarily, the borrower is responsible for any damage that might occur to the thing that is borrowed (this is why apartment owners require a security deposit from renters and why people who rent cars also purchase insurance coverage).

In addition, a borrower loses some of his future freedom, because he must repay the debt instead of putting future income to other uses. This reality is summarized in a brief proverb: "The borrower is the slave of the lender" (Prov. 22:7). Although the borrower is not literally a "slave," the lender does have the right to claim some of the borrower's future earnings, so the borrower's future is controlled to some degree by the lender.

Another danger with borrowing is the possibility of getting into debt so deeply that it begins to appear impossible to repay the debt. Psalm 37 contains this warning:

> *The wicked borrows but does not pay back,*
> but the righteous is generous and gives. (v. 21)

This is a warning against borrowing beyond our ability to repay. Sadly, many Christians (and many non-Christians as well) in modern, wealthy nations borrow far more than is wise or necessary, and suddenly find themselves deeply in debt. Simply paying interest on that debt is a tremendous waste of money, and therefore poor stewardship.

Many Americans are in this predicament. According to the credit rating company Experian, as of September 2016, the average balance on a credit card that usually carries a balance was $7,527. For cards used just to make purchases and that are paid off each month the average balance was much lower, $1,154.[8] But many people have balances on more than one credit card, and one estimate of the average total credit card debt per household that carried a credit card balance in October 2015 was $9,600.[9] According to the Federal Reserve Bank, as of July 2017, total U.S. outstanding consumer debt was $3.75 trillion.[10] By way of comparison, as of July 2017, the total amount of

---

[8] Fred O. Williams, "How Much Is the Average Credit Card Debt in America?" CreditCards.com, Jan. 18, 2017, https://www.creditcards.com/credit-card-news/average-credit-card-debt.php.

[9] Ibid.

[10] "Consumer Credit," Board of Governors of the Federal Reserve System," Sept. 8, 2017, https://www.federalreserve.gov/releases/g19/current/default.htm.

disposable personal income in the United States (total income minus taxes) was $14.4 trillion per year.[11]

Compounding the problem of unwise and excessive borrowing is the fact that some unscrupulous lenders (and credit card companies) will lend to people who have no reasonable expectation of repaying the debt, and then will take advantage of these people in their poverty and distress by charging exceptionally high interest rates.

Yet another danger connected with borrowing is the practice of guaranteeing the repayment of another person's loan:

> Whoever puts up security for a stranger will surely suffer harm,
>> but he who hates striking hands in pledge is secure. (Prov. 11:15)

> Be not one of those who give pledges,
>> who put up security for debts. (Prov. 22:26; see also 6:1–5; 17:18; 20:16;
>> 27:13)

To "put up security" for someone is to guarantee the repayment of someone else's debt. But this can remove much of the sense of responsibility for repayment from the person who borrows the money or other item. Some interpreters may think that these verses prohibit this practice entirely, but it is more likely that they simply caution us that this is usually an unwise practice, without absolutely forbidding it. In any case, what is clear is that when person A agrees to repay a loan taken out by person B, there is a high likelihood of strain or even significant damage to the family relationship or friendship between person A and person B. Thus, "putting up security" is usually unwise.

QUESTIONS FOR PERSONAL APPLICATION

1. How much debt do you have right now? Has it been increasing or decreasing over the past three years? Do you feel that God is pleased with this amount of debt, and that the borrowing that you did was a right decision? Or do you now wish that you had done some things differently in the past with regard to debt?

2. Are you thankful to God for giving us the ability as human beings to borrow and lend things? Is it clear to you how this process multiplies the usefulness of the goods in every society?

3. What abilities did God give to human beings that enable us to borrow and lend things, while even more intelligent animals are unable to do this? How do these abilities reflect something of the glory of God?

---

[11] "US Disposable Personal Income: 14.41T USD for July 2017," https://ycharts.com/indicators/disposable _personal_income.

4. What character traits (see p. 110) would be most helpful in enabling people to avoid accumulating large amounts of credit card debt?

SPECIAL TERMS

interest
security for a debt
usury

BIBLIOGRAPHY

Sections in Other Ethics Texts

(see complete bibliographical data, p. 64)

Frame, 813–18
McQuilkin and Copan, 469–72

Other Works

Burkett, Larry. *Debt-Free Living: Eliminating Debt in a New Economy*. 1999. Revised and expanded ed. Chicago: Moody, 2010.
Chewning, R. C. "Credit." In *New Dictionary of Christian Ethics and Pastoral Theology*, edited by David J. Atkinson and David H. Field, 271–72. Leicester, UK: Inter-Varsity, and Downers Grove, IL: InterVarsity Press, 1995.
———. "Debt." In *New Dictionary of Christian Ethics and Pastoral Theology*, 286–87.
Hunt, Mary. *Debt-Proof Living: How to Get Out of Debt & Stay That Way*. 1999. Revised ed. Grand Rapids, MI: Revell, 2014.

SCRIPTURE MEMORY PASSAGE

Psalm 37:21: The wicked borrows but does not pay back, but the righteous is generous and gives.

HYMN

"Dear Lord and Father of Mankind"

Dear Lord and Father of mankind,
Forgive our feverish ways!
Reclothe us in our rightful mind;
In purer lives Thy service find,
In deeper rev'rence, praise.

In simple trust like theirs who heard,
Beside the Syrian sea,
The gracious calling of the Lord,
Let us, like them, without a word
Rise up and follow Thee.

O Sabbath rest by Galilee!
O calm of hills above,
Where Jesus knelt to share with Thee
The silence of eternity,
Interpreted by love.

Drop Thy still dews of quietness
Till all our strivings cease;
Take from our souls the strain and stress,
And let our ordered lives confess
The beauty of Thy peace.

Breathe thru the heats of our desire
Thy coolness and Thy balm;
Let sense be dumb, let flesh retire;
Speak thru the earthquake, wind, and fire,
O still small voice of calm!

JOHN G. WHITTIER, 1807–1892

BUSINESS ETHICS

Why are buying and selling morally good activities?
Why should we view profit, competition, and the existence of
corporations as morally good things?
Do multinational corporations exploit poor nations?

Christians all over the world work in businesses of one kind or another. Of course, some Christians in every generation will work in full-time church ministry jobs, and others will have teaching positions, military jobs, or other government jobs. But by far the greatest number of Christians will work in the business world. It is important therefore to consider the particular ethical questions that arise in business situations.

Many ethical principles covered in previous chapters are also relevant for business ethics, so I'm assuming the background of the foregoing chapters on property (chap. 34), work (chap. 35), prosperity (chap. 36), poverty and wealth (chap. 37), personal stewardship (chap. 38), and borrowing and lending (chap. 39). But in this chapter I will discuss business ethics from a different perspective, using six core ethical principles from Scripture to address specific questions about business conduct.

Jesus and the New Testament authors were no strangers to business. Jesus began his three years of ministry at about age 30 (Luke 3:23), but prior to that he apparently had followed in the footsteps of his earthly father, Joseph, and worked as a carpenter, because when he returned to his hometown of Nazareth, the people said, "*Is not this the carpenter*, the son of Mary and brother of James and Joses and Judas and Simon? And are not his sisters here with us?" (Mark 6:3; cf. Matt. 13:55). If Jesus began to work as a man at about age fifteen, he must have worked in the business world for fifteen years before he began his three-year ministry. This means that he spent about five times as long working in the business world as he did working in full-time ministry. The apostle Paul worked as a tentmaker to support himself (Acts 18:3; cf. Acts 20:34; 2 Thess. 3:8), and Peter and Andrew worked as fishermen before Jesus called them (Matt. 4:18).

In addition, since the New Testament authors knew that many of the people in the churches to which they were writing worked in various kinds of business or commercial jobs, we can assume that they wrote with the expectation that many listeners and readers would immediately seek to apply their words to real-life situations in the business world.

A. SIX CORE ETHICAL CONVICTIONS ESTABLISH BOUNDARIES FOR MAKING BUSINESS DECISIONS

Many business decisions today can be highly complex, and other books on Christian ethics analyze such decisions in far greater detail than I am able to develop in this one chapter.[1] But I have found that, in teaching about business ethics, the following six "core convictions" are often immensely helpful in clarifying the business decisions that people have to make. These core convictions will not by themselves answer every ethical dilemma, but they do provide useful moral boundaries within which business decisions should be made. Each core principle is derived from a well-known passage of Scripture.

1. Truthfulness: "You Shall Not Bear False Witness" (Ex. 20:16). I discussed truthfulness in speech at some length in chapter 12, and I will assume the background of that discussion here.

God's expectation of truthfulness in speech requires that you will honestly represent your product, not exaggerating its good qualities in a misleading way, and speaking honestly about its shortcomings, just as you would want the other person to do if your situations were reversed (see Matt. 7:12).

I remember once buying a dishwasher and asking if a rebate coupon would still apply, even though it had an expiration date of September 14, which was a week or two earlier. The salesperson replied, "Oh, I'll just give you a receipt dated September 14." I politely declined his offer, because I did not think God would have been honored by such a falsehood in the transaction, nor did I think God would bless the use of the money that I would have saved on account of a lie.

Truthfulness means keeping your word when you agree to something in a business deal. It means not calling in sick when you aren't sick. It means not saying, "I don't remember that," when you do. It means not saying, "Well, I didn't understand you to mean that," when you really did understand exactly what was meant.

> Therefore, having *put away falsehood*, let each one of you *speak the truth* with his neighbor, for we are members one of another. (Eph. 4:25)

2. Not Stealing: "You Shall Not Steal" (Ex. 20:15). I discussed the meaning of stealing at some length in chapter 34 (p. 895), and I will assume that discussion here.

---

[1] See especially the very helpful book by Scott B. Rae and Kenman L. Wong, *Beyond Integrity: A Judeo-Christian Approach to Business Ethics*, 3rd ed. (Grand Rapids, MI: Zondervan, 2012).

The eighth commandment means that we should not take something that doesn't belong to us.

This means you should not bill your company for work time when you're not working for the company, nor should you bill a client for work time when you are not working for that client. It means you should never put personal (nonbusiness-related) items on a business receipt and claim more reimbursement than is due to you. If you have access to proprietary information or some intellectual property belonging to the company you are working for, not stealing means you will never disclose any of that information to another company or use it for personal benefit in a way that is not approved by your company.

Not stealing also obviously means not taking products from your company without paying for them. It also means not giving free or underpriced products (such as food in a restaurant) to your friends without authorization from the owner. The amount of employee theft from companies is sobering, because it shows how little core conviction about honesty many people have today. According to the U.S. Department of Commerce, employees steal $50 billion annually from U.S. businesses.[2] Other sources, including the Association of Certified Fraud Examiners, report that employee theft or fraud results in losses of 7 percent of annual revenue. Seventy-five percent of employees have allegedly stolen at least once from their employers, and 37.5 percent more than twice. Theft and fraud committed by employees has caused 33 percent of all business bankruptcies, with 25.3 percent of the theft or fraud amounting to $1 million or more. Managers have committed 37.1 percent of the total thefts.[3] It was reported that one in every 39.5 employees was apprehended for employee theft in 2013, up 6.5 percent over 2012.[4]

One summer while I was in seminary, I worked at a paper mill in my hometown of Eau Claire, Wisconsin. The first day of work, I was assigned to help a man who had worked many years at that paper mill and who ran a large machine that turned huge rolls of paper into individual small rolls of toilet paper. During the lunch break, we sat near the machine and ate our lunches, and when he was finished he took a roll of toilet paper and put it inside his empty lunch box and closed the box. He looked at me and explained, "I need to get something for a day's work" (as if he wasn't already being paid a fairly substantial union wage). I got the impression that this had been going on every day for many years. Not only did his family never have to buy toilet paper, but he was

---

[2] "Employee Theft," Reference for Business, http://www.referenceforbusiness.com/small/Di-Eq/Employee -Theft.html.

[3] "Employee Theft Statistics," Statistic Brain, April 1, 2017, http://www.statisticbrain.com/employee-theft -statistics/, citing Association of Certified Fraud Examiners, Easy Small Business HR, Institute for Corporate Productivity, and Jack L. Hayes International Inc. Also see "Workplace Theft Statistics—The Latest Statistics and How to Prevent Theft," Easy Small Business HR, http://easysmallbusinesshr.com/2011/06/workplace -theft-statistics-the-latest-statistics-and-how-to-prevent-theft/.

[4] "The 2015 Hiscox Embezzlement Watchlist: A Snapshot of Employee Theft in the United States," Hiscox USA, http://www.hiscoxbroker.com/shared-documents/2015%20Hiscox%20Embezzlement%20 Watchlist.pdf.

probably supplying some friends and relatives with toilet paper as well. To put it bluntly, he was stealing. He was taking something that didn't belong to him.

Paul explicitly tells bondservants not to do this (he calls it "pilfering"):

> Bondservants are to be submissive to their own masters in everything; they are to be well-pleasing, not argumentative, *not pilfering*, but showing all good faith, so that in everything they may adorn the doctrine of God our Savior. (Titus 2:9–10)

3. Honoring Marriage: "You Shall Not Commit Adultery" (Ex. 20:14). I discussed the meaning of this commandment at some length in chapter 28, and I will not repeat that discussion here.

God's requirement that we honor and protect marriages means that managers and owners of businesses should take care that workplace requirements do not put men and women in compromising or tempting situations.

I mentioned in chapter 28 that I am aware of one Christian-owned company, for example, that has a policy that if a man and a woman who are not married to each other travel on company business to another city, they will not have airplane seats together and will not have hotel rooms on the same floor, and they will meet together only in public places such as the hotel lobby. Such guidelines help employees avoid as much as possible the temptation to improper conduct and the appearance of impropriety. Of course, managers in secular companies might think such guidelines to be hopelessly old-fashioned and reactionary, and Christians who work in those situations will have to trust God for wisdom in how to conduct themselves appropriately.

Owners of businesses and company managers can also help to protect marriages by taking thought for how much strain they are putting on their employees' marriages through frequent expectations of extremely long hours or late hours at work. Another way in which business owners and managers can protect marriages is through policies prohibiting the open display of pornography in factories or workplaces.

However, Christians may find themselves working for businesses where cautious policies such as these are not in place. Still, they should seek to maintain personal purity of heart and irreproachable conduct in such difficult situations.

4. Loving Your Neighbor: "You Shall Love Your Neighbor as Yourself" (Matt. 22:39). Many puzzling ethical questions in business can be solved by asking what we would want someone to do if we found ourselves as one of the other parties in the situation. This is an application of the Golden Rule that Jesus proclaimed:

> So whatever you wish that others would do to you, do also to them, for this is the Law and the Prophets. (Matt. 7:12)

Love of neighbor means that we will not go into a store and take a lot of a salesperson's time when we really have no intent to buy a product there at all, but are already planning to buy it online for a lower price. If you were that salesperson or that business owner, would you want to be treated in this way?

In bargaining for a price, love for neighbor means understanding a "good deal" is one that is not only good for you but also allows the other person to make some money and to have some benefit from the transaction. It means that "a good deal is one that benefits both parties." This does not mean that you have to be stupid or wasteful with your money or your product, but it also means you should not be ruthless or driven by greed or the desire to extract the last possible dollar from the bargain.

Love for neighbor also is important when business owners experience a downturn in business and have to lay off some of their employees. If you own a business, I do not think you are obligated to keep on paying people when doing so will eventually drive you out of business (which would do your employees no good either), but love for neighbor does mean acting reluctantly and with a fair and understandable process when you have to lay people off. It means doing so in a way that shows care and respect for the employees, insofar as that is possible.

5. Confidence That There Is Always a Right Decision: "God Is Faithful, and He Will Not Let You Be Tempted beyond Your Ability, but with the Temptation He Will Also Provide the Way of Escape" (1 Cor. 10:13). I discussed this principle in some detail in chapter 7 and I will only summarize that discussion here.

Every time we face a difficult decision, whether in business or in other aspects of life, if no clear solution appears at once, there is always a temptation to give in to despair and to think, "There is no good decision possible in this situation! All of my choices are bad ones!"

But God's Word tells us that this will not be the case for his people. Even Jesus himself faced decisions that, in principle at least, were similar to the difficult choices that we have to make, and the Bible uses that fact to encourage us to go to him in prayer and seek his help:

> For we do not have a high priest who is unable to sympathize with our weaknesses, but one who *in every respect has been tempted as we are, yet without sin*. Let us then with confidence draw near to the throne of grace, that we may receive mercy and find grace to help in time of need. (Heb. 4:15–16)

Paul also assures us that, though we may think we are facing situations that are uniquely difficult, all of those situations of "temptation" (that is, when we are tempted to think there is no good choice and we must disobey some command of Scripture) are actually situations that, in principle at least, have been faced by others as well, and God will always provide a right solution:

> No temptation has overtaken you that is not *common to man*. God is faithful, and he will not let you be tempted beyond your ability, but *with the tempta-*

tion he will also provide the way of escape, that you may be able to endure it. (1 Cor. 10:13)

This passage encourages us to pray and ask God to show us the "way of escape," the way in which we can make a right decision without giving in to the temptation to do something that is morally wrong.

Finally, when facing a difficult decision, it is especially appropriate to follow the advice of James and ask confidently for God to grant us his wisdom for this particular situation:

> *If any of you lacks wisdom, let him ask God*, who gives generously to all without reproach, and it will be given him. But let him ask in faith, with no doubting, for the one who doubts is like a wave of the sea that is driven and tossed by the wind. (James 1:5–6)

When facing a difficult decision in the business world, it should be immensely encouraging, before we know the right answer to the situation, to begin with the confidence that there always will be a right solution and that God encourages us to ask his help in finding it.

6. Trust in God: "Better Is a Little with Righteousness Than Great Revenues with Injustice" (Prov. 16:8). In every business decision we make, it is necessary to maintain a firm trust in God to bless obedience to his commands. He tells us:

> Do not be deceived: God is not mocked, for *whatever one sows, that will he also reap.* (Gal. 6:7)

Every business decision and action should be carried out with the awareness that we do everything in God's presence:

> The eyes of the LORD are in every place,
>   keeping watch on the evil and the good. (Prov. 15:3)

This means that earning a profit of $1,000 with God's blessing is far better than earning a profit of $2,000 through dishonesty and then not having God's blessing.

A Christian who acts with firm confidence in God's promise to the Philippians through Paul will be able to make much better ethical decisions than one who does not:

> And *my God will supply every need of yours* according to his riches in glory in Christ Jesus. (Phil. 4:19)

These six core convictions are not at all complex or difficult to remember, but they are remarkably useful. I have found them relevant again and again in addressing dozens of ethical questions that people have asked me and that have arisen in the business world.

In the next several sections of this chapter, I will discuss a number of core components of business activity and argue that, in each case, the activity is morally good, but it also carries with it temptations to sin. After that, the final three sections of the chapter will discuss ethical questions that apply particularly to corporations.

B. BUYING AND SELLING ARE MORALLY GOOD ACTIVITIES

Several passages of Scripture assume that buying and selling are morally good activities, at least in many situations. Regarding the sale of land in ancient Israel, God's law said:[5]

> If you make a sale to your neighbor or buy from your neighbor, you shall not wrong one another. (Lev. 25:14)

This implies that it is possible and in fact is *expected* that people should buy and sell *without* wronging one another—that is, that both buyer and seller can *do right* in the transaction (see also Gen. 41:57; Lev. 19:35–36; Deut. 25:13–16; Prov. 11:26; 31:16; Jer. 32:25, 42–44).

In fact, buying and selling are necessary for anything beyond subsistence-level living. No individual or family providing for all its own needs could produce more than a very low standard of living (that is, if it could buy and sell *absolutely nothing*, and had to live off only what it could produce itself, which would be a fairly simple range of foods and clothing). But when we can *sell* what we make and *buy* from others who specialize in producing milk or bread, orange juice or blueberries, bicycles or televisions, cars or computers, then, through the mechanism of buying and selling, we can all obtain a much higher standard of living, and thereby we can fulfill God's purpose that we enjoy the resources of the earth with thanksgiving (1 Tim. 4:3–5; 6:17) while we "eat" and "drink" and "do all to the glory of God" (1 Cor. 10:31).

Therefore, we should not look at buying and selling (that is, commercial transactions) as a necessary evil or as only morally neutral. Rather, commercial transactions are *in themselves good* because through them we do good to other people. This is because of the amazing truth that, in most cases, *voluntary commercial transactions benefit both parties.*

If I sell you a copy of my book for $12, then I get something that I want more than that copy of the book: your $12. So I am better off than I was before, when I had too many copies of that book, copies that I was never going to read. And I am happy. But you got something that you wanted more than your $12: a copy of my book, which you

---

[5] This section and the next two are adapted from my book *Business for the Glory of God: The Bible's Teaching on the Moral Goodness of Business* (Wheaton, IL: Crossway, 2003), 35–39, 41–45, 61–66, with permission of the publisher.

did not have. So you are better off than you were before, and you are happy. Thus, by giving us the ability to buy and sell, God has given us a wonderful mechanism through which we can do good for each other. We should be thankful for this process every time we buy or sell something. We can honestly see buying and selling as a means of loving our neighbors as ourselves.

Buying and selling are also activities unique to human beings out of all the creatures that God made. Rabbits and squirrels, dogs and cats, elephants and giraffes know nothing of this activity. Through buying and selling God has given us a wonderful means to glorify him.

We can imitate God's attributes each time we buy and sell, if we practice honesty, faithfulness to our commitments, fairness, and freedom of choice. Moreover, commercial transactions provide many opportunities for personal interaction, as when I realize that I am buying not just from a store but from a person, to whom I should show kindness and God's grace. In fact, every business transaction is an opportunity for us be fair and truthful, and thus to obey Jesus's teaching that we should do to others as we would want them to do to us (Matt. 7:12).

Because of the interpersonal nature of commercial transactions, business activity has a significant stabilizing influence on a society. A farmer may not really like the auto mechanic in town very much, and the auto mechanic may not like the farmer very much, but the farmer *does* want his pickup truck fixed right the next time it breaks down, and the auto mechanic *does* love the sweet corn and tomatoes that the farmer sells, so it is to their mutual advantage to get along with each other, and so their animosity is restrained. In fact, they may even seek each other's good for this reason! So it is with commercial transactions throughout the world and even between nations. This is an evidence of God's common grace, because in the mechanism of buying and selling God has provided us with a wonderful encouragement to love our neighbors by pursuing actions that advance not only our own welfare but also the welfare of others, even as we pursue our own. In buying and selling we also manifest interdependence and thus reflect the interdependence and interpersonal love among the members of the Trinity, and in that way glorify God.

However, commercial transactions provide many temptations to sin. Rather than seeking the good of our neighbors as well as ourselves, our hearts can be filled with greed, so that we seek only our own good and give no thought for the good of others. (This happens, for example, when one person in a business transaction wants 99 percent or 100 percent of the benefit and wants the other person to be reduced to 1 percent or 0 percent of the benefit.) Or our hearts can be overcome with selfishness, an inordinate desire for wealth, and setting our hearts on longing for material gain. Paul says:

> Those who desire to be rich fall into temptation, into a snare, into many senseless and harmful desires that plunge people into ruin and destruction. For the love of money is a root of all kinds of evils. It is through this craving

that some have wandered away from the faith and pierced themselves with many pangs. (1 Tim. 6:9–10)

Because of sin, we can also engage in dishonest practices, such as selling shoddy materials whose defects are covered with glossy paint. Where there is excessive concentration of power or a huge imbalance in knowledge, there will often be oppression of those who lack power or knowledge (as in government-sponsored monopolies in socialist or communist countries, where consumers are only allowed access to poor-quality, high-priced goods from one manufacturer for each product.).

But the distortions of something good must not cause us to think that the thing itself is evil. Buying and selling in themselves are fundamentally right and pleasing to God. They are a wonderful gift from him through which he has enabled us to have many opportunities to glorify him.

C. EARNING A PROFIT IS A MORALLY GOOD ACTIVITY

What is earning a profit? In essence, it is selling a product for more than the cost of producing it. If I have a bakery and bake 100 loaves of bread at a cost of $200, but sell them for a total of $400, I have made $200 profit. If people are willing to pay $4 for each of my loaves of bread, it means that they think that what I have produced is valuable—the bread that cost me $2 is worth $4 to them! Profit is thus an indication that I have made something useful for others, and in that way it can show that I am doing good for others in the goods and services that I sell.

In addition, profit can indicate that I have used resources more efficiently than others, because when my costs are lower my profit is higher. If another baker wasted some flour and yeast, and spent $225 to make 100 loaves, then his profit was less than mine. But using resources more efficiently (not wasting them) is also good, since it leaves more and cheaper resources for others to use as well. Therefore, profit is usually an indication that I am making good and efficient use of the earth's resources, thus obeying God's original "creation mandate" to "subdue" the earth:

> Be fruitful and multiply and fill the earth and *subdue it*, and have dominion over the fish of the sea and over the birds of the heavens and over every living thing that moves on the earth. (Gen. 1:28)

In the parable of the minas (or pounds), Jesus tells of a nobleman calling 10 of his servants, giving them one mina each (about three months' wages), and telling them, "Engage in business until I come" (Luke 19:13). The servant who earned a 1,000 percent profit was rewarded greatly, for when he said, "Lord, your mina has made ten minas more," the nobleman responded:

> Well done, good servant! Because you have been faithful in a very little, you
> shall have authority over ten cities. (Luke 19:16–17)

The servant who made five more minas received authority over five cities, but *the
one who made no profit was rebuked* for not at least putting the mina in the bank to earn
interest (v. 23).

The nobleman of course represents Jesus himself, who has gone to a "far country"
to receive a kingdom and will return to reward his servants. The parable has obvious
applications to stewardship of spiritual gifts and ministries that Jesus entrusts to us, but
in order for the parable to make sense, it has to assume that *good stewardship, in God's
eyes, includes expanding and multiplying whatever resources or stewardship he entrusts to
us.* Surely we cannot exclude money and material possessions from the application of
the parable, for they are part of what God entrusts to each of us, and our money and
possessions can and should be used to glorify him. Seeking profit, therefore, or seeking
to multiply our resources is seen as fundamentally good. Not to do so is condemned by
the master when he returns.

The parable of the talents (Matt. 25:14–30) has a similar point, but the amounts are
larger, for a talent was worth about 20 years' wages for a laborer, and different amounts
are given at the outset.

A similar assumption is behind the approval given to the ideal wife in Proverbs 31:

> She perceives that her merchandise is profitable. (v. 18)

The word translated as "merchandise" (Hebrew, *saḥar*) refers to profit-producing
commercial transactions. This "excellent wife" is commended for selling goods for
a profit.

Some people will object that earning a profit is "exploiting" other people. Why
should I charge you $4 for a loaf of bread if it only cost me $2 to produce? One reason
is that you are paying not only for my raw materials, but also for my work as an "en-
trepreneur"—my time in baking the bread, my baking skill that I learned at the cost
of more of my time, my skill in finding and organizing the materials and equipment
to bake bread, and (significantly) the risk I take in baking 100 loaves of bread each day
before any buyers have even entered my shop!

In any society, some people are too cautious by nature to assume the risks involved
in starting and running a business, but others are willing to take those risks, and it is
right to give them some *profit* as a reward for taking those risks that benefit all the rest
of us. It is the hope of such reward that motivates people to start businesses and assume
such risks. If profit were not allowed in a society, then people would not take such risks,
and we would have very few goods available to buy. Allowing profit, therefore, is a very
good thing that brings benefits to everybody in the society.

Of course, there can be wrongful profit. For example, if there is a great disparity in
power or knowledge between you and me, and I take advantage of that and cheat you,

I would not be obeying Jesus's command to do to others as I would want them to do to me (Matt. 7:12).

Or if I am in charge of a monopoly on a necessary good, so that people can only buy bread, water, or gasoline from me, and I charge an exorbitant price that depletes people's wealth, of course that kind of profit is excessive and wrong. That is where the process of earning a profit provides temptations to sin.

But as I noted above, the distortion of good thing must not cause us to think that the thing itself is evil. If profit is made in a system of voluntary exchange not distorted by monopoly power or greatly unequal knowledge, then when I earn a profit I also help you. You are better off because you have a loaf of bread that you wanted, and I am better off because I earned $2 profit, and that keeps me in business and makes me want to make more bread to sell. Everybody wins; nobody is exploited. Through this process, as my business profits and grows, I continue to glorify God by enlarging the possessions over which I am "sovereign" and over which I can exercise wise stewardship.

The ability to earn a profit thus results in multiplying our resources while helping other people. It is a wonderful ability that God has given us, and it is not evil or morally neutral, but is fundamentally good.

D. COMPETITION IS MORALLY GOOD

As with other aspects of business that we have considered, so it is with competition: the evils and distortions that have sometimes accompanied competition have led people to the conclusion that competition is evil in itself. But this is not true.

We can think of some good examples of competition in other areas of life. To take one example, most people think competition in sports is a good thing, whether in children's soccer leagues, Little League baseball, high school and college competitions, or professional sports. Although we can all think of bad examples of coaches who are overly competitive, for the most part we think competitive sports is a good system and that it is fair for the best team to receive some prize or award at the end. (See 1 Cor. 9:25–26; 2 Tim. 2:5 for some metaphors of athletic competition that Paul uses in a positive way.)

There are several benefits that come from competition:

1. Vocational Guidance by Trying Different Activities. In most school systems, the assigning of grades is a competitive activity in which the best math students, the best English students, and the best art and music students receive higher grades. The "competitive" grading system provides guidance to help students find something they can do well and to help society assign jobs to those who are best suited to those roles. The result is that when I fly in an airplane, I am glad that it was designed by people who got high grades in mathematics and engineering. The grading system was "competitive" and *it guided society in assigning jobs* to those who were best suited to those jobs.

In the business world, competition does that as well. We once hired a careless painter for our house, and he only lasted a day. But then we found a good painter, and we were willing to pay more for his high-quality work. The bad painter needed to find another occupation, and we were helping him see that by asking him not to come back the next day. The world is so diverse, and the economic system has so many needs, that I am sure there is some area in which he can fulfill a need and do well. But it wasn't painting.[6]

So a competitive system is one in which we test our abilities and find if we can do something better than others, and so be paid for it. The system works well when we reward better work and greater quantities of work with greater rewards.

If you have ever shopped around for the lowest price on a shirt, a computer, or a car, that action shows that you approve of competition in the economy, because you were making competition work. You bought from the company who could produce and distribute a computer cheaper than someone else, and you encouraged that more efficient manufacturer to stay in business and discouraged the less efficient, more expensive computer manufacturers from staying in business. This happens every day, so we take it for granted. This should cause us to realize that if we are going to be good stewards of our possessions, we need to have competition in the marketplace.

2. Lower Prices and Higher Quality of Goods. Lower prices are another benefit that affects everybody. One result of competition is that people keep getting better at making things, and the (inflation-adjusted) prices of consumer goods keep falling and falling over the course of decades. As a result, the society continues to obtain a higher standard of living (in economic terms).

For example, computers keep getting better and prices keep falling, so more and more people can afford computers, and everyone who buys one has more money left over than he or she would have had a year before. The first pocket calculators cost around $100, but today I can buy one at the checkout counter at the drugstore for $1. These are examples of how competition brings economic benefit to the society as a whole.

3. An Incentive for Improvement. There is still another benefit to competition. God has created us with a desire to do well and to improve what we are able to do. Competition spurs us on to do better because we see others doing better and decide that we can do better too. An executive from a company that made mail-sorting machines once told me that his engineers thought they had made the fastest, quietest mail-sorting machine possible—until he took them to watch a machine, manufactured by a German company,

---

[6] In every society there will be some people who, because of physical or mental disabilities, are unable to find productive work without help from others, either from charitable organizations or government agencies. Surely we should support such efforts to provide a "safety net" for those unable to care for themselves. In addition, many companies make special efforts to provide opportunities for productive work for adults with disabilities. As a result, in American society (with which I am most familiar) and in many other countries as well, there is productive work available for the vast majority of the population, and competition is the mechanism that helps workers find the jobs for which their interests and abilities best suit them.

that was even faster and quieter! Then the engineers went back to work, determined to do even better. I think that God has made us with such a desire to strive for excellence in our work so that we may imitate his excellence more fully.

A kind of competition to try to do as well as or better than someone else seems to be what Solomon had in mind when he wrote:

> Then I saw that all toil and all skill in work come from a man's *envy* of his neighbor. (Eccles. 4:4)

The term translated as "envy" (in most translations) or "rivalry" (NASB) is the Hebrew word *qin'āh*, which can have either negative or positive moral connotations, depending on the context (much like the English terms "jealousy" and "zeal"). Here it seems to have the sense "competitive spirit."[7] The verse does not say this is good or bad, only that it happens. (A different word, *ḥāmad*, is used in Ex. 20:17, when God says, "You shall not covet.") People see what someone else has and decide to work harder themselves or to gain better skills. In this way, competition spurs people on to better work so that they themselves prosper, and society prospers with them.

There is in fact a sort of mild "competition" implied in the testing of men before they become deacons:

> And let them also be tested first; then let them serve as deacons if they prove themselves blameless. (1 Tim. 3:10)

If these men do well in the time of testing ("if they prove themselves blameless"), then they can become deacons. If not, then they should find some other area of service within the church.[8]

Competition seems to be the system God intended when he gave some people greater talents in one area and gave other people greater talents in another area, and when he established a world where justice and fairness would require giving greater reward for better work.

4. Opportunities to Glorify God and Opportunities to Sin. Competition brings many opportunities to glorify God, as we try to use our talents to their full potential and thus manifest the Godlike abilities that he has granted to us, with thankfulness in our hearts to him. Competition enables each person to find a role in which he or she can make a

---

[7] The definition "competitive spirit" is given for this word in this verse by HALOT, p. 1110. (The NET has "competition" here, but most translations say "envy.")

[8] There also appears to have been some kind of competition among David's "mighty men": "Now Abishai, the brother of Joab . . . was chief of the thirty. . . . He was the most renowned of the thirty and became their commander, but he did not attain to the three" (2 Sam. 23:18–19). Note also Paul's comparison of himself to the other apostles: "I am the least of the apostles, unworthy to be called an apostle, because I persecuted the church of God. . . . I worked harder than any of them, though it was not I, but the grace of God that is with me" (1 Cor. 15:9–10).

positive contribution to society, serving others by doing good for them. Competition is thus a sort of societal functioning of God's attributes of wisdom and kindness, and it is a way society helps people discover God's will for their lives. Competition also enables us individually to demonstrate fairness and kindness toward others, even those with whom we compete.

On the other hand, competition brings many temptations to sin. There is a difference between trying to do a job better than others on the one hand, and trying to harm others and prevent them from earning a living on the other hand. There is nothing wrong with trying to run a better car-repair shop than the one down the street, but there is a lot wrong with lying about the other mechanic, stealing his tools, or otherwise seeking to do him harm.

Competition also brings temptations to pride and to excessive work that allows no rest or time with family or with God. There is also the temptation to so distort life values that we become unable even to enjoy the fruits of our labor.

But the distortions of something that is good must not cause us to think that the thing itself is evil. These temptations to sin should not obscure the fact that competition in itself, within appropriate limits (some of which should be established by government), is good and pleasing to God, and provides many opportunities for glorifying him.

E. ADVERTISING IS MORALLY GOOD

Advertising is publishing information about a product or a service for the purpose of increasing sales. The goal of advertising is to inform others about a product or service, and persuade them that it is valuable enough that they want to buy it.

If you honestly believe that your product will bring benefit to other people, there is nothing inherently wrong with trying to inform them about it. Yes, you will benefit if you sell your product, but advertising your product is also seeking the good of other people. You can seek to accomplish both things (help yourself by making sales and help others by making a good product available to them), and this is possible because a good business transaction brings benefit to both parties.

I have had a role in advertising from time to time. For example, my picture appeared in a magazine advertisement for Phoenix Seminary along with a statement about the excellent work the seminary does in combining a strong mentoring program, care for students' spiritual growth, involvement by local pastors, and solid academic training. I hope that the ad encouraged students to consider Phoenix Seminary and that that process eventually persuaded some of them to enroll as students. I could honestly put my name on that advertisement because I believed what I was saying about the quality of the seminary.

The primary ethical principles to keep in mind regarding advertising are truthfulness and genuinely seeking the good of other people as well as yourself. In other words, in advertising, do not bear false witness and do not fail to love your neighbor as yourself.

There are some dangers to beware of regarding advertising. It would be wrong to speak untruthfully in advertisement, to say that your bakery sells only bread that is "baked fresh every day" if in fact some of what you sell is left over from the previous day. However, I find it interesting that U.S. law allows a fairly wide leeway in ads that say something is the "best," "greatest," "most beautiful," and so forth. If you own a restaurant that sells pizza, it is not a violation of the law to put out a sign that says "Best Pizza in Arizona!" or "World's Best Pizza!" This is legally acceptable because it would be very hard for anyone to determine in a definitive way what constitutes "the best pizza," and, furthermore, customers reading such claims understand them to be a commonly used form of "puffery," that is, language that speaks of a product in a superlative way.[9]

Another wrongful kind of advertising seeks to induce people to purchase things that are harmful or unwise, such as a lottery ticket, which is most likely a colossal waste of money. And yet another wrongful kind of advertising tries to sell products by blatantly flaunting a woman's (or man's) sexuality.

Another question that is frequently asked is this: Does advertising wrongly breed a consumer demand for goods that people don't need, so that the actual result of advertising is an increase in materialism and in irresponsible levels of consumer debt?

I think this is a legitimate objection, but my judgment is that the primary solution to this problem has to come through instructing the hearts and minds of consumers more effectively so that they are not deceived and do not make irresponsible stewardship decisions regarding things they see advertised. Even if there is an increase in materialism as a result of advertising (and I am sure there is), there is also a great benefit that comes from allowing legal freedom of speech and freedom of advertising in a society, so that people can inform others about their products. It seems to me that any proposed government-imposed solution to such harm from advertising would also have to recognize that forbidding or severely restricting advertising would result in a great societal loss of information about products, a loss of some increased quality and lower prices that result through free speech and competition, and a great loss in consumer freedom to choose what to listen to and which claims to believe. Therefore, I think that any objections about the materialism that is incited by advertising should lead in the direction of increased consumer education rather than in the direction of increased government restriction on people's freedoms.

F. ARE CORPORATIONS ETHICALLY LEGITIMATE?

A corporation is an organization that is set up as "a separate legal entity having its own rights, privileges and liabilities distinct from those of its members."[10] Is such a legal entity a morally good thing? I believe that it is.

---

[9] However, if it were my restaurant, I would be personally reluctant to put out a sign like this because I could not be sure that it was true.

[10] *American Heritage Dictionary*, 4th ed. (Boston: Houghton Mifflin, 2006), 410.

CHAPTER 40 · BUSINESS ETHICS

A corporation allows people to own portions of a company (they are the stockholders) and to manage a company (they are the employees who oversee its operations) without being legally liable for the losses that a corporation might incur, especially if it enters bankruptcy and/or goes out of business.

Some people have said that such an arrangement is not ethically right because it encourages personal irresponsibility. This is because (people sometimes claim) corporate officers and managers can avoid responsibility for the decisions that they make—the company can lose money and they don't have to repay it personally.[11] I do not agree with this objection. This is because people who buy stock in a company do so knowing there is a measure of risk involved and knowing that the managers of the company are not putting their personal resources at risk. In addition, people who do business with a corporation also recognize that this kind of risk exists.

The benefit of corporations is that many companies today are far too large for any one individual to assume responsibility for them. They have annual sales of many billions of dollars. Many of the activities carried on by corporations today (especially those with sales across an entire nation or around the world) would probably be impossible unless this type of legal structure existed.

The idea of a corporation is not entirely new. In the ancient world, some enterprises (such as trading with foreign countries through shipping) were very expensive, and therefore many people would purchase "shares" in an enterprise and would share later in its profits or losses. But no one individual would be responsible for all of the losses.[12]

Another objection is that a large corporation of necessity becomes "impersonal" and therefore becomes a dehumanizing place in which to work. But even very large corporations do not need to be impersonal at the level of individual employee interactions, and company policies and practices can certainly establish a corporate culture that is employee-friendly and that values the distinctive contribution of each individual.

Of course, I recognize that corporations can be used by people in morally wrong ways. They can cheat vendors, treat employees harshly and unfairly, sell products by means of deceptive advertising, manufacture defective or harmful products, pollute the environment, and do other harmful things. But these are abuses of the idea of a corporation; they are not inherent in the institution itself.

G. CORPORATE SOCIAL RESPONSIBILITY AND THE QUESTION OF "GIVING BACK"

When corporations make charitable contributions to their communities, this is increasingly referred to as "giving back." I believe there are good reasons for making such contributions, but I think the expression "giving back" is unfortunate and misleading.

---

[11] Of course, if a corporate executive is guilty of intentional wrongdoing or fraud (as opposed to simply mistaken judgments), then he is committing a crime and can be held legally liable for it.

[12] See Jules Toutain, *The Economic Life of the Ancient World* (London: Routledge & Kegan Paul, 1930), 246–49.

1. Good Reasons for Donations to the Community. There are several good reasons why corporations should ordinarily make contributions to charitable organizations in their communities:

1. A pattern of such donations builds good relationships within the community and a spirit of goodwill in the community as a whole.
2. Such donations encourage others similarly to donate to worthy causes.
3. Such donations improve the image of the company in the community and thereby help the company in its business.
4. Such donations tend to make employees proud to work for the company.
5. The charitable organization that receives the money is able to do good for the community.

These are all benefits that come from corporate donations. Just as individuals in the community are *not legally obligated* to contribute to charitable organizations but often *voluntarily* donate time and money, so a corporation, as a responsible member of a community, should not be legally obligated to make such donations, but should, it seems to me, feel some sense of moral obligation to make such donations in a voluntary manner. How much is given, and where it is given, will vary widely from corporation to corporation.[13]

2. "Giving Back" Is an Unfortunate and Misleading Expression. Sometimes when corporations make donations to charitable organizations in a community, people refer to this as "giving back," thus suggesting that the corporation has "taken" its profit in an illegitimate or immoral manner and therefore has some obligation to *give back some of what it has "taken."*

However, as I explained above, profit is not morally evil but is morally good (so long as it is gained legally and for morally good products). Therefore, a company has no obligation to give corporate donations as a way of atoning for its "sin" of making a profit. That is an entirely skewed moral perspective.

Rather, every time the company pays wages to employees, *it is already giving something very valuable to the community.* And every time it produces a product that other people buy and find useful, *it is already giving benefit to the community.* To understand this, imagine what would happen if the company suddenly ceased to operate. There would be no more of its products and no more jobs. Then the benefit that it gives to the community would be entirely lost. This illustrates how wages and products are already giving much to a community. Charitable contributions are not "giving back" but are

---

[13] However, I do not agree with those who speak of all the "stakeholders" within a company (all those who are affected by it or do business with it) having some sort of right or authority to decide how much the company should give to charitable organizations. The legally constituted owners are the only ones who have such authority, though they may find it wise to consult with members of the community, employees, customers, suppliers, and others.

"giving more" than the good jobs and good products that the companies are already providing.

3. It Is Wrong to Think the Only Purpose of a Company Is to Make Profits. Some people have argued that the managers of a corporation are really the employees of the shareholders, and therefore the managers have no right to give donations to the community because that is spending the shareholders' money in ways that they are not authorized to do.[14]

I disagree with this viewpoint. If it is the practice of a company to give some percentage of its profits to the community in charitable donations, anyone who purchases the stock can find that out and can buy the stock with the full knowledge that that is part of what the company is going to do with the profits. There is no dishonesty or deception involved.

In addition, it seems to me that just as individuals and private business owners who live in a community should have some sense of moral responsibility to make charitable contributions to worthy organizations that help others in the community, so corporations, as separate legal entities, should exercise some of the same care as well. This is part of what it means to be a good citizen in a community.

H. DO MULTINATIONAL CORPORATIONS EXPLOIT POOR COUNTRIES?

Sometimes people object to a free-market economic system because they claim that it allows powerful global corporations to exploit people in poor countries.[15] This claim is an important one, and it deserves thoughtful analysis.

1. What Does "Exploit" Mean? In order to analyze this objection, we first have to understand what it means to "exploit" a poor country. It might mean different things:

---

[14] A famous essay advocating this viewpoint is Milton Friedman, "The Social Responsibility of Business Is to Increase Its Profits," *The New York Times Magazine*, Sept. 13, 1970, 33, 122–126. It was reprinted in the first edition of Rae and Wong, *Beyond Integrity* (Grand Rapids, MI: Zondervan, 1996), 241–45. Interestingly, the third edition of *Beyond Integrity* (2012) includes a critique of Friedman's essay by John Mackey, the founder and chief executive officer of Whole Foods, and a forceful reply from Friedman himself (see pp. 147–50).

[15] This section is adapted from Wayne Grudem and Barry Asmus, "Do Global Corporations Exploit Poor Countries?" in *Counting the Cost: Christian Perspectives on Capitalism*, ed. Art Lindsley and Anne R. Bradley (Abilene, TX: Abilene Christian University Press and McLean, VA: Institute for Faith, Work, and Economics, 2017), pp. 277–303, with permission of the publisher. Some sections of that essay were adapted from various sections of Wayne Grudem and Barry Asmus, *The Poverty of Nations: A Sustainable Solution* (Wheaton, IL: Crossway, 2013), and this material is used with permission of the publisher. As we explain in that book, we prefer the term "free market" to the term "capitalism" because for many people "capitalism" carries too many negative connotations, and "free market" better conveys the heart of the economic system that we favor (see pp. 136–38). However, as used in this chapter, "capitalism" should be understood in the positive sense in which it has most commonly been understood in economic literature and discussion.

1. *Robbery*: It might mean taking valuable natural resources from a poor country without paying for them.
2. *Unfair prices*: It might mean buying natural resources or agricultural crops from a poor country for unfairly low prices.
3. *Environmental damage*: It might mean extracting natural resources from a poor country in an environmentally harmful way.
4. *Unfair wages*: It might mean hiring laborers in a poor country for unfairly low wages.
5. *Inhumane working conditions*: It might mean requiring people in poor countries to work in unsafe or inhumane working conditions.

2. Do Corporations Exploit Poor Nations in These Ways? I first need to make clear that Scripture explicitly condemns rich people for defrauding poor laborers by misusing the power that comes with their wealth:

> Come now, you rich, weep and howl for the miseries that are coming upon you. . . . Your gold and silver have corroded, and their corrosion will be evidence against you and will eat your flesh like fire. . . . Behold, *the wages of the laborers* who mowed your fields, *which you kept back by fraud*, are crying out against you, and the cries of the harvesters have reached the ears of the Lord of hosts. . . . You have condemned and murdered the righteous person. He does not resist you. (James 5:1–6)

James also indicates that some rich people in the first-century world were oppressing poor Christians:

> Are not the rich *the ones who oppress you*, and the ones who drag you into court? (James 2:6)

The apostle Paul likewise warns that if people allow themselves to be dominated by a desire to become wealthy, temptations to other wrongdoing will soon follow:

> Those who desire to be rich fall into temptation, into a snare, into many senseless and harmful desires that plunge people into ruin and destruction. (1 Tim. 6:9)

Do these warnings against the evils done by rich people in the first century also apply to some multinational corporations today? Yes, because corporations are made up of *people*, corporate decisions are made by *people*, and there are sinful people in corporations today just as there were sinful people in the first century. Therefore, we would be foolish to deny that global corporations are capable of doing evil things, and sometimes (when their executives think they can get away with it) they do evil things. For specific examples, one needs only to read the business section of a newspaper for a week to find another story of some corporation convicted of wrongdoing.

But that is not the question we are attempting to answer here. The question is *whether a free-market system (sometimes called "capitalism") encourages wrongful behavior by global corporations.* In other words, the correct question is whether wrongful corporate behavior is caused by a free-market economic system or by sin in the human heart.

My answer to that question is that the true cause is sin in the human heart, often aided and abetted by corrupt government officials (as some examples below will indicate). And a free-market system, far from encouraging wrongful behavior, does better than any other economic system at deterring such wrong behavior by bringing legal and economic sanctions against corporate wrongdoers.[16]

With that background, we can now examine the five different ideas that people might have in mind when they say that powerful global corporations exploit people in poor countries.

a. Robbery? If ExxonMobil drilled for oil in Nigeria or Brazil, then took it away without paying anything for it, that would be outright robbery. But that kind of outright robbery simply does not happen today. The Nigerian or Brazilian police would arrest workers from any company that tried to steal their oil. They would board and impound their oil tankers right in the harbor.

I recognize that in past history, such outright plundering of valuable resources did happen. For example, in the early 1500s, Spanish conquerors invaded Mexico and Peru, and carried off immense storehouses of gold. In 1519, Hernando Cortez and his armed troops conquered the Aztec Empire in Mexico, and the Spanish finally found the gold they had long sought. Then in 1532–1539, Francisco Pizarro captured the Incan Empire in Peru, and again the conquerors found fabulous amounts of gold that they took back to Spain. These violent conquests with their plunder were truly robbery, and they were morally wrong. (Spain eventually suffered for centuries from this sudden curse of easy riches—see the analysis by Barry Asmus and me elsewhere.[17])

But the plunder of gold by 16th-century Spain is not a failure of modern global corporations.

Of course, some global corporations today *purchase* natural resources (such as oil, timber, gold, and other minerals) from poor countries. But these are voluntary transactions, and the corporations pay money for the resources, so this practice should not be called "stealing" but rather "*buying*" resources. Because there is a world market for commodities, with many companies competing to purchase the resources of a poor nation, any given company must pay the world market price or the country will seek

---

[16] See chap. 37, p. 970, on scriptural support for a free-market economic system as opposed to a socialist or communist system, in which government officials determine what is produced and what can be bought and sold. See also Grudem and Asmus, *The Poverty of Nations*, chap. 6, on the moral advantages of a free-market system.

[17] See Grudem and Asmus, *The Poverty of Nations*, 79–81.

another buyer that will pay. Such a practice does not exploit a poor nation. It provides a significant input of cash for that nation.

However, what if the government officials in a poor country accept bribes in exchange for granting a multinational company an *exclusive* right to drill for oil, so that no other companies can bid for the oil, and then they give this one company the right to pay the poor country a "special bargain price" for the oil, far below the world market price? The oil company makes a huge profit even after it gives regular payoffs to the government officials.

I agree that this case is a form of robbery, but a robbery carried out by secret agreements between the multinational company and the corrupt officials. This example shows us not the free-market system but a *breakdown* of the system, because the country is not receiving the world market price for its resources, which an open free market would provide. Such a situation is not the fault of a free-market system, but is due to a failure to allow the free market to operate. It shows what happens in an "unfree-market system" imposed by a nation's corrupt government. The blame belongs to the government officials who sold the drilling rights too cheaply and then took the bribes, as well as to the corporation that agreed to pay the bribes and pay far below the rightful market price. On both sides, human greed and not the free market are to be blamed. The solution is not for the country to abandon the free market, but for the country to establish it more firmly with more effective rule of law, including accountability for officials who engage in such criminal wrongdoing.

b. Unfair Prices? The second major claim of "exploitation" against large corporations relates to the prices they pay for goods. Do large global corporations pay unfairly low prices for natural resources or for agricultural crops? This will be a longer discussion, because five distinct points must be made in response to this concern. I will primarily discuss coffee here, but the same arguments apply to hundreds of other items.

(1) No One Can Control Commodity Prices on World Markets: Thousands of large and small companies in the world seek to buy coffee for their customers. These include (in the United States) the companies that market Starbucks, Seattle's Best, Nestlé, Maxwell House, Folgers, Dunkin' Donuts, Yuban, Melitta, and thousands of other coffee brands. These are independent companies, and they are found in nearly every country of the world.

The world price of coffee that these companies must pay is mainly determined by two factors—supply and demand.

How does demand affect prices? When customers around the world drink more coffee, the coffee companies need to buy more, which means that the quantity demanded in coffee markets goes up. This pushes the price upward. But if people drink less coffee, the quantity demanded goes down, and this pushes the price down. With many thousands of buyers throughout the world, no one company or nation can determine the overall *demand* for coffee.

What about the supply? If it is a bad year for coffee crops, less coffee is supplied, coffee is scarce, and customers are willing to pay more or drink less so they do not run out. The smaller amount supplied pushes prices up. But if there is a bumper crop of coffee, then more coffee is supplied, and there is more to sell than the companies were planning to buy. Sellers have to cut their prices in order to sell their coffee. A larger supply drives the price of coffee down.

Every year around the world, thousands upon thousands of small and large coffee growers decide how much they are going to plant and try to bring to harvest. (They have to plan in advance because the coffee tree grows for three to five years before it bears coffee beans.) With so many thousands of growers, no one company or nation can determine the overall *supply* of coffee.

For example, the online price table from the International Coffee Organization showed that on July 25, 2014, the composite world price for coffee was 157.69 cents (or $1.5769 in U.S. currency) per pound.[18] (This is the composite price among several varieties and markets, which I will round to 158 cents in what follows.) In coffee exchanges in various cities around the world, 158 cents per pound was the price at which supply and demand intersected. Farmers were willing to *sell* their coffee at that price (supply), and coffee companies were willing to *buy* it at that price (demand). (In this discussion, I am holding other factors constant and omitting transaction costs for the sake of simplification.)

In such a system, with a world market and with prices determined by hundreds of thousands of individual decisions, there is no way a wealthy company or a wealthy nation could say: "We want to increase our profits, so we are going to pay coffee farmers an unfairly low price because we can get away with it. We don't think they should get 158 cents per pound for coffee. We're just going to pay 130 cents per pound!"

Suppose a powerful company such as Starbucks decided it would pay only 130 cents per pound. Starbucks buyers would go to coffee exchanges in cities around the world and announce, "We are offering to buy coffee at 130 cents per pound!" What would happen?

The traders would laugh them out of the room. No one would sell coffee to the Starbucks buyers. Why should they sell to Starbucks at 130 cents a pound when they can sell to anyone else in the world for 158 cents per pound? If no one sells to Starbucks at that price, Starbucks will soon run out of coffee, and its customers will get fed up and start buying their coffee elsewhere. Starbucks knows this, so its buyers have no choice but to offer 158 cents per pound, the world price for coffee. So no individual, no government, and no powerful company is able to "set" the world price for agricultural products.

(2) Governments of Poor Countries Sometimes Keep Farmers from Receiving the World Price for Their Crops: Governments of poor countries can force poor farmers in these countries to accept unfairly low prices, far below the world market price. They do

---

[18] Current prices are listed by the International Coffee Organization, ICO Indicator Prices, http://www .ico.org/coffee_prices.asp.

this by means of taxes, fees, licensing restrictions, tariffs, quotas, and other distortions of the market. British economist P. T. Bauer explains how this can happen:

> The world prices of coffee and cocoa . . . are determined by market forces and not prescribed by the West. On the other hand, the farmers in many of the exporting countries receive far less than the market prices, because they are subject to very high export taxes and similar government levees.[19]

Bauer adds that after the end of British colonial rule, "the great bulk of agricultural exports from British colonies in Africa, including practically all exports produced by Africans, *was handled by state export monopolies known as marketing boards.* . . . [They] became the most important single instrument of state economic control in Africa."[20] The marketing boards received the world price for a crop, took much of it for themselves, then paid the local farmers a far lower price from what was left over.

Though many such marketing boards have now been abolished, it is still important to determine in each nation whether there are government-imposed tariffs, quotas, or local dealer monopolies that mean that growers receive much less than the world market price for their crops—and whether government officials are skimming off profits from these tariffs, quotas, or monopolies. Sometimes that is still happening.

In such cases, farmers are receiving an unjustly low price for their crops—far below the world market price. But the government officials who collect bribes and exorbitant export fees, or the government-protected monopoly buyers who pay the farmers a horribly low price and then sell the crops on a world market for a huge profit, are the true culprits who are using government power to distort the free market for their own selfish benefit.

Are such practices by governments in poor nations the fault of the large global corporations that buy the coffee from those governments or from local monopoly sellers for the world market price? No. The companies are paying the right price. The injustice is being done by the governments of the poor countries, and those governments should bear the blame. The low prices are not the fault of the free market and not the fault of global corporations.[21]

(3) "Fair-Trade" Coffee Is a Form of Charitable Giving That Cannot Provide a Long-Term Change in World Prices: Although it is a slight detour from the question of

---

[19] P. T. Bauer, *Equality, the Third World, and Economic Delusion* (Cambridge, MA: Harvard University Press, 1981), 68–69. See also 173, 177–82.

[20] Ibid., 177, emphasis added.

[21] On the other hand, if a nation's government is not distorting the market, and growers are receiving something close to the world market price for crops, and if they are still very poor, this should not be blamed on global corporations. Worldwide supply and demand for a product are the result of millions of individual decisions by millions of people throughout the world, not the result of the actions of a few large companies. The only viable solution for such poor coffee growers, difficult as it may seem at first, is to find some other crop that is more profitable, or even find another occupation.

whether global corporations exploit poor countries, I want to comment briefly here on the campaign to encourage people to buy "fair-trade" coffee at higher prices, a topic I touched on in chapter 37 (p. 981). This campaign is widely promoted as an alternative to raw capitalism and the unconstrained actions of the free market. The promise of the fair-trade movement is that coffee growers in poor nations will receive a higher price for coffee if it is produced in better working conditions with higher wages. Then coffee that is marketed as "fair-trade coffee" is sold at a higher price to consumers in wealthy nations.

Here are some of the arguments in favor of fair-trade coffee:

1. *Unfair prices*: Since coffee prices have plummeted in recent years, prices received by small farmers can be less than the costs of production. This is not fair to the farmers, who cannot make any money growing coffee.
2. *Care for nature*: Fair-trade coffee strives to be organic, bird-friendly, and shade-growth-oriented.
3. *Some success*: Thousands of fair-trade coffee growers have already been helped by this kind of program.

However, those arguments are not as persuasive as they first appear.

1. *Unfair prices*: One of the most basic concepts in economics, remembered by Econ 101 students long after they have forgotten everything else, is that prices are determined by the interaction of supply and demand. Prices are not determined by various people's thoughts of what is a "fair" price.

This means that if a small coffee grower cannot pay his production costs and earn a living by growing coffee, there are only two ways to change the price: (1) decrease the world's *supply* of coffee (but it is impossible for the farmer to do this in a significant way) or (2) increase the world's *demand* for coffee (but it is impossible for a single farmer to do this). If the world price cannot be changed by the farmer, then appealing to people to pay more than the world price is like begging; it is asking for a charitable donation. It might raise a bit of money for a few growers, but it will not change the world price. If a small coffee grower cannot earn a living by growing coffee, the best long-term solution is for him to switch to growing another crop that will enable him to earn a living. He might even have to leave farming for another occupation altogether.

Here is an analogy: Suppose a man tries to earn a living by collecting used aluminum cans from trash bins and selling them to a recycling center. After several weeks he says to us, "I'm not getting a fair price for these cans. I work all day and only earn a few dollars."

Should we then say, "We'll help you get a fair price. We'll set up a network of 'fair-trade' recycled aluminum centers that will pay you more than the market price"? No, that would be foolish. If we truly want to help him, we should say, "You need another occupation," and even, "We'll help get you some training in another skill."

2. *Care for nature*: I think that care for nature is an important issue, and I discuss it more fully in chapter 41. But at this point I wish to point out that people can and do

care for the natural world in many ways other than through supporting fair-trade coffee. The fair-trade movement is not necessary to care for nature in effective ways.

3. *Some success*: Campaigns for fair-trade coffee, like all campaigns for charitable contributions, do provide some help for the people to whom the contributions are given. But it is also necessary to consider the harm that comes to all the other coffee growers in the world, who receive lower prices when the fair-trade movement increases production beyond what the world market demands, as indicated by the world price for coffee. In addition, the fair-trade movement keeps its coffee growers working in a crop that can provide them with an adequate living only as long as they keep receiving these charitable contributions from others. It discourages them from changing to another crop or another occupation in which they could support themselves for a lifetime without depending on charity from others.

A number of economists agree with these conclusions. Economist Victor Claar points out, "Fair trade coffee roughly represents just one percent of the coffee markets in the United States and Europe."[22] But Claar identifies an economic harm that comes from an artificial increase of the price of some coffee above what the world market will bear (that is, higher than the price set by world supply and demand). Paying some growers a higher price than the world market price for coffee encourages them *to grow more coffee* than the market actually demands. Claar writes:

> Thus, while there is too much coffee being grown relative to global demand in general, there is also not sufficient demand to purchase, at the fair trade price, all of the coffee being grown as fair trade coffee. In both cases, there is simply too much coffee.[23]

The larger supply of coffee then *depresses the price for other coffee growers* who are not part of the fair-trade movement. As I explain in the next section, this is something like what occurs because of the agricultural subsidies that the United States pays to certain farmers, giving them a price above the world market price for their crops, and then ending up with surplus crops that it "dumps" on the world market, depressing agricultural prices for other countries. In the case of fair-trade coffee, the oversupply comes about not by government price supports but by voluntary contributions from people buying the coffee.

Claar goes on to say that artificially raising the price for coffee only prolongs the problem of too much coffee on the world market:

> If the fundamental problem with the coffee market is that prices are low because there is too much coffee, then it would appear that the fair trade move-

---

[22] Victor Claar, *Fair Trade? Its Prospects as a Poverty Solution* (Grand Rapids, MI: Poverty Cure, 2012), 39. Even if fair-trade coffee represented 3 percent or 4 percent of the coffee market in the United States and Europe, that would not take into account the rest of the world, so it is doubtful that fair-trade coffee accounts for even 1 percent of the world market.

[23] Ibid., 40.

ment may be making matters worse rather than better because it increases the incentives to grow more coffee.[24]

An additional problem is that, by paying a higher price than the world market price for coffee, the fair-trade movement encourages farmers to keep producing coffee when they would be much better off shifting to alternative crops for which there is more demand. Claar shows how Costa Rica shifted its production to new products and significantly increased the value of its exports.[25]

Paul Collier is a professor of economics at Oxford University and former director of development research at the World Bank. He writes the following about fair-trade coffee, but the arguments apply to "fair-trade" campaigns for other products as well:

> The price premium in fair trade products is a form of charitable transfer, and there is evidently no harm in that. But the problem with it, as compared with just giving people the aid in other ways, is that it encourages recipients to stay doing what they are doing—producing coffee. . . . They get charity as long as they stay producing the crops that have locked them into poverty.[26]

I agree with these economic assessments, and therefore I cannot recommend that people support the "fair-trade" movement. Charitable contributions to the poor are more efficiently given by other means, and such charitable transfers will never lead to a long-term solution for world poverty, or even for most growers of a single product, such as coffee.

(4) When Rich Nations "Dump" Excess Agricultural Products on the World Market, This Wrongfully Depresses World Prices:

I discussed above the evil that results when governments of poor countries keep farmers from receiving world market prices for their crops. But "commodity dumping" by wealthy nations can also depress the prices farmers receive.

Commodity dumping happens when governments (usually in wealthier European nations and in the United States) pay huge subsidies to farmers in their countries, which means that many farmers are paid above the world market prices for crops such as wheat, peanuts, sugar beets, and many others. The government makes a "support price" guarantee, so the farmers grow more of a product (for example, wheat) than the world market demands. The government then buys the wheat from these farmers at the promised price and stores it in huge grain silos. This happens in the United States year after year.

What is to be done with this excess wheat? The U.S. government can either give it away to other countries of the world (in which case it would destroy the market for

---

[24] Ibid., 43–44.

[25] Ibid., 53.

[26] Paul Collier, *The Bottom Billion: Why the Poorest Countries Are Failing and What Can Be Done about It* (Oxford: Oxford University Press, 2007), 163.

locally grown wheat in those countries, because the farmers cannot compete with a price of zero) or it can offer the wheat for sale on the world market at less than the world market price (in which case the large influx of supply depresses the world market price for wheat, and again the farmers in poor countries receive less than they otherwise would).

Many economists believe this system of farm subsidies is economically harmful and would like to see it abolished. I agree. When wealthy nations "dump" massive amounts of a crop on the world market, they definitely harm farmers in poor countries. I also think such subsidies are economically harmful for the countries where they occur. However, there are political reasons why these subsidies continue in various nations, which I have written about elsewhere.[27]

But once again, this problem is the fault of wrongful government policies, not the fault of global corporations. It is not the fault of the free market but the fault of governments distorting the free market.[28]

(5) Rich Nations Wrongfully Impose Harmful Tariffs and Quotas on Products That They Import from Poor Nations: There is another harmful practice by rich nations. When wealthy countries place restrictive tariffs or quotas on goods imported from poor countries, they wrongfully hinder those poor countries. If a Latin American country can grow tomatoes more cheaply than producers in the United States, then U.S. consumers benefit from the lower prices, and the Latin American growers benefit from earning more income. The U.S. government should not prevent the Latin American growers from realizing this benefit by forcing them to pay high tariffs when they bring tomatoes into the United States, just so that American tomato growers are protected. Free trade brings benefits to both nations.[29]

But what about the tomato growers in the United States who would be put out of business if cheaper Latin American tomatoes were allowed into the United States without the growers having to pay tariffs? Shouldn't the United States care for its own tomato farmers?

I admit that the businesses of some American tomato growers would be hurt by

---

[27] See the discussion of farm subsidies in Wayne Grudem, *Politics—According to the Bible* (Grand Rapids, MI: Zondervan, 2010), 528–33. See also Barry Asmus and Donald B. Billings, *Crossroads: The Great American Experiment: The Rise, Decline, and Restoration of Freedom and the Market Economy* (Lanham, MD: University Press of America, 1984), 224–27.

[28] Can poor nations today do anything to end such commodity dumping? Quite honestly, it is unlikely that any poor nation or group of poor nations can stop the dumping of excess products on the world market in the foreseeable future. The practice can be changed only by internal political powers within each country that dumps commodities, and that might or might not happen soon. I certainly hope it does. For now the only step that poor countries can take seems to be to adapt to circumstances as they are.

If the world market for wheat is unpredictable, and if growing wheat therefore proves unlikely to provide a farmer with a good income year after year, then the only solution (short of producing much more wheat) is for him to shift to other crops. In other words, poor nations can successfully adapt to foreign dumping of commodities by growing other crops or producing other products that are not subject to such dumping.

[29] Ron Sider, *Rich Christians in an Age of Hunger: Moving from Affluence to Generosity*, 5th ed. (Nashville: Thomas Nelson, 2005), 143–47, 240–44, offers disturbing statistics about the harm that such tariffs impose on poor nations.

lower-priced imports. But on balance, the economic evidence is clear and compelling: while a small group is helped by such tariffs, the rest of the people in a country are be hurt by having to pay higher prices.

Therefore, while high tariffs at first appear to help local growers and can be defended as "job saving," the actual result ends up protecting a few jobs while destroying jobs in other areas because, after paying higher prices for tomatoes, people don't have as much left to spend on other things. The same situation is true for a nation as well as a household: if it pays higher prices than it needs to pay for some products, then it has less money left to spend on other products.

Economists have been making this argument for 240 years. Adam Smith said in his 1776 book *The Wealth of Nations*:

> It is the maxim of every prudent master of a family, never to attempt to make at home what it will cost him more to make than to buy. . . . If a foreign country can supply us with a commodity cheaper than we ourselves can make it, better buy it of them with some part of the produce of our own industry, employed in a way in which we have some advantage.[30]

The conclusion is that it is important for citizens and leaders in rich nations to work to remove such harmful tariffs and quotas that just raise prices for everyone and rob poor farmers in other nations of the right to profit from their lower prices. In fact, the first two legislative recommendations of the HELP Commission's report to the U.S. Congress in 2007 included: "Grant duty-free, quota-free access to U.S. markets" to many poor countries, including especially "those countries with a per capita Gross Domestic Product (GDP) under $2000."[31]

But once again, imposing tariffs and quotas is a harmful action carried out by the governments of some wealthy countries, for the benefit of certain influential people inside their own countries. It is not the fault of global corporations.

c. Environmental Damage? The third major type of "exploitation" sometimes alleged against global corporations is that they damage the environment. Critics of global corporations can point to environmental catastrophes such as the oil spill when the *Exxon Valdez* tanker hit a reef in Prince William Sound, Alaska, on March 24, 1989. The ship spilled over 10 million gallons of its 55 million-gallon cargo of oil into the sea, causing extensive damage to the shoreline and to marine life.[32] Are such events the fault of capitalism or a free-market economic system?

---

[30] Adam Smith, *An Inquiry into the Nature and Causes of the Wealth of Nations*, ed. Edwin Cannan (1776; repr., New York: Modern Library, 1994), Book IV, chap. 2; 485–86.

[31] "Beyond Assistance: The HELP Commission Report on Foreign Assistance Reform," Dec. 7, 2007, 24, http://www.americanprogress.org/wp-content/uploads/issues/2007/12/pdf/beyond_assistance.pdf. HELP stands for Helping to Enhance the Livelihood of People around the Globe.

[32] See "The Exxon Valdez Oil Spill: A Report to the President," by the National Response Team, May 1989, 2.

I agree that nations should protect their natural resources from careless human destruction. But a free-market economy will best meet this need, so long as the government is accountable to the people. In a free-market economy with freedom of the press and genuine governmental accountability to the people, stricter environmental safeguards will soon result from a catastrophe such as that of the *Exxon Valdez* (Exxon was found guilty of negligence and paid huge fees for damages and cleanup efforts, and maritime regulations and procedures were tightened as a result). In a free-market system, those who cause such damages are held responsible for the harm they cause.

In addition to the penalties it paid, Exxon suffered the financial loss of over 10 million gallons of oil, worth approximately $9.7 million.[33] Because Exxon is a corporation, the company had to absorb that loss. It is especially in a free-market system that companies have large financial incentives to protect the environment by preventing such accidents from happening.

Such accountability for damages generally does not happen, however, if the guilty party is the government or a government-owned enterprise, as in strongly socialist or planned economies. In such systems, destruction of the environment is often much worse than in free-market economies because there is less government accountability to the people. Rampant destruction of the environment can persist for decades, unchecked by any governmental concern.

For example, economist P. J. Hill writes:

> With the collapse of the Soviet Union and the coming of democracy to Eastern Europe, information has flowed much more freely, and the extent of ecological disruption has become more widely known.
>
> Children from the Upper Silesia area of Poland have been found to have five times more lead in their blood than children from Western European cities. Half of the children in that area suffer from pollution related illnesses.
>
> The worst air pollution is in the industrial corridor of the southern part of East Germany, across northern Czechoslovakia, and into southern Poland.
>
> In Leuna, in what was formerly East Germany, at any given time 60 percent of the population suffers from respiratory ailments. Four out of five children in Espenhain develop chronic bronchitis or heart ailments by the age of seven. In Telpice, a town in northwest Czechoslovakia, air pollution keeps children inside for about a third of the winter.
>
> Water pollution has also been a significant problem in numerous Eastern European countries. Drinking water in Hungary is seriously contaminated with arsenic. Sewage treatment is nonexistent or very primitive in many large

---

[33] I calculated this approximate value by multiplying 42 gallons per barrel and a world crude oil price of $40.90 per barrel in March 1989, obtained from www.macrotrends.net/1369/crude-oil-price-history-chart. This gives $0.974 per gallon x 10 million gallons = $9.74 million.

cities. Bulgarian agriculture suffers from heavy metals pollution through irrigation water of much of its best farming regions.

As deplorable as conditions are in Eastern Europe, the situation in the former Soviet Union is little better. Air and water pollution abound there also.[34]

Although much of the damage has been cleaned up since freedom came to Eastern Europe, the tragic record of destruction brought by the socialist/communist economy is undeniable.

Excluding accidents (such as the *Exxon Valdez*), does environmental damage ever occur in free-market economies because large companies *intentionally* cut corners and pollute rivers or cut down forests without replanting trees just to reduce their costs? Yes, this happens in some countries, because every economic system in the world has some evil people who are willing to damage the environment for the sake of their own gain. But if they are allowed to do this without any penalty imposed by law, then the government officials who allow it (perhaps for generous bribes) are also responsible. The polluting company and the corrupt government are both at fault.

If the government is not corrupt, but a corporation intentionally damages the environment and just doesn't get caught, this is still the fault of the flawed character of the people running the business. This is not a shortcoming inherent in global corporations or in a free-market system, which actually discourages such wrongdoing better than any other economic system.

d. Unfair Wages? What about the fourth major objection, the claim that large multinational corporations pay unjustly low wages in poor countries, thereby taking advantage of workers in those countries? In answering this question, it is important to distinguish between a labor market in a country that is completely free and a labor market that is constrained by laws and restrictive hiring permits.

Just as the government of a poor country can restrict coffee exports so that local farmers receive much less than the world price for their product (and the government officials pocket the huge difference when they sell the coffee on the world market), so the government can keep wages artificially low. For example, the government might give only one company a permit to build a factory and hire workers in a certain region.

Suppose government officials in a poor country sign a lucrative agreement with World Famous Running Shoes to build a shoe factory in a certain area, and as part of the agreement they guarantee (because of money they receive) that they will deny all other companies permits to build factories in that area. Thus, World Famous Running Shoes gains a monopolistic control on the hiring of local workers (technically called a "monopsony," a market where there is only one buyer), and it can pay extremely low wages and allow horrendous working conditions.

---

[34] P. J. Hill, "Environmental Problems under Socialism," *Cato Journal* 12, no. 2 (Fall 1992): 321–34.

In this situation, much of the blame must be placed with the government officials who set up and protect World Famous's monopoly in the local labor market. The officers of the World Famous company also share in the blame for this wrongdoing.

On the other hand, if there are no such government-imposed restrictions on hiring, then any company in the world is free to come and hire workers, and an element of competition enters the labor market. Then wages are set by the prevailing market price. If World Famous offers people only $1 per hour, then Saucony is free to come and offer people $1.50 per hour, and Jockey is free to build a shirt factory and offer people $1.75 per hour, and so forth. With a free labor market, every company that manufactures any kind of goods in the world is free to compete for local workers.

In such a labor market, local workers are free to work for any company they want, and no one can "set" the price of labor; rather, it is regulated by the interplay of supply and demand in the free market. If a company offers $1.50 per hour for 500 jobs and finds that it has 500 qualified applicants, the labor supply is certainly meeting the demand, and $1.50 is a "fair" and "just" wage. It is the price at which workers are willing to work in that labor market. Presumably they have decided that they are far better off working for $1.50 per hour than not working at all or working at subsistence-level farming.

Does the factory that pays $1.50 per hour *make these workers poor*? No. It makes them more prosperous than they were before, and the increased prosperity of these workers no doubt brings benefits to the rest of the economy as well.

One of the economic advantages that poor nations have today is a supply of inexpensive labor. Low labor costs make it economically attractive for companies to build factories and invest in poor countries, and thereby help those countries to create goods and services, and move toward prosperity.

When people object that companies should not pay such low wages (suggesting that something closer to American or Western European wages would be more "fair"), they fail to understand that any regulation that requires companies to pay higher wages in a poor country tends to take away that country's economic advantage, making it more difficult for that country to compete on the world market and attract the factories and investments needed for economic growth.

In summary, the wages that global corporations pay in poor countries are not unfair if they are determined by the free interaction of supply and demand for labor in the local area, and if any company that wants to is free to establish a factory there. But if corrupt government officials distort the process and give only one company permission to operate in an area, then the artificially low wages are the result of government corruption in the poor country, not the result of the existence of global corporations or a genuinely free-market system.

e. Inhumane Working Conditions? The final major allegation of "exploitation" relates to working conditions. To expand on our shoe factory example above, what if World Famous Running Shoes establishes a factory where the work environment is unsafe, workers regularly suffer major injuries, and work hours and overall working conditions are horribly inhumane?

In large measure this situation is the fault of the World Famous company, which has allowed excessive greed to triumph over a just concern for its workers. In addition, when such inhumane conditions exist in a factory like that of World Famous, it is also the fault of the leaders in the national government (or local officials) who have allowed such abuses. Both the government officials and the World Famous company share the blame for this wrongful suffering, but not the free-market system or the mere fact that multinational corporations exist.

A solution would be found if the leaders who have authority in government and in the business would heed the teaching of the New Testament: "Masters, treat your bondservants justly and fairly, knowing that you also have a Master in heaven" (Col. 4:1).

3. Poor Nations Were Poor before Global Corporations Ever Existed. In addition to the foregoing analysis of five different allegations of "exploitation," I wish to make two further points about the broad sweep of world history.

It is easy today to look at multibillion-dollar corporations operating in poor countries and assume that "these rich companies made this country poor." But that quick assumption is not true, for several reasons.

First, the nations that are poor today were not prosperous in the past.[35] Second, countries that are rich today became so by producing their own goods and services, and by trading with other countries. In general, they did not get rich by making the poor nations poor.[36] Third, the factual evidence of history shows that the accusation that large corporations in rich countries are responsible for poverty in poor countries is simply not true.

Until about 1770, there was very little difference in the lives of ordinary people in the richer and poorer countries of the world. Most of the people worked hard, obtained enough food, clothing, and shelter to survive, and saw little change in their standard of living century after century. Living on less than a dollar a day was common.

But around 1770, the Industrial Revolution began in Britain and soon spread to other countries. David Landes notes that British income per head "doubled between

---

[35] Someone might object that China was relatively rich in the 15th century. That is partially true, because at least a few people in China were quite wealthy; but then China went through centuries of backwardness and poverty before it began to develop rapidly in the late 1970s.

[36] However, I mentioned above that Spanish explorers forcibly stole vast quantities of gold from the Aztec and Inca empires in Latin America in the early 16th century, and Spain gained vast amounts of wealth in the process, which was ultimately destructive not only to the conquered people but also to Spain itself. Spanish explorers also forcibly enslaved natives in Central and South America to work in their mines, inflicting great suffering, and they left behind a destructive legacy that continues to some extent even today. See the comments of Daron Acemoglu and James A. Robinson, *Why Nations Fail: The Origins of Power, Prosperity, and Poverty* (New York: Crown, 2012), 9–19, 114–15, 432–33. These actions were not the *initial* cause of poverty, however, because the common people in Central and South America were extremely poor even before the Spanish arrived.

1780 and 1860, and then multiplied by six times between 1860 and 1990."[37] In short, some nations produced tremendous new prosperity, and other nations stayed poor. Landes says, "The Industrial Revolution made some countries richer and others (relatively) poorer; or more accurately, some countries made an industrial revolution and became rich; and others did not and stayed poor."[38]

Therefore, the poverty of poor nations has not been caused by modern rich nations, by global corporations, or by free-market economic systems. The poor nations were poor long before such things existed.

4. Economic Contacts with Global Corporations in Wealthy Nations Have Mostly Benefitted Poor Nations. Far from causing poverty, contacts with global corporations that want to do business in poor countries have generally been beneficial. Economist P. T. Bauer explains the results of economic transactions between rich and poor nations:

> Far from the West having caused the poverty in the Third World, contact with the West has been the principal agent of material progress there. . . . The level of material achievement usually diminishes as one moves away from the foci of Western impact. The poorest and most backward people have few or no external contacts; witness the aborigines, pygmies and desert peoples.[39]

> The prosperity of the West was generated by its own peoples and was not taken from others.[40]

> The West has not caused the famines in the Third World. These have occurred in backward regions with practically no external commerce. [This backwardness at times] reflects the policies of the rulers who are hostile to traders . . . and often to private property. . . .
> Contrary to the various allegations and accusations . . . the higher level of consumption in the West is not achieved by depriving others of what they have produced. Western consumption is more than paid for by Western production.[41]

Bauer points out that the frequent accusation that wealthy countries have "exploited" the poor nations of the world began with Marxist ideology and has become a standard claim put forth by Marxist scholars. He writes:

---

[37] David S. Landes, *The Wealth and Poverty of Nations: Why Some Are So Rich and Some So Poor* (New York: W. W. Norton, 1999), 194.

[38] Ibid., 169.

[39] Bauer, *Equality, the Third World, and Economic Delusion*, 70.

[40] Ibid., 75.

[41] Ibid., 82.

The notion of Western exploitation of the Third World is standard in publications and statements emanating from the Soviet Union and other communist countries. . . . [According to] Marxist-Leninist ideology . . . any return on private capital implies exploitation. . . . The principal assumption behind the idea of Western responsibility for Third World poverty is that the prosperity of individuals and societies generally reflects the exploitation of others. . . . According to Marxist-Leninist ideology, colonial status and foreign investment are by definition evidence of exploitation.[42]

But Bauer's own conclusion is quite the opposite. He writes:

In fact, foreign private investment and the activities of the multi-national companies have expanded opportunities and raised incomes and government revenues in the Third World. Reference to economic colonialism and neo-colonialism both debase the language and distort the truth.[43]

We must recognize, of course, that some economic interactions between rich and poor nations have caused harm. Sometimes wealthy multinational corporations have bribed government officials in poor nations to secure monopoly privileges that have oppressed those countries' ordinary people and prevented free markets from functioning (I mentioned this above). In such cases, both the companies that paid the bribes and the officials who took them share in the moral blame. But I understand that to be the *breakdown* of free markets, not the fault of the free-market system itself. (And many countries, such as the United States, make such practices illegal for American companies that do business in other countries.) In addition, such bribery is at least as common, if not much more common, in socialist and communist economic systems.

In general terms, however, Bauer has no doubt that the economic interaction between rich and poor nations has been immensely beneficial for the poor nations:

Altogether, it is anomalous or even perverse to suggest that external commercial relations are damaging to development or to the living standards of the people of the Third World. They act as channels for the flow of human and financial resources and for new ideas, methods and crops. They benefit people by providing a large and diverse source of imports and by opening up markets for exports.[44]

The poorest areas of the Third World have no external trade. Their condition shows that the causes of backwardness are domestic and that external

---

[42] Ibid., 74–76.
[43] Ibid., 76.
[44] Ibid., 79.

commercial contacts are beneficial. Even if the terms of trade were unfavorable on some criterion or other, this would only mean that people would not benefit from foreign trade as much as they would if the terms of trade were more favourable. People benefit from the widening of opportunities which external trade represents.[45]

5. Conclusion. Global corporations and a free-market economy, in general, do not exploit poor countries, except where corrupt governments allow unjust practices by evil, greedy leaders of some wealthy corporations. In those cases, the wrongdoing is the fault of the government leaders that allow it, as well as the companies that carry it out. But that kind of wrongdoing is not characteristic of global corporations in general, nor is it essential to the very idea of a global corporation. It is a distortion of what such corporations should be.

QUESTIONS FOR PERSONAL APPLICATION

1. Did the six core ethical convictions at the beginning of this chapter make you think you should have acted differently in any business situation in the past?
2. Do you think these core ethical convictions will help you make right decisions in the future? In what way?
3. Before reading this chapter, had you thought of both buying and selling as morally good activities by which people can do good for one another? How will this idea change your attitudes regarding buying and selling?
4. Did reading this chapter change your view of the moral status of profits?
5. Can you think of some benefits that have come to your life because of competition? Some harmful results?
6. What character traits (see p. 110) will be most helpful in enabling you to have right actions, thoughts, and attitudes in business activities?

SPECIAL TERMS

competition
exploitation
fair-trade coffee
giving back
multinational corporation
pilfering
profit

[45] Ibid., 76.

BIBLIOGRAPHY

Sections in Other Ethics Texts

(see complete bibliographical data, p. 64)

Frame, 798–800
Gushee and Stassen, 377–78
McQuilkin and Copan, 482–84
Rae, 342–53

Other Works

Clements, Philip J., ed. *Business Ethics Today: Foundations*. Philadelphia: Westminster Seminary Press, 2011.

Cramp, A. B. "Economic Ethics." In *New Dictionary of Christian Ethics and Pastoral Theology*, edited by David J. Atkinson and David H. Field, 115–21. Leicester, UK: Inter-Varsity, and Downers Grove, IL: InterVarsity Press, 1995.

Grudem, Wayne. *Business for the Glory of God: The Bible's Teaching on the Moral Goodness of Business*. Wheaton, IL: Crossway, 2003.

Novak, Michael. *Business as a Calling: Work and the Examined Life*. New York: The Free Press, 1996.

Pollard, C. William, ed. *The Heart of a Business Ethic*. Lanham, MD: University Press of America, 2005.

Rae, Scott B., and Kenman L. Wong. *Beyond Integrity: A Judeo-Christian Approach to Business Ethics*. 3rd ed. Grand Rapids, MI: Zondervan, 2012.

Wong, Kenman L., and Scott B. Rae. *Business for the Common Good: A Christian Vision for the Marketplace*. Christian Worldview Integration Series. Downers Grove, IL: IVP Academic, 2011.

SCRIPTURE MEMORY PASSAGE

Matthew 7:12: So whatever you wish that others would do to you, do also to them, for this is the Law and the Prophets.

HYMN

"Be Thou My Vision"

Be Thou my Vision, O Lord of my heart
Nought be all else to me, save that Thou art;
Thou my best thought, by day or by night
Waking or sleeping, Thy presence my light.

Be Thou my Wisdom, and Thou my true Word
I ever with Thee and Thou with me, Lord;
Thou my great Father, I Thy true son
Thou in me dwelling, and I with Thee one.

Riches I heed not, nor man's empty praise
Thou mine inheritance, now and always;
Thou and Thou only, first in my heart
High King of heaven, my Treasure Thou art.

High King of heaven, my victory won,
May I reach heaven's joys, O bright heav'n's Sun!
Heart of my own heart, whatever befall,
Still be my Vision, O Ruler of all.

ELEANOR H. HULL, 1860–1935

Chapter 41

STEWARDSHIP OF THE ENVIRONMENT

Why is the preservation of "untouched nature" not a biblical ideal?
Why should God's creation of a "very good" earth lead us to expect that we will not deplete the earth's resources in the foreseeable future?
Is there a real danger that human use of fossil fuels will create destructive global warming?

The previous several chapters have discussed various aspects of our stewardship of the property and abilities that God entrusts to our care. Now in the final chapter of this unit we will discuss the stewardship of the earth's resources, a responsibility that God has entrusted to the human race. People often refer to this as "stewardship of the environment."[1]

As was the case with several previous ethical issues (such as honoring God's name, truthfulness in speech, abortion, sexual ethics, divorce, or homosexuality), so it is with the environment: the Bible approaches this topic from a far different perspective than is common in much of secular culture today.

A. BIBLICAL TEACHING

1. The Original Creation Was "Very Good." When God completed his work of creation, "God saw everything that he had made, and behold, *it was very good*"

---

[1] Much of this chapter is been adapted from Wayne Grudem, *Politics—According to the Bible: A Comprehensive Resource for Understanding Modern Political Issues in Light of Scripture* (Grand Rapids, MI: Zondervan, 2010), chap. 10, with permission of the publisher. In many places I have reworded material and updated statistics with more recent information.

(Gen. 1:31). He had made a world in which there was no disease and no "thorns and thistles" (see 3:18) to harm human beings. It was a world of great abundance and beauty, far beyond anything we can imagine today. Moreover, Adam and Eve were included in the pronouncement "very good," so they were perfectly free from sin. In addition, they were not subject to disease, aging, or death (see Rom. 5:12; Eccles. 7:29).[2]

But even in this perfect world, God gave Adam and Eve work to do: "The LORD God took the man and put him in the garden of Eden *to work it and keep it*" (Gen. 2:15). God also set before Adam and Eve the entire created earth and told them to develop it and make it useful, with the implication that they would enjoy it and give thanks to him: "And God said to them, 'Be fruitful and multiply and fill the earth *and subdue it, and have dominion* over the fish of the sea and over the birds of the heavens and over every living thing that moves on the earth'" (1:28).

2. Because Adam and Eve Sinned, God Placed a Curse on the Entire Natural World.
When Adam and Eve sinned, many things changed, even the natural world itself. The current state of the natural world is not the same as God created it to be. One of the punishments that God imposed on Adam and Eve was to change the functioning of the natural world so that it was no longer idyllic, but a much more dangerous and difficult place for human beings to live:

And to Adam he said,

"Because you have listened to the voice of your wife
and have eaten of the tree
of which I commanded you,
'You shall not eat of it,'
cursed is the ground because of you;
in pain you shall eat of it all the days of your life;
thorns and thistles it shall bring forth for you;
and you shall eat the plants of the field.
By the sweat of your face
you shall eat bread,
till you return to the ground,
for out of it you were taken;
for you are dust,
and to dust you shall return." (Gen. 3:17–19)

---

[2] For further discussion of the original sinlessness of Adam and Eve, their freedom from disease, aging, and death, and the perfection of the natural world as originally created, see my discussion in Wayne Grudem, "Theistic Evolution Undermines Twelve Creation Events and Several Crucial Christian Doctrines," in *Theistic Evolution: A Scientific, Philosophical, and Theological Critique*, ed. J. P. Moreland, Stephen C. Meyer, Chris Shaw, Ann K. Gauger, and Wayne Grudem (Wheaton, IL: Crossway, 2017), 783–838.

At that point early in the history of mankind, God "cursed" the ground so that Adam could no longer eat food in overwhelming abundance, but would raise crops only with "pain" (Gen. 3:17) and hard toil, for "by the sweat of your face you shall eat bread" (v. 19).

a. The Earth Would Now Contain "Thorns and Thistles" and Many Other Dangerous and Harmful Things: God's words told Adam that now there would be danger and harm on the earth, for "thorns and thistles" (Gen. 3:18) would come forth. Here the expression "thorns and thistles" functions as a figure of speech known as a *synecdoche*, a specific, concrete example that represents a whole category of things—such as poisonous plants, poisonous snakes and insects, hostile wild animals, hurricanes, floods, droughts, earthquakes—that make the earth a place where natural beauty and usefulness are constantly mixed with elements that bring destruction, sickness, and even death. Nature is not now what it was created to be, but is "fallen."

Carl Keil and Franz Delitzsch comment on this passage:

> The curse pronounced on man's account upon the soil created for him, consisted in the fact, that the earth no longer yielded spontaneously the fruits requisite for his maintenance, but the man was obliged to force out the necessaries of life by labour and strenuous exertion. . . . [The effects of sin] spread over the whole material world; so that everywhere on earth there were to be seen wild and rugged wastes, desolation and ruin, death and corruption, or *mataiotēs* [futility] and *phthora* [decay] (Rom. 8:20, 21). Everything injurious to man in the organic, vegetable and animal creation, is the effect of the curse pronounced upon the earth for Adam's sin, however little we may be able to explain the manner in which the curse was carried into effect.[3]

John Calvin likewise says:

> Before the fall, the state of the world was a most fair and delightful mirror of the divine favour and paternal indulgence towards man. Now, in all the elements we perceive that we are cursed.[4]

This component of a Christian worldview has significant implications for how people view the environment today. The creation is *not now perfect*, as it once was and someday will be again. At present, nature still exists in a "fallen" state. Therefore, *what we think of as "natural" today is not always good.* We must protect children from putting their hands in the hole of a cobra or an adder, and we must build floodwalls

---

[3] Carl Friedrich Keil and Franz Delitzsch, *Commentary on the Old Testament*, vol. 1 (Peabody, MA: Hendrickson, 1996), 65–66. See also K. A. Mathews, *Genesis 1–11:26*, vol. 1A, NAC (Nashville: Broadman & Holman, 1996), 252.

[4] John Calvin and John King, *Commentary on the First Book of Moses Called Genesis*, vol. 1 (Bellingham, WA: Logos Bible Software, 2010), 173.

and levies to protect against floods, for example. We irrigate fields to grow crops where "nature" did not decide to grow them. We put screens on windows and spray insect repellant to keep "natural" mosquitoes from biting us. *Fallen nature today is not the garden of Eden!* We improve on nature in thousands of ways to make the world a more suitable place to live.

The fact that nature is not perfect today has many other implications. It means that people with a Christian worldview may decide that it is morally right to use insecticides to kill malaria-bearing mosquitoes, for example. They may decide it is right to clear flammable dead branches in national parks so as to prevent forest fires and to cut down dry trees in residential areas so that homes are not consumed in the next forest fire. It means that it can be morally right, and even pleasing to God, to breed seedless grapes, oranges, and watermelons, or to use biological research and selective breeding of plants to develop varieties of rice or corn that are resistant to insects and mold, even though all of these activities are "tampering with nature." Actually, they involve tampering with *fallen* nature, making natural products better. *That is what God intends us to do*. Part of our God-given task of subduing the earth and having dominion over it (Gen. 1:28) is inventing various measures to overcome the way in which nature is sometimes harmful to man and sometimes less than fully helpful. (God told Adam and Eve to "subdue" even the unfallen world, implying that he wanted them to *improve on* nature as it was originally created—that is, God created it to be investigated, explored, and developed!)

Of course, people can make mistakes in their attempts to subdue the earth, and there can be harmful results (such as polluting the air). But evaluating whether those attempts are "helpful" or "harmful" is *merely a matter of assessing the resulting facts,* not something to be dismissed merely because they are "tampering with nature." Attempting to make such modifications to what is "natural" is, in general, morally right and part of what God wants human beings to do with the earth.[5] Christians should not automatically assume that what is "natural" is probably or always better.

By contrast, some people today, especially among more radical environmental movements, do not understand the "fallen" status of the natural world but think that what is "natural" is the ideal, and therefore they regularly oppose ordinary, beneficial human efforts to improve on the way things exist in the natural world. This tendency leads some people to oppose every new factory, dam, or residential development project, no matter how carefully constructed and how sensitive the plans are to protecting the surrounding environment, all because their highest good—their "god" in some sense—is the earth *in its untouched natural state.* Thus, they oppose everything that "tampers" with the earth, everything that changes an animal habitat or a growth of trees. This is making nature to be God, and it is not consistent with a biblical worldview.

[5] Of course, this does not mean that we should approve of morally wrong uses of technological development, such as creating drugs that cause abortions (see chap. 21) or using IVF in ways that intentionally destroy living embryos (see chap. 30).

It is not wrong *in principle*, as many environmentalists think it is, for human beings to modify the world, from the macro scale (such as hydroelectric dams and huge canals) to the micro scale (genetically modified organisms). God created the earth to be occupied and developed by human beings made in his image. Isaiah says that God "formed the earth and made it (he established it; he did not create it empty, *he formed it to be inhabited!*)" (Isa. 45:18).

b. God Did Not Destroy the Earth after the Fall, but Left Much That Is Good in It: A biblical worldview also recognizes that God did not *completely destroy* the earth when Adam and Eve sinned, nor did he make it *entirely evil and harmful* (not all plants are poisonous, for example). He simply changed it so that it is not perfect now. The earth that God created is still "good" in many ways. And it is *amazingly resourceful* because of the great treasures that he has placed in it for us to discover, enhance, and enjoy.

God did not tell Adam and Eve that they would be unable to eat of the ground, but that their existence on it would be painful. In the same verse in which he said, "thorns and thistles it shall bring forth for you," he added, "and *you shall eat* the plants of the field" (Gen. 3:18). This implies that there would still be much good for human beings to discover, use, and enjoy in the earth.

In fact, many times in the Old Testament God promised abundant blessings on crops and livestock as a reward for the obedience of his people (see Deut. 28:1–14). With regard to various kinds of food, Paul could say, "*Everything created by God is good,* and nothing is to be rejected if it is received with thanksgiving, for it is made holy by the Word of God and prayer" (1 Tim. 4:4–5). Paul also said that God "richly provides us with everything to enjoy" (6:17). This implies that human beings should feel free to use the earth's resources with joy and thanksgiving to God.

c. God Promises a Future Time When the Abundant Prosperity of Eden Will Be Restored to the Earth: The Bible predicts a time—after Christ's return—when "the creation itself will be *set free* from its bondage to corruption and obtain the freedom of the glory of the children of God" (Rom. 8:21). In that day:

> The wolf shall dwell with the lamb,
>   and the leopard shall lie down with the young goat,
> and the calf and the lion and the fatted calf together;
>   and a little child shall lead them. . . .
> *The nursing child shall play over the hole of the cobra,*
>   *and the weaned child shall put his hand on the adder's den.*
> They shall not hurt or destroy
>   in all my holy mountain;
> for the earth shall be full of the knowledge of the LORD
>   as the waters cover the sea. (Isa. 11:6–9)

Therefore, the prophet Amos could say that in this future time, crops will spring up and grow suddenly, just as soon as they are planted, and agricultural land will need no time to lie fallow and recover its productive abilities:

> "Behold, the days are coming," declares the LORD,
>> "when the plowman shall overtake the reaper
>> and the treader of grapes him who sows the seed;
> the mountains shall drip sweet wine,
>> and all the hills shall flow with it." (Amos 9:13)

Other Old Testament prophetic passages also predict this future time of a wonderful renewal of nature, so that "the desert shall rejoice and blossom like the crocus" (Isa. 35:1), and God will make the "desert" of Zion "like the garden of the LORD" (51:3; cf. 55:13). In New Testament times Peter echoed this theme in preaching that in the future there would come "the time for restoring all the things about which God spoke by the mouth of his holy prophets long ago" (Acts 3:21).

I also believe that such restoration of the earth need not completely wait until Christ's return and God's miraculous renewing of the earth, but that the redeeming work of Christ provides the basis for us even now *to work incrementally toward the direction that God shows us is his future good intention for the earth.*[6] Theologian and economist Cal Beisner puts it this way:

> The effects of the atoning death, victorious resurrection, and triumphant ascension of Christ, then, sweep over all of creation, including man, animals, plants, and even the ground itself. They include the restoration of the image of God in the redeemed and through them—and by common grace even through many who are not redeemed—the restoration of knowledge, holiness, and creativity in working out the cultural mandate, including human multiplication, subduing and ruling the earth, transforming the wilderness by cultivation into a garden, and guarding that garden against harm.[7]

3. God Now Wants Human Beings to Develop the Earth's Resources and to Use Them Wisely and Joyfully. As stated earlier, at the very beginning of human history, immediately after God created Adam and Eve, he told them:

---

[6] In the famous Christmas carol "Joy to the World," Isaac Watts saw the connection between the joy of Christ's first coming and our present task of removing "thorns" from the ground that God had cursed in his punishment of Adam:

No more let sins and sorrows grow
Nor thorns infest the ground:
He comes to make his blessings flow
Far as the curse is found.

[7] E. Calvin Beisner, *Where Garden Meets Wilderness: Evangelical Entry into the Environmental Debate* (Grand Rapids, MI: Acton Institute and Eerdmans, 1997), 107.

> Be fruitful and multiply and fill the earth *and subdue it, and have dominion*
> ... over every living thing that moves on the earth. (Gen. 1:28)

He also told them how they were to care specifically for the garden of Eden—primarily "to work it and keep it" (Gen. 2:15).

This responsibility to "subdue" the earth and "have dominion" over it implies that God expected Adam and Eve and their descendants to explore and develop the earth's resources in such a way that they would bring benefit to themselves and other human beings. (The Hebrew word *kābash* in Gen. 1:28 means "to subdue, dominate, bring into servitude or bondage,"[8] and is used later, for example, of the subduing of the land of Canaan so that it would serve and provide for the people of Israel; cf. Num. 32:22, 29; Josh. 18:1.)

a. Subduing the Earth after the Fall: The responsibility to develop the earth and enjoy its resources continued after Adam and Eve's sin, for even then God told them, "You shall eat the plants of the field" (Gen. 3:18).

David also says in Psalm 8:

> What is man that you are mindful of him ... ?
> *You have given him dominion over the works of your hands;*
>   you have put all things under his feet,
> all sheep and oxen,
>   and also the beasts of the field,
> the birds of the heavens, and the fish of the sea,
>   whatever passes along the paths of the seas. (vv. 4–8)

Another evidence that our responsibility to "subdue" the earth continues after the fall is the very necessity of cultivating the earth in order to grow food to eat. We have to "subdue" the earth to some extent or we will all starve!

Moreover, the fact that after the flood God explicitly told Noah, "Every moving thing that lives shall be food for you" (Gen. 9:3) confirms the fact that God still gives human beings the responsibility to exercise dominion over the natural creation, including the animal kingdom. In the New Testament, Paul implies that eating meat is morally right and no one should pass judgment on another person because of this (see Rom. 14:2–3; 1 Cor. 8:7–13; 1 Tim. 4:4; also Mark 7:19, which says that Jesus "declared all foods clean").

Jesus also taught that *human beings are much more valuable in God's sight than animals,* and this tends to confirm our continuing responsibility to "have dominion" over the animal kingdom and to seek to make animals useful for us, since they are God's good provision for the human race. Jesus said, "Of how much *more value* is a man than a sheep!" (Matt. 12:12). He also said, "Look at the birds of the air. . . . Are you not of

---

[8] BDB, 461.

more value than they?" (6:26). And again he said, "You are of *more value* than many sparrows" (10:31).

However, these commands to subdue the earth and have dominion over it do not mean that we should use the earth in a wasteful or destructive way, or that we should intentionally treat animals with cruelty. Rather, God declares, "Whoever is righteous has regard for the life of his beast" (Prov. 12:10), and he told the people of Israel to take care to protect fruit trees during times of war (see Deut. 20:19–20). In addition, the command "You shall love your neighbor as yourself" (Matt. 22:39) implies a responsibility to think of the needs of other human beings, even those who will come in future generations. Therefore, we should not use the earth in such a way that we destroy its resources or make them unusable for future generations. *We should use the resources of the earth wisely, as good stewards*, not wastefully or abusively.

b. Contrasting a Biblical View of the Earth and a Radical Environmentalist View: This biblical principle about the moral goodness of developing and enjoying the earth's resources stands in contrast to the views of radical environmentalists, many of whom hold to "untouched nature" as their ideal and therefore object to activities such as the use of animals (such as guinea pigs or chimpanzees) in medical research. Environmentalists will attempt to block many new building projects through the use of lawsuits claiming that some species of turtle or other small creature, such as the pygmy owl, will be harmed.[9]

For instance, in late 2008 in California's San Joaquin Valley, much of the water that farmers used for growing crops was diverted to the Pacific Ocean to save a three-inch fish called the delta smelt.[10] As a result, unemployment rates hit nearly 50 percent in some parts of the region, which provides much of the produce for the rest of the nation.[11] Thus, this environmentalist action, the result of a wrongheaded policy that hinders responsible use of irrigation for important human food crops, has made minnows more important than human beings and, in addition to the soaring unemployment, has caused food shortages and higher prices, again harming the poor most of all. *The Wall Street Journal* wrote:

> California has a new endangered species on its hands in the San Joaquin Valley—farmers. Thanks to environmental regulations designed to protect the likes of the three-inch long delta smelt, one of America's premier agricultural regions is suffering in a drought made worse by federal regulations.

---

[9] "Pygmy Owl Leaves a Conservation Legacy," *Arizona Star*, Aug. 5, 2005, http://www.biologicaldiversity.org/news/media-archive/Pygmy%20Owl%20Leaves%20a%20Conservation%20Legacy.pdf and Leslie Carlson and Pete Thomas, "Back off, Bambi," *Los Angeles Times*, June 15, 2004, http://articles.latimes.com/2004/jun/15/news/os-deer15.

[10] Peter Fimrite, "U.S. Issues Rules to Protect Delta Smelt," *San Francisco Chronicle*, Dec. 16, 2008, www.sfgate.com/cgi-bin/article.cgi?f=/c/a/2008/12/15/MNDD14OIOF.DTL.

[11] Jonathan Wood, "In California, a Flood of Missed Opportunities," *The Washington Times*, April 19, 2015, http://www.washingtontimes.com/news/2015/apr/19/jonathan-wood-in-california-delta-smelt-gets-water/.

The state's water emergency is unfolding thanks to the latest mishandling of the Endangered Species Act. Last December, the U.S. Fish and Wildlife Service issued what is known as a "biological opinion" imposing water reductions on the San Joaquin Valley and environs to safeguard the federally protected *hypomesus transpacificus*, a.k.a., the delta smelt. As a result, tens of billions of gallons of water from mountains east and north of Sacramento have been channeled away from farmers and into the ocean, leaving hundreds of thousands of acres of arable land fallow or scorched. . . .

The result has already been devastating for the state's farm economy. In the inland areas affected by the court-ordered water restrictions, the jobless rate has hit 14.3%, with some farming towns like Mendota seeing unemployment numbers near 40%. Statewide, the rate reached 11.6% in July, higher than it has been in 30 years. In August, 50 mayors from the San Joaquin Valley signed a letter asking President Obama to observe the impact of the draconian water rules firsthand.[12]

Eight years later, the tragic situation in California's San Joaquin Valley remains unchanged. On April 5, 2017, after massive rainstorms and heavy snowfall finally ended California's long drought period, *The Wall Street Journal* again reported how environmentalists had succeeded in preventing the much-needed water from reaching these same farmers and their parched lands:

Reservoirs and rivers are overflowing as storms have pounded California this winter, and after years of drought that should be good news. The problem is that misguided environmentalism is wasting the water. . . .

Millions of acre-feet will invariably flow into the ocean due to lack of storage capacity and rules to protect endangered fish species. . . . While the state population has increased 70% since 1979, storage hasn't expanded. . . .

Yet environmentalists have opposed every significant surface storage project for three decades. . . .

Regulations intended to protect smelt and salmon have limited pumping at the Sacramento-San Joaquin River Delta. As a result, some 7 million acre-feet of water that was once available for Central Valley farmers and Southern California is flushed into San Francisco Bay each year.[13]

Again and again, "untouched nature" receives a higher priority than human well-being. Secular environmentalists will object to the killing of deer or geese in residential

---

[12]"California's Man-Made Drought," *The Wall Street Journal*, Sept. 2, 2009, A14, http://online.wsj.com /article/SB10001424052970204731804574384731898375624.html.

[13]"California's Wasted Winter Rains," *The Wall Street Journal*, April 6, 2017, A18, https://www.wsj.com /articles/californias-wasted-winter-rains-1491434129.

neighborhoods, even when these animals are so numerous they are a significant public nuisance and even a danger to health (as with the prevalence of ticks that spread Lyme disease).[14] They will object to the killing of mosquitoes with pesticides even when the mosquitoes spread West Nile virus and (in Africa) spread malaria that kills millions of people.[15] It seems to me a correct application of Matthew 10:31 to think that Jesus would have said, "People are of *more value* than many millions of mosquitoes."

Another tendency of secular culture is to view much use of the earth's resources with *fear*—fear that human beings will damage some part of "untouched nature," which seems to be the environmentalists' ideal. Such fear will lead people to oppose hydro-electric dams (they harm fish),[16] windmills (they harm birds),[17] oil and natural gas development (oil rigs ruin the appearance of nature, and there might be a spill),[18] any burning of coal, oil, or gas (doing so might harm the climate),[19] and any use of nuclear energy (it might lead to an accident).[20]

Radical environmentalists repeatedly emphasize the dangers (whether real or imagined) and seldom realistically evaluate an *insignificant risk* of danger in comparison to a *certain promise* of great benefit. Some of them give the impression that they think the major problem with the whole earth is the presence of human beings!

In fact, radical environmentalist Paul Watson of the Sea Shepherd Institute wrote of the threat that he thinks human beings cause to the earth:

> Today, escalating human populations have vastly exceeded global carrying capacity and now produce massive quantities of solid, liquid, and gaseous waste. Biological diversity is being threatened by over-exploitation, toxic pollution, agricultural mono-culture, invasive species, competition, habitat destruction, urban sprawl, oceanic acidification, ozone depletion, global warming, and climate change. It's a runaway train of ecological calamities.
>
> It's a train that carries all the earth's species as unwilling passengers with *humans* as the manically insane engineers unwilling to use the brake pedal.[21]

---

[14] See "Environmental Impacts of Overabundant Deer Populations," Connecticut Coalition to Eradicate Lyme Disease, www.eradicatelymedisease.org/environment.html.

[15] Michael Doyle, "Environmentalists Challenge Pesticide Rule," McClatchy Newspapers, Nov. 29, 2006, http://www.sitnews.us/1106news/112906/112906_shns_pesticides.html.

[16] "How Dams Damage Rivers," "https://www.americanrivers.org/threats-solutions/restoring-damaged -rivers/how-dams-damage-rivers/, and Erik Robinson, "Latest Dam Plan Already under Fire from Groups," *The Columbian*, May 6, 2008, https://www.highbeam.com/doc/1P2-21735032.html (subscription needed to read full article).

[17] John Ritter, "Wind Turbines Take Toll on Birds of Prey," *USA Today*, Jan. 4, 2005, http://www.energybc .ca/cache/wind2/www.usatoday.com/news/nation/2005-01-04-windmills-usat_x.htm.

[18] "Congress Allows Offshore Oil Drilling Ban to Expire," *NBC News*, Sept. 30, 2008, http://www.nbcnew york.com/news/green/Congress_Allows_Offshore_Oil_Drilling_Ban_to_Expire.html.

[19] See "Coal: Dangerous Power," Energy Justice Network, www.energyjustice.net/coal/.

[20] "Nuclear Energy," Greenpeace, http://www.greenpeace.org/usa/global-warming/issues/nuclear/.

[21] Paul Watson, "The Beginning of the End for Life as We Know It on Planet Earth?" Sea Shepherd Conservation Society, May 4, 2007, http://www.seashepherd.org/news-and-commentary/commentary

Watson also called human beings the "AIDS of the Earth" and declared that people must reduce the world's population to less than one billion people (from its then-current 6.8 billion), dwell in communities no larger than "20,000 people and separated from other communities by wilderness areas," and recognize themselves as "earthlings" dwelling in a primitive state with other species. Watson wrote, "Curing a body of cancer requires radical and invasive therapy, and therefore, curing the biosphere of the human virus will also require a radical and invasive approach."[22]

Speaking about the environment in Great Britain, John Guillebaud, cochairman of Optimum Population Trust and emeritus professor of family planning at University College in London, told the *Sunday Times* that parents ought to consider the environment first when they plan to have a child. He said, "The greatest thing anyone in Britain could do to help the future of the planet would be to have one less child"[23]—a view directly contrary to the Bible's understanding of children as a great blessing (see discussion in chap. 29, p. 747). A report by that same trust, entitled *A Population-Based Climate Strategy*, said, "Population limitation should therefore be seen as the most cost-effective carbon offsetting strategy available to individuals and nations."[24]

By contrast, God's perspective in the Bible is that his creation of human beings in his image and placement of them on the earth to rule over it as his representatives is the crowning achievement of his entire work of creation.

A Christian worldview would consider it morally right—and pleasing to God, and no cause for irrational fear—for human beings to wisely exercise widespread and effective dominion over the earth and its creatures. This worldview will present no moral objection to eating meat from various animals or to wearing leather or fur made from animal skins. (God himself clothed Adam and Eve with animal skins in Gen. 3:21, setting a precedent for the beneficial use of animals for human beings.) Such a Christian worldview would also think it morally right—even morally imperative—to use animals (in a reasonably compassionate way) for medical research that can lead to solutions to human diseases.

Another implication of this component of a Christian worldview is that *we should view the development and production of goods from the earth as morally good*, not merely an evil kind of "materialism." God placed in the earth resources that would enable man to develop much more than food and clothing. There are resources that enable the construction of beautiful homes, automobiles, airplanes, computers, and millions of other consumer goods. While these things can be misused, and while

---

/archive/the-beginning-of-the-end-for-life-as-we-know-it-on-planet-earth.html.

[22] Ibid.

[23] Sarah-Kate Templeton, "Having Large Families 'Is an Eco-Crime'," *Sunday Times*, May 6, 2007, https://www.thetimes.co.uk/article/having-large-families-is-an-eco-crime-5fl0tvlr5sk.

[24] Peter J. Smith and Steve Jalsevac, "Environmentalist Extremists Call Humanity 'Virus,' a 'Cancer,' Large Families Guilty of 'Eco-Crime'," LifeSite News, May 8, 2007, www.lifesitenews.com/ldn/2007/may/07050812.html.

people's hearts can have wrongful attitudes about them (such as pride, jealousy, and coveting), *the things in themselves* should be viewed as *morally good* because they are part of God's intention in placing us on the earth to subdue it and have dominion over it.

Therefore, the creation of large amounts of wealth in some of the world's more economically developed nations should not be seen as morally evil in itself, but rather as fundamentally good. It is part of what God intended when he told Adam and Eve to subdue the earth and have dominion over it. This means that wealthy nations and wealthy individuals should not automatically be considered "evil" or even "unspiritual." Rather, we should do what we can to help other nations achieve similar levels of wealth for themselves—as is happening every year in more and more countries around the world. If subduing the earth and making it useful for mankind is a good activity, then it is right to encourage many different kinds of development of the earth's resources and many different kinds of production of material goods from the earth.

God's command to human beings to subdue the earth and have dominion over it also implies that *it was not his intention for all human beings to live in abject poverty or live as subsistence farmers, barely surviving from crop to crop.* Rather, his intention was that all people should enjoy the abundance of the earth's resources with thanksgiving to him. This implies that it is *morally right* for us to seek to overcome poverty wherever it is found. It is also *morally right* for us to help the world's poor to gain the ability to develop and enjoy the earth's good resources in abundance.

4. God Created an Abundant and Resourceful Earth. Did God create an earth that would run out of essential resources because of human development? That is not the picture given in the Bible. God created an earth that he pronounced to be "very good" (Gen. 1:31). Although he cursed the earth after the sin of Adam and Eve, he also promised a future time when *this same earth* would be renewed and bring forth abundant prosperity (see above, p. 1100). That renewed earth will have the same natural resources (I do not believe it will be a *replacement* of this present creation but a *renewed* version of this creation),[25] but the dangers, harmfulness, and painfulness to man will be removed. It will once more become abundantly productive, like the original garden of Eden and original "very good" earth (Gen. 1:31).

Therefore, the Bible's picture of the earth *in general* is that it has abundant resources that God has put there to bring great benefit to us as human beings made in his image. There is no hint that mankind will ever exhaust the earth's resources by developing them and using them wisely.

Does current information about the earth confirm this idea that it has abundant resources? That question is addressed in the next section.

---

[25] See Wayne Grudem, *Systematic Theology: An Introduction to Biblical Doctrine* (Leicester, UK: Inter-Varsity, and Grand Rapids, MI: Zondervan, 1994), 1160–61.

B. THE CURRENT STATE OF THE EARTH'S RESOURCES

Many questions about applying biblical teachings to environmental issues have to do with *correctly evaluating the facts* about the current situation of the earth. What is the current status of the earth's resources, and what can we learn from long-term trend lines on various resources?

1. Are We Destroying the Earth? People often fear that we are about to run out of land for growing food, clean water, or some other essential resource, so that the earth will no longer sustain human life. That fear leads them to live with a faint cloud of continual guilt whenever they drive a car, water their lawn, or use paper cups and paper plates.

However, I believe those feelings of fear and guilt are misleading. In the pages that follow, I present data indicating that *there is no good reason to think we will ever run out of any essential natural resource.* God has created for us an earth that has incredible abundance, and whenever it seems that some resource is becoming scarce, he has given us the wisdom to invent useful substitutes. I will look at data regarding the following factors:

1. World population
2. Land for growing food
3. Water
4. Clean air
5. Waste disposal
6. Global forests
7. Herbicides and pesticides
8. Life expectancy

2. The Importance of Using Information from Long-Term, Worldwide Trends Rather Than Short-Term, Local Stories of Disasters. Through many conversations, I have found that people's *vague impressions* about what is happening to the earth are almost always wrong. People have developed their opinions not from actual data showing the true state of the earth as a whole and showing long-term trends, but from a barrage of media reports about specific local incidents where something has gone wrong—a certain oil spill, or a crop failure and famine in a particular country, or the cutting down of trees and loss of forest area in another country, or a video of a polar bear jumping off a slab of melting ice somewhere in the Arctic, and so forth.

But we should always keep in mind that newspapers need readers and television programs need viewers, and fear is one of the great ways to increase an audience. Therefore, the media have a natural bias toward reporting alarming events—whether an airplane crash, a serial killer, or a water or food shortage in one place or another. But such individual events almost always have specific local causes that may not exist elsewhere.

Many of the statistics I cite below come from one of the most influential books of the past two decades, *The Skeptical Environmentalist* by Bjørn Lomborg.[26] The advantage of Lomborg's book is that, as a former statistics professor and former director of the Environmental Assessment Institute of the government of Denmark, he is an expert in the fair and accurate use of statistics, especially environmental statistics, and he repeatedly bases his arguments on official, publicly available information from sources such as United Nations agencies and the World Bank.[27] He quotes long-term trends, not just isolated bits of data from short periods.

Because Lomborg's book mounted a massive challenge to widely accepted environmentalist views, it was severely criticized by a number of writers and organizations. But Lomborg has responded in an articulate and sensible way to the most serious of these criticisms (anyone can read these exchanges on the Internet). From what I have read of the controversy, it appears clear to me that Lomborg has gotten the best of the arguments and that his critics are careless and emotional in their claims, but not very persuasive. It is not surprising that *Time* magazine named Lomborg one of the world's 100 most influential people in 2004[28] and *Foreign Policy* magazine named him one of the top 100 public intellectuals in 2008.[29] Also in 2008, *Esquire* magazine named him one of the 75 most influential people of the 21st century.[30]

The use of reliable, long-term data is necessary if we are going to rightly assess the state of the world's resources. But a major factor in people's mistaken impressions of resource scarcity today is the existence of a number of special-interest organizations that raise money and keep themselves employed only by putting out news releases declaring that worldwide environmental disaster is just around the corner. Lomborg cites numerous examples of astoundingly blatant dishonesty in the use of data in publications by environmentalist organizations such as the Worldwatch Institute, the World Wide Fund for Nature, or Greenpeace. For example, Lomborg writes that Lester Brown and the Worldwatch Institute make statements such as this:

> The key environmental indicators are increasingly negative. Forests are shrinking, water tables are falling, soils are eroding, wetlands are disappearing, fisheries are collapsing, range-lands are deteriorating, rivers are running dry, temperatures are rising, coral reefs are dying, and plant and animal species are disappearing.

[26] Bjørn Lomborg, *The Skeptical Environmentalist: Measuring the Real State of the World* (Cambridge, UK: Cambridge University Press, 2001), 8–31.

[27] Ibid., 31.

[28] Matt Ridley, "Bjorn Lomborg: Green Contrarian," *Time*, April 26, 2004, www.time.com/time/magazine/article/0,9171,994022,00.html?iid=chix-sphere.

[29] "The Top 100 Public Intellectuals: Bios," *Foreign Policy*, April 2008, http://foreignpolicy.com/2008/04/19/the-top-100-public-intellectuals-bios/.

[30] "The Heretic's New Book," *Esquire*, Sept. 24, 2007, www.esquire.com/news-politics/a3446/global warming1007/.

Lomborg adds, "Powerful reading—stated entirely without references."[31] He goes on to refute these claims. For example, he says that reports from the Food and Agricultural Organization (FAO) of the United Nations show that global forest cover *increased* from 30.04 percent of the global land area in 1950 to 30.89 percent in 1994.[32]

With regard to water shortages, Lomborg writes:

> One of the most widely used college books on the environment, *Living in the Environment*, claims that "according to a 1995 World Bank study, 30 countries containing 40 percent of the world's population (2.3 billion people) now experience chronic water shortages that threaten their agriculture and industry and the health of their people." This World Bank study is referred to in many different environment texts with slightly differing figures. Unfortunately, none mentions a source.
>
> With a good deal of help from the World Bank, I succeeded in locating the famous document. It turns out that the myth had its origin in a hastily drawn up press release. The headline on the press release was "The world is facing a water crisis: 40 percent of the world's population suffers from chronic water shortage." If you read on, however, it suddenly becomes clear that the vast majority of the 40 percent are *not people who use too much water* but those who have *no access to water* or sanitation facilities—the exact opposite point. If one also reads the memo to which the press release relates, it shows that the global water crisis which Lester Brown and others are worried about affects not 40 percent but about 4 percent of the world's population. And, yes, it wasn't 30, but 80 countries the World Bank was referring to.[33]

Therefore, it is important for us to find some reliable data that accurately show the long-term trends in the earth's resources. What is the overall result of human development on the world environment that we live in? Is the presence of mankind actually destroying the earth? Taken as a whole, is human development of the earth's resources helpful or harmful?

These questions are especially important in light of the biblical teachings that I discussed earlier (see beginning of p. 1095), especially the teaching that the earth God created was "very good" (Gen. 1:31) and the teaching that God told Adam and Eve that they were to "be fruitful and multiply and *fill the earth* and *subdue* it, and *have dominion* over the fish of the sea and over the birds of the heavens and over every living thing that moves" (v. 28).

If God created an earth for man to subdue and develop (which he did), then it is

---

[31] Ibid., 16.

[32] Ibid.

[33] Ibid., 20, emphasis added. His point is that the World Bank study was referring to people who don't have wells (even though there is abundant underground water where they live), and this tells us nothing about a worldwide water shortage.

reasonable to think that he created (1) an earth with *abundant resources* that are available to be developed and (2) an earth that would *benefit* from man's developing it, not one that would be destroyed through such development. In addition, if God wanted human beings to "fill the earth" (which he did), then it seems reasonable to expect that the spread of the human population over the earth could happen without necessarily harming or destroying it.

The "curse" that God put on the earth (Gen. 3:17–18) would make development of the earth's resources more difficult and more painful, but it would not change the basic character of such development or turn it into something harmful rather than helpful. Instead, subduing the earth would be even more necessary in a planet filled with "thorns and thistles" that had to be removed before any parcel of land would be a suitable and enjoyable place for human beings.

Our overall viewpoint on these matters affects our basic expectations. Do we basically expect that development of the earth's resources will be *helpful* or *harmful* to the earth? Do we expect that obedience to God's commands will bring benefits to ourselves and to the earth, or bring harm to both? Do we tend to assume that God made an earth that is about to run out of all sorts of resources necessary for human survival, or do we think that he made an incredibly abundant earth with incredibly rich and diverse resources that would be useful for human life and enjoyment?

If it is *God's purpose* for us to develop and enjoy the earth's resources with thanksgiving to him (which it is), then we would also expect it would be *Satan's purpose* to oppose and hinder such developmental activity at every point and in every way possible.

In the following section I will refer to *long-term trends* that show remarkable human progress in making the earth useful for mankind and doing so in a sustainable way. As the teachings of Genesis suggest, modern evidence confirms that *God created an incredibly abundant and resourceful earth*, and he also created human beings with the wisdom and skill to develop and use those resources for his glory and with thanksgiving to him.

3. Long-Term Trends Show That Human Beings Will Be Able to Live on the Earth, Enjoying Ever-Increasing Prosperity, and Never Exhausting Its Resources.

a. World Population: The world's population has grown from 750 million people in 1750 to more than 7.5 billion people today.[34] A rapid increase in growth began around 1950 but is already slowing down and is projected to end at about 11 billion around the year 2100.[35] Other projections show world population stabilizing at even lower levels (such as 8 billion to 9 billion) and then declining, as the population already is doing

---

[34] See "Current World Population," Worldometers, http://www.worldometers.info/world-population/.

[35] United Nations, *World Population Prospects, the 2015 Revision: Key Findings and Advance Tables*, 2, https://esa.un.org/unpd/wpp/Publications/Files/Key_Findings_WPP_2015.pdf.

in Western Europe. In fact, according to data from the United Nations Department of Economic and Social Affairs, populations could also drop in Asia and Latin America.[36]

Of course, estimates of future world population depend on the fertility rates that are used for the projections. The Austrian International Institute for Applied Systems Analysis has released research that the world's population could drop to half of what it is today by 2200, and to one-seventh of today's population by 2300, if fertility rates drop to Europe's current rate of 1.5. The authors write: "By the end of the 22nd century [world population] would then fall below three billion even though under this scenario, life expectancies would continue to increase until they reach 100 years in all parts of the world. Still lower fertility assumptions, based upon the kind of figures currently seen in East Asia, would result in more rapid declines and by 2200 in total world population sizes around one billion or below."[37]

The world population grew quickly in the last 250 years because modern development gave people better access to food, water, medical care, and sanitation, so on average they lived much longer. But the world population will likely stabilize because as nations increase in wealth, their birth rates decline, as is evident in the smaller birth rates in Europe and Japan today, for instance.[38]

But will we run out of space on the earth? No, there is much more available space for people to live. The two largest countries in the world by population are India and China, with the following population densities as of 2017:[39]

Country	Population/Sq. Mile
India	1169[*]
China	389[†]

[*] See "India Population," Worldometers, http://www.worldometers.info/world-population/india-population/.
[†] See "China Population," Worldometers, http://www.worldometers.info/world-population/china-population/.

Table 41.1. Population Densities, India and China

---

[36] Ibid., 1.

[37] Stuart Gietel-Basten, Wolfgang Lutz, and Sergei Scherbov, "Very Long Range Global Population Scenarios to 2300 and the Implications of Sustained Low Fertility," *Demographic Research* 28, Article 39 (May 30, 2013), https://www.demographic-research.org/volumes/vol28/39/default.htm.

[38] The UN Population Division website, https://esa.un.org/unpd/wpp/Download/SpecialAggregates /Geographical/ (under the sub group "Crude Birth Rate"), shows that there has been a significant birth rate decline globally and it is more pronounced in Europe: The world birth rate declined from 36.9 births per 1,000 population in 1950–1955 to 31.6 (1970–1975), then to 27.8 (1980–1985), then 24.5 (1990–1995), then 20.8 (2000–2005), and finally 19.6 (2010–2015). Further declines are predicted in the future. For Europe the birth rate has declined from 21.5 births per 1,000 population in the period 1950–1955 to 10.8 for 2010–2015. See also Mark Henderson, "Europe Shrinking as Birthrates Decline," *London Times*, March 28, 2003, https://www.thetimes.co.uk/article/europe-shrinking-as-birthrates-decline-qkqj68xpwpj.

[39] These figures are converted from square kilometers to square miles.

But some countries in Europe have similar population densities, as shown on the following chart:

Country	Population/Sq. Mile
Belgium	979[*]
United Kingdom	701[†]
Germany	599[‡]
Italy	527[**]
Switzerland	554[††]

[*] See "Belgium Population," Worldometers, http://www.worldometers.info/world-population/belgium-population/.
[†] See "United Kingdom Population," Worldometers, http://www.worldometers.info/world-population/uk-population/.
[‡] See "Germany Population," Worldometers, http://www.worldometers.info/world-population/germany-population/.
[**] See "Italy Population," Worldometers, http://www.worldometers.info/world-population/italy-population/.
[††] See "Switzerland Population," Worldometers, http://www.worldometers.info/world-population/switzerland-population/.

Table 41.2. Population Densities, Other Nations

These figures are much higher than the United States, which has a population density of 91.5 people per square mile.[40] But as anyone who has visited Belgium, the United Kingdom, or Germany can attest, these countries still have large areas of uncrowded farmland and open spaces.

We can compare these densities with a few states in the United States (2015).[41]

State	Population/Sq. Mile
New Jersey	1,218
Rhode Island	1,022
Massachusetts	871
New York	420
Florida	378

[40] "Population Density of the United States from 1790 to 2015 in Residents Per Square Mile of Land Area," Statista, https://www.statista.com/statistics/183475/united-states-population-density/.
[41] "Population Density in the U.S. by Federal States Including the District of Columbia: 2015," Statista, https://www.statista.com/statistics/183588/population-density-in-the-federal-states-of-the-us/.

State	Population/Sq. Mile
Ohio	284
California	251
Illinois	232
Virginia	212
North Carolina	207

Table 41.3. Population Densities, Select States

Certainly the more densely populated states have a number of large cities, but they also have vast amounts of land in forests, parks, and agricultural areas.

In other words, world population is stabilizing, and there is still an immense amount of room left on the earth in which everyone can live comfortably.

b. Land for Growing Food: But will we run out of land to grow enough food to feed the world's population? No, not at all. Out of the total ice-free land surface of the earth, one estimate is that about 24 percent of the land is "arable"[42]—that is, it could produce an acceptable level of food crops. That is about 3.2 billion hectares (7.9 billion acres) of land that could produce food. (The remaining land is in areas that are too cold, too dry, or too rocky or hard, or that have soil that is too poor for crop use.) But this potential cropland is more than three times the area actually used for growing crops in any given year at the present time.[43] That is, we currently grow crops on *less than one-third of the earth's arable land.*

How many people could the available land feed? Roger Revelle, former director of Harvard University's Center for Population Studies, estimated as far back as 1984 that even if this land produced less than half the average production of the "Corn Belt" in the United States, it could feed about 35 billion people "at an average intake of 2,350 kcal per day."[44] Another estimate was that the available land could readily feed about 18 billion people per year.[45] This is still two and a half times the current world population of about 7.5 billion, and it is much more than the best current estimates that world population will stabilize at about 11 billion people. We are not running out of land to grow crops.

In addition, *food production per acre* has increased remarkably in the last 50 years and will likely continue to increase in the future through better farming methods and

---

[42] Roger Revelle, "The World Supply of Agricultural Land," in *The Resourceful Earth: A Response to Global 2000*, ed. Julian Simon and Herman Kahn (New York: Basil Blackwell, 1984), 184.

[43] Ibid., 185.

[44] Ibid., 186. A "kcal" is a kilogram calorie—that is, 1,000 grams of calories.

[45] "Resources Unlimited," National Center for Policy Analysis, Feb. 19, 1996, www.ncpa.org/sub/dpd/index.php ?Article_ID=12935, citing Thomas Lambert, "Defusing the 'Population Bomb' with Free Markets," Policy Study No. 129, February 1996, Center for the Study of American Business, Washington University, St. Louis, Missouri.

greater use of modern technology. Our ability to grow more and more food—and better food—on more kinds of land should continue to increase due to the amazing inventiveness that God has placed in the human mind.

As Figure 41.1 shows, the amount of cereal grain grown per hectare in the world more than doubled between 1961 and 2014.[46] (A "hectare" is a metric unit for measuring area and is equal to 2.47 acres). These gains have come about through higher-yielding seeds, modern fertilizer, increased pest control, new plants that tolerate colder weather, and an earlier start to the growing season.[47]

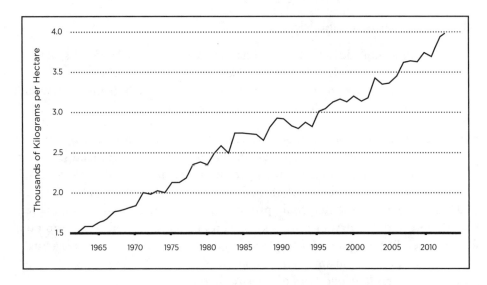

Figure 41.1. World Cereal Yields (Source: Food and Agriculture Organization of the United Nations.)

For these reasons, there has been a steady increase in available food and in the food actually consumed. Lomborg says, "Although there are now twice as many of us as there were in 1961, each of us has *more* to eat, in both developed and developing countries. Fewer people are starving. Food is far cheaper."[48] (Of course, the number of calories consumed has become *too great* for many people in developed countries, but that is another sort of problem!)

This does not mean that there are no remaining problems. Estimates are that the percentage of the population still starving in the world is around 10.9 percent.[49] (The

---

[46]"Cereal yield (kg per hectare)," The World Bank, http://data.worldbank.org/indicator/AG.YLD.CREL.KG?end=2014&start=1961&view=chart. See similar data for various regions of the world in *The State of Humanity*, ed. Julian Simon (Oxford, UK, and Cambridge, MA: Blackwell, 1995), 381.

[47] See further discussion in Dennis Avery, "The World's Rising Food Productivity," in *The State of Humanity*, 376–91.

[48] Lomborg, *The Skeptical Environmentalist*, 60.

[49]"The State of Food Insecurity in the World 2015," Food and Agriculture Organization of the United Nations, 8, http://www.fao.org/3/a-i4646e.pdf.

United Nations defines "starving" as not getting enough food to perform light physical activity.) But the long-term direction of the trend lines is wonderfully encouraging. From 1970 to 2010 (estimate), a period of 40 years, the percentage of the world's people who were starving fell from 35 percent to 12 percent.[50] (In just the developing areas of the world, 13.5 percent of the population, as of 2016, was chronically undernourished.[51])

However, progress has not been uniform in all parts of the world. While most regions of the world have seen a rapid decline since 1970 in the proportion of people living in starving conditions, the progress in sub-Saharan Africa has not kept pace with the progress in the rest of the world. There, 20.0 percent still live in starvation.[52]

c. Water: In a remarkable development over a 45-year period, the percentage of people in developing countries with access to clean drinking water increased from 30 percent in 1970 to 91 percent in 2015![53] However, such encouraging progress is not always recognized and is sometimes concealed. As mentioned above, Lomborg documents how a widely used college textbook on the environment quotes erroneous statistics on water shortages that it claims were from a World Bank study.[54]

But are we using up the world's supply of water too quickly? Not at all. There is a massive amount of water on the earth—71 percent of the earth's surface is covered by water. This is how the water is distributed:

Water in the oceans	97.2 percent
Water in polar ice	2.15 percent
Remaining water, including all freshwater lakes, rivers, and groundwater (water under the ground)	0.65 percent
Total	100 percent

Table 41.4. Distribution of the Earth's Water[55]

---

[50] Lomborg, *The Skeptical Environmentalist*, 61.

[51] "2016 World Hunger and Poverty Facts and Statistics," Hunger Notes, http://www.worldhunger.org/2015-world-hunger-and-poverty-facts-and-statistics/.

[52] Ibid.

[53] Lomborg, *The Skeptical Environmentalist*, 21, and WHO/UNICEF Joint Monitoring Programme (JMP) for Water Supply and Sanitation, "Progress on Sanitation and Drinking Water," 2015 Update and MDG Assessment," 4. The report can be downloaded at https://washdata.org/reports?reports%5B0%5D=date%3A2015&reports%5B1%5D=monitoring-category%3Awater.

[54] Lomborg, *The Skeptical Environmentalist*, 20.

[55] Ibid., 149–50.

Of that 0.65 percent of water that is potentially available for human use, some of it is in areas so remote that it is inaccessible to human beings for all practical purposes. But of the remaining water that is accessible for human use, *we use less than 17 percent of the annually renewable water on the earth.* That is not 17 percent of the fresh water on earth, but just 17 percent of the "readily accessible and renewable water" that is refreshed each year on the earth.[56] The current high-end projections are that just 22 percent of the readily accessible, annually renewed water will be used in 2025.[57]

Who uses most of the water? In terms of global usage, here is the breakdown:

Agriculture	69 percent
Industry	23 percent
Households	8 percent
Total	100 percent

Table 41.5. World Water Usage[58]

Therefore, do we need to be concerned that we will use up the world's water in the future? I do not think so, for at least two reasons:

1. There is an incredible amount of waste in the current usage of water in many countries, both through leakage and through inefficient agricultural usage.[59] But countries such as Israel have developed highly efficient water use, with both a drip irrigation system and effective water recycling.[60] If water prices were allowed to rise so that users were much more responsible in how they used water, much higher efficiencies could be achieved.[61]

2. Desalination of water is becoming more and more economically feasible. The price today for removing the salt from ocean water has fallen below $0.50 per cubic meter in some areas,[62] or less than one-fifth of a cent per gallon. This is significantly less than the $1.15 per cubic meter that I currently pay at my home in Arizona![63] In 2013, the

[56] Ibid., 150–51.
[57] Ibid., 150.
[58] Ibid., 154.
[59] Ibid., 154–56.
[60] Ibid.
[61] Ibid.
[62] In other areas the cost remains around $1 per cubic meter, but the overall trend is a declining price due to improved technology. See Noreddine Ghaffour, Thomas M. Missimer, Gary L. Amy, "Technical Review and Evaluation of the Economics of Water Desalination: Current and Future Challenges for Better Water Supply Sustainability," *Desalination* 309 (January 2013): 197–207, http://www.sciencedirect.com/science/article/pii/S0011916412005723.
[63] My residential water bill at my home in Arizona is based on a sliding price scale that increases with the quantity of water used, but I took my bill from October 2016 (a typical month) and found that I paid $0.0043415 per gallon of water. There are 264.17 gallons in a cubic meter of water (1,000 liters), so my cost per cubic meter was $1.15.

average price of water in the United States was $0.74 per cubic meter, while in the United Kingdom it was $2.37 and in Germany $5.65.[64] (Yet many of these costs reflect not only the raw production costs, but also delivery costs and no doubt other governmental fees.)

According to the International Desalination Association, as of June 2015, 18,426 desalination plants operated worldwide, producing 86.8 million cubic meters per day, providing water for 300 million people from 150 countries.[65] The Middle East contains the most desalinated water plants (53 percent of the total).[66] By 2030, it is estimated that more than 110 million cubic meters per day of desalinated water will be produced, with 70 percent of that water in Saudi Arabia, the United Arab Emirates, Kuwait, Algeria, and Libya.[67] In Malta, 70 percent of the total water consumption is desalinated water.[68]

It is encouraging that a large, new desalination plant opened in Carlsbad, California (near San Diego) on December 14, 2015.[69] It will produce 8 percent of the water needs for the San Diego region.[70] As of 2014, there were more than 20 desalination plants operating or under construction in California, producing 2.6 million cubic meters of desalinated water per day, or 15 percent of the state's total water needs.[71]

When we take into account the stabilization of world population in the future, the increased efficiencies with which more developed countries use their water supply, the more than 80 percent of available and renewable fresh water supplies that are not being used today, and the virtually unlimited supply of water found in the oceans for a slightly higher price, we have no reason to expect that the earth will run out of water *ever*. In providing the earth with water, God truly provided us with a wonderfully abundant resource.

Are there local and regional areas where water supply is scarce and difficult to obtain? Yes, but those are local problems that have to do with *access to water*, not with the total supply of water on the earth. In many cases, local water shortages are due either to lack of economic development of the nation as a whole (and therefore the lack of ability to transport, purify, deliver, and pay for water) or to local or national legal, economic, or political hindrances to water access.

For example, the state of California sits next to the inexhaustible water resources of

[64] Alex Webb, "German Water Charges Second-Highest Rate in Europe, Handelsblatt says," *Bloomberg*, Aug. 7, 2013, https://www.bloomberg.com/news/articles/2013-08-07/german-water-charges-second-highest-in-europe-handelsblatt-says.

[65] "Desalination by the Numbers," International Desalination Association, http://idadesal.org/desalination-101/desalination-by-the-numbers/.

[66] Konstantinos Zotalis, Emmanuel G. Dialynas, Nikolaos Mamassis, and Andreas N. Angelakis, "Desalination Technologies: Hellenic Experience," *Water* 6, no. 5 (April 30, 2014): 1136, http://www.mdpi.com/2073-4441/6/5/1134/htm.

[67] Ibid., citing M. Isaka, *Water Desalination Using Renewable Energy*, Technology Brief I12, International Energy Agency (IEA)-Energy Technology Systems Analysis Program (ETSAP), Paris, France; International Renewable Energy Activity (IRENA), Abu Dhabi, United Arab Emirates, 2012.

[68] Ibid., 1139.

[69] Bradley J. Fikes, "$1-Billion Desalination Plant, Hailed as Model for State, Opens in Carlsbad," *Los Angeles Times*, Dec. 15, 2015, http://www.latimes.com/local/california/la-me-desalination-20151215-story.html.

[70] Zotalis et al, "Desalination Technologies: Hellenic Experience," 1140.

[71] Ibid.

the Pacific Ocean, but local political opposition to constructing desalination plants has for many years hindered Californians from tapping this source of water to meet all their needs. While plants are finally being built, much more could still be done.

d. Clean Air: I remember as a child how unpleasant it was to walk on the sidewalk along any city street when a line of cars was waiting at a stoplight. The air pollution from the exhaust coming from the cars made the very act of breathing unpleasant and on some days even made my eyes sting. But today if I walk on the same sidewalk beside a line of cars waiting at a stoplight, I can breathe freely and the automobile exhaust is almost undetectable. What happened?

The change came about because the people of the United States (collectively, through their elected representatives) decided that it was worth the extra expense to require pollution controls on automobile engines. They did the same for trucks, factories, home furnaces, and many other sources of air pollution. As a result, the air became much cleaner.

This cleanup of the air is the pattern followed by all countries of the world as their economies grow and they become wealthier overall. They begin to spend the extra money that is required to control air pollution.

To take another example, Figure 41.2 (p. 1119) shows the concentrations of sulfur dioxide (SO_2) and smoke in London over a 400-year period. Today these major pollutants are present in London's air in lower concentrations than they have been since before 1585, long before the modern industrial period. Urban pollutants have also decreased 90 percent since 1930.[72]

Another remarkable chart shows that *economic development is the way by which nations can overcome air pollution*. Figure 41.3 (p. 1120) shows that extremely poor countries (the left side of the chart) have almost no particle pollution in their air. This is because they have few cars, trucks, or factories to pollute the air. When nations begin to develop economically, the people drive older cars and trucks that sputter along but pollute more, and they burn fuels in their homes and factories that increase air pollution. But when a nation's annual per capita income reaches about $3,000 (the peak of the lines in the center of the chart), people decide that the polluted air is so harmful to their quality of life that they begin to impose regulations and fees to decrease it. Finally, when nations develop to the point that they have a per capita income of $30,000 per year or higher (the right side of the chart), their air returns to the purity it had when it was an undeveloped nation with essentially no cars or factories.

What is more encouraging about this chart is the progress it reveals between 1972 and 1986. *The entire graph of pollution particles* is lower for every level of economic development. Even the poorer countries were able to develop with less total pollution because of the use of cheaper and cleaner technology (including less-polluting cars and trucks) that could be imported from more developed countries. (The chart also shows

---

[72] Derek M. Elsom, "Atmospheric Pollution Trends in the United Kingdom," in *The State of Humanity*, 476–90.

that pollution reduction can occur at lower levels of income over time, as poorer countries come to use technology developed in wealthier countries.)

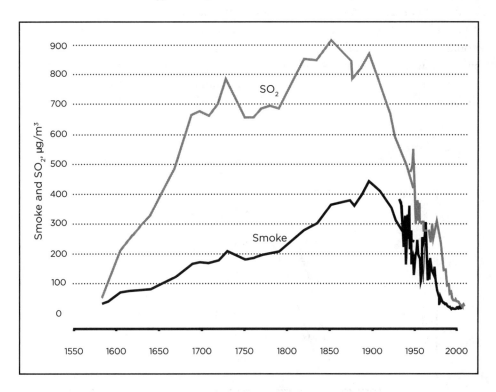

Figure 41.2. Average Concentrations of SO² and Smoke in London, 1585–1994/5. (Adapted from Bjørn Lomborg, *The Skeptical Environmentalist: Measuring the Real State of the World* [Cambridge, UK: Cambridge University Press, 2001], 165, with permission of the publisher.)

As far as future trends in air pollution are concerned, Lomborg points to the example of the United States:

> In the US, the total number of car miles traveled has more than doubled over the past 30 years. The economy has likewise more than doubled, and the population has increased by more than a third. Nevertheless, over the same period emissions have decreased by a third and concentrations by much more. This is why it is reasonable to be optimistic about the challenge from air pollution.[73]

Speaking as a Christian, I am not at all surprised by these findings. It seems to me consistent with the teachings of the Bible, because if God put us on the earth to develop

---

[73] Lomborg, *The Skeptical Environmentalist*, 177.

and use its resources *for our benefit, with thanksgiving,* and *for his glory,* and if God is a good and wise Creator, then it is completely reasonable to think that he would create in the earth the resources that we need and that there would be methods that we could discover by which we could use these resources wisely. It is reasonable to think that he would make it possible for us to use the good resources of the earth in wonderful and enjoyable ways while simultaneously improving human quality of life *and* protecting the environment. We have found that to be true not only with food supplies and water supplies, but also with the increasingly abundant supply of clean air on the earth.

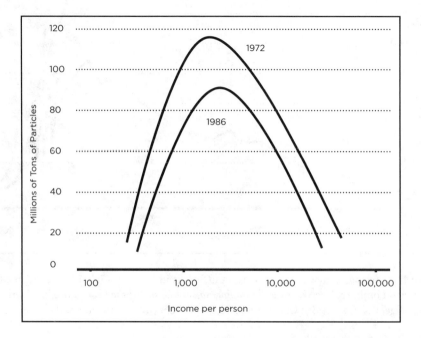

Figure 41.3. Connection between GDP per Capita and Particle Pollution in 48 Cities in 31 Countries, 1972 and 1986. (Adapted from Bjørn Lomborg, *The Skeptical Environmentalist: Measuring the Real State of the World* [Cambridge, UK: Cambridge University Press, 2001], 177, with permission of the publisher.)

e. Waste Disposal: Will nations of the earth continue to produce more and more waste that will eventually overwhelm our cities and make life unpleasant if not actually dangerous? Reliable statistics on waste disposal suggest that the answer is no.

Some of the waste that people generate is recycled or put into compost piles. Another portion of it is incinerated, in some cases in energy-producing incineration plants. Several European countries—especially France, Germany, Denmark, the United Kingdom, and Italy—make considerable use of modern incineration plants with extensive measures to minimize air pollution or waste-disposal pollution from the resulting ashes.

France alone has 225 incineration plants for energy production.[74] In addition, energy production from waste incineration seems to be the cheapest of all methods available, when measured per kilowatt-hour.[75] In France, for instance, just three plants can provide enough energy (200,000 megawatts) to heat 40,000 apartments each year.[76] In addition, "The plants also produce the steam to supply 40 percent of Paris's heating needs, which is currently enough to heat 200,000 apartments, all 24 of the city's hospitals, and dozens of famous tourist sites and museums, including the Louvre."[77] The power generated by the incineration of garbage saves 300,000 tons of fossil fuels and stops the release of 900,000 tons of carbon dioxide into the air each year, the equivalent of taking 200,000 cars off the roads.[78]

But not all waste is burned to produce energy. Most of the rest of the waste that people generate is put into landfills. Modern U.S. landfills are highly regulated by the Environmental Protection Agency and are considered very safe for the groundwater in the area around them.[79]

But landfills are not simply "wasted space." I once went to watch one of my sons run in a beautiful park with rolling hills when he was part of his high school cross-country team in Illinois. Only later did I find out that the park was built on the site of a landfill that had been carefully covered by soil. In fact, the massive Fresh Kills Landfill on Staten Island in New York City is now closed so it can be turned into landscaped public parkland about three times the size of Central Park. The New York City Parks website says:

> The transformation of what was formerly the world's largest landfill into a productive and beautiful cultural destination makes the park a symbol of renewal and an expression of how our society can restore balance to its landscape. In addition to providing a wide range of recreational opportunities, including many uncommon in the city, the park's design, ecological restoration and cultural and educational programming emphasize environmental sustainability and a renewed public concern for our human impact on the earth.[80]

How much space would be required to receive all the garbage being produced in

---

[74] Bernt Johnke, "Emissions from Waste Incineration," *Good Practice Guidance and Uncertainty Management in National Greenhouse Gas Inventories*, Intergovernmental Panel on Climate Change, 456, www.ipcc-nggip.iges.or.jp/public/gp/bgp/5_3_Waste_Incineration.pdf.

[75] The Cornwall Alliance for the Stewardship of Creation, *A Renewed Call to Truth, Prudence, and Protection of the Poor: An Evangelical Examination of the Theology, Science, and Economics of Global Warming* (Burke, VA: The Cornwall Alliance, 2009), 66, Table 3, "Index of lifetime generation costs by generating type," www.cornwallalliance.org/docs/a-renewed-call-to-truth-prudence-and-protection-of-the-poor.pdf.

[76] "How the French are Burning Garbage to Heat Homes," *PBS Newshour*, Nov. 22, 2015, http://www.pbs.org/newshour/bb/how-the-french-are-burning-garbage-to-heat-homes/.

[77] Ibid.

[78] Ibid.

[79] Lomborg, *The Skeptical Environmentalist*, 208.

[80] "The Park Plan," The Freshkills Park Alliance, http://freshkillspark.org/the-park/the-park-plan.

the United States? Even with quite generous assumptions about the amount of waste produced per person and about the size of the growth of the American population, if all the waste generated in the United States for the next hundred years were placed in one landfill, it would fit within an area less than eighteen miles on each side and about a hundred feet high (lower than the Fresh Kills Landfill in New York City). This single landfill would take up less than 0.009 percent of the land area of the United States.[81] And it could be made into another landscaped public park for people to use in centuries to come. To take another comparison, if each state had to handle its own waste, it would have to find simply one site for a single landfill of two and a half miles on each side.[82] When full, those sites too could be covered with soil and turned into beautiful state parks. (This assumes that each of these landfills is filled with waste and dirt over each layer and compacted appropriately, according to modern environmental standards.)

But in actual fact, thousands of local landfills much smaller in size will be used and will be entirely adequate to handle the waste that we generate. Like me, other dads will watch their sons run cross-country meets on the rolling, wooded hills and never know that a landfill lies under the ground.

Another important factor is that with technological advances we continually discover new uses for waste products and new ways to produce goods with less waste. So the amount of waste generated will probably be much less than these current predictions. In any case, we will easily be able to handle that amount of waste. We will never run out of space to store our garbage.

Is recycling worthwhile, then? It does reduce the amount of waste that is put into landfills, but a sensible approach would ask, with respect to each kind of material being recycled, *is it worth the time, effort, and expense it takes to do such recycling?* That is simply a *factual* analysis that needs to be carried out.

For example, should we put resources into recycling paper, or should we simply burn it at incineration plants and produce energy with it? A quick check of the Staples website, where I buy office supplies, shows me that an ordinary package of 12 of the legal pads that I use costs $13.99, while a 12-pack of the same size of legal pads made of recycled paper costs $19.99! That is 43 percent higher! So the recycled paper costs *much more* than newly produced paper. Is there any good reason for me to spend 43 percent more for the paper I use? There is no need to do it to reduce the use of landfills, for which we have abundant space. Should I use recycled paper so we do not have to cut down so many trees? That would make sense only if the world were going to run out of trees to make paper, which is simply not going to happen (see below).

Paper is a *renewable resource*, because trees can be planted and grown, just as oats, wheat, and corn are grown. (Trees take longer, but they *are* a renewable resource.) If the recycled paper costs more, that means that *the total amount of resources* used to produce recycled paper is *greater* than the resources used to produce

[81] Lomborg, *The Skeptical Environmentalist*, 207.
[82] Ibid.

new paper, for the price reflects, in general, the cost of production, and it probably reflects less than the true cost of production because of government subsidies for recycling plants. Buying the recycled paper would waste $6, which I am not going to do. I buy legal pads made of ordinary paper.

f. Global Forests: If we could never grow any more trees in the world, or if we were quickly depleting the amount of trees available for paper and wood production, then of course recycling would make a lot of sense. But is the world running out of trees? Once again, this is simply a question of analysis of *the facts that show worldwide trends.*

About one-third of the earth's land is covered by forests today, and this number has remained relatively stable since World War II. More precisely, forest cover increased from 30.04 percent of the global land area in 1950[83] to 30.825 percent in 2015,[84] an increase of 0.821 percentage point over 65 years. Four countries (Russia, Brazil, the United States, and Canada) together have more than 50 percent of the world's forests, and in the whole world about two to three times as much land is taken up by forests as by agricultural land used for crops.[85]

As for the United States, from its early history until about 1920 a significant amount of the forest cover was cleared, largely for agricultural use. But since 1920, the amount of forest land has remained quite stable.[86]

After a natural forest area where trees are growing randomly is first cleared for wood or paper use, new trees are planted in neat rows so that much more total wood is grown in each land area. The result of this more efficient use of land has been that the amount of wood (in cubic feet) that is actually growing in the United States each year *is three and a half times what it was in 1920.*[87]

As far as the entire world is concerned, we have lost about 20 percent of the original forest cover on the earth since agriculture began,[88] but that percentage has now stabilized. Developing countries tend to clear forests and put more land into agricultural use, but then that trend stabilizes as better agricultural methods are adopted and the food needs of the country are met. Another factor is that less developed societies tend to use wood for fuel in open fires, but with development, other sources of energy are used.

In any case, global use of paper and other products made from wood does not pose a significant threat to worldwide forest cover. Lomborg writes that "our entire consumption of wood and paper can be catered for by the tree *growth* of just 5 percent of the current forest area."[89]

There is still a legitimate concern over loss of tropical rain forests in some countries,

[83] Ibid., 111.

[84] "Forest Area (% of land area)," The World Bank, http://data.worldbank.org/indicator/AG.LND.FRST.ZS.

[85] Lomborg, *The Skeptical Environmentalist*, 112.

[86] Roger A. Sedjo and Marian Clawson, "Global Forests Revisited," in *The State of Humanity*, 331.

[87] Ibid., 331–32.

[88] Lomborg, *The Skeptical Environmentalist*, 112.

[89] Ibid., 115.

because rainforests contain many thousands of diverse biological species and produce much of the world's oxygen. But earlier estimates of an annual loss of 2 percent or more of the tropical rainforests in Brazil have now been shown to be excessively high.[90] The rate of loss of Brazilian tropical forests more recently has been estimated at about 0.2-0.5 percent per year.[91]

By far the largest proportion of tropical rain forest in the world is in Brazil. The Amazon forest makes up about one-third of the world's tropical forest area. About 19 percent of the Amazon rain forest has been cut down since earliest human history, with 81 percent remaining as of 2016.[92] The Brazilian government has wisely imposed restrictions on deforestation in the Amazon area. Ultimately this is a problem that can be solved only by the government of each nation that has tropical forests, including Brazil. But the primary cause of loss of forest area is not wood used for paper, but overuse of wood fuel due to low income in less developed countries.[93] In any case, the world consumption of wood and paper can easily be satisfied without any significant deforestation throughout the world.

g. Herbicides and Pesticides: One of the most significant reasons for increased food production around the world has been the invention of modern herbicides (that kill harmful weeds) and pesticides (that kill harmful insects and bacteria). Herbicides and pesticides improve crop yields and make fruits and vegetables cheaper. If herbicide and pesticide use were restricted or even prohibited, the proportion of income that a family in North America or Europe needs to spend on food might double. People would eat fewer fruits and vegetables, would buy more primary starch, and would consume more fat. The effect on the poor would be the greatest, but these changes might lead to an increase of something like 26,000 additional cancer deaths per year in the United States.[94] In short, herbicides and pesticides create *great health benefits* and significantly *higher food production* while requiring *less use of land*.

But are pesticides harmful? U.S. government agencies such as the Food and Drug Administration (FDA) and the Environmental Protection Agency (EPA) set strict limits on the use of pesticides based on the measurable amounts that get into the food and water that we consume. After extensive testing, a value is established called the NOAEL (No Observed Adverse Effect Level). A level below this is a value called the ADI (Accepted Daily Intake). The ADI limit is usually between one hundred and ten thousand times lower than the NOAEL.[95] These limits apparently prevent any harm from pesticides.

---

[90] Ibid., 114, citing William P. Cunningham and Barbara Woodworth Saigo, *Environmental Science: A Global Concern* (Dubuque, IA: Wm. C. Brown, 1997), 297–98.

[91] Rhett Butler, "Calculating Deforestation Figures for the Amazon," Mongabay, Jan. 27, 2017, http://rainforests.mongabay.com/amazon/deforestation_calculations.html.
Lomborg, *The Skeptical Environmentalist,* 114, gives the 0.5% figure for 1999.

[92] Ibid.

[93] Lomborg, *The Skeptical Environmentalist,* 114.

[94] Ibid., 247–48.

[95] Ibid., 226.

One of the most respected studies of various causes of cancer in the United States, for example, concluded that it could find *no significant percentage of cancers caused by pesticides in the United States*.[96] There are many causes of cancer (such as tobacco, diet, sun exposure, and infections), but pesticides do not even make the list. Lomborg concludes that "virtually no one dies of cancer caused by pesticides."[97] In another place, he summarizes a number of studies by saying, "Pesticides contribute astoundingly little to deaths caused by cancer."[98] He says that a "plausible estimate" for the number of cancer deaths due to pesticide use in the United States is close to 20 per year out of 560,000,[99] or one out of every 28,000 people who die of cancer. When this low death rate is weighed against the immense benefits that come from pesticide use, and the great harm that would come to the world population and world diets if pesticide use were abolished, it appears that there should be no significant objection to their current level of wise and carefully restricted use. More recent research also indicates that low levels of pesticide use do not result in a greater occurrence of cancer.[100]

Once again, this conclusion should not be surprising. Since God wanted us to subdue the earth and develop its resources in useful ways, then it is reasonable to expect that he would give us the ability to discover means of overcoming the "thorns and thistles" that grow on the earth, as well as the pests that tend to destroy food crops. In addition, it must be recognized that many of the pesticides in use are not synthetic chemical compounds but are derived from natural substances that already occur in one place or another in the plant world—substances that already allow some plants to fight off the pests that would attack them.[101]

h. Life Expectancy: Is the earth becoming a safer or more dangerous place for human beings to live? One very important measure is overall life expectancy. When people have better health, when they are able to overcome diseases, when they are able to keep themselves safe from natural disasters, and when they have better nutrition, they will live longer. Therefore, we would expect that people would have a longer life expectancy as they advance in developing the earth's resources and making them useful for human beings, as God intended them to do.

This is in fact what has happened as nations have developed economically and human beings have discovered more ways to make the resources of the earth useful for themselves.

While records from earlier centuries are less detailed, enough information remains to gain a fairly good idea of overall life expectancy in a number of nations. England may be taken as typical of what happens as nations develop economically:

---

[96] Ibid., 229, citing Richard Doll and Richard Petro, "The Causes of Cancer: Quantitative Estimates of Avoidable Risks of Cancer in the United States Today," *Journal of the National Cancer Institute* 66, no. 6: 1,191–1308, 1981.

[97] Ibid., 228–29.

[98] Ibid., 245.

[99] Ibid.

[100] "Agricultural Health Study," National Cancer Institute, June 16, 2011, https://www.cancer.gov/about -cancer/causes-prevention/risk/ahs-fact-sheet.

[101] Lomborg, *The Skeptical Environmentalist*, 232–33.

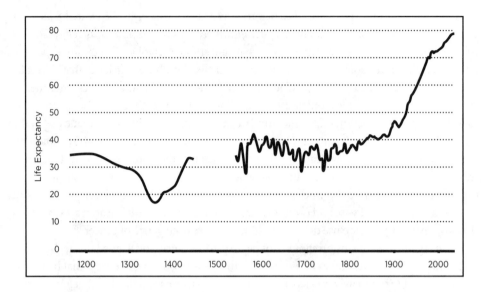

Figure 41.4. Life Expectancy in England and Wales, 1200–1998. (The chart shows life expectancy at birth for male landholders in England, 1200–1450, and for both sexes in England and Wales or the UK, 1541–1998. Adapted from Bjørn Lomborg, *The Skeptical Environmentalist: Measuring the Real State of the World* [Cambridge, UK: Cambridge University Press, 2001], 165, with permission of the publisher.)

Note that life expectancy in the last 200 years has increased from about 38 years to about 78 years. This is an astounding increase. Other countries experienced similar growth so that the average life expectancy in developed countries is now 78.3 years.[102]

In less developed countries, the average life expectancy at the beginning of the 20th century was under 30 years. By 1950 it had reached 41 years and in 2015 was at 68.8 years.[103] It is astounding that life expectancy even in less developed countries has more than doubled in just over a hundred years.[104] The predictions for future development are continually upward for all parts of the world.

These statistics are valuable in that they serve as an overall indicator of human progress in the ability to live productive lives on the earth, overcome dangers, and make the resources of the earth beneficial for our health and well-being. The overall picture is a very encouraging one of continual growth and progress. We are making better use of the environment in which we live and also taking better care of it each year.

God created an abundant and resourceful earth, and we are developing an ever-greater ability to make wise use of the resources that he has placed in it for our benefit, so that we would use these resources with thanksgiving and give glory to him.

---

[102] United Nations, *World Population Prospects, the 2015 Revision: Vol. 1: Comprehensive Tables*, 168, https://esa.un.org/unpd/wpp/Publications/Files/WPP2015_Volume-I_Comprehensive-Tables.pdf.
[103] Ibid.
[104] Ibid.

C. ENERGY RESOURCES AND ENERGY USES

Sometimes people naively assume that we are quickly running out of energy sources, but that is simply not true.

To get an overall picture of world energy production, we first need to understand that energy is derived from several sources. The following diagram shows the distribution of energy sources used in a particular year for the entire world:

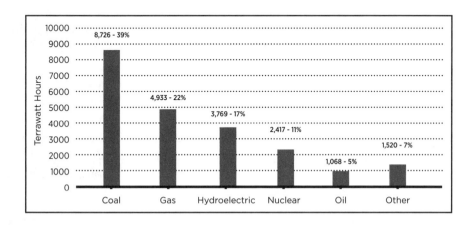

Figure 41.5. World Electricity Production from All Energy Sources, 2014. (Figures are in terawatt hours. Sources: U.S. Energy Information Administration and World Bank.)

A terawatt is equal to one trillion watts of power. One terawatt hour of electricity is enough to power 85,000 to 100,000 homes per year.[105] In total, 22,433 terawatt hours of electricity were produced in 2014.[106]

1. Wind Power. In 2014, according to World Bank development indicators, electricity generated from wind power represented only 3 percent of global electricity production.[107] Wind power accounted for nearly 4 percent of U.S. electricity production in 2014.[108] Wind power has some potential, but its contribution to world energy production will probably remain quite small because it is not dependable in most areas of the world (wind does not blow all the time and varies in intensity) and the energy of

---

[105] U.S. Department of Energy, "Energy Department Invests $16 Million to Harness Wave and Tidal Energy," Aug. 29, 2013, https://energy.gov/articles/energy-department-invests-16-million-harness-wave-and -tidal-energy, and "Opower to Save One Terawatt Hour of Energy by 2012," *BusinessWire*, June 15, 2011, http://www.businesswire.com/news/home/20110615005924/en/Opower-Save-Terawatt-Hour-Energy-2012.

[106] A terawatt-hour refers to getting power at a capacity of 1 terawatt (10^{12} watts) for one hour. One terawatt-hour is equal to a sustained power of approximately 114 megawatts for a period of one year.

[107] "Breakdown of Electricity Generation by Energy Source," The Shift Project, http://tsp-data-portal.org /Breakdown-of-Electricity-Generation-by-Energy-Source#tspQvChart.

[108] Ibid.

the wind is so diffuse that wind farms require huge land areas (or ocean areas) with hundreds of giant windmills that destroy the beauty of the landscape for miles around.

2. Hydroelectric Power. While the United States gets 6.5 percent of its electricity (2016)[109] from hydroelectric dams on rivers, it is unlikely that this capacity can be expanded much because few good locations for new dams remain. The situation is similar in most developed countries, so it is unlikely that the 17 percent of the world's electrical energy that is produced by hydroelectric plants[110] will increase very much.

3. Oil. Because of new technology and further exploration, people are constantly discovering new reserves of oil and other energy sources. For example, Figure 41.6 shows how the world's *known reserves* of oil have multiplied since 1980.

Moreover, when the price of oil increases, oil in more difficult areas becomes economically more feasible to develop. If we factor in the oil available in tar sands and shale oil fields, the amount of oil remaining is equal to the total energy consumption of the entire world for more than 5,000 years![111] But of course we will also be using other energy sources as well, and technological developments in the next 25 to 50 years will likely shift our usage away from even the amount of world energy that oil now produces. In other words, we will never run out of oil.

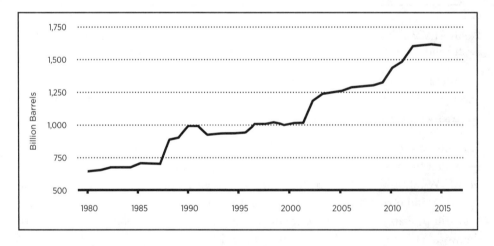

Figure 41.6. World Crude Oil Proved Reserves. (Source: U.S. Energy Information Administration.)

In many cases, oil-based gasoline and diesel fuel are going to remain the preferred fuels for years to come because of their high energy content and easy transportability—

---

[109] "Hydropower Explained," U.S. Energy Information Administration, June 13, 2017, http://www.eia.gov/energyexplained/index.cfm?page=hydropower_home.

[110] "Breakdown of Electrical Generation by Energy Source."

[111] Lomborg, *The Skeptical Environmentalist*, 128.

you can't burn coal in a car or plane engine, and electric batteries do not (presently) deliver enough energy for long enough to power larger trucks or airplanes. Oil is also still relatively cheap and abundant.

4. Coal. Coal is another widely used source of energy, and modern coal-burning power plants are much cleaner and more efficient than in previous years. The total coal resources available in the world will be sufficient for "well beyond the next 1,500 years."[112]

5. Natural Gas. Natural gas is an excellent source of energy for home heating and is also widely used to generate electrical power. Some areas have used natural gas to power automobiles and buses, but the special refueling stations are found only in certain places. The existence of natural gas in a gaseous rather than a liquid state under normal temperatures makes it readily transportable by pipelines. But it has to be kept under pressure to be used in a liquid form, so it requires specially pressurized refueling pumps and thick, heavy, reinforced tanks in cars that use it. It burns very cleanly and is now less expensive than gasoline produced from oil.

6. Nuclear Power.

a. The Benefits of Nuclear Power: Nuclear power is also an excellent source of energy. The energy produced by one gram (that is, 1/28th of an ounce)[113] of uranium-235 is equivalent to the energy produced by almost three tons of coal![114] Nuclear power gives off almost no pollution, a significant benefit. In addition, the energy available from nuclear power is immense. Former U.S. Sen. Pete Domenici of New Mexico, who devoted many years to learning about nuclear energy and was once the chairman of the Energy and Natural Resources Committee of the U.S. Senate, said that nuclear plants could easily provide the energy needs of the entire United States for thousands of years to come if they were not prevented from being built by opposition "based on irrational fear led by Hollywood-style fiction, the Green lobbies and the media. These fears are unjustified, and nuclear energy from its start in 1952 has proved to be the safest of all energy sources."[115]

b. The Disposal of Nuclear Waste: Nuclear power production produces radioactive waste, which needs to be stored safely. This has become a political controversy in the United States, but many nations have already solved this problem for themselves,

---

[112] Lomborg, *The Skeptical Environmentalist*, 127, citing James R. Craig, David J. Vaughn, and Brian J. Skinner, *Resources of the Earth: Origin, Use, and Environmental Impact* (Upper Saddle River, NJ: Prentice Hall, 1996), 159.

[113] A U.S. penny weighs 2.5 grams, so 1 gram is the weight of a little less than half a penny.

[114] Lomborg. *The Skeptical Environmentalist*, 129, citing Craig et al., *Resources of the Earth*, 164.

[115] Pete Domenici, *A Brighter Tomorrow: Fulfilling the Promise of Nuclear Energy* (Lanham, MD: Rowman & Littlefield, 2004), 211. This book contains an abundance of information on the benefits of more nuclear energy, with detailed responses to objections.

and it should not be a problem in the United States either. Domenici pointed out that in France, to dispose of nuclear waste, "a single 150-liter glass canister contains the waste (fission products and actinides) from 360,000 families of four heating their homes with electricity for one year."[116] To give some comparison, 150 liters is about the size of a common 40-gallon steel drum (or the water tank that is inside all the insulation of an ordinary home water heater). This means that the yearly nuclear waste of *over a million people* could be stored in a container of this size. (This would require that the United States adopt a method of reprocessing nuclear fuel that is now used safely in France and other countries.)

According to the U.S. Department of Energy's Civilian Nuclear Waste Management Office, France stores its spent nuclear fuel for one year at its nuclear power plants in specially constructed storage pools. Following storage, spent nuclear fuel is then transported to the La Hague and Marcoule reprocessing plants and stored for two to three years. France has also reprocessed nuclear fuel for Germany, Belgium, Japan, and the Netherlands.[117] The fuel and radioactive waste is buried 400 to 1,000 meters below the ground. In Japan, the waste is buried 300 meters underground.[118] Some 76.8 percent of the electricity generated in France is from nuclear power.[119]

There are currently 100 operable nuclear power plants in the United States (including the Palo Verde Nuclear Generating Station west of Phoenix, the same metropolitan area in which I live). These plants provide 19.7 percent of the electricity generated for the United States.[120]

Several hundred more nuclear power plants had been planned up until about the mid-1970s, but because of endless legal and regulatory barriers, very few new nuclear power plants have been approved for construction in the United States for the last 40 years.[121]

Why is this? Domenici attributed the failure of the United States to change these prohibitive barriers to two causes: (1) "many Americans have an irrational fear of anything 'nuclear,'" and (2) "the policy of deliberate misinformation that opponents of nuclear energy employ with shameless disregard of the truth."[122]

[116] Ibid., 157.

[117] "France's Radioactive Waste Management Program," U.S. Department of Energy, Office of Civilian Nuclear Radioactive Waste Management, https://biotech.law.lsu.edu/Courses/adlawf04/doeymp0411.pdf.

[118] The Federation of Electric Power Companies of Japan. www.japannuclear.com/nuclearpower/program/waste.html. See also "FAQ," Nuclear Waste Management Organization of Japan, www.numo.or.jp/en/faq/main1.html.

[119] "Country Profile: France," Nuclear Energy Agency, www.nea.fr/html/general/profiles/france.html.

[120] See "Nuclear Explained," U.S. Energy Information Agency, Aug. 31, 2017, http://www.eia.gov/energyexplained/index.cfm?page=nuclear_home#tab2.

[121] However, the Watts Bar 2 nuclear power plant in Tennessee came online in 2016. See Chris Mooney, "It's the First New U.S. Nuclear Reactor in Decades: And Climate Change Has Made That a Very Big Deal," *The Washington Post*, June 17, 2016, https://www.washingtonpost.com/news/energy-environment/wp/2016/06/17/the-u-s-is-powering-up-its-first-new-nuclear-reactor-in-decades/.

[122] Domenici, *A Brighter Tomorrow*, xii.

c. Accidents at Nuclear Power Plants: Three accidents at nuclear power plants have become widely known: (1) Three Mile Island in Pennsylvania (1979); (2) Chernobyl in Russia (1986); and (3) Fukushima in Japan (2011). These accidents illustrate that human carelessness or negligence can lead to accidents at nuclear power plants, but they do not show that nuclear power is itself inherently unsafe.

(1) Three Mile Island: Contrary to popular impressions, the accident with a cooling system malfunction at the Three Mile Island Nuclear Generating Station in Pennsylvania on March 29, 1979, involved no human deaths and no injuries to plant workers or nearby residents.[123] The generator that experienced the accident resumed operation in October 1985 after repairs and lengthy litigation.[124]

(2) Chernobyl: In the former Soviet Union, the Chernobyl Nuclear Reactor in Ukraine was destroyed by a terrible accident on April 26, 1986, but that was due to flagrantly poor quality construction and maintenance under the communist government, combined with a blatant disregard for safety that has never been allowed in the United States, France, the United Kingdom, or other countries with significant nuclear power production. According to the U.S. Nuclear Regulatory Commission, "U.S. reactors have different plant designs, broader shutdown margins, robust containment structures, and operational controls to protect them against the combination of lapses that led to the accident at Chernobyl."[125]

(3) Fukushima: On March 11, 2011, an earthquake estimated at 8.9 to 9.1 on the Richter Scale, the largest in Japanese history, took place 231 miles northeast of Tokyo.[126] It was followed by a tsunami with waves as high as 30 feet and several aftershocks that damaged several nuclear reactors.[127] At the time, Japan had 54 nuclear reactors at seventeen power plants that were responsible for generating 30 percent of the nation's electricity.[128] At the Fukushima Daini nuclear plant, three of the four units failed, resulting in radiation near the plant's main gate spiking eight times above the normal level. There were no fatalities, but several dozen people were injured, and eventually 185,000 people had to be evacuated from the area.[129]

---

[123] "Backgrounder on the Three Mile Island Accident," United States Nuclear Regulatory Commission, Dec. 12, 2014, www.nrc.gov/reading-rm/doc-collections/fact-sheets/3mile-isle.html.

[124] See "Three Mile Island Unit 1," www.ucsusa.org/assets/documents/nuclear_power/three-mile-island-1.pdf.

[125] "Background on Chernobyl Nuclear Power Plant Accident," United States Nuclear Regulatory Commission, Dec. 12, 2014, www.nrc.gov/reading-rm/doc-collections/fact-sheets/chernobyl-bg.html.

[126] "2011 Japan Earthquake-Tsunami Fast Facts," CNN, Nov. 22, 2016, http://www.cnn.com/2013/07/17/world/asia/japan-earthquake—-tsunami-fast-facts/index.html.

[127] Motoko Rich, "New Quake Tests Resilience, and Faith in, Japan's Nuclear Plants," *The New York Times*, Nov. 22, 2016, https://www.nytimes.com/2016/11/22/world/asia/japan-earthquake-tsunami-fukushima.html.

[128] "An Overview of Japan's Nuclear Issues," CNN, March 14, 2011, http://www.cnn.com/2011/WORLD/asiapcf/03/13/japan.nuclear.facts/index.html.

[129] "2011 Japan Earthquake-Tsunami Fast Facts."

The problem was caused when poorly trained operators misread a backup system and waited too long to start pumping water to the units. The resulting meltdowns were determined to be a "man-made disaster" that occurred because of collusion between the facility's operator, regulators, and government to avoid the need to properly prepare the plant for such a disaster by playing down safety risks. Three executives of the Tokyo Electrical Power Company would later be indicted for their role in the disaster.[130] However, when another large earthquake (7.4) hit on November 22, 2016, the cooling pump at the Fukushima Daini plant was restored within an hour and half and there were no further problems. This time, the proper safety precautions had been implemented and training had occurred.

But cleanup from the 2011 disaster is still ongoing and has run into difficulties. On February 8, 2017, it was announced that reactor two at the plant was emitting dangerously high radiation levels. The radiation was measured at 530 sieverts (the unit for measuring radiation levels) per hour. In comparison, most dental x-rays are just .01 millisievert. One estimate is that it could take four decades to resolve all the cleanup issues.[131]

Because of the failure of the Fukushima plant and the subsequent cleanup issues, most of Japan's 54 nuclear plants remain closed to this day. Prime Minister Shinzo Abe favors restarting most of them, but groups opposed to nuclear energy are trying to keep them closed and pushing renewable energy such as solar and wind instead.[132]

I do not believe that these three accidents provide sufficient reason to oppose nuclear energy in the future. Yes, human carelessness or corruption can result in failure to follow proper safety procedures, and then accidents can happen. But no kind of energy production is risk-free, because accidents, injuries, and deaths have also occurred (in much larger numbers) in coal mining, oil drilling, and construction of hydroelectric dams. The continuing existence of many hundreds of accident-free nuclear power plants throughout the world is strong testimony to the fact that nuclear power is a remarkably safe and reliable source of energy.

d. Further Developments in Nuclear Energy: With the development of the so-called "fast-breeder" reactor, there is now sufficient uranium for "up to 14,000 years" of energy production.[133] And then there is another method of producing nuclear energy—not from nuclear *fission* (splitting an atom) but from nuclear *fusion* (the joining of atomic nuclei). The fuel for this is not uranium, but is taken from ordinary seawater, and therefore the supply is unlimited. However, this technology has not yet been refined to a level that would make it commercially useful, and it is unknown when a technological breakthrough will occur.

---

[130] Ibid.

[131] "Incredibly High Radiation Levels Discovered at Crippled Fukushima Plant," Fox News, Feb. 8, 2017, http://www.foxnews.com/science/2017/02/08/incredibly-high-radiation-levels-discovered-at-crippled-fukushima-plant.html.

[132] Rich, "New Quake Tests Resilience, and Faith in, Japan's Nuclear Plants."

[133] Lomborg, *The Skeptical Environmentalist*, 129, citing Craig et al., *Resources of the Earth*, 181.

7. Solar Energy. Prices for both wind energy and solar energy have dropped considerably in recent years, but they are still not widely used, primarily because they are not yet economically competitive with coal, natural gas, oil, hydroelectric power, and nuclear energy. For 2015, solar energy produced less than 1 percent of the electricity in the United States,[134] but recent developments with solar cells have made solar energy more affordable, and its use will likely increase. Solar energy is unreliable in many areas that are frequently overcast, and of course it cannot be generated at night, which means that solar energy must be used at once (during the daytime)—unless battery technology improves so that the energy that is generated can be stored in large batteries. Solar energy is by far the greatest source of energy available, however. The amount of solar energy falling on the earth *each year* is equal to about 7,000 times our present global energy consumption.[135]

8. Conclusion. There is an incredible abundance of energy available for human use on the earth. Once again, this is not surprising. God put us on the earth to develop and use his resources wisely, so it is reasonable that he provided us with multiple sources of energy that we could discover in order to perform the tasks he gives us to do.

Therefore, it makes no sense for people to think that there is some virtue in always seeking to "reduce our energy use." Energy is what replaces human physical work (such as walking everywhere and carrying everything by hand rather than driving) and animal work (such as plowing fields or grinding grain with oxen), and energy is what makes economic development possible. When we *increase our use of the energy sources* that God has provided—by using a truck to carry goods hundreds of miles, flying by airplane to a distant city, driving quickly to a meeting 30 miles away, using a tractor to plow a field, turning on the dishwasher or washing machine, or living comfortably in a climate-controlled house in hot summers and cold winters—*we decrease the time we have to spend* on travel or menial labor. Therefore, we *increase the amount of work* we can get done (and thus increase human prosperity), and we *increase human freedom* because we have more time left to devote to more creative and valuable tasks of our own choosing. Using all available energy sources is a wonderful ability that God has provided the human race, and it marks us as far above the animal kingdom, as creatures truly made in the image of God. We should never carelessly *waste* energy, but we should also never be afraid to *use* energy for productive, useful purposes. We should be thankful for the ability of the human race to *use* more and more of the energy resources that God has placed in the world for our benefit and enjoyment.

If people want to reduce their energy use *to save money* (turning off unused lights, for example), that of course is wise. But if reducing energy use means that you will get

---

[134] "Electricity Explained: Electricity in the United States," U.S. Energy Information Administration, May 10, 2017, http://www.eia.gov/energyexplained/index.cfm?page=electricity_in_the_united_states.

[135] Lomborg, *The Skeptical Environmentalist*, 133.

less work done, that you will have to work longer in order to accomplish the same task (washing a large load of dishes by hand when you have a dishwasher), or that you will reduce your quality of life (shivering in a cold, dark room on a winter night to "save energy" when you could easily afford to heat and light your home), then I see no virtue in it. You are just wasting your time and your human energy when God gives you the wonderful gift of abundant nonhuman energy.

We should also realize that during the past hundred years the most significant resource of all has been *human ingenuity* in discovering and developing new sources of energy and finding more efficient ways to carry out various tasks. It is certainly reasonable to expect that human ingenuity will continue to develop new sources of energy and better ways of using energy in the future. Just as past predictions have vastly underestimated the amount of energy remaining on the earth,[136] it is likely that present predictions are also too pessimistic, and as further technological progress is made we will realize that the amount of energy that remains will last even beyond the current predictions.

D. GLOBAL WARMING AND CARBON FUELS

Before we can decide what to do about the question of "global warming" (more recently called "climate change"), it is necessary to understand some of the scientific factors related to the earth's temperature and carbon dioxide.[137]

1. The Earth's Atmosphere Causes Both Warming and Cooling Influences on the Earth.

a. Warming Effects from the Atmosphere: We are able to live on the earth only because the earth's atmosphere retains some heat from the sun. If the earth had no atmosphere, its average surface temperature would be about 0° Fahrenheit—too cold to sustain most life. Yet because there is an atmosphere surrounding the earth, average worldwide temperatures tend to hover around 59°F—but much colder near the poles and much warmer near the equator, cooler at night and warmer in the daytime, cooler in winter and warmer in summer, and so forth. Over most of the earth most of the time, the temperature is well-suited to human life and to plant and animal life of various kinds.

The way the atmosphere warms the earth is often called the "greenhouse effect"— that is, some of the atmosphere retains the heat energy that comes from the sun. Not all of the atmosphere does this, however. Nitrogen (which makes up 78 percent

---

[136] Ibid., 118–36.

[137] I wish to thank my friend E. Calvin Beisner, a leading expert on Christian stewardship of the environment, for writing the initial draft of this section on global warming. However, I have rewritten some portions and added others, and the final responsibility for the content of this section is mine. Beisner is the founder and national spokesman of the Cornwall Alliance for the Stewardship of Creation, http://cornwallalliance.org/.

of the atmosphere) and oxygen (which makes up 21 percent) don't retain the sun's heat. That means 99 percent of the atmosphere does not retain heat or function as a "greenhouse gas."

In the remaining 1 percent of the atmosphere there are fourteen other elements or compounds. Most of these do not have a warming effect either, and these constitute 0.55 percent of the atmosphere. The ones that do have a warming effect are called "greenhouse gases," and they constitute about 0.45 percent of the atmosphere—just under one-half of 1 percent. Water vapor makes up 89 percent of these greenhouse gases, or about 0.4 percent of the entire atmosphere (higher at the earth's surface, but diminishing with altitude). The other greenhouse gases are carbon dioxide (about 0.04 percent of the total atmosphere), methane (about 0.00018 percent), nitrous oxide (about 0.00003 percent), ozone (less than 0.000007 percent), and miscellaneous trace gases. All of these other greenhouse gases (apart from water) total less than 0.05 percent of the atmosphere.

Water vapor, then, is the most important greenhouse gas. It is responsible for about 80 percent of the total warming effect of the entire atmosphere.

Another 15 percent of the warming effect of the atmosphere comes from clouds. (Clouds are not considered to be water vapor because they are actually made of water droplets—liquid, not gas.) But the effect of clouds is complex, because some clouds warm the earth and some cool it. *Low-altitude clouds* mostly *cool* the earth by reflecting the sun's heat back into space before it reaches the surface. (We notice this when a cloud passes in front of the sun on a hot day, and the shade from the cloud leaves us feeling cooler than we did in the direct sunlight.) By contrast, *high-altitude cirrus clouds* tend to *warm* the earth because they retain more heat than they reflect back into space.

For convenience, most scientists just combine water vapor (80 percent of warming) and the net warming effect of warming clouds (15 percent) to say that water causes about 95 percent of "greenhouse warming." The remaining approximately 5 percent of greenhouse warming comes from carbon dioxide (about 3.6 percent), methane (about 0.36 percent), nitrous oxide (about 0.95 percent), and miscellaneous gases including ozone (about 0.072 percent).[138]

How exactly do these greenhouse gases warm the earth? Despite the metaphor, they don't work at all like a greenhouse, because in a greenhouse the glass walls and roof warm the interior by trapping warm air inside—the glass keeps the air that is warmed by incoming sunlight from rising and blowing away. But greenhouse gases don't keep

---

[138] Data on the composition of the entire atmosphere are readily available in standard sources, but precise amounts vary slightly from source to source, the main variations being in percentage of carbon dioxide, which has risen over recent years, so it is lower in older sources and higher in newer ones. The percentages stated here reflect those in *Fundamentals of Physical Geography*, 2nd ed., chap. 7, "Introduction to the Atmosphere," Table 7a–1, online at www.physicalgeography.net/fundamentals/7a.html, updated in the case of carbon dioxide from 360 to 400 ppmv (parts per million by volume). See also John Houghton, *Global Warming: The Complete Briefing*, 3rd ed. (Cambridge, UK: Cambridge University Press, 2004), 16. Greenhouse gas composition data are from "Water Vapor Rules the Greenhouse System," Geocraft, www.geocraft.com/WV Fossils/greenhouse_data.html, Table 4a.

warm air from rising and blowing away. Instead, they *absorb heat energy* and then *radiate* it outward.

Here is what happens: First, energy comes from the sun mostly in the form of light. When that light hits the surface of the earth, the earth absorbs the light energy and then radiates it back in the form of *infrared energy*—what we call heat. If you hold your hand above a rock that has been sitting in the sun, you can feel the heat energy radiating from the warm rock. Now, if you hold your hand above the warm rock for some time, your hand also becomes warm. Your hand has absorbed heat energy from the warm rock, and now your hand is also radiating heat energy. If you put your hand to your cheek, you will feel the heat energy radiating from your hand.

In a similar way, greenhouse gases *absorb* infrared energy (heat) and then, having absorbed it, radiate it outward. Some of it goes up into space, thus cooling the earth by moving the heat away, but some of it radiates back down to the earth's surface and warms the earth.

It is good for us that not all of the sun's energy stays at the earth's surface, or we would cook. It is also good that not all of it bounces back into space, or we would freeze. As Christians, we can be thankful that by God's wise design such infrared absorption by greenhouse gases ensures that the earth retains the right balance of incoming and outgoing energy.

b. Cooling Effects from the Atmosphere: Without the "greenhouse effect," earth's average surface temperature would be about 0°F, and with it, the temperature is about 59°F. But if the atmosphere didn't have any *balancing factors to modify* the greenhouse effect, there would be another problem: the total warming by the greenhouse gases in earth's atmosphere would cause the average surface temperature to be about 140°F—much too hot for most life.[139] So why is the average temperature only 59°F? Because in addition to *warming influences*, the atmosphere also has some *cooling influences* that moderate the greenhouse effect. These fall in the general category of climate "feedbacks" (changes in the atmosphere that are caused by other changes in the atmosphere, which then lead to other changes).

These cooling feedbacks, the net effect of which is to bring cooling influences to the earth, include such things as evaporation, precipitation (rain, snow, dew, and sleet), convection (upward movement of warm air), and advection (sideways movement of air—that is, wind). Together we call these "weather," and they include everything from gentle breezes to hurricanes, from the violent downdrafts of wind shear to the massive, twisting updrafts of tornados, and much more.

There are other feedbacks, too, literally thousands of them, the most important being changes in cloudiness (which can warm or cool the earth), expansion or con-

---

[139] Earth's temperatures with no greenhouse effect, with greenhouse effect but no feedbacks, and with feedbacks are from S. Manabe and R. F. Strickler, "Thermal equilibrium of the atmosphere with a convective adjustment," *Journal of the Atmospheric Sciences* 21 (1964): 361–65.

traction of ice (ice reflects solar energy away from earth and so cools it), expansion or contraction of forests, grasslands, and deserts, and changes in how rapidly plants take up or give off water through their leaves.

Complete understanding of all these feedbacks is not crucial to the global warming debate. What *is* important is knowing whether, on balance, they *increase* or *decrease* the warming caused by greenhouse gases, and by how much. There is a very simple way to answer that question. As noted above, with no greenhouse effect, average surface temperature would be about 0°F; with it but without feedbacks, it would be about 140°F; but with the greenhouse effect plus feedbacks, it is about 59°F. It seems evident, then, that on balance these feedbacks decrease the greenhouse effect. By how much? Well, 59 is about 42 percent of 140, which implies that *the feedbacks considered as a whole eliminate about 58 percent of "greenhouse warming."*

c. Then What Is the Controversy about Carbon Dioxide? The global warming controversy has focused mostly on carbon dioxide (CO_2). The people who warn about the dangers of global warming argue that human activities are causing the concentration of greenhouse gases—primarily carbon dioxide, secondarily methane, and to a much lesser extent ozone and chlorofluorocarbons—to increase, and that this increased concentration could warm the earth enough to cause significant, perhaps even catastrophic, harm to people and ecosystems.

The biggest culprit, according to this position, is carbon dioxide, which is responsible for about 3.6 percent of the total greenhouse effect.

What is carbon dioxide? It is a colorless and nearly odorless gas. It is used to produce the bubbles (carbonation) in carbonated beverages. In a frozen form, it is known as dry ice. When an organic material such as wood burns in a fire, it releases carbon dioxide. Carbon dioxide is also released when coal, gasoline, or natural gas (methane) burns. Therefore, much energy production releases carbon dioxide into the atmosphere.

In our bodies, carbon dioxide plays an important role in regulating our blood flow and rate of breathing. When we breathe, we inhale oxygen and exhale carbon dioxide in every breath. In fact, all insects, animals, and people emit carbon dioxide when they exhale. Indeed, carbon dioxide makes up about 40,000 ppmv (parts per million by volume) of what we exhale—roughly 100 times the current concentration in the atmosphere! In addition, oceans, volcanoes, and other natural sources emit it. Carbon dioxide is part of the natural way God has made the world to function.

Carbon dioxide is also crucial for plants, because they need it for photosynthesis, a process that uses light energy to produce various compounds necessary for a plant to live and grow. During photosynthesis, plants absorb carbon dioxide and release oxygen. Thus, in a wonderful cycle of nature that has been designed by God, animals and people continually use up oxygen and release carbon dioxide for plants to use, and then plants use up that carbon dioxide and release oxygen for people and animals to use. *Carbon dioxide is thus essential to all the major life systems on the earth.* We should not think of carbon dioxide as a pollutant, but as an essential part of God's wise arrangement of life on earth.

Many atmospheric scientists believe the concentration of carbon dioxide in the atmosphere has risen from about 280 to about 400 ppmv, or from about 0.028 percent to 0.040 percent, since preindustrial times (before about 1750).[140] Where did this increase in carbon dioxide come from? Primarily, so goes the theory, from the burning of carbon-based ("fossil") fuels: coal, oil, and natural gas. (Although there are some reasons to question whether atmospheric carbon dioxide has increased that much, and how much of the increase is due to the burning of fossil fuels, answering those questions isn't crucial to our discussion.[141])

What is the effect of increasing carbon dioxide from 280 to 400 ppmv? We can compare that with some estimates of what the temperature effect would be from actually *doubling* carbon dioxide concentration. Doubling carbon dioxide concentration, according to different estimates, would raise earth's average surface temperature, *before feedbacks,* by about 1.8° to 2.16°F.[142] Frankly, that is a relatively small increase in average temperature that does not scare anybody with knowledge of climatology.

What causes some people to fear much greater warming is *the belief that climate feedbacks magnify this warming.* So that belief is built into the computer models that predict global temperatures for many decades into the future. All of the computer models used by the United Nations' Intergovernmental Panel on Climate Change (IPCC) assume that climate feedbacks magnify the warming that comes from greenhouse gases.

It is important to understand here that the fears of future global warming rest on the *predictions of computer models* that give different weights to different factors. The computer programs are not infallible, but will predict whatever is required by the data and formulas fed to them; different data and different formulas, based on different assumptions, will give different predictions.

Therefore, the fears of future global warming rest on *hypotheses* represented by computer models, *not on empirical observations* of the real world. These models, *by assuming various feedbacks that add to the greenhouse effect,* predict that warming from *doubled* carbon dioxide since preindustrial time would result in an increase of from 3.5°F to a midrange estimate of 5.4°F to a high estimate of about 7°F over the whole period.

---

[140] Roy W. Spencer et al., "The Science of Global Warming," in *A Renewed Call to Truth, Prudence, and Protection of the Poor: An Evangelical Examination of the Theology, Science, and Economics of Global Warming* (Burke, VA: The Cornwall Alliance for the Stewardship of Creation, 2009), 27, www.cornwallalliance.org /docs/a-renewed-call-to-truth-prudence-and-protection-of-the-poor.pdf.

[141] Our discussion here will focus on whether it is important to reduce carbon dioxide emissions to reduce global warming. If carbon dioxide has risen less than widely thought since preindustrial times, or if nonfossil fuel sources have contributed more than widely thought, then the case in favor of reducing emissions becomes weaker.

[142] The low figure (1.8°F) is from Spencer et al., "The Science of Global Warming," 27. The high figure (2.16°F) is from Martin L. Weitzman, "On Modeling and Interpreting the Economics of Catastrophic Climate Change," *The Review of Economics and Statistics* 91, no. 1 (February 2009): 1–19, https://dash.harvard .edu/bitstream/handle/1/3693423/weitzman_onmodeling.pdf?sequence=2.

(Global average temperature has already risen by about 1.8°F since the Industrial Revolution, leaving about another 1.7°F to 3.6°F to 5.2°F yet to come, if the models are right.)

Then some *other* computer formulas (other models) have used the *upper range* of this first set of predictions and have gone on to predict serious harm from such warming. (But remember: model results that predict the future are not *evidence*; they are merely *hypotheses*. Only empirical observations about events that have already occurred are evidence.)

Other scientists, however, have raised significant objections to this entire process of making predictions. They point out that climate feedbacks are climate feedbacks, and *there is no reason to think the feedbacks will act differently on man-made "greenhouse gases" than on natural ones.* Since the feedbacks currently eliminate about 58 percent of the warming effect of natural greenhouse gases, it stands to reason that they will do the same to the warming effect of man-made ones.

These scientists say that the proponents of global warming *have the feedbacks backward in their computer formulas.* Appealing to what we already know *by observing the real world,* they say that although some feedbacks tend to warm the earth, *the combined feedback effect* must be negative—very strongly negative—and therefore the feedbacks will tend to have an overall *cooling* effect on additional man-made greenhouse gases.

The result? I mentioned above that *if we did not factor in climate feedbacks,* doubling the amount of carbon dioxide from preindustrial times, so that it would increase from 280 to 560 ppmv, would have a net result of raising earth's average surface temperature by about 1.8°F to 2.16°F. But if we expect climate feedbacks to *subtract* from warming, we can expect they will lower the warming effects by about 58 percent to between 0.76°F to 0.9°F—in other words, actually *doubling* the amount of carbon dioxide from preindustrial times would lead to a total "global warming" of less than 1°F.[143]

An increase in average world temperature of less than 1°F is not dangerous. In fact, in general, such slight warming would be beneficial, especially to agriculture. This is because most of the warming would occur in higher latitudes (near the poles), in the winter, and at night, not in already hot places at hot times. The result would be *longer growing seasons in cooler climates, less crop damage* from frost, and *fewer deadly cold snaps* (which tend to kill about 10 times as many people per day as heat waves). Longer growing seasons would make food more abundant and therefore more affordable, a great benefit to the world's poor.[144]

---

[143] Spencer et al., "The Science of Global Warming," 26–27, figures recalculated using Weitzman's higher (2.16°F) estimate of warming from doubled carbon dioxide. If Spencer's lower estimate (1.8°F) for warming from doubled carbon dioxide is correct, the estimates from the Intergovernmental Panel on Climate Change of the United Nations (IPCC) require much greater added increments—94 percent, 200 percent, or 289 percent—and the net warming after feedbacks is about 0.76°F instead of 0.9°F.

[144] See William Nordhaus, *A Question of Balance: Weighing the Options on Global Warming Policies* (New Haven, CT: Yale University Press, 2008); Bjørn Lomborg, *Cool It: The Skeptical Environmentalist's Guide to*

This way of arguing that there is low climate sensitivity to increases in greenhouse gases—from the big picture of what we know about the effect of overall feedbacks on "greenhouse warming"—isn't the only way to reach this conclusion. More narrowly focused studies have reached it also. For example, Richard Lindzen and Yong-Sang Choi conclude their analysis from the Earth Radiation Budget Experiment by saying that "ERBE data appear to demonstrate a climate sensitivity of about 0.5°C [0.9°F]."[145] So this study also shows less warming than 1°F.

Therefore, should we believe the predictions of dangerous results that will come from increased temperatures? I don't think so, for three reasons: (1) actual empirical data about the effects of climate feedbacks (from observing events that have already occurred) show that they do not multiply the warming effect of greenhouse gases as the global warming computer programs (that predict future events) would have us believe (as explained above); (2) some principles from the Bible make me doubt these global warming predictions; and (3) some important facts from other scientific evidence make me doubt them as well. The material that follows will explain reasons 2 and 3.

2. The Bible's Teaching about the Earth.

a. Did God Design a Fragile Earth or a Resilient One? The predictions of global warming, most prominently from the UN's IPCC, require us to believe that the net climate feedback response to "greenhouse warming" is very strongly positive (or warming) and therefore that dangerous global warming is likely.

But should Christians believe that God has actually designed the earth to be this fragile in response to human activity? This would be analogous to believing that an architect designed a building so that if someone leaned against one wall, the building's structural feedbacks would so magnify the stress of that person's weight that the building would collapse! No one would consider such an architectural design "very good." Yet Genesis 1:31 tells us, "God saw everything that he had made, and behold, it was *very good*."

Global Warming (New York: Knopf, 2007); Robert Mendelsohn, *Climate Change and Agriculture: An Economic Analysis of Global Impacts, Adaptation and Distributional Effects*, New Horizons in Environmental Economics (Northampton, MA: Edward Elgar, 2009).

[145] Richard S. Lindzen and Yong-Sang Choi, in "On the Determination of Climate Feedbacks from ERBE [Earth Radiation Budget Experiment] Data," *Geophysical Research Letters* 36 (Aug. 26, 2009): 5, http://www.leif.org/EOS/2009GL039628-pip.pdf. Stephen E. Schwartz, in "Heat Capacity, Time Constant, and Sensitivity of Earth's Climate System," *Journal of Geophysical Research* 112 (Nov. 2, 2007): 17, www.ecd.bnl.gov/steve/pubs/HeatCapacity.pdf, concludes that climate sensitivity could range from 1.08°F to 2.88°F (1.1 ± 0.5 K). Richard S. Lindzen, Ming-Dah Chou, and Arthur Y. Hou, in "Does the Earth Have an Adaptive Infrared Iris?" *Bulletin of the American Meteorological Society* 82, no. 3 (March 2001): 417–32, www-eaps.mit.edu/faculty/lindzen/adinfriris.pdf, provide evidence that clouds respond to surface warming by allowing more heat to escape into space, thus acting as a strong negative feedback. Roy W. Spencer, William D. Braswell, John R. Christy, and Justin Hnilo, in "Cloud and Radiation Budget Changes Associated with Tropical Intraseasonal Oscillations," *Geophysical Research Letters* 34 (Aug. 9, 2007), http://ruby.fgcu.edu/courses/twimberley/EnviroPhilo/Intraseasonal.pdf, each reached similar conclusions using different methods.

Since the earth is the product of the infinitely wise and omniscient God, and is sustained by his providence, it seems more reasonable to think that the fundamental mechanisms of the earth's climate system are robust, self-regulating, and self-correcting—that they are designed to operate somewhat like a thermostat, cooling the planet when it begins to warm and warming it when it begins to cool.

There is long-term evidence that the earth has warmed and cooled cyclically throughout its history, which is consistent with the expectation of self-correcting temperature mechanisms in the earth and its atmosphere. Fred Singer and Dennis Avery put it this way in the prologue to their book *Unstoppable Global Warming— Every 1,500 Years*:

> The history of Earth's climate is a story of constant change. Through at least the last million years, a moderate 1,500-year warm-cold cycle has been superimposed over the longer, stronger Ice Ages and warm interglacials. In the North Atlantic, the temperature changes about 4°C [7.2°F] from peak to trough during these "Dansgaard-Oeschger cycles."[146]

b. God's Promises to Maintain Stability in Seasons and Oceans: Some other biblical teachings point in this same direction, reflecting details of God's protection of the earth's seasons and oceans. For example, after the great flood of Noah's day, God promised, "While the earth remains, seedtime and harvest, cold and heat, summer and winter, day and night, shall not cease" (Gen. 8:22). This suggests God's commitment to sustain the various cycles on which human, animal, and plant life on earth depend until the final judgment.

Also following the flood, God promised, "Never again shall there be a flood to destroy the earth" (Gen. 9:11; see also v. 15). While that by itself doesn't rule out the possibility of a significant sea level increase (probably the most feared effect predicted from global warming), it does indicate that God controls the sea level. Psalm 104:9 likewise says, regarding the waters of the seas, "*You set a boundary that they may not pass, so that they might not again cover the earth.*" And in Jeremiah, God says:

> I placed the sand as the boundary for the sea,
>   a perpetual barrier that it cannot pass;
> though the waves toss, they cannot prevail;
>   though they roar, they cannot pass over it. (Jer. 5:22)

c. People Displease God When They Fail to Acknowledge His Control of the Weather: In the next verses after Jeremiah 5:22, God rebuked Israel for not acknowledging that he controls the weather:

---

[146] S. Fred Singer and Dennis T. Avery, *Unstoppable Global Warming—Every 1,500 Years*, 2nd ed. (Lanham, MD: Rowman & Littlefield, 2008). (By quoting this material I do not mean to imply any particular viewpoint about the age of the earth. See Grudem, *Systematic Theology*, chap. 15.)

> But this people has a stubborn and rebellious heart;
>> they have turned aside and gone away.
> They do not say in their hearts,
>> "Let us fear the LORD our God,
> who gives the rain in its season,
>> the autumn rain and the spring rain,
> and keeps for us
>> the weeks appointed for the harvest."
> Your iniquities have turned these away [that is, the rains and the harvest
>> seasons],
>> and your sins have kept good from you. (Jer. 5:23–25)

Here Jeremiah rebuked the Jewish people for fearing an out-of-control climate pattern (no rain) that would destroy the earth, but they "do not say in their hearts, 'Let us fear the LORD our God, who gives the rain in its season.'" If there is a parallel regarding people's fear of an out-of-control climate today, this passage suggests that the underlying cause of fears of dangerous global warming might not be science but rejection of trust in God. Has his sovereign control of the earth's weather actually been nullified by human activity? Do we really believe that he controlled the weather in Old Testament times but does not control it today? And did he really create an earth that is so fragile that his sovereignty over nature would be destroyed by human beings discovering and using such portable and powerful sources of energy as coal, oil, and natural gas? And would such nullification of God's control of the weather be so concealed from ordinary people that no one could see it except a small group of highly trained scientists using complex computer predictions?

In the New Testament, the apostle Paul speaks similarly of people who "suppress the truth" about God's existence and attributes (Rom. 1:18). These people "did not honor him as God or give thanks to him, but they became futile in their thinking, and their foolish hearts were darkened" (v. 21). Surely that includes people who did not honor God or give thanks to him for the brilliant order and structure of his creation, and so, "claiming to be wise, they became fools" (v. 22) and "exchanged the truth about God for a lie and worshiped and served the creature rather than the Creator" (v. 25). Such a description could be applied to much of the environmentalist movement, for whom "Mother Earth" rather than the one true God is their highest object of devotion.

Many other passages of Scripture affirm God's control over the earth's weather (see Lev. 26:18–20; Deut. 28:12, 23–24; 2 Sam. 21:1; 1 Kings 17–18; Job 37:9–13; Ps. 107:23–38; 148:8; Amos 4:7–8; Jonah 1:4–16; Matt. 8:24–27).

d. God Did Not Design the Earth So That We Would Destroy It by Obeying His Commands: God originally commanded Adam and Eve (and by implication all mankind):

> Be fruitful and multiply and *fill the earth and subdue it*, and have dominion over the fish of the sea and over the birds of the heavens and over every living thing that moves on the earth. (Gen. 1:28)

This command seems inconsistent with a belief in dangerous, man-made global warming. Do we think God set up the earth *so that we would destroy it by obeying God's commands to develop the earth's resources and use them for our benefit?* Do we really think that he set up the earth so that when we burn wood to warm ourselves or cook food; when we burn gasoline to drive to work, school, or church; when we use diesel fuel to transport food, clothing, and household goods from farm or factory to market; or when we burn oil, coal, or natural gas to produce electricity to cook with, to heat or cool our homes, or to provide light that *the more we do these morally right things*, the more we will *destroy the earth?*

Such questions played a significant role in my thinking when I first began to read about the supposed threat of man-made global warming. Again and again, I reflected that I do not think God made the earth to work that way—so that we would inevitably destroy it by obeying his commands. Rather, I think that God put wood on the earth, and coal, oil, and natural gas in the earth, so that we could have abundant, easily transportable sources of fuel for use in various applications.

Of course, all of these resources can be used foolishly and dangerously—instead of building a safe fire to cook food, someone can carelessly start a forest fire. And carelessly built coal-burning plants and factories can spew out soot and chemicals, polluting the air. I am not advocating reckless, dangerous use of fossil fuels.

But that is not what global warming alarmists are complaining about. They are also warning against *clean and safe uses of all these fuels*. They are saying that there is *no* safe use of these fuels, because even if they are burned with 100 percent pollution-free flames, *they will still necessarily emit carbon dioxide* because that is an unavoidable by-product of combustion. They object not to the *abuse* of fossil fuels that leads to the pollution or destruction of the environment, but to their very *use*. They want to take away from human beings the best, most convenient, and cheapest energy sources we currently have.

Do we really think God created the earth so that its climate system would careen off into catastrophe if carbon dioxide rose from 0.028 percent to 0.056 percent of the atmosphere (that is, from 28 to 56 *thousandths of 1 percent* of the atmosphere)? That is what global warming alarmists imply. Or do we think, by contrast, that God has set up the earth so that it is immensely resilient and will be able to adapt and be useful for human life under a wide variety of conditions?

My own conclusion is that God has placed in the earth and its atmosphere a number of self-regulating, self-correcting mechanisms by which it can manage its own temperature. One example of this is the "global iris" effect of clouds over the oceans.[147] When the surface becomes warmer, high-level clouds diminish, permitting more heat to escape

---

[147] Lindzen et al., "Does the Earth Have an Adaptive Infrared Iris?" 417–32.

into space. When the surface cools, high-level clouds increase, retaining more heat. Christian environmental theologian E. Calvin Beisner writes:

> [Evidence that clouds regulate earth's temperature should lead] Christians to praise God for the way in which the Earth, like the human body, is "fearfully and wonderfully made." In some senses this planet, like the eye, may be fragile. But it may also, by God's wise design, be more resilient than many fearful environmentalists may imagine.[148]

High-level cloud variation certainly looks like a self-correcting mechanism that God built into the earth's system to keep temperatures relatively stable. Who knows whether there are other systems like this that we have not yet discovered, in which a heating factor triggers a balancing cooling factor, and vice versa? It would not be surprising, since the earth's long-term temperature averages tend to go back and forth between warming trends followed by cooling trends followed by warming trends.

e. Global Warming Alarmists Remove Our Motivation to Thank God for His Wonderful Gifts of Affordable, Abundant Energy Resources: The Bible praises God for his creation of the earth:

> And God saw everything that he had made, and behold, *it was very good.* (Gen. 1:31)

> The earth is the LORD's and the fullness thereof,
>   the world and those who dwell therein. (Ps. 24:1)

> *Everything created by God is good*, and nothing is to be rejected if it is received with thanksgiving. (1 Tim. 4:4)

These passages and others tell us that we should give thanks and praise to God for the excellence of the earth that he created. He wants us to develop and use the earth's resources because "he formed it to be inhabited!" (Isa. 45:18). We should use the resources he placed in the earth with thanksgiving to him.

Those who warn that we face dangerous global warming tell us we should feel guilty about using wood, coal, oil, and natural gas to produce energy. Rather than allowing us to use God's good gifts with thanksgiving, they load us with guilt for doing so. Therefore, they rob people of the motivation to thank God for the wonderful things he has given.

3. What Does the Scientific Evidence Say about Global Warming? One response to the arguments above is to say that "scientists agree" that human emissions of greenhouse

---

[148] E. Calvin Beisner, *What Is the Most Important Environmental Task Facing American Christians Today?* Mt. Nebo Papers, No. 1 (Washington: Institute for Religion and Democracy, 2008), 23, in sidebar, "Climate Science and Doxology," http://ecalvinbeisner.com/freearticles/MtNebo.pdf.

gases are causing global warming that could do great harm. For example, that is the message trumpeted endlessly by former Vice President Al Gore, whose video documentary *An Inconvenient Truth* has been shown in thousands of schools and even won an Academy Award, and who with the IPCC received the Nobel Peace Prize for warning the world of impending climate disaster.

But is the scientific consensus really that clear? No, it certainly is not. Every attempt to prove the existence of such a scientific consensus has failed.

a. Scientific Opinion Is Strongly Divided about the Danger of Global Warming:

(1) Many Scientists Reject the Predictions of Catastrophic Global Warming: It is likely that more scientists who have actually studied the issue—possibly many times more— *reject* than embrace the idea of man-made global warming dangerous enough to justify spending literally $1 trillion to $2 trillion per year worldwide (the cost of implementing the 2015 Paris climate treaty) to reduce it by a mere 0.306°F in the year 2100[149] when that money could yield far greater benefits if spent on activities that directly improve human well-being, such as providing electricity, purified drinking water, sewage sanitation, improved nutrition, and infectious disease control. According to one list compiled by a U.S. Senate panel, *more than 700 scientists* have published their rejections of the whole or significant parts of the global warming hypothesis.[150] According to another list, *more than 31,000 degreed scientists*, including over 9,000 with PhDs, have signed the "Global Warming Petition," saying:

> There is *no convincing scientific evidence* that human release of carbon dioxide, methane, or other greenhouse gases is causing or will, in the foreseeable future, cause catastrophic heating of the Earth's atmosphere and disruption of the Earth's climate. Moreover, there is substantial scientific evidence that increases in atmospheric carbon dioxide produce many beneficial effects upon the natural plant and animal environments of the Earth.[151]

The Wall Street Journal reported that a number of well-known scientists, including Nobel Prize winners, have dissented from the idea that man-made global warming constitutes a significant danger:

---

[149] Bjørn Lomborg, "Impact of Current Climate Proposals," *Global Policy* 7, no. 1 (February 2016): 109–18, http://onlinelibrary.wiley.com/doi/10.1111/1758-5899.12295/full.

[150] U.S. Senate Committee on Environment and Public Works, "U.S. Senate Minority Report Update: Over 700 International Scientists Dissent over Man-Made Global Warming Claims," Dec. 11, 2008, https://www .epw.senate.gov/public/index.cfm/press-releases-all?ID=2674e64f-802a-23ad-490b-bd9faf4dcdb7.

[151] "Global Warming Petition Project," Oregon Institute of Science and Medicine, http://petition project.org/, emphasis added. The site includes complete lists of signers and, at http://petitionproject.org /qualifications_of_signers.php, summarizes the numbers from various specialties relevant to the debate.

Ivar Giaever, a 1973 physics Nobel Laureate . . . resigned last week from the American Physical Society in protest over the group's insistence that evidence of man-made global warming is "incontrovertible."

In an email to the society, Mr. Giaever—who works at Rensselaer Polytechnic Institute—wrote that "The claim (how can you measure the average temperature of the whole earth for a whole year?) is that the temperature has changed from ~288.0 to ~288.8 degree Kelvin in about 150 years, which (if true) means to me . . . that the temperature has been amazingly stable, and both human health and happiness have definitely improved in this 'warming' period." Mr. Giaever was an American Physical Society fellow, an honor bestowed on "only half of one percent" of the members, according to a spokesman.

He follows in the footsteps of University of California at Santa Barbara Emeritus Professor of Physics Harold Lewis, a former APS fellow who resigned in 2010, calling global warming "the greatest and most successful pseudoscientific fraud I have seen in my long life as a physicist."

Other dissenters include Stanford University physicist and Nobelist Robert B. Laughlin, deceased green revolution icon and Nobelist Norman Borlaug, Princeton physicist William Happer and World Federation of Scientists President Antonino Zichichi.

Our point is not that all of these men agree on climate change, much less mankind's contribution to it, only that to one degree or another they maintain an open mind about warming or what to do about it. One of the least savory traits of climate-change advocates is how they've tried to bully anyone who keeps an open mind. This is true of many political projects, but it is or ought to be anathema to the scientific method.[152]

Other prominent scientists have publicly dissented from the idea that human use of fossil fuels is causing dangerous levels of global warming. They include Judith Curry, professor emeritus and former chair of the School of Earth and Atmospheric Sciences at the Georgia Institute of Technology;[153] Richard Lindzen, Alfred P. Sloan Professor of Meteorology emeritus at MIT;[154] Roy Spencer, principal research scientist at the Univer-

---

[152] "'High School Physics': Another Nobel Laureate Breaks from the Climate Change Pack," *The Wall Street Journal*, Sept. 18, 2011, https://www.wsj.com/articles/SB10001424053111903927204576572842778437276.

[153] "Full Committee Hearing—Climate Science: Assumptions, Policy Implications, and the Scientific Method," Committee on Science, Space, and Technology, March 29, 2017, https://science.house.gov /legislation/hearings/full-committee-hearing-climate-science-assumptions-policy-implications-and. (Notice in the following list of names how many of the highly-accomplished scientists who publicly disagree with the alarms about global warming have "emeritus" status, indicating that they are largely retired and no longer need to fear that their academic careers will be derailed by speaking truthfully and publicly about the scientific facts related to global warming.)

[154] Marc Morano, "MIT Climate Scientist Dr. Richard Lindzen on 'Hottest Year' Claim: 'Why Lend Credibility to This Dishonesty?'" Climate Depot, Jan. 20, 2016, http://www.climatedepot.com/2016/01/20/mit -climate-scientist-dr-richard-lindzen-on-hottest-year-claim-why-lend-credibility-to-this-dishonesty/.

sity of Alabama in Huntsville, and the U.S. Science Team leader for the Advanced Microwave Scanning Radiometer on NASA's Aqua satellite;[155] John Christy, distinguished professor of atmospheric science and director of the Earth System Science Center at the University of Alabama in Huntsville;[156] and William Happer, Princeton professor of physics, emeritus.[157]

Those scientists who claim that man-caused global warming is a danger have so politicized the atmosphere of climate science that any dissent is met with name-calling and *ad hominem* attacks rather than serious argument. Curry, in testimony before a committee of the U.S. House of Representatives on March 29, 2017, said this:

> The politicization of climate science has contaminated academic climate research and the institutions that support climate research, so that individual scientists and institutions have become activists and advocates for emissions reductions policies. Scientists with a perspective that is not consistent with the consensus are at best marginalized (difficult to obtain funding and get papers published by "gatekeeping" journal editors) or at worst ostracized by labels of "denier" or "heretic." . . .
>
> When the IPCC consensus is challenged . . . these activist scientists and organizations call the questioners "deniers" and claim "war on science." These activist scientists seem less concerned with the integrity of the scientific process than they are about their privileged position and influence in the public debate about climate and energy policy. They do not argue or debate the science—rather, they denigrate scientists who disagree with them. These activist scientists and organizations are perverting the political process and attempting to inoculate climate science from scrutiny—this is the real war on science.[158]

An important resource regarding scientists who disagree about the danger of man-caused global warming is Lawrence Solomon's book *The Deniers: The World-Renowned Scientists Who Stood Up against Global Warming Hysteria, Political Persecution, and*

[155] "About," http://www.drroyspencer.com/about/.

[156] Michael Wines, "Though Scorned by Colleagues, a Climate-Change Skeptic is Unbowed," *The New York Times*, July 15, 2014, https://www.nytimes.com/2014/07/16/us/skeptic-of-climate-change-john-christy-finds-himself-a-target-of-suspicion.html.

[157] Chris Mooney, "Trump Meets with Princeton Physicist Who Says Global Warming Is Good for Us," *The Washington Post*, Jan. 13, 2017, https://www.washingtonpost.com/news/energy-environment/wp/2017/01/13/trump-meets-with-princeton-physicist-who-says-global-warming-is-good-for-us/?utm_term=.e09700f36212, and William Happer, "Global Warming Models Are Wrong Again: The Observed Response of the Climate to more CO2 Is Not in Good Agreement with Predictions," *The Wall Street Journal*, March 27, 2012, https://www.wsj.com/articles/SB10001424052702304636404577291352882984274.

[158] Judith A. Curry, "Statement to the Committee on Science, Space and Technology of the United States House of Representatives," March 29, 2017, https://science.house.gov/sites/republicans.science.house.gov/files/documents/HHRG-115-SY-WState-JCurry-20170329.pdf.

Fraud.[159] He shows that those who reject the global warming alarms include many of the world's top experts in their fields.

(2) The Scientific Literature Is Divided on the Global Warming Hypothesis: Contrary to common claims, the published scientific literature is divided about this issue. A 2003 review, by history professor Naomi Oreskes, of scientific abstracts that purported to demonstrate scientific agreement about global warming was shown to have been badly flawed, and a reexamination of the database found no such consensus.[160] Then a study of the same database covering up to 2007 actually showed a significant shift away from what had earlier (and mistakenly) been claimed as the consensus. As Klaus-Martin Schulte put it in the last of those studies:

> Though Oreskes said that 75% of the papers in her sample endorsed the consensus, fewer than half now endorse it. Only 6% do so explicitly. Only one paper refers to "catastrophic" climate change, but without offering evidence. There appears to be little evidence in the learned journals to justify the climate-change alarm that now harms [medical] patients [whose well-being was adversely affected by fear of global warming].[161]

Since then, similar studies claiming overwhelming consensus have been similarly flawed.[162] For example, a 2009 survey-based study reported that 97.4 percent of scientists "who listed climate science as their area of expertise and . . . have published more than 50% of their recent peer-reviewed papers on the subject of climate change" agreed that "When compared with pre-1800s levels . . . mean global temperatures have generally risen" and "human activity is a significant contributing factor in changing mean global temperatures."[163] A 2010 literature review-based study claimed that "97–98% of the climate researchers most actively publishing in the field" believe that "anthropogenic greenhouse gases have been responsible for 'most' of the 'unequivo-

[159] Lawrence Solomon, *The Deniers: The World-Renowned Scientists Who Stood Up against Global Warming Hysteria, Political Persecution, and Fraud* (Minneapolis: Richard Vigilante Books, 2008), 207–8.

[160] Naomi Oreskes, "The Scientific Consensus on Climate Change," *Science* 306, no. 5702 (Dec. 3, 2004): 1686, www.sciencemag.org/cgi/content/full/306/5702/1686. This was disputed by Benny J. Peiser's letter to *Science*, Jan. 4, 2005, submission ID: 56001, http://www.cfact.org/2005/05/04/dr-benny-peisers-letter-to-science-magazine-and-the-story-of-its-rejection/. The surveys were reported in Dennis Bray and Hans von Storch, *The Perspectives of Climate Scientists on Global Climate Change* (Geesthacht, Germany: GKSS–Forschungszentrum Geesthacht, 2007), http://www.academia.edu/4840717/Perspectives_of_climate_scientists_on_global_climate_change.

[161] Klaus-Martin Schulte, "Scientific Consensus on Climate Change?" *Energy and Environment* 19, no. 2 (July 2008): 281–86, http://scienceandpublicpolicy.org/images/stories/papers/reprint/schulte_two_colmun_fomat.pdf.

[162] Joseph Bast and Roy Spencer, "The Myth of the Climate Change '97%,'" *The Wall Street Journal*, May 27, 2014, http://blog.heartland.org/2014/06/the-myth-of-the-climate-change-97/.

[163] Peter T. Doran and Maggie Kendall Zimmerman, "Examining the Scientific Consensus on Climate Change," *Eos* 90, no. 3 (Jan. 20, 2009): 22–23, http://www.ucsusa.org/sites/default/files/legacy/testfolder/aa-migration-to-be-deleted/assets-delete-me/documents-delete-me/ssi-delete-me/ssi/DoranEOS09.pdf.

cal' warming."[164] A 2013 review of abstracts in refereed literature claimed that "97.1% endorsed the consensus position that humans are causing global warming."[165]

Yet all of these studies define the claim too broadly. Virtually all who challenge the claim that humans are causing *dangerous* global warming would *agree* with the 2009 study's claims that the global mean temperature has risen since 1800 and that human activity has probably contributed significantly. Indeed, one could believe that humans cause only 1 percent of global warming or 100 percent of it and still be counted among the 97 percent. A new review of the same abstracts covered by the 2013 study found only "0.3% endorsement of the standard definition of consensus: that *most* warming since 1950 is anthropogenic."[166] Perhaps most relevant to the question of what, if anything, should be done in response to human-induced warming, none of the studies addressed whether scientists believed human-induced warming would cause more harm than benefit—let alone whether it is likely to be dangerous enough to justify policies costing a trillion dollars or more a year to reduce it.

More rigorous studies weaken the claim of overwhelming scientific consensus that human activity has caused *most* of the warming *and* that it is dangerous—the two conditions needed to justify expensive policies to mitigate it. One 2016 study reported that 87 percent of scientists surveyed agreed that "most of recent or near future climate change is, or will be, the result of anthropogenic causes" and that 86 percent agreed that "climate change poses a very serious and dangerous threat to humanity."[167] But the study did not distinguish whether respondents considered specifically human-induced warming, exclusive of natural warming, a "threat to humanity." A 2016 survey of members of the American Meteorological Society found that about "67% think humans are causing at least 61% of the warming" while 14 percent think human and natural causes are roughly equal, 12 percent think nature causes most of the warming, and 6 percent say they don't know the balance of human and natural causes.[168] But as climatologist Curry pointed out, only 53 percent of AMS members who received the survey responded, and the notoriety of the lead author and the research center that organized the survey as

[164] William R. L. Anderegg et al., "Expert Credibility in Climate Change," *Proceedings of the National Academy of Sciences* 107, no. 27 (July 6, 2010): 12107–9, http://www.pnas.org/content/107/27/12107.full.pdf.

[165] John Cook et al., "Quantifying the Consensus on Anthropogenic Global Warming in the Scientific Literature," *Environmental Research Letters* 8 (2013): 024024, http://iopscience.iop.org/article/10.1088/1748 -9326/8/2/024024/pdf.

[166] David R. Legates et al., "Climate Consensus and 'Misinformation': A Rejoinder to Agnotology, Scientific Consensus, and the Teaching and Learning of Climate Change," *Science & Education* 24, no. 3 (April 2015): 299–318, emphasis added, http://link.springer.com/article/10.1007/s11191-013-9647-9.

[167] D. Bray and H. von Storch, *The Bray and von Storch 5th International Survey of Climate Scientists 2015/2016* (Geesthacht, Germany: Helmholtz-Zentrum Geesthacht, 2016), 10 and 98, https://www.hzg .de/imperia/md/content/hzg/zentrale_einrichtungen/bibliothek/berichte/hzg_reports_2016/hzg_report _2016_2.pdf.

[168] Edward Maibach et al., "A 2016 National Survey of American Meteorological Society Member Views on Climate Change: Initial Findings," George Mason University Center for Climate Change Communication, March 2016, https://gmuchss.az1.qualtrics.com/CP/File.php?F=F_cRR9lW0HjZaiVV3.

entities that demand criminal prosecution of "climate skeptics"[169] could have resulted in an unrepresentative sample skewed toward alarm.[170]

Scientific consensus that arises spontaneously is a legitimate way to depict the views of scientists on a given issue. But the value of a "consensus" intentionally manufactured over time, particularly by government or government-academic partnerships supported by billions of dollars in tax funding, is dubious. And when some government officials and influential scientists call for criminal prosecution of those who reject the alleged consensus, self-preservation is likely to mask dissent, skewing all survey results toward alarm and so invalidating them.

That consensus on climate change has been officially manufactured[171] and that dissenters have been threatened with professional persecution[172] and criminal prosecution is historically certain. Sen. Sheldon Whitehouse (D-RI) actually called for investigations and potential prosecution of "climate skeptics" under the Racketeer Influenced and Corrupt Organizations Act.[173] Congressman Raul Grijalva (D-AZ) wrote to seven universities employing "climate skeptic" scientists demanding information regarding their funding.[174] Sens. Edward Markey (D-MA), Barbara Boxer (D-CA), and Whitehouse wrote letters to one hundred corporations, think tanks, and other organizations, demanding information about funding of "climate skeptic" research and publishing.[175] Attorneys general from seventeen states formed AGs United for Clean Power to investigate and potentially prosecute "climate skeptics."[176] Former U.S. Attorney General

---

[169] "Letter to President Obama, Attorney General Loretta Lynch, and OSTP Director Holdren," Sept. 1, 2015, http://web.archive.org/web/20150920110942/http://www.iges.org/letter/LetterPresidentAG.pdf.

[170] Judith Curry, "New AMS Members Survey on Climate Change," Climate Etc., March 24, 2016, https://judithcurry.com/2016/03/24/new-ams-members-survey-on-climate-change/.

[171] J. A. Curry and P. J. Webster, "Climate Change: No Consensus on Consensus," *CAB Reviews* 8, no. 001, (September 2013), https://www.researchgate.net/publication/274619323_Climate_change_no_consensus _on_consensus; full text at https://curryja.files.wordpress.com/2012/10/consensus-paper-revised-final.doc.

[172] Will Happer discusses two (Patrick Michaels and David Legates) of many examples of academics' suffering persecution in Appendix 3 of the National Association of Scholars' *Sustainability: Higher Education's New Fundamentalism*, March 25, 2015, https://www.nas.org/images/documents/NAS-Sustainability_Appendix_3.pdf.

[173] Sen. Sheldon Whitehouse (D-RI), "The Fossil-Fuel Industry's Campaign to Mislead the American People," *The Washington Post*, May 29, 2015, https://www.washingtonpost.com/opinions/the-fossil -fuel-industrys-campaign-to-mislead-the-american-people/2015/05/29/04a2c448-0574-11e5-8bda -c7b4e9a8f7ac_story.html.

[174] Brad Johnson, "Rep. Grijalva Asks for Conflict-of-Interest Disclosures from GOP's Go-To Climate Science Witnesses," *Hill Heat*, Feb. 24, 2015, http://www.hillheat.com/articles/2015/02/24/rep-grijalva-asks-for -conflict-of-interest-disclosures-from-gops-go-to-climate-science-witnesses. A sample letter is at https:// wattsupwiththat.com/2015/02/26/anatomy-of-a-climate-witch-hunt-letter-from-u-s-representative-raul -m-grijalva/.

[175] "Markey, Boxer, Whitehouse Query Fossil Fuel Companies, Climate Denial Organizations on Science Funding," Ed Markey, United States Senator for Massachusetts, Feb. 25, 2015, https://www.markey.senate.gov /news/press-releases/markey-boxer-whitehouse-query-fossil-fuel-companies-climate-denial-organizations -on-science-funding.

[176] "Al Gore and New York Attorney General Eric Schneiderman Launch AGs United for Clean Power Coalition," The Climate Reality Project, March 30, 2016, https://www.climaterealityproject.org/blog/al-gore -and-new-york-attorney-general-eric-schneiderman-launch-ags-united-clean-power-coalition.

Loretta Lynch told Congress she was considering civil action against "climate skeptics" and had referred the matter to the FBI.[177]

It is impossible to know how many dissenters censor themselves to avoid such persecution—and possible prosecution—but their number is not likely to be small. We can be grateful that thirteen other state attorneys general rebuked AGs United for Clean Power in a letter of their own, accusing its members of bias, of aligning themselves with competitors of their industry targets, and of undermining freedom of speech.[178] Nevertheless, widespread threats, from those in positions to make good on them, of criminal, civil, or professional punishment of those who dissent from the alleged consensus on global warming make all claims of consensus prone to exaggeration.

(3) Consensus Is a Political Value, Not a Scientific Value: As Thomas Kuhn so famously pointed out in *The Structure of Scientific Revolutions*, great advances in science, often involving major paradigm shifts, occur when small minorities patiently—and often in the face of withering opposition—point out anomalies in the data and inadequacies in the reigning explanatory paradigms until their number and weight become so large as to require a wholesale paradigm shift, and what once was a minority view becomes a new majority view. Many theories once embraced by all or almost all scientists have been overturned by new evidence. This is why consensus, though a political value, is not a scientific value. If you want to know who won an election, count votes. If you want to know how much warming comes from adding a given amount of carbon dioxide to the atmosphere, don't count votes; instead, do the hard work of constructing a hypothesis based on your understanding of the myriad geological, oceanographic, atmospheric, and even solar and cosmic systems involved, then make a prediction based on the hypothesis, and finally compare the prediction with observation. As Nobel Prize-winning physicist Richard Feynman famously put it:

> In general we look for a new law by the following process. First we guess it. Then we compute the consequences of the guess to see what would be implied if this law that we guessed is right. Then we compare the result of the computation to nature, with experiment or experience, compare it directly with observation, to see if it works. If it disagrees with experiment it is wrong. In that simple statement is the key to science. It does not make any difference how beautiful your guess is. It does not make any difference how smart you are, who made the guess, or what his name is—if it disagrees with experiment it is wrong. That is all there is to it.[179]

---

[177] Melanie Arter, "AG Lynch: DOJ Has Discussed Whether to Pursue Civil Action Against Climate Change Deniers," CNS News, March 9, 2016, http://www.cnsnews.com/news/article/melanie-hunter/ag-lynch-doj -has-discussed-whether-pursue-legal-action-against-climate.

[178] Alabama Attorney General Luther Strange et al., letter to "AGs United for Clean Power," June 15, 2016, https://assets.documentcloud.org/documents/2862197/AG-Coalition-Resp-Letter-2016-06-15.pdf.

[179] Richard P. Feynman, *The Character of Physical Law* (New York: Modern Library, 1965), 156.

b. Global Average Temperature Measurements Undermine the Credibility of the Computer Models on Which Predictions of Dangerous Warming Rest: As Feynman explained, the normal process in scientific investigation is to propose a hypothesis and then test it by seeing if empirical data confirm or falsify it. What has happened with respect to global warming?

The hypothesis is that recent increases in atmospheric carbon dioxide should be causing a relatively rapid increase in global average temperature. To be specific, had the global average temperature over the period 1979–2016 conformed to the average predicted by the 102 CMIP-5[180] models (on which the IPCC, various national academies, and other researchers who generally believe in dangerous man-made warming rely), it should have risen, on average, by 0.389°F per decade, or a total of 1.44°F.

But according to our most reliable sources for the global average temperature—satellites[181]— there was *no statistically significant upward trend* from early 1997 through late 2015, a period of almost nineteen years,[182] and the measured rate of increase in 1979–2016 was only 0.223°F per decade, or a total of 0.83°F.[183] So even assuming that *all* the warming over the last 37 years was caused by human emissions of carbon dioxide and *none* by other factors, the models exaggerate carbon dioxide's warming effect by about three-fourths (74.4 percent). If some of the warming was natural—which cannot be ruled out and is likely, granted the earth's long-term recovery from the ice age that ended about 12,000 years ago and from the so-called Little Ice Age that ended in the early 19th century—then the exaggeration is greater.

Further, the decadal warming trend calculated from the satellite data 1979–2016 is itself probably misleadingly high. Why? Because an extraordinarily powerful El Niño[184]

---

[180] CMIP-5 stands for "Coupled Model Intercomparison Project Version 5," the state-of-the-art computer climate models.

[181] Satellite data are more reliable than surface measurements for several reasons. First, satellite measurements are randomly (and almost completely) distributed around the globe in longitude, latitude, and altitude, while surface instruments are far fewer, limited to land and sea surface, and distributed with a bias toward urban and other inhabited areas, which have their own localized warming (like the "urban heat island" effect, which may account for about half the apparent global warming; see Ross McKitrick and Patrick J. Michaels, "A Test of Corrections for Extraneous Signals in Gridded Surface Temperature Data," *Climate Research* 26 [2004]: 159–73, http://www.rossmckitrick.com/uploads/4/8/0/8/4808045/mckitrick-michaels-cr04.pdf). Second, satellite measurements are less subject to difference in instrumentation from station to station and year to year. Third, satellite measurements are less subject to improper instrument siting—a widespread problem even for the best-maintained surface stations in the world, those in the United States. See http://surfacestations.org/.

[182] Christopher Monckton, "The Pause Lengthens Again—Just in Time for Paris: No Global Warming at All for 18 Years 9 Months—a New Record," Climate Depot, Nov. 4, 2015, http://www.climatedepot.com/2015 /11/04/no-global-warming-at-all-for-18-years-9-months-a-new-record-the-pause-lengthens-again-just-in -time-for-un-summit-in-paris/.

[183] Email from John R. Christy to E. Calvin Beisner, Jan. 17, 2017. Christy is the distinguished professor of atmospheric science and director of the Earth System Science Center at the University of Alabama in Huntsville. With his research partner Dr. Roy W. Spencer he manages global temperature data collected by NASA satellites. Christy updates the data regularly at http://www.nsstc.uah.edu/data/msu/v6.0/tlt/uahncdc_lt_6.0.txt.

[184] El Niño is one phase of the El Niño Southern Oscillation, a cycle of above-average (the El Niño phase) and below-average (the La Niña phase) sea surface temperatures in the central and eastern tropi-

(like what made 1998 the warmest year in the satellite record) pushed the global average temperature upward starting in 2015.[185] It peaked in early 2016, then began declining slowly in response to La Niña.

Might the slower warming from 1997 to 2016 be explained by a deceleration in the rise of atmospheric carbon dioxide concentration? Theoretically, yes, but in fact the rate of carbon dioxide increase has risen slightly over the period.[186]

Atmospheric carbon dioxide concentration and the global average temperature correlate fairly well. Those who believe in dangerous man-made global warming tend to assume that this is because carbon dioxide drives temperature. While carbon dioxide does contribute somewhat (under 4 percent) to total warming from greenhouse gases—that is, carbon dioxide influences temperature—temperature also influences carbon dioxide. You can observe this easily yourself by noticing the difference between opening a hot can of carbonated soda and opening a cold one. The hot one fizzes a lot more. That is because cold water holds gases (like carbon dioxide) better than warm water. So as the oceans warm, they release carbon dioxide into the atmosphere, and as they cool, they absorb it back. So the correlation could be controlled more by changes in temperature than by changes in carbon dioxide.

How can we know which drives which? We must carefully examine the time sequence of changes in the global average temperature and atmospheric carbon dioxide concentration. Evidence from ice cores obtained in Greenland and Antarctica indicates that over very long periods temperature leads carbon dioxide by 200 to 1,000 years.[187] But might the time sequence have changed due to the rapid increase in carbon dioxide driven by fossil fuel use? Theoretically, yes, but empirical observation finds instead that over the very period when carbon dioxide should, according to the "consensus" theory, have had its most powerful effect on temperature, changes in temperature have preceded changes in carbon dioxide concentration by nine to 12 months.[188]

---

cal Pacific Ocean. El Niño warms the atmosphere over most of the earth, while La Niña cools it. See Michelle L'Heureux, "What Is the El Niño Southern Oscillation (ENSO) in a Nutshell?" May 5, 2014, https://www.climate.gov/news-features/blogs/enso/what-el-ni%C3%B1o%E2%80%93southern-oscillation-enso-nutshell.

[185] See E. Calvin Beisner, "Did the Pause End, or Did El Niño Interrupt It?" The Cornwall Alliance, Feb. 2, 2017, http://cornwallalliance.org/2017/02/did-the-pause-end-or-did-el-nino-interrupt-it/.

[186] Calculated from National Oceanic and Atmospheric Administration data at ftp://aftp.cmdl.noaa.gov/products/trends/co2/co2_mm_mlo.txt. The average decadal rate of increase from 1977 to 2017 was 0.000414 percent. For the decade ending in January 1997 it was 0.000338 percent; for the decade ending in January 2007 it was 0.000438 percent; and for the decade ending in January 2017 it was 0.000504 percent.

[187] H. Fischer et al., "Ice Core Records of Atmospheric CO_2 around the Last Three Glacial Terminations," *Science* 283 (1999): 1712–14, http://science.sciencemag.org/content/283/5408/1712. N. Caillon et al., "Timing of Atmospheric CO_2 and Antarctic Temperature Changes across Termination III," *Science* 299 (2003): 1728–31, http://scrippsscholars.ucsd.edu/jseveringhaus/content/timing-atmospheric-co2-and-antarctic-temperature-changes-across-termination-iii.

[188] O. Humlum, K. Stordahl, and J. Solheim, "The Phase Relation between Atmospheric Carbon Dioxide and Global Temperature," *Global and Planetary Change* 100 (2013): 51–69, http://www.sciencedirect.com/science/article/pii/S0921818112001658.

Finally, other factors seem better able to explain the changes that have been observed in global temperatures, especially changes in ocean currents and solar activity.[189]

c. Should the UN's Intergovernmental Panel on Climate Change (IPCC) Be Trusted to Have the Last Word? Many people refer to the IPCC as the world's most authoritative body on global warming and describe its pronouncements as those of "thousands of climate scientists." The IPCC certainly warns of dangerous global warming. But we need to understand just what the IPCC has said and what kind of organization it is.

The "Summary for Policymakers" that the IPCC publishes does not always accurately represent the detailed science in its Assessment Reports (which have been issued in 1992, 1995, 2001, 2007, and 2013). Instead, the Summary for Policymakers generally exaggerates the actual scientific conclusions. But because few journalists or politicians ever read the actual science, they tend to be unaware of this problem.[190]

In addition, we should not assume that the IPCC is an *objective* body of *objective* scientists not serving particular political agendas. On the contrary, the IPCC is *highly politicized*. Its charter called for it to study *human* influence on global temperature; consequently, it largely ignores *natural* influences. (And hundreds of staff workers now know that their jobs depend on continuing to find and publish evidence supporting the theory of dangerous man-made global warming, which makes for a built-in bias in their data.) The crucial chapter 9 of its 2007 Assessment Report, which assessed likely temperature change from human "greenhouse gas" emissions and on which all the rest of the report depends, relied heavily on the work of a small group of scientists prone to "group think" for lack of adequate interaction with others. Structural flaws seriously reduce the IPCC's credibility.[191]

Finally, the IPCC's authority was deeply undermined by a large number of scandals that surfaced in late 2009 and early 2010. These included particularly "Climategate" and discoveries that the IPCC had based some of its most frightening predictions on unsci-

---

[189] See David R. Legates and G. Cornelis van Kooten, *A Call to Truth, Prudence, and Protection of the Poor 2014: The Case against Harmful Climate Policies Gets Stronger* (Burke, VA: The Cornwall Alliance: 2014), 19–24, http://www.cornwallalliance.org/wp-content/uploads/2014/09/A-Call-to-Truth-Prudence-and-Protection-of-the-Poor-2014-The-Case-Against-Harmful-Climate-Policies-Gets-Stronger.pdf.

[190] Mark W. Hendrickson, "A Closer Look at the IPCC," Center for Vision and Values, Grove City College, May 22, 2009, www.visandvals.org/A_Closer_Look_at_the_IPCC.php.

[191] David Henderson, "Governments and Climate Change Issues: A Flawed Consensus," article can be read in "The Global Warming Debate: Science, Economics, and Policy," Proceedings of a Conference Sponsored by the American Institute for Economic Research, Nov. 2–3, 2007, 61, https://www.aier.org/sites/default/files/Files/Documents/Research/3220/EEB200805.pdf, and Ross McKitrick, "Response to David Henderson's 'Governments and Climate Change Issues,'" *American Institute of Economic Research Economic Education Bulletin* 48, no. 5 (May 2008): 83–104, http://ross.mckitrick.googlepages.com/McKitrick.final.pdf, both in *American Education Bulletin* XLVIII, no. 5 (May 2008); John McLean, *Prejudiced Authors, Prejudiced Findings: Did the UN Bias Its Attribution of "Global Warming" to Humankind?* (Washington: Science & Public Policy Institute, 2008), http://scienceandpublicpolicy.org/images/stories/papers/originals/McLean_IPCC_bias.pdf.

entific sources—such as news releases from environmental advocacy groups—while the actual scientific data refuted them.[192]

The term "Climategate" refers to the November 2009 leak, from the Climatic Research Unit at the University of East Anglia in England, of thousands of emails, computer codes, and other documents. These documents revealed that a core group of climate scientists at a wide range of agencies—the CRU, NASA's Goddard Institute for Space Studies, the National Oceanic and Atmospheric Administration, the National Center for Atmospheric Research, the National Climatic Data Center, the U.K. Meteorological Office, and others—on which the IPCC and national governments relied for data basic to global warming projections had committed serious scientific misconduct. Among the misdeeds were these:

- Fabricating, cherry-picking, suppressing, withholding, and destroying data related to historic and present temperatures
- Failing to keep proper research archives
- Using computer programs intentionally designed to exaggerate recent warming and minimize earlier climate variability (both warming and cooling) to create the appearance that recent warming was unprecedented when it was not
- Refusing to share data and source codes with other scholars on request, as required both by standard scientific practice and, in some cases, by the written standards of journals in which their work was published
- Intimidating dissenting scientists to deter them from publishing research contrary to belief in dangerous man-made global warming
- Corrupting the peer review process to prevent publication of dissenting research
- Attempting to have journal editors who published dissenting research removed from their jobs
- Boycotting journals that published dissenting papers
- Refusing to turn over information subject to freedom of information laws in both the United States and the United Kingdom

This is simply not the way researchers act when they are confident that the actual facts are overwhelmingly on their side. The misconduct was so serious and systemic that *it undercut the credibility of all historic and contemporary temperature data* published in the IPCC's Assessment Reports.[193] But these sets of data were the basis for the claims of

---

[192] Mark Landsbaum, "What to Say to a Global Warming Alarmist," *Orange County Register*, Feb. 12, 2010, www.ocregister.com/articles/-234092—.html, provides a helpful list and summary of such IPCC errors.

[193] Four thorough analyses of "Climategate" are John Costella, *The Climategate Emails*, SPPI Reprint Series, June 8, 2010, from the Washington, D.C.-based Science & Public Policy Institute, http://science andpublicpolicy.org/images/stories/papers/reprint/climategate_analysis.pdf; Steven Mosher and Thomas Fuller, *Climategate: The CRUtape Letters* (Charleston, SC: CreateSpace/Amazon.com, 2010); Brian Suss-

the global warming alarmists! In short, the IPCC's authority on global warming is poor. It is doubtful that it will be able to regain the credibility it had in the scientific world before Climategate. It was using distorted, incorrect data.

A top climate-change official at the United Nations, Yvo de Boer, announced his resignation February 19, 2010. *The Washington Times* reported, "The bureaucrat's departure is no surprise because his pseudo-scientific global warming religion was proved to be a hoax on his watch."[194] In the same article, the *Times* reported the following remarkable disclosure:

> Joseph D'Aleo, the first director of meteorology and co-founder of the Weather Channel, and Anthony Watts, a meteorologist and founder of SurfaceStations.org, are well-known and well-respected scientists. On Jan. 29, they released a startling study showing that starting in 1990, the National Oceanic and Atmospheric Administration (NOAA) began systematically eliminating climate-measuring stations in cooler locations around the world. Eliminating stations that tended to record cooler temperatures drove up the average measured temperature. The stations eliminated were in higher latitudes and altitudes, inland areas away from the sea and more rural locations. The drop in the number of weather stations was dramatic, declining from more than 6,000 stations to fewer than 1,500.[195]

Lawrence Solomon, author of *The Deniers*, had already written that the Climategate scandal made the historical temperature data suspect and that carbon dioxide's "contribution to global warming remains approximately nil."[196] In the years since Climategate, similar data-manipulation scandals have unfolded, including serious questions about the reliability of data "homogenization" techniques used by IPCC-related scientists that consistently raise more recent temperatures while lowering more remote ones, causing the appearance of more rapid warming. Data homogenization is legitimate in principle, since different instruments, in different locations, sited and operated differently, aren't directly comparable, but if errors were random, one would expect corrections of recent and more remote data to raise and lower them about equally often, resulting in no change in the apparent trend.[197]

---

man, *Climategate: A Meteorologist Exposes the Global Warming Scam* (Torrance, CA: WND Books, 2010); and A. W. Montford, *The Hockey Stick Illusion: Climategate and the Corruption of Science* (London: Stacey International, 2010).

[194] "Editorial: More Errors in Temperature Data," *The Washington Times*, Feb. 18, 2010, www.washington times.com/news/2010/feb/18/more-errors-in-temperature-data/?feat=home_editorials.

[195] Ibid.

[196] Lawrence Solomon, "The Ozone Hole Did It," *Financial Post*, Jan. 9, 2010, http://www.odlt.org/dcd/docs /solomon_The%20ozone%20hole%20did%20it.pdf.

[197] For an introduction to and examples of suspect global temperature data homogenization practices, see "On Sunday, Goulburn Got Colder Than the BOM Thought Was Possible (and a Raw Data Record Was 'Adjusted')," JoNova, July 5, 2017, http://joannenova.com.au/tag/adjustments-to-data/, which focuses on

d. Are Glaciers Melting and Sea Levels Rising? For years now, the public has been bombarded with messages that man-made global warming is causing disastrous consequences, such as melting glaciers, endangered polar bears, and rising sea levels. What should we think of these claims?

If we did see glaciers melting and sea levels rising, these might well be due to other factors, such as variations in sun activity, variations in ocean currents, and ordinary long-term weather cycles, and not due to changes in carbon dioxide levels (as explained above). However, none of the claimed disasters is well supported by evidence. Here are some examples:

(1) Glaciers and Ice Caps: Glaciers have been shrinking slowly since the end of the last ice age (perhaps around 12,000 years ago)—during more than 99 percent of which time people did not emit enough greenhouse gas to have any effect on the global average temperature. So the mere fact of their shrinking is nothing new and is not evidence of human-induced warming. During the Holocene era (approximately the last 12,000 years of earth's history), "glaciers around the world have fluctuated broadly in concert with changing climate, at times shrinking to positions and volumes smaller than today," and "mountain glaciers . . . show a wide variety of responses to local climate variation, and do not respond to global temperature change in a simple, uniform way. Tropical mountain glaciers in both South America and Africa have retreated in the past 100 years because of reduced precipitation and increased solar radiation . . . [and] the data on global glacial history and ice mass balance do not support the claims made by the IPCC that CO_2 emissions are causing most glaciers today to retreat and melt."[198]

As for ice caps in the Arctic and Antarctic, short-term observations do not prove much of anything. Ice melts in warmer seasons and freezes in cooler seasons every year, and there are warmer years and colder years, so a video of a polar bear jumping off melting Arctic ice does not prove a long-term trend. Polar bears have jumped off the ice and caught fish for centuries. In addition, it is now clear that, far from dwindling, polar bear populations have grown during the period of alleged man-made global warming and shrinking Arctic sea ice.[199]

Over the relatively short period in which human-induced warming is supposed to

---

practices in Australia. Blogger Paul Homewood has published many critiques of data homogenization, such as "Five Years of GISS Cheating," *Not a Lot of People Know That*, Dec. 17, 2016, https://notalotofpeopleknow that.wordpress.com/2016/12/17/five-years-of-giss-cheating/.

[198] Donald J. Easterbrook, Clifford D. Ollier, and Robert M. Carter, "Observations: The Cryosphere," chap. 5 of *Climate Change Reconsidered II: Physical Science*, ed. Craig D. Idso, Robert M. Carter, and S. Fred Singer (Chicago: Heartland Institute, 2013), 629–712, at 629–30, https://www.heartland.org/_template -assets/documents/CCR/CCR-II/CCR-II-Full.pdf.

[199] Paul Homewood, "As Polar Bear Numbers Continue to Increase, GWPF Calls for Re-assessment of Endangered Species Status," *Not a Lot of People Know That*, Feb. 27, 2017, https://notalotofpeopleknowthat .wordpress.com/2017/02/27/as-polar-bear-numbers-continue-to-increase-gwpf-calls-for-re-assessment-of -endangered-species-status/.

have prevailed, there is no clear trend in the area or mass of *global* sea ice.[200] "Global sea-ice cover remains similar in area to that at the start of satellite observations in 1979, with ice shrinkage in the Arctic Ocean since then being offset by growth around Antarctica."[201] Arctic sea ice has decreased, while Antarctic sea ice has expanded. It appears that fluctuations in sea ice area and mass are driven at least in part by the same El Niño Southern Oscillation that we have already discussed as having driven the exceptionally warm years of 1998 and 2016.[202] It is difficult to know what else might be driving sea ice cycles. One recent theory, yet to be deeply tested, is that Arctic and Antarctic sea (and land) ice oscillate in extent (expanding in the Antarctic while contracting in the Arctic, and vice versa), acting as a thermostat to keep earth's temperature within certain bounds.[203]

(2) Sea Levels: Al Gore, in his book *Earth in the Balance*, dramatically claimed, "Many residents of low-lying Pacific Island nations have already had to evacuate their homes because of rising seas"—a claim illustrated by a photo of Tuvalu (an island nation of 12,000 people between Hawaii and Australia).[204]

But as Marlo Lewis pointed out in his devastating 154-page critique of Gore's book, "Tide gauge records show that sea levels at Tuvalu *fell* during the latter half of the 20th century. Altimetry data from the Topex-Poseidon satellite show that Tuvalu sea levels fell even during the 1990s."[205] Indeed, no one has had to evacuate any Pacific island nations because of rising sea levels. Gore's claim was just misleading.

In the film *An Inconvenient Truth* Gore claimed that melting ice from West Antarctica and Greenland would cause a 20-foot increase in sea levels worldwide. Although he did not specify *when* this would happen, the context makes it clear that he intends the prediction to prompt action *now* to protect our children or perhaps our grandchildren. Clearly he had the remainder of this century in mind.

Yet the IPCC, even with its questionable assumption of high warming from rising greenhouse gases, estimated instead that melt from those two locations would add only about *2.5 inches*—not 20 feet!—to sea levels over the next 100 years.[206] In fact, sea levels, which have been slowly rising ever since the end of the last ice age, rose only about 6.3

---

[200] For graphic depictions of regularly updated data, see the "Sea Ice Page," WUWT, https://wattsupwith that.com/reference-pages/sea-ice-page/.

[201] Easterbrook et al., "Observations: The Cryosphere," 629–712, at 629.

[202] Craig Lindberg, "A Relationship between Sea Ice Anomalies, SSTs, and the ENSO?" WUWT, Feb. 13, 2014, https://wattsupwiththat.com/2014/02/13/a-relationship-between-sea-ice-anomalies-ssts-and-the-enso/.

[203] The theory is that of Herman A. Pope, who explains it at his website, http://www.popesclimatetheory .com/.

[204] Al Gore, *Earth in the Balance: Ecology and the Human Spirit* (New York: Rodale, 2006), 186.

[205] Marlo Lewis Jr., *Al Gore's Science Fiction: A Skeptic's Guide to An Inconvenient Truth*, Congressional Briefing Paper (Washington: Competitive Enterprise Institute, n.d.), 88, http://cei.org/pdf/5820.pdf. See also Cliff Ollier, "Sea Level in the Southwest Pacific is Stable," *New Concepts in Global Tectonics Newsletter* 51 (June 2009), http://nzclimatescience.net/images/PDFs/paperncgtsealevl.pdf.

[206] Christopher Monckton, *35 Inconvenient Truths: The Errors of Al Gore's Movie* (Washington: Science and Public Policy Institute, 2007), 4. http://scienceandpublicpolicy.org/images/stories/press_releases/monckton -response-to-gore-errors.pdf.

inches in the entire 20th century—and the *rate* of increase *declined* in the latter half of the century.[207] While the rate of sea level rise cycles up and down, it appears likely to remain at about 0.08 inch per year, or about 8 inches per century.[208]

Gore's movie was judged by a British court to have so many and such serious errors that it could no longer be shown in British government schools without an accompanying list and refutation of its errors. Otherwise, said the judge, it would violate an act of Parliament prohibiting political indoctrination of children.[209]

e. Is Global Warming Altering the Weather? Has the supposedly warming earth caused more frequent or intense *severe weather*? No.[210] The most common claim—that hurricane frequency and strength have risen with recent global warming—not only has been refuted empirically but also abandoned by the scientist who most strongly promoted it.[211] An attempt by climatologist Michael Mann (author of the discredited "hockey stick" graph that eliminated the Medieval Warm Period and the Little Ice Age to make twentieth-century warming appear extraordinary) to show an increase in hurricanes in recent years brought a devastating rebuttal by Chris Landsea, one of the world's leading hurricane experts.[212]

What about *droughts and floods*? Are they growing more frequent and intense? Even if they were, that alone would not prove that increases in carbon dioxide were to blame. But in fact, droughts and floods are not increasing in frequency or intensity.[213]

4. The Benefits That Come from Increased Carbon Dioxide in the Atmosphere. We should not ignore a completely different aspect of the discussion. Carbon dioxide's

---

[207] S. J. Holgate, "On the Decadal Rates of Sea Level Change during the Twentieth Century," *Geophysical Research Letters* 34 (2007), cited in Craig Idso and S. Fred Singer, *Climate Change Reconsidered: 2009 Report of the Nongovernmental International Panel on Climate Change* (NIPCC) (Chicago: Heartland Institute, 2009), 186–87, http://f1a.fa0.myftpupload.com/climate-change-reconsidered-2009-nipcc-report/.

[208] Willem de Lange and Robert M. Carter, "Observations: The Hydrosphere and Ocean," chap. 6 of *Climate Change Reconsidered II*, 713–808, at 753, https://www.heartland.org/_template-assets/documents/CCR/CCR-II/CCR-II-Full.pdf.

[209] Monckton, *35 Inconvenient Truths*, 3. See also William Lee Adams, "British Court: Gore Film 'Political,'" *Time*, Oct. 12, 2007, www.time.com/time/world/article/0,8599,1670882,00.html.

[210] Idso and Singer, *Climate Change Reconsidered*, 281–360; Randall S. Cerveny, "Severe Weather, Natural Disasters, and Global Change," in *Shattered Consensus: The True State of Global Warming*, ed. Patrick J. Michaels (Lanham, MD: Rowman & Littlefield, 2005), 106–20; Patrick J. Michaels, *Meltdown: The Predictable Distortion of Global Warming by Scientists, Politicians, and the Media* (Washington: Cato Institute, 2004), 111–61.

[211] National Oceanic and Atmospheric Administration, "NOAA Attributes Recent Increase in Hurricane Activity to Naturally Occurring Multi-Decadal Climate Variability," Nov. 29, 2005, http://zfacts.com/metaPage/lib/NOAA-2005-11-Hurricane-Story-184.pdf, Eric Berger, "Hurricane Expert Reconsiders Global Warming's Impact," *Houston Chronicle*, April 12, 2008, www.chron.com/disp/story.mpl/tech/news/5693436.html; Kerry Emanuel, Ragoth Sundararajan, and John Williams, "Hurricanes and Global Warming: Results from Downscaling IPCC AR4 Simulations," *Bulletin of the American Meteorological Society* 89, no. 3 (March 2008): 347–67, http://journals.ametsoc.org/doi/pdf/10.1175/BAMS-89-3-347.

[212] Chris Landsea, untitled letter in response to Michael Mann and coauthors, http://icecap.us/images/uploads/LetterMann.pdf.

[213] Idso and Singer, *Climate Change Reconsidered*, 281–309.

effect on *the global average temperature* is most likely insignificant and benign, as I argued above. But its effect on *plant life*—and therefore on all other life, which depends on plant life—is large and *overwhelmingly beneficial.*

Hundreds and hundreds of peer-reviewed scientific studies have demonstrated that increased atmospheric carbon dioxide leads to enhanced plant growth. Indeed, on average, doubled carbon dioxide increases plant growth efficiency by about 35 percent. With enhanced carbon dioxide, plants grow better, whether they are subjected to higher or lower temperatures, or to drier or wetter soil. Consequently, their geographical range expands, and so does that of the various animals that depend on them. The plants also become more resistant to diseases and pests.[214]

Earth's atmospheric carbon dioxide level is now very low compared with many past geologic periods—periods during which its plant and animal life thrived. The IPCC and other global warming alarmists tend to hide this fact by referring to carbon dioxide's increase only since preindustrial times. As mentioned before, we can see the great variation by comparing earlier periods with our current concentration of 385 ppmv. Many scientists believe the concentration was 270 ppmv in preindustrial times.[215]

But what about much earlier periods? One study says that early in the Paleozoic era (540 million to 250 million years ago[216] [mya], according to time scales used in modern geological studies), carbon dioxide climbed from about 5,000 to 7,000 ppmv and then fell back again, then fell in fits and starts to about 3,000 ppmv late in the Silurian period (440–415 mya), rose to about 4,000 in the first half of the Devonian period (415–360 mya), fell to around 400 in the Carboniferous (360–300 mya) and Permian (300–250 mya) periods, rose again to about 2,000 in the Triassic period (250–200 mya), fell stepwise to about 1,300 by the middle of the Jurassic period (200–145 mya), rose for a while in that period to about 2,800, and then began a long decline through the Cretaceous (145–65 mya) and Tertiary (65–3 mya) periods, reaching around 200 to 300 in the Quaternary period (3 mya to present).

Did these massive changes in carbon dioxide concentrations result in massive temperature changes? Contrary to the view that carbon dioxide drives temperature, throughout geologic history there has been no clear correlation between the two. Sometimes they rose together, sometimes they both fell, and sometimes they went in opposite directions.[217]

---

[214] The Center for the Study of Carbon Dioxide and Global Change, www.co2science.org, maintains an enormous and growing database of published scientific studies on the subject. A review of the findings is in Idso and Singer, *Climate Change Reconsidered*, 361–578.

[215] Spencer et al., "The Science of Global Warming," 27, www.cornwallalliance.org/docs/a-renewed-call-to-truth-prudence-and-protection-of-the-poor.pdf.

[216] See above, p. 1141, note 153, about the age of the earth.

[217] Robert A. Berner and Zavareth Kothavala, "Geocarb III: A Revised Model of Atmospheric CO2 over Phanerozoic Time," *American Journal of Science* 301 (2001): 182–204, summarized in Ian Wishart, *Air Con: The Seriously Inconvenient Truth about Global Warming* (North Shore, NZ: Howling at the Moon Publishing, 2009), 33–36.

What is clear is that the periods of higher carbon dioxide have also been periods of *much more prolific plant growth*. As Ian Plimer puts it:

> The CO_2 content of air has hardly ever been as low as today and ecosystems suffer because of this. Early in the Earth's history, the CO_2 content of air was tens to hundreds of times higher than today and, over time, this CO_2 has been stored as carbon compounds in rocks, oil, gas, coal and carbonate rocks.[218]

The release of carbon dioxide now, by our burning of fossil fuels, is restoring some of it to the atmosphere and greatly benefitting life on earth. It appears to be causing deserts to green, and it has contributed significantly to increasing crop yields since 1950, making food more abundant and less expensive, and therefore reducing the percentage of the human population experiencing hunger and starvation.

Sherwood Idso, one of the world's foremost researchers on the subject, says, "We appear to be experiencing the initial stages of what could truly be called a *rebirth of the biosphere*, the beginnings of a biological rejuvenation that is without precedent in all of human history."[219] For this reason, intentionally forcing people to reduce carbon dioxide emissions would actually do enormous harm, not only to human economies but also to the whole biosphere.

5. The Unacceptable Loss of Human Freedom That Would Come with Government Control of Energy Use. A neglected factor in this discussion is how much we think that governments should control our lives. The controversy over global warming is to a very large degree a controversy over human liberty versus government control.[220] The liberal politicians who continually seek more government control do so because they think that enlightened governing officials can run people's lives better than they can run them themselves. Such people will eagerly flock in large groups to the global warming crusade because it appears to be a wonderful mechanism by which government can control more people's lives.

Regulating people's use of energy is an incredibly effective way of increasing the control of central governments over people's lives. If the government can dictate how far you drive your car, how much you heat or cool your home, how often you use electric lights, computers, or TVs, how much energy your factory can use, and how much jet fuel you can have to fly an airplane, then it can control most of the society.

---

[218] Ian Plimer, *Heaven and Earth: Global Warming, the Missing Science* (Lanham, MD: Taylor Trade Publishing, 2009), 411.

[219] Sherwood B. Idso, *CO2 and the Biosphere: The Incredible Legacy of the Industrial Revolution* (St. Paul, MN: University of Minnesota Department of Soil, Water and Climate, 1995). The Center for the Study of Carbon Dioxide and Global Change offers two excellent video documentaries on the benefits of increased carbon dioxide: *The Greening of Planet Earth* and *The Greening of Planet Earth Continues*, www.co2science.org.

[220] For a discussion of the need for governments to protect a significant amount of human freedom, see Grudem, *Politics—According to the Bible*, 91–95.

Václav Klaus, president of the Czech Republic, said that in his opinion the alarm about global warming and the campaign to reduce carbon dioxide provide the greatest threat to human liberty that has come to the earth since communism. He wrote in the *Financial Times* that "global warming hysteria has become a prime example of the truth versus propaganda problem." He continued:

> As someone who lived under communism for most of his life, I feel obliged to say that I see the biggest threat to freedom, democracy, the market economy and prosperity now in ambitious environmentalism, not in communism. This ideology wants to replace the free and spontaneous evolution of mankind by a sort of central (now global) planning.
>
> The environmentalists ask for immediate political action because they do not believe in the long-term positive impact of economic growth and ignore both the technological progress that future generations will undoubtedly enjoy, and the proven fact that the higher the wealth of society, the higher is the quality of the environment. They are Malthusian pessimists.[221]

This statement is significant because Klaus lived through many years of communism in the former Czechoslovakia. He is also a trained economist.

6. The Unacceptable Costs of Reducing Our Use of Carbon Fuels. Global warming alarmists want the world to drastically reduce the use of fossil fuels to cut carbon dioxide emissions. But the best economic analyses show that trying to reduce fossil fuel use would cause far more harm than good.[222] Why? Because abundant, affordable energy is crucial to economic production, especially to societies that seek to climb out of abject poverty. It is important to remember that when we use energy sources, we reduce the need for human work: plowing a field with a tractor rather than walking behind a horse, driving a car rather than walking huge distances, driving a truck rather than pushing a cart, and so forth. Energy use makes possible all human economic progress and frees us to use our time in higher intellectual endeavors, interpersonal human relationships, or even various Christian ministries. Energy use gives us freedom that we can use as we choose—for good or for ill.

Where can we obtain energy? Fossil fuels are (along with nuclear energy) the most affordable sources of energy available. Forcing people to replace carbon fuels would require them to switch to alternative energy sources. But generating electricity with solar, wind, and biofuels—the sources frequently mentioned—tends to cost *from two*

---

[221] Václav Klaus, "Freedom, Not Climate, at Risk," *Financial Times*, June 13, 2007, www.ft.com/cms/s/2/9deb730a-19ca-11dc-99c5-000b5df10621.html.

[222] Nordhaus, *A Question of Balance*; Lomborg, *Cool It*; Bjørn Lomborg, ed., *Global Crises, Global Solutions* (Cambridge, UK: Cambridge University Press, 2004); *Solutions for the World's Biggest Problems: Costs and Benefits* (Cambridge, UK: Cambridge University Press, 2007); and *How to Spend $50 Billion to Make the World a Better Place* (Cambridge, UK: Cambridge University Press, 2006).

to eight times as much as with fossil fuels.[223] Such a switch would *drastically increase the price of energy* and thus slow economic development, trapping the world's poor in their poverty and perpetuating the high rates of disease and premature death that stem from their poverty.

Human beings already live in widely differing climates, from the freezing Arctic to the searing Sahara. Temperature is not a significant challenge. The wealthier people are, the better they can cope with heat and cold, droughts and floods, storms, diseases, and other challenges. Forced reductions in fossil fuel use would cause economic harm to every person in the world (as prices for everything would rise), but especially immense harm to the world's poor.

Bjørn Lomborg, the respected Danish environmentalist and professor of statistics, convened a series of meetings under the title "the Copenhagen Consensus," beginning in 2004. The participants assumed (for the purpose of their discussions) that man-made global warming is occurring and then asked what the best human response would be. They concluded that "for some of the world's poorest countries, which will be adversely affected by climate change, problems like HIV/AIDS, hunger, and malaria are more pressing and can be solved with more efficacy."

Consequently, after carefully comparing the severity of many challenges and the cost-benefit ratios of proposed solutions, they agreed that the top priorities should be fighting communicable diseases, relieving malnutrition and hunger, and eliminating trade subsidies and barriers—all of which have benefits far outweighing their costs, while proposals to fight climate change were the worst use of funds, with their costs far outweighing their benefits.[224]

As I mentioned earlier in this chapter, Lomborg calculated—using the IPCC's own estimates of how much warming would result from the rise in atmospheric carbon dioxide it predicts through the remainder of this century—that full implementation of the 2015 Paris climate treaty, while costing *over $1 trillion per year* from 2030 to 2100, would reduce global average temperature by a nearly undetectable 0.306°F, an amount that would have no significant effect on any ecosystems or human economy in the year 2100.[225]

Christians who are concerned about alleviating poverty in the world cannot ignore the tremendous economic harm that would come from forcing reductions in

[223] G. Cornelis van Kooten, "The Economics of Global Warming Policy," in *A Renewed Call to Truth, Prudence, and Protection of the Poor*, 66, www.cornwallalliance.org/docs/a-renewed-call-to-truth-prudence-and-protection-of-the-poor.pdf.

[224] Lomborg, *How to Spend $50 Billion to Make the World a Better Place*. The overall premise of this book is to document how spending funds on climate change hurts more worthy efforts to eliminate human suffering and improve society.

[225] Bjorn Lomborg, "We Have a Climate Treaty—But at What Cost?" *Forbes*, Dec. 13, 2015, https://www.forbes.com/sites/bjornlomborg/2015/12/13/we-have-a-treaty-but-at-what-cost/#4f5e4507558c; Lomborg, "Impact of Current Climate Proposals," 109–118, http://onlinelibrary.wiley.com/doi/10.1111/1758-5899.12295/full.

carbon-based energy sources. The policies promoted to fight global warming would harm the poor more than they would the warming itself, even if it were real.

In 2009, I joined with the 29 evangelical scholars who authored and endorsed the statement *A Renewed Call to Truth, Prudence, and Protection of the Poor: An Evangelical Examination of the Theology, Science, and Economics of Global Warming.*[226] It concluded:

> Policies requiring drastic reductions in carbon dioxide emissions are unrealistic and threaten human well-being, especially in developing countries, where, by curtailing use of the most abundant, reliable, and affordable energy sources, they would prolong abject poverty and the miseries of toil, disease, and premature death that accompany it. . . .
>
> The most scientifically, economically, and ethically defensible policy response to alleged dangerous anthropogenic global warming is to promote economic development, especially for the world's poor, through policies that ensure abundant and affordable energy, on the one hand, and reduce specific risks from which the poor suffer regardless of climate change (e.g., undernutrition and malnutrition; waterborne, pest-borne, and communicable diseases; depressed income because of tariffs, trade restrictions, and corrupt governments; high rates of accidental injury and death because of poor transport and industry infrastructure), on the other hand.

Today I find no reason to rescind that endorsement. Rather, I am more firmly convinced of it than ever, which is why in 2015 I joined hundreds of other theologians, scientists, economists, and other scholars in signing "An Open Letter to Pope Francis on Climate Change" that concluded, "We believe it is both unwise and unjust to adopt policies requiring reduced use of fossil fuels for energy. Such policies would condemn hundreds of millions of our fellow human beings to ongoing poverty."[227]

7. Conclusion. The warnings about dangerous man-made global warming are based on poor scientific evidence and poor scientific methods, are not proven by previous empirical data, conflict with the Bible's teachings about the nature of the earth and man's purpose on the earth, and propose solutions that would cripple the world's economies and bring immense harm to the poor. These solutions would also bring unacceptable losses of human freedom[228] and immense increases in government power.

While carbon dioxide does not contribute in any significant measure to danger-

---

[226] See van Kooten, "The Economics of Global Warming Policy," 68, www.cornwallalliance.org/docs/a -renewed-call-to-truth-prudence-and-protection-of-the-poor.pdf. See also the conclusions of Nobel Prize-winning economists of the Copenhagen Consensus Center, http://copenhagenconsensus.com/CCC%20 Home%20Page.aspx.

[227] "An Open Letter to Pope Francis on Climate Change," The Cornwall Alliance for the Stewardship of Creation, June 2015, http://cornwallalliance.org/anopenlettertopopefrancisonclimatechange/.

[228] For a discussion of the needless loss of human life and human freedom of choice brought about by government-imposed Corporate Average Fuel Economy standards (CAFE standards) for motor vehicles man-

ous levels of global warming, increasing its amount in the atmosphere would bring important agricultural benefits in terms of increased plant growth. Slight increases in global temperatures would on the whole bring important agricultural benefits as well, especially in terms of longer growing seasons in cool climates.

In light of these factors, governments should not adopt any policies to regulate the amount of carbon fuel used or to diminish the amount of carbon dioxide in the atmosphere.

QUESTIONS FOR PERSONAL APPLICATION

1. How did this chapter change your view of the proper use of the earth's resources?
2. Do you think we are in danger of running out of any essential natural resource in the next 1,000 years?
3. Do you think that human use of carbon fuels is leading to dangerous levels of man-caused global warming? Whether you think so or not, what do you think is the best argument for the position you oppose?
4. Are you specifically doing anything differently in your own life primarily or only for the purpose of reducing your use of carbon fuels?
5. How often are you consciously thankful to God for the amazingly wonderful resources of the earth that he has put here for our enjoyment? Do you truly *enjoy* using the resources of the earth in a wise manner?
6. What character traits (see p. 110) do you need in order to make wise decisions and have right attitudes about the right use of and care for the environment?

SPECIAL TERMS

anthropogenic global warming
carbon dioxide
carbon fuels
Chernobyl
climate change
Climategate
environmentalism
feedbacks
Fukushima
IPCC

ufactured in the United States, see Grudem, *Politics—According to the Bible*, 383–86. Fear of catastrophic global warming has been the primary motive behind the continuation and even tightening of the CAFE standards.

BIBLIOGRAPHY

Sections in Other Ethics Texts

(see complete bibliographical data, p. 64)

Clark and Rakestraw, 2:381–422
Davis, 258–73
Frame, 743–45
Geisler, 314–34
Gushee and Stassen, 379–95
Kaiser, 211–30
McQuilkin and Copan, 491–93
Rae, 352

Other Works

Bauckham, Richard. *Bible and Ecology: Rediscovering the Community of Creation*. Waco, TX: Baylor University Press, 2010.

———. *Living with Other Creatures: Green Exegesis and Theology*. Milton Keynes, UK: Paternoster, 2012.

Beisner, E. Calvin. *Where Garden Meets Wilderness: Evangelical Entry into the Environmental Debate*. Grand Rapids, MI: Acton Institute and Eerdmans, 1997.

Domenici, Pete V. *A Brighter Tomorrow: Fulfilling the Promise of Nuclear Energy*. Lanham, MD: Rowman & Littlefield, 2004.

Essex, Christopher, and Ross McKitrick. *Taken by Storm: The Troubled Science, Policy, and Politics of Global Warming*. Toronto, ON: Key Porter Books, 2007.

Horner, Christopher C. *The Politically Incorrect Guide to Global Warming*. Washington: Regnery, 2007.

———. *Red Hot Lies: How Global Warming Alarmists Use Threats, Fraud, and Deception to Keep You Misinformed*. Washington: Regnery, 2008.

Houghton, John. *Global Warming: The Complete Briefing*. 4th ed. Cambridge, UK: Cambridge University Press, 2009.

Huber, Peter W. *Hard Green: Saving the Environment from the Environmentalists*. New York: Basic Books, 1999.

Idso, Craig D., R. M. Carter, and S. Fred Singer. *Why Scientists Disagree about Global Warming: The NIPCC Report on Scientific Consensus*. Arlington Heights, IL: Nongovernmental International Panel on Climate Change (NIPCC), 2015.

Laframboise, Donna. *The Delinquent Teenager Who Was Mistaken for the World's Top Climate Expert*. Toronto: Penguin, 2011.

Liederbach, Mark, and Seth Bible. *True North: Christ, the Gospel, and Creation Care*. Nashville: B&H, 2012.

Lin, Johnny Wei-Bing. *The Nature of Environmental Stewardship: Understanding Creation Care Solutions to Environmental Problems.* Eugene, OR: Wipf & Stock, 2016.

Lomborg, Bjørn. *Cool It: The Skeptical Environmentalist's Guide to Global Warming.* New York: Knopf, 2007.

———, ed. *Global Crises, Global Solutions.* Cambridge, UK: Cambridge University Press, 2004.

———. *The Skeptical Environmentalist: Measuring the Real State of the World.* Cambridge, UK: Cambridge University Press, 2001.

———, ed. *Solutions for the World's Biggest Problems: Costs and Benefits.* Cambridge, UK: Cambridge University Press, 2007.

Michaels, Patrick J. *Meltdown: The Predictable Distortion of Global Warming by Scientists, Politicians, and the Media.* Washington: Cato Institute, 2004.

———, ed. *Shattered Consensus: The True State of Global Warming.* Lanham, MD: Rowman & Littlefield, 2005.

Moo, Douglas J. "Nature in the New Creation: New Testament Eschatology and the Environment." *JETS* 49 (2006): 449–88.

Moo, Jonathan. "Continuity, Discontinuity, and Hope: The Contribution of New Testament Eschatology to a Distinctively Christian Environmental Ethos." *Tyndale Bulletin* 61 (2010): 21–44.

Moo, Jonathan A., and Robert S. White. *Let Creation Rejoice: Biblical Hope and Ecological Crisis.* Downers Grove, IL: InterVarsity Press, 2014

Moore, Russell D. "Heaven and Nature Sing: How Evangelical Theology Can Inform the Task of Environmental Protection (and Vice Versa)." *JETS* 57 (2014): 571–88.

Moss, R. P. "Environment." In *New Dictionary of Christian Ethics and Pastoral Theology,* edited by David J. Atkinson and David H. Field, 349–52. Leicester, UK: Inter-Varsity, and Downers Grove, IL: InterVarsity Press, 1995.

Murray, Iain. *The Really Inconvenient Truths: Seven Environmental Catastrophes Liberals Don't Want You to Know About—Because They Helped Cause Them.* Washington: Regnery, 2008.

Nordhaus, William D. *A Question of Balance: Weighing the Options on Global Warming Policies.* New Haven, CT: Yale University Press, 2008.

Plimer, Ian. *Heaven and Earth: Global Warming, the Missing Science.* Lanham, MD: Taylor Trade Publishing, 2009.

Schaeffer, Francis A., and Udo W. Middelmann. *Pollution and the Death of Man.* Wheaton, IL: Crossway, 2011.

Simon, Julian, ed. *The State of Humanity.* Oxford, UK, and Cambridge, MA: Blackwell, 1995.

———. *The Ultimate Resource 2.* Rev. ed. Princeton, NJ: Princeton University Press, 1998.

Simon, Julian, and Herman Kahn, eds. *The Resourceful Earth: A Response to Global 2000.* New York: Basil Blackwell, 1984.

Singer, S. Fred, and Dennis T. Avery. *Unstoppable Global Warming: Every 1,500 Years.* 2nd ed. Lanham, MD: Rowman & Littlefield, 2008.

Smith, Wesley J. *A Rat Is a Pig Is a Dog Is a Boy: The Human Cost of the Animal Rights Movement*. New York: Encounter Books, 2010.

———. *The War on Humans*. Seattle: Discovery Institute, 2014.

Solomon, Lawrence. *The Deniers: The World-Renowned Scientists Who Stood Up against Global Warming Hysteria, Political Persecution, and Fraud*. Rev. ed. Minneapolis: Richard Vigilante Books, 2010.

Spencer, Roy W. *Climate Confusion: How Global Warming Hysteria Leads to Bad Science, Pandering Politicians, and Misguided Policies That Hurt the Poor*. New York: Encounter Books, 2008.

———. *The Great Global Warming Blunder: How Mother Nature Fooled the World's Top Climate Scientists*. New York: Encounter Books, 2010.

Vantassel, Stephen M. *Dominion over Wildlife? An Environmental Theology of Human-Wildlife Relations*. Eugene, OR: Wipf & Stock, 2009.

Wanliss, James. *Resisting the Green Dragon; Dominion, Not Death*. Burke, VA: The Cornwall Alliance, 2010.

Williamson, Kevin D. "What to Think About Global Warming." *National Review*, Dec. 8, 2009, http:// www.nationalreview.com/article/228756/what-think-about-global -warming-kevin-d-williamson.

SCRIPTURE MEMORY PASSAGE

Genesis 1:28: And God blessed them. And God said to them, "Be fruitful and multiply and fill the earth and subdue it, and have dominion over the fish of the sea and over the birds of the heavens and over every living thing that moves on the earth."

HYMN

"This Is My Father's World"

This is my Father's world,
And to my list'ning ears
All nature sings, and round me rings
The music of the spheres.
This is my Father's world!
I rest me in the thought
Of rocks and trees, of skies and seas;
His hand the wonders wrought.

This is my Father's world,
The birds their carols raise;
The morning light, the lily white,

Declare their Maker's praise.
This is my Father's world!
He shines in all that's fair;
In the rustling grass I hear Him pass,
He speaks to me ev'rywhere.

This is my Father's world,
O let me ne'er forget,
That tho the wrong seems oft so strong
God is the Ruler yet.
This is my Father's world!
The battle is not done;
Jesus who died shall be satisfied,
And earth and heav'n be one.

MALTBIE D. BABCOCK, 1858–1901

Part 7

PROTECTING PURITY OF HEART

"You shall not covet."

Chapter 42

PURITY OF HEART

Why is God concerned with purity in our hearts?
How can we attain contentment with what God has given us?

The tenth commandment reads:[1]

> You shall not covet your neighbor's house; you shall not covet your neighbor's wife, or his male servant, or his female servant, or his ox, or his donkey, or anything that is your neighbor's. (Ex. 20:17)

A. THE MEANING OF THE COMMANDMENT

1. The Commandment in the Old Testament. The Hebrew verb translated as "covet" is *ḥāmad*, which simply means "to desire, take pleasure in" something.[2] The verb can be used to speak of a strong desire in either a positive or negative sense. When used in a good sense, the verb describes desire or delight in something that is beautiful or attractive, such as the trees that were "*pleasant* to the sight" when God created them (Gen. 2:9) or God's laws, which are "more to be *desired*" than gold (Ps. 19:9–10). The verb is even used in a positive sense of God desiring Mount Zion for "his abode" (Ps. 68:16). And it is used of the delight of romantic love (Song 2:3).

But in several other passages, the context shows clearly that the verb is used in a negative sense to speak of inordinate, ungoverned, selfish desire that is contrary to God's will. With this negative meaning, this verb is used in Genesis 3 to speak of Eve's perception of

---

[1] I have not skipped the ninth commandment, "You shall not bear false witness." I discussed it in chap. 12, beginning on p. 309 (see my explanation for treating it out of order, p. 310).

[2] The parallel passage in Deut. 5:21 uses this same verb to say, "You shall not *covet* your neighbor's wife," but then it switches to a different verb with similar meaning, *'āwāh* ("to desire, crave"), in the rest of the verse: "And you shall not *desire* your neighbor's house, his field, or his male servant, or his female servant, his ox, or his donkey, or anything that is your neighbor's." The Septuagint translates both verbs in Deut. 5:21 with the Greek *epithymeō*, "to have a strong desire, long for."

the forbidden fruit of the tree of the knowledge of good and evil, which she saw was "to be *desired* to make one wise" (v. 6). Also, Achan used it to describe his response when he saw much silver and gold, as well as a beautiful cloak, among the spoils of the conquest of Jericho (see Josh. 6:19; 7:1); he confessed, "Then I *coveted* them and took them. And see, they are hidden in the earth inside my tent, with the silver underneath" (7:21).

The verb is also used to speak of a wrongful desire for sex outside of marriage, for Proverbs cautions this about the adulteress, "Do not *desire* her beauty in your heart" (6:25). Elsewhere it is used to speak of powerful oppressors who "*covet* fields and seize them, and houses, and take them away" (Mic. 2:2).

2. The Commandment in the New Testament. The tenth commandment is directly quoted twice in the New Testament:

> What then shall we say? That the law is sin? By no means! Yet if it had not been for the law, I would not have known sin. For I would not have known what it is to covet if the law had not said, "*You shall not covet*." (Rom. 7:7)

> For the commandments, "You shall not commit adultery, You shall not murder, You shall not steal, *You shall not covet*," and any other commandment, are summed up in this word: "You shall love your neighbor as yourself." (Rom. 13:9)

In both verses, the Greek verb is *epithymeō*, the same verb used in the Septuagint translation of Exodus 20:17 and Deuteronomy 5:21. This verb means "to have a strong desire, long for" and has a range of meaning similar to *hāmad* in the Old Testament, because it can be used of a strong desire that is either positive or negative.

For example, *epithymeō* is used to convey a positive desire when Jesus says, "I have earnestly *desired* to eat this Passover with you" (Luke 22:15). It is used similarly when Paul says that a man who aspires to the office of overseer "*desires* a noble task" (1 Tim. 3:1). It is also used to depict the desire of good angels when Peter says that they "*long to look*" into the way the gospel is being applied to the lives of his readers (1 Pet. 1:12).

But the verb is also used in several verses in a negative sense to speak of a wrongful desire, a strong desire for something that is contrary to God's will. James says, "You *desire* and do not have, so you murder" (James 4:2). And Paul told the elders at Ephesus that when he was with them, "I *coveted* no one's silver or gold or apparel" (Acts 20:33). Jesus used this verb to speak of wrongful sexual desire when he said, "Everyone who looks at a woman *with lustful intent* [literally, for the purpose of lusting after her] has already committed adultery with her in his heart" (Matt. 5:28).

However, the New Testament also forbids coveting with the use of a different word, *pleonexia* ("greediness, insatiableness, avarice, covetousness"). This word is always used in a negative sense, and it is translated as "covetousness" several times in the New Testament, as in the following verses:

And he said to them, "Take care, and be on your guard against all *covetousness*, for one's life does not consist in the abundance of his possessions." (Luke 12:15)

But sexual immorality and all impurity or *covetousness* must not even be named among you, as is proper among saints. (Eph. 5:3)

For you may be sure of this, that everyone who is sexually immoral or impure, or *who is covetous* (that is, an idolater), has no inheritance in the kingdom of Christ and God. (Eph. 5:5; Paul here uses a cognate noun, *pleonektēs*, "one who is covetous or greedy.")

Put to death therefore what is earthly in you: sexual immorality, impurity, passion, evil desire, and *covetousness*, which is idolatry. (Col. 3:5)[3]

3. Summary of the Meaning. This commandment, then, both in the Ten Commandments and in its reaffirmations in several New Testament passages, refers to desiring or longing for something that is not rightfully yours. "You shall not *covet* your neighbor's house" because the house belongs to your neighbor, not to you. "You shall not *covet* your neighbor's wife" because she is your neighbor's wife, not your wife.

This does not mean that all desires for things you do not now have are wrong. There is a rightful kind of desire that leads to planning and saving for future purchases (such as a child saving to buy a bicycle or a couple saving to buy a house). And there is a rightful desire to be placed in a church office that a person does not now hold, for Paul says, "If anyone aspires to the office of overseer, he *desires* [Greek, *epithymeō*] a noble task" (1 Tim. 3:1).

In order to distinguish these right and wrong desires, here are three helpful questions to ask:

1. Is this desire based on morally right planning for the future acquisition of some item, or is it based on a morally wrong longing for something you could never reasonably hope to acquire in a morally right way (such as your neighbor's wife or a very expensive house or car that you have no reasonable hope of obtaining)?
2. Is this desire for something God wants you to have and has given you an ability to obtain (such as a house you can afford or a church leadership role that you are suited for), or is it longing for something that God does not want you to have and has not given you the ability to obtain?
3. Can you take some morally right actions to begin to move toward obtaining the thing you desire, or are there no morally right actions that would

---

[3] These same two Greek works, *pleonexia* and *pleonektēs*, are also used to refer to "greed" or "one who is greedy" in verses such as 1 Cor. 5:10, 11; 6:10; Eph. 4:19; 1 Thess. 2:5; 2 Pet. 2:3, 14.

reasonably result in obtaining this thing (so that you will just continue to wallow in a covetous desire that has no reasonable hope of fulfillment)?

B. THE OPPOSITE DUTY IS CONTENTMENT

As it is with several other commandments, so it is here: when God prohibits something that is wrong, he implies that there is an opposite responsibility that is morally right and that we should seek to fulfill. In this case, the opposite of coveting is *contentment* with what God has given to us and delighting in it with thanksgiving to him:

> *Be content* with your wages. (Luke 3:14)

> I am [not] speaking of being in need, for I have learned in whatever situation I am *to be content*. (Phil. 4:11)

> Godliness with *contentment* is great gain, for we brought nothing into the world, and we cannot take anything out of the world. But if we have food and clothing, with these *we will be content*. (1 Tim. 6:6–8)

> Keep your life free from love of money, and *be content with what you have*, for he has said, "I will never leave you nor forsake you." (Heb. 13:5)

C. THE BROADER IMPLICATION OF THIS COMMAND: GOD IS CONCERNED WITH PURITY OF HEART

When God told the people of Israel, "You shall not covet your neighbor's house . . . or his ox, or his donkey, or anything that is your neighbor's" (Ex. 20:17), he was teaching them that he required more than simply not stealing their neighbors' property. God also wanted their hearts to be free of the *desire* to steal anything of their neighbors'.

Then when he said, "You shall not covet your neighbor's wife," he was teaching them that merely refraining from the physical act of adultery (the seventh commandment) was not enough, for he expected them also not to *desire* to commit adultery.

Therefore, the tenth commandment has a broader implication: God requires his people to have purity of heart as well as right actions during their daily lives.

This means that, if we understand the implications of the tenth commandment rightly, we will realize that God demands of us that we not desire to have any other gods (the first commandment), not desire to make a carved image (the second commandment), not desire to take God's name in vain (the third commandment), and not desire to profane the Sabbath day (the fourth commandment). He is telling us that we should desire to honor our father and mother (the fifth commandment). And he is demanding that we should not desire to murder (the sixth commandment) commit adultery (the seventh commandment), steal (the eighth commandment), or bear false witness (the ninth commandment). God requires of us purity of heart that is consistent with his moral standards throughout Scripture: "For the LORD sees not as man sees: man looks on the outward appearance, but *the LORD looks on the heart*" (1 Sam. 16:7). God desires for us to have fellowship with him, but he is an omniscient, omnipresent, holy God, and so he requires purity of heart for those who draw near to him:

> Who shall ascend the hill of the LORD?
>> And who shall stand in his holy place?
> He who has clean hands and a pure heart. (Ps. 24:3–4)

> Blessed are the pure in heart, for they shall see God. (Matt. 5:8)

Other passages of Scripture also speak this way:

> Prove me, O LORD, and try me;
>> *test my heart* and my mind. (Ps. 26:2)

> Search me, O God, and *know my heart*!
>> Try me and know my thoughts! (Ps. 139:23)

> I the LORD *search the heart*
>> and test the mind,
> to give every man according to his ways,
>> according to the fruit of his deeds. (Jer. 17:10)

> And all the churches will know that *I am he who searches mind and heart*, and
> I will give to each of you according to your works. (Rev. 2:23)

This perspective shows us that Jesus was interpreting the Ten Commandments rightly, according to their deeper intent, when he connected the sixth commandment ("You shall not murder") to anger against one's brother (Matt. 5:21–22) and when he connected the seventh commandment ("You shall not commit adultery") to looking at a woman "with lustful intent" (vv. 27–28).

D. REASONS FOR THIS COMMAND

We might wonder, what is really wrong with coveting? So long as our coveting does not result in harming anyone else, why does God see it as wrong?

We can suggest several reasons for this commandment, all of which deal with our relationship to God.

1. Coveting Implies That We Do Not Trust God. When we covet things we do not have, we indicate that do not trust God to provide what we need and what is best and right for us. There is a strong correlation between our moment-by-moment relationship with God and our contentment with what we have:

> Keep your life free from love of money, and *be content with what you have, for he has said, "I will never leave you nor forsake you."* (Heb. 13:5)

2. Coveting Implies That We Disagree with God's Laws. To covet suggests that we think God's laws are wrong, and we are unhappy with his laws that protect other people's marriages or property. Eve saw that "the tree was to be *desired* to make one wise" (Gen. 3:6), which implied that God's command was not the best thing for her. If you think of an adulterous woman and "*desire* her beauty in your heart" (Prov. 6:25), it implies that you do not think that God's provision of a wife for you (or of singleness) is wise or good.

3. Coveting Implies That We Dislike God's Provision for Our Lives. If we covet other people's possessions, or perhaps other people's gifts, abilities, and opportunities, the implication is that we think God's provisions for our own lives are wrong. Therefore, the recognition that other people have different gifts and abilities (and therefore end up with different possessions in life) is in many ways a test of our trust in God and the goodness of his provisions for us.

Paul cautioned the Corinthians to remember that all they possessed had come from God:

> For who sees anything different in you? *What do you have that you did not receive?* If then you received it, why do you boast as if you did not receive it? (1 Cor. 4:7)

4. Coveting Implies That We Want Something More Than God. When we covet, we are implying that we want something more on this earth than we want God. It implies that God is not first in our hearts. It implies that we are not obeying the command "love the LORD your God with all your heart and with all your soul and with all your might" (Deut. 6:5), which Jesus said is the first and greatest commandment (Matt. 22:37–38).

That is why Paul says that coveting is "idolatry"—it shows us where our hearts really are: "Put to death therefore what is earthly in you: sexual immorality, impurity, passion, evil desire, and *covetousness, which is idolatry*" (Col. 3:5; see also Eph. 5:5).

When we want something on earth more than God, that desire inevitably leads us into other harmful consequences: "But those who desire to be rich fall into temptation, into a snare, into many senseless and harmful desires [Greek, *epithymia*, the noun that corresponds to the verb *epithymeō*] that plunge people into ruin and destruction" (1 Tim. 6:9).

Though we will never fully obey it in this life, the high standard of perfection that God calls us to is to ultimately desire nothing on earth except him:

> Whom have I in heaven but you?
>> And there is *nothing on earth that I desire besides you.*
> My flesh and my heart may fail,
>> but *God is the strength of my heart and my portion forever.* (Ps. 73:25–26)

5. Coveting Implies That We Are Missing the Purpose of Our Possessions. Covetousness shows that we have missed the purpose of what God has given us in this life. His purpose in giving us good things is not that we would focus all our delight on those things, but that they would draw our hearts to him as the Giver—and reveal God's love to others as we use those gifts to help them. But if the things that God *has already given* us are not drawing us to him, then getting *the things that we do not have* surely will not draw our hearts to him. Coveting shows that we really want the things, not their Maker. We want the gifts, not the Giver!

> As for the rich in this present age, charge them not to be haughty, *nor to set their hopes on* the uncertainty of *riches, but on God, who richly provides us with everything to enjoy.* (1 Tim. 6:17)

6. On a Human Level, Coveting Is Horribly Destructive. Several passages of Scripture show us how horribly destructive coveting can be. For example, James says it leads to fighting and even to murder:

> You desire and do not have, so you *murder.* You covet and cannot obtain, so you *fight* and *quarrel.* You do not have, because you do not ask. (James 4:2)

This verse also has application to the affairs of nations, because many wars have been fought due to one ruler coveting the territory of another ruler or another nation.

The Old Testament also gives some examples of the tragic consequences of coveting, and two of these examples show that not only poor people but also extremely rich people can be guilty of coveting. King Ahab coveted the vineyard belonging to his neighbor Naboth, but Naboth would not sell it to him. "And Ahab went into his house vexed and sullen because of what Naboth the Jezreelite had said to him, for he had said, 'I will not give you the inheritance of my fathers'" (1 Kings 21:4). Ahab's coveting of that vineyard prompted his wife Jezebel to have Naboth falsely accused and put to death (vv. 9–14), and then Ahab took the vineyard that he wanted (v. 16). God then sent a terrible word of judgment to Ahab and Jezebel through Elijah the prophet (vv. 17–24).

The spectacular and tragic sin of King David also came about through coveting—in this case, through coveting (and taking) the wife of his neighbor Uriah the Hittite (2 Sam. 11:2–5). This led eventually to David having Uriah murdered (vv. 14–17). "But the thing that David had done displeased the Lord" (v. 27). It all began with coveting.

It is likely that much of the excessive accumulation of consumer debt in many modern societies is due to people giving in to coveting and purchasing things they neither need nor can afford. Unfortunately, much modern advertising and political rhetoric encouraging people to resent "inequality" also arouse destructive kinds of coveting that do much more harm than good in society.

E. THE WONDERFUL BENEFITS OF THIS COMMANDMENT

The longer we ponder this commandment against coveting, the more we come to realize the significant benefits that it brings to our lives.

1. It Nips Sin in the Bud. Because this commandment speaks to our hearts, it is wonderfully suited to counteract the early stages of sin. If you don't covet your neighbors' possessions, you will certainly never steal them. And if you don't covet your neighbor's wife, you will certainly never commit adultery with her.

Therefore, this commandment serves as an excellent challenge to us and provides an area of beneficial focus as we seek to grow as Christians. If by God's grace and the help of the Holy Spirit we are able to make progress in overcoming covetous habits in our lives, becoming more content with what God has given us, we will have taken a significant step in growth toward maturity as Christians.

If somehow all cities, regions, or countries could experience a significant reduction in coveting, crime would also drop precipitously. If any city or nation could somehow be free of coveting, it would have no theft, no adultery, and no wrongful focus on material possessions. It would probably have no murder either.

2. It Draws Us to God. By teaching us not to focus our desires on earthly things, this command shows us the purpose of all the good gifts that we have received—to increase our contentment in God and our thankfulness and love to him, and even our joy in his presence.

3. It Drives Us to Christ for Help. Who can ever obey this command perfectly? This most demanding of commands, the one that reveals the desires of our hearts, should cause us to despair of making ourselves right before God. This despair should cause us to flee to Christ to forgive us and to cleanse our hearts in a way we cannot do.

> What then shall we say? That the law is sin? By no means! Yet if it had not been for the law, I would not have known sin. For I would not have known what it is to covet if the law had not said, "You shall not covet." But sin, seizing an opportunity through the commandment, produced in me all kinds of covetousness. (Rom. 7:7–8)

> Wretched man that I am! *Who will deliver me from this body of death? Thanks be to God through Jesus Christ our Lord!* (Rom. 7:24–25)

For unbelievers, this command can also serve as a "gospel" message (or more specifically a pregospel message) to show unbelievers their need for Christ. Surely no person on earth can free his heart of all coveting by his own efforts. "Who can say, 'I have made my heart pure; I am clean from my sin'?" (Prov. 20:9). When unbelievers face the impossibility of fulfilling this command, that inability should show them their need of Christ, causing them to turn to him as the only one who can rescue them from failure and despair.

In addition, in the thinking of unbelievers who are studying various systems of ethics, this commandment makes very clear that Christian ethics, rightly understood, is much more than a study of merely human moral laws. This commandment reminds us that Christian ethics must be studied and practiced in the presence of a living God who sees into the depths of our hearts. And this is a God who requires absolute purity of heart.

4. It Promotes Peace, Love, and Unity in the Family of God. When coveting diminishes within a church, then love for one another flourishes, because "love is patient and kind; *love does not envy* or boast" (1 Cor. 13:4). In addition, when coveting diminishes, then believers in a church do not face difficulties or successes alone, but in fellowship with each other, for "if one member suffers, all suffer together; if one member is honored, all rejoice together" (12:26).

5. It Reminds Us That Wealth Does Not Itself Produce Happiness. Too often today people imagine, "If only I could inherit a million dollars, then I would be happy," or, "If only I could win the lottery, then I would be content." But this commandment rebukes those foolish desires and reminds us that true joy comes only when we delight ourselves in God and are content with the provisions he has ordained for our lives. "Godliness with contentment is great gain" (1 Tim. 6:6).

QUESTIONS FOR PERSONAL APPLICATION

1. Have you noticed any changes in your heart as you have read this book? In your pattern of life?
2. Are there people or things that you wrongfully covet? Why do you think that this specific coveting is displeasing to God? What harmful results might possibly come from this coveting?
3. With regard to the way God has created you, are you content or are you coveting what God has not given you regarding your physical appearance? Your intelligence? Your personality? Your athletic ability? Your job? Your responsibilities within the church?
4. Can you think of anything that God might be prompting you to do in order to bring about greater purity of heart in these areas?

5. Are there times when you desire God more than anyone or anything else?

6. Do you like the fact that God commands us not to covet?

7. What character traits (see p. 110) will better enable us to overcome wrongful coveting?

SPECIAL TERMS

contentment

coveting

BIBLIOGRAPHY

Sections in Other Ethics Texts

(see complete bibliographical data, p. 64)

Frame, 844–48

Gushee and Stassen, 365–70

Jones, 37–58

McQuilkin and Copan, 140–41

Other Works

Beale, G. K. *We Become What We Worship: A Biblical Theology of Idolatry.* Downers Grove, IL: InterVarsity Press, 2008.

Bigney, Brad. *Gospel Treason: Betraying the Gospel with Hidden Idols.* Phillipsburg, NJ: P&R, 2012.

Fitzpatrick, Elyse M. *Idols of the Heart: Learning to Long for God Alone.* 2nd ed. Phillipsburg, NJ: P&R, 2016.

Hardyman, Julian. *Idols: God's Battle for Our Hearts.* Leicester, UK: Inter-Varsity, 2010.

Keller, Timothy. *Counterfeit Gods: The Empty Promises of Money, Sex, and Power, and the Only Hope That Matters.* New York: Dutton, 2009

Pigott, G. J. "Covetousness." In *New Dictionary of Christian Ethics and Pastoral Theology*, edited by David J. Atkinson and David H. Field, 267–68. Leicester, UK: Inter-Varsity, and Downers Grove, IL: InterVarsity Press, 1995.

Raymond, Erik. *Chasing Contentment: Trusting God in a Discontented Age.* Wheaton, IL: Crossway, 2017.

Rosner, Brian S. *Greed as Idolatry: The Origin and Meaning of a Pauline Metaphor.* Grand Rapids, MI: Eerdmans, 2007.

SCRIPTURE MEMORY PASSAGE

Exodus 20:17: You shall not covet your neighbor's house; you shall not covet your neighbor's wife, or his male servant, or his female servant, or his ox, or his donkey, or anything that is your neighbor's.

HYMN

"Take Time to Be Holy"

Take time to be holy, speak oft with thy Lord;
Abide in him always, and feed on his Word.
Make friends of God's children; help those who are weak;
Forgetting in nothing his blessing to seek.

Take time to be holy, the world rushes on;
Spend much time in secret with Jesus alone.
By looking to Jesus, like him thou shalt be;
Thy friends in thy conduct his likeness shall see.

Take time to be holy, let him be thy guide,
And run not before him, whatever betide;
In joy or in sorrow, still follow thy Lord,
And, looking to Jesus, still trust in his Word.

Take time to be holy, be calm in thy soul;
Each thought and each motive beneath his control;
Thus led by his Spirit to fountains of love,
Thou soon shalt be fitted for service above.

AUTHOR: WILLIAM D. LONGSTAFF, 1887

SHOULD WE MOVE BEYOND THE NEW TESTAMENT TO A BETTER ETHIC?

An Analysis of William J. Webb, Slaves, Women & Homosexuals: Exploring the Hermeneutics of Cultural Analysis

Author's note: In 2001, William Webb published an influential book advocating "redemptive movement hermeneutics" or "trajectory hermeneutics," a major proposal for a substantially new method of determining which moral commands of Scripture were valid only for the ancient culture in which they were written and which of them God still intends us to obey today. Because of the intricate and extensive nature of Webb's system of interpretation, and because he raises important questions that are relevant to any system of biblical ethics, I thought it appropriate to include my review of Webb's book as an appendix. This review was first published in the *Journal of the Evangelical Theological Society*.[1]

How can Christians today know which parts of the Bible are "culturally relative" and which parts apply to all believers in all cultures throughout history?

---

[1] This review of William J. Webb, *Slaves, Women & Homosexuals: Exploring the Hermeneutics of Cultural Analysis* (Downers Grove, IL: InterVarsity Press, 2001), first appeared in *JETS* 47, no. 2 (June 2004): 299–346, and is reprinted here with permission. All Scripture verses are from the ESV unless otherwise noted.

William Webb has provided an entirely new approach to that question in a book that focuses specifically on the questions of slavery, men's and women's roles, and homosexuality, but that also provides a general approach to the question of cultural relativity, an approach that Webb hopes will prove useful for solving similar questions on other topics as well.

The book provides an extensive and rather complex system of cultural analysis that Webb calls a "redemptive-movement hermeneutic." I expect that most readers will find Webb's explanation of why the Bible regulated but did not prohibit slavery to be a helpful analysis. Readers will also find helpful Webb's explanation of why the Bible's prohibitions against homosexual conduct should not be thought to be culturally relative, but rather transcultural. Webb has read widely in literature that explains historical material concerning slavery and homosexuality in the cultural backgrounds that surrounded the writers of the Old Testament and the New Testament, and his book provides a helpful resource in those areas.

In addition, Webb's book provides a significant new challenge to those who believe that the Bible teaches that wives should be subject to their husbands today (according to several New Testament passages), and that some governing and teaching roles in the church, such as the office of elder or pastor, are restricted to men. In contrast to many egalitarians who have argued that the New Testament does not teach that wives should be subject to their husbands, or that only men should be elders, Webb takes a different approach: he believes that the New Testament *does* teach these things *for the culture in which the New Testament was written*, but that in today's culture the treatment of women is an area in which "*a better ethic than the one expressed in the isolated words of the text is possible*" (p. 36, italics added).

Webb admits that the Old and New Testaments improved the treatment of women when compared with their surrounding cultures, but, he says:

> If one adopts a redemptive-movement hermeneutic, the softening of patriarchy (which Scripture itself initiates) can be taken a considerable distance further. Carrying the redemptive movement within Scripture to a more improved expression for gender relationships ... [today] ends in either ultra-soft patriarchy or complementary egalitarianism. (p. 39)

Later in the book, Webb defines such "ultra-soft patriarchy" as a position in which there are no unique leadership roles for men in marriage or in the church, but men are given "a certain level of *symbolic* honor" (p. 243). He defines "complementary egalitarianism" as a system in which there is full interdependence and "mutual submission" within marriage, and the only differences in roles are "based upon biological differences between men and women," so that Webb would favor "a greater participation of women in the early stages of child rearing" (p. 241). Thus, Webb's "ultra-soft patriarchy" differs from his "complementary egalitarianism" only in the slight bit of "symbolic honor" that ultra-soft patriarchy would still give to men.

Because of its detail, novelty, and the complexity of its approach, this book deserves to be taken seriously by complementarians. However, because of concerns that are detailed below, I do not think that the book succeeds in showing that male headship in the home and the church are culturally relative. Nor do I believe that the book provides a system for analyzing cultural relativity that is ultimately helpful for Christians to use today.

1. Webb's Trajectory Hermeneutic Nullifies in Principle the Moral Authority of the Entire New Testament. At first glance, it may not seem as though Webb "nullifies" the moral authority of the entire New Testament, because he agrees, for example, that homosexual conduct is morally wrong, and that the New Testament condemnations of homosexual conduct are transcultural (pp. 39–41, 250–252, and many other places in the book). He also affirms that the New Testament admonitions for children to be subject to their parents are transcultural (p. 212). Is Webb not then affirming that some aspects of New Testament ethics are transcultural?

The important point to realize is the *basis* on which Webb affirms that these things are transcultural commands. Most evangelicals today would read a text such as "Children, obey your parents in the Lord, for this is right" (Eph. 6:1) and would conclude that children *today* are to obey their parents because the New Testament was written for Christians in the new covenant age (after Christ's death), and since we Christians today are also in the new covenant age (the period of time until Christ returns), this command is binding on us today.

Most evangelicals today would reason similarly about the New Testament texts concerning homosexual conduct (see, for example, Rom. 1:26–27; 1 Cor. 6:9), and would conclude that these are morally binding on us today, because we are part of the new covenant age and these texts were written to new covenant Christians.

But for Webb, *the process is entirely different*, and the basis of authority is different. The commands concerning children and homosexuals are not binding on us today *because we are part of the new covenant age*, for which the New Testament was written (I could not find such a consideration anywhere in Webb's book), but rather *because these commands have passed through the filtering system of Webb's eighteen criteria* and have survived. As a matter of fact, the command concerning children has not entirely survived his filtering process, because Webb believes that the New Testament commands that tell children to obey their parents actually teach that *adult children* should continue to be obedient to their own parents throughout their adult lives, but that this aspect of the command as Paul wrote it was culturally relative and need not be followed by us today (see p. 212).

In this way, I believe it is fair to say that Webb's system invalidates the moral authority of the entire New Testament, at least in the sense that we today should be obedient to the moral commands that were written to new covenant Christians. Instead, only those commands are binding that have passed through his eighteen-part filter. (Webb does not consider the far simpler possibility that first-century readers would have understood the word *children* (Greek, *tekna*) to apply only to people who were not adults, and so we today can say that Ephesians 6:1 applies to modern believers in just the same way that it applied to first-century believers, and no "cultural filters" need to be applied to that command.)

Someone may object at this point, "Doesn't everyone have to use some kind of cultural filter like this? Doesn't everyone have to test the New Testament commands to see if they are culturally relative or transcultural, before deciding whether to obey them?"

I would respond to that question by saying that there is a significant difference in approach. Most evangelicals (including me) would say that we *are* under the moral authority of the New Testament, and we are morally obligated to obey its commands when we are in the same situation as that addressed in the New Testament commands (such as being a parent, a child, a person contemplating a divorce, a church selecting elders or deacons, a church preparing to celebrate the Lord's Supper, a husband, a wife, and so forth). When there is no exact modern equivalent to some aspect of a command (such as "honor the emperor" in 1 Pet. 2:17), then we are still obligated to obey the command, but we do so by *applying* it to situations that are essentially similar to the one found in the New Testament. Therefore, "honor the emperor" would be applied to honoring the president or the prime minister. In fact, in several such cases the immediate context contains pointers to broader applications (such as 1 Pet. 2:13–14, which mentions being subject to "every human institution" including the "emperor" and "governors" as specific examples). (For the small handful of slightly more difficult cases, such as a "holy kiss" and "foot washing," see section 10 below.)

But with Webb the situation is entirely different. He does not consider the moral commands of the New Testament to represent a perfect or final moral system for Christians. They are rather a pointer that "provides the direction toward the divine destination, but its literal, isolated words are not always the destination itself. Sometimes God's instructions are simply designed to get his flock moving" (p. 60).

At the heart of Webb's system is what he calls a "redemptive-movement hermeneutic." He says that some may prefer calling his approach a "progressive" or "developmental" or "trajectory" hermeneutic, and he says "that is fine" (p. 31). Webb explains his hermeneutic by what he calls "the X→Y→Z Principle." The letter Y indicates what the Bible says about a topic. Webb says, "The *central position* (Y) stands for where the isolated words of the Bible are in their development of a subject" (p. 31). The letter X represents "the perspective of the *original culture*," and the letter Z represents "an *ultimate ethic*," that is, God's final ideal that the Bible is moving toward.

Therefore, in Webb's system, what evangelicals have ordinarily understood to be "the teaching of the Bible" on particular subjects is in fact only a point along the way (indicated by letter Y) toward the development of a final or ultimate ethic (Z). Webb says:

> The X→Y→Z Principle illustrates how numerous aspects of the biblical text were *not* written to establish a utopian society with complete justice and

equity. They were written within a cultural framework with limited moves toward an ultimate ethic. (p. 31)

Therefore, Webb discovers a number of points where "our contemporary culture" has a better ethic than what is found in the words of the Bible. Our culture has a better ethic today "where it happens to reflect a better social ethic—one closer to an *ultimate ethic* (Z) than to the ethic revealed in the isolated words of the biblical text" (p. 31).

Webb's approach to Scripture can also be seen in the way he deals with biblical texts regarding slavery. While most evangelical interpreters today would say that the New Testament does not command or encourage or endorse slavery, but rather tells Christians who were slaves how they should conduct themselves within that situation, and also gives principles that would modify and ultimately lead to the abolition of slavery (1 Cor. 7:21–22; Gal. 3:28; Philem. 16, 21), Webb does not take this approach. Instead, Webb believes that the Bible actually endorses slavery; however, it is a kind of slavery with "better conditions and fewer abuses" (p. 37).

Webb's redemptive-movement hermeneutic approaches the slavery question by saying that the original culture (X) approved of "slavery with many abuses" (p. 37). Second, the Bible (Y) endorses "slavery with better conditions and fewer abuses" (p. 37). However, Webb believes that on the issue of slavery "our culture is much closer to an ultimate ethic than it is to the unrealized ethic reflected in the isolated words of the Bible" (p. 37). Today, the ethic of our culture, which is superior to that of the Bible, has "slavery eliminated and working conditions often improved" (p. 37). Webb believes our culture is much closer to an "ultimate ethic" (Z) in which we will see "wages maximized for all" (p. 37).[2]

At the end of the book, Webb recapitulates the results of his analysis regarding slavery:

> Scripture does not present a "finalized ethic" in every area of human relationship. . . . To stop where the Bible stops (with its isolated words) ultimately fails to reapply the redemptive spirit of the text as it spoke to the original audience. It fails to see that further reformation is possible. . . . While Scripture had a positive influence in its time, we should take that redemptive spirit and move to an even better, more fully-realized ethic today. (p. 247)

Therefore, rather than saying that *the New Testament* does not endorse or command slavery, Webb believes that it does approve a system of slavery for the people at the time at which it was written. However, in its modifications and regulations of the institution

---

[2] Webb does not explain what he means by "wages maximized for all," but readers might wonder if it means that profits would be minimized and capital investment would be minimized in order for wages to be maximized? Or does it mean that all would have equal wages, since "all" would have maximized wages and this must mean that none would have lower wages than others? He does not make clear in what sense he thinks wages would be "maximized for all."

of slavery, the Bible starts us along a trajectory that would lead to the ultimate abolition of slavery, though the New Testament never actually reaches that point.

Webb asks why the Bible is this way:

> Why does God convey his message in a way that reflects a less-than-ultimate ethic . . . that evidences an underlying redemptive spirit and some movement in a positive direction, yet often permits its words to stop short of completely fulfilling such a spirit? Why did God not simply give us a clearly laid out blueprint for an ultimate-ethic utopia-like society? How could a God of absolute justice not give us a revelation concerning absolute justice on every page? (p. 57)

Webb's answer to these questions is to see this incomplete movement toward an ultimate ethic as a manifestation of God's wisdom. In showing us that the Bible was making progress against the surrounding culture, but not completely correcting the surrounding culture, we can see God's pastoral wisdom (p. 58), his pedagogical skill (p. 60), his evangelistic care for people who might not have heard the gospel if it proclaimed an ultimate ethic (p. 63), and other aspects of God's wisdom (pp. 64–66).

According to Webb's system, then, Christians can no longer simply go to the New Testament, begin to read the moral commands in one of Paul's epistles, and believe that they should obey them. According to Webb, that would be to use a "static hermeneutic" that just reads the "isolated words of the text" and fails to understand "the spirit-movement component of meaning which significantly transforms the application of texts for subsequent generations" (p. 34). Rather, we must realize that the New Testament teachings simply represent one stage in a trajectory of movement toward an ultimate ethic.

So how can Christians discover this "ultimate ethic"? Webb takes the rest of the book to explain eighteen fairly complex criteria by which Christians must evaluate the commands of the Bible and thereby discover the more just, more equitable ethical system toward which the Bible was heading. Once that ultimate ethic has been discovered, that ultimate ethic is the moral standard that we should follow and obey.

What this means in actual practice, then, is that the moral authority of the New Testament is completely nullified *at least in principle*. There may in fact be some New Testament commands that Webb concludes actually do represent an ultimate ethic, but even then we should obey them *not because they are taught in the New Testament*, but because Webb's system has found that what the New Testament teaches is also the moral standard that is found in his "ultimate ethic."

The implications of this for Christian morality are extremely serious. It means that our ultimate authority is no longer the Bible but Webb's system. Of course, he claims that the "redemptive spirit" that drives his hermeneutic for each area of ethics is derived from the biblical text, but by his own admission this "redemptive spirit" is not the same as the teachings of the Bible, but rather is derived from Webb's own analysis of the interaction between the ancient culture and the biblical text. Here is his key explanation:

> The final and most important characteristic of a redemptive-movement hermeneutic is its focus on the spirit of a text. . . . The coinage "redemptive-movement hermeneutic" is derived from a concern that Christians apply the *redemptive spirit* within Scripture, not merely, or even primarily, its isolated words. *Finding the underlying spirit of a text is a delicate matter. It is not as direct or explicit as reading the words on the page.* In order to grasp the spirit of a text, *the interpreter must listen for how the texts sounds within its various social contexts.* Two life settings are crucial: the broader, foreign ancient Near Eastern and Greco-Roman (ANE/GR) social context and the immediate, domestic Israelite/church setting. One must ask, what change/improvement is the text making in the lives of people in the covenant community? And, how does the text influence the larger ANE/GR world? Through reflecting upon these social-setting questions *the modern reader will begin to sense the redemptive spirit of the text.* Also, a third setting permits one another way of discovering the redemptive spirit, namely, the canonical movement across various biblical epochs. (p. 53; emphasis added)

This paragraph is remarkable for the candor with which it reveals the subjective and indeterminate nature of Webb's ethical system. If the heart of the "most important characteristic" of his hermeneutic is discovered through "reflecting upon" the way the Bible interacts with ancient Near Eastern and Greco-Roman cultures, and through such reflection the interpreter will "begin to sense the redemptive spirit of the text," we have entered a realm so subjective that no two interpreters in the future will probably ever be able to agree on where the "redemptive spirit of the text" that they are beginning to "sense" is leading, and what kind of "ultimate ethic" they should count as God's will for them.

Those with a predisposition toward socialism will no doubt be delighted that Webb has begun "to sense" a "redemptive spirit" that will lead to "wages maximized for all" (p. 37). But those more inclined to capitalism will no doubt "begin to sense" quite another "redemptive spirit" in which the dominant biblical themes of freedom and liberty and fair reward for one's labor lead to an "ultimate ethic" (Z) that encourages investment and a free-enterprise system, one with *maximization of profits* for those worthy individuals who through their business activities best meet the material needs of mankind, and thus by means of the high quality of goods they produce for others best show that they love their neighbors as themselves.

No doubt Arminians will "begin to sense the redemptive spirit" of Arminianism moving against the fatalism of the ancient world in a much more Arminian direction than we find even in the New Testament. And Calvinists, through serious and sober reflection upon the way in which the biblical text corrects the puny, weak gods in the

Greek and Roman pantheon, will "begin to sense the redemptive spirit" of Calvinism moving through the New Testament toward an even higher emphasis on the sovereignty of God than we find in any current New Testament texts.

And on and on it will go. Baptists will "begin to sense the redemptive spirit" of believer's baptism as the New Testament corrects the all-inclusive nature of the religions of the ancient world, and paedobaptists will "begin to sense the redemptive spirit" of inclusion of infants in the covenant community as the New Testament decisively corrects the neglect and abuse of children found in many ancient cultures. People seeking justification for their desire to obtain a divorce will "begin to sense the redemptive spirit" of more and more reasons for divorce, moving from the one reason that Jesus allowed (adultery in Matt. 19:9) to the increasing freedom found in Paul, who allows a second ground for divorce (desertion by an unbeliever in 1 Cor. 7:15) along a trajectory toward many more reasons for divorce as we move toward an "ultimate ethic" (Z) where everyone should be completely happy with his or her spouse.

Now, Webb may object that these hypothetical "redemptive spirit" findings could not be derived from a responsible use of his eighteen criteria. On the other hand, I have lived in the academic world for over 30 years, and I have a great deal of confidence in the ability of scholars to take a set of eighteen criteria like this and make a case for almost anything they desire, through skillful manipulation of the variable factors involved in the criteria. But whether or not these are the result of a proper use of Webb's criteria, the point remains: *the standard is no longer what the New Testament says, but rather the point toward which some biblical scholar thinks the Bible was moving.* And that is why I believe it is correct to say that Webb's redemptive-movement hermeneutic nullifies in principle the moral authority of the entire New Testament.

2. Webb Fails in Nearly Every Section of the Book to Recognize That Christians Are No Longer Bound by Old Covenant Laws, and Thus He Neglects to Use the Fundamental Structural Division of the Entire Bible (the Difference between the Old Testament and the New Testament) as a Means of Determining Moral Obligations for Christians Today. It is remarkable that in section after section, Webb does not distinguish between the teachings of the Old Testament and the teachings of the New Testament. He flattens them all into one large category that he calls "the Bible." Thus, in dealing with slavery, he combines New Testament and Old Testament passages in the same list, without noticing any distinction between them (pp. 44, 74–76, 163–164, and elsewhere). He does the same thing with regard to texts referring to women (pp. 46–47, 76–81, 160, 165–167) and primogeniture (94–95, 136–142), and with respect to other elements of the Mosaic law code.

Although Webb occasionally gives limited attention to what he calls "canonical movement" from the Old Testament to the New Testament (see pp. 77–78 for example), for him these are just two steps along the way in the direction of further redemptive movement in ethical development beyond the New Testament. *He never considers the possibility that the development from Old Testament to New Testament is the end, and that the New Testament itself provides the final ethical standard for Christians in the new covenant.*

When Webb claims that "A redemptive-movement hermeneutic has always been a major part of the historic church, apostolic and beyond" (p. 35), and therefore that all Christians believe in some kind of "redemptive-movement" hermeneutic, he fails to make one important distinction: evangelicals have always held that the redemptive movement within Scripture ends with the New Testament! Webb carries it beyond the New Testament.

Yes, the New Testament explicitly tells us that we are no longer under the regulations of the old covenant (Heb. 8:6–13), so we have clear warrant for saying the sacrificial laws and dietary laws are no longer binding on us. And we do see the apostles in a process of coming to understand the inclusion of the Gentiles in the church (Acts 15; Gal. 2:1–14; 3:28). But *that process was completed within the New Testament*, and the commands given to Christians in the New Testament say nothing about excluding Gentiles from the church! We do not have to progress on a "trajectory" beyond the New Testament to discover that.

Christians living in the time of Paul's epistles were living under the new covenant. And we Christians living in the year 2003 are also living under the new covenant. This is "the new covenant in my blood" (1 Cor. 11:25) that Jesus established and that we affirm every time we take the Lord's Supper. That means that we Christians today are living in *the same period in God's plan for "the history of redemption"* as the first-century Christians. And that is why we can read the New Testament and see it applying directly to ourselves today.

To attempt to go *beyond* the New Testament documents and derive our authority from "where the New Testament was heading" is to reject the very documents that God gave us to govern our life under the new covenant until Christ returns.

When Webb does touch on the subject of the relationship between the Old and New Testaments, he says that he is not going to decide how the Old Testament relates to the New Testament. After saying that he rejects both the idea that "*only* those particulars of the Mosaic law that the New Testament *expressly sanctions* apply to New Testament believers," and the idea that "Christians are bound to obey *all* those particulars in the Mosaic law that the New Testament does not *expressly abrogate*," then Webb tells us:

> Nor am I going to establish a more durable and alternative dictum about how the Old Testament relates to the modern Christian. Such is beyond the scope of this work. (p. 205)

The problem is that throughout the book Webb uses dozens of examples from the Old Testament to establish and support the need to use his eighteen criteria in determining what is culturally relative, and to support the idea that we should abandon what he calls "biblical patriarchy" and move beyond it by "taking . . . a redemptive-movement approach to the present-day application of biblical patriarchy" (p. 172, after appealing to several Mosaic covenant laws regarding the treatment of women on pp. 165–167, for example). Rather than saying, for example, that we should not follow the law that a woman was to be stoned if she was not a virgin at the time of marriage (Deut. 22:20–21) *because we are under the new covenant and no longer subject to the laws of the Mosaic covenant*, Webb uses this law about stoning as one of his examples showing that "the Christian who embraces the redemptive-movement hermeneutic will surely carry the redemptive spirit of *the biblical text* forward in today's setting" (p. 167). What is telling in this statement (and dozens like it throughout the book) is his phrase "the biblical text." Anything found in any part of the Bible for Webb is simply part of "the biblical text," which is heavily affected by its ancient culture and which we need to move beyond today.

When Webb repeatedly gives long lists of Mosaic laws on slavery or wives, and then says it would be foolish to obey what "the Bible" says on these subjects today, unsuspecting readers may think that he has built a persuasive case for his eighteen criteria. But he has not, because the change from old covenant to new covenant means that those dozens of Mosaic laws are not part of what "the Bible" requires of Christians today. We are not under the Mosaic law.[3]

Yet this fundamental omission is pervasive in Webb's book. If someone were to go through his book and remove all the examples he takes from the Old Testament, and all the implications that he draws from those examples, we would be left not with a book by Webb but with a small pamphlet.

Webb's failure to adequately take into account the fact that Christians are no longer bound by Mosaic covenant legislation is an omission of such magnitude as to nullify the value of this book as a guide for hermeneutics.

3. Webb Repeatedly Confuses Events with Commands, and Fails to Recognize That What the Bible Reports as a Background Situation (Such as Slavery or Monarchy, for Example) It Does Not Necessarily Approve or Command. Again and again in his analysis Webb assumes that "the Bible" (in Webb's undifferentiated form, lumping Old Testament and New Testament verses together) supports things such as slavery (see pp. 33, 36–37, 84, 106, 186, 202–203). He also uses monarchy as an example, assuming that the Bible presents monarchy as a favored form of government, one that people should approve or even say that the Bible requires (see, for example, pp. 107, 186, 203).

With respect to slavery, therefore, Webb says that

> a static hermeneutic [this is Webb's term for the hermeneutic used by everyone who does not use his redemptive-movement hermeneutic] would apply this slavery-refuge text by *permitting the ownership of slaves today*, provided

---

[3] Webb does at one point note that Christians are no longer bound to obey laws concerning Old Testament sacrifices, food laws, and circumcision (pp. 201–202), because these are explicitly discontinued in the New Testament, but the recognition of these specific points of discontinuity is nowhere else expanded into a general realization that New Testament Christians are not under the Mosaic law code.

that the church offers similar kinds of refuge for runaway *slaves. . . . Christians would dare not speak out against slavery*. They would support the institution of slavery . . . (p. 33, italics added)

What is rather astonishing is that the only alternative that Webb acknowledges to his position is what he calls a "static hermeneutic." But then he affirms that such a "static hermeneutic" would have to support slavery:

Even more tragic is that, in arguing for or *in permitting biblical slavery today*, a static hermeneutic takes our current standard of human rights and working conditions *backwards* by quantum leaps. We would shame a gospel that proclaims freedom to the captive. . . . A static hermeneutic would not condemn biblical-type slavery if that social order were to reappear in society today." (pp. 34, 36)

In his eyes there are only two choices: do you support Webb's system or do you support slavery? Which will it be? He appears oblivious to the fact that millions of Christians since the time of the apostle Paul have opposed slavery *from the text of Scripture itself*, without using Webb's new system of interpretation, and without rejecting the final moral authority of the New Testament. To say we have to choose between Webb's system and slavery is historically unfounded, is biblically untrue, and is astonishing in its failure to recognize other alternatives.

Webb sometimes appeals to the fact that proponents of slavery or proponents of monarchy in the past appealed to the Bible to prove their case. He says, "slavery proponents frequently argued from theological and christological analogies in the text" (p. 186), and that "in the past, the submission texts cited above were used by Christians to support monarchy as the only appropriate, God-honoring form of government" (p. 107). But the fact that some Christians in the past used the Bible to support slavery does not prove that the Bible supports slavery any more than one can prove that the Bible supports any number of false teachings (such as Arianism, or the Crusades, or the Inquisition, or salvation by works) that were supported in the past by people "using the Bible," but were ultimately rejected by the church.

With regard to slavery, the fact of the matter is that the Bible was used by more Christians to *oppose* slavery than to *defend* it, and eventually their arguments won, and slavery was abolished. But the difference from Webb is that the evangelical, Bible-believing Christians who ultimately brought about the abolition of slavery *did not advocate modifying or nullifying any biblical teaching*, or moving "beyond" the New Testament to a better ethic. They taught the abolition of slavery from the New Testament itself.

The New Testament never commanded slavery, but gave principles that regulated it and ultimately led to its abolition. Paul says to slaves, "*If you can gain your freedom, avail yourself of the opportunity*" (1 Cor. 7:21). And he tells Philemon, regarding his slave Onesimus, that he should welcome him back "*no longer as a slave* but more than a slave, as a beloved brother" (Philem. 16), and that he should "receive him as you would receive me" (v. 17), and that he should forgive anything that Onesimus owed him, or at least that Paul would pay it himself (vv. 18–19), and finally he says, "Confident of your obedience, I write to you, knowing that you will do *even more than I say*" (v. 21). This is a strong and not very subtle hint that Philemon should grant freedom to Onesimus.

When we couple those verses with the realization that every human being is created in the image of God (see Gen. 1:27; 9:6; James 3:9; see also Gal. 3:28), we then see that the Bible, and especially the New Testament, contains powerful principles that would lead to an abolition of slavery. The New Testament never commands people to practice slavery or to own slaves, but rather gives principles that would lead to the overthrow of that institution, and also regulates it while it is in existence by statements such as "Masters, treat your slaves justly and fairly, knowing that you also have a master in heaven" (Col. 4:1).

The Bible does not approve or command slavery any more than it approves or commands persecution of Christians. When the author of Hebrews commends his readers by saying, "You joyfully accepted the plundering of your property, since you knew that you yourselves had a better possession and an abiding one" (Heb. 10:34), that does not mean the Bible *supports* the plundering of Christians' property, or that it *commands theft*! It only means that *if* Christians find themselves in a situation where their property is taken through persecution, they should still rejoice because of their heavenly treasure, which cannot be stolen. Similarly, when the Bible tells slaves to be submissive to their masters, it does not mean that the Bible supports or commands slavery, but only that it tells people who are in a situation of slavery how they should respond.

Webb's mistaken evaluation of the Bible's teaching on slavery forms a fundamental building block in constructing his hermeneutic. Once we remove his claim that "the Bible" condones slavery, Webb's Exhibit A is gone, and he has lost his primary means of supporting the claim that we need his "redemptive-movement hermeneutic" to move beyond the ethic of the Bible itself.

4. Webb Repeatedly Assumes Unlikely Interpretations of Scripture in Order to Present a "Bible" That Is So Clearly Wrong That It Is Impossible to Believe and Obey Today. In numerous sections Webb presents what he claims is the teaching of "the Bible" in order to build up a long list of culturally relative teachings, teachings to which readers will evidently respond by thinking, "Of course we cannot believe or obey those things today!" Webb then uses these lists of "impossible for today" teachings in order to show that his eighteen criteria are necessary and valid to determine cultural relativity.

The problem is, most evangelicals do not need Webb's "redemptive-movement hermeneutic" to know that the Bible does not teach these things. In fact, few if any responsible exegetes of Scripture today would claim that the Bible teaches any of these things as ideas or ethical standards that should be followed by Christians today. When Webb assumes that "the Bible" teaches them apart from interpreting it with his redemptive-movement hermeneutic, he assumes interpretations contrary to the biblical texts themselves.

Here is a list of things that Webb assumes that the Bible teaches:

a. People Should Pursue Farming as an Occupation (pp. 124–125): Webb derives this from the fact that "in the garden man was instructed to till the ground and eat of its produce" (p. 124). The problem here is that Webb takes a *good* thing in the Bible (raising food from the ground) and wrongly makes it into a *requirement for every person*, rather than seeing it as one among several responsibilities that God gave the human race. A more sound application of this text would be to say that God still expects human beings to gain food from the ground, but the diversity of occupations within Scripture shows that this never was an expectation or a requirement of every single person.

b. People Should Use Only Ground Transportation: Webb says that "the mode of transportation within the garden was walking," and he allows for extending that to "transportation by horse and other animals" (p. 125). He says that the creation pattern thus "squares nicely" with the lifestyle of those who restrict their transportation to horse and buggy today. But he says most Christians would see this as a "non-binding pattern within the creation texts" (p. 125). The problem in this case is that even within the first two chapters of Genesis the commands to "subdue" the earth and "have dominion" over it imply an expectation that human beings would develop all sorts of products from the earth, including many different means of transportation. We do not need Webb's redemptive-movement hermeneutic to know that the Bible never presents "ground transportation" as the mode of transportation that people should use exclusively (think of all the journeys by boats in the Bible), nor is this pattern of transportation ever used elsewhere as a basis for commands to God's people.

Once again in this case Webb has taken an event (Adam and Eve walking) and has mistakenly viewed it as a requirement that then has to be overcome by Webb's redemptive-movement hermeneutic.

c. Singleness Is outside the Will of God: Webb says, since Adam and Eve were married in the garden of Eden, "if the creation material provides a tightly ordered paradigm for all of humanity to follow, one might get the impression that singleness was outside the will of God" (p. 124). Here Webb has misread the Genesis narrative. Genesis 1–2 does not present a pattern where marriage is the only acceptable option, for God's command to Adam and Eve to "be fruitful and multiply" (Gen. 1:28) envisions a situation where they would have children, and these children would have to be single for some time before they could be married. What we see rather from the creation narrative is that God created marriage, that marriage is "very good," and that the relationship between Adam and Eve in marriage was not sinful but was good in God's sight. But to say that marriage is *good* does not imply that singleness is *bad*, or that marriage is *required*, nor does the Genesis narrative imply those things.

d. Women Should Be Viewed as Property: Webb says, "Within the biblical text one discovers an ownership mentality in the treatment of women. Women are frequently listed with the cattle and servants (Exod. 20:17; cf. Deut. 5:21; Judg. 5:30)" (p. 165). But Webb oversimplifies when he assumes that listing "with" something implies a similar status. The main verse he cites is Exodus 20:17:

> You shall not covet your neighbor's house; you shall not covet your neighbor's wife, or his male servant, or his female servant, or his ox, or his donkey, or anything that is your neighbor's.

This does not imply an "ownership mentality" toward women any more than it proves that people thought of women as houses! This amazing commandment actually establishes a high level of protection and honor for women and for marriage, for it addresses purity of heart.[4] People were not to covet someone else's house or wife or animals, but this surely also implies that wives were not to covet their neighbors' husbands, and surely the commandment does not also imply that husbands were viewed as property. Hearers could easily distinguish between houses, animals, and wives. Moreover, in the previous verses the seventh commandment (against adultery) is separate from the eighth (against stealing), thus clearly making a distinction between husbands and wives, on the one hand, and property on the other. In any case, it is not hermeneutically legitimate to take aspects of the Mosaic law code as part of what "the Bible" teaches about women, for Christians are no longer under the Mosaic covenant. We do not need Webb's redemptive-movement hermeneutic to understand this, nor do these Mosaic covenant provisions demonstrate the legitimacy of Webb's hermeneutic.

e. Families Should Practice Primogeniture: Webb sees a system of primogeniture, in which the oldest son received "a double portion of the inheritance . . . led in military protection for the family . . . avenged wrongs done against family members . . . performed religious ceremonies" (p. 141), and so forth as a pattern that is found in the ethical system contained in "the Bible." But he says primogeniture is culturally relative and should no longer be practiced today. But in this case again Webb has mistakenly confused *events that are reported by the Bible* with *things that are required in the ethical system taught in the Bible*. Nowhere does the Bible command people to follow primogeniture customs (and Webb himself shows many examples where Scripture deviates from this pattern, pp. 136–139), and therefore we do not need a redemptive-movement hermeneutic to know that such a pattern is not required for people to follow, nor was it ever something that God required everyone to follow, even in the ancient world.

---

[4] Webb mentions other factors, such as a bride price paid to a father, and the fact that a husband is sometimes called a *ba'al* ("master"). But these things do not establish a view of women as property, for the bride price could simply be an expression of the honor and high value that the future husband was attributing to his bride, and the word *ba'al* can simply mean "husband" (BDB, 127).

f. We Should Establish and Support Slavery (pp. 33, 36–37, 84, 106, 186, 202–203).

g. People Should Establish and Support Monarchy as the Right Form of Government (pp. 153, 186).

h. People Should Wash Each Others's Feet (pp. 204, 211).

i. Adult Children Should Obey Their Parents (p. 212).

j. The Earth Is the Center of the Universe: Webb says, "Scripture depicts a geocentric or earth-centered model of the universe. The earth is placed on a stationary foundation in a central location with other luminous bodies revolving above it" (pp. 221–222).

k. The Earth Is Flat: Webb says, "The church had difficulty accepting [that the earth was round] . . . because the Bible incorporated a 'flat earth' view of the world" (p. 223).

l. Wives Should Be Subject to Their Husbands Because Husbands Are Older and Better Educated (pp. 213–216).

m. Husbands Should Be Allowed to Physically Discipline Their Wives (p. 167, 189–190): Webb actually claims that the Bible gives approval to the idea that a husband should "strip his wife" and "physically confine" her (p. 189). Webb bases this on his own misinterpretation of Hosea 2:1–23. He claims that in this passage,

> unless Gomer puts away her sexual promiscuity, Hosea will take action against his wife:
>
> > I [Hosea] will strip her [Gomer] naked
> > and make her as bare as on the day she was born. . . .
> > Therefore I will block her path with thorn bushes;
> > I will wall her in so she cannot find her way. (p. 189)

What Webb does not disclose to readers is that the overwhelming majority of commentators understand this entire chapter to be speaking not of Hosea and Gomer but of God's judgment upon Israel. Speaking in prophetic imagery, as is common among the Old Testament prophets, God says that unless Israel abandons her sins, he will "strip her naked and make her as in the day she was born" (Hos. 2:3), vividly portraying God's judgment on the nation.[5]

---

[5] Thomas McComiskey writes, "It is obvious that the lengthy address in 2:3–25 [English 2:1–23] is directed to the nation and not to Gomer personally." "Hosea," in *The Minor Prophets*, ed. Thomas McComiskey (Grand Rapids, MI: Baker, 1992), 32. See also Keil and Delitzsch, Douglas Stuart and the section heading before chap. 2 in many English Bible translations, which say something similar to the *NIV Study Bible* heading, "Israel Punished and Restored" (p. 1323). McComiskey points out that the phrase in verse 15, "as at the time when she came out of the land of Egypt," cannot apply to Gomer and indicates that the entire passage must have Israel primarily in mind. (Since the passage is an extended allegory, there are elements of it that

n. People Should Greet One Another with a Holy Kiss (pp. 203–204).

o. Women Are Simply "Reproductive Gardens" and Husbands Provide 100 percent of the Baby's New Life: Webb says that the biblical picture is one in which

> a woman provides the "soil" into which a man planted the seed of the minia-
> ture child . . . to grow for nine months. . . . A tight agricultural analogy—the
> man provides the totality of the new life in seedling form while the woman
> provides only the fertile environment for its growth—reflects a culture-based
> component within the text. (pp. 223–224)

p. The Bible Approves Obedience to Many Details of the Old Testament Narrative and the Old Testament Mosaic Laws, Such as "Polygamy and Concubinage, Levirate Marriages, Unequal Value of Men and Women in Vow Redemption . . . the Treatment of Women as Spoils of Battle" and So Forth (pp. 166–167): If readers actually believe Webb when he implies that the Bible teaches these things, then they will be inclined to agree with his argument that we need to go beyond the ethical system of "the Bible" and use Webb's "redemptive-movement hermeneutic" to move closer toward an "ultimate ethic."

But the fact is that the Bible teaches and commands none of these things for Christians today. And that is not because Webb's "redemptive-movement hermeneutic" enables us to move *beyond* the ethics of the Bible. It is rather because new covenant Christians know that the ethical system of the Bible itself does not support or require these things. Webb has given us a pot of stew mixed with Mosaic covenant laws that no longer apply, fragments of narrative history that were never commanded, cultural customs or habits that the Bible never commanded us to follow, and phenomenological observations of the natural world that the Bible never presented as a description of the shape of the earth or the structure of the universe. We do not need a "redemptive-movement hermeneutic" to know that the Bible does not require these things of people today. We simply need the Bible itself, understood in each case with sensitivity to the immediate context and to the larger old covenant-new covenant structure of redemptive history that is found within the Bible itself.

5. Webb Creates an Overly Complex System of Interpretation That Will Require a Class of "Priests" Who Have to Interpret the Bible for Us in the Light of Ancient Near Eastern and Greco-Roman Culture. At the heart of Webb's system is his requirement that the interpreter "must listen for how the text sounds within its various social contexts," especially "the broader, foreign ancient Near-Eastern and Greco-Roman (ANE/GR) social context and the immediate, domestic Israelite/church setting" (p. 53).

---

of course could apply to the situation between Hosea and Gomer as well, but that does not mean that the primary reference is to Gomer, and it certainly does not mean that the passage provides justification for a husband to physically discipline his wife.)

How does one do this? Webb gives eighteen criteria that one must use in order to carry out his redemptive-movement hermeneutics properly. His first criterion of these eighteen is called "preliminary movement," and here is how he says it should happen:

> Assessing redemptive-movement has its complications. Without going into an elaborate explanation, I will simply suggest a number of guidelines: (1) the ANE/GR *real* world must be examined along with its *legal* world, (2) the biblical subject on the *whole* must be examined along with its *parts*, (3) the biblical text must be compared to a number of other ANE/GR cultures which themselves must be compared with each other and (4) any portrait of movement must be composed of broad input from all three streams of assessment—foreign, domestic, and canonical. (p. 82)

And this is just his procedure for the first of eighteen criteria! Who will be able to do this? Who knows the history of ancient cultures well enough to make these assessments?

Speaking from the perspective of over 30 years in the academic world, I will not say that only one percent of the *Christians* in the world will be able to use Webb's system and tell us what moral standards we should follow today. I will not even say that one percent of the *seminary-trained pastors* in the world will be able to follow Webb's system and tell us what moral standards we should obey today. I will not even say that one percent of the *seminary professors* will be able to have the requisite expertise in ancient cultures to use Webb's system and tell us what moral standards we should follow today. That is because the evaluation and assessment of any one ancient culture, to say nothing of all the ancient cultures surrounding the Bible, is a massive undertaking, even with regard to one narrow subject such as laws concerning marriage and divorce, or property rights, or education and training of children, and so forth. It is time-consuming and requires much specialized knowledge and an excellent research library. Therefore, I will not even say that one percent of the *seminary professors who have academic doctorates in Old Testament or New Testament* will be able to use Webb's system and tell us what moral standards we should follow today, for many of them do not have specialized and extensive knowledge in the cultures surrounding God's people at the time the Bible was written. No, *in the end Webb's system as he describes it above can only be used by far less than one percent of the professors of New Testament and Old Testament in the Christian world today*, those few scholars who have the time and the specialized knowledge of rabbinic studies, of Greco-Roman culture, and of ancient Egyptian and Babylonian and Assyrian and Persian cultures, and who have access to a major research library, and who will then be able to use Webb's "redemptive-movement hermeneutic" in the way he describes in the paragraph just quoted. This tiny group of experts will have to tell us what moral standards God wants us to follow today.

And that is only for Criterion 1 in his list of eighteen criteria.

If the evangelical world begins to adopt Webb's system, it is not hard to imagine that we will soon require a new class of "priests," those erudite scholars with sufficient expertise in the ancient world that they can give us reliable conclusions about what kind of "ultimate ethic" we should follow today.

But this will create another problem, one I have observed often as I have lived and taught in the academic world for over 30 years: *scholars with such specialized knowledge often disagree.* Anyone familiar with the debates over rabbinic views of justification in the last two decades will realize how difficult it can be to understand exactly what was believed in an ancient culture on even one narrow topic, to say nothing of the whole range of ethical commands that we find in the New Testament.

Where then will Webb's system lead us? *It will lead us to massive inability to know with confidence anything that God requires of us.* The more scholars who become involved with telling us "how the Bible was moving" with respect to this or that aspect of ancient culture, the more opinions we will have, and the more despair people will feel about ever being able to know what God's requires of us, what his "ultimate ethic" is.

How different from Webb's system is the simple, direct teaching of the New Testament! Consider the following commands:

> Therefore, having put away falsehood, let each one of you speak the truth with his neighbor, for we are members of one another. (Eph. 4:25)

> Let the thief no longer steal, but rather let him labor, doing honest work with his own hands, so that he may have something to share with anyone in need. (Eph. 4:28)

> Let no corrupting talk come out of your mouths, but only such as is good for building up, as fits the occasion, that it may give grace to those who hear. (Eph. 4:29)

> Let all bitterness and wrath and anger and clamor and slander be put away from you, along with all malice. Be kind to one another, tenderhearted, forgiving one another, as God in Christ forgave you. (Eph. 4:31–32)

> But sexual immorality and all impurity or covetousness must not even be named among you, as is proper among saints. (Eph. 5:3)

> And do not get drunk with wine, for that is debauchery, but be filled with the Spirit. (Eph. 5:18)

> Wives, submit to your own husbands, as to the Lord. (Eph. 5:22)

> Husbands, love your wives, as Christ loved the church and gave himself up for her. (Eph. 5:25)

> Children, obey your parents in the Lord, for this is right. (Eph. 6:1)

> Fathers, do not provoke your children to anger, but bring them up in the discipline and instruction of the Lord. (Eph. 6:4)

I do not believe that God gave us a Bible that is so direct and clear and simple, only to require that all believers throughout all history should first filter these commands through a complex system of eighteen criteria before they can know whether to obey them or not. That simply is not the kind of Bible that God gave us, nor is there any indication in Scripture itself that believers have to have some kind of specialized academic knowledge, and some kind of elaborate hermeneutical system, before they can be sure that these are the things that God requires of his children.

6. Webb Creates a System That Is Overly Liable to Subjective Influence and Therefore Is Indeterminate and Will Lead to Significant Misuse. A built-in liability to subjective influence is evident in Webb's own treatment of several subjects, particularly in his treatment of texts relating to the role of women in marriage and in the church. With few exceptions, the selection of materials and the evaluation of the criteria are skewed in order that Webb can show again and again how male leadership in the home and in the church is a culturally relative idea. For example, he places his first three criteria—(1) Preliminary Movement, (2) Seed Ideas, (3) Breakouts—within the category of "persuasive criteria" (p. 73) because all three of these assume that one needs to move to a higher ethic than that of the New Testament. These categories therefore allow him to say that the New Testament teachings on women are only "preliminary," and that the exceptions he finds in Galatians 3:28 and in Deborah and Junia are the truly "persuasive" criteria that point to the "ultimate ethic" that is far better than the New Testament, the ethic toward which the New Testament is heading.

By contrast, when he gets to Criterion 6, which is "Basis in Original Creation, Section 1: Patterns" (p. 123), Webb brings in several bizarre items, such as "farming as an occupation" and "ground transportation," which no responsible interpreter would ever say the Bible requires for everyone today. Why does he do this? These allow him to claim that "original creation patterns do not provide an automatic guide for assessing what is transcultural within Scripture" (p. 126). But when someone brings in such bizarre interpretations in order to be able to say that original creation patterns of marriage are not clearly transcultural, then the reader rightly suspects that a subjective bias has entered into the selection of material.

Similarly, when we reach Criterion 14, "Basis in Theological Analogy" (p. 185), of course the difficulty for egalitarians is going to be the fact that Paul makes an analogy between the relationship of a husband and wife and the relationship between Christ and the church in Ephesians 5:22–33. How does Webb evade the force of the argument that this is obviously a transcultural comparison? He says there are other "theological analogies in Scripture that are not transcultural" and he says that slavery, monarchy, and "*right-handedness*" are also supported by "theological analogy" within Scripture (pp. 186–187). The problem is of course that the examples are not parallel. The Bible never says, "Support monarchy as the best system of government because God is a heavenly king," or "Support slavery as an institution because God is the ultimate slave owner in heaven," or "It is better to be right-handed because Christ sits at God's right hand." So Webb's examples are not parallel to the example of Paul's statement,

> the husband is the head of the wife even as Christ is the head of the church. . . . As the church submits to Christ, so also wives should submit in everything to their husbands. Husbands, love your wives, as Christ loved the church and gave himself up for her. (Eph. 5:23–25)

The fact that Webb brings in what he calls examples of "theological analogy" that are not really parallel is again, it seems to me, evidence of subjective bias in the formulation and development of his criteria. Once he brings in these examples, he is able to classify "Basis in Theological Analogy" as an "inconclusive" criterion (p. 185), one that really cannot rightly be used to prove that a wife's submission to her husband is transcultural.

Webb follows a similar procedure in Criterion 16, "Appeal to the Old Testament" (p. 201). In order to show that this also is an "inconclusive" criterion, Webb brings in examples that are not parallel to the Old Testament quotations concerning the role of women. Webb says that "several slave/master texts within the New Testament rely heavily on the Old Testament for their formulation for their ideas and words" (p. 202), but the passages he mentions (such as 1 Pet. 2:22–25) are simply used by the New Testament authors to show that Christians should trust in God when they are mistreated, and the passages in no way affirm that mistreatment of others is proper or that slavery is a morally right institution. In the same way, when Webb talks about "kings and subjects," he says, "The monarchy texts within the New Testament derive their message largely from the Old Testament" (p. 203), and he mentions particularly 1 Peter 2:13–17 and Romans 13:1–5. But these passages do not support what Webb claims. They tell Christians to be subject to the ruling authority, but they nowhere quote the Old Testament to prove that monarchy as an institution is required. Webb even goes so far in this section as to claim that the "holy kiss" and "foot-washing" are supported from the Old Testament (pp. 203–204), though no Old Testament verses are ever quoted to support them.

Once Webb has claimed that all these things are supported from the Old Testament but are not transcultural, it is the basis on which he claims that the New Testament teachings on the role of women are not transcultural just because they are supported by quotations from the Old Testament—he mentions 1 Corinthians 14:34, 1 Timothy 2:14–15 [sic], and 1 Peter 3:5–6 (p. 204). But because his other "cultural" examples are not parallel, this argument has little force.

Why is it then that Webb brings in these examples that are not parallel in his Criterion 16, "Appeal to the Old Testament"? Readers may well suspect that a subjective bias has entered into the selection of material here. But the same criteria could easily be used by others, with other examples selected, to produce widely divergent results.

7. Webb Tellingly Denies the Historicity of Genesis 2–3 in Order to Deny the Contemporary Validity of the Male Headship That He Finds Recorded in the Text. Webb agrees that "the practice of primogeniture in which the firstborn is granted prominence within the 'creative order' of a family unit" (p. 135) is found in the narrative in Genesis 2. Webb sees this as support for male headship within the text of Genesis 2. He also thinks this is how it is understood by Paul when he says, "For Adam was formed first, then Eve" (1 Tim. 2:13). But Webb sees this "primogeniture" theme in Genesis 2 as a cultural component in that text.

But how could there be changing cultural influence in the prefall garden of Eden? Webb answers this question in three ways. First, he says these indications of male headship may be a literary device that anticipates events in the future rather than accurately recording what was in fact true in the garden:

> A second question is how cultural features could possibly be found in the garden before the influence of culture. Several explanations exist. First, the whispers of patriarchy in the garden may have been placed there in order to anticipate the curse. (pp. 142–143)

Webb then claims that the literary construction of Genesis 2–3 includes at least one other example of "literary foreshadowing of the curse" in the pejorative description of the serpent as "*more crafty* than any of the wild animals" (Gen. 3:1). Webb then asks, "If the garden is completely pristine, how could certain creatures in the just-created animal kingdom reflect craftiness? Obviously, this Edenic material embraces *an artistic foreshadowing of events to come*" (p. 143, italics added).

Webb's analysis here assumes that there was no sin or evil in the garden *in actual fact*, but that by a literary device the author described the serpent as "crafty" (and therefore deceitful and therefore sinful), thus anticipating what he would be later, after the fall.

There are two problems here. First, it makes Genesis 3:1 affirm something that was not true at that time, and this denies the truthfulness of a section of historical narrative in Scripture. Second, it fails even to consider the most likely explanation, namely, that there was sin in the angelic world sometime after the completion of the initial creation (Gen. 1:31) but prior to Genesis 3:1.[6] Because of this rebellion in the angelic world (see 2 Pet. 2:4; Jude 6), Satan himself was somehow speaking through the serpent.[7] So Webb's

---

[6] This is a fairly standard view among evangelical scholars, but Webb does not even consider it. See Wayne Grudem, *Systematic Theology: An Introduction to Biblical Doctrine* (Leicester, UK: Inter-Varsity, and Grand Rapids, MI: Zondervan, 1994), 412, and the relevant pages given for other systematic theologies on pp. 434–435.

[7] The serpent, the act of deception, and Satan are connected in some New Testament contexts. Paul says, "I am afraid that as the serpent deceived Eve by his cunning, your thoughts will be led astray from a sincere and pure devotion to Christ" (2 Cor. 11:3, in a context opposing false apostles whom he categorizes as servants of Satan who "disguise themselves as servants of righteousness," v. 15). Revelation 12 describes Satan as "that ancient serpent, who is called the devil and Satan, the deceiver of the whole world" (v. 9). See also John 8:44 and 1 John 3:8, with reference to the beginning stages of history.

claim that there must be "artistic foreshadowing of events to come" is not persuasive with respect to the serpent in Genesis 3:1.

The same should be said of his claim that "the whispers of patriarchy in the garden may have been placed there in order to anticipate the curse" (pp. 142–143). In this statement Webb is saying that patriarchy did not exist in the garden *in actual fact*, but hints of it were placed in the story by the author as a way of anticipating the situation that would come about after there was sin in the world. This then is also an explicit denial of the historical accuracy of the Genesis 2 account.

Webb goes on with a second explanation for the indications of male headship in Genesis 2:

> Second, Eden's quiet echoes of patriarchy may be a way of *describing the past through present categories*. The creation story may be *using the social categories that Moses's audience would have been familiar with*. God sometimes permits such accommodation in order not to confuse the main point he wants to communicate with factors that are secondary to that overall theme. (p. 143, italics added).[8]

This is another way in which Webb denies the historicity of the Genesis 2 account. He is saying that Moses in the time he wrote was using "present categories" such as patriarchy to describe the past, and this was simply an "accommodation" by God "in order not to confuse the main point." All that is to say that patriarchy did not actually exist in the garden of Eden, but Moses inserted it there in Genesis 2 just the same, so as not to confuse his audience at a later time. Thus, Moses inserted into Genesis 2 facts that were not true.

Finally, Webb gives a third reason:

> Third . . . *the patriarchy of the garden may reflect God's anticipation of the social context into which Adam and Eve were about to venture*. An agrarian lifestyle . . . would naturally produce some kind of hierarchy between men and women. . . . The presentation of the male-female relationship in patriarchal forms may simply be a way of anticipating this first (and major) life setting into which humankind would enter. (p. 144)

Again, Webb believes that the element of primogeniture (Adam being created before Eve) in Genesis 2 may have been written there not because it reflected the actual facts of the situation in the garden of Eden, but *because Adam and Eve after they sinned would enter into a situation where Adam as husband had leadership over his wife*. This again is an explicit denial of the historical accuracy of the headship of Adam and his prior creation as found in Genesis 2. It was simply "a practical and gracious *anticipation* of the

---

[8] Webb explains in a footnote that the "main point" of the creation narrative "is that Yahweh created the heavens and all that is in them, and Yahweh created the earth and all that is in it—God made everything" (p. 143, n. 46).

agrarian setting into which Adam and Eve were headed" (p. 145, italics added; repeated on p. 151, note 55).

It is important to realize how much Webb is denying as historical fact in the Genesis narrative. He is not just denying that there actually was a "crafty" serpent who spoke to Eve (Gen. 3:1). He is also denying the entire *theme of primogeniture* that is found in Genesis 2. That is, he is denying the entire narrative structure that shows the man as created before the woman, for this is the basis for the "primogeniture" theme that Webb sees Paul referring to in 1 Timothy 2:13, "For Adam was formed first, then Eve."

How much of Genesis 2 does that involve? How much inaccurate material has to be inserted into Genesis 2, either as a literary device foreshadowing the fall (reason 1), or as an accommodation to the situation familiar to readers at the time of Moses (reason 2), or as an anticipation of an agrarian society that would be established after the fall (reason 3)? It is no small amount.

According to Webb's view of primogeniture in Genesis 2 as a literary device, the entire narrative of God placing the man in the garden (Gen. 2:8) and putting the man in the garden "to work it and keep it" (2:15) and commanding the man by himself that he may eat of every tree of the garden but not of the tree of the knowledge of good and evil (2:16–17), and saying, "It is not good that the man should be alone, I will make him a helper fit for him" (2:18), and bringing the beasts of the field and the birds of the heavens to the man to see what he would call them (2:19), and the man giving names to all livestock and all the birds of the heavens and every beast of the field (2:20), and there not being found a helper fit for man (2:20), and God causing a deep sleep to fall upon the man and taking one of his ribs and forming it into a woman (2:21–22)—all of this sequence that is summarized by Paul in the statement "For Adam was formed first, then Eve"—all of this is a mere literary device that did not actually happen, according to Webb.

And all of this then enables him to say that Criterion 7, "Basis in Original Creation, Section 2: Primogeniture" is only a "moderately persuasive criterion" (p. 123), so that he can then say that Paul's appeal to the creation of Adam prior to Eve is not proof of a transcultural ethical standard.

8. Webb Fails to Demonstrate That New Testament Teachings on Men and Women in the Home and in the Church Are Culturally Relative. Throughout Webb's book he attempts to dismantle most of the complementarian arguments for male leadership in the home and the church by claiming that the biblical texts on such male leadership are culturally relative, for various reasons. Yet in each case, his attempts to demonstrate cultural relativity for these texts do not turn out to be persuasive. In the following section, I consider each of Webb's claims for culturally relativity in the order in which they occur in his book.

a. Webb Fails to Show That New Testament Commands Regarding Male Headship Are Only a "Preliminary Movement" and That the New Testament Ethic Needs Further

Improvement (Criterion 1): Webb claims that the commands regarding wives submitting to their husbands in Ephesians 5:22–33 are not a final ethic that we should follow today, but are simply an indication of "where Scripture is moving on the issue of patriarchal power" (pp. 80–81). But this claim is not persuasive because it depends on his assumption that the ethical standards of the New Testament are not God's ultimate ethical standards for us, but are simply one step along the way toward a kind of "ultimate ethic" that we should adopt today (pp. 36–39).

b. Webb Fails to Show That Galatians 3:28 Is a "Seed Idea" That Would Ultimately Lead to the Abolition of Male Headship Once Cultural Changes Made It Possible to Adopt a Superior Ethic to That of the New Testament (Criterion 2): Once again, Webb's conception of a "seed idea" is based on his claim that some New Testament commands are inconsistent with that seed idea, and those commands show only that "the biblical author pushed society as far as it could go at that time without creating more damage than good" (p. 73). Webb claims that the "seed idea" is simply a pointer showing that there should be "further movement" toward a "more fully realized ethic" that is "more just, more equitable and more loving . . . a better ethic than the one expressed in the isolated words of the text" (p. 36).

But as I indicated above, it is not necessary to "move beyond" the ethic of the New Testament in order to argue for the abolition of slavery, for the New Testament never condones or approves of slavery as an institution, and never says it was created by God (as marriage was), and the New Testament itself provides statements that would eventually lead to the abolition of slavery *based on the New Testament ethic itself*, not based on some "higher ethic" that would later be discovered. Similarly, Galatians 3:28 should not be seen as a "seed idea" pointing to some future "higher ethic," but as a text that is fully consistent with other things the apostle Paul and other New Testament authors wrote about the relationships between men and women. If we take the entire New Testament as the very words of God for us in the new covenant today, then any claim that Galatians 3:28 should overrule other texts such as Ephesians 5 and 1 Timothy 2 should be seen as a claim that Paul the apostle contradicts himself, and therefore that the Word of God contradicts itself.

c. Webb Fails to Show That 1 Corinthians 7:3–5 Establishes an Egalitarian Model within Marriage (Criterion 3): In 1 Corinthians 7:3–5 Paul says:

> The husband should give to his wife her conjugal rights, and likewise the wife to her husband. For the wife does not have authority over her own body, but the husband does. Likewise the husband does not have authority over his own body, but the wife does. Do not deprive one another, except perhaps by agreement for a limited time, that you may devote yourselves to prayer; but then come together again, so that Satan may not tempt you because of your lack of self-control.

Webb claims that the explanation that John Piper and I gave for this text in our book, *Recovering Biblical Manhood and Womanhood*,[9] nullifies all male headship within marriage. Webb says that Piper and Grudem's approach "ultimately abandons their own position" because "once one has eliminated any power differential and set up mutual deference and mutual consent as the basis for *all* decision making in a marriage (such as Piper and Grudem have done) there is nothing that makes the view substantially different from egalitarianism" (p. 101).

But Webb has misread our argument. In the very section to which he refers, we say:

> What are the implications of this text for the leadership of the husband? Do the call for mutual yielding to sexual need and the renunciation of unilateral planning nullify the husband's responsibility for general leadership in the marriage? We don't think so. But this text . . . makes clear that his leadership will not involve selfish, unilateral choices. (p. 88)

Thus, Piper and I agree that 1 Corinthians 7:3–5 shows that there are areas of mutual obligation between husband and wife, and that we can extrapolate from that and say that the husband's leadership in the marriage should not be a selfish leadership that fails to listen to the concerns of his wife. But in that very context, and in dozens of places throughout the rest of the book, we argue that the husband has an authoritative leadership role in the marriage that the wife does not have. To say that the word *authority* is sometimes misunderstood is not to say that we deny the concept. We qualify and modify the concept of authority, as Scripture does, in many places, but we nevertheless affirm it throughout the rest of the book.

d. Webb Fails to Show That the Only Purpose for the Wife's Submission to Her Husband Is Evangelism, or That This Purpose Is No Longer Valid (Criterion 4): In dealing with his Criterion 4, "Purpose/Intent Statements," Webb says that Peter "tells wives to obey their husbands so that unbelieving husbands 'may be won over without words' (1 Pet. 3:1)," but that today the kind of "unilateral, patriarchy-type submission" that Peter advocates "may actually repulse him and prevent him from being won to Christ." Webb concludes that "the stated evangelistic purpose of the text is not likely to be fulfilled in our contemporary setting" (p. 107–108).

We should be very clear what Webb is saying here. He is saying that wives with unbelieving husbands today should not obey 1 Peter 3:1–2, which says:

> Likewise, wives, be subject to your own husbands, so that even if some do not obey the word, they may be won without a word by the conduct of their wives—when they see your respectful and pure conduct.

---

[9] John Piper and Wayne Grudem, eds., *Recovering Biblical Manhood and Womanhood: A Response to Evangelical Feminism* (Wheaton, IL: Crossway, 1991), 87–88.

One problem with Webb's assertion is that it trivializes the testimony of thousands of Christian women even today whose unbelieving husbands *have* been won by the submissive behavior of their believing wives.

A second problem with Webb's claim is that it makes first-century Christian evangelism into the ultimate "bait-and-switch" sales technique. Webb claims that Peter's command aimed to attract non-Christian husbands by the submissive behavior of their wives, but once these men became Christians and began to grow toward maturity they would discover the "seed ideas" for equality and "mutual submission" in texts such as Galatians 3:28, and then (according to Webb) they would learn that *this command for submission of their wives is a morally deficient pattern* that has to be abandoned in favor of an egalitarian position. Therefore, according to the logic of Webb's position, first-century evangelism was a deceptive maneuver, in which the Word of God told people to use a morally deficient pattern of behavior simply to win unbelievers.

The third problem with Webb's explanation is that it opens the door for people to disobey many other New Testament commands if they think that the reason given for the command will no longer be fulfilled in our modern culture. For example, the command to be subject to human government is also based on an expected good outcome:

> Be subject for the Lord's sake to every human institution, whether it be to the emperor as supreme, or to governors as sent by him to punish those who do evil and to praise those who do good. For this is the will of God, *that by doing good you should put to silence the ignorance of foolish people.* (1 Pet. 2:13–15)

But people today could say that being subject to government might not "put to silence the ignorance of foolish people," because some governments in some societies today are just so hardened against the gospel that it will make no difference to them. Therefore (according to Webb's reasoning), we do not have to obey that command either.[10]

A fourth problem with Webb's approach is that it fails completely to consider the *other reasons* given in the New Testament for a wife's submission to her husband. Paul says:

> Wives, submit to your own husbands, as to the Lord. For the husband is the head of the wife even as Christ is the head of the church . . . (Eph. 5:22–23)

Similarly, when Paul talks about being subject to "the governing authorities" he does not give evangelism as the reason, but rather says that the agent of the government "is the servant of God, an avenger who carries out God's wrath on the wrongdoer. There-

---

[10] Webb says that we should be subject to the law today, not to political leaders (p. 107), but Peter's admonition to be subject to "every human institution" would surely include both the law and the government officials. The fact is that we are subject not just to the law, but to the people who enforce the law and who are representatives of the government and bear its authority today.

fore one must be in subjection, not only to avoid God's wrath but also for the sake of conscience" (Rom. 13:4–5).

It is better to reject Webb's redemptive-movement hermeneutic and see the New Testament as the words of God for us today, words that contain God's morally pure standards for us to obey, and to obey *all* of the New Testament commands *simply because they are the words of God*, who holds us responsible for obeying them. We do not have the right to take it upon ourselves to say, as Webb's position implies, "If a wife today submits to her unbelieving husband according to 1 Peter 3:1, I don't think that will help evangelism in our modern culture, so women should not follow that text today." That is simply setting up our own moral judgment as a higher standard than God's Word.

e. Webb Fails to Show That Adam's Naming of Eve in Genesis 2 Indicates Only Equality (Discussed under Criterion 5): Webb claims that when Adam calls the woman *'ishshah* in Genesis 2:23, because this word for "woman" sounds like the Hebrew word for man (*'ish*), that shows that "Adam pronounces an affinity between the woman and himself. This act of naming places man and woman as partners in the dominion over the animal/plant kingdom" (p. 116).

This argument is not convincing because the names for "man" and "woman" are similar but they are not identical (*'ish* and *'ishshah*), so they are somewhat the same and somewhat different. For Webb to say that this name *only* indicates equality is simply reductionistic—it is taking part of the truth and making it the whole truth. The names signify *both* similarity *and* difference.

Second, Webb fails to consider the strongest reason that this process shows male headship, and that is that throughout the Old Testament the one giving a name to someone else has authority over the one receiving that name. Therefore, just as Adam's prior activity of naming the animals indicated that he had the right to name them because he had authority over them, so Adam's action of giving a name to the woman is an indication of the fact that God had granted to Adam an authority or leadership role with respect to his wife.

f. Webb Fails to Show That There Are Culturally Relative Components in the Pre-fall Garden of Eden (Criterion 6): First, Webb attempts to minimize the significance of the fact that God called Adam to account first after Adam and Eve had sinned (Gen. 3:9). Webb admits that this might qualify as "a quiet whisper of patriarchy" (p. 130), but this is minimizing what is there in Scripture. If this is *God's* action and *God's* call to Adam, it is anything but a whisper! This is the action of the sovereign God of the universe calling the man to account first for what had happened in his family (even though Eve had sinned first). It is an indication that God held Adam primarily responsible for what had happened.

With regard to the pre-fall narrative itself, Webb claims to find some culturally relative elements within the account, such as "farming as an occupation" and "ground transportation" and a "vegetarian diet" (pp. 124–125). But this is hardly a persuasive list of examples, because Webb fails to take account of the nature of the items that he lists. Surely nothing in the text suggests, and no responsible interpreter claims, that these events are presented as the *only* activities human beings can do! So it is unclear why Webb thinks these can be counted as examples of "culturally relative" principles.

The point Webb overlooks is that everything in the garden is *good* because it has been created by God and it was declared by him to be "very good" (Gen. 1:31). Therefore, farming and gaining food from the earth are good. Walking through the garden is good. Vegetables are good. Bearing children is good. None of these things are later superceded by a "superior ethic" that would declare the goodness of these things to be culturally relative, so that farming would no longer be good, or walking on the earth would no longer be good, or vegetables would no longer be good, or bearing children would no longer be good!

Similarly, we have in the garden male-female equality together with male headship in the marriage. That also is *good* and it is *created by God*, and we should not follow Webb in thinking that we can one day create a "superior ethic" that would declare male headship to be something that is *not* good or *not* approved by God.[11]

g. Webb Fails to Show That 1 Timothy 2:13, "For Adam Was Formed First, Then Eve," Is Culturally Relative (Criterion 7): The reason egalitarians find 1 Timothy 2:13 particularly difficult is that Paul uses the original creation account in which "Adam was formed first, then Eve" as the basis for saying, "I do not permit a woman to teach or to exercise authority over a man; rather, she is to remain quiet" (1 Tim. 2:12). If God's original creation of Adam and Eve was very good and free from sin (which it was), and if Paul sees in Adam's creation prior to Eve an indication that some teaching and governing roles in the New Testament church should be reserved for men (which Webb agrees is Paul's reasoning), then it is hard to escape the conclusion that the creation of Adam before Eve indicates a permanent, transcultural principle that supports some kinds of exclusively male teaching and governing roles in the church for all generations.

Webb attempts to avoid this by claiming that there are some culturally relative things in the original creation account. But as I indicated in the previous section, Webb fails to take into account the fact that all the things that are there in the original creation are morally *good* and free from sin, and that includes Adam's headship in the marriage. In addition to that, if Webb's reasoning were correct, then Paul could not have appealed to the creation account in the first century either, because people in the first century were not limited to "farming as an occupation" (Paul was a tentmaker!), and people in the first century were not limited to "ground transportation" (Paul traveled by sea!), and people in the first century were not all married (both Jesus and Paul were single!), and there was no requirement for everyone to have children (both Jesus and Paul were

---

[11] Some things that Webb claims are in the garden, such as keeping the Sabbath or a six-day workweek (pp. 125–126), are doubtful interpretations, and it is not evident that they were present in the garden. Therefore, they do not form a persuasive argument that some things in the garden are culturally relative.

single!), and there was no limitation to being a vegetarian (Paul approved the eating of meat, Rom. 14:2–4; 1 Cor. 10:25–27). Therefore, the apostle Paul himself did not think that any of Webb's supposedly "culturally relative" factors were actually found in the creation account itself, or could be used to prove that it was invalid to appeal to the creation of Adam before Eve for transcultural principles that apply to conduct within the New Testament church. In short, Paul was not persuaded by any of the factors that Webb claims to show cultural relativity in the creation account. Paul knew that all those factors were there, yet he still believed that "Adam was formed first, then Eve" gave a valid ground for affirming an abiding transcultural principle.

Webb's argument that the author of Genesis projected later circumstances back into the account of the garden of Eden and thereby placed primogeniture in the Genesis 2 account, though it did not in fact happen that way (pp. 142–145; see discussion above), is also unpersuasive, because it denies the historical truthfulness of extended sections of the narrative in Genesis 2.

Finally, Webb objects that if complementarians take Paul's argument seriously in 1 Timothy 2:13, then, to be consistent, we should argue that primogeniture should be practiced today as well. He says, "It is interesting that those who appeal to primogeniture in affirming the transcultural status of 1 Timothy 2:13 say very little about the sustained application of other primogeniture texts for our lives" (p. 142).

But here Webb is simply confusing the issue. The Bible never says anything like "All families should give a double portion of inheritance to the firstborn son, because Adam was formed first, then Eve." The Bible never commands any such thing, and Webb himself shows how the Bible frequently overturns such a practice (see pp. 136–139). Webb has imported into the discussion an idea of "consistency" that is foreign to the Bible itself. Webb is basically arguing as follows:

1. The Bible makes one application from Adam's prior creation.
2. If you affirm that the Bible is correct in that first application, then you *have to* say that the Bible makes *other* applications from Adam's prior creation.

But that reasoning does not follow. We are not free to say that the Bible "should" make applications which it does not in fact make! That decision belongs in the hands of God, not us.

Consistency in this matter is simply affirming what the Bible says, and not denying the validity of any of the reasoning processes in Scripture (as Webb attempts to do with 1 Tim. 2:13), as well as not adding to the commands of Scripture (as Webb tries to push complementarians to do with regard to this text). "Consistency" does not imply that we must make all sorts of applications of a biblical principle even when the Bible does not make those applications; rather, consistency is saying that the application Paul made from Genesis 2 is a valid and good one, and Scripture requires us also to affirm it as a transcultural principle today.

Paul is saying in 1 Timothy 2:12–13 that Adam's prior creation does prove at least one thing, and that is that in the assembled church a woman should not "teach" or "exercise authority over a man" (1 Tim. 2:12). Are we to say that Paul was wrong?

h. Webb Fails to Show That Galatians 3:28 Is a "New Creation" Pattern That Overthrows the "Old Creation" Patterns of Male Leadership in the Home and Church (Criterion 8): Webb says that there are several "in Christ" statements like Galatians 3:28, which tells us that "there is neither male nor female, for you are all one in Christ Jesus." These "in Christ" statements, he claims, "should be given prominence over the old-creation patterns" that include what Webb sees as "patriarchy" within the "old creation" patterns. He says, "New-creation theology transforms the status of all its participants . . . into one of equality. . . . It . . . heavily favors an egalitarian position" (p. 152).

In this case again, Webb fails adequately to take into account the fact that the male headship in marriage that was found in the garden was itself "very good" in God's sight, and we should not look for some kind of morally superior ethic to replace it. Moreover, Webb fails to take into account other "new-creation" statements that affirm male headship in marriage, such as Colossians 3:18, "Wives, submit to your husbands, as is fitting *in the Lord.*" This command is part of the new "in Christ" or "in the Lord" creation, just as "Children, obey your parents *in the Lord*, for this is right" (Eph. 6:1) is part of the new creation in Christ. In fact, Paul's commands as an apostle for the New Testament church *are* part of the "new creation" in Christ, and therefore "I do not permit a woman to teach or to exercise authority over a man" *is also part of that new creation*, because it is part of the teaching of the New Testament for the church after Pentecost.

i. Webb Fails to Show That the Bible Adopted Male Leadership Because There Were No Competing Options (Criterion 9): Webb says, "It is reasonably safe to assume, therefore, that the social reality of the biblical writers was the world of patriarchy. . . . This consideration increases the likelihood of patriarchy being a cultural component within Scripture" (pp. 154–155). Webb explains that this was because an egalitarian position regarding marriage or the church was simply not an option, given the surrounding culture.

But this criterion is not persuasive. The New Testament teaches many things that were not found in the surrounding culture. There were no people in the surrounding culture who believed in Jesus as the Messiah before he came. Even Webb admits that the idea that husbands should love their wives as Christ loved the church was revolutionary in terms of the surrounding culture. The idea that there could be a church made up of Jews and Gentiles fellowshipping together on an equal basis was not an option in the surrounding culture.

The fact of the matter is that Scripture often challenges and transforms the societies and cultures into which it speaks. Therefore, if a truly egalitarian model for marriage had been what God wanted for his people, he surely could have proclaimed it clearly through the pages of the New Testament and through the teachings of Jesus and the apostles. But (as Webb admits) the New Testament itself does not teach such a fully egalitarian position. (According to Webb, we have to move "beyond" the ethic of the New Testament to reach full egalitarianism.)

j. Webb Fails to Show That the General Principle of "Justice" Nullifies Specific New Testament Commands Regarding Male Leadership (Criterion 13): Webb asks, "Does the power inequality between men and women violate a theology of justice? Is there a hint of inequity or unfairness about the treatment of women in the Bible?" (p. 181). Webb's answer is that "the general or broad principles of Scripture appear to favor movement from soft patriarchy to an egalitarian position" (p. 184).[12]

The problem with Webb's analysis in this case is that it pits Scripture against Scripture. We are not free to take "general principles" like "justice" or "love" and then say that they take priority over specific teachings of Scripture. Are we to say that the commands of the Bible in Ephesians 5 or 1 Timothy 2 were "unjust"?

Another problem with Webb's entire Criterion 13 (on specific vs. general principles) is that it allows an interpreter to select any "general principle" he wants, and so drive the discussion in one direction or another. Webb chooses the general principles of "justice" and "equality," but why should these be the driving considerations? Why not choose the general principle of "the imitation of Christ" in his subjection to rightful authority and in his submission to the will of his Father? Why not choose the general principle of "submission to rightful authority" which is found in many levels of the Bible, and which is even found in the relationship of the Son to the Father in the Trinity? Of course, Webb does not select that general principle, for it would lead to a complementarian position.

This procedure of arguing that some broad principle overrides specific texts of Scripture is not a new idea with Webb. It is remarkably similar to the procedure used by liberals in the early part of the 20th century when they appealed to the general principle of "the love of God" to override the specific teachings of the Bible about God's wrath, and particularly about God's wrath being poured out on his Son on the cross for our sins. In this way liberals commonly denied the heart of the atonement, that is, the doctrine of Christ's death as a substitute sacrifice who bore God's wrath against sin in our place (the penal substitutionary doctrine of the atonement).

Therefore, this criterion (Webb's Criterion 13, "Specific Instructions versus General Principles") is among the most dangerous of Webb's criteria because it potentially can give legitimacy for disobedience to the specific texts of Scripture on any uncomfortable subject for which people might find some "general principle" that will override it. The "love of God" principle could override the doctrine of hell or could override the idea

---

[12] What Webb calls "soft patriarchy" seems to be the position he thinks the New Testament taught for its time, because he thinks it is the position we should move "from." It is also essentially the position held by me and by the Council on Biblical Manhood and Womanhood, the position I have called a "complementarian" position; see Webb, pp. 26–27.

that not everyone will be saved. The "grace of God" principle could override the need for measuring up to specific character traits for church elders. The "grace and forgiveness of God" principle could be used to override the specific teachings of the New Testament on divorce and remarriage. And so forth.

Webb himself says that this criterion is "susceptible to misuse" (p. 183), to which I certainly agree. But then he says that it is still "extremely helpful" (p. 183), a statement with which I must strongly disagree. Scripture does not contradict Scripture.

k. Webb Fails to Show That a Wife's Submission May Be Culturally Relative Because It Is Based on an Analogy with Christ or with God (Criterion 14): Webb argues that there are a number of culturally relative standards in the Bible, such as "slavery" or "monarchy" or "right-handedness" (pp. 186–187), that are based on an analogy with Christ or with God, and therefore it is not valid to say that New Testament teachings on male headship are transcultural because they are based on an analogy with Christ or with God. Specifically, Webb says that Ephesians 5:22–33 and 1 Corinthians 11:3 should not be seen as transcultural just because they depend on a "theological analogy" (pp. 188–189).

But once again Webb has mixed together things that are not parallel. First Corinthians 11:3 draws a parallel between the headship of the Father with respect to the Son and the headship of a husband with respect to his wife:

> But I want you to understand that the head of every man is Christ, the head of a wife is her husband, and the head of Christ is God.

But the Bible never makes statements like this regarding the other categories that Webb mentions. We do not find anywhere in Scripture statements like these:

> I want you to understand that right-handed people are superior to left-handed people, because Christ sits at the right hand of God.

> But I want you to understand that slavery is the best economic system, because God is the supreme slaveholder and you are all his slaves.

> I want you to understand that monarchy is the form of government that all nations should adopt, because God is the supreme king over the universe and you are all his subjects.

These are all ridiculous statements that the Scripture would never make. Of course God *is* king over the universe and of course Jesus *does* sit at God's right hand, but the Bible never reasons from these things to the kinds of foolish statements that Webb would have to have the Bible make in order to make his argument work regarding the culturally relative nature of some theological parallels.

Another problem with Webb's argument here is that it is once again based on his underlying assumption that it is possible to move to a "better ethic" (p. 32) than the ethic of the New Testament. But consider 1 Corinthians 11:3 once again:

> But I want you to understand that the head of every man is Christ, the head of the wife is her husband, and the head of Christ is God.

Are we to understand that "the head of Christ is God" is only true for certain cultures at certain times? Are we to understand that "the head of every man is Christ" is true only for certain cultures and certain times? Certainly not (unless Webb also thinks these statements to be culturally relative). But if the first and third sentences in this verse are transcultural, then must we not also consider the second sentence to be transcultural, "the head of a wife is her husband"? Paul's reasoning here says that there is a parallel between the eternal relationship of the Father to the Son and the Trinity and the relationship of a wife to her husband. And if Paul is correct that there is such a parallel, then the headship of a husband with respect to his wife is surely transcultural. Webb has shown no passages in the New Testament where such an argument is culturally relative.

The same considerations apply to Ephesians 5:22–33, where Paul says:

> Wives, submit to your own husbands, as to the Lord. For the husband is the head of the wife *even as Christ is the head of the church.*

Paul is basing his command on the fact that the relationship between a husband and wife is analogous to the relationship between Christ and the church. That is also a transcultural truth. Would Webb say that "Christ is the head of the church" is something that is culturally relative? *Webb has produced no examples from the New Testament where a culturally relative command is similarly based on an appeal to the conduct of Christ or his relationship to the church.*

Contrary to Webb's claim on page 186, 1 Peter 2:18–25 does not *endorse* slavery based on Christ's submission to suffering! First Peter 2 tells Christians *how to suffer* based on an imitation of Christ's example, but it does not thereby *encourage persecution* of Christians or say that such persecution or mistreatment is right. Similarly it does not argue, "Slavery is a morally good institution because Christ submitted to mistreatment." The New Testament never makes any such claim.

Webb's other response to Ephesians 5 and 1 Corinthians 11 is to say that if Paul had been addressing a different culture he would have commanded something different:

> If Paul had been addressing an egalitarian culture, he may have used the very same christological analogy (with its transcultural component) and reapplied it to an egalitarian relationship between husband and wife. He would simply have encouraged both the husband and the wife to sacrificially love one another. (pp. 188–189)

This amazing statement reveals how deeply committed Webb is to finding an egalitarian ethic that is "better than" the ethic taught in the New Testament. Even though he admits that *Paul did not teach an egalitarian view of marriage*, he says that *Paul would have taught an egalitarian view of marriage* had he been addressing a different culture such as our egalitarian culture today! Webb is not at all bound by what Paul taught, but here as elsewhere feels free to use his speculation on what Paul "might have" taught in a different situation as a higher moral authority than what Paul actually did teach.

As I mentioned earlier, Webb also claims that the Bible in Hosea 2 endorses the idea of a husband physically disciplining his wife after the analogy of God, who disciplines the people of Israel (pp. 189–190). But here Webb is assuming a very unlikely view of Hosea 2, and he is surely assuming a morally offensive view of God and the Bible, because he is claiming that in its time, Hosea 2 could have rightly been used by husbands within Israel as a justification for stripping their wives naked and confining them physically, thus physically disciplining them for wrongdoing! This is something the Bible nowhere teaches, and certainly it is not taught in Hosea 2, but Webb claims it is taught there in order to find another "theological analogy" text that he can claim as transcultural. This one is a long stretch, and it is anything but persuasive.

l. Webb Fails to Show That New Testament Submission Lists Have Some Culturally Relative Commands and some Transcultural Commands (Criterion 15): Webb says that when he looks at the "submission lists" within the New Testament, two of the items are "culture bound" (monarchy and slavery), while two are "transcultural" (children/parents and congregation/elders) (p. 196). Therefore, he says it is uncertain whether the wife/husband submission command is cultural or transcultural, based on this criterion alone.

The problem with Webb's analysis here is the way he dismisses two of the commands in the New Testament as culturally relative. According to Webb, the command "Be subject for the Lord's sake to every human institution, whether it be to the emperor as supreme, or to governors as sent by him to punish those who do evil and to praise those who do good" (1 Pet. 2:13–14) is "culturally relative" and we need to move to a better ethic than that of the New Testament, an ethic where we no longer have to submit to government leaders. But a better approach, and the one used by evangelicals who don't believe that we can move to a "better ethic" than that of the New Testament, would be to say that we are still to *obey* that command, but we are to *apply it* to the closest parallel in our situation today, which is to be subject to the authorities of the government in which we find ourselves. In fact, Peter allows for this when he talks about "every human institution," and Paul makes the same kind of general statement, not even mentioning an "emperor," but simply saying, "Let every person be subject *to the governing authorities*" (Rom. 13:1). I see no reason why we should try to move beyond this New Testament teaching or see it as culturally relative.

In the same way, Christians today can obey the command "Slaves, obey your earthly masters" (Eph. 6:5) by *applying it* to the nearest parallel situation in our modern culture, namely, a situation of employees being subject to and obedient to their employers. The institution of "slave" (Greek, *doulos*) was, in general, significantly different from the horrible abuses found in American slavery in the 19th century, and it was in fact the most common employment situation found in the ancient world.[13] To make a parallel application to employees in their relationship to their employers is still to be subject to the ethic of the New Testament and obedient to it, and it is far different from Webb's system, in which we are no longer to obey this ethic but move toward a "better ethic" in which employees do not have to obey the directives of their employers, but simply have to "fulfill the terms of their contract to the best of their ability" (p. 38) in the hope that we will move toward Webb's "ultimate ethic," which has "wages maximized for all" (p. 37; he nowhere explains this utopian platitude—must everyone earn $10,000,000?).

m. Webb Fails to Show That Wives Were to Be Subject to Their Husbands Only Because They Were Younger and Less Educated (Criterion 17): Webb says that it made sense for wives to submit to their husbands in an ancient culture because they had less education, less social exposure, less physical strength, and they were significantly younger than their husbands (pp. 213–214). But these reasons, says Webb, no longer apply today, and therefore the command for wives to be subject to their husbands should be seen as culturally relative. A wife today should just give some kind of "honor" and "respect" to her husband (p. 215).

Webb's argument here is not persuasive, however, because these are not the reasons that the Bible gives for wives to be subject to their husbands. The reasons the Bible gives are the parallel with Christ's relationship to the church (Eph. 5:22–24) and the parallel with the relationship between the Father and Son in the Trinity (1 Cor. 11:3). Another reason that Paul gives is that this is what "is fitting in the Lord" (Col. 3:18). Yet another reason is that it is part of "what is good" (Titus 2:3–4), and another reason is that unbelieving husbands may be "won without a word by the conduct of their wives" (1 Pet. 3:1).

Webb's reasons here are merely speculative, and there is no indication that the biblical authors are taking these factors into account when they give these commands. Moreover, these New Testament commands apply to *all* wives, even those who were more intelligent that their husbands, or the same age as their husbands, or physically as strong as their husbands, or who had as much social exposure and social rank as their husbands, or as much wealth as their husbands. Webb's reasons are simply not the reasons that the Bible uses.

In short, Webb says that the Bible teaches a wife's submission because of Webb's own invented reasons. Then he removes these invented reasons for today's culture, and concludes that we can count the command as culturally relative. It would be far better to heed the reasons that the Bible actually gives, and to believe that these are the reasons that the Bible commands wives to be subject to husbands.

---

[13] See the discussion of slavery in chap. 16, p. 441.

n. Webb Fails to Show That 1 Timothy 2:14, "And Adam Was Not Deceived, but the Woman Was Deceived and Became a Transgressor," Is Culturally Relative (Criterion 18, "Scientific and Social-Scientific Evidence"): Webb argues that women were more easily deceived in the ancient world because they were not as well educated as men, were younger, and had less social exposure and less knowledge (p. 229). But Webb goes to great lengths to demonstrate that these factors are not true of women today (he even has an appendix on research showing that gender plays a very small role in differences in ability to detect deception, pp. 269–273). Therefore, he says 1 Timothy 2:14 is culturally relative and does not apply to women today.

This argument is not persuasive because Paul makes no reference to his current culture or to women being susceptible to deception in the first century. Paul is talking again about Adam and Eve, and he says that another reason why women should not "teach" or "exercise authority over a man" is that "Adam was not deceived, but the woman was deceived and became a transgressor" (1 Tim. 2:12–14). However we understand that passage, it is evident that Paul is saying that something is true of Eve in relationship to Adam *that has transcultural significance for women and men generally in the New Testament church.* Paul is not basing his argument on education or age or social exposure or knowledge (for no doubt there were many older and wiser women in the large church at Ephesus when Paul was writing to Timothy), but he is basing his argument on something that he sees to be a transcultural principle that has application to men and women generally. Some complementarians understand this verse to be referring to the fact that Eve wrongfully took leadership in the family and made the decision to eat the forbidden fruit on her own, and other complementarians understand this to refer to a women's "kinder, gentler nature" and the fact that she is therefore less likely to draw a hard line when close friends are teaching doctrinal error and relationships need to be broken.[14] Whatever interpretation we take, Paul is arguing from Eve's action at the fall to a general truth about men and women teaching and governing the church; he is not explicitly arguing from any statement about women in his culture or any other culture.

o. Webb Fails to Ask, "What If I Am Wrong?" about His Entire System, but Asks It Only about One Inconsequential Point: When readers see the title of Webb's last chapter, "What If I Am Wrong?" (p. 236), they will likely expect, from the placement of this chapter at the end of the book, that Webb is raising the question, "What if I am wrong about my entire system?" But when we read this chapter carefully we find that is not at all what Webb is asking. *He does not even raise the possibility that his entire system about moving to a "better ethic" than the New Testament might be wrong.* He only asks, "What if I am wrong?" with respect to one very small point, and that is whether Paul's appeal to primogeniture in 1 Timothy 2:13 should be viewed as transcultural rather than cultural.

---

[14] (For discussion of this verse, see Thomas R. Schreiner, "An Interpretation of 1 Timothy 2:9–15: A Dialogue with Scholarship," in *Women in the Church: A Fresh Analysis of 1 Timothy 2:9–15*, ed. Andreas Kösten-berger, Thomas R. Schreiner, and H. Scott Baldwin (Grand Rapids, MI: Baker, 1995), 140–146.

He says, "I am prepared to ask this chapter's reflective question about one aspect of my findings, namely, my assessment of 1 Timothy 2:13" (p. 236). But he concludes that it does not really make much difference in the end, for even if one sees primogeniture as a transcultural factor, it is "a light (not heavy) value in Scripture" (p. 238), and it is significantly modified by other "culture-based factors" (p. 238), and Galatians 3:28 still has "sociological implications that will modify the application even further" (p. 240).

Therefore, even if Webb finds himself to be "wrong" on primogeniture in 1 Timothy 2:13, he says it will make very little difference at all. If he is right on 1 Timothy 2:13 being entirely culturally relative, then he will end up with a "complementary egalitarianism" in which there is no "power differential based solely on gender" and no "role differentiation related to that power differential" (p. 231). The only difference between the genders would be "based upon biological differences between men and women" and would include, for instance, "a greater participation of women in the early stages of child rearing" because of "the benefits of breast-feeding during early infant formation" (p. 241).

But if Webb is wrong on 1 Timothy 2:13, then he thinks it would lead to an "ultra-soft patriarchy" in which there is "an equal power differential" between men and women in the home and in the church (p. 243), but in which men would be granted "a certain level of *symbolic* honor for their first born status within the human family" (p. 243).

Is there any difference then between Webb's two models, whether he is "right" or "wrong" on 1 Timothy 2:13? Webb himself says there is very little, because in either case:

> The application of 1 Timothy 2 is going to be very similar for both complementary egalitarians and ultra-soft partriarchalists. The only difference is whether there should be a dimension of *symbolic honor* granted to one gender over the other. (p. 241)

What Webb is telling us then is that *the only two options his system will allow are both thoroughgoing egalitarian options.* In both cases, all teaching and governing roles in the church are open to women as well as men. In both situations, marriage is based on "neutral submission" and there is no unique leadership role or authority for the husband in the marriage. *The only difference is no real difference at all*, a mere question of whether some kind of "symbolic honor" should be given to men, a kind of honor that Webb does not further specify. I think it would be hard for anyone to see that "symbolic honor" as anything other than meaningless tokenism.

p. Webb Proposes a Misleading "Forum for Harmony" (p. 243) That Requires the Abandonment of All Gender-Based Leadership for Men and Asks That Both Sides Begin to Dialogue on the Basis of a 99 Percent Capitulation to Egalitarian Claims: At the end of his book, Webb says, "Complementary egalitarianism and ultra-soft patriarchy provide a forum for harmony and healing within the church" (p. 243). His reflections in this final chapter have been included because, he says, "I hope they will awaken a spirit of reconciliation between egalitarians and partriarchalists" (p. 243).

What is the basis on which Webb proposes this "forum for harmony"? It is a forum to discuss whether we should adopt (choice 1) "complementary egalitarianism" (which is Webb's title for a thoroughgoing egalitarian position) or whether we should adopt (choice 2) "ultra-soft patriarchy" (which is Webb's other egalitarian option, the one that gives a token amount of "symbolic honor" to men).

I personally find this somewhat insulting. I fail to understand how Webb expects that his invitation could ever be taken seriously when the only two options offered in his "forum" are to capitulate 99 percent to egalitarian claims or to capitulate 100 percent to egalitarian claims. And even the 99 percent capitulation found in what he calls "ultra-soft patriarchy" in the end is demeaning because it expects men to give up all male leadership roles in the home and the church, and accept in return a token kind of "symbolic honor."

In addition, complementarians will consider Webb's terminology offensive and confusing. As a cofounder of the Council on Biblical Manhood and Womanhood in 1987, and as a coauthor of the complementarian book *Recovering Biblical Manhood and Womanhood: A Response to Evangelical Feminism* (Wheaton, IL: Crossway, 1991), I wish to lodge a fairly strong protest against Webb's use of two terms. His phrase "complementary egalitarianism," which he uses to describe a thoroughgoing egalitarian position, simply confuses the issues by using the word *complementary* for a position that is totally antithetical to what complementarians hold. In 1991, in the preface to *Recovering Biblical Manhood and Womanhood*, John Piper and I wrote:

> If one word must be used to describe our position, we prefer the term *complementarian*, since it suggests both equality and beneficial differences between men and women. We are uncomfortable with the term "traditionalist" because it implies an unwillingness to let Scripture challenge traditional patterns of behavior, and we certainly reject the term "hierarchicalist" because it overemphasizes structured authority while giving no suggestion of equality or the beauty of mutual interdependence. (p. xiv)

Since that time, the term "complementarian" has been the one we have consistently used to describe our position, and it has been widely (and courteously) used by others to describe our position as well. For Webb to apply it to an egalitarian position is needlessly confusing the issues in the minds of readers.

For similar reasons, I find it objectionable that Webb consistently characterizes our position as "patriarchy." That term (which literally means "father-rule") almost uniformly has a pejorative connotation to it in modern society, and it carries nuances of an authoritarian father ruling over several generations of adults and children in an extended family in an ancient culture, none of which we are advocating today. The term by itself says nothing about the equal value that the Bible and our position attribute to men and women alike, nor does it say anything about a leadership role for the *husband* within the marriage (since it focuses on the role of the "father" or *pater* in the relationship). So *it is a singularly inappropriate, pejorative, and misleading term to refer to the position that we represent.* Is it not common courtesy in academic debate to refer to positions by the terms that the representatives of those positions would choose for themselves?

9. Most of Webb's Eighteen Criteria for Determining Cultural Relativity, as He Has Constructed Them, Are Unreliable Guides for Christians Today. As I have argued above, Webb's entire system is based on an assumption that the moral commands we find in the pages of the New Testament represent only a temporary ethical system for that time, and that we should use Webb's "redemptive-movement hermeneutic" to move beyond those ethical teachings to a "better ethic" (p. 32) that is closer to the "ultimate ethic" that God wants us ultimately to adopt. Since all of Webb's criteria are based on that assumption, the entire system seems to me to be unpersuasive and inconsistent with a belief in the absolute moral authority of the teachings of the New Testament themselves.

But at this point it is appropriate to comment specifically on each of the eighteen criteria that Webb produces, because in some cases his analysis produces helpful insight in spite of the fact that it is based on an underlying assumption with which I find myself in disagreement.

In the following material, I offer only brief observations on each of the eighteen criteria.

a. Preliminary Movement (p. 73): I find this criterion unhelpful because it assumes that there can be "further movement" beyond the ethical teachings of the New Testament to a higher or better ethic. However, Webb's discussion is helpful as it applies to a number of Old Testament moral commands, which all interpreters I think would admit are a "preliminary" set of standards and not God's final moral standards for his people today. (All Christians of course see the Old Testament as "preliminary" to the New Testament, but that is far different from seeing the New Testament also as "preliminary" to further ethical development. Another way of saying this is to say that all Christians agree there is "redemptive movement" from the Old Testament to the New Testament, but evangelicals have held that the movement stops with the New Testament! Prior to Webb, only Roman Catholics and liberal Protestants, not evangelicals, have taken developments beyond the New Testament as part or all of their ultimate authority.)

b. Seed Ideas (p. 83): I find this category unhelpful and unpersuasive because it assumes that some ideas in the New Testament (such as Gal. 3:28) are in fact contradictory to other New Testament commands, and these "seed ideas" show us the direction in which we should look for a superior ethic to the New Testament.

c. Breakouts (p. 91): I also find this category unhelpful and unpersuasive because it assumes that there are certain people in the Bible (such as Deborah or Junia) who engage in activities that are contrary to the moral teachings found in the biblical text, but that anticipate a movement to a higher ethic superior to that found in the Bible.

d. Purpose/Intent Statements (p. 105): I find this category unpersuasive and in fact troubling because it implies that we can disobey New Testament commands (such as the command for wives to be subject to their husbands) if we decide that the purpose specified in the command will no longer be fulfilled (for example, if we decide that wives being subject to their husbands will no longer help evangelism). This again assumes that we can move to a higher ethical level than that of the teachings of the New Testament. However, if Webb's analysis did not have the assumption that we could move to a higher ethical system than the New Testament, his explanation of the specific details of application today (such as his explanation of why we need not give a "holy kiss" because it may not make people feel welcomed at all, but should instead give some other kind of warm greeting) is helpful. (See the following section for a discussion of the "holy kiss" and similar physical actions with symbolic purpose.)

e. Basis in Fall or Curse (p. 110): I agree with Webb's argument that moral commands based on the curse that God imposed in Genesis 3 are not valid as a standard for us to obey today. I also agree that the results of the curse continue in the present time, so that we are still subject to death, the ground still brings forth weeds, and women still experience pain in childbirth. I also agree with Webb that today we should attempt to overcome these effects of the curse (because I believe that has been the purpose of God in the history of redemption ever since he in justice imposed the curse in Genesis 3).

f. Basis in Original Creation, Section 1: Patterns (p. 123): I am not persuaded by Webb's argument that a component of a text "may" be transcultural only if it is rooted in the original creation material (p. 123), because I do not think he has discovered anything in the garden before the fall that is not morally good or that we should not see as morally good today. His attempts to find culturally relative components in the Genesis narrative are all based on a misreading of the purpose and intent of that narrative in its original context.

g. Basis in Original Creation, Section 2: Primogeniture (p. 134): I find Webb's analysis here to be unpersuasive, both because his position is based on a denial of the historicity of the story of Adam being created before Eve in Genesis 2, and because he thinks that the principle of primogeniture found in Adam's being created before Eve should not be taken as a transcultural principle unless people are willing to apply primogeniture in other aspects of society today. As I explained above, this assumes that Paul cannot properly make one application of a pattern found in Genesis 2 unless he also makes many other applications of a principle found in Genesis 2. I believe, in contrast to Webb, that it is up to God, not us, to decide what commands to give us based on principles in Genesis, and that we should simply follow the ones that he does in fact give.

h. Basis in New Creation (p. 145): I find this criterion unpersuasive and unhelpful, not because I think that "new creation patterns" in the New Testament are wrong, but because Webb wrongly assumes that these patterns are in conflict with the pattern of male leadership found in God's original creation of Adam and Eve, and because Webb fails to consider other "new creation" commands that encourage wives to be subject to their husbands "in the Lord" (Col. 3:18), and because Webb again assumes that the "new creation" statements found in the New Testament are simply an indicator that leads us along the path to a higher ethical standard than that found in the commands of the New Testament itself.

i. Competing Options (p. 152): I find this criterion helpful with regard to Webb's discussion of why God did not immediately give commands to outlaw slavery (it would have caused massive and destructive economic upheaval), but rather gave principles that would lead to its abolition. But I find this criterion unhelpful in its assumption that the New Testament actually commanded or endorsed slavery, and also I find it unpersuasive in its claim that the New Testament could not have taught an egalitarian position at the time it was written (something that I think Webb has simply failed to prove, and something that I do not think can be proven in light of the clear New Testament willingness to challenge culture at many points).

j. Opposition to Original Culture (p. 157): I find this criterion to be generally helpful, especially as it indicates the ways in which both Old and New Testaments oppose many current cultural attitudes and practices regarding slavery. I am not quite as sure that it is helpful regarding Webb's argument that the commands against homosexuality are transcultural because homosexuality was widely accepted in the ancient world, because I think that Webb underestimates the extent to which there was widespread moral disapproval of homosexual conduct in many sections of ancient society. And I think in this section Webb has not adequately considered the way the New Testament does oppose some cultural values regarding marriage when it strongly emphasizes the need for husbands to love their wives as Christ loved the church. But this shows that the New Testament was willing to stand against cultural views on marriage when it was something that was morally right.

k. Closely Related Issues (p. 162): I find this category to be unhelpful and unpersuasive because Webb deals almost entirely with Mosaic laws regarding women while failing to take into account that Christians are no longer under the Mosaic covenant, and these laws are not what "the Bible" teaches for New Testament Christians in any case. Webb seems in this section to be on a fishing expedition to find deficient elements in Scripture, especially regarding the treatment of women, so that he can argue that we need to move to a higher ethic than that taught in the commands of the biblical text.

l. Penal Code (p. 179): I found this section to be helpful in its observation that most actions that received the severe punishment of the death penalty in the Old Testament still receive divine disapproval today (but there are a couple of exceptions regarding Sabbath breaking and cultic violations, so the analysis is not entirely convincing). This criterion does not have much application to the relationship between husbands and wives, as Webb himself admits (p. 179).

m. Specific Instructions versus General Principles (p. 179): I found this section to be unpersuasive and actually quite dangerous for Christians today, because it could easily give legitimacy to disobedience to many specific texts of Scripture on any uncomfortable subject, simply by enabling people to find a "general principle" of Scripture that could be used to override that specific teaching.

n. Basis in Theological Analogy (p. 185): I found this section to be deeply flawed, because it wrongly assumes that the Bible taught and approved slavery, monarchy, and even "right-handedness"! Then it argues that not all of these theological analogies are transcultural, and therefore the teachings on marriage in Ephesians 5 and 1 Corinthians 11:3 are not necessarily transcultural.

By use of this procedure Webb potentially nullifies all "imitation of Christ" passages in the New Testament. Webb's claim that a command that is based in theological analogy need not be transcultural is based on his claim that some culturally relative commands are based on similar theological analogies, but in fact he has produced no examples that are actually parallel to Ephesians 5 or 1 Corinthians 11:3.

o. Contextual Comparisons (p. 192): I found this category to be unhelpful because Webb incorrectly assumes that the New Testament approves and endorses slavery and monarchy.

p. Appeal to the Old Testament (p. 201): I found this analysis to be unpersuasive and unhelpful because Webb incorrectly brings in a number of texts that do not appeal to the Old Testament to prove the validity of slavery or monarchy, and also because he brings in a number of texts that do not appeal to the Old Testament at all but simply have parallels in the Old Testament (such as foot washing or the "holy kiss"). Therefore, Webb wrongly dismisses texts regarding women that appeal to the Old Testament (such as 1 Cor. 14:33, 36; 1 Tim. 2:11–15; 1 Pet. 3:1–7).

In addition, Webb rightly sees that if the New Testament discontinues a practice it is not required for Christians to obey (p. 201). But he wrongly sees this as an evidence of cultural change rather than an evidence of a change from the old covenant to the new covenant.

q. Pragmatic Basis between Two Cultures (p. 209): I found this criterion to be unpersuasive because in a number of cases (particularly with respect to husbands and wives) Webb assumed that he knew the reasons for a command, then he used his assumed reasons (such as that wives were younger or less educated) to replace the actual reasons that the Bible gave for the command. However, in the rather obvious example of why we do not wash other people's feet today, Webb's discussion of the fact that we don't travel on dirt roads with sandals did give expression to what people instinctively understand about the differences between ancient and modern culture in this regard.

r. Scientific and Social-Scientific Evidence (p. 221): I found this entire section unpersuasive because Webb claims that the Bible teaches many things that it does not actually teach (such as a flat earth and a geocentric model of the universe). He then uses these examples to show that we have to abandon the teaching of the Bible because in a number of cases it goes contrary to present-day scientific evidence. Moreover, if Webb really believes that the Bible teaches these incorrect things, he seems to indicate that he does not believe the Bible is inerrant in everything it affirms (and this is similar to his denial of the historicity of the creation of Adam prior to Eve in Genesis 2).

10. The Difficult Passages for Determining Cultural Relativity Are Few, and Most Evangelicals Have Already Reached a Satisfactory Conclusion about Them. Since Webb's entire book was concerned with principles for determining when some part of Scripture is culturally relative, it is appropriate at the end of this discussion to say something about how most evangelicals have approached this question prior to Webb's book, and prior to his theory of a "redemptive-movement hermeneutic."

I believe that Webb has made the question of determining when something is "culturally relative" into a much bigger problem than it actually is. The main question is not whether the historical sections of the Bible *report* events that occurred in an ancient culture, because the Bible is a historical book, and of course it reports thousands of events that occurred at an ancient time and in a culture significantly different from our own. The question rather is how we should approach the *moral commands* found in the New Testament. Are those commands to be obeyed by us today as well?

I am going to suggest here—and I will be interested to see if others find this suggestion helpful—that the question of which New Testament commands are culturally relative is really not a very complicated question. It is not nearly as complicated as Webb makes it out to be. I am suggesting that the commands that are culturally relative are primarily—or exclusively—those that concern *physical actions that carry symbolic meaning.* When we look at the commands in the New Testament, I think there are only six main examples of texts about which people wonder if they are transcultural or if they are culturally relative:

1. Holy kiss (Rom. 16:16; 1 Cor. 16:20; 2 Cor. 13:12; 1 Thess. 5:26; 1 Pet. 5:14)
2. Foot washing (John 13:14; cf. 1 Tim. 5:10, which is not a command)
3. Head covering for women or wives in worship (1 Cor. 11:4–16)
4. Short hair for men (1 Cor. 11:14)
5. No jewelry or braided hair for women (1 Tim. 2:9; 1 Pet. 3:3)
6. Lifting hands in prayer (1 Tim. 2:8)

The first thing that we notice about this list is that *all of these examples refer to physical actions that carry symbolic meaning.* The holy kiss was a physical expression that conveyed the idea of a welcoming greeting. Foot washing (in the way that Jesus modeled it in John 13) was a physical action that symbolized taking a servantlike attitude toward one another. A head covering was a piece of clothing that symbolized something about a woman's status or role (most likely that she was a married woman, or possibly that she was a woman and not a man; others have proposed other interpretations, but all of them are an attempt to explain what was being symbolized by the head covering). As Paul understands long hair for a man in 1 Corinthians 11:14, it is a "disgrace for him," because it is something (in that culture at least) that was distinctive to women, and therefore it was a physical symbol of a man being like a woman rather than like a man.

For these first four examples, one can still find a few examples of Christians who argue that we should follow those commands literally today, and that they are still applicable to us. But the vast majority of evangelicals, at least in the United States (I cannot speak for the rest of the world), have not needed Webb's "redemptive-movement hermeneutic" to reach the conclusion that the Bible does not intend us to follow those commands literally today. That is because they are not in themselves *fundamental, deep-level actions* that have to do with essential components of our relationships to one another (such as loving one another, honesty with one another, submission to rightful authority, speaking the truth and not lying about others, not committing adultery or murder or theft, and so forth), but they are rather outward, *surface-level manifestations* of the deeper realities that we should manifest today (such as greeting one another in love, or serving one another, or avoiding dressing in such a way as to give a signal that a man is trying to be a woman or that a woman is trying to be a man). Therefore, the vast majority of evangelicals are not troubled by these four "culturally relative" commands in the New Testament because they have concluded that *only the physical, surface manifestation is culturally relative*, and the underlying intent of the command is *not culturally relative* but is still binding on us today.

It is important to realize that in seeing these outward manifestations as culturally relative (long before Webb's book was written), evangelicals have not adopted Webb's viewpoint that we need to move to a "better ethic" than that found in the New Testament commands. Evangelicals who take the Bible as the very words of God, and who believe that God's moral commands for his people are good and just and perfect, have not seen these commands as part of a deficient moral system that is just a "pointer" to a higher ethic, but they have seen these commands as a part of the entire New Testament ethic that they even today must submit to and obey.

For most people in the evangelical world, deciding that a holy kiss is a greeting that could be manifested in another way is not rocket science. It is something that comes almost instinctively as people intuitively realize that there are of course differences in forms of greetings among different cultures.

The last two items on the list need to be treated a bit differently. When we rightly interpret the texts about jewelry and braided hair for women, I do not think that they prohibited such things *even at the time they were written*. Paul says that "women should *adorn themselves* in respectable apparel, with modesty and self control, not with braided hair and gold or pearls or costly attire" (1 Tim. 2:9). Paul is not saying that women should never wear such things. He is saying that those things should not be the things that they consider the source of their beauty. That is not how they should "adorn themselves."

This sense of the prohibition becomes even more clear in 1 Peter 3:3. The very literal English Standard Version translates the passage as follows:

> Do not let your adorning be external—the braiding of hair, the wearing of gold, *or the putting on of clothing*—but let your adorning be the hidden person of the heart with the imperishable beauty of a gentle and quiet spirit, which in God's sight is very precious. (1 Pet. 3:3–4)

If this passage forbids braiding of hair and wearing of gold, then it must also forbid "the putting on of clothing"! But surely Peter was not telling women they should wear no clothes to church! He was rather saying that those external things should not be what they look to for their "adorning," for their source of attractiveness and beauty to others. It should rather be the inner character qualities that he mentions.[15] Therefore, I do not think that the statements about jewelry and braided hair for women, *when rightly understood*, are "culturally relative" commands, but they have direct application to women today as well.[16]

Finally, should men be "lifting holy hands" in prayer today? Personally, I lean toward thinking that this may be something that is transcultural and that we should consider restoring to our practice of prayer (and praise) in evangelical circles today. (I realize that many Christians already do this in worship.) On the other hand, since this is an outward, physical action (and thus some may think that it falls in the same category as a holy kiss or the washing of feet), I can understand that others would conclude that this is simply a variable cultural outward expression of a physical expression of an inward heart attitude toward God and dependence on him and focus on him in our prayers. It seems to me that there is room for Christians to differ on this question, but in any case it certainly is not a complicated enough question that it requires Webb's entire

---

[15] Some translations of 1 Peter 3:3 say that women should not put on "fine clothes" (so NIV; similarly RSV, NRSV, NLT, NKJV), but there is no adjective modifying "clothing" (Greek, *himation*), and the ESV, NASB, and KJV have translated it more accurately.

[16] I realize that others might argue that such braided hair and jewelry in the first century was recognized as an outward symbol of low moral character, and that was the reason that Paul and Peter prohibited it. I'm not persuaded by this because Peter still prohibits the "wearing of clothing," and I cannot think that only women of low moral character wore clothes in the first century. But if someone does take this position, it does not matter much for my argument, for this would then simply be one additional physical action that carries a symbolic meaning, and in this case also the prohibition would not be one that would apply absolutely to women who wanted to wear braided hair or jewelry today, since braided hair and jewelry would not signal that a woman had a low moral character in modern society.

"redemptive-movement hermeneutic" to encourage us to move beyond the ethic of the commands that we find in the New Testament.

Is it really that simple? Are the only matters in dispute about cultural relativity just these simple physical actions, all of which carry symbolic meaning? Perhaps I have missed one or two other examples, but I suspect it really is that simple. I believe God has given us a Bible that he intends believers generally to be able to understand (what has traditionally been called the clarity or the perspicuity of Scripture). Surely the question is not as complex and confusing as Webb's book portrays it.

At this point someone may object, what about all those other passages that Webb lists at the beginning of his book (pp. 14–15), passages which we found so difficult to classify regarding the question of cultural relativity?

My response is that there are other widely accepted principles of biblical interpretation that explain why many other commands in the Bible are not binding today. These principles of interpretation, however, are far different from Webb's principles, because they argue that certain commands are not binding on Christians today because of *theological convictions about the nature of the Bible and its history*, not because of *cultural analysis* or because of convictions about *cultural relativity*, and surely not because of any conviction that the New Testament commands were simply representative of a transitional ethic beyond which we need to move as we find a better ethic in today's society.

The following list gives some kinds of commands in the Bible that Christians do not have to obey in any literal or direct sense today (a fact that is evident apart from Webb's "redemptive-movement hermeneutic"):

1. The details of the Mosaic law code, which were written for people under the Mosaic covenant.[17]
2. Pre-Pentecost commands for situations unique to Jesus's earthly ministry (such as "go nowhere among the Gentiles" in Matt. 10:5).
3. Commands that apply only to people in the same life situation as the original command (such as "bring the cloak . . . and above all the parchments" in 2 Tim. 4:13, and also "no longer drink only water" in 1 Tim. 5:23). I would also put in this category Acts. 15:29, which is a command for people in a situation of Jewish evangelism in the first century: "That you abstain from what has been sacrificed to idols, and from blood, and from what has been strangled" (note that Paul himself explicitly allows the eating of foods sacrificed to idols in 1 Corinthians 10).

---

[17] I realize that many people, including myself, would argue that many of the laws in the Mosaic law code give us guidance on the kinds of things that are pleasing and displeasing to God today. In some ways that question is one of the more difficult questions in biblical interpretation. But I know of no Christians who would say that Christians today are actually under the Mosaic covenant, and therefore bound to obey *all* of the commands in the Mosaic covenant, including the commands about sacrifices, and clean and unclean foods, and so forth.

4. Everyone agrees that there are some passages, especially in Jesus's earthly teaching, that are difficult to understand in terms of how broadly we should apply them. Passages like "Do not refuse the one who would borrow from you" (Matt. 5:42) must be interpreted in the light of the whole of Scripture, including passages that command us to be wise and to be good stewards of what God has entrusted to us. But *these are not questions of cultural relativity*, nor do these difficult passages cause us to think that we must move beyond Jesus's teaching to some kind of higher and better ethic. We agree that we are to be subject to this teaching and to obey it, and we earnestly seek to know exactly how Jesus intends us to obey it.

5. There are differences among Christians today on how much we should try to follow commands regarding the miraculous work of the Holy Spirit, such as "Heal the sick, raise the dead, cleanse lepers, cast out demons" (Matt. 10:8). Some Christians think we should obey those commands directly, and they seek to do exactly what Jesus commanded. Other Christians believe that these commands were given only for that specific time in God's sovereign work in the history of redemption. But the important point here is that these differences are *theological*. This is not a dispute over whether certain commands are *culturally relative* because the point at issue is not one of ancient culture versus modern culture, but is rather a theological question about the teaching of the whole Bible concerning the work of miracles, and concerning God's purpose for miracles at various points in the history of redemption.

After we have made these qualifications, how much of the New Testament is left? Vast portions of the New Testament are still easily and directly applicable to our lives as Christians today, and many other passages are applicable with only minor changes to modern equivalents. As I was preparing to write this analysis of Webb's book, I read quickly through the New Testament Epistles, and I was amazed how few of the commands found in the Epistles raise any question at all about cultural relativity. (I encourage readers to try the same exercise for themselves.)

Where it is necessary to transfer a command to a modern equivalent, this is generally not difficult because there are sufficient similarities between the ancient situation and the modern situation, and Christian readers generally see the connection quite readily. It is not difficult to move from "the wages of the *laborers who mowed your fields*, which you kept back by fraud" (James 5:4) to "the wages of the *employees who work in your factory*, which you kept back by fraud." It is not difficult to move from "honor the *emperor*" (1 Pet. 2:17) to "honor *government officials* who are set in authority over you." It is not difficult to move from "Masters, treat your *slaves* justly and fairly" to "Employers, treat your *employees* justly and fairly." It is not difficult to move from "*Slaves*, obey in everything those who are your earthly masters, not by way of eye-service, as people-pleasers, but with sincerity of heart, fearing the Lord" to "*Employees*, obey your employers" (with the general biblical principle that we are never to obey those in authority over us when obedience would mean disobedience to God's laws). It is not difficult to move from "food offered to idols" (1 Cor. 8:10) to other kinds of things that encourage Christians to violate their consciences. And, to take one Old Testament example of a command that everyone believes tells us what God expects today, it is not difficult to move from "You shall not covet your neighbor's . . . ox" (Ex. 20:17) to "You shall not covet you neighbor's car or boat."

My suggestion, then, about the question of culturally relative commands is that it is not that difficult a question. There are perhaps three to five "culturally relative" commands concerning physical actions that carry symbolic meaning (at least the holy kiss, head covering, and foot washing; perhaps short hair for men and lifting hands in prayer), but we still obey these by applying them in different forms today. There are other broad categories of commands (such as Mosaic laws) that are not binding on us because we are under the new covenant. There are some fine points that require mature reflection (such as to what extent the details of the Old Testament show us what pleases God today). But the rest—especially the commands in the New Testament addressed to Christians in the new covenant—were written for our benefit, and they are not for us to "move beyond," but to obey.

11. Is William Webb's Book Then a Helpful Guide for Christians Today? Although Webb raises many interesting and challenging questions regarding cultural relativity, in the final analysis I believe *Slaves, Women & Homosexuals: Exploring the Hermeneutics of Cultural Analysis* is a deeply flawed book that nullifies in principle the moral authority of the entire New Testament and replaces it with the moral authority of a "better ethic," an ethic that Webb claims to be able to discover through a complex hermeneutical process that is entirely foreign to the way in which God intended the Bible to be read, understood, believed, and obeyed. Because a denial in principle of the moral authority of the New Testament commands is at the heart of the whole system, and because the system denies the historical accuracy of the creation account, I do not believe Webb's "redemptive-movement hermeneutic" should be accepted as a valid system for evangelicals to hold today.

SCRIPTURE VERSIONS CITED

Unless otherwise indicated, all Scripture quotations are from the ESV® Bible (The Holy Bible, English Standard Version®), copyright © 2001 by Crossway, a publishing ministry of Good News Publishers. Used by permission. All rights reserved.

Other Scripture versions cited include the following:

Scriptures marked as CEV are taken from the Contemporary English Version Copyright © 1995 by American Bible Society. Used by permission.

Scripture quotations marked CSB have been taken from the Christian Standard Bible®. Copyright © 2017 by Holman Bible Publishers. Used by permission. Christian Standard Bible® and CSB® are federally registered trademarks of Holman Bible Publishers.

Scripture quotations marked HCSB® are taken from *The Holman Christian Standard Bible®*. Copyright © 1999, 2000, 2002, 2003, 2009 by Holman Bible Publishers. Used by permission. HCSB® is a federally registered trademark of Holman Bible Publishers.

Scripture quotations marked KJV are from the *King James Version* of the Bible.

Scripture quotations marked NASB are from *The New American Standard Bible®*. Copyright © The Lockman Foundation 1960, 1962, 1963, 1968, 1971, 1972, 1973, 1975, 1977, 1995. Used by permission.

Scripture quotations marked NCV are from *The Holy Bible, New Century Version*, copyright © 1987, 1988, 1991 by Word Publishing, Dallas, Texas 75039. Used by permission.

Scripture quotations marked NET are from *The NET Bible®* copyright © 2003 by Biblical Studies Press, L.L.C. www.netbible.com. All rights reserved. Quoted by permission.

GLOSSARY

By Phil Hoshiwara

(Numbers in parentheses at the end of each entry refer to chapters and sections in this book.)

abortifacient: Any birth-control method that causes the death of a newly conceived child. (29D)

abortion: Any action that intentionally causes the death and removal from the womb of an unborn child. (21)

adultery: Voluntary sexual intercourse between a married person and a partner other than the lawful spouse. (28)

advance medical directive: A legal document giving instructions about end-of-life care. (24E.1.b)

anarchy: A situation in which there is no effective civil government. (16A.1.b)

anthropogenic global warming: The theory that human activities are causing the atmospheric concentration of greenhouse gases to increase, and that this increased concentration could warm the earth enough to cause significant, perhaps even catastrophic, harm to people and ecosystems. (41D.1.c)

artificial insemination by donor (AID): The process by which a male donor's sperm is collected and then injected into the cervix or uterus of a woman who is not his wife using a needleless syringe or other medical device with the goal of conception. (30D.2)

artificial insemination by husband (AIH): The process by which the husband's sperm is collected and then injected into the wife's cervix or uterus using a needleless syringe or other medical device with the goal of conception. (30C.1)

asceticism: A teaching that opposes and criticizes the enjoyment of material things that God has placed in this world. (34F.3)

assisted suicide: Suicide committed with the "assistance" of a physician, either by way of information or means. (22C.2–3)

authority of Scripture: A quality of the Bible whereby it is the written Word of God, so that to disbelieve or disobey any part of it is to disbelieve or disobey God. In ethics, this means that the Bible is our only absolute authority for defining moral right and wrong. (3C.1)

bearing false witness: As used in the ninth commandment (Ex. 20:16), this expression narrowly refers to false testimony against one's neighbor in a courtroom, and broadly refers to all lying. (12A)

"Bible and wisdom only" view of guidance: The view that God does not ordinarily use subjective impressions to guide a person into an "individual will," but rather he expects his people to use wisdom from the Bible to evaluate decisions in accordance with his "moral will." (6F.1)

bonds: Certificates issued by a company or government agency stating the amount of money that a person has lent to the company or agency; the amount of interest the company or agency promises to pay the lender; and the date on which the company or agency will return the entire amount of money to the lender. (38B.9.c)

bondservant: In the Roman Empire in the first century AD, a person who was "bound" by law to his or her employer for a certain period of time; "bondservant" is sometimes used to translate the Greek word *doulos*. (17A.1)

canon within the canon: A certain preferred section of Scripture (such as the teachings of Jesus or the writings of Paul) that is used as a person's authority for ethical decisions (a "personal canon") rather than using all the books of the Bible (the whole canon) as one's authority. (1E.3)

capital punishment: The putting to death of a person by the governing authorities for certain especially heinous crimes, such as murder. (18A–B)

carbon dioxide: A greenhouse gas that is claimed to contribute to dangerous amounts of global warming. (41D.1.c)

carbon fuels: Fuels such as wood, coal, oil, and natural gas that produce carbon dioxide when burned. (41D.6)

carved image: An figure that is carved or chiseled out of wood, stone, or metal and used as an object of worship—in other words, an idol. (10A.1)

ceremonial laws: A category used by some interpreters to speak of Old Testament laws that regulated the old covenant institutions of the sacrificial system, the priesthood, and the temple (often distinguished from "civil laws" and "moral laws"). (8E)

Chernobyl: The site of a nuclear power plant accident in Ukraine on April 26, 1986, caused by flagrantly poor quality construction and maintenance. (41C.6.c)

children: As used in the command, "Children, obey your parents" (Eph. 6:1), this term refers only to young people who are not yet considered adults in their society. (14B)

Christian ethics: Any study that answers the question "What does the whole Bible teach us about which acts, attitudes, and personal character traits receive God's approval, and which do not?" (1A.1)

Christians for Biblical Equality (CBE): An organization that advocates the egalitarian position that all leadership roles in marriage and the church should be open to women as well as men. (15B)

civil laws: A category used by some interpreters to speak of Old Testament laws that were enforced by the government authorities in Israel but were not ceremonial laws (often distinguished from "ceremonial laws" and "moral laws"). (8E)

clarity of Scripture: A quality of Scripture whereby it is able to be understood, but not all at once, not without effort, not without ordinary means, not without a willingness to obey it, not without the help of the Holy Spirit, not without some misunderstanding, and never completely. (3C.2)

climate change: Another term for "global warming," but referring more broadly to changes in the world's climate patterns. (41D)

Climategate: The November 2009 leak, from the Climatic Research Unit at the University of East Anglia in England, of thousands of emails, computer codes, and other documents that revealed scientific misconduct among a core group of climate scientists in an attempt to skew global warming projections. (41D.3.c)

cloning: The process of producing an organism that is genetically identical to the organism from which it was derived. (30D.4)

cohabitation: The state of two unmarried people living together in a sexual relationship. (28J)

communism: A societal and economic system in which private ownership of property is abolished and all goods and services, as well as all work responsibilities, are distributed by the government. (34B.3)

competition: A system in which people are encouraged by reward for their efforts to continue and to improve in activities in which they do well, and discouraged by lack of reward from continuing in activities in which they do not do well. (40D)

complementarian: The view that men and women are equal in value before God but have distinct roles in the family and the church. (15B)

conscience: A person's instinctive inward sense of right and wrong. (6C.6)

contentment: A state of satisfaction with what God has given us. (42.B)

Council on Biblical Manhood and Womanhood (CBMW): An organization that advocates the complementarian position that, according to Scripture, men and women are equal in value but have distinct roles in marriage and the church. (15B)

coveting: Desiring or longing for something that is not rightfully yours and that you could not reasonably hope to acquire in a morally right way. (42A.1)

cryopreservation: In the context of in vitro fertilization, the freezing of remaining embryos for potential use by the couple in future treatment cycles or for potential use by other people. (30C.2)

cursing: Expressing a wish that someone would be damned or condemned. (11B)

Danvers Statement: A statement of principles published by the Council on Biblical Manhood and Womanhood in 1988 concerning biblical roles for men and women. (15B)

debt forgiveness: The cancellation of debts that have been incurred by poor nations. (37B.5.d.(4))

deontological systems: Ethical systems based on rules for right and wrong, that is, rules for what ought and ought not to be done. (1B.1)

doulos: A Greek term sometimes translated as "bondservant," "servant," or "slave" in the New Testament. (17A.1)

drunkenness: A debilitating condition induced by alcohol and marked by (1) loss of good judgment, (2) unclear thinking, (3) loss of moral restraint, (4) defaming behavior, or (5) loss of physical coordination. (27A)

earned success: The experience of having a specific responsibility and then doing good work to fulfill that responsibility, in whatever career or field of life one chooses. (35D.1)

egalitarian: The view that no differences in the roles of men and women should be based on their gender alone. In particular, egalitarians deny that there is any unique male leadership role in marriage or in the church. (15B)

elders: In the New Testament, church officers who had governing and teaching responsibilities in local churches. (17B.1)

embryo adoption: The process of adopting the "excess" embryos from someone else's *in vitro* fertilization process, which have been frozen and kept in storage. An embryo is implanted in a woman's womb and allowed to grow and be born as a normal child. (30C.3)

environmentalism: An ideology that claims that "untouched nature" is nearly always the ideal, and that therefore objects to many human economic developments that would affect the environment. (41A.3.b)

ethical investing: The practice of investing only in companies for which one has no moral objection to the products they produce. (38B.9.d.(3))

euthanasia: The act of intentionally ending the life of a person who is elderly, terminally ill, or suffering from an incurable injury or disease. (22)

evangelical feminist: One who advocates an egalitarian position (*see* egalitarian). (15)

exploitation: When used with respect to poor nations, exploitation refers to the alleged practice of powerful corporations or richer nations taking advantage of poorer countries through robbery, unfair prices, environmental damage, unfair wages, or inhumane working conditions. (40H)

fair-trade coffee: Coffee that is purchased from low-income coffee farmers in poor nations at more than the world market price and then sold for a higher price in richer nations. (37B.5.d.(7) and 40H.2.b.(3))

fatherly displeasure: God's displeasure with the sins of his justified and adopted children. (5C.3.b)

fear of God: A healthy fear of God's fatherly displeasure and fatherly discipline, which leads to wisdom but does not include any fear of God's wrath in the final judgment, from which Christ has set Christians free. (6E.3)

feedbacks: Changes in the atmosphere that are caused by other changes in the atmosphere, which then lead to other changes. (41D.1.b)

fornication: Sex between unmarried people. (28F.3)

freedom of religion: A constitutional right (in the United States and elsewhere) by which every person is free to follow whatever religion he or she chooses. (16H.2)

Fukushima: The site of a nuclear power plant accident in Japan on March 11, 2011, which was caused by a tsunami and human error. (41C.6.c)

GDP: *See* gross domestic product.

giving back: The act of corporations making charitable contributions to their communities. The term can be misleading since it implies that corporations must have "taken" their profits in an illegitimate or immoral manner, and therefore are obligated to "give back." (40G)

good works: The good deeds that Christians do in order to please God after they have been justified by faith alone in Christ alone. (5A.4)

gospel: In a narrow sense, "the gospel" refers to the simple message "Believe in the Lord Jesus, and you will be saved" (Acts 16:31). In a broader sense, "gospel" is an English translation of the Greek word *euangelion,* which means "good news," and this good news includes all that God did in past history (since Genesis 1) in preparation for the Messiah, all that he has done in Christ, who is the Messiah, and all that he is doing now and will do in the future in believers' lives and in the whole world as a result of the redemptive work of Christ. (3B.3)

graded absolutism: The view that certain categories of God's moral laws are higher than others; that in some situations it is impossible to obey all of God's moral commands; and that in such situations a person is exempt from obeying the "lower" law in order to obey the "higher" law. (7A.1)

greater sins: Those sins that are more harmful in their effect, that break biblical commands that God considers more weighty, or that are committed by a person entrusted with greater responsibility. (5C.2)

gross domestic product: The total market value of all the final goods and services produced within a country in a given period of time, usually one year (abbreviated GDP). (37B.5.c.(2))

gross world product: The total market value of all the final goods and services produced in the whole world in a given period of time, usually one year. (36A)

head: As used in the New Testament to refer to interpersonal relationships, this term (a translation of the Greek word *kephalē*) means "authority over" in verses such as Ephesians 5:23, "the husband is the head of the wife even as Christ is the head of the church." (15D)

health-and-wealth gospel: The teaching that if a person has enough faith and gives enough money, God will make him or her prosperous and protect him or her from sickness. Also called the "prosperity gospel." (34F.2)

heart: The inward center of a person's deepest moral and spiritual inclinations and convictions, especially in relationship to God. (6C.7)

historical ethics: The study of how Christians in different periods of church history have understood various ethical topics. (1A.2)

homeschooling: An educational method in which the parents of the child do most or all of the training themselves. (14D.3)

honor: As used in the fifth commandment (Ex. 20:12), the practice of treating one's father and mother with respect, deference, and care; treating them as worthy of honor, as important and significant. (14A.2)

human flourishing: The activity of creating useful products from the earth, including technological, artistic, musical, culinary, literary, and other products, and of developing interpersonal relationships in home, church, and community, all for human benefit and enjoyment with thanksgiving to God. (34E)

hyperbole: Exaggerated statements made for rhetorical effect but not intended to be taken as literally true. (12B.2)

illicit drugs: Illegal drugs, especially those used not for medicinal purposes but for the purpose of enjoying the mental and emotional effects they cause. (27G)

impossible moral conflict: A situation so difficult that a person is forced to choose between disobeying one of God's moral commands or another, and thus is forced to choose to commit the "lesser sin." (This book denies that such situations occur.) (7)

in vain: As used in the third commandment (Ex. 20:7), any use of God's name in an irreverent or dishonorable way. (11A.2; 11B.1)

in vitro fertilization: The process of joining together a woman's egg (ovum) and a man's sperm in a laboratory rather than inside a woman's body, and then implanting it in a woman's womb. (The Latin phrase *in vitro* means "in glass.") (30C.2)

inequality: The varying degrees of abilities or stewardships (such as material, vocational, relational, intellectual, educational, or athletic) entrusted to different people by God. (37A)

infertility: The inability of a couple to conceive and bear children, due to a lack of normal function in either the man's or the woman's reproductive system. (30A)

interest: The "rental fee" paid for borrowed money. (39A)

IPCC: The Intergovernmental Panel on Climate Change, an international organization that assesses climate change. (41D.1.c)

"is" statements: Statements of fact about the world (*see* "ought" statements). (2D)

IUD: Abbreviation for "intrauterine device," a medical device that allows a woman's egg to be fertilized by a man's sperm, but prevents the embryo from being implanted in the woman's womb, thus causing a very early abortion. (29D)

just war: A war that is said to be morally right (or "just") because it meets certain criteria and is conducted within the bounds of certain moral restrictions (*see* unjust war). (19C)

killing: In the context of euthanasia, actively doing something to a patient that hastens or causes his or her death. (22B)

kingdom of God: The arrival of the new age of the reign of God in people's hearts and lives, which began to be manifested in Jesus's earthly ministry. (8B.3)

law of Christ: An expression in the New Testament that refers to the entire body of Christian teaching about a life pleasing to God. (8D.4)

legalism: A broad term that can refer to (1) a works-based view of salvation; (2) the addition of man-made moral requirements to Scripture; (3) an overly critical, proud attitude; or (4) an emphasis on minor doctrines or behaviors instead of the major ones. (4E.4)

lesser sins: Sins that are less harmful in their effect, that break biblical commands that God considers less weighty, or that are committed by a person entrusted with less responsibility. (5C.2)

letting die: In the context of euthanasia, passively allowing someone to die from his or her illness or other natural causes, without interfering with that process. (22B)

liberty: The individual human freedom and responsibility to choose one's actions. (16F)

lying: Affirming in speech or writing something you believe to be false. (12B)

major ethical issue: An ethical issue that has a wide and long-lasting effect on one's life and the lives of others. (1D)

marriage: In the Bible, a lifelong relationship between a man and a woman that is established by a solemn covenant before God. (28A.1)

Mayflower Compact: The first governing document written by the American Pilgrims on board the *Mayflower* in 1620, which introduced a pattern of government that was established by the consent of the governed. (16K.6)

medical power of attorney: A legal document that designates the person or persons who are authorized to make medical decisions on a person's behalf if that person becomes unconscious and unable to make decisions for himself or herself. (24E.1.b)

mental image: With respect to the second commandment, an image in one's mind in which God is pictured as having a physical body or looking like a man or some other part of creation. (10F)

minor ethical issue: An ethical issue that has little effect on one's life and the lives of others. (1D)

moral laws: A category used by some interpreters to speak of Old Testament laws that revealed God's moral standards that are applicable to all of mankind for all of history (often distinguished from "ceremonial laws" and "civil laws"). (8E)

moral will of God: The moral standards that God has revealed in Scripture. (6F)

Mosaic covenant: The covenant God made with the people of Israel under Moses at Mount Sinai; it was an administration of detailed written laws given for a time to restrain the sins of the people and to be a custodian to point people to Christ. (8A)

multinational corporation: A business that operates in several nations. (40F)

murder: The unlawful taking of another human life. (18A)

mutual submission: An egalitarian understanding of Ephesians 5:21, "submitting to one another," in which husbands do not exercise any unique authority in marriage, but rather men and women submit to one another "mutually." (15D)

name: In the Bible, the "name" of a person often is a description of the person's character or reputation. (11A.1)

Nashville Statement: A statement published by the Council on Biblical Manhood and Womanhood in 2017 concerning biblical principles regarding homosexuality and transgenderism. (33J)

natural family planning (NFP): A method of birth control based on fertility awareness that avoids "artificial" means of birth control. (29F)

natural law: In ethics, the set of moral conclusions drawn from reason, conscience, and observation of human nature. (3C.3.a)

necessity of Scripture: A quality of Scripture whereby it is necessary for knowing the gospel, for maintaining spiritual life, and for knowing God's declarations of right and wrong, but is not necessary for knowing that God exists or for knowing something about his character and moral laws. (3C.3)

new covenant: The covenant between God and his people that took effect at the death of Christ and remains in effect today. (8A)

nonconflicting biblical commands: The view that Christians will never be forced to choose to commit a "lesser sin," but that God requires people to obey every moral command in the entire Bible that rightly applies to them in their situations rather than just a handful of moral absolutes. (7C)

nonconflicting moral absolutism: The view that Christians will never be forced to choose to commit a "lesser sin," but that in every situation there will be at least one course of action that does not involve disobedience to any of God's commands (when rightly understood and applied). (7C)

nutrition and hydration: Food and fluids supplied to a patient who is unable to feed himself or herself. (22B)

oath: An appeal for God's punishment if your statement is untruthful. (11D)

obscene language: Language that uses offensive or vulgar words to talk about bathroom activities or sexual activities. (11B.3)

old covenant: The Mosaic covenant. (8A)

"ought" statements: Statements of moral right and wrong (*see* "is" statements). (2D)

pacifism: The view that it is always morally wrong for Christians to use military force against others and thus it is wrong for Christians to participate in military combat. A related pacifist view holds that it is wrong for anyone to participate in military combat. (19E)

parachurch organization: A Christian organization that works alongside churches and denominations in a specialized ministry. These organizations include mission agencies; Christian schools, colleges, and seminaries; campus ministries; Christian radio and television stations; book publishers; and so forth. (38A.2)

patriotism: The quality of loving, supporting, and defending one's country, and always seeking its good, even when that requires criticizing its leaders if they act contrary to biblical moral standards. (16L)

per capita income: The standard measurement of how rich or poor the people of a country are, on average, calculated by dividing the total market value of everything produced in a nation in a year (GDP) by the number of people in the nation. (37B.5.c.(1))

philosophical ethics: The study of ethical topics largely without appeal to the Bible, using the tools and methods of philosophical reasoning and analyzing what can be known about moral right and wrong from observing the world. (1A.2)

pilfering: Another term for stealing. (40A.2)

plagiarism: The act of publishing part of another author's work but claiming it as one's own. (12J.2)

postmodern hermeneutics: A viewpoint that claims there is no absolute truth, nor is there any single meaning in a text, but meaning depends on the assumptions and purposes that a reader brings to a text. (3C.2.c)

preemptive war: A war in which one nation discovers overwhelming evidence that another nation is about to launch an attack against it, so it attacks that other nation, not to conquer it but to prevent an attack. (19C)

prefertilization genetic screening: The process of genetically screening a husband prior to fertilization of a woman's egg by in vitro fertilization or prior to artificial insemination by the husband. Such screening can reveal if certain genetically determined diseases will be passed on from the father to the children. (30C.4)

***prima facie* duty:** A duty that people instinctively realize to be valid (the expression *prima facie* here means "self-evident, obvious"). (7A.2.c)

profit: The financial gain that results from selling a product for more than the cost of producing it. (40C)

Prohibition: The period of time (1920–1933) during which the transportation and sale of alcoholic beverages were prohibited in the United States by the Eighteenth Amendment to the U.S. Constitution. (27)

property: Something that belongs to someone. (34B)

prosperity gospel: *See* health-and-wealth gospel. (34F.2)

prosperity: As defined in this book, the accumulation and enjoyment of significantly more material wealth than previous generations. (36)

punctuality: The virtue of being consistently on time for agreed-upon appointments. (12J.3)

racial discrimination: The unfair treatment of people on the basis of their racial backgrounds. (25)

relativism: The belief that there is no absolute right and wrong, and so ethical decisions should be based on what is commonly accepted in each person's culture (*cultural relativism*) or on each individual's personal preferences (*individual relativism*). (1B.3)

rhythm method: A form of natural family planning based on avoidance of sexual intercourse during the days each month when a woman is able to conceive. (29D)

RU-486: A pill that acts as an abortifacient, commonly known as a "morning after" pill. (29D)

rule of law: The principle that all of a country's citizens, including its leaders, are subject to the authority of its laws. (16J)

Sabbatarian position: The view that the Old Testament Sabbath should still be observed today, but that the day of its observance has been moved from Saturday to Sunday. (13B)

Sabbath: In the fourth commandment (Ex. 20:8–11), the seventh day of the week, a day that was blessed by God and in which people were to rest from their labor and draw near to God in worship. (13A)

school choice: A system in which parents are free to choose the type of school to which government funding will be sent to pay for their child's education, including public, charter, private, or religious schools. (14D.4)

security for a debt: A guarantee that one will repay another person's debt if he or she fails to repay it. (39D.3)

seeker-sensitive services: Church services heavily tailored to draw in non-Christians, often at the expense of biblical truth that is perceived as offensive, particularly truth about sin, obedience, and God's holiness. (3B.1)

self-defense: The act of defending oneself from a physical attack, especially through the use of physical force. (20)

separation of powers: A model of governance in which government power is divided among several different groups or persons, not concentrated in only one group or person. (16I)

Seven Deadly Sins: A summary list, developed by Christians, of various vices that oppose God and oppose having a Christlike character in our lives. The list traditionally includes pride, envy, wrath, sloth, avarice, lust, and gluttony. (4C.4)

sexual immorality: In the Bible, a widely inclusive term that refers to any kind of morally prohibited sexual intercourse, especially between people who are not married to each other. (28F.3)

situation ethics: The view that there are no absolutely right or wrong actions, but a person should always do the most loving thing based on the different facts in each new situation. (1B.3)

slippery slope: In the context of euthanasia, the subtle but predictable movement from allowing "the right to die" to the belief that there is "an obligation to die." (22C.2)

sluggard: A term in Scripture used to refer to a lazy person. (35C)

snowflake children: Children who, in the embryonic state, were frozen for preservation and later implanted into a woman's womb, where they grew and were born. (30C.3)

social justice: A vague term used to describe the righting of perceived wrongs in a society. The term is not often employed in this book because of its ambiguous political and economic connotations. (37B.1)

sorcery (in the Bible): The morally prohibited activity of using ancient magic practices, often involving mind-altering drugs and the casting of spells upon people. (27G.5)

sovereign will of God: God's secret will according to which he directs all the detailed events of our lives. (6F.1)

spirit: The nonmaterial part of a person, the part that survives when the person's physical body dies. (6C.8)

stealing: The act of taking something that does not belong to you. (34A)

stewardship: The responsibility of managing whatever has been entrusted to a person by God. (34C; 38)

stocks: Shares of partial ownership of a company. (38B.9.d.(1))

stumbling block: In the Bible, a practice that is morally good in itself, but which becomes morally wrong when it leads other Christians to act contrary to the convictions of their consciences. (27C.2)

subjective impression: A person's instinctive sense of what to do. Subjective impressions can come from a person's conscience, heart, or human spirit, or from the Holy Spirit; they are helpful but not infallible and must be tested by Scripture because they can also come from a person's sinful desires or from demonic influence. (6C.10–11)

sufficiency of Scripture: A quality of Scripture whereby it contains all the words of God we need for salvation, for trusting him perfectly, and for obeying him perfectly. (3C.4.a)

surrogate motherhood: A process in which a woman is impregnated with and carries to term the child of another couple. This can involve in vitro fertilization, using both the egg and the sperm of the original couple, or artificial insemination by donor, using the husband's sperm and the surrogate mother's egg. (30D.3)

teleological systems: Ethical systems based on seeking the best *results* for an action. (1B.2)

theological ethics: A study of ethics that starts with one or a few major Christian doctrines, then reasons from those doctrines to ethical conclusions. (1A.2)

theological liberalism: A view that the Bible is a fallible human record of religious thought and experience rather than a divine revelation of truth and reality. (3C.2.c)

theonomy: The view that the "moral" and "civil" laws of the Mosaic covenant are still in force today, and therefore the civil laws of the Old Testament should be enforced by civil governments today. (8C)

third use of the law: The use of God's moral law in Scripture to instruct believers in obedience. (3B.2)

tithe: In the Old Testament, one-tenth of the Israelites' income, the portion that was to be given to the Lord. (38A.1)

total abstinence: The practice of abstaining completely from all alcoholic beverages. (27C.1)

tragic moral choice: A situation in which no nonsinful choices are available, so that a person is forced to commit a "lesser" sin in order to avoid a "greater" sin. (This book denies that such situations occur). (12F.3)

transgender identity: To think of oneself (or to "identify") as having a gender that is different from one's biological sex. (33I)

tuition vouchers: Certificates of government funding that can be used to enroll children in any school. (14D.4)

unjust war: A war that is said to be morally wrong because it fails to meet certain criteria or is conducted outside the bounds of certain moral restrictions (*see* just war). (19C)

usury: As used in the King James Version of the Bible, the charging of interest (the term is generally considered archaic today). (39C)

vengeance: The punishment inflicted for a wrong. The Bible condemns personal vengeance, but approves of God's just vengeance, which is sometimes carried out by human agents. (18C.4)

vices: Qualities or behaviors that are the opposite of Christlike virtues. (4C.4)

virtue ethics: A study of ethics that places emphasis not on whether specific actions are right or wrong, but rather on the moral character of the individual and the character traits people should strive to exemplify. (1B.4 and 4C)

virtues: Habitual inward dispositions to act, feel, respond, and think in morally good ways. (4C)

Volstead Act: The law passed by Congress in 1919 specifying details of the enforcement of the Eighteenth Amendment (Prohibition). (27)

vow: A promise made to God to perform a certain action or behave in a certain way. (11E)

whole-life ethic: An ethic that opposes all intentional taking of human life, including abortion, euthanasia, capital punishment, and war. (18D.8)

will: A legal document that directs the distribution of one's assets after one's death. (24E.1)

"wisdom only" view of guidance: See "'Bible and wisdom only' view of guidance." (6F.1)

"wise but not required" position: The view that it is a wise practice to observe regular periodic times of rest from work, ordinarily one day per week, but that this is not specifically commanded by God in the new covenant, and therefore working on that day from time to time should not be considered a sin. (13D.2.c)

workaholic: A person who works too much. (35I.3)

NAME INDEX

Lewis, C. S., 523
Lewis, Harold, 1146
Lewis, Julia, 841
Lewis, Robert, 423, 744
Lichter, Daniel T., 740n72
Liederbach, Mark, 1166
Lillback, Peter A., 484
Lin, Johnny Wei-Bing, 1167
Lincoln, Abraham, 447, 533, 545–46
Lindskoog, Kathryn Ann, 340
Lindsley, Art, 1009
Lindzen, Richard, 1140, 1143n147, 1146
Linebarger, D. L., 371n7
Litfin, Duane, 1010
Lockerbie, D. Bruce, 286
Lomborg, Bjørn, 1108–9, 1114–16, 1119–25, 1129, 1139n144, 1163
Longman, Tremper, 548
Loritts, Bryan, 651
Lot, 678
Lott, John R., Jr., 564
Louw, J. P., 690n38
Lovejoy, Elijah, 476
Lovelace, Richard F., 890
Lowrie, Roy W., 387
Lupton, Robert D., 1010
Luther, Martin, 50, 51, 52, 84
Lutzer, Erwin W., 65
Lynch, Loretta, 1150–51

MacArthur, John, 65, 103, 438, 476–77, 484, 840, 890
MacArthur, John D., 1020
Mackey, John, 1075n14
Madison, James, 483
Mahaney, C. J., 30, 338n43, 744, 956
Mahaney, Carolyn, 744
Mains, Karen Burton, 307
Mangalwadi, Vishal, 1010, 1103
Mankiw, N. Gregory, 976n29
Mann, Michael, 1159
Manuel, David, 484
Maranz, David E., 1010
Markey, Edward, 1150
Marshall, I. Howard, 827n60
Marshall, P. A., 938
Marshall, Peter, 484
Martinez, Ernie, 692
Marx, Karl, 899
Mary, 275
Mask, Russell, 1010
Masters, Peter, 346n10, 695
Mathis, David, 123
Maxson, J. Robin, 171n23, 185
Mayer, Lawrence, 878
Mayer, Marissa, 662
Mayhall, Carole, 307
McCloskey, Deirdre N., 1010

McComiskey, Thomas, 1199n5
McConnell, Mez, 1010
McDowell, Josh, 88n16
McDowell, Sean, 88n16, 890
McHugh, Paul, 877–78, 880
McIlroy, David, 484
McKinley, Mike, 1010
McKissic, William Dwight, 651
McKitrick, Ross, 1166
McLawhorn, Richard, 797
McQuilkin, Robertson, 56n33, 64, 77, 103, 122, 146, 163–64n14, 185, 256, 261, 276, 286, 307, 339, 360, 387, 422, 482, 491n6, 495, 500, 523, 548, 558, 563, 575n16, 584, 604, 609n8, 614, 650, 685–87, 694, 726n34, 742, 760, 781, 796, 815n37, 840, 844n3, 888, 917, 937, 955, 962n4, 1009, 1042, 1056, 1093, 1166, 1182
Meese, Edwin III, 791
Meier, Paul D., 695
Meilaender, Gilbert, 781
Melchizedek, 682
Mendelsohn, Robert, 1140n144
Metaxas, Eric, 781
Michael (archangel), 293n4, 902n8
Michael, Robert T., 741n75
Michaels, Patrick J., 1167
Michelangelo, 282
Middelmann, Udo W., 965n10, 1011, 1167
Miller, Arlene B., 604
Miller, Darrow L., 500, 945n6, 956, 965n10, 1011
Miller, Paul E., 123
Miller, Stephen R., 381n30
Miller, Terry, 977n31, 1004n67
Mills, Paul, 990n50
Minirth, Frank B., 695
Minnery, Tom, 484
Miriam, 644
Mitchell, C. Ben, 65, 604, 781, 782
Mitchell, Craig Vincent, 66
Mocan, H. Naci, 519–20
Mohler, R. Albert, Jr., 744, 846–47n11, 890
Moles, Chris, 816n39, 840
Montgomery, John Warwick, 207
Moo, Douglas J., 214n6, 231n36, 246n51, 914n18, 1167
Moo, Jonathan, 1167
Moore, Russell D., 779, 782, 1167
Moore, Stephen, 976n28, 1011
Mordecai, 470
Moreland, James Porter, 523, 614
Morey, Robert A., 340, 635, 695
Morris, Brian, 668
Morris, Leon, 126n1

Morrison, Todd G., 788
Moses, 335, 440, 462, 643–44, 935
Moss, M. J., 635
Moss, R. P., 1167
Mounce, William, 827n60
Moyo, Dambisa, 978–79, 1011
Muhlhausen, David, 519
Murray, Charles A., 484
Murray, David, 674
Murray, Iain, 1167
Murray, John, 56n33, 64, 71, 77, 146, 202n50, 207, 232n38, 239n45, 243n48, 256n56, 261, 314, 339, 346, 360, 482, 523, 528n3, 552n2, 724, 742, 760, 806nn18–19, 814–15, 840, 937
Myers, Jeff, 66

Nadab, 517
Naselli, Andrew David, 103, 119n14, 123, 133n10, 145, 156n5, 185, 373n12, 666n22, 797
Nathan, 459
Nebuchadnezzar, 430, 469, 582
Nehemiah, 469–70
Nelson, Tom, 500, 938
Neuhaus, Richard John, 484
Neumayr, George, 484
Newcombe, Jerry, 475n70, 484
Newheiser, Jim, 841
Newton, Marit, 500
Nicolosi, Joseph, 890
Nicolosi, Linda Ames, 890
Nida, Eugene Albert, 690n38
Niebuhr, H. Richard, 484
Nietzsche, Friedrich, 94
Nieves, Alvaro L., 651
Nitschke, Philip, 594
Noah, 507, 678, 1141
Noebel, David A, 66
Nordhaus, William D., 1139n144, 1167
Novak, Michael, 1011, 1093
Nyquist, J. Paul, 484, 1011

O'Donovan, Oliver, 39, 66, 185
O'Mathúna, Dónal P., 614
Obama, Barack, 541, 662
Oholibah, 785
Olasky, Marvin N., 585, 1011
Olson, Roger E., 484
Olthuis, J. H., 423, 726n34, 744
Oreskes, Naomi, 1148
Ortlund, Raymund C., 400, 401n24, 744
Osborne, Grant R., 94n23
Osten, Craig, 484, 860, 890, 931n4
Ovey, Michael, 484
Owens, Erik C., 523

HYMN INDEX

SCRIPTURE INDEX

SUBJECT INDEX

"karma," 274
keeping one's word, 1059
Keep Sunday Special campaign, 357
kephalē as "head," 408
killing, 527, 1240
   vs. letting die, 590–92
kindness, 111, 338
king, 457, 460
kingdom of God, 225, 902, 1240
   advancing of, 131
   beauty of, 623
   expansion of, 749
   seeking, 115
   and spiritual children, 764
   and the sword, 515
knowing God, 269
knowledge, and wisdom, 168–69
Korah, 517
Korean churches, 648
kosher foods. *See* food laws

landfills, 1121–22
land for growing food, 1113–15
landmarks, prohibition against moving, 896
La Niña, 1153
language, 648–49
lateness, 194, 337–38
Lateran Council (second: 1139), 541
Lateran Council (third: 1179), 1052
Lateran Council (fourth: 1215), 1052
Latin America, wealth and poverty in, 992
laughter, in Scripture, 305–6
law. *See also* ceremonial law; civil law; moral law; Mosaic law
   teaching function of, 447–48
   three uses of, 83–84
   written on hearts, 156, 244–46, 253
"law of Christ," 233–34, 1241
layoffs, 1062
laziness, 661, 691, 792, 925–26, 932–33
leadership, 736, 902
   restoration of, 136
legal ethics, 271
legalism, 53, 54, 117–21, 685, 1241
Legalzoom.com, 629
Lemon v. Kurtzman, 270–71
lending, 1045–49, 1053–55
LensCrafters illustration, 905–6
lesbian intercourse, 854
lesser commandments, 140, 205–6
"lesser sin," 25, 139–41, 187–206, 1241
lethargy, 691
"letting die," 25–26, 596, 1241
   vs. killing, 590–92
Levirate marriages, 1200
Levitical priesthood, 212
libel, 793
libertarianism, 738
liberty, 1241
   restriction of, 444–45
life expectancy, 1125–26

life-support system, 592
lifting hands in prayer, 1227–29, 1232
lights, leaving on in home, 193, 311
literature, 906
locker rooms, separate for boys and girls, 878–80, 886
logic, 58–59
London, history of air pollution in, 1118–19
loneliness, 735, 788, 803
long hair for men, 876
long life, 366
Lord's Day, 352–53
lost blessings, restoration of, 135
lottery, 1035, 1041
love, 111, 338, 379, 859, 871, 887, 907–8
   for God, 127
   for neighbor, 923, 945, 1061–62
   of parents, 372
lower prices, 1069
low-income countries, 975
lust, 113, 716, 726n34, 727, 785, 792
Lutherans, 454
   numbering of Ten Commandments, 259–60
luxury, 991
LYDIA Fund, 779
lying, 309–41, 863–64, 1241
   biblical examples of, 321–26
   definition of, 310–14
   economic harm from, 953
   as lesser sin, 187, 191–94, 202
   and moral character, 330–32
   in order to protect life, 326
   results of, 329–30
"lying spirit," 320n25, 325

Magna Carta, 476
major ethical issues, 50, 1241
"majority religion" and wealth of countries, 951
"making room" for younger workers, 936
mail-sorting machine, 1069
malaria, 1098, 1104
male dominance, 391
male-female equality, 1212
male headship, 394–407, 1205, 1207, 1211, 1212
   and justice, 1215
   and "new creation," 1214
malice, 113
"man" (as name for human race), 398–400
Managing God's Money (ministry), 1032n15
mandatory retirement ages, 936
manhood, 877n69
manipulation, 914
"man of God," 98n30
marijuana, 26, 456
   legalization of, 691–93
   medical, 693
marital rights, 819, 820
market economy. *See* free-market economic system
marketing boards in Africa, 1080
market value, 976
marriage, 50, 338, 699–745, 1241